Mastering VBA for Microsoft® Office 2016

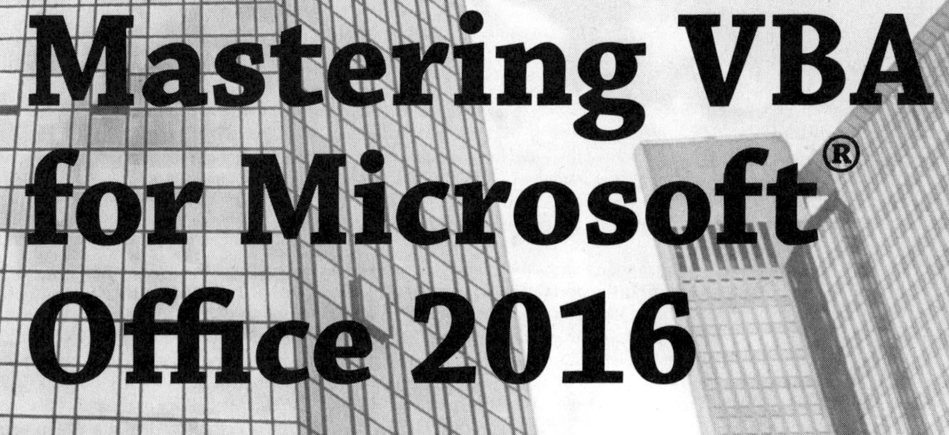

Mastering VBA for Microsoft® Office 2016

Richard Mansfield

SYBEX
A Wiley Brand

Acquisitions Editor: Kenyon Brown
Development Editor: David J. Clark
Technical Editor: Russ Mullen
Production Editor: Joel Jones
Copy Editor: Kathy Grider-Carlyle
Editorial Manager: Mary Beth Wakefield
Production Manager: Kathleen Wisor
Associate Publisher: Jim Minatel
Proofreader: Nancy Bell
Indexer: Nancy Guenther
Project Coordinator, Cover: Brent Savage
Cover Designer: Wiley
Cover Image: ©TimotiSt/iStockphoto

ISBN: 978-1-119-22538-6
ISBN: 978-1-119-22539-3 (ebk.)
ISBN: 978-1-119-22540-9 (ebk.)

Library of Congress Control Number: 2015957032

10 9 8 7 6 5 4 3 2 1

I dedicate this book to my brother John.

Acknowledgments

I'd like to thank all the good people at Sybex who contributed to this book. Senior Acquisitions Editor Kenyon Brown's sponsorship and encouragement made this book possible in the first place, and he also oversaw its progress through the various departments that polish, compose, and complete a book.

I'm also indebted to Development Editor David Clark who, once again, contributed valuable ideas that improved this latest edition. Technical Editor Russ Mullen carefully checked the manuscript for accuracy and ensured that the code examples worked as advertised. Also thanks go to Joel Jones, production editor, who moved the book through its final stages of copy editing, proofing, and design. And, finally, I appreciated the efforts of Nancy Bell, proofreader, who ensured that anomalies in the details were discovered and purged.

About the Author

Mastering VBA for Microsoft Office 2016 is Richard Mansfield's 45th book. His other titles include *Visual Guide to Visual Basic* (Ventana), *CSS Web Design for Dummies* (Wiley), and *Programming: A Beginner's Guide* (McGraw-Hill). Overall, his books have sold more than 500,000 copies worldwide and have been translated into 12 languages. Richard also teaches a course titled Introduction to XML at the online school ed2go.

Contents at a Glance

Contents

Introduction

Visual Basic for Applications (VBA) is a powerful tool that enables you to automate tasks in Microsoft Office applications.

Automating can save you and your colleagues considerable time and effort. Getting more work done in less time is usually good for your self-esteem, and it can do wonderful things for your job security and your career.

Where to Get This Book's Example Code

Throughout this book you'll find many code (programming) examples. Rather than type in the code, you'll save yourself time (and typo-debugging headaches) if you just copy the code from this book's web page and then paste it into the Visual Basic Editor. You can find all the code from this book—accurate, fully tested, and bug-free—at this book's web page:

`www.sybex.com/go/masteringvbaoffice2016`

If You Have Questions

I'm happy to hear from readers, so if you have any difficulty while using this book, write me at `earth@triad.rr.com`.

I'll try to respond the same day. We've all been beginners at some point, so don't feel your question is silly. If you're embarrassed, sign your email *Connie* and I'll think you're Connie.

What Can I Do with VBA?

You can use VBA to automate almost any action that you can perform interactively (manually) with an Office 2016 application. For example, in Word, VBA can create a document, add text to it, format it, edit it, and save it. All without human intervention.

Here are some more examples. In Excel, you could automatically integrate data from multiple workbooks into a single workbook. PowerPoint's VBA can create a custom presentation, including the latest data drawn from a variety of sources with no human intervention. And in Access you can create new tables, populate them with data, and send the table up to the cloud.

VBA is faster, more accurate, more reliable, and far less expensive than any human worker. You can even specify conditions for making a decision and then let VBA make that decision for you in the future. By adding decision-making structures and loops (repetitions) to your code, you can go far beyond the range of actions that any human user can perform. What's more, VBA can finish most jobs in less than a second.

Beyond automating actions you would otherwise perform manually, VBA also gives you the tools to create user interfaces for your code—message boxes, input boxes, and *user forms* (windows containing graphical objects that you can use to create forms and custom dialog boxes to display to the user).

Using VBA, you can create custom applications that run within the host application, too. For example, you could build within PowerPoint a custom application that automatically creates presentations for you.

And VBA can communicate between applications. Let one application assist another. Word can't do much in the way of mathematical calculations on sets of data; that's Excel's specialty. So, you could make Word start Excel running, perform some calculations, and then put the results into a Word document. Similarly, you could send graphs from Excel to PowerPoint or Outlook. You get the picture.

You only have to learn VBA once. Because VBA provides a standard set of tools that differ only in the specializations of the host applications, once you've learned to use VBA in one application, you'll be able to apply that knowledge quickly to using VBA in another application. For example, you might start by learning VBA in order to manipulate Excel and then move on to using your VBA skills with Outlook. You'll need to learn the components particular to Outlook, because they're different from Excel's features, but you'll be up to speed rapidly. It's like shopping. Once you understand the basics, going to a hardware store differs from going to a bookstore only in the particulars.

As with any programming language, getting started with VBA involves a learning curve—but you'll be surprised how many tools VBA provides to help you quickly learn the fundamentals.

The VBA Editor is among the best programming environments available. It includes help features that list programming options while you're typing, that instantly point out problems (and suggest solutions), that prevent you from making some kinds of mistakes, that offer context-sensitive help (with example programming), and that even automatically complete your lines (sentences) of programming code.

Best of all, you can create some VBA programs without even writing a single line of code! You use the Macro Recorder tool built into Word and Excel—a great way to learn VBA more quickly. You turn on the Recorder and do what you want with Word or Excel manually via keyboard and mouse as usual, while the Recorder watches you work and translates all your actions into programming code for you. The Recorder also acts as an assistant. Can't remember the programming code for saving a document? Just turn on the Recorder (click the icon on the lower left of Word's or Excel's status bar), save a document, and then you've got the code it recorded:

```
ActiveDocument.Save
```

Another truly cool thing about VBA: Its words—most of the programming commands that make the language do what you want—are English words. Unlike less efficient programming languages, Basic strives to be human-friendly, understandable, and readable. The programming code that saves Word's current document is `ActiveDocument Save`. For Excel, you use `ActiveWorkbook Save`. Makes sense, doesn't it?

For fun, search "save a document in c++" with Google, and you'll find lots of puzzling explanations attempting to accomplish this straightforward task in unfortunately unstraightforward ways, using often-puzzling diction. If you've tried programming in other languages, you'll find the simplicity and plain English of VBA a great relief. It's easy to learn, easy to use, yet no less powerful than any other programming language.

This book uses the Macro Recorder as the jumping-off point for you to start creating code. You first explore how to record macros (small programs) and then learn to edit this recorded code to make it do other things. After that easy introduction, you go on to explore the essentials of VBA diction and syntax. The book concludes with several ambitious topics.

Word, because it's the most popular Office application and because it has the most sophisticated and efficient programming tools, is used for many of the examples in this book. But there are plenty of examples showing how to program Excel, PowerPoint, Outlook, and even Access. And remember: Code that works in one Office 2016 application will generally work with other applications in the suite—with little or sometimes no modification.

What's in This Book?

This book teaches you how to use VBA to automate your work in Office 2016 applications. For its general examples, the book focuses on Word, Excel, Outlook, and PowerPoint, because those are the Microsoft Office applications that you're most likely to have, and because they have less eccentric programming tools and strategies than Access. The last part of the book continues the discussion of how to program these four applications, but also increases coverage of Access.

Part 1 of the book, "Recording Macros and Getting Started with VBA," contains the following chapters:

- Chapter 1 shows you how to record a macro using the Macro Recorder in Word and Excel. You also learn several ways to run macros and how to delete them.
- Chapter 2 introduces you to the powerful VBA Editor, the application in which you create VBA code (either by editing recorded code or by writing code from scratch) and user forms. The second half of this chapter discusses how you can customize the Visual Basic Editor so that you can work in it more efficiently.
- Chapter 3 shows you how to edit recorded macros, using the macros you recorded in Chapter 1. You learn how to step through (execute in slow motion) and test a macro in the Visual Basic Editor.
- Chapter 4 teaches you how to start writing code from scratch in the Visual Basic Editor. You create a procedure (another word for *macro*) for Word, one for Excel, and a third for PowerPoint.

Part 2, "Learning How to Work with VBA," contains the following chapters:

- Chapter 5 explains the essentials of VBA syntax, giving you a brief overview of the concepts you need to know. You also practice creating statements in the Visual Basic Editor.
- Chapter 6 shows you how to work with variables and constants, which are used to store information for your procedures to work on.
- Chapter 7 discusses how to use arrays. Arrays are like super-variables that can store multiple pieces of information at the same time.

- Chapter 8 teaches you how to find the objects you need to create your macros. You learn how to correctly write code involving objects by employing the Macro Recorder, the Object Browser, and the Help system. And you see how to use object variables to represent objects. Finally, you explore the uses of object models.

Part 3, "Making Decisions and Using Loops and Functions," consists of the following chapters:

- Chapter 9 describes how to use VBA's built-in functions—everything from string-conversion functions through mathematical and date functions to file-management functions.
- Chapter 10 shows you how to create functions of your own to supplement the built-in libraries of functions. You create functions that work in any VBA-enabled application, together with application-specific functions for Word, Excel, and PowerPoint.
- Chapter 11 shows you how to use conditional statements (such as `If` statements) to make decisions in your code. Conditional statements are key to making your code flexible and intelligent.
- Chapter 12 covers how you can use loops to repeat actions in your procedures: fixed-iteration loops for fixed numbers of repetitions, and indefinite loops that repeat until they satisfy a condition you specify. You also learn how to avoid creating infinite loops, which can cause your code to run either forever or until the computer crashes.

Part 4, "Using Message Boxes, Input Boxes, and Dialog Boxes," has the following chapters:

- Chapter 13 shows you how to use message boxes to communicate with the users of your procedures and let users make simple decisions about how the procedures run. You also explore input boxes, which are dialog boxes that give the users a way to supply information the macros need.
- Chapter 14 discusses how to employ VBA's user forms to create custom dialog boxes that enable the users to supply information, make choices, and otherwise interact with your macros.
- Chapter 15 discusses how to build more-complex dialog boxes. These include dynamic dialog boxes that update themselves when the user clicks a button, dialog boxes with hidden zones that the user can reveal to access infrequently used options, dialog boxes with multiple pages of information, and dialog boxes with controls that respond to actions the user takes.

Part 5, "Creating Effective Code," contains the following chapters:

- Chapter 16 illustrates the benefits of reusable modular code and shows you how to create it.
- Chapter 17 explains the principles of debugging VBA code, examines the different kinds of errors that occur, and discusses how to deal with them.
- Chapter 18 explores how to build well-behaved code that's stable enough to withstand being run under the wrong circumstances and civilized enough to leave the user in the best possible state to continue their work after it finishes running.

- Chapter 19 discusses the security mechanisms that Windows and VBA provide for safeguarding VBA code and ensuring that you or your users do not run malevolent code (viruses, trojans, worms, and so on). The chapter discusses digital certificates and digital signatures, how to choose an appropriate security setting for the application you're using, and how to manage passwords.

Part 6, "Programming the Office Applications," consists of these 12 chapters:

- Chapter 20 explains the Word object model and shows you how to work with key objects in Word, including the `Document` object, the `Selection` object, and `Range` objects. You also learn how to set options in Word and manage cloud storage via such systems as Dropbox or Microsoft's OneDrive.
- Chapter 21 discusses how to work with widely used objects in Word, including the objects for Find and Replace; headers, footers, and page numbers; sections, page setup, windows, and views; and tables.
- Chapter 22 introduces you to the Excel object model and shows you how to work with key objects in Excel, including the `Workbook` object, the `Worksheet` object, the `ActiveCell` object, and `Range` objects. You also learn how to set options in Excel.
- Chapter 23 shows you how to work with charts, windows, and the Find and Replace feature in Excel via VBA.
- Chapter 24 gets you started working with the PowerPoint object model and the key objects that it contains. You work with `Presentation` objects, `Window` objects, `Slide` objects, and `Master` objects.
- Chapter 25 teaches you how to go further with VBA in PowerPoint by working with shapes, headers and footers, and the VBA objects that enable you to set up and run a slide show automatically.
- Chapter 26 introduces you to Outlook's object model and the key objects that it contains. You meet Outlook's creatable objects and main interface items; learn general methods for working with Outlook objects; and work with messages, calendar items, tasks and task requests, and searches.
- Chapter 27 shows you how to work with events in Outlook. There are two types of events, application-level events and item-level events, which you can program to respond to both Outlook actions (such as new mail arriving) and user actions (such as creating a new contact).
- Chapter 28 familiarizes you with the Access object model and demonstrates how to perform key tasks with some of its main objects.
- Chapter 29 shows you how to manipulate the data in an Access database via VBA.
- Chapter 30 shows you how to communicate between applications via VBA. You learn which tools are available, how to use Automation, how to work with the `Shell` function, and how to use data objects, DDE, and `SendKeys`.
- Chapter 31 explores the various ways you can customize the Ribbon programmatically. It's not possible to customize it by VBA code alone. Instead, you must write XML code to

modify what the user sees on the Ribbon and write *callbacks* (event-handler procedures in VBA) to respond when the user clicks one of the buttons or other controls you've added to the Ribbon. You see how to modify tabs, groups, and individual controls—in Word, PowerPoint, Excel, and, using different techniques, in Access.

How Should I Use This Book?

This book tries to present material in a sensible and logical way. To avoid repeating information unnecessarily, the chapters build on each other, so the later chapters generally assume that you've read the earlier chapters.

The first five parts of the book offer a variety of code samples using Word, Excel, PowerPoint, and, to a lesser extent, Access. If you have these applications (or some of them), work through these examples as far as possible to get the most benefit from them. While you may be able to apply some of the examples directly to your work, mostly you'll find them illustrative of general VBA techniques and principles, and you can customize them to suit your own needs.

The sixth and last part of this book shows you some more advanced techniques that are useful when using VBA to program Word, Excel, PowerPoint, Outlook, and Access. Work through the chapters that cover the application or applications that you want to program with VBA.

Chapters 30 and 31 are specialized, but quite useful. Chapter 30 shows you how to use one application to control another application; for example, you might use Word to contact Excel and benefit from its special mathematic or graphing capabilities. And Chapter 31 shows you many different ways to program the Ribbon—the primary user interface in Office 2016 applications.

Is This Book Suitable for Me?

Yes.

No programming experience required. This book is for anyone who wants to learn to use VBA to automate their work in Office. Automating your work could involve anything from creating a few simple procedures that would enable you to perform some complex and tedious operations via a single keystroke, to building a custom application with a complete interface that looks quite different from the host application.

This book attempts to present theoretical material in a practical context by including lots of examples of the theory in action. For example, when you learn about loops, you execute short procedures that illustrate the uses of each kind of loop so that you can see how and why they work, and when to use them. And you'll also find many step-throughs—numbered lists that take you through a task, one step at a time. Above all, I've tried to make this book clear and understandable, even to readers who've never written any programming in their life.

Conventions Used in This Book

This book uses several conventions to convey information succinctly:

- ➤ designates choosing a command from a menu. For example, "choose File ➤ Open" means that you should pull down the File menu and choose the Open command from it.
- + signs indicate key combinations. For example, "press Ctrl+Shift+F9" means that you should simultaneously hold down the Ctrl, Shift, and F9 keys. Also, you'll sometimes see this: Press Ctrl+F, I. That means simultaneously press Ctrl and F; then release them and press I.

Some of these key combinations can be confusing at first (for example, "Ctrl++" means that you hold down Ctrl and press the + key—in other words, hold down Ctrl and Shift together and press the = key, because the + key is the shifted =.).

- Likewise, "Shift+click" means that you should hold down the Shift key as you click with the mouse, and "Ctrl+click" means that you should hold down the Ctrl key as you click.
- ↑→↓← represent the arrow keys on your keyboard. These arrows are also represented in the text as "up-arrow," "down-arrow," etc. The important thing to note is that ← does not mean the Backspace key (which on many keyboards bears a similar arrow). The Backspace key is indicated simply by the words "Backspace" or "the Backspace key."
- **Boldface** indicates that you are to type something.
- `Program font` indicates program items, or text derived from program lines. Complete program lines appear offset in separate paragraphs like the example below, while shorter expressions appear as part of the main text.

```
Sub Sample_Listing()
    'lines of program code look like this.
End Sub
```

- *Italics* usually indicate either new terms being introduced or variable information (such as a drive letter that will vary from computer to computer and that you'll need to substitute for your own).
- _ (a continuation underline character) indicates that a single line of code has been broken onto a second or subsequent line in the book (because of the limitations of page size). In the VBA Editor, you should enter these "broken" lines of code as a single line. For example, in this code sample, a single line of VBA Editor code has been broken into three lines when printed in this book:

```
MsgBox System.PrivateProfileString("", _
"HKEY_CURRENT_USER\Software\Microsoft\ _
Office\11.0\Common\AutoCorrect", "Path")
```

- You'll also see sidebars throughout the book. These include asides, notes, tips, and warnings. They're a bit like footnotes, though less tedious. Each sidebar, no matter how small, has a headline—so you can quickly see if you want to read it.
- Finally, each chapter includes one, longer, *Real World Scenario* sidebar: a case study, an important practical technique, or some other useful advice.

The Mastering Series

The Mastering series from Sybex provides outstanding instruction for readers with intermediate and advanced skills in the form of top-notch training and development for those already working in their field and clear, serious education for those aspiring to become pros. Every Mastering book includes the following:

- Real World Scenarios, ranging from case studies to interviews, that show how the tool, technique, or knowledge presented is applied in actual practice

- Skill-based instruction with chapters organized around real tasks rather than abstract concepts or subjects
- Self-review test questions so you can be certain you're equipped to do the job right

For More Information

Sybex strives to keep you supplied with the latest tools and information you need for your work. Please check the website at `www.sybex.com/go/masteringvbaoffice2016`, where we'll post additional content and updates that supplement this book if the need arises.

Part 1

Recording Macros and Getting Started with VBA

Chapter 1

Recording and Running Macros in the Office Applications

In this chapter, you'll learn the easiest way to get started with Visual Basic for Applications (VBA): recording simple *macros* using the Macro Recorder that's built into the Office applications. Then you'll see how to run your macros to perform useful tasks.

I'll define the term *macro* in a moment. For now, just note that by recording macros, you can automate straightforward but tediously repetitive tasks and speed up your regular work. You can also use the Macro Recorder to create VBA code that performs the actions you need and then edit the code to customize it—adding flexibility and power. In fact, VBA is a real powerhouse if you know how to use it. This book shows you how to tap into that power.

IN THIS CHAPTER, YOU WILL LEARN TO DO THE FOLLOWING:

- Record a macro
- Assign a macro to a button or keyboard shortcut
- Run a macro
- Delete a macro

What Is VBA and What Can You Do with It?

Visual Basic for Applications is a programming language created by Microsoft that is built into applications. You use VBA to automate operations in all the main Office applications—Word, Excel, Outlook, Access, and PowerPoint.

Please don't be put off by the notion that you'll be *programming*. As you'll see shortly, working with VBA is nearly always quite easy. In fact, quite often you need not actually write any VBA yourself; you can merely *record* it—letting the Office application write all the VBA "code."

The phrase *automate operations in applications* is perhaps a bit abstract. So here are a few examples of how to use VBA to streamline tasks, avoid burdensome repetition, customize the applications' interfaces, and in general improve your efficiency.

- You can record a macro that automatically carries out a series of actions that you frequently perform. Let's say that you often edit Word documents written by a coworker, but she sets the zoom level to 100. You prefer to zoom to 150. All you need to automatically change the zoom level is this VBA code:

```
ActiveWindow.ActivePane.View.Zoom.Percentage = 150
```

- Don't worry! You do not even need to know the programming terms `ActiveWindow` or `View.Zoom`. Just turn on the Macro Recorder, manually click View, then click Zoom, and then set to 150 percent. The recorder will watch the steps you take and then write the necessary VBA code that can reproduce those steps. You write no code at all!
- You can write code that performs actions a certain number of times and makes decisions depending on the situation in which it is running. For example, you could write code that takes a series of actions on every presentation that's open in PowerPoint.
- You can use VBA to modify the look or behavior of the user interface. VBA can, for example, interact with the user by displaying *forms*, or custom dialog boxes, that enable the user to make choices and specify settings. You might display a set of formatting options—showing captioned controls such as check boxes and option buttons—that the user can select. Then when the user closes the dialog box, your macro takes appropriate actions based on the user's input.
- You can take actions via VBA that you can't do easily, or at all, when directly manipulating the user interface by hand. For example, when you're working interactively in most applications, you're limited to working with the active file—the active document in Word, the active workbook in Excel, and so on. By using VBA, you can access and manage files that aren't active.
- You can make one application control another application. For example, you can make Word place a table from a Word document into an Excel worksheet.

The Difference Between Visual Basic and Visual Basic for Applications

VBA is based on Visual Basic, a programming language derived from BASIC. *BASIC* stands for Beginner's All-Purpose Symbolic Instruction Code. BASIC is designed to be user-friendly because it employs recognizable English words (or variations on them) rather than the abstruse and incomprehensible programming terms found in languages like COBOL. In addition to its English-like diction, BASIC's designers endeavored to keep its punctuation and syntax as simple and familiar as possible as well.

Visual Basic is *visual* in that it offers efficient shortcuts such as drag-and-drop programming techniques and many graphical elements.

Visual Basic for Applications is a version of Visual Basic tailored to manage the Microsoft Office applications. The set of *objects* (features and behaviors) available in each application differs somewhat because no two applications share the exact same set of features and commands.

For example, some VBA objects available in Word are not available in Excel (and vice versa) because some of Word's features, like the Table of Contents generator, are not appropriate in Excel.

However, the large set of primary commands, fundamental structure, and core programming techniques of VBA in Word and VBA in Excel are the same. So you'll find that it's often quite easy to translate your knowledge of VBA in Word to VBA in Excel (or indeed in any VBA-enabled application).

For example, you'd use the `Save` method (a *method* is essentially an action that can be carried out) to save a file in Excel VBA, Word VBA, or PowerPoint VBA. What differs is the object involved. In Excel VBA, the command would be `ActiveWorkbook.Save`, whereas in Word VBA it would be `ActiveDocument.Save` and in PowerPoint it would be `ActivePresentation.Save`.

VBA always works within a host application (such as Access or Word). With the exception of some few stand-alone programs that are usually best created with Visual Basic .NET, a host application always needs to be open for VBA to run. This means that you can't build stand-alone applications with VBA the way you can with Visual Basic. If you like, you can *hide* the host application from the user so that all they see is the interface (typically user forms) that you give to your VBA procedures. By doing this, you can create the illusion of a stand-alone application—but VBA is rarely used for this purpose. If you want to write self-sufficient programs, investigate Visual Basic Express.

WHAT ARE VISUAL BASIC .NET AND VISUAL BASIC EXPRESS?

Visual Basic .NET (VB .NET) is just one version of Microsoft's long history of BASIC language implementations. BASIC contains a vast set of libraries of prewritten code that allow you to do pretty much anything that Windows is capable of doing. Although VB .NET is generally employed to write stand-alone applications, you can tap into its libraries from within a VBA macro should you need to. Just remember, each Office application has its own object library, but the .NET libraries themselves contain many additional capabilities (often to manipulate the Windows operating system). So, if you need a capability that you can't find within VBA or an Office application's object library, the resources of the entire .NET library are also available to you. Visual Basic Express is included in a free version of VB .NET. After you've worked with VBA in this book, you might want to download and explore Visual Studio Express for Desktop at:

`https://www.visualstudio.com/en-us/products/visual-studio-express-vs.aspx`

Visual Studio Express includes several languages, and VB is one of them.

Understanding Macro Basics

A *macro* is a sequence of commands you or a user can repeat at will. That's also exactly the definition of a *computer program*. Macros, however, are generally short programs—dedicated to a single task. Think of it like this: A normal computer program, such as Photoshop or Internet Explorer (IE), has many capabilities. It can prevent pop-up ads, block websites, display full-screen when you press F11, and so on. A macro is smaller, dedicated to accomplishing just one of these tasks, such as displaying full-screen. So a macro would likely add one new feature to the huge collection of features already built into an Office application.

In some applications, you can set a macro to run itself automatically. For instance, you might create a macro in Word to automate basic formatting tasks on a type of document you regularly receive incorrectly formatted. As you'll see in Chapter 6, "Working with Variables, Constants, and Enumerations," in a discussion of the `AutoExec` feature, you can specify that a macro run automatically upon opening a document of that type.

A macro is a type of *subroutine* (sometimes also called a *subprocedure*). Generally, people tend to use the shorter, more informal terms *sub, procedure,* and *routine*. In the Visual Basic Editor, each of your macros starts with the word `Sub`. Note that a macro is a single procedure, whereas a computer program like IE is a collection of many procedures.

In an Office application that supports the VBA Macro Recorder (such as Word or Excel), you can create macros in two ways:

- Turn on the Macro Recorder and just perform by hand the sequence of actions you want the macro to perform. Clicks, typing, dragging, dropping—whatever you do is recorded.
- Open the Visual Basic Editor and type the VBA commands into it to write a macro without first recording it.

There's also a useful hybrid approach that combines recording with editing. First record the sequence of actions, and then later, in the Visual Basic Editor, you can view and edit your macro. You could delete any unneeded commands or type in new commands. You could also use the Editor's Toolbox feature to drag and drop user-interface elements (such as message boxes and dialog boxes) into your macro so users can make decisions and choose options for how to run it. Macros are marvelously flexible, and the VBA Editor is famously powerful yet easy to use. This Editor is to programming what Word is to writing—a very mature, efficient, and well-designed toolbox.

Once you've created a macro, you specify how you want the user to trigger it. In most applications, you can assign a macro to the Ribbon, to the Quick Access Toolbar, or to a shortcut key combination. This makes it very easy to run the macro by merely clicking an icon or pressing a shortcut key (such as Alt+R). You can also optionally assign your macro to a Quick Access Toolbar button or keyboard shortcut when you first record the macro, via a dialog box that automatically appears when you begin a recording. You'll see how all this works shortly. It's simple. (To assign a macro to the Ribbon, first record it, and then right-click the Ribbon and choose Customize The Ribbon. Click the Choose Commands From drop-down box, and then click the Macros entry to display all your macros.)

Recording a Macro

The easiest way to create VBA code is to record a macro using the Macro Recorder. Only Word and Excel include a Macro Recorder.

You switch on the Macro Recorder, optionally assign a trigger that will later run the macro (a toolbar button or a shortcut key combination), perform the actions you want in the macro, and then switch off the Macro Recorder. As you perform the actions, the Macro Recorder translates them into commands—*code*—in the VBA programming language.

Once you finish recording the macro, you can view the code in the Visual Basic Editor and modify it if you want. If the code works perfectly as you recorded it, you never have to look at it—you can just run the macro at any time by clicking the toolbar button or key combination you assigned to the macro.

Displaying the Developer Tab on the Ribbon

Before going any further, ensure that the Developer (programmer) tab is visible in your Ribbon. This tab is your gateway to macros, VBA, and the VBA Editor. By default, Outlook doesn't display this tab. Word, Excel, and PowerPoint do. (Access doesn't even *have* this tab. Word, Excel, PowerPoint and Outlook do.) To add the Developer tab to your Ribbon, click the File tab and then click Options. Click Customize Ribbon. In the list box on the right, click Developer to select it. Click the OK button to close the Options dialog box. You'll now see a new Developer tab to the right of the default tabs.

In the following sections, you'll look at the stages involved in recording a macro. The process is easy, but you need to be familiar with some background if you haven't recorded macros previously. After the general explanations, you'll record example macros in Word and Excel. (Later in the book you'll examine and modify those macros, after you learn how to use the Visual Basic Editor. So don't delete them.)

Planning the Macro

Before you even start the Macro Recorder, it's sometimes a good idea to do a little planning. Think about what you will do in the macro. In most cases, you can just record a macro and not worry about the context. You can just record it with a document open. But in some situations you need to ensure that a special context is set up before you start the recording. For example, you might want to create a macro in Word that does some kind of editing, such as italicizing and underlining a word. To do this, you'll want to first have the blinking "insertion" cursor on a word *that's not italicized or underlined*. You don't want to record the actions of moving the insertion cursor to a particular word. That would make your macro specific to this document and this word in this document. You usually want a macro to work well with more than just one particular document.

Your macro is intended to just italicize and underline whatever word is currently under the blinking cursor in any document. Nevertheless, most simple macros can be recorded without any special planning. Just record whatever you want the macro to do.

Pausing a Macro

Word (but not Excel) lets you pause the Macro Recorder if you need to stop while recording to do something that you do not want to record. This capability allows you to deal with problems you hadn't anticipated when planning the macro—for example, having to open a document that should have been open before you started recording the macro.

Some macros should perform any necessary setup themselves. The setup will be part of the macro. In these cases, you should make sure the application is in the state that the macro expects before you start recording the macro. For example, if, to do its job, a macro needs a blank active workbook in Excel, the macro itself should create that blank workbook rather than using whichever workbook happens to be active at the time. This saves the user a step when the macro runs. To do this, start recording before launching a blank active workbook.

A Warning About Security

Macros are computer programs, albeit usually small. You can even tap into all the features in the Windows operating system itself from within a macro. The result is that viruses and other harmful code can be contained within macros (and such code can execute automatically merely by the user opening an infected document via the `AutoExec` feature discussed in Chapter 6 and via other techniques, such as employing the application's Startup folder). For example, a virus embedded in a macro could delete files on the hard drive if the user opened an infected Word document. This is obviously dangerous.

Office 2016 applications, not to mention the Windows operating systems, contain multiple layers of security to protect against such viruses and harmful code. Specific to macros is a macro "trust" technology that's built into Office applications. To see or modify these trust settings, open the Trust Center dialog box by clicking the Developer tab on the Ribbon, and then click the Macro Security icon (in the Code section of the Ribbon) in Word, Excel, Outlook, or PowerPoint. (Access, as is often the case, does things a bit differently than the other Office applications. Access has no Developer tab. To manage macro security in Access you click the File tab, click the Options link on the left side, click Trust Center, click the Trust Center Settings button, and then click Macro Settings.)

The main point here is that you might have to make some adjustments if you can't run macros or if you get mysterious error messages such as "The Macro Could Not Be Created" or "Access Is denied." If this happens, your first step should be to look at the Trust Center and choose Disable All Macros With Notification. This setting asks the user for permission to run macros. While you're working with macros in this book, you might want to just select Enable All Macros in the Trust Center. Then deselect this option before closing a document that you worked on in this book. The idea is that you can trust your own macros but you don't want to trust *all* macros from *all* documents you might get from outside sources.

If you are working on a document that you created and it contains macros that you wrote, you can trust that document and agree to activate the macros. However, if you open a document from someone else, you have to be careful.

Additional security issues can be solved by managing the various strata of security that now, out of necessity, are embedded within operating systems and applications. One way to deal with security issues is to explore security topics in Windows 7, 8, or 10 applications' Help features. You can also sometimes get good answers by posting questions in online user groups or searching expert websites such as *Wikipedia*. Also, you can find a good overview of Office 2016 security here:

`http://technet.microsoft.com/en-us/library/ee857085(v=office.15).aspx`

Chapter 19, "Securing Your Code with VBA's Security Features," covers Office 2016 security issues in depth.

Starting the Macro Recorder

Start the Macro Recorder by clicking the Developer tab on the Ribbon and then clicking the Record Macro button. You can also click the Macro Record button on the left side of the status bar at the bottom of the application. Note that if you don't see this Macro Record button, right-click the status bar and select Macro Recording from the context menu.

By clicking the Macro Record button, you don't have to open the Developer tab. The button looks like the one shown in Figure 1.1.

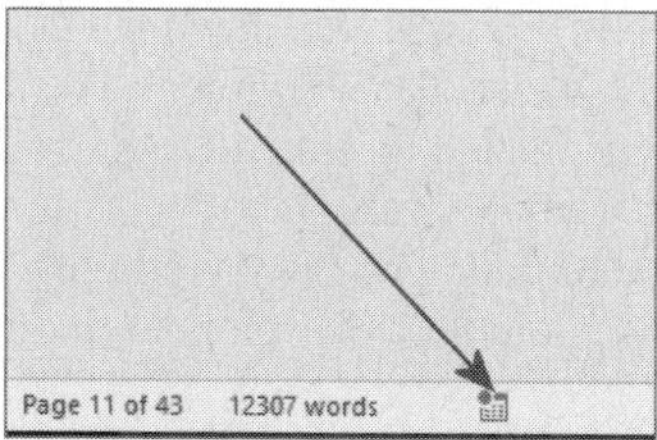

FIGURE 1.1
Find this Record Macro button on the status bar.

As soon as you start the Macro Recorder, the Record Macro dialog box opens. You see that this new macro has been given a default macro name (Macro1, Macro2, and so on). You can accept that default name or change it. There's also an optional description to fill in if you like.

To stop the Macro Recorder, you can click the Stop Recording button in the Developer tab. You can alternatively stop the recording by clicking the square button that appears during recording on the status bar, down on the bottom left of the application's window. Once the Recorder is stopped, the square button is replaced with the icon that you can click to start recording a new macro. In Word for the Mac, click the REC indicator rather than double-clicking it.

The appearance of the Record Macro dialog box varies somewhat in Word and Excel because the dialog box must offer suitable options to accommodate the varying capabilities particular to each application. In each case, you get to name the macro and add a description of it. In most cases, you can also specify where to save the macro—for example, Word offers two options. For *global* use (making the macro available to all Word documents), store it in the file named `Normal.dotm`. If it is merely to be used in the currently active document, choose to store it in a file with the document's name and the `.dotm` filename extension. An ordinary Word template has a `.dotx` filename extension, but macros are stored in a file with the filename extension `.dotm`.

Excel allows you three options: to store macros in the current workbook, in a new workbook, or for use with *all* Excel workbooks, in the Personal Macro Workbook. That's the equivalent of Word's `Normal.dotm` file, and Excel's Personal Macro workbook is saved in a file named `Personal.xlsb`.

WHERE TO STORE MACROS IN POWERPOINT

You can't record macros in the 2016 version of PowerPoint, but you can create them by writing programming code using the Visual Basic Editor. Then you can store macros in the currently active presentation or in any other open presentation or template. PowerPoint also provides a global macro storage container (similar to Word's `Normal.dotm` file). In PowerPoint, choose the All Open Presentations option in the Macro list box, which is found by clicking the Macros icon in the Code section of the Ribbon's Developer tab.

The Record Macro dialog box also lets you specify how you want the macro triggered. Word displays buttons you can click to either open a dialog for entering a shortcut key combination or open the Word Options dialog where you can create a button for this macro that will appear on the Quick Access Toolbar. Excel limits you to Ctrl+ shortcut key combinations as a way of launching macros, so there is no button to display a full keyboard shortcut dialog like the one in Word. Excel has only a small text box where you can enter the key that will be paired with Ctrl as the shortcut.

Most of the Microsoft applications that host VBA have the Developer tab from which you control macro recording, launch the Visual Basic Editor, and otherwise manage macros. Access, however, groups several of its macro-related tools in a Database Tools tab (which is visible by default) and also has a Macro option on its Create tab.

Figure 1.2 shows the Record Macro dialog box for Word with a custom name and description entered. Figure 1.3 shows Word's version of the Developer tab on the Ribbon.

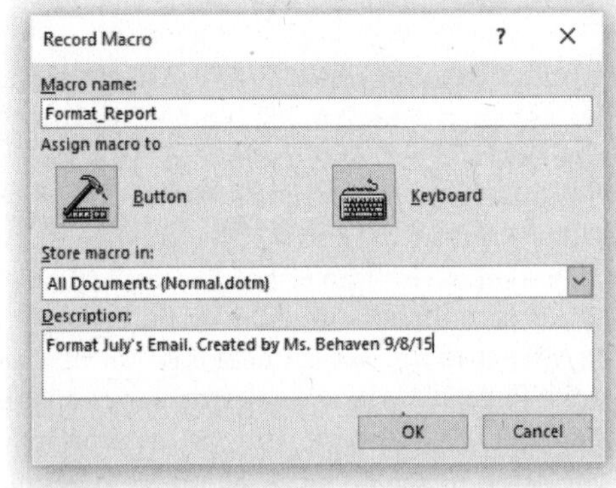

FIGURE 1.2 In the Record Macro dialog box, enter a name for the macro you're about to record. You can type a concise description in the Description box. This is the Record Macro dialog box for Word.

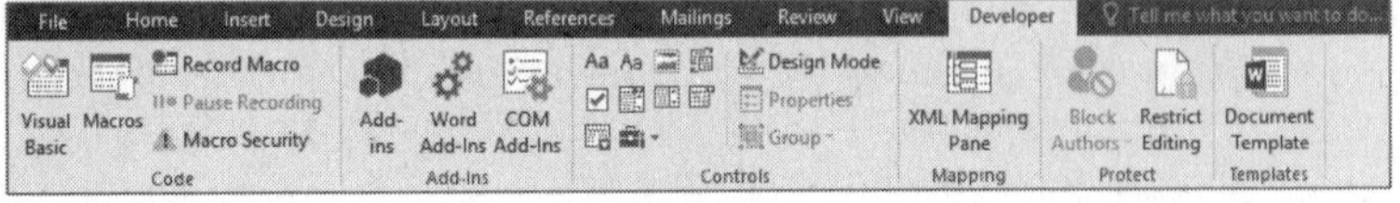

FIGURE 1.3 You can use the Developer tab on the Ribbon to work with macros.

Here's what the primary Visual Basic features on the Ribbon's Developer tab (or Access's Database Tools tab) do:

Run Macro button Only Access has this Ribbon button. It displays a Run Macro dialog box, in which you can choose the macro to execute (run). Many aspects of VBA in Access are unique only to Access, and Chapter 28, "Understanding the Access Object Model and Key Objects," covers them in depth.

Record Macro button Displays the Record Macro dialog box in Word or Excel.

Macro Security button Displays the Trust Center Macro Settings dialog. You'll examine this feature in detail in Chapter 19. This button allows you to specify whether and how you want macros enabled.

Visual Basic button Switches to the Visual Basic Editor. You'll begin working in the Visual Basic Editor in Chapter 2, "Getting Started with the Visual Basic Editor" (and you'll spend most of the rest of the book employing it).

Macros button Opens the classic Macros dialog from which you can run, step into (start the Visual Basic Editor in Break mode; more about this in Chapter 3, "Editing Recorded Macros"), edit, create, delete, or open the macro project organizer dialog. (Not all of these options are available in all applications. For example, PowerPoint has no organizer.) Word and Excel have a similar Macros button in the Ribbon's View tab. This button has the ability to open the Macros dialog but can also start recording a macro. Note that Break mode is also referred to as Step mode.

Add-Ins This is where you can access templates, styles, and specialized code libraries.

Controls A set of control buttons that, when clicked, insert user-interface components—such as a drop-down list box—into an open document. Similar components can also be added to macros that you create in the VBA Editor. Chapter 14, "Creating Simple Custom Dialog Boxes," and Chapter 15, "Creating Complex Forms," explore this user-interface topic.

Design Mode button Toggles between Design mode and Regular mode. When in Design mode, you can add or edit embedded controls in documents. In Regular mode, you can interact normally with controls (controls can accept information from the user via typing or mouse clicks).

Properties button This button is enabled only if you're in Design mode. It allows you to edit the properties of the document (such as removing personal information).

XML button This section of the Developer tab is explored in Chapters 21 through 24.

Restrict Editing button Allows you to specify what formatting or editing others are allowed to perform.

Document Template button Here you can see or modify the current template, or manage add-ins or the global template.

THE EMERGENCE OF XML

XML has become an industry standard for storing and transmitting data. With Office 2007, the Office applications' documents began to employ XML extensively. This switch to XML is the primary reason that documents created in versions of Office 2007, 2010, 2013, and 2016 are not compatible with earlier versions of Office, such as Office 2003 documents. Therefore, you must *convert* old Office documents to the newer Office formats. People still using older versions of Office must install the Microsoft Office Compatibility Pack for Word, Excel, and PowerPoint File Formats. Note that starting with Word 2010, document files are saved with a `.docx` filename extension, the `x` reflecting the underlying XML format on which Office now rests.

Naming the Macro

Next, enter a name for the new macro in the Macro Name text box in the Record Macro dialog box. The name must comply with the following conventions:

- It must start with a letter; after that, it can contain both letters and numbers.
- It can be up to 80 characters long.

- It can contain underscores, which are useful for separating words, such as `File_Save`.
- It cannot contain spaces, punctuation, or special characters, such as ! or *.

Name and Describe Your Macros

Some people insist that to properly manage your set of macros, you must follow some clerical procedures that involve giving your macros descriptive names and also typing in a narrative description of each macro's purpose. They claim that if you create many macros, you should organize them carefully. Recording macros is so easy; you can create code so quickly that you can end up with a *pile* of macros—as Southerners say—making it easy to get confused about which macro does what.

You may be tempted not to assign a macro description when you're in a hurry or when you're playing with different ways to approach a problem and you're not sure which (if any) of your test macros you'll keep.

For simple, obvious code, perhaps using the default names (such as Macro12, Macro13) and omitting a description isn't a problem. Also, if you find it easy to read and understand VBA code, you can usually just look at a macro and see what it does.

Even so, for more complex macros, and for people who find code hard to read—go ahead and enter a few notes for each macro that you record. Otherwise, you can end up with that pile of recorded macros that have the cryptic default names and no descriptions. To figure out what each macro does and which ones you no longer use and can safely delete, you'll have to plow through the code—and a recorded macro's code can be surprisingly long, even if the macro does nothing more than adjust a few options in a couple of dialog boxes.

You might also want to employ a macro-naming convention to indicate which macros are simply tests that you can delete without remorse. Start the name with a word like `Temp`, and then add numeric values sequentially to keep track of the versions—for example, `Scratch` (`Scratch01`, `Scratch02`, and so on) and `Temp` (`Temp01`, `Temp02`, and so on).

Each new macro you record is by default placed at the bottom of the set of macros in the VBA Editor. You can, however, always open the Visual Basic Editor and rename or add a description any time you want because macros are fully editable.

Personally, I like to put a little descriptive note inside more complicated macros' code, right at the top, under the `Sub` line. It looks like this:

```
Sub AltH()
' Applies Heading 1 style
    Selection.Style = ActiveDocument.Styles("Title1")
End Sub
```

Any text following a single-quote symbol `'` on a line of code is ignored by VBA. The single quote indicates that what follows is a *comment* to assist the programmer in understanding the code rather than actual code that VBA should try to execute. (VBA would not know what to make of the words `Applies Heading 1 style`. They are not part of VBA's vocabulary.)

Note that if you type a description in the Description field of the Record Macro dialog when you first start recording, that comment is automatically inserted into your code—complete with the single-quote symbol.

Also, my preferred way to name any macros that are triggered by keyboard shortcuts is to use the name of the keyboard shortcut itself. Therefore, `Sub AltH` tells me that this macro is triggered by the Alt+H keyboard shortcut.

But whatever system you adopt, it's generally better to err on the side of greater description or commenting within the code rather than too little. It only takes a moment to provide an expressive, meaningful name and a clear description of the purpose of the macro.

Invalid Macro Names

Word and Excel raise objections to invalid macro names. If you enter a prohibited macro name in the Record Macro dialog box, these applications let you know—in their own way—as soon as you click the OK button. Word displays a brief, rather cursory message, while Excel gives more helpful info. Figure 1.4 shows how these applications respond to an invalid macro name once it's entered.

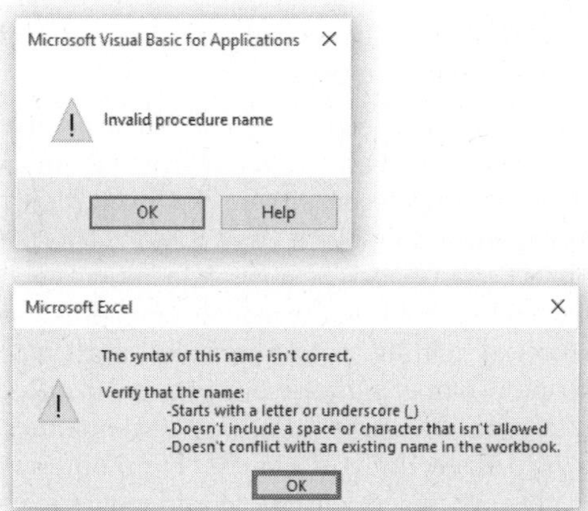

Figure 1.4 The dialog boxes supplied by Word and Excel show invalid macro names.

Describing Your Macros

Type a description for the macro in the Description text box. Recall that this description is to help you (and anyone you share the macro with) identify the macro and understand when to use it. If the macro runs successfully only under particular conditions, you can note them briefly in the Description text box. For example, if the user must make a selection in the document before running the macro in Word, mention that.

You now need to choose where to store the macro. Your choices with Word and Excel are as follows:

Word Recall that in Word, if you want to restrict availability of the macro to just the current template (`.dotm` file) or document (`.docm` file), choose that template or document from the Store Macro In drop-down list in the Record Macro dialog box shown in Figure 1.2. If you want the macro to be available no matter which template you're working in, make sure the default setting—All Documents (`Normal.dotm`)—appears in the Store Macro In combo box. (If you're not clear on what Word's templates are and what they do, see the sidebar "Understanding Word's `Normal.dotm`, Templates, and Documents" later in this chapter).

Excel In Excel, you can choose to store the macro in This Workbook (the active workbook), a new workbook, or Personal Macro Workbook. The Personal Macro Workbook is a special workbook named `Personal.xlsb`. Excel creates this Personal Macro Workbook the first time you choose to store a macro in the Personal Macro Workbook. By keeping your macros and other customizations in the Personal Macro Workbook, you can make them available to any of your procedures. Recall that the Personal Macro Workbook is similar to Word's global macros storage file named `Normal.dotm`. If you choose New Workbook, Excel creates a new workbook for you and creates the macro in it.

Storing Your Macros

Word and Excel automatically store recorded macros in a default location in the specified document, template, workbook, or presentation:

Word Word stores each recorded macro in a *module* named `NewMacros` in the selected template or document, so you'll always know where to find a macro after you've recorded it. This can be a bit confusing because there can be multiple NewMacros folders visible in the Project Explorer pane in the Visual Basic Editor. (This happens because there can be more than one project open—such as several documents open simultaneously, each with its own NewMacros folder holding the macros embedded within each document.) Think of NewMacros as merely a holding area for macros—until you move them to another module with a more descriptive name. (Of course, if you create only a handful of macros, you don't need to go to the trouble of creating various special modules to subdivide them into categories. You can just leave everything in a `NewMacros` module. As always, how clerical you need to be depends on how organized your mind and memory are—and also on the size of the collection with which you're dealing.)

If a `NewMacros` module doesn't yet exist, the Macro Recorder creates it. Because it receives each macro recorded into its document or template, a `NewMacros` module can soon grow large if you record many macros. The `NewMacros` module in the default global template, `Normal.dotm`, is especially likely to grow bloated, because it receives each macro you record unless you specify another document or template prior to recording. Some people like to clear out the `NewMacros` module from time to time, putting recorded macros they want to keep into other modules and disposing of any useless or temp recorded macros. I don't have *that* many macros, so I find no problem simply leaving them within the `NewMacros` module.

Excel Excel stores each recorded macro for any given session in a new module named `Module` *n*, where *n* is the lowest unused number in ascending sequence (`Module1`, `Module2`, and so on). Any macros you create in the next session go into a new module with the next available number. If you record macros frequently with Excel, you'll most likely need to consolidate (copy and paste) the macros you want to keep so that they're not scattered across many modules.

Understanding Word's *Normal.dotm*, Templates, and Documents

Word since version 2007 stores data differently than earlier versions of Word. For one thing, in Word 2003 you could create custom menus and toolbars that you stored in templates. Later versions of Word do not permit menus, nor do they permit any toolbars other than the Quick Access Toolbar. What's more, customizing that toolbar has a *global* impact. In other words, any modifications you make to the Quick Access Toolbar will be visible in all Word documents, no matter which template(s) is currently active.

The versions of Word since 2007 feature three kinds of templates:

- Legacy templates from Word 2003 and earlier versions. These have a `.dot` filename extension. If you are working with one of these templates, the phrase (Compatibility Mode) appears on the Word title bar.
- Templates that contain no macros use a `.dotx` filename extension. You can save macros in a document that employs a `.dotx` template, but the macro will not be saved within the template. This type of template made its first appearance with Word 2010.
- Templates with a `.dotm` filename extension contain macros. Recall that because macros written by malicious people can do damage just like a virus can, Word segregates macros into this special kind of template with a `.dotm` filename extension. A `.dotm` template can do anything that a `.dotx` template can do, but the `.dotm` template features the additional capability of hosting macros.

Word has a four-layer architecture. Starting from the bottom, these layers are the application itself, the global template (`Normal.dotm`), the active document's template, and finally, the active document itself (the text and formatting). Each of the four layers can affect how Word appears and how it behaves, but all four layers are not necessarily active at any given time.

The bottom layer, which is always active, is the Word application itself. This layer contains all the Word objects and built-in commands, such as Open. Also always active are objects such as Word's Quick Access Toolbar, the Ribbon, and so on. This layer is the most difficult to picture because usually you don't see it directly. `Normal.dotm`, the global template, forms the second layer and is also always active.

When you start Word, it loads `Normal.dotm` automatically, and `Normal.dotm` stays loaded until you exit Word. (There's a special switch you can use—`winword /n`—to prevent the macros in `Normal.dotm` from being active if you need to troubleshoot it. Press the Start key [the Windows key] in Windows 8 and 10 [the Start key in earlier versions of Windows], and then type **Run** to launch Word in this special way.)

`Normal.dotm` contains styles (such as the default paragraph style), AutoText entries, formatted AutoCorrect entries, and customizations. These customizations also show up in the other layers unless specifically excluded.

Continues

Continued

Default new blank documents (such as the document that Word normally creates when you start it and any document you create by clicking Ctrl+N or by clicking the Ribbon's File tab and then choosing New and Blank Document) are based on `Normal.dotm`. When you're working in a default blank document, you see the Word interface as it is specified in `Normal.dotm`.

The currently active template sits on top of the Word application and `Normal.dotm`. This template can contain styles, macro modules (if it is a macro-enabled `.dotm` file type), and settings for the template, along with any boilerplate text needed for this particular type of document. This is the third layer, but it is used only if the current document (or *active document*) is attached to a template other than `Normal.dotm`.

On top of the current template sits the current document, which contains the text and graphics in the document, its formatting, and its layout. Documents can also contain macro modules specific to it, along with custom keyboard shortcuts, so the document itself can act as a fourth layer. This layer is always present when a document is open, but it has no effect on Word's interface or behavior unless the document contains its own, local customizations.

Because these layers might contain conflicting information (such as two different font styles with the same name), there has to be an order of precedence to specify which layer "wins" in any such conflict. Customized settings work from the top layer downward, so customized settings in the active document take precedence over those in the active template. Likewise, any settings in the active template take precedence over any global templates (templates that automatically apply to all Word documents) or add-ins other than `Normal.dotm`. Customized settings in those global templates or add-ins take precedence over those in `Normal.dotm`.

As another example, say you have the key combination Ctrl+Shift+K assigned to different actions in `Normal.dotm`, in a loaded global template, in a document's template, and in the document itself. When you press that key combination, only the procedure assigned in the document runs because that is the topmost layer. If you remove the key-combination assignment from the document, the template then becomes the topmost layer containing a definition of this key combination, so the procedure assigned in the template runs. If you remove the key combination from the template as well, the procedure in the loaded global template runs. Finally, if you remove that template's key combination too, the procedure in `Normal.dotm` runs. It is the lowest layer.

Choosing How to Run a New Macro

Continuing our exploration of the Record Macro dialog box shown in Figure 1.2, at this point, after you've named the macro, typed a description, and chosen where to store it, it's time to choose how to trigger the macro. In other words, how do you want the user to *run* the macro: via a shortcut key or via a Quick Access Toolbar button? Good typists generally prefer shortcut keys (they don't have to take their hand off the keyboard to reach for the mouse), but buttons provide at least a visual hint of the macro's purpose, plus hovering your mouse on the button also displays the name of the macro.

Shortcut keys and buttons are handy for people who record a moderate number of macros and don't organize them in complex ways—moving them from one module to another. If you create a great number of macros and feel the need to move them into other modules, assigning a shortcut key or button prior to recording becomes less useful. This is because moving a macro from one module to another disconnects any way you've assigned for running the macro.

This limitation means that it makes sense to assign a way of running a macro—prior to recording—only if you're planning to use the macro in its recorded form (as opposed to, say, using part of it to create another macro) *and* from its module location. If you plan to move the macro or rename it, don't assign a way of running it now. Instead, wait until the macro is in its final form and location, and then assign the means of running it. See "Specifying How to Trigger an Existing Macro," later in this chapter, for details on how to do this.

Personally, I don't have more than a few dozen macros that I use all the time, so I avoid the complications described in the previous paragraph and this chapter's sidebar titled "Manage Your Macros with Modules." Instead, I just add shortcut keys when I first create the macro and leave them all in a single version of `Normal.dotm` template. However, if you face more complicated situations—such as managing a big set of macros for a company—you might want to manage your macros with modules.

MANAGE YOUR MACROS WITH MODULES

By moving your recorded macros into different modules, you can group related macros thereby making it easier to compare the code, edit them, and distribute them.

To assign a way to run the macro, follow the instructions in the next sections.

Remember that you don't have to assign a button or keyboard shortcut prior to recording a macro. You can do it later, or at any time. In Word and Excel, you can use File ➢ Options ➢ Quick Access Toolbar dialog box to assign a button on the Quick Access Toolbar to a macro. You can also use File ➢ Options ➢ Customize Ribbon dialog box to assign a shortcut key to a macro (click the Customize button at the bottom of this dialog box).

Excel limits you to Ctrl+ or Ctrl+Shift key combinations. PowerPoint and Access do not permit you to assign keyboard shortcuts to macros.

RUNNING A MACRO FROM THE RIBBON

Although it's not available in the Record Macro dialog box, you can add a macro to the Ribbon, like this:

1. Right-click anywhere on the Ribbon.
2. Click Customize The Ribbon on the menu. The Word Options dialog box appears.
3. In the Choose Commands From drop-down list, select Macros.
4. Click a macro's name to select it in the list.
5. Click an existing tab in the list of tabs in the right dialog box where you want to locate your macro.
6. Then click the New Group button and specify the name of your custom group.
7. Click the Rename button to give your new group a name.
8. Click OK to close the Rename dialog box.

9. Click the Add button to add your macro.
10. Click the Rename button to give your macro an easily understood name and optionally an icon.
11. Click OK to close the Rename dialog box.
12. Click OK to close the Word Options dialog box.

Running a Macro from the Quick Access Toolbar

Here's how to use the Word Options dialog box to assign a macro to a button on the Quick Access Toolbar:

1. Right-click anywhere on the Quick Access Toolbar (it's the set of icons in the upper-left corner, normally above the Ribbon), and a menu will appear. (This toolbar will be just below the Ribbon if you've previously selected the Show Quick Access Toolbar Below The Ribbon option from this menu.)
2. Click Customize Quick Access Toolbar on the menu. The Word Options dialog box appears.
3. In the Choose Commands From drop-down list, select Macros.
4. Click a macro's name to select it in the list, as shown in Figure 1.5.

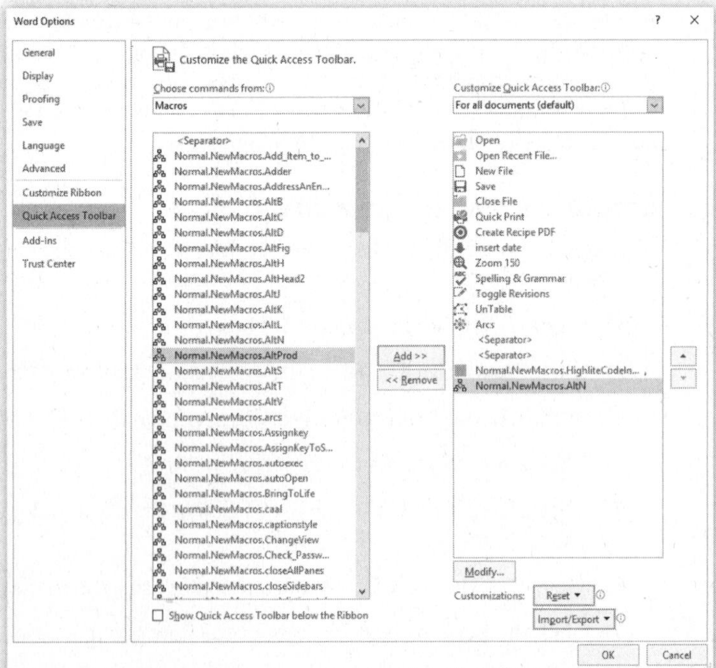

Figure 1.5 Choose a way to run the macro in Word's Options dialog box.

5. Click the Add button to insert this macro's name in the Customize Quick Access Toolbar list, as shown in Figure 1.5.
6. Word adds a button to the toolbar for the macro, giving it the macro's fully qualified name (its location plus its name), such as `Normal.NewMacros.CreateDailyReport`. This name consists of the name of the template or document in which the macro is stored, the name of the module that contains the macro, and the macro's name, respectively. You don't need all this information displayed when you hover your mouse pointer over the button.
7. So rename the button or menu item: Click the Modify button at the bottom of the Customize Quick Access Toolbar list (see Figure 1.5). Whatever macro is highlighted (currently selected) in the list of toolbar items will be the one you're modifying.

Macro Button Labels Need Not Match Their Macros' Official Names

Notice that a macro's button name (displayed as its tooltip caption when you hover your mouse over it) doesn't have to bear any relation to the macro's actual name as it appears in the Visual Basic Editor or the Macro dialog.

8. While you're modifying the macro's name, you might also want to choose a button icon that visually cues you about the macro's purpose. To do that, just double-click whatever icon you want to use, and then click OK (see Figure 1.6).

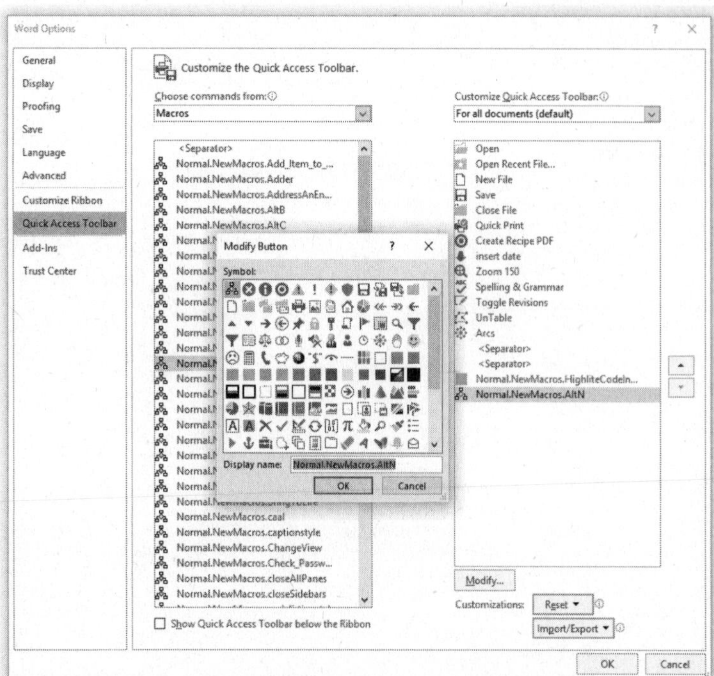

Figure 1.6 Word gives the menu item or toolbar button the full name of the macro. Use this Modify Button dialog to change the name to something shorter and better.

Running a Macro via a Shortcut Key Combination

To assign the macro to a key combination, follow these steps:

1. Right-click the Ribbon and choose Customize The Ribbon from the menu that appears. This opens the Word Options dialog.
2. Click the Customize button next to Keyboard Shortcuts in the bottom left of the Word Options dialog box.
3. Scroll down the Categories list box until you see Macros, and then click Macros to select it.
4. Click to select the name of the macro to which you want to assign a shortcut key combination.
5. Check the Current Keys list box to see if a key combination is already assigned. If it is, you can press the Backspace key to clear the key combination if you want, or you can employ multiple key combinations to launch the macro.
6. In the Press New Shortcut Key field, type the key combination you want to use to trigger the macro (see Figure 1.7).
7. Check to see if this key combination is already used for another purpose. If so, you can reassign it, or you can choose a different combination by pressing the Backspace key in the Press New Shortcut Key field.
8. Be sure to click the Assign button when you're finished. Just closing this dialog does *not* assign the key combination.

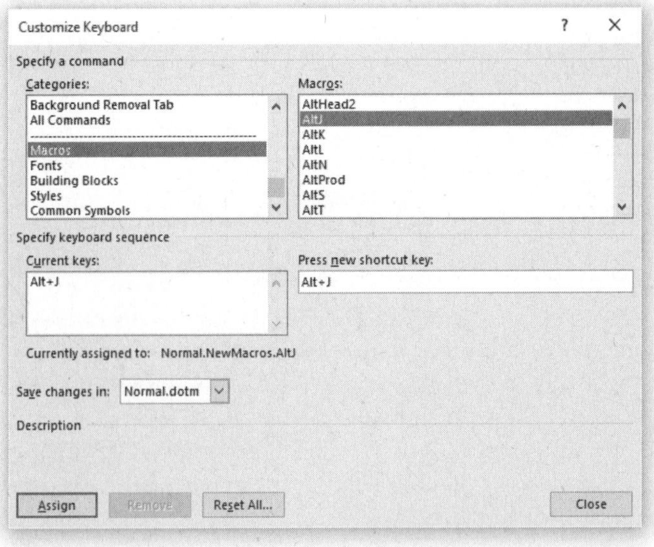

Figure 1.7
Set a shortcut key combination for the macro in the Customize Keyboard dialog box.

Customize Keyboard ? ×

Specify a command

Categories: Background Removal Tab, All Commands, Macros, Fonts, Building Blocks, Styles, Common Symbols

Macros: AltHead2, AltJ, AltK, AltL, AltN, AltProd, AltS, AltT

Specify keyboard sequence

Current keys: Alt+J

Press new shortcut key: Alt+J

Currently assigned to: Normal.NewMacros.AltJ

Save changes in: Normal.dotm

Description

Assign Remove Reset All... Close

YOU CAN POSTPONE ASSIGNING A SHORTCUT KEY COMBINATION

Remember that, as with the other ways of running a macro, you can assign a key combination to run a macro either at the time you record the macro or at any point after you finish recording it. If you intend to move the macro from the `NewMacros` module to another module, remember that you need not assign the key combination until the macro has reached its ultimate destination.

A key combination in Word can be any of the following:

- Alt plus either a function key or a regular key not used as a menu-access key.
- Ctrl plus a function key or a regular key.
- Shift plus a function key.
- Ctrl+Alt, Ctrl+Shift, Alt+Shift, or even Ctrl+Alt+Shift plus a regular key or function key. Pressing Ctrl+Alt+Shift and another key tends to be too awkward for practical use.

SPECIFY TWO-STEP KEY COMBINATIONS

You can set up shortcut keys that have two steps—for example, Ctrl+Alt+F, 1 and Ctrl+Alt+F, 2—by pressing the second key (in this case, the 1 or the 2) after pressing the key combination. However, these shortcuts are probably more trouble than they're worth.

RUNNING A MACRO THE OLD-FASHIONED WAY

A clumsy, rarely used way to run a macro is to click the Developer tab in the Ribbon. To see how this works, follow these steps:

1. Click the Macros icon.
2. Click the name of the macro in a displayed list.
3. Finally, click the Run button.

By the way, you can also run a macro from within the Visual Basic Editor by pressing F5. This is how you test macros while you're editing them. The macro in which the insertion cursor is located (the blinking vertical line) is the one that will execute when you press F5 in the Editor.

ASSIGNING A WAY TO RUN A MACRO IN EXCEL

When you're recording a macro, Excel allows you to assign only a Ctrl shortcut key, not a button, to run it. If you want to assign a Quick Access Toolbar button to the macro, you need to do so *after* recording the macro (using the Customize feature as described shortly).

To assign a Ctrl shortcut key to run the macro you're recording, follow these steps:

1. Start recording the macro to display the Record Macro dialog box, and then click the Shortcut Key Ctrl+text box to display the blinking insertion cursor. Press the shortcut key you want to use. (Press the Shift key at the same time if you want to include Shift in the shortcut.)
2. In the Store Macro In drop-down list, specify where you want the Macro Recorder to store the macro. Your choices are as follows:
    - *This Workbook* stores the macro in the active workbook. This option is useful for macros that belong to a particular workbook and do not need to be used elsewhere.
    - *New Workbook* causes Excel to create a new workbook for you and store the macro in it. This option is useful for experimental macros that you'll need to edit before unleashing them on actual work.
    - *Personal Macro Workbook* stores the macro in the Personal Macro Workbook, a special workbook named `PERSONAL.XLSB`. By keeping your macros and other customizations in the Personal Macro Workbook, you can make them available to any of your procedures—in that way, the Personal Macro Workbook is similar to Word's `Normal.dotm`. If the Personal Macro Workbook does not exist yet, the Macro Recorder creates it automatically.
3. Click the OK button to start recording the macro.

Assigning a Way to Run a Macro in PowerPoint

PowerPoint does not let you record macros, but you can assign a way to run macros written in the Visual Basic Editor, as discussed in the section "Specifying How to Trigger an Existing Macro" later in this chapter.

Assigning a Way to Run a Macro in Outlook

Outlook doesn't let you record macros, and by default macros are disabled. To enable macros in Outlook, click the Developer tab on the Ribbon, and then click the Macro Security icon (it's on the left in the Code section of the Ribbon). The Trust Center dialog box opens. Click the Notification For All Macros option or the Enable All Macros option. To see how to assign a way to run macros, see the section "Specifying How to Trigger an Existing Macro" later in this chapter.

Recording the Actions in a Macro

When you close the Record Macro dialog box in Word or Excel, the Macro Recorder begins recording the macro. The Macro Recorder displays the Stop Recording icon (a dark gray square) in the status bar at the bottom left of the screen (and a Stop Recording button in the Developer tab on the Ribbon). In addition, Word displays a small symbol of a cassette tape with the mouse pointer (these tapes were used in the old days, prior to the invention of the CD).

Now you perform the sequence of actions you want to record. What exactly you can do varies from application to application, but in general, you can use the mouse to select items, make choices in dialog boxes, and select defined items in documents (such as cells in spreadsheets). You'll find a number of things that you can't do with the mouse, such as select items within a document window in Word. To select items in a Word document window, you have to use the keyboard (Shift+arrow keys, for example).

> **THE MACRO RECORDER RECORDS EVERYTHING—THE COMPLETE CURRENT STATUS**
>
> When you make choices in a dialog box and click the OK button, the Macro Recorder records the current settings for all the options on that page of the dialog box. So, for example, when you change the left indentation of a paragraph in the Paragraph dialog box in Word, the Macro Recorder records *all the other settings* on the Indents And Spacing page as well (Alignment, Before and After spacing, and so forth).

In Word, if you need to perform any actions that you don't want recorded, pause the Macro Recorder by clicking the Pause Recording button on the Ribbon. The button changes to Resume Recording. Click the button again to start recording again.

To stop recording, click either the Stop Recording button on the Ribbon or the other one on the status bar.

The Macro Recorder has now recorded your macro and optionally assigned it to a key combination or button.

Running a Macro

To run a macro you've recorded, you can use four methods to run it within the application:

- If you assigned a Quick Access Toolbar button, use that.
- If you added your macro to the Ribbon, you can use that.
- If you specified a shortcut-key-combination macro, use it.
- A less convenient approach is to press Alt+F8 to display the Macros dialog box, select the macro, and then click the Run button. (Alternatively, you could double-click the macro name in the list box.)

> **RUNNING IN THE EDITOR**
>
> You can also run a macro from the Visual Basic Editor, which is useful when you're working in the Editor. Just press F5.

The macro runs, performing the actions in the sequence in which you recorded them. For example, suppose you create a macro in Excel that selects cell A2 in the current worksheet, boldfaces that cell, enters the text **Yearly Sales**, selects cell B2, and enters the number **100000** in it. The Macro Recorder recognizes and saves those five actions. VBA then performs all five actions, step-by-step, each time you run the macro—albeit quite rapidly.

HOW TO STOP AN EXECUTING MACRO

To stop a running macro, press Ctrl+Break (Break is usually the unshifted Pause key on the keyboard). VBA stops running the code and displays a dialog box telling you that code execution has been interrupted. Click the End button to dismiss this dialog box.

Some applications (such as Word) let you undo most actions executed via VBA after the macro stops running (by pressing Ctrl+Z or clicking the Undo button on the Quick Access Toolbar, undoing one command at a time); other applications do not.

MACRO ERRORS ARE OFTEN CAUSED BY INCORRECT CONTEXTS

If running the macro results in an error, often this means that the macro is trying to do something to a file or an object that isn't available. For example, if you record a macro in Excel that works on the active workbook, the macro causes an error if you run it when no workbook is open (therefore, there is no such thing as an active workbook). Likewise, if you write a macro in PowerPoint that works with the third shape on the active slide, that macro fails if you run it on a slide that has no third shape. To get the macro to run properly, re-create the conditions it needs and then try it again.

Recording a Sample Word Macro

In this section, you'll record a sample macro in Word. This macro selects the current word, cuts it, moves the insertion point one word to the right, and pastes the word back in. This is a straightforward sequence of actions that you'll work with later in the book, and view and edit in the Visual Basic Editor.

Follow these steps to record the macro:

1. Create a new document by pressing Ctrl+N.
2. Start the Macro Recorder by clicking the Developer tab on the Ribbon, and then clicking the Record Macro button. Alternatively you could click the Macro Record button on the status bar at the bottom of the application. (With this approach, you don't have to open the Developer tab. Just click the button on the status bar.)
3. In the Macro Name text box, enter **`Transpose_Word_Right`**.

4. In the Store Macro In drop-down list, make sure All Documents (`Normal.dotm`) is selected, unless you want to assign the macro to a different template. (This and future examples in this book assume this macro is located in `Normal.dotm`, so do store it there.)

5. In the Description box, enter a description for the macro (see Figure 1.8). Be fairly explicit and enter a description such as **Transposes the current word with the word to its right. Created 9/14/15 by Toro Selest-Gomes**.

FIGURE 1.8
Creating the sample macro in Word

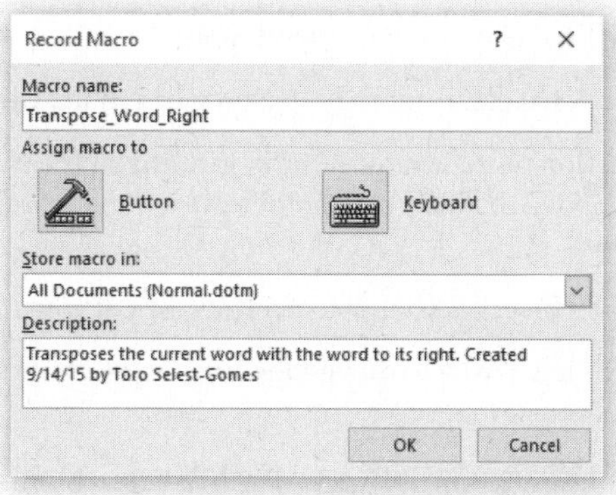

6. Assign a method of running the macro, as described in the previous section, if you like. Create a toolbar button or assign a keyboard shortcut. (The method or methods you choose is strictly a matter of personal preference.) If you'll need to move the macro to a different module (or a different template or document) later, don't assign a method of running the macro at this point.

7. Click the OK button to dismiss the Word Options dialog box or the Customize Keyboard dialog box (or just click the OK button to dismiss the Record Macro dialog box if you chose not to assign a way of running the macro). Now you're ready to record the macro. The Stop Recording option appears on the Ribbon and on the status bar, and the mouse pointer has a cassette-tape icon attached to it.

8. As a quick demonstration of how you can pause recording, click the Pause Recording button on the Ribbon. The cassette-tape icon disappears from the mouse pointer, and the

Pause Recording button changes into a Resume Recording button. Enter a line of text in the document: **The quick brown fox jumped over the lazy dog.** Position the insertion point anywhere in the word *quick*, and then click the Resume Recording button on the Ribbon to reactivate the macro recorder.

9. Record the actions for the macro as follows:
   a. Use Word's extend selection feature to select the word *quick* by pressing the F8 key twice.
   b. Press the Esc key to cancel Extend mode.
   c. Press Shift+Delete to cut the selected word to the Clipboard.
   d. The insertion point is now at the beginning of the word *brown*. Press Ctrl+right arrow to move the insertion point right by one word so that it's at the beginning of the word *dog*.
   e. Press Shift+Insert or Ctrl+V to paste in the cut word from the Clipboard.
   f. Press Ctrl+left arrow to move the insertion point one word to the left. This restores the cursor to its original position.
10. Click the Stop Recording button on the Ribbon or status bar. Your sentence now reads, "The brown quick fox jumped over the lazy dog."

Finding Built-In Keyboard Shortcuts

You can find a complete list of the built-in keyboard shortcuts (such as Ctrl+left arrow) by searching an application's Help system for "Keyboard Shortcuts." (In Office 2016 you can just use the Tell Me What You Want To Do feature on the Ribbon.)

You can now run this macro by using the toolbar button or keyboard shortcut that you assigned (if you chose to assign one). Alternatively, click the Macros button in the Developer tab and run the macro from the Macros dialog box.

At this point, Word has stored the macro in `Normal.dot`. If you don't save macros until you exit Word (or until an automated backup takes place), Word doesn't, by default, prompt you to save them then. It just saves them automatically. But it's best to click the Save button in the File tab to store Normal now. That way, if Word or Windows crashes, you will avoid losing the macro.

You Can Force Word to Prompt You to Save the Normal Template

Word, by default, automatically saves new macros added to the Normal template. But if you prefer to have Word prompt you to save any changes to the Normal template, choose Options on the File tab, click the Advanced button, and then scroll down until you see the section of Save options. Select the Prompt Before Saving Normal Template check box, and then click the OK button.

Recording a Sample Excel Macro

In the following sections, you'll record a sample Excel macro. This macro creates a new workbook, enters a sequence of months into it, and then saves it. You'll work with this macro again in Chapter 3, so don't delete it.

Creating a Personal Macro Workbook

If you don't already have a Personal Macro Workbook in Excel, you'll need to create one before creating this procedure. (If you do have a Personal Macro Workbook, skip to the next section.) Follow these steps:

1. Click the Developer tab in the Ribbon, and then click the Record Macro button on the Ribbon (or just click the Record Macro button on the status bar) to display the Record Macro dialog box.
2. Accept the default name for the macro because you'll be deleting it momentarily.
3. In the Store Macro In drop-down list, choose Personal Macro Workbook.
4. Click the OK button to close the Record Macro dialog box and start recording the macro.
5. Type a single character in whichever cell is active, and press the Enter key.
6. Click the Stop Recording button on the Ribbon or status bar to stop recording the macro.
7. Click the Unhide button on the View tab to display the Unhide dialog box. Select `PERSONAL.XLSB` and click the OK button.
8. Click the Developer tab in the Ribbon, and then click the Macros button on the Ribbon to display the Macros dialog box.
9. Select the macro you recorded and click the Delete button to delete it. Click the Yes button in the confirmation message box.

You now have caused Excel to generate a Personal Macro Workbook that you can use from now on to hold your global macros.

Recording the Macro

To record this macro, start Excel and follow these steps:

1. Create a new workbook by choosing File ➢ New ➢ Blank Workbook.
2. Click the Developer tab in the Ribbon, and then click the Record Macro button on the Ribbon (or just click the Record Macro button on the status bar). This displays the Record Macro dialog box, shown in Figure 1.9, with information entered.
3. Enter the name for the macro in the Macro Name text box: **`Add_Months`**.
4. In the Shortcut Key text box, enter a shortcut key if you like. (Remember that you can always change the shortcut key later, so you're not forced to enter one at this point.)

5. In the Store Macro In drop-down list, choose whether to store the macro in your Personal Macro Workbook, in a new workbook, or in this active workbook. As discussed a little earlier in this chapter, storing the macro in the Personal Macro Workbook gives you the most flexibility because it is Excel's global macro container. For this example, don't store the macro in the active workbook. Instead, store it in your Personal Macro Workbook. Remember, we'll use this macro in future examples.

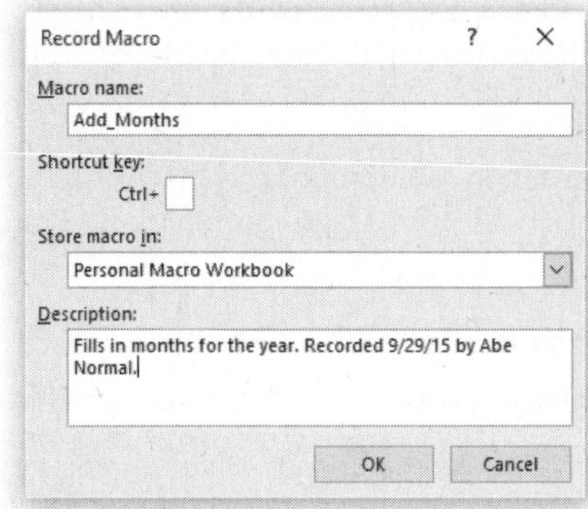

FIGURE 1.9
Display the Record Macro dialog box for Excel and make your choices in it.

6. Type a description for the macro in the Description text box.
7. Click the OK button to dismiss the Record Macro dialog box and start recording the macro. When Excel starts running, it sometimes randomly doesn't open the Personal Macro Workbook. So if you see an error message telling you that your "Personal Macro Workbook in the startup folder must stay open for recording," you'll need to open it by hand. Close the Record Macro dialog box. Choose File ➤ Options ➤ Trust Center. Click the Trust Center Settings button. Click Trusted Locations in the left pane. Click to select Excel Default Location: User Startup, and then look down to where it says Path and you'll find the location you want on the hard drive. It should resemble this: `C:\Users\Yourname\AppData\Roaming\Microsoft\Excel\XLSTART`. Use File Explorer to find this path, and then double-click the `PERSONAL.XLSB` file to open it.
8. Click cell A1 to select it. (It may already be selected; click it anyway because you need to record this click instruction.)
9. Enter **January 2016** and press the right-arrow key to select cell B1. Excel automatically changes the date to your default date format. That's fine.
10. Enter **February 2016** and press the left-arrow key to select cell A1 again.
11. Drag from cell A1 to cell B1 so that the two cells are selected.
12. Drag the fill handle from cell B1 to cell L1 so that Excel's AutoFill feature enters the months March 2016 through December 2016 in the cells. (The fill handle is the small black dot in the lower-right corner of the selection frame. You'll know you're on it when the cursor changes from a white to a black cross.)
13. Click the Stop Recording button on the Ribbon or status bar to stop recording the macro.

Now test the new macro. Create a new workbook by choosing File ➤ New ➤ Blank Workbook. On the Developer tab, click the Macros button to open the Macro dialog box. Double-click `PERSONAL.XLSB!Add_Months`. You should see the months filled into the new workbook. You can delete the two workbooks you created in this session. They're no longer needed. Just click the X in the upper-right corner to close them, and then choose Don't Save. But *do* save the `PERSONAL.XLST` workbook.

Specifying How to Trigger an Existing Macro

If you didn't assign a way of running the macro when you recorded it, you can do that now as described here.

Assigning a Macro to a Quick Access Toolbar Button in Word

To assign a macro to the Quick Access Toolbar, follow these steps:

1. Right-click anywhere on the Quick Access Toolbar (it's the set of icons in the upper-left corner, above the Ribbon). A menu appears.
2. Click Customize Quick Access Toolbar on the menu. The Word Options dialog box appears.
3. In the Choose Commands From drop-down list, select Macros.
4. Click the name of the macro to which you want to assign a button.
5. Click the Add button to copy the macro name into the list of buttons on the right.
6. Click the Modify button if you want to assign a different icon or modify the button's name.
7. Click OK to close the dialog.

Assigning a Macro to a Shortcut Key Combination

The section "Running a Macro via a Shortcut Key Combination," earlier in this chapter, explained how to do this in Word. PowerPoint and Access do not let you assign a macro to a key combination. Excel uses a slightly different approach than Word, limiting you to Ctrl and Shift combinations, as described earlier in this chapter in the section "Assigning a Way to Run a Macro in Excel."

Deleting a Macro

To delete a macro you no longer need, follow these steps:

1. Press Alt+F8 to display the Macros dialog box.
2. Choose the macro in the Macro Name list box.
3. Click the Delete button.
4. In the warning message box that appears, click the Yes button.
5. Click the Close button or the Cancel button to close the Macros dialog box.

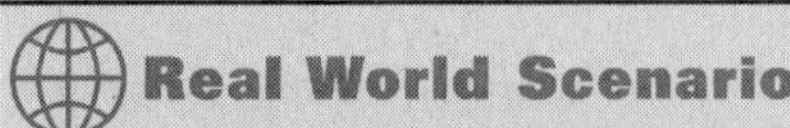

Organizing Macros in Word with the Organizer Dialog Box

Most VBA-enabled applications require you to use the Visual Basic Editor (which is discussed in the next chapter) to move code modules, user forms, and other code items from one file to another file. (A *code module* is a virtual container used for storing macros. A *user form* is a custom dialog box displayed to the user for input.) Word provides a useful tool called the Organizer dialog box that you can use to copy, move, rename, and delete code modules, user forms, and other code items directly in the Word interface without opening the Visual Basic Editor.

To use the Organizer dialog box, follow these steps:

1. In Word, press Alt+F8.
2. Click the Organizer button to display the Organizer dialog box, and click the Macro Project Items tab if the Macro Project Items page (shown here) isn't automatically displayed.

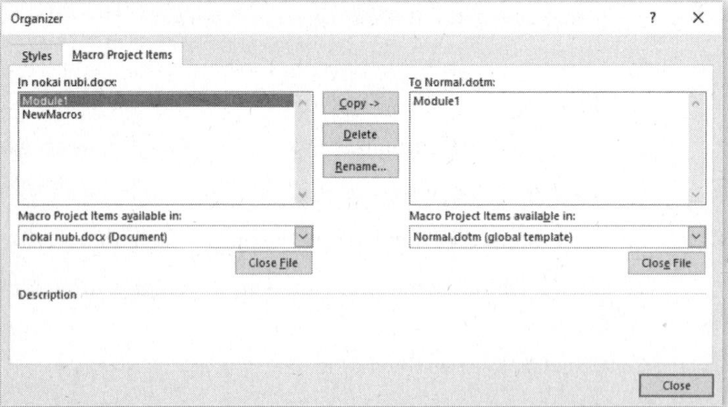

3. Look at the two documents or templates listed in the readouts above the two list boxes. Usually, the left list box shows the active document, and the right one shows `Normal.dotm`. Change these so that one list box shows the document or template that contains the code you want to copy or move and the other list box shows the destination document or template. (If you want only to delete or rename code items, you need only make the Organizer dialog box list the document or template that contains the items.) To change the document or template listed, click the Close File button underneath the list box on the corresponding side. The Close File button changes to an Open File button. Click this button to display the Open dialog box, navigate to and select the document or template you want, and then click the Open button. The Open dialog will automatically default to displaying the Templates folder.

4. You can then delete, rename, copy, and move macro project items. The following list details how to do this:
   - To delete one or more macro project items from a template, choose the item or items from either panel of the Organizer dialog box and click the Delete button. Click the Yes button in the confirmation message box. Any copies of the items in other templates are unaffected.
   - To rename a macro project item, select it from either panel and click the Rename button to open the Rename dialog box. Enter the new name and click the OK button. Any copies of the same item in other templates are unaffected.
   - To copy one or more macro project items from one template to another, open the templates in the Organizer dialog box. Select the item or items to copy in either panel of the dialog box (the arrows on the Copy button change direction to point to the other panel). Then click the Copy button. If the recipient template contains a macro project item of the same name as one you're copying, Word displays a warning message box telling you that it can't copy the item. If you still want to copy the item, rename either the item you're copying or the item with the same name in the destination template, and then perform the copy operation.
   - To move a macro project item from one template to another, copy it as described in the previous paragraph, and then delete the macro project item from the source template.
5. Once you've deleted, renamed, copied, or moved macro project items, click the Close button to close the Organizer dialog box. If Word prompts you to save any changes to affected documents or templates that aren't open in your Word session, click the Yes button.

The Bottom Line

Record a macro. The easiest way to create a macro is to simply record it. Whatever you type or click—all your behaviors—are translated into VBA automatically and saved as a macro.

Master It Turn on the macro recorder in Word and create a macro that moves the insertion cursor up three lines. Then turn off the macro recorder and test the new macro.

Assign a macro to a button or keyboard shortcut. You can trigger a macro using three convenient methods: clicking an entry on the Ribbon, clicking a button in the Quick Access Toolbar, or using a keyboard shortcut. You are responsible for assigning a macro to any or all of these methods.

Master It Assign an existing macro to a new Quick Access Toolbar button.

Run a macro. Macros are most efficiently triggered via a Ribbon entry, by clicking a button on the Quick Access Toolbar, or by pressing a shortcut key combination such as Alt+N or Ctrl+Alt+F. When you begin recording a macro, the Record Macro dialog has buttons that allow you to assign the new macro to a shortcut key or toolbar button. However, if you are using the Visual Basic Editor, you can run a macro by simply pressing F5.

Master It Execute a macro from within the Visual Basic Editor.

Delete a macro. It's useful to keep your collection of macros current and manageable. If you no longer need a macro, remove it. Macros can be directly deleted from the Visual Basic Editor or by clicking the Delete button in the Macros dialog (opened by pressing Alt+F8).

Master It Temporarily remove a macro, and then restore it using the Visual Basic Editor.

Chapter 2

Getting Started with the Visual Basic Editor

In this chapter, you'll start learning how to use the Visual Basic Editor, a powerful tool bundled with Office 2016 for working with VBA. This programming editor is the culmination of more than 20 years of modifications and improvements. It is highly effective.

All applications that host VBA use the Visual Basic Editor, so the interface and the Editor's tools are much the same no matter which application you're using.

This chapter covers the fundamentals of the Visual Basic Editor: its components, what they do, and how you use them. You'll learn more advanced maneuvers as you work with VBA throughout this book.

This chapter also shows you how to customize the Visual Basic Editor to make it more comfortable and more in tune with your preferences. This customization doesn't take long, and you'll find the resulting ease of use more than worth the time invested.

IN THIS CHAPTER, YOU WILL LEARN TO DO THE FOLLOWING:

- Open the Visual Basic Editor
- Open a macro in the Visual Basic Editor
- Understand the Visual Basic Editor's main windows
- Set properties for a project
- Customize the Visual Basic Editor

Opening the Visual Basic Editor

You open the Visual Basic Editor from within the host application you're using. For example, if you're working in Word, you open the Visual Basic Editor from inside Word. The instance of the Visual Basic Editor that you open is then associated with Word.

However, you can open more instances of the Visual Basic Editor. For example, if you've already opened an instance of the Visual Basic Editor in Word, you could open another instance in Excel and then another in Access.

You can open the Visual Basic Editor in two ways:

- Select a macro that you want to edit. The host application then opens the Visual Basic Editor and displays that macro so that you're ready to work with it.
- Open the Editor directly and then locate the macro code with which you want to work.

The next two sections demonstrate the two ways of opening the Visual Basic Editor, and the third section shows you how to navigate to a macro.

Opening the Visual Basic Editor with a Macro Selected

If you know the name of the macro you want to work with, use this method to open the Visual Basic Editor and also display the macro at the same time. This example uses Word to open the `Transpose_Word_Right` macro that you recorded in Chapter 1, "Recording and Running Macros in the Office Applications":

1. Open Word if it's not already running.
2. Press Alt+F8 to display the Macros dialog box.
3. Select the `Transpose_Word_Right` macro and click the Edit button. Word opens the Visual Basic Editor with the macro displayed and ready for editing, as shown in Figure 2.1.

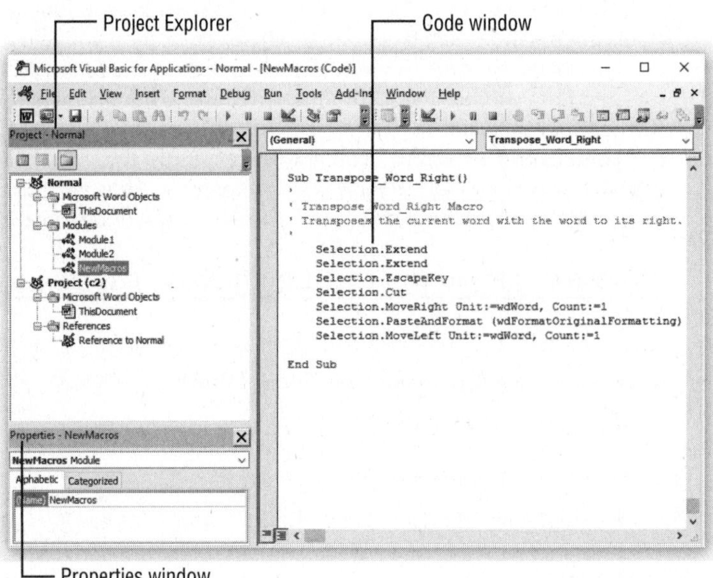

FIGURE 2.1 The Visual Basic Editor with the `Transpose_Word_Right` macro open in the Code window

4. Choose File ➢ Close to close the Visual Basic Editor for the moment so that you can open it using the method described in the next section.

Opening the Visual Basic Editor Directly

To open the Visual Basic Editor directly, follow these steps:

1. Open or activate the host application. In this case, open or switch to Word.
2. Press Alt+F11. The Visual Basic Editor opens.

The Visual Basic Editor Remembers Its Code Window

Depending on the state of the Visual Basic Editor the last time it was closed, you may see one or more Code windows open. For example, if you left the Code window for the `NewMacros` module open in the previous section, the Visual Basic Editor will display this Code window again.

If you don't see the Properties window (see Figure 2.1), press F4. You'll learn more about this important window shortly.

Navigating to a Macro

After opening the Visual Basic Editor directly, use the Project Explorer pane (shown on the left side in Figure 2.1) to navigate to your macro. You also use the Project Explorer to navigate among open projects and modules when you're working in the Visual Basic Editor.

The Project Explorer Resembles the Windows File Explorer Folder View

The Project Explorer pane works like a standard Windows File Explorer tree when you're viewing folders and subfolders. Depending on the application you're using, you'll see different projects displayed in the tree (more on this later in the chapter).

To navigate to the `Transpose_Word_Right` macro, follow these steps:

1. In the Project Explorer pane in the upper-left corner of the Visual Basic Editor, expand the entry for Normal (which represents `Normal.dotm`, the Normal template) by clicking the + sign to the left of its name. (If the Normal entry is already expanded, skip this step.)
2. Double-click the Modules entry to expand it.
3. Double-click the `NewMacros` module. (This is the global module in which Word automatically stores the macros you record unless you specify a different location in the Record Macro dialog box.) The Visual Basic Editor displays the contents of the module in the Code window on the right side, as you can see in Figure 2.1.

If the module contains more than one macro, you'll also need to select the macro you want to work with—in this case, the `Transpose_Word_Right` macro. (If you've recorded only the `Transpose_Word_Right` macro, only this macro appears in the Code window.) To select a macro, use one of these methods:

- In the Code window, select the macro from the Procedure drop-down list, as shown in Figure 2.2. (If you hover the mouse pointer over the list before dropping it down, you'll see a tooltip that gives its name: Procedure.)

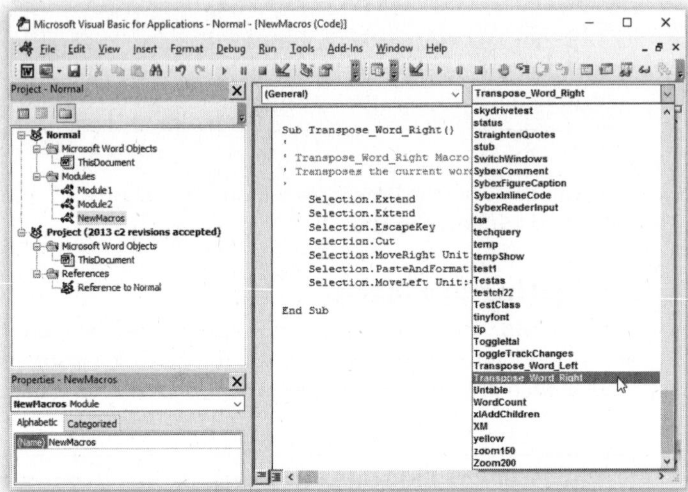

FIGURE 2.2 If the module contains two or more macros, scroll to the macro you want to edit or select it from this Procedure drop-down list.

- Use the scroll bar to scroll to the macro you want to edit, which is identified by the word `Sub`, the name you gave it, and a pair of parentheses—in this case, `Sub Transpose_Word_Right()`.

> **MAXIMIZE YOUR CODE WINDOW**
>
> By default, the Code window is displayed in a "normal" window size. In other words, there is a gray background around it and it doesn't fill the Code window area. This allows you to open other Code windows in the Code window area. However, that's a bit too much micro-multitasking for me, so I'll always display the Code window maximized, as shown in Figures 2.1 and 2.2. That makes it easier to see the code. To display only one, maximized Code window, click the Code window's Maximize button, just to the left of the red X button that closes the window.

Using the Visual Basic Editor's Main Windows

In the following sections, you'll learn how to use the main windows of the Visual Basic Editor.

The Project Explorer

The Project Explorer is the tool for navigating among the various objects in the Visual Basic Editor. Figure 2.3 shows the Project Explorer for a Visual Basic Editor session with Word as the host application.

Depending on the host application and its capabilities, each project can contain some or all of the following elements. (But don't worry now about such items as class modules, link libraries, and so on—we'll explore them in later chapters.)

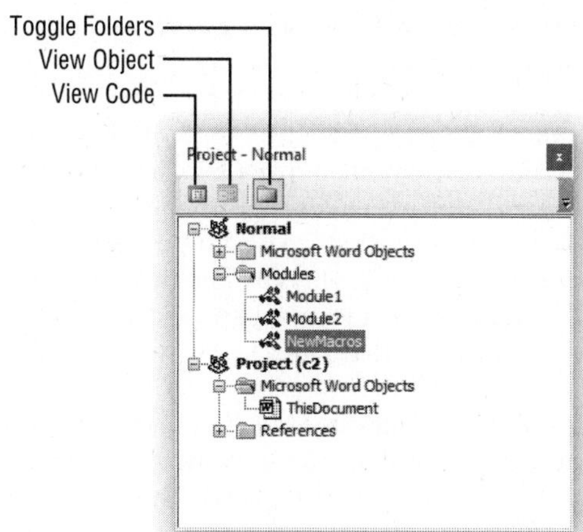

FIGURE 2.3 Use the Project Explorer to navigate to the module with which you want to work.

- User forms (windows that make up part of the macro's user interface, such as a custom dialog box that accepts user input).
- Modules containing macros, procedures, and functions.
- Class modules (specialized modules that define objects, their properties, and their values).
- References to other projects or to library files (such as DLLs—Dynamic Link Libraries).
- Objects related to the application. For example, each Word document and template contains a Microsoft Word Objects folder that holds a class object named `ThisDocument`. `ThisDocument` gives you access to the properties and *events* (actions the object can react to, such as a click event) for the document or template. Each Excel workbook contains a class object named `ThisWorkbook` that gives you access to the properties and events for the workbook and a `Sheet` object (named `Sheet1`, `Sheet2`, and so on) for each worksheet.

For most host applications, each open document and template is considered a separate project and is displayed as a root in the project tree. The project tree also contains any global macro storage containers—such as the `Normal.dotm` template in Word or the Personal Macro Workbook in Excel—and any add-ins that are loaded.

As an example, in Figure 2.3, `Normal.dotm` is identified as Normal, and the active document is identified as Project (C2): the document named C2.

CHANGE A PROJECT'S NAME AT ANY TIME

You can change the name of a project by using the Project Properties dialog box (discussed later in this chapter) or by selecting the project and entering a new name in the Properties pane, shown directly below the Project Explorer pane (as shown earlier in Figure 2.1).

Once you change the name, the project is identified by that name in the Project Explorer, followed by the name of the document or template. For example, if you change the project name of document 2 to **Testing**, the document project is identified as Testing(2) in the Project Explorer rather than Project(2).

You navigate the Project Explorer by clicking the boxed plus sign to the left of a project item to expand the view and display the items contained in the project, and click the resulting boxed minus sign to collapse the view and hide the items again. Double-click a module to display its code in the Code window. Double-click a user form to display it in the Code window.

The Visual Basic Editor displays the Project Explorer by default, and because the Project Explorer provides fast and efficient navigation among the various elements of your VBA projects, it's usually easiest to just leave it displayed unless you're short on screen space or you're working for long periods in the Code window and don't need to switch to other elements. However, most people don't create document-specific macros or large, complicated programs spanning multiple projects. As a result, they just leave all their macros in the `NewMacros` module.

To close the Project Explorer, click its close button (the X button in its title bar). To display the Project Explorer again, press Ctrl+R or choose View ➤ Project Explorer. As you'll see later in this chapter, you can also undock the Project Explorer. This lets you push it aside when you need more room. But it doesn't take up much room, so, again, many people just leave it tucked up there in the upper left.

In Figure 2.3, three buttons appear on a toolbar at the top of the Project Explorer:

View Code Displays the Code window for the selected object. For example, if you select a user form in the Project Explorer and click the View Code button, the Visual Basic Editor displays a Code window containing any code attached to the user form. If you select a module or a class module in the Project Explorer and click the View Code button, the Visual Basic Editor displays a Code window containing the code in the module. You can also right-click an item in the Project Explorer and choose View Code from the context menu.

Code is merely a synonym for programming—the series of commands you type in (or record) to make the computer behave a certain way. Code is sometimes called *programming code* or *source code.*

Note that the words used in programming—terms such as `Selection` or `End Sub` employed by a computer-programming language such as VBA—are referred to by a variety of synonyms: statements, keywords, commands, and so on. In this book, I'll frequently simply use the generic term *commands.*

DOUBLE-CLICK MODULES TO VIEW THEIR CODE

For a module or a class module, you can also double-click the object to view its code. This is usually faster than selecting it and then clicking the View Code button. For a user form or a file, however, double-clicking displays the View Object option (discussed next) rather than the View Code option.

View Object Displays a window containing the selected object. The View Object button remains dimmed and disabled until you select an object (such as a user form or a file or object within a file) that can be displayed. If the selected object is a user form, clicking the View Object button displays the user form; if the selected object is a file or an object within a file, clicking the View Object button displays that object in the host application's window.

For example, selecting the `ThisDocument` object for a Word document and clicking the View Object button just switches to the actual Word document in the Word window. Selecting a `Sheet1` object in an Excel workbook and clicking the View Object button displays that worksheet in the Excel workbook in the Excel window.

VIEWING AN OBJECT

You can also trigger the View Object mode by right-clicking an object and choosing View Object from the shortcut menu or by double-clicking an object that supports the View Object feature. (If the object doesn't support the View Object feature, double-clicking it triggers the View Code mode instead.)

Toggle Folders Toggles the view of the objects in the Project Explorer between *folder view* (a view that shows the objects grouped within their projects and folders) and *contents view* (which displays only the objects within their projects—no folders are shown).

The left part of Figure 2.4 shows the Project Explorer for an application session sorted by folder view, and the right part shows the Project Explorer for the same situation in contents view. Whether you spend more time in folder view or contents view will depend on the size of your screen, the number of objects you put in any given project, and the way your mind works—not necessarily in that order. For many purposes, you'll want to toggle between folder view and contents view to locate objects most easily.

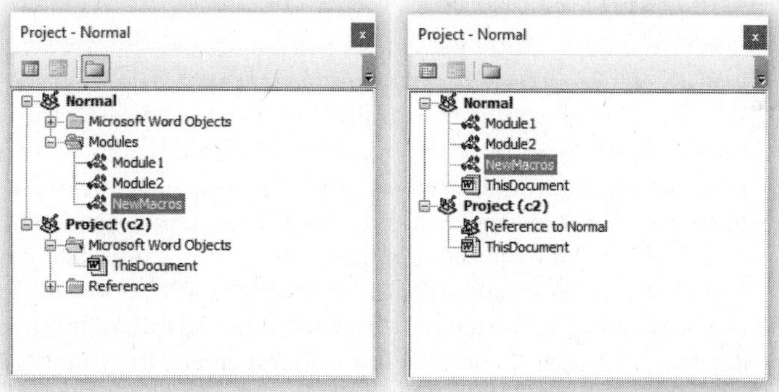

FIGURE 2.4 Folder view (left) displays the objects separated into folders beneath the projects that contain them. Contents view (right) displays only the objects and the projects that contain them.

The Project Explorer has several uses, which is a good reason to keep it open all the time. Apart from navigating to the items you need to work with, you can perform the following additional tasks with the Project Explorer:

- Add components to or remove them from a project. For example, you can use the Project Explorer to add a module or a user form to a project.
- Compare the components of one project to the components of another project. Such a comparison can be useful when you need to establish the differences between two or more

projects quickly (for example, your reference copy of a company template and the copies to which users have been adding).

- Move or copy items from one project to another. You can drag a code module, class module, or user form from one project to another in the Project Explorer to copy it or from the Project Explorer in one instance of the Visual Basic Editor to a project in the Project Explorer in another instance. For example, you could drag a user form from a Visual Basic Editor instance hosted by Excel to a Visual Basic Editor session hosted by PowerPoint to copy the user form. You can't, however, copy or move objects that are specific to a particular application's object model; for example, you can't drop an Excel sheet into Word's Project Explorer because Word doesn't support that type of object.
- Import or export a code module or a user form to or from a project.

THE PROJECT EXPLORER IS YOUR BEST VIEW

Many actions that you can perform through the Project Explorer you can also perform through the Visual Basic Editor's menu items. In general, though, the Project Explorer provides the easiest way to navigate in the Visual Basic Editor, especially if you ever have several complex projects open at the same time. You can access the most commonly used features for an object by right-clicking it in the Project Explorer to display the context menu.

The Object Browser

The Visual Basic Editor provides a full Object Browser for working with objects in VBA. You'll look at the Object Browser in detail in Chapter 8, "Finding the Objects, Methods, and Properties You Need," and when you examine the object models for the various Office applications in the final part of this book. In the meantime, take a quick look at Figure 2.5, which shows the Object Browser for a Word VBA session. The `Document` object is selected in the left-hand panel, and a list of its properties appears in the right-hand panel. (To see this in your VBA Editor, press F2.)

You'll find that a number of these properties immediately make sense from your general knowledge of Word documents. For example, as you would expect, the `AttachedTemplate` property tells you the template to which the document is currently attached. Likewise, the `Bookmarks` property contains information on any bookmarks in the document. The property information is displayed at the bottom of the Object Browser. One of the great things about the BASIC language, of which VBA is a variant, and the libraries of objects underlying the Office applications is that they generally use ordinary English terminology.

The Code Window

You'll do most of the actual work of testing and editing your macros in the Visual Basic Editor's Code window. (Because code is written in plain text, you could simply write it in Notepad, and then paste it into the Code Editor for testing and debugging. However, the Visual Basic Editor offers so many useful programming tools that only the brilliant few can easily get good results by trying to wing it without any assistance from the Editor.)

FIGURE 2.5
The Object Browser provides a quick way to look up objects and their properties. Here, you can see the properties contained in the `Document` object.

The Visual Basic Editor provides an individual Code window for each open project, for each document section within the project that can contains code, and for each code module and user form in the project. Each Code window is identified by the project name, the name of the module within the project, and the word *Code* in parentheses. Figure 2.6 shows the Visual Basic Editor Code window with the `Transpose_Word_Right` macro open in it.

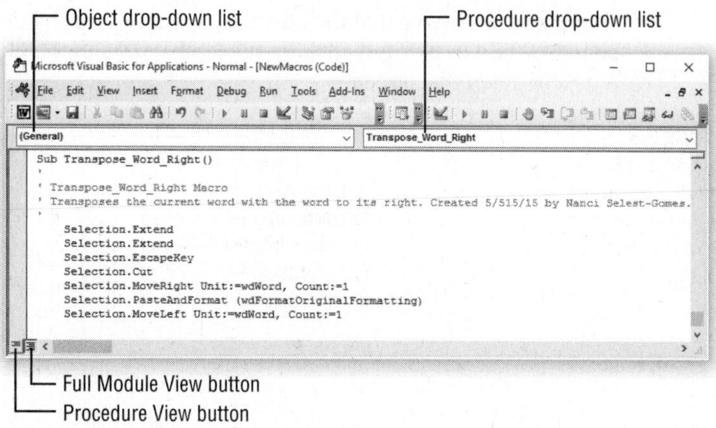

FIGURE 2.6
You edit macros in the Code window.

As you can see from the figure, two drop-down list boxes appear just below the title bar of the Code window:

- The Object drop-down list box at the upper-left corner of the Code window provides a quick way of navigating between different objects.
- The Procedure drop-down list box at the upper-right corner of the Code window lets you move quickly from procedure to procedure within the current module. Click the down-arrow button to display the drop-down list of procedures. You'll see that the first procedure is (Declarations). Clicking this item in the list takes you to the Declarations area at the top of the current code sheet, which is where you declare public variables and other VBA information that multiple procedures need to know.

The Visual Basic Editor Code window provides a half dozen features that help you edit code efficiently and accurately, as discussed in the following sections.

Complete Word

The Complete Word feature can complete the word you're typing into the Code window, once you've typed enough letters to distinguish that word from any other. If you haven't typed enough letters to distinguish the word, the Visual Basic Editor gives you the closest possibilities (see Figure 2.7). You can either "type down" (continue typing to narrow the selection) or scroll through the displayed list to find the one you want.

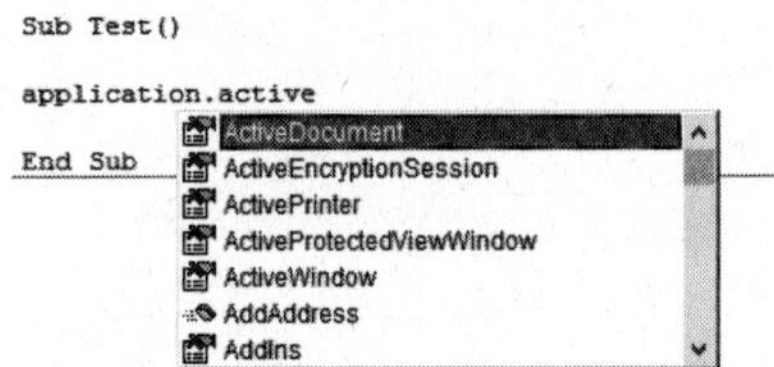

Figure 2.7 The Complete Word feature automatically completes a term when you've typed enough to identify it. If you haven't typed enough, you can choose from a short list.

The easiest way to activate Complete Word when you're typing code is to press Ctrl+spacebar. You can also choose Edit ➤ Complete Word or click the Complete Word button on the Edit toolbar (see Figure 2.8). Note that the Edit toolbar isn't visible by default. Open it by choosing View ➤ Toolbars ➤ Edit or by right-clicking the toolbar area in the Editor, and then choosing Edit from the shortcut menu that appears.

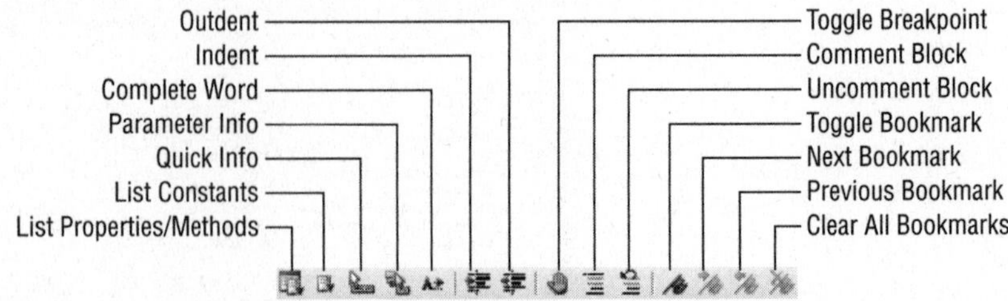

Figure 2.8 The Edit toolbar contains features used when working in the Code window.

Quick Info

The Quick Info feature displays a ScreenTip showing syntax information about the currently selected variable, function, method, command, or sub. (*Selected* here just means the word in the code that's under or adjacent to the blinking cursor insertion point.) If you type in a command like **MsgBox** and then press the spacebar, the ScreenTip pops up to help you complete typing in the command. The tip shows both the required and optional elements of that command. Optional elements are enclosed in square brackets.

Figure 2.9 shows an example of a Quick Info ScreenTip.

Figure 2.9
Use the Editor's Quick Info feature to see a VB language command's syntax or a quick readout of status.

```
msgbox |
MsgBox(Prompt, [Buttons As VbMsgBoxStyle = vbOKOnly], [Title], [HelpFile], [Context]) As VbMsgBoxResult
```

To display Quick Info, use one of these methods:

- Just type a space following a VB command. For example, type **msgbox** `(space).`
- Click the Quick Info icon on the Edit toolbar.
- Right-click a VB command and choose Quick Info from the shortcut menu.
- Position the insertion point in the command and press Ctrl+I.
- Position the insertion point in the term and choose Edit ➢ Quick Info.
- If you're typing in actual commands from the VBA language (as opposed to, say, variables or objects), the easiest way to see Quick Info is just to type the command's name (such as **MsgBox**), and then press the spacebar key. Note that VB doesn't pay any attention to capitalization, so you can type in **msgbox** or **MsgBox** or whatever variation you want. Once you finish typing in the line of code (by pressing Enter), the Editor will automatically capitalize the command the standard way: `MsgBox`.

Auto List Members

Many VB commands have properties (qualities) and methods (behaviors). Taken together, the properties and methods of an object are called its *members*.

For example, a message box can display various icons (such as question mark, exclamation point, and so on) to cue the user about the purpose of the message (question, warning, etc.). This icon is called the *Buttons property* of the message-box object. And this property is specified right after the text message in the line of code. Therefore, when I type a comma to indicate that I'm now going to specify the icon for my message box, the Auto List Members feature opens a drop-down list of the choices available. As you can see in Figure 2.10, I'm choosing `vbOKOnly`, but there are a number of other possible choices, such as `vbOKCancel`, `vbQuestion`, and so on.

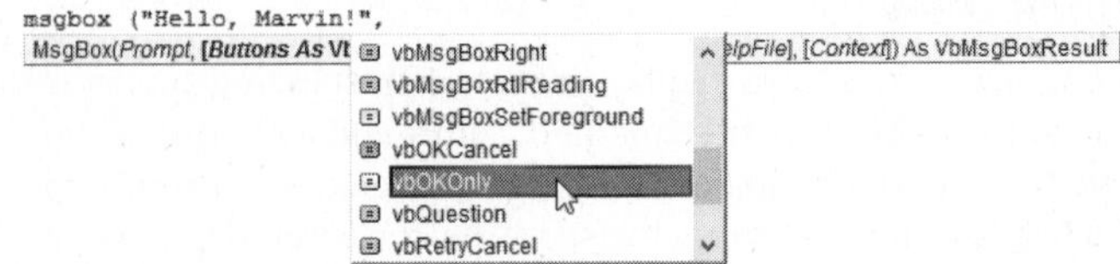

FIGURE 2.10 Use the Auto List Members command to enter code items quickly and accurately.

The Auto List Members list allows you to quickly complete the line of code. Auto List Members is switched on by default and is automatically displayed when you type a period in an object description or a comma, parentheses, or other punctuation in a line of code. Notice in Figure 2.10 that I've typed in a message-box command followed by the text `Hello, Marvin!` and then a comma. As soon as I typed the comma, the list of settings for the Buttons appeared. (These settings are called *constants*.)

Alternatively, you can display the list box by clicking the List Properties/Methods button on the Edit toolbar.

To use Auto List Members to insert your choice into your code, follow these steps:

1. Press the down-arrow key to scroll down to the property or method, or scroll down with the mouse (see Figure 2.10). You can also type the first few letters of the property or method's name to jump to it.
2. Enter the property or method into the code by doing one of the following:
    a. Press Tab, or double-click the property or method, if you want to continue adding to this line of code after entering the property or method. (There might be additional optional properties you want to specify on this line.)
    b. Press Enter if you want to start a new line after entering the property or method.

LIST CONSTANTS

The List Constants feature displays a pop-up list box containing constants for a property you've typed so that you can quickly complete the expression. List Constants is switched on by default. Alternatively, you can display the list box by clicking the List Constants button on the Edit toolbar.

To use List Constants (see Figure 2.11), follow these steps:

1. Type **`Assistant.Animation =`** in the Code window. The constants list will be displayed as shown in Figure 2.11.
2. Press the ↓ (down-arrow) to scroll down to the constant you're after, or type its first letter (or first few letters), or scroll down with the mouse.
3. Enter the constant in the code by doing the following:
    a. Press Tab, or double-click the constant, if you want to continue working on the same line after entering the constant.
    b. Press Enter if you want to start a new line after entering the constant.

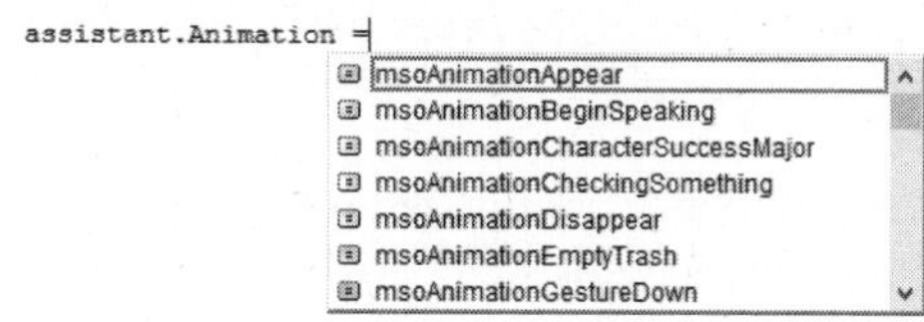

FIGURE 2.11
The List Constants feature saves you time and effort, especially when typing complex constant names.

DATA TIPS

The Data Tips feature displays a ScreenTip containing the value of a variable the mouse pointer moves over when the Visual Basic Editor is in Break mode (a mode you use for testing and debugging macros, described later in this book). Figure 2.12 shows an example. The Data Tips feature is switched on by default, but you can switch it, and other features, off by choosing Tools ➤ Options.

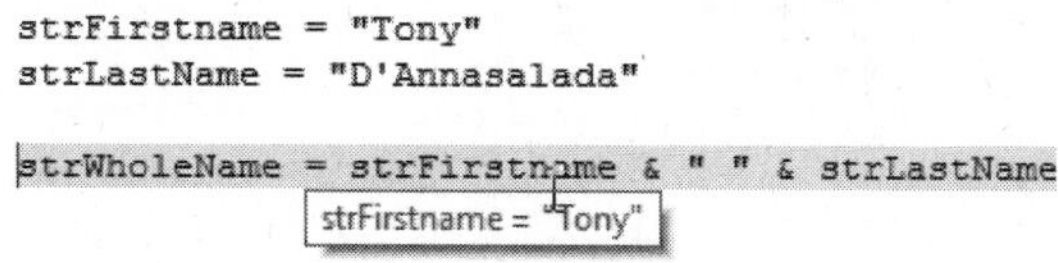

FIGURE 2.12
Use the Data Tips feature to check the value of a variable when you're running or stepping through code.

MARGIN INDICATORS

The Margin Indicators feature lets you quickly set a breakpoint, the next statement, or a bookmark by clicking in the margin of the Code window. You'll look at setting breakpoints, setting the next statement, and setting bookmarks later. (You can just right-click the gray margin on the left side of the Code window, and then choose Toggle from the shortcut menu to manipulate breakpoints or bookmarks. You can also just left-click to toggle breakpoints.)

OTHER EDITING FEATURES

Apart from these features, the Code window includes standard Office editing features such as copy and move, cut and paste, and drag and drop. You can drag code from one procedure or module to another, for example.

The Properties Window

The Visual Basic Editor provides a Properties window you can use to view and modify the properties of an object in VBA, such as a project, a module or class module, a user form, or a *control* (a button or check box in a dialog box, for example). If the Properties window isn't visible in the Editor, press F4.

In the drop-down list at the top of the Properties window, you can select the object with the properties you want to view or modify. Or you can select an entry in the Project Explorer window. The Alphabetic option displays an alphabetical list of the properties in the item, and the

Categorized option presents a list of the properties broken down into categories. Generally, I find the categorization less than useful because many properties don't really fit neatly into any particular category.

Figure 2.13 shows the Alphabetic option with the properties for an Excel workbook on the left and the Categorized page on the right. (Showing the Categorized page for the Excel workbook or worksheet isn't very helpful because all of the properties belong to a Misc category—miscellaneous. There's no categorization here at all.)

FIGURE 2.13
Use the Properties window to view the properties of a project, user form, module, class module, or control.

The purpose of most of the workbook properties is easy to grasp. For example, if the `HasRoutingSlip` property is set to `False`, it means the workbook does not have an email routing slip attached to it, and if the `Saved` property is set to `True`, that indicates that the workbook does not contain any unsaved changes. You'll learn about the properties for user forms in Chapter 14, "Creating Simple Custom Dialog Boxes," and Chapter 15, "Creating Complex Forms."

Understanding Design Mode, Run Mode, and Break Mode

The Visual Basic Editor can be in one of three modes, reflecting three fundamental phases of programming—writing the code, locating a bug, and fixing a bug:

Design mode Also known as *design time*. Any time you're working in the Visual Basic Editor on your code, you're in Design mode. You don't have to be actively designing anything visually—such as a user control or form—although you often will be. You will also often just be typing in *source code*—the commands that Visual Basic will execute when you switch to Run mode, or you might be editing code you've recorded.

Run mode Also known as *runtime*. When code is running, you're in Run mode. The macro will be executed just as if it had been launched from within an application like Word (using a shortcut key combination or via clicking a Quick Access Toolbar button). The purpose of Run mode in the Visual Basic Editor is to allow you to test and observe the code's behavior and interact with it if necessary, to see that it works as it's supposed to. This is known as *debugging*. If you do find any problems during runtime testing, you can stop the execution by pressing Ctrl+Break and then check the values in variables or otherwise attempt to track down *where* in your code the error is located. VBA itself can also throw you into Break mode if it detects an error condition.

Break mode When code is running but execution is temporarily suspended, you're in Break mode. Among other things, Break mode lets you step through your code one command or one procedure at a time (rather than running all the commands at once at full speed). Stepping is a very handy tool when you're debugging or otherwise critiquing your code. You'll explore debugging techniques in detail in Chapter 17, "Debugging Your Code and Handling Errors."

To change a property, click the cell containing the property's name. If a down-arrow button appears in the value cell, click it to choose a new value from a drop-down list. If no button appears, click the value cell to display the blinking insertion cursor and type in a new value.

You'll be able to choose different values from drop-down lists, depending on the type of property. For a `True/False` property, you'll be limited to those two choices in the drop-down list. For a text property such as `Name`, you can enter any valid VBA name.

By default, the Properties window is docked below the Project Explorer. You can adjust the relative heights of the Properties window or the Project Explorer window by dragging the border between them. You can also widen both at once by dragging the border to their right. If you undock the Properties window (drag it or double-click its title bar), you can resize it by dragging its borders or corners to display more properties or to shrink the window so it takes up less space in the Visual Basic Editor. Undock interior windows (also called *panes*, such as the Properties pane) by dragging them by their title bar or by double-clicking their title bar. Redock by double-clicking their title bar.

The Immediate Window

Beyond the Project Explorer and the Code window, the Visual Basic Editor includes a number of other windows that it doesn't display by default. Three of these windows are key: the Properties window and the Object Browser (both described earlier in this chapter) and the Immediate window, shown in Figure 2.14. The Immediate window is a small, unadorned window you can use as a virtual scratch pad to enter lines of code you want to test without entering them in an actual macro. When you type a line of code into the Immediate window and press the Enter key, the Visual Basic Editor executes that code. You'll use the Immediate window during the discussion of the VBA language in Chapter 5, "Understanding the Essentials of VBA Syntax."

Figure 2.14
Use the Immediate window for on-the-fly work and information.

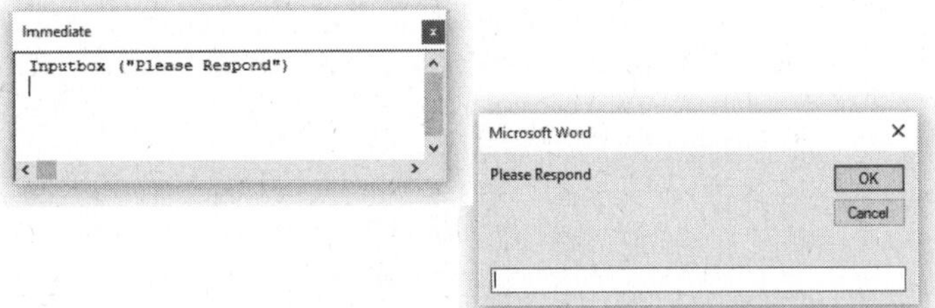

To display the Immediate window, press Ctrl+G or choose View ➤ Immediate Window.

Display the Status of Variables During Debugging

You can also use the Immediate window to display information to help you check the values of variables and expressions while code is executing. That is done by using the `Debug.Print` command, as in this example, which displays the value of the variable *x* in the Immediate window:

```
Sub ShowDebug()

Dim x As Integer
x = 12

Debug.Print x

End Sub
```

Setting Properties for a Project

Each VBA project has several properties of its own that you can set, including its project name, its description, and whether it is locked against viewing. To examine or set the properties for a project, right-click the project or one of its components in the Project Explorer and choose the Project Properties item in the context menu to display the Project Properties dialog box.

Both the menu item and the resulting dialog box are identified by the description of the project—for example, the properties dialog box for a template in Word is identified as TemplateProject – Project Properties, and the properties dialog box for an Excel workbook is identified as VBAProject – Project Properties. Figure 2.15 shows the Project Properties dialog box for an Excel workbook project.

FIGURE 2.15
Use the Project Properties dialog box to view and set the properties for a project and to lock a project against change.

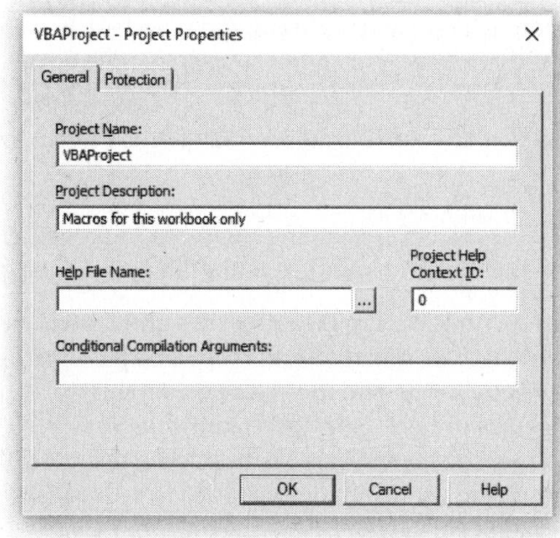

Here's what you can do on the General tab of the Project Properties dialog box:

- Set the project name in the Project Name text box. This name identifies the project in the Object Browser and, when necessary, in the Windows Registry. Make sure the name is unique to avoid confusion with any other project. Technically, the project name is the name of the type library for the project (a *type library* describes the objects—such as modules and user forms—that the project contains); it is used to build the fully qualified class name of classes in the project (more on this later in the book). The project name can contain underscores but cannot contain spaces.
- Enter a description of the project in the Project Description text box. This description appears in the Description pane in the Object Browser to help the user understand what the project is. So be as concise, yet descriptive, as possible.
- Designate the Help file for the project by entering the name and path of the Help file in the Help File Name text box. Click the button marked with the ellipsis (…) to the right of the Help File Name text box to display the Help File dialog box. Then select the file and click the Open button to enter the name of the Help file in the text box. (Alternatively, you can type or paste in the name and path.)
- Specify the Help context for the project in the Project Help Context ID text box. The *Help context* refers to a location in the Help file. The default Help context is 0, which causes the Help file to display its opening screen (the same screen you'll see if you run the Help file from the Run dialog box or by double-clicking the file in Explorer). You can specify a

different help context to take the user to a particular topic—for example, one more relevant to the project on which they're seeking help.

- Specify any conditional compilation arguments needed for the project. Some find conditional compilation useful, but most don't. It allows you to create different versions of a VBA project based on what you specify in this dialog box. Personally, I find that more trouble than it's worth—and confusing too. I'd rather just create more than one version of a project instead. If you're interested in this topic, take a look here:

```
https://msdn.microsoft.com/en-us/library/x435tkbk(v=vs.90).aspx
```

Here's what you can do on the Protection tab of the Project Properties dialog box, shown in Figure 2.16:

- Select the Lock Project For Viewing check box to prevent other people from opening the project, viewing it, and changing it without knowing the password.
- In the Password To View Project Properties group box, enter a password for the project in the Password text box, and then enter the same password in the Confirm Password text box. Click the OK button and then close the project. Now nobody can open and view (let alone change) the project if they don't know the password. That said, Office's password security has been weak and was easily cracked prior to Office 2007. Now superior encryption techniques are used, but the password is still crackable, albeit with far greater difficulty. More on this in Chapter 19, "Securing Your Code with VBA's Security Features."

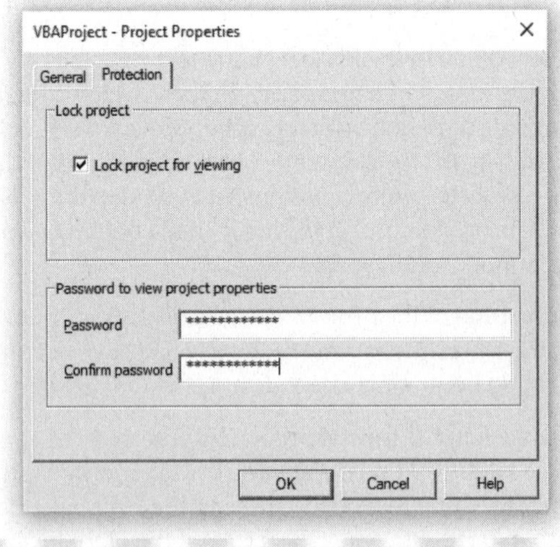

FIGURE 2.16
The Protection page of the Project Properties dialog box lets you lock your project with a password so that nobody can view or edit it

Select Lock Project For Viewing If You Want to Prevent Others from Opening It

If you enter a password in the Password text box and the Confirm Password text box but you don't select the Lock Project For Viewing check box, the Visual Basic Editor will prompt you for the password the next time you try to display the Project Properties dialog box. However, you'll be able to open and view the project and its contents without supplying the password.

Customizing the Visual Basic Editor

Given how much time you're likely to spend in the Visual Basic Editor, you ought to customize it so you can work as efficiently and comfortably as possible. You can customize it as follows:

- Choose Editor and View preference settings in the Visual Basic Editor to control how it interacts with you.
- Choose which windows to display in the Visual Basic Editor, and organize their layout so you can use your workspace as effectively as possible.
- Customize the toolbar and menus in the Visual Basic Editor so the commands you need are at hand (without cluttering up your workspace).
- Customize the Toolbox so it contains the tools you need to build your user forms.

The following sections explain your options.

Customization Is Global Across Applications

Any customizing you do to the VBA Editor applies across all Office applications using the version of VBA you are customizing. For example, if you change the font in an instance of the Visual Basic Editor hosted by Excel, the font also changes for Editor instances hosted by Word, PowerPoint, Outlook, and so on.

Choosing Editor and View Preferences

To begin choosing Editor and View preferences, choose Tools ➤ Options to open the Options dialog box (see Figure 2.17).

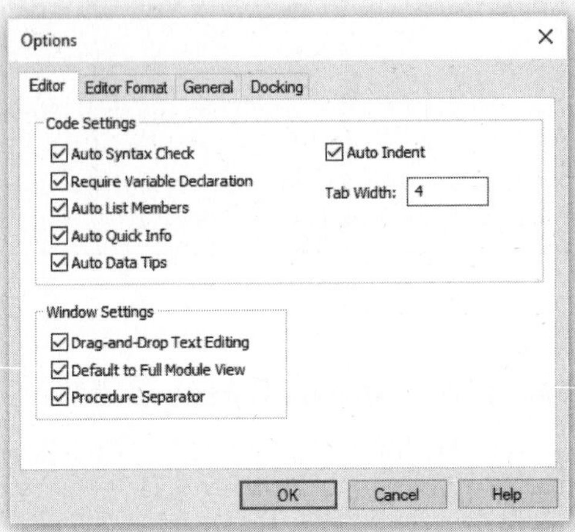

FIGURE 2.17
The Editor page of the Options dialog box

EDITOR PAGE OPTIONS

The Editor page of the Options dialog box includes the following settings:

Auto Syntax Check Controls whether VBA displays warning message boxes when it discovers errors while automatically checking your syntax as you type lines of code. (At the time of this writing, this feature is not working in Office 2016.)

Some people find this feature helpful because VBA instantly points out errors that could otherwise remain unnoticed until you try to run or debug your code. But if your style is to move from one unfinished line of code to another (and ultimately finish all the lines at your convenience), you may want to turn off this feature to prevent the Visual Basic Editor from bombarding you with message boxes for errors you're aware of but prefer to fix later. This choice is similar to the difference between writers who like to fix spelling errors while they're typing (and, therefore, leave Word's Check Spelling As You Type option active) and those who prefer to keep their eye on the ball and deal with minutiae such as spelling after finishing their thoughts.

> **YOU'LL ALWAYS GET A CODE RED ON LINES WITH ERRORS**
>
> Even if you turn off Auto Syntax Check, the Visual Basic Editor still turns any offending lines of code red to draw your attention to them. It simply stops interrupting you with message boxes displaying error warnings each time you mistype something.

Require Variable Declaration Governs whether you must declare variables explicitly. Declaring variables explicitly is a little more work than declaring them implicitly, but many people believe that it's a good practice and will save you time down the road—so make sure that this check box is selected unless you have a strong preference otherwise. (Chapter 6, "Working with Variables, Constants, and Enumerations," discusses how to work with variables.)

Auto List Members Described earlier in this chapter, this option controls whether the Auto List Members and List Constants features automatically suggest properties, methods, and constants as you work in the Code window. Most people find these features helpful, but some experienced programmers turn off these features because they know pretty much all the properties, methods, and constants they need and prefer not to be distracted by a busy interface.

Auto Quick Info This option controls whether the Quick Info feature automatically displays information about functions and their parameters as you work with functions in the Code window.

Auto Data Tips This option controls whether the Visual Basic Editor displays ScreenTips when you hover the mouse pointer over a variable or expression in Break mode, enabling you to check the value of a variable or expression quickly. (Alternatively, you can use the Locals, Immediate, or Watch window, but they take up more screen space.)

Auto Indent Determines whether the Visual Basic Editor automatically indents subsequent lines of code after you've indented a line. When Auto Indent is switched on, the Visual Basic Editor starts each new line of code indented to the same level (the same number of tabs or spaces or the same combination of the two) as the previous line. When Auto Indent is switched off, the Visual Basic Editor starts each new line of code at the left margin of the Code window. Usually, automatic indentation is a time-saver, although it means that each time you need to decrease a new line's level of indentation, you must press Shift+Tab, click the Outdent button on the Edit toolbar, or delete the tabs or spaces.

Tab Width Sets the number of spaces in a tab. You can adjust this setting from 1 to 32 spaces. The default setting is 4 spaces, which works well for the default font. If you choose to use a proportional font (such as Times or Arial) rather than a monospaced font (such as the default New Courier) for your code, you may want to increase the number of spaces a tab represents in order to clarify the levels of indentation in your code.

Drag-And-Drop Text Editing Controls whether the Visual Basic Editor supports drag-and-drop. Most people find this feature helpful. You can drag portions of your code around the Code window or from one Code window to another. You can also drag code into the Immediate window or drag an expression into the Watch window.

Default To Full Module View Controls whether the Visual Basic Editor displays all the procedures in a module in one list (Full Module view) or displays them one at a time (Procedure view). If you're working with short procedures, you may find Full Module view useful. However, the individual view can provide a less cluttered and more workable context for lengthy procedures. When working in Procedure view, you open the procedure you want to work with by choosing it from the Procedure drop-down list at the top of the Code window. To toggle between Full Module view and Procedure view, click the Full Module View button or the Procedure View button in the lower-left corner of any Code window.

Use a Drop-Down List to Quickly Move Procedures

When working in Full Module view, you can also use the Procedures drop-down list to quickly move to a procedure by name.

Procedure Separator Controls whether the Visual Basic Editor displays horizontal lines to separate the procedures within a module shown in Full Module view in the Code window. Usually these lines are helpful, providing a quick visual cue showing where one procedure ends and the next begins. (If you're using Procedure view, this check box has no effect.)

EDITOR FORMAT PAGE OPTIONS

The Editor Format page of the Options dialog box, shown in Figure 2.18, controls how code appears in the Visual Basic Editor.

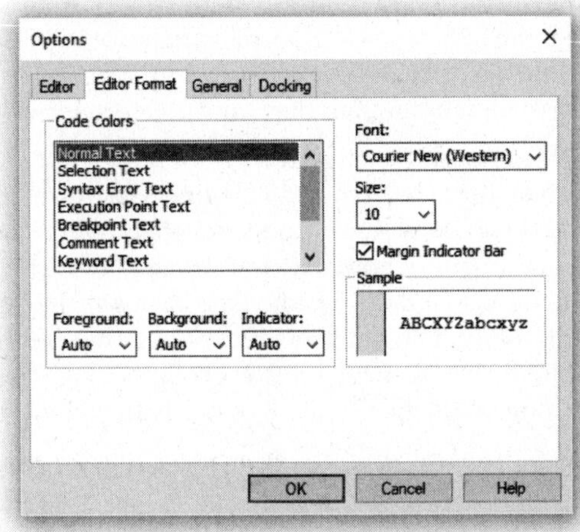

FIGURE 2.18 The Editor Format page of the Options dialog box

By default, comments in your code are rendered in green. This helps you easily recognize that type of text in the Code window. You can change the default colors for various types of text by choosing a type of text in the Code Colors list box and then specifying its colors and typeface (font). You have control over Foreground, Background, and Indicator options via drop-down lists. However, I find the default choices sensible, so I don't change them.

Here's what the Code Colors choices mean:

Normal Text Takes care of much of the text in a typical procedure. You'll probably want to make this a conventional color (such as black, the default).

Selection Text Affects the color of selected (highlighted) text.

Syntax Error Text Affects the color VBA uses for offending lines. The default color is red.

Execution Point Text Affects the color VBA uses for the line currently being executed in Break mode. You'll usually want to make this a highlighter color (like the fluorescent yellow the Visual Basic Editor uses as the default) so you can immediately see the current line.

Breakpoint Text Affects the color in which VBA displays breakpoints (points where code execution is forced to stop).

Comment Text Affects the color of comment lines. The default color is dark green.

Keyword Text Affects the color of keywords (words recognized as part of the VBA language). Recall that in this book I'm using the term *command* for the words in the VBA language.

Such text accounts for a sizable portion of each procedure. You may want to display keywords in a different color than normal text because some people find it helpful to be able to distinguish keywords without needing to read the entire code. The default color is dark blue, which is a good choice—not so intrusive that the characters look like confetti, yet not so hard to see that you can't quickly visualize the underlying syntax of a line of code.

Identifier Text Affects the color VBA uses for identifiers. Identifiers include the names of variables, constants, and procedures you define.

Bookmark Text Affects the color VBA uses for the bookmarks in your code.

Call Return Text Affects the color VBA uses for calls to other procedures. By default, the Visual Basic Editor uses lime green for call return text.

You can change the font and size of all the types of text in the Code window by using the Font and Size drop-down lists on the Editor Format page. You can also prevent the display of the margin indicator bar (the zone in which items such as the Next Statement and Breakpoint icons appear) by clearing the Margin Indicator Bar check box. (Usually, these icons are helpful, but removing this bar slightly increases the code area onscreen.)

General Page Options

The General page of the Options dialog box contains several categories of settings. The following sections discuss them in groups. I always leave these options set to the default settings, which are shown in Figure 2.19.

FIGURE 2.19
The General page of the Options dialog box

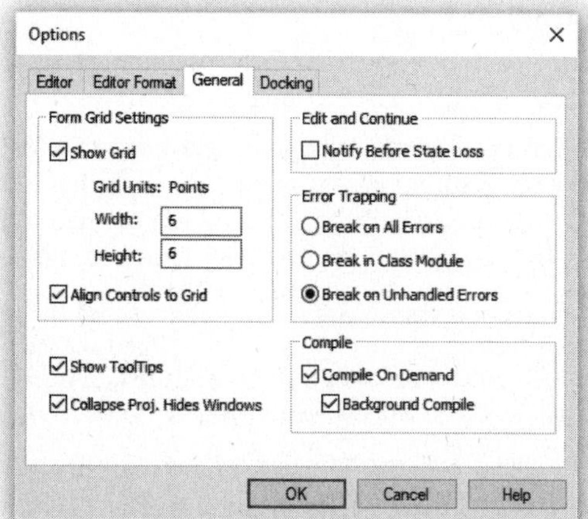

Form Grid Settings Group Box

The Form Grid Settings options control how the Visual Basic Editor handles user forms:

- The Show Grid check box controls whether the Visual Basic Editor displays a grid pattern of dots on the user form in Design mode to help you place and align controls. This check box is selected by default.
- The Width and Height text boxes set the spacing of the dots that make up the grid. You can set any value from 2 points to 60 points (the default setting is 6 points). If you display the grid onscreen, you'll see the dots; if you don't display the grid, it still affects the Align Controls To Grid feature, which is discussed next. Experiment and find the coarseness of grid that is easiest to work with for you.
- The Align Controls To Grid check box governs whether the Visual Basic Editor automatically snaps the edges of controls you place or move to the nearest grid line. This option lets you place controls in approximately the right positions rapidly and easily, but it prevents you from making extremely fine positional adjustments. The grid enforces certain positions, and you might find it frustrating when trying to improve the layout of controls you've already placed on a user form. (If so, one option is to clear the Align Controls To Grid check box; another is to leave it selected but to decrease the size of the grid—to allow finer adjustments.)

Edit and Continue Group Box

The Edit And Continue group box contains only one control—the Notify Before State Loss check box. This option controls whether the Visual Basic Editor warns you, when you're running code, if you try to take an action that requires VBA to reset the values of all variables in the module.

Error Trapping Group Box

The Error Trapping group box contains three option buttons you use to specify how VBA handles errors that occur when you're running code:

Break On All Errors Tells VBA to enter Break mode when it encounters any error, no matter whether an error handler (a section of code designed to handle errors) is active or whether the code is in a class module. Break On All Errors is useful for pinpointing where errors occur, which helps you track them down and remove them. But if you've included an error handler in your code, you probably won't need this option.

Break In Class Module This is arguably the most useful option for general use. When VBA encounters an unhandled error in a class module (a module that defines a type of object), VBA enters Break mode at the offending line of code.

Break On Unhandled Errors The default setting, this is useful when you've constructed an error handler to deal with predictable errors in the current module. If there is an error handler, VBA allows the handler to trap the error and doesn't enter Break mode, but if there is no handler for the error generated, VBA enters Break mode on the offending line of code. An unhandled error in a class module, however, causes the project to enter Break mode on the line of code that invoked the offending procedure of the class, thereby enabling you to identify (and alter) the line that caused the problem.

Compile Group Box

The Compile group box controls when VBA compiles the code for a project into executable code. Before any code can be executed, it needs to be compiled, but not all the code in a project must necessarily be compiled before the Visual Basic Editor can start executing the first parts of the code.

You can select the Compile On Demand check box if you want VBA to compile the code only as needed. VBA compiles the code in the procedure you're running before starting to execute that procedure, but it doesn't compile code in other procedures in the same module unless the procedure you're running *calls* them (transfers execution to them, a technique you'll learn later in this book).

As a result, execution of the procedure you run first in a module can begin as soon as VBA finishes compiling the code for that procedure. If the procedure then calls another procedure in the module, VBA compiles the code for the second procedure when the first procedure calls it, not when you begin running the first procedure.

Compile On Demand is usually a good choice. It's especially useful when you're building a number of procedures in a module and have unfinished code lying around in some of them. In contrast, if you clear the Compile On Demand check box, VBA compiles *all* the code in *all* the procedures in the module before starting to execute the procedure you want to run. This means that not only does the procedure start a little later (more code takes more time to compile, although most computers today are so fast you won't notice), but any language error or compile error in *any* procedure in the entire module prevents you from running and testing the current procedure, even if the code in that procedure contains no errors. This is a problem when you've only sketched in some of the procedures, so they remain unfinished.

Suppose you have a module named `Compilation` that contains two procedures, `GoodCode` and `BadCode`, which look like this:

```
Sub GoodCode()
  MsgBox "This code is working."
End Sub

Sub BadCode()
  Application.Delete
End Sub
```

`GoodCode` simply displays a message box to indicate that it's working, whereas `BadCode` contains an invalid statement (`Application` objects don't have a `Delete` method). `GoodCode` runs without causing a problem, but `BadCode` causes an error every time.

If you try to run `GoodCode` with Compile On Demand switched on, the procedure runs fine: VBA compiles only the programming in the `GoodCode` procedure, finds no errors, and runs it. But if you try to run `GoodCode` with Compile On Demand switched off, VBA also compiles the code in `BadCode` before starting to run `GoodCode`—and VBA stops with a compile error at the bogus `Application.Delete` statement. This thorough checking before running any code is good for finished modules that work together, but it can slow you down and be annoying when you're just "sketching" code—experimenting with code in a module.

On the other hand, you can see the advantage of compiling all the code in the module when GoodCode calls BadCode, as in the third line of this version of the procedure:

```
Sub GoodCode()
  MsgBox "This code is working."
  BadCode
End Sub
```

Here, compiling the code in BadCode before starting to run GoodCode is a good idea because doing so prevents GoodCode from running if BadCode contains an error. If you run this version of GoodCode with Compile On Demand switched on, VBA compiles GoodCode and starts to run it, displaying the message box in the second line. The BadCode call in the third line then causes VBA to compile BadCode, at which point VBA stops with the compile error. You don't want this to happen in the middle of a complex procedure; in such a case, you'd want Compile On Demand switched off.

The Background Compile check box, which is enabled only when the Compile On Demand check box is selected, controls whether the Visual Basic Editor uses idle CPU time to compile further code while it's running the code that it has already compiled. Keep Background Compile switched on unless you notice and are bothered by any slowing of the execution of your code. With current computer speeds, and if your projects aren't huge, you'll likely be unaware of any bothersome difference in execution rate.

Show ToolTips and Collapse Proj. Hides Windows

The final two options on the General page of the Options dialog box are Show ToolTips and Collapse Proj. Hides Windows. Also known as ScreenTips, ToolTips are text descriptions that appear when you hover the mouse pointer over a button or icon. The Show ToolTips check box controls whether the Visual Basic Editor displays ToolTips for its toolbar buttons. ToolTips tend to be useful unless you're desperate to save the memory and processor cycles they consume—which is very unlikely.

The Collapse Proj. Hides Windows check box controls whether the Visual Basic Editor hides the Code window and other project windows that you collapse in the Project Explorer's tree. This check box is selected by default, and in general it's a useful choice. When you collapse a project in the Project Explorer, the Visual Basic Editor hides any Code windows or user form windows belonging to that project and removes them from the list that appears on the Window menu. When you expand the project again, the Visual Basic Editor displays the windows in their previous positions and restores them to the Window menu's list.

Docking Page Options

The Docking page of the Options dialog box, shown in Figure 2.20, controls whether the various windows in the Visual Basic Editor are dockable—that is, whether they snap automatically and magnetically to a side of the window when you move them there. Keeping windows dockable usually makes for a more organized interface. However, you may want to make the windows undockable so you can drag them outside the Visual Basic Editor if necessary and arrange them as you like on the screen. Contemporary monitors are becoming quite large, so you might have plenty of room to display various windows outside the primary Editor window.

At the time of this writing, this feature isn't working in Windows 10.

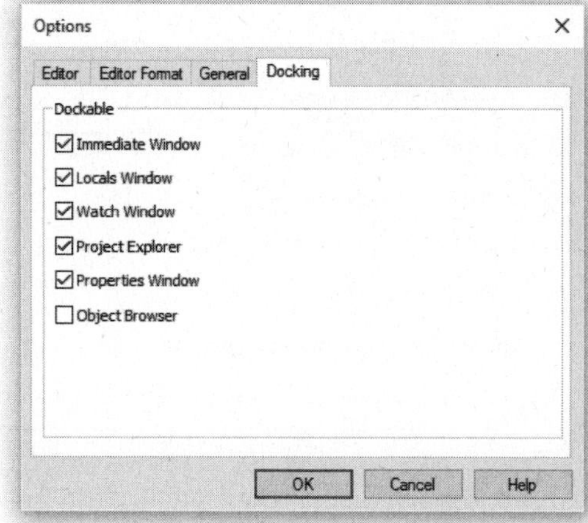

FIGURE 2.20
The Docking page of the Options dialog box

Choosing and Laying Out the Editor Windows

You can reposition the various windows (or *panes*) within the Visual Basic Editor. Your choice of layout depends largely on the size and resolution of your screen and your personal preferences, but here are a couple of suggestions:

- Always make the Code window large—maximize it within the Editor. If you write long lines of code, you'll want to have as much space in the Visual Basic Editor window as possible. That way your lines won't wrap and the code will be easier to read.
- Some people find that much of the time they're actively writing code, they can dispense with the Project Explorer, displaying it only when needed. As a handy way of restoring it, you can put the Project Explorer display command on the Code window, Code window break, Watch window, Immediate window, and Locals window context menus. (You'll learn how to customize the Editor's menus in the next section.) You can also quickly display the Project Explorer by pressing its shortcut key, Ctrl+R.

Customizing the Toolbar and Menu Bar

There are no menus at all in Word, Excel, Access, and the other Office applications. And the lone toolbar is the Quick Access Toolbar. The Ribbon replaced menus and most toolbars back in 2007.

But the Visual Basic Editor retains the older interface style—no Ribbon, but instead the classic menus and toolbars, and you can customize them to a limited extent. To do this, choose View

➤ Toolbars ➤ Customize (or right-click a toolbar or the menu bar and choose Customize from the context menu). You'll see the Customize dialog box, shown in Figure 2.21.

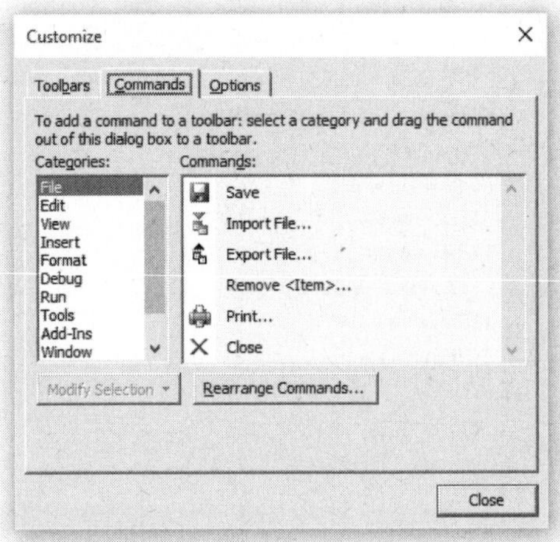

FIGURE 2.21
Use the Customize dialog box to tailor the Visual Basic Editor's menus, toolbars, and context menus.

Customizing the Toolbox

You can also customize the Toolbox, a special pane that contains controls for building user forms. It can be made visible only when a user form is visible in the Code window. (Chapters 14 and 15 show you how to build user forms.)

You can customize this Toolbox by adding and removing controls and adding new Toolbox pages of your own. Some programmers put their most-used controls on the Toolbox, all on one page, to save themselves time. These controls can include customized variations on the regular Toolbox controls, and by putting them on the Toolbox, you avoid having to customize them again.

For example, many dialog boxes you create need an OK button that dismisses the dialog box, implements some code, and then continues execution of the procedure. Each OK button needs its `Name` property set to `cmdOK`, its `Caption` property set to `OK`, its `Default` property set to `True`, and its `Height` and `Width` properties set to a size smaller than the clunky dimensions the Visual Basic Editor assigns by default. Once you've customized a command button by modifying all these properties, you can place a copy of the special button on the Toolbox and easily just reuse it for subsequent forms. Another control that's a candidate for this kind of customization is the TextBox. The default TextBox displays only a single line of text, and uses a nearly unreadable tiny font size of 8. To avoid having to modify these default properties each time you use a TextBox, create a custom TextBox that has multiple lines and is set to a font size of 11 or so.

Another reason to customize the Toolbox is to add advanced controls that extend the things you can do with dialog boxes and user forms.

ADDING CONTROLS TO THE TOOLBOX

The first way you'll probably want to add controls to the Toolbox is directly from a user form. For example, create your custom TextBox, and then copy it from the user form to the Toolbox.

To copy one of your custom controls from a displayed user form to the Toolbox, just drag it and drop it, as shown in Figure 2.22. (Chapter 14 shows you how to put controls onto user forms you create yourself.)

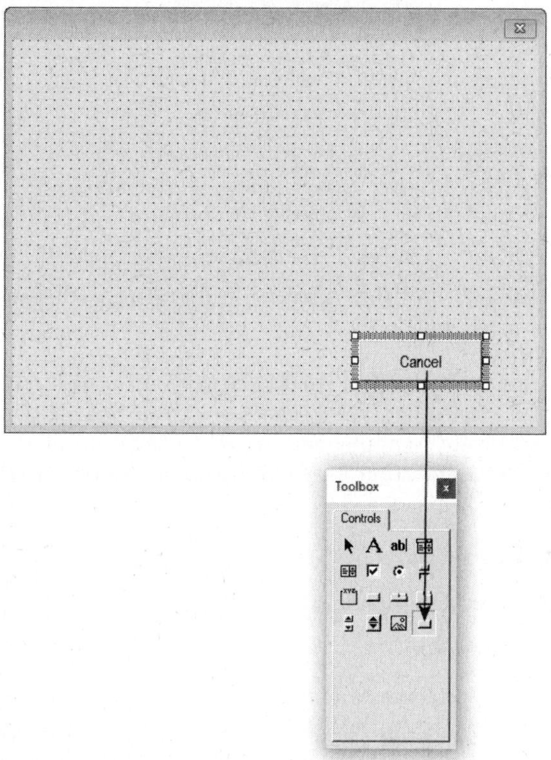

FIGURE 2.22
The quickest way to add a control to the Toolbox is to drag it there from a user form.

Microsoft and other vendors also provide a variety of prewritten controls you can add to your Toolbox. To add these controls, follow these steps:

1. Right-click in the Toolbox page (not the tab itself) where you want to add controls. (You'll learn how to add new pages to the Toolbox in the section "Adding Pages to the Toolbox" a little later in this chapter.)
2. Choose Additional Controls from the context menu to display the Additional Controls dialog box shown in Figure 2.23.

3. In the Available Controls list box, click the check boxes for the controls you want to add to the Toolbox, and then click the OK button.

FIGURE 2.23
In the Additional Controls dialog box, select the check boxes for the controls you want to add and then click the OK button.

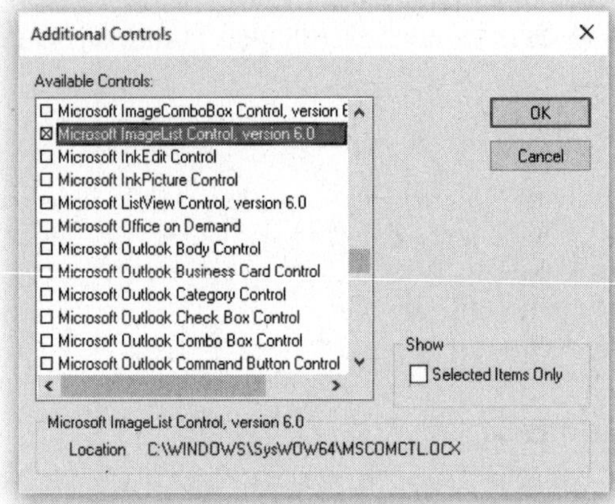

Once you are finished, if you would like to collapse the list to see only the currently selected items, click the Selected Items Only check box in the Show group box.

Depending on your computer and what software is installed on it, you may find a variety of interesting and useful controls. There are numerous controls, but these are among the most noteworthy:

- A set of Microsoft Outlook controls
- A control for Apple's QuickTime
- A status-bar control

Some of these controls can add important functionality to your macros. You can also search the Internet for additional specialized controls such as calendars, security locks, and so on. Adding prebuilt controls is quite convenient: You simply drag and drop functionality onto your user forms—functionality that doesn't require you to spend days writing code.

You can move a control from one page of the Toolbox to another by dragging it from the page it's on and moving the mouse pointer (still dragging) over the tab of the destination page to display that page. Then, move the mouse pointer down (again, still dragging) into the body of that page and drop the control.

RENAMING A TOOLBOX CONTROL

When you move the mouse pointer over a control in the Toolbox, a ScreenTip appears, showing the name of that control. To rename a control, right-click it in the Toolbox and choose the Customize option from the context menu to display the Customize Control dialog box.

Type the name for the control in the Tool Tip Text box in the Customize Control dialog box (delete or change the existing name as necessary). This name appears as a ScreenTip when the user moves the mouse pointer over the control in the Toolbox. Then, if you like, assign a different picture to the control's Toolbox icon, as described in the next section. Otherwise, click the OK button to close the Customize Control dialog box.

Assigning a Picture to a Control's Toolbox Icon

Each control in the Toolbox is identified by a picture. You can assign a new picture to the control by displaying the Customize Control dialog box, clicking the Load Picture button, and selecting the picture or icon in the resulting dialog box. If you add a personalized control (like the button control we added earlier in this chapter), you might want to use a different icon to distinguish your control from the default VBA button.

You can edit the picture assigned to some controls by displaying the Customize Control dialog box, clicking the Edit Picture button, and using the Edit Image dialog box to color the pixels that make up the picture.

Removing Controls from the Toolbox

To remove a control from the Toolbox, right-click it and choose Delete from the context menu. The item is identified by the name of the control—for example, if you right-click a control named Company Name Combo Box, the menu item is named Delete Company Name Combo Box.

If the item is a custom control you created, this action gets rid of the control and you can't restore it (unless you have a copy elsewhere). If the item is one of the Microsoft-supplied controls that come with the Microsoft Forms 2.0 package (which is automatically used by VBA), you can restore it to the Toolbox using the Additional Controls dialog box. Just select the check box for the appropriate object (for example, Microsoft Forms 2.0 CommandButton).

You can also remove controls from the Toolbox by deleting the entire page on which they appear. See "Removing Pages from the Toolbox," later in this chapter.

Adding Pages to the Toolbox

To add a page to the Toolbox, right-click the tab at the top of a page (or the label on the tab) and choose New Page from the context menu. The Visual Basic Editor adds a new page named New Page, to which it adds the Select Objects control. You'll probably want to rename the new page immediately.

By the way, the Select Objects control (its icon is a black arrow) appears on *every* page in the Toolbox, and you can't remove it. This is strange since you can go years without ever clicking it. This "control" is unlike others. It isn't added to a form. Instead, it must be selected in the Toolbox when you're resizing or repositioning, or when you otherwise need to select a true control on the form. However, when you merely click a control (and following many other actions), VBA automatically activates this "select object" feature—so you'll find that you never actually click it.

Renaming Pages in the Toolbox

To change the name of a Toolbox page, right-click its tab or label and choose Rename from the context menu to display the Rename dialog box. Type the name in the Caption text box, type any control tip text in the Control Tip Text box, and click the OK button to close the dialog box.

Removing Pages from the Toolbox

To remove a page from the Toolbox, right-click its tab or label and choose Delete Page from the context menu. The Visual Basic Editor removes the page from the Toolbox without any confirmation, regardless of whether the page contains controls.

Importing and Exporting Toolbox Pages

If you want to share Toolbox pages, you can save them as separate files and distribute them to your colleagues. Toolbox pages have a `.pag` filename extension.

To import a Toolbox page, right-click the tab or label on an existing page in the Toolbox and choose Import Page from the context menu to display the Import Page dialog box. Select the page you want to import and click the Open button in the dialog box. The Visual Basic Editor adds the new page after the last page currently in the Toolbox and names it New Page.

Right-click the page's tab or label, choose Rename, type a new name and description, and then click the OK button.

Likewise, you can export a Toolbox page by right-clicking its tab or label and choosing Export Page from the context menu to display the Export Page dialog box. Type a name for the page, choose the folder in which to save it, and then click the Save button to save it. Now anyone can import your page into their Editor as described previously.

Moving Pages in the Toolbox

To move a page in the Toolbox, right-click its tab or label and choose Move from the context menu to display the Page Order dialog box. In the Page Order list box, select the page or pages you want to move (Shift+click to select multiple contiguous pages, Ctrl+click to select multiple pages individually) and use the Move Up and Move Down buttons to rearrange the pages as desired. Click the OK button to close the Page Order dialog box when you've finished.

The Bottom Line

Open the Visual Basic Editor. When you want to create a new macro by hand-programming (as opposed to recording) or need to modify or test a macro, the Visual Basic Editor is a powerful tool.

Master It Open the Visual Basic Editor in Word and create a simple macro.

Open a macro in the Visual Basic Editor. You edit and test macro code in the Code window of the Visual Basic Editor.

Master It Open the Visual Basic Editor and display a particular macro in the Code window.

Understand the Project Explorer's two views. The Project Explorer window displays a tree of current projects. You can choose between viewing only the files or the folders and files.

Master It Switch between folder and contents view in the Project Explorer.

Set properties for a project. You can specify a project's name, an associated Help file, and other qualities of a project.

Master It Lock a project so others can't modify or even read its contents.

Customize the Visual Basic Editor. The Visual Basic Editor can be customized in many ways, including personalizing classic menus and toolbars.

Master It Undock the Properties window and change its size. Then redock it.

Chapter 3

Editing Recorded Macros

In this chapter, you'll use the Visual Basic Editor to edit the Word and Excel macros you recorded with the Macro Recorder in Chapter 1, "Recording and Running Macros in the Office Applications." In addition, you'll create a new macro in PowerPoint and see how to edit it. Even if you're working with an application that doesn't include the Macro Recorder (such as PowerPoint), you may still want to read through this chapter because it shows you how to use some of the key editing features of the Visual Basic Editor.

There are three reasons for using the Visual Basic Editor to work with macros:

- First, to fix any problems in the behavior of a macro you recorded. For example, if you accidentally hit the Enter key while recording the macro, the macro will keep performing that wrong instruction every time you run it unless you remove or change the instruction. You would want to delete this line of code in your macro:

  ```
  Selection.TypeParagraph
  ```

  (Alternatively, it's sometimes easier to just rerecord a macro than it is to repair it manually.)
- Second, to add further instructions to the macro to make it behave differently. This is a great way to get started learning the VBA language. And sometimes by just making relatively small or simple changes to a recorded macro, you can greatly increase its power and flexibility.
- Third, to create new macros by writing them in the Visual Basic Editor instead of recording them. You can write a new macro from scratch or paste in parts of an existing macro, as appropriate.

IN THIS CHAPTER, YOU WILL LEARN TO DO THE FOLLOWING:

- Test a macro in the Visual Basic Editor
- Set breakpoints and use comments
- Edit the recorded Word macro
- Edit the recorded Excel macro
- Edit a new PowerPoint macro

Testing a Macro in the Visual Basic Editor

If a macro fails when you try to run it from the host application, the quickest way to find out what's going wrong is to open the macro in the Visual Basic Editor, run it, and see where in the code it fails:

1. In the host application, press Alt+F8 or choose View ➤ Macros to display the Macros dialog box.
2. Select the macro, and then click the Edit button. The host application opens an instance of the Visual Basic Editor and displays the macro for editing.
3. Start the macro running by pressing F5. Alternatively, you could choose Run ➤ Run Sub/UserForm or click the Run Sub/UserForm button (a green arrow) on the Standard toolbar in the Visual Basic Editor (see Figure 3.1).

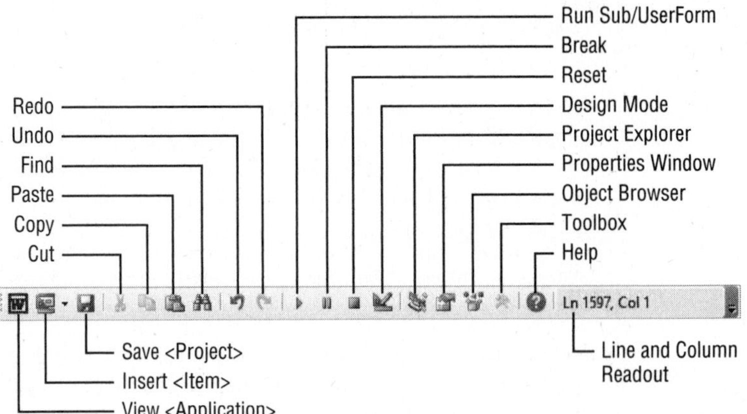

FIGURE 3.1 Click the Run Sub/UserForm button on the Standard toolbar to start running the code.

4. If the macro encounters an error and halts execution (goes into *Break mode*), VBA displays an error-message box onscreen and selects the offending statement in the Code window (displays white letters on a blue background). You can then edit the statement to fix the problem. Once you've done so, step through the macro as described in the next section.

UNDERSTANDING THE VBA EDITOR MODES

The VBA Editor is always in one of three modes:

- *Design mode* when you're designing a user form or writing code
- *Execution mode* when you've pressed F5 and are running your code, usually to see how it behaves to test it
- *Break mode* when execution has been halted (so you can examine variables or otherwise take a look at what's going on in the code)

The Editor halts execution and enters Break mode in several ways: when you press Ctrl+Break, each time you press F8 to single-step through the code, when the Editor encounters a breakpoint that you've set within the code (discussed shortly), or when certain types of errors occur.

You can tell if you're in Break mode by looking at the Editor's title bar (at the very top of the Editor). If you see the word [*break*], you're in Break mode. You'll also see the line of code that's next to be executed highlighted in yellow.

When you're in Break mode, you can return to normal Design (editing) mode (so you can type in the Code window to revise and retest the macro) by clicking the Reset button on the Standard toolbar in the Visual Basic Editor (it's the blue square next to the Break button—a pause symbol). If you ever find yourself unable to type in the Editor, or the Editor is otherwise behaving strangely, remember to click this Reset button to get out of Break mode and restore normalcy.

TEST MACROS ONLY ON FILES YOU DON'T CARE ABOUT

Always test your macros on documents or files (or copies of them) that you don't care about. There are few better ways to lose valuable work than to unleash an untested macro on a document and watch it get mangled or worse.

Also, try to store your code in a central location (such as `Normal.dotm` in Word or the Personal Macro Workbook in Excel) so that it's accessible to all your files rather than only the file that contains it. If you create a macro in the wrong file, export it from that file and import it into your centralized storage. To export a macro, right-click its module in the Project Explorer, choose Export File from the context menu, use the Export File dialog box to specify the folder and filename, and then click the Save button. To import a module, right-click the destination project in the Project Explorer, choose Import File, select the file in the Import File dialog box, and then click the Open button.

Stepping Through a Macro

To see exactly what a macro does (and what it does wrong), you can *step through* the macro—go through the macro, executing one command at a time, like watching a football replay in slow motion. This way you can see the effect of each command. Stepping through a macro can be time-consuming, but it's one of the best ways to identify problems and fix them. You can, for example, switch at any time to the document, presentation, or spreadsheet to see the effect of the just-executed line in the code.

Usually debugging is a matter of finding out *where* in the code something goes wrong. Although you generally already know *what* goes wrong, you still need to figure out the location of the problem in your code; then you can determine how the error happens.

To step through a macro, follow these steps:

1. Open the host application, and then open the macro for editing by pressing Alt+F8. Select the macro, and then click the Edit button.

2. Sometimes it's helpful to arrange the Visual Basic Editor window and the host application's window so that you can see them both simultaneously. Either arrange the windows manually or use a Windows command to do so. For example, stack the windows by right-clicking in open space on the Windows Taskbar and choosing Show Windows Stacked from the context menu. Alternatively, you can select Show Windows Side By Side. If you have any other applications currently running, minimize them so they won't be included in your stack. (If you have two monitors, you can dedicate one to the Editor and one to the application.) In Windows 7 or Windows 8, the quickest way to display two windows is to drag one of them to the far left (drop it, and it will snap to that location and automatically resize so it takes up 50 percent of the screen). Drag the other window to the right. In Windows 10, press Windows Key+←, or Windows Key+→.
3. Now set up any conditions the macro expects. Perhaps you need to have a document open. For example, to run properly, a macro that applies a style to the current paragraph requires that a paragraph is actually available.
4. Click somewhere in the macro code. The location of the blinking vertical line (insertion cursor) is how the Editor determines which macro you want to work with.
5. Press F8 to step through the macro command by command. Each time you press F8, one line of your VBA code will be executed. The Visual Basic Editor highlights in yellow each command as it's executed, and you can switch to the application to watch the effect and try to catch errors.

Pressing F8 Is the Easiest Way to Step Through Macros

You can also step through a macro by choosing Debug ➤ Step Into or by clicking the Step Into button on the Debug toolbar, but the F8 key is easiest to use. After all, you'll often need to step repeatedly until you locate the problem. Pressing a single key is quite a bit more efficient than repetitively opening a menu.

Figure 3.2 provides an example of stepping through a macro recorded in Word.

Figure 3.2 Stepping through a macro recorded in Word

```
Sub closeAllPanes()

'ctrlx
' closeAllPanes Macro
'
'
    CommandBars("Navigation").Visible = False
    CommandBars("Styles").Visible = False
    CommandBars("Research").Visible = False
    With ActiveWindow.View
        .ShowFormatChanges = False
        .ShowComments = False
    End With

End Sub
```

You'll learn about debugging macros in detail in Chapter 17, "Debugging Your Code and Handling Errors." However, let me briefly introduce two additional important techniques that can help you locate bugs in your macros: setting breakpoints and commenting out lines.

Setting Breakpoints

A *breakpoint* can be specified for a line of code to tell VBA to stop executing the macro there. By using a breakpoint, you can first press F5 to quickly execute known functional parts of a macro at full speed, and then the Editor automatically stops at the breakpoint. You put a breakpoint just before where you suspect a bug is located in the code. That way, you don't have to step through *all* your code. You can execute the macro at normal, rapid speed—but then halt near the suspicious location and begin pressing F8 to step through the code, executing it slowly, statement by statement, to closely observe the behaviors. You can set as many breakpoints as you want.

To toggle a breakpoint on or off, right-click in a line of executable code (not a comment line, described in the following section) and choose Toggle ➤ Breakpoint from the context menu or click the Toggle Breakpoint button on the Edit toolbar. Even easier, just click in the gray margin-indicator bar to the left of the line of code.

A line of code on which you set a breakpoint is shaded red by default. The breakpoint itself is designated by a red circle in the margin indicator bar (see Figure 3.3).

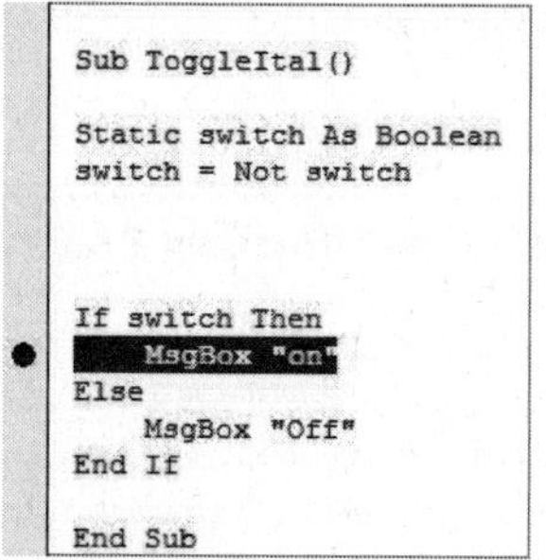

Sub ToggleItal()
Static switch As Boolean
switch = Not switch
If switch Then
MsgBox "on"
Else
MsgBox "Off"
End If
End Sub

FIGURE 3.3
Use a breakpoint (the red circle that appears in the margin indicator bar) to stop code execution at a line of your choice.

BREAKPOINTS ARE NOT PERSISTENT

Breakpoints are temporary—the Visual Basic Editor doesn't save them with your code. You must specify them for each editing session.

Commenting Out Lines

Like most programming languages, VBA lets you add comments to your code so that it's easier to understand. Comments can be invaluable both while you're creating code and when you're revisiting your own code long enough after you've forgotten what it does—or, worse, when you're trying to figure out what someone else's code does.

However, there's another use for commenting. You can also *comment out* lines of code to prevent the Visual Basic Editor from executing them. In other words, comments are normally just notes to self that are not part of the macro proper. They are not written in VBA, nor does the Editor pay any attention to them when examining the code for errors, or executing the code. So, sometimes while debugging you'll want to comment out a line or lines of executable code in your macro. That way during execution, this line is simply not executed. It's ignored.

This can be a useful technique for temporarily skipping over suspect lines of code without actually removing them from the macro. Then you run the code and see what the difference is with the commented lines ignored. If the bug goes away, it's probably located within the lines that are commented out. For example, if the macro suddenly and wrongly deletes some lines in the document and then doesn't do that when some lines are commented out, you've found the bug!

To comment out a line manually, type an apostrophe (`'`) at the very beginning of the line. Alternatively, you can use the `Rem` command instead of the apostrophe. (`Rem` is short for `remark`, and comment lines are sometimes called remark lines.) To uncomment the line manually, just delete the apostrophe or `Rem`.

The Visual Basic Editor provides convenient Comment Block and Uncomment Block commands for commenting out multiple lines automatically. Select the target lines of code, and then click the Comment Block button on the Edit toolbar to place an apostrophe at the beginning of each line; to uncomment a line or a group of selected lines, click the Uncomment Block button, and the Visual Basic Editor removes an apostrophe from each line.

The Comment Block command uses only apostrophes, not with `Rem` lines. If you prefer to use `Rem`, you must comment and uncomment lines manually. Few people, though, use `Rem` these days.

COMMENT BLOCK COMMANDS CAN BE EFFICIENT

The Comment Block command adds an apostrophe to the beginning of each line in the selected block, even for lines that are already commented (this does no harm). Likewise, the Uncomment Block command removes apostrophes one at a time from each line in the selected block rather than removing all apostrophes at once. This behavior helps preserve comment lines and enables you to use different levels of commenting.

Stepping Out of a Macro

Once you've identified and fixed the problem with a macro, you probably won't want to step through the rest of the macro command by command. To run the rest of the macro and the rest of any macro that called it (triggered it), you can again press the F5 key. Alternatively, you can click the Run Sub/UserForm button on the Standard toolbar or the Debug toolbar (see Figure 3.4), or you can choose Run ➢ Continue.

If you want to run only the rest of *this* macro, and then return to stepping through the macro that called (triggered) this one, use the Step Out command. The Step Out command finishes executing the current macro or procedure at full speed, but if the code then continues with another procedure, the Visual Basic Editor reverts to Break mode so you can examine that procedure's code. We'll explore what it means to *call* procedures later in this book.

To issue the Step Out command, press Ctrl+Shift+F8, click the Step Out button on the Debug toolbar, or choose Debug ➢ Step Out.

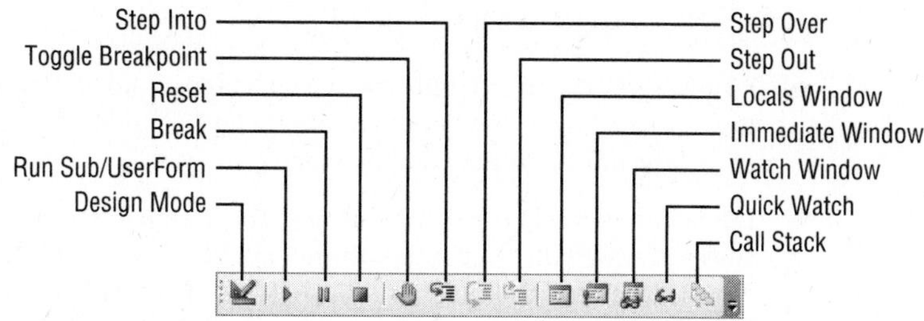

FIGURE 3.4 The Debug toolbar contains commands for running code, stepping into it and out of it, and displaying key windows for debugging.

Editing a Word Macro

Now try editing the `Transpose_Word_Right` macro that you recorded in Word in Chapter 1, and also build another macro out of it. To begin, open the macro in the Visual Basic Editor:

1. Start Word if it's not already running, or activate it.
2. Press Alt+F8.
3. Select the `Transpose_Word_Right` macro, and then click the Edit button.

In the Code window, you should see code similar to Listing 3.1, except for the line numbers, which I'm using here to identify the lines of code.

LISTING 3.1: The recorded transpose-words macro

```
Sub Transpose_Word_Right()
'
' Transpose_Word_Right Macro
' Transposes the current word with the word to its right. _
'Created 5/5/13 by Nanci Selest-Gomes.
'
    Selection.Extend
    Selection.Extend
    Selection.EscapeKey
    Selection.Cut
    Selection.MoveRight Unit:=wdWord, Count:=1
    Selection.PasteAndFormat (wdFormatOriginalFormatting)
    Selection.MoveLeft Unit:=wdWord, Count:=1
End Sub
```

Here's what the macro does:

- Line 1 starts the macro with the `Sub Transpose_Word_Right()` statement, and line 14 ends the macro with the `End Sub` statement. The `Sub` and `End Sub` lines mark the beginning and end of the macro (as they do any macro).
- Lines 2 and 6 are blank comment lines the Macro Recorder inserts to make your macro easier to read. You can use any number of blank lines or blank comment lines in a macro to help separate statements into groups. (A blank line doesn't have to be commented out—it can just be blank—but the Macro Recorder has added commenting to these blank lines to make it clear what they are.)
- Lines 3 through 5 are comment lines that contain the name of the macro and its description. The Macro Recorder entered these lines from the information you typed into the Record Macro dialog box.
- Line 7 records the first keystroke of the F8 key, which starts Extend mode—a way of selecting text in a Word document.
- Line 8 records the second keystroke of the F8 key, which continues Extend mode and thereby selects the current word.
- Line 9 records the keystroke of the Esc key, which cancels Extend mode.
- Line 10 records the Cut command, which cuts the selection (in this case, the selected word) to the Clipboard.
- Line 11 records the Ctrl+→ command, which moves the insertion point one word to the right.
- Line 12 records the Paste command, which pastes the selection into the document at the current position of the insertion point. Whatever formatting was originally applied to the selection is retained (rather than applying the formatting in effect at the new location).
- Line 13 records the Ctrl+← command, which moves the insertion point one word to the left.

Stepping Through the *Transpose_Word_Right* Macro

Now try stepping through this macro in Break mode using the Step Into command:

1. Arrange your screen so you can see both the active Word window and the Visual Basic Editor window (for example, by right-clicking the Taskbar and choosing Show Windows Stacked from the context menu or by snapping each window to a side of the screen).
2. Click in the Visual Basic Editor, and then click to place the blinking insertion point at the start (on the `Sub`) of the `Transpose_Word_Right` macro in the Code window.
3. Press F8 to step through the code one active line at a time. You'll notice that VBA skips the blank lines and the comment lines because they're supposed to be ignored by the computer during execution. VBA highlights the current statement each time you press F8, and you see the actions taking place in the Word window.

The Visual Basic Editor leaves Break mode when it reaches the end of the macro (in this case, when you press F8 to execute the `End Sub` statement in line 14). The Editor returns to Design mode. You can also exit Break mode at any time by clicking the Reset button (blue square) on the Standard or the Debug toolbar, or by choosing Run ➤ Reset. Unfortunately, there's no key on the keyboard you can press to halt execution. You must use the mouse.

Running the *Transpose_Word_Right* Macro

If the macro works fine when you step through it, you may also want to run it from the Visual Basic Editor. Just press F5. In Break mode, F5 executes the macro, starting from the current instruction (where the insertion cursor is located).

Creating a *Transpose_Word_Left* Macro

At this point we'll modify the macro. We'll create a `Transpose_Word_Left` macro by making minor adjustments to the `Transpose_Word_Right` macro. Follow these steps.

1. In the Code window, select all the code for the `Transpose_Word_Right` macro, from the `Sub Transpose_Word_Right()` line to the `End Sub` line. You can select in three ways: by dragging with the mouse, by holding down Shift and using the arrow keys to extend the selection, or by positioning the insertion point at one end of the macro and then Shift+clicking the other end.
2. Copy the code by issuing a Copy command (for example, by right-clicking and choosing Copy from the context menu or by pressing Ctrl+C or Ctrl+Insert).
3. Click to move the insertion point to the line below the `End Sub` statement for the `Transpose_Word_Right` macro in the Code window.
4. Paste the code by issuing a Paste command (by right-clicking and choosing Paste from the context menu or by pressing Ctrl+V or Shift+Insert). The Visual Basic Editor automatically enters a horizontal line between the `End Sub` statement for the `Transpose_Word_Right` macro and the new macro you've pasted.
5. Change the name of the second `Transpose_Word_Right` macro to `Transpose_Word_`**`Left`** by editing the `Sub` line:

   ```
   Sub Transpose_Word_Left()
   ```

6. Edit the comment lines at the beginning of the macro accordingly—for example,

   ```
   'Transpose_Word_Left Macro
   'Transposes the current word with the word to its left. _
   'Created 5/5/13 by Nanci Selest-Gomes.
   ```

7. Now all you need to do is replace the `MoveRight` method with the `MoveLeft` method. This will move the insertion point one word to the left instead of one word to the right. While you could do that by typing the correction or by using Cut and Paste to replace the `Selection.MoveRight` line with the commented-out `Selection.MoveLeft` line, try using the List Properties/Methods feature instead. Just for practice, follow these steps:
   a. Click to place the insertion point in the word `MoveRight`.

b. Click the List Properties/Methods button on the Edit toolbar to display the list of properties and methods. It's the first button on the far left. Or just press Ctrl+J. (If the Edit toolbar isn't visible, right-click one of the existing toolbars and choose Edit from the context menu.)

c. Double-click the `MoveLeft` method in the list to make it replace the `MoveRight` method in the code line.

8. Now that you no longer need it, delete the line `Selection.MoveLeft Unit:=wdWord, Count:=1` from the end of the macro.

You should end up with a macro that looks like Listing 3.2.

LISTING 3.2: The edited transpose-words macro

```
Sub Transpose_Word_Left()
'
' Transpose_Word_Left Macro
' Transposes the current word with the word to its left. _
' 'Created 5/5/13 by Nanci Selest-Gomes.
'
    Selection.Extend
    Selection.Extend
    Selection.EscapeKey
    Selection.Cut
    Selection.MoveLeft Unit:=wdWord, Count:=1
    Selection.PasteAndFormat (wdFormatOriginalFormatting)
End Sub
```

Try stepping through this macro to make sure it works. If it does, you're ready to save it—and perhaps to create a Quick Access Toolbar button, or keyboard shortcut, for it—in Word if you plan to use it in your writing.

Saving Your Work

When you finish working with this or any other macro, choose File ➤ Save (Ctrl+S) from the Visual Basic Editor to save the document or template that contains the macro and the changes you've made to it. Then press Alt+Q or choose File ➤ Close And Return To Microsoft Word to close the Visual Basic Editor and return to Word.

Editing the Excel Macro

In the following sections, you'll edit the Excel macro that you recorded in Chapter 1. This time, you won't create a new macro—instead, you'll just add to the existing one.

Unhiding the Personal Macro Workbook

Before you can edit the Excel macro, you'll need to unhide the Personal Macro Workbook if it's currently hidden:

1. Open the View tab on the Ribbon.
2. If the Unhide button is gray (disabled) in the Window group, then no workbooks are hidden, including Personal. You can skip the following steps. However, if the Unhide button is black (enabled), click it to display the Unhide dialog box.
3. Select `PERSONAL.XLSM` or `PERSONAL.XLSB` and click the OK button. If you stored the macro from Chapter 1 in another workbook, open that workbook before trying to proceed. To hide the Personal Macro Workbook again after editing the macro, click the Hide button on the Ribbon while the Personal Macro Workbook is active (visible).

Creating a Backup Copy of Your Files

Eventually, you'll have a collection of macros in the Personal workbook. It's a good idea to keep a backup copy of these files in case something happens—such as a general collapse of your hard drive. You don't want to lose your macro collection. To create a backup file, just locate `PERSONAL.XLSB` in Windows 8 by pressing the Windows key+F (or in Windows 7, just by pressing the Windows key) to open the Windows Search field and typing in its name. Then right-click `PERSONAL.XLSB` in the search-results list and choose Open File Location.

In Windows 10, type **PERSONAL.XLSB** into the Cortana search field where it says "Ask Me Anything" on the left side of the taskbar. Then click the "My Stuff" option just about the search field to see the list.

It's likely to be found here in any version of Windows: `C:\Users\Your Name\AppData\Roaming\Microsoft\Excel\XLSTART\PERSONAL.XLSB`.

Now you can copy the file, save it to another location, and rename it something like **PERSONAL.BAK**.

Also make a backup copy of any other important macro collections, such as Word's `Normal.Dotm` file.

Opening a Macro for Editing

Now take the following steps to open the Excel macro you recorded in Chapter 1 for viewing and editing:

1. Press Alt+F8 to display the Macros dialog box.
2. Select the macro named `Add_Months`.
3. Click the Edit button to display the macro for editing in the Visual Basic Editor. Listing 3.3 shows code similar to what you should be seeing.

LISTING 3.3: New "workbook with months added" macro

```
1.  Sub Add_Months()
2.  '
3.  ' Add_Months Macro
4.  ' Fills in months for the year. Recorded 9/29/15 by Abe Normal.
5.  '
6.  '
7.  '
8.      Range("A1").Select
9.      ActiveCell.FormulaR1C1 = "Jan-2016"
10.     Range("B1").Select
11.     ActiveCell.FormulaR1C1 = "Feb-2016"
12.     Selection.AutoFill Destination:=Range("B1:L1"), Type:=xlFillDefault
13. End Sub
```

Here's what happens in the macro in Listing 3.3:

- Line 1 starts the macro with the `Sub New_Workbook_with_Months()` statement, and line 16 ends the macro with the `End Sub` statement.
- Lines 2 through 7 are comment lines that the Macro Recorder automatically adds. (The comment lines that are blank are merely to make the code easier to read. Delete any blank or comment lines you want. They'll have no effect on the behavior of the macro, although removing them could make it less readable in the Editor. It's your call.)
- Line 3 is a comment line that gives the macro's name and describes it as a macro, and line 4 contains the description from the Record Macro dialog box.
- Line 8 selects the `Range` object `A1`, making cell A1 active.
- Line 9 enters `Jan-2016` in the active cell. Notice that the Macro Recorder has stored the parsed date value rather than the text that you typed in (January 2016). Also, keep in mind that the date displayed in the cell may be in a different format than *`MMM`*.
- Line 10 selects the `Range` object B1, making cell B1 active, and line 11 enters `Feb-2011` in that cell.
- Line 12 performs a default AutoFill operation on the range A1:L1.

Editing a Macro

Now modify the macro by following these steps:

1. Select lines 8 through 12.
2. Copy these lines by pressing Ctrl+C or right-clicking in the selection and choosing Copy from the context menu.
3. Press the Enter key to insert a new blank line just above the `End Sub` line.

4. Paste the copied lines by pressing Ctrl+V, choosing Edit ➤ Paste, or right-clicking at the insertion point and choosing Paste from the context menu.

Your new macro should look like Listing 3.4.

LISTING 3.4: New extended version

```
1.  Sub Add_Months()
2.  '
3.  ' Add_Months Macro
4.  ' Fills in months for the year. Recorded 9/29/15 by Abe Normal.
5.  '
6.  '
7.  '
8.      Range("A1").Select
9.      ActiveCell.FormulaR1C1 = "Jan-2016"
10.     Range("B1").Select
11.     ActiveCell.FormulaR1C1 = "Feb-2016"
12.     Selection.AutoFill Destination:=Range("B1:L1"), Type:=xlFillDefault
13.     Range("A1").Select
14.     ActiveCell.FormulaR1C1 = "Jan-2016"
15.     Range("B1").Select
16.     ActiveCell.FormulaR1C1 = "Feb-2016"
17.     Selection.AutoFill Destination:=Range("B1:L1"), Type:=xlFillDefault
18. End Sub
```

Now, change the macro to display a second row of autofilled values by taking the following steps:

1. Change line 13 to select cell A2 instead of cell A1:

   `Range("A2").Select`

2. Change line 14 so that it enters the value `1` instead of `Jan-2016`:

   `ActiveCell.FormulaR1C1 = 1`

3. Change line 15 to select cell L2 instead of cell B1:

   `Range("L2").Select`

4. Change line 16 so that it enters the value `12` instead of `Feb-2016`:

   `ActiveCell.FormulaR1C1 = 200`

5. Change line 17 so that it performs the `AutoFill` operation on the range A2:L2, and change the fill type to `xlFillSeries`:

   `Selection.AutoFill Destination:=Range("A2:L2"), Type:=xlFillSeries`

6. Click the Save button or choose File ➤ Save to save the changes you made.

The macro should now read like Listing 3.5.

LISTING 3.5: Streamlined macro

```
Sub Add_Months()
'
' Add_Months Macro
' Fills in months for the year. Recorded 9/29/15 by Abe Normal.
'
'
'
    Range("A1").Select
    ActiveCell.FormulaR1C1 = "Jan-2016"
    Range("B1").Select
    ActiveCell.FormulaR1C1 = "Feb-2016"
    Selection.AutoFill Destination:=Range("B1:L1"), Type:=xlFillDefault
    Range("A2").Select
    ActiveCell.FormulaR1C1 = "1"
    Range("L2").Select
    ActiveCell.FormulaR1C1 = "12"
    Selection.AutoFill Destination:=Range("A2:L2"), Type:=xlFillSeries
End Sub
```

To see this in action, choose File ➤ New Blank Workbook. Make sure you're seeing this new workbook (this makes it the active workbook, the one where our macro will do its job). Now step through the macro and watch what happens: As before it enters the months, but then it enters the values 1 through 12 in the second row of cells. This one is fun to watch on a split screen because you watch the cells fill with data as you step through it.

Editing a PowerPoint Macro

In this section, you'll edit a PowerPoint macro. PowerPoint has no Macro Recorder, so you'll either have to type in the code for the following example or, better, just copy and paste it from this book's web page at `www.sybex.com/go/masteringvba2016`.

Start by opening the PowerPoint Visual Basic Editor:

1. Open PowerPoint, and choose the blank presentation template. Now add a shape by clicking the Insert tab on the Ribbon and then clicking the Shapes icon in the Illustrations section.
2. Click to select a rectangle shape of your choice, and click somewhere in the slide to create it. This will be object 1 in the Shapes collection, so we can refer to it in the code like this:

   ```
   ActiveWindow.Selection.SlideRange.Shapes(1).Select
   ```
3. Open the PowerPoint Visual Basic Editor by pressing Alt+F11.

4. Create a new, empty module by choosing Insert ➤ Module in the Editor. Now you're ready to add some code.

5. Type in (or paste from this book's web page) the code shown in Listing 3.6.

LISTING 3.6: Add a slide in PowerPoint

```
Sub Add_Slide_and_Format_Placeholder()
'
' Sample macro that adds a slide, formats its placeholder,
' and adds text to it. Recorded 6/16/15 by Batfield Dial.
'
    ActiveWindow.View.GotoSlide Index:= _
        ActivePresentation.Slides.Add(Index:=2, _
        Layout:=ppLayoutText).SlideIndex
    ActiveWindow.Selection.SlideRange.Layout = ppLayoutTitle
    ActiveWindow.Selection.SlideRange.Shapes(1).Select
    With ActiveWindow.Selection.ShapeRange
        .IncrementLeft -6#
        .IncrementTop -125.75
    End With
    ActiveWindow.Selection.ShapeRange.ScaleHeight 1.56, msoFalse, _
        msoScaleFromTopLeft
    ActiveWindow.Selection.SlideRange.Shapes(1).Select
    ActiveWindow.Selection.ShapeRange.TextFrame.TextRange.Select
    ActiveWindow.Selection.ShapeRange.TextFrame.TextRange.Characters _
        (Start:=1, Length:=0).Select
    With ActiveWindow.Selection.TextRange
        .Text = "The quick brown dog jumped over the lazy fox"
        With .Font
            .Name = "Arial"
            .Size = 44
            .Bold = msoFalse
            .Italic = msoFalse
            .Underline = msoFalse
            .Shadow = msoFalse
            .Emboss = msoFalse
            .BaselineOffset = 0
            .AutoRotateNumbers = msoFalse
            .Color.SchemeColor = ppTitle
        End With
    End With
    ActiveWindow.Selection.ShapeRange.TextFrame.TextRange.Characters _
        (Start:=1, Length:=42).Select
    With ActiveWindow.Selection.TextRange.Font
        .Name = "Impact"
```

```
34.             .Size = 54
35.             .Bold = msoFalse
36.             .Italic = msoFalse
37.             .Underline = msoFalse
38.             .Shadow = msoFalse
39.             .Emboss = msoFalse
40.             .BaselineOffset = 0
41.             .AutoRotateNumbers = msoFalse
42.             .Color.SchemeColor = ppTitle
43.         End With
44.     End Sub
```

Press F5 to run the macro and see what it does to PowerPoint.

Here's what happens in the macro:

- Line 1 starts the macro, and line 44 ends it.
- Lines 2 and 4 are blank comment lines used to set off the description of the macro, which appears in line 3.
- Line 5 adds the slide to the presentation. This statement is a little complicated, but don't worry about it too much just yet. For now, note two things: First, the statement uses the `Add` method with the `Slides` collection object to add a slide to the collection (in other words, to create a new slide in this case). This is similar to the way the Excel macro explored earlier in this chapter used the `Add` method to add a workbook to its `Workbooks` collection. Second, the layout of the slide is `ppLayoutText`, the VBA constant for the Text slide layout that PowerPoint uses for a default new slide.
- Line 6 applies the Title layout (`ppLayoutTitle`) that you chose when recording the macro. (If you chose a different slide layout, you'll see a different constant than `ppLayoutTitle`.)
- Line 7 selects the first shape in the `Shapes` collection on the active slide. (For the moment, don't worry about how you get to the active slide.)
- Lines 8 to 11 are a `With` block. This block begins with a `With` statement that specifies properties or behaviors (*methods*) for the shape that has been selected (`ActiveWindow.Selection.ShapeRange`). A `With` statement is a way of simplifying object references, and everything between the `With` statement and the `End With` statement refers to the objects that the `With` statement first mentions. In this case, line 9 uses the `IncrementLeft` method with a negative value to move the shape to the left, and line 10 uses the `IncrementTop` method with a negative value to move the shape up the slide.

The *With* Command Has Two Uses

`With` statements have two benefits: They simplify code (because you don't need to specify the object in each of the lines between the `With` and `End With` lines), and they make code run faster.

- Line 13 selects the first shape in the `Shapes` collection, and line 14 selects the `TextRange` object in the `TextFrame` object in the shape. When you're working interactively, PowerPoint makes this selection process seamless: You click in a shape displaying the legend "Click To Add Title" (or whatever), and PowerPoint selects the text range in the shape's text frame—but all you see is that the text in the shape becomes selected. In VBA, you have to go through a couple of unseen layers in the object model before getting to the text.
- When you select the placeholder text, PowerPoint gets rid of it. The same thing happens when you select the placeholder text via VBA. So line 15 makes a new selection at the beginning of the first character in the text range. The `Length` of the selection is `0`, meaning that the selection is collapsed to an insertion point rather than containing any characters. Line 16 starts a `With` statement that continues until line 30. The `With ActiveWindow .Selection.TextRange` statement in line 16 lets line 17 reference the `Text` property of the `TextRange` object in the `ActiveWindow` object's `Selection` object much more simply (instead of `ActiveWindow.Selection.TextRange.Text`), and it lets line 18 reference the `Font` property of the `TextRange` object in the `Selection` object in the `ActiveWindow` object easily (instead of `ActiveWindow.Selection.TextRange.Font`).
- Line 17 sets the `Text` property of the `ActiveWindow.Selection.TextRange` object to the text typed.
- Line 18 then begins a nested `With` statement that sets the properties of the `Font` object for the `TextRange` object. Line 19 sets the `Name` property of the `Font` object to `Arial`; line 20 sets the `Size` property of the `Font` object to `44`; line 21 sets the `Bold` property of the `Font` object to `msoFalse`, the Microsoft Office (`mso`) constant for `False`; and so on. These statements are not necessary for our purposes in this macro. But they're harmless, so you can leave them in your code or, if you like, delete this entire `With` block (as we'll do shortly). Line 29 ends the nested `With` statement.

With Blocks Can Be Nested

A nested `With` statement is one that is placed within another `With` statement and specifies an object within the object specified in the outer `With` statement. You can nest multiple-level `With` statements when necessary. You can see that the `With` block that begins on line 18 is nested within the outer `With` block that begins on line 16.

- Line 31 uses the `Select` method to select characters 1 through 42 in the text range. This is the same as pressing the Ctrl+Shift+Home key combination. Because this statement specifies the characters to select, you'll need to change it if you change the text that this macro inserts. (If you run the statement on a text range that has fewer than 42 characters, it will return an error. If you run it on a text range that has more than 42 characters, it will select only the first 42 characters in the text range—not what you want.)

- Line 32 begins another `With` statement that works with the `Font` object of the `TextRange` object. This `With` statement imitates what happens if the user opens and modifies the Font dialog box.
- Line 43 ends the `With` statement, and line 44 ends the macro.

Now try editing this macro by slimming it down a little and changing the text it inserts:

1. Delete the unnecessary `With` statement in lines 18 through 29.
2. Delete line 30.
3. Change lines 16 and 17 into a single statement without `With`:

   ```
   ActiveWindow.Selection.TextRange.Text = _
       "The quick brown dog jumped over the lazy fox"
   ```

4. Now change the text that the new line 16 inserts. Type any text of your choice between the double quotation marks.
5. Change line 31 to use the `Select` method on the text *range* rather than specifying which characters to select. Delete `Characters(Start:=1, Length:=42)` to leave this statement:

   ```
   ActiveWindow.Selection.ShapeRange.TextFrame.TextRange.Select
   ```

   By specifying a range rather than a particular character count, you avoid the problem discussed earlier of having to count characters any time you change the message. Specifying a character count is called *hard-coding* and it's to be avoided whenever possible. If there's a way—as there is here with the `TextRange` property—let the computer figure out the count rather than specifying it in your code.

6. Click the Save button on the Standard toolbar or choose File ➤ Save to save the changes you've made to the presentation. In the Save As dialog box, locate the Save As Type drop-down list and change it from the default `.pptx` type (which cannot contain macros) to the `.pptm` type (which can).

You should now have code that reads like Listing 3.7.

LISTING 3.7: The macro slimmed down and modified

```
1.  Sub Add_Slide_and_Format_Placeholder()
2.  '
3.  ' Sample macro that adds a slide, formats its placeholder, and adds text
4.  ' to it.        Recorded 12/4/15 by Rodney Converse.
5.  '
6.      ActiveWindow.View.GotoSlide Index:= _
7.          ActivePresentation.Slides.Add(Index:=2, _
8.          Layout:=ppLayoutText).SlideIndex
9.      ActiveWindow.Selection.SlideRange.Layout = ppLayoutTitle
10.     ActiveWindow.Selection.SlideRange.Shapes(1).Select
11.     With ActiveWindow.Selection.ShapeRange
12.         .IncrementLeft -6#
```

```
        .IncrementTop -125.75
    End With
    ActiveWindow.Selection.ShapeRange.ScaleHeight 1.56, msoFalse, _
        msoScaleFromTopLeft
    ActiveWindow.Selection.SlideRange.Shapes(1).Select
    ActiveWindow.Selection.ShapeRange.TextFrame.TextRange.Select
    ActiveWindow.Selection.ShapeRange.TextFrame.TextRange.Characters _
        (Start:=1, Length:=0).Select
    ActiveWindow.Selection.TextRange.Text = "Welcome to Acme Industries"
    ActiveWindow.Selection.ShapeRange.TextFrame.TextRange.Select
    With ActiveWindow.Selection.TextRange.Font
        .Name = "Impact"
        .Size = 54
        .Bold = msoFalse
        .Italic = msoFalse
        .Underline = msoFalse
        .Shadow = msoFalse
        .Emboss = msoFalse
        .BaselineOffset = 0
        .AutoRotateNumbers = msoFalse
        .Color.SchemeColor = ppTitle
    End With
End Sub
```

Now step through the changed macro and make sure it works the way you expect.

Saving Your Work

When you finish working with this macro, choose File ➢ Save from the Visual Basic Editor to save the presentation that contains the macro and the changes you've made to it. Be sure to change the file type from the default `.pptx` to the macro-enabled `.pptm` file type. Then press Alt+Q or choose File ➢ Close And Return To Microsoft PowerPoint to close the Visual Basic Editor and return to PowerPoint.

Real World Scenario

WHEN SHOULD YOU USE THE MACRO RECORDER?

As you've seen so far in this book, you can create VBA code two ways. First, you can use the Macro Recorder (in the two applications—Word and Excel—that provide one) to record a series of actions when working interactively in the application. Or, second, you can type VBA statements into the Code window in the Visual Basic Editor. You're probably wondering when you should record a macro and when you should create code from scratch. Writing a procedure from scratch is clearly more difficult and more advanced than recording a procedure—so should you always record if a Recorder is available?

Continues

Continued

Using the Macro Recorder has advantages and disadvantages. The advantages are as follows:

- The Macro Recorder creates usable code every time (provided you run the macro under suitable conditions).
- It is quick and easy to use.
- It can help you discover which VBA objects, methods, and properties correspond to which part of an application's interface.

And here are the disadvantages:

- Code created in the Macro Recorder may contain unnecessary statements because the Macro Recorder records *everything* you do in the application—including all the options in every built-in dialog box you use when recording the macro. For example, if you start the Macro Recorder from Word, choose Tools ➤ Options to display the View page of the Options dialog box, click the Edit tab to display the Edit page, and change the Auto-Keyboard Switching setting, the Macro Recorder will record all the settings on the Edit page as well as all those on the View page. The result is about 40 lines of unnecessary code. (If you visit any other pages in the Options dialog box on the way to the Edit page, the Macro Recorder will record all the settings in those pages as well.) If you create the code manually in the Visual Basic Editor, you can achieve the same effect by using one statement rather than dozens. However, extraneous or redundant code causes no problems—it runs the same as an edited, pared down version. It's just harder to read and maintain. There's noise in the code.
- Code created by the Macro Recorder can work only in the active document (the one that's visible at the time) because whichever document you're working with interactively automatically becomes the active document. Later in this book, you'll learn how to use objects in the applications' object models to work with documents other than the active document. Working with other documents can have advantages; for example, you can make your code run faster, or you can hide from the user the manipulations you're performing so as not to disturb them.
- The Macro Recorder can create VBA code for only *some* of the actions you perform in the host application. For example, if you want to display a dialog box or a user form in the course of a procedure, you need to write the appropriate statement manually—you can't record it. The subset of VBA actions available through the Macro Recorder is similar to the set of actions you can take in the host application when working interactively, so you can get a lot done with it. Still, you'll find it's limited compared to the full range of actions you can perform through VBA.

However expert you become with VBA, consider the Macro Recorder a useful tool for creating either rough-and-ready macros or the basis of more complex procedures. You'll often find it makes sense to have the Macro Recorder handle as much of the strain of creating a procedure as possible. If you can save time by using the Macro Recorder to quickly identify the VBA object or property that you need, then do so.

In addition, the Macro Recorder can teach you how to write code that you can't figure out how to write on your own. The Recorder always gets the syntax right.

The Bottom Line

Test a macro in the Visual Basic Editor. When you need to modify or debug a macro, the Visual Basic Editor is your best friend. It's filled with tools to make your job easier.

Master It Open a macro; then step through it to see if anything goes wrong.

Set breakpoints and use comments. Setting breakpoints allows you to press F5 to execute a macro, but forces the Editor to enter Break mode when execution reaches the line where the breakpoint resides. Comments help you understand the purpose of code—they describe it but are ignored during execution of the macro's code. "Commenting out" a line of code allows you to temporarily render it inactive to see what effect this has during execution. This is sometimes a good way to see if that line is causing the bug you're tracking down.

Master It Set a breakpoint in, and add a comment to, a macro.

Edit a recorded macro. Make some changes to a Word macro.

Master It With the Visual Basic Editor open, choose a macro and modify it.

Chapter 4

Creating Code from Scratch in the Visual Basic Editor

In this chapter, you'll practice creating macros (procedures) from scratch in the Visual Basic Editor. The examples walk you through the process of creating a macro in Word, Excel, and PowerPoint.

For the examples in this book, the Visual Basic Editor should be set up a certain way visually, and set to require explicit declarations of variables (considered a good programming practice), so we'll start off this chapter by ensuring that these conditions are met.

The purpose of this chapter is to give you a feel for creating code in the Visual Basic Editor before you study the details of the language in future chapters. Here you'll work briefly with VBA elements (such as objects, properties, methods, variables, and constants) that you'll learn about more fully later in this book. Along the way, you'll meet several of the many helpful tools that the Visual Basic Editor provides, including the Macro Recorder, the Object Browser, and the Help system. You'll explore these tools, too, more thoroughly later in this book.

IN THIS CHAPTER, YOU WILL LEARN TO DO THE FOLLOWING:

- Set up the Visual Basic Editor to create macros
- Create a macro for Word
- Create a macro for Excel
- Create a macro for PowerPoint
- Create a macro for Access

Setting Up the Visual Basic Editor to Create Macros

You'll find it easiest to follow the instructions in the following macros—and in the rest of the book—if you have the Visual Basic Editor set up in a default configuration. (Any changes you make to the VBA Editor will be in effect across all VBA-enabled Office applications.) So, if you set up the Editor as described next, it will look like this whether you open it in Excel, Word, Access, Outlook, or PowerPoint.

The following steps describe how to set up the Visual Basic Editor so it looks like Figure 4.1:

1. Open the Visual Basic Editor.
2. If the Project Explorer isn't displayed, choose View ➢ Project Explorer or press Ctrl+R to display it.

3. If the Properties window isn't displayed, choose View ➤ Properties Window or press the F4 key to display it.
4. Unless you really prefer things otherwise, dock the Project Explorer in its conventional position at the upper-left corner of the main Visual Basic Editor area. Dock the Properties window below the Project Explorer, again in its default position. (To change docking, choose Tools ➤ Options, click the Docking tab, and select the Docking options.) To dock an undocked (floating) window, double-click its title bar.
5. Set up the Visual Basic Editor to require variables to be declared explicitly. The Editor will then enforce a rule that says you must declare each variable formally before you can use it in the code. Choose Tools ➤ Options to display the Options dialog box, ensure the Require Variable Declaration check box on the Editor page is checked, and then click the OK button. We'll discuss variable declaration in greater detail later in the book, but here's a brief summary. This setting makes the Visual Basic Editor automatically enter an `Option Explicit` statement for all code modules and user forms you create from now on. And *that* statement causes the Editor to check during runtime for any implicitly declared variables (considered bad practice) and remind you that you must declare them *explicitly*, like this:

```
Dim txtName As String
```

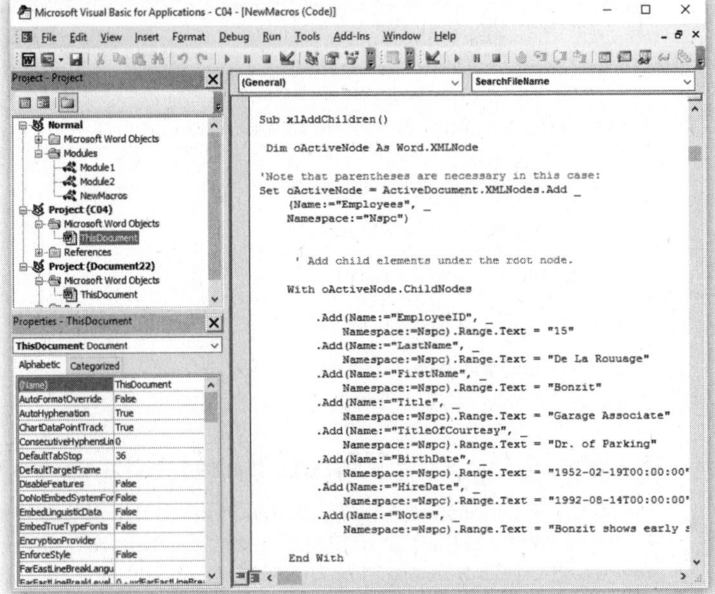

FIGURE 4.1
The default configuration for the VBA Editor

Creating a Procedure for Word

The macro you'll create for Word causes the Track Changes feature to toggle how deleted text will be displayed (whether Strikethrough or Hidden). In other words, using this macro, you'll be able to switch instantly between having deleted text remain onscreen with a line through it or having it simply disappear.

Start by using the Macro Recorder to provide the necessary object qualifications. Then you can modify the code by hand in the Editor to create the toggle behavior.

Follow these steps to record the macro:

1. Start Word. If Word is already running, exit it and restart it.
2. Record a macro to get to the object qualifications (properties and settings) you need. (Remember that to some, recording may feel like cheating, but the Macro Recorder is truly a gift when it comes to finding objects and getting complicated syntax correctly coded.) Follow these substeps:
   a. Click the Developer tab on the Ribbon; then click the Record Macro button in the Code section to display the Record Macro dialog box.
   b. Either accept the macro name that the Macro Recorder automatically assigns (`Macro1`, `Macro2`, and so on) or create a scratch name of your own, such as `Temp`, that will remind you to delete the macro if you forget to do so.
   c. Leave the Store Macro In drop-down list set to All Documents (Normal.dotm). Leave the description blank. This is a temporary macro just for practice, so we won't add it to our permanent collection.
   d. Click the OK button to start recording the macro.
   e. Click the Review tab on the Ribbon, and then click the small arrow in the lower-right corner of the Tracking section. The Track Changes Options dialog box opens. In that box, click the Advanced Options button. (Note that the Advanced Track Changes Options dialog box looks somewhat different in Office 2010 and earlier versions. And you open the first dialog box by clicking the bottom half of the Track Changes icon.) Now ensure that Strikethrough is selected in the Deletions drop-down list (see Figure 4.2), and then click OK twice to close the two Track Changes Options dialog boxes. (Strikethrough is the default, so it's probably already selected—but we want the Recorder to show us how this option is coded in VBA. Clicking OK to close a dialog box records all the current settings in that box.)
   f. Repeat the preceding step (e) to reopen the Track Changes Options dialog box. Now, select Hidden in the Deletions drop-down list, and again click OK twice to close the dialog boxes.
   g. Stop recording the macro by clicking the white recording button in the status bar or by clicking the Stop Recording button on the Developer tab on the Ribbon.

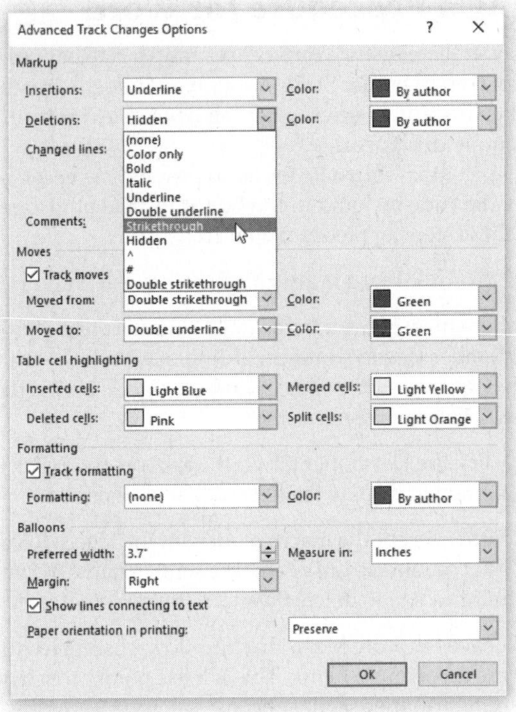

FIGURE 4.2
The Advanced Track Changes Options dialog box in Word

3. Press Alt+F8 to display the Macros dialog box. Select the *Temp* macro you just recorded and click the Edit button to open it for editing in the Visual Basic Editor. Your code should look like this:

```
Sub temp()
'
' temp Macro
'
'
    With Options
        .InsertedTextMark = wdInsertedTextMarkUnderline
        .InsertedTextColor = wdRed
        .DeletedTextMark = wdDeletedTextMarkStrikeThrough
        .DeletedTextColor = wdRed
        .RevisedPropertiesMark = wdRevisedPropertiesMarkNone
        .RevisedPropertiesColor = wdByAuthor
        .RevisedLinesMark = wdRevisedLinesMarkOutsideBorder
        .CommentsColor = wdRed
        .RevisionsBalloonPrintOrientation = _
wdBalloonPrintOrientationPreserve
    End With
```

```
    ActiveWindow.View.RevisionsMode = wdMixedRevisions
    With Options
        .MoveFromTextMark = wdMoveFromTextMarkDoubleStrikeThrough
        .MoveFromTextColor = wdGreen
        .MoveToTextMark = wdMoveToTextMarkDoubleUnderline
        .MoveToTextColor = wdGreen
        .InsertedCellColor = wdCellColorLightBlue
        .MergedCellColor = wdCellColorLightYellow
        .DeletedCellColor = wdCellColorPink
        .SplitCellColor = wdCellColorLightOrange
    End With
    With ActiveDocument
        .TrackMoves = False
        .TrackFormatting = True
    End With
    With Options
        .InsertedTextMark = wdInsertedTextMarkUnderline
        .InsertedTextColor = wdRed
        .DeletedTextMark = wdDeletedTextMarkHidden
        .DeletedTextColor = wdRed
        .RevisedPropertiesMark = wdRevisedPropertiesMarkNone
        .RevisedPropertiesColor = wdByAuthor
        .RevisedLinesMark = wdRevisedLinesMarkOutsideBorder
        .CommentsColor = wdRed
        .RevisionsBalloonPrintOrientation = _
wdBalloonPrintOrientationPreserve
    End With
    ActiveWindow.View.RevisionsMode = wdMixedRevisions
    With Options
        .MoveFromTextMark = wdMoveFromTextMarkDoubleStrikeThrough
        .MoveFromTextColor = wdGreen
        .MoveToTextMark = wdMoveToTextMarkDoubleUnderline
        .MoveToTextColor = wdGreen
        .InsertedCellColor = wdCellColorLightBlue
        .MergedCellColor = wdCellColorLightYellow
        .DeletedCellColor = wdCellColorPink
        .SplitCellColor = wdCellColorLightOrange
    End With
    With ActiveDocument
        .TrackMoves = False
        .TrackFormatting = True
    End With
End Sub
```

4. That's a daunting amount of code for the few rather simple actions you took. Remember that this is because the Macro Recorder records the settings for *all* of the possible options

in the Track Changes Options dialog box that you visited, not just the single option you selected and modified. Look over the code briefly to see the many settings that were recorded from the options inside the dialog box displayed in Figure 4.2.

If you look at the figure, you can see how the code reflects the settings. For example, see the `.SplitCellColor = wdCellColorLightOrange` line of code and locate the setting it refers to in the dialog box.

5. A second set of nearly identical settings in the code represents your second visit to the dialog box. Notice lines 9 and 35 in particular; these are key. Line 35 reflects the change made on your second visit—specifying a hidden rather than strikethrough property for the `DeletedTextMark` property of the `Options` object. Notice, too, the two values for this property: `wdDeletedTextMarkStrikeThrough` (when you recorded the Deletions drop-down specifying Strikethrough) and `wdDeletedTextMarkHidden` (when you set it to Hidden).
6. Now in the Editor, select the entire recorded macro, from the `Sub temp` statement down to the `End Sub` statement, and press the Delete key to get rid of it.
7. Make sure the Visual Basic Editor is set up as described in the section "Setting Up the Visual Basic Editor for Creating the Macros," earlier in this chapter.
8. In the Project Explorer window, right-click anywhere in the `Normal` item and choose Insert ➢ Module from the context menu. The Visual Basic Editor inserts a new module in the `Normal.dotm` global template and displays a Code window for it.
9. Press the F4 key to activate the Properties window for the new module. (By *activate* I mean *give the focus to*—whatever window has the focus is the one where typing will be displayed or mouse clicks will have an effect.) The Visual Basic Editor selects the `(Name)` property, the only property available for this new module. (Confusingly, the property's name is enclosed in parentheses.)
10. Type a name for the new module in the Properties window. For this example, delete the default name (`Module 1` or `Module 2` or whatever it is) and type the name **`Procedures_to_Keep_1`**.
11. Press the F7 key or click in the Code window to activate it.
12. Verify that the Visual Basic Editor has entered the `Option Explicit` statement in the declarations area at the top of the code sheet (the code area) in the Code window. If not, go back and complete step 4 in the list at the start of this chapter.
13. Below the `Option Explicit` statement, type the `Sub` statement for the procedure and press the Enter key. Name the procedure **`Toggle_Track_Changes_between_Hidden_and_Strikethrough`**:

```
Sub Toggle_Track_Changes_between_Hidden_and_Strikethrough
```

14. When you press the Enter key, the Visual Basic Editor inserts for you the required parentheses at the end of the `Sub` statement, a blank line, and the `End Sub` statement and places the insertion point on the blank line, ready for you to start typing in some programming:

```
Sub Toggle_Track_Changes_between_Hidden_and_Strikethrough()

End Sub
```

15. Press the Tab key to indent the first line below the `Sub` statement.
16. Type **`if options.`** (in lowercase, and be sure to end with the period). Now the Editor displays the List Properties/Methods drop-down list.
17. Type down through the list (type **`d`**, **`e`**, and then **`l`**) and use the ↓ key, or simply scroll with the mouse, to select the `DeletedTextMark` entry.
18. Now just type **=** (the equal sign). The Visual Basic Editor enters the `DeletedTextMark` command for you, followed by the equal sign, and then displays the List Properties/Methods list of constants that can be used with the `DeletedTextMark` property (see Figure 4.3).

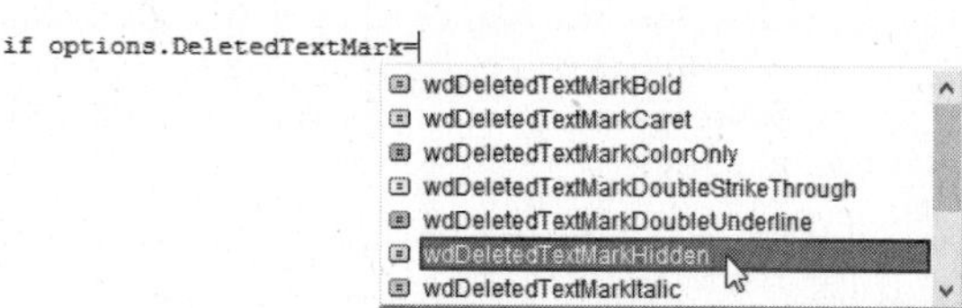

FIGURE 4.3 The Visual Basic Editor's List Properties/Methods list displays the constants available for the `DeletedTextMark` property.

19. Select the `wdDeletedTextMarkHidden` item and enter it into your code by pressing the Tab key or by double-clicking it.
20. Type **`Then`** and press the Enter key. Note that when you start the next line of code (by pressing Enter), the Visual Basic Editor checks the line of code for errors. If you used lowercase for the `If Options` part of the statement, the Visual Basic Editor applies capitalization (this is just for show—VBA pays no attention to capitalization when executing code). If there are no space characters on either side of the equal sign, the Visual Basic Editor adds them too.
21. Enter **`Options.DeletedTextMark=wdDeletedTextMarkStrikethrough`**, using the assistance offered by the Visual Basic Editor's Auto List Members features (described earlier, in steps 16 through 18), and then press Enter.
22. Press the Backspace key or Shift+Tab to unindent the new line of code by one tab stop.
23. Type the **`ElseIf`** keyword, and then enter the rest of the procedure as follows:

```
ElseIf Options.DeletedTextMark = wdDeletedTextMarkStrikeThrough Then
    Options.DeletedTextMark = wdDeletedTextMarkHidden
End If
```

24. Make sure your completed procedure looks like this:

```
Sub Toggle_Track_Changes_between_Hidden_and_Strikethrough()
    If Options.DeletedTextMark = wdDeletedTextMarkHidden Then
        Options.DeletedTextMark = wdDeletedTextMarkStrikeThrough
    ElseIf Options.DeletedTextMark = wdDeletedTextMarkStrikeThrough Then
        Options.DeletedTextMark = wdDeletedTextMarkHidden
    End If
End Sub
```

25. Press Alt+F11 to switch to Word, and then type in a line or two of text.
26. Arrange the Word window and the Visual Basic Editor window side by side. In Word, click the Review tab on the Ribbon, and click the upper half of the Track Changes button (the graphic icon) to activate the feature that marks up (or otherwise handles) revisions. Delete a word in your text. Notice whether it is struck through or is simply hidden. You have a macro that toggles between these two behaviors, so in the Visual Basic Editor, press the F5 key or click the Run Sub/UserForm button (on the Standard and Debug toolbars) to run the macro. Back in Word, see what effect the deletion has now. You can also take a look at the Track Changes Options dialog box to see that the Deletions setting has changed.
27. Click the Save button on the Standard toolbar in the Visual Basic Editor.

Note that you could alternatively write this macro using a `With` statement for the `Options` object so that it looks like this:

```
Sub Toggle_Track_Changes_between_Hidden_and_Strikethrough_2()
    With Options
        If .DeletedTextMark = wdDeletedTextMarkHidden Then
            .DeletedTextMark = wdDeletedTextMarkStrikeThrough
        ElseIf .DeletedTextMark = wdDeletedTextMarkStrikeThrough Then
            .DeletedTextMark = wdDeletedTextMarkHidden
        End If
    End With
End Sub
```

There are usually several ways to code a given behavior in VBA. Although formal (professional) programmers learn a set of "best practices," if you're just a hobbyist writing VBA for your own personal use, go ahead and code however you wish. Use whatever works.

Creating a Macro for Excel

The procedure you'll create for Excel is short but helpful. When the user runs Excel, the procedure maximizes the Excel window and opens the last file used. The procedure also illustrates some useful techniques, including these:

- Writing a macro that executes when an application first starts up
- Working with events
- Using the Object Browser to find the objects, methods, and properties you need

Follow these steps to create the procedure:

1. Start Excel if it's not already running.
2. Press Alt+Tab to cycle through your workbooks to locate `Personal.xlsb`. If your Personal Macro Workbook is currently hidden, click the Unhide button in the Window section of

the View tab on the Ribbon. Select `PERSONAL.XLSB` in the Unhide Workbook list box, and then click the OK button.

3. Press Alt+F11 to open the Visual Basic Editor.
4. Make sure the Visual Basic Editor is set up as described in the section "Setting Up the Visual Basic Editor for Creating the Procedures" earlier in this chapter.
5. In the Project Explorer window, expand `VBAProject (PERSONAL.XLSB)` if it's collapsed. To expand it, either double-click its name or click the + sign to its left.
6. Expand the Microsoft Excel Objects folder.
7. Double-click the `ThisWorkbook` item to open its code sheet in a Code window. The `ThisWorkbook` object represents the current workbook.
8. Verify that the Visual Basic Editor has entered the `Option Explicit` statement in the declarations area at the top of the code sheet. If not, go back and complete step 4 in the list at the start of this chapter. However, note that at the time of this writing, even if you select the Require Variable Declaration option (via the Tools ➤ Options menu in the Excel version of the VBA Editor), `Option Explicit` is not automatically inserted into your Code window. So go ahead.
9. In the Code window, if it's not already there, type

```
Private Sub Auto_Open
```

and then press the Enter key. The Editor will add the required parentheses and the `End Sub` line.

MACROS HAVE SCOPE

The `Private` keyword limits the scope of a macro—the area in which it can operate. Private scope makes the macro available to all procedures in the module that contains it, but not to procedures in other modules. Chapter 6, "Working with Variables, Constants, and Enumerations," explains scope in more detail.

10. Open the Object Browser: Press the F2 key, or choose View ➤ Object Browser, or click the Object Browser button on the Standard toolbar to display the Object Browser window (see Figure 4.4).
11. The first action we want to take in this macro is to maximize the Excel's application window. As in any application, VBA uses the `Application` object to represent the Excel application, but you need to find the correct property of this object to utilize. Select Excel in the Project/Library drop-down list (see the label in Figure 4.4), type **`maximize`** in the Search Text box, and either click the Search button or press the Enter key. The Object Browser displays the result of the search (see Figure 4.5) in its Search Results pane (which

was collapsed and not visible in Figure 4.4). The constant `xlMaximized` is a member of the class `XlWindowState`.

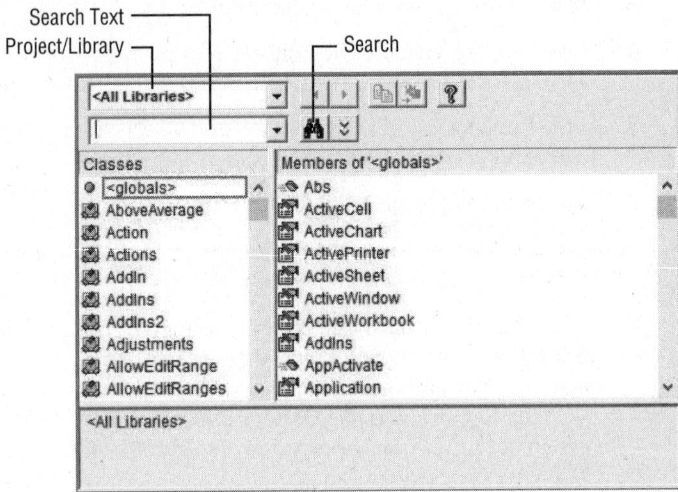

FIGURE 4.4 Use the Object Browser to find the objects, methods, and properties you need for a procedure.

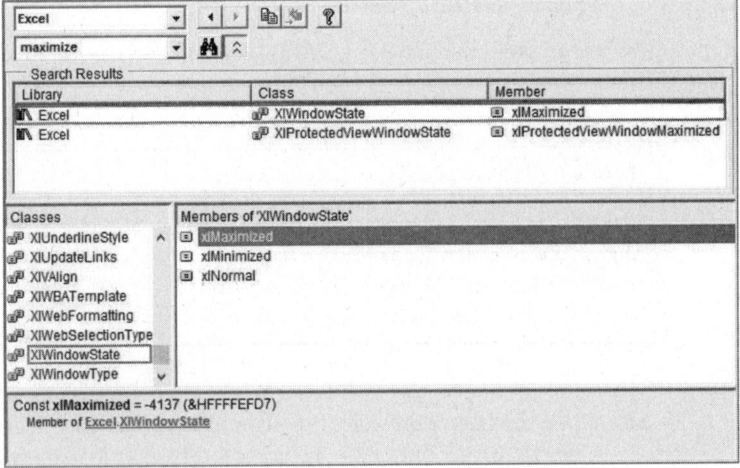

FIGURE 4.5 The result of the search for "maximize" in the Object Browser

12. Press the F7 key to activate the Code window. (Alternatively, click the Code window, choose View ➤ Code, or choose the Code window from the Window menu.)
13. Type **`application.`** (in lowercase and including the period) so that the Visual Basic Editor displays the drop-down list, type **`w`** to jump to the items beginning with *W*, and select the `WindowState` item.

14. Type = to enter the `WindowState` item in your code and to display the list of constants available for `WindowState` (see Figure 4.6).

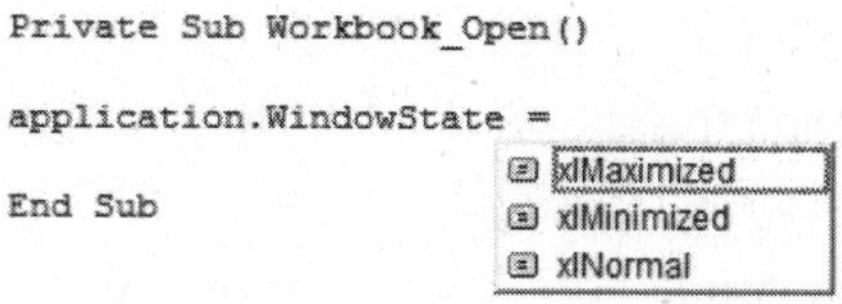

FIGURE 4.6
Use the list of constants to enter the constant quickly and easily.

```
Private Sub Workbook_Open()

application.WindowState =
                          xlMaximized
End Sub                   xlMinimized
                          xlNormal
```

15. Select the `xlMaximized` item and press Enter to insert that property in the code, and move down a line to start writing a new statement.

16. The second action for the macro is to open the last file used—file 1 on the recently used files list (this is the list that appears in the Recent Documents list when you click the Recent item in the File tab on the Ribbon). Press the F2 key to activate the Object Browser again.

17. Leave Excel selected in the Project/Library drop-down list, type **`recent`**, and either press the Enter key or click the Search button. The Object Browser displays the results of the search (see Figure 4.7). The item you need is the `RecentFiles` property of the `Application` object. The `RecentFiles` property returns the `RecentFiles` *collection*, an object that knows the information about the files in the recently used files list.

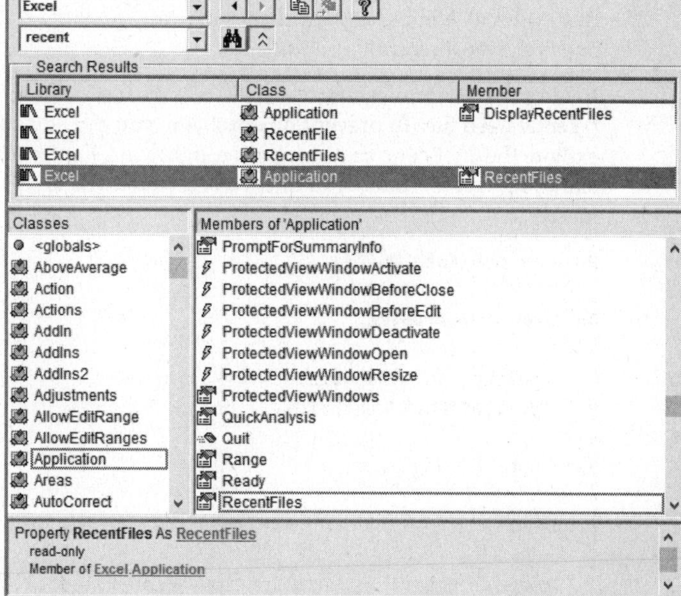

FIGURE 4.7
The result of the search for “recent” in the Object Browser

18. Press the F7 key to return to the Code window. Type **`application.`** and select `RecentFiles` from the List Properties/Methods drop-down list. Then type **`(1).`** to indicate the first item in the `RecentFiles` collection, and select the `Open` method from the List Properties/Methods list:

    ```
    Application.RecentFiles(1).Open
    ```

19. That's it. Your procedure should look like this:

    ```
    Private Sub Auto_Open()

        Application.WindowState = xlMaximized
        Application.RecentFiles(1).Open

    End Sub
    ```

20. Press Alt+Q or choose File ➢ Close And Return To Microsoft Excel to return to Excel.
21. Click the File tab on the Ribbon and choose Save.
22. Click the Hide button in the Window section of the View tab on the Ribbon. This hides `PERSONAL.XLSB` from view.
23. Open a sample document, type something into one of the cells, save it, and close it.
24. Press Alt+F4 to exit Excel. If you are asked if you want to save the changes you made to the current workbook and your Personal Macro Workbook, choose Yes.
25. Restart Excel. Notice how Excel automatically maximizes the application window and opens the most recently used file.

    If you see an error message, it most likely means that you've renamed or moved the most recently used file. To prevent this problem, you can add some error-trapping code. We'll explore the `On Error` command thoroughly in Chapter 17, "Debugging Your Code and Handling Errors," but if you like, you can make the following changes to your `Auto_Open` macro:

    ```
    Private Sub Auto_Open()

    On Error GoTo Problem

        Application.WindowState = xlMaximized
        Application.RecentFiles(1).Open

    Exit Sub

    Problem:

        MsgBox "Error: " & Application.RecentFiles(1).Path & " can't be opened."

    End Sub
    ```

The `Auto_Open` name is special. When you name a macro `Auto_Open`, VBA knows that whatever actions are in the macro code should be executed when Excel starts running. This is one of a handful of special names called Excel's *events*—things that happen to an object, in this case the `Open` event of the Excel application. (Notice that an object's *methods* are actions it can take, such as a print method sending a document to the printer. Conversely, an object's *events* are things that can happen to it, such as a user clicking a button or opening an application.)

How to Turn Off Default Templates

The following section describes how to use a template that comes with PowerPoint. You've likely noticed that when you start Office 2016 applications, they display a set of templates. Some users are likely to never use these templates and would prefer the traditional Office applications' behavior: starting with a blank document and bypassing this display of templates. To turn this off, choose File ➤ Options, and then uncheck Show The Start Screen When This Application Starts.

Creating a Procedure for PowerPoint

The procedure you'll create for PowerPoint is short and straightforward, but it can save the user enough effort over the long run to make it worthwhile. It adds a title slide to the active presentation, inserting a canned title that includes the current date and the company's name as the presenter.

Follow these steps to create the procedure:

1. Start PowerPoint. If PowerPoint is already running, close it and restart it.
2. Click to open the Blank Presentation template.
3. Press Alt+F11 to open the Visual Basic Editor.
4. Make sure the Visual Basic Editor is set up as described in the section "Setting Up the Visual Basic Editor for Creating the Procedures" earlier in this chapter.
5. In the Project Explorer window, right-click `VBAProject(Presentation1)` and choose Insert ➤ Module from the context menu. The Visual Basic Editor inserts a new module in the project, displays a Code window containing the code sheet for the module, and expands the project tree in the Project Explorer.
6. Verify that the Visual Basic Editor has entered the `Option Explicit` statement in the declarations area at the top of the code sheet. If not, go back and complete step 4 in the list at the start of this chapter.
7. Press the F4 key to activate (move to) the Properties window.
8. Delete the default name `Module 1` and replace it by typing **`General_Procedures`**.
9. Press the F7 key or click in the Code window to activate it.
10. Below the `Option Explicit` statement, type the `Sub` statement for the procedure and press the Enter key:

```
Sub Add_Title_Slide
```

11. When you press Enter, the Visual Basic Editor enters the parentheses at the end of the Sub statement, a blank line, and the End Sub statement for you, and places the insertion point on the blank line:

```
Sub Add_Title_Slide()

End Sub
```

12. Press the Tab key to indent the first line below the Sub statement. This is strictly for your benefit. It makes the code a little easier to read.

13. Let's identify which objects we need for this macro. You'll be working with the active presentation, which is represented by the `ActivePresentation` object. As you'll see in Part 6 of this book, "Programming the Office Applications"—which is all about objects—there are several ways to get information when programming with objects. For now, let's try searching online help rather than using the Editor's built-in Object Browser. Using Google or Bing, search for **`object model reference powerpoint 2016`**. If you only see the 2013 version, that's OK. That version will work fine for this exercise.

    Now you can locate the details about the application object's `ActivePresentation` property object, as shown in Figure 4.8.

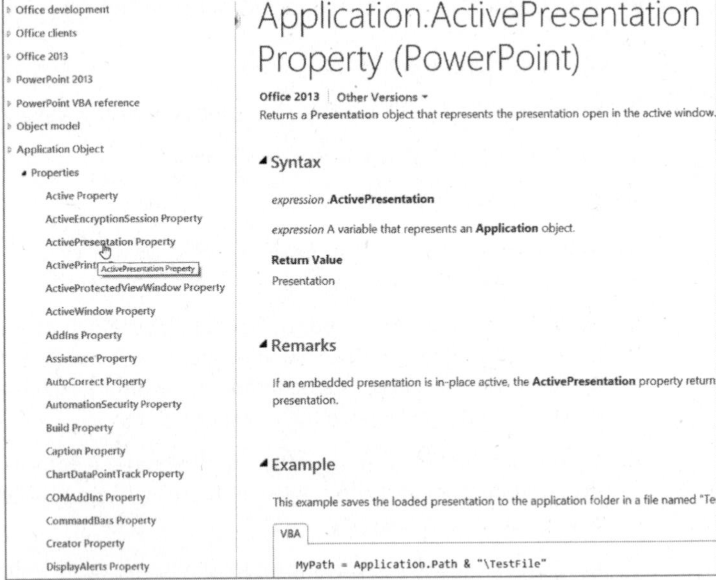

FIGURE 4.8
The ActivePresentation property screen

14. Click the `Presentation` link in "Returns a Presentation object…" near the top, as shown in Figure 4.8. This link will take you to the `Presentation` object's Help screen. We're drilling down in this Help system to find example code and other assistance that will show us how to work with slides and related objects. All this will become much clearer to you in Part 6. For now, just follow along to get the general idea.

15. Now on the Presentation object's Help page, click the Presentation Object Members link (scroll to find it near the bottom of this web page), and then scroll way down to locate the

`Slides` object in the properties list. Click the Slides link (click Slides in the right column, see the pointing finger in Figure 4.9). Now you see the information about the `Slides` Collection object, as shown in Figure 4.10.

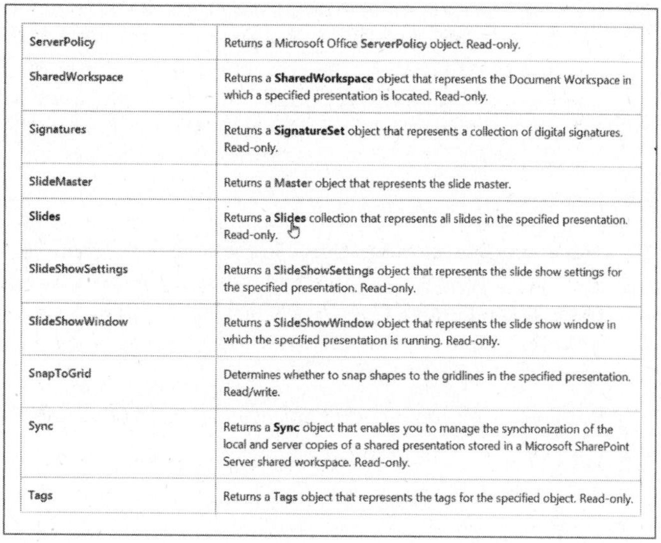

FIGURE 4.9
Select the `Slides` object from the list.

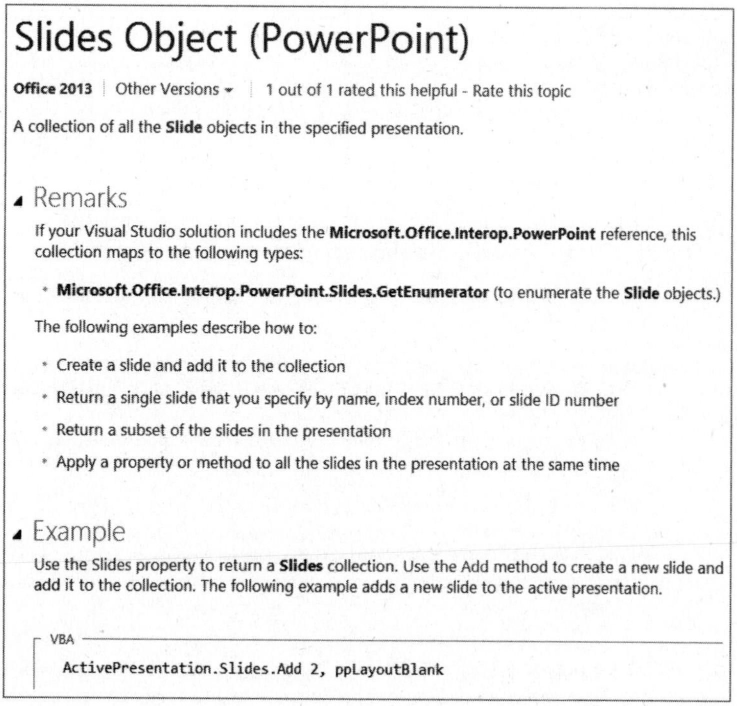

ServerPolicy	Returns a Microsoft Office **ServerPolicy** object. Read-only.
SharedWorkspace	Returns a **SharedWorkspace** object that represents the Document Workspace in which a specified presentation is located. Read-only.
Signatures	Returns a **SignatureSet** object that represents a collection of digital signatures. Read-only.
SlideMaster	Returns a **Master** object that represents the slide master.
Slides	Returns a **Slides** collection that represents all slides in the specified presentation. Read-only.
SlideShowSettings	Returns a **SlideShowSettings** object that represents the slide show settings for the specified presentation. Read-only.
SlideShowWindow	Returns a **SlideShowWindow** object that represents the slide show window in which the specified presentation is running. Read-only.
SnapToGrid	Determines whether to snap shapes to the gridlines in the specified presentation. Read/write.
Sync	Returns a **Sync** object that enables you to manage the synchronization of the local and server copies of a shared presentation stored in a Microsoft SharePoint Server shared workspace. Read-only.
Tags	Returns a **Tags** object that represents the tags for the specified object. Read-only.

FIGURE 4.10
The `Slides` Collection Object Help screen

Slides Object (PowerPoint)

Office 2013 | Other Versions ▾ | 1 out of 1 rated this helpful - Rate this topic

A collection of all the **Slide** objects in the specified presentation.

Remarks

If your Visual Studio solution includes the **Microsoft.Office.Interop.PowerPoint** reference, this collection maps to the following types:

- **Microsoft.Office.Interop.PowerPoint.Slides.GetEnumerator** (to enumerate the **Slide** objects.)

The following examples describe how to:

- Create a slide and add it to the collection
- Return a single slide that you specify by name, index number, or slide ID number
- Return a subset of the slides in the presentation
- Apply a property or method to all the slides in the presentation at the same time

Example

Use the Slides property to return a **Slides** collection. Use the Add method to create a new slide and add it to the collection. The following example adds a new slide to the active presentation.

VBA

```
ActivePresentation.Slides.Add 2, ppLayoutBlank
```

16. From this screen, you learn two pieces of information: first, that a slide is represented by a `Slide` object (stored in a `Slides` collection), and second, that you use the `Add` method to create a new slide.

17. Here's a shortcut when writing code. Type the following code line. It's a declaration for an object variable of the `Slide` object type, that will be used to represent the slide created in this Sub. Notice that after you type **as** and a space, the Visual Basic Editor displays the list of available objects. Type **s** and **l** to move down the list until you see `Slide` selected (highlighted) and then press the Enter key to complete the code line and move down to the next line:

```
Dim sldTitleSlide As Slide
```

18. Here's another shortcut. Use a `Set` statement to assign to the `sldTitleSlide` object a new slide you create by using the `Add` method. Type **set sld** and then press Ctrl+spacebar to make the Editor's Complete Word feature enter `sldTitleSlide` for you. Then type **= activepresentation.slides.add(**, using the Visual Basic Editor's assistance, so that the line reads as shown here:

```
Set sldTitleSlide = ActivePresentation.Slides.Add(
```

19. When you type the parenthesis, the Auto Quick Info feature displays the syntax for the `Add` method, as shown in Figure 4.11.

FIGURE 4.11 The Auto Quick Info feature displays the syntax for the `Add` method when you type the parenthesis after the `Add` method.

```
Dim sldTitleSlide As Slide

Set sldTitleSlide = ActivePresentation.Slides.Add(
                    Add(Index As Long, Layout As PpSlideLayout) As Slide
```

20. Type the **Index** argument, a colon, an equal sign, the value **1** (because the title slide is to be the first slide in the presentation), and a comma:

```
Set sldTitleSlide = ActivePresentation.Slides.Add(Index:=1,
```

CHOOSING BETWEEN LABELED AND IMPLIED ARGUMENT LISTS

When a method uses arguments, as the `Add` method does here, you can choose between specifying the argument names or omitting them and letting VBA infer the arguments from the order of the values or constants. For example, in this case you can specify either `Add(Index:=1, Layout:=ppLayoutTitle)` or `Add(1, ppLayoutTitle)`. The latter is more concise and easier to type in, but the former is much clearer to read.

21. Break the statement to the next line with a line-continuation character (an underscore preceded by a space). Then type a tab to indent the new line, type the **Layout** argument, a

colon, and an equal sign, and pick the ppLayoutTitle constant from the List Properties/Methods drop-down list, as shown in Figure 4.12.

22. Type the parenthesis to end the statement:

```
Set sldTitleSlide = ActivePresentation.Slides.Add(Index:=1, _
    Layout:=ppLayoutTitle)
```

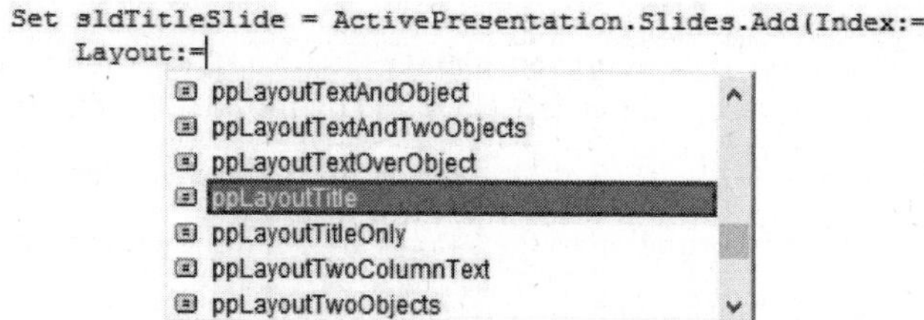

FIGURE 4.12 Choose the ppLayoutTitle constant for the Layout argument.

23. Press the Enter key to start a new line, and then press either the Backspace key or Shift+Tab to unindent the new line by one tab stop.

24. You'll be working with the sldTitleSlide from here on, so create a With statement using it, and place the insertion point on the line between the With statement and the End With statement:

```
With sldTitleSlide

End With
```

25. Next, the macro will manipulate the two items on the slide. To make it do so, you need to know the objects that represent them. You could use the Macro Recorder to find the objects, but this time try a more direct method: Place the insertion point on the line within the With statement and type **.** (a period) to display the List Properties/Methods drop-down list of available properties and methods for the Slide object.

26. Sometimes the List Properties/Methods drop-down list is of little help because it displays so many possibly relevant properties and methods that you can't identify the property you need. But if you scan the list in this case, you'll see that the Shapes property (which returns the Shapes collection) is the only promising item.

27. Press Ctrl+G, choose View ➢ Immediate, or click the Immediate Window button on the Debug toolbar to display the Immediate window for a bit of testing.

28. Type the following test statement into the Immediate window and press the Enter key to execute this statement:

```
ActivePresentation.Slides(1).Shapes(1).Select
```

(The Immediate window is a sometimes helpful and quick way to test individual lines of code without having to run the entire macro.) Now switch to the PowerPoint to see if the item was, in fact, selected (whether it has a frame drawn around it). Press Alt+F11 or click the View Microsoft PowerPoint button on the Standard toolbar to display the PowerPoint window to verify that VBA has selected the first Shape object on the slide.

29. Okay, this is the right object to start with, but now you need to find out how to add text to the shape. Go back to the Code window (click in the Code window or press the F7 key). Press the Backspace key to delete the period, and then type it again to redisplay the list. Type **te** to jump down to the items in the list whose names start with *text*. Select the `TextFrame` item in the list, and then type a period to enter the term and display the next list. Scroll down the list, select the `TextRange` object, and type a period to enter the term and display the next list. In the next list, select the `Text` property. Type an equal sign to enter the term. Then type double quotation marks followed by the text to assign to the text property **Pollution Update:** (with a space after it), double quotation marks, an ampersand, and the date (supplied by the `Date` function):

    ```
    Shapes(1).TextFrame.TextRange.Text = "Pollution Update: " & Date
    ```

30. Assign information to the second `Shape` in the same way:

    ```
    .Shapes(2).TextFrame.TextRange.Text = "JMP Industrials."
    ```

31. The finished procedure should look like this:

    ```
    Sub Add_Title_Slide()
        Dim sldTitleSlide As Slide
        Set sldTitleSlide = ActivePresentation.Slides.Add(Index:=1, _
            Layout:=ppLayoutTitle)
        With sldTitleSlide
            .Shapes(1).TextFrame.TextRange.Text = _
                "Pollution Update: " & Date
            .Shapes(2).TextFrame.TextRange.Text = _
                "JMP Industrials"
        End With
    End Sub
    ```

32. Press F5 to test the procedure. Look at the slides in PowerPoint. There should be a new first slide in the collection of slides on the left. Delete all slides from the presentation (select slides by pressing Shift while clicking a range of slides in the left pane, and then press Delete).

33. If you want, right-click on the Quick Access Toolbar in the upper-left corner of PowerPoint's screen, and then choose Customize Quick Access Toolbar. Then add a Quick Access Toolbar button for the `Add_Title_Slide` macro.

34. Save the presentation under a name such as `Procedures.pptm`. You might see a warning about personal-information risks. Click OK to close that Be Careful! message box.

35. Create a new presentation; then test the toolbar button or menu item for the procedure. If you see a security warning, read the sidebar titled "A Warning About Security" in Chapter 1. Close the presentation without saving changes.

Creating a Procedure for Access

Access has a long tradition of autonomy from the other Office applications, and this applies as well to its implementation of macros. It has no Recorder, for example, nor does it permit you to assign macros to shortcut key combinations.

In addition, Access includes a legacy "Macro Builder," which you can take a look at by clicking the Macro button on the Create tab of the Ribbon. (Note that in Access there is no Developer tab on the Ribbon. You open the Visual Basic Editor from the Database Tools tab or press Alt+F11.)

The Macro Builder utility has been generally unpopular over the years because the Visual Basic Editor offers far more options, objects, and features. The Builder is for nonprogrammers—a way to create simple macros via lists rather than actual programming. However, the Builder was somewhat improved in Access 2007, including provisions for error handling and the ability to embed macros within individual forms. Additional improvements were made for Access 2010, enough improvements that Microsoft renamed it the Macro Designer. But a dead rose by any other name is still a dead rose. If you're interested in details about the Macro Designer and its curious, some might say simplistic, reliance on repeated `If…Then` structures, see the sidebar titled "Using the Macro Builder" in Chapter 28, "Understanding the Access Object Model and Key Objects."

For the reasons I mentioned, you will likely prefer to use the Visual Basic Editor rather than the Builder/Designer for any but the most elementary macros. After all, relying on a list of `If` queries is not only limiting, it's downright dated.

Let's get a feel for writing real VBA macros in Access. In this example, you'll write a macro that displays today's date and time:

1. Start Access.
2. Double-click the Blank Desktop Database icon (in Access 2010 and earlier, double-click the Blank Database button).
3. Press Alt+F11 to open the Visual Basic Editor.
4. Right-click the database name in the Project Explorer, and then choose Insert Module to open a new module in the Code window, where you can write macros.
5. In the Code window, type the following macro:

   ```
   Sub ShowDate()

   MsgBox ("It is: " & Now)

   End Sub
   ```

6. Click anywhere within this code, and then press F5 to execute the macro. You should see a message box that displays the current date and time. (Note that you don't type the `End Sub`; Access automatically inserts it for you.)

We'll cover Access macro programming in depth in Chapter 28 and Chapter 29, "Manipulating the Data in an Access Database via VBA." Also, you might have noticed that the Editor automatically inserted a line of code at the top: `Option Compare Database`. This specifies a particular way to go about comparing text strings.

The Bottom Line

Set up the Visual Basic Editor to create macros. How you arrange the various components of the Visual Basic Editor is your personal choice, but while using this book, it's easiest if you set up the Editor to resemble the way it appears in the book's figures. Besides, this arrangement is quite close to the default layout, which has proven to be the most effective one for the majority of programmers (according to various focus groups and polls) for the decades that Visual Basic has been used.

Master It Press a single key to toggle (to display and then hide), the Properties window.

Create a macro for Word. Using the Help feature in any VBA-enabled application allows you to find code examples that you can copy and paste into your own code.

Master It Open the Code window and use Help to find a code example.

Create a macro for Excel. Certain procedure names are special. In a previous Excel exercise, you added line numbering and gave that procedure a name of your own choice. But some procedure names have a special meaning—they are triggered by an *event* in Excel itself. They will execute automatically when that event takes place (you don't have to run events by choosing Run from the Macro dialog box or by assigning the macro to a keyboard shortcut or Quick Access Toolbar button). One such event is Excel's `Auto_Open` procedure.

Master It Display a message to the user when Excel first executes.

Create a macro for PowerPoint. As you type a procedure, the Visual Basic Editor provides you with lists of objects' members (the Auto List Members feature) and with syntax examples, including both required and optional arguments (the Auto Quick Info feature). These tools can be invaluable in guiding you quickly to the correct object and syntax for a given command.

Master It Use the Auto List Members and Auto Quick Info features to write a macro that saves a backup copy of the currently active presentation.

Create a procedure for Access. Although Access includes a variety of macro-related features that are unique (such as its Macro Builder/Designer), its Visual Basic Editor is quite similar to the Visual Basic Editors in the other Office applications.

Master It Open the Visual Basic Editor in Access and write a macro that displays today's date using the `Date` function rather than the `Now` function. Use the Access Visual Basic Editor Help system to understand the difference between these two functions.

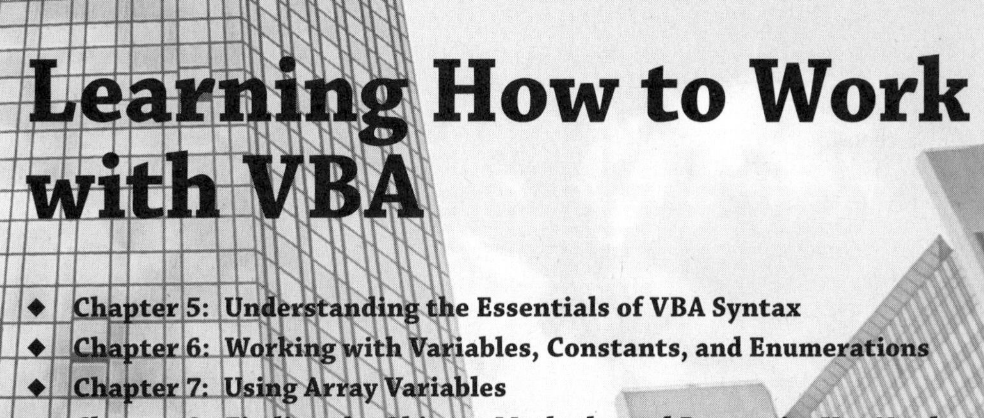

Part 2

Learning How to Work with VBA

Chapter 5

Understanding the Essentials of VBA Syntax

In this chapter, you'll learn the essentials of VBA syntax, building on what you learned via practical examples from the previous chapters. This chapter defines the key terms you need to know about VBA to get going with it, and you'll practice using some of the features in the Visual Basic Editor.

If You Don't Understand a Programming Term, Look Ahead

You'll find lots of definitions of programming terms as you work your way through this chapter. If you come across something that doesn't yet make sense to you, just keep going; you'll most likely find an explanation in the next few pages.

IN THIS CHAPTER, YOU WILL LEARN TO DO THE FOLLOWING:

- Understand the basics of VBA
- Work with subs and functions
- Use the Immediate window to execute statements
- Understand objects, properties, methods, and events

Getting Ready

To learn most efficiently in this next section, arrange the Visual Basic Editor in Word by performing the following steps. This chapter focuses on Word because it's the most widely distributed of the VBA-enabled applications. If you don't have Word, read along anyway without performing the actions on the computer; the examples are easy to follow. (Much of this code will work on any VBA host application, although many of the commands shown here are specific to Word.) Here are the steps:

1. Start Word.
2. Launch the Visual Basic Editor by pressing Alt+F11 or by clicking the Developer tab on the Ribbon and then clicking the Visual Basic button.

3. Arrange the Word window and the Visual Basic Editor window so that you can see both of them at once. For example, if these are the only two open windows that are not minimized, right-click the Taskbar and choose Show Windows Stacked or Show Windows Side By Side from the context menu to arrange the windows, or just drag them by their title bars to the right or left side. In Windows 10, you can press Windows Key+← or Windows Key+→.

4. Display the Immediate window in the Visual Basic Editor by pressing Ctrl+G, choosing View ➤ Immediate Window, or clicking the Immediate Window button on the Debug toolbar. Your setup should look like Figure 5.1.

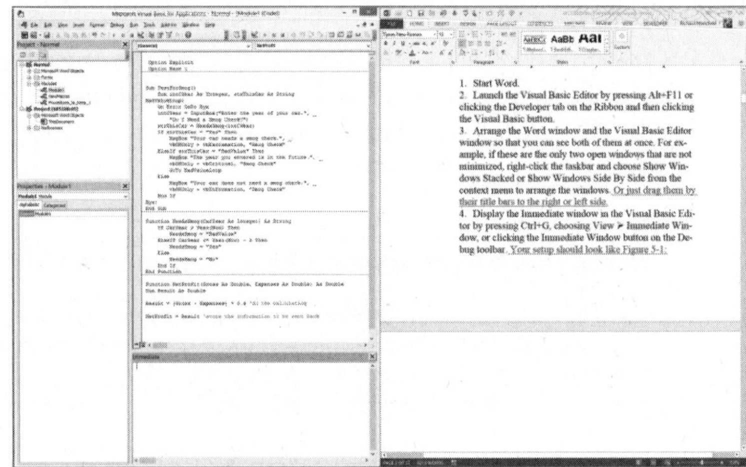

FIGURE 5.1 The Visual Basic Editor set up alongside a Word document. This is a good way to edit or debug macros. You can see where you are in the code and, often, the effect the macro is having.

> **USING DUAL MONITORS**
>
> If you're using a multiple-monitor setup, you can dedicate one monitor to Word and another to the Visual Basic Editor.

Procedures

A *procedure* in VBA is a named unit of code that contains a sequence of statements to be executed as a group. You can write your own procedures (subs or functions), but VBA itself has a library of prewritten procedures you can use as well.

For example, VBA contains a function (a type of procedure) named `Left`, which returns the left portion of a text string that you specify. For example, `hello` is a string of text five characters long. The statement `Left("hello", 3)` returns the leftmost three characters of the string: `hel`. (You could then display this three-character string in a message box or use it in code.) The name assigned to the procedure gives you a way to refer to the procedure in your code.

When you write a macro, you are writing a procedure of your own (as opposed to a procedure built into VBA already).

Your macro in VBA must be contained in a procedure (between a `Sub` and an `End Sub`) or within a function. If it isn't, VBA can't execute it and an error occurs. (The exception is a statement you execute in the Immediate window, which takes place outside a procedure. However, the contents of the Immediate window exist only during the current VBA editing session and are used for testing code. They cannot be executed from the host application via buttons, ribbons, or keyboard shortcuts, nor will they be there when you restart the application.)

A macro—in other words the code inside `Sub` to `End Sub`—is a procedure. Procedures are contained within modules, which in turn are contained within project files, templates, or other VBA host objects, such as user forms.

There are two types of procedures: functions and subprocedures (usually called just *subs*).

Functions

A *function* in VBA is one of the two types of procedures. Like a sub, a function is a procedure designed to perform a specific and limited task. For example, the built-in VBA `Left` function returns the left part of a text string, and the `Right` function, its counterpart, returns the right part of a text string. Each function has a clear task that you use it for, and it doesn't do anything else. `Left` just does its one, simple job.

You can create your own function procedures (in addition to the normal macro subprocedures) as well. You'll create your own functions later in the book. They will begin with a `Function` statement and end with an `End Function` statement.

Each function returns a value. For example, the `Left` function returns the left part of the string. Other functions return different kinds of results. Some, for example, just test a condition and return `True` if the condition is met and `False` if it is not met. Just remember that what distinguishes a function is that it returns some value. Subs don't.

Subprocedures

A *subprocedure* (also called a *subroutine*), like a function, is a complete procedure designed to perform a specific task, but remember that, unlike a function, a sub *does not return a value.*

Note that many tasks need not return a result. For example, the `Transpose_Word` macros you created earlier in this book merely switch a pair of words in a document. There's no need for any value to be returned to VBA for further use. On the other hand, if your procedure calculates sales tax, there *is* a result (the amount of tax), so that figure must be returned by the procedure for display to the user or other uses in the VBA code.

All the *macros* you record using the Macro Recorder are subs, as are many of the procedures you'll look at in the rest of this book.

Each sub begins with a `Sub` statement and ends with an `End Sub` statement.

FUNCTIONS AREN'T DISPLAYED IN THE MACROS DIALOG BOX

Only subs appear in the Macros dialog box. Should you choose to write a function, it will not appear in that box.

Statements

When you create a macro in VBA, you're writing statements, which are similar to sentences in ordinary speech. A *statement* is a line of code that describes an action, defines an item, or gives the value of a variable. VBA usually has one statement per line of code, although you can put more than one statement on a line by separating them with colons. (This isn't usually a good idea because it makes your code harder to read. Most programmers stick to one statement per line.)

You can also break a lengthy line of code onto a second line or a subsequent line to make it easier to read (although this isn't usually necessary). You continue a statement onto the next line by using a line-continuation character: an underscore (_) preceded by a space (and followed by a carriage return—in other words, press the Enter key). You continue a line strictly for visual convenience on your monitor. VBA still reads a continued line as a single "virtual" line of code. In other words, no matter how many line continuations you use for easy-to-read formatting, during execution it's still a single statement to VBA. Here's an example. Note the underscore that tells VBA to read this as a single, continuous line of code, even though it's broken into two visual lines:

```
Selection.InsertSymbol Font:="Wingdings", CharacterNumber:=-3880, Unicode _
:=True
```

So, think of VBA code as a series of sentences, each on its own line (or continued), that are usually executed one by one down from the top. Just like a list of steps to take when following a recipe in a cookbook.

YOU CAN'T BREAK STRINGS WITH THE LINE-CONTINUATION CHARACTER

You can't break a *string* (text enclosed in quotation marks) with the line-continuation character. If you need to break a line that involves a long string in quotes, break the string into shorter strings and concatenate them using the & operator: `"This" & "that"`.

VBA statements vary widely in length and complexity. A statement can range in length from a single word (such as `Beep`, which makes the computer beep, or `Stop`, which halts the execution of VBA code) to very long and complicated lines involving many components. To make it easy to read your code, though, try to make your lines as brief as possible.

That said, let's examine the makeup of several sample VBA statements in Word. Most of these will use the `ActiveDocument` object, which represents the currently active (the one that's visible) document in the current session of Word. However, a couple of these statements use the `Documents` collection, which represents all open documents (including the active document). One example uses the `Selection` object, which represents the current selection within a document (selected text or the location of the blinking insertion cursor). Don't worry if some of these statements aren't immediately comprehensible—you'll understand them soon enough.

Here are some example statements for you to try:

```
Documents.Open "c:\temp\Sample Document.docm"
MsgBox ActiveDocument.Name
```

```
ActiveDocument.Words(1).Text = "Industry"
ActiveDocument.Close SaveChanges:=wdDoNotSaveChanges
Documents.Add
Selection.TypeText "The quick brown fox jumped over the lazy dog."
Documents.Close SaveChanges:=wdDoNotSaveChanges
Application.Quit
```

Let's look at each of these statements in turn. The statement

```
Documents.Open "c:\temp\Sample Document.docm"
```

uses the `Open` method of the `Documents` collection to open the specified document—in this case, `Sample Document.docm`. Try it: Type this statement in the Immediate window, substituting a path and filename of a document that exists on your computer for ***`\temp\Sample Document.docm`***.

Press the Enter key, and VBA opens the target document in the Word window. Just as when you open a document by hand while working interactively in Word, this statement in the macro makes this document the active document (the document with the window that has the *focus*—in other words, the window you can see and that will, therefore, take input from keystrokes or mouse activity).

The statement

```
MsgBox ActiveDocument.Name
```

uses the `MsgBox` function (built into VBA) to display to the user the `Name` property of the `ActiveDocument` object (in this example, `Sample Document.docm`). As an experiment, type this `MsgBox` statement into the Immediate window (type in lowercase, and use VBA's Help features as you choose) and press the Enter key. VBA displays a message box over the Word window. Click the OK button to dismiss the message box.

Now you see how useful the Immediate window can be when you just want to quickly test a statement to see its effects. You don't have to execute its entire macro. You can just try out a single statement (a single line of code) in the Immediate window if you want to see what it does.

Next, the statement

```
ActiveDocument.Words(1).Text = "Industry"
```

uses the *assignment operator* (the equal [=] sign) to assign the value `Industry` to the `Text` property of the first item in the `Words` collection in the `ActiveDocument` object. Enter this statement in the Immediate window and press the Enter key. You'll see the word *Industry* displayed in the current typeface at the beginning of the document you opened.

Note that after this line executes, the blinking insertion point appears at the *beginning* of this word rather than at the end of the word, where it would be if you'd typed the word. This happens because VBA manipulates the properties of the document (in this case, the `Words` collection) directly rather than imitating "typing" into it.

The statement

```
ActiveDocument.Close SaveChanges:=wdDoNotSaveChanges
```

uses the `Close` method to close the `ActiveDocument` object. It uses one argument, `SaveChanges`, which controls whether Word saves the document that's being closed (if the document contains unsaved changes). In this case, the statement uses the constant `wdDoNotSaveChanges` to specify that Word shouldn't save changes when closing this document. Enter this statement in the Immediate window and press the Enter key, and you'll see VBA make Word close the document.

An *argument* is information you send to a procedure. For example, in this next statement the argument is the text string `show`, which is sent to the built-in VBA `MsgBox` function:

```
MsgBox ("show")
```

A `MsgBox` function will display *any* text, so you send it an argument: the particular text you want it to display. You'll learn more about arguments shortly.

Now try entering this statement in the Immediate window:

```
Documents.Add
```

This statement uses the `Add` method of the `Documents` collection to add a new `Document` object to the `Documents` collection. In other words, it creates a new document. Because the statement doesn't specify which template to use, the new document is based on the default template (`Normal.dotm`). When you enter this statement in the Immediate window and press Enter, Word creates a new document. As usual, this new document becomes the active document.

The statement

```
Selection.TypeText "The quick brown fox jumped over the lazy dog."
```

uses the `TypeText` method of the `Selection` object to type text into the active document at the position of the insertion point or current selection. (The `Selection` object represents the current selection, which can be either a "collapsed" selection—a mere insertion point with nothing actually selected, as in this example—or one or more selected objects, such as one or more words.)

If text is selected in the active document, that selection is overwritten—unless you've cleared the Typing Replaces Selected Text check box by pressing Alt+F, then pressing I, and then clicking the Advanced option in the left pane of the Word Options dialog box. In that case, the selection is collapsed to its beginning and the new text is inserted before the previously selected text.

However, in this example—because you just created a new document—nothing is selected. Enter the previous `Selection.TypeText` statement in the Immediate window and press the Enter key, and Word enters the text. Note that this time the insertion point ends up *after* the inserted text; the `TypeText` method of the `Selection` object *is* analogous to typing something into Word yourself.

The statement

```
Documents.Close SaveChanges:=wdDoNotSaveChanges
```

is similar to an `ActiveDocument.Close SaveChanges:=wdDoNotSaveChanges` statement except that it works on the `Documents` collection rather than the `ActiveDocument` object. The `Documents` collection represents *all* open documents in the current Word session. So this statement closes all open documents and doesn't save any unsaved changes in them. Enter this statement in the Immediate window and press Enter, and you'll see that Word closes all the open documents.

The statement

```
Application.Quit
```

uses the `Quit` method of the `Application` object to close the Word application. Enter the statement in the Immediate window and press the Enter key. Word closes itself, also closing the Visual Basic Editor in the process because Word is the host for the Visual Basic Editor.

Getting Help in Visual Basic for Applications

The Visual Basic Editor offers comprehensive help for the Visual Basic for Applications programming language. To view it, choose Help ➤ Microsoft Visual Basic For Applications Help from the Visual Basic Editor. You're taken to a website devoted to the current application (in this case, at this time, it's Word 2013, although that will eventually be replaced with Word 2016).

Pressing F1 works two ways. If your blinking cursor is on a blank space or an empty line in the Code window, F1 displays a generic Office Help page. This page contains the link "Welcome to the Visual Basic for Applications language reference for Office 2013." Click that link and take a look.

Here's a second way to press F1 for help and it's great. Often the quickest way to get help is to click a keyword in your code, such as `ActiveWindow` or `MsgBox`. By clicking, you put the blinking insertion cursor in that command, "selecting" it. Now when you press F1, the Editor tries to locate online help for that particular command.

Most of the built-in VBA statements and functions are illustrated with code examples, which can be particularly useful when you're creating and troubleshooting your own code. The samples show you how it's done.

The Visual Basic Help files use a couple of conventions you should know about before you try to use them:

- Italics denote variables or values you'll need to change yourself. Like this, where you replace this italicized file path with a path to some document on your hard drive:

  ```
  Documents.Open "c:\temp\Sample Document.docm"
  ```

- Brackets—`[fonttype]`—denote optional arguments.

This book uses the same conventions, so you'll see them in use soon.

If you don't find what you need by searching the Microsoft Visual Basic Help web pages, choose Help ➤ MSDN On The Web. That's a more generic help site, with links to searchable code samples and many other useful items.

Keywords

A *keyword* is a word that is part of the built-in VBA language. It's part of VBA diction. Here are some examples:

- The `Sub` keyword indicates the beginning of a sub, and the `End Sub` keywords mark the end of a sub.
- The `Function` keyword indicates the beginning of a function, and the `End Function` keywords mark the end of a function.
- The `Dim` keyword starts a declaration (for example, of a variable), and the `As` keyword links the item declared to its type, which is also a keyword. For example, in the statement `Dim strExample As String`, there are three keywords: `Dim`, `As`, and `String`.

The names of functions and subs are not keywords (neither the built-in procedures nor procedures you write). Note that in this book I often use the term *command* as a synonym for *keyword*.

IDENTIFYING KEYWORDS BY COLOR

The Visual Basic Editor displays all keywords in blue. If you like, you can specify a different color for keyword text on the Editor Format tab of the Options dialog box (choose Tools ➤ Options from the Visual Basic Editor). If you're not sure whether an item is a keyword, check if the color the Visual Basic Editor gives the item is the same color as keywords such as `Sub`.

Expressions

An *expression* involves multiple words. It consists of a combination of keywords, operators, variables, and/or constants that results in (or *resolves to*) a string, number, or object. For example, you could use an expression to do a math calculation or to compare one variable against another. Here's an example of a numeric expression (it's shown in boldface) that compares the variable *N* to the number 4 by using the > (greater than) operator:

```
If N > 4 Then
```

The result of this expression will depend on whatever value is currently held in the variable *N*. If it holds 12, the expression will result in `TRUE` because 12 is greater than 4. You'll learn more about expressions later.

Operators

An *operator* is a symbol you use to compare, combine, or otherwise work with values in an expression. VBA has four kinds of operators:

- *Arithmetic operators* (such as + and -) perform mathematical calculations.
- *Comparison operators* (such as < and >, less than and greater than, respectively) compare values.
- *Logical operators* (such as `And`, `Not`, and `Or`) build logical structures.
- The *concatenation operator* (&) joins two strings together.

You'll look at the different kinds of operators and how they work in Chapter 11, "Making Decisions in Your Code."

Variables

Variables are very important in programming. A *variable* is a location in memory set aside for storing a piece of information—information that can change while a procedure is running. (Think of it as a named, resizable compartment within the memory area. Like a small file folder.)

For example, if you need the user to input their name via an input box, you'll typically store the name in a variable so you can work with it further down in some later statement in the macro.

Perhaps you want to get a total of several numbers that the user types in. You would have a variable that holds the current sum total—which keeps changing (varying) as the user types in more numbers.

VBA uses several types of variables, including these:

Strings store text characters or groups of characters.

Integers store whole numbers (numbers without fractions).

Objects store objects.

Variants can store any type of data. Variant is the default type of variable.

Either you can let VBA create Variant variables as the default type, or you can specify another data type if you want. Specifying the types of variables has certain advantages that you'll learn about in due course.

For the moment, try creating a variable in the Immediate window. Type the following line and press Enter:

```
myVariable = "Some sample text"
```

Nothing visible happens, but VBA has created the `myVariable` variable. It has set aside some memory and labeled that area `myVariable`. It also stored the text string `Some sample text` in that variable. Now, type the following line into the Immediate window and press Enter:

```
MsgBox myVariable
```

This time, you can see the result: VBA goes to the memory area you specified (that was labeled with the variable name `myVariable`) and retrieves the value, the string. A message box appears containing the text you had stored in the variable.

You can declare variables either explicitly or implicitly. An *explicit declaration* is a line of code that specifies the name you want to give the variable, and usually its type, before you use the variable in your code. Here's an explicit variable declaration:

```
Dim myVariable As String
```

An *implicit declaration* means that you don't bother with that explicit declaration statement. Instead, you just use the variable name in some other statement. VBA then stores the data in a Variant variable type because you didn't specify the type.

In other words, if you *just use* a variable in your code without declaring it, it's implicit.

Here's an example of implicit declaration:

```
myVariable = "Some sample text"
```

You never *explicitly* declared this variable. The first time it appeared in your code, you just assigned some data, the text, to it. Therefore, VBA assumes that you want to create the variable implicitly.

In the next few chapters, you'll use a few implicit variable declarations to keep things simple. In other words, you won't have to type in lines of code to declare implicit variables. VBA will create them for you when you first use them in an assignment or other statement.

However, many educators and professional programmers insist on explicit declaration, so we'll do that for the most part in the later sections of this book. Explicit variable declarations make your code run faster and make it easier to understand. What's more beneficial, some types of errors can be avoided if you explicitly declare all your variables. So declaring is a good habit to get into. And when you or VBA include this line at the top of your Code window, you *must* declare all variables:

```
Option Explicit
```

Constants

A *constant* is similar to a variable. It's a named item that keeps a constant value while a program is executing. The constant's meaning *doesn't change* during the macro's execution (so in this way, it's unlike a variable.) Some programmers use more constants than others—I rarely use them. Variables are just fine for holding most data, even data that doesn't vary. The choice is yours.

VBA uses two types of constants: *intrinsic constants*, which are built into the VBA language itself (and individual Office applications' implementations of VBA), and *user-defined constants*, which you can create. For example, the built-in constant `vbOKCancel` is always available in VBA to be used with the `MsgBox` function. This constant creates a message box that contains an OK and a Cancel button. There are sets of built-in constants for colors, printing (`vbTab`, for example), and other properties. I *do* use intrinsic constants. They're convenient.

Concerning constants that you define, you might want to create one to store a piece of information that doesn't change, such as the name of a procedure or the distance between Boston and New York. In practice, the built-in *intrinsic constants* are used quite often in VBA programming; user-defined constants not so much. I repeat: It's just as easy to put the distance between those cities in a variable, even though it won't vary.

Arguments

An *argument* is a piece of information—supplied by a constant, a variable, a literal, or an expression—that you pass to a procedure (a function or sub), or a method. Some arguments are required; others are optional. The text `hello there` in this `MsgBox` function is an argument:

```
MsgBox ("hello there")
```

Arguments often must be enclosed in parentheses, but not always. Here's another example. As you saw earlier, the following statement uses the optional argument `SaveChanges` to specify whether Word should save any unsaved changes while closing the active document:

```
ActiveDocument.Close SaveChanges:=wdDoNotSaveChanges
```

This optional argument uses the built-in constant `wdDoNotSaveChanges`.

Understanding Literals

A *literal* can be used in your code instead of a constant or variable, if you like. With a literal, you just type the actual value into the argument. For example, you could display a message box that says "Hi there" by using a variable:

```
txtMsg = "Hi there!"
MsgBox (txtMsg)
```

Or you could simply avoid using the variable and employ a literal (the actual text string) as the argument:

```
MsgBox ("Hi there!")
```

Both of these approaches have the same result.

The Visual Basic Editor's helpful prompts and the Visual Basic Help file show the list of arguments for a function, a sub, or a method in parentheses, with any optional arguments enclosed in brackets. If you have its Auto Quick Info feature activated, the Editor displays the argument list for a function, sub, or method after you type its name followed by a space.

Figure 5.2 shows the argument list for the `Document` object's `Open` method. Type **`Documents.Open`**, and then press the spacebar to see the argument list.

FIGURE 5.2
Optional arguments are enclosed within brackets.

```
Documents.Open
    Open(FileName, [ConfirmConversions], [ReadOnly], [AddToRecentFiles],
    [Visible], [OpenAndRepair], [DocumentDirection], [NoEncodingDialog], [X
```

The `FileName` argument is required, so it isn't surrounded by brackets. All the other arguments (`ConfirmConversions`, `ReadOnly`, `AddToRecentFiles`, and so on) are optional and, therefore, are surrounded by brackets.

If you don't supply a value for an optional argument, VBA uses the default value for the argument. (To find out the default value for an argument, consult the VBA Help file. The default is usually the most commonly employed value.) The Visual Basic Editor uses boldface to indicate the current argument in the list; as you enter each argument, the next argument in the list becomes bold.

Specifying Argument Names vs. Omitting Argument Names

You can add arguments in either of two ways:

- Enter the name of the argument (for example, `ConfirmConversions`), followed by a colon, an equal sign (`ConfirmConversions:=`), and the constant or value you want to set for it (`ConfirmConversions:=True`). For example, the start of the statement might look like this:

  ```
  Documents.Open FileName:="c:\temp\Example.docm", _

      ConfirmConversions:=True, ReadOnly:=False
  ```

- Or enter the constant or value in the appropriate position in the argument list for the method, without entering the name of the argument. The previous statement would look like this:

  ```
  Documents.Open "c:\Temp\Example.docm", True, False
  ```

When you use the first approach—naming the arguments—you don't need to put them in order because VBA looks at their names to identify them. The following statements are functionally equivalent:

```
Documents.Open ReadOnly:=False, FileName:= "c:\temp\Example.docm", _
    ReadOnly:=False, ConfirmConversions:=True
```

```
Documents.Open FileName:="c:\temp\Example.docm", _
    ConfirmConversions:=True, ReadOnly:=False
```

You also don't need to indicate to VBA which optional arguments you're omitting.

By contrast, when you don't employ argument names, you're specifying which argument is which simply by its position in the list. Therefore, *the arguments must be in the correct order* for VBA to recognize them accurately. If you choose to omit an optional argument but to use another optional argument that follows it, enter a comma (as a placeholder) to denote the omitted argument. For example, the following statement omits the `ConfirmConversions` argument and uses a comma to denote that the `False` value refers to the `ReadOnly` argument rather than the `ConfirmConversions` argument:

```
Documents.Open "c:\temp\Example.docm",, False
```

Remember that when you type the comma in the Code window or the Immediate window, Auto Quick Info moves the boldface to the next argument in the argument list to indicate that it's next in line for your attention.

REQUIRED ARGUMENTS PRECEDE OPTIONAL ARGUMENTS

Typically, required arguments are listed first in the argument list—before optional arguments. That way, you don't have to use commas to indicate the omission of optional arguments if you only want to enter the required arguments. You can just leave out all the rest of the items in the argument list.

Including Parentheses Around the Argument List

Most programmers enclose argument lists within parentheses. It makes the code easier to read. However, parentheses can be omitted in some circumstances. When you're assigning the result of a function to a variable or other object, you *must* enclose the whole argument list in parentheses. For example, to assign to the variable `objMyDocument` the result of opening the document `c:\temp\Example.docm`, use the following statement:

```
objMyDocument = Documents.Open(FileName:="c:\temp\Example.docm", _
    ConfirmConversions:=True, ReadOnly:=False)
```

However, when you aren't assigning the result of an operation to a variable or an object, you don't need to use the parentheses around the argument list, even though it's common practice to do so. The following examples illustrate how you can either use or leave out parentheses when not assigning a result to a variable or other object:

```
MsgBox ("Hi there!")
MsgBox "Hi there!"
```

Objects

To VBA, each application consists of a series of *objects*. Here are a few examples:

- In Word, a document is an object (the `Document` object), as is a paragraph (the `Paragraph` object) and a table (the `Table` object). Even a single character is an object (the `Character` object).
- In Excel, a workbook is an object (the `Workbook` object), as are the worksheets (the `Worksheet` object) and charts (the `Chart` object).
- In PowerPoint, a presentation is an object (the `Presentation` object), as are its slides (the `Slide` object) and the shapes (the `Shape` object) they contain.

Most of the actions you can take in VBA involve manipulating objects. For example, as you saw earlier, you can close the active document in Word by using the `Close` method on the `ActiveDocument` object:

```
ActiveDocument.Close
```

Collections

A *collection* is an object that contains other objects, the way an umbrella-stand object contains umbrella objects. Collections provide a way to access all their members at the same time. For example, the `Documents` collection contains all the open documents, each of which is an object. Instead of closing `Document` objects one by one, you can close all open documents by using the `Close` method on the `Documents` collection:

```
Documents.Close
```

Likewise, you can use a collection to change the properties of all the members of a collection simultaneously.

Here's an example of some code that displays, in the Immediate window of the Editor, all the names of the objects in Word's `CommandBars` collection:

```
'fetch the number of commandbars
    n = CommandBars.Count

'display all their names
    For i = 1 To n
        Debug.Print CommandBars(i).Name
    Next i
```

Properties

Each object has a number of *properties*. Think of properties as the qualities of an object, such as its color, size, and so on.

For example, the current document in Word has properties such as the number of sentences in the document. Type this into the Immediate window, and then press Enter:

```
MsgBox (ActiveDocument.Sentences.Count)
```

Here you're using the `Count` property of the `Sentences` collection to find out how many sentences are in the document.

Likewise, even a single character has various properties, such as its font, font size, and various types of emphasis (bold, italic, strikethrough, and so on).

Methods

A *method* is something an object can *do*—a capability. Different objects have different methods, just as different people have different talents. For example, here's a list of some of the methods of the `Document` object in Word (many of these methods are also available to objects such as the `Workbook` object in Excel and the `Presentation` object in PowerPoint):

`Activate`

Activates the document (the equivalent of selecting the document's window with the keyboard or mouse)

`Close`

Closes the document (the equivalent of pressing Alt+F and then C, or clicking the Close button after clicking the File tab on the Ribbon)

`Save`

Saves the document (the equivalent of pressing Alt+F and then S, or clicking the Save button after clicking the File tab on the Ribbon)

`SaveAs`

Saves the document under a specified name (the equivalent of pressing Alt+F and then A, or clicking the Save As button after clicking the File tab on the Ribbon)

Events

When an *event* occurs, VBA is aware that something happened, usually something that happened *to* an object. For example, the opening of a file on the hard drive (either by a user or by a macro procedure) typically generates an event. The user clicking a button in the toolbar generates a Click event. Another way to put it is that when you click a button, you trigger that button's Click event, and VBA becomes aware that this has happened.

By writing code for an event, you can cause VBA to respond appropriately when that event occurs. For example, let's say you display a user form (a window). You might write some code in an OK button's Click event. This code might check that all necessary settings were specified by the user when the user clicked the OK button to close the user form and apply the settings. You might write more code within that button's Click event that responded (perhaps by displaying a message box) if the user had failed to type in some required information. In essence, you can write code in an event to tell VBA what to do if that event is triggered. You don't have to write code for all events in any given macro. Sometimes you'll write code in only one of them. But if you put a button captioned "Display Results" on a user form, you'd better at least write some code in that button's Click event to display some results. If you don't, your user will be baffled when they click this button and nothing happens.

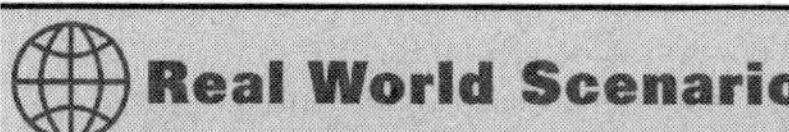

OBJECTS AND THEIR COMPONENTS

I'll have much more to say about objects throughout the rest of this book. For now, see if you can identify the three primary parts of a typical object: properties (its qualities), methods (ways you can make the object behave), and events (something that happens to an object while a program or application is executing). Collectively, these three components of an object are called the object's *members*.

Take a look at the following Code window. See if you can spot the members of the `Document` object—its properties, its methods, and an event.

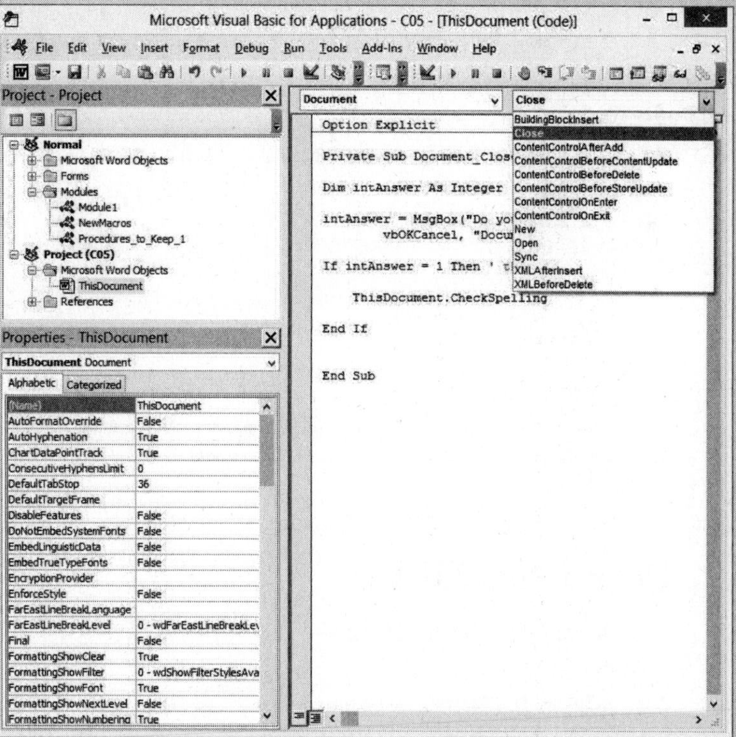

Continues

Continued

Here, you can see that the ThisDocument object is selected in the Project Explorer on the left. This object has available to it the many properties in the long list displayed in the Properties window on the left side. You can either modify those properties directly in the Visual Basic Editor or write code that modifies them on the fly while the macro executes.

On the right side is a drop-down list of events—actions that can happen to a Document object, or at least happen while the document is in existence within the computer. You can write code in any of these events (in the Code window, each event will be a separate sub, enclosed within the Sub and End Sub statements). Here, you can see that we're writing code that will execute when the Document_Close event is triggered:

```
Private Sub Document_Close()
```

In this example, I'm writing code to query users if they attempt to close the document. This code will execute any time this document's Close event is triggered (when the user clicks the X button in the upper-right corner of the window, for instance).

Only one *method* is shown in the Code-window illustration. Can you spot it? It's in boldface in the following code example:

```
Private Sub Document_Close()

Dim intAnswer As Integer

intAnswer = MsgBox("Do you want to check the spelling?", _
        vbOKCancel, "Document Is Being Closed")

If intAnswer = 1 Then ' they clicked OK. 1 = OK  2 = Cancel

ThisDocument.CheckSpelling
End If

End Sub
```

As you can see, CheckSpelling is a method (a task that an object is able to carry out).

The Bottom Line

Understand the basics of VBA. VBA includes two types of procedures, used for different purposes.

Master It Name the two types of procedures used in VBA (and indeed in most computer languages), and describe the difference between them.

Work with subs and functions. A procedure (a sub or function) is a container for a set of programming statements that accomplish a particular job.

Master It Write a sub in the Visual Basic Editor that displays a message to the user. Then execute that sub to test it.

Use the Immediate window to execute individual statements. When you're writing code, you often want to test a single line (a statement) to see if you have the syntax and punctuation right or if it produces the expected result.

Master It Open the Immediate window, type in a line of code, and then execute that line.

Understand objects, properties, methods, and events. Object-oriented programming (OOP) means working with objects in your programming. OOP has become the fundamental paradigm upon which large programming projects are built. Generally speaking, macros are not large and, therefore, they usually don't profit from the clerical, security, and other benefits that OOP offers—these features particularly benefit people who write large applications as a team.

However, in your programming, you'll make frequent use of code libraries. All VB's commands are part of these libraries, such as the vast VBA set of objects and their members (not to mention the even vaster .NET libraries that tap into the power of the operating system itself). These libraries *are* written by large groups of people, and they are written at different times. What's more, the libraries themselves are huge. They are so big that there must be a way to organize their objects and functions—to categorize them and allow you to execute the methods and manage their properties and arguments in your own macros. As a result, another aspect of OOP—taxonomy—is quite valuable even when writing brief macros. It's a way to quickly locate the members you're interested in.

Master It Look up the `Document` object in the Visual Basic Editor's Help system; then look at its methods.

Chapter 6

Working with Variables, Constants, and Enumerations

This chapter covers the basics of working with variables, constants, and enumerations. *Variables* are used often in programming—they provide a way of storing and manipulating information. Variables come in several types, such as String variables for storing text, various numeric data types for storing numbers (for example, Integer variables for storing integer values), Date variables for storing dates and time, Boolean variables for storing `True`/`False` values, and even Object variables for storing objects.

A *constant* is a named item that stores a value that doesn't change. Constants, like variables, exist only while a program is executing. Most programmers rarely create their own constants; they just use variables instead. However, there is another kind of constant that the programmer does not create but sometimes uses. Many useful constants are built into VBA to represent elements in Access, text color options in Excel, styles in Word, and so on.

For our purposes, the term *enumeration* means a numbered list—like a list of all the items you need to buy to paint a room. The list contains both the numbers and the names of the items so you can refer to each item either by its number in the list or by its name. Essentially, an enumeration is a group of related, predefined constants, but constants are more commonly identified by their names rather than their numbers. That's because the name `AnimationFlyIntoFromLeft` is easier to use in your programming than its number, 1312.

The one type of variable that this chapter doesn't discuss is the Array variable, which is used to store a set of multiple pieces of related information at the same time. It's similar to an enumeration. Arrays are so important in computer programming that I'll devote an entire chapter to them: Chapter 7, "Using Array Variables."

IN THIS CHAPTER, YOU WILL LEARN TO DO THE FOLLOWING:

- Understand what variables are and what you use them for
- Create and use variables
- Specify the scope and lifetime of a variable
- Work with constants
- Work with enumerations

Working with Variables

Variables are used in nearly all computer programs, even short programs like macros. Think of a variable as a named area in the computer's memory that you use for storing data while a procedure is running. For example, in Chapter 5, "Understanding the Essentials of VBA Syntax," you created a variable that stored a simple string of text that you then displayed in a message box:

```
myVariable = "Sample variable text"
MsgBox myVariable
```

The first statement sets aside an area in memory, names it `myVariable`, and assigns the string `Sample variable text` to it. The second statement retrieves the contents (called the *value*) of `myVariable` from memory and uses the `MsgBox` function to display it in a message box. The contents of `myVariable` remain in memory, so you can use the value again if necessary while the macro is running. Or you can even change the contents. In other words, the value in a variable can *vary* while the program runs. A *constant*, by contrast, doesn't vary during program execution.

Choosing Names for Variables

VBA imposes several constraints on how you name your variables:

- Variable names must start with a letter and can be up to 255 characters in length. Usually, you'll want to keep them much shorter than this so that you can easily type them into your code and so that your lines of code don't rapidly reach awkward lengths.

  The Visual Basic Editor's AutoComplete feature helps make long variable names a little more manageable: Type enough of the variable's name to distinguish it from any keywords and other variable names, and press Ctrl+spacebar. If you've typed enough letters to uniquely identify the variable, the Visual Basic Editor inserts its name; if not, the Visual Basic Editor displays the drop-down list of keywords and names starting with those letters.

- Variable names can't contain characters such as periods, exclamation points, mathematical operators (+, -, /, *), or comparison operators (=, <>, >, >=, <, <=), nor can they internally contain type-declaration characters (@, &, $, #). (You'll learn about the type-declaration characters later in this chapter.)

- Variable names can't contain spaces but can contain underscores, which you can use to make the variable names more descriptive by combining words. `User_Response` is one example. However, it's more common to just omit the underscore and let capitalization segregate the words, as in `UserResponse`.

As a general rule, you're pretty safe if you stick with straightforward alphanumerics enlivened with the occasional underscore if you like underscores.

For example, all of the following variable names are fine, although the last one is awkwardly long:

- `i`
- `John`

- `MyVariable`
- `MissionParameters`
- `The_String_the_User_Entered_in_the_Input_Box`

On the other hand, these variable names are not usable:

- `My Variable`—Contains a space
- `My!Variable`—Contains an exclamation point
- `Time@Tide`—Contains a type-declaration character (@)
- `1_String`—Does not start with a letter

Each variable name must be unique within the scope in which it's operating (to prevent VBA from confusing it with any other variable). Typically, the scope within which a variable operates is a procedure, but if you declare the variable as public or private (discussed later in this chapter), its scope is wider.

The other constraint on variable names is that you should avoid assigning to a variable a name that VBA already uses in its own language or the name of a built-in function, statement, or object member. Doing so is called *shadowing* a VBA keyword. It doesn't necessarily cause problems, but it may prevent you from using that function, statement, or method without specifically identifying it to VBA by prefacing its name with `VBA`. For example, instead of `Date`, you'd have to use `VBA.Date`—it's no big deal, but worth avoiding. After all, why add this complexity when it's simpler to just make up your own, unique variable names? Why do things that provide you with no real benefit and have drawbacks such as making your code harder to read? On top of that, if you forget to prepend the *VBA*, shadowing can cause bugs.

There's no reason to shadow a VBA keyword, but VBA has so many keywords that it's surprisingly easy to do so. But don't worry about accidentally creating a variable name that violates one of the rules listed in this section. VBA will throw you an error message if you use @ or start your variable name with 6 or try any other illegal moves. VBA will either report "Invalid Character" or separate your variable name into multiple words, such as changing `56nin` into `56 nin`, thinking you are trying to use line numbers in your code. (You can, if you like, number your lines, and VBA will execute the code by just ignoring the line numbers. I number the lines in the code in this book so I can reference them in the text.)

Declaring a Variable

Recall from Chapter 5 that VBA lets you declare variables either implicitly or explicitly. As you'll see shortly, each approach has its pros and cons. However, *explicit* declarations are almost always the best approach, and when you've been working with VBA for even a little while, you'll probably be explicit all the time. For this reason, it's best to declare your variables explicitly right from the beginning. This chapter also illustrates how to make implicit declarations so you know that technique if that's your preference.

Declaring a Variable Implicitly

Declaring a variable implicitly means that you just use it in your code without first declaring it explicitly. When you declare a variable implicitly, VBA checks to make sure that there isn't already an existing variable with that name. It then automatically creates a variable with that name for you and assigns it the *Variant* data type, which can contain any type of data except a fixed-length string.

For example, in the previous chapter, you declared the variable `myVariable` by using the following implicit declaration:

```
myVariable = "Sample variable text"
```

Here, `myVariable` is implicitly declared as a variable—because it is used in a statement rather than first being declared explicitly (usually with the `Dim` command, which we'll get to shortly).

VBA assigns an implicitly declared variable to the Variant data type, which has a dozen or so subtypes. In the previous example, the variable's subtype is a string because it contains text. VBA usually assigns the variable the value `Empty` (a special value used to indicate Variant variables that have not yet been used during execution) when it creates it, but in our example the variable receives a value immediately (because the string of text is assigned to it). VBA then assigns the string type because it can see you're storing a string in the variable.

The advantage of declaring a variable implicitly is that you write less code. When you want a variable, you simply declare it on the spot by using it in a statement. But declaring a variable implicitly also has a couple of rather serious disadvantages:

- It's easier to make a mistake when you're typing the variable's name elsewhere in your code. For example, suppose you implicitly declare the variable `FilesToCreate` and then later type `FllesToCreate` instead. VBA doesn't query the latter spelling (with its double `ll` typo). No error messages are displayed. VBA merely creates another, new, different variable with the `ll` name.

When you're working with many variables, it can be difficult and time-consuming to catch little typo mistakes like this. A mistake like this (having two variables when you think you have only one) causes errors. The problem in this example is that you think you're referring to the `FilesToCreate` variable, but you're not. VBA can detect this kind of error, but only if *explicit declaration* is enforced. (*Enforced* here means that if you try to get away with using an undeclared variable, the Visual Basic Editor displays an error message and halts execution.)

- The Variant variable type takes up more memory than other types of variables because it has to be able to store various types of data. This difference is negligible under most normal circumstances, particularly if you're using only a few variables or writing only short procedures. However, if you're using many variables in a huge program running on a computer with limited memory, the extra memory used by Variant variables might slow down a procedure or even run the computer out of memory. What's more important on an underpowered computer is that manipulating Variants takes longer than manipulating the other data types. This is because VBA has to keep checking to see what sort of data is in the variable. Memory and speed are less significant issues than they used to be, but some special-purpose computers (built into a forklift for instance) can even today be small and slow.

You can get around this second disadvantage in a couple of ways: first, by using a type-declaration character to specify the data type when you declare a variable implicitly or, second (as you will see in the next section), by simply telling VBA to force you to declare variables explicitly—and to display an error message if you don't. However, this technique is rarely employed.

A *type-declaration character* is a character that you add to the end of a variable's name in an implicit declaration to tell VBA which data type to use for the variable. Table 6.1 lists the type-declaration characters.

TABLE 6.1: Type-declaration characters

CHARACTER	DATA TYPE OF VARIABLE	EXAMPLE
%	Integer	`Quantity%`
&	Long	`China&`
@	Currency	`Profits@`
!	Single	`temperature!`
#	Double	`Differential#`
$	String (variable length)	`myMessage$`

You could implicitly declare the String variable `UserName` with the following statement, which assigns the value `Jane Magnolia` to the variable:

```
UserName$ = "Jane Magnolia"
```

You could implicitly declare the currency variable `Price` by using this statement:

```
Price@ = Cost * Margin
```

You use the type-declaration character only when declaring the variable. Thereafter, you can refer to the variable by its name—`UserName` and `Price` in the previous examples.

DECLARING A VARIABLE EXPLICITLY

Declaring a variable explicitly is the best practice. It means telling VBA that the variable exists before you use it. VBA allocates memory space to that variable and registers it as a known quantity. You can also declare the variable type at the same time, which is a good idea but not obligatory.

You can declare a variable explicitly at any point in code before you use it, but custom and good sense recommend declaring all your variables at the beginning of the procedure that uses them. (Or, to give a variable greater scope, declare it in the General Declarations area up at the top of the Code window. You'll learn more about *scope* later.)

Locating all your declarations at the top of a procedure makes them easy to find, which helps anyone reading the code.

Declaring variables explicitly offers the following advantages:

- Your code is easier to read and to debug, both for you and other programmers. When you write complex code, this is an important consideration.
- Making the Editor enforce explicit variable declarations is accomplished by adding an `Option Explicit` statement at the top of a module—in the General Declarations section of the Code window. This enforcement makes it more difficult for you to create new variables unintentionally by mistyping the names of existing variables.
- It is more difficult for you to wipe out the contents of an existing variable unintentionally when trying to create a new variable.

- VBA can catch some data-type errors at design time or compile time that, with implicit declaration, wouldn't surface until runtime.

> **STORE THE CORRECT TYPE OF VALUE IN A VARIABLE**
>
> A data-typing error occurs when you assign the wrong type of information to a variable. For example, if you declare an Integer variable and then assign a string of text to it, VBA notifies you of an error because it can't store string information in an Integer variable.

- Your code runs a fraction faster because VBA won't need to determine each variable's type while the code is running.

The disadvantage of declaring variables explicitly is that doing so takes a little more time, effort, and thought. For most code, however, this disadvantage is far outweighed by the advantages.

To declare a variable explicitly, you use one of the following keywords: `Dim`, `Private`, `Public`, or `Static`.

For example, the following statement declares the variable `MyValue`:

```
Dim MyValue
```

`Dim` is the most common keyword to use for declaring a variable, and you'll probably want to use it for most of your variable declarations. You use the other keywords to specify a different scope, lifetime, and data type for the variable in the declaration. In the previous example, the `MyValue` variable receives the default scope and lifetime and the Variant data type, which makes it suitable for general-purpose use.

You can also declare multiple variables on the same line by separating the variable statements with commas:

```
Dim Supervisor As String, ControllerCode As Long
```

This can help you keep down the number of declaration lines in your code, but it makes the declarations harder to read, so it's not usually a good idea.

Be warned that when you declare multiple variables on the same line, you must specify the data type for each, as in the previous example. You might be tempted to try a little abbreviation, like this, hoping for a couple of String variables:

```
Dim strManager, strReportingEmployee As String
```

This statement doesn't create two String variables: `strReportingEmployee` is a String variable, but `strManager` is a Variant because the `As String` part of the code applies only to `strReportingEmployee`.

Choosing the Scope and Lifetime of a Variable

The *scope* of a variable is the area where it can operate. Think of it as similar to your scope of activity at work: those areas in which you perform tasks and those areas in which you don't. Your scope might be the office-cubicles area of the building, but if you were found slinking around inside the walk-in safe, there would be trouble. Entering the safe is not part of your job description.

The default scope of a variable is the procedure in which that variable is declared. In other words, the scope is between the `Sub` and `End Sub` (or `Function` and `End Function`) that define the start and end of a given procedure. Macros are most often fairly short; therefore, their code is most often contained within a single procedure. For the typical macro, there's no reason for a variable to have a scope any larger than its own procedure.

Here's an example of procedure-level scope. Suppose you have two macros called `Breakeven_Table` and `Profit_Analysis_Table`. Would there be a problem for VBA if you used a variable named `Expenses` in *both* of these procedures? No. The variables in each procedure are distinct from the variables in the other procedure, so there is no danger of VBA confusing the two when the macros are executed. Each instance of `Expenses` is walled off, its scope limited to its own procedures. It doesn't leak out into other procedures. It's said to be *local* to its procedure.

The *lifetime* of a variable is the period during which VBA *remembers* the value of the variable (to put it a different way, the period during which the variable even exists). You need different lifetimes for your variables for different purposes. A variable's lifetime is tied to its scope. *Lifetime*, here, refers to how long during program execution the variable is in existence. Variables declared within a procedure have the briefest lifetime: They only exist while that procedure is executing. For most macros, however, this is the usual lifetime because macros are typically self-contained and need not pass data to other macros.

Sometimes you do need to access a variable from outside the procedure in which it's declared, however. In these cases, you need to declare a different, wider scope for the variable. You can do this by declaring a variable up top, above the first procedure in the module. Such a variable is said to have *global* rather than *local* scope. Likewise, a global variable exists for any of the procedures within the module—so its lifetime is greater than a local variable.

In practice, though, we're dealing here with macros and they rarely act in concert with other macros, so the need for a global variable to communicate data between them is equally rare. In fact, if you *do* need to send data from one macro to another, making them functions is preferable. Functions are designed to transmit data outside their own procedure.

That said, you'll find an example in Listing 6.1 later in this chapter that shows how to use a global variable to communicate between two different macros.

Real World Scenario

REQUIRING EXPLICIT DECLARATIONS FOR VARIABLES

Most experts urge you to explicitly declare variables. You can make VBA require you to declare variables explicitly. Most programmers and developers find this feature useful because it prevents them from declaring any variables implicitly, whether intentionally or otherwise.

To require variable declarations globally—so explicit declaration is automatically enforced in any new module you create—choose Tools ➤ Options in the Visual Basic Editor to display the Options dialog box, select the Require Variable Declaration check box in the Code Settings area, and then click the OK button. (The Require Variable Declaration check box is cleared by default, enabling you to declare variables implicitly, which is usually the easiest way to learn how to work with variables.) The Visual Basic Editor then adds an `Option Explicit` statement to each *new* module that you create. This statement enforces explicit variable declarations for the module it's in.

Continues

Continued

When you select the Require Variable Declaration check box, the Visual Basic Editor doesn't add the `Option Explicit` statement to your existing modules. You must type the `Option Explicit` statement into your existing modules manually if you want to force explicit declarations in them.

To require variable declarations only for specified modules, put an `Option Explicit` statement at the beginning of each module for which you want to require declarations. The `Option Explicit` statement must go before the `Sub` or `Function` statement for the first procedure in the module—if you put it inside a procedure, or between procedures, VBA gives an error when you try to run any of the code in the module. This zone—above the first procedure in a module—is called the General Declarations area.

If you've set `Option Explicit` either globally or for an individual module, VBA tests the procedure before running it. More precisely, VBA protests when it tries to compile the code and discovers that you haven't declared one or more of the variables, and it warns you if a variable isn't explicitly declared, as shown here in this screenshot. VBA also highlights the variable in your code.

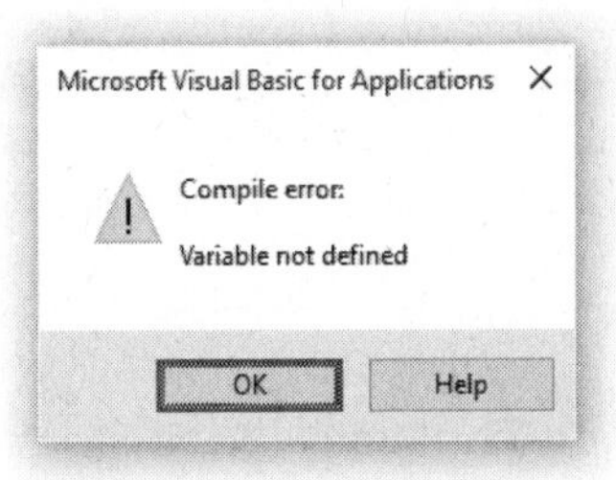

If you get this message box, you can solve the problem either by declaring the variable or by turning off the requirement of variable declarations for the module. To turn off the requirement, remove the `Option Explicit` statement from the module by selecting and deleting the line that contains it or by commenting out this line by putting a single-quote symbol (`'`) at the start of the line.

A variable can have three types of scope:

- Procedure
- Private
- Public

Procedure Scope

Recall that a variable with *procedure scope* (also known as *procedure-level scope* or *local scope*) is available only to the procedure that contains it. As a result, the lifetime of a *local variable* is limited to the duration of the procedure that declares it. As soon as that procedure stops running, VBA removes all local variables from memory and reclaims the memory that held them. This is true even if later on that same procedure is executed again. Local variables don't *persist* if execution moves outside their procedure. But again, macros are usually only a single procedure, so local variables are usually all you need.

Procedure scope is all you'll need for variables that operate only in the procedure in which they're declared. For example, say you declare a Variant variable named `Supervisor`, like this:

```
Dim Supervisor = "Paul Smith"
```

You can then use this `Supervisor` variable in the rest of that procedure—for example, retrieving the text stored in it or changing that text. But when the procedure stops running, VBA removes the variable. VBA forgets it.

Implicitly Declared Variables Are Always Local

When you declare a variable implicitly, it's automatically assigned procedure scope.

To explicitly declare a local variable, use the `Dim` keyword and place the declaration inside the procedure, like this:

```
Sub Create_Weekly_Report()
    Dim strSupervisor As String
    Dim lngController As Long
...
End Sub
```

Here, the second line declares the variable `strSupervisor` as the String data type, and the third line declares the variable `lngController` as the Long data type. (The section "Specifying the Data Type for a Variable," a bit later in this chapter, goes through the variable types.)

On the other hand, if you need to pass any of these variables to another procedure that you call from the current procedure, procedure scope isn't sufficient—you need to use either private scope or public scope.

Private Scope

A variable declared with private scope is available to all the other procedures in the module that contains it, but not to procedures in other modules. Using private variables enables you to pass the value of a variable from one procedure to another. Unlike local variables, which retain their value only as long as the procedure that contains them is running, private variables retain their value as long as *any procedure* in the project that contains them is executing.

To declare a variable with private scope, you can use either the `Dim` keyword or the `Private` keyword, but use it up at the beginning of a module, placing it up top before the `Sub` statement for the first procedure in the module, like this:

```
Dim strSupervisor As String
Private blnConsultantAssigned As Boolean

Sub Assign_Personnel()
. . .
End Sub
```

The Visual Basic Editor displays the private declarations above the dividing line that appears between the General Declarations area and the code below it (see Figure 6.1).

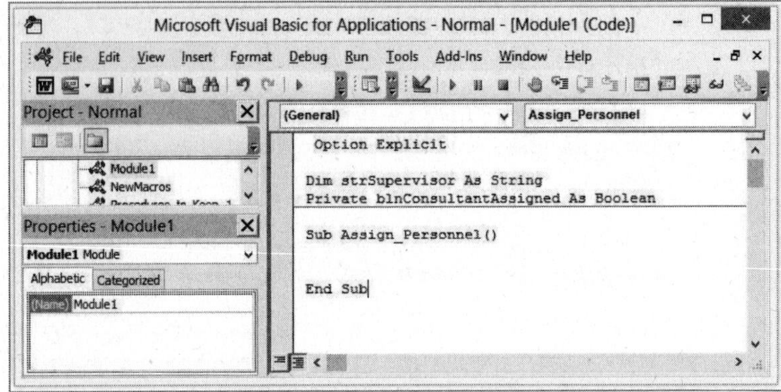

FIGURE 6.1 Private variable declarations appear in the declarations area.

You'll notice that the `Dim` statement here uses exactly the same syntax as the earlier declaration for the local variable. The only difference is that here you place the `Dim` statement in the declarations area of a module (up top) rather than within a procedure. Because the `Private` statement has the same effect as the `Dim` statement for declaring private variables and can't be used within a procedure, it's clearer to use the `Private` statement rather than the `Dim` statement for declaring private variables. (The term *private* is a bit confusing because they're not private to a procedure, only private to their module.)

PUBLIC SCOPE

A variable declared with *public* scope is available anywhere in a project. It's accessible by all procedures in all modules in the project that contains it.

To declare a public variable, you use the `Public` keyword in the General Declarations area at the beginning of a module (up above the `Sub` statement for the first procedure in the module). Here's an example:

```
Option Explicit
Public intMyVar As Integer
```

The second statement declares the public variable `intMyVar` as the Integer type.

Like private variables, public variables retain their value as long as the project that contains them is open (still running). For example, if you want to track the user's name through a series of operations in Word, you can create an `AutoExec` procedure that prompts users to enter their name when they start Word. (`AutoExec` is the built-in name for a procedure that runs automatically when Word starts. Word, when you start it, searches to see if there is a `Sub` named `AutoExec` and, if so, executes that procedure.)

The Declarations Area Appears at the Top of the Code Window as Necessary

The General Declarations area appears at the beginning of each module that contains declarations. For example, if you choose to use explicit variable declarations (by selecting the Require Variable Declaration check box on the Editor page of the Tools ➤ Options dialog box), the Visual Basic Editor automatically enters the `Option Explicit` declaration at the start of each new module you create. If not, the Visual Basic Editor creates the declarations area when you first enter a statement there manually.

By storing the result of the user's input in a public variable, you can retrieve the value for use any time later in the same Word session. You can see how this would be handy if several macros needed the information contained in a variable. Remember that local variables (those declared inside a procedure) are destroyed as soon as that procedure reaches its `End Sub` statement and shuts down.

Use Prefixes to Identify Variable Types

You'll likely notice in the various examples in this chapter that prefixes identify a variable's data type (more on this later in the chapter). For instance, instead of naming a variable `CurrentUser` in Listing 6.1, I named it `strCurrentUser`. This `str` prefix identifies `CurrentUser` as a variable that holds text strings. These prefixes make your code easier to read and modify because each variable, everywhere in the code, is identified as a particular type. Prefixes commonly used include `str` for String, `int` for Integer, `var` for Variant, `lng` for Long, `obj` for Object, and so on. As you'll see later in this book, a similar set of prefixes is used to identify controls you place on a user form: `txt` for Text, `btn` for Button, and so on. If you're interested in following this convention, you can find lists of prefixes at this location in *Wikipedia*:

`http://en.wikipedia.org/wiki/Leszynski_naming_convention`

Listing 6.1 shows an `AutoExec` procedure.

Listing 6.1: An AutoExec procedure

```
Public strCurrentUser As String

Sub AutoExec()
    strCurrentUser = InputBox("Please enter your name.", _
        "Current User Identity")
```

```
5.  End Sub
6.
7.  Sub Identify_Current_User()
8.      MsgBox "The current user is " & strCurrentUser, _
            vbOKOnly + vbInformation, "Current User"
9.  End Sub
```

This code consists of three different parts:

- Line 1 declares the public String variable `strCurrentUser`.
- Lines 3 through 5 contain the `AutoExec` procedure. This procedure runs each time the user starts Word. Line 4 displays an input box that prompts the user to enter their name and stores their response in the public variable `strCurrentUser`.
- Lines 7 through 9 contain the `Identify_Current_User` procedure, which simply displays a message box that gives the name of the user, along with lead-in text and an information icon and title bar for completeness.

You can test these procedures by stepping through (by pressing the F8 key) first the `AutoExec` procedure and then the `Identify_Current_User` procedure in the Visual Basic Editor. To see their effect, you'll have to create the procedures and then exit Word. When you restart Word, the `AutoExec` procedure displays the input box for you to enter your name. At any point thereafter (until you exit Word), you can access the value in the `strCurrentUser` variable. For example, you could run the `Identify_Current_User` procedure at any time (until you close Word itself), and VBA displays a message box with the name you entered. A public variable is said to *persist*.

A Large Number of Public Variables Can Clog Memory

Why not just make all variables public? When writing short programs like macros, this wouldn't cause as much difficulty as when writing large programs or programming professionally in a team. However, there are a variety of reasons to limit the scope of variables to as local as possible. For an interesting take on the advantages and disadvantages of public (global) variables, see this website:

`http://c2.com/cgi/wiki?GlobalVariablesAreBad`

Using Static Variables

Besides declaring variables with `Dim`, `Private`, and `Public`, you can also use the `Static` keyword, which is special. You can use it to cause even a *local* variable to persist. Use `Static` instead of `Dim` when you want to declare a *static* variable—a variable whose values you want to preserve between calls to the procedure in which they are declared.

Static variables are similar to public variables in that their lifetime is not limited to the duration of the procedure that declares them. The difference is that static variables, once declared, are available only to the procedure that declared them, whereas public variables are available to all procedures once they've been declared. So, a static variable has the *scope* of a local variable but the *lifetime* of a public or private variable. To be practical, there is one particular situation where static variables come in handy: *toggling*.

Static variables are useful for maintaining information on a process that you need to run a number of times during a session of the application, either to maintain a running total (for example, a count of the times you performed a procedure) or to keep at hand a piece of information that may prove useful when you run a procedure a second or subsequent time. Typically, you employ a static variable in a procedure that *toggles* something between two states. For example, you could create a procedure that when first executed turns on italics, then when next executed turns italics off, then back on, and so on. Such a toggle would look something like this:

```
Sub ToggleItal()

Static switch As Boolean

switch = Not switch

If switch Then
    MsgBox "on"
Else
    MsgBox "Off"
End If

End Sub
```

You can test this by stepping through it (pressing F8 after clicking the first line of the procedure). Each time you execute the procedure, you get a different message. The `Not` command switches a Boolean variable type back and forth between `True` and `False`. A Boolean variable has only those two possible values.

The following statement declares the static String variable `strSearchTerm1`:

```
Static strSearchTerm1 As String
```

Specifying the Data Type for a Variable

Table 6.2 explains the data types that VBA supports and the amount of memory each variable type requires.

TABLE 6.2: VBA variable data types

VARIABLE	SHORT DESCRIPTION	MEMORY REQUIRED
Boolean	`True` or `False`	2 bytes
Byte	An integer from 0 to 255	1 byte

TABLE 6.2: VBA variable data types *(CONTINUED)*

VARIABLE	SHORT DESCRIPTION	MEMORY REQUIRED
Currency	A positive or negative number with up to 15 digits to the left of the decimal point and 4 digits to the right of it	8 bytes
Date	A floating-point number with the date to the left of the decimal point and the time to the right of it	8 bytes
Decimal	An unsigned integer scaled by a power of 10	12 bytes
Double	A floating-point number with a negative value between –1.79769313486231570E+308 and –4.94065645841246544E-324 or a positive value between 4.94065645841246544E-324 and 1.79769313486231570E+308	8 bytes
Integer	An integer from –32,768 to 32,767	2 bytes
Long	An integer from –2,147,483,648 to 2,147,483,647	4 bytes
Object	A reference to an object	4 bytes
Single	A floating-point number with a negative value between –3.4028235E+38 and –1.401298E-45 and a positive value between 1.401298E-45 and 3.4028235E+38	4 bytes
Variable-Length String	A string of text	10 bytes plus the storage for the string
Fixed-Length String	A string whose length doesn't change	Whatever size is specified for the length
Variant	Any type of data except a fixed-length string in a subtype of the Variant	Variants containing numbers: 16 bytes; Variants containing characters: 22 bytes plus the storage for the characters

The next few pages discuss these data types in detail.

DO YOU NEED TO SPECIFY THE DATA TYPE?

Specifying the data type for each variable you create is a good idea, but it's not compulsory. You're permitted to use the default Variant data type (as you've done a couple of times so far in this book's examples) and let VBA figure out which subtype to assign to the Variant. But remember that even though something is possible, it might not be wise. You can drive with your legs crossed, but it's a bad idea.

There are four disadvantages to using the Variant data type like this:

- Sometimes VBA makes a mistake when trying to interpret which kind of subtype you intended. This can cause rather obscure bugs.
- Using the Variant data type causes your code to run more slowly. However, with short procedures (or long procedures involving relatively few variables), memory and speed are rarely an issue.
- Your code is harder for humans to read and to debug. This can be more of a concern than memory or speed issues.
- The Variant data type takes up more memory than any of the other data types except long strings.

To sum up, most programming experts frown on the Variant and suggest that it's better to always specify the data types when you declare your variables. So let's now take a look at the data types in VBA.

Boolean

A Boolean variable can be set only to `True` or `False`. You can use the keywords `True` and `False` to set the value of a Boolean variable, as in the second line in the following code (the first declares the Boolean variable `blnProduct_Available`):

```
Dim blnProduct_Available As Boolean
blnProduct_Available = True
```

You can then retrieve the result of the Boolean variable and take action accordingly:

```
If blnProduct_Available = True Then
    MsgBox "The product is available."
Else             'blnProduct_Available = False
    MsgBox "The product is not available."
End If
```

When you convert a Boolean variable to another data type (such as a numeric value), `True` returns `-1` and `False` returns `0`. When you convert a numeric value to a Boolean value, `0` returns `False` and all other numbers (whether positive or negative) return `True`.

Boolean variables take up 2 bytes each in memory.

Byte

A Byte variable takes up the least memory of any data type—just 1 byte—and can store a number from 0 to 255.

Currency

The Currency data type is designed for use with money. It allows for positive and negative numbers with up to 15 digits to the left of the decimal point and 4 digits to the right of it. Unlike the Single and Double data types, the Currency data type is exact, not rounded.

To implicitly declare a Currency variable, use the type-declaration character `@`. For example, you could work out your weekly salary with a little simple math:

```
Sub Calculate_Weekly_Salary()
    Salary@ = InputBox("Enter your salary.", _
        "Calculate Weekly Salary")
    WeeklySalary@ = Salary / 52
    MsgBox WeeklySalary
End Sub
```

Currency variables take up 8 bytes each.

Date

The Date data type is relatively complex. VBA works with dates and times as floating-point numbers, with the date displayed to the left of the decimal point and the time to the right. VBA can handle dates from 1 January 100 to 31 December 9999 and times from 0:00:00 to 23:59:59.

> **Fixed-Point Numbers Are More Efficient**
>
> Computer programming typically stores a number in either of two ways: as a floating-point number or as a fixed-point number. A floating-point number is a number in which the quantity is given by one number multiplied by a power of the number base (for example, 10): the decimal point "floats" to different locations. A fixed-point number is one in which the decimal place remains in the same location. Fixed-point numbers should be used whenever practical because the computer can calculate with them more quickly, for the same reason that addition, multiplication, and subtraction are easier to learn in school than long division and fractions.

You can enter date variables as literal date values—such as **6/30/36** or **June 30, 1936**—by placing a # sign before and after the literal date value:

```
#June 30, 1936#
```

When you move the insertion point from the line in the Code window in which you've entered a literal date value between # signs, VBA converts the data to a number and changes the display to the date format set in your computer. For example, if you enter **June 30, 1936**, VBA will probably display it as `6/30/36`. Likewise, you can enter a literal time value (for example, **#10:15PM#**), and VBA converts it to a number and displays it according to the current time format (for example, `10:15:00 PM`).

Date variables take up 8 bytes each.

> **Always Specify the Century When Managing Date Data**
>
> Always specify the century of the dates you use (such as 1909 or 2009), because VBA may supply the wrong century if you don't. Earlier versions of VBA (for example, in Office 2000 and Office 97) used to assign any year from 1 through 29 to the twentieth century and any year from 30 through 00 to the twenty-first century.

Decimal

The Decimal data type stores unsigned integers, scaled by powers of 10. *Unsigned* means that the integers carry no plus or minus designation. Note that you can't declare a Decimal variable directly: you can use the Decimal data type only within a Variant data type (discussed later in this section).

Decimal variables take up 12 bytes each.

Double

The Double data type is for floating-point numbers and can handle negative values from –1.79769313486231570E+308 to –4.94065645841246544E-324 and positive numbers from 4.94065645841246544E-324 to 1.79769313486231570E+308

Some numbers in this range cannot be represented exactly in binary, so VBA rounds them.

Double here stands for double-precision floating point—the way in which the number is handled by the computer. *Single* (discussed later) stands for single-precision floating point.

You can use the # type-declaration character to declare a Double variable implicitly. Double variables take up 8 bytes each.

Integer

The Integer data type is the most efficient way of handling numbers within its range (from 32,768 to 32,767), a range that makes it useful for many procedures. For example, if you wanted to repeat an action 300 times, you could use an Integer variable for the counter, as in the following lines:

```
Dim intMyVar As Integer
For intMyVar = 1 to 300
    'repeat actions
Next intMyVar
```

Integer variables take up 2 bytes each. The Integer is the most commonly used numeric data type for many programming tasks. This is because unless you're working with something like moon rockets or the national debt, most math will fall within the Integer type's range.

Long

The Long data type is for the national debt. A Long can hold integer values larger or smaller than those the Integer data type can handle: long variables can handle numbers from –2,147,483,648 to 2,147,483,647. (For numbers even larger or smaller than these, use the Double data type, but beware of its rounding.)

Long variables use the type-declaration character & for implicit declarations and take up 4 bytes each.

Object

The Object data type is for storing addresses that reference objects (for example, objects in an application's object model), providing an easy way to refer to an object.

Object variables take up 4 bytes each.

SINGLE

The Single data type, like the Double data type, is for working with floating-point numbers. Single can handle negative values from –3.4028235E+38 through –1.401298E-45 and positive values from 1.401298E-45 through 3.4028235E+38

Some numbers in this range cannot be represented exactly in binary, so VBA rounds them.

Use the exclamation point type-declaration character to declare a Single variable implicitly (if you must use implicit declarations). Single variables take up 4 bytes each.

STRING

The String data type is for handling text:

- Variable-length String variables can contain up to about 2 billion characters. They take up 10 bytes plus the storage required for the string.
- Fixed-length String variables can contain from 1 to about 64,000 characters. They take up only the storage required for the string. If the data assigned to the String variable is shorter than the fixed length, VBA pads the data with trailing spaces to make up the full complement of characters. If the data assigned to the String variable is longer than the fixed length, VBA truncates the data after the relevant character. VBA counts the characters from the left end of the string—for example, if you assign the string `Output` to a fixed-length String variable that's four characters long, VBA stores `Outp`. Fixed-length String variables are rarely used in most programming, with the exception of managing certain databases where there's a rule that a string cannot be longer than a specified length.
- Strings can contain letters, numbers (digits), spaces, and punctuation, not to mention special characters like `@` and `*`.
- You can use the `$` type-declaration character to declare a String variable implicitly, but (as usual) you'll do best to declare your String variables explicitly, along with all your other variables.

VARIANT

The Variant data type, as mentioned earlier in this chapter, is the default type. It's assigned by VBA to any variable whose data type isn't specified by you—so a declaration such as `Dim myUntypedVariable` creates a Variant. However, `Dim intVariable As Integer` creates a variable of the Integer data type. (You can also declare a Variant variable explicitly: `Dim myVariant As Variant`, for example.)

Variants can handle most of the different types of data, but there are a couple of characteristics of Variants to keep in mind:

- Variants can't contain fixed-length string data. If you need to use a fixed-length string, you must specify a fixed-length String data type.
- Variant variables can contain four special values: `Empty` (which means the variable hasn't yet been initialized), `Error` (a special value used for tracking errors in a procedure),

`Nothing` (a special value used for disassociating a variable from the object it was associated with), and `Null` (which you use to indicate that the variable deliberately contains no data).

Variant variables take up more memory than other types. Variant variables that contain numbers take up 16 bytes, and Variant variables that contain characters take up 22 bytes plus the storage required for the characters.

Deciding Among Types for Variables

If you found the details of the different types of variables confusing, relax. You'll mostly use strings and integers. Here are some straightforward rules to direct your choices:

- If the variable will contain only the values `True` and `False`, you can declare it as the Boolean data type.
- If the variable will always contain an integer (if it will never contain a fraction), declare it as the Integer data type. (If the number may be too big for the Integer data type, declare it as the Long data type instead, which is like an integer only bigger.)
- If the variable will be used for calculating money, or if you require no-rounding fractions, use the Currency data type.
- If the variable may sometimes contain a fraction, declare it as the Single or Double data type.
- If the variable will always contain a string, declare it as the String data type.

If You're Unsure, Test a Variable's Type Using a Variant

If you aren't sure what type of variable will best contain the information you're planning to use, start by declaring the variable as a Variant. Then step through the procedure in Break mode with the Locals window displayed (View ➤ Locals Window). The Locals window displays local variables, their value, and their type. As you press F8 to step through your procedure, see what Variant subtype VBA assigns to the variable. You'll see the type, such as Variant/Double or Variant/String, in the Type column. Test the procedure a couple more times to make sure this subtype is consistent, and then try declaring the variable as the data type indicated by the subtype. Run the code a few times to make sure the new data type works.

Working with Constants

A constant is a named item that keeps a constant value during execution of a program. VBA provides many built-in constants, but you can also declare your own constants to help you work with information that stays constant through a procedure. Recall that many programmers simply use variables rather than constants, even for values that won't change (such as the number of eggs in a dozen). However, constants are available if you or your superiors find them of value.

Declaring Your Own Constants

To declare your own constants, use the `Const` statement. By declaring a constant, you can simplify your code when you need to reuse a set value a number of times in your procedures.

Syntax

The syntax for the `Const` statement is as follows:

```
[Public/Private] Const constant [As type] = expression
```

Here, `Public` and `Private` are optional keywords used for declaring public or private scope for a constant. You'll learn how they work in a moment. *`constant`* is the name of the constant, which follows the normal rules for naming variables. *`type`* is an optional argument that specifies the data type of the constant. *`expression`* is a literal (a value written into your code), another constant, or a combination of the two.

As with variables, you can declare multiple constants in the same line by separating the statements with a comma:

```
Const conPerformer As String = "Carmen Singer", _
    conTicketPrice As String = "$34.99"
```

Example

Declaring a constant in VBA works in a similar way to declaring a variable explicitly, but you declare the value of the constant when you declare the constant (rather than at a later point of your choosing). You can't change its value afterward.

As an example, take a look at the following statements:

```
Const conVenue As String = "Davies Hall"
Const conDate As Date = #December 31, 2016#
MsgBox "The concert is at " & conVenue & " on " _
& conDate & "."
```

The first line declares the constant `conVenue` as a String data type and assigns it the data `Davies Hall`. The second line declares the constant `conDate` as a Date string type and assigns it the date `December 31, 2016`. (When you finish creating this line of code and move the insertion point to another line, VBA changes the date to the date format set in your computer's clock—`#12/31/2016#`, for example.) The third line displays a message box containing a string concatenated from the three text items in double quotation marks, the `conVenue` string constant, and the `conDate` date constant.

Choosing the Scope or Lifetime for Your Constants

Scope works the same way for constants as it does for variables. The default scope for a constant declared in a procedure is local—that is, its scope is the procedure that declares it. Consequently, its lifetime is the time for which the procedure runs. But you can set a different scope and lifetime for your constants by using the `Public` or `Private` keyword.

- To declare a private constant, place the declaration at the beginning of the module in which you want the constant to be available. A private constant's lifetime isn't limited, but it's available only to procedures in the module in which it's declared:

  ```
  Private Const conPerformer As String = "Carmen Singer"
  ```

- To declare a public constant, place the declaration at the beginning of a module. A public constant's lifetime isn't limited, and it's available to all procedures in all modules in the project in which it's declared:

```
Public Const conTicketPrice As String = "$34.99"
```

Working with Enumerations

In addition to the constants you can create in your code, VBA includes sets of predefined constants. An *enumeration* is a predefined list of unique integers (numbers) that have individual names. It's a set of items, related in some way.

Here's an enumeration, a set of items that you need to paint a room. Note that another way to describe this is that it's a numbered list:

1. Brushes
2. Paint
3. Masking tape
4. Drop cloth
5. Sandpaper

You could now refer to any of these items by either their number in the enumeration or by their name.

An enumeration is typically used in your programming to specify a property of an object. Each integer in the enumeration has a meaning to VBA and a name that allows you to refer to it easily. The names that correspond to the integers in the enumeration are called *enumerated constants.*

For example, when you use the `MsgBox` function to display a message box using VBA, you can pick one of the enumerated constants in the `VbMsgBoxStyle` enumeration to specify the type of message box you want to show. If you require an icon in the message box, you can specify which icon from the list of available built-in icons. For example, one of the icons—a stop sign—is the enumerated constant `vbCritical` (or the integer `16`). The enumerated constant `vbQuestion` (integer `32`) displays a question-mark icon, and the enumerated constant `vbExclamation` (`48`) displays an exclamation-point icon. The enumerated constant `vbInformation` (`64`) refers to an information icon. However, in practice, the integers are rarely used. The enumerated constants (names like `vbQuestion`) are far easier for humans to grasp, read, and remember than the values (the various integers like `16`, `32`, `64`, and so on) to which they are mapped. So, although you *could* use the integers in your code, it's better to stick with the enumerated constants like `vbQuestion`.

VBA includes many built-in enumerations, and the Visual Basic Editor displays the list of available enumerated constants to help you select the appropriate integer value when you're creating code. To see such a list, type this into a procedure:

```
msgbox("inga",
```

As soon as you type the comma, up pops the list of enumerated constants, all the available button styles for a message box, including `vbQuestion`, `vbYesNo`, `vbOKOnly`, and so on. As you might guess, the `vbOKOnly` style displays only a single button, captioned OK. The `vbYesNo` style displays two buttons, one captioned Yes, the other No.

You just click one of these button styles in the list of enumerated constants to enter it into your code. If you don't see the list, choose Tools ➤ Options in the Visual Basic Editor, and then select the Auto List Members check box.

You can also define your own enumerations in custom objects that you create.

The Bottom Line

Understand what variables are and how you use them. Variables are a cornerstone of computer programming; they are extremely useful for the same reason that files are useful in the real world. You give a name to a variable for the same reason that you write a name to identify a file folder. A file can, over time, contain various different papers, just as the value contained in a programming variable can vary. In both cases, the contents vary; the name remains the same. It's good practice to always specifically name a variable before using it in your code. This is called *explicit declaration.*

Master It Explicitly declare a variable named `CustomersAge`.

Create and use variables. When creating (declaring) a new variable, you should avoid using words or commands that are already in use by VBA, such as `Stop` or `End`. There are other restrictions too, such as not using special characters.

Master It The following variable name cannot be used, for two reasons. Fix it so it is a legitimate variable name:

```
Dim 1Turn! as Integer
```

Specify the scope and lifetime of a variable. Variables have a range of influence, depending on how you declare them.

Master It Create a variable named `AnnualSales` that will be available to any procedure within its own module but not to other modules.

Work with constants. Constants, like variables, are named locations in memory that contain a value. Unlike with variables, however, the value in a constant does not change during program execution.

Master It Define a string constant using the `Dim` command. Name your constant `FirstPrez`, and assign it the value `George Washington`.

Work with enumerations. Enumerations provide a handy name for each item in a list, often a list of properties.

Master It In the Project Explorer, click the `ThisDocument` object to select it. Then locate the `JustificationMode` property in the Properties window, and choose one of that property's enumerated constants by clicking the small down arrow that appears and then clicking one of the constants in the drop-down list.

Chapter 7

Using Array Variables

In this chapter, you'll learn how to use arrays—containers that can store multiple values at the same time. An array is a kind of super-variable.

You'll start by examining what arrays are and what you use them for. You'll then examine how to create them, populate them, and erase them. Along the way, you'll look at how to resize an array to make it contain more (or fewer) values, how to specify the scope for an array, and how to determine while your macro executes whether a particular variable name represents an array or a just an ordinary, single-value variable.

IN THIS CHAPTER, YOU WILL LEARN TO DO THE FOLLOWING:

- Understand what arrays are and what you use them for
- Create and use arrays
- Redimension an array
- Erase an array
- Find out whether a variable is an array
- Sort an array
- Search an array

What Is an Array?

An *array* is a variable on steroids—a variable that can contain multiple values (but they must be of the same data type).

You can access the array itself as a whole to efficiently work with all the values it contains at once. Or you can also access any individual value stored within the array by specifying its index number, which indicates its position within the array.

If you're having difficulty visualizing what this means, try picturing an array as a numbered list, similar to an enumeration (as described in Chapter 6, "Working with Variables, Constants, and Enumerations"). Each item in the list is located in its own row and is identified by an index number, so you can access the value of the item by just specifying its index number. It's like houses on a street: They all share the same name, such as Maple Drive, but each has a distinguishing number all its own. You'll see visual examples of arrays later in this chapter.

The previous description is of a simple array—a numbered list like a row of houses on a street. Such an array is said to have only one *dimension*. However, later in this chapter you'll see that you can construct more complicated arrays, which are called *multidimensional*. They're more like a crossword puzzle with both rows *and columns*.

For now, though, let's look at the qualities of the most common and most easily visualized array structure, the *one-dimensional array*.

Variant Arrays Can Store Values of Differing Data Types

An array with the Variant data type can store multiple subtypes of data. That's because a Variant permits any kind of data: strings, integers, and so on. Remember that a Variant is a shape-shifter, unique among data types in that it can contain data of all types.

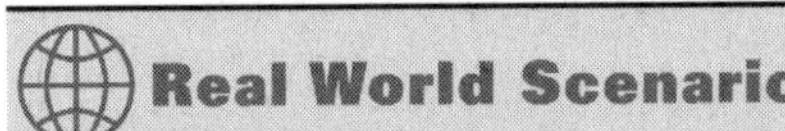

Use Option Base 1 to Simplify Indexes

Although your code will be less portable—and other programmers who use other computer languages might object—if you're writing macros for your own private use, you might want to employ the controversial `Option Base 1` statement.

An array is *delimited* (or bounded) by a lower bound and an upper bound. In other words, the array's index numbers start with 1 (the lower bound) and end with whatever number of items are in the array (the upper bound). An array representing the eggs in an egg carton would have a lower bound of 1 and an upper bound of 12. That's the simple way to construct and visualize an array, but there's a catch: Many computer languages, including VBA, employ by default a lower bound of zero rather than one.

This means that the first item in an array is indexed as zero—it's the zeroth item. This can obviously be confusing, because it means that you're always working with an index number that's one lower than the item's actual position in the array. In such an array, January would be the zeroth month; February would be the first month, with array index number 1; March would be given index 2; and so on. It's as if your shopping list looked like this:

0. Brushes
1. Paint
2. Masking tape
3. Drop cloth
4. Sandpaper

Nobody writes lists with a zeroth item, but this is just one of the kinks in computer programming caused by carelessness when programming languages were first constructed.

`http://www.cs.utexas.edu/users/EWD/transcriptions/EWD08xx/EWD831.html`

However, *unlike* most other computer languages, VBA allows you to normalize the way array indexes work: beginning them with index 1, the way humans count items in sets or lists.

VBA lets you make 1 the default index number of the first item in an array by entering an `Option Base 1` statement at the beginning of a module. Type this option up in the General Declarations section of your Code window, and the index number for each item in the array will then be the same as the item's position in the array, so the array is easier to work with—easier to visualize.

Why does the first item in an array default to zero anyway? Forty years ago, people who wrote the programming languages decided to do this, and it has persisted. The major exception was the BASIC language, VBA's ancestor. It defaulted, sensibly, to 1 as the lower bound of any array. Eventually (with version 6 of Visual Basic), BASIC was modified to make it conform to the other languages and those in charge changed VBA's lower bound to zero. BASIC did, however, preserve the programmer's option to specify the lower bound as 1 with this `Option Base` statement.

Arrays are lists, and we humans don't start lists with zero. We have a first birthday party, not a zeroth one. A winning team comes in first place, not zeroth place. Nonetheless, computer programmers have been wrestling with zero-based array indexing for several decades now—and introducing countless bugs into their code as a result. You're fortunate to be working with VBA, where you have an option to avoid this problem if it bothers you. But note that if you are studying programming or plan to use other languages or program professionally, you will have to accustom yourself to the types of error messages generated by this zero index hitch. Then you can say, "Oh, this is probably an indexing problem," and fiddle with an index number to fix it. Generally, you'll subtract 1 from the index number and that'll do the trick.

Declaring an Array

An array is a kind of variable, so you declare an array by using the familiar keywords: `Dim`, `Private`, `Public`, and `Static`. However, to indicate that it's an array rather than a normal variable, you add a pair of parentheses after the array's name. For example, the following statement declares an array named `curMonthProfit`:

```
Dim varMonthProfit()
```

If you had left off the parentheses, you would have created an ordinary variable capable of holding only a single value:

```
Dim varMonthProfit
```

Because no data type was specified in the declaration (`Dim`) of the preceding array example, this example creates a Variant array. VBA then assigns the appropriate data types (String, Integer, and so on) when you store data in the array.

However, you can specify the data type of an array, just as you would for an ordinary variable. For example, the following statement declares the array named `curMonthProfit` and makes it the Currency data type:

```
Dim curMonthProfit() As Currency
```

You can also specify the number of items in the array by using an *array subscript*. For example, the following statement declares the array named `curMonthProfit`, assigns the Currency data type, and specifies that the array contains 12 items:

```
Dim curMonthProfit(11) As Currency
```

Now you can see one aspect of the zeroth problem. This array holds 12 items, but in its declaration we must specify 11! The array *subscript* in the `Dim curMonthProfit(11) As Currency` statement is `11` rather than `12` because by default an array's index starts at 0 rather than 1. That 0 index number gives this list *an extra element*. The first item is `curMonthProfit(0)`, the second is `curMonthProfit(1)`, and the twelfth is `curMonthProfit(11)`. (Remember that you can avoid this counterintuitive approach by using the `Option Base 1` statement.)

Figure 7.1 shows a simple representation of the single-dimensional array created by the `Dim curMonthProfit(11) As Currency` statement.

FIGURE 7.1
The single-dimensional array created by the statement `Dim curMonthProfit(11) As Currency` can be thought of as looking like this.

Element #	Name	Contents
0	curMonthProfit(0)	—
1	curMonthProfit(1)	—
2	curMonthProfit(2)	—
3	curMonthProfit(3)	—
4	curMonthProfit(4)	—
5	curMonthProfit(5)	—
6	curMonthProfit(6)	—
7	curMonthProfit(7)	—
8	curMonthProfit(8)	—
9	curMonthProfit(9)	—
10	curMonthProfit(10)	—
11	curMonthProfit(11)	—

To make numbering start at 1, add an `Option Base` statement to the declarations area at the beginning of the module in which you declare the array. Here is an example:

```
Option Base 1   'at the beginning of the code sheet

Dim curMonthProfit(12) As Currency
```

Figure 7.2 shows a simple representation of how this array would look.

VARIANTS CAN BE INEFFICIENT UNDER EXTREME CIRCUMSTANCES

Recall that omitting the data type when declaring an array (thereby making VBA automatically use the Variant data type) causes slightly increased memory usage, which could (under extreme circumstances) slow the performance of the computer. Because an array needs storage for each item it contains, a very large array can consume a significant amount of memory. This is particularly true with multidimensional arrays discussed later in this chapter.

You can also specify both the lower and upper bounds of an array explicitly. This example code states that the lower bound is to be 1 and the upper bound is 12:

```
Option Base 1   'at the beginning of the code sheet

Dim curMonthProfit(1 To 12) As Currency
```

Because learning to use arrays is much easier for beginners if we start with an index of 1, the examples in the rest of this chapter use `Option Base 1` statements.

FIGURE 7.2 The single-dimensional array created by the statement `Dim curMonthProfit(12) As Currency` with the `Option Base 1` statement. Compare this to Figure 7.1.

Element #	Name	Contents
1	curMonthProfit(1)	—
2	curMonthProfit(2)	—
3	curMonthProfit(3)	—
4	curMonthProfit(4)	—
5	curMonthProfit(5)	—
6	curMonthProfit(6)	—
7	curMonthProfit(7)	—
8	curMonthProfit(8)	—
9	curMonthProfit(9)	—
10	curMonthProfit(10)	—
11	curMonthProfit(11)	—
12	curMonthProfit(12)	—

Storing Values in an Array

To assign a value to an item in an array, you use each item's index number to identify it. For example, the following statements assign the values `London`, `Hong Kong`, and `Taipei` to the first three items in an array named `strLocations`:

```
Option Base 1

Dim strLocations(6) As String

strLocations(1) = "London"
strLocations(2) = "Hong Kong"
strLocations(3) = "Taipei"
```

Figure 7.3 shows how this array can be envisioned.

FIGURE 7.3
A simple String array with three values assigned

Element #	Name	Contents
1	`strLocations(1)`	London
2	`strLocations(2)`	Hong Kong
3	`strLocations(3)`	Taipei
4	`strLocations(4)`	—
5	`strLocations(5)`	—
6	`strLocations(6)`	—

Multidimensional Arrays

The `curMonthProfit` example in the previous section is a one-dimensional array, which is the easiest kind of array to use. VBA supports arrays with up to 60 dimensions—enough to tax the visualization skills of anyone without a PhD in multidimensional modeling. You probably won't want to get this complicated with arrays—two, three, or four dimensions are enough for most purposes. In fact, one dimension is enough for many purposes.

To declare a multidimensional array, you separate the dimensions with commas. For example, the following statements declare a two-dimensional array named `MyArray` with three items in each dimension:

```
Option Base 1
Dim MyArray(3, 3)
```

Figure 7.4 shows how you might represent the resulting array. Note that inside each item in this figure's table you can see the pair of index numbers you would use to access it, such as item `1,2` or item `3,2`.

FIGURE 7.4
You can think of a two-dimensional array as consisting of rows and columns.

Column 1	Column 2	Column 3
1,1	2,1	3,1
1,2	2,2	3,2
1,3	2,3	3,3

Multidimensional arrays sound forbidding, but a two-dimensional array is quite straightforward if you think of it basically as a *table* that consists of rows and columns.

In this example, the first series of three elements appears down the first column of the table, the second series of three elements appears down the second column, and so on.

The information in any series doesn't need to be related to information in the other series, although it does need to be of the same data type. For example, you could assign three folder names to the first dimension of a String variable array (they would be in column 1), the names of your three cats to the second dimension (more strings), a list of the names of the Three Stooges to the third dimension (the third column in the table), and so on. You could then access the information in the array by specifying the position of the item you want to access—for instance, the second item in the first column of the table (item 1,2). You'll learn how to do this in just a minute.

Similarly, you could picture a three-dimensional array as being something like a workbook of spreadsheets—rows and columns, with further rows and columns in the third dimension (down, or away from you).

But that's about the limit of easily pictured arrays—four-dimensional and larger arrays start to tax the imagination. A row of honeycombs, a set of apartment buildings? It gets difficult.

Declaring a Dynamic Array

You can declare both *fixed-size* arrays and *dynamic* arrays. The examples you've seen so far were fixed-size arrays. For instance, the `curMonthProfit` array was specified as having 12 items.

Dynamic arrays are useful when the number of values you need to store will vary. For example, for a procedure that arranges windows side by side, you might create an array to contain the name of each open window. However, while writing the code, you can't know how many windows might want to open while the macro runs. You'll probably want to use a dynamic array to contain the information. That way the array can be sized to fit the situation.

To declare a dynamic array, you use a declaration statement *without* specifying the number of items (you include the parentheses but leave them empty). For example, the following statement declares a dynamic array named `arrTestArray` and causes VBA to assign it the Variant data type (because no data type is specified):

```
Dim arrTestArray()
```

Redimensioning an Array

You can change the size of, or *redimension*, a dynamic array by using the `ReDim` statement. For example, to redimension the dynamic array `arrTestArray` declared in the previous example and assign it a size of five items, you could use the following statement:

```
ReDim arrTestArray(5)
```

When you use `ReDim` to redimension an array like this, you lose the values currently in the array. If so far you've only declared the array as a dynamic array and it contains nothing, losing its contents won't bother you. There are no contents.

But in other situations an array might be full of data, so you'll want to increase the size of an array while keeping its current contents. To preserve the existing values in an array when you raise its upper bound, use a `ReDim Preserve` statement instead of a straight `ReDim` statement:

```
ReDim Preserve arrTestArray(5)
```

If you use `ReDim Preserve` to reduce the size of the array (to lower its upper bound), you, of course, lose the information stored in any items not included in the redimensioned array. For example, if you have a five-subscript (five-item) array with information in each item and you redimension it using `ReDim Preserve` so that it has only three subscripts, you lose the information in the fourth and fifth subscripts.

Note that `ReDim Preserve` works only for the last dimension of a multidimensional array. You can't preserve the data in other dimensions in a multidimensional array.

Returning Information from an Array

To get information from an array, you use an index number to specify the position of the information you want to return. For example, the following statement returns the fourth item in the array named `arrMyArray` and displays it in a message box:

```
Option Base 1
MsgBox arrMyArray(4)
```

The following statement returns the fifth item in the second dimension of a two-dimensional array named `arrMy2DArray` and displays it in a message box:

```
Option Base 1
MsgBox arrMy2DArray(2,5)
```

To return multiple items from an array, specify each item individually.

Erasing an Array

To erase the contents of an array, use the `Erase` command with the name of the array. This command reinitializes the items in a fixed-size array and frees the memory taken by items in dynamic arrays (completely erasing the array). For example, the following statement erases the contents of the fixed-size array named `arrMyArray`:

```
Erase arrMyArray
```

Determining Whether a Variable Is an Array

Because an array is a type of variable, you may occasionally need to check whether a particular variable name denotes an array or an ordinary variable (sometimes called a *Scalar variable*). To find out whether a variable is an array, use the `IsArray` function with the variable's name. For example, the following statements check the variable `MyVariable` and display the results in a message box:

```
If IsArray(MyVariable) = True Then
    Msg = "MyVariable" & " is an array."
Else
    Msg = "MyVariable" & " is not an array."
End If
MsgBox Msg, vbOKOnly + vbInformation, "Array Check"
```

Finding the Bounds of an Array

To find the bounds of an array, you use the `LBound` function and the `UBound` function. `LBound` returns the *lower bound*, the index number of the first item; `UBound` returns the upper bound, the index number of the last item.

The LBound function and the UBound function have the following syntax:

```
LBound(array [, dimension])
UBound(array [, dimension])
```

Here, *array* is a required argument specifying the name of the array, and *dimension* is an optional Variant specifying the dimension that has the bound you want to return—1 for the first dimension, 2 for the second, and so on. (If you omit the *dimension* argument, VBA assumes you mean the first dimension.)

For example, the following statement returns the upper bound of the second dimension in the array named arrMyArray and displays it in a message box:

```
MsgBox UBound(arrMyArray, 2)
```

Sorting an Array

You'll sometimes need to sort an array, especially when you load information into the array from an external source rather than assigning values one by one in your code. Unfortunately, VBA has no built-in command to sort an array.

Sorting is easy to understand conceptually: You simply rearrange things into the desired order. For example, you could sort the strings in one array into alphabetical order or reverse alphabetical order, or the numbers in another array into ascending order or descending order. However, writing a program that sorts is much more difficult, so don't write it. Just copy it from examples on the Internet or from the following example.

This section shows you a simple form of sorting—the *bubble sort*, so called because the items being sorted to the earlier positions in the array gradually bubble up to the top. The bubble sort consists of two *loops* that compare two items in the array; if the second item belongs further up the list than the first item, the sort reverses their positions, and the comparisons continue until the whole list is sorted into order. The bubble sort is a relatively inefficient method of sorting items, but it's easy to grasp, and processor cycles are comparatively cheap these days. The bubble sort itself hasn't become any more efficient over the years, but processor speeds have sure ramped up.

This example also introduces you to a major element of programming: the *loop*. Loops are an important tool found in many procedures and projects. In effect, a loop repeats some action until a condition is met. It's like saying, "Keep rearranging these attendance cards until the stack is alphabetized." Chapter 12, "Using Loops to Repeat Actions," shows you how to work with loops.

Listing 7.1 contains the code for the bubble sort.

LISTING 7.1: A bubble sort

```
Option Explicit
Option Base 1

```

```
Sub Sort_an_Array()

    'declare the array and other variables
    Dim strArray(12) As String
    Dim strTemp As String
    Dim strMsg As String
    Dim X As Integer, Y As Integer, i As Integer

    'assign strings to the array
    strArray(1) = "nihilism"
    strArray(2) = "defeatism"
    strArray(3) = "hope"
    strArray(4) = "gloom"
    strArray(5) = "euphoria"
    strArray(6) = "despondency"
    strArray(7) = "optimism"
    strArray(8) = "pessimism"
    strArray(9) = "misery"
    strArray(10) = "happiness"
    strArray(11) = "bliss"
    strArray(12) = "mania"

    strMsg = "Current items in array:" & vbCr & vbCr
    For i = 1 To UBound(strArray)
        strMsg = strMsg & i & ":" & vbTab & strArray(i) & vbCr
    Next i
    MsgBox strMsg, vbOKOnly + vbInformation, "Array Sorting: 1"

    For X = LBound(strArray) To (UBound(strArray) - 1)
        For Y = (X + 1) To UBound(strArray)
            If strArray(X) > strArray(Y) Then
                strTemp = strArray(X)
                strArray(X) = strArray(Y)
                strArray(Y) = strTemp
                strTemp = ""
            End If
        Next Y
    Next X

    strMsg = "Items in sorted array:" & vbCr & vbCr
    For i = 1 To UBound(strArray)
        strMsg = strMsg & i & ":" & vbTab & strArray(i) & vbCr
    Next i
    MsgBox strMsg, vbOKOnly + vbInformation, "Array Sorting: 2"

End Sub
```

Go ahead and read through this code and the explanation of it that follows to see how much of it you can understand. At this point, you might not grasp much at all. Don't worry, though; things will become clearer as you progress through this book. What's more, you never need to write a bubble sort from scratch anyway—just copy this one, modifying it a little to sort whatever array you're dealing with. And remember, you can copy all the code in this book from this book's website at `www.sybex.com/go/masteringvba2016`.

How to Locate Line Numbers in the Editor

In this book, code examples more than a few lines long are given line numbers so the lines can be referenced easily in the explanatory text. If you're following along with a code description in this book, you'll sometimes want to know what line the blinking cursor is on in the Editor code. Just look at the field at the far right of the Editor's Standard toolbar, right next to the blue Help question mark. This field always displays the current line number and character number, as you can see in this screenshot.

Ln 15, Col 14

Here's what happens in Listing 7.1:

- Line 1 contains an `Option Explicit` statement to force explicit declarations of variables, and line 2 contains an `Option Base 1` statement to make array index numbers start at 1 rather than `0`. These two statements appear in the General Declarations zone of the code sheet, above any other procedure in the Code window. Line 3 is a spacer—a blank line inserted just to make the code easier to read. You can remove it if you like, or add more spacers—it's your call. VBA ignores blank lines.
- Line 4 begins the `Sort_an_Array` procedure. Line 5 is a spacer.
- Line 6 is a comment line prefacing the declaration of the array and the variables. Line 7 declares the String array `strArray` with 12 subscripts (array items). Line 8 declares the String variable `strTemp`. Line 9 declares the String variable `strMsg`. Line 10 declares the Integer variables `X`, `Y`, and `i`. Line 11 is a spacer.
- Line 12 is a comment line explaining that the next 12 statements (lines 13 through 24) assign strings to the array. The strings used are words describing various moods. Line 25 is a spacer.
- Lines 26 through 30 build a string out of the strings assigned to the array and then display it in a message box. This section of code is included to help users easily see what's going on if they run the procedure rather than stepping through it. Line 26 assigns introductory text and two carriage returns (two `vbCr` characters) to the String variable `strMsg`. Line 27 starts a `For… Next` loop that runs from `i = 1` to `i = UBound(strArray)`—in other words, once for each item in the array. (The loop could also have run to `i = 12` because the upper bound of the array is set, but using the upper bound is more flexible than hard-coding values.) Line

28 adds to `strMsg` the value of the counter variable `i`, a colon, a tab (`vbTab`), the contents of the array item currently referenced (`strArray(i)`), and a carriage return (`vbCr`). Line 29 concludes the loop, and line 30 displays a message box containing `strMsg`, as shown in Figure 7.5. Line 31 is a spacer.

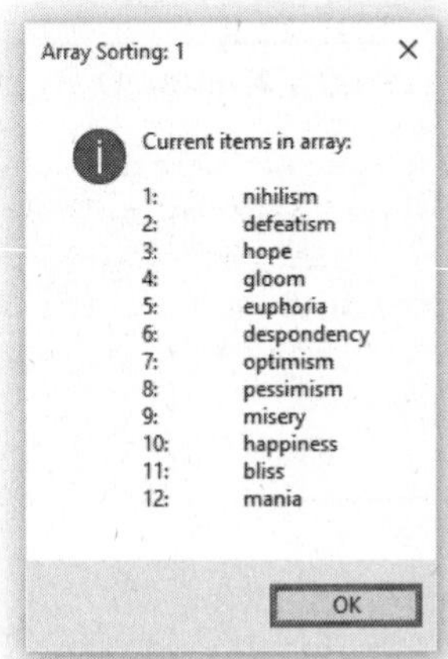

FIGURE 7.5
The `Sort_an_Array` procedure displays a message box of the unsorted terms so that the user can see how things start.

- The sorting part of the procedure takes place in lines 32 through 41. Here are the details:
  - Line 32 begins a set of nested loops: one inside another. There's an outer loop and an inner loop. The outer `For... Next` loop ends in line 41 with the `Next X` statement. This loop runs from `X = LBound(strArray)` (in other words, X = 1) to `X = (UBound(strArray) - 1)` (in other words, X = 11, the upper bound of the array, minus 1).
  - Line 33 begins the inner (nested) `For... Next` loop, which runs from `Y = (X + 1)` to `Y = UBound(strArray)`. Line 40 ends this loop.
  - Line 34 compares `strArray(X)` to `strArray(Y)`. If `strArray(X)` is greater than `strArray(Y)`—in other words, if `strArray(X)` should appear after `strArray(Y)` in the alphabetized array—line 35 assigns `strArray(X)` to `strTemp`, line 36 assigns `strArray(Y)` to `strArray(X)`, and line 37 assigns `strTemp` to `strArray(Y)`, thereby switching the values. Line 38 restores `strTemp` to an empty string. Line 39 ends the `If` statement. Line 40 ends the inner loop, line 41 ends the outer loop, and line 42 is a spacer.
- Lines 43 through 47 essentially repeat lines 26 through 30, displaying a message box (shown in Figure 7.6) of the now-sorted array so that the user can see that the sort has worked.
- Line 48 is a spacer, and line 49 ends the procedure.

FIGURE 7.6
When the `Sort_an_Array` procedure has finished sorting, it displays the sorted list in a second message box.

Searching an Array

Another task you sometimes need to perform with an array is searching to find a particular value in it. This is similar to rifling through a box of recipe cards until you find *Ralph's Jailhouse Chili.*

The following sections show you two methods of sorting—a linear search, which you can perform on either a sorted array or an unsorted array, and a binary search, which is faster but works only on a sorted array. However, speed, particularly when dealing with the usually small tasks performed by macros, is rarely an issue.

Performing a Linear Search Through an Array

A *linear* search is a simple kind of search: You start at the beginning of the array and check each item until you find your target, or until you reach the end of the array and must report *not found.*

Before executing this code, display the Immediate window in the Editor by pressing Ctrl+G or choosing View ➤ Immediate Window. This procedure prints information in the Immediate window so that you can see what's going on—and determine whether the code is running as intended. Using the Immediate window like this to check output is often preferable to displaying message boxes as we did in the previous section. With the Immediate window, you don't have to click the message boxes closed, and the window can also be scrolled, displaying as much information as you want.

Listing 7.2 contains the code for a simple linear search through a one-dimensional array.

LISTING 7.2: A simple linear search

```
Option Explicit
Option Base 1

```

```
 4.  Sub Linear_Search_of_Array()
 5.
 6.      'declare the array and the variables
 7.      Dim intArray(10) As Integer
 8.      Dim i As Integer
 9.      Dim varUserNumber As Variant
10.      Dim strMsg As String
11.
12.      'add random numbers between 0 and 10 to the array
13.      'and print them to the Immediate window for reference
14.      For i = 1 To 10
15.          intArray(i) = Int(Rnd * 10)
16.          Debug.Print intArray(i)
17.      Next i
18.
19.  Loopback:
20.      varUserNumber = InputBox _
             ("Enter a number between 1 and 10 to search for:", _
             "Linear Search Demonstrator")
21.      If varUserNumber = "" Then End
22.      If Not IsNumeric(varUserNumber) Then GoTo Loopback
23.      If varUserNumber < 1 Or varUserNumber > 10 Then GoTo Loopback
24.
25.      strMsg = "Your value, " & varUserNumber & _
             ", was not found in the array."
26.
27.      For i = 1 To UBound(intArray)
28.          If intArray(i) = varUserNumber Then
29.              strMsg = "Your value, " & varUserNumber & _
                     ", was found at position " & i & " in the array."
30.              Exit For
31.          End If
32.      Next i
33.
34.      MsgBox strMsg, vbOKOnly + vbInformation, "Linear Search Result"
35.
36.  End Sub
```

Here's what happens in Listing 7.2:

- As in the previous listing, line 1 contains an `Option Explicit` statement to force explicit declarations of variables, and line 2 contains an `Option Base 1` statement to make the index numbers of arrays start at 1 rather than `0`. These two statements appear in the declarations part of the code sheet, before any other procedure. Line 3 is a spacer.
- Line 4 begins the `Linear_Search_of_Array` procedure. Line 5 is a spacer.

- Line 6 is a comment line prefacing the declaration of the array and the other variables that the code uses. Line 7 declares the Integer array `intArray` with 10 subscripts. Line 8 declares the Integer variable `I` (traditionally programmers use the name `I` for a loop's counter variable—*I* for *increment* or *iteration*).
- Line 9 declares the Variant variable `varUserNumber`, which the code uses to store the user's input from an input box. (More on this control in a moment.) Line 10 declares the String variable `strMsg`. Line 11 is a spacer.
- The procedure declares the variable `varUserNumber` as a Variant rather than an Integer. This way, Visual Basic doesn't automatically halt execution and display an error message if the user enters something other than an integer (for example, text) in the input box.
- Lines 12 and 13 contain an extended comment line on the code in lines 14 through 17. (These two lines could be combined into one logical line by adding a continuation character at the end of the first line and omitting the apostrophe at the beginning of the second line, but the code is easier to read when the second line begins with the comment character as well.)
- Line 14 begins a `For... Next` loop that repeats 10 times: from `i = 1` to `1 = 10`. Line 15 assigns to the current item in the `intArray` array the integer result of a random number multiplied by 10: `intArray(i) = Int(Rnd * 10)`. (The `Rnd` function generates a random number between 0 and 1 with a good number of decimal places. Therefore, the procedure multiplies that random number by 10 to get a number between 0 and 10 and then takes the integer portion of the number. In other words, the `Int` command strips off any fractional result, any values to the right of the decimal point.) Line 16 then uses the `Print` method of the `Debug` object to print the current item in `intArray` to the Immediate window. This is an easy way for you, the programmer, to examine the values generated randomly for the array. The user never sees the Immediate window. Line 17 ends the loop with the `Next i` statement. Line 18 is a spacer.
- Line 19 contains a *label*, named `Loopback`, used to return execution to this point in the code if the user's input does not meet required conditions (If it's not between 1 and 10).
- Line 20 assigns to the Variant variable `varUserNumber` the result of the user's input. An input box (shown in Figure 7.7) prompts the user to enter a number between 1 and 10.
- Line 21 then compares the contents of `varUserNumber` to an empty string—the result you get if the user clicks the Cancel button in the input box or clicks the OK button without entering anything in the text box. If `varUserNumber` is an empty string, the `End` statement ends execution of the procedure.
- Line 22 uses the `IsNumeric` function to see whether the contents of `varUserNumber` are numeric. If they're not, the `GoTo Loopback` statement returns execution to the `Loopback` label, after which the input box is displayed again for the user to try their luck once more. Line 23 checks to see if `varUserNumber` is less than 1 or greater than 10. If either is the case, another `GoTo Loopback` statement returns execution to the `Loopback` label, and the input makes another appearance. Line 24 is a spacer.

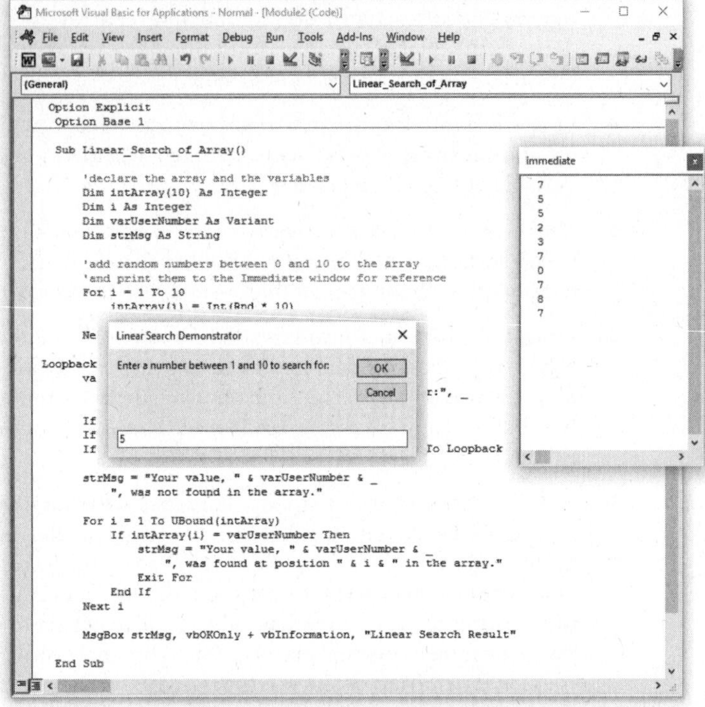

FIGURE 7.7 The `Linear_Search_of_Array` procedure displays an input box prompting the user to enter a number between 1 and 10. The array itself is printed in the Immediate window.

VBA IS FLEXIBLE

Note the flexibility of VBA here: The code solicits user input and makes sure that it's a number between 1 and 10 (inclusive). Although that number is still stored in a Variant rather than explicitly converted to an Integer, VBA still performs the comparison needed.

- Line 25 assigns to the String variable `strMsg` a preliminary message stating that the value (which it specifies) was not found in the array. (If the code finds the value in the array, it changes the message before displaying it.) Line 26 is a spacer.
- Lines 27 through 32 contain the searching part of the procedure. Line 27 begins a `For...` `Next` loop that runs from `i = 1` to `i = UBound(intArray)`—once for each subscript in the array. Line 28 compares `intArray(i)` to `varUserNumber`; if there's a match, line 28 assigns to `strMsg` a string telling the user at which position in the array the value was found, and line 29 uses an `Exit For` statement to exit the `For... Next` loop. (If line 28 does not match, the `Next i` statement in line 32 causes the code to loop.)
- Line 33 is a spacer. Line 34 displays a message box containing `strMsg` to convey to the user the result of the linear search operation. Figure 7.8 shows the result of a successful search. Line 35 is a spacer, and line 36 ends the procedure.

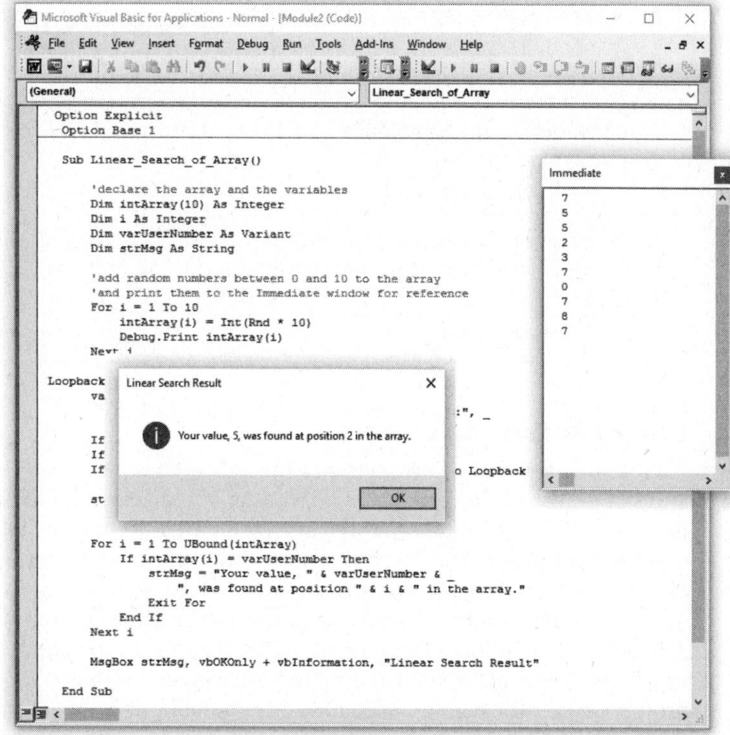

FIGURE 7.8 Line 34 of Listing 7.2 displays a message box showing the user the result of the linear search operation.

HOW TO GENERATE RANDOM NUMBERS

Sharp-eyed readers will notice that a 0 sometimes appears in the array in the previous example—and what's more, 10 never appears. In other words, the code `Int(Rnd * 10)` randomly produces numbers ranging from 0 to 9. (This is a byproduct of the rounding performed by the `Int` command.) Here's how to use the `Rnd` command to produce the exact range of numbers you want.

When asking VBA for a random number, you specify the upper limit of the range of numbers you want and then multiply that number by `Rnd`. For example, if you want to simulate rolling dice, you need random numbers from 1 to 6, so 6 is the upper limit. You multiply the result that `Rnd` gives you by 6. *Then you must add 1* in your code to make the result range from 1 to this upper limit. (Otherwise, the result is a range between 0 and the upper limit, minus 1, as in the code in Listing 7.2, which provided numbers from 0 to 9 rather than 1 to 10.)

The `Int` function must be used because `Rnd` provides only fractions. Here are some typical results when the `Rnd` function executes:

- `0.4542078`
- `0.3570231`
- `0.1499811`

- `0.7043958`
- `0.928786`

Because these are fractions, you need to multiply to get whole numbers. However, the `Int` command rounds off any fractional part of the final result, so here is how you would get a random number from 1 to 50:

```
X = Int(Rnd * 50 + 1)
```

To get a range from 0 to an upper limit, specify as the upper limit a number 1 higher than you actually want. Don't add 1 inside the parentheses. This example provides a random number from 0 to 50:

```
X = Int(Rnd * 51)
```

Binary Searching an Array

As you saw in the previous section, a linear search is easy to perform, but it's pretty simple and slow—it starts looking at the beginning of the array and then checks each element, each item, in turn. This approach works fine for small searches, such as the 10-subscript array you searched in the last example, but you wouldn't want to try it on anything the size of a list of all the people in the USA. For serious, heavy-duty searching, you need a smarter approach.

For conventional purposes, a *binary search* is a good way to approach searching a sorted array. A binary search imitates the approach you probably use when searching for something like a lost TV remote control. You expect it to be in a given location—somewhere in the living room, probably near the couch—so you focus your attention on the relevant area and search there. (With a *linear search*, by contrast, you search everywhere in the house, from start to finish, without any attempt to intelligently narrow the search area.)

The binary search technique (technically called an *algorithm*) determines the most likely target area by dividing the sorted array in half, establishing which half will contain the search item, and then repeating the divide-and-interrogate procedure until it either finds the search item or reaches the last subdivisible unit of the array without finding it. Remember, this array is presorted, so if the algorithm is looking for the number 12 in a list from 1 to 20, the target must be in the second half of the list.

Here's another example. Say that a binary search is looking for the value 789,789 in a million-subscript array that contains the numbers 1 through 1,000,000 in ascending order. It divides the array into two halves, each of which contains a half million subscripts. It establishes whether the search item is in the first half or the second half and then narrows the search to the appropriate half and divides it into new halves. It establishes whether the search item is in the first of these halves or the second and then focuses on that half, dividing *it* into halves—and so on until it finds the term or has gotten down to a single subscript.

This is a simple example, but a million is still a hefty number. Listing 7.3 makes things even simpler by using an array of a thousand subscripts that contains the numbers 1 through 1000 in order. The first subscript contains the number 1, the second subscript contains the number 2, and so on up to 1000. The example is unrealistic, but it makes it easy to see what's happening in the code.

LISTING 7.3: Searching through a large array

```
Option Explicit
Option Base 1

Sub Binary_Search_of_Array()

    'declare the array and the variables
    Dim intThousand(1000) As Integer
    Dim i As Integer
    Dim intTop As Integer
    Dim intMiddle As Integer
    Dim intBottom As Integer
    Dim varUserNumber As Variant
    Dim strMsg As String

    'populate the array with numbers 1 to 1000, in order
    For i = 1 To 1000
        intThousand(i) = i
    Next i

    'prompt the user for the search item
Loopback:
    varUserNumber = InputBox _
        ("Enter a number between 1 and 1000 to search for:", _
        "Binary Search Demonstrator")
    If varUserNumber = "" Then End
    If Not IsNumeric(varUserNumber) Then GoTo Loopback

    'search for the search item
    intTop = UBound(intThousand)
    intBottom = LBound(intThousand)

    Do
        intMiddle = (intTop + intBottom) / 2
        If varUserNumber > intThousand(intMiddle) Then
            intBottom = intMiddle + 1
        Else
            intTop = intMiddle - 1
        End If
    Loop Until (varUserNumber = intThousand(intMiddle)) _
        Or (intBottom > intTop)

    'establish whether the search discovered the search item _
     or not and add the appropriate information to strMsg
    If varUserNumber = intThousand(intMiddle) Then
```

```
41.         strMsg = "The search found the search item, " _
                & varUserNumber & ", at position " & intMiddle _
                & " in the array."
42.     Else
43.         strMsg = "The search did not find the search item, " _
                & varUserNumber & "."
44.     End If
45.
46.     MsgBox strMsg, vbOKOnly & vbInformation, "Binary Search Result"
47.
48. End Sub
```

Here's what happens in Listing 7.3:

- Line 1 contains an `Option Explicit` statement to force explicit declarations of variables, and line 2 contains an `Option Base 1` statement to make the numbering of arrays start at 1 rather than `0`. These two statements appear in the declarations part of the code sheet, before any procedure.
- Line 3 is a spacer. Line 4 declares the `Binary_Search_of_Array` procedure, and line 5 is another spacer.
- Line 6 is a comment line prefacing the declaration of the array (the thousand-subscript Integer array `intThousand`, declared in line 7) and the other variables that the procedure uses: the Integer variables `i` (line 8), `intTop` (line 9), `intMiddle` (line 10), and `intBottom` (line 11); the Variant variable `varUserNumber` (line 12); and the String variable `strMsg` (line 13). Line 14 is yet another spacer.
- Line 15 is a comment line announcing that lines 16 through 18 populate the array with the numbers 1 to 1000 in order. To do so, these lines use a `For...Next` loop that runs from `i = 1` to `i = 1000`, assigning the current value of `i` to the subscript in the array referenced by `i`—in other words, assigning to each subscript the number that corresponds to its position in the array. Line 19 is a spacer.
- Line 20 is a comment line introducing the section of code (lines 21 through 24) that uses an input box (shown in Figure 7.9) to prompt users to enter a number to search for, and checks that they do so. As in the previous listing, this section of code checks to make sure users don't enter an empty string in the input box (line 23) and terminates execution of the procedure if they do. It also uses a label named `Loopback` (in line 21), to which the code returns if what a user entered in the input box (in line 22) turns out not to be numeric when line 24 checks. Because this time you know which numbers the array will contain, you don't need to check to make sure that users enter a suitable value. If they want to enter a value that doesn't appear in the array, so be it.
- Line 25 is a spacer, and line 26 is a comment that introduces the section of code that searches for the search item the user entered. Line 27 assigns to the `intTop` variable the upper bound of the array, and line 28 assigns to `intBottom` the lower bound. Line 29 is a spacer.

FIGURE 7.9
The `Binary_Search_of_Array` procedure prompts the user to enter a number between 1 and 1000.

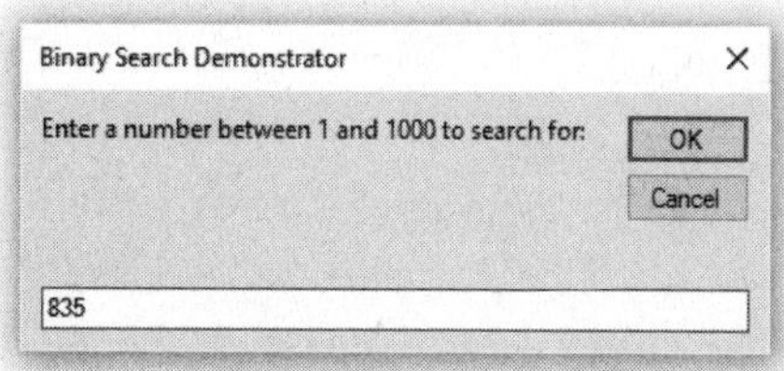

- Lines 30 through 37 contain a `Do… Loop Until` loop that performs the bulk of the binary searching. Here are the details:
    - Line 30 starts the `Do… Loop Until` loop with the `Do` keyword, and line 37 ends it with the `Loop Until` keywords and the condition `((varUserNumber = intThousand(intMiddle)) Or (intBottom > intTop))`. You'll look at loops in detail in Chapter 12; for now, all you need to know is that a `Do… Loop Until` runs once and then evaluates the condition in the `Loop Until` statement to determine whether it should end or run again. The condition here specifies that the loop continue until either the value of the subscript in the array identified by `intMiddle` —`intThousand(intMiddle)`—matches the value in `varUserNumber` or the value of `intBottom` is greater than the value of `intTop` (`intBottom > intTop`).
    - Line 31 sets the value of the Integer variable `intMiddle` to the sum of `intTop` and `intBottom` divided by 2: `(intTop + IntBottom) / 2`. Doing so gives the midpoint for dividing the array. For example, in the thousand-subscript array, `intTop` has a value of `1000` on the first iteration of the loop, and `intBottom` has a value of `0`, so `intMiddle` receives the value `500` (`1000` divided by 2).
    - Line 32 tests whether `varUserNumber` is greater than the value stored in the subscript identified by `intMiddle`—`intThousand(intMiddle)`, the midpoint of the current section of the array. If it is, the search needs to work on the top half of the array, so line 33 resets `intBottom` to `intMiddle + 1`. If it's not, the `Else` statement in line 34 kicks in, and line 35 resets `intTop` to `intMiddle – 1` so that the search works on the lower half of the array.
    - Line 36 ends the `If` statement, and line 37 tests the condition and continues or terminates the loop, as appropriate.
- Line 38 is a spacer. Line 39 contains a two-line comment introducing the code in lines 40 through 44, which establish whether the search found the search item and assign suitable information to the `strMsg` String variable. Line 40 compares `varUserNumber` to `intThousand(intMiddle)`; if it matches, line 41 assigns to `strMsg` a string telling the user where the search item was found in the array. If it doesn't match, line 43 assigns a string telling the user that the search did not find the search item. Line 45 is a spacer, and line 46 displays a message box telling the user the result of the search. Figure 7.10 shows examples—one successful, one otherwise—of the message box.
- Line 47 is another spacer, and line 48 ends the procedure.

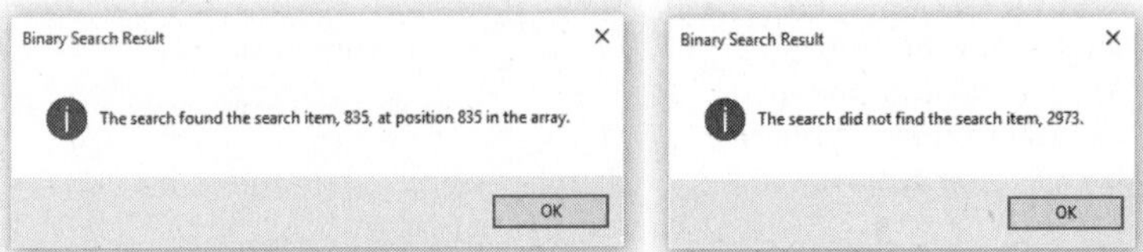

FIGURE 7.10 The `Binary_Search_of_Array` procedure tells the user whether the search was successful (left) or not.

The most complex part of the procedure is what happens in the loop. Download the code from the book's website at `www.sybex.com/go/masteringvba2016`.

Copy the code, and paste it into the Visual Basic Editor (this code will work in any VBA-enabled application). Then open up the module and follow these steps:

1. Display the Locals window (View ➢ Locals Window) so that you can track the values of the variables `intTop`, `intMiddle`, and `intBottom`. Figure 7.11 shows the Locals window while the procedure is running.

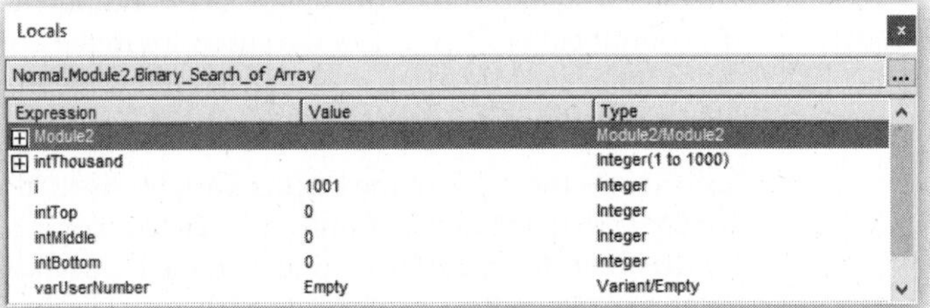

FIGURE 7.11 Use the Locals window to track the values of the `intTop`, `intMiddle`, and `intBottom` variables as the procedure runs.

2. Set a breakpoint in the procedure on line 22 by clicking in the margin indicator bar next to the statement that begins `varUserNumber = InputBox`. (Because the statement is broken onto three lines, the Visual Basic Editor displays three red dots rather than one in the margin indicator bar, to indicate the breakpoint.)

3. Press the F5 key (or choose Run ➢ Run Sub/UserForm) to run the code up to the breakpoint. VBA creates and populates the array and then stops at line 22.

4. Press the F8 key to step through the next statements. The first press displays the input box. Enter the value 67 for this example and click the OK button.

5. As the code enters the `Do` loop and cycles through it, watch the values of the variables `intTop`, `intMiddle`, and `intBottom` in the Locals window. You'll see them change, as shown in the following list:

ITERATION	intTop	intMiddle	intBottom
0	1000	—	1
1	499	500	1
2	249	250	1

ITERATION	intTop	intMiddle	intBottom
3	124	125	1
4	124	62	63
5	93	94	63
6	77	78	63
7	69	70	63
8	69	66	67
9	69	68	67
10	67	67	67

At the end of the tenth iteration of the loop, `intThousand(intMiddle)` is equal to `varUserNumber`, so the loop ends. As you can see, breakpoints, single-stepping, and the Locals window are excellent debugging tools. Chapter 17, "Debugging Your Code and Handling Errors," further explores these and other debugging techniques.

The Bottom Line

Understand what arrays are and what you use them for. Arrays play an important role in computer programming. In some ways, they resemble a mini-database, and organized data is central to computing. Computers are sometimes called data processors for good reason, and arrays make it easier for you to manipulate variable data.

Master It. What is the difference between an array and an ordinary variable?

Create and use arrays. When you create a new array, you *declare* it and, optionally, specify the number of values it will contain.

Master It There are four keywords that can be used to declare arrays. Name at least three of them.

Redimension an array. If you want to resize an existing dynamic array, you can redimension it.

Master It Redimensioning an array with the `ReDim` statement causes you to lose any values that are currently in that array. However, you can preserve these values using a special keyword. What is it?

Erase an array. You can erase all the values in a fixed-size array or completely erase a dynamic array.

Master It Write a line of code that erases the contents of an array named arrMyArray.

Find out whether a variable is an array. An array is a type of variable, and you may occasionally need to check whether a particular variable name denotes an array or an ordinary *Scalar variable* (a variable that isn't an array).

Master It Which built-in function can you use in VBA to find out whether a variable is an array or an ordinary, single-value variable?

Sort an array. Visual Basic .NET includes array objects with built-in search and sort methods. In VBA, however, you must write a bit of code to search and sort the values in an array.

Master It Name a popular, understandable, but relatively inefficient sorting technique.

Search an array. Searching through an array can be accomplished in two primary ways. If you have a relatively small array, you can use the simpler, but less efficient technique. With large amounts of data, though, it's best to use the more robust approach.

Master It Name two common search algorithms.

Chapter 8

Finding the Objects, Methods, and Properties You Need

In this chapter, you'll learn how to find the objects you need in the applications you're using. To learn the material in this chapter, you'll build on what you learned in the earlier chapters. You'll start by examining the concepts involved: what objects and collections are, what properties are, and what methods are. You'll then learn how to find the objects, collections, properties, and methods you need to make your code work. To identify these items, you'll use a number of tools you've already read about, including the Object Browser (which you used briefly in Chapter 4, "Creating Code from Scratch in the Visual Basic Editor") and the VBA online Help resources.

Along the way, this chapter explains how to use Object variables to represent objects in your code.

IN THIS CHAPTER, YOU WILL LEARN TO DO THE FOLLOWING:

- Understand and use objects, properties, and methods
- Use collections of objects
- Find objects, properties, and methods
- Use Object variables to represent objects

What Is an Object?

VBA-enabled applications (and many other modern applications) consist of a number of discrete objects, each with its own characteristics and capabilities.

The Benefits of OOP

Building an application out of objects is called *object-oriented programming (OOP)*. In theory, object-oriented programming offers a number of benefits to programmers—for example, the code is easier to build and maintain (update) because you break it down into objects of a manageable size.

Object-oriented programs should also be easier to understand than monolithic programs because it's less difficult for most people to grasp the concept of individual objects with associated characteristics and actions than to remember a far longer list of capabilities for the application as a whole.

Figuring out which commands to use to accomplish your programming goals can also be faster thanks to OOP taxonomy. For example, a table in Word is represented by a `Table` object, and a column is represented by a `Column` object. The `Column` object has a `Width` property that sets or returns its width. It's simpler to manage this information when it's broken down into these small pieces than to deal with some more complex command such as `WordTableSetColumnWidth` or `WordTableGetColumnWidth`.

A third benefit of object-oriented programming is that the VBA language itself can be extended. The programmer can build custom objects to implement functionality that the language itself didn't originally contain. For example, you can use VBA to build your own objects that do things that the Office applications themselves can't do.

Another, rather different, use for OOP is somewhat clerical: OOP can be of help when a group of programmers are working together on a single program. They can easily step on each other's toes in various ways—using the wrong version, changing each other's code, and so on. At the end of this chapter, we'll look at the ways OOP is employed to prevent these problems in team programming.

Objects can—and frequently do—contain other objects. Typically, the objects in an object-oriented application are arranged into a hierarchy called the *object model* of the application. This hierarchy is intended to make it easier to figure out where—within a large library of objects—you'll find a particular object that you want to use in your macros. It's similar to the way a biography is likely to be found in the library's nonfiction area.

Object Models Covered in Depth Later in the Book

This chapter discusses object models only a little, at the conceptual level. You need to know what an object model is in order to make sense of what you'll be learning in the following chapters, but you don't need to know the specifics of each object model to manipulate the objects used in the examples. Part 5 of this book, "Creating Effective Code," examines the object models of each of the applications covered in this book in enough detail to get you started exploring these object models more broadly on your own.

Most VBA host applications, including all the major Office applications, have an `Application` object that represents the application as a whole. The `Application` object itself has properties and methods for things that apply to the application as a whole. For example, many applications have a `Quit` method that exits the application and a `Visible` property that controls whether the application is visible or hidden.

In a typical object model, the `Application` object essentially *contains* all the other objects (and collections—groups—of objects) that make up the application. For example, Excel has an `Application` object that represents the Excel application, a `Workbook` object (grouped into the `Workbooks` collection) that represents a workbook, and a `Worksheet` object (grouped into the `Sheets` collection) that represents a worksheet. The `Workbook` object is contained within the `Application` object because you normally need to have the Excel application open to work with an Excel workbook.

In turn, the `Worksheet` object is contained within the `Workbook` object because you need to have an Excel workbook open to use a worksheet. Walking further down the object model, the `Worksheet` object contains assorted other objects, including `Row` objects that represent the individual rows in the worksheet, `Column` objects that represent columns in the worksheet, and `Range` objects that represent ranges of cells. And these objects in turn contain further objects.

To get to an object, you typically walk down through the hierarchy of the object model until you reach the object you're looking for.

To get to a `Range` object in Excel, for example, you would go through the `Application` object to the `Workbook` object, through the `Workbook` object to the appropriate `Sheet` object, and then finally to the `Range` object. The following statement shows how to select the range A1 in the first worksheet in the first open workbook (more on this in a minute):

```
Application.Workbooks(1).Sheets(1).Range("A1").Select
```

Understanding Creatable Objects

The `Application` object, however, is optional and is usually left out of code. Why? Because you'd have to go through the `Application` object to get to pretty much *anything* in the application, most applications *expose* (make available to you) a number of *creatable* objects. Creatable merely means that you can access something without having to type the word `Application` in your code. It's assumed. This is similar to the fact that you don't have to include the word *Earth* when addressing an envelope. There's only that one possibility. So far.

These creatable objects are usually the most-used objects for the application, and, by going through them, you can access most of the other objects without having to refer to the `Application` object. For example, Excel exposes the `Workbooks` collection as a creatable object, so you can use the following statement, which doesn't require that you type in `Application`. See the alternative example a couple of paragraphs earlier in this chapter.

```
Workbooks(1).Sheets(1).Range("A1").Select
```

Any object can have properties and methods. The next sections discuss these items in detail.

Properties

In VBA, a *property* is an attribute or characteristic of an object. Think of it as a quality of an object, such as its color. Most objects have multiple properties that specify each aspect of that object.

Each property has a specific data type for the information it stores. For example, the objects that represent files (such as documents, workbooks, or presentations) typically have a Boolean property named `Saved` that stores a value denoting whether all changes in the object have been saved (a value of `True`) or not (a value of `False`). These two values encompass the entire range of possibilities for the saved status of the object: it can either contain unsaved changes or not contain unsaved changes. There is no third state. A Boolean data type can, therefore, be used because that type has only two possible values.

Similarly, most objects that represent files have a `Name` property that contains the name of the file in question. The `Name` property contains a String data type because it needs to contain text. That text can be just about anything, limited only by the 255-character path that Windows permits for files and by certain characters—such as colons and pipe (|) characters—that Windows forbids in filenames.

To work with a property, you *get* (fetch or return) it to find out its current value or *set* (change) it to a value of your choosing. Many properties are *read/write*, meaning that you can both *get* and *set* their values, but some properties are *read-only*, meaning that you can view their values but not change them.

The Saved property is read/write for most applications, so you can set it. This means that you can tell the application that a file contains unsaved changes when it really doesn't or that it contains no unsaved changes when it actually has some. (Changing the Saved property can be useful when you're manipulating a file without the user's knowledge.) However, the Name property of a file object is read-only—you'll typically set the name by issuing a Save As command, after which you cannot change the name from within the application while the file is open. Therefore, you can get (read, return, or fetch) the Name property but not set it. You'll also encounter some *write-only properties*, properties that you can set but not get.

When an object contains another object, or contains a collection, it typically has a property that you *call* (invoke) to return the contained object or collection. For example, the Word Document object includes a PageSetup property that returns the PageSetup object for the document (the PageSetup object contains settings such as paper size, orientation, lines per page, and margins for the document) and a Tables property that you call to return the Tables collection. Here's how you can call the PageSetup object (which is contained in the Document object):

```
Sub GetLinesPage()

    Dim sngLinesPerPage As Single

    sngLinesPerPage = ActiveDocument.PageSetup.LinesPage

    MsgBox sngLinesPerPage


    End Sub
```

Each object of the same type has the same set of properties but stores its own particular values for them. For example, if you're running PowerPoint and have three Presentation objects open, each has its own Name property. The value in each Name property is specific to each Presentation object. In other words, the value in a property in one object has nothing to do with the value in that property in another object: Each object is independent of the other objects.

Methods

A *method* is an action that an object can perform, a capability an object has. For example, the Document object in various applications has a Save method that saves the document. You can use the Save method on different Document objects—Documents(1).Save saves the first Document object in the Documents collection, and Documents(2).Save saves the second Document object—but the Save method does the same thing in each case. An object can have one or more methods associated with it. Some objects have several dozen methods to implement all the functionality they need.

The Save method is very common. It appears in many applications' objects, as do other methods, such as SaveAs (which saves the file with a different name, location, or both) and Close (which closes the file).

Other methods are unique to each application. For example, the Presentation object in PowerPoint has an AddBaseline method that applies a baseline (consisting either of the active presentation or of a specified presentation file) that enables you to track changes for a merge. The Document object in Word has no AddBaseline method, but it has an AcceptAllRevisions method that accepts all revisions in the document. PowerPoint doesn't have an `AcceptAllRevisions` method.

Just as methods such as `Save` are common to multiple applications, some methods are found in more than one object. For example, the `Delete` method is associated with many different objects. As its name suggests, the `Delete` method usually deletes the specified object. However, other implementations of the Delete method behave somewhat differently, depending on the object with which they're working. Therefore, even if you're familiar with a method from using it with one object, you need to make sure that it will have the effect you expect when you use it with another object.

Some methods take no arguments. Other methods take one or more arguments (to supply necessary information). Just as with built-in VBA functions such as `MsgBox`, some arguments are required, while others are optional.

When a method applies to multiple objects, it may have different syntax for different objects. Again, even if you're familiar with a method, you need to know exactly what it does with the object for which you're planning to use it.

To use a method, you access it through the object involved. For example, to close the `ActivePresentation` object, which represents the active presentation in PowerPoint, you use the `Close` method (but you must specify the `ActivePresentation` object, like this):

```
ActivePresentation.Close
```

Real World Scenario

MAX THE DOG: VISUALIZING OBJECTS, METHODS, AND PROPERTIES

If you have a hard time getting a grip on objects, their properties, and methods, here's a somewhat strained comparison between the virtual objects, properties, and methods in VBA and physical objects, properties, and actions in the real world. Consider this example.

Let's say you have a massive dog named Max—a Pyrenean mountain dog, white, 200 pounds, four years old, male, and not *fixed*.

Max performs all the usual dog actions—sleep, run, eat, bark, growl, chew things, various unmentionable actions that we'll skip over—but also has a couple of unusual (for dogs) actions built in, such as slobbering on command, knocking people down, and biting mail carriers.

If Max were implemented in VBA, he'd be a `Dog` object in a `Dogs` collection. The `Dog` object for Max would have properties such as these:

`Name` This is a read-only String with a value of `Max`.

`Sex` This is a read-only String with a value of `Male`.

`Fixed` This is a read/write Boolean with a value of `False`.

`Height` This is a read/write Long with a value of `36`.

`Weight` This is a read/write Long with a value of `200`.

`Age` This is a read/write Integer with a value of `4`.

`Type` This is a read/write String with a value of `Pyrenean Mountain`.

`Color` This is a read/write String with a value of `White`.

Further, Max would have methods such as `Slobber`, `Bark`, `KnockDown`, `Intimidate`, `Chew`, `Run`, and so on. Some of these methods would require arguments. The `Slobber` method would definitely need arguments like this, probably using `Dog`-specific constants that start with the `dog` designation:

```
Dogs("Max").Slobber OnWhat:="MyKnee", How:= Disgustingly
```

The `Dog` object would contain other objects representing the many components of the dog—ears, eyes, tongue, brain, stomach, legs, tail, and so on. Each of these objects in turn would have its own properties and methods as appropriate. For example, the `Tail` object would need a `Wag` method, which you would probably invoke *(call)* something like this:

```
Dogs("Max").Tail.Wag Direction:=dogWagHorizontal, Frequency:=200
```

Working with Collections

When an object contains more than one object of the same type, the contained set of objects is said to be grouped into a *collection*. For example, Word uses `Document` objects, which are grouped into the `Documents` collection; PowerPoint has a `Presentations` collection for `Presentation` objects, and Excel has the `Workbooks` collection.

As in these examples, the names of most collections are simply the plural of the outer, container object. There *are* some exceptions, such as the `Sheets` collection in Excel that contains the `Worksheet` objects. But by and large the names of most collections are easy to derive from the name of the objects they contain—and vice versa.

A collection—taken as a whole—is itself an object, too, and can have its own properties and methods. For example, many collections have a `Count` property that tells you how many objects are in the collection. This next example tells you how many documents are in the `Documents` collection:

```
Sub GetDocCount()

  Dim lngCount As Long

  lngCount = Documents.Count

  MsgBox lngCount

End Sub
```

Collections tend to have fewer properties and methods than individual objects. Most collections have an `Add` method for adding another object to the collection. Some collections, however, are read-only and do not have an `Add` method. Most collections have an `Item` property (the default property) for accessing an item within the collection.

Most collections in VBA have the core group of properties listed in Table 8.1.

TABLE 8.1: Core properties for collections in VBA

PROPERTY	EXPLANATION
`Application`	A read-only property that returns the application associated with the object or collection—the root of the hierarchy for the document. For example, the `Application` property for objects in PowerPoint returns `Microsoft PowerPoint`.
`Count`	A read-only Long property that returns the number of items in the collection—for example, the number of `Shape` objects in the `Shapes` collection in a PowerPoint slide.
`Creator`	In Microsoft applications, a read-only Long property that returns a 32-bit integer indicating the application used to create the object or collection.
`Item`	A read-only property that returns a specified member of the collection. `Item` is the default property of every collection, which means that you seldom need to specify it.
`Parent`	In Microsoft applications, a read-only String property that returns the parent object for the object or collection. The *parent* object is the object that contains the object in question; the contained object is the *child* object. For example, a `Document` object is a child of the `Documents` collection.

Working with an Object in a Collection

To work with an object in a collection, you identify the object within the collection either by its name or by its position in the collection. For example, the following statement returns the first `Document` object in the `Documents` collection and displays its `Name` property in a message box:

```
MsgBox Documents(1).Name
```

MOST COLLECTIONS ARE ZERO-BASED

Recall that arrays are zero-based by default in VBA. They employ a 0 index number for the first item in the array (unless you use the `Option Base 1` statement to force the first index number to 1 as we did in Chapter 7, "Using Array Variables").

Fortunately, most VBA collections default to the more sensible 1 for the first item in the collection. This makes it easy to identify the object you need. For example, `Documents(1)` gives you the first document, `Workbooks(2)` gives you the second workbook, and so on.

But notice the word *most*. Sadly, there are exceptions to this rule. Be warned that *some* collections in VBA implementations are zero-based—their numbering starts at 0 (zero) rather than 1. For example, Access—nearly always the special case in VBA—employs zero-based collections. If you're not sure whether a particular collection is one- or zero-based, consult the Help topic for that collection.

You can optionally use the `Item` property to return an object from the collection, but because `Item` is the default property of a collection, you don't need to use it. It's assumed. The following two statements have the same effect, so there's no advantage to using the `Item` method:

```
strName = Documents(1).Name
strName = Documents.Item(1).Name
```

Adding an Object to a Collection

To create a new object in a collection, you add an object to the collection. In many cases, you use the `Add` method to do so. For example, the following statement creates a new `Document` object in Word:

```
Documents.Add
```

Finding the Objects You Need

The Visual Basic Editor provides a number of tools for finding the objects you need:

- The Macro Recorder, which you used to record macros in some Microsoft Office applications in Chapter 1, "Recording and Running Macros in the Office Applications"
- The Object Browser, which you used briefly in Chapter 4
- The online Help system, which can provide detailed help on the objects in the application
- The Auto List Members feature in the Visual Basic Editor

The following sections show you how to use these tools to find objects.

Using the Macro Recorder to Add Code for the Objects You Need

If you're using a Microsoft application, chances are that the easiest way to find the objects you need is to run the Macro Recorder to record a quick macro using the objects that interest you. While you perform various actions in the application, the Macro Recorder creates code that you can then open in the Visual Basic Editor, examine, and modify if necessary.

In spite of its advantages, the Macro Recorder does have two drawbacks:

- First, you can't record *every* action that you might want. Let's say you're working in Excel and want to create a statement that performs an action on a specified workbook in the `Workbooks` collection rather than on the currently active workbook. With the Macro Recorder, you can record only actions performed on the active workbook. (This is the case because the Macro Recorder can record only those actions you can perform interactively in Excel, and you can't work interactively with any workbook other than the active one. The same thing is true for Word documents.) Here's another example: Some Ribbon actions are not recorded. In Word, clicking the Review ➤ Show Markup Formatting feature to deselect it results in no recorded code. You would need to write the following code in the Editor yourself:

  ```
  ActiveWindow.View.ShowFormatChanges = False
  ```

- Second, the Macro Recorder is apt to include more statements than you actually need, particularly when you're trying to record a setting in a dialog box.

You saw an example of the second problem in Chapter 4. Here's another example. This time we'll record a macro to create an AutoCorrect entry. Let's say that you often have to type the word *references* in your job—dozens of times every day. You can speed up your work by merely typing **reffs** (or some other abbreviation of your choice). Then Word will automatically replace *reffs* with *references* as you type. Here's how to create this macro:

1. Start Word.
2. Click the Record Macro button on the status bar, or click the Developer tab on the Ribbon and then click the Record Macro button in the Code section. This displays the Record Macro dialog box. Type **Add_Item_to_AutoCorrect** in the Macro Name text box, and type a description in the Description text box. Make sure All Documents (Normal.dotm) is selected in the Store Macro In drop-down list, and then click the OK button to start recording.
3. Press Alt+F and then press I. Then click the Proofing button and the AutoCorrect Options button to display the AutoCorrect dialog box. Type **reffs** in the Replace box and **references** in the With box, and click the Add button. Then click OK twice to close both open dialog boxes.
4. Click the Stop Recording button on the Ribbon or the status bar to stop the Macro Recorder.

Now press Alt+F8 to display the Macros dialog box, select the `Add_Item_to_AutoCorrect` entry, and click the Edit button to open the macro in the Visual Basic Editor. The code should look like this:

```
Sub Add_Item_to_AutoCorrect()
'
' Add_Item_to_AutoCorrect Macro
' Change reffs to references
'
    AutoCorrect.Entries.Add Name:="reffs", Value:="references"
    With Options
        .AutoFormatAsYouTypeApplyHeadings = False
        .AutoFormatAsYouTypeApplyBorders = True
        .AutoFormatAsYouTypeApplyBulletedLists = True
        .AutoFormatAsYouTypeApplyNumberedLists = True
        .AutoFormatAsYouTypeApplyTables = True
        .AutoFormatAsYouTypeReplaceQuotes = True
        .AutoFormatAsYouTypeReplaceSymbols = True
        .AutoFormatAsYouTypeReplaceOrdinals = True
        .AutoFormatAsYouTypeReplaceFractions = True
        .AutoFormatAsYouTypeReplacePlainTextEmphasis = False
        .AutoFormatAsYouTypeReplaceHyperlinks = True
        .AutoFormatAsYouTypeFormatListItemBeginning = True
        .AutoFormatAsYouTypeDefineStyles = False
        .TabIndentKey = True
    End With
    With AutoCorrect
        .CorrectInitialCaps = True
```

```
            .CorrectSentenceCaps = True
            .CorrectDays = True
            .CorrectCapsLock = True
            .ReplaceText = True
            .ReplaceTextFromSpellingChecker = True
            .CorrectKeyboardSetting = False
            .DisplayAutoCorrectOptions = True
            .CorrectTableCells = True
        End With
        With OMathAutoCorrect
            .UseOutsideOMath = False
            .ReplaceText = True
        End With
        With Options
            .AutoFormatApplyHeadings = True
            .AutoFormatApplyLists = True
            .AutoFormatApplyBulletedLists = True
            .AutoFormatApplyOtherParas = True
            .AutoFormatReplaceQuotes = True
            .AutoFormatReplaceSymbols = True
            .AutoFormatReplaceOrdinals = True
            .AutoFormatReplaceFractions = True
            .AutoFormatReplacePlainTextEmphasis = True
            .AutoFormatReplaceHyperlinks = True
            .AutoFormatPreserveStyles = True
            .AutoFormatPlainTextWordMail = True
        End With
        Options.LabelSmartTags = False
    End Sub
```

Here, the Recorder has created dozens of lines of unnecessary code. The only statement you actually need to accomplish your task is this:

```
AutoCorrect.Entries.Add Name:="reffs", Value:="references"
```

This line shows you that to add an AutoCorrect entry, you need to work with the `Entries` collection object in the `AutoCorrect` object. You use the `Add` method on the `Entries` collection to add an AutoCorrect entry to the list.

All the other lines of code specifying the status of various options are unnecessary because you are not interested in changing any of them in this macro.

By removing these extraneous lines from this recorded macro, you can reduce it to just the single line it needs to contain (together with the comment lines, which you can also remove if you want):

```
Sub Add_Item_to_AutoCorrect()
'
' Add_Item_to_AutoCorrect Macro
' Change reffs to references
'
    AutoCorrect.Entries.Add Name:="reffs",Value:="references"
End Sub
```

You used the Recorder to see the correct syntax for adding an entry to the AutoCorrect feature. There's no point to leaving in lines of code unrelated to your purposes.

What's more, such extraneous code would make it harder at some future date to read and understand the macro's purpose.

Worst of all, these extra lines can set properties to conditions that you, or someone else using this macro, might not want. Let's say you run this macro in the future and you are working in a document that must not have any bullet symbols in it. You've clicked the File tab on the Ribbon, chosen File ➢ Options ➢ Proofing ➢ AutoCorrect Options ➢ AutoFormat As You Type, and turned off bullets. However, when you run this macro, bullets are turned back on by this unneeded line in the code:

```
.AutoFormatAsYouTypeApplyBulletedLists = True
```

In spite of its limitations, the Macro Recorder does provide quick access to the objects you need to work with, and you can always modify the resulting code in the Visual Basic Editor. What's more, the code that the Recorder generates is, if nothing else, guaranteed to execute without bugs.

Using the Object Browser

For many programmers, the primary tool for writing code for objects is the Object Browser, which you used briefly in Chapter 4. In the following sections, you'll get to know the Object Browser better and learn to use it to find the information you need about objects. To see the Object Browser, press F2 in the Editor.

Components of the Object Browser

The Object Browser provides the following information about both built-in objects and custom objects you create:

- Classes (formal definitions of objects)
- Properties (the attributes of objects or aspects of their behavior)
- Methods (actions you can perform on objects)
- Events (for example, the opening or closing of a document)
- Constants (named items that keep a constant value while a program is executing)

Figure 8.1 shows the components of the Object Browser.

Here's what the different elements of the Object Browser do:

- The Project/Library drop-down list provides a list of object libraries available to the current project. (An *object library* is collection of objects made available to programs. There can be several libraries in use at a given time. For example, one library might contain objects that specialize in rendering graphics, a second library might contain objects that assist with security features, and so on.) Use the drop-down list to choose the object libraries you want to view. For example, you might choose to view only objects in Outlook by choosing Outlook in the Project/Library drop-down list. Alternatively, you could stay with the default choice of <All Libraries>.

FIGURE 8.1
The Object Browser provides information on built-in objects and custom objects. Here, the application is Excel.

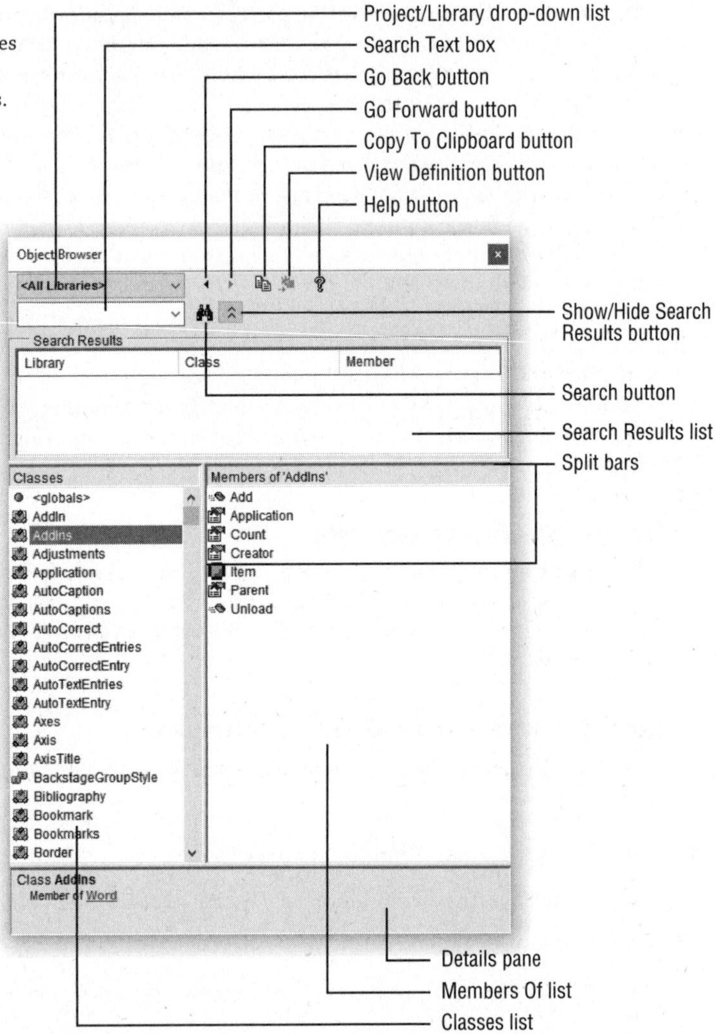

- In the Search Text box, enter the string you want to search for: Either type it in or choose a previous string in the current project session from the drop-down list. Then either press Enter or click the Search button to find members containing the search string.

IMPROVE YOUR SEARCHES WITH THESE TECHNIQUES

To make your searches in the Object Browser less specific, you can use wildcards such as ? (to represent any single character) and * (to represent any group of characters). You can also choose to search for a whole word only (rather than matching your search string with part of another word) by right-clicking anywhere in the Object Browser (except in the Project/Library drop-down list or in the Search Text box) and choosing Find Whole Word Only from the context menu. The Find Whole Word Only choice has a check mark next to it in the context menu when it's active; to deactivate it, choose Find Whole Word Only again on the context menu.

- Click the Go Back button to retrace one by one your previous selections in the Classes list and the Members Of list. Click the Go Forward button to move forward through your previous selections one by one. The Go Back button becomes available when you go to a class or member in the Object Browser; the Go Forward button becomes available only when you've used the Go Back button to go back to a previous selection.
- Click the Copy To Clipboard button to copy the selected item from the Search Results list, the Classes list, the Members Of list, or the Details pane to the Clipboard so that you can paste it into your code.
- Click the View Definition button to display a Code window containing the code for the object selected in the Classes list or the Members Of list. The View Definition button is available (undimmed) only for objects that contain code, such as procedures and user forms that you've created.
- Click the Help button to display any available help for the currently selected item. Alternatively, press the F1 key.
- Click the Search button to search for the term entered in the Search Text box. If the Search Results pane isn't open, VBA opens it at this point.
- Click the Show/Hide Search Results button to toggle the display of the Search Results pane on and off.
- The Search Results list in the Search Results pane contains the results of the latest search you've conducted for a term entered in the Search Text box. If you've performed a search, the Object Browser updates the Search Results list when you use the Project/Library drop-down list to switch to a different library. Choosing a different library in the Project/Library drop-down list is a handy way of narrowing, expanding, or changing the focus of your search.
- The Classes list shows the available classes in the library or project specified in the Project/Library drop-down list.
- The Members Of list displays the available elements of the class selected in the Classes list. A method, constant, event, property, or procedure that has code written for it appears in boldface. The Members Of list can display the members either grouped into their different categories (methods, properties, events, and so on) or ungrouped as an alphabetical list of all the members available. To toggle between grouped and ungrouped, right-click in the Members Of list and choose Group Members from the context menu; click either to place a check mark (to group the members) or to remove the check mark (to ungroup the members).
- The Details pane displays the definition of the member selected in the Classes list or in the Members Of list. For example, if you select a procedure in the Members Of list, the Details pane displays its name, the name of the module and template or document in which it's stored, and any comment lines you inserted at the beginning of the procedure. The module name and project name contain hyperlinks (jumps) so that you can quickly move to them. You can copy information from the Details pane to the Code window by using either copy and paste or drag and drop.
- Drag the three split bars to resize the panes of the Object Browser to suit yourself. (You can also resize the Object Browser window as needed or maximize it so that it docks itself in the Code window.)

The Object Browser uses different icons to indicate the various types of object that it lists. Figure 8.1 shows several icons; Table 8.2 shows the full range of icons and what they represent.

A blue dot in the upper-left corner of a Property icon or a Method icon indicates that that property or method is the default.

TABLE 8.2: Object Browser icons

ICON	MEANING
	Property
	User-defined type
	Method
	Global
	Constant
	Library
	Module
	Project
	Event
	Built-in keyword or type
	Class
	Enum (enumeration)

ADDING AND REMOVING OBJECT LIBRARIES

The default object libraries are sufficient for most typical macros, so you generally need not worry about adding any specialized libraries. If you get into some kinds of advanced macro programming, however, you will need to add other libraries (you'll modify the Ribbon in Chapter 31, "Programming the Office 2016 Ribbon," and to do that you do have to add a special library). You can add and remove object libraries by choosing Tools ➤ References in the Editor and using the References dialog box to make your selections:

- By adding object libraries, you can make available additional sets of objects with which to work.
- By removing object libraries that you don't need to view or use, you can reduce the number of object references that VBA needs to resolve when it is compiling the code in a project. This allows the code to run faster, although as I've mentioned before, today's computers are so fast that finding ways to increase the speed of macro execution is never an issue for most people.

When you start the Visual Basic Editor, it automatically loads the object libraries required for using VBA and user forms with the host application. You don't have to change this set of object libraries until you need to access objects contained in other libraries. For example, if you create a procedure in Word that needs to employ a feature found in Excel, you'll have to add to Word's VBA Editor a reference to an Excel object library to make Excel's objects available.

You can adjust the priority (or *order of precedence*) of different references by adjusting the order in which the references appear in the References dialog box. The priority of references matters when you use in your code an object that's listed in more than one reference: VBA checks the References list to determine the order of the references that contain that object name and uses the first one unless specifically told to do otherwise by use of an unambiguous name.

To add or remove object libraries, follow these steps:

1. In the Visual Basic Editor, choose Tools ➢ References to display the References dialog box (see Figure 8.2). You can also display the References dialog box by right-clicking in the Object Browser and choosing References from the context menu.

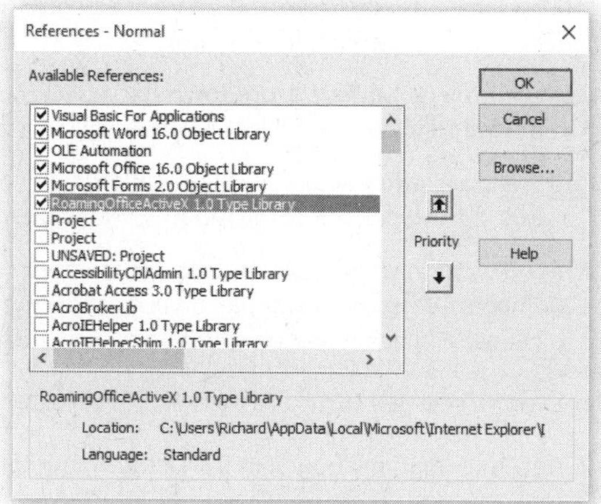

FIGURE 8.2
You add and remove object libraries by using the References dialog box.

2. In the Available References list box, select the check boxes for the object libraries you want to have access to, and clear the check boxes for the references you want to remove because you don't need them. You should find a reference for an object library for each application that supports automation and is installed on your computer. *Automation*, in this context, means that an application permits the automation of tasks (in other words, macros). Another way to put this is an application that supports automation *exposes its objects*, meaning that the application makes its objects available to programmers.
3. The references that are in use appear together at the top of the Available References list box, not in alphabetical order (in order of precedence, as described earlier in this chapter).
4. Adjust the order of precedence of the references if you want by selecting a reference and using the up- and down-arrow Priority buttons to move it up or down the list. Usually, you'll want to keep Visual Basic for Applications and the object library of the application you're working with at the top of your list.

Adding a Reference Library

You can even add new reference libraries to the list of available references in the References dialog box by clicking the Browse button to display the Add Reference dialog box, selecting the library file, and then clicking the Open button.

5. Click OK to close the References dialog box and return to the Object Browser.

Navigating with the Object Browser

To browse the objects available to a project, follow these steps:

1. First, activate a code module by double-clicking it in the editor's Project Explorer.
2. Display the Object Browser by choosing View ➤ Object Browser, by pressing the F2 button, or by clicking the Object Browser button on the Standard toolbar. (If the Object Browser is already displayed, make it active by clicking it or by selecting it from the list at the bottom of the Window menu.)
3. In the Project/Library drop-down list, select the name of the project or the library that you want to view. The Object Browser displays the available classes in the Classes list.
4. In the Classes list, select the class with which you want to work. For example, if you chose a project in step 3, select the module you want to work with in the Classes list.
5. If you want to work with a particular member of the class or project, select it in the Members Of list. For example, if you're working with a template project, you might want to choose a specific procedure or user form with which to work.

Once you've selected the class, member, or project, you can do the following things with it:

- View information about it in the Details pane at the bottom of the Object Browser window.
- View the definition of an object by clicking the View Definition button. Alternatively, right-click the object in the Members Of list and choose View Definition from the context menu. The View Definition button and the View Definition command are enabled (available, undimmed) only for objects that contain code, such as procedures and user forms that you've created.

A *Definition* Is Contained Code

The definition of a *procedure* is the code that it contains. The definition of a *module* is all the code in all the procedures that it contains. The definition of a *user form* is the code in all the procedures attached to it. To see how the View Definition button works, type the name of one of your macros in the Object Browser's Search field (to the left of the icon). Then click the icon to locate this macro. Then click the View Definition button, and the Code window will open, displaying this macro's code.

- Copy the text for the selected class, project, or member to the Clipboard by clicking the Copy button or by issuing a standard Copy command (pressing Ctrl+C or Ctrl+Insert).

Using Help to Find the Object You Need

VBA's online Help system provides another easy way to access the details of the objects you want to utilize. The Help files provide a hyperlinked reference to all the objects, methods, and properties in VBA, including graphics that show how the objects are related to each other, and plenty of code samples to show you the correct syntax.

The quickest way to access VBA Help is to press the F1 key while working in the Visual Basic Editor.

Pressing F1 to Go to a General VBA Help Page

F1 works two different ways. Press F1 with the cursor (the blinking vertical line) on a blank line in the Code window, and you're taken to the VBA portal shown in Figure 8.3. However, press F1 with the cursor on a language keyword in your code, such as `Variant` or `InputBox`, and you're taken to a Help page with specific information about that particular keyword.

First, try clicking a blank line in the Code window, and then press F1. Your browser opens a generic Office website like the one shown in Figure 8.3.

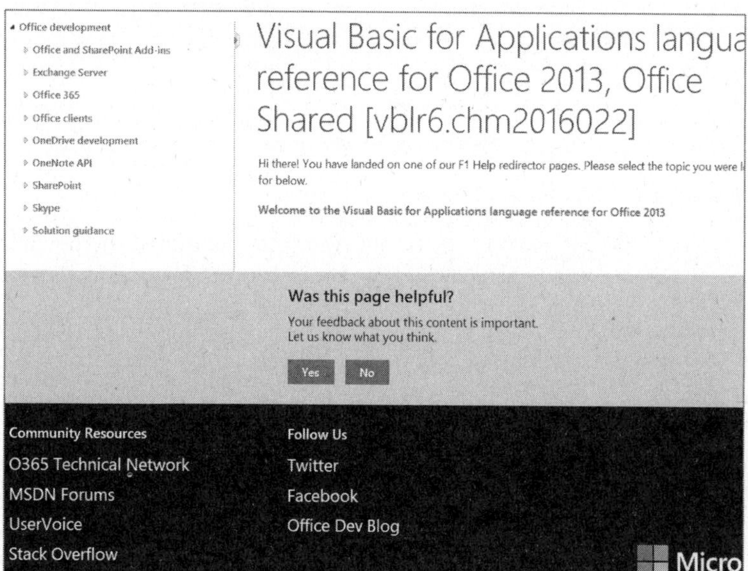

Figure 8.3
The generic VBA portal

Several links appear along the left side (both top and bottom) of the web page shown in Figure 8.3. Try some of these links, including the Office and SharePoint Add-ins and the MSDN Forums links. Click the Stack Overflow link and you're taken a Q & A site with loads of useful code samples.

Also try the *Welcome to the Visual Basic for Applications language reference for Office 2013* link shown in the middle of the page. (Note that Microsoft will likely change "2013" to "2016" at some point.)

Pressing F1 to Go Directly to a Command's Help Page

The second way to use F1 takes you directly to the Help page for the keyword that interests you. If you want to see how to manipulate the active window, for example, just type **`activewindow`** into the Editor's Code window, and then, with the blinking insertion cursor somewhere in that word, press F1. See Figure 8.4.

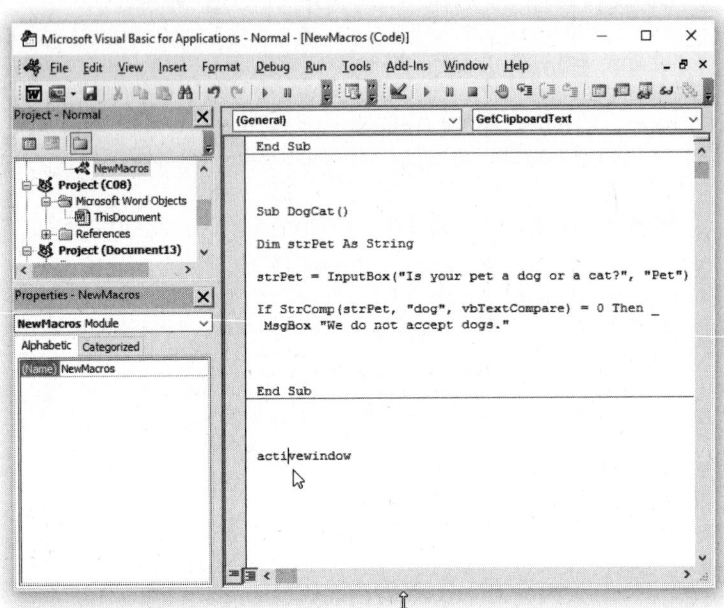

FIGURE 8.4
Put your insertion cursor on a command, and then Press F1 to get context-sensitive help.

After you press F1 on the `activewindow` command, as shown in Figure 8.4, the Help page for this command opens, as you can see in Figure 8.5.

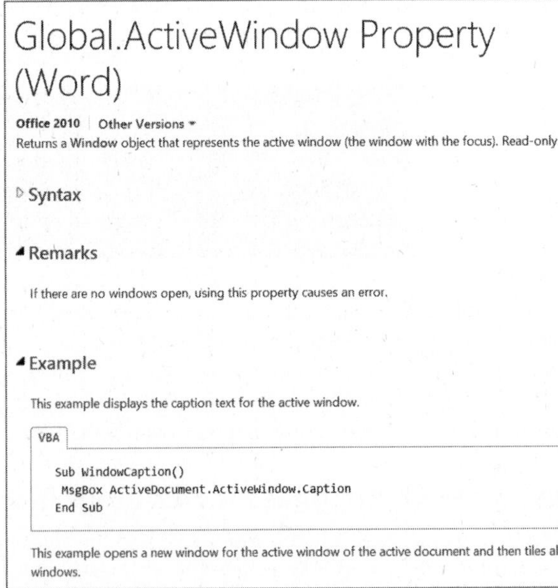

Global.ActiveWindow Property (Word)

Office 2010 | Other Versions

Returns a **Window** object that represents the active window (the window with the focus). Read-only.

Syntax

Remarks

If there are no windows open, using this property causes an error.

Example

This example displays the caption text for the active window.

VBA

```
Sub WindowCaption()
 MsgBox ActiveDocument.ActiveWindow.Caption
End Sub
```

This example opens a new window for the active window of the active document and then tiles all windows.

FIGURE 8.5
The main Help page for the `ActiveWindow` property

Notice in Figure 8.5 that it shows Office 2010, but provides you with an Other Versions link. Click that to get the latest information. (Why they don't just display the other version links rather than requiring you to click this is a mystery.)

Apart from the regular Help information you'll find in the Help pages online, here are a few additional ways to find help:

- At the top of most Microsoft Help windows, you'll see a search field (look for the magnifying glass symbol). Try typing **Word 2016 selection object** into the search field (you may have to type **2013**). A page is displayed with plenty of links.
- When looking for help, you can also try clicking the Help menu in the Editor and then choosing one of the two help options listed: Microsoft Visual Basic Applications Help or MSDN On The Web. These two options open different entrees into the Help system, from which you can drill down until you locate the explanations or code samples you're after. (Note that although the first option listed displays F1, you are *not* taken to the same web page you get when actually pressing F1.)
- Finally, when looking for help with objects, remember that you can press F2 to display the built-in Object Browser.

Using the Auto List Members Feature

You've already used the Auto List Members feature a couple of times in the previous chapters. To recap, in VBA code—as with most other programming languages—objects and their *members* (properties and methods) are separated by periods. This punctuation helps you see the relationships between parent objects, child objects, and, at the end of the line, the members. Notice the two periods in this code:

```
sngLinesPerPage = ActiveDocument.PageSetup.LinesPage
```

When you're entering a statement in the Visual Basic Editor and you type the period, the Auto List Members feature displays a list of properties and methods appropriate to the object. (If necessary, turn this feature on in the Visual Basic Editor by choosing Tools ➢ Options, and then selecting the Auto List Members check box.)

Technically, there's a distinction between Auto List Members and a somewhat similar List Properties/Methods feature. The former feature is triggered by typing a period (.) following the name of an object in a line of code. The latter is triggered by pressing Ctl+J or by right-clicking the name of an object in a line of code and choosing List Properties/Methods from the menu that appears. Of the two, I find Auto List Members more useful.

The Auto List Members feature provides a quick way of completing statements, but you need to know which object you should work with before you can work with its members. Sometimes using this feature is a bit like finding your way through a maze and being given detailed directions that end with the phrase, "But you can't get there from here."

Once you know the object from which to start, though, you can easily find the property or method you need. For example, to put together the statement `Application.Documents(1).Close` (to close the first document in the `Documents` collection in Word), you could work as follows:

1. Place the insertion point on a fresh line in an empty procedure (between the `Sub` and `End Sub` statements). Create a new procedure if necessary.

2. Type the word **application**, or type **appl** and press Ctrl+spacebar to have the Complete Word feature complete the word for you.
3. Type the period (.) after Application. The Auto List Members feature displays the list of properties and methods available to the `Application` object.
4. Choose the `Documents` item in the Auto List Members list. You can scroll to it using the mouse and then double-click it to enter it in the Code window, scroll to it by using the arrow keys and enter it by pressing Tab, or type the first few letters of its name (to automatically locate it) and then enter it by pressing Tab. The latter method is shown in Figure 8.6, which uses Word.

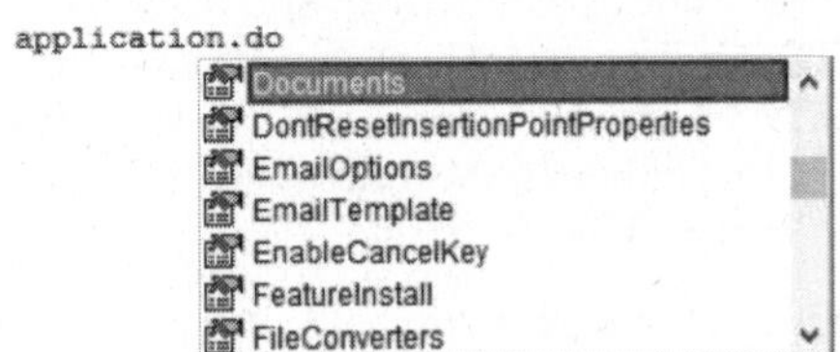

FIGURE 8.6
Using the Auto List Members feature to enter code

5. Type **(1).** after `Documents`. When you type this period, the Auto List Members feature displays the list of properties and methods available to a `Document` object. Note that without the `(1)`, you're working with the documents collection, but as soon as you add the `(1)`, you're then working with a specific document, namely the first one in the collection.
6. Choose the `Close` method in the Auto List Members list by scrolling to it with the mouse or with the down-arrow key. Because this is the end of the statement, press the Enter key to enter the method and start a new line (rather than pressing the Tab key, which enters the method but continues the same line of code).

AUTOMATIC SELECTION LETS YOU KEEP YOUR HANDS ON THE KEYBOARD

For most people, the quickest way to enter statements in the Code window is to keep their hands on the keyboard. After all, you're *typing* your programming. To help you do this, the Visual Basic Editor automatically selects the current item in the Auto List Members list when you type a period or an opening parenthesis. In the previous example, you can type **Application.** to display the list, **Do** to select the `Documents` item, and **(** to enter the `Documents` item.

Using Object Variables to Represent Objects

As you learned in Chapter 6, "Working with Variables, Constants, and Enumerations," one of the data types available for variables in VBA is the *Object* type. You use an Object variable to represent an object in your code: Instead of referring to the object directly, you can employ the Object variable to access or manipulate the object it represents.

Here's one major benefit of this approach: Using Object variables makes your code easier to read. It's simpler to see which object a section of code is working with, especially when you're working with multiple objects in the same section of code. Plus, you can give descriptive names to these variables that are easily understood. What's more, Object variables are often a necessity when you need to manipulate collections of objects.

For example, say you create a procedure that manipulates the three open workbooks in Excel, copying a range of cells from one to the other two. If you have only those three workbooks open, you'll be able to refer to them directly as `Workbooks(1)`, `Workbooks(2)`, and `Workbooks(3)`, respectively, because they'll occupy the first (and only) three slots in the `Workbooks` collection.

But if your procedure changes the order of the workbooks, closes one or more workbooks, or creates one or more new workbooks, things rapidly get confusing. If, however, you've created Object variables (named, say, `xlWorkbook1`, `xlWorkbook2`, and `xlWorkbook3`) to refer to those specific workbooks, it will be much easier to keep them straight. This is because no matter which workbook moves to first position in the `Workbooks` collection, you'll be able to refer to the object represented by the Object variable `xlWorkbook1` and know that you'll be accessing the workbook you're after. In other words, when you create Object variables, you get to *name them*, using words that are more easily understood than index numbers. More important, once it's named, an Object variable's name does not change. Index numbers can change.

To create an Object variable, you declare it in almost exactly the same way as you declare any other variable, using a `Dim`, `Private`, or `Public` statement. However, you specify the type `As Object`. For example, the following statement declares the Object variable `objMyObject`:

```
Dim objMyObject As Object
```

As usual when using the `Dim` statement, if you use this declaration within a procedure, it creates a variable with local scope. If you use it in the declarations section at the top of a code sheet, it creates a variable with module-level private scope. Similarly, the `Private` and `Public` keywords create module-level private and public Object variables, respectively.

Once you've declared the Object variable, you can assign an object to it. (Assigning objects works a bit differently from the way you use just an equal sign to assign a value to an ordinary variable.) To assign an object to an Object variable, you use a `Set` statement. The syntax for a `Set` statement is as follows:

```
Set objectvariable = {[New] expression|Nothing}
```

Here's how that syntax breaks down:

- *`Objectvariable`* is the name of the Object variable to which you're assigning the object.
- `New` is an optional keyword that you can use to implicitly create a new object of the specified class. However, usually it's better to create objects *explicitly* and then assign them to Object variables rather than use `New` to create them implicitly.
- *`expression`* is a required expression that specifies or returns the object you want to assign to the Object variable.
- `Nothing` is an optional keyword that you assign to an existing Object variable to obliterate its contents and release the memory they occupied.

For example, the following statements declare the Object variable `objMyObject` and assign to it the active workbook in Excel:

```
Dim objMyObject As Object
Set objMyObject = ActiveWorkbook
```

The following statement uses the `Nothing` keyword to release the memory occupied by the `objMyObject` Object variable:

```
Set objMyObject = Nothing
```

What's different about declaring an Object variable versus declaring other types of variables is that not only can you declare the Object variable as being of the type `Object` and then use the `Set` command, but you can also specify which type of object it is. For example, if an Object variable will always represent a `Workbook` object, you can declare it as being of the Workbook data type. The following statement declares the Object variable `xlWorkbook1` as being of the Workbook data type:

```
Dim xlWorkbook1 As Workbook
```

Strongly associating a type with an Object variable like this has a couple of advantages. First, once you've *strongly typed* (as it's called) the Object variable, the Visual Basic Editor can provide you with full assistance for the Object variable, just as if you were dealing with the object directly. For example, once you've created that Object variable `xlWorkbook1` of the `Workbook` object type, the Visual Basic Editor displays the Auto List Members drop-down list when you type that Object variable's name followed by a period, as shown in Figure 8.7.

Second, when you strongly type an Object variable, you make it a bit harder to get things wrong in your code. If you try to assign the wrong type of object to a strongly typed Object variable, VBA gives an error. For example, if you create a `Worksheet` Object variable in Excel, as in the first of the following statements, but assign to it a `Workbook` object, as in the second statement, VBA displays a "Type Mismatch" error message when you execute this code—as well it should:

```
Dim wksSheet1 As Worksheet
Set wksSheet1 = ActiveWorkbook
```

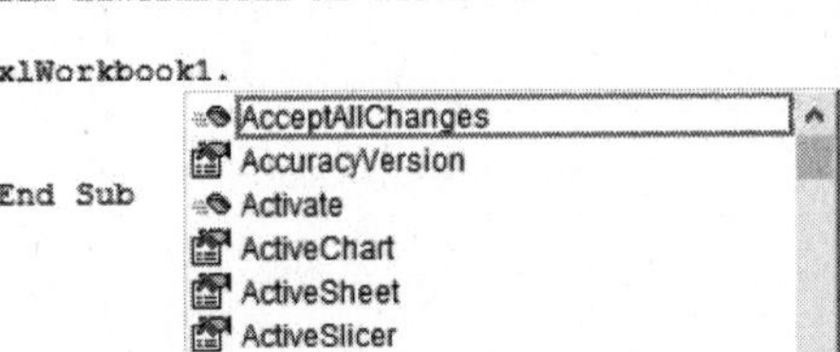

FIGURE 8.7
When you strongly type your Object variables, you get the full benefit of the Visual Basic Editor's code-completion features for those Object variables.

Finding out at this testing stage that you've created a problem is usually preferable to finding out later (for example, when you go to manipulate the `wksSheet1` object and discover it doesn't behave as you expect it to).

The main argument for *not* strongly typing an Object variable is that you might not be sure ahead of time (while writing the code) what kind of object that variable will eventually reference during execution or if the kind of object it will store may vary from one execution of the code to another. (If either is the case, your code will need to be flexible enough to accommodate objects of different types for the same Object variable.) Usually, though, you'll want to strongly type all your Object variables.

If you're not sure which object type to use for an Object variable, start by declaring the Object variable as being of the Object data type. Then run through the code a couple of times with the Locals window (View ➤ Locals Window) displayed, and note the data type that VBA assigns to the Object variable. For example, if you press F8 repeatedly to step through the following statements in a Visual Basic Editor session hosted by Excel, the readout in the Locals window at first identifies the Object variable `wks` only as `Object`.

That's not too useful. However, press F8 again to execute the `Set` command, and you see loads of information (press the + icon next to `wks`). You now see `Object/Sheet1` (as shown on the right in Figure 8.8) when executing the second statement assigns the first sheet in the active workbook to it. You also can see all the members, their current values, and their type.

```
Dim wks As Object
Set wks = ActiveWorkbook.Sheets(1)
```

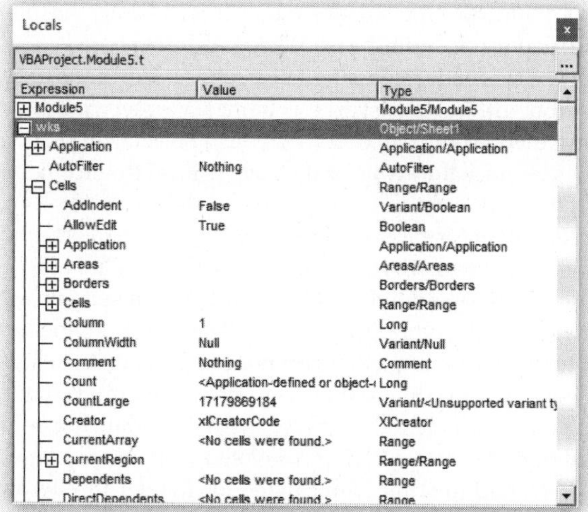

FIGURE 8.8
You can use the Locals window to help identify the object type that an Object variable will contain.

THERE ARE DRAWBACKS TO WEAKLY TYPED VARIABLES

As you learned earlier in the book, you can avoid specifying data types altogether by using the Variant type. For example, the statement `Dim varMyVariant` creates a Variant variable because the statement does not specify a data type. Variant variables can contain objects as well as other data types—but as before, using Variants requires VBA to do a little more work each time it encounters the variable (because VBA has to determine what data type the variable currently is) and denies you the benefits of strongly typing your variables. Weak typing also makes your code harder to read.

Team Programming and OOP

VBA is used by individual programmers as well as teams. OOP can offer some special advantages when you are trying to manage a group of programmers working together on a large, complex VBA solution. OOP can help people avoid stepping on each other's toes—duplicating global variable names, creating version problems, and so on—because everyone's individual copy of the code is *their* latest version but not the latest official version of the group (and other kinds of interference.)

Group programming needs management, and OOP, among its other benefits, assists in avoiding chaos when a team needs to work together on a common goal.

One feature of OOP is *encapsulation*. This means that an object is self-contained and sealed off. It's like a so called "black box" that you plug into your video system to improve the picture. You don't open the box. Nobody is supposed to modify the innards. You just use it.

As an example, say that the boss wants all documents from now on to emphasize the company's name. You give Sandra the task of creating an object that is supposed to italicize and capitalize all references to *ACME WINDOWORKS* in all company documents. You ask Joe to create an object that ensures that any use of the company name is displayed in green rather than the normal black letters. (In reality, you would likely want to code these simple manipulations into *functions*—see Chapter 10, "Creating Your Own Functions,"—rather than *objects*. Objects can perform multiple related jobs rather than a single, simple job like turning something green, but this is just an example, so we'll keep it simple here.)

When this code is encapsulated into sealed-off objects, nobody has to worry that Sandra and Joe might use the same variable names or otherwise interfere with each other's code. Instead, within their totally separate, sealed-off objects, they can go ahead and write code as they please. This is because the scope of the code is local to the object, and also, neither Joe nor Sandra can view, much less modify, each other's code.

A document is passed to Sandra's `ItalAndCap` object, and the document comes out the other end (returns) with all instances of *ACME WINDOWORKS* italicized and capitalized. Then the document is passed to Joe's object and in turn spit out with *ACME WINDOWORKS* in green. Therefore, each component of the overall solution, the larger program, does its own job without interference from any other component (object). As a result, you avoid a lot of problems if people are working on individual tasks with the assurance that nobody else will be able to mess with their code or accidentally interact with it in some unpredictable way. Also, it's easier to track down bugs because each job is isolated from other jobs—and if the company name is only turning green half the time, you can tell Joe to take another look at his object.

It's true that over the years some elements of OOP theory have grown quite arcane and abstract. OOP can be, in the upper reaches of universities, a terribly complex subject of study. In fact, they say that, like quantum mechanics, advanced OOP theory is understood by only 12 people in the world—and they're fooling themselves.

Nonetheless, if you are in charge of a team that's responsible for building a large application for Office, take some time to employ OOP's clerical features. Each individual programmer will be responsible for how their object works. The other programmers can merely use that object without worrying about debugging it. They are not even allowed to see its internal code. Consider the objects that are built into VBA itself, such as Word's `Selection` object. It was written by somebody at Microsoft. You can put this object in your code and ask it to do things for you, such as move the cursor one word to the left:

```
Selection.MoveLeft Unit:=wdWord, Count:=1
```

However, you never see the actual code within the `Selection` object that does the moving left. You aren't allowed to modify it, and its code does not interact with your code's variables or cause other unwanted side effects. In other words, the built-in VBA objects are encapsulated—usable as black boxes, but sealed off.

To create your own encapsulated objects in VBA, you can add *class modules* to a project, which are distinct from regular code modules. You'll see how to do this in Chapter 16, "Building Modular Code and Using Classes."

The Bottom Line

Understand and use objects, properties, and methods. Contemporary programming employs a hierarchical method of organization known as object-oriented programming (OOP). At the very top of the hierarchy for any given application is the `Application` object. You go through this object to get to other objects that are lower in the hierarchy.

Master It By using *creatable* objects, you can often omit the `Application` object when referencing it in code. What are creatable objects?

Use collections of objects. Collections are containers for a group of related objects, such as the `Documents` collection of `Document` objects.

Master It Are collections objects? Do they have their own methods and properties?

Find objects, properties, and methods. The Visual Basic Editor offers several ways to locate objects' members and add them to your programming code. There's an extensive Help system, the Object Browser, a List Properties/Methods tool, and the Auto List Members tool.

Master It How do you employ Auto List Members to find out which properties and methods are available for Word's `Document` object?

Use Object variables to represent objects. You can create variables that contain objects rather than typical values like strings or numbers.

Master It What keywords do you use to declare an Object variable?

Part 3

Making Decisions and Using Loops and Functions

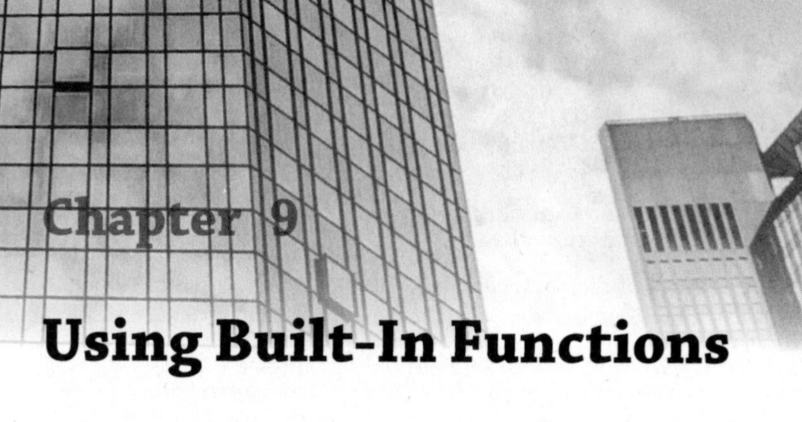

Chapter 9

Using Built-In Functions

VBA comes with a large number of built-in functions that perform commonly needed operations—everything from determining whether a file exists to returning the current date and converting data from one format to another. (For example, you can use a function to convert numeric data into a text string.)

In this book, I generically refer to most VBA language components (VBA's diction) as *commands*. But in this chapter, though, we'll call them *functions*. Other names that are sometimes used—more or less accurately—for these built-in commands include: operations, methods (with objects), routines, procedures, and stored procedures.

This chapter demonstrates what functions are, what they do, and how to use them. Along the way, you'll get to know some of the key functions built into VBA—including functions that convert data from one data type to another, functions that manage file operations, functions that do math, and many others.

You can also create custom functions of your own to supplement VBA's built-in functions. The next chapter tells you how to build your own when VBA's functions don't meet your special needs.

IN THIS CHAPTER, YOU WILL LEARN TO DO THE FOLLOWING:

- Understand what functions are and what they do
- Use functions
- Use key VBA functions
- Convert data from one type to another
- Manipulate strings and dates

What Is a Function?

A *function* is a type of procedure. In the BASIC language (of which VBA is a descendant), a function differs from a subroutine (subprocedure) in that a function always returns a value and a subroutine doesn't. And in common practice, a function almost always takes one or more arguments. Although subroutines *can* be written to take arguments, most programmers don't write their code this way.

Other computer languages don't make a distinction between function and subroutine. So, to sum up, here are the key differences between functions and subroutines in VBA:

Subroutines These never return values and are rarely sent arguments. Subs are also generally self-contained.

Functions These communicate more with code outside their own, accepting incoming data from arguments, processing that data in some way, and sending back a result to other code.

You'll often use the functions that are built into VBA. Typically, you feed information into a built-in function by sending it arguments. The built-in function then processes that info and returns a value for you to use.

Built-in functions are so essential to VBA that you've already used several in examples in this book. However, we'll now explore them more fully. For example, in Chapter 7, "Using Array Variables," you used the `Rnd` function to generate random numbers to fill an array named `intArray`, and the `Int` function to turn the random numbers into integers:

```
intArray(i) = Int(Rnd * 10)
```

`Rnd` is one of the rare functions that does not have to take one or more arguments. (`Rnd` *can* take one optional argument, but the previous example doesn't use it.)

The `Int` function, on the other hand, requires an argument—the number or expression that you want turned into an integer. The argument in this example is supplied by the expression `Rnd * 10`. Here the `Rnd` function returns a value that the `Int` function uses. The `Int` function then returns a value to the procedure, which uses it to populate a subscript in the array.

An *argument* is a piece of information that gets passed to a function. (Arguments are also passed to objects' methods and other commands.) You can tell when arguments are optional in Help descriptions because they're shown enclosed within brackets. When they are optional, you can either provide or omit the arguments displayed in the brackets. For example, the full Help syntax for the `Rnd` function looks like this:

```
Rnd([number]) As Single
```

The brackets indicate that the *`number`* argument is optional, and the `As Single` part of the syntax denotes that the value *returned* by the function will be of the Single data type.

Different functions return different data types suited to their jobs: Many functions return a Variant, but yes/no functions, such as the `IsNumeric` function used in Chapter 7, return a Boolean value, either `True` or `False`. When necessary, VBA may even sometimes convert the result of a function to a different data type needed by another function in the expression.

If any pair of brackets contains two arguments, you have to use both of them at once (blessedly, this is quite rare). For example, the `MsgBox` function displays a message box. The syntax for the `MsgBox` function is as follows:

```
MsgBox(prompt[, buttons] [, title][, helpfile, context])
```

Here, *`prompt`* is the only required argument: *`buttons`*, *`title`*, *`helpfile`*, and *`context`* are all optional, they're bracketed. But notice that *`helpfile`* and *`context`* are enclosed within a single set of brackets instead of each having its own pair, meaning that you need to use either both of these arguments or neither of them. You cannot use one without the other. Chapter 13, "Getting User Input with Message Boxes and Input Boxes," shows you how to use the `MsgBox` function in your code.

Using Functions

To use a function, you *call* (execute) it from a procedure in your code.

To call a function, you can use a `Call` statement, either with the optional `Call` keyword or by just using the name of the function. Using the `Call` keyword allows you to search through all calls in your project by searching for "call " (*call* followed by a space). However, using the `Call` keyword is overkill for everyday functions; programmers rarely use it.

The syntax for the `Call` statement is as follows:

```
[Call] name [argumentlist]
```

Here, *`name`* is a required String argument giving the name of the function or procedure to call, and *`argumentlist`* is an optional argument providing a comma-delimited list of the variables, arrays, or expressions to pass to the function or procedure. When calling a function, you'll almost always need to pass arguments (except for those few functions that take no arguments).

The brackets around the `Call` keyword indicate that it is optional. If you do use this keyword, you need to enclose the *`argumentlist`* argument in parentheses. In most cases, it's easier to read the code if you don't use the `Call` keyword when calling a function.

For example, the following statement calls the `MsgBox` function, supplying the required argument *`prompt`* (in this example, it's the string `Hello, World!`):

```
MsgBox "Hello, World!"
```

You could use the `Call` keyword instead, as shown in the following statement, but there's little advantage in doing so:

```
Call MsgBox "Hello, World!"
```

(Note that the `MsgBox` function is one of the few with which you can omit the parentheses around the argument list.)

You can assign to a variable the result returned by a function. For example, consider the following code fragment. The first two of the following statements declare the String variables `strExample` and `strLeft10`. The third statement assigns a string of text to `strExample`. The fourth statement uses the `Left` function to return the leftmost 10 characters from `strExample` and assign them to `strLeft10`, which the fifth statement then displays in a message box (see Figure 9.1):

```
Dim strExample As String
Dim strLeft10 As String
strExample = "Technology is interesting."
strLeft10 = Left(strExample, 10)
MsgBox strLeft10
```

If you prefer, you can assign the result of a function to a variable, as in this next example. Here the first String variable, `str1`, is assigned the leftmost 13 characters from the string `This is Pride and Patriotism`. So after its code line executes, `str1` holds the value `This is Pride`. Then `str2` is assigned the rightmost five characters from `str1`, resulting in `Pride`.

```
Dim str1 As String
Dim str2 As String
```

```
str1 = Left("This is Pride and Patriotism", 13)
str2 = Right(str1, 5)

MsgBox str2
```

FIGURE 9.1 Using the `Left` function to take the left part of a string—in this case, the first 10 characters of the string

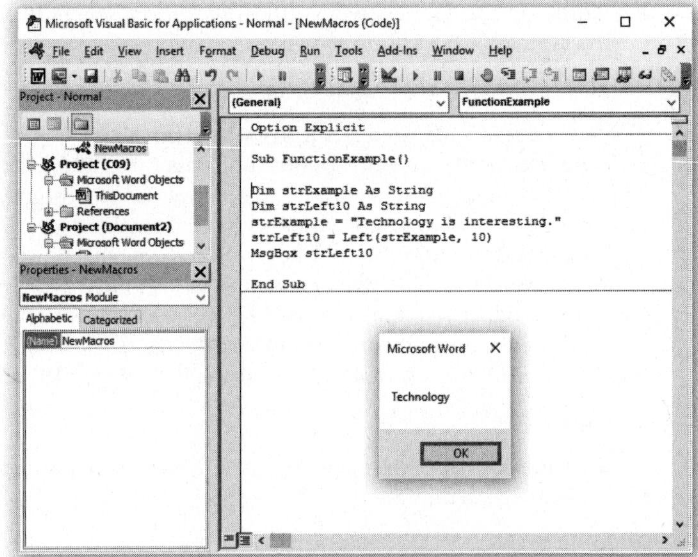

However, after you become accustomed to working with functions, you can collapse them in various ways in your code. Instead of assigning the result of a function to a variable, you can insert it directly in your code or pass it (as an argument) to another function. This is a common shortcut. Take a look at the following statement. It does the same thing as the previous example but collapses the code into one line, avoiding the use of variables altogether:

```
MsgBox Right(Left("This is Pride and Patriotism", 13), 5)
```

This statement uses three functions: the `MsgBox` function, the `Left` function, and the `Right` function. (The `Right` function is the counterpart of the `Left` function and returns the specified number of characters from the right side of the specified string.)

When you have multiple sets of parentheses in a VBA statement, the code is executed starting from the innermost pair of parentheses and working outward. This is the same way that nested parentheses are handled in math.

Therefore, in the previous example the `Left` function is evaluated first, returning the leftmost 13 characters in the string: `This is Pride` (the spaces are characters too). VBA passes this new string to the `Right` function, which in this case returns the rightmost five characters from it: `Pride`. VBA then passes this second new string to the `MsgBox` function, which displays it in a message box.

LIMIT YOUR NESTING

You can nest functions to many levels without giving VBA any trouble, but multilevel nesting can become hard for us humans to read and troubleshoot. For most practical purposes, it's a good idea to limit nesting to only a few levels, if that.

Passing Arguments to a Function

When a function takes more than one argument, you can pass the arguments to it in any of three ways:

- By supplying the argument values, without their names, *positionally* (in the order in which the function expects them)
- By supplying the arguments, with their names, in the order in which the function expects them
- By supplying the arguments, with their names, in any order you choose

The first method, supplying the arguments positionally without using their names, is usually the quickest way to proceed. The only disadvantage to doing so is that someone reading your code might not know immediately which value corresponds to which argument—although they can look this up without trouble. To omit an optional argument, you place a comma where it would appear in the sequence of arguments.

It does take extra time to type in argument names, but it makes your code easier to read. And when you omit an argument from a named argument list, you don't need to use the comma to indicate that you're skipping it.

There's no advantage to using named arguments out of order over using them in order unless you happen to find doing so easier.

For example, the `DateSerial` function returns a Variant/Date containing the date for the given year, month, and day. The syntax for `DateSerial` is as follows:

```
DateSerial(year, month, day)
```

Here, *`year`* is a required Integer argument supplying the year, *`month`* is a required Integer argument supplying the month, and *`day`* is a required Integer argument supplying the day.

The following statement supplies the arguments positionally without their names:

```
MsgBox DateSerial(2016, 12, 31)
```

This statement is equivalent but supplies the arguments positionally with their names:

```
MsgBox DateSerial(Year:=2016, Month:=12, Day:=31)
```

The following statement supplies the arguments, with their names, out of order:

```
MsgBox DateSerial(Day:=31, Year:=2016, Month:=12)
```

All three of these statements work fine and achieve the same result. You'll cause a problem only if you list out-of-order arguments that you're supplying without names (positionally), if you name some arguments and don't name others, or if you omit required arguments. Figure 9.2 shows one of the errors you may encounter. In this case, I left out the required `month` argument.

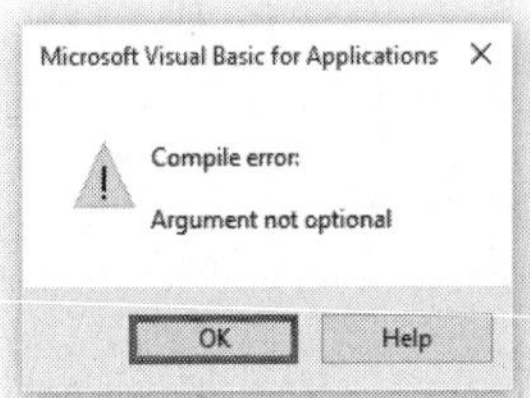

FIGURE 9.2 An "Argument not optional" error occurs when you omit a required argument.

Using Functions to Convert Data

In VBA you don't often have to convert data types, but you might as well at least understand what it does. Some computer languages are pretty strict about requiring explicit data typing (sometimes called *strong data typing*). And there *are* a few specialized situations even in VBA where you will need to convert one variable type into another. For example, you might be using the `InputBox` command to get some information from the user. The user is typing on a keyboard, so all the data they input will be characters (text string) data. But if your macro needs to do any math with this input, such as using the + command to add numbers, you would first want to convert the string data into numeric variables (or use the default Variant type). To convert a string to an integer number, you could use the `Cint` command. This same issue arises if you are importing data from another source, such as a database that stores everything as a String variable.

VBA provides a full set of simple functions for converting data from one data type to another. Table 9.1 lists VBA's functions for simple data conversion.

TABLE 9.1: VBA's functions for simple data conversion

FUNCTION (ARGUMENTS)	DATA TYPE RETURNED
`CBool(`*`number`*`)`	Boolean
`CByte(`*`expression`*`)`	Byte
`CCur(`*`expression`*`)`	Currency
`CDate(`*`expression`*`)`	Date
`CDec(`*`expression`*`)`	Decimal

FUNCTION (ARGUMENTS)	DATA TYPE RETURNED
`CDbl(`*expression*`)`	Double
`CInt(`*expression*`)`	Integer
`CLng(`*expression*`)`	Long
`CSng(`*expression*`)`	Single
`CStr(`*expression*`)`	String
`CVar(`*expression*`)`	Variant

For example, the following statements declare the untyped variable `varMyInput` and the Integer variable `intMyVar` and then display an input box prompting the user to enter an integer. In the third statement, the user's input is assigned to `varMyInput`, which automatically becomes a Variant/String. The fourth statement uses the `CInt` function to convert `varMyInput` to an integer, assigning the result to `intMyVar`. The fifth statement compares `intMyVar` to `10`, converts the result to Boolean by using the `CBool` function, and displays the result (`True` or `False`) in a message box.

```
Dim varMyInput
Dim intMyVar As Integer
varMyInput = InputBox("Enter an integer:", "10 Is True, Other Numbers Are False")
intMyVar = CInt(varMyInput)
MsgBox CBool(intMyVar = 10)
```

Recall that a Boolean variable is either `True` or `False`. So, in the final line of this example, you're saying in effect, "If the value in the variable `intMyVar` is 10, the Boolean result will be `True`. If the value is anything other than 10, the result will be `False`."

VBA also has a set of functions that manipulate data in more complicated ways. Only two of these more complex manipulation functions—`Format` and `Chr`—are used much in VBA programming, so we'll explore them in depth in this chapter.

Table 9.2 lists VBA's functions for more complex data manipulation.

TABLE 9.2: VBA's functions for complex data conversion

FUNCTION (ARGUMENTS)	RETURNS
`Asc(`*string*`)`	The ANSI character code for the first character in the string.
`Chr(`*number*`)`	The string for the specified character code (a number between 0 and 255).

TABLE 9.2: VBA's functions for complex data conversion *(CONTINUED)*

FUNCTION (ARGUMENTS)	RETURNS
`Format(`*`expression, format`*`)`	A Variant containing *`expression`* formatted as specified by *`format`*. (You'll see how `Format` works in "Using the `Format` Function to Format an Expression" later in the chapter.)
`Hex(`*`number`*`)`	A string containing the hexadecimal value of *`number`*.
`Oct(`*`number`*`)`	A string containing the octal value of *`number`*.
`RGB(`*`number1, number2, number3`*`)`	A Long integer representing the color value specified by *`number1`*, *`number2`*, and *`number3`*.
`QBColor(`*`number`*`)`	A Long containing the RGB value for the specified color.
`Str(`*`number`*`)`	A Variant/String containing a string representation of *`number`*. Use the superior `CStr` function instead.
`Val(`*`string`*`)`	The numeric portion of *`string`*; if *`string`* does not have a numeric portion, `Val` returns 0. Use the superior `CInt` function instead.

Using the *Asc* Function to Return a Character Code

This function isn't used much. `Asc` tells you which numeric value has been assigned to a particular letter according to the ANSI character code that's used in Windows. A *character code* is a list of numbers by which computers refer to letters of the alphabet. For example, the character code used in Windows for a capital *A* is 65 and for a capital *B* is 66; a lowercase *a* is 97, and a lowercase *b* is 98.

The syntax for the `Asc` function is straightforward:

```
Asc(string)
```

Here, `string` is any string expression. For example, `Asc("A")` returns 65.

The following statements use the `Asc` function to return the character code for the first character of the current selection in the active document and display that code in a message box:

```
strThisCharacter = Asc(Selection.Text)
MsgBox strThisCharacter, vbOKOnly, "Character Code"
```

Using the *Val* Function to Extract a Number from the Start of a String

The `Val` function, like `Asc`, is not used much, but for completeness, I've included it. The `Val` function converts the numbers contained in a text string into a numeric value. `Val` follows these rules:

- It reads only numbers in a string.
- It starts at the beginning of the string and reads only as far as the string contains characters that it recognizes as numbers (digits).

- It ignores tabs, line feeds, and blank spaces.
- It recognizes the period as a decimal separator, but not the comma.

This means that if you feed `Val` a string consisting of tabbed columns of numbers, such as the second line here, it will read them as a single number (in this case, 445634.994711):

```
Item#   Price  Available   On Order  Ordered
 4456   34.99       4          7         11
```

If, however, you feed it something containing a mix of numbers and letters, `Val` will read only the numbers and strings recognized as numeric expressions (for example, `Val("4E5")` returns 400000 because it reads the expression as exponentiation). For example, if fed the address shown in the next example, `Val` returns 8661, ignoring the other numbers in the string (because it stops at the *L* of *Laurel*, the first character that isn't a number, a tab, a line feed, or a space):

```
8661 Laurel Avenue Suite 3806, Oakland, CA 94610
```

The syntax for `Val` is straightforward:

```
Val(string)
```

Here, *`string`* is a required argument consisting of any string expression.

The following statement uses `Val` to return the numeric variable `StreetNumber` from the string `Address1`:

```
StreetNumber = Val(Address1)
```

USING *CINT* INSTEAD OF *VAL*

You should generally use the `CInt` function rather than the `Val` function when converting text to numbers. The reason is that CInt takes into account where you are located (the *regional settings* in Windows). In America, for example, we use a comma to indicate thousands: 12,000. The `CInt` function can handle this; `Val` cannot (and converts "12,000" into 12):

```
Dim StrVar As String
StrVar = "12,000"
MsgBox "Val = " & Val(StrVar) & "  CInt = " & CInt(StrVar)
```

When you execute this code, you'll see the result shown in the following message box. This illustrates why you should use `CInt` rather than `Val`.

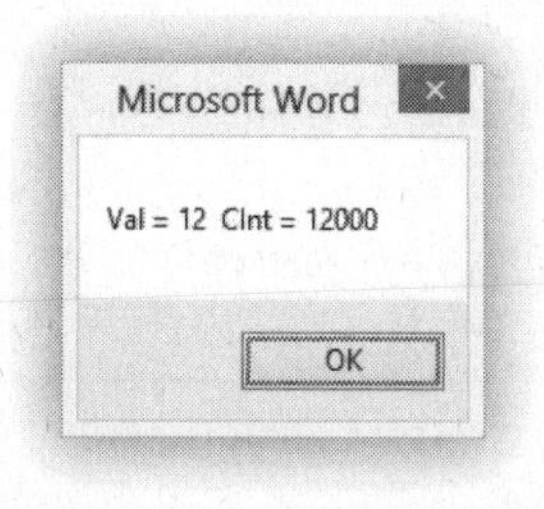

Remember that `Val` stops when it reaches the first nondigit character. So that comma trips it up when trying to convert 12,000.

Using the *Str* Function to Convert a Number into a String

Just as you can use `CInt` to convert a text string into a numeric value as described in the previous section, you can also convert a numeric value to a string with the `Str` function. But you should use the newer `CStr` function rather than the `Str` function, for the same reasons that `CInt` is superior to the older `Val` command.

You'll need to convert a number to a string when you want to *concatenate* the information contained in a value with a string. Concatenation means appending one string to another, as in `"123" & "654"`, which results in the text `"123654"`. This result is quite distinct from adding these two numbers together mathematically.

Concatenation cannot be accomplished by simply using the + operator because VBA would attempt to perform the mathematical operation addition rather than the string operation you want: concatenation.

A text string is just that: text. It's one or more alphanumeric characters, such as "55"—and that's quite different from the number 55. You can't concatenate "55" and 55. They're not the same kind of data at all.

Here's an example. Suppose you've declared a String variable named `strYourAge` and a numeric variable named `intAge`. You can't use a `strYourAge + intAge` statement to concatenate them because they're different data types. You first need to create a string from the `intAge` variable and then concatenate that string with the `strYourAge` string. (Alternatively, you can use the & operator to concatenate the two variables.)

To convert a value to a string, use the `CInt` function. The syntax for the `CInt` function is this:

```
CInt(number)
```

Here, *`number`* is a variable containing a numeric expression (such as an Integer data type, a Long data type, or a Double data type).

The following short procedure provides an example of converting a value to a string:

```
Sub Age()
    Dim intAge As Integer, strYourAge As String
    intAge = InputBox("Enter your age:", "Age")
    strYourAge = "Your age is " & CInt(intAge) & "."
    MsgBox strYourAge, vbOKOnly + vbInformation, "Age"
End Sub
```

Using a Declaration Shortcut

Notice in the example `Sub Age` how the `Dim` statement uses a kind of shorthand. Two different variables, separated by a comma, are declared on the same line using the same `Dim` command. This is equivalent to:

```
Dim intAge As Integer
Dim strYourAge As String
```

Using the *Format* Function to Format an Expression

The `Format` function is a powerful tool for changing numbers, dates and times, and strings into a format that you prefer.

The syntax for the `Format` function is as follows:

```
Format(expression[, format[, firstdayofweek[, firstweekofyear]]])
```

These are the components of the syntax:

- *`expression`* is any valid expression.
- *`format`* is an optional argument specifying a named format expression or a user-defined format expression. More on this in a moment.
- *`firstdayofweek`* is an optional constant specifying the day that starts the week (for date information): The default setting is `vbSunday` (`1`), but you can also set `vbMonday` (`2`), `vbTuesday` (`3`), `vbWednesday` (`4`), `vbThursday` (`5`), `vbFriday` (`6`), `vbSaturday` (`7`), or `vb UseSystem` (`0`; uses the system setting).
- *`firstweekofyear`* is an optional constant specifying the week considered first in the year (again, for date information), as shown in Table 9.3.

TABLE 9.3: Constants that specify how a year starts

CONSTANT	VALUE	YEAR STARTS WITH WEEK
`vbUseSystem`	`0`	Use the system setting.
`vbFirstJan1`	`1`	The week in which January 1 falls (the default setting).
`vbFirstFourDays`	`2`	The first week with a minimum of four days in the year.
`vbFirstFullWeek`	`3`	The first full week (seven days) of the year.

You can define your own formats for the `Format` function as described in the following sections if none of the predefined numeric formats (described next) suit your needs.

USING PREDEFINED NUMERIC FORMATS

Table 9.4 lists the predefined numeric formats that you can use with the `Format` function.

TABLE 9.4: Predefined numeric formats

FORMAT NAME	EXPLANATION	EXAMPLE
General Number	The number is displayed with no thousand separator.	`124589`
Currency	The number is displayed with two decimal places, a thousand separator, and the currency symbol appropriate to the system locale.	`$1,234.56`
Fixed	The number is displayed with two decimal places and at least one integer place.	`5.00`
Standard	The number is displayed with two decimal places, at least one integer place, and a thousand separator (when needed).	`1,225.00`
Percent	The number is displayed multiplied by 100, with two decimal places and with a percent sign.	`78.00%`
Scientific	The number is displayed in scientific notation.	`5.00E+00`
Yes/No	A nonzero number is displayed as `Yes`; a zero number is displayed as `No`.	`Yes`
True/False	A nonzero number is displayed as `True`; a zero number is displayed as `False`.	`False`
On/Off	A nonzero number is displayed as `On`; a zero number is displayed as `Off`.	`Off`

For example, the following statement returns $123.45:

```
Format("12345", "Currency")
```

CREATING A NUMERIC FORMAT

If none of the predefined numeric formats suit your needs, you can create your own numeric formats by using your choice of a combination of the characters listed in Table 9.5.

TABLE 9.5: Characters for creating your own number formats

CHARACTER	EXPLANATION
`[None]`	Displays the number without any formatting. (You won't usually want to use this option.)
`0`	Placeholder for a digit. If there's no digit, VBA displays a zero. If the number has fewer digits than you use zeroes, VBA displays leading or trailing zeroes as appropriate.

CHARACTER	EXPLANATION
`#`	Placeholder for a digit. If there's no digit, VBA displays nothing.
`.`	Placeholder for a decimal. Indicates where the decimal separator should fall. The decimal separator varies by locale (for example, a decimal point in the United States, a comma in Germany).
`%`	Placeholder for a percent character. VBA inserts the percent character and multiplies the expression by 100.
`,`	Thousand separator (depending on locale, a comma or a period).
`:`	Time separator (typically a colon, but again this depends on the locale).
`/`	Date separator. (Again, what you'll see depends on the locale.)
`E- E+ e- e+`	Scientific format: `E-` or `e-` places a minus sign next to negative exponents. `E+` or `e+` places a minus sign next to negative exponents and places a plus sign next to positive exponents.
`- + $ ( )`	Displays a literal character.
`\[character]`	Displays the literal character.
`"[string]"`	Displays the literal character. Use `Chr(34)` (the character code for double quotation marks) to provide the double quotation marks.

For example, the following statement returns a currency formatted with four decimal places:

```
Format("123456", "$00.0000")
```

Creating a Date or Time Format

Similarly, you can create your own date and time formats by mixing and matching the characters listed in Table 9.6.

TABLE 9.6: Characters for creating your own date and time formats

CHARACTER	EXPLANATION
`:`	Time separator (typically a colon, but this depends on the locale).
`/`	Date separator (also locale-dependent).
`C`	Displays the date (if there is a date or an integer value) in the system's short date format and the time (if there is a date or a fractional value) in the system's default time format.

TABLE 9.6: Characters for creating your own date and time formats *(CONTINUED)*

CHARACTER	EXPLANATION
D	Displays the date (1 to 31) without a leading zero for single-digit numbers.
Dd	Displays the date with a leading zero for single-digit numbers (01 to 31).
Ddd	Displays the day as a three-letter abbreviation (Sun, Mon, Tue, Wed, Thu, Fri, Sat) with no period.
Dddd	Displays the full name of the day.
Ddddd	Displays the complete date (day, month, and year) in the system's short date format.
Dddddd	Displays the complete date (day, month, and year) in the system's long date format.
aaaa	Displays the full, localized name of the day.
w	Displays an integer from 1 (Sunday) to 7 (Monday) containing the day of the week.
ww	Displays an integer from 1 to 54 giving the number of the week in the year. The number of weeks is 54 rather than 52 because most years start and end with partial weeks rather than having 52 start-to-finish weeks.
m	Displays an integer from 1 to 12 giving the number of the month without a leading zero on single-digit months. When used after h, returns minutes instead of months.
mm	Displays a number from 01 to 12 giving the two-digit number of the month. When used after h, returns minutes instead of months.
mmm	Displays the month as a three-letter abbreviation (except for May) without a period.
mmmm	Displays the full name of the month.
oooo	Displays the full localized name of the month.
q	Displays a number from 1 to 4 giving the quarter of the year.
y	Displays an integer from 1 to 366 giving the day of the year.
yy	Displays a number from 00 to 99 giving the two-digit year.
yyyy	Displays a number from 0100 to 9999 giving the four-digit year.
h	Displays a number from 0 to 23 giving the hour.
Hh	Displays a number from 00 to 23 giving the two-digit hour.
N	Displays a number from 0 to 60 giving the minute.
Nn	Displays a number from 00 to 60 giving the two-digit minute.

CHARACTER	EXPLANATION
S	Displays a number from 0 to 60 giving the second.
Ss	Displays a number from 00 to 60 giving the two-digit second.
ttttt	Displays the full time (hour, minute, and second) in the system's default time format.
AM/PM	Uses the 12-hour clock and displays AM or PM as appropriate.
am/pm	Uses the 12-hour clock and displays am or pm as appropriate.
A/P	Uses the 12-hour clock and displays A or P as appropriate.
a/p	Uses the 12-hour clock and displays a or p as appropriate.
AMPM	Uses the 12-hour clock and displays the AM or PM string literal defined for the system.

For example, the following statement returns `Saturday, April 01, 2016`:

```
Format(#4/1/2016#, "dddddd")
```

CREATING A STRING FORMAT

The `Format` function also lets you create custom string formats using the options shown in Table 9.7.

TABLE 9.7: Characters for creating your own string formats

CHARACTER	EXPLANATION
@	Placeholder for a character. Displays a character if there is one, and a space if there is none.
&	Placeholder for a character. Displays a character if there is one, and nothing if there is none.
<	Displays the string in lowercase.
>	Displays the string in uppercase.
!	Causes VBA to fill placeholders from left to right instead of from right to left (the default direction).

For example, the following statement assigns to `strUser` a string consisting of four spaces if there is no input in the input box:

```
strUser = Format(InputBox("Enter your name:"), "@@@@")
```

Using the *Chr* Function and Constants to Enter Special Characters in a String

To insert special characters (such as a carriage return or a tab) into a string, specify the built-in constant (for those special characters that have built-in constants defined) or enter the appropriate character code using the `Chr` function. The syntax for the `Chr` function is straightforward:

```
Chr(charactercode)
```

Here, *charactercode* is a number that identifies the special character you want to add.

Table 9.8 lists the most useful character codes and character constants.

TABLE 9.8: VBA character codes and character constants

CODE	BUILT-IN CHARACTER CONSTANT	CHARACTER
`Chr(9)`	`vbTab`	Tab
`Chr(10)`	`vbLf`	Line feed
`Chr(11)`	`vbVerticalTab`	Soft return (Shift+Enter)
`Chr(12)`	`vbFormFeed`	Page break
`Chr(13)`	`vbCr`	Carriage return
`Chr(13) + Chr(10)`	`vbCrLf`	Carriage return/line feed combination
`Chr(14)`	—	Column break
`Chr(34)`	—	Double straight quotation marks (")
`Chr(39)`	—	Single straight quotation mark/apostrophe (')
`Chr(145)`	—	Opening single smart quotation mark (‘)
`Chr(146)`	—	Closing single smart quotation mark/apostrophe (’)
`Chr(147)`	—	Opening double smart quotation mark (“)
`Chr(148)`	—	Closing double smart quotation mark (”)
`Chr(149)`	—	Bullet
`Chr(150)`	—	En dash
`Chr(151)`	—	Em dash

Here's a practical example exploiting the Chr function. Say you want to build a string containing a person's name and address from individual strings containing items of that information. You also want the individual items separated by tabs in the resulting string so that you could insert the string into a document and then easily convert it into a table.

To do this, you could use the following code:

```
Sub FormatTabular()

Dim i As Integer
Dim strFirstName As String
Dim strLastName As String
Dim strAddress As String
Dim strCity As String
Dim strState As String
Dim strAllInfo As String

strFirstName = "Phil"
strLastName = "Mortuqye"
strAddress = "12 Batwing Dr."
strCity = "Tulsa"
strState = "OK"

    strAllInfo = strFirstName & vbTab & strLastName _
        & vbTab & strAddress & vbTab & strCity _
        & vbTab & strState & vbCr

    Selection.TypeText strAllInfo
End Sub
```

String variables are assigned to the string strAllInfo by concatenating the strings strFirstName, strLastName, and so on with tabs—vbTab characters—between them. The final character added to the built string is vbCr (a carriage-return character), which creates a new paragraph.

The final line enters the strAllInfo string into the current document, thereby building a tab-delimited list containing the names and addresses. This list can then be easily converted into a table with columns that each contain one item of information: The first column contains the strFirstName string, the second column the strLastName string, and so on.

Using Functions to Manipulate Strings

String variables are often useful for holding text. You can use them to store any quantity of text, from a character or two up to a large number of pages from a Word document or other text document. You can also use strings to store specialized information, such as filenames and folder names. Once you've stored text in a string, you can manipulate it according to your needs.

Table 9.9 lists VBA's built-in functions for manipulating strings. Because many of these functions are useful and some are complex, you'll find detailed examples after the table.

TABLE 9.9: VBA's string-manipulation functions

FUNCTION (ARGUMENTS)	RETURNS
`InStr(`*`start, string1, string2, compare`*`)`	A Variant/Long giving the position of the first instance of the search string (*string2*) inside the target string (*string1*), starting from the beginning of the target string
`InStrRev(`*`stringcheck, stringmatch, start, compare`*`)`	A Variant/Long giving the position of the first instance of the search string (*stringmatch*) inside the target string (*stringcheck*), starting from the end of the target string
`LCase(`*`string`*`)`	A String containing the lowercased *string*
`Left(`*`string, number`*`)`	A Variant/String containing the specified number of characters from the left end of *string*
`Len(`*`string`*`)`	A Long containing the number of characters in *string*
`LTrim(`*`string`*`)`	A Variant/String containing *string* with any leading spaces trimmed off it
`Mid(`*`string, start, length`*`)`	A Variant/String containing the specified number of characters from the specified starting point within *string*
`Right(`*`string, number`*`)`	A Variant/String containing the specified number of characters from the right end of *string*
`RTrim(`*`string`*`)`	A Variant/String containing *string* with any trailing spaces trimmed off it
`Space(`*`number`*`)`	A Variant/String containing *number* of spaces
`StrComp(`*`string1, string2, compare`*`)`	A Variant/Integer containing the result of comparing *string1* and *string2*
`StrConv(`*`string, conversion, LCID`*`)`	A Variant/String containing *string* converted as specified by *conversion* for the (optional) specified Locale ID (*LCID*)
`String(`*`number, character`*`)`	A Variant/String containing *number* of instances of *character*
`StrReverse(`*`expression`*`)`	A String containing the characters of *expression* in reverse order
`Trim(`*`string`*`)`	A Variant/String containing *string* with any leading spaces or trailing spaces trimmed off it
`UCase(`*`string`*`)`	A String containing the uppercased *string*

Using the *Left*, *Right*, and *Mid* Functions to Return Part of a String

Sometimes you'll need to use only part of a string in your macros. For example, you might want to take only the first three characters of the name of a city to create a location code.

VBA provides several functions for returning from strings the characters you need:

- The `Left` function returns a specified number of characters from the left end of the string.
- The `Right` function returns a specified number of characters from the right end of the string.
- The `Mid` function returns a specified number of characters starting from a specified location inside a string.

SOME STRING FUNCTIONS COME IN TWO FLAVORS

VBA provides two versions of a number of string functions, including the `Left`, `Right`, and `Mid` functions: the versions shown here, which return String-type Variant values, and versions whose names end with `$` (`Left$`, `Right$`, `Mid$`, and so on), which return pure String values.

The functions that return the pure Strings run faster (though you're not likely to notice any difference in normal use) but return an error if you use them on a `Null` value. The functions that return the String-type Variants can deal with `Null` values with no problem. Which approach you employ can depend on, for example, the type of data you're manipulating. Some databases employ `Null`, some do not.

USING THE *LEFT* FUNCTION

The `Left` function returns the specified number of characters from the left end of a string. The syntax for the `Left` function is as follows:

```
Left(string, length)
```

Here, the *`string`* argument is any string expression—that is, any expression that returns a sequence of contiguous characters. `Left` returns `Null` if *`string`* contains no data. The *`length`* argument is a numeric expression specifying the number of characters to return. *`length`* can be a straightforward number (such as 4, or 7, or 11) or it can be an expression that results in a number. For example, if the length of a word were stored in the variable named `LenWord` and you wanted to return two characters fewer than `LenWord`, you could specify the expression `LenWord - 2` as the *`length`* argument; to return three characters more than `LenWord`, you could specify `LenWord + 3` as the *`length`* argument.

One way to use the `Left` function would be to separate the area code from a telephone number that was provided as an unseparated 10-digit number from a database. In the following statements, the telephone number is stored in the String variable `strPhone`, which the code assumes was created earlier:

```
Dim strArea As String
strArea = Left(strPhone, 3)
```

These statements create the variable `Area` and fill it with the leftmost three characters of the variable `strPhone`.

USING THE *RIGHT* FUNCTION

The `Right` function is the mirror image of the `Left` function. `Right` returns a specified number of characters from the right end of a string. The syntax for the `Right` function is as follows:

```
Right(string, length)
```

Again, the *`string`* argument is any string expression, and *`length`* is a numeric expression specifying the number of characters to return. And, again, `Right` returns `Null` if *`string`* contains no data, and *length* can be a number or an expression that results in a number.

To continue the previous example, you could use the `Right` function to separate the last seven digits of the phone number stored in the string `strPhone` from the area code:

```
Dim strLocalNumber As String
strLocalNumber = Right(strPhone, 7)
```

These statements create the variable `strLocalNumber` and fill it with the rightmost seven characters from the variable `strPhone`.

USING THE *MID* FUNCTION

The `Left` and `Right` functions extract a substring from the left or right side of a string. The `Mid` function fetches a substring out of the middle of a string.

The `Mid` function returns a specified number of characters from inside a given string. You specify a starting position in the string and the number of characters (to the right of the starting position) that you want extracted.

The syntax for the `Mid` function is as follows:

```
Mid(string, start[, length])
```

Here are the elements of the syntax:

- As in `Left` and `Right`, the *`string`* argument is any string expression. `Mid` returns `Null` if *`string`* contains no data.
- *`start`* is a numeric value specifying the character position in *`string`* at which to start the *`length`* selection. If *`start`* is larger than the number of characters in *`string`*, VBA returns a zero-length string. In code, an empty string is typed as two quotation marks with nothing inside: `strState = ""`.
- *`length`* is an optional numeric expression specifying the number of characters to return. If you omit *`length`* or use a *`length`* argument greater than the number of characters in *`string`*, VBA returns all the characters from the *`start`* position to the end of *`string`*. *`length`* can be an ordinary literal number or an expression that results in a number.

Using the phone-number example, you could employ `Mid` to pluck the local exchange code out from within a 10-digit phone number (for instance, extract the 555 from 510**555**1212), like this:

```
Dim strPhone As String
```

```
strPhone = "5105551212"
MsgBox Mid(strPhone, 4, 3)
```

This statement displays three characters in the variable `strPhone`, starting at the fourth character.

Real World Scenario

DON'T TORTURE YOUR USERS—ACCEPT A VARIETY OF FORMATS

All too often programmers, for no good reason, make it hard for users to succeed. How many times have you tried to type your phone number in a website and been told that the only acceptable format is xxx-xxx-xxxx? Or (xxx) xxx-xxxx? Or numbers only? No spaces for you! You *will* do things our way. Well...why?

Why? Because the programmer was too lazy to spend a few extra minutes writing friendly code that would permit a variety of input.

People write down their phone number various ways. Some type it in like this: (xxx) xxx-xxxx; others favor variations like xxx xxx-xxxx. Have you seen those instructions that say "use no hyphens" or "you must use hyphens"?

This is simply slothful programming. The programmer doesn't want to take a little extra time to deal with varying input, so they transfer the work to the user. Instead, make life easier for your users by writing a little extra code to translate various typical formats into whatever your program expects. Don't force the users to provide data "just so."

Write some code that tests the user's input, yes—but also *you* translate that input into whatever format you need. Here are a few easy solutions:

Use the `InStr` function (described later in this chapter) to check for parentheses or hyphens. You can also use `Mid` to extract only the numeric values in the user's string entry—ignoring whatever blank spaces or nonnumeric characters the user might have typed in. Your program's goal is to end up with 5105551212. After extracting the non-digits, you can then show the user a *useful* error message if they have not entered the necessary 10 digits. Your program can't translate missing digits, so in this case you must require more input from the user.

Test the number with the `Len` function to see if there are 10 digits. If not, tell the user they made a mistake and to please reenter the phone number because there are not enough (or too many) digits.

Your error message should also display the user's entry so they can see the problem. But you're just being annoying if you tell them they can't use parentheses or hyphens or they *must* use those punctuation marks—to satisfy *you*. Who are you?

Always remember: Your code should accept several predictable variations of user input. There's no need to reject legitimate user input simply because that input is punctuated in a different way than your data store or your code prefers. After all, why waste the time of perhaps thousands of users when it only takes a little extra coding to accommodate them?

You've seen how to extract a substring using `Mid`, but this function has another use as well. You can also use `Mid` to *find* the location of a character within a string. In the following snippet, the `Do Until`...loop walks backward through the string `strFilename` (which contains the

`FullName` property of the template attached to the active document in Word) until it reaches the first backslash (\), storing the resulting character position in the Integer variable `intLen`. The message box then displays that part of `strFilename` to the right of the backslash (determined by subtracting `intLen` from the length of `strFilename`)—the name of the attached template without its path:

```
Dim strFilename As String, intLen As Integer
strFilename = ActiveDocument.AttachedTemplate.FullName
MsgBox strFilename

intLen = Len(strFilename)
Do Until Mid(strFilename, intLen, 1) = "\"
    intLen = intLen - 1
Loop
MsgBox Right(strFilename, Len(strFilename) - intLen)
```

This example is more illustrative than realistic for two reasons: First, you can get the name of the template more easily by just using the `Name` property rather than the `FullName` property. Second, there's a function called `InStrRev` (discussed next) that returns the position of one string within another by walking backward through it.

Using *InStr* and *InStrRev* to Find a String Within Another String

You can use the `Mid` function to find an individual character within a string, but what if you need to find a set of characters within a string? The `InStr` function is designed to find one string within another string. For example, you could check, say, the current paragraph to see if it contained a particular word. If it did, you could take action accordingly—for instance, replacing that word with another word or selecting the paragraph for inclusion in another document. Maybe your company has changed its name and you need to do a search and replace in a large number of document templates.

The `InStrRev` function is the counterpart of the `InStr` function, working in a similar way but in the reverse direction.

The syntax for `InStr` is as follows:

```
InStr([start, ]string1, string2[, compare])
```

Here are the arguments:

- *`start`* is an optional argument specifying the starting position in the first string, *`string1`*. If you omit *`start`*, VBA starts the search at the first character in *`string1`* (which is usually where you want to start). However, you do need to use *`start`* when you use the *`compare`* argument to specify the type of string comparison to perform.
- *`string1`* is a required argument specifying the string expression in which to search for *`string2`*.

- `string2` is a required argument specifying the string expression for which to search in `string1`.
- `compare` is an optional argument specifying the type of string comparison you want to perform. Text can be compared two ways: a *binary comparison*, which is case sensitive, or a *textual comparison*, which is not case sensitive. The default is a binary comparison, which you can specify by using the constant `vbBinaryCompare` or the value `0` for `compare`. Although specifying this value isn't necessary (because it's the default), you might want to include it to make your code ultra-clear. To specify a textual, case-insensitive comparison, use the constant `vbTextCompare` or the value `1` for `compare`.

Use Textual Comparisons with Unpredictable String Data

A textual comparison is a useful weapon when you're dealing with data that may arrive in a variety of ways, like the telephone-number punctuation problem described in this chapter's Real World Scenario. Here's another example: If you wanted to search a selection for instances of a name, you'd probably want to find *all* instances of the name—uppercase, lowercase, or title case (initial caps). Otherwise, you'd find only the name with exactly the same capitalization as you specified in the `String2` argument.

Another way to use `InStr` is to find the *location* of a certain string within another string so that you can then *change* that substring. You might want to do this if you needed to move a file from its current position in a particular folder or subfolder to another folder that had a similar subfolder structure. For instance, suppose you work with documents stored in a variety of subfolders beneath a folder named In (such as `z:\Documents\In\`), and after you're finished with them, you save them in corresponding subfolders beneath a folder named Out (`z:\Documents\Out\`). The short procedure shown in Listing 9.1 automatically saves the documents in the subfolder Out.

Listing 9.1: Changing a file path

```
Sub Save_in_Out_Folder()
    Dim strOName As String, strNName As String, _
        intToChange As Integer
    strOName = ActiveDocument.FullName
    intToChange = InStr(strOName, "\In\")
    strNName = Left(strOName, intToChange - 1) & "\Out\" _
        & Right(strOName, Len(strOName) - intToChange - 3)
    ActiveDocument.SaveAs strNName
End Sub
```

The code in Listing 9.1 works as follows:

- Line 1 begins the procedure, and line 7 ends it.
- Line 2 declares the String variable `strOName` (as in *original name*), the String variable `strNName` (as in *new name*), and the Integer variable `intToChange`. Line 3 then assigns `strOName` the `FullName` property of the `ActiveDocument` object: the full name of the active document, including the path to the document (for example, `z:\Documents\In\Letters\My Letter.docm`).
- Line 4 assigns to the variable `intToChange` the value of the `InStr` function that finds the string `\In\` in the variable `strOName`. Using the example path from the previous paragraph, `intToChange` will be assigned the value 13 because the first character of the `\In\` string is the thirteenth character in the `strOName` string.
- Line 5 assigns to the variable `strNName` the new filename created in the main part of the statement. This breaks down as follows:
  - `Left(strOName, intToChange - 1)` takes the left section of the `strOName` string, returning the number of characters specified by `intToChange - 1`—the number stored in `intToChange` minus one.
  - `& "\Out\"` adds to the partial string specified in the previous bullet item (to continue the previous example, `z:\Documents`) the characters `\Out\`, which effectively replace the `\In\` characters, thereby changing the directory name (`z:\Documents\Out\`).
  - `& Right(strOName, Len(strOName) - intToChange - 3)` completes the partial string by adding the right section of the `strOName` string, starting from after the `\In\` string (`Letters\My Letter.docm`), giving `z:\Documents\Out\Letters\My Letter.docm`. The number of characters to take from the right section is determined by subtracting the value stored in `intToChange` from the length of `strOName` and then subtracting 3 from the result. Here, the value 3 comes from the length of the string `\In\`; because the `intToChange` value stores the character number of the first backslash, you need count only the *I*, the *n*, and the second backslash to reach its end.
- Line 6 saves the document using the name in the `strNName` variable.

The syntax for `InStrRev` is similar to that of `InStr`:

```
InStrRev(stringcheck, stringmatch[, start[, compare]])
```

These are the arguments:

- *`stringcheck`* is a required String argument specifying the string in which to search for *`stringmatch`*.
- *`stringmatch`* is a required String argument specifying the string for which to search.
- *`start`* is an optional numeric argument specifying the starting position for the search. If you omit *`start`*, VBA starts at the last character of *`stringcheck`*.
- *`compare`* (as for `InStr`) is an optional argument specifying how to search: `vbTextCompare` for text, `vbBinaryCompare` for a binary comparison.

Using *LTrim*, *RTrim*, and *Trim* to Remove Spaces from a String

Often you'll need to trim strings before concatenating them to avoid ending up with extra spaces in inappropriate places, such as in the middle of eight-character filenames. Recall the telephone number example above where your program wanted no spaces, but the user is certainly permitted to input them without penalty.

Data can contain appended or prepended spaces, and always remember that users might randomly type spaces in various ways when entering data. You never know. Your programming (and databases), however, need data in a predictable format (so the data can easily be searched, sorted, and otherwise manipulated).

For example, if 500 users entered their zip codes, some might type a space before entering the digits. Any such entries would be placed at the start of a list after the list was alphabetically sorted (the space character is seen as "lower" than ordinary characters by a sorting function). So, the sort would produce an inaccurate result. It's easy, though, to use the `Trim` functions to get rid of spaces.

As you saw in Table 9.9, VBA provides three functions specifically for trimming leading spaces and trailing spaces from strings:

- `LTrim` removes leading spaces from the specified string.
- `RTrim` removes trailing spaces from the specified string.
- `Trim` removes both leading and trailing spaces from the specified string.

Trim Is Often the Only Space-Removal Function You Need

In many cases, you can simply use `Trim` instead of figuring out whether `LTrim` or `RTrim` is appropriate for what you expect a variable to contain. At other times, you'll need to remove either leading or trailing spaces while *retaining* spaces on the other end. In those special cases, you'll need to use either `LTrim` or `RTrim`. `RTrim` is especially useful for working with fixed-length String variables, which will contain trailing spaces if the data assigned to them is shorter than their fixed length.

The syntax for the `LTrim`, `RTrim`, and `Trim` functions is straightforward:

```
LTrim(string)
RTrim(string)
Trim(string)
```

In each case, `string` is any string expression.

You could use the `Trim` function to remove both leading and trailing spaces from a string derived from the current selection in the active document in Word. The first line in this next code example declares `strUntrimmed` and `strTrimmed` as String variables. The second line assigns the data in the current selection to the `strUntrimmed` string. The third line assigns the trimmed version of the `strUntrimmed` string to the `strTrimmed` string:

```
Dim strUntrimmed As String, strTrimmed As String
strUntrimmed = Selection.Text
strTrimmed = Trim(strUntrimmed)
```

Using *Len* to Check the Length of a String

To find out how long a string is, use the Len function. The syntax for the Len function is straightforward:

```
Len(string)
```

Here, *string* is any valid string expression. (If *string* is Null, Len also returns Null.)

One use for Len is to make sure a user's entry in an input box or in a text box on a form is of a suitable length. A United States phone number must be 10 digits, for instance.

The CheckPassword procedure shown in Listing 9.2 uses Len to make sure a password the user enters is long enough to be difficult to guess, but not too long.

LISTING 9.2: Testing password length with the Len function

```
1.  Sub CheckPassword()
2.      Dim strPassword As String
3.  BadPassword:
4.      strPassword = InputBox _
            ("Enter the password to protect this item from changes:" _
            , "Enter Password")
5.      If Len(strPassword) = 0 Then
6.          End
7.      ElseIf Len(strPassword) < 6 Then
8.          MsgBox "The password you chose is too short." _
                & vbCr & vbCr & _
                "Choose a password between 6 and 15 characters in length.", _
                 vbOKOnly + vbCritical, "Unsuitable Password"
9.          GoTo BadPassword
10.     ElseIf Len(strPassword) > 15 Then
11.         MsgBox "The password you chose is too long." _
                & vbCr & vbCr & _
                "Choose a password between 6 and 15 characters in length.", _
                vbOKOnly + vbCritical, "Unsuitable Password"
12.         GoTo BadPassword
13.     End If
14. End Sub
```

Listing 9.2 ensures that a password contains between 6 and 15 characters (inclusive). Here's how the code works:

- Line 2 declares a String variable named strPassword.
- Line 3 contains the label BadPassword, to which the GoTo statements in line 9 and line 12 redirect execution if the password fails either of the checks. Labels are locations within code that you might need to jump to during execution. A label is a word on its own line in the code that ends with a colon. Labels are discussed in Chapter 11, "Making Decisions in Your Code."

- Line 4 assigns to `strPassword` the result of an input box that invites the user to enter the password for the item.
- Lines 5 through 13 then use an `If` statement to check that the password is an appropriate length. First, line 5 checks `strPassword` for zero length, which would mean that the user clicked either the Cancel button or the Close button on the input box or clicked the OK button with no text entered in the input box. If the length of `strPassword` is zero, the `End` statement in line 6 terminates the procedure. If the password passes that test, line 7 checks to find out if its length is less than six characters; if so, the procedure displays a message box alerting the user to the problem and then redirects execution to the `BadPassword` label. If the password is six or more characters long, line 10 checks to see if it's more than 15 characters long; if it is, the user is shown another message box and another trip to the `BadPassword` label.

Using *StrConv*, *LCase*, and *UCase* to Change the Case of a String

If you need to change the case of a string, use the `StrConv` (short for *string conversion*), `LCase`, and `UCase` functions. Of these, the easiest to use is `StrConv`, which can convert a string to a variety of different formats varying from straightforward uppercase, lowercase, or *propercase* (as VBA refers to initial capitals, also known as title case) to the Japanese *hiragana* and *katakana* phonetic characters.

Using *StrConv*

The `StrConv` function has the following syntax:

```
StrConv(string, conversion)
```

Here, the *`string`* argument is any string expression, and the *`conversion`* argument is a constant or value specifying the type of conversion required. The most useful conversion constants and values are shown in Table 9.10.

Table 9.10: The most common conversion constants

Constant	Value	Effect
`vbUpperCase`	1	Converts the given string to uppercase characters
`vbLowerCase`	2	Converts the given string to lowercase characters
`vbProperCase`	3	Converts the given string to propercase (aka title case—the first letter of every word is capitalized)

TABLE 9.10: The most common conversion constants *(CONTINUED)*

CONSTANT	VALUE	EFFECT
`vbUnicode`	64	Converts the given string to Unicode using the system's default code page
`vbFromUnicode`	128	Converts the given string from Unicode to the system's default code page

For example, suppose you received from a database program a string called `strCustomerName` containing a person's name. You could use `StrConv` to make sure that it was in title case by using a statement such as this:

```
strProperCustomerName = StrConv(strCustomerName, vbProperCase)
```

STRCONV IGNORES THE CAPITALIZATION YOU FEED IT

Note that `StrConv` doesn't care about the case of the string you feed it—it simply returns the case you requested. For example, feeding `StrConv` uppercase and asking it to return uppercase doesn't cause any problem.

USING *LCASE* AND *UCASE*

If you don't feel like using `StrConv`, you can alternatively use the `LCase` and `UCase` functions, which convert a string to lowercase and uppercase, respectively. `LCase` is frequently used to avoid case-sensitivity in languages like XML that make a distinction (in their variable names) between upper- and lowercase letters. In other words, *`ThisVariableName`* and *`ThisVariablename`* are considered entirely different variables. If you try to use two variable names with different capitalization, the VBA Code Editor will automatically force them to be the identically capitalized.

VBA, however, *is* case-sensitive when comparing string data.

`LCase` and `UCase` have the following syntax:

```
LCase(string)
UCase(string)
```

Here, *`string`* is any string expression.

For example, the following statement lowercases the string `MyString` and assigns it to `MyLowerString`:

```
MyLowerString = LCase(MyString)
```

Using the *StrComp* Function to Compare Apples to Apples

As you've seen already, you can compare one item to another item by simply using the = operator:

```
If 1 = 1 Then MsgBox "One is one."
```

This straightforward comparison with the = operator also works with two strings, as shown in the second line here:

```
strPet = InputBox("Is your pet a dog or a cat?", "Pet")
If strPet = "Dog" Then MsgBox "We do not accept dogs."
```

The problem with this code as written is that the strings need to match exactly in capitalization for VBA to consider them equal. If the user enters `dog` or `DOG` (not to mention `dOG`, `doG`, `dOg`, or `DoG`) rather than `Dog`, the condition isn't met. Again, permit your users a variety of correct responses—don't enforce pointless capitalization and punctuation rules.

To accept variations of capitalization, you could use the `Or` operator to hedge your bets:

```
If Pet = "Dog" Or Pet = "dog" Or Pet = "DOG" Or Pet = "dogs" _
    Or Pet = "Dogs" or Pet = "DOGS" Then MsgBox _
    "We do not accept dogs."
```

As you can see, such code rapidly becomes clumsy, even omitting some variations such as `dOG`. Or you could change the case of one or both strings involved to make sure their case matched, but it's simpler to just use the `StrComp` function, which is designed to permit you to ignore case. The syntax for `StrComp` is as follows:

```
StrComp(string1, string2 [, compare])
```

Here, *`string1`* and *`string2`* are required String arguments specifying the strings to compare, and *`compare`* is an optional argument specifying textual comparison (`vbTextCompare`) or binary comparison (`vbBinaryCompare`).

The following statement uses `StrComp` to settle the pet question once and for all:

```
If StrComp(Pet, "dog", vbTextCompare) = 0 Then _
    MsgBox "We do not accept dogs."
```

Using VBA's Mathematical Functions

VBA provides a solid suite of functions for standard mathematical operations. Table 9.11 lists these functions with examples.

TABLE 9.11: VBA's mathematical functions

FUNCTION(ARGUMENT)	RETURNS	EXAMPLE
`Abs(`*`number`*`)`	The absolute value of *`number`*—the unsigned magnitude of the number.	`Abs(-100)` returns `100`.
`Atn(`*`number`*`)`	The arctangent of *`number`* in radians.	`Atn(dblMyAngle)`
`Cos(`*`number`*`)`	The cosine of angle *`number`*.	`Cos(dblMyAngle)`
`Exp(`*`number`*`)`	e, the base of natural logarithms, raised to the power of *`number`*.	`Exp(5)` returns `148.413159102577`.
`Fix(`*`number`*`)`	The integer portion of *`number`* (without rounding). If *`number`* is negative, returns the negative number greater than or equal to *`number`*.	`Fix(3.14159)` returns 3. `Fix(-3.14159)` returns -3.
`Int(`*`number`*`)`	The integer portion of *`number`* (again, without rounding). If *`number`* is negative, returns the negative number less than or equal to *`number`*.	`Int(3.14159)` returns 3. `Int(-3.14159)` returns -4.
`Log(`*`number`*`)`	The natural logarithm of *`number`*.	`Log(dblMyAngle)`
`Rnd([`*`number`*`])`	A random number (with no argument) or a number based on the given initial seed.	`Rnd(1)` returns a random number.
`Sgn(`*`number`*`)`	`-1` if *`number`* is negative, `0` if *`number`* is `0`, `1` if *`number`* is positive.	`Sgn(7)` returns 1. `Sgn(-7)` returns -1. `Sgn(0)` returns `0`.
`Sin(`*`number`*`)`	The sine of the angle specified by *`number`* (measured in radians).	`Sin(dblMyAngle)`
`Sqr(`*`number`*`)`	The square root of *`number`*. If *`number`* is negative, VBA gives a runtime error.	`Sqr(9)` returns 3.
`Tan(`*`number`*`)`	The tangent of the angle specified by *`number`* (measured in radians).	`Tan(dblMyAngle)`

Using VBA's Date and Time Functions

VBA provides a full complement of date and time functions, as listed in Table 9.12. The table provides brief examples of working with the functions. The sections after the table provide longer examples showing how to use some of the more complex functions.

TABLE 9.12: VBA's date and time functions

FUNCTION (ARGUMENTS)	RETURNS	EXAMPLE
`Date`	A Variant/Date containing the current date according to your computer	`MsgBox Date` might display `04/01/2016`. (The format depends on your Windows date settings.)
`DateAdd(`*`interval`*`, `*`number`*`, `*`date`*`)`	A Variant/Date containing the date of the specified interval after the specified date	`DateAdd("m", 1, "6/3/06")` returns `7/3/2016`.
`DatePart(`*`interval`*`, `*`date`*`)`	The part (specified by *`interval`*) of the specified date	See the example in the next section.
`DateSerial(`*`year`*`, `*`month`*`, `*`day`*`)`	A Variant/Date containing the date for the specified year, month, and day	`dteCompanyFounded = DateSerial(1997, 7, 4)`.
`DateValue(`*`date`*`)`	A Variant/Date containing the specified date	`dteDeath = "July 2, 1971"`
`Day(`*`date`*`)`	A Variant/Integer between 1 and 31, inclusive, representing the day of the month for *`date`*	`If Day(Date) = 1 And Month(Date) = 1 Then MsgBox "Happy new year!"`
`Hour(`*`time`*`)`	A Variant/Integer between 0 and 23, inclusive, representing the hour for *`time`*	`dteHour = Hour(dteLoggedIn)`
`Minute(`*`time`*`)`	A Variant/Integer between 0 and 59, inclusive, representing the minute for *`time`*	`dteMinute = Minute(dteLoggedIn)`
`Month(`*`date`*`)`	A Variant/Integer between 1 and 12, inclusive, representing the month for *`date`*	`strThisDate = Month(Date) & "/" & Day(Date)`
`MonthName(`*`month`*`)`	A String containing the name of the month represented by *`month`*	`MsgBox MonthName(Month(Date))` displays a message box containing the current month.
`Now`	A Variant/Date containing the current date and time according to your computer	`MsgBox Now` might display `04/01/2016 9:25:15PM`. (The format of date and time will depend on your Windows date settings.)

TABLE 9.12: VBA's date and time functions *(CONTINUED)*

FUNCTION (ARGUMENTS)	RETURNS	EXAMPLE
`Second(time)`	A Variant/Integer between 0 and 59, inclusive, representing the second for *time*	`dteSecond = Second(dteLoggedIn)`
`Time`	A Variant/Date containing the current time according to your computer	`MsgBox Time` might display `9:25:15PM`. (The time format and time will depend on your Windows date settings.)
`Timer`	A Single giving the number of seconds that have elapsed since midnight	`If Timer > 43200 Then MsgBox _ "This code only works in the morning.": End`
`TimeSerial(hour, minute, second)`	A Variant/Date containing the time for the specified hour, minute, and second	`TimeSerial(11, 12, 13)` returns `11:12:13AM`. (The format will depend on your Windows date settings.)
`TimeValue(time)`	A Variant/Date containing the time for *time*	`TimeValue(Now)`
`Weekday(date)`	A Variant/Integer containing the day of the week represented by *date*	See the next entry.
`WeekdayName (weekday)`	A String containing the weekday denoted by *weekday*	`WeekdayName(Weekday (#4/1/2016#))` returns `Friday`, the day of the week for April Fool's Day 2016.

Using the *DatePart* Function to Parse Dates

The `DatePart` function lets you take a date and separate it into its components. You can often achieve the same results by using other date functions, but `DatePart` is a good tool to have in your VBA toolbox.

The syntax for `DatePart` is as follows:

```
DatePart(Interval, Date[,FirstDayOfWeek[, FirstWeekOfYear]])
```

The components of the syntax are as follows:

- *`Interval`* is a required String expression giving the unit in which you want to measure the interval: `yyyy` for year, `q` for quarter, `m` for month, `y` for the day of the year, `d` for day, `w` for weekday, `ww` for week, `h` for hour, `n` for minute (because `m` is for month), and `s` for second.
- *`Date`* is a required Variant/Date giving the date you want to examine.

- `FirstDayOfWeek` is an optional constant specifying the day that starts the week (for date information). The default setting is `vbSunday` (1), but you can also set `vbMonday` (2), `vbTuesday` (3), `vbWednesday` (4), `vbThursday` (5), `vbFriday` (6), `vbSaturday` (7), or `vb UseSystem` (0; this uses the system setting).
- `FirstWeekOfYear` is an optional constant specifying the week considered first in the year. Table 9.13 shows the options for this constant.

TABLE 9.13: The options for the FirstWeekOfYear constant

CONSTANT	VALUE	YEAR STARTS WITH WEEK
`vbUseSystem`	0	Use the system setting.
`vbFirstJan1`	1	The week in which January 1 falls (the default setting).
`vbFirstFourDays`	2	The first week with a minimum of four days in the year.
`vbFirstFullWeek`	3	The first full week (7 days) of the year.

For example, the following statement assigns the current year to the variable `dteThisYear`:

```
dteThisYear = DatePart("yyyy", Date)
```

Calculating Time Intervals Using the *DateDiff* Function

The `DateDiff` function returns the interval (the number of days, weeks, hours, and so on) between two specified dates. The syntax for `DateDiff` is as follows:

```
DateDiff(interval, date1, date2[, firstdayofweek[, firstweekofyear]])
```

Here are the components of the syntax:

- `interval` is a required String expression giving the unit in which you want to measure the interval: `yyyy` for year, `q` for quarter, `m` for month, `y` for the day of the year, `d` for day, `w` for weekday, `ww` for week, `h` for hour, `n` for minute (because `m` is for month), and `s` for second.
- *`date1`* and *`date2`* are the dates between which you're calculating the interval.
- *`firstdayofweek`* is an optional constant specifying the day that starts the week (for date information). The default setting is `vbSunday` (1), but you can also set `vbMonday` (2), `vbTuesday` (3), `vbWednesday` (4), `vbThursday` (5), `vbFriday` (6), `vbSaturday` (7), or `vb UseSystem` (0; this uses the system setting).
- *`firstweekofyear`* is an optional constant specifying the week considered first in the year. Table 9.13 shows the options for this constant.

For example, the following statement returns the number of weeks between June 3, 2009, and September 30, 2009:

```
MsgBox DateDiff("ww", "6/3/2009", "9/30/2009")
```

Using the *DateAdd* Function to Add or Subtract Time from a Date

The DateAdd function lets you easily add an interval of time to, or subtract an interval of time from, a specified date, returning the resulting date. The syntax for DateAdd is as follows:

```
DateAdd(interval, number, date)
```

Here are the components of the syntax:

- *interval* is a required String expression giving the unit of measurement for the interval: yyyy for year, q for quarter, m for month, y for the day of the year, d for day, w for weekday, ww for week, h for hour, n for minute, and s for second.
- *number* is a required numeric expression giving the number of intervals to add (a positive number) or to subtract (a negative number). If *number* isn't already of the data type Long, VBA rounds it to the nearest whole number before evaluating the function.
- *date* is a required Variant/Date or literal date giving the starting date.

For example, the following statement returns the date 10 weeks from May 27, 2016:

```
DateAdd("ww", 10, #5/27/2016#)
```

Using File-Management Functions

The following sections demonstrate how to use a couple of key VBA file-management functions: the Dir function, which you use to find out whether a file exists, and the CurDir function, which returns the current path.

Checking Whether a File Exists Using the *Dir* Function

Often when managing files, you'll need to first check whether a particular file already exists. For instance, if you're about to save a file, you may want to make sure the save operation won't overwrite an existing file—a file with the same name in the same location on the hard drive.

If you're about to open a file, you might want to see if that file exists before you use the Open method; otherwise, VBA will give an error.

To test whether a file exists, you can use a straightforward procedure such as the one shown in Listing 9.3.

LISTING 9.3: Checking if a file exists with the `Dir` function

```
1.  Sub Does_File_Exist()
2.      Dim strTestFile As String, strNameToTest As String, _
            strMsg As String
3.      strNameToTest = InputBox("Enter the file name and path:")
4.      If strNameToTest = "" Then End
5.      strTestFile = Dir(strNameToTest)
6.      If Len(strTestFile) = 0 Then
7.          strMsg = "The file " & strNameToTest & _
                " does not exist."
8.      Else
9.          strMsg = "The file " & strNameToTest & " exists. "
10.     End If
11.     MsgBox strMsg, vbOKOnly + vbInformation, _
          "File-Existence Check"
12. End Sub
```

This procedure in Listing 9.3 uses the `Dir` function to check whether a file exists and displays a message box indicating whether it does or doesn't. Figure 9.3 shows examples of the message box. This message box is for demonstration purposes only. In a real-world macro you'd likely use the result of the test to branch (execute different code blocks) based on whether the file exists. Branching is covered in Chapter 11.

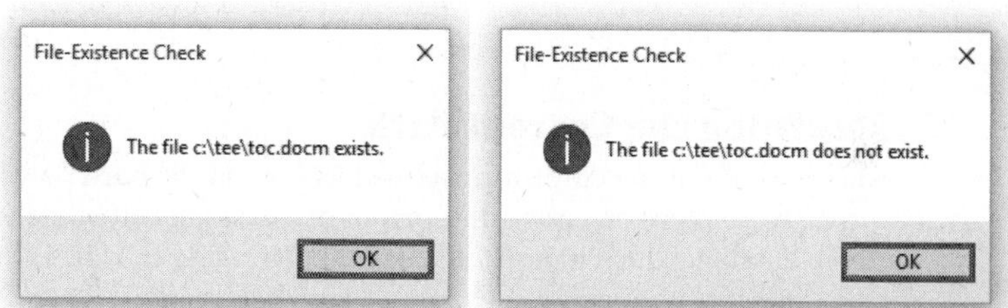

FIGURE 9.3 You can use the `Dir` function to check whether a file exists so that you don't accidentally overwrite it or cause an error by trying to open a nonexistent file.

Here's how the code works:

- Line 2 declares the String variables `strTestFile`, `strNameToTest`, and `strMsg`.
- Line 3 then displays an input box prompting the user to enter a filename and path; VBA assigns the result of the input box to `strNameToTest`.
- Line 4 compares `strNameToTest` to a blank string (which means the user clicked the Cancel button in the input box or clicked the OK button without entering any text in the text box) and uses an `End` statement to end the procedure if it gets a match.

- Line 5 assigns to `strTestFile` the result of running the `Dir` function on the `strNameToTest` string. If `Dir` finds a match for `strNameToTest`, `strTestFile` will contain the name of the matching file; otherwise, it will contain an empty string.
- Line 6 begins an `If...Then` statement by testing the length of the `strTestFile` string. If the length is 0, the statement in line 7 assigns to `strMsg` text saying that the file doesn't exist; otherwise, VBA branches to the `Else` statement in line 8 and runs the statement in line 9, assigning text to `strMsg` saying that the file does exist. Line 10 ends the `If` statement.
- Line 11 displays a message box containing `strMsg`. Line 12 ends the procedure.

GARBAGE IN, GARBAGE OUT

The code shown in Listing 9.3 isn't bulletproof because the `Dir` command is designed to work with wildcards as well as regular characters. As long as you're working with a simple text filename in `strNameToTest`, you'll be fine because `Dir` compares that text to the existing filenames on the hard drive and the result lets you know whether you have a match. But if `strNameToTest` contains wildcards (say the string is `c:\temp\*.*`; the asterisks specifying *any filename*), `Dir` reports that the file exists. However, there's no file by that name, just one or more files that match the wildcard. You can check on line 5 whether the name returned by `Dir` is exactly the same as the input name and make sure you do a case-insensitive comparison. This literalness of `Dir` is a nice illustration of GIGO (garbage in, garbage out)—from the computer's (and VBA's) point of view, it's doing what you asked it to, but the result is far from what you intended.

Returning the Current Path

You can find out the current path (the location on the hard drive to which the host application is currently pointed) on either the current drive or a specified drive by using the `CurDir` function. Often, you'll need to change the current path (using the `ChDir` function) to make sure the user is saving files in, or opening files from, a suitable location.

To return the current path, use `CurDir` without an argument:

```
CurDir
```

To return the current path for a specified drive, enter the drive letter as an argument. For example, to return the current path on drive D, use this statement:

```
CurDir("D")
```

The Bottom Line

Understand what functions are and what they do. A function is a unit of code, a procedure, that performs a task *and returns a value.*

You can write your own functions by writing code between `Function` and `End Function` in the VBA Editor. Chapter 10, "Creating Your Own Functions," explores how to write such custom functions. In addition to functions you might write, there are many functions already prewritten in VBA—ready for you to call them from your macros to perform various tasks.

Master It A function in VBA is quite similar to a subroutine, but there is a significant difference. What is it?

Use functions. In a macro, you can call a built-in function by merely typing in its name and providing any required arguments.

Master It You can combine multiple functions in a single line of code. The `MsgBox` function displays a message box containing whatever data you request. The only required argument for this function is the *`prompt`*. The `Now` function returns the current date and time. Write a line of code that calls the `MsgBox` function and uses the `Now` function as its argument.

Use key VBA functions. VBA offers the services of hundreds of built-in functions. You'll find yourself using some of them over and over. They are key to programming.

Master It What built-in function is used quite often to display information in a dialog box to the user while a procedure runs?

Convert data from one type to another. It's sometimes necessary to change a value from one data type to another. Perhaps you used an input box to ask the user to type in a String variable, but then you need to change it into an Integer type so you can do some math with it. (You can't add pieces of text to each other.)

Master It What built-in function would you use to convert a string such as `"12"` (which, in reality, is two text *characters*, the digits 1 and 2) into an Integer data type, the actual *number* 12, that you can manipulate mathematically?

Manipulate strings and dates. VBA includes a full set of functions to manage text and date data.

Master It Which built-in function would you use to remove any leading and trailing space characters from a string? For example, you want to turn

```
"  this         "
```

into

```
"this"
```

Chapter 10

Creating Your Own Functions

In Chapter 9, "Using Built-In Functions," you learned how to use VBA's built-in functions. In this chapter, you'll learn how to create your own functions.

You create a function the same way you create a subprocedure: by typing in the Code window. (You can't *record* a function in Excel and Word—the applications that include a Macro Recorder. Instead, you have to write functions yourself because the Recorder creates only subprocedures.)

It's important to recall that, although both are procedures, in VBA functions differ from subs. The primary difference is that functions interact more with other procedures. Functions accept arguments (incoming data) from the procedure that calls them, and they return a value (outgoing data) back to the procedure that calls them. Subs, by contrast, normally don't require arguments and *never* return any data.

But functions are used in VBA far less often than subs. Most macros are self-contained subs. That's because most macros are small, brief automations: They perform simple, quick jobs such as inserting a date into a document or saving a document using a particular filename. In these situations, there is no need for the procedure to return any data.

But you aren't limited to brief macros. You are free to create more complex, larger, and more sophisticated programs in VBA. And if you do create a large project, you'll want to use multiple procedures, not just one sub. This allows you to divide your work into multiple logical units that can each be individually tested and more easily modified. When you're using multiple procedures, however, they must work together and sometimes need to communicate among themselves. This is why you often use functions in large projects. Remember that the key feature of a function is that it facilitates *communication*—sending values back and forth—among multiple procedures.

This chapter will cover several ways to employ functions with the various Office 2016 applications. I'll start by explaining the components of a function and showing you how to put them together. You'll then create some functions that work in any VBA host and some functions that are specific to Word, Excel, and PowerPoint.

IN THIS CHAPTER, YOU WILL LEARN TO DO THE FOLLOWING:

- Understand the components of a function statement
- Create a generic function
- Create a function for Word
- Create a function for Excel
- Create a function for PowerPoint
- Create a function for Access

Components of a Function

To create a function, you use a `Function` statement. This is essentially the same way you create a Sub: Just type in the word **`Function`** followed by the name you're giving the function.

The syntax for the `Function` statement is as follows:

```
[Public | Private] [Static] Function function_name [(argument_list)] [As type]
     [statements]
     [function_name = expression]
     [Exit Function]
     [statements]
     [function_name = expression]
End Function
```

This syntax, most of which is optional, breaks down like this:

- `Public` is an optional keyword that you can use to make the function publicly accessible—accessible to all other procedures in all loaded modules. (If you need to limit the function's scope to the project that contains it, you can override this public availability by putting an `Option Private Module` statement in the module that contains the function.)
- `Private` is an optional keyword that you can use to make the function accessible to the other procedures in the module that contains it. The function is hidden from procedures in any other module.
- `Static` is an optional keyword that you can use to make local variables in the function retain their value between calls to the function.
- *`function_name`* is required. It specifies a name for the function so you can refer to it elsewhere in your project (so you can call the function—in other words, start it running). Functions follow the same naming rules as other VBA items, such as the rules for variable names: Alphanumerics and underscores are fine, but no spaces, symbols, or punctuation. Note that a function *passes data back* to whatever procedure called (executed) the function. It passes data back by assigning a value to its (the function's) name. If the function's name is `AddStateTax`, you could have it do some calculations to add the tax, and then assign the result to the function's name:

```
Function AddStateTax(SubTotal)

 AddStateTax = SubTotal * 1.07 'do the math and assign the result
                               'to the function name so it gets passed back

 End Function
```

- Then the code outside the function that called it could use the information returned by the function.
- *`argument_list`* is an optional argument supplying the list of variables that represent arguments passed to the function when it is invoked. *`argument_list`* takes the syntax shown here:

```
[Optional] [ByRef | ByVal] [ParamArray] variable_name[( )] [As type]

[= default_value]
```

Here's a description of the elements of the `argument_list`:

- `Optional` is an optional keyword that you can use to denote that an argument is optional—in other words, that it is not required. Once you've used `Optional` to declare an optional argument, any subsequent arguments in the `argument_list` also have to be optional. That means you must put any *required* arguments before the optional arguments, the same way VBA does with its built-in functions' argument lists. Also, it's a good idea to give optional arguments a default value.
- `ByRef` is an optional keyword that you can use to specify that an argument be passed *by reference*; `ByVal` is an optional keyword that you can use to specify that an argument be passed *by value*. You can pass an argument either by reference or by value.
- `ParamArray` is an optional keyword you can use as the last argument in `argument_list` to denote an optional array of Variants. You can't use `ParamArray` with `ByVal`, `ByRef`, or `Optional`.

YOU CAN PASS TO A FUNCTION EITHER A VALUE'S ADDRESS OR A COPY OF THE ACTUAL VALUE

When a procedure (either a function or a subroutine) passes an argument to a function *by reference*, the recipient procedure gets access to the actual memory location where the original variable is stored and can thereby *change* the value held in the original variable. By contrast, when an argument is passed *by value*, the function gets only a copy of the information in the variable and, therefore, can't change the value held in the original variable (the recipient procedure doesn't even know where the original variable is located). By reference is the default way to pass an argument, and there is rarely any reason to pass by value, so just use the default.

- *`variable_name`* is the name of the variable that you want to use for this argument. When the function is called and a value is supplied for this argument, this variable can be used in your code.
- *`type`* is an optional keyword giving the data type of the argument (Byte, Boolean, Currency, Date, Decimal, Double, Integer, Long, Object, Single, variable-length String, or Variant). For mandatory arguments, you can also specify an object type (for example, a `Worksheet` object) or a custom object (one you've created).
- *`default_value`* is an optional *literal* (the value itself spelled out, such as "Sacramento") constant, or constant expression that you use to specify a default value for optional parameters. You'll see how to provide a default value shortly.

- *`type`* is an optional argument specifying the data type of the value that the function returns: Byte, Boolean, Currency, Date, Decimal, Double, Integer, Long, Object, Single, variable-length String, Variant, or a custom type.
- `statements` represents the statement or statements in the function (the code that does the job the function is supposed to accomplish). In theory, `statements` is optional, but in practice, most functions will need one or more statements.
- *`expression`* represents the value the function returns. *`expression`* is also optional.

Creating a Function

The following sections walk you through the process of creating a function.

Starting a Function Manually

The easiest way to start creating a function is to type into the VBA Code window the word **Function** followed by the name you want to give to the function and any necessary arguments in parentheses, and then press Enter. VBA automatically enters a blank line and an `End Function` statement for you and places the insertion point on the blank line ready for you to create the programming code inside the new function.

For example, if you type the following line and press Enter, the Visual Basic Editor displays what you see in Figure 10.1:

```
Function MyFunction(MaxTemp, MinTemp)
```

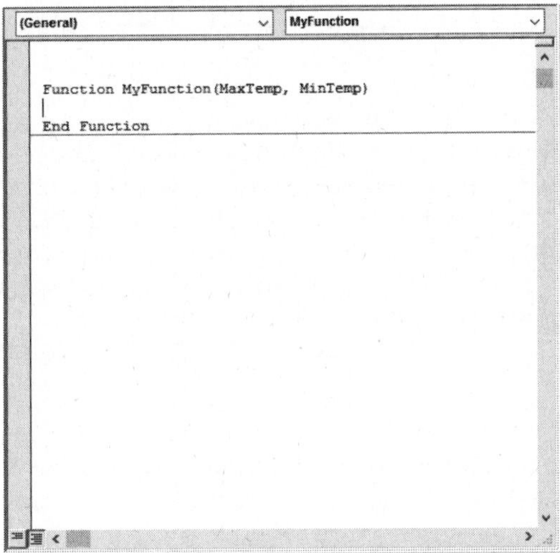

FIGURE 10.1 When you type a `Function` statement and press Enter, the Visual Basic Editor automatically inserts a blank line and an `End Function` statement for you.

Starting a Function by Using the Add Procedure Dialog Box

If you like to make the Visual Basic Editor work for you as much as possible (and prefer the slow way of doing things), you can also start creating a new function by using the Add Procedure dialog box:

1. Choose Insert ➤ Procedure to display the Add Procedure dialog box (see Figure 10.2).
2. Type the name for the procedure in the Name text box.
3. Select the Function option button in the Type group box.

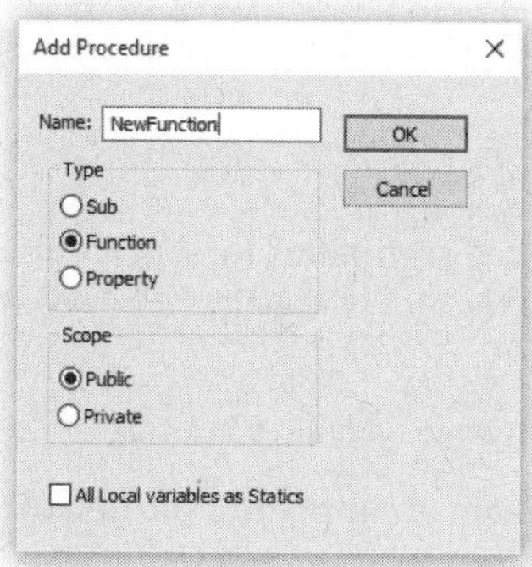

FIGURE 10.2
You can also use the Add Procedure dialog box to specify elements of a new function.

4. Select the Public option button or the Private option button (as appropriate) in the Scope group box.
5. If you want all local variables in the function to be of the static type (which you usually won't), select the All Local Variables As Statics check box.
6. Click OK to enter the stub for the function, and then enter any arguments for the function in the parentheses manually.

Passing Arguments to a Function

The arguments that will be passed to a function are listed in parentheses, separated by commas. In the following example code, the function states that it requires an argument named `MaxTemp` and an argument named `MinTemp`. These data must be passed to (sent to) this function for it to work:

```
Function GetTemps(MaxTemp As Double, MinTemp As Double)
```

If somewhere in your code you attempt to call this function without passing the data it requires, VBA will display the error message "Argument Not Optional."

You can also specify the data type of the arguments if you want by including an `As` statement with the data type after the argument's name. For example, you could use the following statement to set the `MaxTemp` and `MinTemp` arguments to the Double numeric data type:

```
Function GetTemps(MaxTemp As Double, MinTemp As Double)
```

Passing an argument by reference (the default) is useful when you want to manipulate the variable in the recipient procedure and then return the variable to the procedure from which it originated. Alternatively, passing an argument by value is useful when you want to use the information stored in the variable in the recipient procedure and at the same time ensure that the original information in the variable doesn't change (but this is rare; it typically isn't necessary).

Because by *reference* is the default way of passing an argument, both of the following statements pass the argument `MyArg` by reference:

```
Function PassByReference(MyArg)
Function PassByReference(ByRef MyArg)
```

As you see, you can omit the default ByRef command. However, to pass an argument by value, you must use the ByVal keyword. The following statement passes the ValArg argument by value:

```
Function PassByValue(ByVal ValArg)
```

If necessary, you can pass some arguments for a procedure by reference and others by value. The following statement passes the MyArg argument by reference and the ValArg argument by value:

```
Function PassBoth(ByRef MyArg, ByVal ValArg)
```

In practice, though, you're likely to simply use the default ByRef approach for most, if not all, of your programming.

Declaring the Data Types of Arguments

You can explicitly declare the data types of arguments. This conserves memory (although this is rarely an issue anymore) and ensures that the outside (calling) procedures are passing the correct type of information to your function. For this second reason, it's always a good idea to specify the data type. You avoid some kinds of errors that way.

When passing an argument, you want to ensure that the data type of the argument you're passing matches the data type expected in the procedure. For example, if you declare a string and try to pass it as an argument when the receiving function specifies that it is expecting a Variant, VBA displays an error message.

To declare the data type of an argument, just include the usual data-type declaration in the argument list. The following statement declares MyStrArg, specifying with As that a string must be passed and specifying a variant with VarArg:

```
Function PassType(MyStrArg As String, VarArg As Variant)
```

Specifying an Optional Argument

Sometimes a function may not always require a particular argument. You can specify that an argument is optional by using the Optional keyword:

```
Function PassBoth(ByRef MyArg As String, ByVal ValArg As Variant, _
    Optional ByVal strName As String)
```

When you specify an optional argument, it's a good idea to assign a default value to it. Doing so makes the code less susceptible to errors and gives the programmer a clue as to what kind of information is used here. To assign the default value, type an equal sign after the variable's definition, and then type the default value (use double quotation marks for a String value). For example, the following function statement declares the strName optional argument and assigns the default value if no value is passed:

```
Function PassBoth(ByRef MyArg As String, ByVal ValArg As Variant, _
    Optional ByVal strName As String = "Sacramento")
```

What happens here is that this macro is being used by a company located in Sacramento, so they most often use that city's name for the literal value in this particular macro. Your default literal will of course differ, depending on what your macro is supposed to accomplish.

Controlling the Scope of a Function

Like a subroutine, a function can have private or public scope. Private scope makes the function available only to procedures in the module that contains it, and public scope makes the function available to all open modules in your project.

If you don't specify whether a function is private or public, VBA makes it public by default, so you don't need to specify the scope of a function unless you want it to have private scope. However, if you do use explicit `Public` declarations for those functions you want to be public, your code will be somewhat easier to read:

```
Private Function MyFunction(MaxTemp, MinTemp)
Public Function AnotherFunction(Industry, Average)
```

Examples of Functions for Any VBA-Enabled Office Application

This part of the chapter contains two examples of functions that will work in any application that hosts VBA. That's because these functions don't access objects particular to any specific Office application.

Later in this chapter, you'll see examples of functions that employ resources or features particular to the specific Office applications.

To start, first declare the function and its arguments. The following statement declares a function named `NetProfit`:

```
Function NetProfit(Gross As Double, Expenses As Double) As Double
```

`NetProfit` uses two arguments, `Gross` and `Expenses`, declaring each as the Double data type; it's a floating-point (has a decimal point) number.

At the end of this statement, we have specified that our function returns a Double value type. It's important to explicitly specify the variable types of the arguments and the type of the value that the function returns to the caller. This avoids unpleasant surprises (bugs) in your code because VBA catches and reports any attempt to pass the wrong data type to the function or send the wrong type of data back to whatever code called (executed) your function.

Armed with the arguments (and their type, if you *explicitly type* them as I'm suggesting you do), you call your `NetProfit` function the same way you would execute a prewritten function that's built into VBA (such as `MsgBox`). You simply use the function's name and supply the two arguments it needs, like this:

```
MyProfit = NetProfit(44000, 34000)
```

Here, the variable `MyProfit` is assigned the value of the `NetProfit` function. In other words, after this function finishes its job and execution resumes in the *caller* (the procedure that invoked the function), the returned value is assigned to the variable `MyProfit`.

In this example, the `NetProfit` function is provided with a `Gross` argument of `44000` and an `Expenses` argument of `34000`.

Once you've created a function, the Visual Basic Editor displays its argument list when you type the name of the function in a caller procedure, as shown in Figure 10.3.

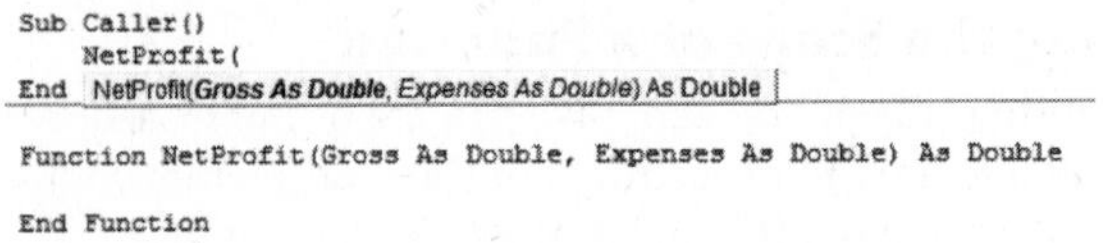

FIGURE 10.3 The Visual Basic Editor displays a ToolTip of Auto Quick Info for functions you create as well as for its built-in functions.

```
Sub Caller()
    NetProfit(
End  NetProfit(Gross As Double, Expenses As Double) As Double

Function NetProfit(Gross As Double, Expenses As Double) As Double

End Function
```

Listing 10.1 contains an example of calling a function: The `ShowProfit` procedure calls the `NetProfit` function and displays the result in a message box.

LISTING 10.1: How to call a function

```
1.  Sub ShowProfit()
2.      MsgBox (NetProfit(44000, 34000)),, "Net Profit"
3.  End Sub
4.
5.  Function NetProfit(Gross As Double, Expenses As Double) As Double
6.      NetProfit = (Gross - Expenses) * 0.9
7.  End Function
```

In Listing 10.1, lines 1 through 3 contain the `ShowProfit` procedure, which simply calls the `NetProfit` function in line 2, passes it the arguments `44000` for `Gross` and `34000` for `Expenses`, and displays the result in a message box titled `Net Profit`. Notice that in line 2 we have employed a shortcut: using the function call inside an argument list. Line 2 does the same thing as this longer version:

```
Dim result as double
Result = NetProfit(44000, 34000)
MsgBox (Result),, "Net Profit"
```

Lines 5 through 7 contain the `NetProfit` function. Line 5 declares the function as working with two Double arguments, `Gross` and `Expenses`, telling VBA what to do with the two arguments that line 2 has passed to the function.

Line 6 calculates `NetProfit` to be 90 percent (`0.9`) of the value of `Gross` minus `Expenses`.

How Functions Return Information

It's important to notice what else happens in line 6: The information calculated by the function is being assigned to the name of the function. This is *how the information gets passed back* to the `ShowProfit` procedure that called the function.

To make this process a bit clearer, let's write the code in a more verbose way. We'll do this the long way, without using the shortcut of doing both the calculating and assigning all on the same line. Here's how a function goes about its business.

There are three main steps: calculation, assignment, and return. They are labeled as lines 1, 2, and 3 in the following listing.

The function first does some computing—in this case, calculating a net profit. Then, second, it assigns the results of the calculation to its own name (`NetProfit`, in this case). This assignment is how the data gets passed back to the caller. And finally, third, with the `End` command, it sends the results back to whatever procedure called the function:

```
Function NetProfit(Gross As Double, Expenses As Double) As Double
Dim Result As Double

1.  Result = (Gross - Expenses) * 0.9 'do the calculating

2.  NetProfit = Result 'store the information to be sent back

3.  End Function 'send the information back
```

Returning Text Data from a Function

Listing 10.2 contains a function that returns a String argument.

LISTING 10.2: A function that returns a string

```
Sub TestForSmog()
    Dim intCYear As Integer, strThisCar As String
BadValueLoop:
    On Error GoTo Bye
    intCYear = InputBox("Enter the year of your car.", _
        "Do I Need a Smog Check?")
    strThisCar = NeedsSmog(intCYear)
    If strThisCar = "Yes" Then
        MsgBox "Your car needs a smog check.", _
        vbOKOnly + vbExclamation, "Smog Check"
    ElseIf strThisCar = "BadValue" Then
        MsgBox "The year you entered is in the future.", _
        vbOKOnly + vbCritical, "Smog Check"
        GoTo BadValueLoop
    Else
        MsgBox "Your car does not need a smog check.", _
        vbOKOnly + vbInformation, "Smog Check"
    End If
Bye:
End Sub

Function NeedsSmog(CarYear As Integer) As String
    If CarYear > Year(Now) Then
        NeedsSmog = "BadValue"
    ElseIf CarYear <= Year(Now) - 3 Then
```

```
22.             NeedsSmog = "Yes"
23.         Else
24.             NeedsSmog = "No"
25.         End If
26.     End Function
```

Listing 10.2 contains the procedure `TestForSmog` (lines 1 through 16) and the `NeedsSmog` function (lines 18 through 26). The `TestForSmog` procedure calls the `NeedsSmog` function, which returns a value indicating whether the user's car needs a smog check. `TestForSmog` uses this value to display a message box (see Figure 10.4) informing users whether or not their car needs a smog check.

Here's how the code works:

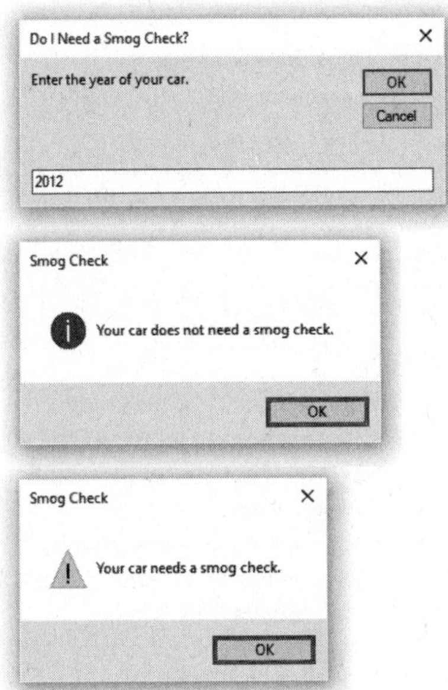

Figure 10.4
The `TestForSmog` procedure prompts for the car's year and then displays a message box stating whether the car needs a smog test.

- `TestForSmog` starts by declaring the Integer variable `intCYear` and the String variable `strThisCar` in line 2.
- Line 3 contains the `BadValueLoop` label, to which execution returns from line 11 if the user has entered an unsuitable value for the year of the car. We'll want to display the input box again, to see if they can get it right this time. Note that if you want execution to jump to a particular zone in your code, you just type in a name for the location, such as `BadValueLoop` here, and end with a colon. This name-plus-colon is called a *label* and it provides a way for you to transfer execution to a specific location within your macro. Then elsewhere in your code you can transfer execution to this label by using the `GoTo` command like this:

```
GoTo BadValueLoop
```

- Line 4 contains an `On Error` statement to transfer execution to the `Bye` label in line 15 if an error occurs. An error occurs if the user cancels the upcoming input box or clicks its OK button with no value entered in its text box.
- Line 5 displays an input box prompting the user to enter the year of the car. This line assigns to the `intCYear` variable the value the user enters in the input box.
- Line 6 then sets the value of the String variable `strThisCar` to the result of the `NeedsSmog` function running on the `intCYear` integer variable.
- Execution now shifts to the `NeedsSmog` function (line 18), which evaluates `intCYear` and returns the value for `strThisCar`. Line 18 declares the function, assigning its value to `NeedsSmog`. The function takes one argument, `CarYear`, which is declared as the Integer data type.
- Line 19 checks to see whether `CarYear` is greater than the value of the current year using `Year(Now)`. If so, line 20 sets the value of `NeedsSmog` to `BadValue`, which is used to indicate that the user has entered a date in the future. If not, the `ElseIf` statement in line 21 runs, checking if the value of `CarYear` is less than or equal to `Year(Now) - 3`, the current year minus three. If so, line 22 sets the value of `NeedsSmog` to `Yes`; if not, the `Else` statement in line 23 runs, and line 24 sets the value of `NeedsSmog` to `No`. Line 25 ends the `If` statement, and line 26 ends the function.
- Execution then returns to the calling line (line 6) in the `TestForSmog` procedure, to which the `NeedsSmog` function returns the value it has assigned to the `strThisCar` variable.
- The rest of the `TestForSmog` procedure then works with the `strThisCar` variable. Line 7 compares `strThisCar` to `Yes`. If it matches, line 8 displays a message box stating that the car needs a smog check. If `strThisCar` doesn't match `Yes`, line 9 compares `ThisCar` to `BadValue`. If it matches, line 10 displays an alert-message box, and line 11 returns execution to the `BadValueLoop` label in line 3. If `strThisCar` doesn't match `BadValue`, the `Else` statement in line 12 runs, and line 13 displays a message box stating that the car doesn't need a smog check.
- Line 14 ends the `If` statement, line 15 contains the `Bye` label, and line 16 ends the procedure.

Functions can be more complex than the simple, stand-alone examples shown here. For instance, you can include a function as part of a larger expression. This code snippet illustrates how to do this. Here we add the results of two functions—`NetProfit` and `CurrentBalance`—by using an expression:

```
CurrentEstimate = NetProfit(44000, 33000) + CurrentBalance(MainAccount)
```

Creating a Function for Word

Functions such as those shown in the previous section work in any VBA-hosting application because they do not call any application-specific features. This section and the following three sections show you examples of functions that are specific to applications.

The task accomplished by the example program shown in Listing 10.3 is to remove some special types of formatting (hyperlinks, bookmarks, and fields) but retain any text in those special zones.

CREATING CUSTOM FUNCTION LIBRARIES

Some programmers like to keep functions they write (that aren't application-specific) in separate modules in the Editor. These little libraries store your own collections of tested, useful, generic procedures. Need to calculate sales tax? Don't reinvent the wheel. Just import your library of math functions, among which is just this procedure. You can export a module as a file with the `.bas` filename extension and import it into whichever application needs the functions. Choose File ➤ Export File (or press Ctrl+E). For example, you might maintain separate modules that contain your math equations, your string-manipulation functions, and other custom functions that work in any VBA host. A `.bas` file is merely an ordinary text file containing a module's source code (its subroutines and functions). You can read it in Notepad, but you can also use the File Import feature to add it to a VBA project. When imported, it will appear in the Project Explorer as a new module.

The function shown in Listing 10.3 is for Word and—unusually for a function—returns no information (technically, it returns a null value). The function's main purpose is to perform several operations on the specified document, so no data needs to be returned to the caller.

LISTING 10.3: A function that returns a null value

```
Option Explicit

Function Strip_Hyperlinks_Bookmarks_Fields()
    Dim myLink As Hyperlink
    Dim myBookmark As Bookmark
    Dim myField As Field
    With ActiveDocument
        For Each myLink In .Hyperlinks
            myLink.Delete
        Next myLink
        For Each myBookmark In .Bookmarks
            myBookmark.Delete
        Next myBookmark
        For Each myField In .Fields
            myField.Unlink
        Next myField
    End With
End Function

Sub Clean_Up_Document_for_Conversion()
```

```
21.         Call Strip_Hyperlinks_Bookmarks_Fields
22.         'other cleanup functions here
23.     End Sub
```

Here's how the code works:

- Line 1 contains the `Option Explicit` statement for the module to force explicit declarations of all variables. Line 2 is a spacer.
- Line 3 starts the function named `Strip_Hyperlinks_Bookmarks_Fields`, which removes all hyperlinks, bookmarks, and fields from the active document. The function continues until the `End Function` statement in line 18.
- Line 4 declares a variable named `myLink` as being of the `Hyperlink` type. Line 5 declares a variable named `myBookmark` as being of the `Bookmark` type. Line 6 declares a variable named `myField` as being of the `Field` type.
- Line 7 begins a `With` statement that works with the `ActiveDocument` object and continues until the `End With` statement in line 17. This `With` statement contains three `For Each...Next` loops.
- The first `For Each...Next` loop, in lines 8 through 10, goes through each `myLink` object in the current document's `Hyperlinks` collection. Line 9 uses the `Delete` method to delete each of the links in turn. Deleting a hyperlink removes the link from the document but leaves the text that was displayed for the hyperlink.
- The second `For Each...Next` loop, in lines 11 through 13, works with each `myBookmark` object in the `Bookmarks` collection. Line 12 uses the `Delete` method to delete each of the bookmarks in turn. Deleting a bookmark removes the marker from the document but leaves any text or other object that the bookmark contained.
- The third `For Each...Next` loop, in lines 14 through 16, works with each `myField` object in the `Fields` collection. Line 15 uses the `Unlink` method to unlink each of the fields in turn. Unlinking a field leaves the field's contents in the document as text or as an object, but removes the field link.
- Line 17 contains the `End With` statement that ends the `With` statement, and line 18 contains the `End Function` statement that ends the function. Line 19 is a spacer.
- Lines 20 through 23 contain a short subprocedure that simply calls the `Strip_Hyperlinks_Bookmarks_Fields` function. Line 22 contains a comment stating that the subprocedure would call other cleanup functions, but the code to call other functions hasn't yet been written. It's a reminder.

Creating a Function for Excel

This section shows you a function for Excel. The function in Listing 10.4 checks whether a workbook contains any unused sheets.

LISTING 10.4: An Excel function

```
1.  Option Explicit
2.
3.  Function BlankSheetsInWorkbook(ByRef WorkbookToTest As Workbook) As Boolean
4.      Dim objWorksheet As Worksheet
5.      BlankSheetsInWorkbook = False
6.      For Each objWorksheet In WorkbookToTest.Worksheets
7.          If Application.WorksheetFunction.CountBlank _
                (objWorksheet.Range("A1:IV65536")) = 16777216 Then
8.              BlankSheetsInWorkbook = True
9.              Exit Function
10.         End If
11.     Next objWorksheet
12. End Function
13.
14. Sub Check_Workbook_for_Blank_Worksheets()
15.     If BlankSheetsInWorkbook(ActiveWorkbook) = True Then
16.         MsgBox "This workbook contains one or more blank worksheets." & _
                vbCr & vbCr & "Please remove all blank worksheets before" & _
                " submitting the workbook.", vbOKOnly & vbExclamation, _
                "Check Workbook for Blank Worksheets"
17.     End If
18. End Sub
```

Here's how the code works:

- Line 1 contains the `Option Explicit` statement for the module to force explicit declarations of all variables. Line 2 is a spacer.
- Line 3 starts the function named `BlankSheetsInWorkbook`, which it declares as a Boolean function. The function works on an object named `WorkbookToTest`, which has the type `Workbook`—in other words, it's a workbook.
- Line 4 declares a variable named `objWorksheet` that is of the `Worksheet` type.
- Line 5 sets the value of the `BlankSheetsInWorkbook` function to `False`.
- Line 6 starts a `For Each...Next` loop that runs for each `objWorksheet` object (each worksheet) in the `Worksheets` collection in the `WorkbookToTest` object—that is, with each worksheet in the workbook that is passed to the function.
- Line 7 uses the `CountBlank` worksheet function to count the number of blank cells in the range A1:IV65536 in the worksheet being tested by the loop. If the number of blank cells is 16777216, the worksheet is blank because this is the number of cells in a worksheet. Line 8 then sets the value of the `BlankSheetsInWorkbook` function to `True`, and line 9 uses an `Exit Function` statement to exit the function. You quit the function because there is no need to test any more worksheets once the function has found that at least one worksheet is blank.
- Line 10 contains the `End If` statement that ends the `If` statement. Line 11 contains the `Next objWorksheet` statement that ends the `For Each...Next` loop. And line 12 contains the `End Function` statement that ends the function. Line 13 is a spacer.

- Line 14 begins a short subprocedure named `Check_Workbook_for_Blank_Worksheets`. Line 15 runs the `BlankSheetsInWorkbook` function on the `ActiveWorkbook` object, which represents the active workbook in the Excel session. If the `BlankSheetsInWorkbook` function returns `True`, line 16 displays a message box that points out to the user that the workbook contains one or more blank worksheets and tells the user to remove them.

Creating a Function for PowerPoint

This section includes an example function for PowerPoint. The function in Listing 10.5 checks that all the text on a slide is at least the minimum font size specified and displays an error-message box if any font is too small. (If, when you press Alt+F11 to open the VBA Editor, you see nothing in the Code window, choose Insert ➢ Module so you'll have a container for your code.)

LISTING 10.5: A function in PowerPoint

```
Option Explicit

Function CheckMinFontSize(objPresentation As Presentation) As Boolean

    Dim objSlide As Slide
    Dim objShape As Shape

    CheckMinFontSize = True

    For Each objSlide In objPresentation.Slides
        objSlide.Select
        objSlide.Shapes.SelectAll
        For Each objShape In Windows(1).Selection.ShapeRange
            If objShape.Type = msoPlaceholder Then
                If objShape.TextFrame.TextRange.Font.Size < 14 Then
                    CheckMinFontSize = False
                    Exit Function
                End If
            End If
        Next objShape
    Next objSlide
End Function

Sub Font_Check()
    If CheckMinFontSize(ActivePresentation) = False Then
        MsgBox "Some of the fonts in this presentation are too small." _
        & vbCr & vbCr & "Please change all fonts to 14 points or larger.", _
        vbCritical + vbOKOnly, "Font Size Check"
    End If
End Sub
```

Here's how the code works:

- Line 1 contains the `Option Explicit` statement for the module to force explicit declarations of all variables. Line 2 is a spacer.
- Line 3 declares the function named `CheckMinFontSize` as Boolean and specifies that it works on a variable named `objPresentation`, which is of the `Presentation` type. Line 4 is a spacer.
- Line 5 declares a variable named `objSlide` that is of the `Slide` type. Line 6 declares a variable named `objShape` that is of the `Shape` type. Line 7 is a spacer.
- Line 8 sets the value of the `CheckMinFontSize` function to `True`. This indicates that the font sizes are the minimum size or larger. Line 9 is a spacer.
- Line 10 starts a `For Each...Next` loop that continues until line 21 and works with each `objSlide` object in the `Slides` collection in the `objPresentation` object. This loop makes the function examine each of the `Slide` objects in the presentation that is passed to the function.
- Line 11 selects the current `objSlide` object, and line 12 uses the `SelectAll` method of the `Slides` collection.
- Line 13 starts a nested `For Each...Next` loop that runs once for each of the `objShape` objects in the `ShapeRange` object in the `Selection` object in the first window using `Windows(1)`. The `ShapeRange` object contains all of the `Shape` objects within the selection. Here, the `Shape` objects are represented by the `objShape` variable.
- Line 14 uses an `If` statement to see if the `Type` property of the current `Shape` object is `msoPlaceholder`, the type that indicates a placeholder used for text. If the shape is a placeholder, line 15 checks if the font size used in the `TextRange` object within the `TextFrame` object within the `Shape` object is smaller than 14 points. If so, line 16 assigns the value `False` to the `CheckMinFontSize` function, and line 17 uses an `Exit Function` statement to stop execution of the function. This is because once a font smaller than the minimum permitted size has been found, there is no need to check further.
- Line 18 contains the `End If` statement that ends the nested `If` structure, and line 19 contains the `End If` statement that terminates the outer `If` structure.
- Line 20 contains the `Next objShape` statement that ends the nested `For Each...Next` loop, and line 21 contains the `Next objSlide` statement that ends the outer `For Each... Next` loop.
- Line 22 contains the `End Function` statement that ends the function. Line 23 is a spacer.
- Lines 24 through 28 contain a subroutine named `Font_Check` that runs the `CheckMinFontSize` function on the `ActivePresentation` object. If the function returns `False`, the subprocedure displays a message box alerting the user to the problem.

Creating a Function for Access

You can create functions for Access the same way you do for any other VBA-enabled Office 2016 application—just type in the word **Function** and give this function a name.

However, recall that Access doesn't have the same history as the other Office programs (which are more similar to each other). Thus, Access often has special ways of programming, and it has several unique aspects to its object model. The first thing you'll notice is a general-purpose object named `DoCmd`. This object has no properties, but it has lots of methods that accomplish such common tasks as launching other applications, locating records, and opening reports and forms.

Before we create a macro to illustrate how to use the `DoCmd` object, it's necessary to have a little database set up that you can experiment with. Access comes with several templates, so we'll use one of them. Follow these steps:

1. Run Access.
2. In Office 2016, the various applications such as Word and Access by default display on startup a set of common templates.
3. Double-click *Desktop* Contacts to open that database template. (Don't choose the Contacts template, which includes online features that will complicate this example.)
4. If you see a security warning message (a yellow strip below the Ribbon), click the Enable Content button.
5. Click Create. If you see an offer to watch some videos from Microsoft at this point, click the X in the upper-right corner to close that window.
6. Type in some random data by clicking the (New) link in the Open column on the left side, as shown in Figure 10.5. A Contacts Details dialog box opens (not shown in the figure).
7. Click the Save And New button in the Contact Details dialog box each time you add a new contact. Add about three contacts.

Now you can use the `DoCmd` to locate a particular record by its ID number. Press Alt+F11 to open the Visual Basic Editor in Access; and then right-click the database name (it's the one in boldface) in the Project Explorer. Choose Insert ➤ Module from the context menu. In your new module, type the following code, which will move the insertion pointer to a new record:

```
Function MoveToNew()

    DoCmd.OpenForm "Contact List"
    DoCmd.GoToRecord , , acNewRec

End Function
```

To test this macro, click somewhere in one of the existing records so the blinking insertion cursor is located above the New record line. Then switch to the VBA Editor and click inside the `MoveToNew` function to place the Editor's cursor there. Press F5. Then go back to Access, and you should see that the blinking cursor has moved to the New record.

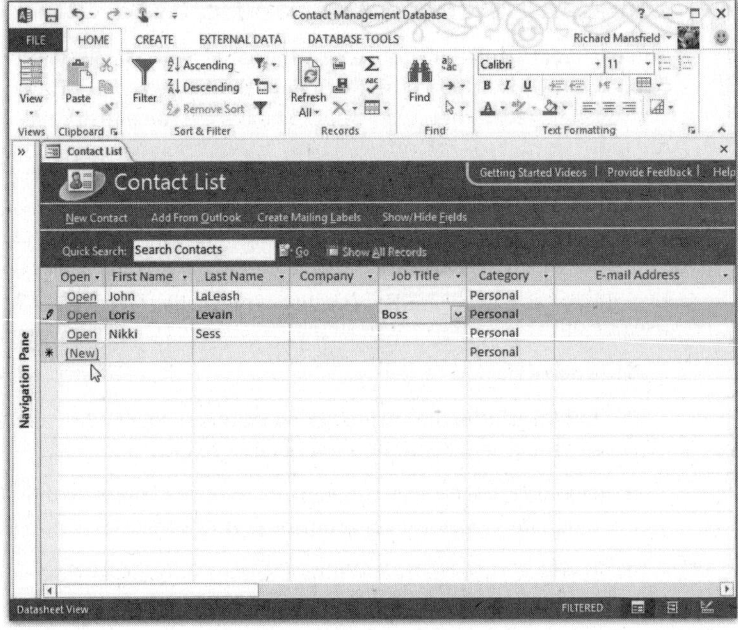

FIGURE 10.5 Type in some data—any data will do—so you can experiment with Access's `DoCmd` object.

Here's how the code works:

- Line 3 ensures that the correct form is open. Because you've just started working with this Contacts database and filled in some information in the Contact List form, the correct form is open and has the focus. However, it's possible that later additional forms will be added. It's always a good idea to specify which form, table, or other object you want to work with. You can't assume that a macro will always be executed in a specific context (such as with the correct form having the focus). In other words, if you omit line 3, this macro will act on whatever form is currently open in Access.
- Line 4 employs the `GoToRecord` method of the `DoCmd` object. The `acNewRec` constant specifies a new, rather than an existing, record.

The Bottom Line

Understand the components of a function statement. Arguments can be passed from the calling code to a function in one of two ways: by reference or by value.

Master It Describe the difference between passing data by reference and passing data by value.

Create a generic function. You can write, and save (File ➤ Export File) sets of generic functions that work in any VBA-enabled application.

Master It Create a function that displays the current year in a message box. This function will require no arguments, nor will it return any value.

Create a function for Word. Word contains a whole set of objects and members unique to word-processing tasks. Functions that are specific to Word employ one or more of these unique features of the Word object model.

Master It Write a function that displays the number of hyperlinks in the currently active document. Use Word's `Hyperlinks` collection to get this information.

Create a function for Excel. Excel uses an `ActiveWorkbook` object to represent the currently selected workbook. You can employ a full set of built-in methods to manipulate the features of any workbook.

Master It Using the `Sheets` collection of Excel's `ActiveWorkbook` object, write a function that displays the number of sheets in the current workbook.

Create a function for PowerPoint. PowerPoint's object model includes an `ActivePresentation` object, representing the currently selected presentation. Functions can make good use of this object and its members.

Master It Write a function that returns how many slides are on a presentation. Pass the `ActivePresentation` object as an argument to this function; then display the number of slides the presentation contains. Call this function from a subroutine.

Create a function for Access. Access often works a little differently from other VBA-enabled Office applications. For example, some common tasks are carried out by using methods of the special `DoCmd` object rather than methods of a `Form` or `Table` object.

Master It Write a function that closes Access by using the `DoCmd` object's `Quit` method. Ensure that all data is saved by employing the `acQuitSaveAll` constant as an argument for the `Quit` method.

Chapter 11

Making Decisions in Your Code

Computers behave intelligently in large part because programming languages offer a way to test conditions. Then based on the results of that test, the code jumps (*branches*) to an appropriate area within the program. This is similar to human decision-making: If it's raining, then take an umbrella. If not, leave it at home.

This chapter covers what are called *conditional* expressions. VBA uses them to create decision structures to direct the flow—the path of execution—of your procedures.

By using decision structures, you can cause your procedures to branch to different sections of code depending on such things as the value of a variable or expression or whether the user clicks the OK or Cancel button in a message box.

VBA offers two types of decision structures: `If` blocks and `Select Case` blocks. And there is a subset of various kinds of `If` statements suitable for making a variety of different kinds of decisions.

However, for more complicated decision-making, you'll want to use the heavy-duty `Select Case` block structure. It's more efficient when working with truly involved decisions.

The chapter starts by introducing you to the comparison operators and logical operators you can use when building conditional expressions and logical expressions. Then it covers the different types of `If` blocks, which take up the bulk of the chapter. At the end of the chapter, you'll learn how to use `Select Case`.

IN THIS CHAPTER, YOU WILL LEARN TO DO THE FOLLOWING:

- Use comparison operators
- Compare one item with another
- Test multiple conditions
- Use `If` blocks
- Use `Select Case` blocks

How Do You Compare Things in VBA?

To compare things in VBA, you use *comparison operators* to specify what type of comparison you want: whether one variable or expression is equal to another, whether one is greater than another, whether one is less than or equal to another, and so on.

VBA supports the comparison operators shown in Table 11.1.

TABLE 11.1: VBA's comparison operators

OPERATOR	MEANING	EXAMPLE
=	Equal to	If strMyString="Hello" Then
<>	Not equal to	If x <> 5 Then
<	Less than	If y < 100 Then
>	Greater than	If strMyString > "handle" Then
<=	Less than or equal to	If intMyCash <= 10 Then
>=	Greater than or equal to	If Time >= 12:00 PM Then MsgBox "It's afternoon." Else MsgBox "It's morning." End If
Is	Is the same object variable as	If Object1 **Is** Object2 Then

The first six comparison operators shown in Table 11.1 are straightforward. Numeric expressions are evaluated as you would expect. Alphabetical expressions are evaluated in alphabetical order: For example, because *ax* comes before *handle* in alphabetical order, it's considered "less than" *handle*.

So, "ax" < "handle" would evaluate to True. And whether an evaluation results in True or False determines what happens in an If…Then block. (In other words, the code in the Then section is executed when something is True. And it is not executed if something is False. Think of it this way: If it's raining, Then take an umbrella. Otherwise, don't.)

Mixed expressions (numbers and letters) are evaluated in alphabetical order as well: *Office 97* is "greater than" *Office 2016* because 9 is greater than 2.

Is, the seventh comparison operator, is less familiar and less often used. You use Is to compare object variables to establish whether two object variables represent the same object (a named object, not an object such as a document or a range).

For example, the following statements declare two objects—objTest1 and objTest2—and assign to each ActiveDocument.Paragraphs(1).Range, the range consisting of the first paragraph in the active document in Word. The next statement then compares the two objects to each other, returning False in the message box because the two objects are different even though their contents are the same:

```
Dim objTest1 As Object
Dim objTest2 As Object
Set objTest1 = ActiveDocument.Paragraphs(1).Range
```

```
Set objTest2 = ActiveDocument.Paragraphs(1).Range
'the next statement returns False because the objects are different
MsgBox objTest1 Is objTest2
```

However, if both object variables refer to the same object, the `Is` comparison returns `True`, as in the following example in which both `objTest1` and `objTest2` refer to the object variable `objTest3`:

```
Dim objTest1 As Object
Dim objTest2 As Object
Dim objTest3 As Object
Set objTest3 = ActiveDocument.Paragraphs(1).Range
Set objTest1 = objTest3
Set objTest2 = objTest3
'the next statement returns True because
'objTest1 and objTest2 refer to the same object
MsgBox objTest1 Is objTest2
```

When using `Is`, keep in mind that it isn't the specific *contents* of the object variables that are being compared, but which *object* they refer to.

Testing Multiple Conditions by Using Logical Operators

Often, you'll need to test two or more conditions before taking an action: If statement X is `True` and statement Y is `True`, then do this; if statement X is `True` or statement Y is `True`, then do the other; if statement X is `True` and statement Y isn't `True`, then find something else to do; and so on. For example, if it's raining *and* you have a cold, put on your warmest rain gear.

To test multiple conditions, you use VBA's logical operators to link the conditions together. Table 11.2 lists the logical operators that VBA supports, with short examples and comments.

TABLE 11.2: VBA's logical operators

OPERATOR	MEANING	EXAMPLE	COMMENTS
`And`	Conjunction	`If ActiveWorkbook.FullName = "c:\temp\Example.xlsm" And Year(Date) >= 2005 Then`	If both conditions are `True`, the result is `True`. If either condition is `False`, the result is `False`.
`Not`	Negation	`ActivePresentation.Saved = Not ActivePresentation.Saved`	`Not` reverses the value of `x` (`True` becomes `False`; `False` becomes `True`). The `Saved` property used in this example is Boolean.
`Or`	Disjunction	`If ActiveWindow.View = wdPageView Or ActiveWindow.View = wdOutlineView Then`	If either the first condition or the second is `True`, or if both conditions are `True`, the result is `True`.

Table 11.2: VBA's logical operators *(continued)*

Operator	Meaning	Example	Comments
`XOr`	Exclusion	`If Salary > 55000` **`XOr`** `Experienced = True Then`	Tests for different results from the conditions. Returns `True` if one condition is `False` and the other is `True`; returns `False` if both conditions are `True` or both conditions are `False`.
`Eqv`	Equivalence	`If blnMyVar1` **`Eqv`** `blnMyVar2 Then`	Tests for logical equivalence between the two conditions. If both values are `True`, or if both values are `False`, `Eqv` returns `True`. If one condition is logically different from the other (that is, if one condition is `True` and the other is `False`), `Eqv` returns `False`.
`Imp`	Implication	`If blnMyVar1` **`Imp`** `blnMyVar2 Then`	Tests for logical implication. Returns `True` if both conditions are `True`, both conditions are `False`, or the second condition is `True`. Returns `Null` if both conditions are `Null` or if the second condition is `Null`. Otherwise, returns `False`.

Of these six logical operators, you'll probably use the conjunction (`And`), disjunction (`Or`), and negation (`Not`) operators the most, with the other three thrown in on special (in other words, rare) occasions. (If the `Imp` logical operator doesn't make sense to you at this point, you probably don't need to use it.)

VBA Doesn't Employ Short-Circuit Evaluation

Here's something to beware of when evaluating multiple conditions: VBA doesn't do *short-circuit evaluation* in logical expressions (unlike other programming languages, such as C and C++).

Short-circuit evaluation is the formal term for a simple logical technique most people use several times a day when making decisions in their daily lives: If the first of two or more dependent conditions is false, you typically don't waste time evaluating any additional conditions contingent upon it.

For example, suppose your most attractive coworker says they'll take you to lunch if you get the product out on time *and* get a promotion. If you don't get the product out on time, you've blown your chances—it doesn't much matter if you get the promotion because even if you do, your lunch will still be lonely. There's no point in evaluating the second condition because the result requires both conditions be met, and the first condition wasn't met. So, you can just short-circuit (skip) any further condition testing.

VBA doesn't think that way. It evaluates the second condition (and any subsequent conditions) whether or not it needs to. Evaluating all conditions takes a little more time (which isn't usually an issue), but it *can* introduce unexpected complications in your code (which can be an issue).

For example, the following snippet produces an error when the selection is only one character long. The error occurs because the code ends up running the `Mid` function on a zero-length string (the one-character selection minus one character)—even though you wouldn't expect this condition to be evaluated when the first condition is not met (because the length of the selection is not greater than 1):

```
Dim strShort As String
strShort = Selection.Text
If Len(strShort) > 1 And _
  Mid(strShort, Len(strShort) - 1, 1) = "T" Then
  MsgBox "The second-last character is T."
End If
```

To avoid problems such as this, use *nested* `If` blocks. In the following code example, the first condition isn't met (again, for a one-character selection), so the second condition isn't evaluated. Notice that one of the `If` blocks here is nested within (contained within) the other `If` block:

```
If Len(strShort) > 1 Then
  If Mid(strShort, Len(strShort) - 1, 1) = "T" Then
    MsgBox "The second-last character is T."
  End If
End If
```

Using *Not* to Toggle Boolean Properties

Here's a useful tip. The `Not` command is a handy way of turning `True` to `False` and `False` to `True`. By using `Not` with a Boolean variable or property, you can toggle the state of the variable or property without needing to check what the current state is. For example, in Excel, you could create an `If` structure to toggle the value of the Boolean property `Saved` (which controls whether Excel thinks the document in question contains unsaved changes) by using code such as this:

```
If ActiveWorkbook.Saved = True Then
  ActiveWorkbook.Saved = False
Else
  ActiveWorkbook.Saved = True
End If
```

But you can achieve the same toggling effect much more simply by using `Not` as shown in the following code:

```
ActiveWorkbook.Saved = Not ActiveWorkbook.Saved
```

If Blocks

As in most programming languages, `If` blocks in VBA are among the most immediately useful and versatile commands for making decisions.

In the sections that follow, you'll look at three variations on the `If` statement:

- `If...Then`
- `If...Then...Else`
- `If...Then...ElseIf...Else`

If...Then

`If...Then` statements tell VBA to make the simplest of decisions. If the condition is met, execute the following statement (or statements). If the condition isn't met, skip to the line immediately following the *conditional block.*

An `If` statement block begins with `If` and concludes with `End If`. (However, a short `If...Then` statement can be written entirely on a single line, in which case the `End If` is omitted.)

SYNTAX

Simple `If...Then` statements can be expressed entirely on a single line. A one-line `If...Then` statement looks like this:

```
If condition Then Code to be executed goes here
```

If the condition is met, VBA executes the statement or statements that follow *on that same logical line.* If the condition isn't met, VBA doesn't execute the statement or statements.

But you can also write multiline `If...Then` blocks. A multiple-line `If...Then` statement (the lines of code between `If` and `End If` are more properly known as a *block*) looks like this:

```
If condition Then
Code to be executed goes here
End If
```

If the condition is met, VBA executes all the code within the block (the statements enclosed between the `If` and `End If`). If the condition isn't met, VBA skips over the enclosed line or lines of code and resumes execution at the line after the `End If` statement.

SINGLE-LINE *IF* STATEMENTS DON'T USE *END IF*

Remember that a single-line `If...Then` statement has no `End If` to end it, whereas the `If` block requires an `End If`. VBA knows that a single-line `If` condition will end on the same line on which it starts. But an `If` block needs to have its end clearly specified so VBA knows which code to skip over if the condition evaluates to `False`. `If` blocks tend to be easier for humans to read.

EXAMPLES

In the previous chapters, you've already encountered a number of If blocks—this if…then testing process is so necessary in programming (not to mention in life itself) that it's hard to get anything done without them. The following sections show you some further examples.

One-Line **If** *Statements*

Here's an example of a one-line If statement:

```
Dim bytAge As Integer
bytAge = InputBox("Enter your age.", "Age")
If bytAge < 21 Then MsgBox "You may not purchase alcohol.",, "Underage"
```

The first line declares the Integer variable bytAge. The second line prompts the user to enter their age in an input box and stores the answer in the variable. The third line checks the value held in bytAge and displays an Underage message box if bytAge is less than 21.

You can include multiple statements on a single line if you separate the statements by a colon. A single-line If statement can sometimes be a good candidate for a multistatement line of code. What you are doing is specifying that more than one action should be taken if the expression in the If…Then statement evaluates to True.

For example, let's say you wanted to halt the macro after displaying the Underage message box. You could include the End statement after a colon on the same line, as shown here:

```
If bytAge < 21 Then MsgBox "You may not purchase alcohol.",, "Underage": End
```

VBA executes this as follows:

1. First, it evaluates the condition.
2. If the condition is met, it executes the first statement after Then—in this case, it displays the Underage message box. Then it proceeds to execute any further statements on that line. Notice that *all* statements on a single-line If structure are conditionally based on (dependent on) that If statement. They are executed (or not) based on whether the condition is true or false.
3. Once the user has dismissed the Underage message box (by clicking the OK button, the only button it has), VBA executes the statement after the colon: End.

If you wanted, you could even add several more statements on the same "logical" line, separated by colons. End would have to be the last one because it ends the procedure. (By the way, a *logical* line means that VBA sees this as a single line of code to be executed, no matter how many real-world, *physical* lines the code takes up on your monitor.)

You could even add another If statement if you felt like it:

```
If bytAge < 21 Then If bytAge > 18 Then MsgBox _
  "You may vote but you may not drink.",, "Underage": End
```

As you'll see if you're looking at this line in the Visual Basic Editor, there are a couple of problems with this approach:

- First, you need to break long lines of code with the line-continuation character or else they go off the edge of the Code window in the Editor, forcing you to scroll horizontally to read the ends of each line. You *could* hide all windows except the Code window, use a minute font size for your code, or buy a larger monitor, but you're probably still not going to have any fun working with long lines of code. So, in practice, you don't want to pile statements onto a single code line. The brief `End` statement is probably the most you'll want to add.
- Second, long lines of code (broken or unbroken) that involve a number of statements tend to become visually confusing. Even if everything is obvious to you when you're entering the code, you may find the code hard to read when you have to debug it a few months later. Usually, it's better to use `If` blocks rather than complex one-line `If` statements.

If *Blocks*

Block `If` constructions work the same way as one-line `If` statements except blocks contain multiple lines—typically with one command to each line—and they require an `End If` statement at the end. For example, the one-line `If` statement from the previous section could also be constructed as an `If` block like this:

```
If bytAge < 21 Then
  MsgBox "You may not purchase alcohol.",, "Underage"
  End
End If
```

If the condition in the first line (the line with the `If` command) is `True`, VBA executes the statements within the block `If`. VBA displays the message box and then executes the `End` statement.

As you can see from this example, `If` blocks are much easier to read (and, therefore, easier to debug) than complicated one-line `If` statements. This is especially true when you nest `If` statements within one another, which you'll need to do fairly often.

To make `If` blocks easier to read, the convention is to press the Tab key to indent the lines within the block (VBA ignores the indentation during execution). You can see this indentation in the previous code example.

With short `If` blocks, like the ones shown in this section, indentation doesn't make a great deal of difference. But with complex `If` statements, it can make all the difference between clarity and incomprehensibility, as you'll see in "Nesting `If` Blocks" later in this chapter.

If...Then...Else Statements

`If...Then` statements are good for taking a single course of action based on a condition, but often you'll need to decide between two courses of action. To do so, you use the `If...Then...Else` statement.

By using an `If...Then...Else` statement, you can take one course of action if a condition is `True` and another course of action if it's `False`. It's the equivalent of ordinary language, such as `If` it's raining, `Then` take an umbrella, `Else` wear sunscreen.

For example, `If...Then... Else` statements are a great way to deal with two-button message boxes. If the user clicks the OK button, the code will do one thing. If they click the Cancel button, it will do something different.

USE *IF...THEN...ELSE* WITH CLEAR-CUT TRUE/FALSE SITUATIONS

The `If...Then...Else` statement is best used with clear-cut binary conditions—those that lend themselves to a true/false analysis. (Recall that a binary condition is like a two-position light switch—if it's not switched on, it must be switched off.) For more complex conditions, such as switches that can have three or more positions, you need to use a more complex logical statement, such as `If...Then...ElseIf...Else` or `Select Case`. We'll get to these structures later in this chapter.

SYNTAX

The syntax for the `If...Then...Else` statement is as follows:

```
If condition Then
statements1
Else
statements2
End If
```

If the condition is `True`, VBA executes *`statements1`*, the first group of statements. If the condition is `False`, VBA moves execution to the `Else` line and executes *`statements2`*, the second group of statements.

Again, you have the option of creating one-line `If...Then...Else` statements or block `If...Then...Else` statements. However, it makes more sense to create block `If...Then...Else` statements because they're much easier to read and debug, and because an `If...Then...Else` structure is inherently longer than an `If...Then` structure and thus certain to result in an awkwardly long line.

EXAMPLE

As a straightforward example of an `If...Then...Else` statement, consider the `Electronic_Book_Critic` procedure shown in Listing 11.1.

LISTING 11.1: A simple `If...Then` example

```
Sub Electronic_Book_Critic()

   Dim intBookPages As Integer

   intBookPages = InputBox _
    ("Enter the number of pages in the last book you read.", _
    "The Electronic Book Critic")
   If intBookPages > 1000 Then
     MsgBox "That book is seriously long.", vbOKOnly _
       + vbExclamation, "The Electronic Book Critic"
   Else
```

```
9.      MsgBox "That book is not so long.", vbOKOnly _
          + vbInformation, "The Electronic Book Critic"
10.   End If
11.
12. End Sub
```

Here's what happens in Listing 11.1:

- Line 1 starts the procedure, and line 12 ends it. Lines 2, 4, and 11 are spacers.
- Line 3 declares the Integer variable `intBookPages`. Line 5 then assigns to `intBookPages` the result of an input box prompting users to enter the number of pages in the last book they read.
- Line 6 checks to see if `intBookPages` is greater than 1000. If it is, the statement in line 7 runs, displaying a message box that states that the book is long.
- If `intBookPages` is not greater than 1000, VBA branches to the `Else` statement in line 8 and executes the statement following it, which displays a message box telling the user that the book wasn't so long.
- Line 10 ends the `If` condition.

If…Then…ElseIf…Else Statements

The last variation of the `If` command that you'll look at here is the `If…Then…ElseIf…Else` block, which you can use to help VBA decide between multiple courses of action. You can use any number of `ElseIf` lines, depending on how complex the condition is that you need to check.

Again, you could create either one-line `If…Then…ElseIf…Else` statements or `If…Then…ElseIf…Else` blocks. However, in almost all cases, `If…Then…ElseIf…Else` blocks are easier to construct, to read, and to debug. As with the other `If` statements, one-line `If…Then…ElseIf…Else` statements don't need an `End If` statement, but `If…Then…ElseIf…Else` blocks do need one.

Syntax

The syntax for `If…Then…ElseIf…Else` is as follows:

```
If condition1 Then
statements1
ElseIf condition2 Then
statements2
[ElseIf condition3 Then
statements3]
[Else
statements4]
End If
```

If the condition expressed in *condition1* is True, VBA executes *statements1*, the first block of statements, and then resumes execution at the line after the End If clause. If *condition1* is False, VBA branches to the first ElseIf clause and evaluates the condition expressed in *condition2*. If this is True, VBA executes *statements2* and then moves to the line after the End If line; if it's False, VBA moves to the next ElseIf clause (if there is one) and evaluates its condition (here, *condition3*) in turn.

If *all* the conditions in the ElseIf statements prove False, VBA branches to the Else statement (if there is one) and executes the statements after it (here, statements4). The End If statement then terminates the conditional statement, and execution resumes with the line after the End If.

The Else clause is optional, although in many cases it's a good idea to include it to let VBA take a different course of action if none of the conditions specified in the If and ElseIf clauses turns out to be True. You, the programmer, can't always predict the conditions when your program runs, so it helps to have an Else at the end of your list of If's. This is how you can handle a situation you didn't account for in the list.

You can have any number of ElseIf clauses in an If block, each with its own condition. But if you find yourself needing to use If statements with large numbers of ElseIf clauses (say, more than 5 or 10), you may want to try using the Select Case command instead, which you'll look at toward the end of the chapter.

Examples

This section shows you two examples of If…Then…ElseIf…Else statements:

- A simple If…Then…ElseIf…Else statement for taking action based on which button the user clicks in a three-button message box
- An If…Then…ElseIf statement without an Else clause

A Simple If…Then…ElseIf…Else Statement

A simple If…Then…ElseIf…Else statement, as used in Listing 11.2, is perfect for dealing with a three-button message box.

Listing 11.2: Understanding the **If…Then…ElseIf…Else** structure

```
Sub Creating_a_Document()

  Dim lngButton As Long
  Dim strMessage As String

  strMessage = "Create a new document based on the " & _
   "VP Report project?" & vbCr & vbCr & _
   "Click Yes to use the VP Report template." & vbCr & _
   "Click No to use a blank document." & vbCr & _
   "Click Cancel to stop creating a new document."
```

```
7.
8.    lngButton = MsgBox _
       (strMessage, vbYesNoCancel + vbQuestion, "Create New Document")
9.
10.   If lngButton = vbYes Then
11.     Documents.Add Template:= "z:\public\template\vpreport.dotm"
12.   ElseIf lngButton = vbNo Then
13.     Documents.Add
14.   Else  'lngButton is vbCancel
15.     End
16.   End If
17.
18. End Sub
```

The `Creating_a_Document` procedure in Listing 11.2 displays a Yes/No/Cancel message box inviting the user to create a new document based on the VP Report project. The user can choose the Yes button to create such a document, the No button to create a blank document, or the Cancel button to cancel out of the procedure without creating a document at all.

Here's what happens:

- Line 1 starts the procedure, and line 18 ends it.
- Line 2 is a spacer, after which line 3 declares the Long variable `lngButton` and line 4 declares the String variable `strMessage`. Line 5 is another spacer.
- Line 6 assigns to the String variable `strMessage` a long string that contains all the text for the message box. Line 7 is another spacer.
- Line 8 displays the message box, using `strMessage` as the prompt, specifying the `vbYesNoCancel` constant to produce a Yes/No/Cancel message box, and applying a suitable title (Create New Document). It assigns the result of the message box to the Long variable `lngButton`. Line 9 is a spacer.
- Line 10 starts the `If`...Then...`ElseIf`...`Else` statement, comparing the value of `lngButton` to `vbYes`.

  If line 10 matches, line 11 uses the Add method of the `Documents` object to create a new document based on the `vpreport.dotm` template. If not, the `ElseIf` condition in line 12 is evaluated, comparing the value of `lngButton` to `vbNo`. If you run this procedure and choose the Yes button in the message box, you will need to have a template named `vpreport.dotm` in the folder `z:\public\template\` for line 11 to run. If you don't have the template, you'll get an error. Given that you're unlikely to have this template, you might want to change the path and filename to a template that you *do* have.
- If this second comparison matches, line 13 uses the Add method of the `Documents` object to create a new blank document. If not, the `Else` statement in line 14 is activated because the user must have chosen the Cancel button in the message box. The End statement in line 15 ends execution of the procedure.
- Line 16 ends the `If` statement. Line 17 is a spacer.

This example is a little unusual in that the Else statement is limited to three possible branches because that's the number of possible responses from a message box—Yes, No, and Cancel.

Because the If statement checks for the vbYes response and the ElseIf statement checks for the vbNo response, only the vbCancel response will trigger the Else statement.

In other circumstances, the Else statement can serve as a catchall for *anything* not caught by the If and ElseIf statements above the Else, so you need to make sure the If and ElseIf statements cover all the contingencies you want evaluated *before* the Else statement kicks in. So, put the Else statement at the bottom of the block.

For example, if you quiz the reader about the colors of the US flag, you must provide If and ElseIf statements for red, white, and blue. If you omit, for example, *white* (one of the possibilities), and the user types in *white,* your code will fall through to the Else statement, which might display an incorrect message such as "The color you entered is not on the flag."

An If...Then...ElseIf *Statement Without an* Else *Clause*

You can use an If...Then...ElseIf statement without an Else clause when you don't need to take an action if none of the conditions in the If statement proves True. In the previous example, the situation had three clearly defined outcomes: The user could choose the Yes button, the No button, or the Cancel button in the message box. So, you were able to use an If clause to test whether the user chose the Yes button, an ElseIf clause to test whether the user chose the No button, and an Else clause to test whether neither was chosen (meaning that the Cancel button was chosen). (Clicking the Close button [X] on the title bar of a message box is the equivalent of choosing the Cancel button in the message box.)

As an example of a situation in which you don't need to take action if no condition is True, consider the If statement in the Check_Password procedure in Listing 11.3. This procedure checks to ensure that the password a user enters to protect an item is of a suitable length.

LISTING 11.3: Taking no action when no condition is true

```
Sub Check_Password()

  Dim strPassword As String

BadPassword:

  strPassword = InputBox _
   ("Enter the password to protect this item from changes:", _
   "Enter Password")

  If Len(strPassword) = 0 Then
    End
  ElseIf Len(strPassword) < 6 Then
    MsgBox "The password you chose is too short." & vbCr _
     & vbCr & "Please choose a password between " & _
     "6 and 15 characters in length.", _
    vbOKOnly + vbCritical, "Unsuitable Password"
    GoTo BadPassword
```

```
14.     ElseIf Len(strPassword) > 15 Then
15.         MsgBox "The password you chose is too long." & vbCr _
            & vbCr & "Please choose a password between " & _
            "6 and 15 characters in length.",
            vbOKOnly + vbCritical, "Unsuitable Password"
16.         GoTo BadPassword
17.     End If
18.
19. End Sub
```

This procedure forces users to enter an acceptable password. Here's what happens:

- Line 1 starts the procedure, and line 19 ends it.
- Line 2 is a spacer, after which line 3 declares the String variable `strPassword`.
- Line 4 is a spacer. Line 5 contains a label, `BadPassword`, to which VBA will loop if the password the user enters proves to be unsuitable. Line 6 is another spacer.
- Line 7 displays an input box prompting the user to enter a password, which VBA stores in the variable `strPassword`. Line 8 is a spacer.
- Line 9 checks `strPassword` to see if its length is zero, which means it's an empty string. This could mean that either the user clicked the Cancel button in the input box or the user clicked the OK button without entering any text in the text box of the input box. Either of these actions causes VBA to branch to line 10, where it executes the `End` statement that ends execution of the procedure.
- If the length of `strPassword` isn't zero (that is, the user has entered text into the text box of the input box and clicked the OK button), the `If` clause in line 9 is `False` and VBA moves to line 11, where it checks to see if the length of `strPassword` is less than six characters.
- If the length of `strPassword` is zero, VBA executes the code in lines 12 and 13. Line 12 displays a message box telling the user that the password is too short and specifying the length criteria for the password. This message box contains only an OK button, so when the user clicks it to continue, VBA continues with line 13, which returns execution to the `BadPassword` label on line 5. From there the procedure repeats itself, redisplaying the input box so that the user can try again.
- If the length of `strPassword` isn't more than 15 characters, execution passes from line 11 to the second `ElseIf` clause in line 14, where VBA checks to see if the length of `strPassword` is more than 15 characters.
- If the length of `strPassword` is more than 15 characters, VBA executes the code in lines 15 and 16: Line 15 displays a message box (again, with only an OK button) telling the user that the password is too long, and line 16 returns execution to the `BadPassword` label, again displaying the input box.

There's no need for an `Else` statement in this case because once the user has supplied a password that doesn't trigger the `If` clause or either of the `ElseIf` clauses, execution moves out of the `If` block and continues at the line after the `End If` statement.

Creating Loops with *If* and *GoTo*

So far in this book, you've seen several examples of For...Next loops and For Each...Next loops. (Chapter 12, "Using Loops to Repeat Actions," shows you how to construct these types of loops and other types, such as Do loops.) You can also create loops with If statements and the GoTo statement, as you did in the last example.

But many teachers and programmers frown upon making loops with If and GoTo. It's bad practice because If...GoTo loops can create "spaghetti code" (execution paths that jump around in a haphazard way and are hard to visualize). Such paths can be not only grotesque in themselves, but also a nightmare to debug.

However, *simple* versions of If and GoTo loops can work perfectly well, so even if you choose not to use this technique yourself, you should at least know how such loops work. Whether or not to ban GoTo from your code is a matter of personal preference, company policy, or your teacher's beliefs.

If nothing else, you might one day be responsible for working with someone else's code—someone whose standards aren't as rigorous as yours regarding the notorious GoTo command. So, let's take a brief look at how GoTo can be used.

Syntax

The GoTo statement is straightforward and can be useful—it's already been used several times in the examples you've looked at so far in this book (in Listings 7.2 and 9.2, for example). The syntax is as follows:

```
GoTo line
```

Here, the line argument can be a line label (or, rarely these days, a line number) within the current procedure.

A line number is simply a number placed at the beginning of a line to identify it. For example, consider this demonstration of GoTo:

```
Sub Demo_of_GoTo()
1
  If MsgBox("Go to line 1?", vbYesNo) = vbYes Then
    GoTo 1
  End If
End Sub
```

The second line here contains only the line number 1, which identifies the line. The third line displays a message box offering the choice of going back to line 1; if the user chooses the Yes button, VBA executes the GoTo 1 statement and returns to the line labeled 1, after which it displays the message box again. (If the user chooses the No button, the If block is exited.)

However, it's usually better to use a line *label* than a line number. A line label is a name for a line. A label starts with a letter and ends with a colon. Between the letter and the colon, the label can consist of any combination of characters. For example, earlier in this chapter you saw the label BadPassword: used to loop back to an earlier stage in a procedure when certain conditions were met. Perhaps the quintessential example of a label is the Bye: label traditionally placed at the end of a procedure for use with this GoTo statement:

```
GoTo Bye
```

When this label is placed just above the End...Sub command, it simply exits the macro.

GoTo is usually used with a condition. If you use it without a condition to go back to a line earlier in the code than the GoTo statement, you're apt to create an *infinite loop* (this bug is discussed in Chapter 12). And if you were to use the GoTo Bye statement without a condition, you would guarantee that your procedure would stop executing—no statement after this line would ever be executed. You would be jumping to the end of the macro.

EXAMPLE

As an example of a GoTo statement with a condition, you might use a GoTo Bye statement together with a message box that makes sure that the user wants to run a certain procedure:

```
Response = MsgBox("Do you want to create a daily report for " & _
  "the head office from the current document?", _
  vbYesNo + vbQuestion, "Create Daily Report")
If Response = vbNo Then GoTo Bye
```

If the user chooses the No button in the message box that the first line displays, VBA executes the GoTo Bye statement, branching to the Bye: label located at the end of the subroutine.

Another good reason to avoid using line numbers as targets is that you might later insert some code prior to the target line, which would likely result in an error (because the correct target line number will have changed because of your insert).

Nesting *If* Blocks

You can *nest* If blocks (put one inside another) as needed to manage any contortions required in your code. Each nested If block must be complete in and of itself. (This means each nested block must start with an If and conclude with its own End...If.)

For example, if you nest one If block within another If block (but forget the End If that concludes the nested If), VBA assumes that the End If line for the outer If actually pairs with the nested If. That's so wrong.

To make your If blocks easy to read, indent them to different levels. This is particularly important when nesting If blocks. Indenting provides you with visual cues, making it clear which If line is paired with each End If line. In other words, indentation makes the various If blocks stand out.

To see how this is done, check out the following nested If statements:

```
If condition1 Then       'start of first If
  If condition2 Then      'start of second If
    If condition3 Then    'start of third If
      statements1
    ElseIf condition4 Then 'ElseIf for third If
      statements2
    Else            'Else for third If
      statements3
    End If          'End If for third If
  Else              'Else for second If
    If condition5 Then    'start of fourth If
      statements4
```

```
13.     End If          'End If for fourth If
14.   End If            'End If for second If
15. Else                'Else for first If
16.   statements5
17. End If              'End If for first If
```

By following the layout, you can easily trace the flow of execution. For example, if `condition1` in line 1 is `False`, VBA branches to the `Else` statement in line 15 and continues execution from there. If `condition1` in line 1 is `True`, VBA evaluates the nested `condition2` in line 2, and so on.

The indentation is for visual clarity only. It makes comprehension easier for us humans—VBA pays no attention to it. The previous nested `If` commands are also annotated with comments so that you can see which `Else`, `ElseIf`, and `End If` line belongs with which `If` line. However, with the indentation, commenting is unnecessary.

By contrast, check out the unindented version of these nested blocks. This version is hard for the human eye to follow—and is even harder when it's buried in a morass of other code:

```
1. If condition1 Then
2. If condition2 Then
3. If condition3 Then
4. statements1
5. ElseIf condition4 Then
6. statements2
7. Else
8. statements3
9. End If
10. Else
11. If condition5 Then
12. statements4
13. End If
14. End If
15. Else                '
16. statements5
17. End If
```

There's seldom a pressing need to nest multiple `If` blocks. Often, you'll need only to nest a simple `If…Then` statement within an `If…Then…Else` statement or within an `If…Then…ElseIf…Else` statement. Listing 11.4 shows an example using Word.

LISTING 11.4: Nesting an `If…Then` block

```
Selection.HomeKey Unit:=wdStory
Selection.Find.ClearFormatting
Selection.Find.Style = ActiveDocument.Styles("Heading 5")
Selection.Find.Text = " "
Selection.Find.Execute
If Selection.Find.Found Then
  lngResponse = MsgBox("Make this into a special note?", _
    vbOKCancel, "Make Special Note")
```

```
 8.    If lngResponse = vbOK Then
 9.       Selection.Style = "Special Note"
10.    End If
11. End If
```

The code in Listing 11.4 searches through the active document for the Heading 5 style and, if it finds the style, displays a message box offering to make it into a special note by applying the Special Note style. Here's what happens:

- Line 1 starts by returning the insertion point to the beginning of the document.
- Line 2 clears formatting from the `Find` command (to make sure that it isn't searching for inappropriate formatting).
- Line 3 sets Heading 5 as the style for which the `Find` command is searching, and Line 4 sets the search string as an empty string (" ").
- Line 5 then runs the `Find` operation.
- Lines 6 through 11 contain the outer `If…Then` loop. Line 6 checks to see if the `Find` operation in line 5 found a paragraph in Heading 5 style. If it did, VBA runs the code in lines 7 through 10.
- Line 7 displays a message box asking if the user wants to make the paragraph into a special note.
- Line 8 begins the nested `If…Then` statement and checks the user's response to the message box.
- If the user's response is a `vbOK`—if the user chose the OK button—VBA executes the statement in line 9, which applies the Special Note style (which I'll assume is included in the styles available to the current document or template) to the paragraph.
- Line 10 contains the `End If` statement for the nested `If…Then` block, and line 11 contains the `End If` statement for the outer `If…Then` block.

If you expect a document to contain more than one instance of the Heading 5 style, use a `Do While…Loop` loop to search for each instance. See Chapter 12 for details on `Do While…Loop` loops.

Select Case Blocks

The `Select Case` block provides an effective alternative to complex multiple `If…Then` blocks or multiple `ElseIf` statements. `Select Case` combines the same decision-making capability of `If` constructions with tighter and more readable code.

Use the `Select Case` statement when the decision you need to make is complicated because it involves more than two or three different values that are being evaluated

`Select Case` blocks are easier to read than complex `If…Then` blocks, mostly because there's less code. This also makes `Select Case` blocks easier to modify: when you need to adjust one or more of the values used, you have less code to wade through.

Syntax

The syntax for `Select Case` is as follows:

```
Select Case TestExpression
  Case Expression1
Statements1
  [Case Expression2
Statements2]
  [Case Else
StatementsElse]
End Select
```

Here's how the syntax breaks down:

- `Select Case` starts the block, and `End Select` ends it.
- *`TestExpression`* is the expression that determines which of the `Case` statements executes.
- *`Expression1`*, *`Expression2`*, and so on are the expressions against which VBA matches `TestExpression`.

For example, you might test to see which of a number of buttons in a user form the user chose. The *`TestExpression`* would be tied to a button that's been chosen; if it were the first button, VBA would match that to *`Expression1`* and would run the statements in the lines following `Case` *`Expression1`*; if it were the second button, VBA would match that to *`Expression2`* and would run the statements in the lines following `Case` *`Expression2`*; and so on for the rest of the `Case` blocks.

`Case Else` is similar to the `Else` clause in an `If` block. `Case Else` is an optional clause that (if it's included) runs if none of the given expressions are matched.

Example

As an example of a `Select Case` block, consider Listing 11.5, which prompts users to enter their typing speed and then displays an appropriate response.

LISTING 11.5: Working with a `Select Case` structure

```
Sub Check_Typing_Speed()

    Dim varTypingSpeed As Variant
    Dim strMsg As String

    varTypingSpeed = InputBox _
      ("How many words can you type per minute?", "Typing Speed")
    Select Case varTypingSpeed
      Case " "
        End
      Case Is < 0, 0, 1 To 50
        strMsg = "please learn to type properly before " & _
        "applying for a job."
```

```
12.      Case 50 To 60
13.        strMsg = "Your typing could do with a little brushing up. "
14.      Case 60 To 75
15.        strMsg = "We are satisfied with your typing speed."
16.      Case 75 To 99
17.        strMsg = "Your typing is more than adequate. "
18.      Case 100 To 200
19.        strMsg = "You wear out keyboards with your blinding speed."
20.      Case Is > 200
21.        strMsg = "I doubt that's true."
22.    End Select
23.
24.    MsgBox strMsg, vbOKOnly, "Typing Speed"
25.
26. End Sub
```

Here's what happens in the `Check_Typing_Speed` procedure in Listing 11.5:

- Line 1 starts the procedure, and line 26 ends it.
- Line 2 is a spacer. Line 3 declares the Variant variable `varTypingSpeed`, and line 4 declares the String variable `strMsg`. Line 5 is another spacer.
- Line 6 displays an input box prompting the user to enter their typing speed. It stores this value in the variable `varTypingSpeed`.
- Line 7 begins the `Select Case` block, predicating it on the variable `varTypingSpeed`.
- Next, VBA evaluates each of the `Case` clauses in turn until it finds one that proves `True`. The first `Case` clause, in line 8, compares `varTypingSpeed` to an empty string (`" "`) to see if the user chose the Cancel button in the input box or clicked the OK button without entering a value in the text box. If `Case " "` is `True`, VBA executes the `End` statement in line 9, ending the procedure.
- If `Case " "` is `False`, VBA moves execution to the next `Case` clause—line 10 in this example—where it compares `varTypingSpeed` to three items: less than 0 (`Is < 0`), 0, and the range 1 to 50 words per minute. Notice three things here:
    1. You can include multiple comparison items in the same `Case` statement by separating them from each other with commas.
    2. Using the `Is` keyword with the comparison operator (here, the *less than* operator) checks the relation of two numbers to each other.
    3. The `To` keyword denotes the range of values.
- If `varTypingSpeed` matches one of the comparison items in line 10, VBA assigns to the String variable `strMsg` the text on line 11 and then continues execution at the line after the `End Select` statement.

- If `varTypingSpeed` isn't within this range, VBA moves to the next `Case` clause and evaluates it in turn. When VBA finds a `Case` clause that's `True`, it executes the statement following that clause (in this case, assigning a text string to the `strMsg` variable) and then continues execution at the line after the `End Select` statement.
- For any case other than that in line 8 (which ends the procedure), line 24 displays a message box containing the text stored in the statement `strMsg`.

A `Select Case` block can be a good way of specifying which action to take based on the user's choice from a ListBox or ComboBox control (these controls are explored in Chapter 14, "Creating Simple Custom Dialog Boxes").

Typically, a list box or combo box displays a list of many different options, such as all the states in the USA. Then, after the user clicks to select an item within a ListBox or ComboBox control, the chosen item appears in the control's `Value` property. Your macro could then check this `Value` property as the test expression in your `Select Case` block and take action accordingly.

When Order Matters

One final point about complex test structures. You need to ensure that your `Select Case` and `If...Then...Else` statements (or other multiple `If` structures) evaluate their test conditions in the appropriate order. This means that each condition to be evaluated must *exclude* all the conditions that follow it.

Let's say you're asking the user how old they are, and you set up your test cases like this:

```
1.  Age = InputBox ("How old are you?")
2.
3.  Select Case Age
4.
5.    Case < 50
6.      strMsg = "You're nearing retirement."
7.
8.    Case < 12
9.      strMsg = "Hello, youngster."
```

This is a logic bug, and a bad one. Line 8 can never execute because everyone under 50, including those younger than 12, will trigger line 5. (The expression "less than 50" *includes* "less than 12.")

To work properly, these tests must be reversed, like this:

```
Case < 12
   strMsg = "Hello, youngster."

Case < 50
  strMsg = "You're nearing retirement."
```

You can avoid this problem entirely by testing for equality or a range, as illustrated in Listing 11.5:

```
Case 50 To 60
```

The Bottom Line

Use comparison operators. Comparison operators compare items using such tests as *greater than or not equal to.*

Master It Write a line of code that uses a *less than* comparison to test whether a variable named `Surplus` is less than 1200.

Compare one item with another. You can compare strings using *less than* and *more than* comparison operators.

Master It What symbol do you use to determine if `VariableA` is lower in the alphabet than `VariableB`?

Test multiple conditions. To test multiple conditions, you use VBA's *logical operators* to link the conditions together.

Master It Name two of the most commonly used logical operators.

Use `If` blocks. `If` blocks are among the most common programming structures. They are often the best way to allow code to make decisions. To test two conditions, use `If...Else...EndIf`.

Master It Write an `If...Else...End If` block of code that displays two message boxes. If the temperature (the variable `Temp`) is greater than 80, tell the user that it's hot outside. Otherwise, tell the user that it's not that hot.

Use `Select Case` blocks. `Select Case` structures can be a useful alternative to `If` blocks.

Master It When should you use a `Select Case` structure?

Chapter 12

Using Loops to Repeat Actions

As in life, so in macros. Sometimes, you'll want to repeat an action a predetermined number of times: break six eggs to make an omelet, write two letters, nap for 20 minutes.

More often, though, you'll just repeat an action until a certain condition is met: break eggs until the pan is full, or buy two lottery tickets a week until you hit it big, or subtract five from every instance of a value in an Excel spreadsheet. In these situations, you don't know in advance when you'll triumph against the wretched odds of the lottery or how many times the value will appear in the spreadsheet—your code must simply carry on until the condition is met. These, then, are the two types of loops: keep doing something until 1) you've done it a particular number of times or 2) you've finished the job.

In VBA, you use *loops* to repeat actions. VBA provides a number of ways to use loops in your code. In this chapter, you'll learn about the different types of loops and typical uses for each.

IN THIS CHAPTER, YOU WILL LEARN TO DO THE FOLLOWING:

- Understand when to use loops
- Use `For`...loops for fixed repetitions
- Use `Do`...loops for variable numbers of repetitions
- Nest one loop within another loop
- Avoid infinite loops

When Should You Use a Loop?

To repeat an action or a series of actions in VBA, you could record the repetition itself into a macro by using the Macro Recorder (if the application you're using supports the Macro Recorder—remember that only Word and Excel do).

Or you could copy some code and paste it back into the macro multiple times to repeat the behavior. For example, you could record a macro containing the code for creating a new Word document based on the default template, open the macro in the Visual Basic Editor, and then copy this new-document code and paste it five times to create a procedure that makes six new documents.

It's almost always much better, however, to just write a loop block (structure) to repeat the commands as necessary.

Loops have several straightforward advantages over repetitive, redundant code:

- Your procedures are shorter—they contain less code and fewer instructions—and are, therefore, easier to understand.
- Your procedures are more flexible: Instead of hard-coding the number of repetitions, you can vary the number as necessary. (*Hard-coding* means writing fixed, unchanging code as opposed to flexible, variable code. An example of fixed code would be *Create six new documents;* whereas an example of flexible would be *Create x number of new documents,* thereby allowing the user or the code to supply the value of *x*.)
- Your procedures are easier to test, debug, and modify, particularly by people other than you.

That said, if you just need to repeat one or more actions two or three times in a procedure and that procedure will *always* need to repeat the action this same number of times, there's nothing wrong with hard-coding the procedure by repeating the code. It'll work fine, it's easy to do, and you won't have to spend time considering the logic of loops. The code will be longer and a tad harder to maintain, but that's no big deal in simple situations.

Understanding the Basics of Loops

In VBA, a loop is a structure (block of code) that repeats a number of statements, looping back to the beginning of the structure once it has finished executing the code lines within. Each cycle of execution of a loop is called an *iteration*.

Here's another way to describe the two basic categories of loops:

- *Fixed-iteration loops* repeat a set number of times (six eggs).
- *Indefinite loops* repeat a flexible number of times (enough eggs to fill whatever pan is being used).

The execution of either type of loop is controlled by the *loop invariant*, also called the *loop determinant*. This can be either a numeric expression or a logical expression. Fixed-iteration loops typically use numeric expressions, whereas indefinite loops typically use logical expressions. For example, a fixed-iteration loop might specify that the loop will iterate five times, while an indefinite loop might continue iterating until the end of a document is reached.

Table 12.1 explains the types of loops that VBA provides.

TABLE 12.1: VBA's loop types

LOOP	TYPE	EXPLANATION
`For...Next`	Fixed	Repeats an action or a sequence of actions a given number of times.
`For Each...Next`	Fixed	Repeats an action or a sequence of actions once for each object in a VBA collection.
`Do While...Loop`	Indefinite	Performs an action or a sequence of actions if a condition is `True` and continues to perform it until the condition becomes `False`.

TABLE 12.1: VBA's loop types *(CONTINUED)*

LOOP	TYPE	EXPLANATION
`While...Wend`	Indefinite	Performs an action or a sequence of actions if a condition is `True` and continues to perform it until the condition becomes `False`. This type of loop is similar to `Do...Loop While` but is now almost obsolete.
`Do Until...Loop`	Indefinite	Performs an action or sequence of actions while a condition is `False` and continues to perform it until the condition becomes `True`.
`Do...Loop While`	Indefinite	Performs an action or a sequence of actions once and then repeats it while a condition is `True` until it becomes `False`.
`Do...Loop Until`	Indefinite	Performs an action or a sequence of actions once and repeats it while a condition is `False` until it becomes `True`.

Using *For*...Loops for Fixed Repetitions

`For`...loops execute for a fixed number of times. `For...Next` loops repeat for the number of times of your choosing, while `For Each...Next` loops execute once for each element in a specified VBA collection.

For...Next Loops

A `For...Next` loop repeats an action or a sequence of actions a given number of times. How many times it loops is specified by a *counter variable*. The counter variable can be hard-coded into the procedure, passed from an input box or dialog box, or passed from a value generated either by a different part of the procedure or by a different procedure.

SYNTAX

The syntax for `For...Next` loops is as follows:

```
For counter = start To end [Step stepsize]
   [statements]
[Exit For]
   [statements]
Next [counter]
```

Here's what happens in a `For...Next` loop (refer to the syntax):

1. When VBA enters the loop at the `For` statement, it assigns the *`start`* value to *`counter`*. It then executes the statements in the loop. When it reaches the `Next` statement, it increments *`counter`* by 1 or by the specified *`stepsize`* and loops back to the `For` statement.
2. VBA then checks the *`counter`* variable against the *`end`* variable. When *`stepsize`* is positive, if *`counter`* is greater than *`end`*, VBA terminates the loop and continues execution

of the procedure with the statement immediately after the `Next` statement (which could be any action or the end of the procedure). If *counter* is less than or equal to *end*, VBA repeats the statements in the loop, increases *counter* by 1 or by *stepsize*, and loops back to the `For` statement again. (For a loop in which *stepsize* is negative, the loop continues while *counter* is greater than or equal to *end* and ends when *counter* is equal to or less than *end*. In other words, when the *stepsize* is negative, the loop counts *down* rather than up.)

3. The `Exit For` statement exits the `For...`loop early. You'll look at how to use the `Exit For` statement, and examples of the different uses of `For...Next` loops, later in this chapter.

Table 12.2 explains the components of the `For...Next` loop syntax. As usual, brackets enclose optional items and italicized words are placeholders—elements in the code that are to be replaced by you, the programmer.

TABLE 12.2: Components of the syntax for a `For...Next` loop

COMPONENT	DESCRIPTION
Counter	A numeric variable or an expression that produces a number. By default, VBA increases the *counter* value by an increment of 1 with each iteration of the loop, but you can change this increment by using the optional `Step` keyword and *stepsize* argument. *counter* is required in the `For` statement and is optional in the `Next` statement, but it's a good idea to also include *counter* in the `Next` statement to make your code easy to read. This is particularly important when you're using multiple `For...Next` statements in the same procedure or nesting `For...Next` statements within each other.
Start	A numeric variable or numeric expression giving the starting value for *counter*.
End	A numeric variable or numeric expression giving the ending value for *counter*.
Stepsize	A numeric variable or numeric expression specifying how much to increase or decrease the value of *counter*. To use *stepsize*, use the `Step` keyword and specify the *stepsize* variable. *stepsize* is 1 by default, but you can use any positive or negative value.
`Exit For`	A statement for exiting a `For...`loop.
`Next`	The keyword indicating the end of the loop. Again, you can specify the optional *counter* here to make your code clear.

STRAIGHTFORWARD *FOR...NEXT* LOOPS

In a simple `For...Next` loop, you first specify a *counter* variable and the starting and ending values for it:

```
Dim i As Integer
For i = 1 to 200
```

Here, `i` is the *counter* variable, 1 is the starting value, and 200 is the ending value. Because VBA by default increases the *counter* variable by 1 with each iteration of the loop, the counter variable in this example will count 1, 2, 3, and so on up to 200. Once the loop iterates enough times so the value in counter is 201, the looping ends and execution continues in the line below the loop's `End` statement.

You can also use the `Step` keyword to specify a different increment, either positive or negative. You'll learn more on this in the next section.

The Traditional Counter Variable Name for *For...Next* Loops

`i` is the classic integer *counter* variable used in a `For`...`Next` loop; after using `i`, the convention is to use `j`, `k`, `l`, `m`, and `n` for any subsequent *counter* variables (if you're adding nested loops within an `i` loop). These short variable names derive from the days of key-card computation, when memory was at a premium and longer names represented a significant extravagance. These days, computer memory is abundant, so using long variable names is common practice for *most* variables, but not with loop counters. Using `i` as the loop counter is pervasive, even in languages like Java and C++, so stick with `i`.

After the previous two statements (`Dim` and `For`), you specify whatever actions you want carried out within the loop, followed by the `Next` keyword to end the loop:

```
Application.StatusBar = _

    "Please wait while Excel checks for nonuniform prices: " & i & "..."
Next i
```

This code displays (on the status bar) Excel's progress in checking your spreadsheet for improbable values.

Here's another example: Say you need to check every paragraph in Word documents you receive from contributors to make sure there's no unsuitable formatting. By using a loop that runs from 1 to the total number of paragraphs in the active document, you can check each paragraph in turn and let the user view the progress in the status bar. The number of paragraphs in a document is stored in the `Count` property of the `Paragraphs` collection in the `ActiveDocument` object:

```
Dim i As Integer
For i = 1 To ActiveDocument.Paragraphs.Count

    'CheckParagraphForIllegalFormatting

    DoEvents

Application.StatusBar = _
        "Please wait while Word checks the formatting in " _
        & " this document: Paragraph " & i & " out of " _
        & ActiveDocument.Paragraphs.Count & "..."
Selection.MoveDown Unit:=wdParagraph, _
        Count:=1, Extend:=wdMove
Next i
```

This code snippet executes a `CheckParagraphForIllegalFormatting` procedure. We've not yet written this procedure, so I just wrote a comment line indicating that the procedure needs to be called from inside this loop.

Next, we use the `DoEvents` command. This improves multitasking. It interrupts the loop to see if something else is going on in the computer (the user typing something, the status bar in Word being updated, or whatever). This prevents your loop from hogging the computer's microprocessor.

Then the loop continues executing. The message is displayed in the status bar, indicating which paragraph out of the total number it's working on, and then the loop moves down a paragraph. When VBA reaches the `Next` statement, it increases the `i` counter by the default value, 1 (because no *`stepsize`* variable is specified in the `For` statement) and loops back to the `For` statement, where it compares the value of `i` to the value of `ActiveDocument.Paragraphs.Count`. The procedure continues to loop until `i` has reached the value of `ActiveDocument.Paragraphs.Count`, which is the final iteration of the loop. Notice here how the `counter` variable is used twice: first to keep track of the loop's iterations, but it's also used later *within* the loop to display the current paragraph number:

```
Paragraph " & i &
```

In a similar way, you could use a simple `For…Next` loop to quickly build the structure of a timesheet or work log in Excel. The following statements use a `For…Next` loop to insert the labels 1.00 through 24:00 in the current column in the active sheet of the active workbook:

```
Dim i As Integer
For i = 1 To 24
    ActiveCell.FormulaR1C1 = i & ":00"
    ActiveCell.Offset(RowOffset:=1, ColumnOffset:=0).Select
Next i
```

Here, the `ActiveCell.FormulaR1Ci` statement inserts the automatically increased string for the counter `i` together with a colon and two zeroes (to create a time format). The `ActiveCell.Offset(RowOffset:=1, ColumnOffset:=0).Select` statement selects the cell in the next row and the same column. The loop runs from `i = 1` to `i = 24` and stops when the automatic increase takes `i` to 25. Again, the counter variable is used within the loop. This is quite common.

For...Next Loops with Step Values

If increasing the *`counter`* variable by the default 1 doesn't suit your purpose, you can use the `Step` keyword to specify a different increment or decrement.

For example, the following statement increases the *`counter`* variable by 20, so the sequence is 0, 20, 40, 60, 80, 100:

```
For i = 0 to 100 Step 20
```

You can also decrement by specifying a negative `Step` value:

```
For i = 1000 to 0 Step -100
```

This statement produces the sequence 1000, 900, 800, and so on, down to 0.

Instead of the "x out of y" countdown given in the example in the previous section, you could produce a countdown running from `ActiveDocument.Paragraphs.Count` to zero:

```
Dim i As Integer
For i = ActiveDocument.Paragraphs.Count To 0 Step -1
```

```
        CheckParagraphForIllegalFormatting
        Application.StatusBar = _
            "Please wait while Word checks the formatting in this document: " & i
        Selection.MoveDown Unit:=wdParagraph, Count:=1, Extend:=wdMove
    Next i
```

Using an Input Box to Drive a *For...Next* Loop

Sometimes you'll be able to hard-code the number of iterations into a `For...Next` loop (six eggs). You'll know the number of iterations when writing your code, so you can just type in the end condition number, like the 100 here:

```
For i = 0 to 100
```

Other times, though, you can't know in advance how many loop iterations are needed. This information only becomes available during program execution (called *runtime*) rather than when you're writing the code (called *design time*).

Often you'll take a number from another operation during execution, such as the `ActiveDocument.Paragraphs.Count` property in the previous example.

You want to use this macro with many documents in the future. The number of paragraphs in various documents is different; it varies. So, you can't know when writing your code how many times it should loop. Your macro itself has to gather that information at runtime.

Frequently, you ask the user to specify the number of loop repetitions. The easiest way of doing this is to display an input box, requesting the user to enter a value.

For example, Listing 12.1 contains a simple procedure named `CreatePresentations` that displays an input box prompting users to enter the number of presentations they want to create. It then uses a `For...Next` loop to create the documents in PowerPoint.

Listing 12.1: Letting the user specify the number of iterations

```
1.  Sub CreatePresentations()
2.      Dim intPresentations As Integer
3.      Dim i As Integer
4.      intPresentations = InputBox _
            ("Enter the number of presentations to create:", _
            "Create Presentations")
5.      For i = 1 To intPresentations
6.          Presentations.Add
7.      Next i
8.  End Sub
```

Here's what happens in the `CreatePresentations` procedure in Listing 12.1:

- Line 2 declares the Integer variable `intPresentations`, and line 3 declares the Integer variable `i`.
- Line 4 displays an input box prompting users to enter the number of presentations they want to create.

- Lines 5 through 7 contain a `For…Next` loop that runs from `i = 1` to `i = intPresentations` with the default increment of `1` per iteration. Each iteration of the loop executes the `Presentations.Add` statement in line 6, creating a new presentation based on the default template.

Real World Scenario

CONTROL A *FOR...NEXT* LOOP WITH USER INPUT VIA A DIALOG BOX

An input box returns only a single value. Sometimes you need multiple values from the user. So, for those occasions when an input box won't suffice, you can easily get input from a dialog box to drive a `For…Next` loop. This book hasn't yet shown you how to create dialog boxes, but in this section you'll get a sneak preview by looking at a procedure named `Create_Folders`. You aren't expected to build and test this example; just read the code to get an idea of how it accepts user input and then employs that information in the loop.

This example procedure reduces the tedium of creating multiple folders with predictable names, such as when I had to create 31 folders, a folder for each chapter in this book.

Say that you're using a four-digit number to identify the project, the letter *s* for section, and a two-digit number to identify the section, so you'd end up with folders named 1234s01, 1234s02, 1234s03, and so on. This is simple enough to create manually, but tedious if you need more than a dozen or so.

In its simplest form, this dialog box would provide a text box for the number of folders to be created (although you could also use a drop-down list for this or even a spinner control) and a text box for the project number. The following illustration is an example of how this dialog box might look.

Create Folders

Number of folders to create:

Number of folders to create:

Number of folders to create:

OK Cancel

You display a dialog box by using the `Show` method in a separate macro, perhaps using a `Load` statement first, like this:

```
Sub makefolders()

    Dialogs(wdDialogFileSaveAs).Show

    Load frmCreateFolders

    frmCreateFolders.Show

End Sub
```

You might have noticed the `Dialogs` command in this code. It's quite useful, but we'll discuss it at the end of this sidebar. For now, our focus is on looping techniques.

I named the example dialog box `frmCreateFolders`. However, any valid VBA name will work. The first text box—identified with the Number Of Folders To Create label—is named `txtFolders`; the second text box is named `txtProjectNumber`.

The Cancel button here has an End statement attached to its Click event so that if the user clicks it, VBA ends the procedure:

```
Private Sub cmdCancel_Click()
    End
End Sub
```

The OK button in the dialog box has the following code attached to its Click event:

```
Private Sub cmdOK_Click()

    Dim strMsg As String
    Dim strFolder As String
    Dim i As Integer

    frmCreateFolders.Hide
    Unload frmCreateFolders
    strMsg = "The Create_Folders procedure has created " _
        & "the following folders: " & vbCr & vbCr

    For i = 1 To txtFolders.Value
        strFolder = txtProjectNumber.Value & "p" & Format(i, "0#")
        MkDir strFolder
        strMsg = strMsg & "    " & strFolder & vbCr
    Next i

    MsgBox strMsg, vbOKOnly + vbInformation, _
        "Create Folders"

End Sub
```

Continues

Continued

Let's pause here a minute for a pep talk. You might read the preceding code and say, "Hey! I'll never be able to remember all this stuff about `Format` and `Hide` and `vbCr` and `vbOKOnly`." Don't pout. Nobody memorizes all the variations of the `Format` command or all the `vb` constants like `vbCr`. Remember, there are tons of sample code examples on the Internet and in books like this one. What's more, the VBA Editor itself displays lists of constants and object members as you type in a line of code. (Look up "Auto List Members" in this book's index, or search the VBA Editor's Help index to locate online resources.)

Now back to our regular programming. Notice that the `Value` properties of the two text boxes are used in this loop. The value in `txtFolders` specifies the loop's number of iterations. The `txtProjectNumber` specifies the first part of the name for each newly created folder.

The `cmdOK_Click` procedure runs when the user clicks the OK button in the dialog box:

- Line 1 declares the `cmdOK_Click` subroutine, and line 19 ends it.
- Line 3 declares the String variable `strMsg`, which is used to contain a string to display in a message box at the end of the procedure.
- Line 4 declares the String variable `strFolder`, which will contain the name of the current folder to create in each iteration of the loop.
- Line 5 declares the Integer variable `i`, which will be the *`counter`* variable for the `For...Next` loop.
- Line 7 hides `frmCreateFolders`.
- Line 8 unloads `frmCreateFolders` from memory.
- Line 9 assigns some introductory text to `strMsg`, ending it with a colon and two `vbCr` carriage-return characters to make the start of a list.
- Lines 11 through 15 contain the `For...Next` loop that creates the folders. Line 11 causes the loop to run from `i = 1` to `i = txtFolders.Value`, the value supplied by the user in the Number Of Folders To Create text box. Line 12 assigns to the `strFolder` String variable the `Value` property of the `txtProjectNumber` text box, the letter *p*, and the value of `i` formatted via the `Format` function to include a leading zero if it's a single digit (so that 1 will appear as 01, and so on). Line 13 uses the `MkDir` command with `strFolder` to create a folder (that is, make a directory—the old DOS command `mkdir` lives on in VBA) of that name. Line 14 adds some spaces (for an indent), the contents of `strFolder`, and a `vbCr` character to `strMsg`. Line 15 then loops back to the `For` statement, incrementing the `i` counter. VBA then compares the `i` counter to `txtFolders.Value` and repeats the loop as necessary.

This procedure creates a set of new subfolders within whatever is the current folder, without giving the user a choice of location. Chances are you won't want to do this in real-life situations. You might want to change a folder to a set location (so as to keep all the project files together), but more likely you'll want to let the user choose a suitable location—for example, by displaying a common dialog box, such as the Save As dialog box used by most Windows applications. These built-in dialog boxes can be very useful because everyone who uses Windows is familiar with them and because they contain quite a bit of functionality. You display, for example, the classic Windows `SaveAs` dialog box like this:

```
Dialogs(wdDialogFileSaveAs).Show
```

When the user closes this dialog box, whatever folder the user specifies becomes the current folder and the document is automatically saved. You can find out more about how to use common dialog boxes in Chapter 14, "Creating Simple Custom Dialog Boxes," and also at this Microsoft web page:

`http://msdn.microsoft.com/en-us/library/bb208857.aspx`

I wanted you to be aware that common dialog boxes exist because they can be so useful. However, in this example, perhaps a more direct way of allowing the user to specify the path for the new directories would be to use the `ChDir` (change directory) command, like this:

```
Dim strDir As String

strDir = InputBox("Type the full path where you want new folders to be stored")

ChDir (strDir)
```

For Each...Next Loops

The `For Each...Next` loop (which by the way is unique to the various versions of Visual Basic, including VBA) is similar to the `For...Next` loop. However, it works with collections. The iterations are based on the number of objects in a collection, such as the `Slides` collection in a presentation or the `Documents` collection of Word documents. So, using `For Each` means that you, the programmer, don't necessarily know the number of loop iterations in advance, but VBA will know during execution because it will query an object's `Count` property.

For example, let's assume you want to do something to each `Slide` object in a presentation. During design time while writing your macro you don't need to know how many slides are in the collection. (If there are none, nothing happens.)

Syntax

The syntax for the `For Each...Next` statement is straightforward:

```
For Each object In collection
    [statements]
    [Exit For]
    [statements]
Next [object]
```

VBA starts by evaluating the number of objects in the specified collection. It then executes the statements in the loop for the first of those objects. When it reaches the `Next` keyword, it loops back to the `For Each` line, reevaluates the number of objects, and performs further iterations as appropriate.

Here's an example: The `Documents` collection contains the open documents in Word. So, you could create a straightforward procedure to close all the open documents by using a `For Each...Next` loop like this:

```
Dim Doc As Document
For Each Doc in Documents
```

```
        Doc.Close SaveChanges:=wdSaveChanges
    Next
```

VBA closes each open document in turn by using the `Close` method. The statement uses the `wdSaveChanges` constant for the `SaveChanges` argument to specify that any unsaved changes in the document be saved when the document is closed. As long as there are open documents in the `Documents` collection, VBA repeats the loop, so it closes all open documents and then terminates the procedure.

This example provides a straightforward illustration of how a `For Each...Next` loop works, but you probably wouldn't want to use the example in practice. Instead, you'd probably use the `Close` method with the `Documents` collection (this collection contains all the open documents) to close all the open documents. It's a simpler approach. However, you might use a `For Each...Next` loop to check each document for certain characteristics before closing it.

Using an *Exit For* Statement

As you saw earlier in this chapter when looking at the syntax for `For` statements, you can use one or more `Exit For` statements to exit a `For...`loop if a certain condition is met. `Exit For` statements are optional and are seldom necessary; in fact, they're generally frowned upon as poor coding practice. If you find yourself needing to use `Exit For` statements in all your procedures, there's probably something wrong with the way you're constructing your loops.

That said, you may sometimes find `Exit For` statements useful—for example, to respond to an error that happens within a loop or if the user chooses to cancel a procedure.

On those occasions when you do need `Exit For` statements to exit a loop early, you'll typically use them with straightforward conditions. For example, in Word, if you wanted to close open windows until you reached a certain document that you knew to be open, you could use an `Exit For` statement like this:

```
Dim Doc As Document
For Each Doc in Documents
    If Doc.Name = "Document1" Then Exit For
    Doc.Close
Next Doc
```

This `For Each...Next` statement checks the `Name` property of the document to see if it's `Document1`; if it is, the `Exit For` statement causes VBA to exit the loop. Otherwise, VBA closes the document and returns to the start of the loop.

USE MULTIPLE *EXIT FOR* STATEMENTS IF YOU WANT

You can also use multiple `Exit For` statements if you need to. For example, you might need to check two or more conditions during the actions performed in the loop.

Using *Do*...Loops for Variable Numbers of Repetitions

`Do` loops give you more flexibility than `For`…loops in that you can test for conditions and direct the flow of the procedure accordingly. VBA includes several types of `Do` loops:

- `Do While…Loop`
- `Do…Loop While`
- `Do Until…Loop`
- `Do…Loop Until`

These loops break down into two categories:

- Loops that test a condition at the start of the loop, before executing any of the statements contained inside the loop. `Do While…Loop` and `Do Until…Loop` loops fall into this category. In other words, if the test fails, the loop's code within the loop block will not execute even once.
- Loops that test a condition at the end of the loop. This type of loop executes the code within the loop block before testing a condition. `Do…Loop While` and `Do…Loop Until` fall into this category. This type of loop will execute at least one time.

The difference between the two types of loop in each category is that each `While` loop repeats itself *while* a condition is `True` (until the condition becomes `False`), whereas each `Until` loop repeats itself *until* a condition becomes `True` (while the condition remains `False`).

This means that you can get by to some extent using only the `While` loops or only the `Until` loops—you'll just need to set up some of your conditions the other way around. For example, you could use a `Do While…Loop` loop with a condition of `x < 100` or a `Do Until…Loop` loop with a condition of `x = 100` to achieve the same effect. Put another way: *loop while x is less than 100 is equivalent to loop until x = 100*—as long as you start looping below 100.

The following sections describe all the different kinds of `Do` loops so that you can know when to use each.

Do While...Loop Loops

In a `Do While…Loop` loop, you specify a condition that has to remain `True` for the actions (statements) inside the loop to be executed. If the condition isn't `True`, the actions aren't executed and the loop ends. When a loop ends, the code *below* the loop block then executes.

For example, you might want to search a document for an instance of a particular word or phrase and take action after you find it. Figure 12.1 shows a `Do While…Loop` loop.

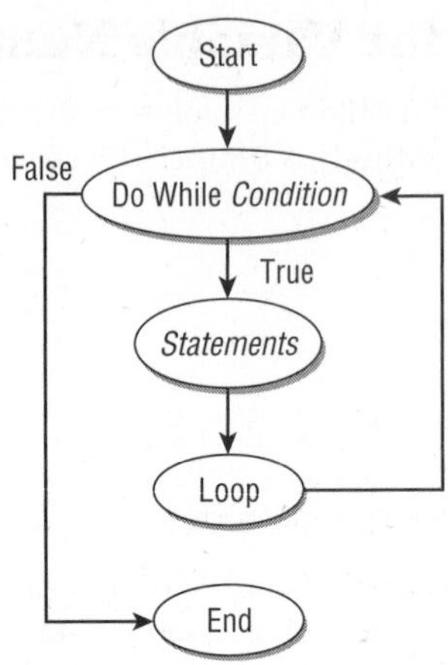

FIGURE 12.1 A Do While…Loop loop tests for a condition before performing the actions contained in the loop.

SYNTAX

The syntax for the Do While…Loop loop is straightforward:

```
Do While condition
    [statements]
    [Exit Do]
    [statements]
Loop
```

While the *condition* is met (Do While the condition remains True), the statements in the loop are executed. The Loop keyword returns execution to the Do While line, which is then reevaluated. If the *condition* is still True, the loop continues—it iterates again.

However, if the *condition* is False, execution jumps to the code below the loop block, starting with the statement on the line after the Loop keyword.

You can use one or more optional Exit Do statements if you want to exit the loop without waiting until the condition turns False.

Say you wanted to construct a glossary from a lengthy Word document that highlights the main terms by italicizing them. These terms are located in the body text as well as within bulleted or numbered lists. However, you want to avoid picking up italicized terms used in other elements of the document, such as headings or captions. In this situation, body text is in the Times New Roman font, but the captions and headlines are in other fonts.

You could command Word to search for Times New Roman text with the italic attribute. If Word found instances of the text, it would take the appropriate actions, such as selecting the sentence containing the term, together with the next sentence (or the rest of the paragraph), and copying it to the end of another document. Then it would continue the search, performing the loop until it no longer found instances of italic Times New Roman text.

Listing 12.2 shows an example of how such a procedure might be constructed with a Do While…Loop structure. This listing includes a number of commands that you haven't learned about yet, but you should be able to see how the loop portion of this code works.

LISTING 12.2: Understanding how `Do While` works

```
Sub GenerateGlossary()

    Dim strSource As String
    Dim strDestination As String
    Dim strGlossaryName As String

    strSource = ActiveWindow.Caption
    strGlossaryName = InputBox _
        ("Enter the name for the glossary document.", _
        "Create Glossary")
    If strGlossaryName = "" Then End

    Documents.Add
    ActiveDocument.SaveAs FileName:=strGlossaryName, _
        FileFormat:=wdFormatDocument
    strDestination = ActiveWindow.Caption
    Windows(strSource).Activate

    Selection.HomeKey Unit:=wdStory
    Selection.Find.ClearFormatting
    Selection.Find.Font.Italic = True
    Selection.Find.Font.Name = "Times New Roman"
    Selection.Find.Text = ""
    Selection.Find.Execute

    Do While Selection.Find.Found
        Selection.Copy
        Selection.MoveRight Unit:=wdCharacter, _
            Count:=1, Extend:=wdMove
        Windows(strDestination).Activate
        Selection.EndKey Unit:=wdStory
        Selection.Paste
        Selection.TypeParagraph
        Windows(strSource).Activate
        Selection.Find.Execute
    Loop

    Windows(strDestination).Activate
    ActiveDocument.Save
    ActiveDocument.Close

End Sub
```

The `GenerateGlossary` procedure in Listing 12.2 copies italic items in the Times New Roman font from the current document and inserts them in a new document that it creates and saves. Here's what happens:

- Line 1 begins the procedure.
- Lines 3, 4, and 5 declare the String variables `strSource`, `strDestination`, and `str GlossaryName`, respectively.
- Line 7 assigns the `Caption` property of the active window to the String variable `strSource`. The procedure uses this variable to activate the document when it needs to work with it.
- Line 8 displays an input box asking the user to enter a name for the document that will contain the glossary entries pulled from the current document. It stores the string the user enters in the String variable `strGlossaryName`.
- Line 9 then compares `strGlossaryName` to an empty string (`""`) to make sure the user hasn't clicked the Cancel button to cancel the procedure or clicked the OK button in the input box without entering a name in the text box. If `GlossaryName` is an empty string, line 9 uses an `End` statement to terminate execution of the procedure.
- Provided line 9 hasn't stopped the procedure in its tracks, the procedure rolls on. Line 11 then creates a new blank document. (This document is based on the `Normal.dotm` global template because no `Template` argument is used to specify a different template.) This document will become the glossary document.
- Line 12 saves the document with the name the user specified in the input box.
- Line 13 stores the `Caption` property of this document in the `strDestination` variable, again making it available to activate this document as necessary throughout the procedure. You now have the source document identified by the `strSource` variable and the destination document identified by the `strDestination` variable.
- Line 14 uses the `Activate` method to activate the `strSource` window. Line 16 uses the `HomeKey` method of the `Selection` object with the `wdStory` unit to move the insertion point to the beginning of the document, which is where the procedure needs to start working to catch all the italicized words in Times New Roman.
- Lines 17 through 20 detail the `Find` operation the procedure needs to perform: Line 17 removes any formatting applied to the current `Find` item, line 18 sets the `Find` feature to find italic formatting, line 19 sets `Find` to find Times New Roman text, and line 20 specifies the search string, which is an empty string (`""`) that causes `Find` to search only for the specified formatting.
- Line 21 then performs the `Find` operation by using the `Execute` method. Lines 23 through 32 implement the `Do While...Loop` loop. Line 23 expresses the condition for the loop: `While Selection.Find.Found` (while the `Find` operation is able to find an instance of the italic Times New Roman text specified in the previous lines). While this condition is met (is `True`), the commands contained in the loop will execute.
- Line 24 copies the selection (the item found with italic Times New Roman formatting).
- Line 25 moves the insertion point one character to the right, effectively deselecting the selection and getting the procedure ready to search for the next instance in the document.

You need to move the insertion point off the selection to the right so that the next `Find` operation doesn't find the same instance. (If the procedure were searching up through the document instead of down, you'd need to move the insertion point off the selection to the left instead by using a `Selection.MoveLeft` statement.)

- Line 26 activates the `strDestination` window, putting Word's focus on it.
- Line 27 then moves the insertion point to the end of the glossary document, and line 28 pastes the copied item in at the position of the insertion point. Moving to the end of the document isn't strictly necessary here, provided that the `Normal.dotm` global template doesn't contain any text—if `Normal.dotm` is empty, the new document created in line 11 will be empty too, and the start and end of the document will be in the same position. And after each `paste` operation, Word positions the insertion point after the pasted item. However, if `Normal.dotm` *does* contain text, then this step is necessary.
- Line 29 uses the `TypeParagraph` method of the `Selection` object to enter a paragraph after the text inserted by the `paste` operation.
- Line 30 activates the `strSource` document once more, and line 31 repeats the `Find` operation.
- The `Loop` statement in line 32 then loops execution of the procedure back to line 23, where the `Do While Selection.Find.Found` condition evaluates whether this latest `Find` operation was successful (`True`).
- If it was successful, the loop continues; if it wasn't, execution of the procedure continues at line 34, which activates the glossary document again. Line 35 saves the active document (the glossary document, because it was just activated), and line 36 closes it.

Do...Loop While Loops

A `Do…Loop While` block is similar to a `Do While…Loop`, except that in the `Do…Loop While` loop, the statements contained within the loop are executed at least once.

Whether the condition is `True` or `False`, the loop executes at least the first time through because the condition isn't tested until the end of the loop block.

If the condition is `True`, the loop continues to run until the condition becomes `False`. Figure 12.2 shows a `Do…Loop While` loop.

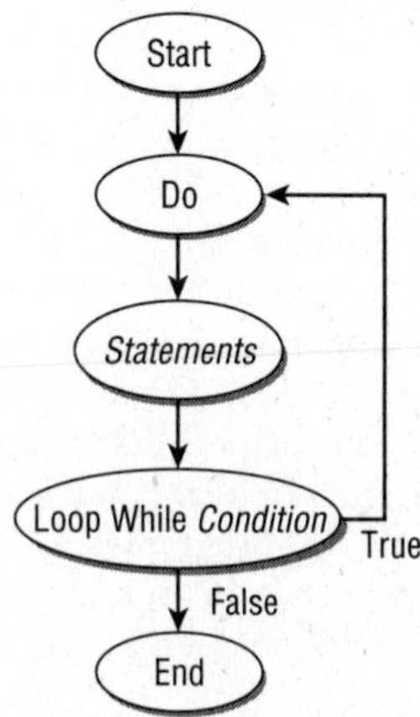

FIGURE 12.2
In a `Do…Loop While` loop, the actions in the loop run once before the condition is tested.

The Do While...Loop block described earlier probably made immediate sense to you, but this Do...Loop While block may seem odd. You're going to execute the contained statements *before* checking the condition?

But you'll find that Do...Loop While loops can be very useful, although they lend themselves to different situations than Do While...Loop loops.

Consider the lottery example from the beginning of the chapter. In that situation, you execute the action before you check the condition that controls the loop. First you buy a lottery ticket, and then you check to see if you've won. If you haven't won, or you've won only a small sum, you loop back and buy more tickets for the next lottery. (Actually, this is logically a Do...Loop Until loop rather than a Do...Loop While loop because you continue the loop while the condition is False; when you win a suitably large amount, the condition becomes True.)

Likewise, in programming it's not uncommon to take an action and then check whether you need to repeat it. For example, you might want to apply special formatting to the current paragraph and then check to see if other paragraphs need the same treatment.

SYNTAX

The syntax for a Do...Loop While loop is as follows:

```
Do
    [statements]
    [Exit Do]
    [statements]
Loop While condition
```

VBA performs the statements included in the loop, after which the Loop While line evaluates the condition. If it's True, VBA returns execution to the Do line and the loop continues to execute; if it's False, execution continues at the line after the Loop While line.

As an example of a Do...Loop While loop, consider this crude password checker that you could use to prevent someone from executing a macro without supplying the correct password:

```
Dim varPassword As Variant
VarPassword = "corinth"
Do
    varPassword = InputBox _
        ("Enter the password to start the procedure:", _
        "Check Password 1.0")
Loop While varPassword <> "CorrectPassword"
```

Here the Do...Loop While loop first displays an input box for the user to enter the password. The Loop While line compares the value from the input box, stored in varPassword, against the correct password (here, CorrectPassword). If the two aren't equal (varPassword <> "CorrectPassword"), the loop continues, displaying the input box again.

This loop is just an example—you wouldn't want to use it as it is in real life. Here's why: Choosing the Cancel button in an input box causes it to return a blank string, which also doesn't match the correct password, causing the loop to run again. The security is perfect; the problem is that the only way to end the loop is for users to supply the correct password. If they're unable to do so, they will see the input box again and again. There's no way out of the loop. This is called an *endless loop* and it's really bad programming. The user can get hopelessly trapped within an endlessly repeating loop. Such loop traps are also called *infinite* or *endless loops*. You'll learn more about these at the end of this chapter.

You should instead build a friendlier password-checking procedure. You might specify a number of incorrect password guesses that the user could enter (perhaps three) and then if they still haven't gotten it right, make the procedure terminate itself. Or you could simply use an `End` statement to terminate the procedure if the user entered a blank string, like this:

```
Do
    varPassword = InputBox _
        ("Enter the password to start the procedure:", _
         "Check Password 1.0")
    If varPassword = "" Then End
Loop While varPassword <> "CorrectPassword"
```

Do Until...Loop Loops

A `Do Until...Loop` loop is similar to a `Do While...Loop` loop. The difference is how the condition works. In a `Do Until...Loop` loop, the loop runs while the condition is `False` and stops running when it's `True`. So, this is the opposite of the way that the condition works in a `Do While...Loop` loop.

Figure 12.3 shows a `Do Until...Loop` loop.

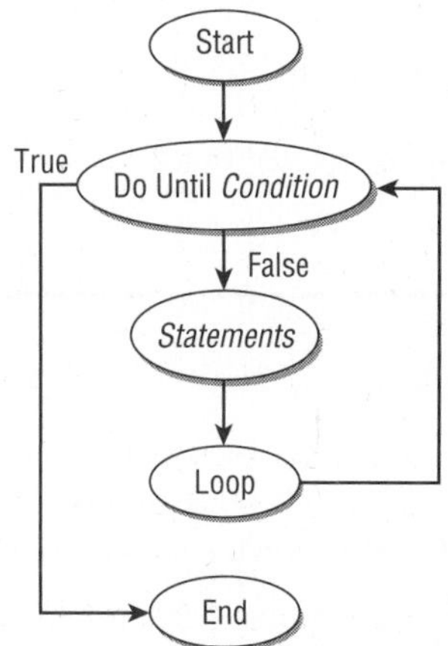

FIGURE 12.3 A `Do Until...Loop` loop runs while the condition is `False` and stops running when the condition becomes `True`.

DO UNTIL...LOOP BLOCKS EXECUTE UNTIL A CONDITION BECOMES FALSE

Note that `Do Until...Loop` loops are useful if you prefer to work with a condition that's `True` and keep it looping until the condition becomes `False`. Otherwise, you can achieve the same effects using `Do While...Loop` loops and inverting the condition. In other words, these two approaches to looping are functionally the same; it's just a matter of how you want to manage the condition. It's the difference between "sweep the porch *until* it's clean" versus "sweep the porch *while* it's still dirty." It's the same idea expressed differently.

SYNTAX

The syntax for `Do Until...Loop` loops is as follows:

```
Do Until condition

statements
    [Exit Do]
    [statements]
Loop
```

When VBA enters the loop, it checks the *`condition`*. If the *`condition`* is `False`, VBA executes the statements in the loop, encounters the `Loop` keyword, and loops back to the beginning of the loop, reevaluating the *`condition`* as it goes. If the *`condition`* is `True`, VBA terminates the loop and continues execution at the statement after the `Loop` line.

For example, here's the lottery example once again, but now employing a `Do...Until` loop in Listing 12.3.

LISTING 12.3: Using `Do...Until` loops

```
1.  Sub Lottery_1()
2.      Dim intWin As Integer
3.      Do Until intWin > 2000
4.          intWin = Rnd * 2100
5.          MsgBox intWin, , "Lottery"
6.      Loop
7.  End Sub
```

Here's how Listing 12.3 works:

- Line 2 declares the Single variable `intWin`. Line 3 then starts a `Do Until...Loop` loop with the condition that `intWin > 2000`—the value of the `intWin` variable must be larger than 2000 for the loop to end. Until then, the loop will continue to run.
- Line 4 assigns to `intWin` the result of 2100 multiplied by a random number produced by the `Rnd` function, which generates random numbers between 0 and 1. (This means that the loop needs to receive a random number of a little more than .95 to end—a chance of a little less than 1 in 20, considerably better than most lotteries.)
- Line 5 displays a simple message box containing the current value of the `Win` variable so that you can see how lucky you are.
- Line 6 contains the `Loop` keyword that completes the loop.
- Line 7 ends the procedure.

Listing 12.4 shows a more useful example of a `Do Until...Loop` loop in Word.

LISTING 12.4: A practical example showing how to employ `Do Until` in Word

```
1.  Sub FindNextHeading()
2.      Do Until Left(Selection.Paragraphs(1).Style, 7) = "Heading"
3.          Selection.MoveDown Unit:=wdParagraph, _
                Count:=1, Extend:=wdMove
4.      Loop
5.  End Sub
```

Listing 12.4 contains a short procedure that moves the insertion point to the next heading in the active document in Word. Here's how it works:

- Line 2 starts a `Do Until...Loop` loop that ends with the `Loop` keyword in line 4. The condition for the loop is that the seven leftmost characters in the name of the style for the first paragraph in the current selection—`Left(Selection.Paragraphs(1).Style, 7)`—match the string `Heading`. This will match any of the Heading styles (the built-in styles Heading 1 through Heading 9, or any style the user has defined whose name starts with *`Heading`*).
- Until the condition is met, VBA executes the statement in line 3, which moves the selection down by one paragraph.

Do...Loop Until Loops

The `Do...Loop Until` loop is similar to the `Do Until...Loop` structure except that in the `Do...Loop Until` loop, the statements contained within the loop block are executed at least once, whether the condition is `True` or `False`. If the condition is `False`, the loop continues to run until the condition becomes `True`. Figure 12.4 shows a `Do...Loop Until` loop.

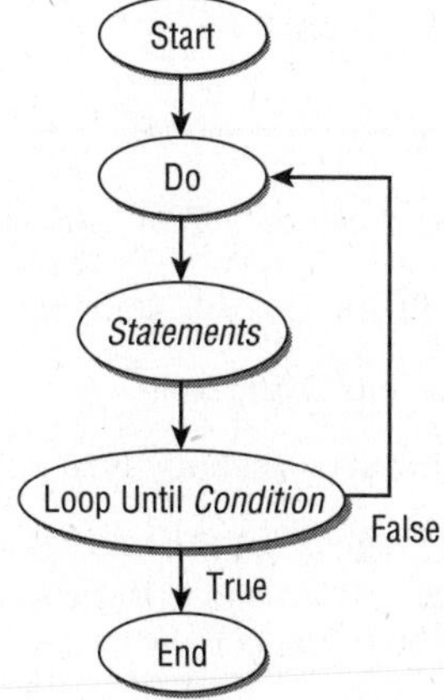

FIGURE 12.4 In a `Do...Loop Until` loop, the actions in the loop are run once before the condition is tested.

SYNTAX

The syntax for Do…Loop Until loops is as follows:

```
Do
    [statements]
    [Exit Do]
    [statements]
Loop Until condition
```

VBA enters the loop at the Do line and executes the *statements* in the loop. When it encounters the Loop Until line, it checks the *condition*. If the condition is False, VBA loops back to the Do line and again executes the *statements*. If the condition is True, VBA terminates the loop and continues execution at the line after the Loop Until line.

As an example, say you want to repeatedly display an input box that adds new worksheets to a workbook until the user clicks the Cancel button or enters an empty string in the text box. You could use code like that shown in Listing 12.5.

LISTING 12.5: Use Do Loop to execute the code at least once

```
 1.  Sub Create_Worksheets()
 2.      Dim strNewSheet As String
 3.      Do
 4.          strNewSheet = InputBox _
                 ("Enter the name for the new worksheet " _
                 & "(31 characters max.):", "Add Worksheets")
 5.          If strNewSheet <> "" Then
 6.              ActiveWorkbook.Worksheets.Add
 7.              ActiveSheet.Name = strNewSheet
 8.          End If
 9.      Loop Until strNewSheet = ""
10.  End Sub
```

Here's what happens in the Create_Worksheets procedure:

- Line 2 declares the String variable strNewSheet.
- Line 3 begins a Do…Loop Until loop.
- Line 4 displays an input box asking the user to enter the name for the new worksheet.
- Line 5 uses an If statement to make sure that strNewSheet is not an empty string. If it's not, line 6 adds a new worksheet to the active workbook, and line 7 assigns the value of strNewSheet to the active sheet (the new sheet). Line 8 ends the If statement.
- Line 9 contains a Loop Until strNewSheet="" statement that causes the procedure to loop back to the Do line until the user enters an empty string in the input box. The user can enter an empty string either by leaving the text box in the input box blank and clicking the OK button or by clicking the Cancel button.
- Line 10 ends the procedure.

Using an *Exit* Do Statement

As with an `Exit For` statement in a `For`...loop, you can use an `Exit Do` statement to exit a `Do` loop without executing the statements below the `Exit` line. The `Exit Do` statement is optional, and you'll probably seldom want to use `Exit Do` statements in your loops—at least if the loops are properly designed.

When you do need an `Exit Do` statement, you'll generally use it with its own condition. The example shown in Listing 12.6 makes the lottery a little more interesting by adding an `If` condition with an `Exit Do` statement to take effect if the win is less than $500.

LISTING 12.6: How to use the `Exit Do` command

```
1.  Sub Lottery_2()
2.      Dim intWin As Integer
3.      Do Until intWin > 2000
4.          intWin = Rnd * 2100
5.          If intWin < 500 Then
6.              MsgBox "Tough luck. You have been disqualified.", _
                    vbOKOnly + vbCritical, "Lottery"
7.              Exit Do
8.          End If
9.          MsgBox intWin, , "Lottery"
10.     Loop
11. End Sub
```

The procedure in Listing 12.6 works in the same way as the example in Listing 12.3 except that line 5 introduces a new `If` condition. If the variable `intWin` is less than 500, the statements in lines 6 and 7 run. Line 6 displays a message box announcing that the player has been disqualified from the lottery, and line 7 exits the `Do` loop.

Is the *Exit Do* Statement Bad Practice?

Some programmers consider using an `Exit Do` statement to exit a `Do` loop a tactic of last resort, or at least clumsy programming. Others disagree. Many reckon that it's always acceptable to use an `Exit Do` statement to respond to an error or to the user clicking a Cancel button.

VBA executes `Exit Do` statements with no problem, so it's there if you want to use it. However, you can often rewrite your code to avoid using an `Exit Do` statement.

For example, a condition that you check in the middle of the loop to decide whether to exit the loop can often be built into the main condition of the loop by using an operator such as `And`, `Or`, or `Not`, as shown in Listing 12.7:

LISTING 12.7: How to avoid the `Exit Do` command

```
Sub Lottery_3()

Dim intWin As Integer

```

```
5.  Do
6.      intWin = Rnd * 2100
7.      MsgBox intWin, , "Lottery"
8.  Loop Until intWin > 2000 Or intWin < 500
9.
10.
11. If intWin < 500 Then
12.     MsgBox "Tough luck. You have been disqualified.", _
13.                 vbOKOnly + vbCritical, "Lottery"
14. End If
15.
16. End Sub
```

Listing 12.7 is a revision of the example in Listing 12.6. Listing 12.7 shows you how to use the `Or` operator to specify two conditions for the loop to iterate. In this way, you can omit the `Exit Do` command entirely.

In line 8 of Listing 12.7, we are saying that the loop should end if the variable is greater than 2000 `Or` less than 500. This makes it somewhat clearer what the loop is doing.

We must also make two other changes. First, we have to move the condition test from the top of the loop to the bottom. The `Do Until` command in Listing 12.6 must be changed to the `Loop Until` command in Listing 12.7. If we leave the condition test at the top of the loop, the condition will *always* prevent the loop from executing. This is because the `intWin` variable will always hold zero when this loop first executes. So, we move the condition test to the bottom of the loop, allowing the variable to be assigned some value in line 6.

The final change we need to make is to move the `If…Then` block down to the bottom of the procedure.

If the code is simple like this example, you might be better off rewriting it to employ an operator. But if the code is complex and lengthy, there's no good reason to force yourself to use operators when an `Exit Do` statement will do the trick instead.

While...Wend Loops

In addition to the `For…Next` loop, the `For Each…Next` loop, and the four flavors of `Do` loops examined so far in this chapter, VBA includes the `While…Wend` loop. `While…Wend` is VBA's version of the `While…Wend` looping structure used by earlier programming languages, such as the WordBasic programming language used with versions of Word up to and including Word 95. VBA includes `While…Wend` more for compatibility with those earlier versions than as a recommended technique. But you can use it if you choose to. The various `Do` loops have replaced `While…Wend`, but `While…Wend` still works fine.

The syntax of a `While…Wend` loop is as follows:

```
While condition
    [statements]
Wend
```

While the *`condition`* is `True`, VBA executes the *`statements`* in the loop. When it reaches the `Wend` keyword (which is a contraction of `While End`), it returns to the `While` statement and evaluates the *condition* again. When the *condition* evaluates as False, the statements in the loop are no longer executed and execution moves to the statement after the Wend statement.

The following statements create a simple While…Wend loop for Word:

```
While Documents.Count < 10
    Documents.Add
Wend
```

While the number of documents in the Documents collection (specified here by the Count property of the Documents collection) is smaller than 10, the loop runs. Each time through, the Documents.Add statement in the second line creates a new document based on the Normal— template (because no other template is specified). After the new document is created, the Wend statement in the third line returns execution to the first line, where the While condition is— evaluated again.

AVOID BRANCHING INTO THE MIDDLE OF A *WHILE...WEND* LOOP

If you do use a While…Wend loop, make sure the only way to enter the loop is by passing through the gate of the While condition. Branching into the middle of a While…Wend loop (for example, by using a label and a GoTo statement) can cause errors.

Nesting Loops

You can nest one or more loops within another loop to create the pattern of repetition you need: You can nest one For…loop inside another For…loop, a For…loop inside a Do loop, a Do loop inside a For…loop, or a Do loop inside a Do loop.

VBA PERMITS UP TO 16 LEVELS OF NESTING, BUT WHO COULD UNDERSTAND SUCH COMPLEXITY?

You can nest up to 16 levels of loops in VBA, but you'll be hard-pressed to comprehend even half that number of levels as you read over your code. If you find your code becoming this complicated, consider whether you can take a less tortuous approach to solve the problem.

For example, if you need to create a number of folders, each of which contains a number of subfolders, you could use a variation of the Create_Folders procedure you looked at earlier in the chapter. But such a task cries out for nesting.

The dialog box for the procedure will need another text box to contain the number of sub-folders to create within each folder. The new dialog box is named frmCreateFoldersAnd SubFolders and the text box for the number of subfolders is named txtHowManySubFolders. Figure 12.5 shows the dialog box.

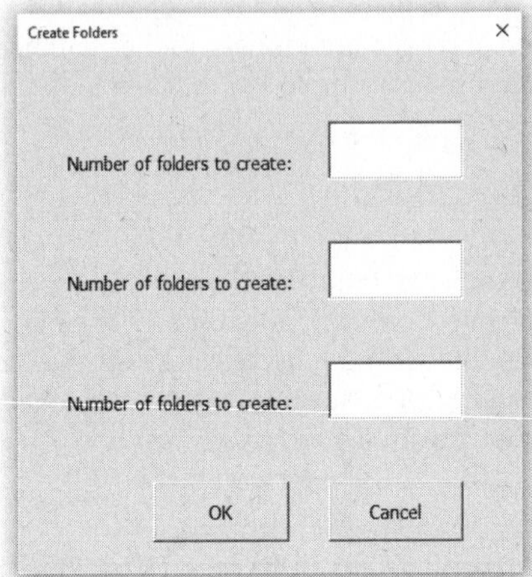

FIGURE 12.5 The dialog box to create folders and subfolders

Listing 12.8 shows the code triggered by the Click event on the `cmdOK` button of the form.

LISTING 12.8: Employing a nested loop

```
Private Sub cmdOK_Click()

    Dim strStartingFolder As String
    Dim strFolderName As String
    Dim strSubfolderName As String
    Dim intSubfolder As Integer
    Dim intLoopCounter As Integer

    frmCreateFoldersAndSubfolders.Hide
    Unload frmCreateFoldersAndSubfolders

    strStartingFolder = CurDir

    For intLoopCounter = 1 To txtHowManyFolders.Value
        strFolderName = txtProjectNumber.Value & "s" & _
            Format(intLoopCounter, "0#")
        MkDir strFolderName
        ChDir strFolderName
        For intSubfolder = 1 To txtHowManySubfolders.Value
            strSubfolderName = "Subsection" & intSubfolder
            MkDir strSubfolderName
        Next intSubfolder
        ChDir strStartingFolder
    Next intLoopCounter

End Sub
```

Here's what the code in Listing 12.8 does:

- Line 1 begins the procedure, and line 25 ends it.
- Lines 3 through 5 declare three String variables: `strStartingFolder`, `strFolderName`, and `strSubfolderName`, respectively.
- Line 6 declares the Integer variable `intSubfolder`, and line 7 declares the Integer variable `i`.
- Line 9 hides the user form, and line 10 unloads it.
- Line 12 stores the name of the current folder in the String variable `strStartingFolder`. You'll need this variable to make sure everything happens in the appropriate folder later in the procedure. Lines 14 through 16 and line 23 are essentially the same as in the previous procedure. They build the folder name out of the `Value` property of the `txtProjectNumber` text box, the letter *s*, a two-digit number, and the `i` variable and then use the `MkDir` statement to create the folder.
- Line 17 uses a `ChDir` statement to change folders to the folder that was just created, `strFolderName`.
- In line 18, the nested `For...Next` loop starts. This loop is controlled by the loop counter `intSubfolder` and will run from `intSubfolder = 1` to `intSubfolder = txtHowMany-SubFolders.Value`, which is the value entered by the user in the Number Of Subfolders To Create text box in the dialog box.
- Line 19 builds the String variable `strSubfolderName` out of the word *Subsection* and the value of the `intSubfolder` *`counter`* variable. For this procedure, you can assume that there will be fewer than 10 subsections for each of the sections, so single-digit numbering is adequate.
- Line 20 creates the subfolder by using a `MkDir` statement with the `strSubfolderName` String variable.
- Line 21 uses the `Next Subfolder` statement to loop back to the beginning of the nested `For...Next` loop. VBA reevaluates the condition and repeats the loop as necessary.
- Line 22 changes folders back to `strStartingFolder` for the next iteration of the outside loop. (Otherwise, the next folder would be created within the current folder, `strFolderName`.)
- Line 23 then loops back to the beginning of the outer loop.

Use the Counter Variable with *Next* when Nesting *For...*Loops

Using counter variables with the `Next` command is optional (in Listing 12.8, the counter variables are named `intLoopCounter` and `intSubfolder`). You could simply use `Next` by itself and VBA will figure out what you mean. But when nesting `For...`loops, it's a good idea to include a counter variable to make it easier to see which loop is ending with the `Next` command (in other words, use `Next intLoopCounter`, for example, rather than just the shorthand version `Next`). Using a counter variable makes your procedures much easier to read and may prevent unpleasant surprises (bugs). Your nested loops must end in the exact reverse order of their starting, and the counters need to match.

Avoiding Infinite Loops

If you create an infinite (aka endless) loop in a procedure, it will happily run forever, unless the user knows enough to press Ctrl+Break, presses Ctrl+Alt+Del to use the Task Manager to shut down the frozen application, restarts the computer, or pulls the plug. The machine won't smolder, but the user might.

For example, one type of loop you haven't yet encountered is the `Do...Loop`. As you can see in the example in Listing 12.9, without a condition attached to it, this structure is an infinite loop. There's no condition that can stop the looping.

LISTING 12.9: An example of an endless loop

```
1.  Sub InfiniteLoop()
2.      Dim x
3.      x = 1
4.      Do
5.          Application.StatusBar = _
                "Your computer is stuck in an endless loop: " & x
6.          x = x + 1
7.      Loop
8.  End Sub
```

In Listing 12.9, line 2 declares the variable *x*, and line 3 assigns it the value `1`. Line 4 begins the `Do` loop, which displays a status-bar message and increases the value of *x* by `1`. The effect of this loop is to display a message and an ever-increasing number on the status bar until you press Ctrl+Break to stop the procedure or until the value overflows the variable's maximum value. This is all thoroughly pointless (except perhaps as a way to burn in a new computer) and is perhaps a good reason not to use the `Do...Loop` structure—at least not without a condition attached to one end of it.

No matter what type of loop you use, to avoid creating an infinite loop, you need to make sure the condition that will terminate the loop can be satisfied at some point. For example, for an editing or cleanup procedure, you'll often want to perform an action until the end of the document is reached and then stop. Or you'll want to include some form of counting mechanism to make sure a `Do` loop doesn't exceed a certain number of iterations.

The Bottom Line

Understand when to use loops. Loops come in very handy when you need to perform a repetitive task, such as searching through a document for a particular word.

> **Master It** What is the alternative to looping if you are carrying out repetitive tasks in a macro?

Use `For`...loops for fixed repetitions. `For`...loops are the most common loop structures in programming. You specify the number of iterations the loop must make, and the loop is exited when that number is reached.

Master It Write a `For...Next` loop that counts up to 100, but use the `Step` command to increment by twos.

Use `Do`...loops for variable numbers of repetitions. A `Do`...loop iterates until or while a condition exists, and then exits from the loop when the condition no longer exists.

Master It There are two categories of `Do`...loops. `Do While...Loop` and `Do Until...Loop` loops test a condition before performing any action. What is the other category?

Nest one loop within another loop. You can put loops inside other loops.

Master It Think of a programming task where nested loops would be useful.

Avoid infinite loops. An infinite loop causes your macro to continue execution indefinitely—as if the macro had stopped responding and was "frozen."

Master It How can you avoid creating an infinite loop?

Part 4

Using Message Boxes, Input Boxes, and Dialog Boxes

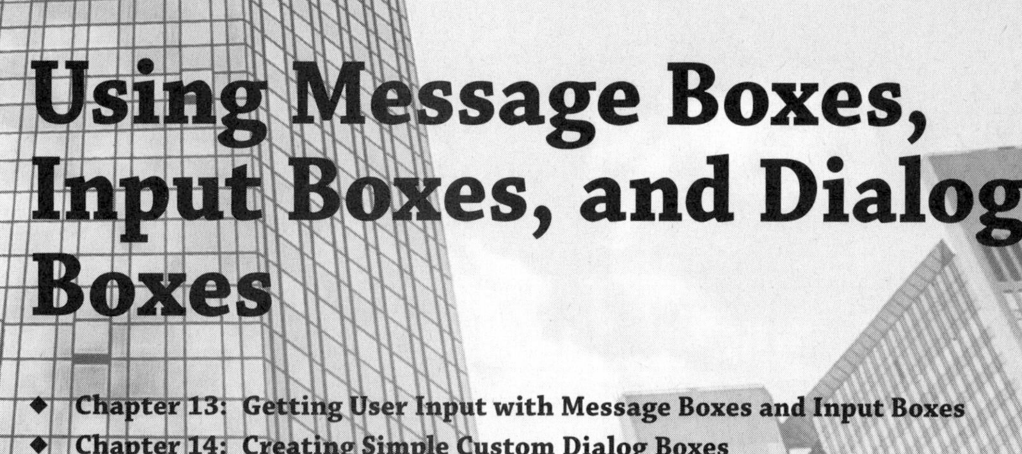

Chapter 13

Getting User Input with Message Boxes and Input Boxes

This chapter shows you how to start adding a user interface to recorded or written code in order to increase the power and functionality of your macros or applications.

You'll learn the three easiest ways of communicating with the user of your macro, the two easiest ways of enabling the user to provide information to your code, and the easiest way of soliciting input from the user. Along the way, you'll see how to decide what the best way to communicate with the user is in any given set of circumstances. This will set the scene for starting an examination of more complex interactions with the user via custom dialog boxes, later in the book.

In most Office applications, VBA offers you a choice of up to five ways of communicating with the user of a macro:

- Displaying a message on the status bar at the bottom of the window (if the application provides a status bar). This is a bit limited, but it can be effective. And it's not intrusive—users can easily ignore the status bar if they like.
- Displaying a message box (usually in the middle of the screen). Message boxes are useful both for providing some information to users and for giving them the means to make a single choice based on the information you give them. You'll spend the bulk of this chapter working with message boxes.
- Displaying an input box (again, usually shown in the middle of the screen). You can use input boxes the same way you use message boxes—to communicate some information to users. But the primary purpose of an input box is input: to solicit one item of information from the user. Input boxes also provide users with the means of making a single choice to direct the flow of a macro, although the mechanism for presenting this choice is much more limited than that in a message box. You'll look at input boxes toward the end of this chapter.
- Displaying a dialog box (once again, usually in the middle of a screen). You can use dialog boxes both to display information to the user and to let them make a variety of choices that are communicated back to your code. Dialog boxes are best reserved for those times when other forms of communication won't suffice; in other words, there's no point in using a dialog box when a simple message box or input box will do. You'll look at creating your own custom dialog boxes by using VBA user forms later in the book.
- Displaying an application's built-in dialog box, such as Word's FileOpen dialog box. This approach is explored in Chapter 14, "Creating Simple Custom Dialog Boxes."

IN THIS CHAPTER, YOU WILL LEARN TO DO THE FOLLOWING:

- Display messages on the status bar
- Display message boxes
- Display input boxes
- Understand the limitations of message boxes and input boxes

Opening a Macro

First you need to ensure that you're all set to edit in the Code window in the VBA Editor:

1. Start the application for which you're creating code.
2. Launch the Visual Basic Editor from the host application by pressing Alt+F11.
3. Open a macro for editing in the Code window: Use the Project Explorer to navigate to the module that holds the macro, and then either scroll to the macro in the Code window or choose it from the Procedures drop-down list in the Code window.

YOU CAN LOCATE MACROS USING THE MACRO DIALOG BOX

Alternatively, in the VBA Editor, choose Tools ➢ Macros to display the Macros dialog box. Or to display this dialog box from an application such as Word, click the Developer tab on the Ribbon, and then click the Macros icon. Once the Macros dialog box is open, you can select a macro you've created from the Macro Name list box and click the Edit button to display the Visual Basic Editor with the macro open in the Code window.

If you've opened an existing macro, test its code by using the F8 key to step through the statements or by clicking F5 (the Run Sub/UserForm) to run it without stepping. (You can also run it by typing the macro's name into the Editor's Immediate window and pressing Enter.)

Nevertheless, it's probably best to work in a new macro rather than in an existing one because that way you won't do any damage to a macro you may want to use in the future.

So, create a new macro in the Visual Basic Editor Code window by typing the **Sub** keyword, giving the macro a name on a blank line in a module, and then pressing Enter. VBA adds the parentheses and `End Sub` statement. For example, you could type the following and press the Enter key:

```
Sub Experimentation_Zone
```

VBA adds the parentheses and `End Sub` statement, together with a separator line to separate the macro from any adjacent macros in the Code window:

```
Sub Experimentation_Zone()
End Sub
```

Displaying Status-Bar Messages in Word and Excel

Word and Excel let you display information on the status bar. This is often a convenient way to tell the user what's happening in a macro without halting execution of the code (or, more important, without interrupting the user's work and requiring them to click a button to get rid of your message box).

By displaying status information on the status bar as the macro works, you can indicate to the user not only what the macro is doing, but also that it's still, in fact, running. Of course, the user might not notice the status bar. So if you are displaying crucial information, you must use a message box or one of the other types of boxes, such as an input box. These approaches *force* the user to pay attention because no further work can be done within the application until that box is dismissed.

How to Avoid Alarming the User

A problem you'll sometimes encounter is that the user thinks a macro has frozen, crashed, gone into an infinite loop, or failed to work because no changes are visible onscreen, whereas in fact your macro is working properly in the background. If you have a macro that takes a long time to execute, updates on the status bar will let the user see that the macro is still working. To see example code that illustrates how to update the status bar, take a look at the sidebar entitled "The Traditional Counter Variable Name for `For...Next` Loops" in Chapter 12, "Using Loops to Repeat Actions."

But remember that the main disadvantage of displaying messages on the status bar is that users may miss them if they're not paying attention, if they've hidden the status bar, or if they're not expecting to see messages there.

How to Hide the Status Bar

When I mentioned hiding the status bar in the previous paragraph, you might have launched an effort to do just that. You looked all over the Ribbon, paying particular attention to the View tab. Then you clicked the File tab to open the Options dialog box. But you didn't find a way, anywhere, to hide the status bar. Well, this is yet one more reason to learn VBA. As I've mentioned, you can do things with VBA that are not possible any other way. Here's the code that will hide the status bar:

```
Sub HideStatusBar()

    Application.CommandBars("Status Bar").Visible = False

End Sub
```

If an application uses the status bar extensively to give the user information (as Word and Excel do), displaying your message there might not be a problem for attentive users. But if there's any doubt, you could notify the user that information will be displayed on the status bar. For example, you might display a message box at the beginning of a macro to tell the user to watch the status bar for updates.

To display a message on the status bar in Excel, you set the `StatusBar` property of the `Application` object to an appropriate string of text. The following example displays the status-bar information shown in Figure 13.1:

```
Application.StatusBar = "Excel is busy formatting. Please wait…"
```

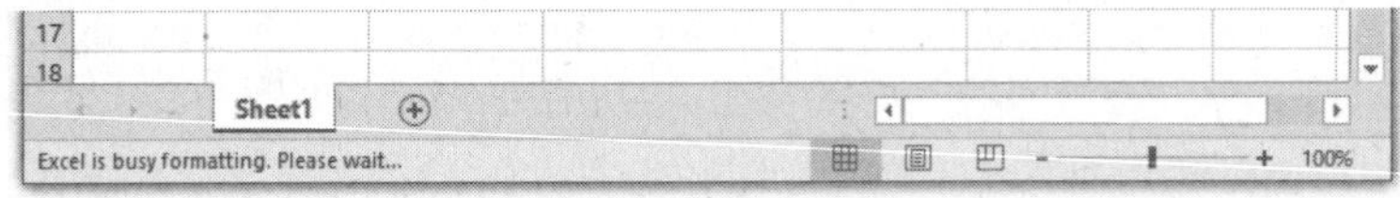

FIGURE 13.1 In some applications, you can display information on the status bar.

Typically, any information you display on the status bar remains displayed there until you change it, until the user clicks something, or until the application displays a message there itself.

For example, if you display a message on the status bar and then invoke the Copy command in Excel, Excel displays its normal Copy message, "Select destination and press ENTER or choose Paste," on the status bar, wiping out your message. Application messages trump user-created messages.

If you display a message on the status bar while a macro executes, you should update it later in the macro to avoid leaving a now-obsolete and potentially misleading message on the status bar after the macro has finished running. For example, you might display another message saying that the macro has finished or clear the status bar by displaying a blank string on it.

To clear the status bar, assign an empty string to it, as in the following statement:

```
Application.StatusBar = ""
```

To see the effect of this statement, run it from the Visual Basic Editor (click the upper-right corner to ensure that the Editor window isn't maximized) with the Word or Excel window (or at least its status bar) visible at the same time. You'll see the effect best if you run a statement that displays information on the status bar (such as `Application.StatusBar = "Hello, World!"`) first so that the status bar has information for the `Application.StatusBar = ""` statement to clear:

```
Application.StatusBar = "Hello, World!"
Application.StatusBar = ""
```

PROGRESS INDICATORS CAN BE WRITTEN VARIOUS WAYS

It's especially helpful to display a progress indicator on the status bar during lengthy processes so that the user can tell the process is still running and making progress. Progress indication is usually coded within a loop block. For example, you might display a readout of the progress, such as "Excel is working on sheet 9 out of 150." Even more simply, adding increasing numbers of periods to the end of the status message gives an indication of progress, although it doesn't give an idea of how much longer the task will take. Here's how you can add periods to a string:

```
strPeriod = strPeriod & "."
```

Message Boxes

Another way to display information to the user is the message box. You've probably seen examples of it in almost every Windows application you've used. Message boxes are simple and limited, but they play an important role.

Here are some typical uses of message boxes:

- Telling users what a macro is about to do (and giving them the chance to exit the macro if it isn't what they thought it was).
- Presenting users with an explanation of what a macro will do next and asking them to make a simple decision (usually, to let it proceed or to send it on a different course).
- Warning users of an error that the macro encountered and allowing them to take action on it.
- Informing users that a macro ran successfully and that it has finished. This message is particularly useful for macros that turn off screen updating or otherwise hide from users what they are doing. Such macros may leave users unsure of whether they are still running or have finished. You can also use the message box to report what a macro has done—for example, that it changed particular items, made a certain number of changes, or discovered problems in the document that require attention.

This chapter shows you how to create a message box suitable for each of these tasks. In later chapters, you'll create specific message boxes to enhance various macros.

The Pros and Cons of Message Boxes

These are the advantages of using a message box:

- Users can't miss seeing the message box. Users are prevented from continuing to use the application until they close the message box. (If you want, you can even display a message box that the user can't escape by pressing Alt+Tab to switch to another application. You'll look at this a little later in the chapter.)
- You can present the user with a simple choice among two or three options.

These are the disadvantages of using a message box:

- A message box can present only one, two, or three buttons, which means it can offer only a limited set of options to the user.
- The buttons in message boxes are predefined in sets—you can't put a custom button in a message box. (For that, you have to use a dialog box.)
- Within message boxes you can't use user-interface features such as text boxes, group boxes, or list boxes.

Message-Box Syntax

The basic syntax for message boxes is as follows:

```
MsgBox(prompt[, buttons] [, title][, helpfile, context])
```

Here's what the elements of this syntax mean:

MsgBox The function that VBA uses to display a message box. You typically use it with a number of arguments enclosed in parentheses after it.

Prompt A required argument for the MsgBox function that specifies what text is displayed in the message box. *prompt* is a String argument, meaning you need to type in the text of your choice; it can be up to 1023 characters long, although it's usually a good idea to be more concise than this. (Any *prompt* longer than 1023 characters is truncated to 1023 characters without warning.)

Buttons An optional argument that controls the type of message box that VBA displays by specifying which buttons it contains. For example, as you'll see in a couple of pages, you can display a message box with just an OK button; with OK and Cancel buttons; with Abort, Retry, and Ignore buttons; and so on. You can also add arguments to the *buttons* argument that control the icon in the message box and the modality of the message box. You'll also look at these options later in this chapter.

Title An optional argument that controls the title bar of the message box. This, too, is a String argument. If you don't specify *title*, VBA uses the application's title—Microsoft Word for Word, Microsoft Excel for Excel, Microsoft PowerPoint for PowerPoint, and so on. Usually, it's best to specify the title because the application name on its own isn't helpful (unless the user has become confused as to which application is running the macro).

Helpfile An optional argument that controls which Help file VBA displays when the user presses F1 within the message box to get help (or clicks the Help button in a message box that contains a Help button).

Context An optional argument that controls which topic in the Help file VBA jumps to. If you specify the helpfile argument, you must specify the *context* argument as well.

In the following sections, you'll first look at how you can build the simplest of message boxes and then explore how to add arguments to it to make it more complex.

Displaying a Simple Message Box

You can display the simplest message box by specifying only the *prompt* as a text string enclosed in double quotation marks:

```
MsgBox "This is a simple message box."
```

Run from Excel, this statement produces the simple message box shown in Figure 13.2. With *prompt* as the only argument supplied, VBA produces a message box with only an OK button and with the application's name in the title bar. This message box does nothing except display information.

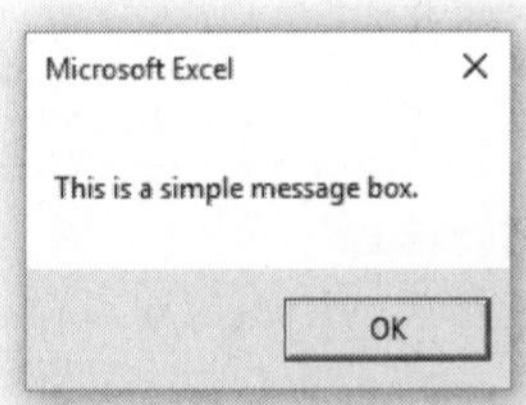

FIGURE 13.2 When you specify only the *prompt* argument to display a simple message box, VBA uses the application's name as the title.

You can enter this `MsgBox` statement on any blank line within a macro. After you type the `MsgBox` keyword, VBA's Auto Quick Info feature prompts you with the syntax of the function, as shown in Figure 13.3.

FIGURE 13.3 VBA's Auto Quick Info feature prompts you with the syntax for the message box.

```
Sub tMessage()

MsgBox (
MsgBox(Prompt, [Buttons As VbMsgBoxStyle = vbOKOnly], [Title], [HelpFile], [Context]) As VbMsgBoxResult

End Sub
```

Once you've entered the `MsgBox` statement with its required argument (*`prompt`*), you can display the message box by stepping through the code (by pressing the F8 key or clicking the Step Into button on the Editor's Debug toolbar) or by running the macro (by pressing the F5 key, by clicking the Run Sub/UserForm button, or by choosing Run ➢ Run Sub/UserForm).

Instead of entering a literal text string for the *`prompt`* argument, you could use a String variable. The following example uses a String variable named `strMsg`:

```
Dim strMsg As String
strMsg = "This is a simple message box."
MsgBox strMsg
```

This approach can be useful when you're working with long strings (you can build a big string by concatenating several shorter strings with the & operator). Using a variable is also useful when you need to display a string that has been defined earlier in the macro or a string dynamically created by the macro (for example, after having gotten the user's name via an input box).

Displaying a Multiline Message Box

By default, VBA displays short message strings as a single line in a message box and wraps longer strings onto two or more lines as necessary, up to the limit of 1024 characters in a string. You can deliberately break a string into more than one line by including line-feed and carriage-return characters in the string as follows:

- `Chr(13)` or `vbCr` represents a carriage return.
- `Chr(10)` or `vbLf` represents a line feed.
- `Chr(10) + Chr(13)` or `vbCrLf` represents a line-feed/carriage-return combination.

In message boxes, these three characters all have the same effect—moving down one line. Your code is easier to read if you use a built-in constant (`vbCr`, `vbLf`, or `vbCrLf`) rather than the corresponding `Chr()` construction; it's also quicker to type. Usually, it's clearest to use the `vbCr` constant.

You can add a tab to a string by using `Chr(9)` or `vbTab`. Again, `vbTab` is easier to read and to type.

The following code displays the Word message box shown in Figure 13.4. Note that each part of the text string is enclosed in double quotation marks (to tell VBA that they're part of the string). The `Chr(149)` characters are bullets, so the text after them starts with a couple of spaces to give the bullets some room:

```
Dim strMsg As String
strMsg = "Word has finished formatting the report you requested." _
```

```
        & vbCr & vbCr & "You can now run the following procedures:" & vbCr _
        & vbCr & Chr(149) & " Distribute_Report will email the report to " _
        & "the head office." & vbCr & vbCr & Chr(149) & _
        " Store_Report will copy the report to the holding directory." _
        & vbCr & vbCr & Chr(149) & " Backup_Report will create a backup " _
        & "of the report on the file server."
    MsgBox strMsg
```

FIGURE 13.4
You can display a multiline message box by using line-feed and carriage-return characters within the *prompt* string.

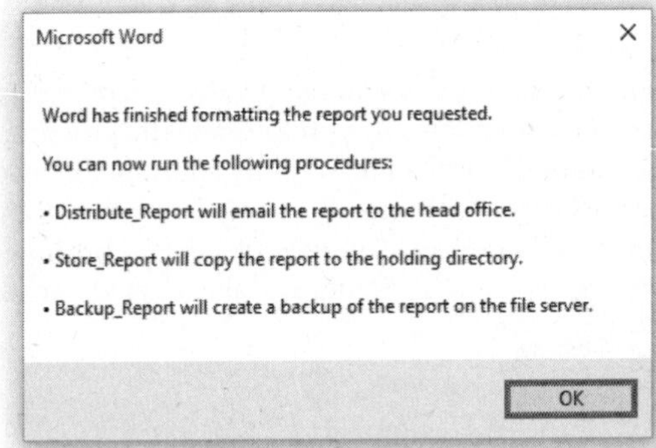

> **VBA AUTOMATICALLY HELPS YOU PUNCTUATE YOUR CODE**
>
> You'll notice that in this example, a space appears on either side of each of the ampersands (&) and the equal sign. You can enter these spaces yourself or have VBA enter them for you when you move the insertion point to another line by pressing Enter or clicking the mouse. (Moving the insertion point to another line causes VBA to check the line you've just been working on and make various automatic changes if necessary. For example, some characters may be capitalized, or if you typed `EndIf`, VBA will make it two words as it's supposed to be.)

Choosing Buttons for a Message Box

The *buttons* argument controls which buttons a message box contains. VBA offers the types of message boxes shown in Table 13.1, controlled by the *buttons* argument.

TABLE 13.1: Message-box types, controlled by the *buttons* argument

VALUE	CONSTANT	BUTTONS
0	vbOKOnly	OK
1	vbOKCancel	OK, Cancel
2	vbAbortRetryIgnore	Abort, Retry, Ignore

TABLE 13.1: Message-box types, controlled by the *buttons* argument *(CONTINUED)*

VALUE	CONSTANT	BUTTONS
3	vbYesNoCancel	Yes, No, Cancel
4	vbYesNo	Yes, No
5	vbRetryCancel	Retry, Cancel

You can specify these message-box types in your code by using either the numeric value or the constant. For example, you can specify either `1` or `vbOKCancel` to produce a message box with OK and Cancel buttons. The value is easier to type; the constant is easier to read. Either of the following statements produces the message box shown in Figure 13.5 when run from PowerPoint:

```
Dim lngR As Long
lngR = MsgBox("Apply standard formatting to the slide?", vbYesNo)
lngR = MsgBox("Apply standard formatting to the slide?", 4)
```

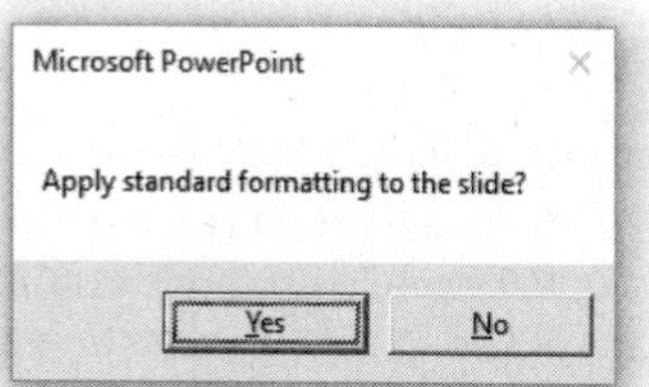

FIGURE 13.5
The `vbYesNo` constant produces a message box with Yes and No buttons.

From VBA's point of view, it doesn't matter whether you use values or constants in the message boxes for your macros. For the human, though, the text constants are far more preferable. Even if you're the only person who ever sees your code, the code is much easier to read if you use the constants.

Choosing an Icon for a Message Box

You can also add an icon to a message box by including the appropriate value or constant argument. Table 13.2 shows the options.

TABLE 13.2: Arguments for message-box icons

VALUE	CONSTANT	DISPLAYS
16	vbCritical	Stop icon
32	vbQuestion	Question-mark icon
48	vbExclamation	Exclamation-point icon
64	vbInformation	Information icon

Again, you can refer to these icons by using either the value or the constant: Either 48 or `vbExclamation` will produce an exclamation-point icon. Again, the constant is much easier to read.

To link the value or constant for the message box with the value or constant for the icon, use a plus sign (+). For example, to produce a message box containing Yes and No buttons together with a question-mark icon (see Figure 13.6), you could enter **`vbYesNo + vbQuestion`** (or **`4 + 32`**, **`vbYesNo + 32`**, or **`4 + vbQuestion`**):

```
lngR = MsgBox("Apply standard formatting to the slide?", _
    vbYesNo + vbQuestion)
```

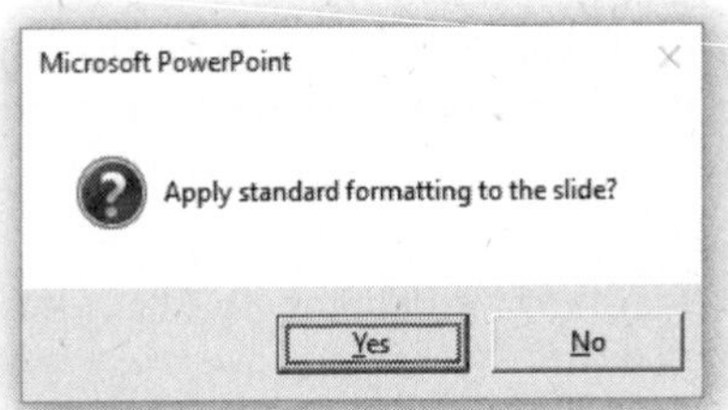

FIGURE 13.6
Adding an icon gives a message box greater visual impact.

Setting a Default Button for a Message Box

As usual in the Windows interface, the user is cued to a default button in a message box. It's the one with a blue border around its outside and a dotted line around its text area. (See the Yes button in Figure 13.6.) The user can move the selection to another button by using Tab or Shift+Tab or the →, ←, ↑, or ↓ key.

However, you can specify in your code which button you want to be the default.

Real World Scenario

THE PRACTICAL USE OF DEFAULT BUTTONS

You can set a default button for a message box by specifying a particular button in the `MsgBox` statement. Specifying a default button can be a wise move when you give macros that take drastic action to users who may be unfamiliar with what's going to happen. (The user might accidentally hit the Enter key or click the highlighted button—the default button.)

For example, consider a macro that deletes the current document without the user having to close it and then switches to a file-management program (such as Windows Explorer) or messes around in one of the common dialog boxes (such as the Open or the Save dialog box). Common dialog boxes are demonstrated in the Real World Scenario sidebar titled "Control a `For...Next` Loop with User Input via a Dialog Box" in Chapter 12.

Because such macros can destroy someone's work if they run it inadvertently, you'd probably want to set a default button of No or Cancel in a confirmation message box so that the user has to actively choose to run the rest of the macro. The message box halts execution, allows the user to agree or disagree with the action, and then carries out the user's wishes based on which button is clicked in the message box.

Why does VBA include a default button at all? This makes it easy for the user to choose the ordinary VBA default button (captioned Yes or OK) by simply pressing Enter. Having the appropriate default button on a message box or dialog box can help the user deal with the message box or dialog box more quickly. But you as the programmer should decide if there is a different, more appropriate, default button. VBA automatically sets the first button in a message box to be the default button. But there are times that you will want to specify that the default button be a different button than the first. If you are doing something potentially dangerous in a macro—such as deleting the current document without saving it—it would be a good idea to make the second button (the No button) the default. This way, if the user simply presses Enter, nothing happens; the macro exits without deletion. Using this technique, you force the user to make a deliberate decision to move the mouse and click the Yes button. Table 13.3 shows you how to adjust which button is the default by using various built-in constants. And the short code example that ends the section demonstrates this technique.

Table 13.3 lists the arguments for default buttons.

TABLE 13.3: Arguments for default message-box buttons

VALUE	CONSTANT	EFFECT
0	`vbDefaultButton1`	The first button is the default button.
256	`vbDefaultButton2`	The second button is the default button.
512	`vbDefaultButton3`	The third button is the default button.
768	`vbDefaultButton4`	The fourth button is the default button.

All the message boxes mentioned so far have only one, two, or three buttons, but you can add a Help button to any of the message boxes, thereby displaying a fourth button. You'll see how to add the Help button in the section "Adding a Help Button to a Message Box" later in this chapter.

In VBA, unless you specify otherwise, the first button on each of the message boxes is automatically the default button—for example, the OK button in a `vbOKCancel` message box, the Abort button in a `vbAbortRetryIgnore` message box, the Yes button in a `vbYesNoCancel` message box, the Yes button in a `vbYesNo` message box, and the Retry button in a `vbRetryCancel` message box. VBA counts the buttons in the order they're presented in the constant for the type of message box (which in turn is the left-to-right order in which they appear in the message box onscreen). So in a `vbYesNoCancel` message box, Yes is the first button, No is the second button, and Cancel is the third button.

To make a different button the default, specify the value or constant as part of the *`buttons`* argument. When run in PowerPoint, this statement produces the message box shown in Figure 13.7:

```
Dim lngQuery As Long
lngQuery = MsgBox("Do you want to delete this presentation?", _
    vbYesNo + vbCritical + vbDefaultButton2)
```

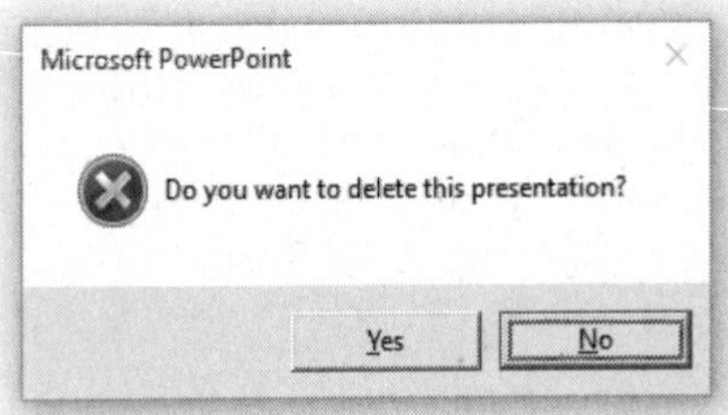

FIGURE 13.7 Specify a default button to steer the user toward a particular button in a message box.

Controlling the Modality of a Message Box

VBA can display both application-modal message boxes and system-modal message boxes—at least in theory. *Application-modal* message boxes stop you from doing anything in the current application until you dismiss them, whereas *system-modal* message boxes stop you from doing anything *on your entire computer* until you dismiss them.

Most message boxes are application modal, allowing the user to switch to another application by pressing Alt+Tab (or switching via the Taskbar). The user can then work in the other application even though they haven't gotten rid of the message box. This gives them freedom and flexibility. In contrast, some message boxes (most often used during an installation process) are system modal, insisting that users concentrate their attention on them and them alone. Windows's critical system errors and "you must restart your computer now" messages are system modal to prevent you from avoiding them.

You probably know from your own experience how frustrating system-modal message boxes can be. So when you're designing macros, use system-modal message boxes only when absolutely necessary—for example, when an action might result in data loss or system instability. For most conventional purposes, application-modal message boxes will do everything you need them to—and won't confuse or vex your users.

In theory, you can control the modality of a message box by using the two *`buttons`* arguments shown in Table 13.4.

TABLE 13.4: Arguments for message-box modality

VALUE	CONSTANT	RESULT
`0`	`vbApplicationModal`	The message box is application modal.
`4096`	`vbSystemModal`	The message box is system modal.

In practice, even if you use the `vbSystemModal` argument, the user can switch to another application (provided that one is running) and continue working. However, the message box does stay "on top," remaining displayed—enough to annoy users but not totally prevent them from accessing another application.

By default, message boxes are application modal, so you need to specify modality only on those rare occasions when you need a system-modal message box. When you do, add the `vbSystemModal` constant or `4096` value to the *`buttons`* argument:

```
Response = MsgBox("Do you want to delete this document?", _
    vbYesNo + vbCritical + vbDefaultButton2 + vbSystemModal)
```

Please note that system-modal message boxes look the same as application-modal message boxes.

Specifying a Title for a Message Box

The next component of the message box is its title bar, which is controlled by the optional *`title`* argument. If you omit *`title`*, VBA displays the application's name as the title, but users of your macros will benefit from your providing a more helpful title.

The string expression *`title`* can be up to 1024 characters in length, in theory (longer strings are truncated with no warning or error message), but in practice, any title longer than about 75 characters gets truncated with an ellipsis. If you want people to read the title bars of your message boxes, 25 characters or so is a reasonable maximum.

Title Bars Can Provide Useful Information

The title bar is usually the first part of a message box that the user notices, so make your title bars as helpful as possible. Conventional etiquette is to put the name of the macro in the title bar of a message box and then use the `prompt` argument to explain what actions the buttons in the message box will trigger.

In addition, if you expect to revise your macros, you may find it helpful to include their version number in the title so that users can easily check which version of the macro they're using (and update to a more current version as appropriate). For instance, the Delete Workbook macro is identified as version 12.39 in the message box shown in Figure 13.8.

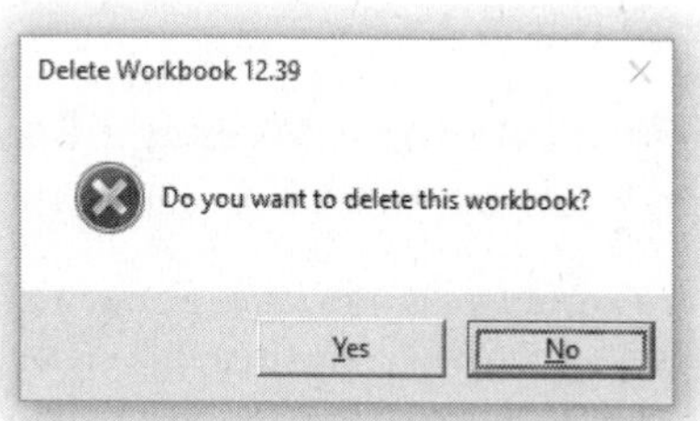

FIGURE 13.8 Usually, you'll want to specify the *`title`* argument for your message boxes. You may also want to include a version number.

Specify the *`title`* argument after the *`buttons`* argument like this:

```
Dim lngQuery As Long
lngQuery = MsgBox("Do you want to delete this workbook?", vbYesNo _
    + vbCritical + vbDefaultButton2, "Delete Workbook 12.39")
```

You can use a string variable as the `title` argument. For example, you could declare a single string variable and use it to supply the title for each message box that a macro calls. Or you might need to display in the title of the message box a string created or stored in the macro.

> **AVOID USING SPECIAL CHARACTERS IN TITLES**
>
> Don't try putting line-feed, carriage-return, or Tab characters in the title argument. VBA just ignores them.

Adding a Help Button to a Message Box

To add a Help button to a message box, use the `vbMsgBoxHelpButton` constant. You add this argument to whichever buttons you're specifying for the message box:

```
lngQuery = MsgBox("Do you want to delete this workbook?", vbYesNo _
    + vbCritical + vbDefaultButton2 + vbMsgBoxHelpButton, _
    "Delete Workbook")
```

Adding the `vbMsgBoxHelpButton` argument simply places the Help button in the message box—it doesn't make the Help button display a Help file if the user clicks it. You must also specify which Help file and topic you want shown (see the next section for details). Figure 13.9 shows the message box that this statement produces.

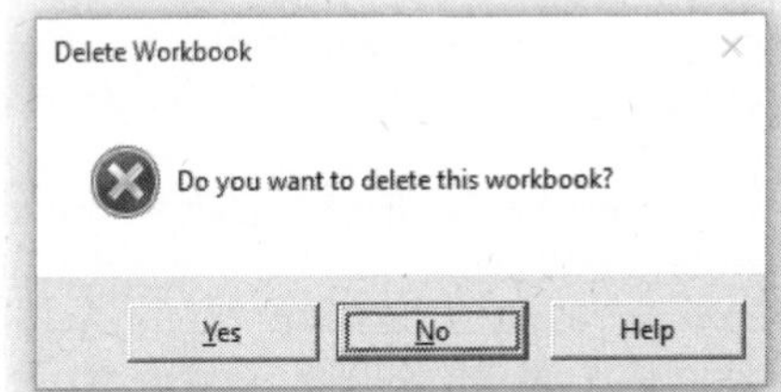

FIGURE 13.9 Use the `vbMsgBoxHelpButton` constant to add a Help button to a message box.

Specifying a Help File for a Message Box

The final arguments you can use for a message box are the `helpfile` and `context` arguments:

- The `helpfile` argument is a string argument specifying the name and location of the Help file that VBA displays when the user summons help from the message box.
- The `context` argument is a Help context number within the Help file. The Help context number controls which Help-file topic is displayed.

The `helpfile` and `context` arguments are primarily useful if you're writing your own Help files, because otherwise it's difficult to access the Help context numbers, which are buried in the official Help files.

If you're writing your own Help files, the syntax for specifying the *helpfile* and *context* arguments is simple:

```
Dim lngQuery As Long
lngQuery = MsgBox("Do you want to delete this workbook?", vbYesNo _
    + vbCritical + vbDefaultButton2 + vbMsgBoxHelpButton, _
    "Delete Workbook", "c:\Windows\Help\My_Help.chm", 1012)
```

In this case, the Help file is specified as `My_Help.chm` in the `\Windows\Help\` folder. VBA displays the Help topic numbered 1012.

When the user clicks the Help button in the message box, VBA displays the specified topic in the Help file. The message box stays onscreen so that when users have finished consulting the Help file, they can make their choices in the message box.

The Help context number for the opening screen of a Help file is 0. Use 0 when you need to display a Help file for which you don't know the Help context number. Users must then locate the information they need on their own.

Three Unusual Constants for Special Effects

VBA provides three special constants for use with message boxes. You probably won't need to use these often, but if you do, they'll come in handy. Specify them as the first argument in the *buttons* arguments:

`vbMsgBoxSetForeground` Tells VBA to make the message box the foreground window. You shouldn't need to use this constant often, because message boxes are displayed in the foreground by default (so that you can see them).

`vbMsgBoxRight` Tells VBA to right-align the text in the message box.

`vbMsgBoxRtlReading` Tells VBA to arrange the text from right to left on Hebrew and Arabic systems. It has no effect on non-BiDi (bidirectional) systems.

Using Some Arguments Without Others

Recall that optional arguments are just that, optional. So, when displaying a message box, you can either specify or omit optional arguments. If you want to specify arguments later in the argument list without specifying the ones before them, use a comma to indicate each unused optional argument. (This technique can be used with any argument list.) For example, if you wanted to display the message box shown in the previous example without specifying *buttons* and *title* arguments, you could use the following statement:

```
Response = MsgBox("Do you want to format the report?",,, _
    "c:\Windows\Help\Macro Help.chm", 1012
```

Here, the triple comma indicates that the *buttons* and *title* arguments are omitted (which will cause VBA to display defaults—a `vbOKOnly` message box with a title bar containing the application's name), preventing VBA from confusing the *helpfile* argument with the *buttons* argument. Alternatively, you could use named arguments, which makes for less-concise but easier-to-read code:

```
Response = MsgBox("Do you want to format the report?", _
    HelpFile:="c:\Windows\Help\Macro Help.chm", Context:=1012)
```

Retrieving a Value from a Message Box

If you display a vbOKOnly message box, you know which button the user clicks because the message box contains only that single OK button. But when you use one of the other message-box styles, which can have two, three, or four buttons, how can your code know which button was clicked? To do that, you must retrieve a value from the message box code that tells you which button the user clicked. (You can then branch execution to respond appropriately to the user's choice.)

To retrieve a value from a message box, declare a variable for it (just as we've been doing throughout this chapter). You can do so quite simply by telling VBA that the variable name is equal to the message box (so to speak), like this:

```
Dim lngResponse As Long
lngResponse = MsgBox("Do you want to create the daily report?", _
    vbYesNo + vbQuestion, "Create Daily Report")
```

You first declare a variable of the appropriate type (a Long variable) to contain the user's choice, as in the examples throughout this chapter.

When you run the code, VBA stores which button the user clicked as a value in the variable. You can then check the value and take action accordingly.

Table 13.5 shows the full list of buttons the user may choose. You can refer to the buttons by either the constant name or the value number. As usual, the constant is easier to read than the value.

TABLE 13.5: Constants for selected buttons

VALUE	CONSTANT	BUTTON SELECTED
1	vbOK	OK
2	vbCancel	Cancel
3	vbAbort	Abort
4	vbRetry	Retry
5	vbIgnore	Ignore
6	vbYes	Yes
7	vbNo	No

For example, to check a vbYesNo message box to see which button the user chose, you can use a straightforward If…Then…Else statement:

```
Dim lngUserChoice As Long
lngUserChoice = MsgBox("Do you want to create the daily report?", _
    vbYesNo + vbQuestion, "Create Daily Report")
If lngUserChoice = vbYes Then
    Goto CreateDailyReport
Else
    Goto Bye
EndIf
```

Here, if the user chooses the Yes button, VBA goes to the line of code identified by the CreateDailyReport label and continues running the macro from there; if not, it terminates the macro by going to the Bye label at the end. The If condition checks the response generated by the choice the user made in the message box to see if it's a vbYes (generated by clicking the Yes button or pressing Enter with the Yes button selected). The Else statement runs if the response was not vbYes—that is, if the user clicked the No button or pressed Esc.

Input Boxes

Message boxes tell VBA which button the user clicked. But sometimes you want the user to supply your macro with some text, such as their name or birthday.

When you want to retrieve one simple piece of text information from the user, use an input box. You'll be familiar with input boxes by sight if not by name: They usually look something like the example shown in Figure 13.10.

FIGURE 13.10
Use an input box to retrieve a single piece of information from the user.

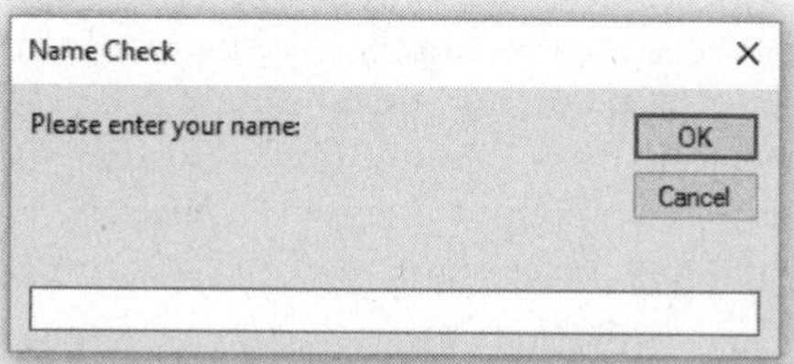

> **CREATE CUSTOM BOXES FOR COMPLEX INTERACTION**
>
> To retrieve two or more pieces of information from the user, you could use two or more input boxes in succession, but it's usually easier for the user if you create a custom dialog box. You'll start building custom dialog boxes in Chapter 14.

Input-Box Syntax

The syntax for displaying an input box is straightforward and similar to the syntax for a message box:

```
InputBox(prompt[, title] [, default] [, xpos] [, ypos] [, helpfile, context])
```

Here's what the arguments mean:

`Prompt` A required string that specifies the prompt that appears in the input box. As with `MsgBox`, *`prompt`* can be up to about 1024 characters long, and you can use the carriage-return constant (`vbCr`) to force separate lines. Like the `MsgBox` *`prompt`* argument, the `InputBox` *`prompt`* automatically wraps if the prompt is longer than about 35 characters.

`Title` A string that specifies the text in the title bar of the input box. If you don't specify a *`title`* argument, VBA supplies the application's name.

`Default` A string that you can use to specify text that will appear in the text box. Entering a *`default`* argument can be a good idea both for cases when the default text is likely to be suitable (so the user can just press Enter to accept that default) or when you need to display sample text so that the user can understand what type of response you're looking for.

Here's an example of suitable default text to cue the user: If you display an input box asking for the user's name, you could enter the Name value by fetching it from the `BuiltInDocumentProperties` collection of the `ActiveDocument` object, like this:

```
Dim strAuthor As String
  strAuthor = _
  ActiveDocument.BuiltInDocumentProperties(wdPropertyLastAuthor)
```

`xpos` and `ypos` These are optional numeric values for specifying the onscreen position of the input box. The *`xpos`* value governs the horizontal position of the left edge of the input box from the left edge of the screen (not of the Word window), whereas *`ypos`* governs the vertical position of the top edge of the input box from the top of the screen. Each measurement is in *`twips`*, described in the sidebar "Input Boxes Are Usually Best Displayed in the Center of the Screen" in this chapter. If you omit these two arguments, VBA displays the input box at the default position of halfway across the screen and one-third of the way down it.

`helpfile` and `context` Optional arguments for specifying the Help file and context in the Help file to jump to if the user summons help from the input box. If you use *`helpfile`*, you must also use *`context`*.

Input Boxes Are Usually Best Displayed in the Center of the Screen

A *twip* is 1/1440 inch. Although there is a fair amount of variation, the average computer screen uses 96 dots per inch (dpi). This works out to 15 twips per pixel, and a computer screen at 1024 × 768 resolution is 15,360 × 11,520 twips. If you need to position your input boxes and dialog boxes precisely, experiment with twips at different screen resolutions until you achieve satisfactory results. Generally, it's most effective to display an input box in the default center position. Your users are likely to have a variety of screen resolutions.

You can omit any of the optional arguments for an input box. But if you want to use another argument later in the syntax sequence, remember that you need to indicate the omission with a spacer comma (or use named arguments as described earlier in this chapter).

Unlike message boxes, input boxes come with a predefined set of buttons—OK and Cancel, plus a Help button if you specify the *helpfile* and *context* arguments—so there's no need to specify the main buttons for an input box. The following example declares the String variable `strWhichOffice` and assigns to it the result of the input box shown in Figure 13.11:

```
Dim strWhichOffice As String
strWhichOffice = InputBox( _
    "Enter the name of the office that you visited:", _
    "Expense Assistant", "Madrid", , , _
    "c:\Windows\Help\Procedure Help.chm", 0)
```

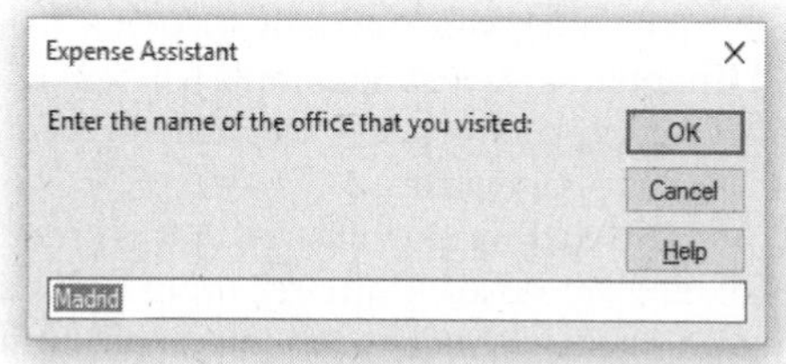

FIGURE 13.11
The input box comes with a predefined set of buttons.

Retrieving Input from an Input Box

To retrieve the user's input from an input box, declare the numeric variable or String variable that will contain it. Here, the variable `strWhichOffice` will contain what the user types into the input box:

```
Dim strWhichOffice
strWhichOffice = _
    InputBox("Enter the name of the office that you visited:", _
    "Expense Assistant 2000", "Madrid", , , _
    "c:\Windows\Help\Procedure Help.chm", 0)
```

Once the user has entered a value or a string and clicked the OK button, your code can then use the returned value as usual in VBA. To make sure the user has clicked the OK button, check that the input box hasn't returned a zero-length string (which it also returns if the user chooses the OK button with the text box empty), and take action accordingly:

```
strWhichOffice = InputBox _
    ("Enter the name of the office that you visited:", _
    "Expense Assistant 2000", "Madrid", , , _
    "c:\Windows\Help\Procedure Help.chm", 0)
If strWhichOffice = "" Then End
```

Forms: When Message Boxes and Input Boxes Won't Suffice

As you've seen in this chapter, a message box can greatly enhance a macro by enabling the user to make a choice at a turning point or by presenting the user with important information. But once you've used message boxes for a while, you're apt to start noticing their shortcomings:

- You can present only a limited amount of information, and you're constrained in the way you can display it (to whatever layout you can conjure up with new paragraphs, line breaks, tabs, and spaces).
- You can use only seven sets of buttons, which limits the amount of information that a user can return to your code via message boxes.

While you can get creative and enter complex messages in message boxes to make the most use of the buttons they offer, you'll usually do better to just create a custom dialog box instead. As you'll see in Chapter 14, "Creating Simple Custom Dialog Boxes," and Chapter 15, "Creating Complex Forms," custom dialog boxes are relatively simple to create, and they are more powerful and flexible than message boxes.

You'll also want to avoid writing macros that present the user with a number of choices via a sequence of message boxes. Similarly, input boxes are useful for retrieving a single piece of information from the user, but beyond that, their limitations quickly become apparent too. If you find yourself planning to use two or more input boxes in immediate succession, create a custom dialog box instead. That way you display a single form for the user to fill in all the needed information, instead of several boxes. You'll see how to create forms in Chapter 14.

The Bottom Line

Display messages on the status bar. The information bar at the bottom of the window in many applications is a useful, unobtrusive way of communicating with the user. The status bar is frequently used by applications to indicate the current page, zoom level, active view (such as *datasheet* in Access), word count, and so on. However, you, too, can display information on the bar.

Master It Write a small sub in the Visual Basic Editor that displays the current date and time in the status bar.

Display message boxes. Message boxes are commonly used to inform or warn the user. By default, they appear in the middle of the screen and prevent the user from interacting with the host application until a button on the message box is clicked, thereby closing it.

Master It Write a small sub in the Visual Basic Editor that displays the current date and time using a message box.

Display input boxes. An input box is similar to a message box, except the former can get more information from the user. An input box allows the user to type in a string, which is more data than the simple information provided by which button the user clicked in a message box.

Master It Write a small sub in the Visual Basic Editor that asks users to type in their name. Use the `InStr` function to see if there are any space characters in the returned string. If not, it means either they are Madonna or they have typed in only one name—so display a second input box telling them to provide both their first and last names.

Understand the limitations of message boxes and input boxes. For even moderately complex interaction with the user, message and input boxes are often too limited. They return to the VBA code, for example, only a single user response: a button click or a single piece of text. So, you can't conveniently use an input box to ask for multiple data—such as an address *and* a phone number—without displaying multiple input boxes. That's ugly and disruptive.

Master It In addition to the limitations on the amount of information you can retrieve from the user, what are the two other major limitations of message boxes and input boxes?

Chapter 14

Creating Simple Custom Dialog Boxes

In this chapter, you'll start looking at Visual Basic for Applications' tools for creating custom dialog boxes that interact with the user. The terms *dialog box* and *form* (or *user form*) are generally used interchangeably. Technically, a dialog box is a quite simple, small window, such as a message box or input box. Forms, generally, are larger windows featuring richer and more complex interaction with the user. These terms, though, are equivalent in common usage.

Dialog boxes and forms are among the most powerful and feature-packed elements of VBA. We will spend quite a bit of time exploring their uses as the primary communication path between users and procedures.

This chapter covers the most common and straightforward components (called *controls*) that you can put on a form. The next chapter shows you how to create more elaborate forms, such as those with tabbed pages and those that update themselves when the user clicks a control.

IN THIS CHAPTER, YOU WILL LEARN TO DO THE FOLLOWING:

- Understand what you can do with a custom dialog box
- Create a custom dialog box
- Add controls to a dialog box
- Link dialog boxes to procedures
- Retrieve the user's choices from a dialog box

When Should You Use a Custom Dialog Box?

You'll sometimes want to use a *form* (another word for *dialog box* or *window*) when simpler methods of interacting with the user fall short. Sometimes, the limited buttons provided in message boxes are insufficient for getting needed information from the user. Similarly, the single text field available in an input box would be inadequate if you need the user to provide multiple data (name, address, phone number, and so on). In other words, sometimes you need the user to fill in a *form*.

You'll also want to use a custom dialog box for specialized input. For example, you might need the user to choose nonexclusive options by selecting or clearing check boxes, or to choose from among mutually exclusive choices via option buttons (also called *radio buttons*), or to select an item within a list that you show them in a list box. Or perhaps you need to show users a picture. In other words, simple message boxes or input boxes cannot handle complex user input.

Custom dialog boxes can include the full range of interface elements (controls) that the user is probably familiar with from working with Windows applications. You can create custom dialog boxes that look and function almost exactly like the dialog boxes built into applications (such as the File Save dialog box). Or you can build even larger constructions that approach the sophistication of typical application windows.

You'll use forms often in your more sophisticated macros. For example, when the user starts a procedure, you can have the procedure display a form presenting options—such as choosing the files for the procedure to manipulate. The user's choices determine what the procedure will then do.

You can also create dialog boxes that VBA triggers in response to events in the computer system—for example, an event that runs at a specific time or runs when the user takes a specific action (such as creating, opening, or closing a document).

Making your own dialog boxes is *not* that hard, but it can be time-consuming if you're building a complicated form. Because creating forms is not the fastest programming job, you might want to consider any practical alternatives to using them.

You've already looked at message boxes and input boxes, which provide a simple alternative for some of the relatively easy tasks for which you might want to create a custom dialog box.

Also, some applications, such as Word and Excel, even let you use their built-in dialog boxes for your own purposes. If users are familiar with the application, they're probably familiar with these built-in dialog boxes and can immediately use them to perform standard actions—for example, to open or save files. These are called *common dialog boxes*. How to use common dialog boxes in your macros is demonstrated briefly in the Real World Scenario titled "Control a `For... Next` Loop with User Input via a Dialog Box" in Chapter 12, "Using Loops to Repeat Actions," and more fully later in this chapter in the section titled "Using an Application's Built-In Dialog Boxes from VBA."

Creating a Custom Dialog Box

If you want to employ a custom dialog box or window in VBA, you use a visual object called a *user form*. A user form (also sometimes just referred to as a *form*) is a blank sheet on which you can place controls, such as check boxes, buttons, and text boxes, to create a made-to-order dialog box.

As you'll see, a user form contains its own code page where you, the programmer, write code to manage the various controls in the form. You can attach code to any of the controls, or to the user form itself, and that code is stored in the Code *window*. You can work with that code as you would macro code. You can also run and test a user form as you would any macro (for example, by pressing F5 with the user form selected), and the VBA Editor will execute the code behind the form.

You can display a user form (a dialog box) for the user to interact with, and you can then retrieve information from the user form and manipulate it with VBA code. It's in this sense that code supporting a form is said to be *behind* a form. The user sees and interacts with a form, but behind the scenes you have written code to intelligently react to whatever the user might input.

Each user form is itself an object and can contain a number of other objects that you can manipulate individually.

User Forms Aren't Always Dialog Boxes

You can also create user forms that aren't dialog boxes. The distinction between a dialog box and a full window is imprecise, but it's usually easiest to define a resizable form as a window (you can resize it by dragging its borders or by clicking its Maximize button), while a dialog box has a fixed size. Some dialog boxes, such as the Find And Replace dialog box in Word, have an initially hidden part that the user can display (in the case of the Find And Replace dialog box, by clicking a More button).

But apart from this simple resizing, the bounds of the dialog box are fixed—you can't grab the corner of the dialog box with the mouse and drag it to enlarge it. But remember that you, the programmer, can create very large user forms that have the complexity and dimensions of a typical application window.

For example, you could create a simple dialog box with two option buttons, an OK button, and a Cancel button. Each option button would be an object, the OK button would be a third object, and the Cancel button would be a fourth object. You could set properties individually for each object—such as the action to take when the Cancel button is clicked or the ScreenTip (also called a ToolTip) to display when the user moves the mouse pointer over each of the option buttons. (ToolTips help make the components of your form understandable for the user.) The point is to consider the components of a form—the *controls* you place on the form—as objects. This is another use of the concept of objects. Controls are visual objects, but like purely programmatic objects, controls have members such as properties.

You can specify most properties of an object either at design time (when you're creating the user form) or at runtime (while the code is executing, either before or after you display the user form). For example, consider the `Value` property of a check-box control. Your code (or the user) can set it to `True` to display the check box in its selected state or to `False` to display the check box in its cleared state. You can set the `Value` property three different ways:

- When building the user form, you can use the Editor's Properties window to specify values. For example, you can make a check box that will default to its selected (checked) state each time the user form is displayed.
- You can write code that sets the check box before the form gets displayed to the user while the macro is running.
- You can write code that sets the check box while the user is interacting with the form. Note that the user can click the check box to toggle it between its selected and deselected states, but your code can also do this.

The next sections explain the process of creating a dialog box. Later in this chapter, you'll find examples that step through creating a procedure and adding a dialog box to it.

Designing a Dialog Box

It's possible to whip together a half-decent dialog box without much planning. Some programmers like to just "sketch" the user interface in a dialog box by dragging and dropping controls from the Toolbox onto the form, then positioning the controls so they look good and, finally, modifying their properties.

Other programmers prefer to adopt a more methodical approach and plan what they need to include in the dialog box before they start creating it. If you fall into this latter category, consider the intended purpose of the dialog box and list the elements it will need in order to achieve this goal. Then sketch on paper a rough diagram of the dialog box to get an approximate idea of where you'll want to locate each of the elements (the controls you place on the form).

Try Basing Custom Dialog-Box Designs on Existing Dialog Boxes

Another option is to base the design for your custom dialog box on an existing dialog box—either a dialog box built into an application (called a common dialog box) or a custom dialog box that your company or organization has already implemented. Leveraging previous development efforts can not only help you avoid reinventing the wheel, but can also produce a custom dialog box that users find familiar and intuitive.

Inserting a User Form

Once you have a design in mind, the first step in creating a custom dialog box is to insert a user form in the appropriate template or document:

1. Press Alt+11 to display the Visual Basic Editor if it's not already open.
2. In the Project Explorer window, right-click the appropriate project and choose Insert ➤ UserForm from the context menu.

Other Ways to Add a User Form

You can also insert a user form by clicking the Insert UserForm button on the far left of the Editor's Standard toolbar.

The Visual Basic Editor opens a new user form like that shown in Figure 14.1, named `UserForm1` (or the next available number if the project already contains other user forms).

The Visual Basic Editor also displays the Toolbox. (If you've previously hidden the Toolbox while working on a user form, the Visual Basic Editor doesn't display it. Choose View ➤ Toolbox or click the Toolbox button on the far right of the Standard toolbar.)

VBA automatically inserts the user form in the `Forms` object (the collection of forms) for the project. If the project you chose didn't already contain a `Forms` collection, VBA adds one to contain the new user form. You'll see the `Forms` object displayed in the Project Explorer.

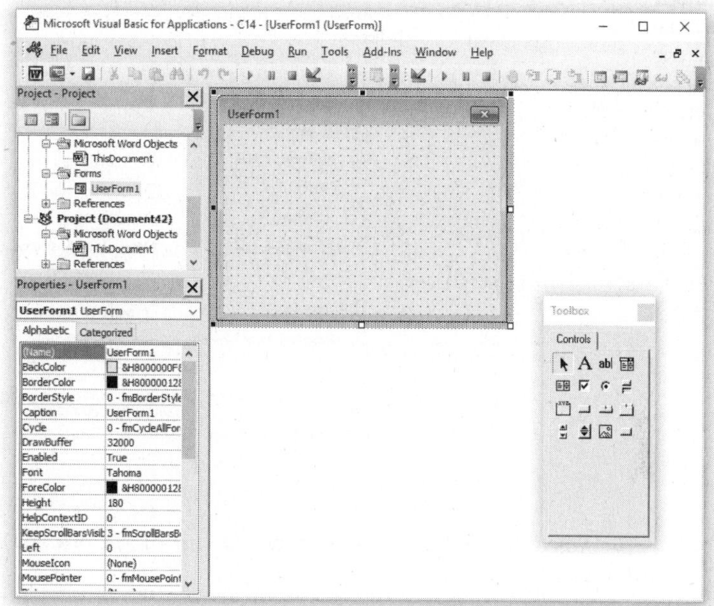

FIGURE 14.1 The first step in creating a new dialog box is to start a new user form. The Visual Basic Editor displays the Toolbox when a user form is the active window.

CHOOSING USER-FORM GRID SETTINGS

The Visual Basic Editor displays a grid in each user form to help you place controls relative to the dialog box and to align controls relative to each other so they look neat instead of random.

I can't think why you would want to do this, but to switch off the display of this grid or to switch off the Visual Basic Editor's automatic alignment of controls to the grid, follow these steps:

1. Choose Tools ➤ Options to display the Options dialog box.
2. Click the General tab to display the General page (see Figure 14.2).
3. Choose the settings you want:
    a. Clear the Show Grid check box if you want to turn off the display of the grid. (The grid continues to function, but the dots are not displayed.)
    b. Clear the Align Controls To Grid check box if you want to stop using the grid whether it's visible or not. This feature is usually a timesaver, but if the grid is too coarse for the layout you're trying to achieve, just reduce the sizing of the grid from the default 6 to perhaps 3 or 4.
    c. Change the number of points in the Width and Height text boxes to adjust the sizing of the grid's units.

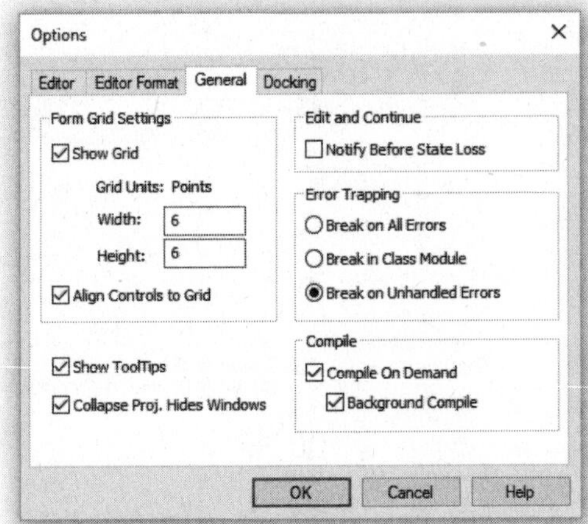

FIGURE 14.2
The General page of the Options dialog box includes options for toggling the display of the grid, resizing the grid, and toggling whether VBA aligns the controls to the grid.

4. Click the OK button to close the Options dialog box and apply your choices.

NAMING CONVENTIONS IN VISUAL BASIC FOR APPLICATIONS

Assigning names to controls in VBA is similar to naming variables. Names for controls can be up to 40 characters long, must begin with a letter, and after that can be any combination of letters, numbers, and underscores. You can't use spaces or symbols in the names, and each name must be unique in its context—for example, each user form must have a unique name within a project, but within any user form or dialog box, a control can have the same name as another control in a different form.

Those are the rules; you can also use conventions to make the names of your VBA objects as consistent and easy to understand as possible. Recall the conventions you've used in previous chapters for identifying the variable type with a prefix: `str`, `lng`, `int`, and so on. The prefixes widely used when naming controls identify the control. For example, by using the convention of prefixing a text box control's name with `txt`, you can be sure that anyone else reading your code will immediately identify the name as belonging to a text box—and that you yourself will easily identify the name when you revisit your old code.

Here's an example showing conventional prefixes for several controls:

```
Private Sub cmbSelectEmployee_Change()
  lblEmployeeName = cmbSelectEmployee.Text
  fraStep2.Enabled = True
  lblInstructions = "Enter text in the Step 2 text box. " & _
    "For example, you might include brief biographical " & _
    "information on the employee, details of their position, " & _
    "or your hopes for their contribution to the company."
  cmdClearEmployeeName.Enabled = True
End Sub
```

Some popular naming conventions for the most-used VBA objects are shown in the following list. You'll encounter the naming conventions for other VBA objects later in the book. This list includes the control's name, the standard prefix, and finally an example showing how the control can be named in code:

Check box The standard prefix is `chk`, as in `chkReturnToPreviousPosition`.

Command button The standard prefix is `cmd`, as in `cmdOK`.

Form (user form) The standard prefix is `frm`, as in `frmMoveParagraph`.

Frame The standard prefix is `fra`, as in `fraMovement`.

List box The standard prefix is `lst`, as in `lstConferenceAttendees`.

Combo box The standard prefix is `cmb`, as in `cmbColor`.

Menu The standard prefix is `mnu`, as in `mnuProcedures`.

Option button The standard prefix is `opt`, as in `optSpecialDelivery`.

Label The standard prefix is `lbl`, as in `lblUserName`.

Text box The standard prefix is `txt`, as in `txtUserDescription`.

Just as with variable names, the naming convention for controls begins with three lowercase letters and then starts the rest of the object's name with an uppercase letter to make it a little easier to read. For example, a text box in which the users are to type their last names might be named `txtLastName`.

Naming conventions can seem awkwardly formal at first, and there's a strong temptation to avoid them. But if you plan to distribute your macros or expect others to work with them, it's usually worth the trouble to follow the naming conventions. Plus, they help you when debugging. It's just another way to make reading code easier for everybody.

Renaming a User Form

Next, change the user form's name property from the default (`UserForm1`) to a more descriptive name. The following steps show how to do this. (For advice on choosing names, refer to the sidebar "Naming Conventions in Visual Basic for Applications" in this chapter.)

1. If the Properties window isn't displayed, press F4 to display it. Figure 14.3 shows the two pages of the Properties window: Alphabetic and Categorized. Alphabetic displays an alphabetical listing of the properties of the currently selected object. Categorized displays the same properties but separated into categories, such as Appearance, Behavior, Font, Misc., Picture, and Position. (Some controls have more categories than those listed here.) You can expand a category by clicking the plus (+) sign beside it to display the properties it contains, and collapse it by clicking the resulting minus (–) sign. If the Alphabetic tab isn't selected, click it to select it.

   The Categorized option is not, in my view, very helpful because many of the properties are simply too difficult to fit into categories that make any sense. The `Caption` property, for example, is assigned to the Appearance category, but the `(Name)` property is contained in the Misc. collection. The very existence of a "miscellaneous" category demonstrates that the categorization effort has broken down. I suggest you stick with the default Alphabetic option instead.

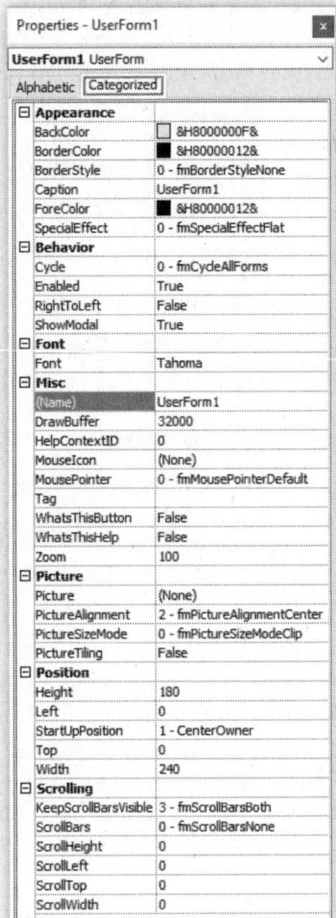

FIGURE 14.3
You can choose either an alphabetized or a categorized list in the Properties window.

2. Make sure the drop-down list (at the top of the Properties window) is displaying the default name of the user form. If it isn't, select the user form from the drop-down list.

3. Select the user form's default name (such as `UserForm1` or `UserForm2`) in the cell to the right of the Name cell (you can double-click the name to select it quickly). Now type a new, more descriptive name for the user form. This name can be anything you want, with the standard VBA limitations:

    - It must start with a letter.
    - It can contain letters, numbers, and underscores but no spaces or symbols.
    - It can be up to 40 characters long.

4. Click the Caption cell to select the user form's default name and type the caption for the user form—that is, the text label that you want the user to see in the title bar of the dialog

box. This name has no restrictions beyond the constraints imposed by the length of the title bar. You can enter a name longer than will fit in the title bar, but VBA truncates it with an ellipsis at its maximum displayable length. As you type, the name appears in the user-form title bar as well, so it's easy to see what's an appropriate length—at least, for the current size of the user form.

5. Press Enter or click elsewhere in the Properties window (or elsewhere in the Visual Basic Editor) to set (make official) the user form's name. (Assigning names to controls works the same way as assigning names to forms.)

Dealing with the "Name Conflicts with Existing Module" Error

If you run into the "Name *name* conflicts with existing module, project, or object library" error (shown here), chances are you've just tried to give a user form the same name already assigned to something else.

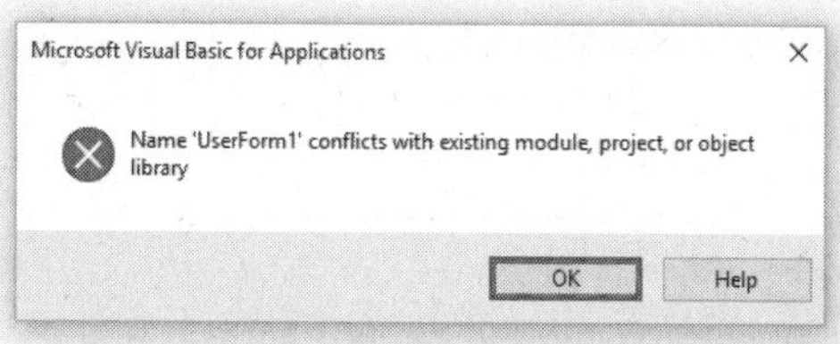

You've tried to reuse the name of a VBA project or object library.

Adding Controls to the User Form

Now that you've renamed the user form, you're ready to add controls to it from the Toolbox, shown in Figure 14.4. VBA automatically displays the Toolbox when a user form is active, but you can also display the Toolbox when no user form is active by choosing View ➤ Toolbox.

Removing the "Roaming Office" Control in VBA 2013

Obviously an oversight on Microsoft's part, they included in the VBA 2013 Toolbox an obscure and—even in VBA's MSDN help system—essentially ignored control called the RoamingOffice control (not shown in Figure 14.4). Its use is beyond the scope of this book (the control isn't included in the VBA 2016 Toolbox)—not to mention beyond the scope of the VBA Help system and even Google. Perhaps Microsoft intended to make it useful in the future. It clearly doesn't belong among the default controls on the Toolbox. It's a small, gray crosshatched square icon next to the Image control. If you like, you can remove the RoamingOffice control from the 2013 Toolbox by right-clicking its crosshatched icon, and then choosing Delete RoamingOffice from the context menu.

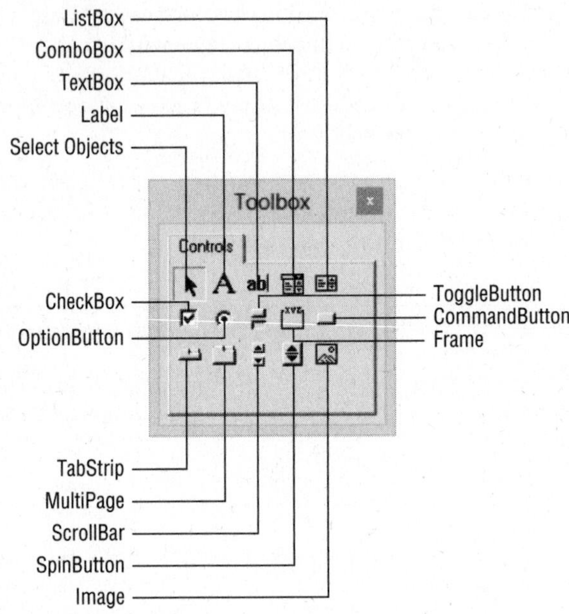

FIGURE 14.4 Use the Toolbox to add controls to the user form.

Here's what the buttons on the Toolbox do:

Select Objects This first control, the arrow symbol, has a very specialized purpose, and you might never need to use it. First, it's not an ordinary control (it doesn't appear on a form; you can't drag and drop it onto a form). Its job is to restore the mouse pointer to Selection mode. However, the mouse pointer *automatically* returns to Selection mode after you've dropped a control onto a form. Usually, you'll need to click the Select Objects button only when you've selected another control and then changed your mind and decided not to use it, so you need to restore the pointer to its normal state. Alternatively, if you double-click a control (such as the check box), you trigger a technique that allows you to quickly add multiple versions of the same control repeatedly. (Every time you click in the form, a new check box is added to it—for example, while the Editor is in this state.) To stop this repetitive behavior, you click the Select Objects button.

Label Creates a *label*, which is text used to identify a part of the dialog box or to explain information the user needs to know in order to use the dialog box effectively.

TextBox Creates a text box (also sometimes called an *edit box*), a field into which the user can type text. You can also use a text box to display text to the user or to provide text for the user to copy and paste elsewhere. A text box can contain either one line (the default) or multiple lines and can display a horizontal scroll bar, a vertical scroll bar, or both.

ComboBox Creates a combo box, a control that combines a text box with a list box. The user can either choose a value from the list box or enter a new value in the text box.

ListBox Creates a list box, a control that lists a number of values. Users can pick one value from the list but can't enter a new value of their own (unlike with a combo box). The list box is good for presenting closed sets of data.

CheckBox Creates a check box and an accompanying label. The user can select or clear the check box to turn the associated action on or off.

OptionButton Creates an option button (also known as a *radio button*) and an accompanying label to identify the purpose of the button. This button is usually a circle that contains a black dot when selected. The user can select only one option button out of any group of option buttons. (The name radio button comes from radios with push buttons for stations; you can select only one button at a time. Push one, and the others pop out.)

ToggleButton Creates a toggle button, a button that shows whether or not an item is selected. A toggle button can be defined with any two settings, such as On/Off or Yes/No. You can add a picture to a toggle button, which provides a graphical way of letting a user choose between options.

Frame Creates a frame, an area of a user form or dialog box surrounded by a thin line and an accompanying label. You can use frames (also known as *group boxes*) to group related elements in your forms. As well as cordoning off elements visually, frames can separate elements logically. For example, VBA treats a group of option buttons contained within a frame as separate from option buttons in other frames or option buttons loose in the dialog box. This separation makes it easier to use multiple sets of option buttons in a form.

CommandButton Creates a command button. This is the typical, ordinary Windows button that users click to communicate their wishes. Most dialog boxes contain command buttons such as OK and Cancel, or Open and Cancel, or Save, or Apply and Close.

TabStrip Creates a tab strip for displaying multiple sets of data in the same set of controls. Tab strips are especially useful for presenting records in a database for review or modification: Each record in the database contains the same fields for information, so they can be displayed in the same group of controls. The tab strip provides an easy way of navigating between records.

MultiPage Creates a multipage control for displaying multipage dialog boxes that have different layouts on each of their tabs. An example of a multipage dialog box is the Options dialog box (Tools ➤ Options), which has multiple pages (often referred to incorrectly as tabs) in most of the Office applications.

ScrollBar Creates a stand-alone scroll bar. Stand-alone scroll bars are of relatively little use in dialog boxes. Combo boxes and list boxes have built-in scroll bars.

SpinButton Creates a spin-button control to use along with another control, such as a text box. Spin buttons (also known as *spinners*) are typically small, rectangular buttons with one arrow pointing up and one down (or one arrow pointing left and the other pointing right). Spin buttons are useful for presenting sequential values with consistent intervals that fall between a predictable range, such as times or dates. For example, if you want the user to increment or decrement a price in a text box in 25-cent steps, you could use a spinner to adjust the price rather than letting the user type directly into the text box.

Image Creates an image control for displaying a picture within a form. For example, you might use an image control to show a corporate logo or a picture of some sort. (If you want to display a photo, texture, or other graphic on the background of the form itself, set the form's Picture property.)

Adding Controls to the Visual Basic Editor Toolbox

The Toolbox shown in Figure 14.4 contains the basic set of tools provided by VBA. As discussed in "Customizing the Toolbox" in Chapter 2, "Getting Started with the Visual Basic Editor," you can customize the Toolbox in various ways: by adding other controls to it, creating additional pages for the controls, moving controls from page to page, and creating customized controls of your own making so that you can avoid having to repeatedly adjust properties each time you add those controls.

Click one of the controls in the Toolbox to select it. Then click in the user form to insert the control on the form, as illustrated in Figure 14.5. VBA places the top-left corner of the control where you click. As you place a control, it snaps to the grid on the user form (unless you've turned off the Align Controls To Grid feature as described in "Choosing User-Form Grid Settings," earlier in this chapter).

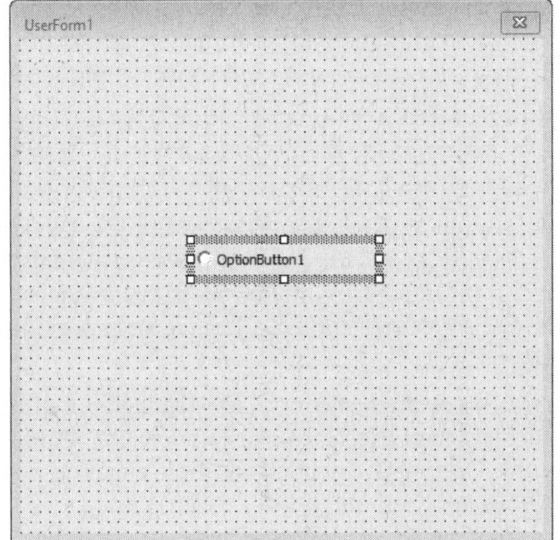

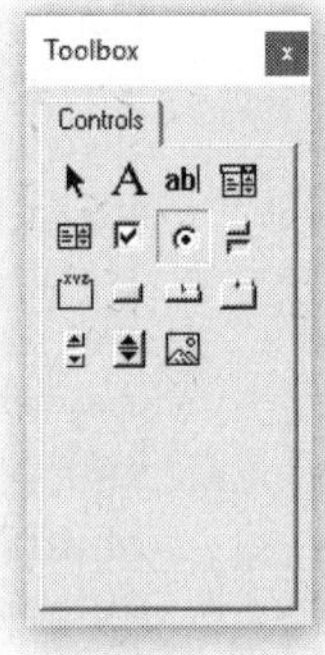

Figure 14.5 When you click in the user form, VBA places a standard-size control of the type you chose. If the Align Controls To Grid feature is switched on (as it is by default), VBA automatically aligns the control with the grid on the user form.

You can resize the control as desired by selecting it and then clicking and dragging one of the selection handles (the white squares) that appear around it, as shown in Figure 14.6. The mouse pointer changes to a double-arrow icon when you've correctly positioned it to drag. When you drag a corner handle, VBA resizes the control on both sides of the corner. When you drag the handle at the midpoint of one of the control's sides, VBA resizes the control only in that dimension. In either case, VBA displays a dotted outline indicating the size that the control will be when you release the mouse button.

To resize the user form itself, click its title bar, or click in any blank space in the form (anywhere outside a control). This selects the user form. Then click and drag one of the selection handles that appear around the form.

To delete a control, right-click it in the user form and choose Delete from the context menu. Alternatively, click it to select it and then press the Delete key or choose Edit ➤ Delete. Restore it by pressing Ctrl+Z.

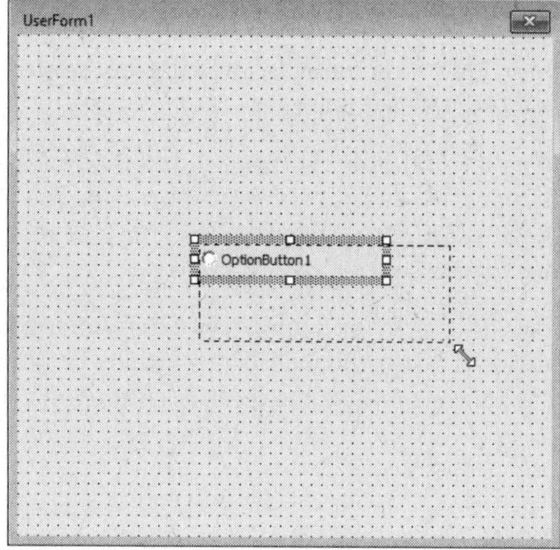

FIGURE 14.6
Once you've placed a control, you can resize it as necessary by dragging one of its selection handles.

RANDOM ADDITIONAL DEFAULT TOOLBOX CONTROLS

Now and then Microsoft adds application-specific or novel controls to the default Toolbox. This not only causes confusion, but it also means that the VBA Editor's Toolboxes are not standardized across the Office applications. This is a recent development—and unwelcome. Recall that Word 2013 arbitrarily included a "Roaming Office" control. For more on this peculiar feature, see the sidebar "Removing the 'Roaming Office' Control" earlier in this chapter.

Excel's VBA Editor includes a RefEdit control that mimics Excel's reference-edit boxes.

Nobody objects to Microsoft providing additional controls to us programmers. (You can easily add controls to the Toolbox by right-clicking within the Toolbox and choosing Additional Controls from the context menu.) What's problematic is randomness in the default Toolboxes.

Grouping Controls

Sometimes it's quite efficient to temporarily select several controls as a group in the Editor. This allows you to manipulate all the grouped controls as a unit. For example, if you want to change the font size of three text boxes, two option buttons, and four labels, just group them and change the font-size property in the Properties window only once. The whole group will have all their font sizes changed automatically. (This trick is not related to grouping controls within a Frame control as described earlier in this chapter.)

We'll explore this useful grouping technique later in this chapter in the section titled "Working with Groups of Controls." For now, I'll just briefly introduce the concept.

To delete, move, resize, or change the properties of multiple controls at once, first select them into a group. You can then delete them all at once by using the methods just described. Or you can move, resize, or modify the properties of the group as a whole.

Here's how to group controls:

- To select multiple contiguous controls, click the first control, hold down Shift, and then click the last control in the sequence.
- To select multiple noncontiguous controls—or to add additional controls to a group after you've selected multiple contiguous controls by using the Shift key—hold down the Ctrl key as you click each additional control. (With the Ctrl key pressed, you can deselect any control in a group by clicking it a second time.)
- To select multiple controls in the same area of the user form, click in the form's background outside the controls and drag the resulting selection box until it encompasses at least part of each control. When you release the mouse button, the Visual Basic Editor selects the controls as a group.

Renaming Controls

As with user forms, VBA automatically gives each control that you add to a form a default name consisting of the type of control plus a sequential number. When you add the first text box in a user form, VBA names it `TextBox1`. When you add another text box, VBA names it `TextBox2`, and so on. (Each control in a dialog box must have a unique name so that you can refer to it specifically in code.)

You'll usually want to change the controls' default names to names that describe their purposes so you can remember what they do for the macro.

For example, if `TextBox2` is used for entering the user's organization name, you might want to rename it `txtOrganizationName`, `txtOrgName`, `txtO_Name`, or something similar.

To rename a control, follow these steps:

1. Click the control in the user form to select it and thereby display its properties in the Properties window.
    - If the Properties window is already displayed, you can, if you prefer, select the control from the drop-down list at the top of the Properties window instead of selecting it in the user form. VBA then visually highlights (selects) the control in the user form, which helps you make sure that you've selected the control you want to affect.
    - If the Properties window isn't displayed, you can quickly display it with the properties for the appropriate control by right-clicking the control in the user form and choosing Properties from the context menu. Or just press F4. (If the Toolbox disappears, just click the form to bring it back.)
2. In the Properties window, double-click to select the default name in the cell to the right of the `Name` property.
3. Type the new name for the control.
4. Press Enter to set the control name, or click elsewhere in the Properties window or in the user form.

If You Rename a Control, You May Have to Modify Your Code

You can rename a control any time. But if you do, you must also change any existing references to it in the code that drives the user form. This gives you a strong incentive to choose suitable names for your controls before you write the code.

Moving a Control

To move a control, click anywhere in it to select it, and then drag it to where you want it to appear, as shown in Figure 14.7.

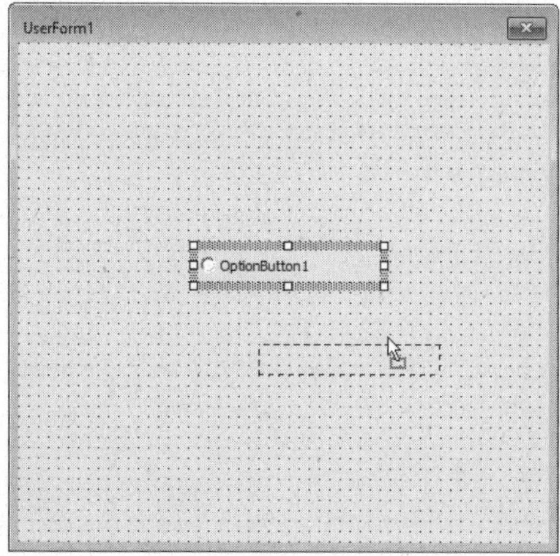

Figure 14.7
If a control isn't currently selected, you can move it by clicking it and dragging it.

To move a selected control, move the mouse pointer over the selection border around it so that the mouse pointer turns into a four-headed arrow (as shown in Figure 14.8), and then click and drag the control to where you want it to appear.

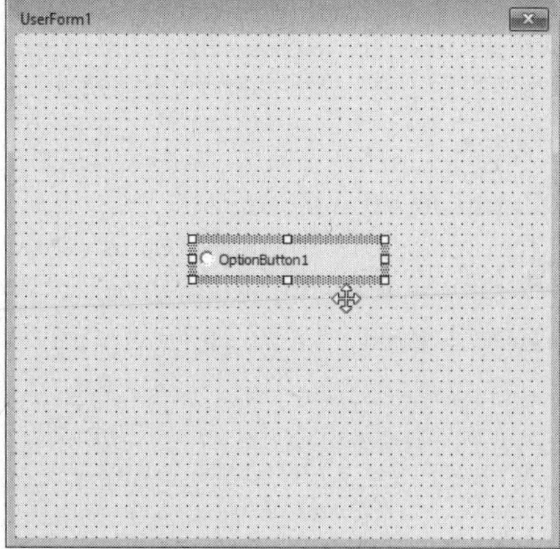

Figure 14.8
If a control is selected, move the mouse pointer over its selection border, and then click and drag the control.

Real World Scenario

USEFUL COPY-AND-PASTE TECHNIQUES WITH CONTROLS

You can use the Copy and Paste commands (from the Standard toolbar, the Edit menu, or the context menu; or by using the easiest approach, the keyboard, such as pressing Ctrl+X and Ctrl+V) to move a control.

Copy and Paste isn't that efficient when moving a *single* control; the Paste command places the control right in the middle of the user form, so you have to drag it to its new position anyway.

However, when creating multiple, similar control sets—such as a group of text boxes with accompanying labels—copying and pasting can be quite useful. It's a quick way to build a whole set of fields for the user to fill in, for example. This way, you don't have to position and align each label/text box pair. Nor do you have to adjust each control's properties because they are copied too. Align the first label/text pair, set the Font property the way you want it (usually larger, changing it from the default 8 pt. size to 11 works well on most monitors), resize the controls as you want them, change any other properties to suit yourself, and then copy and paste (clone) the pair as often as necessary by repeatedly pressing Ctrl+V.

Be aware, though, that the VBA Editor unfortunately places each new clone directly on the center of the form, thereby hiding any other clones you've just added. In other words, when you paste, you can't actually see the new clone—it's in a pile on the center of the form. So, you have to drag the clones away from the center to reveal the others beneath.

Here's a related technique: Sometimes you want to copy the entire set of controls from one form to another. Select all the controls on Form1, then press Ctrl+C to copy them, then click Form2 to select it, and press Ctrl+V to paste the entire set of controls into the new form.

The advantage of using Copy and Paste for creating new controls is that the new controls inherit all the characteristics of the original controls, so you can save time by creating a control, setting its properties, and then cloning it.

You don't even need to change the names of the copies you paste to another user form—they just need to be named suitably for the code with which they work.

As an alternative to using the Copy and Paste commands, you can also copy a control by holding down the Ctrl key as you click and drag the control. VBA displays a plus (+) sign attached to the mouse pointer to indicate that you're copying the control rather than moving it. Drop the copy where you want it to appear on the user form.

Changing the Caption on a Control

Some controls—such as option buttons and check boxes—have built-in text captions to let the user understand their purposes. You can change these captions like this:

1. Click the control to select it.
2. Click the caption itself to select it. VBA displays the blinking insertion cursor and a faint dotted border around the text, as shown in Figure 14.9.

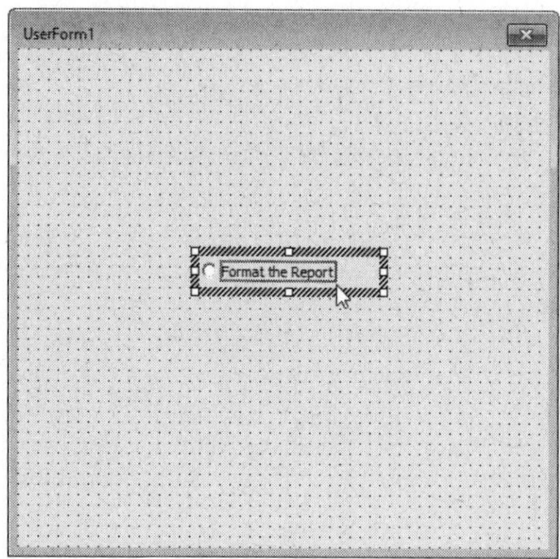

FIGURE 14.9
To change the caption on a control, select the control, and then click in the text so that it displays this faint dotted border.

DOUBLE-CLICKING OPENS THE CODE WINDOW RATHER THAN SELECTS A CONTROL

When you click a label to select it and click again to position the insertion point to change the caption, make sure you click slowly enough that Windows doesn't interpret this as a double-click. A double-click displays the code sheet for the user form and automatically adds a procedure for the `Click` event of the control. If this happens, you can easily get back to viewing the form (it's called Design view, as opposed to Code view). Just press Shift+F7, double-click the module's name in the Project Explorer, or choose View ➢ Object to view the form again.

3. Now click in the label to position the insertion point for editing it, or drag through the label to select all of it.
4. Edit the text of the label as desired.
5. Press Enter or click elsewhere in the user form to effect the change to the label. (You can alternatively change the label by changing its `Caption` property in the Properties window.)

WHEN SHOULD YOU SET PROPERTIES OF A CONTROL?

You can set (specify) many properties of a control either at design time (while you're creating the user form) or at runtime (while the form's code is executing). There's a time and a place for each approach, a time when either is a reasonable course of action.

Generally speaking, the more static the property, the more likely you'll want to set it at design time. Some properties, such as the `Name` property of a user form, *have* to be set at design time—you can't change such properties at runtime for a user form. You'll also usually want to name your controls at design time, though you can add controls at runtime and set their `Name` properties during execution.

Continues

Continued

In most cases, you'll want to set the properties that govern the position and size of the user form itself and its controls at design time. The advantages are clear: You can make sure that the user form looks as you intend it to, that it's legible, and so on.

Occasionally, you may want to change the properties of a user form or the size or position of some of the controls on it at runtime. For example, you might need to add a couple of option buttons to the form to take care of eventualities not included in the basic design of the form. Alternatively, you might create a form that had two groups of option buttons sharing the same space—one group, in effect, positioned on top of the other. At runtime, you could modify their `Visible` properties in your code and thus display one group and hide the other group. If each group contained the same number of option buttons, you could even make do with only one group of option buttons, assigning the appropriate properties to each at runtime. However, there's no particular advantage in trying to simultaneously make just the one group do double duty like that. It can make your code more confusing.

Given the flexibility that many properties of controls provide, you can often design your user forms to handle several circumstances by displaying and hiding different groups of controls at runtime rather than having to add or remove controls at runtime. Creating the complete set of controls for a user form at design time avoids most of the difficulties that can arise from adding extra controls at runtime. That said, you may sometimes need to create a user form on the fly to present information about the situation in which users have placed themselves.

As you'll see as you continue to work with controls, you have to set values for *some* controls at runtime. For example, you sometimes can't assign the list of items to a list box or combo box at design time. If a list displays items from a database, the list can vary depending on which dataset the user selects. So, you would have to write code that fills the list box during execution. (Often, you'll fill a list box during a `UserForm_Initialize` procedure that runs as the user form is being initialized for display.) The set of items in some lists can be known in advance and specified in your code during design time, such as a list box displaying all the countries in the world, from which the user selects the country of residence.

Key Properties of the Toolbox Controls

The following sections discuss the key properties of the controls in the default Toolbox.

First, I'll explain the common properties used to manipulate many of the controls effectively. After that, I'll go through the controls one by one, listing the properties particular to each control.

If you're new to VBA and find this section heavy going, just skip it for the time being and return to it when you're creating code and need to reference information about the properties of the controls.

Common Properties

Table 14.1 lists the properties shared by all or most controls, grouped by category.

Table 14.1: Properties common to most or all controls

Property Information	**Applies To**	**Explanation**
General Properties		
`BoundValue`	All controls except Frame, Image, and Label	Contains the value of the control when the control receives the focus in the user form.
`HelpContextID`	All controls except Image and Label	Returns the context identifier of the Help file topic associated with the control.
`Name`	All controls	Contains the name for the control.
`Object`	All controls	Enables you to assign to a control a custom property or method that uses the same name as a standard property or method.
`Parent`	All controls	Returns the name of the user form that contains the control.
`Tag`	All controls	Used for assigning extra information to the control. This is rarely used.
`Value`	CheckBox, ComboBox, CommandButton, ListBox, MultiPage, OptionButton, ScrollBar, SpinButton, TabStrip, TextBox, ToggleButton	One of the most varied properties, `Value` specifies the current state or value of the control. A CheckBox, OptionButton, or ToggleButton can have an integer value of `-1` (`True`), indicating that the item is selected, or a value of `0` (`False`), indicating that the item is cleared. A ScrollBar or SpinButton returns a value containing the current value in the control. A ComboBox or ListBox returns the currently selected row's (or rows') `BoundColumn` value. A MultiPage returns an integer indicating the active page, and a TextBox returns the text in the text box. The value of a CommandButton is `False` because choosing the command button triggers a `Click` event. However, you can set the value of a CommandButton to `True`, which has the same effect as clicking it. In other words, the value property is similar to the value of a variable, but the property's possible values are highly specific to each control.

TABLE 14.1: Properties common to most or all controls *(CONTINUED)*

PROPERTY INFORMATION	APPLIES TO	EXPLANATION
SIZE AND POSITION		
`Height`	All controls	The height of the control, measured in points.
`LayoutEffect`	All controls except Image	Indicates whether a control was moved when the layout of the form was changed.
`Left`	All controls	The distance of the left border of the control in pixels from the left edge of the form or frame that contains it.
`OldHeight`	All controls	The previous height of the control, measured in pixels.
`OldLeft`	All controls	The previous position of the left border of the control, measured in pixels.
`OldTop`	All controls	The previous position of the top border of the control, measured in pixels.
`OldWidth`	All controls	The previous width of the control, measured in points.
`Top`	All controls	The distance of the top border of the control in pixels from the top edge of the form or frame that contains it.
`Width`	All controls	The width of the control, measured in points.
APPEARANCE		
`Alignment`	CheckBox, OptionButton, ToggleButton	Specifies how the caption is aligned to the control.
`AutoSize`	CheckBox, ComboBox, CommandButton, Image, Label, OptionButton, TextBox, ToggleButton	A Boolean (`True` or `False` only) property that controls whether the object resizes itself automatically to accommodate its contents. The default setting is `False`, which means that the control doesn't automatically resize itself.
`BackColor`	All controls	The background color of the control. This property contains a number representing the color.

TABLE 14.1: Properties common to most or all controls *(CONTINUED)*

PROPERTY INFORMATION	APPLIES TO	EXPLANATION
`BackStyle`	CheckBox, ComboBox, CommandButton, Frame, Image, Label, OptionButton, TextBox, ToggleButton	Specifies whether the background of the object is transparent (`fmBackStyleTransparent`) or opaque (`fmBackStyleOpaque`, the default). You can see through a transparent control—anything behind it on the form will show through. You can use transparent controls to achieve interesting effects—for example, by placing a transparent command button on top of an image or another control.
`BorderColor`	ComboBox, Image, Label, TextBox, ListBox	Specifies the color of the control's border. You can choose a border color from the System drop-down list or the palette or enter `BorderColor` as an eight-digit integer value (such as 16711680 for mid-blue). VBA stores the `BorderColor` property as a hexadecimal value (for instance, 00FF0000). For `BorderColor` to take effect, `BorderStyle` must be set to `fmBorderStyleSingle`.
`BorderStyle`	ComboBox, Frame, Image, Label, ListBox, TextBox, UserForm	Specifies the style of border on the control or user form. Use `BorderStyle` with the `BorderColor` property to set the color of a border.
`Caption`	CheckBox, CommandButton, Label, OptionButton, ToggleButton	A text string containing the description that appears for a control—the text that appears in a label, on a command button or toggle button, or next to a check box or option button.
`Font` (object)	All controls except Image, SpinButton, and ScrollBar	`Font`—an object rather than a property—controls the font in which the label for the object is displayed. For TextBox, ComboBox, and ListBox controls, `Font` controls the font in which the text in the control is displayed.
`ForeColor`	All controls except Image	The foreground color of the control (often the text on the control). This property contains a number representing the color.
`Locked`	CheckBox, ComboBox, CommandButton, ListBox, OptionButton, TextBox, ToggleButton	A Boolean property that specifies whether the user can change the control. When `Locked` is set to `True`, the user can't change the control, though the control can still receive the focus (that is, be selected) and trigger events. When `Locked` is `False` (the default value), the control is open for editing.

TABLE 14.1: Properties common to most or all controls *(CONTINUED)*

PROPERTY INFORMATION	APPLIES TO	EXPLANATION
`MouseIcon`	All controls except MultiPage	Specifies the image to display when the user moves the mouse pointer over the control. To use the `MouseIcon` property, the `MousePointer` property must be set to `99`, `fmMousePointerCustom`.
`MousePointer`	All controls except MultiPage	Specifies the type of mouse pointer to display when the user moves the mouse pointer over the control.
`Picture`	CheckBox, CommandButton, Frame, Image, Label, OptionButton, Page, ToggleButton, UserForm	Specifies the picture to display on the control. By using the `Picture` property, you can add a picture to a normally text-based control, such as a command button.
`PicturePosition`	CheckBox, CommandButton, Label, OptionButton, ToggleButton	Specifies how the picture is aligned with its caption.
`SpecialEffect`	CheckBox, ComboBox, Frame, Image, Label, ListBox, OptionButton, TextBox, ToggleButton	Specifies the visual effect to use for the control. For a CheckBox, OptionButton, or ToggleButton, the visual effect can be flat (`fmButtonEffectFlat`) or sunken (`fmButtonEffectSunken`). For the other controls, the visual effect can be flat (`fmSpecialEffectFlat`), raised (`fmSpecialEffectRaised`), sunken (`fmSpecialEffectSunken`), etched (`fmSpecialEffectEtched`), or a bump (`fmSpecialEffectBump`).
`Visible`	All controls	Indicates whether the control is visible; expressed as a Boolean value.
`WordWrap`	CheckBox, CommandButton, Label, OptionButton, TextBox, ToggleButton	A Boolean property that specifies whether the text in or on a control wraps at the end of a line. For most controls, `WordWrap` is set to `True` by default; you'll often want to change this property to `False` to prevent the text from wrapping inappropriately. If the control is a TextBox and its `MultiLine` property is set to `True`, VBA ignores the `WordWrap` property.

Table 14.1: Properties common to most or all controls *(continued)*

Property Information	Applies To	Explanation
Behavior		
`Accelerator`	CheckBox, CommandButton, Label, OptionButton, Page, Tab, ToggleButton	The accelerator key (or *access key*, or *mnemonic*) for the control—the key the user presses (typically, in combination with Alt) to access the control. For example, in many dialog boxes, the user can access the Cancel button by pressing Alt+C. The accelerator key for a label applies to the next control in the tab order rather than to the label itself. The accelerator character must be one of the characters in the control's text caption, usually the first (the *C* in Cancel, for example). But if some other control is already using the first character, you must, of course, choose a different one. Once you specify the accelerator character, VBA automatically underlines that character in the caption to cue the user that they can press, for example, Alt+C to select the Cancel button. For additional information on tab order, see the section titled "Adjusting the Tab Order of a Form" later in this chapter.
`ControlSource`	CheckBox, ComboBox, ListBox, OptionButton, ScrollBar, SpinButton, TextBox, ToggleButton	The cell or field used to set or store the `Value` of the control. The default value is an empty string (`""`), indicating that there is no control source for the control.
`ControlTipText`	All controls	The text of the ScreenTip displayed when the user holds the mouse pointer over the control. The default value of `ControlTipText` is a blank string, which means that no ScreenTip is displayed.
`Enabled`	All controls	A Boolean value that determines whether the control can be accessed (either interactively or programmatically).
`TabIndex`	All controls except Image	The position of the control in the tab order of the user form, expressed as an integer from 0 (the first position) through the number of controls on the user form.
`TabStop`	All controls except Image and Label	A Boolean value establishing whether the user can select the control by pressing the Tab key. If `TabStop` is set to `False`, the user can select the control only with the mouse. The `TabStop` setting doesn't change the tab order of the dialog box.

Label

The Label control simply displays text on the screen. It's most often used to identify the purpose of another control, so you frequently see a Label control placed on a form to the left of a text box whose purpose the label describes. Use the `Caption` property to type in the text that you want the label to display. Use the `TextAlign` property as shown in Table 14.2 to align the text of the label with the borders of the Label control.

Table 14.2: `TextAlign` property values for the Label control

`fmTextAlign` Constant	Value	Text Alignment
`fmTextAlignLeft`	1	With the left border of the control
`fmTextAlignCenter`	2	Centered on the control's area
`fmTextAlignRight`	3	With the right border of the control

TextBox

The TextBox is one of the most commonly used controls. Recall that it can be a single-line control (often employed to display a field the user must fill in). Single-line is the default. Or it can be a multiline control, for displaying lots of text, as in a diary program where the user determines how many lines they want to write. Adjust this feature with the `MultiLine` property, which can be set to True or False. Also, the defaults for a TextBox are a size of 8 pt. (too small usually) and a sans serif font called `Tahoma` (sans serif type is generally thought more appropriate for headlines than body text). So, you'll usually find yourself employing the `Font` property to choose a larger font size and more readable font (such as Times New Roman).

Table 14.3 lists the key properties of the TextBox control.

Table 14.3: Key properties of the TextBox control

Property	Description
`AutoTab`	A Boolean property that determines whether VBA automatically moves to the next field when the user has entered the maximum number of characters in the text box or combo box.
`AutoWordSelect`	A Boolean property that determines whether VBA automatically selects a whole word when the user drags the mouse through text in a text box or a combo box.
`DragBehavior`	Enables or disables drag-and-drop for a text box or combo box: `fmDragBehaviorDisabled` (`0`) disables drag-and-drop; `fmDragBehaviorEnabled` (`1`) enables drag-and-drop.

TABLE 14.3: Key properties of the TextBox control *(CONTINUED)*

PROPERTY	DESCRIPTION
`EnterFieldBehavior`	Determines whether VBA selects the contents of the edit area of the text box or combo box when the user moves the focus to the text box or combo box: `fmEnterFieldBehaviorSelectAll` (0) selects the contents of the text box or current row of the combo box; `fmEnterFieldBehaviorRecallSelection` (1) doesn't change the previous selection.
`EnterKeyBehavior`	A Boolean property that determines what VBA does when the user presses Enter with the focus on a text box. If `EnterKeyBehavior` is `True`, VBA creates a new line when the user presses Enter; if `EnterKeyBehavior` is `False`, VBA moves the focus to the next control on the user form. If `MultiLine` is `False`, VBA ignores the `EnterKeyBehavior` setting.
`HideSelection`	A Boolean property that determines whether VBA displays any selected text in a text box or combo box. If `HideSelection` is `True`, VBA displays the text without indicating the selection when the control doesn't have the focus. If `HideSelection` is `False`, VBA indicates the selection both when the control has the focus and when it doesn't.
`IMEMode`	Determines the default runtime mode of the Input Method Editor (IME). This property is used only in Far Eastern applications (for example, those using Japanese hiragana or katakana or Korean hangul).
`IntegralHeight`	A Boolean property that determines whether a list box or a text box resizes itself vertically to display any rows that are too tall to fit into it at its current height (`True`) or not (`False`).
`MultiLine`	A Boolean property that determines whether the text box can contain multiple lines of text (`True`) or only one line (`False`). When `MultiLine` is `True`, the text box adds a vertical scroll bar when the content becomes more than will fit within the current dimensions of the text box. VBA defaults to `Multiline = False`.
`PasswordChar`	Specifies the placeholder character to display in place of the characters the user types (so somebody peeping won't see the actual password). The common password character is the asterisk (*). This property is normally used for entering passwords and other information that needs to be obscured so that it cannot be read.
`ScrollBars`	Specifies which scroll bars to display on the text box. Usually, you'll do best to set the `WordWrap` property to `True` and let VBA add the vertical scroll bar to the text box as needed rather than using the `ScrollBars` property.
`SelectionMargin`	A Boolean property that determines whether the user can select a line of text in the text box or combo box by clicking in the selection bar to the left of the line.

TABLE 14.3: Key properties of the ComboBox and ListBox controls *(CONTINUED)*

PROPERTY	DESCRIPTION
`ShowDropButtonWhen`	Determines when to display the drop-down button for a combo box or a text box. `fmShowDropButtonWhenNever` (`0`) never displays the drop-down button and is the default for a text box. `fmShowDropButtonWhenFocus` (`1`) displays the drop-down button when the text box or combo box has the focus. `fmShowDropButtonWhenAlways` (`2`) always displays the drop-down button and is the default for a combo box.
`TabKeyBehavior`	A Boolean property that specifies whether the user can enter tabs in the text box. If `TabKeyBehavior` is `True` and `MultiLine` is `True`, pressing Tab enters a tab in the text box. If `MultiLine` is `False`, VBA ignores a `TabKeyBehavior` setting of `True`. If `TabKeyBehavior` is `False`, pressing Tab moves the focus to the next control in the tab order.

COMBOBOX AND LISTBOX

These controls are similar. From the user's point of view, a key distinction is that a list box simply provides a list of options the user can choose from, whereas a combo box offers that list and also includes a field where the user can type in items.

Table 14.4 shows the key properties of the ComboBox control and the ListBox control. These two controls are similar and share many properties. They do, however, differ somewhat in behavior and features; these differences are described in the entries marked "List box only" and "Combo box only" in the table.

TABLE 14.4: Key properties of the ComboBox and ListBox controls

PROPERTY	DESCRIPTION
`AutoTab`	See Table 14.3.
`AutoWordSelect`	See Table 14.3.
`BoundColumn`	A Variant property that determines the source of data in a combo box or a list box that has multiple columns. The default setting is `1` (the first column). To assign another column, specify the number of the column (columns are numbered from 1, the leftmost column). To assign the value of `ListIndex` to `BoundColumn`, use `0`.
`ColumnCount`	A Long (data type) property that sets or returns the number of columns displayed in the combo box or list box. If the data source is unbound, you can specify up to 10 columns. To display all available columns in the data source, set `ColumnCount` to `-1`.

TABLE 14.4: Key properties of the ComboBox and ListBox controls *(CONTINUED)*

PROPERTY	DESCRIPTION
`ColumnHeads`	A Boolean property that determines whether the combo box or list box displays headings on the columns (`True`) or not (`False`).
`ColumnWidths`	A String (data type) property that sets or returns the width of each column in a multicolumn combo box or list box.
`ListRows`	(Combo box only.) A Long (data type) property that sets or returns the number of rows displayed in the combo box. If the number of items in the list is greater than the value of `ListRows`, the combo box displays a scroll bar so that the user can scroll to the unseen items.
`ListStyle`	Determines the visual effect the list uses. For both a combo box and a list box, `fmListStylePlain` displays a regular, unadorned list. For a combo box, `fmListStyleOption` displays an option button to the left of each entry, allowing the user to select one item from the list. For a list box, `fmListStyle-Option` displays option buttons for a single-select list and check boxes for a multiselect list.
`ListWidth`	(Combo box only.) A Variant property that sets or returns the width of the list in a combo box. The default value is `0`, which makes the list the same width as the text area of the combo box.
`MatchEntry`	Determines which type of matching the combo box or list box uses when the user types characters with the focus on the combo box or list box. `fmMatch EntryFirstLetter` (`0`) matches the next entry that starts with the letter or character typed: If the user types *t* twice, VBA selects the first entry beginning with *t* and then the second entry beginning with *t*. `fmMatchEntryComplete` (`1`) matches each letter the user types: If the user types *te*, VBA selects the entry that starts with *te*. `fmEntryMatchNone` (2) specifies no matching: The user can't select an item by typing in the list box or combo box but must use the mouse or the arrow keys instead. The default `MatchEntry` setting for a combo box is `fmMatchEntryComplete`. The default setting for a list box is `fmMatchEntryFirstLetter`.
`MatchRequired`	(Combo box only.) A Boolean property determining whether the user must select an entry from the combo box before leaving the control (`True`) or not (`False`). This property is useful for making sure that if the user types a partial entry into the text-box area of the combo box, they don't forget to complete the selection in the drop-down list area. If `MatchRequired` is `True` and the user tries to leave the combo box without making a selection, VBA displays an "Invalid Property Value" message box.

TABLE 14.4: Key properties of the ComboBox and ListBox controls *(CONTINUED)*

PROPERTY	DESCRIPTION
`MultiSelect`	(List box only.) Controls whether the user can make a single selection in the list or multiple selections. `fmMultiSelectSingle` (0) lets the user select only one item. `fmMultiSelectMulti` (1) lets the user select multiple items by clicking with the mouse or by pressing the spacebar. `fmMultiSelectExtended` (2) lets the user use Shift+click, Ctrl+click, and Shift with the arrow keys to extend or reduce the selection.
`RowSource`	A String property that specifies the source of a list to be displayed in a combo box or a list box.
`SelectionMargin`	See Table 14.3.
`ShowDropButtonWhen`	See Table 14.3.

CHECKBOX

Check boxes are similar to option buttons—a set of choices presented to the user. However, option buttons permit the user to select only one from among the displayed options (like a set of radio pushbuttons). By contrast, users can select as many check boxes as they want.

Most of the properties of the CheckBox control have been discussed already. The key property of the CheckBox that you haven't come across yet is `TripleState`, which is a feature of the OptionButton and ToggleButton controls as well.

`TripleState` is a Boolean property that determines whether the check box, option button, or toggle button can have a null state as well as `True` and `False` states. When a check box or other control is in the null state, it appears with a small black square in its box.

You can see the null state in the Font dialog box in Word when one of the check-box-controlled properties—such as the Strikethrough check box in Figure 14.10—is true for some but not all of the current selection. For example, select some text where part of it is struck through but other characters are not struck. This will trigger the null state for the Strikethrough check box, as shown in Figure 14.10. Normally, a check box is either checked or not, but when in a null state, it contains a small black square, indicating it's neither true nor false. (In earlier versions of Office, the null state in a check box was indicated by filling the box with gray or black.)

A couple of properties described briefly in the context of other controls deserve more detail here:

- The `SpecialEffect` property controls the visual appearance of the check box. The default value is `fmButtonEffectSunken (2)`, which displays a sunken box—the norm for 3D Windows dialog boxes. You can also choose `fmButtonEffectFlat(0)` to display a box with a flat effect, but why? To me, it doesn't look as good as the default 3D, shadowed box. The flat version is less subtle, crude actually. But, it fits in well with the "Modern" aesthetic introduced and promoted by Microsoft in Windows 8—no gradients, opacity, dimensional effects, shadows, subtle colors, highlights, reflections, serif typefaces, and so on. In other words, flatland.

Figure 14.11 shows a sunken check box and a flat check box. The `Value` property, which indicates whether the check box is selected (`True`) or cleared (`False`), is the default property of the check box. Recall that the default property need not be specified in code. It's assumed. Thus, you can either write `CheckBox1.Value` or just `CheckBox`. The following three statements have the same effect:

```
If CheckBox1.Value = True Then
   If CheckBox1 = True Then
   If CheckBox1 Then
```

This sentence is ~~only partially~~ Struck through.

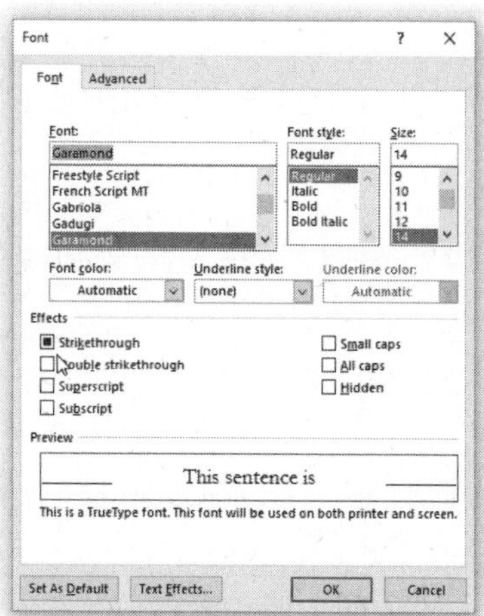

FIGURE 14.10 By setting the `TripleState` property of a check box to `True`, you can display a check box in a null state. Here Word's Font dialog box shows the Strikethrough check box in a null state (containing a small black square, but not checked).

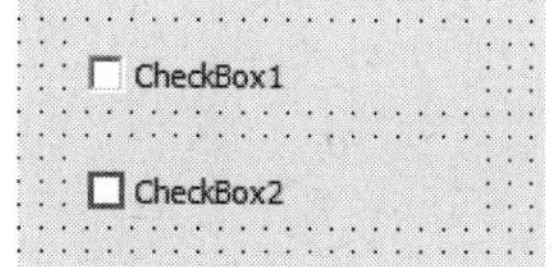

FIGURE 14.11 Use the `SpecialEffect` property to display a flat check box (bottom) rather than the traditional sunken check box.

- The `Accelerator` property provides quick access to the check box. Assign a unique accelerator key to check boxes so that the user can swiftly toggle them on and off from the keyboard.

OptionButton

OptionButtons are useful when you want the user to choose one item in a group. A group of OptionButtons displays a set of mutually exclusive options. Only one of the buttons in a group can be selected at a given time. For instance, you could have two OptionButtons under the heading Sex: Male and Female. (Recall that a set of CheckBoxes permits multiple options to be chosen simultaneously. CheckBoxes are useful for choosing more complex options. For example, under the heading Typeface, you could have Italic, Bold, and Underlined options, all of which could be selected simultaneously.)

Like the CheckBox, the OptionButton control has a straightforward set of properties, almost all of which you've seen already in this chapter. This section shows you the `GroupName` property, which is unique to the OptionButton, and some of the key properties for working with option buttons.

The `GroupName` property is a String data type that assigns the option button to a group of option buttons. Alternatively, you can create a group by placing a set of option buttons on a Frame control. The key idea here is that, once grouped, the buttons become mutually exclusive. However, there can be more than one group (or set) on a form—as long as you employ a Frame control or the `GroupName` property to isolate the various groups of buttons.

The default setting for `GroupName` is a blank string (`""`), which means that an option button isn't assigned to a group until you explicitly assign it. When you enter the group name, the group is created. By using the `GroupName` property, you can have multiple groups of option buttons on the same form without using frames to specify groups, but you must somehow distinguish the logical groups of option buttons from each other so that the user can tell which option buttons constitute a group. Using a Frame control is the easiest way of segregating groups of option buttons both visually and logically—but it's useful to have the flexibility that `GroupName` provides when you need it. Also, a Frame has a built-in `Caption` property you can use to describe the group's purpose.

These are the other key properties of the OptionButton control:

- The `Value` property, which indicates whether the option button is selected (`True`) or cleared (`False`), is the default property of the option button. So, you can set or return the state of the option button by setting either the `OptionButton` object or its `Value` to `True` or `False`, as appropriate. Setting the `Value` of one OptionButton to `True` sets the `Value` of all other OptionButton controls in the same group or frame to `False`.
- The `Accelerator` property provides quick access to the option button. Assign a unique accelerator key to each option button so that the user can toggle it on and off from the keyboard.
- The `SpecialEffect` property controls the visual appearance of the option button. The default value of `fmButtonEffectSunken` (2) displays a sunken button, while `fmButtonEffectFlat` (`0`) displays a flattened button. Figure 14.11 shows a sunken option button and a flat option button.
- The `TripleState` property (discussed in the previous section, "CheckBox") lets you create an option button that has three states: selected (`True`), cleared (`False`), and null (which appears selected but grayed out). The `TripleState` property is disabled so that the user can't set the null state interactively, but you can set it programmatically as needed.

ToggleButton

This button is like a light switch; essentially, it's either on or off. When it's not selected, the ToggleButton control appears raised, but it looks pushed in when it's selected. The key properties for the ToggleButton control are the same as those for the CheckBox and CommandButton:

- The `Value` property is the default property of the ToggleButton.
- The `TripleState` property is rarely used, but lets you create a ToggleButton that has three states: selected (`True`), cleared (`False`), and null. The user can set a triple-state ToggleButton to its null state by clicking it. In its null state, a ToggleButton appears selected, but gray.
- The `Accelerator` property provides quick access to the toggle button.

FRAME

The Frame control is relatively straightforward, but it has several properties worth mentioning; they're shown in Table 14.5. The Frame control shares a couple of these properties with the `Page` object.

TABLE 14.5: Properties of the Frame control

PROPERTY	DESCRIPTION
`Cycle`	Determines the action taken when the user leaves the last control in the frame or on the page. `fmCycleAllForms` (0) moves the focus to the next control in the tab order for the user form or page, whereas `fmCycle CurrentForm` (2) keeps the focus within the frame or on the page until the focus is explicitly moved to a control in a different frame or on a different page. This property applies to the `Page` object as well.
`InsideHeight`	A read-only property that returns the height (measured in points) of the area inside the frame, not including the height of any horizontal scroll bar displayed. This property applies to the `Page` object as well.
`InsideWidth`	A read-only property that returns the width (in points) of the area inside the frame, not including the width of any vertical scroll bar displayed. This property applies to the `Page` object as well.
`KeepScrollBarsVisible`	A property that determines whether the frame or page displays horizontal and vertical scroll bars when they aren't required for the user to be able to navigate the frame or the page. `fmScrollBarsNone` (0) displays no scroll bars unless they're required. `fmScrollBarsHorizontal` (1) displays a horizontal scroll bar all the time. `fmScrollBarsVertical` (2) displays a vertical scroll bar all the time. `fmScrollBarsBoth` (3) displays a horizontal scroll bar and a vertical scroll bar all the time. `fmScrollBarsNone` is the default for the `Frame` object, and `fmScrollBarsBoth` is the default for the `Page` object. This property applies to the `Page` object as well.

TABLE 14.5: Properties of the Frame control *(CONTINUED)*

PROPERTY	DESCRIPTION
PictureTiling	A Boolean property that determines whether a picture displayed on the control is tiled (True) so that it takes up the whole area covered by the control or not (False). To set the tiling pattern, you use the PictureAlignment and PictureSizeMode properties. This property applies to the Page object and the Image control as well.
PictureSizeMode	Determines how to display the background picture. fmPictureSizeModeClip (0), the default setting, crops (removes) any part of the picture too big to fit in the page, frame, or image control. Use this setting to show the picture at its original dimensions and in its original proportions. fmPictureSizeModeStretch (1) stretches the picture horizontally or vertically to fill the page, frame, or image control. This setting is good for colored backgrounds and decorative effects but tends to be disastrous for pictures that need to be recognizable. It also overrides the PictureAlignment property setting. fmPictureSizeModeZoom (3) zooms the picture proportionately until the horizontal dimension or the vertical dimension reaches the edge of the control but doesn't stretch the picture so that the other dimension is maximized as well. This is good for maximizing the size of a picture while retaining its proportions, but you'll need to resize the nonmaximized dimension to remove blank spaces. This property applies to the Page object and the Image control as well.
PictureAlignment	Determines where a picture is located. fmPictureAlignmentTopLeft (0) aligns the picture with the upper-left corner of the control. fmPictureAlignmentTopRight (1) aligns the picture with the upper-right corner of the control. fmPictureAlignmentCenter (2), the default setting, centers the picture in the control (both horizontally and vertically). fmPictureAlignmentBottomLeft (3) aligns the picture with the lower-left corner of the control. fmPictureAlignmentBottomRight (4) aligns the picture with the lower-right corner of the control. This property applies to the Page object and the Image control as well.

CommandButton

The CommandButton is used quite often. This control has three unique properties, listed in Table 14.6.

TABLE 14.6: Unique properties of the CommandButton control

PROPERTY	DESCRIPTION
`Cancel`	A Boolean property that determines whether the command button is the Cancel button for the user form (`True`) or not (`False`). The Cancel button for a user form can bear any name. What distinguishes it is that its `Cancel` property is set to `True`. The Cancel button is activated by the user's pressing Esc, or clicking the button, or putting the focus on the button and pressing Enter. Only one command button on a form can be the Cancel button at any given time. Setting the `Cancel` property for a command button to `True` causes VBA to set the `Cancel` property to `False` for any button for which it was previously set to `True`.
`Default`	A Boolean property that determines whether the command button is the default button for the user form (`True`) or not (`False`). Only one command button on a form can be the default button at any given time. Setting the `Default` property for a command button to `True` causes VBA to set the `Default` property to `False` for any button for which it was previously set to `True`. The default button is activated by the user pressing Enter when the focus isn't on any other command button.
`TakeFocusOnClick`	A Boolean property that determines whether the command button takes the focus when the user clicks it (`True`) or not (`False`). The default setting for this property is `True`, but you may want to set it to `False` when you need the focus to remain on another control in the user form even when the user clicks the command button. However, if the user uses the Tab key or the arrow keys to move to the command button, the command button will take the focus even if the `TakeFocusOnClick` property is set to `False`.

Note that it's useful to set the `Accelerator` property for each command button on a form. This way, the user can quickly access it from the keyboard.

SOMETIMES THE CANCEL BUTTON SHOULD BE THE DEFAULT BUTTON

Sometimes you'll make the Cancel button the default on a form. This offers an obvious benefit for forms that offer irreversible actions, such as deleting text or deleting a file, but it can confuse accessibility aids (such as screen readers) and make it difficult for users with cognitive difficulties to work with the form. For these reasons, it's usually best to make some other button on a form the default rather than the Cancel button.

TabStrip and MultiPage

TabStrip controls allow you to create a multipage dialog box. Click the Home tab in Word and then click the small arrow icon in the lower-right corner of the Font area on the Ribbon. Word's Font dialog box will open and you'll see a two-tab dialog box. One tab is labeled Font and the other tab is labeled Advanced. This is a good way to organize a dialog box when you have quite a few options to present to the user.

The TabStrip control has several unique properties and a number of properties that it shares with the MultiPage control. Table 14.7 lists these properties.

Table 14.7: Properties of the TabStrip and MultiPage controls

Property	Description
`ClientHeight`	(Tab strip only.) A Single (data type) property that sets or returns the height of the display area of the tab strip, measured in points.
`ClientLeft`	(Tab strip only.) A Single property that returns the distance, measured in points, between the left border of the tab strip and the left border of the control inside it.
`ClientTop`	(Tab strip only.) A Single property that returns the distance, measured in points, between the top border of the tab strip and the top border of the control inside it.
`ClientWidth`	(Tab strip only.) A Single property that sets or returns the width of the display area of the tab strip, measured in points.
`SelectedItem`	Sets or returns the tab currently selected in a tab strip or the page currently selected in a MultiPage control.
`TabFixedHeight`	A Single property that sets or returns the fixed height of the tabs, measured in points. Set `TabFixedHeight` to `0` to have the tabs automatically size themselves to fit their contents.
`TabFixedWidth`	A Single property that sets or returns the fixed width of the tabs, measured in points. Set `TabFixedWidth` to `0` to have the tabs automatically size themselves to fit their contents.
`TabOrientation`	Determines the location of the tabs in the tab strip or multipage. `fmTabOrientationTop` (`0`), the default, displays the tabs at the top of the tab strip or multipage. `fmTabOrientationBottom` (`1`) displays the tabs at the bottom of the tab strip or multipage. `fmTabOrientationLeft` (`2`) displays the tabs at the left of the tab strip or multipage, and `fmTabOrientationRight` displays the tabs at the right of the tab strip or multipage.

ScrollBar and SpinButton

A SpinButton allows the user to easily increment or decrement numbers, dates, and so on. The ScrollBar and SpinButton share a number of properties that you haven't yet encountered. Table 14.8 lists these properties.

TABLE 14.8: Properties of the ScrollBar and SpinButton controls

Property	Description
`Delay`	A Long (data type) property that sets the delay in milliseconds between clicks registered on the control when the user clicks and holds down the mouse button. The default delay is 50 milliseconds. The control registers the first click immediately, the second click after `Delay` x 5 (the extra delay is to assist the user in clicking only once), and the third and subsequent clicks after `Delay`.
`LargeChange`	(Scroll bar only.) A Long property that determines how much the item is scrolled when the user clicks in the scroll bar between the thumb (the small square within the scroll bar) and the scroll bar's arrow. Set the `LargeChange` property after setting the `Max` and `Min` properties of the scroll bar.
`SmallChange`	A Long property that determines how much movement occurs when the user clicks a scroll arrow in a scroll bar or spin button. `SmallChange` needs to be an integer value; the default value is `1`.
`Max`	A Long property that specifies the maximum value for the `Value` property of the scroll bar or spin button. `Max` must be an integer. The default value is `1`.
`Min`	A Long property that specifies the minimum value for the `Value` property of the scroll bar or spin button. `Min` must be an integer. The default value is `1`.
`ProportionalThumb`	(Scroll bar only.) A Boolean property that determines whether the thumb is a fixed size (`False`) or is proportional to the size of the scrolling region (`True`), thereby giving the user an approximate idea of how much of the scrolling region is currently visible. The default setting is `True`.

Image

By now, you've seen all the properties of the Image control. Most of the time when you use an Image control, you'll want to adjust the following properties:

- Use the `Picture` property to assign the picture file you want to appear in the Image control. Click in the Picture row in the Properties window, and then click the ellipsis button

(...) that the text box displays. In the Load Picture dialog box, select the picture and click the OK button to add it. The Image control can display `.BMP`, `.CUR` (cursor), `.GIF`, `.ICO` (icon), `.JPG`, and `.WMF` files, but not other graphics files, such as `.TIF`. Most graphics applications, however, can easily convert one graphics file type into another.

An Easy Way to Capture a Graphic Image

The easiest way to display part of a Windows screen in an Image control is to capture it by pressing the Print Screen key (to capture the entire screen) or the Alt+Print Screen key combination (to capture the currently active window). Then paste it into an application such as the Windows Paint accessory, trim (crop) it there as necessary, and save it as a `.BMP` file. Windows 8 introduced a third option: Press the Windows key plus the Print Screen key to capture and automatically save the screen to disk. The captured image will be saved in your Libraries folder in a subfolder named Screenshots. The image is saved as a `.PNG` graphics filetype—widely considered to be the best way to grab screen images.

- Use the `PictureAlignment` property to set the alignment of the picture.
- Use the `PictureSizeMode` property to set whether the picture is clipped, stretched, or zoomed to fill the Image control. Adjust the height and width of the Image control as necessary.
- Use the `PictureTiling` property if you need to tile the image to take up the full space in the control.

Page

The `Page` object is one of the pages contained within a `MultiPage` object. You've already seen all its properties (in the context of other controls) except for the `Index` property, which it shares with the `Tab` object.

The `Index` property is an Integer data type that determines the position of the `Page` object in the `Pages` collection in a MultiPage control or the position of a `Tab` object in the `Tabs` collection in a TabStrip. The first `Page` object or `Tab` object is numbered 0 (zero), the second `Page` or `Tab` object is numbered 1, and so on. You can change the `Index` property of a tab or page to change the position in which the tab or page appears in the collection.

Tab

The `Tab` object is one of the tabs contained within a `TabStrip` object. You've already learned about all its properties in the context of other controls.

Working with Groups of Controls

As mentioned briefly earlier in this chapter, when you're designing a form, it's often handy to *group* controls. By grouping two or more controls, you can work with them as a single unit to size, reposition, format, or delete them. (Recall that this form-design grouping technique has nothing to do with creating a set of option buttons within a Frame control. That creates a mutually exclusive collection of radio buttons to display to the user during runtime.)

Grouping Controls

To group controls, select them by Shift+clicking, Ctrl+clicking, or dragging around them, and then right-click and choose Group from the context menu. Alternatively, select the controls, and then click the Group button on the UserForm toolbar (you'll need to display this toolbar—it's not displayed by default) or choose Format ➢ Group. VBA creates a new group containing the controls and places a shaded border with handles around the whole group, as shown on the right in Figure 14.12.

Figure 14.12
You can work with multiple controls simultaneously by grouping them. VBA indicates a group of controls by placing a border around the entire group, as shown on the right.

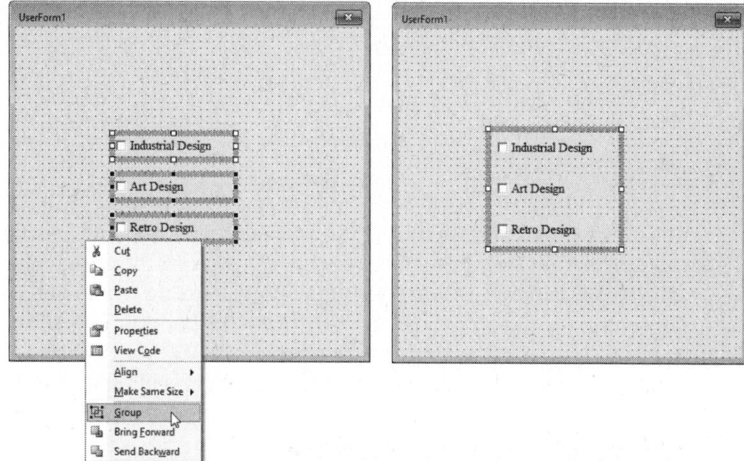

When you merely select a set of controls (by Shift+clicking, Ctrl+clicking, or dragging around them), you have only temporarily grouped them. You can still manipulate them as a group, but as soon as you deselect them—by, for example, clicking the background of the form itself—the grouping disappears. However, when you right-click and choose Group from the context menu, they will remain grouped until you right-click and choose Ungroup.

Ungrouping Controls

To ungroup controls, right-click any of the controls contained in the group and then choose Ungroup from the context menu. Alternatively, select the group of controls by clicking in any control in the group and then click the Ungroup button on the UserForm toolbar, or choose Format ➢ Ungroup. VBA removes the shaded border with handles from around the group and displays the normal border and handles around each individual control.

Sizing Grouped Controls

You can quickly size all controls in a group by selecting the group and then dragging the sizing handles on the surrounding border. For example, you could select the middle handle on the right side and drag it inward to shorten the controls, as shown in Figure 14.13. The controls will be resized proportionately to the change in the group outline.

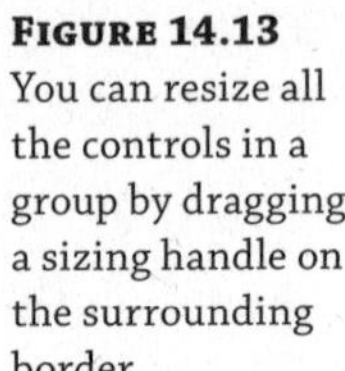

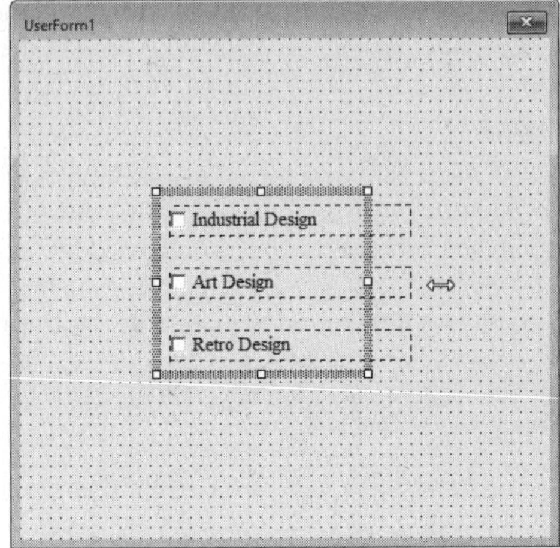

FIGURE 14.13
You can resize all the controls in a group by dragging a sizing handle on the surrounding border.

When the controls are grouped, you can then use the Properties window to quickly modify any properties they have in common (such as Font). But resizing a group can present problems—the results can be ugly. Generally speaking, resizing works fine when you've grouped a number of controls of the same type, as in Figure 14.13. For example, sizing a group that consists of several command buttons or option buttons works well, whereas sizing a group that consists of a text box, a command button, and a combo box is seldom a good idea.

DELETING GROUPED CONTROLS

You can quickly delete a whole group of controls by right-clicking any of them and choosing Delete from the context menu or by selecting the group and pressing the Delete key.

WORKING WITH ONE CONTROL IN A GROUP

Even after you've grouped a number of controls, you can still work with them individually if necessary. To do this, first click any control in the group to select the group as a whole, as shown on the left in Figure 14.14. Then click the control you want to work with. As shown on the right in Figure 14.14, VBA displays a dark shaded border around the group (indicating that the group still exists) and displays the lighter shaded border around the individual control, indicating that that control is selected.

You can then modify the selected individual control as if it were not grouped. Change its ForeColor property to blue, for instance, and only the caption in that particular control will turn blue. When you've finished working with it, click another control in the group to individually select it, or click the background of user form to deselect all individual controls and restore the group.

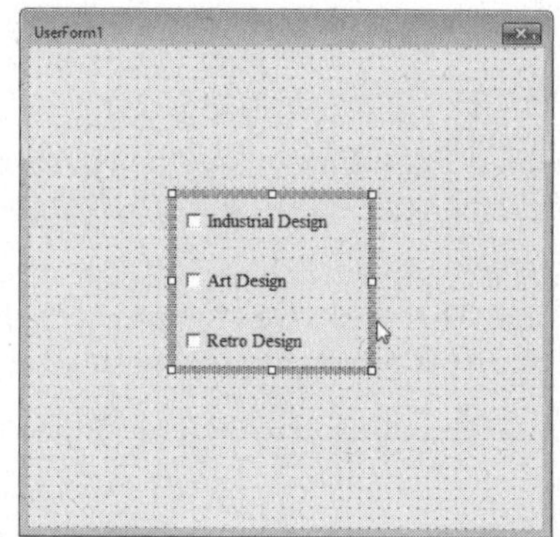

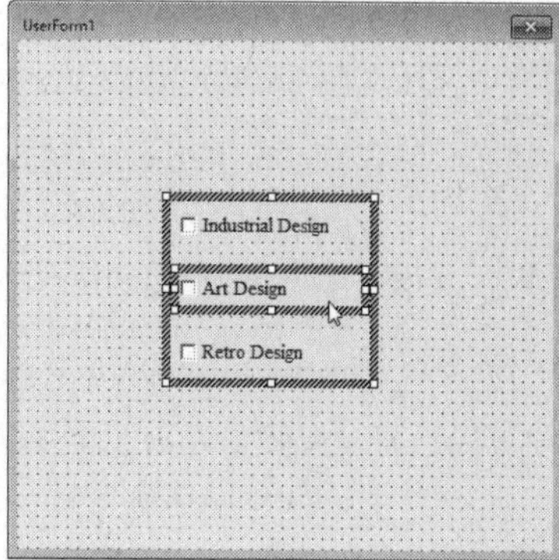

FIGURE 14.14
To work with one control in a group, start by selecting the group (as shown on the left) and then select the control (as shown on the right).

Aligning Controls

Even if you use the Snap To Grid feature, you'll often need to align controls manually. They must be ungrouped for this feature to work. The easiest way to align controls is to select two or more, then right-click in any one of them, and choose an option from the Align submenu: Lefts, Centers, Rights, Tops, Middles, Bottoms, or To Grid. These options work as follows:

Lefts aligns the left borders of the controls.

Centers aligns the horizontal midpoints of the controls.

Rights aligns the right borders of the controls.

Tops aligns the tops of the controls.

Middles aligns the vertical midpoints of the controls.

Bottoms aligns the bottoms of the controls.

To Grid aligns the controls to the grid.

VBA aligns the borders or midpoints to the current position of that border or midpoint on the dominant control—the control that has white sizing handles around it rather than black sizing handles. After selecting the controls you want to align, make dominant the one that is already in the correct position by clicking it so that it takes on the white sizing handles. Then choose the alignment option you want.

ENSURE THAT YOU CHOOSE APPROPRIATE ALIGNMENT OPTIONS

Make sure the alignment option you choose makes sense for the controls you've selected. VBA will happily align controls in an inappropriate way if you tell it to. For example, if you select a number of option buttons or text boxes and choose Tops from the Align submenu, VBA will obligingly stack all the controls on top of each other, rendering them unusable. (To recover from such minor mishaps, press Ctrl+Z.)

Placing Controls

The VBA Editor offers several placement commands on the Format menu:

- On the Format ➤ Make Same Size submenu, use the Width, Height, and Both commands to make two or more controls the same size in one or both dimensions.
- Use the Format ➤ Size To Fit command to have VBA decide on a suitable size for an element based on the size of its label. This works well for, say, a toggle button with a medium-length label, but VBA will shrink an OK button to a size so small as to be unusable.
- Use the Format ➤ Size To Grid command to increase or decrease the size of a control to the nearest gridpoints.
- On the Format ➤ Horizontal Spacing and Format ➤ Vertical Spacing submenus, use the Make Equal, Increase, Decrease, and Remove commands to set the horizontal spacing and vertical spacing of two or more controls. The Remove option removes extra space from between controls, which works well for, say, a vertical series of option buttons (which look good close together) but isn't a good idea for command buttons (which need a little space between them).
- On the Format ➤ Center In Form submenu, use the Horizontally and Vertically commands to center a control or a group of controls in the form. Centering controls vertically is seldom a good idea, but you'll often want to center a frame or a group of command buttons horizontally.
- On the Format ➤ Arrange Buttons submenu, use the Bottom and Right commands to reposition command buttons in a form quickly.

Adjusting the Tab Order of a Form

The *tab order* of a user form (or of a Frame control within a form) is the order in which VBA selects controls in the form or frame when the user moves through them by pressing the Tab key (to move forward) or the Shift+Tab key combination (to move backward).

Put another way, it's a Windows convention that when the user presses the Tab key, the *focus* moves to the next control in a window.

Only one control at a time can have the focus. For example, if a form has five text boxes, only one of these text boxes, the one that currently has the focus, will display characters as the user types. In addition, a button in a set of buttons can also have the focus, and when the user presses the Enter key, the button with the focus will be triggered. Or the user can click a different button to move the focus to that button.

VBA displays a visual cue to indicate which control currently has the focus. You'll see a dotted frame around a button or option button and a blinking insertion cursor in a text box.

Each frame you add to a user form has a separate tab order for the controls it contains: The frame itself appears in the tab order for the form, and the controls within the frame appear in the tab order for the frame.

Set the tab order for the controls on a form or in a frame to make it as easy as possible for the user to work with your form. Generally, for English-speaking users, it's best to arrange the tab order from left to right and from top to bottom in the dialog box or frame. For international users, you may want to arrange the tab order from right to left. You may also need to arrange the tab order to move from one control to a related control that would not normally be next in the tab order.

The whole point of managing the tab order is that you simplify things for your user. Employing the Tab key in this way allows the user to fill in a whole form without once having to move their hand off the keyboard to keep selecting, with a mouse click, each next text box.

This kind of tabbing is particularly useful when the user is asked to fill in several fields by typing into multiple text boxes (such as Name, Address, Phone, and so on). As soon as users finish filling in one field, they can press Tab to move on to the next. (Even easier, pressing the Enter key while in a text box moves users to the next control in the tab order.) At the end, after they've filled in the last field, they can quickly close the dialog box if you make the OK button the next control in the tab order.

VBA assigns the tab order to the controls in a dialog box or frame on a first-come, first-served basis as you add the controls. Unless you add all the controls in perfect order, this default order will seldom produce the optimal tab order for a dialog box, so usually you'll want to adjust the tab order—or at least check to ensure that it's right. You're likely to place fewer controls on a frame than on a form, so you have a better chance of adding them in a suitable order, but you should check these controls too before unleashing the dialog box on users.

Just press F5 and then repeatedly press the Tab key to examine your current tab order. Alternatively, you can open a Tab Order dialog box (shown in Figure 14.15) by right-clicking in the open space in the background of the form or frame and choosing Tab Order from the context menu. Or you can select the user form or frame and then choose View ➤ Tab Order.

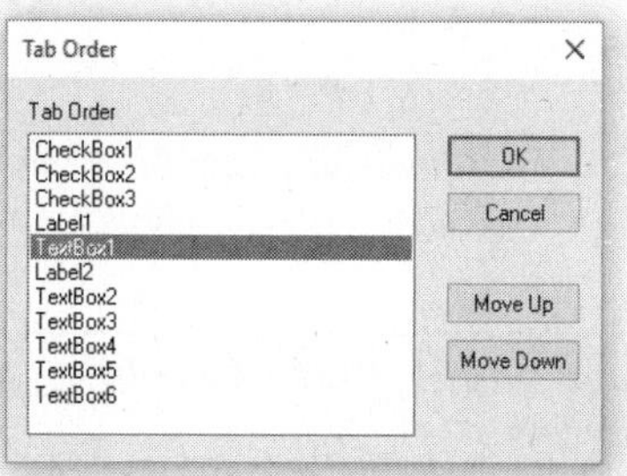

FIGURE 14.15 Use the Tab Order dialog box to arrange the controls in your user form or frame into a logical order for the user.

It's best to adjust the tab order after you've finished creating your form (adding a control later will require that you go back and modify the tab order). Here's how to change the tab order in a dialog box or frame:

1. Rearrange the controls into the order in which you want them to appear by selecting them in the Tab Order list box and clicking the Move Up button or Move Down button as appropriate. You can Shift+click or drag to select a range of controls, or Ctrl+click to select two or more noncontiguous controls. (Or you can just change the controls' TabIndex properties in the Properties window.)
2. Click the OK button to close the Tab Order dialog box.

Linking a Form to a Procedure

Designing a custom form is only the first step in getting it to work in a procedure. The other step is writing the code to display the form to the user and make it perform its tasks.

Typically, the code for a form consists of the following:

- A macro procedure that displays the dialog box by loading it and using the `Show` method. Usually, this procedure can be assigned to a Quick Access Toolbar button or to a shortcut key combination so that the user can conveniently invoke it. However, a procedure can also be designed to run automatically in response to a system event (such as running at a specified time or when a worksheet is opened).
- The user form that represents the form and its controls.
- The code attached to the user form. This code consists of procedures for designated controls. For example, for a simple dialog box containing two option buttons and two command buttons (an OK button and a Cancel button), you'd typically write one procedure for the OK button and one for the Cancel button. The procedure for the OK button is executed when the user either clicks the button with the mouse or presses the Enter key while the focus is on that button. Either of these user actions triggers the button's `Click` event, and whatever code you, the programmer, have written within this event is then executed. Remember that the easiest way to create an event (procedure) for a control is to just double-click the control on the form. The Editor then switches to Code view and writes the necessary `Sub…End Sub` envelope for that event, like this:

```
Private Sub btnOK_Click()

End Sub
```

Notice that the Editor automatically combines the `Name` property of the control with the name of the event as the procedure's name, separated by an underscore character: `btnOK_Click`.

In Static Dialog Boxes, Click Events Are Usually Employed with Command Buttons

Most controls have quite a few events available to them. Some of the events might seem inappropriate or useless at first. For example, option buttons have a `Click` event. But why? It makes sense to *trap* (to respond in code to an event such as a user's mouse click) using command buttons in a static dialog box. (A static dialog box is the most common type. The controls aren't animated; they don't change or move.) However, as you'll see in the next chapter, in a dynamic dialog box, you may want to trap the click on an option button and display further controls to get additional input from the user.

Once the code attached to a button has run, execution returns to the form (if it's still displayed) or to the procedure that called the form.

Note that code that runs directly in response to an event is called an *event procedure* or *event handler.* An event procedure can call other procedures as necessary, so multiple procedures can be run indirectly when a single event handler Sub is triggered.

Loading and Unloading a Form

You load a form by using the Load statement, and unload it by using the Unload statement. The Load statement loads the form into memory so that it's available to the program but doesn't display the form. For that you use the Show method (discussed in the next section). The Unload statement unloads the form from memory and releases any memory associated with that object. If the form is displayed when the Unload statement runs, VBA removes the form from the screen.

The syntax for the Load and Unload statements is straightforward:

```
Load UserForm1
Unload UserForm1
```

Here, *UserForm1* is the name of the user form or dialog box. For example, the following statement loads the dialog box named frmMyDialog:

```
Load frmMyDialog
```

Displaying and Hiding a Form

To display a form, you use the Show method; to hide a form, you use the Hide method. For example, the following statement displays the form named frmMyDialog:

```
frmMyDialog.Show
```

If you execute a procedure containing this line, the frmMyDialog form appears onscreen so the user can interact with it: enter text in its text boxes, select or clear its check boxes, use its drop-down lists, click its buttons, and so on.

When the user closes the form (by clicking the Close button on its title bar or by clicking a command button that dismisses it), the form disappears from the screen and the procedure continues to run. But until you retrieve settings from the form and take action on them, the form has no effect beyond its graphical display.

You can display a form by using the Show method without explicitly loading the form with a Load command first. VBA takes care of the implied Load command for you. There's no particular advantage to including the Load command, but it might make your code easier to read and to debug. For example, the two procedures shown here have the same effect:

```
Sub Display_Dialog()
    Load frmMyDialog     'loads the form into memory
    frmMyDialog.Show     'displays the form
End Sub

Sub Display_Dialog()
    frmMyDialog.Show     'loads the form into memory and displays it
End Sub
```

If you run a `Hide` method without having loaded the form into memory by using the `Load` statement or the `Show` method, VBA loads the form but does not display it onscreen.

Once you've displayed the form, take a moment to check its tab order by pressing F5 and then moving through it using the Tab key. When you first open the form, is the focus on the appropriate control, the control the user is most likely to want to interact with first? When you move forward from that control, is the next control that is selected the next control that the user will typically need to use? Adjust the tab order as necessary, as described in "Adjusting the Tab Order of a Form" earlier in this chapter.

Setting a Default Command Button

To specify a default command button in a form, set that command button's `Default` property to `True`. VBA selects the default button when it displays the form so that if the user simply presses the Enter key to dismiss the dialog box, this button receives the keystroke.

Only one button can be the default button at any given time. If you set the `Default` property of any button to `True`, VBA automatically changes to `False` the `Default` property of any other button previously set to `True`.

Retrieving the User's Choices from a Dialog Box

To make a form do something, your code will usually respond to the user's input. The following sections first cover the VBA commands for retrieving information from a dialog box. Then you'll see an example of how to retrieve the user's choices from both a relatively simple dialog box and then a more complex form.

Returning a String from a Text Box

To *return* (retrieve, for use in your code) a string from a text box, your code can check its `Value` property or `Text` property after the user has clicked an OK or Cancel button or otherwise dismissed the dialog box.

For example, if you have a text box named `txtMyText`, you could return its value and display it in a message box by using the following line:

```
MsgBox txtMyText.Value
```

THE TEXT PROPERTY OF A TEXT BOX IS UNIQUE

For a text box, the `Value` property and the `Text` property return the same information. For most other VBA objects, the `Value` property and the `Text` property return different information.

Recall that VBA supports both one-line and multiline text boxes. To create a multiline text box, select the text box in the user form or in the drop-down list in the Properties window and set its `MultiLine` property to `True`. The user can then enter multiple lines in the text box and start new lines by pressing Shift+Enter.

QUICK CHANGES FOR TWO-STATE PROPERTIES

Here's a tip: If you're changing a Boolean (two-state, `True` versus `False`) property—such as `Enabled`, `Visible`, or `Multiline`—just double-click the value in the Properties window. For example, to change the default `False` setting for `Multiline`, double-click `False` in the Properties window. It changes to `True`. (This doesn't work with the `Value` property.)

To add a horizontal or vertical scroll bar to a text box, set its `ScrollBars` property to `1 - fmScrollBarsHorizontal` (for a horizontal scroll bar), `2 - fmScrollBarsVertical` (for a vertical scroll bar, which is usually more useful), or `3 - fmScrollBarsBoth` (for both).

Returning a Value from an Option Button

A regular option button is a binary control, so it can have only two values: `True` and `False`. `True` indicates that the button is selected, `False` that it's unselected. You can check an option button's value with a simple `If`...`Then` structure. For example, if you have two option buttons, named `optSearchForFile` and `optUseThisFile`, you can check their values and find out which was selected by using the following code:

```
If optSearchForFile = True Then
  'optSearchForFile was selected; take action on this
Else   'optSearchForFile was not selected, so optUseThisFile was
  'take action for optUseThisFile
End If
```

Remember that `Value` is the default property of the OptionButton control. The previous code checks the value of the default property of the control, so you need not specify the property in your code. Default properties can be omitted as a kind of shorthand programming. The first line of code could be written out more fully as `If optSearchForFile`**`.Value`**` = True Then`. But in the code example, I chose to write it more succinctly, with `= True` implied: `If optSearchForFile Then`.

With more than two option buttons, use an `If`...`Then`...`ElseIf` condition or a `Select Case` statement to determine which option button is selected.

YOU CAN'T DIRECTLY TEST FOR A NULL VALUE

This is a bit esoteric, but as you saw earlier in this chapter, an option button or a check box can also have a null value if its `TripleState` property is set to `True`. Null means basically "neither completely true nor false"—a selected paragraph is *partially* boldface, so its FontStyle is neither bold nor regular, it's both. If you allow your option buttons or check boxes to have a null state, you'll need to check for that as well in your procedures. You can't directly check for the control's value being `Null` (for example, `If opt1.Value = Null` causes an error), so use an `If` statement or `Select Case` statement to test `True` and `False` first. If the `Value` of the control is neither `True` nor `False`, it `Else` must be `Null`.

Returning a Value from a Check Box

Like an option button, a regular check box can only be either True or False, so you can use an If...Then structure to check its value. Here's an example:

```
If chkDisplayProgress = True Then
    'take actions for chkDisplayProgress
End If
```

Again, you're checking the default property of the control here—the Value property. The first line of code could also be written as `If chkDisplayProgress.Value = True Then`.

Sometimes you'll need to take an action if the check box was cleared (deselected) rather than selected. For example, if the user clears the check box, you may need to turn off a configuration option.

Returning a Value from a List Box

List boxes start out empty. So, before you can ask the user to choose an item in a list box, you must first fill the box with items from which the user can choose—you must tell VBA which items to display. To do so, you create a procedure to *initialize* (prepare) the user form and add the items to the list box before displaying it:

1. Right-click the name of the user form in the Project Explorer and choose View Code from the context menu to display (in the Code window) the code for the controls assigned to the dialog box. Or you can just double-click somewhere in the background on the user form to go to Code view. Recall that you can toggle between the Code window (press F7) and the form-design window (Shift+F7).

2. In the Object drop-down list (on the top left of the Code window), make sure UserForm is selected.

3. Choose Initialize from the Procedure drop-down list (on the top right of the Code window). The Visual Basic Editor creates a new procedure named `Private Sub UserForm_Initialize` for you, inserting it at the end of the procedures currently displayed in the Code window:

   ```
   Private Sub UserForm_Initialize()
   End Sub
   ```

   Here's a tip: VBA runs a `UserForm_Initialize` procedure every time the user form is brought to life. This procedure is a good place to add items to a list box or combo box or to set properties of other controls on the user form. In other words, this `Initialize` event is where you write code to do any necessary preliminary housekeeping before displaying the form to the user.

4. To add items to a list box, you can use the `AddItem` method for the list box object (here the box is named `lstBatteries`) with a text string in quotation marks to display the ID number of each battery in the list box:

   ```
   lstBatteries.AddItem "Battery #A4601"
   lstBatteries.AddItem "Battery #A4602"
   lstBatteries.AddItem "Battery #A4603"
   lstBatteries.AddItem "Battery #A4604"
   ```

The Initialize Event Is Flexible

By adding items when you initialize the form, you can add different numbers of items as appropriate. For example, if you wanted the user to pick a document from a particular folder, you could create a list of the documents in that folder on the fly in your code during runtime and fill the list box with the documents' names.

To retrieve the user's choice from a single-select-style list box, check the `Value` property in your code, as in this example:

```
MsgBox "You chose this entry from the list box: " & lstBattery.Value
```

Single-select list boxes are like a set of option buttons—the user is allowed to select only one of them.

When you use the `MultiSelect` property to create a list box capable of multiple selections, you can no longer use the `Value` property to return the items selected in the list box. When `MultiSelect` is set to `True`, `Value` always returns a null value. Instead, you use the `Selected` property to determine which rows in the list box are selected and the `List` property (it's an array) to return the contents (the values) of each selected row.

The following statements use a `For…Next` loop to build a string named `strMsg` containing the entries selected from a multiselect list box:

```
strMsg = "You chose the following entries from the list box: " & vbCr
For i = 1 To lstBatteries.ListCount
  If lstBatteries.Selected(i - 1) = True Then
    strMsg = strMsg & lstBatteries.List(i - 1) & vbCr
  End If
Next i
MsgBox strMsg
```

Returning a Value from a Combo Box

To return a value from a combo box (a control that is, in effect, a combination list box and text box), you add items to the combo box list in an `Initialize` procedure and then check the `Value` of the combo box after the user has dismissed the dialog box. (The combo box control doesn't offer multiple-selection capabilities, so `Value` is the property to check.)

For example, you would use the following code to add items to a combo box named `cmbColor`:

```
Private Sub UserForm_Initialize()
  cmbColor.AddItem "Red"
  cmbColor.AddItem "Blue"
  cmbColor.AddItem "Yellow"
End Sub
```

To return the item the user chose in the combo box, retrieve the `Value` property:

```
Result = cmbColor.Value
```

The item retrieved from a combo box can be either one of the items assigned in the `Initialize` procedure or one that the user has typed into the text-box portion of the combo box.

Examples of Connecting Forms to Procedures

The following sections show you two examples of how you can create a procedure and then design a form that works with it to make the procedure more useful and powerful. In the first example, you'll record a macro in Word and then link a form to that code. In the second example, which will work with any VBA-enabled application, you'll create a user form and its associated code from scratch.

Word Example: The Move-Paragraph Procedure

This first example moves the current paragraph up or down within the document by one or two paragraphs in Word.

Recording the Procedure

Start by recording a procedure in Word to move the current paragraph. In the procedure, you need to record the commands for the following actions:

- Selecting the current paragraph
- Cutting the selection and then pasting it
- Moving the insertion point up and down the document
- Inserting a bookmark, moving the insertion point to it, and then deleting the bookmark

We want our finished procedure to display a dialog box with option buttons for moving the current paragraph up one paragraph, up two paragraphs, down one paragraph, or down two paragraphs. The dialog box should also include a check box that indicates the user wants the insertion point returned to its original position at the end of the procedure. Because this is presumably desirable default behavior for the procedure, this check box is selected by default. Users can clear the check box if they don't want to return the insertion point to its original position.

First, start Word and create a new, blank, scratch document (press Ctrl+N), and enter three or four paragraphs of text—just about anything will do, but it'll be easier to have actual text, not random nonsense. That way you can make sure the procedure is moving paragraphs as it should. Then place the insertion point in one of the paragraphs you've just entered and start recording a macro as discussed in Chapter 1, "Recording and Running Macros in the Office Applications":

1. Click the Record Macro icon on the status bar or the Record Macro icon in the Code section of the Ribbon's Developer tab. Either way, you see the Record Macro dialog box.
2. Type the name for the macro, **`Move_Paragraph`**, in the Macro Name text box and a description in the Description text box.
3. Choose a template or document, if necessary, in the Store Macro In drop-down list. (You probably don't want to add this to the global `NewMacros` module in the `Normal.dotm` file. Why clutter it up with practice macros?)

4. If you want, use the Button or Keyboard button to create a Quick Access Toolbar button or keyboard shortcut for the macro.
5. Click the OK button to start recording the macro.

Record the following actions in the macro:

1. Insert a bookmark at the current position of the insertion point by clicking the Bookmark icon in the Links section of the Ribbon's Insert tab. This displays the Bookmarks dialog box. Enter a name for the bookmark, and click the Add button. In this example, the bookmark is named `Move_Paragraph_Temp` to indicate that it's a temporary bookmark used for the `Move_Paragraph` procedure.
2. Select the current paragraph by pressing F8 four times. The first press of F8 activates Extend mode, the second selects the current word, the third selects the current sentence, and the fourth selects the current paragraph. Press the Esc key to turn off Extend mode once the paragraph is selected.
3. Cut the selected paragraph by using one of the variations of the Cut command (for example, press either Ctrl+X or Shift+Delete, or click the Cut icon in the Ribbon's Clipboard section).
4. Move the insertion point up one paragraph by pressing Ctrl+↑.
5. Paste the cut paragraph back in by using a Paste command (for example, press Ctrl+V or Shift+Insert, or click the Paste button on the Home tab of the Ribbon).
6. Move the insertion point down one paragraph by pressing Ctrl+ ↓.
7. Move the insertion point up two paragraphs by pressing Ctrl+ ↑ twice.

   Note that if you started with the insertion point at the beginning of the first paragraph in the document, you'll only be able to move the insertion point up one paragraph. This doesn't matter—press the keystroke anyway to record it. If Word beeps at you, ignore it.
8. Move the insertion point down two paragraphs by pressing Ctrl+↓ twice. (If in doing so you hit the end of the document after the first keystroke, don't worry—perform the second keystroke anyway to record it. Word may sound a beep.)
9. Open the Bookmarks dialog box again (click the Bookmark icon in the Links section of the Ribbon's Insert tab), select the `Move_Paragraph_Temp` bookmark, and click the Go To button to go to it. Then click the Delete button to delete the `Move_Paragraph_Temp` bookmark. Click the Close button to close the Bookmarks dialog box.
10. Stop the Macro Recorder by clicking the Stop Recording icon on the status bar or the Stop Recording icon in the Code section of Ribbon's Developer tab.

Open the recorded macro in the Visual Basic Editor by pressing Alt+F8, selecting the macro's name in the Macros dialog box, and clicking the Edit button.

You should see a macro that looks something like this:

```
Sub Move_Paragraph()
'
```

```
 3. ' Move_Paragraph Macro
 4. ' Move a paragraph up or down
 5. '
 6.     With ActiveDocument.Bookmarks
 7.         .Add Range:=Selection.Range, Name:="Move_Paragraph_Temp"
 8.         .DefaultSorting = wdSortByName
 9.         .ShowHidden = False
10.     End With
11.     Selection.Extend
12.     Selection.Extend
13.     Selection.Extend
14.     Selection.Extend
15.     Selection.EscapeKey
16.     Selection.Cut
17.     Selection.MoveUp Unit:=wdParagraph, Count:=1
18.     Selection.Paste
19.     Selection.MoveDown Unit:=wdParagraph, Count:=1
20.     Selection.MoveUp Unit:=wdParagraph, Count:=2
21.     Selection.MoveDown Unit:=wdParagraph, Count:=2
22.     Selection.GoTo What:=wdGoToBookmark, Name:="Move_Paragraph_Temp"
23.     ActiveDocument.Bookmarks("Move_Paragraph_Temp").Delete
24.     With ActiveDocument.Bookmarks
25.         .DefaultSorting = wdSortByName
26.         .ShowHidden = False
27.     End With
28. End Sub
```

You can probably read this macro code easily enough by now:

- Line 1 starts the macro, and line 28 ends it. Lines 2 and 5 are blank comment lines around the comment lines showing the macro's name (line 3) and description (line 4).
- Lines 6 through 10 contain a `With` statement that adds the `Move_Paragraph_Temp` bookmark. Lines 7 and 8 are unnecessary here, but the Macro Recorder records all the settings in the Bookmarks dialog box, including the setting for the Sort By option button and the Hidden Bookmarks check box.
- Lines 11 through 15 use the Extend Selection feature to select the current paragraph.
- Lines 17, 19, 20, and 21 record the syntax for moving the insertion point up and down one paragraph and two paragraphs, respectively.
- Line 16 records the Cut command and Line 18 the Paste command.
- Line 22 moves the insertion point to the `Move_Paragraph_Temp` bookmark, and line 23 deletes the bookmark. Lines 24 through 27 again record the settings in the Bookmarks dialog box, which you don't need here either.

If you like, you can quickly delete unnecessary lines of code, and collapse the first `With` structure, to create a more succinct, more easily understood, version of the code:

```
Sub Move_Paragraph()
    ActiveDocument.Bookmarks.Add Range:=Selection.Range, _
        Name:="Move_Paragraph_Temp"
    Selection.Extend
    Selection.Extend
    Selection.Extend
    Selection.Extend
    Selection.EscapeKey
    Selection.Cut
    Selection.MoveUp Unit:=wdParagraph, Count:=1
    Selection.Paste
    Selection.MoveDown Unit:=wdParagraph, Count:=1
    Selection.MoveUp Unit:=wdParagraph, Count:=2
    Selection.MoveDown Unit:=wdParagraph, Count:=2
    Selection.GoTo What:=wdGoToBookmark, _
        Name:="Move_Paragraph_Temp"
End Sub
```

Creating the Dialog Box

Next, create the dialog box for the procedure (see Figure 14.16):

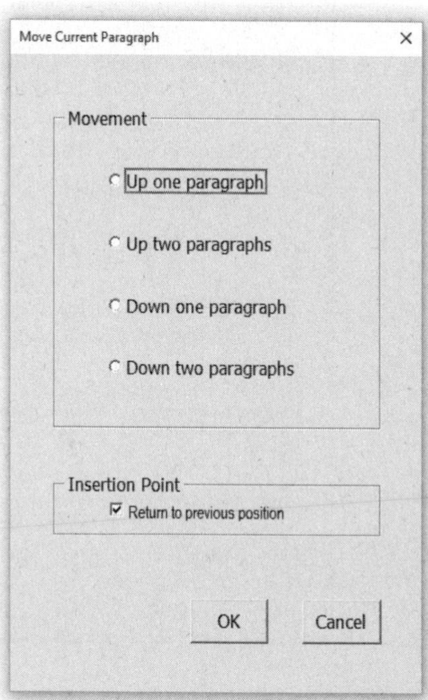

Figure 14.16 The Move Current Paragraph dialog box that you will connect to the `Move_Paragraph` macro

1. Start a user form in the Visual Basic Editor by clicking the Insert button's drop-down list and choosing UserForm (or just click the Insert button if it's already showing the UserForm icon) or by choosing Insert ➢ UserForm.
2. Use the Properties window for the user form to set its `Name` and `Caption` properties. Click in the cell next to the `Name` cell and enter the `Name` property there, and then click in the cell next to the `Caption` cell and enter the `Caption` property. The example user form is named `frmMoveParagraph` and has the caption `Move Current Paragraph` so that the name of the form is closely related to the text the user will see in the title bar of the dialog box but different from the procedure name (`Move_Current_Paragraph`).
3. Place two frames in the user form, as shown in Figure 14.17, to act as group containers in the dialog box:
   a. Double-click the Frame tool in the Toolbox, and then click and drag in the user form to place each frame.
   b. Align the frames by selecting them both and choosing Format ➢ Align ➢ Lefts.
   c. With the frames still selected, verify that they are the same width by choosing Format ➢ Make Same Size ➢ Width. (Don't choose Format ➢ Make Same Size ➢ Height or Format ➢ Make Same Size ➢ Both. The top frame will need to be taller than the bottom frame.)
   d. Caption the top frame **`Movement`** and the bottom frame **`Insertion Point`** by selecting each in turn and then setting the `Caption` property in the Properties window. Then name the top frame **`fraMovement`** and the bottom frame **`fraInsertionPoint`**.

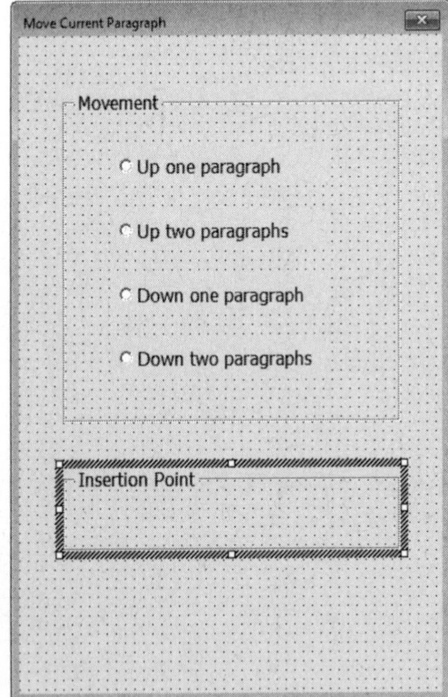

FIGURE 14.17
Start by placing two frames in the user form.

4. Place four option buttons in the Movement frame, as shown in Figure 14.18:

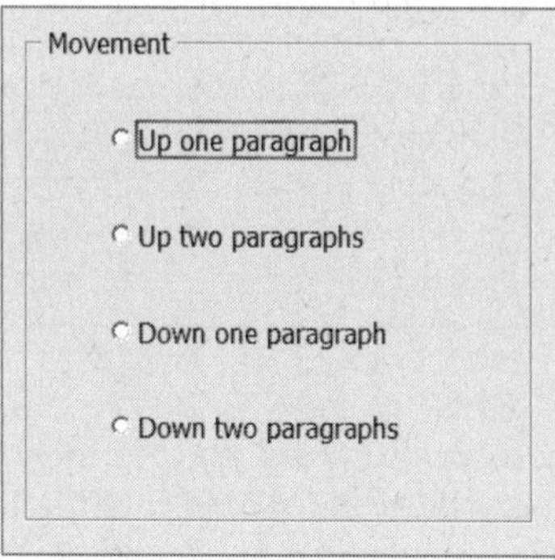

FIGURE 14.18 Place four option buttons in the Movement frame like this.

   a. Double-click the OptionButton tool in the Toolbox, and then click in the Movement frame to place each option button. This time, don't click and drag—just click to place a normal-width option button.

   b. When you've placed the four option buttons, click the Select Objects button in the Toolbox to restore the selection pointer. Then select the four option buttons and align them with each other by choosing Format ➤ Align ➤ Lefts. Even out any disparities in spacing by choosing Format ➤ Vertical Spacing ➤ Make Equal. If necessary, use the other items on the Format ➤ Vertical Spacing submenu—Increase, Decrease, and Remove—to adjust the amount of space between the option buttons. (You can do all these things freehand if you prefer by just eyeballing. Drag them around until you have them neatly positioned and sized.)

   c. Change the caption for each option button by setting the `Caption` property in the Properties window. Caption them as illustrated in Figure 14.18: **`Up one paragraph`**, **`Up two paragraphs`**, **`Down one paragraph`**, and **`Down two paragraphs`**. These option buttons will control the number of paragraphs the procedure moves the current paragraph.

   d. If you need to resize the option buttons to make all the text in the captions visible, select them and group them by right-clicking and choosing Group from the context menu, by choosing Format ➤ Group, or by clicking the Group button on the UserForm toolbar. Then select the group and drag one of the handles to resize all the option buttons evenly. For example, to reveal hidden text that's cut off on the right side, drag the handle at the right midpoint of the group outward.

   e. Name the option buttons **`optUpOne`**, **`optUpTwo`**, **`optDownOne`**, and **`optDownTwo`**, respectively, by changing the `Name` property of each in turn in the Properties window.

Option Buttons Are Mutually Exclusive

By default, all the option buttons on a user form (if they're not contained within a frame) are part of the same option group. This means that only one of these option buttons can be selected at any given time. If you want to provide more than one group of option buttons on a user form, you need to specify the separate groups. The easiest way to do this is to position each group within a separate Frame control as you did in this example. Alternatively, you can specify a different `GroupName` property for each option button.

f. Next, set the first option button's `Value` property to `True` by selecting the default `False` value in the Properties window and entering **`True`** instead. Doing so will select the option button in the user form you're designing, and when the dialog box is displayed, that option button will be selected as the default choice for the option group. Set its accelerator key to *U* by entering **`U`** as its `Accelerator` property. Set the `Accelerator` property of the second option button to *t*, the third to *D*, and the fourth to *w*. The `Accelerator` property is case-sensitive only when the caption for the control contains both the uppercase and lowercase versions of the same letter.

5. Place a check box in the Insertion Point frame, as shown in Figure 14.19:

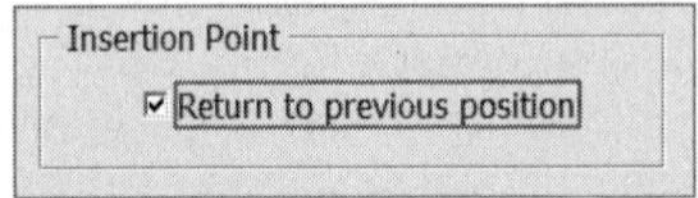

Figure 14.19 Place a check box in the Insertion Point frame.

a. Click the CheckBox tool in the Toolbox and then click in the Insertion Point frame in the user form to place a check box of the default size.

b. In the Properties window, set the name of the check box to **`chkReturnToPreviousPosition`** (a long name but a descriptive one). Then set its `Caption` property to **`Return to previous position`**. Set its accelerator key to *R* by entering **`R`** as its `Accelerator` property. Finally, set the check box to be selected by default by entering **`True`** as its `Value` property.

6. Next, insert the command buttons for the form (see Figure 14.20):

Figure 14.20 Add two command buttons and set their properties.

a. Double-click the CommandButton tool on the Toolbox and click to place the first command button at the bottom of the user form. Click to place the second command button, and then click the Select Objects button to restore the selection mouse pointer.

b. Size and place the command buttons by using the commands on the Format menu. For example, group the buttons, and then use the Format ➤ Center In Form ➤ Horizontally command to center the pair horizontally. You must group the buttons before doing this—if you simply select both of them, VBA centers one button on top of the other so that only the uppermost button is visible.

c. Set properties of the command buttons as follows: For the left-hand button (which will become the OK button), set the `Name` property to **`cmdOK`**, the `Caption` property to **`OK`**, the `Accelerator` property to **`O`** (that's *O* as in OK, not a zero), and the `Default` property to **`True`**. For the right-hand button (which will become the Cancel button), set the `Name` property to **`cmdCancel`**, the `Accelerator` property to **`A`**, the `Caption` property to **`Cancel`**, and the `Cancel` property to **`True`**. Leave the `Default` property set to `False`.

7. Now we attach our code to this form. Dive down into the Code window by double-clicking the Cancel button to display a procedure associated with it:

```
Private Sub cmdCancel_Click()

End Sub
```

Recall that the Editor chooses to create a procedure for the most common event for whatever control (or the form) you double-click to get down into the Code window. For most controls, this will be the `Click` event, as it is for the CommandButton control.

Type an `End` statement between the lines:

```
Private Sub cmdCancel_Click()
    End
End Sub
```

This `End` statement removes the form from the screen and ends the current procedure—in this case, the `Move_Current_Paragraph` procedure.

Now you'll attach code to the OK button, which is where things get interesting. When the user clicks the OK button, the procedure needs to continue executing and do all of the following:

- Remove the dialog box from display by hiding it or by unloading it (or, preferably, both). As discussed earlier in the chapter, the choice is yours, but using both commands is usually clearest.
- Check the `Value` property of the check box to see whether it was selected or cleared.
- Check the `Value` property of each option button in turn to see which of them was selected when the OK button was clicked.

Now continue creating the Move Current Paragraph dialog box:

8. Double-click the OK button to display the code attached to it. (If you're still working in the Code window, select cmdOK in the Object drop-down list (on the top left of the Code window). The Editor automatically creates the `Click` event procedure for this button.

First, enter the following two lines between the `Private Sub` and `End Sub` lines:

```
frmMoveParagraph.Hide
Unload frmMoveParagraph
```

The `frmMoveParagraph.Hide` line activates the `Hide` method for the `frmMoveParagraph` user form, hiding it from display on the screen. The `Unload frmMoveParagraph` line unloads the dialog box from memory.

Removing a Form Can Prevent Confusion

It isn't necessary to hide or unload a form to continue execution of a procedure, but if you don't, users may become confused. For example, if you click the OK button on a Print dialog box in a Windows application, you expect the dialog box to disappear and the Print command to be executed. If the dialog box didn't disappear (but it launched the printing job in the background), you'd probably think it hadn't registered your click, so you'd click again and again until it went away. Then you'd print multiple copies, which is so wrong.

9. Next, the procedure needs to check the `Value` property of the `chkReturnToPrevious-Position` check box to find out whether to insert a bookmark in the document to mark the current position of the insertion point. To do this, enter a straightforward `If…Then` statement:

```
If chkReturnToPreviousPosition = True Then
End If
```

If the `chkReturnToPreviousPosition` statement is set to `True`—that is, if the check box is selected—the code in the lines following the `Then` statement runs. The `Then` statement consists of the lines for inserting a bookmark that you recorded earlier. Cut these lines from the procedure and paste them into the `If…Then` statement like this:

```
If chkReturnToPreviousPosition = True Then
    With ActiveDocument.Bookmarks
        .Add Range:=Selection.Range, Name:=" Move_Paragraph_Temp"
    End With
End If
```

If the check box is selected, the procedure inserts a bookmark. If the check box is cleared, the procedure passes over these lines.

10. Next, right after the `End If`, paste in the code for selecting the current paragraph and cutting it to the Clipboard:

```
Selection.Extend
Selection.Extend
Selection.Extend
Selection.Extend
Selection.Cut
```

11. After this, you need to retrieve the Value properties from the option buttons to see which one was selected when the user chose the OK button in the dialog box. For this, you can again use an If condition—this time, an If…Then ElseIf…Else condition, with the relevant insertion-point-movement lines from the recorded procedure pasted in:

```
If optUpOne = True Then
    Selection.MoveUp Unit:=wdParagraph, Count:=1
ElseIf optUpTwo = True Then
    Selection.MoveUp Unit:=wdParagraph, Count:=2
ElseIf optDownOne = True Then
    Selection.MoveDown Unit:=wdParagraph, Count:=1
Else
    Selection.MoveDown Unit:=wdParagraph, Count:=2
End If
Selection.Paste
```

Here, optUpOne, optUpTwo, optDownOne, and optDownTwo (which uses the Else statement here and, therefore, isn't specified by name in the listing) are the four option buttons from the dialog box, representing the choice to move the current paragraph up one paragraph, up two paragraphs, down one paragraph, or down two paragraphs, respectively.

The condition is straightforward: If optUpOne is True (that is, if this option button is selected), the first Then condition executes, moving the insertion point up one paragraph from its current position (after the current paragraph is cut, the insertion point will be at the beginning of the paragraph that was after the current one). If optUpOne is False, the first ElseIf condition is evaluated. If the condition evaluates to True, the second Then condition runs. And if the condition evaluates to False, the next ElseIf condition is evaluated. If that condition, too, turns out to be False, the Else code is run. In this case, the Else statement means that the optDownTwo option button was selected in the dialog box, so the Else code moves the insertion point down two paragraphs.

Wherever the insertion point ends based on which option button the user chose, the next line of code (Selection.Paste) pastes in the cut paragraph from the Clipboard.

12. Finally, the procedure must return the insertion point to where it was originally if the chkReturnToPreviousPosition check box is selected. Again, you can test for this with a simple If…Then condition that incorporates the go-to-bookmark and delete-bookmark lines from the recorded procedure:

```
If chkReturnToPreviousPosition = True Then
    Selection.GoTo What:=wdGoToBookmark, _
        Name:=" Move_Paragraph_Temp"
    ActiveDocument.Bookmarks("Move_Paragraph_Temp").Delete
End If
```

If the chkReturnToPreviousPosition check box is selected, VBA moves the insertion point to the temporary bookmark and then deletes that bookmark.

Listing 14.1 shows the full listing for the cmdOK button.

LISTING 14.1: The full listing for the cmdOK_Click macro

```
Private Sub cmdOK_Click()
    frmMoveParagraph.Hide
    Unload frmMoveParagraph
    If chkReturnToPreviousPosition = True Then
        With ActiveDocument.Bookmarks
            .Add Range:=Selection.Range, _
                Name:="Move_Paragraph_Temp"
        End With
    End If
    Selection.Extend
    Selection.Extend
    Selection.Extend
    Selection.Extend
    Selection.Cut
    If optUpOne = True Then
        Selection.MoveUp Unit:=wdParagraph, Count:=1
    ElseIf optUpTwo = True Then
    Selection.MoveUp Unit:=wdParagraph, Count:=2
    ElseIf optDownOne = True Then
        Selection.MoveDown Unit:=wdParagraph, Count:=1
    Else
        Selection.MoveDown Unit:=wdParagraph, Count:=2
    End If
    Selection.Paste
    If chkReturnToPreviousPosition = True Then
        Selection.GoTo What:=wdGoToBookmark, _
            Name:="Move_Paragraph_Temp"
        ActiveDocument.Bookmarks("Move_Paragraph_Temp").Delete
    End If
End Sub
```

Go ahead and try it. To test this example properly, you should remove the bookmark you inserted while recording the macro earlier in this chapter. To remove it, click the Bookmark item in the Links section in the Insert tab on Word's Ribbon. In the Bookmarks dialog box that opens, select `Move_Paragraph_Temp` and click the Delete button.

Now, open the scratch document in Word that you created earlier in this chapter and filled with several paragraphs of text. Press Alt+F11 to open the Visual Basic Editor. Double-click `frmMoveParagraph` in the Project Explorer to display the user form. Press F5 to run this procedure. Click the OK button in your user form and observe that the paragraphs were rearranged in the document.

General Example: Opening a File from a List Box

This next example displays a user form that employs a list box from which the user can select a file to open. The user form is simple, as is its code. The macro includes a loop and an array to gather the names of the files in a folder and then displays the filenames in the list box. The user gets to select a file and click the Open button to open it. Figure 14.21 shows the user form in action, displaying Excel files.

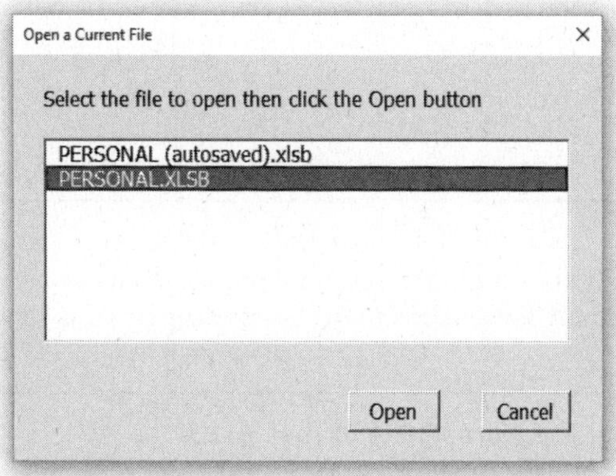

FIGURE 14.21 The user form you'll build in this example contains a list box that gives the user quick access to all current files.

You can adapt this example to any of the Office 2016 applications discussed in this book by changing the filename to an appropriate type for that application and also modifying a couple of the key statements. The version of this example we'll look at now shows you how to create the procedure in Excel.

BUILDING THE USER FORM

Follow these steps to build the user form:

1. Start the application you want to work in. The example uses Excel.
2. Display the Visual Basic Editor by pressing the Alt+F11 key or by clicking the Visual Basic icon in the Ribbon's Developer tab.
3. In the Project Explorer, right-click the project to which you want to add the user form and choose Insert ➤ UserForm from the context menu to insert a default-size user form in the project.
4. Drag the handle at the lower-right corner of the user form to the right to make the user form a bit wider.
5. Set the `Name` property of the form to **`frmOpen_a_Current_File`** and its `Caption` to **`Open a Current File`**. Check the `Width` property. You want it to be about 350 pixels wide.
6. Click the Label button in the Toolbox, and then click in the upper-left corner of the user form to place a default-size label there. Activate the Properties window and set the properties of the label as shown in Table 14.9.

TABLE 14.9: Set these properties of your label.

PROPERTY	VALUE
(Name)	lblInfo
AutoSize	True
Caption	Choose the file to open and click the Open button.
Left	10
Top	6
WordWrap	False

7. Click the ListBox button in the Toolbox, and then click below the label in the user form to place a default-size list box there. Set its properties as shown in Table 14.10.

TABLE 14.10: Set these properties of the ListBox.

PROPERTY	VALUE
(Name)	lstifles
Height	100
Left	10
Top	25
Width	300

8. Double-click the CommandButton button in the Toolbox, and then click twice at the bottom of the user form to place two default-size command buttons there. Set their properties as shown in Table 14.11.

TABLE 14.11: Set these properties of the CommandButton.

PROPERTY	FIRST BUTTON VALUE	SECOND BUTTON VALUE
(Name)	cmdOpen	cmdCancel
Cancel	False	True
Caption	Open	Cancel
Default	True	False

TABLE 14.11: Set these properties of the CommandButton. *(CONTINUED)*

PROPERTY	FIRST BUTTON VALUE	SECOND BUTTON VALUE
`Height`	21	21
`Width`	55	55

9. Arrange the command buttons as follows:
   - a. Click the cmdCancel button to select it, and then drag it close to the cmdOK button.
   - b. With the cmdCancel button still selected, Ctrl+click the cmdOK button to add it to the selection.
   - c. Choose Format ➢ Group to group the buttons.
   - d. Choose Format ➢ Center In Form ➢ Horizontally to center the buttons horizontally in the form.
   - e. Drag the group up or down as necessary.

   (Or just drag them around and eyeball them into a pleasing position.)

Creating the Code for the User Form

Follow these steps to create the code for the user form:

1. With the user form selected, press the F7 key to display the user form's code sheet.
2. In the declarations portion of the code sheet (just keep pressing the up-arrow key until you move to the very top of the Code window), enter an `Option Base 1` statement to make the array numbering start at `1` instead of at `0`:

   ```
   Option Base 1
   ```

3. Make sure that UserForm is selected in the Object drop-down list (top left of the code sheet), and then pull down the Procedure drop-down list (top right) and choose Initialize from it. The Visual Basic Editor enters the stub of an `Initialize` procedure in the code sheet, like this:

   ```
   Private Sub UserForm_Initialize()

   End Sub
   ```

4. Enter the statements for the `Initialize` procedure shown in Listing 14.2.
5. In the Object drop-down list, select cmdCancel. The Visual Basic Editor enters the stub of a `Click` procedure, as shown here. (`Click` is the default event for the CommandButton control, so the Visual Basic Editor assumes that you want to create a `Click` procedure.)

   ```
   Private Sub cmdCancel_Click()

   End Sub
   ```

6. Enter the statements for the `cmdCancel_Click` procedure shown in Listing 14.2.
7. In the Object drop-down list, select cmdOpen. The Visual Basic Editor enters the stub of a `Click` procedure.
8. Enter the statements for the `cmdOpen_Click` procedure shown in Listing 14.2.
9. Customize line 9 (in the `Initialize` procedure) and line 32 (in the `cmdOpen_Click` procedure) so that the code will work with the application you're using, as shown in the following list. The procedure as shown is set up to run for Excel, but you'll probably need to change the path to reflect where the target files are on your computer.

   - For Word, change the `Workbooks.Open` statement to `Documents.Open`:

     ```
     If lstFiles.Value <> "" Then Documents.Open _
         Filename:="c:\transfer\" & lstFiles.Value
     ```

   - For PowerPoint, change the `Workbooks.Open` statement to `Presentations.Open`:

     ```
     If lstFiles.Value <> "" Then Presentations.Open _
         Filename:="c:\transfer\" & lstFiles.Value
     ```

Listing 14.2 shows the full version of the code behind the Open a Current File user form.

LISTING 14.2: Using a ListBox to open a file

```
1.  Option Base 1
2.
3.  Private Sub UserForm_Initialize()
4.
5.      Dim strFileArray() As String
6.      Dim strFFile As String
7.      Dim intCount As Integer
8.
9.      strFFile = Dir("c:\transfer\spreads\*.xlsb")
10.     intCount = 1
11.
12.     Do While strFFile <> ""
13.         If strFFile <> "." And strFFile <> ".." Then
14.             ReDim Preserve strFileArray(intCount)
15.             strFileArray(intCount) = strFFile
16.             intCount = intCount + 1
17.             strFFile = Dir()
18.         End If
19.     Loop
20.
21.     lstFiles.List() = strFileArray
22.
```

```
23.  End Sub
24.
25.  Private Sub cmdCancel_Click()
26.      Me.Hide
27.      Unload Me
28.  End Sub
29.
30.  Private Sub cmdOpen_Click()
31.      Me.Hide
32.      If lstFiles.Value <> "" Then Workbooks.Open _
             Name:="c:\transfer\spreads" & lstFiles.Value
33.      Unload Me
34.  End Sub
```

Listing 14.2 contains all the code that appears on the code sheet for the `frmOpen_a_Current_File` user form: a declarations section and three event procedures.

In the declarations section, line 1 contains the `Option Base 1` statement, which makes any array used on the code sheet begin at 1 rather than at `0`. Line 2 is a spacer.

Here's what happens in the `UserForm_Initialize` procedure (lines 3 to 23):

- Line 3 begins the `Initialize` procedure for the user form. Line 4 is a spacer.
- Line 5 declares the String array variable `strFileArray`. Line 6 declares the String variable `strFFile`. Line 7 declares the Integer variable `intCount`. Line 8 is a spacer.
- Line 9 assigns to `strFFile` the result of a directory operation on the designated folder (here, `c:\transfer\spreads\`), but substitute your own path to a folder on your computer that contains files with an `.xlsb` filename extension. Enter your own path in line 32 as well.
- Line 10 sets the `intCount` counter to `1`. Note that if you don't use the `Option Base 1` declaration for this procedure, you need to set `Count` to `0` (or the corresponding value for a different option base that you use). The first call to `Dir`, which specifies the pathname in an argument, returns the first file it finds in the folder (assuming it finds at least one file). Each subsequent call without the argument returns the next file in the folder, until `Dir` finds no more files.
- Line 11 is a spacer. Lines 12 through 19 contain a `Do While...Loop` loop that runs while `strFFile` isn't an empty string (`""`):
  - Line 13 makes sure that `strFFile` isn't a folder by comparing it to the single period and double period used to denote folders. If `strFFile` isn't a folder, line 14 uses a `ReDim Preserve` statement to increase the dimensions of the `strFileArray` array to the number in `intCount` while retaining the current information in the array, thus building the list of files in the folder.
  - Line 15 assigns to the `intCount` index of the `strFileArray` array the current contents of `strFFile`.

- Line 16 then adds `1` to `intCount`, and line 17 sets `strFFile` to the result of the `Dir` function (the first filename matching the `*.xlsb` pattern in the designated folder).
- Line 18 ends the `If` condition. Line 19 contains the `Loop` keyword that will continue the loop as long as the `Do While` statement is `True`.

- When the loop ends, line 21 sets the `List` property of the `lstFiles` list box in the dialog box to the contents of `strFileArray`, which now contains a list of all the files in the folder.
- Line 22 is a spacer, line 23 ends the procedure, and line 24 is another spacer.

Here's what happens in the `cmdCancel_Click` procedure (lines 25 through 28):

- Line 25 starts the `cmdCancel_Click` procedure, and line 28 ends it.
- Line 26 hides the user form, using the `Me` keyword to reference it.
- Line 27 unloads the user form from memory.

Here's what happens in the `cmdOpen_Click` procedure (lines 30 through 34):

- Line 30 starts the `cmdOpen_Click` procedure, and line 34 ends it.
- Line 31 hides the user form, again by using the `Me` keyword.
- Line 32 checks to make sure the `Value` property of the `lstFiles` list box is not an empty string (`""`) and, if it is not, uses the `Open` method of the `Documents` collection to open the file selected in the list box. The statement adds to the path (`c:\transfer\spreads\`) the `Value` property of the list box to produce the full filename. Substitute your own path for `c:\transfer\spreads\`.
- Line 33 unloads the user form from memory.

Remember that to test this example, you'll need to adjust lines 9 and 32 to include a file path on your machine where some XLSB files are stored. For Excel 2016, try this location: `C:\Users\`*`YourName`*`\AppData\Roaming\Microsoft\Excel\XLSTART`.

Using an Application's Built-In Dialog Boxes from VBA

Some applications, such as Word and Excel, let you use their built-in dialog boxes via VBA. If a built-in dialog box offers the functionality you need, using it can be a great solution: You don't have to build a custom dialog box, just reference the built-in dialog box in your code.

You shouldn't even need to debug a built-in dialog box, and users of your procedures will probably be familiar with the dialog box from their work in the application. These built-in dialog boxes are called *common dialog boxes*, and we explored them briefly in the Real World Scenario sidebar titled "Control a `For…Next` Loop with User Input via a Dialog Box" in Chapter 12.

Displaying a Built-In Dialog Box

To display a built-in dialog box, you need to know its name and constant. You also must decide which method to use to display the dialog box.

Finding the Dialog Box Name and Constant

Although Office 2016 no longer uses menus (with some exceptions, such as the Visual Basic Editor), built-in dialog boxes (in Word and other applications) are still identified by constants derived from the older, pre-Ribbon menu-style interface. These constants start with the letters `wdDialog` (as in *Word dialog*), followed by the name of the dialog box.

The names of common dialog boxes are derived from the pre–Office 2010 menu commands that displayed the dialog boxes prior to the introduction of the Ribbon interface (with Office 2007). For example, to refer to the Open dialog box, you use the constant `wdDialogFileOpen`, because in previous versions of Word, you would have chosen File ➢ Open to display that dialog box.

Or to display the Print dialog box (the old File ➢ Print options), you use the constant `wdDialogFilePrint`, and to display the Options dialog box (Tools ➢ Options), you use the constant `wdDialogToolsOptions`.

So, although the user interface has evolved beyond classic menus, the menu structure itself remains as part of the classification system for internal objects—such as these constants used to identify various dialog boxes.

Excel follows a similar but less rigid taxonomic convention. Built-in Excel dialog boxes are (for backward compatibility with older macro code) still identified by constants starting with the letters `xlDialog` followed by the name of the dialog box. The name of the dialog box is derived either from the classic menu commands that were required to display it or from the dialog box's title. For example, to refer to the Open dialog box, you use the constant `xlDialogOpen` (rather than `xlDialogFileOpen`).

Anyway, the easiest way to find the name for the built-in dialog box you need is to search the Visual Basic Editor's Help system for "Built-In Dialog Box Argument Lists" in Word or Excel. (Access employs a whole different system for common dialog boxes, requiring the importation of object libraries using its Visual Basic Editor's Tools ➢ References menu and the employment of specialized objects.)

You can also view a list of Word or Excel built-in dialog boxes by displaying the Object Browser (press F2 in the Editor) and typing **`wddialog`** (for Word) or **`xldialog`** (for Excel) in the Search textbox.

You use these constants with the `Dialogs` property, which returns the `Dialogs` collection object, which in turn contains all the built-in dialog boxes in the host application.

For example, to display Word's Save As dialog box, you use the `Show` method, as illustrated in the following statement:

```
Dialogs(wdDialogFileSaveAs).Show
```

It's as simple as that. To display Word's Replace dialog box, just substitute `wdDialogEditReplace` for `wdDialogFileSaveAs`.

THE Dialogs COLLECTION IS CREATABLE IN WORD, BUT NOT IN EXCEL

In Word, the `Dialogs` collection is a "creatable object," meaning you can access it directly without going through the `Application` object. In Excel, however, the `Dialogs` collection is not creatable, so you must always add the `Application` object to this code, like this:

```
Application.Dialogs (xlDialogOptionsGeneral).Show
```

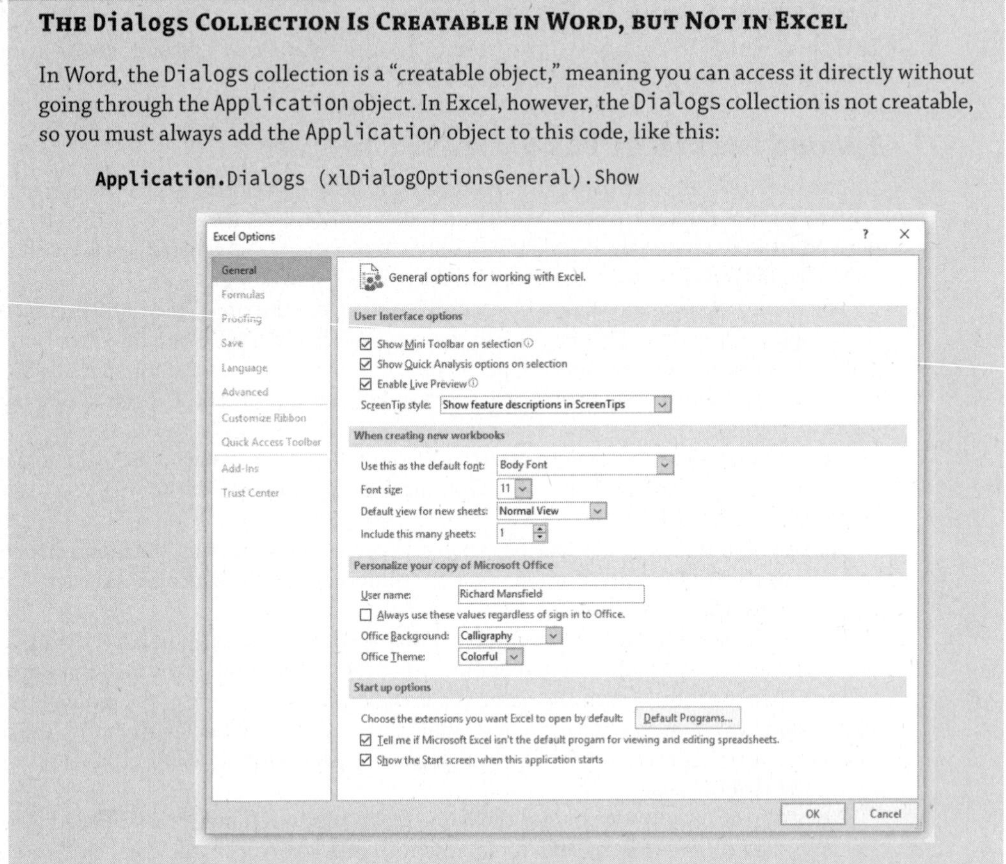

CHOOSING BETWEEN THE *SHOW* METHOD AND THE *DISPLAY* METHOD

VBA provides two methods of displaying built-in dialog boxes onscreen: `Show` and `Display`:

- The `Show` method shows the specified `Dialog` object and then uses functions built into the `Dialog` object to carry out the user's requests. You don't need to write any code of your own. For example, if you use the `Show` method to display the `wdDialogFileSaveAs` dialog box and the user enters a name for the file in the File Name box and clicks the Save button, VBA itself automatically saves the file with the given name in the specified folder (and with any other options the user chose). You didn't write any programming to save this file.
- The `Display` method merely displays the dialog box onscreen, but it does *not* execute the actions the user requests in the dialog box. Instead, it allows you to fetch the settings (the user's requests and selections) from the dialog box once the user dismisses it, but then you must write your own code to carry out what the user requested.

Displaying a Particular Tab of a Word Dialog Box

If the dialog box you want to display has tabs, you can display the tab of your choice by specifying the `DefaultTab` property. You refer to a tab by the name of the dialog box plus the word Tab and the name of the tab. For example, the constant for the Bullets And Numbering dialog box is `wdDialogFormatBulletsAndNumbering`, and the constant for its Outline Numbered tab is `wdDialogFormatBulletsAndNumberingTabOutlineNumbered`. Likewise, the Font dialog box is referred to as `wdDialogFormatFont`, and its Character Spacing tab is referred to as `wdDialogFormatFontTabCharacterSpacing`. You could display this tab by using the following statements:

```
With Dialogs(wdDialogFormatFont)
    .DefaultTab = wdDialogFormatFontTabCharacterSpacing
    .Show
End With
```

To see a list of all Word's tab constants, search for `wdWordDialogTab` in the VBA Editor's Object Browser (press F2). You'll find loads of them.

Using the *Show* Method to Display and Execute a Dialog Box

The Show method displays the specified dialog box and automatically responds to whatever actions the user takes in it. Show is useful when your user is merely going to perform a conventional interactive action. As a simple example, in a procedure that's supposed to perform certain formatting tasks on the current document, you could check to make sure a document is open before attempting to perform the formatting. Then, if no document is open, you could display the built-in Open dialog box so that the user could open a file. (You might precede the Open dialog box with a message box explaining the problem.) Listing 14.3 shows the code for this part of the procedure.

Listing 14.3: Using a common dialog box

```
If Documents.Count = 0 Then
    Proceed = MsgBox("There is no document open." _
        & vbCr & vbCr & _
        "Please open a document for the procedure to work on.", _
        vbOKCancel + vbExclamation, "Format Report")
    If Proceed = vbOK Then
        Dialogs(wdDialogFileOpen).Show
        If Documents.Count = 0 Then End
    Else
        End
    End If
End If
'rest of procedure here
```

Here's how the code works:

- Line 1 checks the `Count` property of the `Documents` collection to see if no documents are open; if that's the case, the statements in lines 2 through 8 run.
- Line 2 displays a message box informing users that no document is open and asking them to open one for the procedure to work on. The message box has OK and Cancel buttons and stores the button chosen in the variable `Proceed`.
- Line 3 checks to see if the OK button was chosen; if it was, line 4 displays the Open dialog box so that users can select the file, which VBA will open when they click the Open button in the Open dialog box.
- Users can cancel the procedure at this point by clicking the Cancel button in the Open dialog box, so line 5 checks the `Count` property of the `Documents` collection again and uses an `End` statement to terminate execution of the procedure if there is still no document open.
- If the OK button was not chosen, execution moves from line 3 to the `Else` statement in line 6, and the `End` statement in line 7 ends execution of the procedure.
- Line 8 contains the `End If` statement for the nested `If` statement, and line 9 contains the `End If` statement for the outer `If` statement.
- Line 10 contains a comment to indicate that you'd write more code here—the rest of the procedure would run from this point, which is reached only if a document is open.

USING THE *DISPLAY* METHOD TO DISPLAY A DIALOG BOX

Remember that unlike the `Show` method, the `Display` method displays a built-in dialog box but doesn't respond to any actions the user takes in the dialog box. Instead, you must write code that checks the settings that the user chose in the dialog box and then write more code to carry out the user's wishes. When you use the `Display` method, the user gets to work with familiar dialog boxes, but you totally control the behavior that results from that interaction.

For example, you'll often need to find out which folder a procedure should be working in, such as when you need the location of a number of documents that the user wants to manipulate. To get the folder, you *could* display a straightforward input box and prompt the user to type in the correct path to the folder—if the user knows the path and can type it in correctly.

Perhaps a better solution is to display a list box containing the tree of drives, folders, and files on the user's hard drive, but to do this you need to dimension an array and fill it with the folders and filenames, and you need to refresh the display every time the user moves up or down the tree—quite a lot of programming work.

So why not just borrow all this functionality from a built-in common dialog box? It's already part of the Office applications. You can achieve the same result much more easily by using a built-in dialog box that has the tree built in (for example, the Open dialog box) and then retrieving the user's responses for your own purposes.

If you need to execute the settings (user choices) in a built-in dialog box, you can use the `Execute` method. But you might want to check the user's selections in the dialog box before implementing them. If you find a problem, you could then, for example, display a dialog box of your own, such as an input box, asking for clarification.

Setting and Restoring Options in a Built-In Dialog Box

Most of the built-in Word and Excel dialog boxes have arguments that you can use for retrieving or setting values in the dialog box. For example, the Open dialog box in Word has arguments for `Name`, `ConfirmConversions`, `ReadOnly`, `LinkToSource`, `AddToMru` (adding the document to the Most Recently Used document list on the Recent section of the File tab on the Ribbon), `PasswordDoc`, and more. Some of these are options that you'll see in the Open dialog box itself. Others are associated options that you'll find on the various tabs of the Options dialog box. You can guess some argument names from the names of the corresponding controls in the dialog box, but other names aren't directly related. To learn the names, search for "Built-In Dialog Box Argument Lists" in the VBA Editor's Help system (choose MSDN on the Web, and then search with Bing).

For example, the following statements set the contents of the File Name text box in the Save As dialog box in Word and then display the dialog box:

```
With Dialogs(wdDialogFileSaveAs)
    .Name = "Yellow Paint Primer"
    .Show
End With
```

Be aware that some arguments that applied to dialog boxes displayed by Office 2003 are not used in later versions of Office dialog boxes. So, you may need to experiment a bit to see if a particular legacy argument is still useful in the Office 2016 interface.

If you change the settings in a dialog box that uses *sticky* (persistent) settings, it's a good idea to change them back at the end of your procedure so that users don't get unexpected results the next time they open the dialog box.

Which Button Did the User Choose in a Dialog Box?

To find out which button the user clicked in a dialog box, check the return value of the `Show` method or the `Display` method. The return values are shown in Table 14.12.

TABLE 14.12: Click return values

RETURN VALUE	BUTTON CLICKED
`-2`	Close
`-1`	OK
`0`	Cancel
`1`	The first command button
`2`	The second command button
`>2 (greater than 2)`	Subsequent command buttons

For example, you might want to cancel your whole procedure if the user clicks the Cancel button in a dialog box, like this:

```
If Dialogs(wdDialogFileOpen).Show = 0 Then End
```

Specifying a Time-Out for a Dialog Box

In some applications, including Word, you can display some built-in dialog boxes for a specified time rather than having them stay open until the user dismisses them by clicking OK or Cancel or some other button. To do so, you use the `TimeOut` Variant argument with the `Show` method or the `Display` method. You specify `TimeOut` as a number of units, each of which is approximately a thousandth of a second. (If the system is busy with many other tasks, the actual result might be a slightly longer delay.) So, you could display the General page of the Word Options dialog box for about 10 seconds—long enough for the user to check the Name setting and change it if necessary—by using the following statements:

```
With Dialogs(wdDialogToolsOptions)
     .DefaultTab = wdDialogToolsOptionsTabUserInfo
     .Show (10000)
End With
```

THE *TIMEOUT* ARGUMENT DOESN'T WORK WITH CUSTOM DIALOG BOXES

`TimeOut` doesn't work with custom dialog boxes you create, only with the built-in Word dialog boxes. Also, some built-in Word dialog boxes—such as the New dialog box (`wdDialogFileNew`) and the Customize dialog box (`wdDialogToolsCustomize`)—don't recognize the `TimeOut` option either.

Timing out a dialog box is especially useful for noncritical information, such as the username in this example, because it allows the procedure to continue even if the user has left the computer. Likewise, you might want to time out a Save As dialog box in which the procedure suggested a viable filename but allowed users to override it if they were present. However, for a procedure in which the user's input is essential, you won't want to use the `TimeOut` argument. You want to compel the user to respond by at least clicking a button. In this context, the dialog box should not disappear all by itself via this timeout technique.

The Bottom Line

Understand what you can do with a custom dialog box. Custom dialog boxes—user interfaces you design as forms in the Visual Basic Editor—are often needed in macros and other kinds of Office automation. You might, for example, want to display a dialog box that allows the user to specify whether to let a macro continue beyond a certain point in its code or cease execution. Perhaps your macro is searching through a document for a particular phrase; then when it finds that phrase, it displays a dialog box to users asking if they want to continue further.

Master It Which VBA statement would you use to stop a macro from continuing execution?

Create a custom dialog box. You use the Visual Basic Editor to both design a custom dialog box (form) and write code for macros. You can attach the various controls to a form and then enter code *behind* the dialog box.

Master It How do you switch between the form-design window (sometimes called the object window) and the Code window in the Visual Basic Editor?

Add controls to a dialog box. It's easy in the Visual Basic Editor to add various controls—such as command buttons and text boxes—to a user form (a custom dialog box).

Master It How do you add a command button to a custom dialog box?

Link dialog boxes to procedures. Buttons, check boxes, option buttons—displaying various controls to the user is fine, but unless you write some code *behind* these various user-interface objects, what's the point? Your macro's user shouldn't discover that clicking a button *does nothing.*

Dialog boxes often display objects with which users can communicate their wants to your code. Therefore, you write code that reads the values the user enters into controls, and responds.

Master It Create a small custom dialog box that displays a message in a label control saying, "Would you like to know the current date and time?" Put an OK button and a Cancel button on this form. Write code that simply ends the procedure if the user presses the Cancel button but that displays the date and time in the label if the user clicks the OK button. If the user clicks OK a second time, end the procedure.

Retrieve the user's choices from a dialog box. A major task of most dialog boxes is retrieving values that the user has specified in various controls by selecting check boxes and so on. Then you write code to carry out the user's wants based on these retrieved values. This interaction via dialog box is the typical way that a user communicates with your procedures, and vice versa.

Master It Create a new dialog box that contains three option buttons captioned Small, Medium, and Large and named `optSmall`, `optMedium`, and `optLarge`. Write code in each option button's `Click` procedure to change the button's caption to boldface when the button is clicked.

Chapter 15

Creating Complex Forms

While simple dialog boxes tend to be static, more complex dialog boxes can be *dynamic*: They can change when the user clicks certain elements in them. Such changes can include the following:

- The application changes the information in the dialog box to reflect choices that the user has made. For example, if a user selects a particular check box, the application may make other check boxes unavailable (hidden or disabled) because the options offered by the other check boxes cannot be simultaneously chosen along with the first check box.
- The dialog box displays a hidden section of secondary, less frequently used options when the user clicks a button in the primary area of the dialog box.
- The application uses the dialog box to keep track of a procedure and to guide the user to the next step by displaying appropriate instructions and by activating relevant controls. In this chapter, you'll look at an example of this technique.

In this chapter, you'll start by investigating how to create dynamic forms. Such dialog boxes require a little more work than static dialog boxes, but they're a great way to both present information and allow the user to make choices. (Note that the terms *form* and *dialog box* can be used interchangeably, though dialog boxes tend to be smaller and simpler than forms.)

From dynamic dialog boxes you'll move on to multipage dialog boxes, which you use to present more information or options to the user than the eye and mind can comfortably encompass at once.

You'll then look at how to create a *modeless* dialog box (one that users can leave onscreen while they continue to work in their application, similar to the way Word's Research pane displays results from the thesaurus, though you can continue to edit the document).

The chapter ends by showing you how to work with the many events supported by the `UserForm` object and the controls you use on it. By using events, you can monitor what the user does and take action accordingly, or even prevent the user from doing something that doesn't seem like a good idea.

IN THIS CHAPTER, YOU WILL LEARN TO DO THE FOLLOWING:

- Understand what a complex dialog box is
- Reveal and hide parts of a dialog box
- Create multipage dialog boxes
- Create modeless dialog boxes
- Explore all the form and control events

Creating and Working with Complex Dialog Boxes

You should avoid using a complex dialog box when a simple one will do the trick and will be easier for users to work with. If all a macro needs is a pair of check boxes and a group of option buttons, there's no need to employ multiple pages of dynamically updating controls. But often, you will want to create complex dialog boxes (like the examples given at the beginning of this chapter) to provide users with the flexibility your procedures demand.

Updating a Dialog Box to Reflect the User's Choices

You'll find it relatively easy to change a form to reflect the options the user chooses. Your primary tool for doing this is the `Click` event, to which most controls placed on a form react and to which you can code in the Code window that's "behind" (associated with) your form.

When you double-click a control on a form, the Code window for that form opens and a default `Sub` procedure is displayed. This procedure is associated with the clicked control. The procedure is automatically named after the control and the control's default event. If you double-click a command button, for example, the Code window opens with this button's default `Click` event:

```
Private Sub CommandButton1_Click()

End Sub
```

Whatever code you put into this procedure will be executed when the user clicks this particular command button.

Some controls have different default events than `Click`; you'll learn about the `Change` event as you work with complex dialog boxes, and you'll see the full slew of other events in the second half of the chapter.

Listing 15.1 in the next section shows you an example of code that updates a dialog box should the user click a button captioned More.

Revealing a Hidden Part of a Form

Hiding part of a complex form is a great way to simplify the user's interaction with the dialog box. Consider the Find And Replace dialog box in Word: When you first see it (by pressing Ctrl+H, or by clicking the Replace icon in the Editing section of the Ribbon's Home tab), you're shown only the part of the dialog box (see the top box in Figure 15.1) for the most common type of search and replace—just the target and the replacement, along with the option to replace them one by one or *en masse.*

But, should you need less common or more advanced options that the abbreviated version of the Find And Replace dialog box doesn't display by default, you can click the More button to reveal the bottom part of the dialog box, as shown at the bottom in Figure 15.1. Here are more rarely used options, such as matching prefix or case.

You may want to take a similar approach with your own dialog boxes, hiding a subset of actions that most users won't need most of the time. To do so, you can use two techniques, either separately or in tandem:

- Set the `Visible` property to `False` to hide controls that are located in a displayed part of the dialog box. Set the `Visible` property to `True` when you want to display these controls (after the user presses a More button or some such trigger).
- Increase the height or width (or both) of the dialog box to reveal an area containing further controls. The Find And Replace dialog shown in Figure 15.1 uses the technique of increasing the `Height` property of the box.

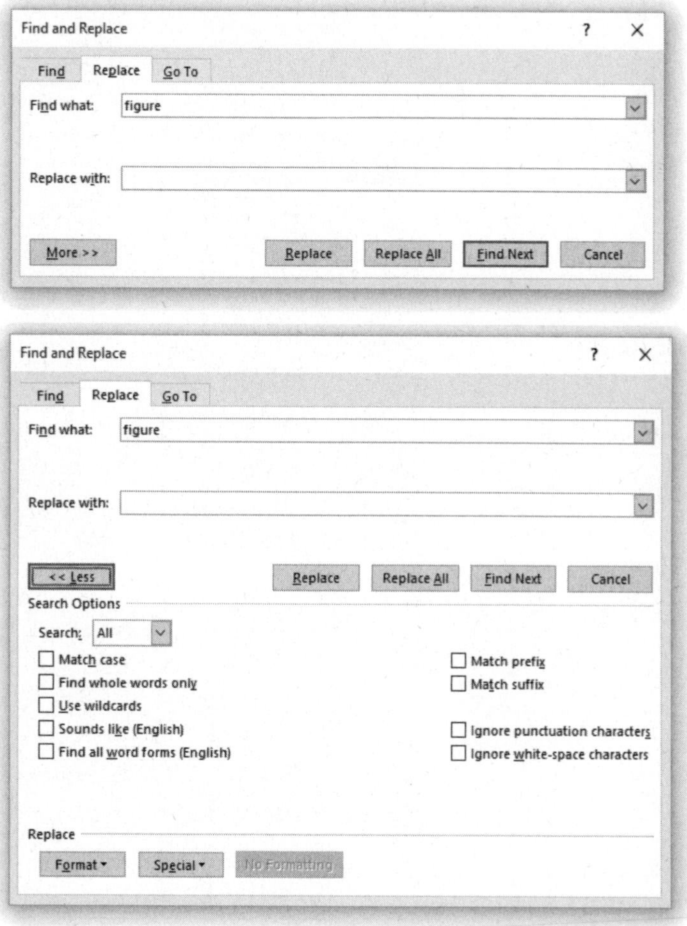

FIGURE 15.1
Word's Find And Replace dialog box hides some of its options (top) until you click the More button to display its lower half (bottom).

As a simple example of the latter technique, consider the dialog box shown in Figure 15.2. When you display the dialog box, only the top part is visible; when you click the More button, the bottom part is displayed. Listing 15.1 contains the code behind the dialog box that makes all this happen.

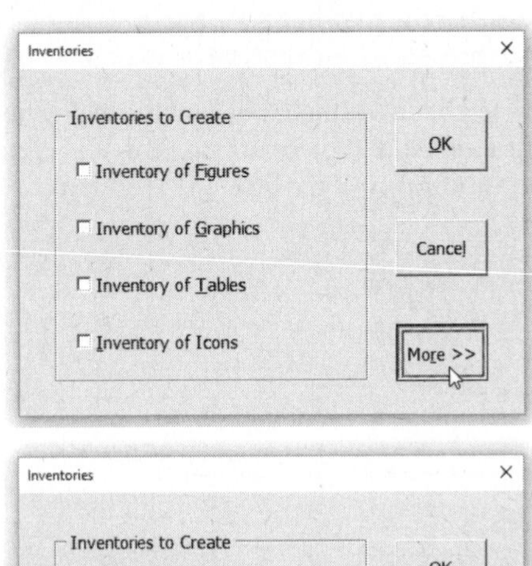

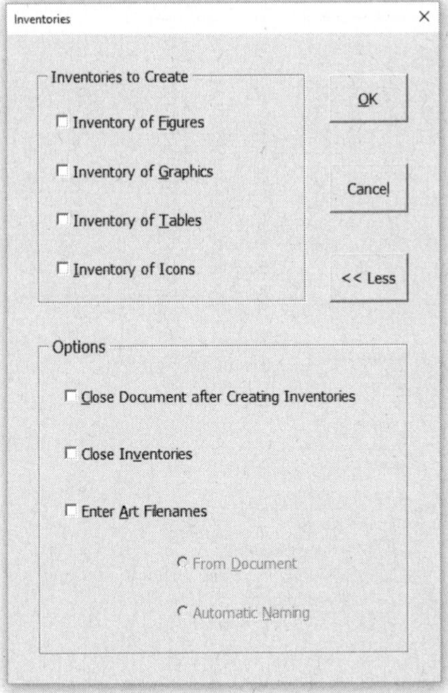

FIGURE 15.2 The top part of this Inventories form offers the most frequently used options. Clicking the More button reveals the rest of the dialog box (shown on the bottom), which contains less-often-used controls.

LISTING 15.1: Revealing part of a dialog box

```
Private Sub UserForm_Initialize()
    frmInventories.Height = 120
End Sub
```

```
Private Sub cmdMore_Click()
    If cmdMore.Caption = "< < Less" Then
        cmdMore.Caption = "More > >"
        cmdMore.Accelerator = "M"
        frmInventories.Height = 120
    Else
        frmInventories.Height = 240
        cmdMore.Caption = "< < Less"
        cmdMore.Accelerator = "L"
        fraOptions.Enabled = True
    End If
End Sub

Private Sub chkArtNames_Click()
    If chkArtNames = True Then
        optFromDocument.Enabled = True
        optFromDocument = True
        optAutoNames.Enabled = True
    Else
        optFromDocument.Enabled = False
        optFromDocument = False
        optAutoNames.Enabled = False
        optAutoNames = False
    End If
End Sub

Private Sub cmdOK_Click()
    frmInventories.Hide
    Unload frmInventories
    'create inventories here
End Sub

Private Sub cmdCancel_Click()
    End
End Sub
```

Listing 15.1 contains five short procedures that control the behavior of the dialog box:

`UserForm_Initialize` Initializes the dialog box before it's displayed.

`cmdMore_Click` Runs when the `cmdMore` button is chosen. This button bears the caption More when only the top half of the dialog box is displayed, and the caption Less when the full dialog box is displayed.

`chkArtNames_Click` Runs when the Enter Art Filenames check box is chosen.

`cmdOK_Click` Runs when the OK button is chosen.

`cmdCancel_Click` Runs when the Cancel button is chosen.

Here's what happens in the code.

- The UserForm_Initialize procedure sets the Height property of the frmInventories user form to 120, which is enough to display only the top part of the dialog box. (To find the appropriate height for your dialog box, drag it to the height that looks right and note the Height property in the Properties window.) This procedure is necessary only if the user form is set to its full height at design time. By setting the user form to a height of 120 at design time, you could avoid having to use a UserForm_Initialize procedure. However, for a user form that has three or more different sizes—or for a user form with two different sizes, one of which needs to be chosen at runtime depending on environmental conditions—you'll need to use a UserForm_Initialize procedure.
- The cmdMore_Click procedure starts by checking in line 6 whether the Caption property of the cmdMore command button is <<Less. If so, that means that the whole dialog box is displayed. Line 7 then sets the Caption property of the cmdMore command button to More > >, the button that will be used to display the bottom part of the dialog box again if necessary. Line 8 sets the Accelerator property of the cmdMore command button to M (to make the *M* in *More* the accelerator key for the button). Line 9 sets the Height property of frmInventories to 120, which is the depth required to show only the top part of the dialog box.

The *Caption* Property Works, but Using a State Variable Is Considered More Elegant

Checking the Caption property of the cmdMore button is an effective way of determining the current state of this form (whether it's expanded or not), but this isn't the most elegant of techniques. It's a form of *hard coding*, considered by many to be a sleazy way of programming. Instead, you could maintain an internal state variable (a Static toggle) in which you store information about whether the dialog box is displayed in its full state or its partial state. Using an internal state variable avoids assuming that this caption will always remain the same. The code would fail to work correctly, for example, if the form were at some point *localized* (adapted for a different language locale, where the words more and less are not used).

If the condition in line 6 is False, execution shifts from line 6 to the Else statement in line 10. This must mean that the Caption property of the cmdMore button is already set to More > >, so the dialog box is displayed in its smaller version and the More > > button is being clicked to expand the dialog box again. Line 11 sets the Height property of the user form to 249, thus displaying the lower part of the dialog box. Line 12 changes the Caption property of the cmdMore command button to < < Less. Line 13 sets the Accelerator property of the cmdMore command button to L.

Line 14 enables the fraOptions frame (identified as Options in the dialog box and disabled in the user form, as are the optFromDocument option button and the optAutoNames option button), making it and the controls it contains available to the user. Line 16 ends the cmdMore_Click procedure.

- The chkArtNames_Click procedure (lines 18 to 29) runs when the Enter Art Filenames check box is clicked. This procedure enables and disables the option buttons below it, as appropriate. Line 19 checks to see if the chkArtNames check box is selected. If it is, the statements in lines 20 through 22 run. Line 20 sets the Enabled property of the optFromDocument option button (identified as From Document in the dialog box) to True, thus making it available, and line 21 selects this option button as the default choice. Line 22 enables optAutoNames, the option button identified as Automatic Naming in the dialog box.

If the chkArtNames check box isn't selected, execution shifts to the Else statement in line 23, which directs execution to line 24. This line sets the Enabled property of the optFromDocument option button to False, disabling it. Line 25 then deselects this option button (whether it's selected or not). Line 26 disables the optAutoNames option button, and line 27 deselects it (again, whether it's selected or not). The End If statement in line 28 ends this If statement, and line 29 ends this procedure.

- The cmdOK_Click procedure in lines 31 to 35 shows the beginning of the procedure that runs once the OK button is clicked. Line 32 hides the Inventories dialog box, and line 33 unloads it from memory. Line 34 contains a comment indicating that the instructions for creating the inventories appear here.
- The cmdCancel_Click procedure contains only an End statement to end execution of the procedure if the user chooses the Cancel button.

Tracking a Procedure in a Form

The next level of complexity in working with forms is using them to track the different stages of a procedure and to guide the user as to how to continue.

Take a look at the Create New Employee Web Page dialog box shown in Figure 15.3. This dialog guides the user through a four-stage procedure to create a web page for a new employee. The first step is to identify the employee deserving of this honor by using either the drop-down list or the Select Other Employee command button in the step 1 frame. The second step is to enter suitable introductory, critical, or laudatory text about the employee. The third step is to select the most (or perhaps least) flattering photo of the employee to include in the web page. The fourth step is to save the web page to a folder on the company's intranet.

When the user first displays the Create New Employee Web Page dialog box, they will see the version of the dialog box shown in Figure 15.3, with steps 2, 3, and 4 disabled and instructions for step 1 shown in the Instructions box at the top.

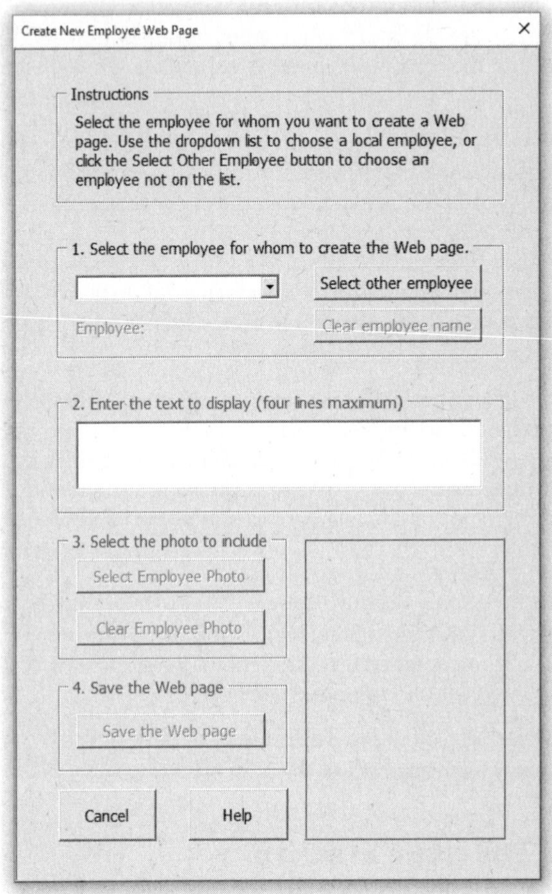

FIGURE 15.3 The Create New Employee Web Page form provides users with instructions that are dynamically updated as they work their way through the procedure.

When the user follows the instructions and selects the employee by using either the combo box drop-down list or the Select Other Employee command button, the code attached to the combo box drop-down list or the command button enables the step 2 frame, making its text box available to the user, as shown in Figure 15.4. Here is the code for the `Change` event of the `cmbSelectEmployee` combo box; the code for the `Click` event of the `cmdSelectOtherEmployee` command button is similar, although a little more complex.

```
Private Sub cmbSelectEmployee_Change()
  lblEmployeeName = cmbSelectEmployee.Text
  fraStep2.Enabled = True
  lblInstructions = "Enter text in the Step 2 text box. " & _
    "For example, you might include brief biographical " & _
    "information on the employee, details of their position, " & _
    "or your hopes for their contribution to the company."
  cmdClearEmployeeName.Enabled = True
End Sub
```

AN ELLIPSIS SIGNALS THAT A DIALOG BOX CAN BE DISPLAYED

The Select Other Employee button in the Create New Employee Web Page dialog box ends with an ellipsis (...), as do some of the other command buttons. This ellipsis is the Windows convention for indicating that the choice (here a command button, but also other contexts) results in a dialog box being displayed rather than an action being taken immediately.

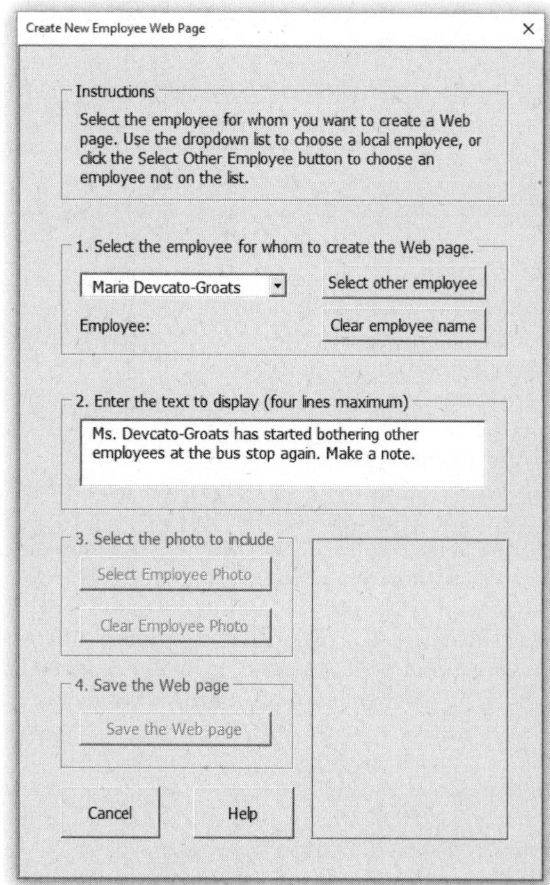

FIGURE 15.4
The second stage of the Create New Employee Web Page dialog box. Notice the changes from the first stage: The instructions in the Instructions frame have changed, and the use of the step 1 combo box drop-down list has enabled the step 2 frame.

These are the changes that occur when the user completes step 1 of the dialog box:

- The text of the label in the Instructions box at the top of the dialog box is changed to contain information about step 2 of the procedure.
- The name of the employee selected by the user is listed above the Employee label in the step 1 frame.
- The frame for step 2 is enabled (the text box it contains is enabled along with the frame).

Using Multipage Dialog Boxes and TabStrip Controls

VBA includes a MultiPage control, which enables you to create multipage dialog boxes, and a TabStrip control, which lets you create dialog boxes driven by TabStrips (similar to the tabs on the Office applications' Ribbon). You've almost certainly used multipage dialog boxes (if you're not sure what they are, press Ctrl+D in Word to open the Font dialog box and see an example of one). You can access any page (one at a time) by clicking the tab at the top of the page. Each page contains a different set of controls and can have a different layout appropriate to the page's purpose.

A TAB IS NOT A PAGE

The tab is the little thing that sticks out from the top of the page, not the whole page itself. Many people refer to the pages as "tabs" because the tab is the part you click to access the page. It's perfectly okay to use these terms interchangeably, but this discussion uses *tab* to mean only the tab component and *page* to refer to the page qua page.

Multipage dialog boxes are great for packing a lot of information into a single form without having it take up the whole screen with a bewildering embarrassment of options. You'll need to divide the information into discrete sets of related information to fit it onto the pages. Each page can (and should) have a different layout of controls that govern the behavior of discrete items; the pages are normally separate in theme or purpose. Again, the Font dialog boxes in the Office applications have a Font tab and an Advanced tab. Look at the Tools ➤ Options dialog box in the VBA Editor for another example.

A dialog box that uses a TabStrip differs from a multipage dialog box in that it contains a TabStrip control containing multiple *tabs* but not multiple *pages*. To the user, it looks as if different pages are being displayed, but the actual layout of the controls in the dialog box doesn't change. No matter which tab on the TabStrip is selected, the set of controls remains the same, although the data displayed in the controls does change. This approach is useful for displaying records from a database. The tabs merely switch to a different record.

TabStrips are useful when you need to display consistent sets of information, such as the records you might maintain on your company's customers. Each customer record has the same set of fields (analogous to the columns in a database): an account number, a name (perhaps several), an address, phone numbers, email addresses, URLs, an order history, an account balance, and so on. Therefore, you can use the same set of controls (text boxes and labels, for example) to display the information for each record. The TabStrip control governs which customer's set of information is displayed in them. Because few databases have a small and fixed number of records, you'll need to populate the TabStrip on the fly (during execution) with tabs and captions, but it works fine.

Table 14.7 in Chapter 14, "Creating Simple Custom Dialog Boxes," explains the properties unique to the TabStrip control and MultiPage control.

Using Multipage Dialog Boxes

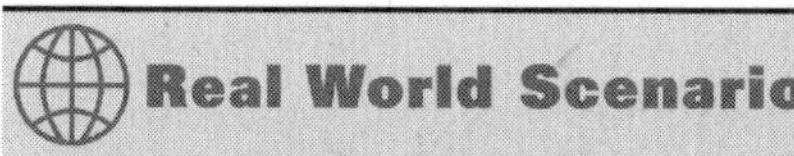

Limit the Number of Pages in Your Multipage Dialog Boxes

You can create dialog boxes containing dozens of tabs or dozens of pages. And if you run out of horizontal space to display the tabs, the VBA Editor adds a scroll bar to enable the user to scroll through the tabs. However, gigantic tab dialog boxes are impractical in the real world. As you doubtless know, not everything that's possible is also desirable.

You'll probably want to avoid creating multipage dialog boxes with more than 10 or 12 pages because the wealth of information such a dialog box will contain is likely to overwhelm the user.

If you need more than a dozen pages to organize the information in a dialog box, you're probably trying to present the user with too much data at once. Consider an alternative way of displaying it. (Most likely, you should subdivide the information into smaller, easier-to-manage categories.) For example, Microsoft spends countless hours spread over several years testing focus groups, quizzing users, and observing people's behavior when using Word. One result is that Microsoft's designers subdivide tasks and user interaction into various subcategories. Click the Layout tab in the Word Ribbon. Notice that the many tasks within this category are subdivided into logical areas: Page Setup, Paragraph, and Arrange. What's more, two of these subcategories—Page Setup and Paragraph—display small icons (a box with a black arrow) in the lower-right corner. Clicking these icons opens a separate dialog box with additional, less frequently used, options.

Tabs are a different matter. If you use a TabStrip to move through the records in a database recordset, you may need to use quite a few tabs in a given TabStrip. Unless the number of tabs is absurdly large, this shouldn't normally be a problem. However, a better solution if you're attempting to manage a database might be to switch to one of the more robust, specialized database-related user interface controls available in Access, Visual Basic Express, or Visual Basic .NET. For more information about various Visual Studio 2015 products, see

`www.visualstudio.com/en-us`

To create a multipage dialog box, click the MultiPage icon in the Toolbox, and then click in the user form where you want the control to appear. The VBA Editor places a two-page MultiPage control with tabs that have the labels `Page 1` and `Page 2`. You can then move and size the control as usual. In typical usage, you'll want to create a MultiPage control that's only a little smaller than the user form it inhabits (like most of the multipage dialog boxes you'll see in Windows applications).

Once you've created a MultiPage control, you work with a page on it by right-clicking its tab and using the resulting context menu:

- To add a page, right-click the label and choose New Page from the context menu. VBA will add a new page of the default size and will name it `Page`*n*, where *n* is the next number after the current number of pages (even if the other pages have names other than `Page1`, `Page2`, and so on).
- To rename a page in a MultiPage control, right-click the label and choose Rename from the context menu. In the Rename dialog box (see Figure 15.5), enter the caption (the label text) for the page in the Caption text box, the accelerator key in the Accelerator Key text box, and any control-tip text (the tip the user sees when they move the mouse pointer over the tab for the page) in the Control Tip Text text box. Click the OK button to close the Rename dialog box.

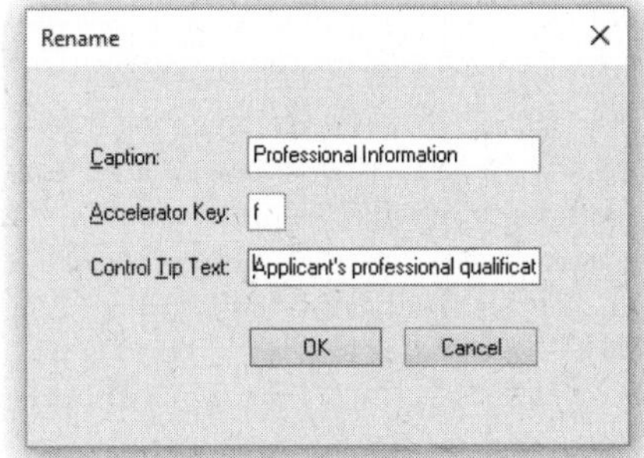

FIGURE 15.5 Use the Rename dialog box to set the caption, accelerator key, and control-tip text for a page.

- To delete a page from a MultiPage control, right-click the label and choose Delete Page from the context menu. The VBA Editor will remove the page without prompting for confirmation.
- To move a page to a different place in the MultiPage control, right-click the label and choose Move from the context menu to display the Page Order dialog box (see Figure 15.6). In the Page Order list box, select the page or pages that you want to move (Shift+click to select multiple contiguous pages, Ctrl+click to select multiple, noncontiguous pages), and then use the Move Up and Move Down buttons to rearrange the page or pages as desired. When you've finished, click the OK button to close the Page Order dialog box.

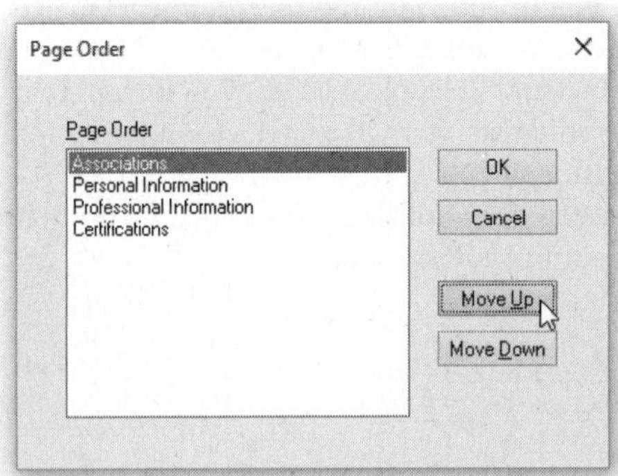

FIGURE 15.6 Use the Move Up and Move Down buttons in the Page Order dialog box to change the order of pages in a MultiPage control.

- To specify which page of a multipage dialog box to display by default, use the `Value` property of the MultiPage control. You can set this property either at design time or at runtime. For example, you could use an initialization procedure such as the one shown here to display the third page (identified by the value 2, because the page numbering starts at 0) of a dialog box with a MultiPage control called `MyMulti` at runtime:

```
Sub UserForm_Initialize()
  MyMulti.Value = 2
End Sub
```

Once you've created a multipage dialog box, you can populate its pages with controls using the techniques you learned in Chapter 14. Each control must have a unique name in the entire form (not just within the page on which it appears).

When designing a multipage dialog box, keep the following issues in mind:

- What's the best way to divide the information or options in the dialog box? What belongs on which page? Which information or options will the user expect to find grouped together?
- Which controls should appear on each page? Most dialog boxes need at least a pair of command buttons—such as OK and Cancel (or End or Close)—available from each page to allow the user to dismiss the dialog box from whichever page they happen to end up on. In rare instances, you may want to force the user to return to a particular page in order to close a dialog box. In these cases, make sure each page that doesn't contain a command button to dismiss the dialog box tells the user where they will find such a command button.
- For settings, do you need to have an Apply button (as well as an OK button) to apply the changes on a particular page without closing the dialog box?

Because each control in a multipage form has a unique name, when returning information from a multipage dialog box you need specify only the relevant object—you don't need to specify which page it's on.

Figure 15.7 shows an example of a multipage dialog box. The first page contains the customer's personal contact information; the second, the customer's professional information; the third, the associations the customer belongs to; and the fourth, the certifications the customer holds.

Most of the properties of the MultiPage control are straightforward, but a few deserve special mention:

- The `Style` property offers `fmStyleTabs` (the default setting, showing tabs for navigating between the pages), `fmStyleButtons` (which gives each page a rectangular button, with the button for the current page appearing pushed in), or `fmStyleNone` (which provides no means of navigating between the pages and no indication of the borders of the multipage dialog box). `fmStyleNone` can be useful for creating user forms that have two or more alternative layouts of which the user will only ever need to see one at a time. By including one set of controls on one page of the multipage dialog box and another set of controls on another page, you can present two seemingly different dialog boxes by doing nothing more than changing which page of the MultiPage control is displayed. For example, you can use this technique to create one of those "wizards" that guides the user through a multistep process. Just add a Next button that they click to move to each subsequent step.

- The `TabOrientation` property controls where the tabs (or buttons) for the pages appear on the control. Your choices are `fmTabOrientationTop` (the default setting, placing the tabs at the top of the control), `fmTabOrientationBottom`, `fmTabOrientationLeft`, and `fmTabOrientationRight`. Experiment with the effects that the bottom, left, and right orientations offer, but unless they provide significant advantages over the more normal top orientation, use them sparingly—if at all. Users won't thank you for deviating from the traditional, familiar interface unnecessarily.
- The `MultiRow` property controls whether a MultiPage control has one row of tabs for its pages (`False`) or multiple rows (`True`). When you have `MultiRow` set to `True`, the VBA Editor adds the second or subsequent rows of tabs when you run out of space on the first or current row.

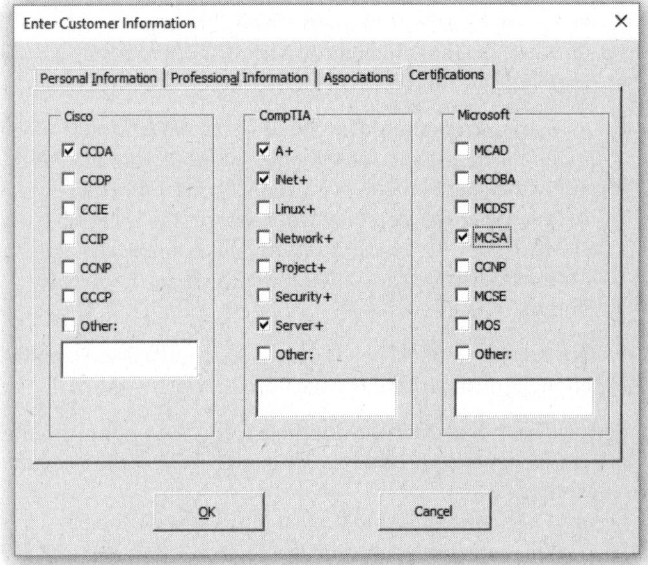

FIGURE 15.7 By using multiple pages in a dialog box, you can achieve a clean and uncluttered look that's also easily navigable.

The MultiPage control doesn't have to take up the whole dialog box—in fact, most dialog boxes keep the key command buttons such as OK and Cancel outside the multipage area so that they're available to the user no matter which page the user is on.

That said, it is usually a good idea to make a MultiPage control the *dominant* part of a dialog box. In a complex and busy dialog box, a small MultiPage control can appear to be little more than a group box, and the user may miss the tabs, particularly if they're just skimming the controls looking for a particular option.

USING THE TABSTRIP CONTROL

Forms that use a TabStrip are substantially different from multipage dialog boxes. A TabStrip control can be used not to rearrange other controls, but to just change the data that appears in them as the user moves from one set of data to another. In other words, the layout of the controls remains static. Only the values displayed in the controls change from page to page on the strip.

For instance, you might use a dialog box driven by a TabStrip to view and update the records in a data source such as a Word table, an Excel spreadsheet, or an Access database. This next example uses an Excel workbook in which information is stored on a number of worksheets. Figure 15.8 shows the DataSurfer dialog box, which is driven by a TabStrip.

The actual strip of tabs in a TabStrip control can appear above, below, or beside the controls that it contains. Above is the conventional—and default—position, just as it is in real-world recipe-card boxes and file drawers. But vertical and bottom tabs have shown up in eccentric Windows applications from time to time. As with the MultiPage control, use the `TabOrientation` property of the TabStrip control to specify whether the TabStrip should appear at the top, bottom, left, or right of its control. But be sure to have a pretty good reason if you're departing from convention. The top position is expected and makes the most sense.

FIGURE 15.8
Using a TabStrip control to create a multitab dialog box. The TabStrip is used to control which set of information is displayed in the other controls in the dialog box.

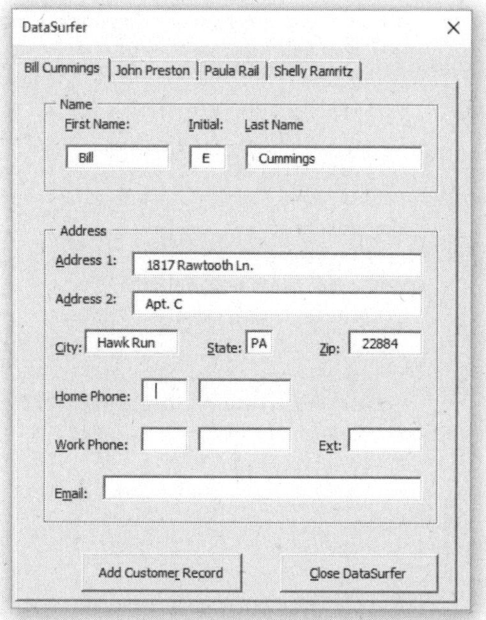

The TabStrip can contain zero, one, or more tabs. For most purposes, there's little point in having only one tab on a TabStrip, and even less in having no tab at all. But if you dynamically populate the TabStrip with tabs in your procedures (as you're about to do in this next example) and create one tab for each record found, you may run into situations with only one record and, thus, a dialog box with only one tab—or even a TabStrip without any tabs at all.

Click the TabStrip button on the Toolbox, click in the user form to place the TabStrip, and then drag it to an appropriate size. Bear in mind that a TabStrip is only a visual display for the user's benefit. Unlike the MultiPage control, you establish the logical connection between the

TabStrip and the other controls through code. You can then add, rename, move, and delete tabs in the same way as you can pages in a MultiPage control.

If you haven't placed the other controls for the dialog box, do so now.

Once everything's in place, you write the code that will enable the TabStrip to display the contents of the other controls. Listing 15.2 shows the code for the TabStrip in the DataSurfer dialog box. This TabStrip is named `tabSurfer`, and the code works with its `Change` event—the event procedure that *fires* (is triggered and executes its code) when the user clicks a new tab on the strip.

LISTING 15.2: Programming a TabStrip

```
Private Sub tabSurfer_Change()
    If blnInitializing = False Then
        With ActiveWorkbook.Sheets(tabSurfer.Value + 1)
            'load the contents of the worksheet that corresponds _
             to the tab chosen
            .Activate
            txtFirstName.Text = .Cells(1, 2).Text
            txtInitial.Text = .Cells(2, 2).Text
            txtLastName.Text = .Cells(3, 2).Text
            txtAddress1.Text = .Cells(4, 2).Text
            txtAddress2.Text = .Cells(5, 2).Text
            txtCity.Text = .Cells(6, 2).Text
            txtState.Text = .Cells(7, 2)
            txtZip.Text = .Cells(8, 2).Text
            txtHomeArea.Text = .Cells(9, 2).Text
            txtHomePhone.Text = .Cells(10, 2).Text
            txtWorkArea.Text = .Cells(11, 2).Text
            txtWorkPhone.Text = .Cells(12, 2).Text
            txtWorkExtension.Text = .Cells(13, 2).Text
            txtEmail.Text = .Cells(14, 2).Text
        End With
    End If
End Sub
```

After specifying the worksheet, the code in Listing 15.2 essentially repeats itself for each of the text boxes that appear in the DataSurfer dialog box. This dialog box works with a data source implemented as Excel spreadsheets in the active workbook.

Each worksheet in the workbook holds one customer's record, with the name of the customer appearing on the worksheet's tab and the customer's data appearing in the second column: the first name in the first cell of the second column, the middle initial in the second cell, the last name in the third cell, and so on for the address, phone numbers (both home and work), and email address. So, to get at any piece of information, you need to know the sheet of the record in question and the appropriate cell in the second column.

Here's how the code works:

- Line 1 declares the procedure `tabSurfer_Change`, which executes automatically whenever the `Change` event of the `tabSurfer` TabStrip fires. The `Change` event fires each time the user clicks a new tab, so you use this event to control the information displayed in the text boxes.
- The `Change` event also fires when a tab is added to (or removed from) the TabStrip. Because the DataSurfer user form uses the `Initialize` event procedure to populate the TabStrip with tabs (one per worksheet in the workbook), you do need to prevent the `Change` event procedure from running unnecessarily during the initialization phase of your program. So, the user form declares a private Boolean variable named `blnInitializing` that the `Initialize` procedure sets to `True` while it's running and to `False` just before it ends. Line 2 of the `Change` event procedure checks to make sure that `blnInitializing` is `False`. If it's not, the `Initialize` procedure has fired the event, and the `Change` procedure does not need to load the information into the cells—so execution continues at line 21, just before the end of the procedure. But once the `Initialize` procedure has finished running, `blnInitializing` will be set to `False`, and the `Change` event procedure will run each time the user changes tabs in the TabStrip.
- Line 3 begins a `With` statement that works with the appropriate worksheet in the active workbook: (`ActiveWorkbook.Sheets(tabSurfer.Value + 1)`. The `Value` property of the `tabSurfer` TabStrip tells us which tab in the TabStrip is selected. Because the first tab in the TabStrip is numbered 0 and the first worksheet in the workbook is numbered 1, you need to add 1 to the `Value` of the TabStrip to even the numbers.
- Line 4 is a comment. Line 5 uses the `Activate` method to activate the worksheet in question.
- Lines 6 through 19 then set the `Text` property of each text box in the user form to the contents of the corresponding cell in the second column on the worksheet. For example, line 6 sets the `Text` property of the `txtFirstName` text box (which appears under the First Name label in the dialog box) to the contents of the first cell in the second column: `.Cells(1, 2).Text`.
- Line 20 ends the `With` statement, line 21 ends the `If` statement, and line 22 ends the procedure.

Using Pictures in Forms

VBA includes extensive graphics capabilities that allow you to make your forms look pretty much any way you want them to. This book doesn't go into design aesthetics in any detail, but there's much you can do to make your forms look good. You can fiddle with Format ➢ Order to pile controls on top of each other. Controls like the command button have their own Picture properties, as do forms themselves. Take a look at Figure 15.9. It shows an image control displaying a photo, a background texture (loaded into the form's Picture property), and a command button that blends into the background (because its BackStyle property is set to Transparent).

To use an Image control, click the Image button in the Toolbox, and then click in the user form where you want the Image control to appear. Once you've placed the Image control, you can size and move the picture just as you would any other control.

Ensure That You Include Any Necessary Graphics Files When You Deploy a Macro

Make sure the picture you choose for an Image control or a user form's background is available to all computers that will display the dialog box. If the picture isn't available, it fails to appear in the dialog box, which spoils the effect.

Figure 15.9
VBA includes extensive graphics features—you can make your forms look any way you want them to.

To choose the picture that will appear in the Image control, select the `Picture` property in the Properties window and click the ellipsis button that then appears to the right of the entry. The VBA Editor displays the Load Picture dialog box. Select the picture file and choose the Open button. The `Picture` property in the Properties window registers the type of picture you selected—such as `Bitmap`—but not its filename, and the picture appears in the Image control so that you can see if it's an appropriate size.

LOADING A PICTURE INTO AN IMAGE CONTROL PROGRAMMATICALLY

When specifying the picture for an Image control *programmatically* (the picture is loaded while the macro is executing, during runtime), you need to use a `LoadPicture` statement. Compare that to how, when programming (design time) you can simply use the Properties window to assign a picture to the `Picture` property of the Image control. `LoadPicture` has the following syntax:

```
LoadPicture filename, [WidthDesired], [HeightDesired]
```

`filename` is a String argument specifying the name of the picture file to be loaded into the Image control. *`WidthDesired`* is an optional Long argument specifying the width of the picture in twips, and *`HeightDesired`* is an optional Long argument specifying the height of the picture.

For example, the following statement loads the picture named `Rose.jpg` that's located in the `C:\` root directory

```
Image1.Picture = LoadPicture("C:\rose.jpg")
```

Once you've chosen the picture, you have various options for positioning it and formatting it:

- If necessary, set the alignment of the picture by using the `PictureAlignment` property. (If the picture fully fills the Image control—neither overlapping it nor leaving parts of it empty—you may not need to set the alignment for it.) Table 15.1 shows the constants and values for the `PictureAlignment` property.
- If necessary, clip, stretch, or zoom the picture by using the `PictureSizeMode` property: `fmPictureSizeModeClip` (`0`) clips the picture to fit the Image control; `fmPictureSize-ModeStretch` (1) stretches or squeezes the picture so that it fits the Image control (this option often makes for strange effects); and `fmPictureSizeModeZoom` (2) enlarges or reduces the picture so that its nearest dimension exactly fits the width or height of the Image control without changing the picture's proportions (this option usually leaves an unfilled gap on the other side).
- If you need to tile the image to take up the remaining space in the control, set the `PictureTiling` property to `True`. This option is rarely used with database work.
- If you need to adjust the position of the picture relative to its caption, set the `PicturePosition` property of the check box, command button, label, option button, or toggle button in question. Table 15.2 shows the constants and values for `PicturePosition`.

TABLE 15.1: Constants and values for the `PictureAlignment` property

CONSTANT	VALUE	PICTURE ALIGNMENT IN IMAGE CONTROL
`fmPictureAlignmentTopLeft`	0	Top left
`fmPictureAlignmentTopRight`	1	Top right

TABLE 15.1: Constants and values for the PicturePosition property *(CONTINUED)*

CONSTANT	VALUE	PICTURE ALIGNMENT IN IMAGE CONTROL
`fmPictureAlignmentCenter`	2	Centered
`fmPictureAlignmentBottomLeft`	3	Bottom left
`fmPictureAlignmentBottomRight`	4	Bottom right

TABLE 15.2: Constants and values for the `PicturePosition` property

CONSTANT	VALUE	PICTURE POSITION	CAPTION ALIGNMENT
`fmPicturePositionLeftTop`	0	Left of the caption	With top of picture
`fmPicturePositionLeftCenter`	1	Left of the caption	Centered on picture
`fmPicturePositionLeftBottom`	2	Left of the caption	With bottom of picture
`fmPicturePositionRightTop`	3	Right of the caption	With top of picture
`fmPicturePositionRightCenter`	4	Right of the caption	Centered on picture
`fmPicturePositionRightBottom`	5	Right of the caption	With bottom of picture
`fmPicturePositionAboveLeft`	6	Above the caption	With left edge of picture
`fmPicturePositionAboveCenter`	7	Above the caption	Centered below picture (the default setting)
`fmPicturePositionAboveRight`	8	Above the caption	With right edge of picture
`fmPicturePositionBelowLeft`	9	Below the caption	With left edge of picture
`fmPicturePositionBelowCenter`	10	Below the caption	Centered above picture
`fmPicturePositionBelowRight`	11	Below the caption	With right edge of picture
`fmPicturePositionCenter`	12	In center of control	Centered horizontally and vertically on top of picture

Once you've placed, sized, and formatted a picture, there are various possibilities for what you can do with it, such as using a picture's `Click` event to trigger an action. For example, you could display two graphics illustrating a choice of two formats for a document. Then the user could click the appropriate picture to signal their choice.

Creating a Modeless Dialog Box

We're using VBA version 7.1, and ever since version 6 the language has offered the programmer an option to create a *modeless* dialog box—one that users can leave onscreen while they continue to work in their application. In other words, with a modal dialog box, the user must click an OK or Cancel button or otherwise dismiss the dialog box before they can regain the ability to interact with their application.

You're doubtless familiar with modeless dialog boxes from working with Office. For example, the Find And Replace dialog box in Access, Word, and Excel is modeless, as is the Replace dialog box in PowerPoint.

When you display one of these modeless dialog boxes, it takes the *focus* just as any modal dialog box does (whatever you type on the keyboard goes into the window with the current focus).

But you can click in the application window to transfer the focus back to that window. For example, you can continue typing in a Word document, even while the Find And Replace dialog box remains visible.

Creating a modeless dialog box is as simple as setting the `ShowModal` property of the user form to `False` from its default setting of `True`.

There are various situations where you might want to use a modeless dialog box rather than a modal one. As a simple example, you might create a procedure and dialog box in Word that collects information from the user for a memo or a report. By making the dialog box modeless, you could allow the user to copy information from an open document (or open other documents and gather information from them) and paste it into the dialog box—saving users from having to copy the information before invoking the dialog box and allowing them to copy multiple separate items easily. Likewise, you could create a modeless user form (perhaps shaped like a toolbar) that users could keep onscreen and use to automatically enter text into predefined sections of three or four other documents without losing their place in the current document.

You can also use modeless dialog boxes to display complex sets of interrelated user forms in which the user needs to copy and paste information from one user form to another or at least to access different areas of two or more displayed user forms at the same time. Displaying multiple forms at once can be confusing to the user, but you may sometimes find it necessary.

Most of the time, you'll probably want to use modal dialog boxes in your VBA procedures. With modal dialog boxes, users must deal with the dialog box before they can continue to work in the application, and there's no risk that they'll end up with multiple dialog boxes scattered around the screen in assorted states of disuse.

You Can Use Serial Modal Dialog Boxes

You can't display both modal and modeless user forms at the same time, but you can display one modal dialog box from another modal dialog box. When users close the second modal dialog box, VBA returns them to the first modal dialog box by default. However, you can write code to make the second modal dialog box automatically close the first dialog box after it closes itself.

Specifying a Form's Location Onscreen

By default, VBA centers a dialog box on the middle of the application window as much as possible, which is the normal behavior for Windows applications. If you want to position a form elsewhere on the screen (for example, to avoid obscuring important data onscreen), set the `StartUpPosition` property for the user form. Table 15.3 explains the settings you can use.

TABLE 15.3: `StartUpPosition` property settings

PROPERTY	VALUE	EFFECT
`Manual`	0	Displays the user form in the upper-left corner of the Windows Desktop.
`CenterOwner`	1	Centers the user form horizontally and vertically in the *owner* application—the application to which the user form belongs.
`CenterScreen`	2	Centers the user form horizontally and vertically on the Desktop. In a multimonitor arrangement, this value centers the user form on the monitor containing the active window.
`WindowsDefault`	3	Displays the user form in the default position for Windows dialog boxes.

Using Events to Control Forms

This section discusses the events built into VBA for use with forms and with individual controls to give the programmer fine control over how user forms look and behave.

So far in this chapter, you've used three of the most useful events:

- You used the `Initialize` event to add items to list boxes just before a form is loaded and to adjust the number of tabs on a TabStrip.
- You used the `Click` event to take action when the user clicks a particular control in a user form. So far you've been using `Click` mostly for command buttons, but you can use it for just about any control—including the user form itself.
- You used the `Change` event to control what happens when the user changes the tab displayed on a TabStrip.

Table 15.4 lists the events that VBA supports and the objects and controls with which each can be used.

Table 15.4: Events that VBA supports and the objects and controls associated with them

Event	Occurs	Applies to These Controls and Objects
`Activate`	When the user form becomes the active window	UserForm
`Deactivate`	When the user form ceases to be the active window	UserForm
`AddControl`	When a control is added at runtime	Frame, MultiPage, UserForm
`AfterUpdate`	After the user has changed data in a control	CheckBox, ComboBox, CommandButton, Frame, Image, Label, ListBox, MultiPage, OptionButton, ScrollBar, SpinButton, TabStrip, TextBox, ToggleButton, UserForm
`BeforeDragOver`	When the user is performing a drag-and-drop operation	CheckBox, ComboBox, CommandButton, Frame, Image, Label, ListBox, MultiPage, OptionButton, ScrollBar, SpinButton, TabStrip, TextBox, ToggleButton, UserForm
`BeforeDropOrPaste`	When the user is about to release a dragged item or about to paste an item	CheckBox, ComboBox, CommandButton, Frame, Image, Label, ListBox, MultiPage, OptionButton, ScrollBar, SpinButton, TabStrip, TextBox, ToggleButton, UserForm
`BeforeUpdate`	When the user has changed data in the control before the new data appears in the control	CheckBox, ComboBox, ListBox, OptionButton, ScrollBar, SpinButton, TextBox, ToggleButton
`Change`	When the `Value` property of a control changes	CheckBox, ComboBox, ListBox, MultiPage, OptionButton, ScrollBar, SpinButton, TabStrip, TextBox, ToggleButton
`Click`	When the user clicks a control or object with the left mouse button	CheckBox, ComboBox, CommandButton, Frame, Image, Label, ListBox, MultiPage, OptionButton, TabStrip, ToggleButton, UserForm
`DblClick`	When the user double-clicks a control or object with the left mouse button	CheckBox, ComboBox, CommandButton, Frame, Image, Label, ListBox, MultiPage, OptionButton, TabStrip, TextBox, ToggleButton, UserForm

TABLE 15.4: Events that VBA supports and the objects and controls *(CONTINUED)*

EVENT	OCCURS	APPLIES TO THESE CONTROLS AND OBJECTS
`DropButtonClick`	When the user displays or hides a drop-down list	ComboBox, TextBox
`Enter`	Just before one control on a user form receives the focus from another control	CheckBox, ComboBox, CommandButton, Frame, ListBox, MultiPage, OptionButton, ScrollBar, SpinButton, TabStrip, TextBox, ToggleButton
`Exit`	Just before one control on a user form loses the focus to another control	CheckBox, ComboBox, CommandButton, Frame, ListBox, MultiPage, OptionButton, ScrollBar, SpinButton, TabStrip, TextBox, ToggleButton
`Error`	When a control or object encounters an error	CheckBox, ComboBox, CommandButton, Frame, Image, Label, ListBox, MultiPage, OptionButton, ScrollBar, SpinButton, TabStrip, TextBox, ToggleButton, UserForm
`Initialize`	After a user form is loaded but before it's displayed	UserForm
`KeyDown`	When the user presses a key on the keyboard	CheckBox, ComboBox, CommandButton, Frame, ListBox, MultiPage, OptionButton, ScrollBar, SpinButton, TabStrip, TextBox, ToggleButton, UserForm
`KeyUp`	When the user releases a key they've pressed on the keyboard	CheckBox, ComboBox, CommandButton, Frame, ListBox, MultiPage, OptionButton, ScrollBar, SpinButton, TabStrip, TextBox, ToggleButton, UserForm
`KeyPress`	When the user presses an ANSI key on the keyboard	CheckBox, ComboBox, CommandButton, Frame, ListBox, MultiPage, OptionButton, ScrollBar, SpinButton, TabStrip, TextBox, ToggleButton, UserForm
`Layout`	When the size of a frame, multipage, or user form changes	Frame, MultiPage, UserForm
`MouseDown`	When the user presses the left mouse button	CheckBox, ComboBox, CommandButton, Frame, Image, Label, ListBox, MultiPage, OptionButton, ScrollBar, SpinButton, TabStrip, TextBox, ToggleButton, UserForm

TABLE 15.4: Events that VBA supports and the objects and controls *(CONTINUED)*

EVENT	OCCURS	APPLIES TO THESE CONTROLS AND OBJECTS
`MouseUp`	When the user releases the left mouse button (after pressing it)	CheckBox, ComboBox, CommandButton, Frame, Image, Label, ListBox, MultiPage, OptionButton, ScrollBar, SpinButton, TabStrip, TextBox, ToggleButton, UserForm
`MouseMove`	When the user moves the mouse	CheckBox, ComboBox, CommandButton, Frame, Image, Label, ListBox, MultiPage, OptionButton, TabStrip, TextBox, ToggleButton, UserForm
`QueryClose`	When a user form is about to close	UserForm
`RemoveControl`	When a control is deleted	Frame, MultiPage, UserForm
`Resize`	When a user form is resized	UserForm
`Scroll`	When the user moves the scroll box	Frame, MultiPage, ScrollBar, UserForm
`SpinDown`	When the user clicks the Down button on a SpinButton control	SpinButton
`SpinUp`	When the user clicks the Up button on a SpinButton control	SpinButton
`Terminate`	When a user form has been unloaded from memory	UserForm
`Zoom`	When the `Zoom` property of the control or user form changes	Frame, MultiPage, UserForm

The `ByVal` keyword is used to pass arguments between procedures. When used with forms, it can return `ReturnBoolean`, `ReturnEffect`, `ReturnInteger`, and `ReturnString` objects.

As you can see, VBA's events fall into several categories, which are discussed in the following sections in descending order of usefulness:

- Events that apply only to the `UserForm` object
- Events that apply to the `UserForm` object and other container objects (such as the Frame control and the MultiPage control)
- Events that apply to many or most of the controls, sometimes including the `UserForm` object as well
- Events that apply only to a few controls

Events Unique to the *UserForm* Object

This section discusses the events that are unique to the UserForm object. These are the Initialize, QueryClose, Activate, Deactivate, Resize, and Terminate events.

Initialize Event

An Initialize event occurs when the user form is loaded but before it appears onscreen.

VBA's syntax for the Initialize event is as follows, where *userform* is a valid UserForm object:

```
Private Sub userform_Initialize()
```

Typical uses for the Initialize event include retrieving information—from a database, a set of worksheets, or whatever—that the user form or application needs and assigning information to the controls on the user form (especially ListBox and ComboBox controls, to which you often need to add the information at runtime rather than at design time).

Depending on the style and complexity of your user forms, you may also want to use the Initialize event to resize the user form, resize controls on the user form, display or hide particular controls, and in general make sure the user form is as closely suited as possible to the user's needs before displaying it.

QueryClose Event

The QueryClose event applies to the UserForm object only. This event fires just before the user form closes.

The syntax for the QueryClose event is as follows:

```
Private Sub UserForm_QueryClose(Cancel As Integer, CloseMode As Integer)
```

Here, Cancel is an integer, typically 0 (zero). A nonzero value prevents the QueryClose event from firing and stops the user form (and the application) from closing.

CloseMode is a value or a constant giving the cause of the QueryClose event. Table 15.5 shows the values and constants for CloseMode.

Table 15.5: Values and constants for the CloseMode argument

Constant	Value	Cause of the QueryClose Event
vbFormControlMenu	0	The user has closed the user form by clicking its Close button or by invoking the Close command from the user form's control menu (for example, by right-clicking the title bar of the user form and choosing Close from the context menu).
vbFormCode	1	An Unload statement in code has closed the user form.
vbAppWindows	2	Windows is closing down and is closing the user form.
vbAppTaskManager	3	The Task Manager is closing the application and, thus, is also closing the user form.

At first glance, QueryClose may appear to have few uses beyond double-checking that users really want to close a user form that they're attempting to close. Say that you have established that users had entered a lot of data in a form they were about to close. You might want to check that they hadn't clicked the user form's Close button or Cancel button by mistake, as illustrated in the following code fragment for Word:

```
Private Sub UserForm_QueryClose(Cancel As Integer, _
    CloseMode As Integer)
    'make sure the user wants to close the user form
    'if they have entered information in it
    Select Case CloseMode
        Case 0
            'user has clicked the close button or invoked an Unload statement
            'if text box contains more than 5 characters, ask to save it
            If Len(txtDescription.Text) > 5 Then
                If MsgBox("The Description text box contains " & _
                    "a significant amount of text." & vbCr & _
                    "Do you want to save this text?", vbYesNo + _
                    vbQuestion, "Close Form") <> 0 Then
                    Documents.Add
                    Selection.TypeText txtDescription.Text
                    ActiveDocument.SaveAs _
                        "c:\temp\Temporary Description.docm"
                    MsgBox "The contents of the Description text " & _
                        "box have been saved in " & _
                        "c:\temp\Temporary Description.docm.", _
                        vbOKOnly + vbInformation, _
                        "Form Information Saved"
                End If
            End If
```

However, QueryClose comes into its own when the whole application, rather than just the user form, is closing. If the user form is modeless, users may not be aware that it's still open and that they're about to lose data they've typed into it or options they've selected in it.

Sometimes you may be able to use QueryClose to save information from a user form when the application has stopped responding and is being closed by Windows or the Task Manager. Be warned that QueryClose's record isn't perfect on this—the code sometimes won't run.

To stop an application from closing, set the Cancel property of the QueryClose event to True.

Activate Event

The Activate event fires when the user form becomes the active window. Typically, this means the event fires when the user form is displayed, occurring just after the Initialize event if the user form is loaded by a Show statement rather than a Load statement.

Note that if the user form is loaded by using a Load statement before being displayed with the Show statement, the Initialize event fires after the Load statement. The Activate event, firing after the Show statement, fires later.

However, the Activate event also fires when the user form is reactivated after first having been deactivated. For example, if you create a modeless user form with an Activate event procedure, the code is executed each time the user reactivates the user form after having deactivated it (for example, by working in the application window). Likewise, if you display one user form from another and then close the second user form, returning the focus to the first user form and reactivating it, the `Activate` event fires again.

The syntax for the `Activate` event is as follows:

```
Private Sub UserForm_Activate()
```

BUG ALERT: YOU MAY FACE PROBLEMS USING *DEACTIVATE* AND *ACTIVATE* IN IMMEDIATE SUCCESSION

VBA can't always execute the event procedures for the `Deactivate` event of one user form and the `Activate` event of another user form in immediate succession. Sometimes things work as they should, but more often they don't.

For example, say you have two user forms, named One and Two, each with an `Activate` event procedure and a `Deactivate` event procedure. If you display form Two by activating it from code in form One, the `Deactivate` event code from One should run, followed by the `Activate` event code from Two. This doesn't usually happen: Often, the `Deactivate` code of One will run, but the `Activate` code of Two won't. Run it again, and you may get the `Activate` code of Two to run but not the `Deactivate` code of One. However, if you remove or comment out the `Deactivate` event procedure from One and try again, Two's `Activate` code will run consistently each time One displays Two, indicating that the `Activate` event is firing but the `Activate` event procedure's code isn't running when the `Deactivate` event procedure is present.

DEACTIVATE EVENT

The `Deactivate` event fires when the user form loses the focus after having been the active window, but it doesn't fire when the user form is hidden or unloaded. For example, if you display a user form that contains a `Deactivate` event procedure and then close the user form, the `Deactivate` event doesn't fire. However, if you display one user form from another, the `Deactivate` event for the first user form fires as the focus is transferred to the second user form. With modeless user forms, the `Deactivate` event is triggered each time the user leaves one user form by clicking on another.

The syntax for the `Deactivate` event is as follows:

```
Private Sub UserForm_Deactivate()
```

See the previous sidebar for details on a bug in using the `Deactivate` and `Activate` events in immediate succession.

RESIZE EVENT

The `Resize` event fires when a user form is resized either manually by the user or programmatically by you.

The syntax for the `Resize` event is as follows:

```
Private Sub UserForm_Resize()
```

The main use for the Resize event is to move, resize, display, or hide controls to respond to a resized form. For example, you might resize a text box so that it occupies most of the width of the user form it resides on (see Figure 15.10) by using code such as that shown in Listing 15.3.

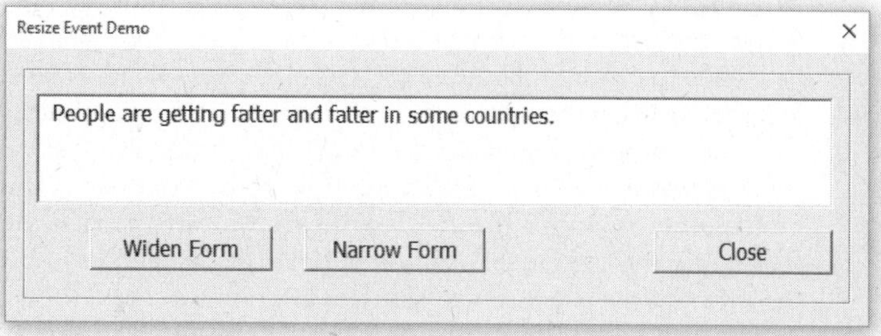

FIGURE 15.10 You can use the Resize event of a user form to resize or reposition the controls it contains.

LISTING 15.3: Resizing via code

```
Private Sub cmdWidenForm_Click()
    With frmResize
        If .Width < 451 Then
            .Width = .Width + 50
            If cmdNarrowForm.Enabled = False Then _
                cmdNarrowForm.Enabled = True
            If .Width > 451 Then _
                cmdWidenForm.Enabled = False
        End If
    End With
End Sub

Private Sub cmdNarrowForm_Click()
    With frmResize
        If .Width > 240 Then
            .Width = .Width - 50
            If cmdWidenForm.Enabled = False Then _
                cmdWidenForm.Enabled = True
            If .Width < 270 Then _
                cmdNarrowForm.Enabled = False
        End If
    End With
End Sub

Private Sub cmdClose_Click()
    Unload Me
End Sub

Private Sub UserForm_Resize()
    txt1.Width = frmResize.Width - 30
End Sub
```

Listing 15.3 contains four short procedures: one for the `Click` event of the `cmdWidenForm` command button, one for the `Click` event of the `cmdNarrowForm` command button, one for the `Click` event of the `cmdClose` command button, and one for the `Resize` event of the user form.

The `cmdWidenForm_Click` procedure shown in lines 1 through 9 increases the width of the user form by 50 points (1 point is 1/72 inch) when the user clicks the Widen Form button, as long as the `Width` property of the user form is less than 451 points. Line 5 enables the `cmd NarrowForm` command button if it isn't already enabled. (The `cmdNarrowForm` command button is disabled when the user form is displayed at its original narrow width.) Line 6 disables the `cmdWidenForm` command button if the `Width` property of the user form is more than 451 points.

The `cmdNarrowForm_Click` procedure shown in lines 11 through 19 narrows the user form by 50 points as long as the `Width` of the user form is greater than 240 points (its original width), reenabling the `cmdWidenForm` button if it's disabled and disabling the `cmdNarrowForm` button if the `Width` of the user form is less than 270 points.

The `cmdClose_Click` procedure shown in lines 21 through 23 simply unloads the user form. The `Me` keyword always refers to the current form, the form in which the `Me` command is located. So it's easy to understand that the code `Unload Me` simply tells the form it close itself.

The `UserForm_Resize` event procedure in lines 25 through 27 sets the `Width` property of `txt1`, the text box in the user form, to 30 points less than the `Width` of the user form. If you step through the code (repeatedly pressing F8) in the user form, you'll notice that the `Resize` event fires when the size of the user form changes. For example, when line 4 of the `cmdWidenForm_ Click` procedure is executed, execution branches to the `Resize` event procedure in line 25, and this procedure is executed before the code in line 5.

TERMINATE EVENT

The `Terminate` event fires when the user form has been unloaded—or, more precisely, when all references to an instance of the user form have been removed from memory or have gone out of scope.

The syntax for the `Terminate` event is as follows:

```
Private Sub UserForm_Terminate()
```

Events That Apply to Both *UserForms* and Container Controls

This section discusses the events that apply to the `UserForm` object *and* to the container controls—the MultiPage control and the Frame control. Container controls can have other controls placed inside of them. (The `Scroll` event applies to the ScrollBar control as well as to MultiPage, Frame, and UserForm.) These events are `Scroll`, `Zoom`, `Resize`, `Layout`, `AddControl`, and `RemoveControl`.

SCROLL EVENT

The `Scroll` event applies to the Frame control, the MultiPage control, the ScrollBar control, and the `UserForm` object. This event occurs when the user moves the scroll box (the thumb) on a scroll bar on a frame, MultiPage control, scroll bar, or user form.

The syntax for the `Scroll` event varies for the three controls and the `UserForm` object. The syntax for the `Scroll` event with the `UserForm` object is as follows:

```
Private Sub UserForm_Scroll(ByVal ActionX As MSForms.fmScrollAction, ByVal
ActionY
As MSForms.fmScrollAction, ByVal RequestDx As Single, ByVal RequestDy As Single,
ByVal ActualDx As MSForms.ReturnSingle, ByVal ActualDy As MSForms.ReturnSingle)
```

The syntax for the `Scroll` event with the ScrollBar control is as follows:

```
Private Sub scrollbar_Scroll()
```

The syntax for the `Scroll` event with the MultiPage control is as follows:

```
Private Sub multipage_Scroll(index As Long, ActionX As fmScrollAction, ActionY As
fmScrollAction, ByVal RequestDx As Single, ByVal RequestDy As Single, ByVal
ActualDx As MSForms.ReturnSingle, ByVal ActualDy As MSForms.ReturnSingle)
```

The syntax for the `Scroll` event with the Frame control is as follows:

```
Private Sub frame_Scroll(ActionX As fmScrollAction, ActionY As fmScrollAction,
ByVal RequestDx As Single, ByVal RequestDy As Single, ByVal ActualDx As MSForms
.Return Single, ByVal ActualDy As MSForms.ReturnSingle)
```

In these last three syntax statements, *`scrollbar`* is a valid `ScrollBar` object, *`multipage`* is a valid `MultiPage` object, and *`frame`* is a valid `Frame` object.

Here are the arguments for the `Scroll` event:

`Index` A required argument specifying the page of the `MultiPage` with which the event procedure is to be associated.

`ActionX` and `ActionY` Required arguments determining the user's horizontal and vertical actions (respectively), as shown in Table 15.6.

`RequestDx` The distance to move the scroll box horizontally, specified in points.

`RequestDy` The distance to move the scroll box vertically, specified in points.

`ActualDx` The distance the scroll box moved horizontally, measured in points.

`ActualDy` The distance the scroll box moved vertically, measured in points.

TABLE 15.6: `ActionX` and `ActionY` constants and values for the `Scroll` event

CONSTANT	VALUE	SCROLL BOX MOVEMENT
`fmScrollActionNoChange`	0	There was no change or movement.
`fmScrollActionLineUp`	1	The user moved the scroll box a short way upward on a vertical scroll bar (equivalent to pressing the ↑ key) or a short way to the left on a horizontal scroll bar (equivalent to pressing the ← key).
`fmScrollActionLineDown`	2	The user moved the scroll box a short way downward on a vertical scroll bar (equivalent to pressing the ↓ key) or a short way to the right on a horizontal scroll bar (equivalent to pressing the → key).

TABLE 15.6: `ActionX` and `ActionY` constants and values for the `Scroll` event *(CONTINUED)*

CONSTANT	VALUE	SCROLL BOX MOVEMENT
`fmScrollActionPageUp`	3	The user moved the scroll box up one page on a vertical scroll bar (equivalent to pressing the Page Up key) or one page to the left on a horizontal scroll bar (also equivalent to pressing the Page Up key).
`fmScrollActionPageDown`	4	The user moved the scroll box down one page on a vertical scroll bar (equivalent to pressing the Page Down key) or one page to the right on a horizontal scroll bar (also equivalent to pressing the Page Down key).
`fmScrollActionBegin`	5	The user moved the scroll box to the top of a vertical scroll bar or to the left end of a horizontal scroll bar.
`fmScrollActionEnd`	6	The user moved the scroll box to the bottom of a vertical scroll bar or to the right end of a horizontal scroll bar.
`fmScrollActionPropertyChange`	8	The user moved the scroll box, changing the value of either the `ScrollTop` property or the `ScrollLeft` property.
`fmScrollActionControlRequest`	9	The scroll action was requested by a control in the container in question.
`fmScrollActionFocusRequest`	10	The user moved the focus to a different control. This movement scrolls the user form if necessary so that the selected control is fully displayed in the available area.

ZOOM EVENT

Changing the `Zoom` property is like using a magnifying glass. The form's controls all grow larger if the `Zoom` value is greater than 100, and they grow smaller if the value is less than 100. However, the form itself doesn't change size. To change the size of the form, you must adjust its `Height` and `Width` properties.

The `Zoom` event fires when the `Zoom` property of the object changes at runtime. The `Zoom` property can be changed either automatically through code or by the user's manipulating—dragging a scroll bar's thumb, for example—a control that changes the property because you've written code that responds this way.

The `Zoom` property uses this syntax for the control and the `UserForm` object:

```
Private Sub object_Zoom(Percent As Integer)
```

Here, *object* is a Frame control or a `UserForm` object. `Percent` is an Integer argument used to specify the percentage (from 10 percent to 400 percent) the user form is to be zoomed to. By default, user forms and controls are displayed at 100 percent zoom—full size.

The `Zoom` property uses this syntax for the MultiPage control:

```
Private Sub multipage_Zoom(ByVal Index As Long, Percent As Integer)
```

`Index` is the index (name or number) of the `Page` object in the MultiPage control with which the `Zoom` event procedure is associated.

Zooming a user form zooms all the controls that are on it. For example, say a user form named `frmEventsDemo` includes a combo box named `cmbZoom` that offers a selection of zoom percentages. When the user selects an item in the combo box, the `Change` event for `cmbZoom` applies the combo box's `Value` property to the `Zoom` property of the user form, zooming it to the percentage selected. Zooming the user form triggers the `Zoom` event, whose procedure in this example sets the `Width` and `Height` of the user form to new values suited to the new zoom percentage:

```
Private Sub cmbZoom_Change()
'change the size of the controls:
    frmEventsDemo.Zoom = cmbZoom.Value
End Sub
Private Sub UserForm_Zoom(Percent As Integer)
' change the size of the form itself:
    frmEventsDemo.Width = 300 * cmbZoom.Value / 100
    frmEventsDemo.Height = 350 * cmbZoom.Value / 100
End Sub
```

Layout Event

A `Layout` event is triggered when the size of the frame, MultiPage control, or user form is changed, either by the user or programmatically (automatically by an autosized control's becoming resized).

By default, the `Layout` event automatically calculates the new position for any control that has been moved and repaints the screen accordingly. However, you can also use the `Layout` event for your own purposes if you need to.

The syntax for the `Layout` event with a Frame control or a `UserForm` object is as follows:

```
Private Sub object_Layout()
```

Here, *object* is a Frame control or a `UserForm` object.

The syntax for using the `Layout` event with a MultiPage control is as follows:

```
Private Sub multipage_Layout(index As Long)
```

Here, *`multipage`* is a MultiPage control and `index` is the `Page` object in the MultiPage control.

VBA Automatically Saves Height and Width Properties

When a control is resized, VBA automatically stores its previous height and width in the `OldHeight` and `OldWidth` properties, while the `Height` and `Width` properties take on the new height and width values. It allows you to restore a control to its previous size by retrieving the `OldHeight` and `OldWidth` properties and assigning them to the `Height` and `Width` properties.

ADDCONTROL EVENT

The AddControl event is triggered when a control is added programmatically to a Frame control, a MultiPage control, or the user form at runtime; it isn't triggered when you add a control manually at design time. The event isn't triggered when the user form is initialized unless the Initialize event adds a control to the user form.

The syntax for the AddControl event varies depending on the object or control. The syntax for the UserForm object and the Frame control is as follows:

```
Private Sub object_AddControl(ByVal Control As MSForms.Control)
```

Here, *object* is a UserForm object or Frame control, and Control is the control that's being added.

The syntax for the MultiPage control is as follows:

```
Private Sub multipage_AddControl(ByVal Index As Long, ByVal Control As MSForms
.Control)
```

Here, Index is the index number or name of the Page object that will receive the control.

For example, the following cmdAddControl_Click procedure adds three option buttons (opt1, opt2, and opt3, respectively) to the frame fraOptions and sets properties for the first option button. (A comment indicates where the code would go on to set properties for the second and third option buttons.) The fraOptions_AddControl event procedure displays a message box giving the number of controls the frame now contains. Because the cmdAddControl_Click procedure adds three controls, the AddControl event fires three times, and the fraOptions_AddControl procedure runs three times:

```
Private Sub cmdAddControl_click()
    Dim opt1 As OptionButton
    Dim opt2 As OptionButton
    Dim opt3 As OptionButton
    Set opt1 = fraOptions.Controls.Add("Forms.OptionButton.1")
    Set opt2 = fraOptions.Controls.Add("Forms.OptionButton.1")
    Set opt3 = fraOptions.Controls.Add("Forms.OptionButton.1")
    With opt1
        .Left = 10
        .Top = 10
        .Name = "optDomestic"
        .Caption = "Domestic"
        .AutoSize = True
        .Accelerator = "D"
    End With
    'set properties for opt2 and opt3 here
End Sub

Private Sub fraOptions_AddControl(ByVal Control As MSForms.Control)
    MsgBox "The frame now contains " & _
        fraOptions.Controls.Count & " controls."
End Sub
```

RemoveControl Event

The RemoveControl event fires when a control is deleted from a frame control, a MultiPage control, or a user form, either programmatically or manually at runtime. (To remove a control manually, the user would typically use a control built into the user form for that purpose. There has to be some programming here—users can't simply delete controls all by themselves.)

The syntax for the RemoveControl event is as follows for all controls but the MultiPage control:

```
Private Sub object_RemoveControl(ByVal Control As MSForms.Control)
```

Here, *object* is a valid object, and Control is a valid control.

The syntax for the RemoveControl event is as follows for the MultiPage control:

```
Private Sub multipage_RemoveControl(ByVal Index As Long, ByVal Control As
MSForms.Control)
```

Here, *multipage* is a valid MultiPage object. For a MultiPage control, Index specifies the Page object in the MultiPage control that contains the control to be deleted.

Events That Apply to Many or Most Controls

This section discusses the events that apply to many or most controls. Some of these events apply to the UserForm object as well. These events are Click; Change; Enter and Exit; BeforeUpdate and AfterUpdate; KeyDown, KeyUp, and KeyPress; MouseDown, MouseUp, and MouseMove; BeforeDragOver; BeforeDropOrPaste; DblClick; and Error.

Click Event

The most common event of all in VBA, the Click event services the CheckBox, ComboBox, CommandButton, Frame, Image, Label, ListBox, MultiPage, OptionButton, TabStrip, and ToggleButton controls. It is not available to the TextBox, ScrollBar, or SpinButton controls, but it *is* a member of the UserForm object.

A Click event occurs when the user clicks a control with the left mouse button, or when the user selects a value for a control that has more than one possible value. For most controls, this means that the event fires every time the user clicks the control. But there are a few exceptions:

- Clicking a disabled control fires the Click event of the user form (as if the user were clicking the user form *through* the control).
- The Click event of an OptionButton control fires when the user clicks the option button to select it. If the option button is already selected, clicking it has no effect. (On the other hand, the Click event of a CheckBox control fires each time the user clicks the check box—either to select it or to clear it.)
- The Click event of a ListBox control or ComboBox control fires when the user clicks to select an item from the list (not when the user clicks on the drop-down arrow or in the undropped portion of the combo box). If the user clicks an already-selected item, the Click event doesn't fire again.

- The `Click` event of a ToggleButton control occurs whenever the toggle button is clicked and when its `Value` property is changed. This means that it isn't a good idea to use the `Click` event of the ToggleButton control to toggle its `Value`.
- The `Click` event of a selected CommandButton control fires when you press the spacebar.
- The `Click` event of the default command button (the button with its `Default` property set to `True`) fires when the user presses Enter with no other command button selected.
- The `Click` event of the command button with its `Cancel` property set to `True` fires when the user presses Esc. The `Click` event for a control with an accelerator key set also fires when the user presses the accelerator key.

For all controls except the TabStrip control and the MultiPage control, the `Click` event needs no arguments, as follows:

```
Private Sub object_Click()
```

For a TabStrip control or a MultiPage control, your code must react to the `Index` argument, a required Long (data type) argument that VBA passes to indicate the affected tab or page of the control:

```
Private Sub object_Click(ByVal Index As Long)
```

Here, *`object`* is a valid MultiPage control or TabStrip control.

Sequence of Events: What Happens When the User Clicks (and Clicks Again)

The order in which events trigger can sometimes be important to the programmer. If you don't understand the order in which events take place, you can write code that causes events to conflict—or even trigger each other.

When the user clicks a command button, the `Enter` event for this button occurs before its `Click` event if the click transfers the focus to the command button. When the `Enter` event for the command button fires, it usually prevents the `Click` event from firing.

When the user clicks a control, the first event triggered is the `MouseDown` event, which fires when the user presses the mouse button. Then the `MouseUp` event fires when the user releases the mouse button. A `Click` event occurs after a `MouseUp` event. If the user clicks again within the double-click timeframe set in Windows, the `DblClick` event fires, followed by another `MouseUp` event.

Change Event

The `Change` event applies to the CheckBox, ComboBox, ListBox, MultiPage, OptionButton, ScrollBar, SpinButton, TabStrip, TextBox, and ToggleButton controls. This event fires when the

Value property of a control changes. This change can occur either through an action of the user's (such as typing text into a text box, selecting an option button, selecting or clearing a check box, clicking a toggle button, or changing the page displayed on a MultiPage control) or through an action taken programmatically at runtime.

Bear in mind that when the Change event is fired by an action of the user's, that action may also trigger a Click event. (Even when this happens, Change is regarded as a better way of determining the new Value of the control than Click—although for many purposes, Click will work satisfactorily as well.) Changing the Value property of a control manually at design time doesn't fire a Change event.

The syntax for the Change event is as follows:

```
Private Sub object_Change()
```

The Change event is useful for updating other controls after the user changes a control. For example, if the user enters the name for a new report into a text box (here, txtReportName), you could use the Change event to automatically insert into another text box (here called txtFileName) the name of the file in which to save the report:

```
Private Sub txtReportName_Change()
    txtFileName.Text = txtReportName.Text & ".txt"
End Sub
```

Enter and *Exit* Events

The Enter and Exit events apply to CheckBox, ComboBox, CommandButton, Frame, ListBox, MultiPage, OptionButton, ScrollBar, SpinButton, TabStrip, TextBox, and ToggleButton controls.

The Enter event fires when the focus is moved from one control on a user form to another control. The event fires just before the second control receives the focus.

Like the Enter event, the Exit event fires when the focus is moved from one control on a user form to another control. However, the Exit event fires just before the first event loses the focus.

The syntax for the Enter event is as follows:

```
Private Sub object_Enter()
```

The syntax for the Exit event is a little more complex:

```
Private Sub object_Exit(ByVal Cancel As MSForms.ReturnBoolean)
```

Here, Cancel is a required argument specifying event status. The default setting is False, which specifies that the control involved should handle the event and that the focus will pass to the next control; a setting of True specifies that the application handle the event, which keeps the focus on the current control.

By using the Enter and Exit events, you can track the user's progress through the controls on a user form.

The Exit event is useful for checking to see if the user has made an appropriate selection in the control or has entered a suitable value. For example, you could check the user's entry in the control and, if you find it inappropriate, display a message box alerting the user to the problem and then return the focus to the control so that the user can try again.

OTHER WAYS TO TRAP USER INPUT

Other events that you might use for checking the contents of a control after the user has visited it include `AfterUpdate` and `LostFocus`. Similarly, you might use the `BeforeUpdate` and `GotFocus` events instead of the `Enter` event. A significant difference between `Enter` and `GotFocus` and between `Exit` and `LostFocus` is that `GotFocus` and `LostFocus` fire when the user form receives or loses the focus, respectively, but `Enter` and `Exit` don't fire.

BeforeUpdate Event

The `BeforeUpdate` event applies to the CheckBox, ComboBox, ListBox, OptionButton, ScrollBar, SpinButton, TextBox, and ToggleButton controls. This event occurs as the value or data in the specified control is changed; you can use the event to evaluate the change and decide whether to implement it.

The syntax for the `BeforeUpdate` event is as follows:

```
Private Sub object_BeforeUpdate(ByVal Cancel As MSForms.ReturnBoolean)
```

Here, *`object`* is a valid object, and `Cancel` is a required argument indicating the status of the event. The default setting of `False` makes the control handle the event; `True` prevents the update from being executed and makes the application handle the event.

Here's the sequence in which events fire as you move focus to a control, update it, and move on:

1. The `Enter` event for the control fires when you move the focus to the control.
2. The `BeforeUpdate` event for the control fires after you've entered the information for the update (for example, after you've pressed a key in a text box) but before the update is executed. By setting `Cancel` to `True`, you can prevent the update from taking place. (If you don't set `Cancel` to `True`, the update occurs and the `AfterUpdate` event can't prevent it from occurring.)
3. The `AfterUpdate` event for the control fires after you've entered the information in the control and the update has been executed. If you set the `Cancel` argument for `BeforeUpdate` to `True`, the `AfterUpdate` event doesn't fire.
4. The `Exit` event for the control fires when you move from this control to another control. (After the `Exit` event fires for the control you've left, the `Enter` event fires for the control to which you have moved the focus.)

AfterUpdate Event

The `AfterUpdate` event applies to the CheckBox, ComboBox, ListBox, OptionButton, ScrollBar, SpinButton, TextBox, and ToggleButton controls. This event fires after the user changes information in a control and after that update has been executed.

The syntax for the `AfterUpdate` event is the same for all the controls and objects it applies to:

```
Private Sub object_AfterUpdate()
```

KeyDown and *KeyUp* Events

The KeyDown event and KeyUp event work with the CheckBox, ComboBox, CommandButton, Frame, ListBox, MultiPage, OptionButton, ScrollBar, SpinButton, TabStrip, TextBox, and ToggleButton controls and to the UserForm object. These events are not available to the Image and Label controls.

The KeyDown event fires when the user presses a key on the keyboard. The KeyUp event fires when the user releases the key. The KeyDown and KeyUp events also occur when a key is sent to the user form or control programmatically by using the SendKeys statement. These events don't occur when the user presses Enter when the user form contains a CommandButton control with its Default property set to True, nor when the user presses Esc when the user form contains a CommandButton control with its Cancel property set to True.

When the keystroke moves the focus to another control, the KeyDown event fires for the original control, while the KeyPress and KeyDown events fire for the control to which the focus is moved.

The KeyPress event fires after the KeyDown event and before the KeyUp event.

The syntax for the KeyDown event is as follows:

```
Private Sub object_KeyDown(ByVal KeyCode As MSForms.ReturnInteger, ByVal Shift As
Integer)
```

The syntax for the KeyUp event is as follows:

```
Private Sub object_KeyUp(ByVal KeyCode As MSForms.ReturnInteger, ByVal Shift As
Integer)
```

Here, *object* is an object name and is required. KeyCode is a required Integer argument specifying the key code of the key pressed. For example, the key code for the letter *t* is 84. The key code isn't an ANSI value—it's a special number that identifies the key on the keyboard.

Shift is a required argument specifying whether the Shift, Ctrl, or Alt key was pressed. Use the constants or values shown in Table 15.7.

Table 15.7: Shift constants and values

Constant	Value	Description
fmShiftMask	1	Shift key pressed
fmCtrlMask	2	Ctrl key pressed
fmAltMask	4	Alt key pressed

KeyPress Event

The KeyPress event is a member of the CheckBox, ComboBox, CommandButton, Frame, ListBox, MultiPage, OptionButton, ScrollBar, SpinButton, TabStrip, TextBox, and ToggleButton controls. It also is a member of the UserForm object. The Label control has no KeyPress event.

The KeyPress event fires when the user presses a printable character, Ctrl plus an alphabetic character, Ctrl plus a special character (symbols), the Esc key, or the Backspace key while the control or object in question has the focus. Pressing the Tab key, the Enter key, or an arrow key doesn't cause the KeyPress event to fire, nor does a keystroke that moves the focus to another control from the current control.

Technically, only ANSI keys fire the KeyPress event. The Delete key isn't an ANSI key, so pressing the Delete key to delete, say, text in a text box doesn't fire the KeyPress event. But deleting the same text in the same text box using the Backspace key does because Backspace is an ANSI key.

The KeyPress event fires after the KeyDown event and before the KeyUp event. It also fires when you use SendKeys to send keystrokes to a user form programmatically.

The syntax for the KeyPress event is as follows:

```
Private Sub object_KeyPress(ByVal KeyAscii As MSForms.ReturnInteger)
```

Here, *object* is a required argument specifying a valid object, and KeyAscii is a required Integer argument specifying an ANSI key code. To get the ANSI key code, use the Asc function. For example, Asc("t") returns the ANSI key code for the letter *t* (the code is 116).

By default, the KeyPress event processes the code for the key pressed—in humble terms, what you press is what you get. For example, if you press the *t* key, you get a *t*; if you press the Delete key, you get a Delete action; and so on. By using a KeyPress event procedure, you can perform checks such as filtering out all nonnumeric keys when the user must enter a numeric value.

MouseDown Event and *MouseUp* Event

The MouseDown and MouseUp events apply to the CheckBox, ComboBox, CommandButton, Frame, Image, Label, ListBox, MultiPage, OptionButton, ScrollBar, SpinButton, TabStrip, TextBox, and ToggleButton controls and to the UserForm object. The MouseDown event fires when the user presses a button on the mouse, and a MouseUp event occurs when the user releases that button. A Click event fires after a MouseUp event occurs.

The syntax for the MouseDown and MouseUp events is as follows for all controls except for MultiPage and TabStrip:

```
Private Sub object_MouseDown(ByVal Button As Integer, ByVal Shift As Integer,
ByVal X As Single, ByVal Y As Single)

Private Sub object_MouseUp(ByVal Button As Integer, ByVal Shift As Integer,
ByVal X As Single, ByVal Y As Single)
```

The syntax for the MouseDown and MouseUp events with the MultiPage and TabStrip controls adds an Index argument to specify the index of the page or the tab involved:

```
Private Sub object_MouseUp(ByVal Index As Long, ByVal Button As Integer, ByVal
Shift As Integer, ByVal X As Single, ByVal Y As Single)
Private Sub object_MouseDown(ByVal Index As Long, ByVal Button As Integer, ByVal
Shift As Integer, ByVal X As Single, ByVal Y As Single)
```

Here, *object* is a valid object for the statement.

Index returns –1 if the user clicks outside the page or tab area of the control but still within the control (for example, to the right of the rightmost tab in a top-tab TabStrip).

`Button` is a required Integer argument specifying the mouse button that triggered the event. Table 15.8 lists the possible values for `Button`.

TABLE 15.8: `Button` values and constants

CONSTANT	VALUE	DESCRIPTION
`fmButtonLeft`	1	Left (primary)
`fmButtonRight`	2	Right (non-primary)
`fmButtonMiddle`	4	Middle

`Shift` is a required argument specifying whether the Shift, Ctrl, or Alt key was pressed. Table 15.9 lists the values for `Shift`.

TABLE 15.9: `Shift` values

VALUE	KEY OR KEYS PRESSED
1	Shift
2	Ctrl
3	Shift+Ctrl
4	Alt
5	Alt+Shift
6	Alt+Ctrl
7	Alt+Shift+Ctrl

You can also detect a single key by using the key masks listed in Table 15.7.

`X` is a required Single argument specifying the horizontal position in points from the left edge of the user form, frame, or page. `Y` is a required Single argument specifying the vertical position in points from the top edge of the user form, frame, or page.

MouseMove Event

The `MouseMove` event is available to the CheckBox, ComboBox, CommandButton, Frame, Image, Label, ListBox, MultiPage, OptionButton, TabStrip, TextBox, and ToggleButton controls and to the `UserForm` object. This event fires when the user moves the mouse pointer over the control or object in question.

The syntax for the `MouseMove` event is different for the MultiPage control and the TabStrip control than for the other controls and for the `UserForm` object. The syntax for the other controls is as follows:

```
Private Sub object_MouseMove(ByVal Button As Integer, ByVal Shift As Integer,
ByVal X As Single, ByVal Y As Single)
```

The syntax for the MultiPage control and the TabStrip control is as follows:

```
Private Sub object_MouseMove(ByVal Index As Long, ByVal Button As Integer,
ByVal Shift As Integer, ByVal X As Single, ByVal Y As Single)
```

Here, *`object`* is a required argument specifying a valid object.

For the MultiPage and TabStrip controls, `Index` is a required argument that returns the index of the `Page` object in the MultiPage control or the `Tab` object in the TabStrip control associated with the event procedure.

`Button` is a required Integer argument that returns which mouse button (if any) the user is pressing. Table 15.10 lists the values for `Button`.

TABLE 15.10: `Button` values

VALUE	BUTTON PRESSED
0	No button
1	Left
2	Right
3	Left and right
4	Middle
5	Left and middle
6	Middle and right
7	Left, middle, and right

`Shift` is a required Integer argument that returns a value indicating whether the user is pressing the Shift, Alt, and/or Ctrl keys. Refer back to Table 15.9 for the list of `Shift` values.

`X` is a required Single argument that returns a value specifying the horizontal position in points from the left edge of the user form, frame, or page. `Y` is a required Single argument specifying the vertical position in points from the top edge of the user form, frame, or page.

As with the `MouseDown` and `MouseUp` events, you can also detect a single key by using the key masks listed in Table 15.7.

Like most windows in the Windows operating system, user forms largely experience life as a nonstop sequence of mouse events. `MouseMove` events monitor where the mouse pointer is on the screen and which control has captured it. `MouseMove` events fire even if you use the keyboard to move a user form from under the mouse pointer because the mouse pointer ends up in a different place in relation to the user form even though it hasn't moved in the conventional sense.

One use for the MouseMove event is to display appropriate text or an image for a control at which the user is pointing. For example, suppose a user form provides a list of available products, with each product's title appearing in a label. When the user positions the mouse pointer over a title in the label, you could use the MouseMove event to load a picture of the product into an Image control and a short description into another label.

MOUSEMOVE EVENTS MAY NOT TRIGGER BETWEEN CLOSE CONTROLS

The user form traps MouseMove events when the mouse pointer isn't over any control. However, if the user moves the mouse pointer quickly from one control to another very close to it, the user form may fail to trap the movement over the short intervening space.

BEFOREDRAGOVER EVENT

The BeforeDragOver event applies to the UserForm object itself and to the following controls: CheckBox, ComboBox, CommandButton, Frame, Image, Label, ListBox, MultiPage, OptionButton, ScrollBar, SpinButton, TabStrip, TextBox, and ToggleButton. A BeforeDragOver event is triggered when the user is performing a drag-and-drop operation.

The syntax for the BeforeDragOver event depends on the object or control in question. The basic syntax for the UserForm object and all controls except the Frame, TabStrip, and MultiPage is as follows, where *object* is a valid UserForm or control:

```
Private Sub object_BeforeDragOver(ByVal Cancel As MSForms.ReturnBoolean, ByVal
Control As MSForms.Control, ByVal Data As MSForms.DataObject, ByVal X As Single,
ByVal Y As Single, ByVal State As MSForms.fmDragState, ByVal Effect As MSForms.
ReturnEffect, ByVal Shift As Integer)
```

The syntax for the BeforeDragOver event with the Frame control is as follows, where *frame* is a valid Frame control:

```
Private Sub frame_BeforeDragOver(ByVal Cancel As MSForms.ReturnBoolean, ByVal
Control As MSForms.Control, ByVal Data As MSForms.DataObject, ByVal X As Single,
ByVal Y As Single, ByVal State As MSForms.fmDragState, ByVal Effect As MSForms.
ReturnEffect, ByVal Shift As Integer)
```

The syntax for the BeforeDragOver event with the MultiPage control is as follows, where *multipage* is a valid MultiPage control:

```
Private Sub multipage_BeforeDragOver(ByVal Index As Long, ByVal Cancel As
MSForms.
ReturnBoolean, ByVal Control As MSForms.Control, ByVal Data As MSForms.
DataObject, ByVal X As Single, ByVal Y As Single, ByVal State As MSForms.
fmDragState, ByVal Effect As MSForms.ReturnEffect, ByVal Shift As Integer)
```

The syntax for the `BeforeDragOver` event with the TabStrip control is as follows, where `tabstrip` is a valid TabStrip control:

```
Private Sub tabstrip_BeforeDragOver(ByVal Index As Long, ByVal Cancel As MSForms
.ReturnBoolean, ByVal Data As MSForms.DataObject, ByVal X As Single, ByVal Y As
Single, ByVal DragState As MSForms.fmDragState, ByVal Effect As MSForms
.ReturnEffect, ByVal Shift As Integer)
```

These are the different parts of the statements:

- `Index` is the index of the `Page` object in a MultiPage control (or the `Tab` object in a TabStrip control) that is affected by the drag-and-drop.
- `Cancel` is a required argument giving the status of the `BeforeDragOver` event. The default setting is `False`, which makes the control handle the event. A setting of `True` makes the application handle the event.
- `Control` is a required argument specifying the control that is being dragged over.
- `Data` is a required argument specifying the data being dragged.
- `X` is a required argument specifying the horizontal distance in points from the left edge of the control. `Y` is a required argument specifying the vertical distance in points from the top of the control.
- `DragState` is a required argument specifying where the mouse pointer is in relation to a target (a location at which the data can be dropped). Table 15.11 lists the constants and values for `DragState`.
- `Effect` is a required argument specifying the operations the source of the drop is to support, as listed in Table 15.12.
- `Shift` is a required argument specifying whether the Shift, Ctrl, or Alt key is held down during the drag-and-drop operation, as listed in Table 15.7.

TABLE 15.11: `DragState` constants and values

CONSTANT	VALUE	POSITION OF MOUSE POINTER
`fmDragStateEnter`	0	Within range of a target
`fmDragStateLeave`	1	Outside the range of a target
`fmDragStateOver`	2	At a new position, but remains within range of the same target

TABLE 15.12: `Effect` constants and values

CONSTANT	VALUE	DROP EFFECT
`fmDropEffectNone`	0	Doesn't copy or move the source to the target
`fmDropEffectCopy`	1	Copies the source to the target
`fmDropEffectMove`	2	Moves the source to the target
`fmDropEffectCopyOrMove`	3	Copies or moves the source to the target

You use the `BeforeDragOver` event to control drag-and-drop actions that the user performs. Use the `DragState` argument to make sure that the mouse pointer is within range of a target.

BeforeDropOrPaste Event

The `BeforeDropOrPaste` event applies to the CheckBox, ComboBox, CommandButton, Frame, Image, Label, ListBox, MultiPage, OptionButton, ScrollBar, SpinButton, TabStrip, TextBox, and ToggleButton controls and to the `UserForm` object.

A `BeforeDropOrPaste` event fires just before the user drops or pastes data onto an object.

The syntax for the `BeforeDropOrPaste` event is different for the MultiPage and TabStrip controls than for the `UserForm` object and for the other controls. The basic syntax is as follows:

```
Private Sub object_BeforeDropOrPaste(ByVal Cancel As MSForms.ReturnBoolean, ByVal
Control As MSForms.Control, ByVal Action As MSForms.fmAction, ByVal Data As
MSForms.DataObject, ByVal X As Single, ByVal Y As Single, ByVal Effect As
MSForms.ReturnEffect, ByVal Shift As Integer)
```

The syntax for the MultiPage control is as follows, where *`multipage`* is a valid MultiPage control:

```
Private Sub multipage_BeforeDropOrPaste(ByVal Index As Long, ByVal Cancel  As
MSForms.ReturnBoolean, ByVal Control As MSForms.Control, ByVal Action As MSForms.
fmAction, ByVal Data As MSForms.DataObject, ByVal X As Single, ByVal Y As
Single, ByVal Effect As MSForms.ReturnEffect, ByVal Shift As Integer)
```

The syntax for the TabStrip control is as follows, where *`tabstrip`* is a valid TabStrip control:

```
Private Sub tabstrip_BeforeDropOrPaste(ByVal Index As Long, ByVal Cancel  As
MSForms.ReturnBoolean, ByVal Action As MSForms.fmAction, ByVal Data As MSForms.
DataObject, ByVal X As Single, ByVal Y As Single, ByVal Effect  As MSForms.
ReturnEffect, ByVal Shift As Integer)
```

Here are the parts of the syntax:

- *`object`* is a required object specifying a valid object.
- For the MultiPage control, `Index` is a required argument specifying the `Page` object involved.

- Cancel is a required argument giving the status of the event. The default setting of False makes the control handle the event; True makes the application handle the event.
- Control is a required argument specifying the target control.
- Action is a required argument specifying the result of the drag-and-drop operation. Table 15.13 shows the constants and values for Action.
- Data is a required argument specifying the data (contained in a DataObject) being dragged and dropped.
- X is a required argument specifying the horizontal distance in points from the left edge of the control for the drop. Y is a required argument specifying the vertical distance in points from the top of the control.
- Effect is a required argument specifying whether the drag-and-drop operation copies the data or moves it, as listed in Table 15.12.
- Shift is a required argument specifying whether the user has pressed the Shift, Ctrl, and/ or Alt keys, as listed in Table 15.7.

TABLE 15.13: Action constants and values

CONSTANT	VALUE	ACTION TAKEN
fmActionPaste	2	Pastes the object into the target.
fmActionDragDrop	3	The user has dragged the object from its source and dropped it on the target.

The BeforeDropOrPaste event fires when a data object is transferred to a MultiPage or TabStrip control and just before the drop or paste operation occurs on other controls.

DBLCLICK EVENT

The DblClick event works with the CheckBox, ComboBox, CommandButton, Frame, Image, Label, ListBox, MultiPage, OptionButton, TabStrip, TextBox, and ToggleButton controls, as well as the UserForm object.

A DblClick event occurs when the user double-clicks a control or object with the left mouse button. The double-click must be fast enough to register as a double-click in Windows (this speed is controlled by the setting on the Buttons tab in the Mouse Properties dialog box in Control Panel) and occurs after the MouseDown event, the MouseUp event, and the Click event (for controls that support the Click event).

The DblClick event has a different syntax for the MultiPage and TabStrip controls than for the other controls or for the user form.

For the MultiPage and TabStrip controls, the syntax is as follows:

```
Private Sub object_DblClick(ByVal Index As Long, ByVal Cancel As MSForms
.ReturnBoolean)
```

The syntax for the `DblClick` event for other controls is as follows:

```
Private Sub object_DblClick(ByVal Cancel As MSForms.ReturnBoolean)
```

Here, *`object`* is a required argument specifying a valid object. For the MultiPage control and the TabStrip control, `Index` is a required argument specifying the `Page` object within a MultiPage control or the `Tab` object within a TabStrip control to be associated with the event procedure.

`Cancel` is a required argument specifying the status of the event. The default setting of `False` causes the control to handle the event; `True` causes the application to handle the event instead and causes the control to ignore the second click.

In controls that support both the `Click` event and the `DblClick` event, the `Click` event occurs before the `DblClick` event. If you take an interface action (such as displaying a message box) with the `Click` event procedure, it blocks the `DblClick` event procedure from running. In the following example, the `DblClick` event procedure doesn't run:

```
Private Sub CommandButton1_Click()
    MsgBox "Click event"
End Sub

Private Sub CommandButton1_DblClick _
    (ByVal Cancel As MSForms.ReturnBoolean)
    MsgBox "Double-click event"
End Sub
```

However, you can execute non-interface statements in the `Click` event procedure without blocking the `DblClick` event procedure. The following example declares a private String variable named `strMessage` in the declarations portion of the code sheet for the user form. The `Click` event procedure for the `CommandButton1` command button assigns text to `strMessage`. The `DblClick` event procedure assigns more text to `strMess` and then displays a message box containing `strMessage` so that you can see that both events have fired. Don't step into this code by pressing F8 in the VBA Editor—instead, press F5 to run it, or it won't work:

```
Private strMess As String
Private Sub CommandButton1_Click()
    strMess = "Click event" & vbCr
End Sub

Private Sub CommandButton1_DblClick _
    (ByVal Cancel As MSForms.ReturnBoolean)
    strMessage = strMessage & "Double-click event"
    MsgBox strMessage
End Sub
```

For most controls you won't want to use both a `Click` event procedure and a `DblClick` event procedure—you'll choose one or the other as appropriate to the control's purpose.

Error Event

The `Error` event applies to the CheckBox, ComboBox, CommandButton, Frame, Image, Label, ListBox, MultiPage, OptionButton, ScrollBar, SpinButton, TabStrip, TextBox, and ToggleButton controls. It also applies to the `UserForm` object. The `Error` event fires when a control encounters an error and is unable to return information about the error to the program that called the control. We will explore error handling in depth in Chapter 17, "Debugging Your Code and Handling Errors."

The syntax for the `Error` event for the `UserForm` object and for all controls except the MultiPage control is as follows:

```
Private Sub object_Error(ByVal Number As Integer, ByVal Description As MSForms.
ReturnString, ByVal SCode As Long, ByVal Source As String, ByVal HelpFile As
String, ByVal HelpContext As Long, ByVal CancelDisplay As MSForms.ReturnBoolean)
```

The syntax for the `Error` event for the MultiPage control is as follows, where *`multipage`* is a valid MultiPage control:

```
Private Sub multipage_Error(ByVal Index As Long, ByVal Number As Integer, ByVal
Description As MSForms.ReturnString, ByVal SCode As Long, ByVal Source As String,
ByVal HelpFile As String, ByVal HelpContext As Long, ByVal CancelDisplay As
MSForms.ReturnBoolean)
```

These are the components of the syntax:

- *`object`* is the name of a valid object.
- For a MultiPage control, `Index` is the index of the `Page` object in the MultiPage control associated with the event.
- `Number` is a required argument that returns the value used by the control to identify the error.
- `Description` is a required String argument describing the error.
- `SCode` is a required argument giving the OLE (Object Linking and Embedding) status code for the error.
- `Source` is a required String argument containing the string identifying the control involved.
- `HelpFile` is a required String argument containing the full path to the Help file that contains the `Description`.
- `HelpContext` is a required Long argument containing the context ID for the `Description` within the Help file.
- `CancelDisplay` is a required Boolean argument that controls whether VBA displays the error message in a message box.

Events That Apply Only to a Few Controls

This section discusses the three events that apply only to one or two controls. The first of the three is the `DropButtonClick` event, which applies only to the ComboBox and TextBox controls; the second and third are the `SpinUp` and `SpinDown` events, which apply only to the SpinButton control.

DropButtonClick Event

The `DropButtonClick` event fires when the user displays or hides a drop-down list on a ComboBox by clicking the drop-down button or by pressing the F4 key when the ComboBox has the focus (is selected). `DropButtonClick` also fires when the user presses the F4 key with a TextBox control selected, though this manifestation of the event is arcane enough to be singularly useless. It also fires when the `DropDown` method is executed in VBA to display the drop-down list, and it fires again when the `DropDown` method is executed again to hide the drop-down list.

The syntax for the `DropButtonClick` event is as follows:

```
Private Sub object_DropButtonClick( )
```

Here, *`object`* is a valid ComboBox or TextBox control.

One use for the `DropButtonClick` event is to add items to a ComboBox control rather than adding them at load time via the `Initialize` event. By adding these items only on demand (I'm assuming the user might not use the ComboBox control at all or might type information into its text-box area), you can cut down on load time for the user form. You can also load the ComboBox with data relevant to the other choices the user has made in the dialog box, allowing for more targeted information than you could have provided by loading the ComboBox with the `Initialize` event.

SpinDown and *SpinUp* Events

The `SpinDown` and `SpinUp` events apply only to the SpinButton control. `SpinDown` and `SpinUp` are used to control what happens when the user clicks either the down-arrow button and up-arrow button, respectively, of a vertical SpinButton control or the right-arrow button and left-arrow button, respectively, of a horizontal SpinButton control. The `SpinDown` event fires when the user clicks the down-arrow or right-arrow button, and the `SpinUp` event fires when the user clicks the up-arrow or left-arrow button.

The syntax for the `SpinUp` event and the `SpinDown` event is as follows:

```
Private Sub spinbutton_SpinDown()
Private Sub spinbutton_SpinUp()
```

Here, *`spinbutton`* is a SpinButton control.

By default, the `SpinDown` event decreases and the `SpinUp` event increases the `Value` property of the SpinButton by the `SmallChange` increment.

The Bottom Line

Understand what a complex dialog box is. Simple dialog boxes tend to be static, but complex dialog boxes are dynamic—they change during execution in response to clicks or other interaction from the user.

Master It Describe two types of dynamic behavior typical of complex dialog boxes.

Reveal and hide parts of a dialog box. Dialog boxes need not display everything at once. Word's Find And Replace dialog box illustrates how useful it can be to display an abbreviated dialog box containing the most common tasks and expand the box to reveal less-popular options if the user needs access to them.

Master It Name the two most common techniques you can use to display additional options in a dialog box.

Create multipage dialog boxes. VBA includes the MultiPage control, which enables you to create multipage dialog boxes. Word's Font dialog box is an example of one. You can access any page (one at a time) by clicking its tab at the top of the page.

Master It How does the TabStrip control differ from the MultiPage control? What are the typical uses for each?

Create modeless dialog boxes. A *modeless* dialog box can be left visible onscreen while the user continues to work in an application. For example, the Find And Replace dialog box in Access, Word, and Excel is modeless, as is the Replace dialog box in PowerPoint. A *modal* dialog box, by contrast, must be closed by users before they can continue to interact with the application.

Master It How do you make a user form modeless?

Work with form events. Events are actions that happen to controls (or the form itself) while a program is executing. By using events, you can monitor what the user does and take action accordingly or even prevent the user from doing something that doesn't seem like a good idea.

Master It Name two of the three most commonly used events in VBA programming.

Part 5

Creating Effective Code

Chapter 16

Building Modular Code and Using Classes

This chapter shows you how to start building *modular code*—code broken up into individual components rather than all built together into a monolithic mass. You'll also see how to create *reusable code* that you can use in future procedures.

The second part of this chapter discusses how you can build and use your own classes in VBA to implement custom objects, store information in them, and return information from them.

IN THIS CHAPTER, YOU WILL LEARN TO DO THE FOLLOWING:

- Arrange your code in modules
- Call a procedure
- Pass information from one procedure to another
- Understand what classes are and what they're for
- Create an object class

Creating Modular Code

The code that you've created so far in this book has been effective—it *worked*—but some of it has been less concise, organized, or elegant than it might be. The following sections show you how to refine your code.

> **WHAT IS ELEGANCE IN CODE?**
>
> *Elegance* in computer programming means not only that your code is bug-free and well organized and that your user interface is thoughtfully designed, but also that the code contains nothing unnecessary—it has been stripped down to the minimum required to achieve the desired effect.

What Is Modular Code?

Modular code is code composed of different procedures that you can use in combination. The name doesn't specifically come from the fact that VBA code is stored in modules.

For example, suppose you're working in Word. You *could* take a monolithic approach and create a single giant macro that does a lot of things: creates a document based on the user's choice of template, inserts text and formats it, saves it in a particular folder under a name of the user's choice, prints it to a specific printer, and then closes it. Whew!

Or…you can take the more practical, *modular* approach and subdivide this lengthy series of tasks into several separate macros—one for each task. If these macros need to work together as a team, you could then create a kind of master macro that runs each of these individual task procedures (macros). In this way, you can achieve the same results as using a large, monolithic macro. But subdivided code is easier to read, test, and even sometimes reuse. Think of it as using multiple small subs rather than a single large sub.

Advantages of Using Modular Code

Modular code has several advantages over code that lumps everything together in one huge macro. For one thing, it's often easier to write modular code because you create a number of short procedures, each of which performs a specific task. You stay focused on the single task at hand.

You can also debug small procedures relatively more easily too, because their shorter length makes it simpler to identify, locate, and eliminate bugs. Debugging often involves finding out exactly *where* the problem is. So, the fewer lines of code that hide the bug, the easier it will be to track it down.

The procedures will also be more readable and more easily modified because they're less complex and you can more easily follow what they do.

Modular code is also more efficient, for four reasons:

- By breaking code into multiple, single-purpose macros, you can repeat their tasks at different points in a sequence of procedures without needing to repeat the lines of code. Having less code should make your procedures run faster.
- By reusing whole procedures, you can reduce the amount of code you have to write. And by writing less code, you give yourself less chance to write new errors into your program.
- If you need to change an item in the code, you can make a single change in the appropriate procedure instead of having to make changes at a number of locations in a long procedure (and perhaps missing some of them). This change then also applies to any procedures that call the procedure.
- You can call individual procedures from other procedures without having to assimilate them into the other procedures. Just think how tedious it would be if you had to create each of VBA's many built-in functions from scratch instead of being able to invoke them at will. You can do much the same with functions you create—reuse them rather than reinvent the wheel.

How to Approach Creating Modular Code

The usefulness of modular coding will vary from person to person, from project to project, and from procedure to procedure. For example, if you record a macro to perform a simple, one-time task on a number of presentations, there's no need to worry about breaking it down into its components and formalizing them as procedures. Just go ahead and use a single macro.

However, if you sit down to plan a large procedure that's going to automate the creation of your company's budget-estimate spreadsheets, you can benefit greatly from dividing the code into a set of several procedures. This automation job is complex and requires a lot of code, and it's also a program that must be reused every time there's a new budget proposal.

You can go about creating modular code in two main ways:

- Record (if the application you're using supports the VBA Macro Recorder) or write a procedure as usual and then examine it and break it into modules as necessary. This is a great way to start creating modular code, but it's usually less efficient: You'll end up spending a lot of time retrofitting your original, large procedure as you break it into smaller, separate procedures.
- List the different actions that your project requires, and then code each action (or set of actions) as a separate procedure. This method requires a bit more planning but usually proves more efficient in the long run.

Arranging Your Code in Modules

Once you've created a set of procedures, you can move them to a new module within the same project or even to a different project. By grouping your procedures in modules, you can easily distribute the procedures to your colleagues without including any they don't need. In addition, you can remove from your immediate working environment any modules of code that you don't need.

> **GIVE DESCRIPTIVE NAMES TO YOUR MODULES**
>
> Give your modules descriptive names so that you can instantly identify them in the VBA Editor Project Explorer and other module-management tools. Avoid leaving modules named the default `Module1`, `Module2`, and so on.

Calling a Procedure

When one of your procedures needs to use another procedure you wrote, it calls it (by name) in the same way that you learned in Chapter 9, "Using Built-In Functions," to call a built-in function such as `MsgBox`.

To call a procedure in the same project, either enter the name of the procedure to be called as a statement or use a `Call` statement with the name of the procedure.

The syntax for the `Call` statement is the same for procedures as for functions:

```
[Call] name[, argumentlist]
```

Here, *`name`* is a required String argument giving the name of the procedure to call. Meanwhile, *`argumentlist`* is an argument (or list of several arguments) providing a comma-delimited list of the variables, arrays, or expressions to pass to the procedure. You use an argument list only for procedures that require arguments.

Calling involves two procedures, the caller and the called. For example, the following `CreateReceiptLetter` procedure (the caller) calls the procedure `FormatDocument` (the called):

```
Sub CreateReceiptLetter()
    'other actions here
    Call FormatDocument
    'other actions here
End Sub
```

Most programmers omit the `Call` keyword, using just the name of the procedure. This next code does the same thing as the previous code example:

```
Sub CreateReceiptLetter()
    'other actions here
    FormatDocument
    'other actions here
End Sub
```

However, as with calling built-in functions, some programmers believe that using the `Call` keyword can make it clearer that your code is calling a procedure, and it enables you to search more easily for your calls. (When debugging, you can see what procedures are calling others by choosing the Call Stack option on the Editor's View menu. This feature is available only in Break mode, however, not during design time.)

In the following example, a procedure named `Caller` calls a procedure named `Called`, which takes the String argument `strFeedMe`. Note that when you use `Call`, you need to enclose the argument list in parentheses:

```
Sub Caller()
    Call Called("Hello")
End Sub

Sub Called(ByVal strFeedMe As String)
    Msgbox strFeedMe
End Sub
```

Again, you can omit the `Call` keyword and, if you want, the parentheses, and achieve the same result:

```
Sub Caller()
    Called "Hello"
End Sub
```

As well as calling a procedure in the same project, you can call a procedure in another open project in the same host application (but usually not in another application). Typically, the syntax used to call a procedure in another project is as follows, although it can vary by application and version:

```
Project.Module.Procedure
```

To call a procedure in another project, you need to add a reference to that project in the VBA Editor's References dialog box. Choose Tools ➤ References, select the project (click the Browse button if you need to browse to it) and then click the OK button. Once this reference is in place, you can call the procedure.

> **CIRCULAR REFERENCES ARE NOT ALLOWED**
>
> You can't add to the current project a reference to a project that itself contains a reference to the current project. If you attempt a "circular" reference like that, when you add the reference and close the References dialog box, the VBA Editor will display a message box with the warning "Cyclic reference of projects not allowed" and the Editor will refuse to insert the reference. (It does close the References dialog box, though.)

Let's turn our attention to another benefit of modular code: you can refine your code and make it run faster by making logical improvements and visual improvements.

Making Logical Improvements to Your Code

Breaking a large procedure into several smaller procedures can improve the logic of your code by forcing you to consider each set of actions the procedure takes as *modular,* which means they're separate from other sets of actions. And you can improve the logic of your code in other ways: by using explicit variable declarations, by stripping out unnecessary statements to simplify recorded code, and by using `With` statements to eliminate repetitive object references. The following sections describe ways to improve the quality of your code.

DECLARING VARIABLES EXPLICITLY INSTEAD OF IMPLICITLY

This has been mentioned before, but it's important so let's revisit it here. Instead of declaring variables implicitly, declare all your variables explicitly:

```
Dim strName As String
strName = "Lola Montez"
```

Be explicit rather than implicit (implicit skips declaring the variable and merely assigns a value to it, which *implicitly* creates it):

```
strName = "Lola Montez"
```

Explicit declaration allows VBA to allocate only as much memory as that variable type needs. But memory these days is extremely cheap, so that's not really important. What *is* important is that explicit declaration allows you to avoid the risk of unintentionally storing the wrong type of data in the variable. When a variable is explicitly typed, VBA displays an error message if you attempt to store the wrong type of data in that variable. Implicit variables are *Variant* types, and with them VBA will store the wrong data and simply change the variable type to match.

Table 16.1 shows the details on the amounts of memory that the different types of variables require.

TABLE 16.1: Memory consumed by the different types of variables

VARIABLE	MEMORY NEEDED (BYTES)
Boolean	2
Byte	1
Currency	8
Date	8
Variant/Decimal	12
Double	8
Integer	2
Long	4
Object	4
Single	4
String	Variable-length strings: 10 bytes plus the storage required for the string, which can be up to about two billion characters; fixed-length strings: the number of bytes required to store the string, which can be from 1 to about 64,000 characters
Variant	Variants that contain numbers: 16 bytes; Variants that contain characters: 22 bytes plus the storage required for the characters

How much memory you save by specifying data types, and how much difference choosing variable types makes to your procedures, depends on the type of work you're doing. For example, if you store a million characters in a Single variable, the 12 bytes you save by specifying that it's a String variable rather than a Variant variable make little difference.

But if you use many variables on a computer with limited memory, specifying the appropriate data types for your variables might save enough memory to enable your procedure to run where it otherwise wouldn't be able to, or it might at least enable it to run faster. Of course, hardware is continually improving—and memory is hardware. Now that RAM is becoming cheap and plentiful, conserving memory is not much of an issue for programmers.

A second reason for declaring your variables explicitly rather than implicitly is to make your code easier to read and to debug. And a third reason is that you can implement some runtime range-checking. If you *know* something will be less than 32,768 and you, therefore, declare it as being the Integer data type (rather than the Long type), you'll automatically get a helpful error if a Long-size value creeps into it somehow at runtime.

Real World Scenario

SIMPLIFY RECORDED CODE

Recall that the Macro Recorder (available only in Word and Excel) offers an excellent way to get started writing code for a project. Just turn on the Recorder and carry out the actions you want your code to accomplish. The Recorder can write code for many tasks. It can't create conditional branches, loops, or a few other code features, but it nevertheless can do quite a bit.

The Macro Recorder provides a great way to kick-start creating code by letting you identify quickly the built-in objects the procedure will need to work with and the methods and properties you'll need to use with them.

But as you've seen, one drawback of the Macro Recorder is that it tends to record a lot of code that you don't actually need in your procedures. It records the *state* of a context—the status of *all* the options in the current context. And you're probably interested in only one or two options.

It's like taking a photo. The camera records *everything* that you point it at. But often you don't want to see everything, just a particular object. You took a picture of the school play. The photo contains all the kids on the stage, but you're only really interested in little Darla's lovely smile and her costume. So you use a graphics program to *crop* out (cut away) everything but Darla.

Here's an example of "cropping" code: When you record a procedure that changes one setting in a dialog box (such as switching to italic in the Font dialog box in Word), recall that the Macro Recorder nonetheless records *all* the other settings on not only that page, but also on all the other Font dialog box's pages (Character Spacing and things like that)—just in case you wanted them. But you don't. You're only interested in the italic feature.

Once you've finished recording the procedure, you'll often want to open it to make minor adjustments; to add loops, decisions, or user interface items (message boxes, input boxes, or user forms); or even to lift parts of the code for use in other procedures. When you do this, first examine the code the Macro Recorder has recorded, and where possible, strip out the statements unrelated to your purpose. Leave only the recorded pieces of code that you need. Make the code focus on what you're actually doing—the task you're carrying out. Later, you'll thank yourself if you have to examine or reuse this code: You'll be able to easily see what the code is doing: not superscript, not boldface, or any of the other settings—just italic.

Take this Word example. Compare the Applying_Arial_Font procedure that follows with the Stripped_Down_Procedure_Applying_Arial_Font procedure that comes after it:

```
Sub Applying_Arial_Font()
'
' Applying_Arial_Font Macro
' Applies the Arial font to the selected text
'
    With Selection.Font
        .Name = "Arial"
```

Continues

Continued

```
                .Size = 13
                .Bold = False
                .Italic = False
                .Underline = wdUnderlineNone
                .UnderlineColor = wdColorAutomatic
                .StrikeThrough = False
                .DoubleStrikeThrough = False
                .Outline = False
                .Emboss = False
                .Shadow = False
                .Hidden = False
                .SmallCaps = False
                .AllCaps = False
                .Color = wdColorAutomatic
                .Engrave = False
                .Superscript = False
                .Subscript = False
                .Spacing = 0
                .Scaling = 100
                .Position = 0
                .Kerning = 0
                .Animation = wdAnimationNone
            End With
        End Sub

        Sub Stripped_Down_Procedure_Applying_Arial_Font()
            Selection.Font.Name = "Arial"
        End Sub
```

As you can see, the `Stripped_Down_Procedure_Applying_Arial_Font` code has the same effect as the recorded procedure, but it contains 2 lines instead of the recorded procedure's 31.

Using *With* Statements to Simplify Your Code

When you're performing multiple actions with an object, you can often use `With` statements to avoid repeating the object reference for each action. This simplifies your code. It becomes easier to read. And it may make it run marginally faster.

For example, the following statements contain multiple references to the first `Paragraph` object—`Paragraphs(1)`—in the `ActiveDocument` object in Word:

```
ActiveDocument.Paragraphs(1).Range.Font.Bold = True
ActiveDocument.Paragraphs(1).Range.Font.Name = "Times New Roman"
ActiveDocument.Paragraphs(1).LineSpacingRule = wdLineSpaceSingle
ActiveDocument.Paragraphs(1).Borders(1).LineStyle = wdLineStyleDouble
ActiveDocument.Paragraphs(1).Borders(1).ColorIndex = wdBlue
```

You can replace this redundancy by employing a `With` structure that references the `Paragraphs(1)` object in the `ActiveDocument` object to simplify the number of references involved:

```
With ActiveDocument.Paragraphs(1)
    .Range.Font.Bold = True
    .Range.Font.Name = "Times New Roman"
    .LineSpacingRule = wdLineSpaceSingle
    .Borders(1).LineStyle = wdLineStyleDouble
    .Borders(1).ColorIndex = wdBlue
End With
```

When you need to work with multiple child objects contained within a single parent object, you can either use separate `With` statements or pick the lowest common denominator of the objects you want to work with and use an outer `With` statement along with nested `With` statements for the child objects.

If you like, you can further reduce the number of object references in the previous code example by using nested `With` statements for the `Font` object in the `Range` object and for the `Borders(1)` object, like this:

```
With ActiveDocument.Paragraphs(1)
    With .Range.Font
        .Bold = True
        .Name = "Times New Roman"
    End With
    .LineSpacingRule = wdLineSpaceSingle
    With .Borders(1)
        .LineStyle = wdLineStyleDouble
        .ColorIndex = wdBlue
    End With
End With
```

DON'T USE *WITH* STATEMENTS POINTLESSLY

`With` statements are great for reducing repetitive object references and making your code easier to read, but don't use them just because you can. If you have only one statement within a `With` statement, as in the following example (which again uses Word), you're probably wasting your time typing the extra code to set up the `With` structure:

```
With ActiveDocument.Sections(1).Headers(wdHeaderFooterPrimary) _
    .Range.Words(1)
    .Bold = True
End With
```

Likewise, don't nest `With` statements unless you need to—it gets confusing, like this bizarre example:

```
With ActiveDocument
    With .Sections(1)
```

```
            With .Headers(wdHeaderFooterPrimary)
                With .Range
                    With .Words(1)
                        With .Font
                            .Italic = True
                            .Bold = False
                            .Color = wdColorBlack
                        End With
                    End With
                End With
            End With
        End With
    End With
```

This code is better when written like this:

```
With ActiveDocument.Sections(1).Headers(wdHeaderFooterPrimary).Range. _
    Words(1).Font
    .Italic = True
    .Bold = False
    .Color = wdColorBlack
End With
```

Optimizing Your *Select Case* Statements

When you use a `Select Case` statement, arrange the `Case` statements so that the most likely ones appear first. This saves VBA some work and time—VBA goes down through the list of `Case` statements until it finds a match, so the earlier in the list it scores a match, the quicker the execution of the statement.

Don't Check Things Senselessly

If you need to implement a setting (especially a Boolean one) every time a particular procedure runs, there's no point in checking the current value.

For example, suppose you wanted to make sure the `EnableAutoRecover` property (a Boolean property that sets or returns whether the AutoRecover feature is on for the current workbook) of the `ActiveWorkbook` object in Excel is set to `True`. You could check the current value of `EnableAutoRecover` and, if it is `False`, set it to `True` like this:

```
If ActiveWorkbook.EnableAutoRecover = False Then _
    ActiveWorkbook.EnableAutoRecover = True
```

But that wastes code. Instead, simply set the property to `True`:

```
ActiveWorkbook.EnableAutoRecover = True
```

Removing Unused Elements from Your Code

To improve the efficiency of your code, try to remove all unused elements from it. When creating a complex project with many interrelated procedures, it's easy to end up with some procedures that are almost or entirely useless. You were trying out various approaches and perhaps sketched in a couple of procedures that ended up never being used, for example.

You'll find it easier to remove superfluous procedures if you've commented your code comprehensively while creating it so you can be sure that what you're removing is unused rather than used. If you're in doubt as to which procedure is calling which, display the Call Stack dialog box (see Figure 16.1); choose View ➢ Call Stack or press Ctrl+L to see what's happening. Recall that the Call Stack dialog box is available in Break mode (while you're single-stepping through a procedure, or the Editor has halted execution at a breakpoint, and so on). If one procedure has called another one during execution, they will both be listed.

Figure 16.1 reveals that the procedure named `Identify_Current_User` called the procedure named `ToggleItal` and that `ToggleItal` then called `GetClipboardText`, which, in turn, called `DocumentOpen`. Execution is currently halted (is in Break mode) within the `DocumentOpen` procedure.

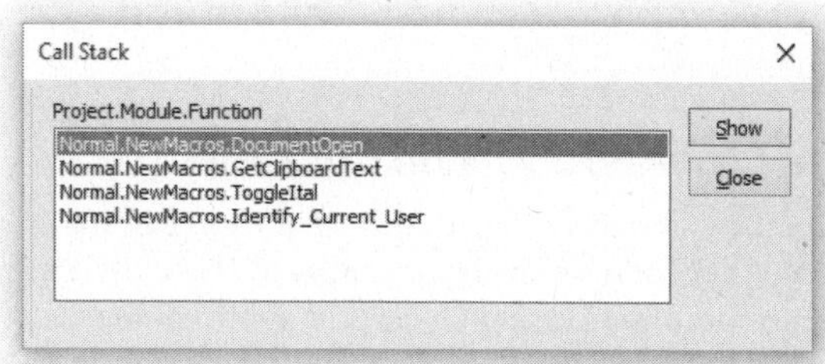

FIGURE 16.1
The Call Stack dialog box lets you see which procedure has called which.

Alternatively, try one of these techniques:

- Set a breakpoint at the beginning of a suspect procedure so that you'll be alerted when it's called.
- Display message boxes at decisive junctures in your code so you can see what's happening: Is the procedure ever called?
- Use a `Debug.Print` statement at an appropriate point (again, perhaps the beginning of a procedure) to temporarily log information in the Immediate window.

Before you remove an apparently dead procedure from your code, make sure not only that it's unused in the way the code is currently being run, but also that it's not used in ways in which the procedure *might* be run were circumstances different. If you think that the procedure might still be used, try moving it to a project from which you can easily restore it rather than deleting it altogether.

Once you've removed any unused procedures, examine the variables in the procedures. Even if you're using the `Option Explicit` declaration and declaring every variable explicitly, check that you haven't declared variables that end up not being used. For simple projects, you'll be able to catch the unused variables by using the Locals window to see which of them never get assigned a value. For more complex projects, you may want to try some of the available third-party tools that help you remove unneeded elements from your code.

If in doubt, just use the Editor's Find feature (Ctrl+F) to see if the variable name appears only once: when the variable is declared.

Removing unused procedures and variables isn't crucial. They do no real harm; they're just debris. But they do clutter up your code, potentially making it harder to understand and modify if you come back to it later for maintenance or reuse.

> **Back Up Your Modules, Forms, and Class Modules**
>
> Before removing an entire module, use the File ➤ Export File command to export a copy of the module to a `.BAS` file in a safe storage location in case the module contains anything you'll subsequently discover to be of value. Similarly, export your user forms to `.FRM` files and your classes to `.CLS` files.

Making Visual Improvements to Your Code

Another way to improve your code is to format it so it's as easy as possible to read, maintain, and modify.

Indenting the Different Levels of Code

As you've seen in the examples so far in this book, you can make code much easier to follow by indenting some lines of code with tabs or spaces to show their logical relation to each other or to visually illustrate subordination and structures such as loops.

You can click the Indent and Outdent buttons on the Editor's Edit toolbar or press Tab and Shift+Tab to quickly indent or unindent a selected block of code, with the relative indentation of the lines within the block remaining the same.

> **Labels Can't Be Indented, But That's a Good Thing**
>
> You can't indent a label—a word ending with a colon (:) and used as the target of a `GoTo` statement. If you try to indent a label, the VBA Editor won't let you. The Editor removes all spaces to the left of the label as soon as you press Enter or otherwise move the insertion point off the line containing the label. A label is a target and *should* be on the far left of its code line so you can easily see it.

Using Line-Continuation Characters to Break Long Lines

Use the line-continuation character (a space followed by an underscore, like this: _) to break long lines of code into two or more shorter lines. Breaking lines makes long statements fit within the Code window on an average-size monitor at a readable point size and enables you to break the code into more logical segments.

Using the Concatenation Character to Break Long Strings

You can't use the line-continuation character to break strings, however. If you want to break a long string, you must divide the string into smaller strings and then use the concatenation character (&) to attach the parts again. You *can* separate the parts of the divided string (which are merely separated by the line-continuation character). For example, consider a long string such as this:

```
strMessageText = "The macro has finished running. Please check your presentation
to ensure that all blank slides have been removed."
```

Instead, you could divide the string into two, and then rejoin it like this:

```
strMessageText = "The macro has finished running. " & _
    "Please check your presentation to ensure that " & _
    "all blank slides have been removed."
```

For Legacy Reasons, You Can Employ the + Character for Concatenation

Alternatively, you can use the addition character (+) to concatenate one string with another, but not to concatenate a string and a numeric variable (do that, and VBA will try to *add* them mathematically instead of concatenating them). However, your code is easier to read if you just stick with the ampersand concatenation character (&) when concatenating strings. Leave the + character for math.

Using Blank Lines to Break Up Your Code

To make your code more readable, use blank lines to separate statements into logical groups. For example, you might segregate all the variable declarations in a procedure as shown in the following example so that they stand out more clearly:

```
Sub Create_Rejection_Letter

    Dim strApplicantFirst As String, strApplicantInitial As String, _
        strApplicantLast As String, strApplicantTitle As String
    Dim strJobTitle As String
    Dim dteDateApplied As Date, dteDateInterviewed As Date
    Dim blnExperience As Boolean

    strApplicantFirst = "Shirley"
    strApplicantInitial = "P"
    strApplicantLast = "McKorley"
]
```

Using Variables to Simplify Complex Syntax

You can use variables to simplify and shorten complex syntax. For example, you could display a message box by using an awkwardly long statement such as this one:

```
If MsgBox("The document contains no text." & vbCr & vbCr _
    & "Click the Yes button to continue formatting the document." & _
```

```
    " Click the No button to cancel the procedure.", _
    vbYesNo & vbQuestion, _
    "Error Selecting Document: Cancel Procedure?") Then
```

Alternatively, you could use one String variable for building the message and another String variable for the title:

```
Dim strMsg As String
Dim strTBar As String
strMsg = "The document contains no text." & vbCr & vbCr
strMsg = _
  strMsg & "Click the Yes button to continue formatting the document. "
strMsg = strMsg & "Click the No button to cancel the procedure."
strTBar = "Error Selecting Document: Cancel Procedure?"
If MsgBox(strMsg, vbYesNo & vbQuestion, strTBar) Then
```

At first sight, this code looks more complex than the straightforward message-box statement, mostly because of the explicit variable declarations that increase the length of the code segment. But in the long run, this approach is much easier to read and modify.

In the previous example, you could also replace the `vbYesNo & vbQuestion` part of the `MsgBox` statement with a variable (preferably a Long rather than a Variant). But doing so would make the code harder to read and is seldom worthwhile.

Passing Information from One Procedure to Another Using Arguments

Often when you call another procedure, you'll need to pass information to it from the calling procedure. And you sometimes go the other way: When the called procedure has finished executing, it needs to pass back info to the caller.

Recall that the preferred way to pass information from a caller procedure to a called procedure is by using *arguments*. You declare the arguments to pass in the declaration line of the procedure that passes them. The arguments appear in the parentheses after the procedure's name. You can pass either a single argument (as the first of the following statements does) or multiple arguments separated by commas (as the second does):

```
Sub PassOneArgument(MyArg)
Sub PassTwoArguments(FirstArg, SecondArg)
```

As with functions (discussed in Chapter 9), you can pass an argument either *by reference* or *by value*. When a procedure passes an argument to another procedure by reference, the recipient procedure gets access to the memory location where the original variable is stored and can change the original variable. By contrast, when a procedure passes an argument to another procedure by value, the recipient procedure gets only a copy of the information in the variable and can't change the information in the original variable.

Passing an argument by reference is useful when you want to manipulate the variable in the recipient procedure and then return the variable to the procedure from which it originated. Passing an argument by value is useful when you want to use the information stored in the variable in the recipient procedure and at the same time make sure the original information in the variable doesn't change.

By reference is the default way to pass an argument, but you can also use the ByRef keyword to state explicitly that you want to pass an argument by reference. Both of the following statements pass the argument MyArg by reference:

```
Sub PassByReference(MyArg)
Sub PassByReference(ByRef MyArg)
```

To pass an argument by value, you must use the ByVal keyword. The following statement passes the ValArg argument by value:

```
Sub PassByValue(ByVal ValArg)
```

In practice, however, you'll rarely, if ever, need to employ ByVal. I've never done it in my decades of VBA programming. Arguments are nearly universally passed by reference, the default.

If necessary, you can pass some arguments for a procedure by reference and others by value. The following statement passes the MyArg argument by reference and the ValArg argument by value:

```
Sub PassBoth(ByRef MyArg, ByVal ValArg)
```

You can explicitly declare the data type of arguments you pass in order to take up less memory and ensure that your procedures are passing the type of information you intend. But when passing an argument by reference, you need to make sure that the data type of the argument you're passing matches the data type expected by the called procedure. For example, if you declare a String in the caller procedure and try to pass it as an argument when the called procedure is expecting a Variant, VBA gives an error.

To declare the data type of an argument, include a data-type declaration in the argument list. The following statement declares MyArg as a String and ValArg as a Variant:

```
Sub PassBoth(MyArg As String, ValArg As Variant)
```

You can specify an optional argument by using the Optional keyword. Place the Optional keyword before the ByRef or ByVal keyword if you need to use ByRef or ByVal:

```
Sub PassBoth(ByRef MyArg As String, ByVal ValArg As Variant, _
    Optional ByVal MyOptArg As Variant)
```

Listing 16.1 shows a segment of a procedure that uses arguments to pass information from one procedure to another.

LISTING 16.1: Passing arguments from one procedure to another

```
Sub GetCustomerInfo()
    Dim strCustName As String, strCustCity As String, _
        strCustPhone As String
    'Get strCustName, strCustCity, strCustPhone from a database
    CreateCustomer strCustName, strCustCity, strCustPhone
End Sub
```

```
7.  Sub CreateCustomer(ByRef strCName As String, _
        ByRef strCCity As String, ByVal strCPhone As String)
8.      Dim strCustomer As String
9.      strCustomer = strCName & vbTab & strCCity _
            & vbTab & strCPhone
10.     'take action with strCustomer string here
11. End Sub
```

Listing 16.1 contains two minimalist procedures—`GetCustomerInfo` and `CreateCustomer`—that show how to use arguments to pass information between procedures:

- The first procedure, `GetCustomerInfo`, explicitly declares three String variables in line 2: `strCustName`, `strCustCity`, and `strCustPhone`.
- Line 3 contains a comment indicating that you would write additional code here to obtain the data and assign information to the variables.
- Line 4 calls the `CreateCustomer` procedure and passes to it the variables `strCustName`, `strCustCity`, and `strCustPhone` as arguments. Because this statement doesn't use the `Call` keyword, the arguments aren't enclosed in parentheses.
- Execution then switches to line 7, which starts the `CreateCustomer` procedure by declaring the three String arguments it uses: `strCName` and `strCCity` are to be passed by reference, and `strCPhone` is to be passed by value.
- Line 8 declares the String variable `strCustomer`. Line 9 then assigns to `strCustomer` the information in `strCName`, a tab, the information in `strCCity`, another tab, and the information in `strCPhone`.
- Line 10 contains a comment indicating where the procedure would take action with the `strCustomer` string (for example, dumping it into some kind of primitive database), and line 11 ends the procedure.

Passing Information Back from a Called Procedure

Just a reminder: Functions, not subs, are used to pass information *back* to a caller. Both functions and subs are procedures, but functions are specifically designed to send information back to a caller.

This code example calls a function that adds state tax to a purchase price, and then passes back the resulting total cost:

```
Sub FindTotalCost()

Dim OriginalCost, TotalCost ' declare two variant types
OriginalCost = 155 'this sweater is expensive

TotalCost = AddTax(OriginalCost) 'call the AddTax function
MsgBox TotalCost 'show the final cost including 7% tax


```

```
10. End Sub
11.
12. Function AddTax(SubTotal)
13.
14. AddTax = SubTotal * 1.07 'do the math and assign the result
15.                          'to the function name so it gets passed back
16.
17. End Function
```

Data is passed from the caller to the called in line 6. Data is passed back from the called to the caller by assigning a value to the name of the function in line 14.

Passing Information from One Procedure to Another Using Private or Public Variables

Another way to pass information from one procedure to another is to use either private variables or public variables (also known as *global* variables, as opposed to variables that are local to individual procedures). You can use private variables if the procedures that need to share information are located in the same module. If the procedures are located in different modules, you'll need to use public variables to pass the information.

> **Avoid Using Global Variables to Pass Data**
>
> Using private or public variables to pass information from one procedure to another is widely considered poor programming practice. Doing so makes it harder to track the flow of information between procedures, especially when several procedures are involved. However, you may sometimes find this way of passing information helpful—or you may be required to work with someone else's code that uses this approach.

Listing 16.2 contains an example of passing information by using private variables.

Listing 16.2: Passing data using a private variable

```
Private strPassMe As String

Sub PassingInfo()
    strPassMe = "Hello."
    PassingInfoBack
    MsgBox strPassMe
End Sub

Sub PassingInfoBack()
    strPassMe = strPassMe & " How are you?"
End Sub
```

Listing 16.2 begins by declaring the private String variable `strPassMe` at the beginning of the code sheet for the module. `strPassMe` is then available to all the procedures in the module.

- The `PassingInfo` procedure (lines 3 to 7) assigns the text `Hello.` (with the period) to `strPassMe` in line 4 and then calls the `PassingInfoBack` procedure in line 5.
- Execution then shifts to line 9, which starts the `PassingInfoBack` procedure.
- Line 10 adds `How are you?` with a leading space to the `strPassMe` String variable.
- Line 11 ends the `PassingInfoBack` procedure, at which point execution returns to the `PassingInfo` procedure at line 6, which displays a message box containing the `strPassMe` string (now *`Hello. How are you?`*).
- Line 7 ends the procedure.

Creating and Using Classes

A *class* is the formal definition of an object—typically, a custom object. By defining classes, you can build your own custom objects. A class is essentially a template for an object: Once you've defined the class in your code, VB will then create objects based on it when the code executes.

The relationship between class and object is sometimes described as similar to a cookie cutter and a cookie or a blueprint and the houses based on that blueprint. The former is a description, the latter is the description brought to life.

Another way to think of the distinction between class and object is to recall the distinction between design time and runtime. You create a *class* during design time by writing code that describes the *object* (or multiple objects). The class will come into being during runtime when the class code executes.

The phrase *come into being* is more formally expressed as follows: an object is *instantiated*. (An *instance*—the object—of the class comes into existence during runtime.) Got it?

What Can You Do with Class Modules?

Programming means telling the computer how to process some information.

Information to be processed can be stored in various places. For example, you can store it in a database that your code accesses. Or you can type it into your code, such as storing the information *`Donald`* in a string variable:

```
MyString = "Donald"
```

The second half of information-processing is executing code that manipulates the information (the data). You've been doing this throughout this book. Here we process some data by computing the length of a string:

```
MsgBox Len(myString)
```

One thing that is interesting about objects is that they not only can process information; they can also *contain* it. They can hide their data (properties) or their processing (methods) from outside programming. This hiding is called *encapsulation*.

You can use objects to store information, to process information, and to make information selectively accessible (hide it or not, as the programmer specifies) to the various other objects in an application.

Consider what is to me the most successful application of object-oriented programming (or OOP): the controls you can put on a user form, such as the TextBoxes or Labels that we explored in Chapter 14, "Creating Simple Custom Dialog Boxes," and Chapter 15, "Creating Complex Forms."

A Label is an object that has a set of *properties*, which can be visualized as both data and as processing capabilities. When you assign the value 33, say, to a Label's `Left` property, the Label automatically moves to that location on the form.

You did no programming to make this move happen. You merely passed a desired position to the object and the object's internal capability to move itself took over and carried out the necessary tasks to make this happen. This is encapsulation: The programming that moves a Label is hidden from the outside world (put another way: hidden from other programmers). The object has its own capabilities. And it contains its own internal data as well (the kind of line that frames a Label, its default width, the color of its background, and so on).

When OOP is applied to more abstract concepts such as translating procedural programming (subs and functions) into OOP (objects), the results are mixed. Some programmers swear by OOP; others demur. OOP has become quite popular in many professional programming circles, but even after decades of implementation, OOP still causes controversy. For small jobs like simple macros, OOP is clearly overkill. For large projects, you might like the organizational and security features of OOP. And, if you intend to go into professional programming, you must understand how to use it.

A Brief Overview of Classes

To create a class in VBA, you insert a *class module* in a project (Insert ➤ Class Module) and give the class the name by which you'll access it. You then use the Code window to create the code (constant and variable declarations, subroutines, and functions) that defines the properties and methods the class will have. When you've finished, the class contains all the information the custom object needs to perform its tasks and store data.

A major distinction between a class module and a regular code module is that you don't directly execute code in a class module. Instead, in a regular code module you declare an object variable of the class's type. You then use this variable to access the class's members (its properties and methods) in your regular code.

The concept of classes can be difficult to grasp, so the following sections present a simple example of a class that relates to something physical—the book you're holding. The example describes a class named `Book` that contains the salient information about a book. During runtime, after creating the `Book` object, the example's code adds this book's information to the `Book` object.

Entire books endeavor to explain OOP and its uses. But I'll give you just a taste of it here. The following example class works in any VBA host application.

Planning Your Class

Before you start creating a class, decide the following:

- A class describes an object, so...what does this object *do*?
- What information does the class need to contain for the object to do what it's supposed to do? You use variables and properties to store this information. You use *variables* to store information used privately, internally inside the object, and *properties* to make available

pieces of that information that need to be accessed from outside the object. You can create both read-only and read/write properties.

- What capabilities should this object have? Things a class can do, its behaviors, are called its *methods*. You create subroutines and functions to implement the class's methods—subroutines for the methods that return no value after doing their job and functions for the methods that do return a value after executing.

Objects based on our `Book` class will contain information about a book project. Note that I said *objects*, plural. A single class can create as many objects during runtime as the programmer wants, just as a single cookie cutter can stamp out multiple cookies. Or as a single blueprint can be used to build many townhouses.

If you're a librarian programmer, you might use the `Book` class to generate thousands of Book objects.

The class we'll construct will need properties for storing information such as the title, author, and price, and it will need a method that displays all this book information.

Creating a Class Module

The first step in creating your class is to insert a class module into your project. You create a class module in much the same way you create a regular module.

In the Project Explorer, right-click the target project or one of the items it contains and choose Insert ➤ Class Module from the context menu. Alternatively, choose Insert ➤ Class Module from the Editor's menu bar, or click the Insert button on the Standard toolbar and choose Class Module from the drop-down list.

The VBA Editor creates a new class module named `Class`*n* (where *n* is the next-higher consecutive number not yet employed to name a class module) and opens a Code window for it. If the project doesn't already contain a Class Modules folder, VBA adds one, and it appears in the Project Explorer.

If you have the Require Variable Declarations option selected (on the Editor page of the Tools ➤ Options dialog box in the VBA Editor), the VBA Editor automatically places an `Option Explicit` statement in the declarations area at the top of the code sheet for the class, just as it does for an ordinary module.

If you don't have the Require Variable Declarations option selected, it's still a good idea to type in the `Option Explicit` statement to force yourself to declare variables explicitly.

Naming the Class

Now change the name of the class to something more descriptive than `Class`*n*. Press F4 to display the Properties window (if it's not already displayed) and enter the new name in the `(Name)` text box. Make the name descriptive, because you'll be using it in your code and you'll want its purpose to be easily grasped. We can name our example class `Book`. Press Enter or click elsewhere in the Visual Basic Editor window to make the change take effect.

Setting the *Instancing* Property

The `Instancing` property determines whether a class module is visible (can be instantiated—brought into existence) from an outside project.

Recall that an outside project must first reference the project that the class module is in before any access to another project's objects is even possible. Referencing is accomplished by Tools ➤ References in the Editor.

The default setting, `1 - Private`, prevents other projects from seeing the class module and from working with instances (objects) of that class. In other words, the object is encapsulated, hidden.

The other setting is `2 - PublicNonCreatable`, and it allows an outside project to see the class. The outside project, even with a reference, however, still can't create instances (create objects) from the class by itself. *The instantiation must take place in the project that hosts the class.*

So, for one project to access an object in another, three conditions must be met:

- The Instancing property in the project containing the object must be set to `PublicNonCreatable`.
- The project containing the object must have instantiated that object.
- The outside project must have established a reference to the project containing the object.

To permit an outside project access to instances of a class (objects), set the `Instancing` property to `2 - PublicNonCreatable`. Otherwise, leave the default setting of `1 - Private` intact. With the default `Private` setting, only the project that has the class can access objects instantiated from that class.

Declaring Variables and Constants for the Class

After setting the `Instancing` property, you should declare the variables and constants that the class will need for its internal operations.

These declarations work just like the declarations you've seen so far in the book, except that you'll probably want to use a naming convention to indicate that the variables and constants belong to a class rather than to a procedure. We'll use the prefix `book` on the constants and variables to make it easy for the programmer to see that they're part of the `Book` class.

The `Book` class uses the declarations shown in the following code snippet to declare one constant (`bookName`) and five variables (`bookTitle`, `bookAuthor`, `bookPages`, `bookPrice`, and `bookPublicationDate`) of assorted data types:

```
Const BookName = "Book Project"
Dim BookTitle As String
Dim BookAuthor As String
Dim BookPages As Long
Dim BookPrice As Currency
Dim BookPublicationDate As Date
```

Adding Properties to the Class

Now add the properties to the class. Table 16.2 lists the properties that the `Book` class uses.

TABLE 16.2: Properties of the Book class

PROPERTY	DESCRIPTION
Title	A read/write String property that sets or returns the formal title of the book
Author	A read/write String property that sets or returns the author's name
Pages	A read/write Long property that sets or returns the page count of the book
Price	A read/write Currency property that sets or returns the price of the book
PublicationDate	A read/write Date property that sets or returns the publication date of the book

You can create properties for a class in either of two ways. The first way is less formal than the second but provides you with less control over the properties.

CREATING A PROPERTY BY USING A PUBLIC VARIABLE

One way to create a property in your code is to declare a public variable in the class module. Doing this creates a read/write property with the name of the variable. For example, the following statement (when typed into a class module) creates a read/write Boolean property named `HardCover`:

```
Public HardCover As Boolean
```

Using a public variable like this is a quick way to create a property, but it's a bit limited: It must be read/write. You can't choose to make the property read-only (or write-only). What's more, you can't execute any other code when the program's code sets or returns the value of the property.

After declaring a public variable, your code can then set and return the property's value in the usual way. For example, say we've created the Boolean property `HardCover` in an instance named `MastVBA` of the `Book` class. The following statements *set* (store, write data in) the property and then display a message box *returning* (reading the value from) the property:

```
MastVBA.HardCover = False
MsgBox MastVBA.HardCover
```

Something special is illustrated here. The name of the *class* is `Book`, but notice that the name of an object instantiated from this class is `MastVBA`. Objects—there can be many derived from a given class—will each have its individual object name. Instantiated objects should not have the same name as the class from which they spring.

CREATING A PROPERTY BY USING PROPERTY PROCEDURES

The second and more formal and flexible way to create a property is to use property procedures. There are three types of property procedures—`Property Let`, `Property Get`, and `Property Set`:

- A `Property Let` procedure assigns a value to a property. It *writes*.
- A `Property Get` procedure returns the value from a property. It *reads*.
- A `Property Set` procedure creates a reference to an object. (This is similar to how you create an object variable in ordinary, non-object procedures.)

You typically use these procedures in pairs, pairing a `Property Get` procedure with a `Property Let` procedure. That creates a read/write capability. Or you pair a `Property Set` procedure with a `Property Let` procedure. If you use a `Property Get` procedure on its own, that property will be read-only.

Assigning a Value to a Property with a Property Let *Procedure*

To permit outside code to assign a value to an object's property, you use a `Property Let` procedure. The syntax for a `Property Let` procedure is as follows:

```
Property Let name ([arglist,] value)
    [statements]
End Property
```

These are the components of the syntax:

- The `Property` keyword starts the procedure, and the `End Property` keywords end the procedure.
- *`name`* is a required argument specifying the name of the property procedure being created. If you also create a paired `Property Get` procedure as well for this property, use the same name as the `Property Let` procedure.
- *`arglist`* is a required argument listing the arguments that are passed to the procedure. An argument list is required here because a `Let` procedure is designed to assign a value or values to this property. So, the outside code must provide at least one value. If *`arglist`* contains multiple arguments, you separate them with commas.

For example, the following `Property Let` procedure creates the String property `Title`, assigning the argument `NewTitle` and passing its value to the variable `bookTitle`:

```
Property Let Title(NewTitle As String)
    bookTitle = NewTitle
End Property
```

If you don't add a `Property Get` procedure for this `Title` data, the property named `Title` will be write-only. Write-only properties aren't widely useful, so the next step is to write code that reads the value in the property. Then it becomes a read/write property.

Returning a Value from a Property with a Property Get *Procedure*

To return a value from a property, you use a `Property Get` procedure. The syntax for a `Property Get` procedure is as follows:

```
Property Get name [(arglist)] [As type]
    [statements]
End Property
```

The components of the syntax are the same as for the `Property Let` procedure, except for two things:

- First, `Property Get` adds the optional *`type`* argument, which specifies the data type for the property.

- Second, for `Property Get`, the *`arglist`* argument is optional. You *can* have arguments for `Property Get` procedures, but you won't usually need to. If you do use arguments, their names and data types must match those in the corresponding `Property Let` procedure.

For example, the following `Property Get` procedure creates the String property `Title`, assigning to it the contents of the `bookTitle` variable:

```
Property Get Title() As String
    Title = bookTitle
End Property
```

If this `Property Get` procedure existed alone (without being paired with a corresponding `Property Let` procedure), it would be a read-only property. Use `Property Get` alone if you don't want to allow outside code to modify this property in any way.

However, because we've paired it with the `Property Let Title` procedure shown in the previous section, you now have a read/write property.

Assigning an Object to a Property with a Property Set *Procedure*

Instead of assigning a value to a property, you can assign an object to it. To do so, you use a `Property Set` procedure rather than a `Property Let` procedure. The syntax for a `Property Set` procedure is as follows:

```
Property Set name ([arglist,] reference)
    [statements]
End Property
```

The components of the syntax are the same as for the `Property Let` procedure, except that `Property Set` uses the *`reference`* argument rather than the `value` argument. *`reference`* is a required argument specifying the object to reference.

For example, the following `Property Set` procedure creates the object property `Where` that references a range:

```
Property Set Where(rngR As Range)
    bookRange = rngR
End Property
```

> **BOTH *SET* AND *LET* CAN BE USED WITH OBJECT VARIABLES**
>
> For an object variable, you can use both a `Property Set` procedure and a `Property Let` procedure, but in most cases it makes more sense to use only a `Property Set` procedure.

THE PROPERTIES FOR THE BOOK CLASS

Listing 16.3 shows the full listing of properties for the `Book` class.

LISTING 16.3: All the properties of the Book class

```
Option Explicit

Const BookName = "VBA Book Project"
Dim BookTitle As String
Dim BookAuthor As String
Dim BookPages As Integer
Dim BookPrice As Currency
Dim BookPublicationDate As Date

Public Property Let Title(strT As String)
    BookTitle = strT
End Property

Public Property Get Title() As String
    Title = BookTitle
End Property

Public Property Let Author(strA As String)
    BookAuthor = strA
End Property

Public Property Get Author() As String
    Author = BookAuthor
End Property

Public Property Let Pages(intPages As Integer)
    BookPages = intPages
End Property

Public Property Get Pages() As Integer
    Pages = BookPages
End Property

Public Property Let Price(curP As Currency)
    BookPrice = curP
End Property

Public Property Get Price() As Currency
    Price = BookPrice
End Property

Public Property Let PublicationDate(dtePD As Date)
    BookPublicationDate = dtePD
End Property

Public Property Get PublicationDate() As Date
    PublicationDate = BookPublicationDate
End Property
```

In Listing 16.3, each property for the `Book` class is declared as Public so that it is publicly accessible.

The code illustrates how you should organize your paired procedures by putting each `Property Let` procedure next to the corresponding `Property Get` procedure: The `Property Let Title` procedure in lines 10 through 12 is matched by the `Property Get Title` procedure in lines 14 through 16, and so on for the `Author`, `Pages`, `Price`, and `PublicationDate` property procedures.

Pairing the procedures makes it easy to read the code to make sure each procedure that should have a counterpart does have one, and to make sure the arguments match.

Adding Methods to a Class

Now that we've created internal variables (properties) as places to store data in our object, it's time to add some internal programming that will process that data, or data passed to the object. It's time to add the class's *methods*. You do this by adding subroutines and functions as necessary. As you'll see at the end of this chapter, the VBA Editor will display a list of the members—properties and methods—of an object you create, or objects built into VBA

Subroutines and functions you create within a class are like the subroutines and functions you use in ordinary, non-object code modules.

Our example `Book` class uses only one method, `ShowInfo`, which displays a message box showing the properties of the book. Listing 16.4 displays the `ShowInfo` procedure.

LISTING 16.4: The `ShowInfo` method of the `Book` class

```
1.  Sub ShowInfo()
2.      Dim strM As String
3.      strM = "Title:" & vbTab & BookTitle & vbCr
4.      strM = strM & "Author:" & vbTab & BookAuthor & vbCr
5.      strM = strM & "Pages:" & vbTab & BookPages & vbCr
6.      strM = strM & "Price:" & vbTab & "$" & BookPrice & vbCr
7.      strM = strM & "Date:" & vbTab & Me.PublicationDate & vbCr
8.          MsgBox strM, vbOKOnly + vbInformation, BookName _
9.          & " Information"
10. End Sub
```

The `ShowInfo` procedure builds a string containing the information from the class and then displays the string in a message box. Here's what happens:

- Line 2 declares the String variable `strM`, which the procedure uses to store the information for the `prompt` argument in the message box.
- Line 3 adds to `strM` the text `Title:`, a tab, the contents of the `bookTitle` variable (which contains the title of the book in the object), and a carriage return.
- Line 4 builds on `strM`, adding the author information. Likewise, line 5 adds the information on the page count, and line 6 adds the price information (including a dollar sign for completeness).

- Line 7 also builds on `strM`, adding the date information. However, instead of using the class's internal variable (`bookPublicationDate`) to return the date stored, it calls the `PublicationDate` property of the object (which is identified by the `Me` keyword). This is by way of an example—returning `bookPublicationDate` works fine too. But you'll see the difference when you retrieve information from the object: Instead of supplying the variable, VBA runs the `Property Get PublicationDate` procedure to return the information.
- Line 9 displays an OK-style message box containing the string `strM`. The message-box title is set to `bookName` (the constant that contains the text `Book Project`) and `Information`, and the message box uses an Information icon.

Using Your Class

Recall that you can't execute class code directly. You can't put your insertion point inside the `ShowInfo` procedure and press F5 to run the code or F8 to step through the code.

A class is a description of an object not yet in existence. Again, think blueprint for a house.

So, before you can execute or test a class, you must create an instance of the class. You can't test the plumbing in a house by just looking at the blueprints before the house has been built. In other words, you must create an object based on the class template and then test the object.

To instantiate an object, you write code in an ordinary, non-object code module (like the modules we've been using throughout this book so far, such as the `Module1` or `NewMacros` module).

To use the class you created, you create a new instance of the object by using a `New` keyword. The `New` keyword can be employed in either a `Dim` statement or a `Set` statement. For example, the following statement creates a new object variable based on the `Book` class:

```
Dim myBook As New Book
```

The following statements declare an Object variable named `bookAnotherBook` and then assign to it a new instance of the `Book` object:

```
Dim bookAnotherBook As Object
Set bookAnotherBook = New Book
```

You can then access the properties and methods of the `Book` object as you would any other VBA object's properties and methods (note the syntax: `objectVariableName.Property`). For example, the following statement sets the `Price` property of the `bookAnotherBook` object:

```
bookAnotherBook.Price = 54.99
```

Listing 16.5 contains a short procedure called `Class_Test` that shows the `Book` class in action. Type this procedure into an ordinary code module (not a class module). And be sure the module you type this into is in the *same project* as the `Book` class module you created earlier.

LISTING 16.5: Testing the `Book` class

```
Sub Class_Test()
    Dim myBook As New Book
```

```
 4.
 5.        myBook.Title = "Mastering VBA for Microsoft Office 2016"
 6.        myBook.Price = 49.99
 7.        myBook.Author = "Richard Mansfield"
 8.        myBook.Pages = 880
 9.        myBook.PublicationDate = #8/17/2016#
10.
11.        myBook.ShowInfo
12.
13.    End Sub
```

The listing shows an example of how to use a class in your programming. Here's what happens:

- Line 1 begins the `Class_Test` procedure, and line 13 ends it.
- Line 2 is a spacer. Line 3 declares a new object variable named `myBook` of the `Book` class. Line 4 is another spacer.
- Lines 5 through 9 set the five properties of the `myBook` object—`Title`, `Price`, `Author`, `Pages`, and `PublicationDate`—as you'd set the properties for any other object. Note that the object name (the object variable name) is separated by a period from the properties and methods of that object.
- Line 10 is a spacer. Line 11 invokes the `ShowInfo` method of the `myBook` object—again, as you'd invoke a method for any other object.

You can now test your object, clicking inside this procedure to put the blinking insertion cursor there and then pressing F5 (run) or F8 (single-stepping). Try single-stepping to see how the instantiation takes place and how the inner workings of the object add info to the properties and carry out the `ShowInfo` method.

Here's another quick experiment. Notice that the VBA Editor's Auto List Members feature works with objects you create, as well as objects built into VBA itself, such as Excel's `Workbooks` object. Remember that if in Excel's VBA Editor Code window you type **`workbooks.`** (you must type the period), suddenly a list drops down showing you all the members—the properties and methods—of the `workbooks` object. To then add one of these members to your code, just click it or use the down-arrow key to select it and then press Enter.

Similarly, when you are programming with the `MyBook` object, typing **`MyBook`** followed by a period drops that object's members list down, as shown in Figure 16.2:

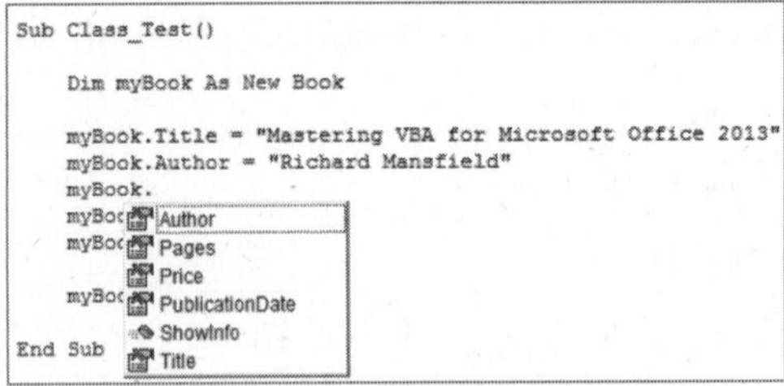

Sub Class_Test()
Dim myBook As New Book
myBook.Title = "Mastering VBA for Microsoft Office 2013"
myBook.Author = "Richard Mansfield"
myBook.
Author
Pages
Price
PublicationDate
ShowInfo
Title
End Sub

FIGURE 16.2 VBA's helpful Auto List Members feature shows the properties and methods of your objects.

The Bottom Line

Arrange your code in modules. Rather than use a single lengthy, complex procedure that accomplishes many tasks at once, programmers usually subdivide their code into smaller, self-contained procedures—dedicated to a single, discrete task.

Master It Shorter, self-contained, single-task procedures offer the programmer several advantages. Name three.

Call a procedure. You execute a procedure by calling it from within your programming code.

Master It How do you call a procedure?

Pass information from one procedure to another. Sometimes a procedure requires that you pass it some information. For example, a procedure that searches text and makes some style changes to it will require that you pass the text you want to modify.

Sometimes a procedure passes back information to the procedure that called it. For example, it might pass back a message describing whether the actions taken in the procedure were (or were not) accomplished successfully.

Master It What kind of procedure can pass back information to the caller?

Understand what classes are and what they're for. Contemporary computer programs employ classes for various reasons—to help organize large programs, to make code more easily reusable, to provide certain kinds of security, or as a substitute for the frowned-upon public variables. But beginners sometimes have a hard time wrapping their minds around OOP concepts, particularly the relationship between classes and objects.

Master It What is the difference between a class and an object?

Choose the correct answer (only one answer is correct):

1. A class is like a cookie and an object is like a cookie cutter.
2. A class is like a programmer and an object is like a module.
3. A class is like a blueprint and an object is like a house built from that blueprint.

Create a class. The VBA Editor employs a special kind of module for containing classes.

Master It How do you create a class module in the VBA Editor?

Chapter 17

Debugging Your Code and Handling Errors

In this chapter, you'll learn some of the things that can go wrong in your VBA code and what you can do about them. You'll examine the types of errors that can occur, from simple typos to infinite loops to errors that occur only once in a while (intermittent bugs are usually the hardest to locate).

The chapter starts by explaining the basics of debugging. Then you'll work with the debugging tools available in VBA and practice using these tools to get the bugs out of some examples. The chapter concludes with a discussion of various ways to have your program itself respond to errors that happen during runtime.

IN THIS CHAPTER, YOU WILL LEARN TO DO THE FOLLOWING:

- Understand the basic principles of debugging
- Recognize the four different types of errors you'll create
- Employ VBA's debugging tools
- Deal with runtime errors

Principles of Debugging

A *bug* is an error in hardware or software that causes a program to execute other than as intended. *Debugging* means removing the bugs from hardware or software.

WHERE DID THE TERM *BUG* COME FROM?

There are various explanations of the etymology of the word *bug* as used in computer programming, ranging from apocryphal stories of moths being found in the circuit boards of malfunctioning computers to musings that the word came from the mythological *bugbear*, an unwelcome beast. But in fact, the term *bug* has been used to mean something troublesome for centuries. For more information, see the "bug" entry in the *Free On-line Dictionary of Computing* at a site such as `http://foldoc.org/`.

Your goal when debugging should be to remove all bugs from your code. Your order of business will probably go something like this:

1. First, test your code to see whether it works as it should. Put it through its paces. Test it by running the procedure once or twice using suitable files or other appropriate data. Try all the options the macro makes available to the user. Even if it seems to work, continue testing for a reasonable period with various data from various sample documents before unleashing the procedure on the world (or your colleagues).
2. If your code doesn't work as you expected it to, you'll need to debug it. That means following the techniques described in this chapter to locate the bugs and then remove them. Once you've removed all the bugs that you can find, retest the code as described in the first step. This is important, because sometimes the act of debugging itself introduces new bugs.
3. When testing your code, try to anticipate unusual, perhaps exotic ways that users might employ your code. For example, you might write a sophisticated procedure for manipulating a Word document on the (perfectly reasonable) assumption that the document will be open when the user starts the procedure running. You can test it on sample documents until you're blue in the face and it'll work fine every time. But if a user tries to run the procedure without first opening a document, it crashes.

   And don't make fun of this user. It might seem sensible to users that the procedure *should* be launched before a file is loaded. Users might expect the procedure to display an input box asking them which document they want to manipulate. And more important, users also expect that you will anticipate and handle unexpected errors without crashing your programming. There are ways to *trap* unanticipated user behavior or other runtime errors and respond to them gracefully. What does your program do if the user attempts to save a file to a disk that's full, for example? Just crash and thereby lose all the information they've spent time typing in?
4. When you're ready to distribute your procedure, you may want to write instructions for its use. In these instructions, you may also need to document any bugs that you can't squash or circumstances under which the procedure shouldn't be run. But it's better to build instructions, responses to unanticipated problems, and other kinds of *error trapping* into the macro itself. Try to make your code bulletproof.

Debugging a procedure tends to be idiosyncratic. There's no magic wand that you can wave over your code to banish bugs (although the VBA Editor does its best to help you eliminate certain types of errors from your code as you create it). Moreover, such simple things as forgetting to initialize a variable can wreak havoc on your code.

You'll probably develop your own approach to debugging, partly because your programming will inevitably be written in your own style. But when debugging, it helps to focus on understanding what the code is supposed to do. You then correlate this with your observations of what the code actually does. When you reconcile the two, you'll probably have worked out how to debug the procedure.

Also, the longer and more complex your code, the higher the probability that it will contain bugs. Certain kinds of bugs occur because of interactions among the parts of a project. And obviously, the larger the project, the more parts with potential side effects, so keep your code as simple as possible by breaking it into separate procedures and modules, as discussed in Chapter

16, "Building Modular Code and Using Classes." Small code sections with distinct, small tasks to accomplish are almost always easier to debug than large lumps of code that try to do several things all at once. Remember that most debugging is a matter of locating *where* in your code the problem occurs. If you're testing a small module of code with a very easily specified objective, locating a bug is that much easier.

The Different Types of Errors

You'll encounter four basic kinds of errors in your programming:

- Language errors
- Compile errors
- Runtime errors
- Program logic errors

The following sections look at these kinds of errors in turn and discuss how to prevent them. After that, you'll examine the tools VBA provides for debugging.

Language Errors

The first type of error is a *language error* (also known as a *syntax error*). When you mistype a word in the Code window, omit a vital piece of punctuation (and in programming, all punctuation is vital), scramble a statement, or leave off the end of a construction, that's a language error. If you've worked your way through the book to this point, you've probably already made dozens of language errors as part of the learning process and through simple typos.

VBA helps you eliminate many language errors as you create them, as you'll see later in this chapter. Those language errors that the VBA Editor doesn't catch as you type them in usually show up as *compile errors* during runtime testing, so the next section shows you examples of both language errors and compile errors.

Compile Errors

Compile errors occur when VBA can't compile a statement correctly—that is, when VBA can't turn a statement that you've entered into viable code.

For example, if your programming tells VBA to use a certain property for an object that doesn't have that property, a compile error results. Compilation is the act of turning your *source code* (the programming you type into the Editor) into the lower-level commands understandable by the computer. For example, when you press F5 to execute your program, VBA starts off by compiling your programming. If it finds a problem during compilation, it displays an error message.

The good news is that the VBA Editor detects many language errors and some compile errors as soon as you move the insertion point from the offending line. You don't even have to press F5 in many cases. For example, try typing the following statement in the Code window and pressing Enter to create a new line (or pressing ↑ or ↓ to move to another line, or clicking the mouse in another line in the macro):

```
If X > Y
```

The VBA Editor displays the compile error "Expected: Then or GoTo" (see Figure 17.1) to tell you that the statement is missing a vital element: it should say `If X > Y Then` or `If X > Y GoTo`. (If you don't see the error message, there are two possibilities: Either you have turned off the Auto Syntax Check option [Tools ➤ Options] or you didn't actually type it in by hand and press Enter.)

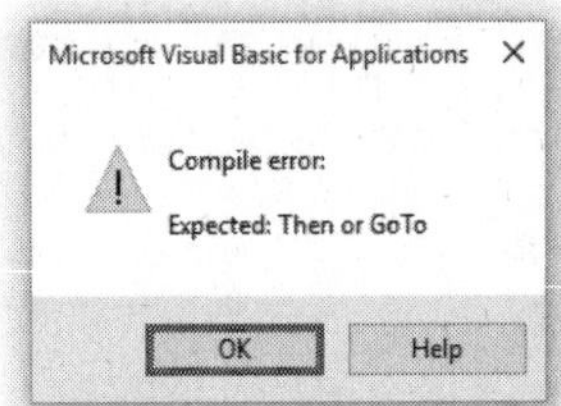

FIGURE 17.1
The VBA Editor helps debug your code by identifying many compile errors as it checks the statements you enter.

Every time you enter a line of code, the Editor examines that line for completeness and accuracy. In this example, VBA knows that when the code contains an `If` command, there must be a subsequent `Then` or `GoTo` command. And so the Editor rejects the line and informs you what the problem is.

This vigilance on the part of the VBA Editor prevents you from running into this type of error deep in the execution of your code.

Real World Scenario

DECIDE FOR YOURSELF IF YOU LIKE THE AUTO SYNTAX CHECK FEATURE

This chapter assumes that you're keeping VBA's Auto Syntax Check feature and other features switched on. If you have Auto Syntax Check turned off (Tools ➤ Options ➤ Editor tab), you won't see the error message displayed in Figure 17.1. Instead, the only warning you will get about that incomplete line of code will be that the VBA Editor turns the line red. Code turned red is the Editor's way of telling you that it's choking on your inadequate programming. You can either try to fix the error right then or keep on coding—putting off the debugging process until you've sketched in more code in the procedure.

Some developers choose to turn off Auto Syntax Checking because they don't want to be nagged as they type in their code—it can interfere with their focus on the larger goals of the program they're writing. Working without automatic, immediate syntax checking can prove a cure worse than the disease for some programmers. But others find error message interruptions about typos annoying.

Ultimately, whether you use the Auto Syntax Check feature is a matter of personal taste. For example, some people like to be told *right away* if they make a spelling error in a Word document; others consider spelling errors rather tedious issues best left for later during an editing phase. They write, focusing on the main points they're trying to make, and then at some later time they turn on the spell checker and fix any typos and punctuation blunders. You find a similar choice when you work at most any task. Consider woodworking: Should you hang each tool back on the wall in its appropriate place when you finish using it, or is it better to just let the saws and screwdrivers pile up around you, putting them away all at once after the coat rack is finished?

The VBA Editor notices blunders like the previous `If X > Y` problem easily enough, but you can also make language errors that the VBA Editor *cannot* identify when you move the insertion point from the line in which the blunder resides. Instead, VBA identifies these errors as compile errors later when you press F5 and it compiles the code. For example, if you enter the following statement in the Code window when working with Word, the VBA Editor won't detect anything wrong. But when you run the procedure by pressing F5, VBA will compile the code, discover the error, and object to it (see Figure 17.2):

```
ActiveDocument.SaveAs FileMame:="My File.docm"
```

FIGURE 17.2
Other errors appear only when you try to run the code.

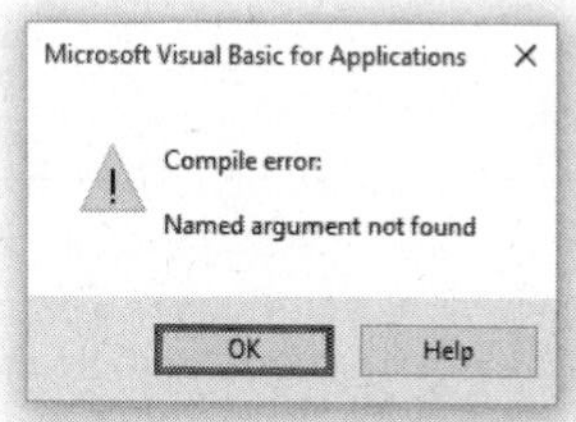

This error is a straightforward typo—`FileMame` instead of `FileName`—but VBA won't see this particular kind of problem until it runs the code and fails to find any `FileMame` property.

The VBA Editor sometimes indirectly helps you to notice errors of this kind while you're writing code. Say you're trying to enter a `Documents.Close` statement in Word and mistype `Documents` as `Docments`. In this case, the VBA Editor won't display the Properties/Methods list (Auto List Members) as it normally does if you have this feature turned on. You haven't entered a valid object. VBA doesn't, therefore, have a members list to display.

Not seeing the Properties/Methods list should alert you that something is wrong. If you continue anyway and enter the `Docments.Close` statement, the VBA Editor won't spot the mistake—it will show up as a "Run-time error 424: Object required" message (if you don't have `Option Explicit` on) when you try to run the procedure. (If you do have `Option Explicit` on, you will get a "Variable not defined" compile error instead.)

The Editor gives you yet another clue that `Docments.Close` is an error. When you press Enter to leave this line of code, you see this:

```
docments.Close
```

Does anything here look odd to you? VBA will automatically capitalize valid object names. But `docments` is not capitalized.

Another kind of problem is caused if you specify a property or method for an object to which that property or method doesn't apply. In this situation, VBA displays a compile error. For example, say you forget that the proper method here is `Add` and you enter `Documents.Create` instead. VBA highlights the offending word and gives the compile error "Method or data member not found" (see Figure 17.3), which tells you there's no `Create` method for the `Documents` collection. This message is displayed only during runtime, not design time (design time means when you're typing in code lines).

FIGURE 17.3
The "Method or data member not found" error tells you that you've used a method or property that isn't available for the object in question.

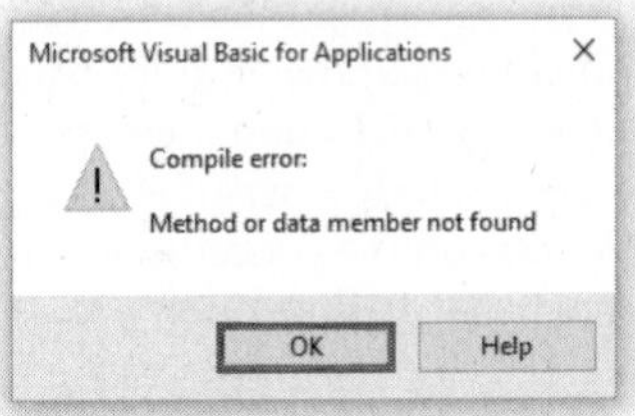

Runtime Errors

The third type of error is the *runtime error,* which occurs while code is executing. You will cause a runtime error if you write code that forces VBA to try to perform an impossible operation, such as opening a document that doesn't exist, closing a file when no file is open, or performing something mathematically impossible, such as dividing by zero.

The diction, punctuation, and syntax of your code is error-free, but you're asking VBA to do something that can't be done. An unhandled runtime error results in a crash that manifests itself as a Microsoft Visual Basic dialog box displaying a runtime error number, such as the one shown in Figure 17.4.

FIGURE 17.4
An unhandled runtime error causes VBA to display a message box such as this one.

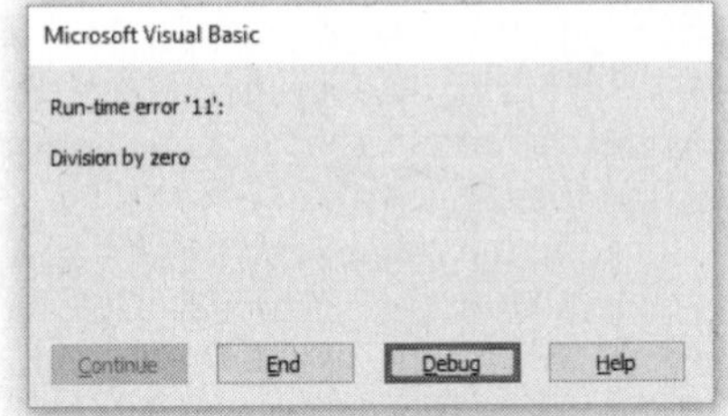

As an example of an impossible operation, consider the archetypal division by zero. The following statements give a "Run-time error '11': Division by zero" message:

```
Dim x As Integer
x = 1 / 0
```

You're unlikely to enter anything as obviously wrong as this in your code (you're not *nuts*). A line of code like this will inevitably produce a division-by-zero error because the divisor is zero. But it's easy to enter a valid equation, such as `MonthlyPay = Salary/Months`, and forget to assign any value to `Months` (if a numeric variable is empty, it counts as a zero value) or to produce a zero value for `Months` by addition or some other math. Or the user can type zero into a dialog box, and your code later tries to use that as a divisor. And so on.

One way to check for runtime errors is to track the values of your variables by using VBA's Watch window (discussed later in this chapter). To avoid possible user-input errors, have your code check their input after they close a dialog box. You can, for example, display a message explaining that zero isn't an acceptable input for their age, and then display the dialog box again, expecting valid input this time around.

Program Logic Errors

The fourth type of error is the *program logic error*. The code is valid, but it nonetheless produces incorrect results. With program logic errors, the code is technically fine. VBA is able to compile and run it without noticing any errors—but you get a different result than you intended. These errors can be tough to fix.

Program logic errors range in scope from the relatively obvious (such as performing manipulations on the wrong workbook in Excel because your code doesn't check which window is active) to the subtle (such as extending a range to the wrong character or cell). In the first example, the procedure is likely to run perfectly, but the resulting workbook will bear little resemblance to what you were trying to accomplish. In the second example, you might get a result that is almost correct—or the error might cause you to get perfect results sometimes and slightly wrong results at other times.

Program logic errors tend to be the hardest bugs to solve. To nail them down, you need to trace the execution of your code and pinpoint where things start to go wrong. To do that, you almost always need to employ the debugging tools discussed in the next section.

A friend of mine wrote a very nice program to format and print forms. But while he was testing it he noticed that after working fine about five times, it suddenly sent only one-third of the form to the printer during a trial run. He couldn't get it to repeat this behavior. So he surrounded the code with a loop and let it run continuously (dumping the sample form repeatedly into a log file rather than wasting paper printing it over and over). He discovered that the error only occurred once every 256 times the program ran. He never could locate this bug, but when he gave the program to other people, he just told them that it worked fine "almost always."

WHEN ERRORS AREN'T YOUR FAULT

There are two other types of errors that you may run into—even though perhaps you shouldn't. The first type is where Microsoft has documented a VBA item differently than it actually works. This shouldn't happen, but because of the complexity of VBA, it does. If you find that your code absolutely won't work even though it follows the Microsoft documentation to the letter, consider the possibility that the documentation may be incorrect. Search the Web using the VBA keywords involved to find if others have encountered this problem and learn how they've worked around it. The second type of error, a distant relation of the first type, is where one version of VBA behaves differently than another version. For example, you might create a procedure that works perfectly in Word 2013, but you have to change it to make it work with Word 2016. In an ideal world, this shouldn't happen—but as you know, this world is far from ideal. These two errors are blessedly quite rare. For one thing, VBA has been extensively used for decades, so it's a very mature language with few surprises.

VBA's Debugging Tools

VBA provides a solid assortment of debugging tools to help you remove the bugs from your procedures. The main windows you'll employ for debugging are the Immediate window, the Locals window, and the Watch window. You can access these tools in various ways, one of which is by using the Debug toolbar (shown in Figure 17.5). Four of the buttons—Design Mode, Run Sub/UserForm, Break, and Reset—are shared with the Standard toolbar. You'll learn about most of the others later in this chapter.

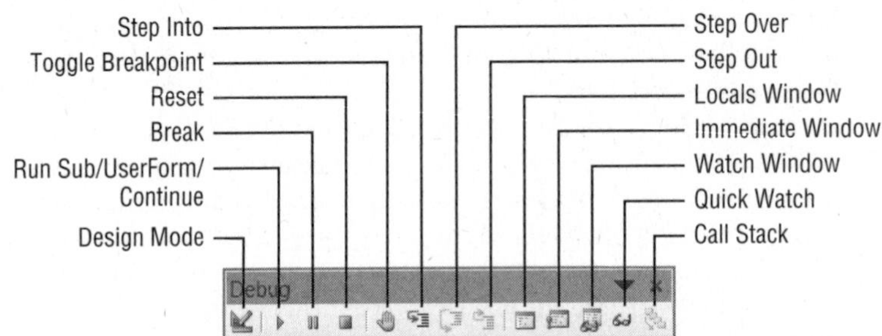

FIGURE 17.5 The Debug toolbar provides 13 commands for debugging your procedures.

HEISENBUGS, BOHR BUGS, AND OTHER UNCATCHABLE CRITTERS

The more complex and lengthy your code, the more likely you are to create bugs that are exceptionally difficult to catch. Usually, with determination and ingenuity, you can track down even the tougher bugs located in a single procedure. But bugs that depend on several unforeseen and improbable circumstances occurring simultaneously can be tough to isolate.

For example, an error that occurs in a procedure when the user makes a certain choice in a dialog box is relatively easy to catch. But if the error occurs only when the user has made two particular choices in the dialog box, it's much harder to locate. And if the error is contingent on a particular combination of three choices the user has made in the dialog box, or if it depends on an element in the particular file from which the procedure is getting its data, you'll likely have a much harder time pinpointing it.

Programmer folklore defines various kinds of rare bugs by assigning them names derived from such disciplines as philosophy and quantum physics. For instance, a *heisenbug* is defined as "a bug that disappears or alters its behavior when one attempts to probe or isolate it." Heisenbugs are frustrating, as are Bohr bugs and mandelbugs (search online for details if you're curious). But the worst kind of bug is the *schroedinbug*, which is a design or implementation bug that remains quiescent until someone reads the code and notices that it shouldn't work, whereupon it stops working until the code is made logically consistent.

These bugs are, of course, ridiculous—until you start to discover bit rot at work on your code and have to explain the problem to your superiors.

Break Mode

Break mode is a vital tool for debugging your procedures because it lets you watch your code execute step by step—line by line—in the Code window (by repeatedly pressing F8). This technique is called *single-stepping.*

For example, if an `If…Then…ElseIf…Else` statement appears to be executing incorrectly, you can step through it in Break mode and watch exactly which statements are executing, and which are being skipped, to produce the bad result.

These are the easiest ways to enter Break mode:

- Click to place the blinking insertion cursor in the procedure you want to run in the Code window and press the F8 key (or click the Step Into button on the Debug toolbar, or choose Debug ➢ Step Into) to start stepping through it. Repeatedly press F8 to step down through the code.
- Set one or more breakpoints in the procedure to cause VBA to halt execution and enter Break mode when it reaches one of the marked lines. A breakpoint allows you to stop execution at a particular point in your code. The easiest way to set a breakpoint is to click beside the line where you want to stop. You click in the gray margin-indicator bar to the left of the Code window. (You could also right-click in the line of code and choose Toggle ➢ Breakpoint from the context menu.) You can set any number of breakpoints. They're especially useful when you need to track down a bug that you suspect is located in a particular procedure because a breakpoint allows you to run the parts of a procedure that have no problems at full speed and then stop the procedure where you think there might be problems. From there, you can step through the suspicious statements and watch closely how they execute.

You can also enter Break mode in a couple of other ways:

- Interrupt your code by pressing Ctrl+Break and then click the Debug button in the resulting dialog box (see Figure 17.6). Normally, the only reason to enter Break mode this way is if your code gets stuck in an endless loop (which you'll typically recognize when the code appears to be doing nothing for a long time or is repeating itself when you think it shouldn't be). VBA highlights the statement that was executing when you pressed Ctrl+Break, but (depending on your timing) it's unlikely to be the statement that's causing the problem in your code—it'll just be one of the statements in the offending loop. You'll then need to step through the loop to identify the aberrant statement.

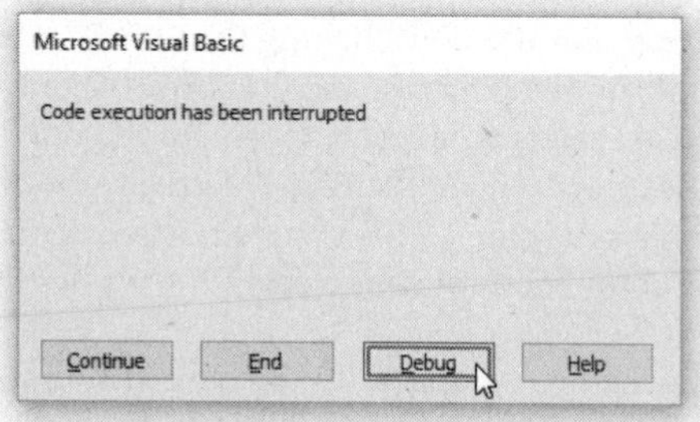

FIGURE 17.6
You can enter Break mode by pressing Ctrl+Break and then clicking the Debug button in this dialog box.

- Click the Debug button in a runtime-error dialog box such as the one shown in Figure 17.7. In the Code window, VBA highlights the statement that caused the error. (You can also click the Help button in the runtime-error dialog box to get an explanation of the error before clicking the Debug button.)

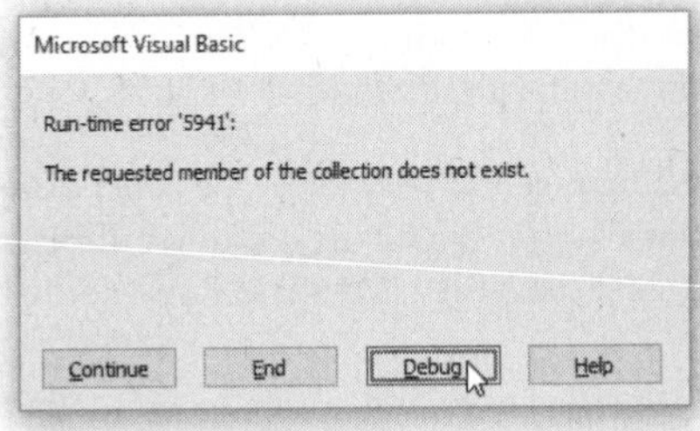

FIGURE 17.7 Entering Break mode from a runtime-error dialog box like this one takes you straight to the offending statement in your code. The problem code will be highlighted in yellow.

> **ACCESS'S *SINGLESTEP* METHOD**
>
> In addition to hosting a full version of VBA, Access includes a unique, legacy macro-design tool called the Macro Builder. This book doesn't spend much time with the Builder feature because Access's VBA offers much more capability and flexibility than its Builder. However, if you want to experiment with the Macro Builder, in Access click on the Ribbon's Create tab, and then click the Macro icon on the far right. One interesting command (added to the Builder in Access 2007) is the `SingleStep` method of the `DoCmd` object. This operates somewhat like a breakpoint, dropping you into Break mode during execution and displaying Access's specialized Macro Single Step dialog box. You can insert `DoCmd.SingleStep` into a VBA macro as well. VBA recognizes it as a legitimate line of code. However, VBA just ignores this statement during runtime. Only macros created in the Access Builder will respond to this `SingleStep` method.

The Step Over and Step Out Commands

In Chapter 3, "Editing Recorded Macros," you learned how to step through a procedure by repeatedly pressing the F8 key to issue the Step Into command, going down the lines one at a time. (You can also issue this command by clicking the Step Into button on the Debug toolbar or choosing Debug ➢ Step Into, but F8 is ever so much more efficient.)

Stepping into lets you see exactly what each statement in your code does, but you'll often find that you need to get past sections of code that you're sure are working fine so that you can step through a section that seems suspicious. This situation is particularly true of loop structures, which can have you going round and round—a real time-waster if you know the bug you're tracking down isn't within the loop.

Break mode offers three features to speed up stepping through your code: the Step Over command, the Step Out command, and the Run To Cursor command. The Step Over and Step

Out commands aren't available until you enter Break mode (for example, by using the Step Into command).

The Step Over command (which you can trigger by pressing Shift+F8, clicking the Step Over button on the Debug toolbar, or choosing Debug ➤ Step Over) executes the whole Sub or function called from the current procedure instead of stepping through the called procedure statement by statement as the Step Into command would do. (It "steps over" that procedure or function.) Use the Step Over command when you're debugging a procedure that calls another procedure or function that you know to be error-free and that you don't need to test step by step.

The Step Out command (which you can issue by Ctrl+Shift+F8, clicking the Step Out button on the Debug toolbar, or choosing Debug ➤ Step Out) runs the rest of the current procedure at full speed. Use the Step Out command to quickly execute the rest of a procedure once you've gotten through the part that you needed to watch step by step.

The Run To Cursor command (which you can issue by pressing Ctrl+F8 or choosing Debug ➤ Run To Cursor) runs the code at full speed until it reaches the statement where the blinking cursor currently is in the Code window, whereupon it enters Break mode. Click to position the cursor in the appropriate statement before invoking this command.

The Locals Window

The Locals window provides a quick readout of the values and types of all variables or expressions in the currently active procedure. It displays a collapsible tree view (see Figure 17.8).

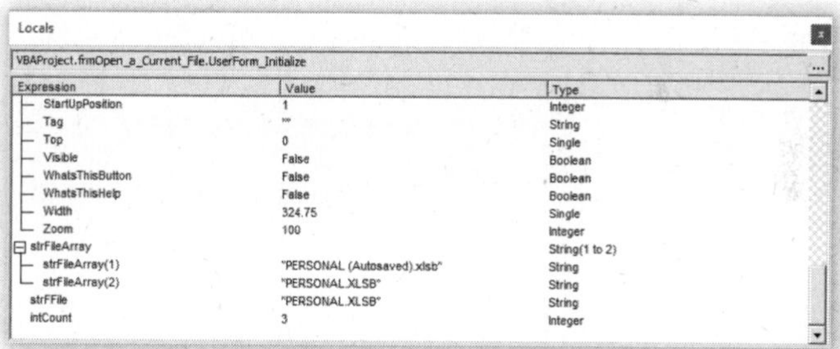

FIGURE 17.8
Use the Locals window to see at a glance all the expressions in the active procedure.

An *expression* is a combination of keywords, operators, variables, and/or constants. *Variables* are one kind of expression; but more complex expressions involve more than a single variable: `x > y`, for example, is an expression stating that `x` is greater than `y`. This expression might be `True` or `False`, depending on what's happening during runtime.

The Expression column displays the name of each expression, listed under the name of the procedure in which it appears. The Value column displays the current value of the expression (including `Empty` if the expression is empty, or `Null` or `Nothing` as appropriate). And the Type column displays the data type of the expression, with Variants listed as "Variant" along with their assigned data type (for example, "Variant/String" for a Variant assigned the String data type).

To display the Locals window, click the Locals Window button on the Debug toolbar or choose View ➤ Locals Window. To hide the Locals window, click its Close button.

From the Locals window, you can also click the button marked with an ellipsis (...) to display the Call Stack dialog box, discussed later in this chapter. This button is available only in Break mode.

> **HOW TO FLOAT AND DOCK WINDOWS**
>
> Remember that you can make panes (interior windows such as the Locals window) *float* (move away from the default "docked" location within the larger window). You can either drag them or double-click their title bar. Restore them to their default docking location by double-clicking their title bar a second time.

The Watch Window

The Watch window (identified as Watches in Figure 17.9) is a separate window that you use to track the values of variables and expressions as your code executes. To display the Watch window, click the Watch Window button on the Debug toolbar or choose View ➤ Watch Window in the VBA Editor. To hide the Watch window again, click its Close button (clicking the Watch Window button or choosing View ➤ Watch Window again doesn't hide it).

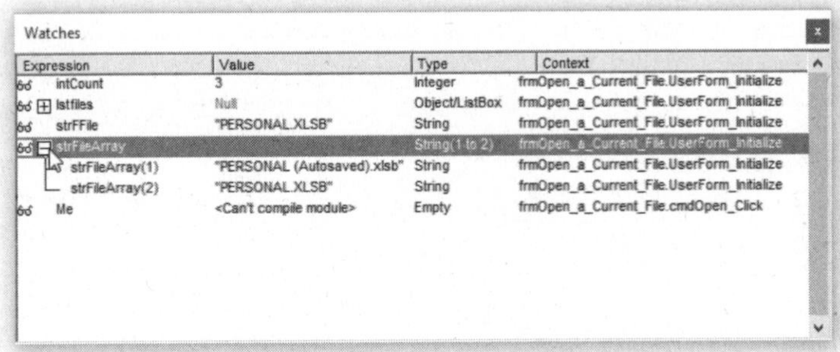

FIGURE 17.9
Use the Watch window to track the values of variables and expressions in your code.

The Watch window displays *watch expressions*—expressions in your code that you specify ahead of time. You want to view a dynamic display of the values in these variables or expressions.

Watch-expression information can help you to pinpoint where an unexpected value for a variable or an expression occurs as your code executes. The Watch window lists the names of the watched expressions or variables in the Expression column, their values in the Value column, their type (Integer, Byte, String, Long, and so on) in the Type column, and their context (the module and procedure in which they're operating) in the Context column. So to track the value of a given variable, you need only look at the Watch window at any given point while in Break mode.

If a variable or expression listed in the Watch window hasn't been initialized, the Watch window displays "< Out of Context >" in the Value column and "Empty" (for a variable other than a Variant) or "Variant/Empty" (for a Variant) in the Type column.

The VBA Editor updates all watch expressions in the Watch window whenever you enter Break mode and whenever you execute a statement in the Immediate window. So if you step through a procedure in the Code window by pressing the F8 key (which keeps you in Break mode), you can watch the value in a variable, or of an expression, as each statement executes. This is a great way to pinpoint where an error or an unexpected value occurs—and is much easier than moving the mouse over each variable or expression in question to check its value by using the Auto Data Tips feature.

Here's a typical debugging scenario. Let's say your code is producing a preposterous result, such as asserting that your annual salary is $2,200,000. As usual with most debugging, you're trying to figure out *where* in your code this sudden and massive gain in income is being calculated. Observe the Watch window while single-stepping through your code to see in which line of code the variable `MySalary` goes from 50,000 to 2,200,000. Now you're right there close to where the bug is and you can examine the preceding lines of code very carefully to see what's impacting the `MySalary` variable.

Because watch expressions slow down the execution of your code, the VBA Editor doesn't save them with the code—you need to redo them for each editing session. However, the Editor *does* store watch expressions during the current editing session, so you can move from procedure to procedure without losing your watch expressions.

SETTING WATCH EXPRESSIONS

Sometimes referred to as *conditional breakpoints*, watch expressions give you considerable flexibility when debugging. You can ask the VBA Editor to halt execution on most any kind of situation you can think up, such as break on any line that causes a variable to exceed a certain value, go below zero, change to a shorter string length, and so on. In other words, you specify a condition, an expression such as `MySalary > 50000`, and the VBA Editor automatically halts execution and displays the line where your salary increases beyond the expected 50,000. As you can imagine, the conditional breakpoint is one of the best tools a debugger has.

To set a watch expression, add it to the list in the Watch window by following these steps:

1. Select the variable or expression in your code, right-click it, and choose Add Watch from the context menu to display the Add Watch dialog box (see Figure 17.10). The variable or expression in which you right-clicked appears in the Expression text box.

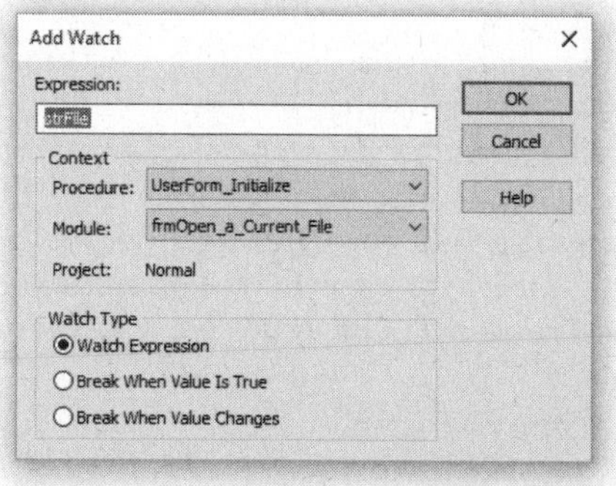

FIGURE 17.10
In the Add Watch dialog box, specify the watch expression you want to add.

You can also select the variable or expression you're interested in and choose Debug ➤ Add Watch to display the Add Watch dialog box. If you choose Debug ➤ Add Watch *without*
selecting the variable or expression, you must type it in the Expression text box, which is a waste of time.

2. If necessary, adjust the settings in the Context group box. The Procedure drop-down list is set to the current procedure, and the Module drop-down list is set to the current module.
3. In the Watch Type group box, adjust the option-button setting if necessary:
   - The default setting—Watch Expression—adds the variable or expression in the Expression text box to the list in the Watch window. However, conditional breakpoints are more useful if you do more than merely observe the status of variables or expressions. The following two list items describe the true benefit of these breakpoints.
   - Break When Value Is True causes VBA to enter Break mode whenever the value of the variable or expression changes to `True`.
   - Break When Value Changes causes VBA to enter Break mode whenever the value of the watch expression changes. Use this setting when dealing either with a watch expression that has a value you don't expect to change but that appears to be changing (such as `MySalary` in the previous example) or when you want to be alerted every time an expression changes.
4. Click the OK button to add the watch expression to the Watch window.

USE THESE TWO IMPORTANT CONDITIONAL BREAK TECHNIQUES

The Break When Value Is True option button allows you to run your code without stepping through each statement that doesn't change the value of the watch expression to `True`. This allows you to specify that Break mode should be entered, for example, when your variable exceeds a certain value (such as `X > 10000`) or equals another variable (such as `x = y`). Employing this kind of conditional break can be extremely helpful when tracking down elusive bugs.

The Break When Value Changes option button allows you to run your code and stop at each location where the value changes in the code.

You can also drag a variable or an expression from the Code window to the Watch window; doing so sets a default watch expression in the current context. To set Break When Value Is True or Break When Value Changes, edit the watch expression after dragging it to the Watch window.

EDITING WATCH EXPRESSIONS

To edit a watch expression, right-click it in the Watch window and choose Edit Watch from the context menu, or select it in the Watch window and choose Debug ➤ Edit Watch. Either action will display the Edit Watch dialog box with the watch expression selected in the Expression box, as shown in Figure 17.11. Change the context or watch type for the watch expression by using the settings in the Context group box and the Watch Type group box, and then click the OK button to apply your changes.

FIGURE 17.11
You can edit your watch expressions in the Edit Watch dialog box.

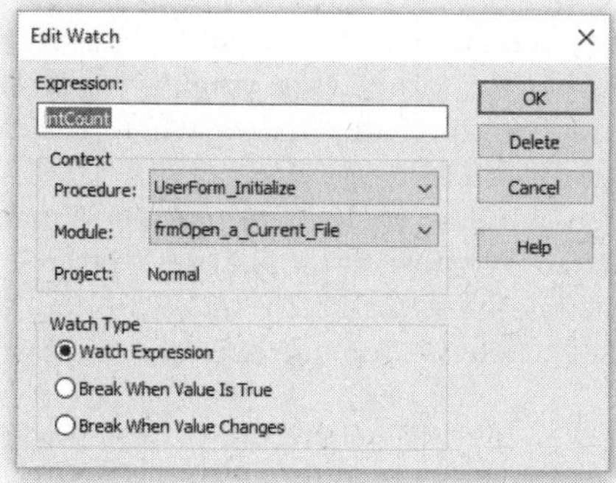

DELETING WATCH EXPRESSIONS

To delete a watch expression, right-click it in the Watch window and choose Delete Watch from the context menu. You can also delete the current watch expression by clicking the Delete button in the Edit Watch dialog box.

USING THE QUICK WATCH FEATURE

For those times when you don't need to create a watch expression for an expression or a variable, when you merely want to observe the value, you can use the Quick Watch feature, which displays the Quick Watch dialog box (see Figure 17.12) containing the context and value of the selected expression.

To use Quick Watch, while in Break mode select the expression or variable in the Code window and then click the Quick Watch button on the Debug toolbar, choose Debug ➤ Quick Watch, or press Shift+F9. (If you're already working in the Quick Watch dialog box, you can click the Add button to add the expression to the Watch window.)

FIGURE 17.12
Use the Quick Watch dialog box to get quick information on a variable or expression for which you don't want to set a watch expression in the Watch window.

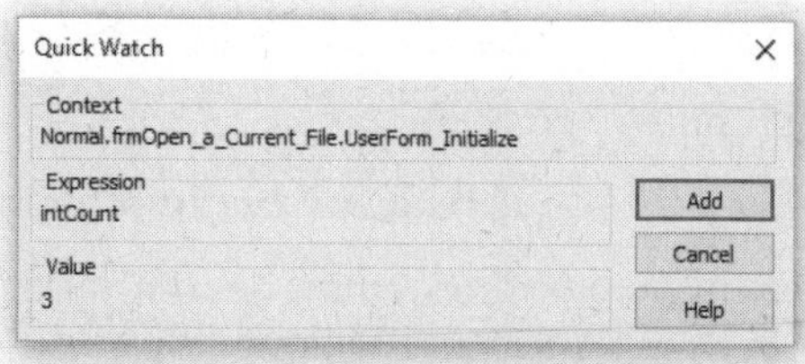

The Immediate Window

One use for the Immediate window is as a virtual scratchpad. In the Immediate window you enter lines of code that you want to test quickly, without having to enter them in a procedure and then testing the entire procedure. A second major use of the Immediate window is to display information to help you check the values of variables while a procedure is executing.

In the first case, you type code into the Immediate window, and then press Enter to see the results immediately (get it?). In the second case, you insert in your code `Debug.Print` statements that display information in the Immediate window, where you can easily view it. We'll explore both of these techniques in the following sections.

To display the Immediate window, click the Immediate Window button on the Debug toolbar, choose View ➤ Immediate Window, or press Ctrl+G. To hide the Immediate window again, click its Close button. (Clicking the Immediate Window button, choosing View ➤ Immediate Window, or pressing Ctrl+G when the Immediate window is displayed does not hide the Immediate window.)

You can execute code in the Immediate window in both Break mode and Design mode.

What You Can't Do in the Immediate Window

There are a number of restrictions on the code you can use in the Immediate window:

- You can't use declarative statements (such as `Dim`, `Private`, `Public`, `Option Explicit`, `Static`, or `Type`) or control-flow statements (such as `GoTo`, `Sub`, or `Function`). These statements cause VBA to return an "Invalid in Immediate Pane" error.
- You can't use multiline statements (such as block `If` statements or block `For...Next` statements) because there's no logical connection between statements on different lines in the Immediate window: Each line is treated in isolation.
- You can't place breakpoints in the Immediate window.

Entering Code in the Immediate Window

The Immediate window supports a number of standard Windows editing keystrokes and key combinations, such as Ctrl+X (Cut), Ctrl+C (Copy), Ctrl+V (Paste), Ctrl+Home (move the insertion point to the start of the window), Ctrl+End (move the insertion point to the end of the window), Delete (delete the current selection), and Shift+F10 (display the context menu).

The Immediate window also supports the following VBA Editor keystrokes and key combinations:

- F5 continues running a procedure.
- Alt+F5 runs the error-handler code for the current procedure.
- F8 single-steps through code (executing one statement at a time).
- Shift+F8 procedure-steps through code (executing one procedure at a time).
- Alt+F8 steps into the error handler for the current procedure.
- F2 displays the Object Browser.

Finally, the Immediate window has a couple of commands of its own:

- Pressing Enter runs the current line of code.
- Pressing Ctrl+Enter inserts a carriage return.

Printing Information to the Immediate Window

As well as entering statements in the Immediate window for quick testing, you can use this window for a different debugging technique. To include in your procedures statements that print information to the Immediate window, use the `Print` method of the `Debug` object. Printing like this allows you to create a log during execution, a log you can later examine for errors or strange behavior. You don't single-step or display message boxes containing the value of a variable. Instead you print data for later study.

The syntax for the `Print` method is as follows:

```
Debug.Print [outputlist]
```

`outputlist` is an optional argument specifying the expression or expressions to print. You'll almost always want to include *`outputlist`*—if you don't, the `Print` method prints a blank line, which is of little use. Construct your *`outputlist`* using the following syntax:

```
[Spc(n) | Tab(n)] expression
```

Here, `Spc(`*`n`*`)` inserts space characters and `Tab(`*`n`*`)` inserts tab characters, with *`n`* being the number of spaces or tabs to insert. Both are optional arguments, and for simple output, you'll seldom need to use them.

`expression` is an optional argument specifying the numeric expression or String expression to print:

- To specify multiple expressions, separate them with either a space or a semicolon.
- A Boolean value prints as either `True` or `False` (as appropriate).
- If *`outputlist`* is `Empty`, `Print` doesn't print anything. If *`outputlist`* is `Null`, `Print` prints `Null`.
- If *`outputlist`* is an error, `Print` prints it as `Error` *`errorcode`*, where *`errorcode`* is the code specifying the error.

As an example, you could log the contents of the String variables (expressions) `CustName`, `Address1`, `Address2`, `City`, `State`, and `Zip` to the Immediate window in an address format by using the following statements:

```
Debug.Print CustName
Debug.Print Address1 & "," & Address2
Debug.Print City & "," & State & " " & Zip
```

As another example, the following procedure prints the names and paths of all open workbooks in Excel to the Immediate window:

```
Sub See_All_Workbook_Names()
    Dim oBook As Workbook
```

```
        For Each oBook In Workbooks
            Debug.Print oBook.FullName
        Next
    End Sub
```

In practice, `Debug.print` is used by many programmers as a sometimes-quick, efficient alternative to debugging with the Watch windows, message boxes, or breakpoints. You need to see if something is going wrong with a variable (its value is wrong, but where does it go wrong?). So you insert some `Debug.Print` statements to display the variable's value while executing a procedure. Then you can see if the value is wrong in that location or somewhere else in the code.

If your program contains multiple procedures, you might also want to `debug.print` the name of the procedure. This example identifies both the procedure and variable name within the `Debug.Print` statement:

```
Debug.Print "In the Sub Add_Tax the variable intLocal is: " & intLocal
```

This results in the following line in the Immediate window:

```
In Sub Add_Tax the variable intLocal is: 7
```

The Call Stack Dialog Box

When working in Break mode, you can summon the Call Stack dialog box (see Figure 16.1 in Chapter 16) to display a list of the active *procedure calls*—the outside procedures being triggered by the current procedure. It shows the history of your code's execution path.

When you begin running a procedure, that procedure is added to the call-stack list in the Call Stack dialog box. If that procedure then calls another procedure, the name of the second procedure is added to the call-stack list, but only while the procedure is executing; it's then removed from the list. By using the Call Stack dialog box in Break mode, you can find out what procedures are being called by another procedure; this can help you establish which parts of your code you need to check for errors.

To display the Call Stack dialog box, click the Call Stack button on the Debug toolbar, press Ctrl+L, or select View ➤ Call Stack. To display one of the procedures listed in the Call Stack dialog box, select it in the Project.Module.Function list box and click the Show button.

Dealing with Infinite Loops

You'll probably find it easy to tell when a procedure gets stuck in an infinite loop: You'll notice that the procedure simply doesn't stop executing. If you open Windows's Task Manager, it will report that your application has "stopped responding." To interrupt an infinite loop, press Ctrl+Break. The VBA Editor then displays a Code Execution Has Been Interrupted dialog box. Infinite loops are also known as *endless loops*.

There are several ways to get stuck in infinite loops, such as using `GoTo` statements without `If` conditions or `Do` loops without `While` or `Until` constraints. These are easy enough to avoid, but even if you do, it's still possible for infinite loops to occur in your code because of conditions you haven't been able to anticipate.

The best way to approach detecting and eliminating an infinite loop is to use breakpoints or a watch expression to pinpoint where the procedure enters the infinite loop. Once you've reached it, use the Step Into command to step into the procedure. Then use the Watch window or the Locals window to observe the variable and expressions in the loop, which should indicate when something is going wrong and causing the loop to be endless.

If your code contains a loop that should execute only a set number of times but you suspect it's running endlessly, you can insert a counter variable in the loop in an `If...Then` structure that triggers either an `Exit For` statement or an `Exit Do` statement to exit the loop if it runs more than a certain number of times.

Dealing with Runtime Errors

Despite the help that VBA provides by checking for language errors and compile errors, *runtime* errors remain an unpleasant fact of life. Sooner or later, you will get runtime errors in your code, but you don't have to take them lying down. The best tactic to deal with them is to add *error handlers*—pieces of code that trap errors that occur during execution, analyze them, and take action to deal with the problem.

An error handler is a preventative measure, allowing your code to manage problems gracefully rather than crashing in front of a user's alarmed or bemused face.

When Should You Write an Error Handler?

Consider writing an error handler in the following circumstances:

- When a runtime error can cause your code to fail disastrously. For a procedure that tweaks a couple of objects on a slide in PowerPoint, you're unlikely to need an error handler. By contrast, for a procedure that creates, deletes, or moves files, you'll probably want an error handler.
- After you've done everything possible to ensure the best coding and error handling, you should also try to do your best to anticipate the user doing something unexpected. And build in error-handling for user errors. Users can do some very unusual things when running macros.
- When your program accesses peripherals or objects outside the application itself—the status of which is unpredictable during design time. In this situation, you can identify particular errors that are likely to occur and that can be trapped. For example, when the user tries to open a file, certain well-known errors can occur—perhaps the file doesn't exist, or is currently in use by another computer, or is on a network drive, floppy drive, CD-ROM drive, or removable drive that isn't available at the time. You'll also run into errors if the user tries to use a printer or other remote device (say, a scanner or a digital camera) that's not present, not connected, turned off, or not configured correctly. Similarly, any procedure that deals with a particular object in a document (for example, a chart in Excel) will run into trouble if that object is not available.

CONSIDER TRAPPING ERRORS RATHER THAN ANTICIPATING THEM

In some instances, you may find it simpler to trap a resulting error from a procedure than to anticipate and try to forestall the many and various conditions that might lead to the generation of the error. For example, instead of checking to make sure a file exists before you try to open or manipulate the file, just trap any kind of error that results if the file isn't detected.

Trapping an Error

Trapping an error means catching it in your code during runtime so that you can write programming that handles the error.

VBA's `On Error` statement triggers when there is a runtime error, allowing you to write code that responds to the error.

Usually, you'll want to prevent an error from stopping your VBA code, but you can also anticipate particular errors and use them to determine a suitable course of action to follow from the point at which they occur.

To trap an error, you use the `On Error` statement. The usual syntax for `On Error` is as follows:

```
On Error GoTo line
```

Here, *`line`* is a label specifying the line to which execution is to branch when a runtime error occurs. For example, to branch to the label named `ErrorHandler`, you could use a structure like this:

```
Sub ErrorDemo()
    On Error GoTo ErrorHandler
    'ordinary code statements here

Exit Sub
ErrorHandler:
            'error-handling statements here
End Sub
```

The label you use to identify the error handler can be named with any valid label name—you don't have to call it `ErrorHandler` or anything similar. Some people find that a descriptive label (perhaps one that identifies the type or types of error expected, such as `HandleErrorNoFileOpen`) is clearer in the long run than a generic name; others prefer to go with a generic name such as `HandleErr`.

Usually, you'll want to place the error trap early, near the top of a procedure so that it's active and ready to trap errors for all the lines of code below it throughout the whole procedure. If necessary, you can place several different error traps in a procedure by entering multiple `On Error` statements where they're needed—but only one can be enabled at a time. (*Enabled* means that an error trap has been switched on by an `On Error` statement. When an error occurs and execution branches to the error handler, that error handler is *active*.)

Inserting multiple error handlers in a procedure can be useful when you're dealing with statements that can cause different types of errors that may need to be trapped. In the following example, the first `On Error` statement directs execution to `ErrorHandler1`, and the second `On Error` statement directs execution to `ErrorHandler2`:

```
Sub ErrorDemo2()
    On Error GoTo ErrorHandler1
    'statements here
    On Error GoTo ErrorHandler2
    'statements here
```

```
    Exit Sub
ErrorHandler1:
    'statements for first error handler here
ErrorHandler2:
    'statements for second error handler here
End Sub
```

Each error handler is limited to the procedure in which it appears, so you can create different error handlers for different procedures and have each enabled in turn as the procedures run.

Because the error handler appears as code in the procedure, you need to make sure that it doesn't run when no error has occurred. You can do this by using either an `Exit Sub` statement in the line just above the error-handler statement (this ends execution of the procedure) or a `GoTo` statement that directs execution to a label beyond the error-handling code. The `Exit Sub` statement is better if you choose to place your error handler at the end of its procedure, which is standard practice and usually makes sense. The `GoTo` statement may prove easier to use if you choose to place your error handler elsewhere in the procedure.

For a function, use an `Exit Function` statement rather than an `Exit Sub` statement. For a property in a class module, use an `Exit Property` statement.

The following example uses an `Exit Sub` statement to cause execution to end before the error handler if no error occurs:

```
Sub ErrorDemo3()
    On Error GoTo ErrorHandler
    'statements that might cause an error
    Exit Sub
ErrorHandler:
    'statements that handle the error
End Sub
```

This next example uses a `GoTo` statement to skip the error handler—which is placed within the code of the procedure—unless an error occurs. When execution reaches the `GoTo SkipErrorHandler` statement, it branches to the `SkipErrorHandler` label, thus bypassing the code in the error handler:

```
Sub ErrorDemo4()
    On Error GoTo ErrorHandler
    'statements that might cause an error
    GoTo SkipErrorHandler
ErrorHandler:
    'statements that  handle the error
SkipErrorHandler:
    'statements
End Sub
```

You read earlier in this book that some people don't like `GoTo` statements for uses such as the second example here. Given that this `GoTo` statement makes the flow of the procedure a little harder to follow, you may be inclined to agree with them in this case. (The use of `GoTo` in the `On Error` statement itself is, however, unavoidable.)

Disabling an Error Trap

Recall that an error trap works only for the procedure in which it appears, and VBA disables it when the code in the procedure has finished executing. You can also disable an error trap before the end of a procedure in which it appears if you want by using the following statement:

```
On Error GoTo 0
```

Why would you do this? You might want to disable an error trap while testing a procedure to enable yourself to pinpoint errors that occur after a certain point while at the same time retaining error trapping for the first part of the procedure.

Resuming After an Error

You use the `Resume` statement to resume execution of a procedure after trapping an error or handling an error with an error-handling routine. The `Resume` statement takes three forms: `Resume`, `Resume Next`, and `Resume` *`line`*.

Using a *Resume* Statement

The `Resume` statement causes execution to resume at the same line that caused the error. Use `Resume` with an error-handling routine that detects and fixes the problem that caused the offending statement to fail. For example, look at the error handler in Listing 17.1, which runs when VBA is unable to apply a specified style in Word.

Listing 17.1: Trapping a style error

```
Sub StyleError()

    On Error GoTo Handler

    Selection.Style = "Executive Summary"

    'the rest of the procedure happens here

    'exit the procedure once execution gets this far
    Exit Sub

Handler:

    If Err = 5834 Then
        ActiveDocument.Styles.Add _
            Name:="Executive Summary", Type:=wdStyleTypeParagraph
        Resume
    End If

End Sub
```

Here's how the `StyleError` procedure in Listing 17.1 works:

- Line 1 starts the procedure, and line 19 ends it. Lines 2, 4, 6, 8, 11, 13, and 18 are spacers.
- Line 3 uses an `On Error` statement to enable the imaginatively named error handler, which is identified by the `Handler` label in line 12.
- Line 5 applies the style named Executive Summary to the current selection. If this operation succeeds, execution will continue at line 7, which in this example contains only a comment indicating that this is where the rest of the procedure would take place.
- Line 9 is a comment introducing line 10, which holds the `Exit Sub` statement to end execution of the procedure before the error handler.
- If the `Selection.Style` statement in line 5 causes an error, execution branches to the `Handler` label in line 12, and the error handler is activated. Line 14 compares the error value to 5834, the error that occurs if the specified style doesn't exist. If it matches, line 15 then adds the missing style to the document, and the `Resume` statement in line 16 causes execution to resume where the error occurred, on line 5. Because the specified style is now available, the `Selection.Style` statement runs without an error.

HOW TO FIND VBA ERROR NUMBERS AND THEIR EXPLANATIONS

To find error numbers, here are three approaches:

- Go to this Web page:

`http://msdn2.microsoft.com/en-us/library/Aa264975(VS.60).aspx`

- Search the VBA Help system for *trappable errors*.
- Deliberately cause the error yourself and note the number and description in the resulting error-message dialog box that VBA displays.

USING A *RESUME NEXT* STATEMENT

`Resume Next` causes execution to resume with the next statement after the statement that caused the error. You can use `Resume Next` in either of the following circumstances:

- With an error-handling routine that ignores the error and allows execution to continue without executing the offending statement
- As a straightforward `On Error Resume Next` statement that causes execution to continue at the next statement after the statement that caused an error, without using an error handler to fix the error

As an example of the first circumstance, if the style specified in the previous example isn't available, you can use a `Resume Next` statement to skip applying it:

```
Sub StyleError2()
    On Error GoTo Handler

    Selection.Style = "Executive Summary"

    'the rest of the procedure happens here

    'exit the procedure once execution gets this far
  Exit Sub

Handler:
    Resume Next

End Sub
```

The descriptions of `Resume` and `Resume Next` apply if the error occurred in the procedure that contains the error handler. But if the error occurred in a different procedure from the procedure that contains the error handler, `Resume` causes execution to resume with the last statement that transferred execution (called) out of the procedure where the handler is located; `Resume Next` causes execution to resume with the statement *after* the last statement to call out of the procedure that contains the error handler.

USING A *RESUME LINE* STATEMENT

`Resume` *`line`* causes execution to resume at the specified line. Use a label to indicate the line, which must be in the same procedure as the error handler.

For example, if a procedure tried to open a particular file, you could create a simple error handler that uses a `Resume line` statement, as shown in Listing 17.2. This procedure works with Word. To make it work with other applications, substitute the appropriate error numbers in line 15.

LISTING 17.2: Resuming execution at a specified line

```
1.  Sub Handle_Error_Opening_File()
2.
3.      Dim strFName As String
4.
5.  StartHere:
6.
7.       On Error GoTo ErrorHandler
8.       strFName = InputBox("Enter the name of the file to open.", _
             "Open File")
9.       If strFName = "" Then End
10.      Documents.Open strFName
11.      Exit Sub
12.
13. ErrorHandler:
```

```
14.
15.     If Err = 5174 Or Err = 5273 Then MsgBox _
            "The file " & strFName & " does not exist." & vbCr & _
            "Please enter the name again.", _
            vbOKOnly + vbCritical, "File Error"
16.       Resume StartHere
17.
18.  End Sub
```

Here's how Listing 17.2 works:

- Line 1 starts the procedure, and line 18 ends it.
- Line 2 is a spacer. Line 3 declares the String variable `strFName`. Line 4 is another spacer.
- Line 5 contains the `StartHere` label, to which execution will return from the `Resume` statement in line 16. Line 6 is a spacer.
- Line 7 uses an `On Error` statement to enable the error handler `ErrorHandler`.
- Line 8 displays an input box prompting users for the name of the file they want to open, and stores the name in the variable `strFName`, which line 9 then tries to open. Line 10 checks `strFName` against an empty string and ends execution if it matches.
- If the file exists and can be opened, execution passes to line 11, where an `Exit Sub` statement exits the procedure, ending its execution. Otherwise, an error is generated, and execution branches to the `ErrorHandler` label in line 13, where the error handler becomes active.
- Line 14 is a spacer. Line 15 then compares the value of the error to 5174 (the error that occurs if VBA can't find the file) and to 5273 (the error that occurs if the document name or path isn't valid in Word). If either of these comparisons matches, line 15 displays a message box advising users of the error and prompting them to enter the correct filename.
- The `Resume` statement in line 16 then returns execution to the `StartHere` label in line 5. Line 17 is a spacer.

Try Inserting a Counter Variable to Deal with Repetitious User Errors

For some procedures, you may want to build in a counter mechanism to prevent users from repeating the same error endlessly because they don't grasp what's wrong. By incrementing a counter variable each time the error handler is invoked and checking the resulting number, you can choose to take a different action after a number of unsuccessful attempts to execute a particular action.

You can't use a `Resume` statement anywhere other than in an error-handling routine (or an `On Error Resume Next` statement). If you do, VBA reports an error.

Getting a Description of an Error

To see the description of the current error, return the `Description` property of the `Err` object:

```
MsgBox Err.Description
```

In general, operating-system and programming-language error messages tend to be terse, cryptic, and of less help to the end user than to the people who built the OS or language. Think twice before displaying one of these error messages to an end user. The error message shown in Figure 17.7 says "Run-time error '5941': The requested member of the collection does not exist." As you can imagine, most users would be baffled by this message; some would panic.

Usually, it's more effective, not to mention kinder, to write and display a more verbose error message of your own devising. It should explain in ordinary English what the problem is—and, preferably, what (if anything) the user can do to solve it.

Raising Your Own Errors

As part of your testing, you may want to deliberately simulate errors so that you can see how well your error handler handles them. (Programming lingo sometimes substitutes the word *`raise`* for *cause* or *trigger*. Nobody knows why.)

To cause an error to be triggered, use the `Raise` method of the `Err` object, specifying only the *`number`* argument. *`number`* is a Long argument giving the number of the error that you want to cause. For example, the following statement "raises" error 5121:

```
Err.Raise 5121
```

Suppressing Alerts

Many of the procedures you build will use message boxes or dialog boxes to allow the user to choose options for the procedure. In some applications—such as Word, Excel, PowerPoint, and Access—you can use the `DisplayAlerts` property of the `Application` object to suppress the display of message boxes and errors while a procedure is running:

- In Word, `DisplayAlerts` can be set to `wdAlertsNone` (`0`) to suppress alerts and message boxes, `wdAlertsMessageBox` (`-2`) to suppress alerts but display message boxes, or `wdAlertsAll` (`-1`, the default) to display all alerts and message boxes. `DisplayAlerts` is a sticky setting. You need to set `DisplayAlerts` explicitly back to one of four things: to `True` or to `wdAlertsAll` when you want to see alerts again after setting it to `False`, to `wdAlertsNone`, or to `wdAlertsMessageBox`. VBA resets the default value when you restart Word.
- In Excel, `DisplayAlerts` is a read/write Boolean property that can be set to `True` to display alerts and `False` to suppress them. The setting sticks until you change it or restart Excel, at which point VBA resets it to `True`.
- In PowerPoint, `DisplayAlerts` is a read/write property that can be set to `ppAlertsAll` to display all alerts and `ppAlertsNone` to suppress all alerts. The setting sticks until you change it or until you restart PowerPoint, at which point VBA resets it to `ppAlertsNone`.
- In Access, you use the pervasive `DoCmd` object's `SetWarnings` method, like this:

  ```
  DoCmd.SetWarnings False
  ```

Handling User Interrupts in Word, Excel, and Project

Errors may seem quite enough of a problem, but you also need to decide what will happen if a user tries to interrupt your code by pressing Ctrl+Break during execution. Some VBA hosts, including Word and Excel, offer you three options:

- You can allow a user interrupt to stop your code. This is the easy way to proceed (and, as the default condition, needs no effort on your part), but in complex procedures, it may cause problems. For example, the user may have spent five minutes typing in data, only to lose it because the data wasn't saved due to the early termination of the program.
- You can prevent user interrupts by disabling user input while the procedure is running. This is simple to do, but you run the risk of creating unstoppable code if a procedure enters an endless loop. The user would have to power down the machine or, at least, invoke Task Manager and kill your task. Any unsaved work in the procedure or even the host application will be lost. The user might have been typing for *hours* without saving their work. Losing this much work can send some people *right over the edge.*
- As a compromise between the first two options, you can allow user interrupts during certain parts of a procedure and prevent user interrupts during more critical parts of a procedure.

Disabling User Input While a Procedure Is Running

To disable user input while a procedure is executing, disable the Ctrl+Break key combination by setting the `EnableCancelKey` property of the `Application` object to `wdCancelDisabled` (in Word) or `xlDisabled` (in Excel):

```
Application.EnableCancelKey = wdCancelDisabled      'Word
Application.EnableCancelKey = xlDisabled            'Excel
```

VBA automatically enables user input again when the procedure stops executing. You can also re-enable user input during a procedure by setting the `EnableCancelKey` property to `wdCancelInterrupt` (in Word) or `xlInterrupt` (in Excel):

```
Application.EnableCancelKey = wdCancelInterrupt      'Word
Application.EnableCancelKey = xlInterrupt            'Excel
```

Excel offers a third setting, `xlErrorHandler`, that traps the Ctrl+Break keystroke as error 18. You can deal with this error as you would any other error. Here's a quick example:

```
Sub CancelKey_Example()
    Dim i As Long
    On Error GoTo EH
    Application.EnableCancelKey = xlErrorHandler
    For i = 1 To 100000000 ' time-consuming loop
        Application.StatusBar = i
    Next i
EH:
    If Err.Number = 18 Then
        If MsgBox("Do you want to stop the procedure?" _
```

```
                & vbCr & vbCr & "If not, stop pressing Ctrl+Break!", _
                vbYesNo + vbCritical, "User Interrupt Detected") = vbYes Then End
        End If
    End Sub
```

Disabling User Input While Part of a Macro Is Running

You may want to temporarily disable user input while a procedure is executing a sensitive task that must not be interrupted. Then when the task is complete, you can re-enable user input because at that point it's again safe for the user to stop the procedure.

For example, say you have a procedure in which a section of code moves a number of files from one folder to another. You don't want the user to interrupt the code that moves the files. That could cause problems because if the user stopped the procedure in mid-task, it might leave some files still in the source folder and some in the destination folder.

Here's an example using Word:

```
'interruptible actions up to this point
Application.EnableCancelKey = wdCancelDisabled
For i = 1 to LastFile
     SourceFile = Source & "\Section" & i
    DestFile = Destination & "\Section" & i
    Name SourceFile As DestFile
Next i
Application.EnableCancelKey = wdCancelInterrupt
'interruptible actions after this point
```

Documenting Your Code

Some musicians can read a symphonic score and more or less "hear" the music. Likewise, some programmers can read raw code and visualize what it does. But most programmers need comments to help them understand what code is doing, particularly if they wrote the code months before or if it was written by another programmer.

Many programmers also find it easier to debug their procedures if they've previously documented their code. The best way to document your code is to add comments to it, either as you create the code or after you've finished creating it: This procedure does this. It expects this data as input and provides this as its output. This line does this. And so on.

Some experts advise that you document your code as you create it in any procedure in which you're exploring your way and trying different methods to reach your goal. Add comments to explain what action each group of statements is trying to achieve. Once you've gotten the procedure to work, go through the code and delete the statements you didn't use, using the comments to identify which sections are now useless and which are still worthwhile and leaving only the comments that are relevant to how the remaining code functions.

Also consider adding comments when you're modifying an existing procedure so that you don't lose track of your changes. Once you have the procedure working to your liking, remove any unnecessary comments and reword any verbose or unclear comments.

Other experts suggest documenting your code when you've finished writing it. This allows you to enter only the comment lines that you want to be there permanently. This is the way to go when you're fairly sure of the direction of your code when you start writing the procedure and the procedure needs only a few pointers to make its code clear once it's complete.

To document your code, use comments prefaced by either the single quote (`'`) or the `Rem` keyword (short for *remark*).

USING BLOCK-COMMENTING AS A DEBUGGING TOOL

Remember that commenting can also be employed as a debugging technique—when you want to see how code runs with some lines inactivated. In other words, does the bug disappear when the commented-out lines are not executed? If so, the bug is probably located somewhere in those lines of code. You can "comment out" a group of lines, a whole line, or part of a line: Anything to the right of an apostrophe or the `Rem` keyword is commented out. See the section in Chapter 3 titled "Commenting Out Lines" for details on this tactic.

Few programmers use `Rem` anymore. When you're trying to comment out only a part of a line, the apostrophe is usually the better choice anyway. If you do choose to use the `Rem` keyword, you'll need to add a colon before it to make it work consistently (some statements accept a `Rem` without a colon at their end; others generate a compile error):

```
Rem This is a comment line.
Documents.Add: Rem create a document based on Normal.dotm
```

Generally, apostrophe-commented remarks are separated by a few spaces or tabs from any statement the line contains (as in the second line here). This makes the code and comments easier to read than comments using `Rem`:

```
'This is a comment line
Documents.Add     'create a document based on Normal.dotm
```

It's tempting to think that you don't need to document your code because you'll be able to recall what it does. But once you've written a lot of code, you probably won't be able to remember. Coming back to a procedure six months after writing it, you'll find it as unfamiliar as if someone else had written it. And if you've become a VBA whiz, you may even find it hard to visualize the clumsy techniques you were using at that time.

Most programmers have a distinct aversion to documenting their code; for some, the dislike of documenting is almost pathological. You can see why: When you're writing the code, documenting what each line does slows you down and distracts you from your larger purpose. And documenting after the code is finished and tested is tedious work. Besides, anyone who's competent should be able to read the code and see what it does, shouldn't they?

Maybe so, but consider this: It's likely that you won't always be the person working with your code—at times, others may work with it too, and they'll appreciate all the help they can get in understanding its purposes and behaviors. Likewise, the code on which you work won't always be your own—you may at times have to debug code that others have written, and in such cases, you'll be the one grateful for comments.

The Bottom Line

Understand the basic principles of debugging. A major aspect of programming is testing your code. Debugging can be enjoyable if you think of it as a puzzle you can solve. But whether or not you enjoy it, debugging is essential if you want to preserve a reputation as a professional.

> **Master It** When testing your code, try to imagine ways that the code could fail. Describe a situation that can produce unanticipated results.

Recognize the four different types of errors you'll create. Experts have concluded that there are four primary categories of error in programs.

> **Master It** Name two of the four basic types of programming errors.

Employ VBA's debugging tools. The VBA Editor and VBA include a generous assortment of debugging tools to help you track down and remove bugs from your procedures. The main windows you'll employ for debugging are the Immediate window, the Locals window, and the Watch window.

> **Master It** The Watch window is especially useful because you can set watch expressions (also known as conditional breakpoints). Describe this debugging tactic.

Deal with runtime errors. You can trap some runtime errors (errors that show up while a procedure is executing) while debugging your code. But others show up only while your user is interacting with your program—and you're probably not there to help them. There is a way, though, to soften the blow and, in some cases, even fix a problem by adding error handlers to your programs.

> **Master It** Error handlers are special statements and sections of code that detect and then manage runtime errors. What VBA statement detects a runtime error?

Chapter 18

Building Well-Behaved Code

This chapter concentrates on the principles of good code behavior. Once you've built a macro that's useful and that works consistently as intended, you'll probably want to distribute it to some friends and coworkers, or even to a wider audience on the Internet.

Before you distribute it, though, you should make sure the procedure behaves in a civilized manner. It should be sensitive in its interaction with users and with the settings they may have chosen on their computers. It's all too easy to distribute an apparently solid, useful procedure that nevertheless runs roughshod over a user's preferences or that fails unexpectedly under certain circumstances. In this chapter, you'll look at how to avoid such problems and how to construct your procedures so that the user will have no problem interacting with them.

The specifics of good macro behavior vary from application to application, so you will need to apply the principles of the application with which you're working. This chapter gives some examples.

IN THIS CHAPTER, YOU WILL LEARN TO DO THE FOLLOWING:

- Understand the characteristics of well-behaved procedures
- Retain and restore the user environment
- Let the user know what's happening
- Check that the procedure is running under suitable conditions
- Clean up after a procedure

What Is a Well-Behaved Procedure?

A well-behaved procedure leaves no trace of its actions beyond those the user expected it to perform. This means the following:

- Making no detectable changes to the user environment or, if the procedure does need to make changes (for example, in order to do its job), restoring the previous settings
- Presenting the user with relevant choices for the procedure and relevant information once the procedure has finished running
- Showing or telling the user what is happening while the procedure is running
- Making sure (if possible) that conditions are appropriate for the procedure to run successfully—before the procedure takes any actions

- Anticipating or trapping errors wherever possible so the procedure doesn't crash or, if it does crash under exceptional circumstances, so that it does so as gracefully as possible, minimizing damage to the user's work
- Leaving users in the optimal position to continue their work after the procedure finishes executing
- Deleting any scratch documents, folders, or other detritus that the procedure created in order to perform its duties but that are no longer needed

You can probably think of a couple of examples of applications you use that don't exactly do these things. For example, do you use Word? Then you're probably familiar with the less-than-inspiring behavior of the Page Up and Page Down feature. While working in a document, press the Page Down key three times, and then press the Page Up key three times. Your blinking insertion point should be back in the exact location where it was before you paged down and then back up, right? Unfortunately, the insertion point doesn't always (let's be honest, it will *rarely*) return to the exact point in the document it should.

So if you page through your document to look at some paragraph but then try to return to where you were last, you always need to check that the insertion point is in the right place before you start typing—otherwise, the characters are very likely to land in the wrong place. Word was first released in October 1983, *so Microsoft has had time to fix this.* Right? It would be simple for Word to note the insertion point before the paging, but why that's never done remains a mystery. However, I will show you how to do this in your macros in the section titled "Leaving the User in the Best Position to Continue Working" later in this chapter.

Such weaknesses in commercial applications' interfaces provoke two main reactions among developers. First, if users are accustomed to such niggles as having to reposition the selection or change the view when they shouldn't need to, they're unlikely to get too annoyed with having to perform similar actions after running one of our procedures. This is particularly true if your macro saves them plenty of time and effort, for which they should be grateful rather than picky. Besides, they mostly likely didn't pay for your macro, did they?

The second reaction is an impressive (and sometimes overzealous) determination on the part of macro programmers to restore the user environment absolutely perfectly even if major software corporations seem incapable of producing software that does so.

The first approach tends to be more economical in its code and the second more inventive. To get your work done and retain your sanity, you'll probably want to steer a course between the two extremes.

Retaining or Restoring the User Environment

In many cases, your macros will run without even needing to change the user environment—but if not, restore it as closely as possible to its previous state. What exactly this means depends on the host application, but here are some examples of environment changes in Word, Excel, and PowerPoint:

- In Word: Changing the revision-marking (Track Changes) setting so that you can change the text without the changes being marked as revisions.
- In Word or PowerPoint: Changing the view to a different view so that you can perform certain operations that cannot be performed in the original view.

- In Excel: Creating a temporary worksheet on which you can manipulate data secure in the knowledge that you don't need to check whether any ranges are already occupied by user data.
- In any application that lets you manipulate its Find and Replace feature: Using the Find and Replace feature to identify and/or modify parts of a document, and then restoring users' last search (and replace, if necessary) so that they can perform it again seamlessly. The problem here is that most applications have "sticky" Find and Replace settings to allow the user to perform the same search or replacement operation again quickly without reentering the parameters. If you've replaced users' search and replacement parameters, they'll get a rude shock the next time they try to search or replace. This is particularly true if you've turned on some esoteric feature such as Match Case. The next time the user tries to search for *florida*, they will find no matches, even if the document is about Miami and is jam-packed with the word *Florida*. Why? Because your macro left the Match Case filter turned on, and the user didn't capitalize *Florida* when initiating the search. Fail.

You'll want to save information about the user's environment so that you can restore it at the end of the procedure. If your procedure will mess around with the Match Case property of the Word's Find and Replace feature, at the start of this procedure you save the user's current value in this property in a private variable, public variable, or custom object as appropriate.

Then at the end of your macro, fetch the saved value and restore it to the property you temporarily modified. Here's an example:

```
Dim CaseStatus As Boolean 'match case is either on or off

    CaseStatus = Selection.Find.MatchCase 'save the user's setting

    Selection.Find.MatchCase = True 'our macro needs to be case-sensitive

    ' execute statements in the macro

    Selection.Find.MatchCase = CaseStatus 'restore the user's preference
```

Leaving the User in the Best Position to Continue Working

After your macro finishes running, users need to be in the best possible position to pick up where they left off to continue their work. What exactly this best possible position entails depends on the situation, but here are three simple suggestions:

- Usually, you'll want to leave users viewing the same document they were working on when they started running your macro. There are some obvious exceptions to this, such as when the procedure creates a new file for the user and the user is expecting to work in that file, but the general principle applies in most situations.
- If a file is essentially untouched (at least from the user's point of view) by your macro, the blinking insertion cursor (selection) should probably be placed back where it was when the user started running the procedure. To restore the selection, you may want to define a

range at the start of your procedure and then move the selection back to it at the end of the procedure. In some applications, you could also use a bookmark or a named range—but if you do, be sure to remove it afterward. Remember, leave no debris behind.

Listing 18.1 is an example macro that you can try out. It saves a Word document's current blinking insertion-cursor location in a bookmark. Next, it moves the cursor down a few lines and shows you a message box so you can see the new location of the cursor. Finally, it restores the cursor to its original location:

LISTING 18.1: Restoring the cursor

```
1.  Sub SaveAndRestoreCursor()
2.
3.  'save the current cursor location in a bookmark
4.     ActiveDocument.Bookmarks.Add Name:="OriginalInsertionPoint", _
       Range:=Selection.Range
5.
6.  'move down eight lines
7.     Selection.MoveDown Unit:=wdLine, Count:=8
8.
9.     MsgBox "moved to here (look for insertion line; it's moved down 8 lines
from where it        was.)"
10.
11. 'fetch the saved bookmark and go to it
12.    Selection.GoTo what:=wdGoToBookmark, Name:="OriginalInsertionPoint"
13.
14.    MsgBox "Now the insertion line has been restored to where it was when this
macro        started.)"
15.
16. 'remove the bookmark to leave no debris behind
17.
18.    ActiveDocument.Bookmarks("OriginalInsertionPoint").Delete
19.  End Sub
```

Notice in line 18 that we delete our bookmark when we've finished using it. Don't leave rubbish behind.

- If the procedure has created a new object in the file, and the user will be expecting to work with it, you may want to have that object selected at the end of the procedure.

Keeping the User Informed During the Procedure

A key component of a well-behaved procedure is keeping the user adequately informed throughout the process. In a macro that performs a basic if tedious task, adequate information may require only a clear description in the macro's Description field to assure users that they're choosing the right procedure from the Macros dialog box.

With a more complex procedure, adequate information will probably have to be more extensive: You may need to display a starting message box or dialog box, show information on the status bar during the procedure, display an ending message box, or create a log file of information so that the user has a record of what took place during execution of the procedure.

You must first decide whether to disable user input during the procedure. In Word and Excel, you can disable user input to protect sensitive sections of your procedures by setting the `EnableCancelKey` property of the `Application` object (as discussed in "Disabling User Input While a Procedure Is Running" in Chapter 17, "Debugging Your Code and Handling Errors"). When you do so, it's a good idea to indicate to the user at the beginning of the procedure that input will be disabled and explain why. Otherwise, a user may react to a procedure that seems not to be executing in the same way they would respond to an application that had hung—by trying to close the application forcibly via Task Manager. To keep the user informed about other aspects of the procedure, you have several options, which are discussed in the following sections. But first, the sidebar "Disabling Screen Updating" examines how you can *hide* information from the user (and the reasons for doing so) by disabling screen updating in Word and Excel.

Real World Scenario

DISABLING SCREEN UPDATING

Access, Word, and Excel let you disable screen updating—that is, stop the redrawing of the information in the document area. The other parts of the application window—the title bar, command bars, status bar, scroll bars, and so on—continue to update, but these items are usually relatively static compared to the document area and so don't take much updating. Still, if the user resizes the application window or the document window, they will see these other parts of the application window change, even with screen updating disabled.

There are two advantages to disabling screen updating while your procedure is running:

- You can speed up the execution of your procedures somewhat. This improvement was quite noticeable in the early days of personal computing, and it is still perceptible with underpowered computers that have slow graphics cards. Most computers built since 2000 or so have relatively capable graphics cards, so turning off screen updating makes little visible difference. Any speed improvement from disabling screen updating applies especially to procedures that cause a lot of changes to the onscreen display. For example, suppose a procedure in Word strips a certain type of information out of the current document, pastes it into a new document, creates a table out of it, and applies assorted formatting to the table. The computer will expend a fair amount of effort updating what's appearing on the monitor. This is wasted effort if the user isn't hanging on every operation, so you might as well turn off screen updating.
- You can hide from users any parts of the procedure that you don't want them to see. This sounds totalitarian, but it's usually more like a cross between a benevolent dictatorship and public television: People shouldn't see certain things that might really upset them, and there's a lot that most people don't *really* need to know about. It's the same when you write programs: If users don't know about the operations that a procedure will routinely perform to achieve certain effects, they may be surprised or dismayed by what they see onscreen. For example, in a procedure that moves an open file, you might want to hide from the user the fact that the procedure closes the open file, moves it, and then reopens the file from its new location. By disabling screen updating, you can achieve this.

Continues

Continued

The major disadvantage to disabling screen updating is that doing so prevents users from seeing information that might be useful to them. In the worst case, users may assume from the lack of activity onscreen that either the procedure has entered an endless loop or the computer has hung, and so they may try to stop the procedure by pressing Ctrl+Break or Ctrl+Alt+Delete to use Task Manager to close the application. (Task Manager typically lists the host application as "Not responding" for much of the time VBA code is running, which doesn't help.)

To forestall users from disrupting a procedure, warn them in advance that a procedure will disable screen updating. For instance, you might mention the fact in a message box at the beginning of the procedure, or you might display a dialog box that allows the user to choose whether to disable screen updating and have the procedure run faster or to leave screen updating on and have the procedure run at its normal speed and provide a performance possibly worth watching.

If you don't display a message box or dialog box at the beginning of a procedure, you may want to display information on the status bar to tell the user what's going on during the procedure. Word and Excel update the status bar and the title bar of the application even if screen updating is turned off—provided the status bar and the title bar are visible. To display information on the status bar, assign a suitable string to the `StatusBar` property of the `Application` object:

```
Application.StatusBar = _
    "Word is creating 308 new documents for you to edit. Please wait …"
```

Alternatively, you can disable screen updating for parts of a procedure and turn it back on, or refresh it, for other parts. Consider a procedure that creates and formats a number of documents from an existing document. If you turn off screen updating at the beginning of the procedure and then refresh it once each document has been created and formatted, the user will see each document in turn (which conveys the progress the procedure is making) without seeing the details of the formatting. What's more, the procedure will run faster than if the screen were showing all of the formatting taking place.

To turn off screen updating, set the `ScreenUpdating` property of the `Application` object to `False`:

```
Application.ScreenUpdating = False
```

To turn screen updating back on, set `ScreenUpdating` to `True` again:

```
Application.ScreenUpdating = True
```

In Access, use the `Echo` method of the `DoCmd` object to turn screen updating on or off, respectively:

```
DoCmd.Echo True  'turns updating on
DoCmd.Echo False 'turns updating off
```

In Word, to refresh the screen with the current contents of the video memory buffer, use the `ScreenRefresh` method of the `Application` object:

```
Application.ScreenRefresh
```

Manipulating the Cursor

Word and Excel permit you to manipulate the cursor (the mouse pointer). You may need to do this because VBA automatically displays the busy cursor (an hourglass in Windows XP, a rotating ring in Windows versions since then) while a VBA procedure is running and then restores the normal cursor when it has finished. Sometimes, however, you may need or want to specify the cursor's appearance in your code.

> **Stick with the Familiar Cursor Cues**
>
> After using computers for even a few months, users tend to develop almost Pavlovian reactions to the cursor, with the busy cursor signifying (in ascending order) a momentary breather (or a slow computer), a chance to grab a cup of coffee or chat with a colleague, or the onset of panic that the computer has hung before they've saved the last three hours of work. You usually won't want to mess with these reactions. So it's a mistake to display an I-beam insertion cursor or "normal" arrow cursor when the system is in fact busy—or to display the busy cursor after the procedure has in fact finished running and is again ready to respond to keypresses (a status that calls for the I-beam symbol).

Manipulating the Cursor in Word

Word implements the cursor via the `System` object. To manipulate the cursor, you set the `Cursor` property. This is a read/write Long property that can be set to the following values: `wdCursorIBeam` (1) for an I-beam cursor, `wdCursorNormal` (2) for a normal cursor, `wdCursorNorthWestArrow` (3) for a left-angled resizing arrow (pointing up), and `wdCursorWait` (`0`) for the busy cursor. The exact appearance of the cursor depends on the cursor scheme the user has selected.

For example, the following statement displays a busy cursor:

```
System.Cursor = wdCursorWait
```

Note that a user can customize the cursors by clicking the Mouse icon in Control Panel to open the Mouse Properties dialog box and then selecting the Pointers tab.

Manipulating the Cursor in Excel

Excel lets you manipulate the cursor through the `Cursor` property of the `Application` object. `Cursor` is a read/write Long property that can be set to the following values: `xlIBeam (3)` for an I-beam cursor, `xlDefault (-4143)` for a default cursor, `xlNorthwestArrow (1)` for the arrow pointing up and to the left, and `xlWait (2)` for the busy cursor.

For example, the following statement displays the busy cursor:

```
Application.Cursor = xlWait
```

When you explicitly set the `Cursor` property of the `Application` object in Excel, remember to reset it to something appropriate before your code stops executing. Otherwise, the cursor stays as you left it.

Displaying Information at the Beginning of a Procedure

At the beginning of many procedures, you'll probably want to display a message box or a dialog box. For this purpose, you'll typically use a Yes/No or OK/Cancel message-box style.

The message box tells users what the procedure will do and gives them the chance to cancel the procedure without running it any further.

Alternatively, a dialog box can present options for the procedure (for example, mutually exclusive options via option buttons or nonexclusive options via check boxes), allowing users to enter information (via text boxes, list boxes, or combo boxes) and, of course, letting them cancel the procedure if they've cued it by accident. If you have time to create a Help file to accompany the procedures and user forms you create, you might add a Help button to each message box or dialog box, linking it to the relevant topic in the Help file.

You can also use a message box or dialog box to warn the user that the procedure is going to disable user interrupts for part or all of its duration.

Communicating with the User via a Message Box or Dialog Box at the End of a Procedure

With some procedures, you'll find it useful to collect information on what the procedure is doing so that you can display that information to the user in a message box or dialog box after the procedure has finished its work. As you saw in Chapter 13, "Getting User Input with Message Boxes and Input Boxes," message boxes are easier to use but are severely limited in their capabilities for laying out text—you're limited to the effects you can achieve with spaces, tabs, carriage returns, and bullets. With dialog boxes, however, you can lay out text however you need to (by using labels or text boxes) and even include images if necessary.

The easiest way to collect information while running a procedure is to build one or more strings containing the information you want to display. For an example of this, look back to the sidebar titled "Control a `For…Next` Loop with User Input via a Dialog Box" in Chapter 12, "Using Loops to Repeat Actions," in which a `cmdOK_Click` procedure collects information while creating a series of folders and then at the end displays a message box telling the user what the procedure has accomplished.

Creating a Log File

If you need to collect a lot of information during the course of running a procedure and either present it to the user once the procedure has finished or just make it available for reference if needed, consider using a log file rather than a message box or dialog box. Log files are useful for lengthy procedures that manipulate critical data: By writing information periodically to a log file (and by saving it frequently), you create a record of what the procedure achieves in case it crashes.

Make a Log File Useful for Both Average and Sophisticated Users

If you want a log file to be useful for ordinary users as well as for the technically inclined, make its entries readable and helpful while including any technical information required for advanced troubleshooting. For example, a message such as "*The data files for the 'Madrid' office (madrid060430.xlsm) and the 'Taos' office (taos060430.xlsm) were not found in the expected location, '\\server2\data\dayfiles\', so the information could not be included*" is usually more widely helpful than a cryptic "Error code 44E: Required Data Missing."

Say you wrote a procedure for Word that collects information from a variety of sources each day and writes it into a report. You might want to keep a log file that tracks whether information from each source was successfully transferred and at what time. Listing 18.2 provides an example of such a procedure. At the end of the procedure, you could leave the log file open so that the user could check whether the procedure was successful in creating the report or leave the summary file open so that the user could read the report itself.

LISTING 18.2: Creating a log file

```
Sub Create_Log_File()

    Dim strDate As String
    Dim strPath As String
    Dim strCity(10) As String
    Dim strLogText As String
    Dim strLogName As String
    Dim strSummary As String
    Dim strFile As String
    Dim i As Integer

    On Error GoTo Crash

    strCity(1) = "Chicago"
    strCity(2) = "Toronto"
    strCity(3) = "New York"
    strCity(4) = "London"
    strCity(5) = "Lyons"
    strCity(6) = "Antwerp"
    strCity(7) = "Copenhagen"
    strCity(8) = "Krakow"
    strCity(9) = "Pinsk"
    strCity(10) = "Belgrade"

    strDate = Month(Date) & "-" & Day(Date) & "-" _
        & Year(Date)
    strPath = "f:\Daily Data\"
    strLogName = strPath & "Reports\Log for " _
        & strDate & ".docm"
    strSummary = strPath & "Reports\Summary for " _
        & strDate & ".docm"
    Documents.Add
    ActiveDocument.SaveAs strSummary

    For i = 1 To 10
        strFile = strPath & strCity(i) & " " & strDate & ".docm"
        If Dir(strFile) <> "" Then
```

```
35.             Documents.Open strFile
36.             Documents(strFile).Paragraphs(1).Range.Copy
37.             Documents(strFile).Close _
38.                 SaveChanges:=wdDoNotSaveChanges
39.             With Documents(strSummary)
40.                 Selection.EndKey Unit:=wdStory
41.                 Selection.Paste
42.                 .Save
43.             End With
44.             strLogText = strLogText & strCity(i) _
                    & vbTab & "OK" & vbCr
45.         Else
46.             strLogText = strLogText & strCity(i) _
                    & vbTab & "No file" & vbCr
47.         End If
48.     Next i
49.
50. Crash:
51.
52.     Documents.Add
53.     Selection.TypeText strLogText
54.     ActiveDocument.SaveAs strLogName
55.     Documents(strLogName).Close
56.     Documents(strSummary).Close
57.
58. End Sub
```

The procedure in Listing 18.2 creates a new document that contains a summary, opens a number of files in turn, copies the first paragraph out of each and pastes it into the summary document, and then closes the file. As it does this, the procedure maintains a string of log information from which it creates a log file at the end of the procedure or, if an error occurs, during the procedure. Here's what happens in the code:

- Lines 3 through 9 declare six String variables—`strDate`, `strPath`, `strLogText`, `strLogName`, `strSummary`, and `strFile`—and one String array, `strCity`, containing 10 items. (The procedure uses an `Option Base 1` statement that doesn't appear in the listing, so `strCity(10)` produces 10 items in the array rather than 11.) Line 10 declares the Integer variable `i`, which the procedure will use as a counter.
- Line 11 is a spacer. Line 12 uses an `On Error GoTo` statement to start error handling and direct execution to the label `Crash:` in the event of an error. Line 13 is a spacer.
- Lines 14 through 23 assign the names of the company's 10 offices to the `strCity` array. Line 24 is a spacer.
- Line 25 assigns to `strDate` a string created by concatenating the month, the day, and the year for the current date (with a hyphen between each part) by using the `Month`, `Day`, and

`Year` functions, respectively. For example, January 21, 2007, will produce a date string of `1-21-2007`. (The reason for creating a string like this is that Windows can't handle slashes in filenames—slashes are reserved for indicating folders.)

- Line 26 sets `strPath` to the `f:\Daily Data\` folder. Line 27 then builds a filename for the log file in the `\Reports\` subfolder, and line 28 creates a filename for the summary file, also in the `\Reports\` subfolder.
- Line 29 creates a new document based on `Normal.dotm`, and line 30 saves this document under the name stored in the `strSummary` variable. Line 31 is a spacer.
- Line 32 begins a `For...Next` loop that runs from `i = 1` to `i = 10`. Line 33 assigns to the String variable `strFile` the filename for the first of the cities stored in the `strCity` array: `strPath & strCity(i) & " " & strDate & ".docm"`.
- Line 34 then begins an `If` statement that checks whether `Dir(strFile)` returns an empty string. If not, line 35 opens the document specified by `strFile`, line 36 copies its first paragraph, and line 37 closes it without saving changes. The procedure doesn't make any changes to the document, but if the document contains any dynamic "hot fields" (such as date fields or links that automatically update themselves when the document is opened), it may have become dirty (modified). Including the `SaveChanges` argument ensures that users don't get an unexpected message box prompting them to save a document they know they haven't changed. (An alternative would be to set the `Saved` property of the document to `True` and then close it without using the `SaveChanges` argument.)
- Lines 39 through 43 contain a `With` statement that works with the `Document` object specified by `strSummary`. Line 40 uses the `EndKey` method with the `Unit` argument `wdStory` to move the selection to the end of the document. Line 41 pastes in the material copied from the document just opened, and line 42 saves the document. Line 43 ends the `With` statement.
- Line 44 adds to `strLogText` the contents of `strCity(i)`, a tab, the text `OK`, and a carriage return, which will produce a simple tabbed list of the cities and the status of their reports.
- If the condition posed in line 34 isn't met, execution branches to the `Else` statement in line 45, and line 46 adds to `strLogText` the contents of `strCity(i)`, a tab, `No file`, and a carriage return. Line 47 ends the `If` statement, and line 48 ends the `For...Next` loop, returning execution to line 32.
- Line 49 is a spacer. Line 50 contains the `Crash:` label and marks the start of the error handler. Unlike in many procedures, you don't want to stop execution before entering the error handler—as it happens, you want to execute these statements (to create the log file) even if an error occurs. Line 51 is a spacer.
- Line 52 creates a new document based on the default template; line 53 types the contents of `strLogText` into the new document; and line 54 saves it under the name `strLogName`. Line 55 closes this new document (alternatively, you could leave the document open so that the user could view it). Line 56 closes the summary document (which has remained open since it was created. Again, you might want to leave this open so that the user can view it, or even offer the user the option of keeping it open). Line 57 is a spacer, and line 58 ends the procedure.

Making Sure a Procedure Is Running Under Suitable Conditions

Another important consideration when creating a well-behaved procedure is to check that it's running under suitable conditions. This ideal is nearly impossible to achieve under all circumstances, but you should take some basic steps, such as the following:

- Make sure a file is open in a procedure that needs a file to be open—otherwise, you'll get an error every time. For example, in Excel, you might check the `Count` property of the `Workbooks` collection to make sure at least one workbook is open:

```
If Workbooks.Count = 0 Then _
    MsgBox "This procedure will not run without a " _
    & "workbook open. Open one, then run the procedure again.", _
vbOKOnly + vbExclamation, _
    "No Workbook Is Open"
```

- Check that the procedure is referencing an appropriate item, if the procedure has definable requirements. For example, in an Excel procedure that applies intricate formatting to a chart the user has selected, make sure the user has, in fact, actually selected a chart. Trying to manipulate another object with chart-related commands is likely to cause an error or at least unwanted side effects.
- Make sure a file contains the element required by the procedure. (If it doesn't, an error will likely result.) Alternatively, trap the error that will result from the element's absence.

Cleaning Up After a Procedure

Like your children or housemates, your procedures should learn to clean up after themselves. Cleaning up involves the following:

- Undoing any changes that the procedure had to make
- Closing any files that no longer need to be open
- Removing any scratch files or folders that the procedure has created to achieve its effects

Undoing Changes the Procedure Has Made

In some cases, you'll need to make changes to a document in order to run a procedure successfully. Here are a couple of examples:

- In Word, you might need to apply some formatting to half of a table but not to the rest of it. In this case, it might be easier to split the table into two tables so that you can select columns in the relevant part and format or change them without affecting the columns in the other half of the original table. If you do this, you'll want to join the tables together again afterward by removing the break you've inserted between the original table's two halves.

The easiest way to do this is to bookmark the break that you insert. You can then go back to the bookmark and delete it and the break at the same time. Alternatively, you could use a `Set` statement to define a range for the break and then return to the range and remove the break.

- In Excel, you may need to define named ranges in a workbook so that you can easily reference them from the code. (Usually, you'll do better to use ranges via VBA, which won't leave unwanted named ranges in the workbook.) Delete these named ranges when you've finished with them.

Removing Scratch Files and Folders

During a complex procedure, you may need to create scratch files in which to temporarily store or manipulate data, or scratch folders in which to store temporary files.

For example, if you need to perform complex formatting on a few paragraphs of a long document in Word, you may find it easier to copy and paste those paragraphs into a new blank document and manipulate them there than to continue working in the original document and risk unintentionally affecting other paragraphs as well. Likewise, in PowerPoint, you might need to create a new presentation that you could use for temporary or backup storage of intricate objects.

Creating scratch files, while often necessary for the safe and successful operation of a procedure, can be intrusive. You're cluttering up the user's hard drive with information that's probably of no use to that user. Creating scratch folders in which to save the scratch files is even worse. Always go the extra distance to clean up any temporary items that you've stored on the user's hard drive. If you're thinking that commercial applications don't always do this, not even Microsoft's applications, you're right. But that doesn't mean you should follow their example.

If your procedure is going to remove any scratch files it creates, you may be tempted to conceal from the user their creation and subsequent deletion. This usually isn't a good idea—in most cases, the best thing is to warn the user that the procedure will create scratch files. You might even let the user specify or create a suitable folder for the scratch files or present the user with a list that logs the files created and whether they were successfully deleted. Doing so will allow users to easily delete any scratch files left on their computer if your procedure goes wrong or is interrupted during execution.

Another approach is to use the API (application programming interface) commands `GetTempDir` and `GetTempFileName` to find out the location of the computer's temporary folder and a temporary filename that you can use. (How to make an API call is illustrated in Chapter 30, "Accessing One Application from Another Application," in the sidebar titled "Using the `Sleep` Function to Avoid Problems with Shell's Asynchrony.") But even if you use the default temporary folder, you should delete any files that you create in it when your procedure is finished. Again, a disappointing number of commercial software developers fail to do this.

Using Your Own Scratch Folder

You can use the `MkDir` command to create a folder. For example, the following statement creates a folder named `Scratch Folder` on the `C:` drive:

```
MkDir "c:\Scratch Folder"
```

Before creating a folder, use the `Dir` command to check to see that the name isn't already in use. (If a folder with that name already exists, an error results.) Here's how:

```
Dim s As String
s = "c:\TempDir"

If Len(Dir(s, vbDirectory)) = 0 Then
    MkDir s
End If
```

For temporary storage, you may want to use a folder name based on the date and time to lessen the chance that a folder with that name already exists. You could also use VBA's `Rnd` function to generate a random number to use as part of the folder name.

DELETING A SCRATCH FOLDER

You can use the `RmDir` statement to remove an empty folder. (Make sure that you've deleted all files in the folder first—otherwise `RmDir` will fail.) For example, the following statement removes the scratch folder named `Scratch Folder` on the `C:` drive:

```
RmDir "c:\Scratch Folder"
```

The Bottom Line

Understand the characteristics of well-behaved procedures. Well-behaved procedures don't annoy or alarm the user either during or after their execution.

Master It Name two ways programmers can write procedures that don't annoy users.

Retain and restore the user environment. Users quite rightly don't appreciate it if your procedure leaves the state of their application's or operating system's environment modified. Find ways to restore the user environment before your procedure finishes execution.

Master It Assume that you are writing a procedure that employs Word's Search and Replace feature. This feature retains its settings between uses so the user can repeatedly trigger the same search or replace actions. How can you temporarily store the status of the user's last search or replace so that you can restore this data after your procedure is finished executing?

Let the user know what's happening. Particularly when a procedure is doing a lengthy "batch job" such as updating dozens of files, it's important to let the user know that the computer hasn't frozen. People need to be told that execution is continuing as expected even though nothing appears to be happening.

Master It Describe a way to let the user know that a procedure isn't frozen—that activity is taking place during execution.

Check that the procedure is running under suitable conditions. Another important element of creating a well-behaved procedure is to check that it's running under suitable conditions. This ideal is nearly impossible to achieve under all circumstances, but you should take some basic steps.

Master It If a procedure accesses data from a file, name an error that could occur and, thus, should be trapped.

Clean up after a procedure. A well-behaved procedure avoids leaving unneeded files or other temporary items behind. In other words, a procedure should clean up after itself.

Master It Cleaning up involves three major tasks. Name one.

Chapter 19

Exploring VBA's Security Features

This chapter discusses how to use the security tools that VBA provides for distributing and implementing macros and VBA code. VBA security falls into three categories: securing your applications against rogue VBA code; establishing that your VBA code isn't itself rogue so that it can be run; and securing your code against theft, alteration, or snooping.

IN THIS CHAPTER, YOU WILL LEARN TO DO THE FOLLOWING:

- Understand how VBA implements security
- Sign a macro project with a digital signature
- Get a digital certificate
- Choose the appropriate security level
- Lock your code

Understanding How VBA Implements Security

Macros are computer programs, albeit usually rather small ones. But because macros can access the user's hard drive and exploit other features of a computer, macros can do damage.

Office and the Windows operating systems include a variety of security features designed to protect the user from malicious code—macro, virus, Trojan horse, or whatever. But some security features are specific to Office documents and the macros, dialog boxes, and user forms they can contain.

It's scary but true: An evil macro can do its damage *automatically*. It's not even necessary for the user to deliberately launch a macro from the Macros dialog box or from within the VBA Editor. Some procedures (with certain special names such as `Open`) automatically launch themselves. For example, if you name one of your macros `Document_Open`, all the code within that sub executes spontaneously when the user opens its host document:

```
Private Sub Document_Open()
```

This can be handy, of course. Perhaps you'll want to write some code in this procedure that automatically sets up your preferred zoom level or completes some other housekeeping task that you always perform when opening any document. But the fact that the user doesn't need to specifically choose to run this macro means that a virus can be put into this procedure. And whammo—your computer is infected.

Malicious code can enter a user's Office applications via three primary vehicles: macros, ActiveX controls, and add-ins. Microsoft provides users with various approaches to VBA security, including the following:

- Certain Office document file types that simply cannot contain any embedded macros at all. That's the difference between, for example, saving a file using the Word `.docx` option, which cannot contain macros, and the `.docm` file type, which can. *M* stands for macro; *X* stands for XML, (a computer language and data storage system employed internally by Office products).
- Documents that are loaded from a trusted area on the hard drive.
- Trust Center settings the user can specify, such as completely preventing the execution of any ActiveX controls, macros, or add-ins without even notifying or querying the user. Alternatively, the user can be prompted for permission before potentially dangerous code is allowed to execute.
- A list of user-modifiable "trusted publishers"—companies whose documents are considered safe.
- The ability to digitally sign your own documents or templates, thereby making you a "trusted publisher."

Office 2007 introduced the concept of two types of documents. For the first time, the user could save documents that simply cannot contain any macros or other potentially malicious code. By default, any new Word document is of the `.docx` type, not the `.docm` (macro-enabled) type. In other words, a document must be deliberately created as a macro-enabled document. And because it also must have a `.docm` filename extension, everybody else (including Word when opening the document) knows that it contains possibly dangerous code. Administrators can use Group Policy to enforce rules concerning which file types are permitted. But the default `.docx` file type is free of potentially risky executables (files or procedures that can execute).

Other Office applications also have pairs of macro-disabled, macro-enabled file types. Excel has `.xlsx` and `.xlsm` files, and PowerPoint has `.pptx` and `.pptm` files.

Office includes various security tools and features that ordinary users, administrators, and IT professionals can employ to further safeguard Office applications from attack:

- An Office ActiveX kill bit that allows administrators to forbid certain ActiveX controls from executing.
- File-type blocking that can be implemented via Group Policy settings or individually via the Office Trust Center. The types of files that an application can access can be specifically controlled.
- A Trusted Documents feature that allows users to specify individual documents as reliable, thereby obviating whatever macro settings the user has enforced in the Trust Center.
- A scanning feature that searches for format exploits before a file can be opened by an Office application.
- A sandbox named Protected View. A *sandbox* isolates an executing program so it can't damage other programs, introduce viruses into the operating system, or store nasty surprises

on the hard drive. Figure 19.1 shows the Protected View options and the warning you get if you're about to open a document from a potentially dangerous source. This is similar to starting Windows in Safe mode. In Protected View, executables are disabled. The protected document is in effect quarantined, so it theoretically can't do any harm to your computer or its contents. I say *theoretically* because as we all know, no security is perfect. Note that in its description of Protected View in Figure 19.1, Microsoft carefully states that this mode will "help minimize harm"—there is no claim of invulnerability. All the Protected View options are turned on by default, so files you get from the Internet and Outlook attachments, for example, are automatically tossed into the sandbox when opened.

FIGURE 19.1
Suspect sources trigger this security warning when opened in Office applications.

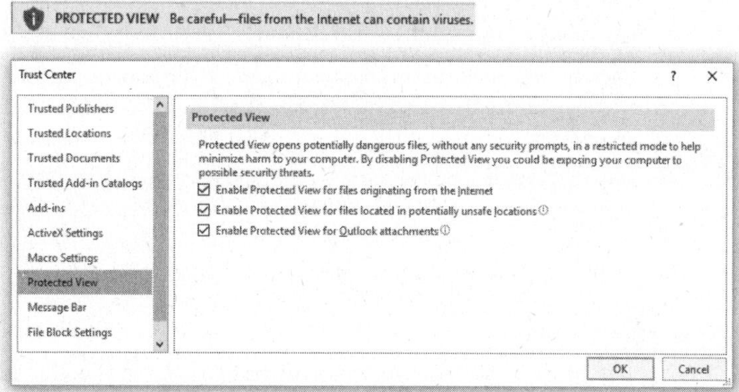

- Various under-the-hood features, including password security and encryption to protect the privacy of user information.

Doubtless there are additional hardening tactics that Microsoft is not mentioning. After all, why tell the bad people everything that's being done to prevent their incursions?

Real World Scenario

REAL SECURITY IN AN INSECURE WORLD

All the virus-detection software, firewalls, digital signatures, and other security efforts in the world won't protect you or your colleagues if somebody on your network opens email attachments, downloads dodgy executables, or otherwise invites trouble into your environment.

Even if everybody is aware of the dangers and follows the best security practices, viruses and other troubles can *still* get in. After all, antivirus applications are always playing catch-up. A new virus is released, and then the antivirus forces identify it and send out a new update.

Continues

Continued

On the plus side, currently it's pretty rare to find macros employed as a vehicle for spreading viruses. And, of course, if you're writing the VBA code yourself—as a reader of this book—you can certainly trust the source of *your* macros. It's you!

However, because threats are constant, and because it's ultimately impossible to guarantee that you will never get a virus (in spite of taking great pains to prevent them), you should ensure that you are taking additional precautions to at least mitigate damage.

Malicious software falls into two broad categories:

- Code that attempts to do damage by, for example, erasing files or slowing your computer down so much that it becomes painful to use. The goal here is to create a mess you have to clean up—or pay culprits to clean up, such as the notorious viruses that lock your files until you send money.
- Code that attempts to find out your secrets to do damage by, for example, stealing your identity to ruin your credit or to drain your bank account. The issue here is violation of your person and an invasion of privacy, a different kind of mess to clean up.

If you're concerned about privacy, you should encrypt any documents containing sensitive information. Fortunately, with Office 2007 the formerly weak Office encryption scheme was replaced with a highly secure one. And Microsoft continues to toughen built-in encryption schemes and has added integrity-checking technologies for encrypted files. PowerPoint, Word, and Excel all permit you to encrypt files and then decrypt them by providing a password. Click File on the Ribbon; then on the Info page, click Protect Document and then Encrypt With Password.

If you're worried about a virus attack, be sure to back up your documents (you should do this anyway, in case of a drive crash, fire, theft, or other havoc). These days, with three-terabyte external drives selling for around $100, it's practical to store your entire computer system (a *system image*)—documents, programs, inbox email, everything—as an image on an external drive. That way, you won't have to reinstall applications in the event of a serious problem. You can use third-party backup systems. Or, if you use Windows 7, you can use Windows's built-in backup system by choosing Start ➢ Control Panel, and then clicking Backup And Restore.

If you use Windows 8 or 10 and just want to back up your data files, press Windows key+S and type **`Save Backup`** to use the File History utility. If you want to use the traditional Windows backup, it's possible even in Windows 8 or 10. To invoke this utility, press Windows key+W and type **`Backup and Restore`** (or in Windows 8 type: **`Windows 7 File Recovery`**). From there, you can create an image, a repair disk, or a traditional Windows-style backup.

To secure an application against rogue VBA code, you can use the Office Trust Center to choose the level of security you want the application to use when running VBA code. Click the File tab and choose Options. Click the Trust Center button in the left pane, and click the Trust Center Settings button.

You can also specify which sources to trust and how much to trust them. A trusted source might be someone who works for the same company as you or someone who has a digital certificate from a third party you trust, such as the VeriSign certification authority. Because you (in this example) trust VeriSign, you, therefore, trust the third party to whom VeriSign has issued a digital certificate. Office also has a trusted time-stamping feature with the digital signature technology.

To establish that your own code is fine for the Office applications to trust, you can sign a document or template project that contains customizations or macro project items (code modules, class modules, or user forms) with a digital signature generated by a digital certificate that uniquely identifies you or your company. We'll look at this technique first because it sets the stage for specifying the level of security to use.

You can also lock a macro project with a password so that nobody can open the code. This prevents anyone from tinkering with your code and either stopping it from working or rendering it harmful. It also protects your intellectual property: If nobody can see your code, nobody can steal your ideas. The section in this chapter titled "Locking Your Code" shows you how to do this.

Signing Your Macro Projects with Digital Signatures

VBA provides a security mechanism for securing macro projects with digital signatures. The digital signatures provide a means of establishing the provenance of the projects, which can help you decide whether to trust the code. If you trust the source of the code to produce benevolent programming, you can open the project and run the code. If you suspect the source or the information of being malignant, you can either avoid opening the project or open the project with the code disabled.

The same goes for other people: If others are concerned about your macros, you may need to sign your projects so that other people know where they come from and who created them. Once you've signed the projects, the code is available to any application that has specified you as a trusted source for macro projects. (This assumes users have chosen one of the Disable options in the Macro Settings dialog box. You'll see how to set the security level later, in the section "Specifying a Suitable Security Setting.")

The following sections discuss what digital certificates are, what they mean in practical terms, how you obtain them, and how you use them to create digital signatures.

TRUSTING A PUBLISHER IS GLOBAL FOR VBA-ENABLED APPLICATIONS

VBA's security mechanism, and the list of certificates, is shared across the range of VBA-enabled applications on your computer. So if you designate a trusted publisher in one application, all the other applications that support VBA security will trust that source as well. For example, if you open a document that contains code in Word and choose to trust the source of the code, Excel and Outlook also gain that trust and open projects from that source without having to prompt you.

What Is a Digital Certificate?

A *digital certificate* is an encrypted datum that uniquely identifies its holder. Rather like a driver's license, it provides a level of trust that you are who you say you are and that your code can be trusted.

You use your digital certificate to create a digital signature for a project. This project can be a document project, a template project, or an add-in. The project doesn't have to contain macros, procedures, user forms, classes, or VBA code for you to sign it, although these contents are the usual reason for signing a project.

A digital signature applies to a whole macro project, typically a document project or a template project. You can't apply a digital signature to just part of a project—say, just to one module of code or to one user form. Each macro project item in that macro project—each module, user form, class, and reference—is covered by the digital certificate.

But digital signatures, while usually reliable, have sometimes been compromised.

Getting a Digital Certificate

There are three types of digital certificates: those you create yourself ("self-signed"), those you get from your company or organization, and those you get from a commercial certification authority, or certificate authority (CA).

A digital certificate you create yourself is the weakest form of identification and is of little use to people beyond you and those who use your machine, whereas a certificate from a commercial certification authority should be good enough for general use in the world. Self-signed code will generate a security warning if someone opens a file containing this code. Office applications will not allow this code to run on any but the machine on which the certificate was created.

A certificate issued by your company falls in the middle range of trustworthiness: In many cases, the company will have obtained the certificate from a commercial certification authority that has established to its satisfaction that the company is trustworthy. Whom the company chooses to trust with the certificate is another matter, and also introduces another complicating link into the chain of trust. However, server software such as Windows Server includes independent certification-authority services that do not require a certificate from a commercial certification authority, so you should be careful which certificates you trust. See the section "Whose Certificate Is It, and What Does It Mean?" later in this chapter for a discussion of how to discern a certificate's provenance and meaning.

Creating a Digital Certificate of Your Own

The quickest and easiest way of getting a digital certificate is to create one yourself. It's easy, but remember that this kind of certification only works on the computer on which the certificate was created. So, its usefulness is very limited.

To understand how digital certificates work, you'll probably want to create several of your own and practice with them on sample files. By designating some of your files as originating from trusted publishers and leaving others untrusted, you can get a clear idea of how digital certificates work without having to actually mess around with suspect code on your system.

To open the Create Digital Certificate dialog box (see Figure 19.2) in Windows 10, use File Explorer to locate, and then double-click to launch this SELFCERT program:

```
"C:\Program Files (x86)\Microsoft Office\root\office16\SELFCERT.EXE"
```

If you're using the 64-bit version of SELFCERT, it will be found instead in the `C:\Program Files\Microsoft Office\root\office16\SELFCERT.EXE` path.

In Windows 8, press the Windows key and type **`digital certificate`**. Press Enter when you see Digital Certificate for VBA projects. You'll see the form you can "sign," as shown in Figure 19.2.

If you're using Windows 7, choose Start ➤ All Programs ➤ Microsoft Office ➤ Microsoft Office 2013 Tools ➤ Digital Certificate For VBA Projects.

Tip: Microsoft appears to be deprecating (moving away from) self-certification. With each version of Windows, they're making it a little more difficult to find the tool. As you see, they keep moving it around, and now with Windows 10, they're really hiding it. Even the search feature built into Windows can't locate it any more.

Type the name for the certificate in the text box, and then click the OK button. The SELFCERT application creates the certificate and installs it automatically.

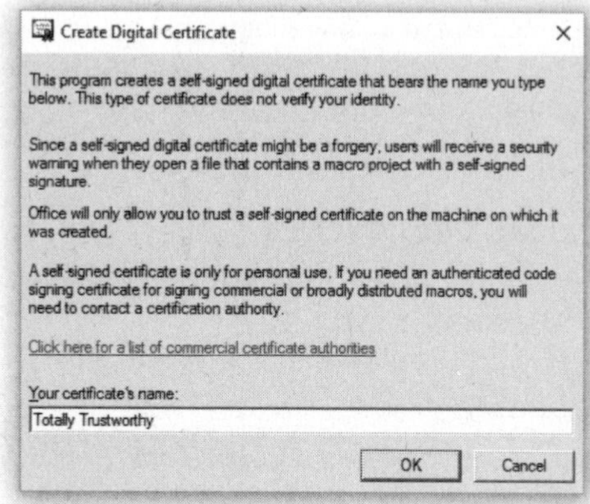

FIGURE 19.2
You can self-sign a certificate, but Office only permits such certification to be trusted within the computer where the certificate was created.

GETTING A DIGITAL CERTIFICATE FROM YOUR COMPANY

Your second option is to get a digital certificate from a digital certificate server that your company has. The details of this procedure vary from company to company. The certificates the company provides via its digital certificate server are generated in the same fashion as the digital certificates distributed by the commercial certification authorities discussed in the next section. However, a company distributes the certificates from a pool that it has allocated, without needing to apply to the certification authority for each certificate as it's needed, or it creates the certificates of its own accord without getting them from a certification authority. Clearly this isn't all that safe. A rogue employee can *pose* as trustworthy, obtain a company certificate, and then run totally wild. Totally.

GETTING A DIGITAL CERTIFICATE FROM A COMMERCIAL CERTIFICATION AUTHORITY

Your third choice is to get a digital certificate from a commercial certification authority such as these:

- Comodo (`https://www.comodo.com/`)
- Symantec (was VeriSign) (`www.symantec.com/products-solutions/`)
- GlobalSign (`www.globalsign.com/en/`)
- Go Daddy (`www.godaddy.com`)

Several types of certificates are available, depending on what you want to do. If you're creating and distributing software, you'll probably want to consider one of the certificates targeted at developers.

The procedure for proving your identity varies depending on the CA and the type of certificate you want. Generally speaking, the greater the degree of trust that the certificate is intended to inspire, the more proof you'll need to supply. For example, you can get a basic certificate on the strength of nothing more than a verifiable email address, but this type of certificate is unlikely to make smart people trust you. Other certificate types require you to appear in person before a registration authority with full documentation (such as a passport, driver's license, or other identity documents). Such certificates obviously inspire more trust.

Installing a Digital Certificate

Once you have a digital certificate, you need to install it so that Windows and the applications that will use it know where it's located.

To install a digital certificate, follow these steps (you must be logged on as Administrator to view the Certificates dialog box):

1. In Windows 8 or 10, from the Desktop, press the Windows key and type **`certmgr.msc`**.

> **Self-Certifications Are Automatically Registered**
>
> The Office SelfCert program automatically registers the certificates it creates on the computer on which it creates them. If you created a digital certificate for yourself, you shouldn't need to install it on the same computer.

   In Windows 7, click the Start button. A Search Programs And Files field opens just above the Start button. In the Search Programs And Files field, type **`certmgr.msc`**.

2. When `certmgr.msc` appears in the Programs list, click it. You'll possibly be asked if you want to give yourself permission to take this step. Unless you are not you, go ahead and grant the permission by clicking the Continue button. (From this point on, Windows 7 will take a different path and display different dialogs than those shown here.)

   You now see the Certificates dialog box shown in Figure 19.3.

   As you can see in Figure 19.3, I, identifying myself as an entity named *TotallyTrustworthy*, granted code-signing certification to myself, also TotallyTrustworthy, as described earlier in this chapter in the section "Creating a Digital Certificate of Your Own."

3. Click the Trusted Publishers folder in the left pane of the Certificates dialog box.

4. Choose Action ➤ All Tasks ➤ Import from the Certificates dialog box's menu. The Certificate Import Wizard opens, as shown in Figure 19.4.

FIGURE 19.3
Windows provides the Certificates dialog box to manage digital certificates.

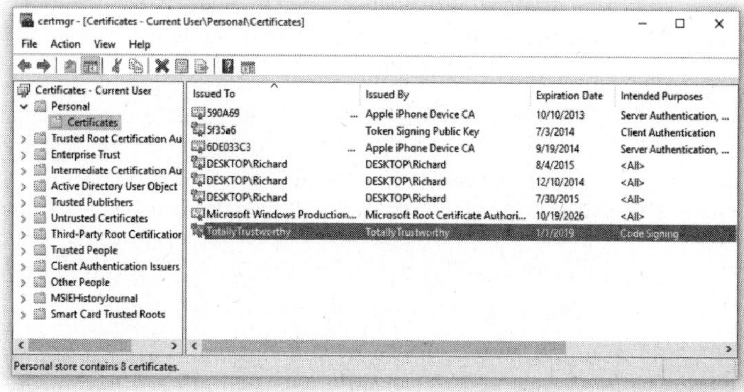

FIGURE 19.4
Windows includes the Certificate Import Wizard to manage digital certificates.

5. Click the Next button in the wizard to locate the file you want to import. You can search your hard drive for filenames ending in `.cer` or `.crt`.
6. Click Next to display the Certificate Store page of the wizard, shown in Figure 19.5.
7. Choose how to store the certificate:

- To have Windows store each certificate automatically in the default certificate store for the certificate's type, select the Automatically Select The Certificate Store Based On The Type Of Certificate option button.
- To control where Windows stores the certificates, select the Place All Certificates In The Following Store option button. To specify the store, click the Browse button to display the Select Certificate Store dialog box, shown in Figure 19.6. Choose the certificate store (for example, Personal) and click the OK button. To specify a particular location within a certificate store, select the Show Physical Stores check box, and then click the plus (+) sign next to the store in question to display its subfolders. Select the folder you want, and then click the OK button.

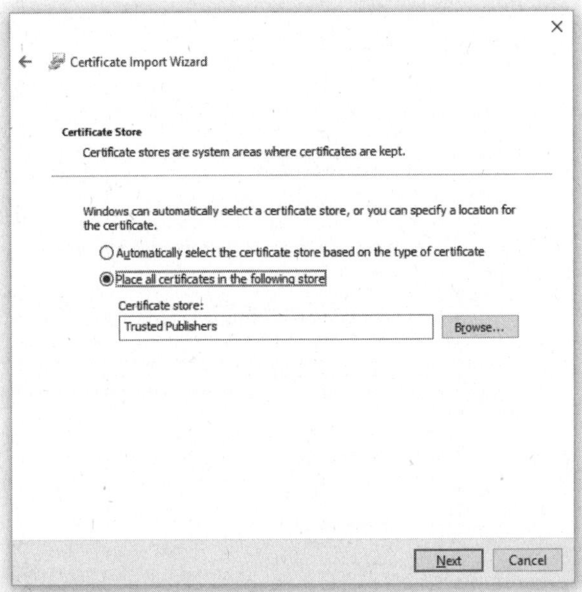

FIGURE 19.5 On the Certificate Store page of the Certificate Import Wizard, choose the certificate store in which to store the certificate you're importing.

8. Click the Next button to finish setting up the import procedure. The Completing The Certificate Import Wizard dialog box is displayed to confirm the choices you've made.
9. Review your choices, and then click the Finish button. The Certificate Import Wizard imports the certificate and then confirms that the operation was successful.

Now that you've imported the certificate, it appears in the Certificates dialog box on the appropriate page.

EXPORTING A DIGITAL CERTIFICATE

You may need to export a certificate either for backup or to install it on another computer. For security, you should not store the digital certificate on your hard drive after you install it, because that's an unnecessary security risk.

To export a certificate, right-click it in the Certificates dialog box, and then choose All Tasks ➤ Export. Windows starts the Certificate Export Wizard, which walks you through the process of exporting the certificate. If you choose to export the private key with the certificate, be sure to protect it with a password.

FIGURE 19.6 Use the Select Certificate Store dialog box to specify the certificate store in which you want to keep the certificate. The screen on the left shows the categories of stores; the screen on the right shows the physical stores.

REMOVING A DIGITAL CERTIFICATE

To remove a digital certificate from Windows's digital certificate store, follow these steps:

1. Display the certmgr.msc Certificates dialog box (follow steps 1 and 2 in the section earlier in this chapter on installing a certificate).
2. Click the folder in the left pane that contains the digital certificate in question, and then select the certificate you want to remove.
3. Click the red X icon on the toolbar, or choose Action ➤ Delete. Windows displays a dialog box warning you of the consequences of deleting the digital certificate and asking you to confirm the deletion. Figure 19.7 shows the warning you get when removing a certification authority certificate (top) or a personal certificate (bottom). Click the Yes button to delete the certificate.

SIGNING A MACRO PROJECT WITH A DIGITAL SIGNATURE

Once you've completed a macro project and have it ready for distribution, you sign it with a digital signature so that applications that use a high level of security can use it.

To sign a macro project digitally, follow these steps:

1. In the VBA Editor, navigate to the document or template project that contains the macro project you want to sign.
2. Select the project in the Project Explorer.
3. Choose Tools ➤ Digital Signature to display the Digital Signature dialog box (see Figure 19.8).

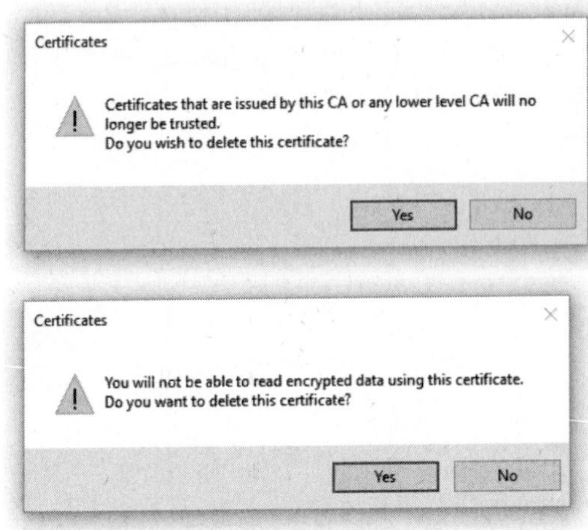

FIGURE 19.7 Two of the warnings the Certificate Manager displays when you're about to remove a digital certificate

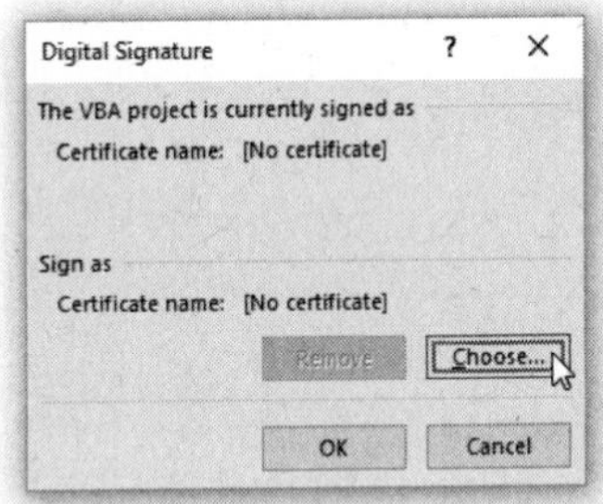

FIGURE 19.8 Use the Digital Signature dialog box to specify the digital signature for a macro project.

If the Digital Signature dialog box lists the certificate you want in the Sign As area, simply click the OK button to use that certificate.

4. Click the Choose button. If you have more than one certificate, you'll see a Select Certificate dialog box. (If you have only one certificate, you'll see the Windows Security dialog box where you can confirm your choice, as shown in Figure 19.9. You should then skip to step 7.)
5. Click the certificate you want to use for the macro project.
6. Click the OK button to apply the selected certificate and close the Select Certificate dialog box.
7. Click the OK button to close the Digital Signature dialog box.
8. Click the Save button on the Standard toolbar, press Ctrl+S, or choose File ➤ Save to save the document or template project with the digital signature applied to it.

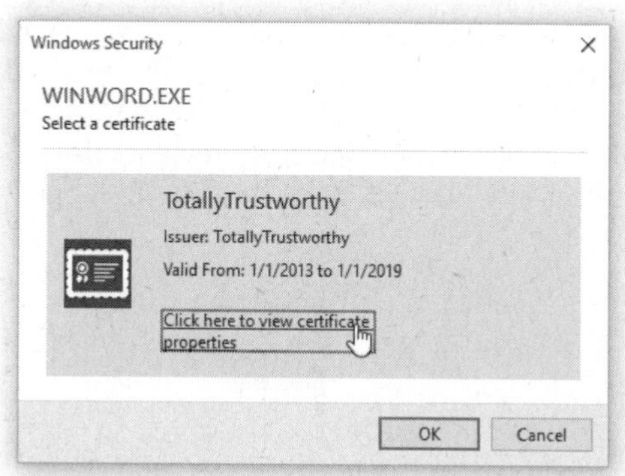

FIGURE 19.9 Use this Windows Security dialog box to confirm your choice of certificate with which to sign the macro project.

REMOVING A DIGITAL SIGNATURE FROM A MACRO PROJECT

To remove a digital signature from a macro project, follow these steps:

1. In the VBA Editor, navigate to the document or template project that contains the macro project.
2. Select the project in the Project Explorer.
3. Choose Tools ➤ Digital Signatures to display the Digital Signature dialog box.
4. Click the Remove button. Both the Certificate Name readout in the area labeled The VBA Project Is Currently Signed As and the Certificate Name in the Sign As area of the Digital Signature dialog box will display [No Certificate] to indicate that the project no longer has a digital certificate assigned to it.
5. Click the OK button to close the Digital Signature dialog box.

You can always reapply the digital signature to the project whenever you want, as described earlier in this chapter.

WHOSE CERTIFICATE IS IT, AND WHAT DOES IT MEAN?

When you receive a digitally signed project, you'll probably want to find out just who has signed it and just what type of digital certificate they used. To view the details of a digital certificate, follow these steps:

1. In the VBA Editor, navigate to the document or template project that contains the macro project.
2. Select the project in the Project Explorer.
3. Choose Tools ➤ Digital Signature to display the Digital Signature dialog box.
4. For an official (VeriSign or other) certification, click the Details button to see information about the source.

If you want to view the details of one of your own, dodgy, *self-signed* certificates, click the Choose button in the Digital Signature dialog box, and then click the Click Here To View Certificate Properties link to display the Certificate Details dialog box shown in Figure 19.10.

By examining Figure 19.10 close up, you'll see the Official Certificate icon with the Gold Seal and the Blue Ribbon (they inspire trust), but there is, alas, also a Red X symbol! Chilling. This X means that the project in question *cannot be trusted whatsoever.*

FIGURE 19.10
Use the Certificate Details dialog box to examine the properties of a certificate.

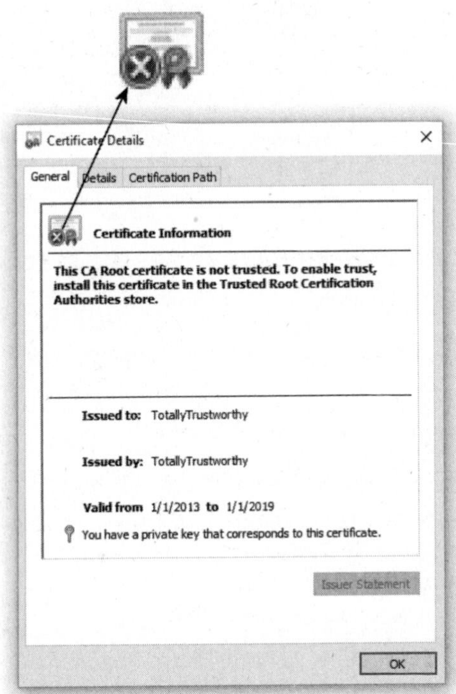

The Certificate Details dialog box has three pages:

- The General page displays basic information about the certificate: for what purpose the certificate is intended, to whom it's issued, by whom it's issued, and the period for which it's valid.
- The Details page of the Certificate Details dialog box, shown in Figure 19.11, contains specifics about the certificate. Click one of the fields in the list box to display its value in the text box below.
- The Certification Path page of the Certificate Details dialog box shows the path by which the certificate has been issued from the issuing authority to the current holder. To check one of the links in the chain, select it in the Certification Path list box and click the View Certificate button (if it's available). You'll see the Certificate Details dialog box for the

certificate in question. You can then follow the certification path for that certificate if you choose or click the OK button to dismiss the second (or subsequent) Certificate Details dialog box and return to the previous one.

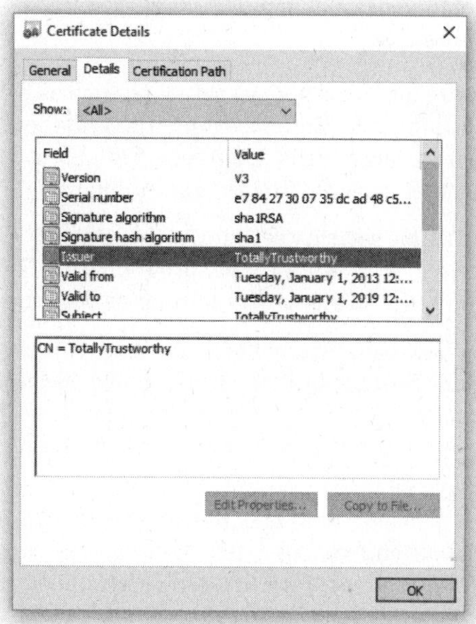

FIGURE 19.11 The Details page of the Certificate Details dialog box contains a host of details about the certificate.

Choosing a Suitable Level of Security

To use VBA macros safely, you or a user of your code must open the Office Trust Center and choose a suitable level of security—high enough to avoid the threats posed by malicious or incompetent code but low enough that it doesn't prevent you from running useful, safe code.

Understanding the Security Threats Posed by VBA

The VBA macro language is formidable. It can accomplish sophisticated and valuable tasks. But its capabilities also pose a threat when misused. Using relatively simple VBA commands, you can create files, delete files, manipulate existing data, and even control other applications.

Also, even code developed with the best of intentions can accidentally do damage if run under unsuitable circumstances. For example, a procedure might mistakenly delete valuable data or delete critical files, making the computer crash. Such inadvertent damage happens frequently enough, but what tends to make the headlines is damage caused intentionally by malicious code in macro viruses and other malicious software (or *malware*).

A *macro virus* is simply a computer virus written in a macro language such as VBA. Currently, the bad guys are focusing on using email as their vector for nuisance, but macros can play a part here. Open a `.doc` file containing an auto-executing macro and your machine is at the mercy of whatever evil code the jerk inserted into the document.

Protecting Against Macro Viruses

Protecting your computer (and computers connected to it in a network) against macro viruses requires three main steps:

1. Install and run quality antivirus software, such as Kaspersky or Malwarebytes. And use the Windows Defender that's built into Windows. Update the antivirus software frequently with the latest virus definitions. Scan your computer often. (Most antivirus software offers automatic updating and scanning.)
2. Configure suitable security settings in the applications you use, especially in those applications that host VBA or other programming languages or scripting languages. For example, configure VBA security settings as described in the next section.
3. Be careful when opening any file that might contain code or arrived as an email attachment. Most modern applications warn you when there might be a problem with a file. However, many macro viruses attempt to obviate such warnings by a tactic called *social engineering*—conning the user—rather than by sophisticated programming.

   For example, a macro virus may transmit itself as an email attachment to all the addresses in a friend's email application. The message and attachment suggest that the contents of the attachment are interesting or amusing—jokes or compromising pictures. And because the file appears to come from a friend, someone you know and trust, many users will open the file and ignore any security warnings. Remember that merely opening a file can cause code within a macro embedded in the file to execute. Simply opening a Word `.docm` file can execute a macro. And after it's open, it could be too late. Creepy code robots could be multiplying exponentially throughout your system.

Specifying a Suitable Security Setting

First, set a suitable level of security for your purposes. To open the Options dialog box in Access, Word, Excel, or PowerPoint, click the File tab, and then choose Options. Click the Trust Center button in the left pane. Then click the Trust Center Settings button, and click Macro Settings (see Figure 19.12).

The various macro security settings are self-explanatory. However, if you are working in documents that you've created yourself and saved as the `.docm` type, having written your own macros you can temporarily choose the Enable All Macros option. At least while you're practicing with the examples in this book, you can trust your own documents. However, if you are opening macro-enabled document files (`.docm` or the other files from PowerPoint or Excel with an `m` appended to the filename extension), you should specify a less risky setting in your Trust Center macro settings.

There's an easier way to deal with this problem, though. You can alternatively (and more safely) employ one of the disable options shown in Figure 19.12, but while doing development work with VBA (such as experimenting with the code in this book), just ensure that you save your `.docm` documents in one of the trusted locations. You can see the list of trusted locations by clicking the Trusted Locations button shown in the left pane in Figure 19.12.

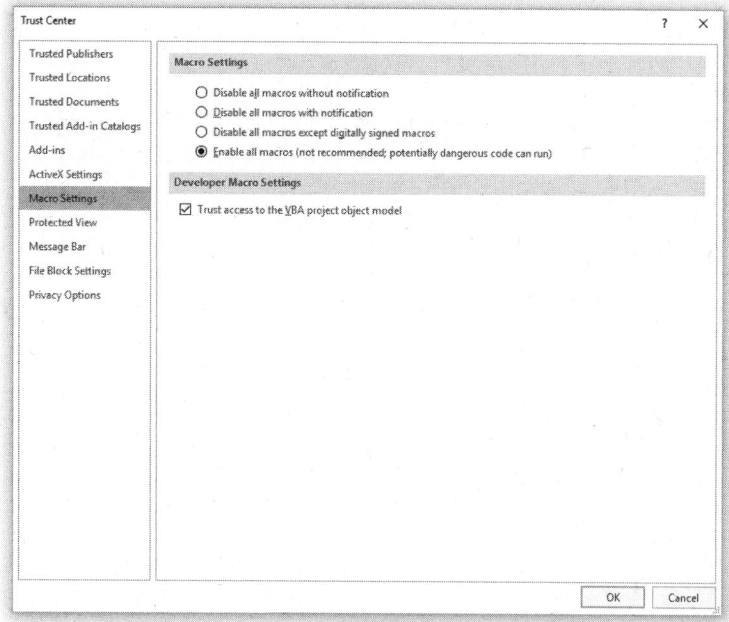

FIGURE 19.12 On the Macro Settings page of the Trust Center dialog box, choose the level of security you want to use when running macros.

If you choose the Disable All Macros Except Digitally Signed Macros option, any unsigned macros in your documents won't work. They are blocked from executing. However, you can get them to work again by simply moving the document files to a trusted location.

Additional Office Security Features

Microsoft is currently encouraging (by the pricing structure if nothing else) Office customers to move from one-purchase, disk-based Office installations to a downloaded, pay-yearly subscription model called Office 365.

What's more, there are multiple versions of Office 365, each with its own variations on security features, such as whether or not it supports Group Policy settings.

For a survey of Office 2016 security features, see this website:

`http://blogs.technet.com/b/in_the_cloud/archive/2015/09/23/the-launch-of-office-2016-the-most-secure-office-ever.aspx`

To see the variations for Office 2013, visit this page:

`http://technet.microsoft.com/en-us/library/jj851145.aspx`

Notice also a security feature listed in the left pane in Figure 19.12 that was new in Office 2013: Trusted Add-in Catalogs.

Open the Trusted Add-In Catalogs page in the Trust Center dialog box and you'll see the options illustrated in Figure 19.13.

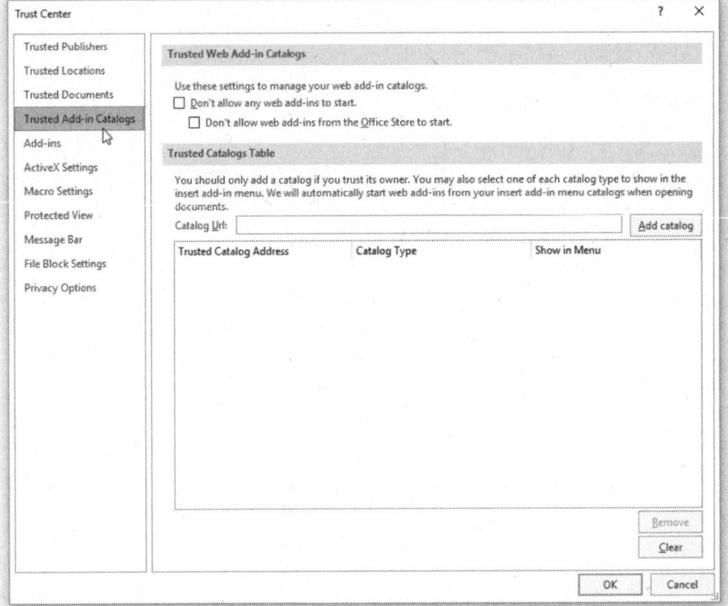

FIGURE 19.13
On this page of the Trust Center dialog box, choose whether you want to trust web add-in catalogs.

OFFICE WEB ADD-INS

What is an Office web add-in? When they were introduced in 2013, Microsoft described them like this: "...a region inside an Office application that contains a web page that can interact with the document to augment content and provide new interactive content types and functionality. apps [*sic*] for Office can be obtained by users from the new Office marketplace or from a private catalog in the form of stand-alone apps or subcomponents of a document template solution, or a SharePoint application." In other words, an online image-search tool or grammar checker could be embedded in Word as a command-bar pane, like Word's own built-in Navigation or Thesaurus command bars.

If you're interested, you can try some free apps that are available in the Office Store. Click the Insert tab on the Ribbon; then in the Add-ins section, click Store. You'll see various apps you can add to whatever Office application you're currently viewing.

A key feature of Office Web add-ins is that they cannot be written in VBA. You must use "web technologies like HTML5, XML, CSS3, JavaScript, and REST APIs" instead.

When you set the option to trust a catalog of Office Web add-ins, you're telling Office that it can stop notifying you or otherwise blocking executable content (such as macros or ActiveX controls) from this source. Thus, you can override on a case-by-case basis the macro and other security settings that you've specified (see Figure 19.12 and Figure 19.13).

File Block Settings

The File Block Settings page, shown in Figure 19.14, gives you the ability to block individual file types from opening or to open them in Protected View. Here you can also specify which types of files can be saved. Notice at the bottom of this page that you specify what choosing the Open option means:

- Do Not Open Selected File Types means documents are totally blocked.
- Open Selected File Types In Protected View means you can open documents in the sandbox for reading only.
- Open Selected File Types In Protected View And Allow Editing means you can open documents in the sandbox for editing.

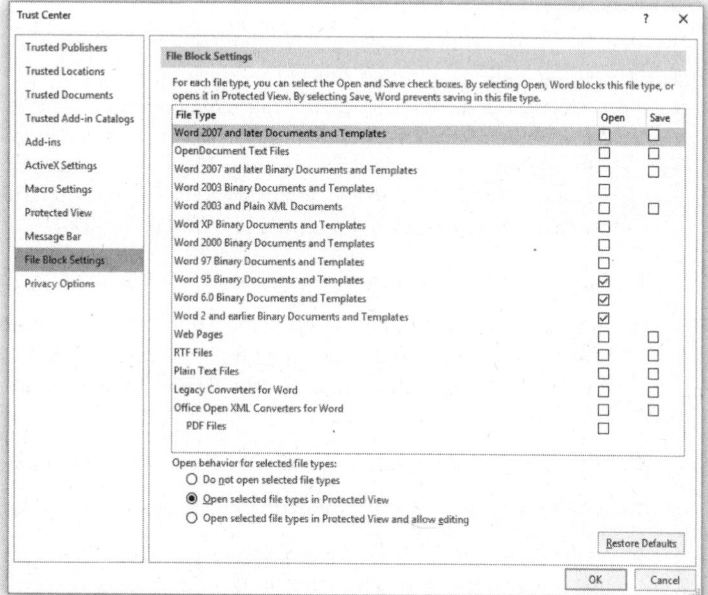

Figure 19.14
File Block Settings specify what types of documents you want blocked or sandboxed.

CAN A SIMPLE .TXT FILE HARBOR A VIRUS?

You might wonder why the Plain Text Files option is included in the File Block Settings page shown in Figure 19.14. It would seem that a simple Notepad `.txt` file couldn't contain any dangerous executable code (any more than a stop sign could fire a bullet at you). After all, text is just words, right?

Nope. Even opening simple `.txt` files can install a virus. How? The bad guys sometimes use trick filename extensions. So, even though it says `.txt`, it might only be masquerading as a text file. Executable files (programs or viruses) usually have a `.exe` filename extension, but by default Windows *hides* filename extensions so you see `Word`, not `Word.exe` in File Explorer. Also, Windows files can be named with multiple extensions. So, you can have a dangerous file named `OpenMe.txt.exe`, but thanks to Windows's default extension-hiding, the filename that you actually see in this case is `OpenMe.txt`. You go ahead and double-click it thinking it will open in Notepad like most `.txt` files. Your hard drive explodes. Well, maybe not a detonation, but all your files could be wiped or there could be some other nasty virus surprise. `OpenMe.txt` was merely *posing* as a harmless `.txt` file, but inside was a monster.

Locking Your Code

To prevent anyone from viewing the contents of a macro project, you can lock it with a password. You'll usually want to do this before distributing a project to your colleagues. If your workplace is particularly volatile, you might even want to lock projects while they are merely under development on your own Desktop. The argument against locking a project on which you're still actively working is that the lock adds a step to accessing the modules and forms in the project—but if you need the security, it's well worth the small amount of effort involved.

Follow these steps to lock a document or template project:

1. Press Alt+F11 to display the VBA Editor.
2. In the Project Explorer, right-click the project that you want to lock, and choose Project Properties from the context menu to display the Project Properties dialog box. Alternatively, select the project in the Project Explorer and choose Tools ➤ Project Properties.
3. Click the Protection tab to display the Protection page (see Figure 19.15).
4. Select the Lock Project For Viewing check box in the Lock Project group box.
5. In the Password To View Project Properties group box, type a password in the Password text box and the same password in the Confirm Password text box. Setting a password is compulsory: You can't lock a project without specifying a password. Without a password, how could you unlock it?
6. Click the OK button to apply the locking to the project. The VBA Editor closes the Project Properties dialog box but leaves the contents of the project open for you to view and work with at this time.
7. Switch back to the application, save your work, and close the application.

Once you've done that, the project is locked and can't be viewed or edited without the password. When you choose to edit a procedure in the project from the application or try to expand the project in the Project Explorer in the VBA Editor, the project Password dialog box appears, as shown in Figure 19.16 (unless you have macros disabled in the Trust Center settings).

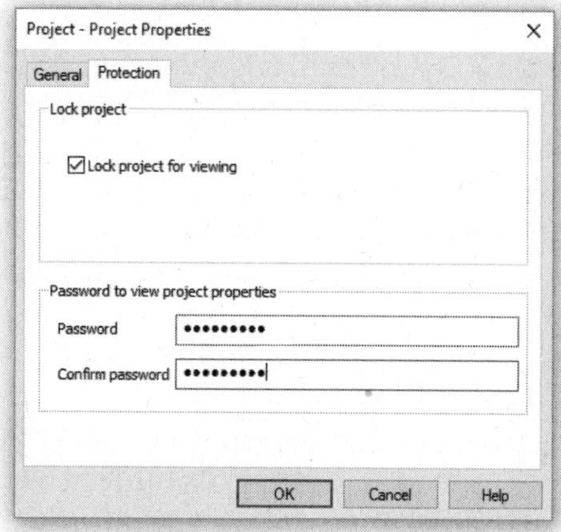

FIGURE 19.15
Use the Protection page of the Project Properties dialog box to lock the project.

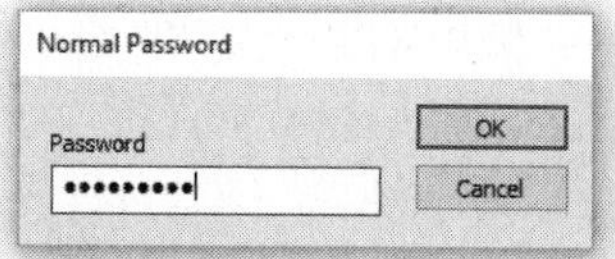

FIGURE 19.16
When you open a locked project, you need to enter the password for the project in this project Password dialog box.

Type the password in the Password text box and click the OK button to display the contents of the project. (If you enter the wrong password, the application or the VBA Editor displays a Project Locked message box followed by the Project Password dialog box for you to try again.)

To unlock a project, open it in the VBA Editor (supplying the password), display the VBA Project Properties dialog box (by right-clicking the project's name in the Project Explorer, and then choosing the Project Properties option from the context menu), clear the Lock Project For Viewing check box on the Protection page, and click the OK button. Save the file that contains the project.

The Bottom Line

Understand how VBA implements security. Microsoft takes a multipronged approach to protecting users from malicious VBA code embedded in documents and capable of launching itself when the user simply opens the document.

Master It Name two ways that users are protected from malicious VBA code.

Sign a macro project with a digital signature. You can add a digital signature to your projects by creating your own certification, getting it from your company, or getting it from certification authorities such as VeriSign.

Master It Describe the limitations of self-certifying a VBA macro project—without obtaining a certificate from your company or a commercial certification authority.

Get a digital certificate. Commercial certification authorities provide the greatest level of security, but their certification is also more difficult to attain than self-certification or certification from your company.

Master It Name some of the ways you may be required to prove your identity when obtaining a digital signature from a commercial certification authority.

Choose the appropriate security level. When choosing the right security level to use VBA macros safely, you or a user of your code must achieve a balance. The security level must be set high enough to avoid malicious or incompetent code but low enough that it doesn't prevent you from running useful, safe code.

Master It To set a suitable level of security for your purposes, open the Trust Center in Access, Word, Excel, or PowerPoint. You'll see four settings. Which one of the following five settings is *not* available:

- Disable All Macros Without Notification
- Disable All Macros With Notification
- Disable All Macros Except Digitally Signed Macros
- Enable All Macros With Notification
- Enable All Macros

Lock your code. You can protect your source code in the VBA Editor from others. You can add a password to a project (projects are in boldface in the Project Explorer) so that others can't open your VBA procedures for reading or modifying.

Master It What is one drawback to locking your code?

Part 6

Programming the Office Applications

Chapter 20

Understanding the Word Object Model and Key Objects

In this chapter, you'll become familiar with the Word object model and the architecture underlying Word. You'll see how to perform common tasks with the most frequently useful Word objects. These objects include the `Documents` collection and the `Document` object, the `Selection` object, `Range` objects, and the `Options` object.

IN THIS CHAPTER, YOU WILL LEARN TO DO THE FOLLOWING:

- Understand the Word object model
- Understand Word's creatable objects
- Work with the `Documents` collection and the `Document` object
- Work with the `Selection` object
- Create and use ranges
- Manipulate options

Examining the Word Object Model

You don't need to understand how the entire Word object model fits together in order to work with VBA in Word, but most people find it helpful to have a general idea of how to research the components and structure of the object model. Some VBA programming involves managing objects, and for this the Help system's code examples are often invaluable. To see Word's online object model reference, follow these steps:

1. Launch or activate Word, and then press Alt+F11 to launch or activate the VBA Editor.
2. Choose Help ➢ Microsoft Visual Basic For Applications Help. (Pressing F1 is not an alternative, alas; it currently takes you to an entirely different page.) You should see a web page similar to the one shown in Figure 20.1 (this figure shows a part of the web page). If you don't see this web page, type this URL into your browser's address field:

   `https://msdn.microsoft.com/en-US/library/fp179696(v=office.15).aspx`

3. Click the Word VBA Reference link on the left side of the web page (see the pointing hand icon in Figure 20.1).

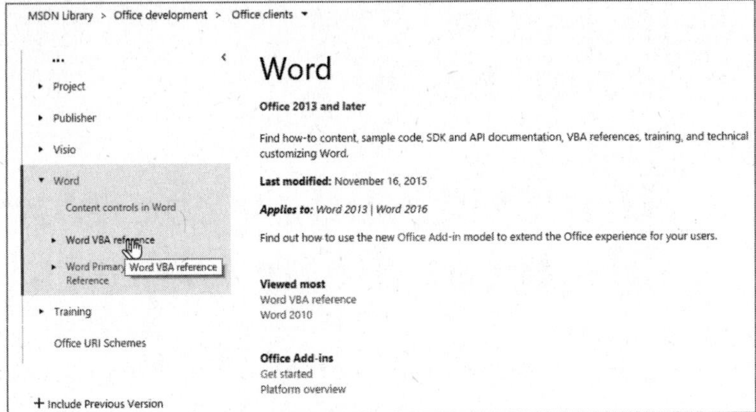

FIGURE 20.1 A Word Help website (partial view)

You now see the page shown in Figure 20.2.

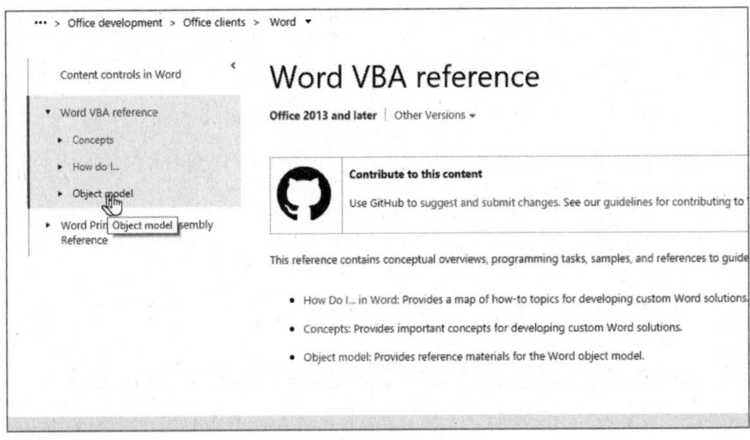

FIGURE 20.2 Drilling down in the Word Help site (partial view)

4. Now click the link named *Object model,* as shown in Figure 20.2 with the pointing hand cursor.

You now see the Object Model Reference, shown partially in Figure 20.3.

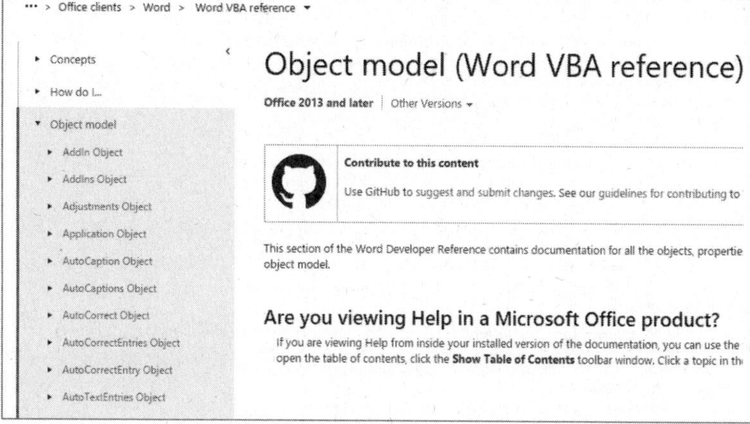

FIGURE 20.3 The entries in the Word Object Model Reference will help you write your own VBA code.

(In the past, the object model reference was specific to the various versions of Office. Now, however, it's become generic. So, you don't see Office 2016 mentioned in Figure 20.3. Nonetheless, you can click the Other Versions link shown in that figure to see the 2010 version of this reference. And the 2013 version is available via searching. However, the Office objects generally remain stable, with few changes in most applications.)

HELP WHEN MIGRATING LEGACY CODE FROM EARLIER OFFICE PROJECTS

If you've inherited VBA code written in earlier versions of Office, those procedures might contain objects, methods, and properties that have since been changed. It's unlikely, but possible. Remember that modifications to object models are generally few, but some incompatibilities can crop up and "break" the code so it won't run correctly. Fortunately, you can download a free utility, the Office Code Compatibility Inspector, that will flag objects and their members that have changed. It does a text comparison of the current Office object model against VBA code written in earlier versions of Office. You can download the Compatibility Inspector from this web page:

`www.microsoft.com/en-us/download/details.aspx?id=15001`

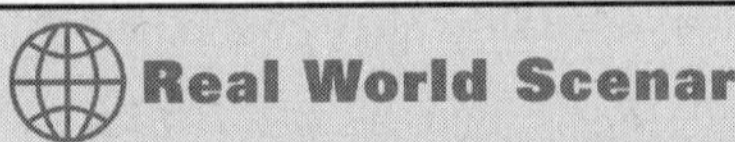

A Shortcut: Understanding *Creatable* Objects

Like most VBA-enabled applications, Word has a number of *creatable objects*. This merely means that you don't have to type in the full qualification. In other words, you don't need to mention the `Application` object in your code. For example, the `Documents` collection object is creatable, so you can omit its parent, the `Application` object, when using the collection in code, like this:

```
Dim x As Integer
x = Documents.Count
MsgBox x
```

The `Application` object is simply understood, for the same reason that you don't have to add Planet Earth when addressing an envelope. The post office assumes that Mother Earth is the parent—the context—of all addresses.

However, you can, if you like, use the longer ("fully qualified") version:

```
x = Application.Documents.Count
```

Both versions have the same effect.

The following are the most useful of these creatable objects:

- The `ActiveDocument` object returns a `Document` object that represents the active document (the one the user is currently interacting with).
- The `ActiveWindow` object returns a `Window` object that represents the active window.
- The `Documents` collection contains the `Document` objects, each of which represents an open document.
- The `Options` object represents Word options and document options, including most of the options that appear in the Options dialog box.
- The `Selection` object represents the selection in the active document. `Selection` represents the selection (containing text or other objects) or collapsed selection (containing nothing—merely the blinking insertion point) in the document.
- The `Windows` collection contains the `Window` objects that represent all open windows.

The following sections show you how to work with some of the most useful Word objects, starting with the `Documents` collection and the `Document` object. You'll see how to use the `ActiveWindow` object and the `Windows` collection in the next chapter.

Working with the *Documents* Collection and the *Document* Object

In many of your Word procedures, you'll likely work with documents: creating, saving, opening, closing, and printing them. To do so, you work with the `Documents` collection, which contains a `Document` object for each open document in Word.

Creating a Document

To create a new document, use the Add method of the Documents collection. The syntax is as follows:

```
expression.Add Template, NewTemplate, DocumentType, Visible
```

Here, *expression* is a required expression that returns a Documents collection. Typically, you'll want to use the Documents collection itself (**Documents**.Add).

Template is an optional Variant argument that specifies the template on which to base the new document. If you omit Template, Word uses the Normal template (this process is the same as if you'd clicked the File tab on the Ribbon and then clicked the New button to open a blank document). So, you need specify a Template argument only when you want to base the new document on a template other than the default Normal.dotm.

NewTemplate is an optional Variant argument that you can set to True to create a template file (.dotx) rather than a document. NewTemplate is set to False by default, so you can safely omit this argument unless you're creating a template.

DocumentType is an optional Variant argument that you can use to specify the type of document to create: wdNewBlankDocument (the default), wdNewEmailMessage, wdNewFrameset (for a frameset), or wdNewWebPage.

Visible is an optional Variant argument that you can set to False to have the document created in a window that isn't visible. The default setting is True, making the document window visible.

There are two ways to create a document:

Creating a document based on Normal.dotm The following statement creates a new document based on the Normal.dotm global template:

```
Documents.Add
```

Creating a document based on a template The following statement creates a new document based on the template named Company Report.dotm stored in the network folder designated \\server\public\templates:

```
Documents.Add Template:= "\\server\public\templates\Company Report.dotm"
```

Creating a Template

The following statements declare a new object variable of the Document class named myTemplate, create a new template based on the template named Fancy.dotx, and assign it to myTemplate:

```
Dim myTemplate As Document

Set myTemplate = Documents.Add(Template:="c:\MyTemplates\fancy.dotx", _
    NewTemplate:=True, Visible:=True)
```

In this example, the file path (c:\MyTemplates*and so on*) to the template is specified because this template is not located in one of the default template folders. The result is a new .dotx file, based on the Fancy.dotx template.

> **CHANGING THE DEFAULT FILE LOCATIONS**
>
> Word has two templates folders: the user templates folder and the workgroup templates folder. To change the locations of these folders, click the File tab on the Ribbon and then click the Options button to open the Word Options dialog box. Then click the Advanced button in the left pane. Scroll all the way down in the General Options section, and click the File Locations button located at the bottom. Then click to select the default folder you want to change and click the Modify button.

Saving a Document

Just as when a user is saving a newly created document via the keyboard and mouse, when executing VBA code you must specify a filename and path the first time you save a new document. After that, you can save it under the same name or specify a different name or format. This is the difference between the Save and Save As options.

SAVING A FILE FOR THE FIRST TIME OR AS A DIFFERENT FILE

To save a file for the first time, or to save a file under a different name or in a different format, use the `SaveAs2` method. The syntax is as follows:

```
expression.SaveAs2(FileName, FileFormat, LockComments, Password, AddToRecentFiles,
WritePassword, ReadOnlyRecommended, EmbedTrueTypeFonts, SaveNativePictureFormat,
SaveFormsData, SaveAsAOCELetter, Encoding, InsertLineBreaks, AllowSubstitutions,
LineEnding, AddBiDiMarks, CompatibilityMode
```

With Word 2010, the traditional `SaveAs` command was replaced by the `SaveAs2` command, which is identical except for the addition of a `CompatibilityMode` argument. Documents can be saved five different ways with respect to their compatibility with earlier versions of Word. Based on how you set the `CompatibilityMode` argument, Word saves your document in one of these ways:

- `0` is the default if you don't specify any of the other CompatibilityMode options in this list. The document will be saved using whatever compatibility mode is currently used by this document.
- `wdCurrent` is a compatibility mode equivalent to the latest version of Microsoft Word.
- `wdWord2003` is a mode that's compatible with Word 2003. Any features new in Word 2013 are disabled.
- `wdWord2007` is essentially the same as 2003 mode, but features compatible with the 2007 version of Word are enabled.
- `wdWord2010` is the mode where the Word 2010 features are enabled.

The traditional `SaveAs` command will still work, but the Editor has a tendency to automatically replace it with `SaveAs2`. Spooky, but no real harm done.

In the syntax, *expression* is an expression that returns a `Document` object. For example, you might use the `ActiveDocument` object or an object in the `Documents` collection.

`FileName` is an optional Variant argument that specifies the name for the document. If you omit `FileName`, VBA uses the current folder and the default filename of `Doc`*n*`.docx` (or `Doc`*n*`.docm`) or a document and `Dot`*n*`.dotx` (or `.dotm`) for a template, where *n* is the next available number (for example, `Doc5.docx` for a macro-free document or `Dot2.dotm` for a macro-enabled template).

AVOID ACCIDENTALLY OVERWRITING A FILE

When writing code that saves a document, you should first check whether a document with this name and location already exists. If you don't check, VBA overwrites an existing file without warning, potentially causing data loss.

`FileFormat` is an optional Variant argument that specifies the format in which to save the document. Table 20.1 lists the `wdSaveFormat` constants for specifying commonly used formats.

TABLE 20.1: `WdSaveFormat` constants

CONSTANT	SAVES DOCUMENT AS
`wdFormatDocument`	A Word document
`wdFormatDocument97`	The Word version 97 document format
`wdFormatDocumentDefault`	The Word document default (the `docx` file type)
`wdFormatDOSText`	A DOS text file (the pre-Windows OS)
`wdFormatDOSTextLineBreaks`	A DOS text file with carriage returns
`wdFormatEncodedText`	A text file with encoding
`wdFormatFilteredHTML`	A filtered HTML file (Word 2003 and XP only)
`wdFormatFlatXML`	An unindexed XML document
`wdFormatFlatXMLMacroEnabled`	An unindexed XML document with macro capability
`wdFormatFlatXMLTemplate`	An unindexed XML template
`wdFormatFlatXMLTemplateMacroEnabled`	An unindexed XML template with macro capability
`wdFormatHTML`	An HTML file
`wdFormatOpenDocumentText`	An XML file format developed by Sun Microsystems

TABLE 20.1: `WdSaveFormat` constants *(CONTINUED)*

CONSTANT	SAVES DOCUMENT AS
`wdFormatPDF`	Adobe's Portable Document Format
`wdFormatRTF`	A Rich Text format file
`wdFormatStrictOpenXMLDocument`	An XML document standard promoted for several years by Microsoft
`wdFormatTemplate`	A Word template
`wdFormatTemplate97`	The Word version 97 template format
`wdFormatText`	A text file (plain ASCII)
`wdFormatTextLineBreaks`	A text file with carriage returns
`wdFormatUnicodeText`	A text file with Unicode characters
`wdFormatWebArchive`	A web archive file
`wdFormatXML`	An XML file (Word 2003 only)
`wdFormatXMLDocument`	XML document format
`wdFormatXMLDocumentMacroEnabled`	XML document format with macros enabled
`wdFormatXMLTemplate`	XML template format
`wdFormatXMLTemplateMacroEn`	XML template format with macros enabled
`wdFormatXPS`	XPS format

A QUICK WAY TO SEE OBJECTS AND THEIR CONSTANTS

If you're writing code and you want to quickly see a list of constants, such as the `WdSaveFormat` constants shown in Table 20.1, just press F2 to open the Object Browser in the Editor. Then, for example, type **`wdsaveformat`** in the Object Browser's search field and press Enter. You'll see the complete list of constants as shown in the illustration.

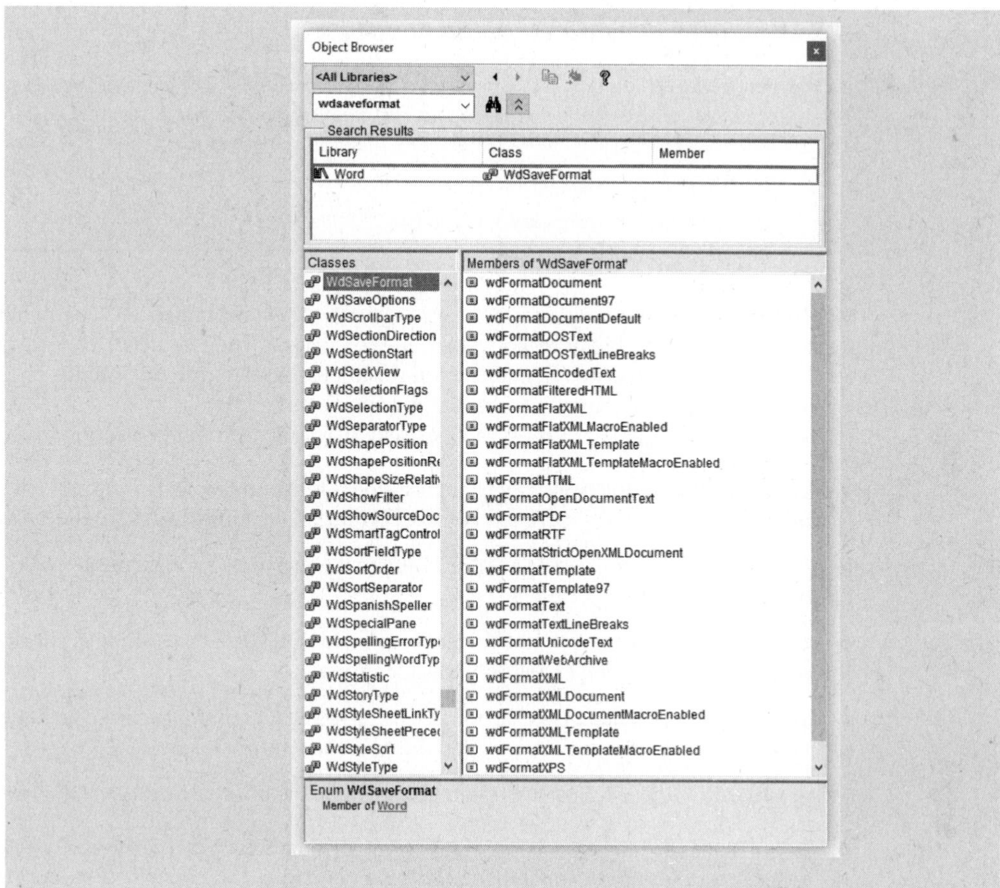

As an example of how to use one of these constants, the following statement saves the active document as a filtered HTML file under the name `Example.html` in the current folder:

```
ActiveDocument.SaveAs2 FileName:="Example.html", _
    FileFormat:=wdFormatFilteredHTML
```

After you run this example code, use Windows Explorer to locate this new `Example.html` file and click on it. It will open in Internet Explorer as if it were a web page, because it's stored using the HTML format (if Internet Explorer is the default application in which your machine opens `.html` files). Or, take a look at it in Notepad if you want to see the full horror of HTML markup.

Save Documents Using File Converters

In addition to the wdSaveFormat constants described in Table 20.1, you can save documents in other formats for which you have file converters installed by specifying the appropriate value for the SaveFormat property of the FileConverter object. For example:

```
ActiveDocument.SaveAs2 FileFormat:=FileConverters(15).SaveFormat.
```

See the FileConverters property entry in the VBA Help file for more information.

AddToRecentFiles is an optional Variant argument that you can set to True to have Word add the document to the list of recently used files displayed when you click the File tab on the Ribbon and then click Recent. (Generally, you'll want to avoid listing documents on this Recent list, leaving the user's previous list of recent files undisturbed.)

To protect the document as you save it, you can use four different protection features:

- LockComments is an optional Variant argument that you can set to True to lock the document so that reviewers can enter comments but can't change the text of the document.
- Password is an optional Variant argument that you can use to set a password required before opening the document.
- WritePassword is an optional Variant argument that you can use to set a password required before saving changes to the document.
- ReadOnlyRecommended is an optional Variant argument that you can set to True to have Word recommend that the user open the document as read-only.

Finally, there are these following optional arguments you'll use infrequently, if ever:

- EmbedTrueTypeFonts is an optional Variant argument that you can set to True to save TrueType fonts with the document. (This is a good idea only if you're distributing the document to someone you know doesn't have the TrueType fonts installed to view the document correctly.)
- SaveNativePictureFormat is an optional Variant argument that you can set to True to have graphics imported from another platform saved as Windows graphics.
- SaveFormsData is an optional Variant argument that you can set to True to save the data entered in a form as a data record (as opposed to saving the whole form, including its static text).
- SaveAsAOCELetter is an optional Variant argument that you can set to True to save the document as an AOCE (Apple Open Collaboration Environment) letter (a mailing format for routing documents).
- Encoding is an optional Variant argument for using a different code page than the system code page. For example, you might need to save a document using a Cyrillic code page.
- InsertLineBreaks is an optional Variant argument that you can set to True when saving a document as a text file to make Word insert a line break at the end of each line of text.

- `AllowSubstitutions` is an optional Variant argument that you can set to `True` when saving a document as a text file to make Word substitute some symbol characters with similar text. For example, Word substitutes (TM) for a trademark symbol (™).
- `LineEnding` is an optional Variant argument that you can use when saving a document as a text file to control how Word marks line breaks and paragraph breaks.
- `AddBiDiMarks` is an optional Variant argument that you can set to `True` to make Word add control characters to the file to maintain bidirectional layout.

Usually, when saving a file for the first time, you'll need to specify only its name and path; if you want to save it in a format other than a Word document, specify that too. The following statement saves the active document under the name `Beehives.doc` in the folder `C:\temp`:

```
ActiveDocument.SaveAs2 _
    "C:\temp\Beehives.doc"
```

Saving a Document That Has Already Been Saved

After a document has been first saved, you can save it in the future under the same name by using the `Save` method. For a `Document` object, the `Save` method takes no arguments (all the document's current formats are saved unchanged). For example, the following statement saves the document named `Guns01.doc`:

```
Documents("Guns01.doc").Save
```

Saving All Open Documents

To save all open documents, use the `Save` method with the `Documents` collection. The syntax is as follows:

```
expression.Save(NoPrompt, OriginalFormat)
```

Here, *`expression`* is an expression that returns a `Documents` collection. Often, you'll use the `Documents` collection itself.

`NoPrompt` is an optional Variant argument that you can set to `True` to make Word save all open documents containing unsaved changes and any attached templates containing unsaved changes without prompting the user. The default setting is `False`, which causes Word to prompt the user whether to save each document and template. Even if you set `NoPrompt` to `True`, Word will prompt the user to save changes to `Normal.dotm` if the Prompt Before Saving Normal Template check box is selected in the Save section of the Advanced tab of the Options dialog box.

`OriginalFormat` is an optional Variant argument that you can set to `wdOriginalDocumentFormat` to save the documents in their original formats, `wdWordDocument` to force each document to be saved as a Word document, or `wdPromptUserX` to prompt the user about which format to use.

For example, the following statement saves all open documents and templates without prompting the user:

```
Documents.Save NoPrompt:=True
```

Checking Whether a Document Contains Unsaved Changes

To find out whether a document contains unsaved changes, check its Saved property. Saved is a read/write Boolean property that returns False if the document contains unsaved changes and True if it does not. A new document contains no unsaved changes, even though it has never been saved.

> **The Dangers of Cloud Storage and How to Send Files into the Cloud**
>
> With mobility now a primary trend in personal computing, people increasingly expect their files to be available anywhere, not just on their hard drives at home or in the office. They also want them available on their various portable devices: the Surface tablet, the phone, the laptop, whatever.
>
> So, to make files within reach everywhere and on whatever kind of computer, data is being moved to the cloud. Never mind that if you read their EULAs (End User License Agreements) you'll discover that cloud storage providers nearly universally refuse to guarantee either the safety or security of your data. It could be lost in a fire at their server farm; it could be captured by snoops. To protect yourself, it is a wise precaution to keep your own backup copies in your own house, bank, or office and also to encrypt sensitive information. The cloud is useful, but dicey. Who *are* these people storing your data? And where, exactly, are their servers located? You don't really know.
>
> Nonetheless, if you want to know the code that saves Word files to the cloud on Microsoft's OneDrive, it's pretty straightforward. Just save a document to your OneDrive folder. This example saves the current document to OneDrive (change my name, *Richard*, to your name in the file path in this example code):
>
> ```
> ActiveDocument.SaveAs ("C:\Users\Richard\Onedrive\CloudTest")
> ```
>
> Similarly, to save to Dropbox:
>
> ```
> ActiveDocument.SaveAs2 ("C:\Users\Richard\Dropbox\CloudTest")
> ```

Opening a Document

To open a document, use the Open method with the appropriate Document object. The syntax for the Open method is as follows:

```
expression.Open FileName, ConfirmConversions, ReadOnly,
AddToRecentFiles, PasswordDocument, PasswordTemplate,
Revert, WritePasswordDocument,  WritePasswordTemplate,
Format, Encoding, Visible, OpenConflictDocument,
OpenAndRepair, DocumentDirection, NoEncodingDialog
```

The arguments are as follows:

- *expression* is a required expression that returns a Documents collection. Usually, you'll want to use the Documents collection itself.
- FileName is a required Variant argument specifying the name (and path, if necessary) of the document to open.

- `ConfirmConversions` is an optional Variant argument that you can set to `True` to have Word display the Convert File dialog box if the file is in a format other than Word.
- `ReadOnly` is an optional Variant argument that you can set to `True` to open the document as read-only.
- `AddToRecentFiles` is an optional Variant argument that you can set to `True` to have Word add the filename to the list of recently used files at the foot of the File menu.
- `PasswordDocument` is an optional Variant argument that you can use to set a password for opening the document.
- `PasswordTemplate` is an optional Variant argument that you can use to set a password for opening the template.
- `Revert` is an optional Variant argument that specifies what Word should do if the `FileName` supplied matches a file that's already open. By default (that is, if you don't include the `Revert` argument), `Revert` is set to `False`, which means that Word activates the open instance of the document and doesn't open the saved instance. You can set `Revert` to `True` to have Word open the saved instance of the document and discard any changes to the open instance.
- `WritePasswordDocument` is an optional Variant argument that indicates the password for saving changes to the document.
- `WritePasswordTemplate` is an optional Variant argument that specifies the password for saving changes to the template.
- `Format` is an optional Variant argument that you can use to specify the file converter with which to open the document. Table 20.2 lists the `WdOpenFormat` constants you can use specify the file converter.
- `Encoding` is an optional Variant argument specifying the document encoding (the code page or the character set) for Word to use when opening the document.
- `Visible` is an optional Variant argument that you can set to `False` to have Word open the document in a window that isn't visible. (The default setting is `True`, specifying a visible window.)
- `OpenAndRepair` is an optional Variant that, when `True`, repairs the document to prevent corruption.
- `OpenConflictDocument` is an optional Variant that specifies whether you want to open the conflict file for a document that has an offline conflict.
- `DocumentDirection` is an optional `WdDocument` Direction variable type, indicating the horizontal flow of text in the document. The default is `wdLeftToRight`.
- `NoEncodingDialog` is an optional Variant that defaults to `False`. But if it's set to `True`, the Encoding dialog box is not displayed when Word cannot recognize text encoding.
- `XMLTransform` is mysterious. The only explanation I could find is in MSDN, and it merely says, "Specifies a transform to use." So your guess is as good as mine about what this option accomplishes.

TABLE 20.2: `WdOpenFormat` constants for opening a document

CONSTANT	EFFECT
`wdOpenFormatAllWord`	Word opens the document in any recognized Word format as a Word document.
`wdOpenFormatAllWordTemplates`	Word opens the document in any recognized Word format as a Word template.
`wdOpenFormatAuto`	Word chooses a converter automatically. This is the default setting.
`wdOpenFormatDocument`	Word opens the document as a Word document.
`wdOpenFormatDocument97`	Microsoft Word 97 document format.
`wdOpenFormatEncodedText`	Word opens the document as a text file with encoding.
`wdOpenFormatOpenDocumentText`	Word opens the document in an XML file format developed by Sun Microsystems.
`wdOpenFormatRTF`	Word opens the document as a Rich Text format file.
`wdOpenFormatTemplate`	Word opens the document as a template.
`wdOpenFormatTemplate97`	Word 97 template format.
`wdOpenFormatText`	Word opens the document as a text file.
`wdOpenFormatUnicodeText`	Word opens the document as a Unicode text file.
`wdOpenFormatWebPages`	Word opens the document as a web page.
`wdOpenFormatXML`	Word opens the document in XML format.
`wdOpenFormatXMLDocument`	XML document format.
`wdOpenFormatXMLDocumentMacroEnabled`	XML document format with macros enabled.
`wdOpenFormatXMLDocumentMacroEnabledSerialized`	Word opens an XML document with macros enabled by reconstructing the original document from a one-dimensional stream of bits.
`wdOpenFormatXMLDocumentSerialized`	Word opens an XML document by reconstructing the original document structure from a one-dimensional stream of bits.
`wdOpenFormatXMLTemplate`	XML template format.

TABLE 20.2: `WdOpenFormat` constants for opening a document *(CONTINUED)*

CONSTANT	EFFECT
`wdOpenFormatXMLTemplateMacroEnabled`	XML template format with macros enabled.
`wdOpenFormatXMLTemplateMacro-EnabledSerialized`	Word opens an XML template with macros enabled by reconstructing the original document from a one-dimensional stream of bits.
`wdOpenFormatXMLTemplateSerialized`	Word opens an XML template by reconstructing the original document from a one-dimensional stream of bits.

The following statement opens the document `Times.docx` found in the `C:\My Documents\` folder:

```
Documents.Open "C:\My Documents\Times.docx"
```

The following statement opens the file `notes.docm` in the folder `C:\temp` as read-only and adds it to the list of most recently used files (the list you see when you click the File tab on the Ribbon and then click Recent):

```
Documents.Open "C:\temp\notes.docm", ReadOnly:=True, _
    AddToRecentFiles:=True
```

HOW TO LOOK UP OFFICE 2016 MEMBERS IN MSDN

Recall that Microsoft's MSDN online help system can sometimes be difficult to search because it is so huge; it's perhaps *too* complete. Among other issues, MSDN includes *enumerations* (a fancy word for *numbered list*, such as a list of properties and methods, or constants, for example) for older versions of Office applications, such as 2007, 2010, or 2013, as well as those for the current version 2016.

Although these lists usually don't change much between versions, they *can* change. To preserve backward-compatibility—so you don't have to rewrite your macros every time a new version of Office comes out—few enumerations ever *lose* members. But new capabilities are added. Word 2013, for example, added `wdFormatStrictOpenXMLDocument` to the enumeration list for `wdSaveFormat` shown in Table 20.1. (Word 2016 didn't change this enumeration. However, in a rare object model deletion, the XMLTransform argument was *removed* from the Open method of the Documents collection in Word 2016.)

To search MSDN for the latest enumerations, you can click the magnifying glass icon in the top right of the MSDN online web pages (see Figure 20.3). This opens a search field where you can type in what you're searching for. Then type something like this: **`wdDefaultFilePath`**. In the list of hits displayed by Bing, choose the enumeration you're interested in. Note that *wd* specifies Word.

Alternatively, you could Google something like this to locate, for example, the `Close` method of the document object: **`msdn document close`**.

Closing a Document

To close a document, use the `Close` method with the application `Document` object. The syntax is as follows:

```
expression.Close(SaveChanges, OriginalFormat, RouteDocument)
```

Here, *`expression`* is a required expression that returns a `Document` object or a `Documents` collection. Typically, you use the `ActiveDocument` object or, to close all documents, the `Documents` collection object.

`SaveChanges` is an optional Variant argument you can use to specify how to handle unsaved changes. Use `wdDoNotSaveChanges` to discard changes, `wdPromptToSaveChanges` to have Word prompt the user to save changes, or `wdSaveChanges` to save changes without prompting.

`OriginalFormat` is an optional Variant argument you can use to specify the save format for the document. Use `wdOriginalDocumentFormat` to have Word use the original document format, `wdPromptUser` to have Word prompt the user to choose a format, or `wdWordDocument` to use the Word document format.

`RouteDocument` is an optional Variant argument that you can set to `True` to route a document that has a routing slip attached.

For example, the following statement closes the active document without saving changes:

```
ActiveDocument.Close SaveChanges:=wdDoNotSaveChanges
```

The following statement closes all open documents (but not the Word application itself) and saves changes automatically:

```
Documents.Close SaveChanges:=wdSaveChanges
```

Changing a Document's Template

To change the template attached to a document, set the `AttachedTemplate` property of the `Document` object you want to affect to the path and name of the appropriate template. For example, the following statement attaches the template named `SalesMarket02.dotm` to the active document. In this example, the template is assumed to be stored in one of the Word templates folders, so the path need not be specified:

```
ActiveDocument.AttachedTemplate = "SalesMarket02.dotm"
```

Printing a Document

To print a document, use the `PrintOut` method for the appropriate `Document` object. The syntax for the `PrintOut` method is as follows:

```
expression.PrintOut(Background, Append, Range, OutputFileName, From, To, Item,
Copies, Pages, PageType, PrintToFile, Collate, ActivePrinterMacGX,
ManualDuplexPrint, PrintZoomColumn, PrintZoomRow, PrintZoomPaperWidth,
PrintZoomPaperHeight)
```

These are the components of the `PrintOut` method:

- *`expression`* is a required expression specifying an `Application`, `Document`, or `Window` object. Usually, you'll print a `Document` object such as `ActiveDocument`.
- `Background` is an optional Variant argument that you can set to `True` to have Word print the document in the background, allowing the procedure to continue running.
- `Append` is an optional Variant argument that you can set to `True` to append the document being printed to file to the print file specified.
- `Range` is an optional Variant argument specifying the selection or range of pages to print: `wdPrintAllDocument` (`0`, the default), `wdPrintCurrentPage` (2), `wdPrintFromTo` (3; use the `From` and `To` arguments to specify the pages), `wdPrintRangeOfPages` (4), or `wdPrint-Selection` (1).
- `OutputFileName` is an optional Variant argument used to specify the name for the output file when printing to file.
- `From` is an optional Variant argument used to specify the starting page number when printing a range of pages.
- `To` is an optional Variant argument used to specify the ending page number when printing a range of pages.
- `Item` is an optional Variant argument used to specify the item to print: `wdPrintAutoText-Entries` (4), `wdPrintComments` (2), `wdPrintDocumentContent` (`0`, the default), `wdPrint-KeyAssignments` (5, shortcut key assignments for the document or its template), `wdPrint-Properties` (1), or `wdPrintStyles` (3).
- `Copies` is an optional Variant argument used to specify the number of copies to print. (If you omit `Copies`, Word prints one copy.)
- `Pages` is an optional Variant argument used to specify the pages to print—for example, `1, 11-21, 31`.
- `PageType` is an optional Variant argument used to specify whether to print all pages (`wdPrintAllPages`, `0`, the default), odd pages (`wdPrintOddPagesOnly`, `1`), or even pages (`wdPrintEvenPagesOnly`, `2`).
- `PrintToFile` is an optional Variant argument that you can set to `True` to direct the output of the print operation to a file.
- `Collate` is an optional Variant argument used when printing multiple copies of a document to specify whether to collate the pages (`True`) or not (`False`).
- `ActivePrinterMacGX` is an optional Variant argument used on the Macintosh to specify the printer if QuickDraw GX is installed.

- `ManualDuplexPrint` is an optional Variant argument that you set to `True` for two-sided printing on a printer that doesn't have duplex capabilities. When `ManualDuplexPrint` is `True`, you can use the `PrintOddPagesInAscendingOrder` property or the `PrintEvenPagesInAscendingOrder` property of the `Options` object to print odd or even pages in ascending order to create a manual duplex effect (reloading the odd-page-printed paper into the printer the other way up to print the even pages). The `ManualDuplexPrint` argument is available only in some languages.
- `PrintZoomColumn` and `PrintZoomRow` are optional Variant arguments that you use to specify the number of pages to print on a page horizontally (`PrintZoomColumn`) and vertically (`PrintZoomRow`). Each property can be `1`, `2`, or `4`.
- `PrintZoomPaperWidth` is an optional Variant argument that you can use to specify the width (measured in twips) to which to scale printed pages.
- `PrintZoomPaperHeight` is an optional Variant argument that you can use to specify the height (measured in twips) to which to scale printed pages.

For example, the following statement prints three collated copies of the active document in the background:

```
ActiveDocument.PrintOut Background:=True, Copies:=3, Collate:=True
```

The following statement prints pages 2 through 5 of the active document:

```
ActiveDocument.PrintOut Range:=wdPrintFromTo, From:=2, To:=5
```

The following statement prints the active document at two virtual pages per sheet of paper:

```
ActiveDocument.PrintOut PrintZoomColumn:=2, PrintZoomRow:=1
```

Working with the *ActiveDocument* Object

The `ActiveDocument` object returns a `Document` object that represents the current document you're working with—in other words, whichever document has the focus in the Word window. The `ActiveDocument` object behaves like a `Document` object, but watch out for the following two possible problems when working with it.

First, you may have problems locating information about the `ActiveDocument` object in the Help system. It's actually a *property* of the `Application` object, so its status as an actual object is somewhat iffy. Object taxonomy is an evolving clerical system and, as you see, remains in places odd.

To find the `ActiveDocument` object in the Help system, MSDN system, or VBA Editor Object Browser, you need to first locate the `Application` object and then look at its properties (or members). Just remember, `ActiveDocument` is found only *under* the `Application` object. It's a clerical error. It's as if you were looking for *California* in a geography book's index, but the index is wacky because you find *most* states listed under their own names (Hawaii is under *H*, for example), but for some reason, California is not listed under C. You're puzzled. It's a big, important state. Then you stumble upon the solution: In this bizarre index, *California* is only found under the entry for *United States.*

The second oddity about the `ActiveDocument` "property" is that it can be evanescent. The first problem is that if there's no document open in Word, there's no `ActiveDocument` object, and, therefore, any code that tries to work with the ActiveDocument object returns an error. So, if you want to use the ActiveDocument object, remember to have your code first check the Count property of the Documents collection to make sure there's actually a document currently open (Count will be at least 1). Here's an example that tests to see if there is an open document:

```
If Documents.Count = 0 Then
    If MsgBox("No document is open." & vbCr & vbCr & _
        "Do you want to create a new blank document?", _
        vbYesNo + vbExclamation, "No Document Is Open") = vbYes Then
        Documents.Add
    Else
        End
    End If
End If
```

A second problem caused by ActiveDocument's evanescence is that a different document may be active than your code assumes is active. This problem tends to occur when a procedure starts with the active document and then creates a new document to work in. A new document automatically becomes the active document, and from this point on, confusion may result.

If you know the *name* of the document you want to be active, you can check to see if the name of the active document matches it, to verify that you'll be working with the right document.

If there's any doubt about which document you're working with, declare a Document object variable and employ that object variable in your code rather than the ActiveDocument object.

For example, the following statements declare a Document object and assign the ActiveDocument object to it so that subsequent code can work with the Document object:

```
Dim myDocument As Document
Set myDocument = ActiveDocument
With myDocument
    'actions here
End With
```

Or, if you know the name of the document you want to work with:

```
Dim myDocument As Document
Set myDocument = ActiveDocument
If myDocument.Name = "CorrectFile.docx" Then
    'actions here
End If
```

Working with the *Selection* Object

Up to now in this chapter, we've worked with programming that affects an entire document. But when you need to write code that works with only part of a document (a word, paragraph, or whatever), you can access these zones in three ways:

- By using the Selection object
- By directly accessing the object you want to affect
- By defining a range that encompasses the object

Using the `Selection` object is analogous to working interactively with Word and is effective with procedures that require the user to select an object or position the blinking insertion cursor to denote what content in the document the procedure should access.

Using the `Selection` object is also effective when you're learning to use VBA with Word, because many actions that you record using the Macro Recorder use the `Selection` object.

The `Selection` object represents the current selection in the active document in Word. The selection can be very small (collapsed to the blinking cursor insertion point), in which case nothing is selected. Or, a `Selection` object can contain one or more objects—one or more characters, one or more words, one or more paragraphs, a graphic, a table, the entire document. Or, the selection can be a combination of these objects. Whatever's selected.

Even if the selection is collapsed to an insertion point, you can use it to refer to objects outside the selection. For example, `Selection.Paragraphs(1).Range.Words(10).Text` returns the tenth word in the paragraph in which the insertion point is located (or, if a paragraph or multiple paragraphs are selected, the tenth word in the first paragraph).

Checking the Type of Selection

Word recognizes nine different kinds of selections. When you're working in the active document, you'll often need to check what kind of selection is active so that you know whether you're dealing with no selection (just the insertion point), a block of ordinary text, or a special type of text like a table or a graphic.

Depending on the current selection, you may not be able to take certain actions in your procedure, and you may not *want* to take other actions. You can't, for example, insert a table row into an ordinary text paragraph.

Table 20.3 lists the types of selections that Word differentiates.

TABLE 20.3: Selection types in Word

WDSELECTIONTYPE CONSTANT	VALUE	MEANING
`wdNoSelection`	0	There's no selection. (This state seems impossible to achieve. You'd think it'd be when no document is open, but then `Selection` statements return runtime error 91. Stay tuned...)
`wdSelectionIP`	1	The selection is collapsed to a plain insertion point—nothing is selected. But the insertion cursor is blinking as usual.
`wdSelectionNormal`	2	A "normal" selection, such as a selected word or sentence.
`wdSelectionFrame`	3	A frame is selected.
`wdSelectionColumn`	4	A column or part of a column (two or more cells in a column or one cell in each of two or more columns) is selected.
`wdSelectionRow`	5	A full row in a table is selected.

TABLE 20.3: Selection types in Word *(CONTINUED)*

WDSELECTIONTYPE CONSTANT	VALUE	MEANING
wdSelectionBlock	6	A block is selected (a vertical part of one or more paragraphs, selected by holding down the Alt key and dragging with the mouse or by using column-extend mode).
wdSelectionInline-Shape	7	An inline shape or graphic (a shape or graphic that's in the text layer rather than floating over it) is selected.
wdSelectionShape	8	A Shape object is selected. (A text box counts as a Shape object.)

To find out what type of selection you currently have, look at the Type property of the Selection object. The following statements check that the current selection is merely an insertion point before inserting a text literal. The text will not be inserted if the user has dragged to select, for example, some characters, a word, or a paragraph:

```
If Selection.Type = wdSelectionIP Then
    Selection.TypeText "This is inserted."
End If
```

Checking the Story Type of the Selection

Beyond the type of selection, you'll sometimes need to find out which "story" the selection is in—the main text story, the comments story, the primary header story, and so on. Microsoft uses the word *story* (instead of *zone*, *type*, or other perhaps more descriptive terms) to mean a distinct type of content.

Checking the story can help you avoid problems, such as trying to do something to a header or footer story that Word can only do to the main text story.

The story is the zone of the document within which the current selection is located. So, most of the time the story is the *main text story* (wdMainTextStory). That's the document and the items within it. But alternative "stories" are things like footnotes, frames, headers, and footers—as you can see in Table 20.4, which lists the wdStoryType constants and the stories to which they correspond.

You may notice another whimsical, enigmatic feature of Table 20.4. It starts the enumeration value with 1. Compare that to Table 20.3 which starts with 0. Inconsistencies like this make programming more challenging.

TABLE 20.4: Word story types

WDSTORYTYPE CONSTANT	VALUE	MEANING
wdMainTextStory	1	Main (body) text of the document
wdCommentsStory	4	Comments section

TABLE 20.4: Word story types *(CONTINUED)*

WDSTORYTYPE CONSTANT	VALUE	MEANING
`wdEndnotesStory`	3	Endnotes section
`wdFootnotesStory`	2	Footnotes section
`wdTextFrameStory`	5	Text in frames
`wdPrimaryFooterStory`	9	Main footer
`wdEvenPagesFooterStory`	8	Even-page footer
`wdFirstPageFooterStory`	11	First-page footer
`wdPrimaryHeaderStory`	7	Main header
`wdEvenPagesHeaderStory`	6	Even-page header
`wdFirstPageHeaderStory`	10	First-page header
`wdFootnoteSeparatorStory`	12	Footnote separator
`wdFootnoteContinuationSeparatorStory`	13	Footnote continuation separator
`wdFootnoteContinuationNoticeStory`	14	Footnote continuation notice
`wdEndnoteSeparatorStory`	15	Endnote separator
`wdEndnoteContinuationSeparatorStory`	16	Endnote continuation separator
`wdEndnoteContinuationNoticeStory`	17	Endnote continuation notice

Here's a code example that displays a message box if the selection isn't in the main text of a document:

```
If Selection.StoryType <> wdMainTextStory Then
    MsgBox "This range is not in the main text."
End If
```

Getting Other Information About the Current Selection

To work effectively with a selection, you'll often need to know what it contains and where it's positioned. To find out, use the `Information` property to learn the details you need. Table 20.5 lists examples of useful information available in the `Information` property.

Here's an example showing how to use the `Information` property:

```
If Selection.Information(wdCapsLock) = True Then
    MsgBox "The caps lock is ON."
End If
```

Sharp-eyed readers will notice a capricious inconsistency in this code. In the other code examples in this section, no parentheses were used around a constant, and the operator (= or <> or whatever) is placed between the property and the constant, as shown in this example:

```
Selection.Type = wdSelectionIP
```

But with the `Information` property, you *do* use parentheses, and you move the operator to the right of the constant:

```
Selection.Information(wdCapsLock) =
```

This syntax and punctuation irregularity is yet another of those fun exceptions to the rule. You should, therefore, remember that if the expected or typical syntax results in an error message from the Editor, you should try a different syntax and see if that works.

To see the complete list of all members, open the Object Browser (F2) and scroll down in the Classes list until you see `wdInformation`. Double-click it, and its members will be listed in the Members of "WdInformation" list on the right.

TABLE 20.5: Information available in the `Information` property

CONSTANT	RETURNS THIS INFORMATION
ENVIRONMENT INFORMATION	
`wdCapsLock`	`True` if Caps Lock is on.
`wdNumLock`	`True` if Num Lock is on.
`wdOverType`	`True` if Overtype mode is on. (You can turn Overtype mode on and off by changing the `Overtype` property.)
`wdRevisionMarking`	`True` if Track Changes is on.
`wdSelectionMode`	A value that specifies the current selection mode: `0` indicates a normal selection, 1 indicates an extended selection (Extend mode is on), and 2 indicates a column selection.
`wdZoomPercentage`	The current zoom percentage.
SELECTION AND INSERTION POINT INFORMATION	
`wdActiveEndAdjustedPageNumber`	The number of the page containing the active end of the selection or range. This number reflects any change you make to the starting page number; `wdActiveEndPageNumber`, the alternative, doesn't.
`wdActiveEndPageNumber`	The number of the page containing the active end of the selection or range.

TABLE 20.5: Information available in the `Information` property *(CONTINUED)*

CONSTANT	RETURNS THIS INFORMATION
`wdActiveEndSectionNumber`	The number of the section containing the active end of the selection or range.
`wdFirstCharacterColumnNumber`	The character position of the first character in the selection or range. If the selection or range is collapsed to an insertion point, this constant returns the character number immediately to the right of the insertion point. (Note that this "column" is relative to the currently active left margin and doesn't have to be inside a table.)
`wdFirstCharacterLineNumber`	In Print Layout view and Print Preview, this constant returns the line number of the first character in the selection. In nonlayout views (e.g., Normal view), it returns `-1`.
`wdFrameIsSelected`	`True` if the selection or range is a whole frame or text box.
`wdHeaderFooterType`	A value that specifies the type of header or footer containing the selection or range: `-1` indicates that the selection or range isn't in a header or footer; `0` indicates an even page header; 1 indicates an odd page header in a document that has odd and even headers and the only header in a document that doesn't have odd and even headers; 2 indicates an even page footer; 3 indicates an odd page footer in a document that has odd and even footers and the only footer in a document that doesn't have odd and even headers; 4 indicates a first-page header; and 5 indicates a first-page footer.
`wdHorizontalPositionRelativeToPage`	The horizontal position of the selection or range—the distance from the left edge of the selection or range to the left edge of the page, measured in twips.
`wdHorizontalPositionRelativeToTextBoundary`	The horizontal position of the selection or range—the distance from the left edge of the selection or range to the text boundary enclosing it, measured in twips.
`wdInCommentPane`	`True` if the selection or range is in a comment pane.
`wdInEndnote`	`True` if the selection or range is an endnote (defined as appearing in the endnote pane in Normal view or in the endnote area in Print Layout view).
`wdInFootnote`	`True` if the selection or range is in a footnote (defined as appearing in the footnote pane in Normal view or in the footnote area in Print Layout view).

TABLE 20.5: Information available in the `Information` property *(CONTINUED)*

CONSTANT	RETURNS THIS INFORMATION
`wdInFootnoteEndnotePane`	`True` if the selection or range is in a footnote or endnote.
`wdInHeaderFooter`	`True` if the selection or range is in a header or footer (defined as appearing in the header or footer pane in Normal view or in the header or footer area in Print Layout view).
`wdInMasterDocument`	`True` if the selection or range is in a master document (a document containing at least one subdocument).
`wdInWordMail`	A value that specifies the WordMail location of the selection or range: `0` indicates that the selection or range isn't in a WordMail message; 1 indicates that it's in a WordMail message you're sending; 2 indicates that it's in a WordMail you've received.
`wdNumberOfPagesInDocument`	The number of pages in the document in which the selection or range appears.
`wdReferenceOfType`	A value that specifies where the selection is in relation to a footnote reference, endnote reference, or comment reference. `-1` indicates the selection or range includes a reference. `0` indicates the selection or range isn't before a reference. 1 indicates the selection or range is before a footnote reference, 2 that it's before an endnote reference, and 3 that it's before a comment reference.
`wdVerticalPositionRelativeToPage`	The vertical position of the selection or range—the distance from the top edge of the selection to the top edge of the page, measured in twips.
`wdVerticalPositionRelativeToText-Boundary`	The vertical position of the selection or range—the distance from the top edge of the selection to the text boundary enclosing it, measured in twips.
TABLE INFORMATION	
`wdWithInTable`	`True` if the selection is in a table.
`wdStartOfRangeColumnNumber`	The number of the table column containing the beginning of the selection or range.
`wdEndOfRangeColumnNumber`	The number of the table column containing the end of the selection or range.

TABLE 20.5: Information available in the `Information` property *(CONTINUED)*

CONSTANT	RETURNS THIS INFORMATION
`wdStartOfRangeRowNumber`	The number of the table row containing the beginning of the selection or range.
`wdEndOfRangeRowNumber`	The number of the table row containing the end of the selection or range.
`wdAtEndOfRowMarker`	`True` if the selection or range is at the end-of-row marker in a table (not the end-of-cell marker).
`wdMaximumNumberOfColumns`	The largest number of table columns in any row in the selection or range.
`wdMaximumNumberOfRows`	The largest number of table rows in the table in the selection or range.
MACINTOSH	
`wdInClipboard`	Used with Microsoft Office Macintosh Edition

Inserting Text at a Selection

You can insert text at the selection by using the `TypeText` method of the `Selection` object, insert text before the selection by using the `InsertBefore` method, or insert text after the selection by using the `InsertAfter` method.

The `TypeText` method merely inserts a text string into the document if the selection is collapsed (if it's just the blinking insertion cursor with nothing actually selected). But if something *is* selected, such as a word or phrase, that selection is *replaced* by the string when you execute the `TypeText` method. However, the `InsertBefore` and `InsertAfter` methods do not replace a selection. They merely insert the new string.

The syntax is as follows:

```
Selection.TypeText string
Selection.InsertAfter string
Selection.InsertBefore string
```

Here, *`string`* is a required String expression containing the text you want to insert in double quotation marks, as in this example:

```
Selection.TypeText "Please come to the meeting next Friday at 9:00 A.M."
Selection.InsertBefore "Dr. "
Selection.InsertAfter vbCr & Address
```

When you use the `InsertAfter` or the `InsertBefore` method, VBA extends the selection to include the text you inserted. (You can see selected text, cells, or other items in a document because Word changes the background from the default white to the document frame color.) When you use the `TypeText` method, the result is a collapsed selection—whether you are replacing a selection or a collapsed selection. (Recall that a collapsed selection means nothing is selected—merely the blinking insertion point.)

A Selected Paragraph Includes an Ending Paragraph Mark

When you have a whole paragraph selected that ends in a paragraph mark, the selection includes the paragraph mark. This causes any text you try to add to the end of the selection appear at the beginning of the next paragraph rather than at the end of the selected paragraph.

Inserting a Paragraph in a Selection

You can insert paragraphs using the following methods:

- To insert a paragraph at the current selection, use the `InsertParagraph` method.
- To insert a paragraph before the current selection, use the `InsertParagraphBefore` method.
- To insert a paragraph after the current selection, use the `InsertParagraphAfter` method.

You can also have VBA type a paragraph by using the `Selection.TypeParagraph` command.

Applying a Style

To apply a style to a paragraph, set the `Style` property of the `Paragraph` object:

```
Selection.Style = "Heading 3"
```

View the styles available to the current document by pressing Ctrl+S, or click the Home tab on the Ribbon.

Similarly, you can apply a character style to the current selection or (as in the following example) to a specific range of words or characters. This example changes the fifth word in the second paragraph of the current document to boldface:

```
ActiveDocument.Paragraphs(2).Range.Words(5).Style = "Bold"
```

Note that a character style must always be applied to a range rather than directly to a paragraph. Also, depending on what styles are defined for the current document, you might see an error message "Item with specified name does not exist." This means the style you're trying to describe isn't in the list of styles. To fix this, look at the styles and, for example, change *Bold* to whatever's listed for bold, such as *Strong*:

```
ActiveDocument.Paragraphs(2).Range.Words(5).Style = "Strong"
```

Extending a Selection

To extend a selection programmatically (through programming rather than by the user), use the `EndOf` method for a `Range` or `Selection` object. The syntax for the `EndOf` method is as follows:

```
expression.EndOf(Unit, Extend)
```

Here, *`expression`* is a required expression that returns a `Range` or `Selection` object, such as an object in the `Characters`, `Words`, `Sentences`, or `Paragraphs` collection. `Unit` is an optional Variant specifying the unit of movement (see Table 20.6).

TABLE 20.6: Units of movement for the `EndOf` method

UNIT	MEANING
`wdCharacter`	A character.
`wdWord`	A word. (This is the default setting if you omit the argument.)
`wdSentence`	A sentence.
`wdLine`	A line. (This unit can be used only with `Selection` objects, not with ranges.)
`wdParagraph`	A paragraph.
`wdSection`	A section of a document.
`wdStory`	The current story—for example, the document story or the header and footer story.
`wdCell`	A cell in a table.
`wdColumn`	A column in a table.
`wdRow`	A row in a table.
`wdTable`	A whole table.

`Extend` is an optional Variant specifying whether to move or extend the selection or range. `wdMove` moves the selection or range and is the default setting; `wdExtend` extends the selection or range.

For example, the following statement extends the current selection to the end of the paragraph:

```
Selection.EndOf Unit:=wdParagraph, Extend:=wdExtend
```

The following statement moves the selection to the end of the paragraph:

```
Selection.EndOf Unit:=wdParagraph, Extend:=wdMove
```

The following statement selects from the current selection to the end of the current Word story:

```
Selection.EndOf Unit:=wdStory, Extend:=wdExtend
```

To select the whole active document, use `ActiveDocument.Content.Select`. This command has the same effect as pressing Ctrl+A when working interactively.

Collapsing a Selection

When you've finished working with a selection larger than a blinking cursor insertion point, you often want to deselect it. In other words, you may want to force the selection into a collapsed state (just the blinking cursor) when your procedure ends. (If you don't do this and the user just starts typing, whatever is selected will be *replaced* by the user's typing.)

The easiest way to do so is to use the `Collapse` method of the `Selection` object to collapse the selection to its start or its end:

```
Selection.Collapse Direction:=wdCollapseStart
Selection.Collapse Direction:=wdCollapseEnd
```

Alternatively, you can reduce the selection to just one point by setting the selection's end selection equal to its start (collapsing the selection to its start) or by setting the selection's start equal to its end (collapsing the selection to its end):

```
Selection.End = Selection.Start
Selection.Start = Selection.End
```

Creating and Using Ranges

In Word, a *range* is a contiguous area of a document with a defined starting point and ending point. For example, if you define a range that consists of the first two paragraphs in a specified document, the range's starting point is at the beginning of the first paragraph, and its ending point is at the end of the second paragraph (after the paragraph mark).

Although similar to a selection, a range is more flexible. And, it's important to note that a range is *named* in your code, so you can refer to it by name at any time. There can be multiple ranges, but there can be only one selection at a time, and it has no name.

The typical use of ranges in Word VBA is similar to how you use bookmarks when working interactively with Word: to mark a location in a document that you want to be able to access quickly or manipulate easily.

Like a bookmark, a range can contain any amount of text in a document, from a single character to the entire contents of the document. A range can even have the same starting point and ending point, which gives it no contents and makes it, in effect, an invisible mark in the document that you can use to insert text. (This is similar to a collapsed selection.)

Once you've created a range, you can refer to it, access its contents or insert new contents in it, or format it—all by using the methods and properties of the range object.

HOW A RANGE DIFFERS FROM A BOOKMARK

The main difference between a range and a bookmark is that the lifetime of a range is limited to the VBA procedure that defines it. Once the procedure finishes executing, the range vanishes. By contrast, a bookmark persists. It is saved with the document or template that contains it and can be accessed at any time (whether or not a procedure is running).

Defining a Named Range

To create a Range object, you use a Set statement and either the Range *method* (with the Document object) or the Range *property* for a different object—for example, the Selection object, the Paragraphs collection, or a Paragraph object classify Range as a property. You might be excused for thinking that a range is always a property of something, but it's how you view the timing. Before a range exists, you can think of it as an action that creates the range, so it's a method. However, after a range exists, it's clearly a property, like an object's color. As I say, object classification is a work in progress. And likely always will be.

The syntax for using the Range *method* is as follows:

```
Set RangeName = Document.Range(Start, End)
```

Here, RangeName is the name you are assigning to the range, and Start and End are optional arguments specifying the starting and ending points of the range.

The syntax for using the Range property on an object is as follows:

```
Set RangeName = object.Range
```

For example, the following statement uses the Range property of the Paragraphs collection to define a range named FirstPara that consists of the first paragraph of the active document. This statement doesn't use Start and End arguments because the starting point and ending point of the paragraph are clearly understood:

```
Set FirstPara = ActiveDocument.Paragraphs(1).Range
```

The following code changes to uppercase the first three words at the start of a document:

```
Dim InitialCaps As Range
Set InitialCaps = ActiveDocument.Range _
(Start:=ActiveDocument.Words(1).Start, _
    End:=ActiveDocument.Words(3).End)
InitialCaps.Case = wdUpperCase
```

The first statement defines a Range object named InitialCaps. The second statement assigns InitialCaps to a range in the active document, from the beginning of the first word to the end of the third word. The third statement changes the case of the InitialCaps Range object to uppercase.

Because InitialCaps is now defined as a Range object for the duration of the procedure that declares it, you can return to InitialCaps and manipulate it later in the procedure if you want to.

Redefining a Range

To redefine a range to make it refer to another part of a document, use the SetRange method. The syntax is as follows:

```
expression.SetRange(Start, End)
```

Here, *expression* is a required expression that returns a Range or Selection object, and Start and End are optional arguments specifying the starting and ending points of the range.

For example, the following statement redefines the range named InitialCaps so it now refers to the first two characters of the document:

```
InitialCaps.SetRange Start:=0, End:=2
```

You can also redefine a range by reusing the Set method, creating the range again from scratch.

Using the *Duplicate* Property to Store or Copy Formatting

You can use the Duplicate property to store or copy a range so that you can apply it to another range. For example, the following statements declare two ranges, Range1 and Range2; store the duplicate of the current selection's range in Range1; assign to Range2 the Range of the first bookmark in the active document; and then apply to Range2 the contents of Range1:

```
Dim Range1 As Range, Range2 As Range
Set Range1 = Selection.Range.Duplicate
Set Range2 = ActiveDocument.Bookmarks(1).Range
```

Manipulating Options

In your macros, you'll often need to check the status of options in the Word application or in a particular document. In VBA, many of the options are controlled by the Options object, which has dozens of properties, but no methods.

Let's look at four brief examples that show how to set options. Three of them use the Options object and one uses a property of the Document object. To see the full list of properties available for the Options object, look in MSDN:

```
https://msdn.microsoft.com/EN-US/library/office/ff822397.aspx
```

Making Sure Hyperlinks Require Ctrl+Clicking

Hyperlinks in Word documents have proved a mixed blessing—especially since Microsoft's changes to the way Word handles hyperlinks have left users unsure whether to just click or to Ctrl+click the hyperlink to follow it. You can set the CtrlClickHyperlinkToOpen property of the Options object to True to ensure that hyperlinks require Ctrl+clicking:

```
Options.CtrlClickHyperlinkToOpen = True
```

Setting this option to False means you can trigger links by merely clicking them—no Ctrl key required.

Turning Off Overtype

To make sure your procedures behave as expected, you may need to check that Word is using Insert mode rather than Overtype mode. (In Insert mode, Word inserts the characters you type at the insertion point, moving right any existing text to make room. In Overtype mode, each character you type replaces the character to the right of the insertion point.)

Overtype mode is controlled by the `Overtype` property of the `Options` object. When `OverType` is `True`, Overtype mode is on; when `Overtype` is `False`, Insert mode is on. The following statements store the user's current `Overtype` setting in a Boolean variable named `blnOvertypeOn`, set `Overtype` to `False`, perform its actions, and then restore the user's `Overtype` setting:

```
Dim blnOvertypeOn As Boolean
blnOvertypeOn = Options.Overtype
Options.Overtype = False   'write more code here to perform actions
Options.Overtype = blnOvertypeOn
```

Setting a Default File Path

When configuring Word on a computer, you may need to make sure that its default file paths are set to the correct folders. You can do so by working with the `DefaultFilePath` property of the `Options` object. The syntax is as follows:

```
expression.DefaultFilePath(Path)
```

Here, *`expression`* is a required expression that returns an `Options` object. Often, it's easiest to use the `Options` object itself. `Path` is one of the self-explanatory enumerated constants shown in the following list:

`wdAutoRecoverPath`	`wdStyleGalleryPath`
`wdBorderArtPath`	`wdTempFilePath`
`wdCurrentFolderPath`	`wdTextConvertersPath`
`wdDocumentsPath`	`wdToolsPath`
`wdGraphicsFiltersPath`	`wdTutorialPath`
`wdPicturesPath`	`wdUserOptionsPath`
`wdProgramPath`	`wdUserTemplatesPath`
`wdProofingToolsPath`	`wdWorkgroupTemplatesPath`
`wdStartupPath`	

For example, the following statements set the user templates path and the workgroup templates path:

```
Options.DefaultFilePath(wdUserTemplatesPath) = _
"c:\users\richard\appdata\roaming\microsoft\templates"
```

```
Options.DefaultFilePath(wdWorkgroupTemplatesPath) = _
"\\server\users\templates"
```

Turning Off Track Changes

Before running a procedure that adds, deletes, or formats text, you may need to turn off the Track Changes feature so that the changes the procedure makes are not marked up in the text. If the user had Track Changes on, you should turn it back on at the end of the procedure so that changes the user makes are tracked again. Remember that it's usually a good practice when changing options to first store the user's current setting in a variable, carry out your procedure's task, and then restore the user's original setting. The following example illustrates this technique.

This example saves the user's setting for the `TrackRevisions` option in the `ActiveDocument` object in a Boolean variable named `blnTrackChangesOn`, sets `TrackRevisions` to `False`, performs its actions, and then restores the user's `TrackRevisions` setting:

```
Dim blnTrackChangesOn As Boolean
blnTrackChangesOn = ActiveDocument.TrackRevisions
ActiveDocument.TrackRevisions = False
' write more code here to perform actions
ActiveDocument.TrackRevisions = blnTrackChangesOn
```

Accessing OneNote

Earlier in this chapter you saw how to access the cloud: OneDrive, Dropbox, and so on. It's uncomplicated. But dealing with OneNote is another matter because its contents are stored in XML format.

When you write code to manage an ordinary text document, it's pretty simple because of VBA's string-manipulation features. Even managing a Word document is easy enough because VBA has so many built-in functions involving the `Range`, `Selection`, and other objects. Word effectively hides its internal formatting and other complexities, allowing you the option of handling the text simply as text.

However, as you'll see, just getting the metadata (information such as the name of a notebook) can be heavy going. A lot depends on who constructed the XML and how capable they were of clarity and logic.

Why bother to explore this topic then? Although VBA is not built into the OneNote application itself, VBA code in other Office 2016 applications can directly manipulate OneNote. And, because Microsoft has been promoting OneNote for several years now, attempting to make it more popular as a repository of your ideas and memories, I'm including this example demonstrating how to access it from the other Office applications.

OneNote *is* useful; it's actually quite rich in features and well integrated into the Windows and Office platforms.

Versions of OneNote are available on everything from iOS to Android devices. So, if you should ever need to know how to contact OneNote from Word or some other Office application, read on.

The following example fetches metadata from the user's OneNote. Before you try this code, choose Tools ➢ References in the Editor and ensure that both Microsoft OneNote 15.0 Object

Library and Microsoft XML, v6.0 are both checked in the References dialog box. They're not checked (included in VBA) by default.

```
1.  Sub GetMetaData()
2.
3.  'If it's not currently running, OneNote will be launched
4.  Dim ONote As oneNote.Application
5.  Set ONote = New oneNote.Application
6.
7.  Dim strXML As String
8.
9.  ONote.GetHierarchy "", hsNotebooks, strXML, xs2013 'note that this fails if
you use xs201610.
11. MsgBox strXML
12. End Sub
```

Lines 4 and 5 create an instance of OneNote and assign it to the `ONote` object variable. Next, we create a string variable in line 7 to hold the metadata. Line 9 uses the `GetHierarchy` method to fill `strXML` with the metadata. `hsNotebooks` represents the collection of notebooks in OneNote. The message box displays the results, as illustrated in Figure 20.4.

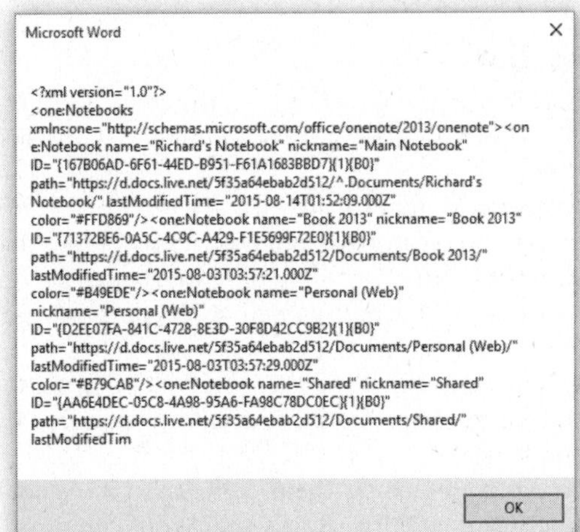

FIGURE 20.4
Metadata fetched from OneNote

The Bottom Line

Understand Word's creatable objects. Word contains a set of creatable objects that VBA programmers will frequently employ in their code.

Master It What is a creatable object?

Work with the `Documents` collection and the `Document` object. The `Documents` collection represents all the currently open documents. Using VBA, you can manipulate this collection in a variety of ways.

Master It Here is the syntax for adding a new document to the `Documents` collection:

```
Documents.Add Template, NewTemplate, DocumentType, Visible
```

If you merely want to add a new, empty document (based on the default `Normal.dotm` template) to the documents currently open in Word, the code is quite simple. What is the code that you would write in VBA to accomplish this?

Work with the `Selection` object. The `Selection` object represents the current selection in the active document in Word. A zone can be selected by the user by dragging the mouse or by using various key combinations (such as pressing Shift and an arrow key). A selection can include one or more objects—one or more characters, one or more words, one or more paragraphs, a graphic, a table, and so on. Or, it can include a combination of these objects.

Master It One kind of selection is described as a *collapsed selection*. What is that?

Create and use ranges. In Word, a *range* is a named area of a document with a defined starting and ending point. The typical use of ranges in Word VBA is similar to how you use bookmarks when working interactively with Word: to mark a location in a document that you want to be able to access quickly or manipulate easily.

Master It Although a range is similar to a bookmark, what is the significant difference between them?

Manipulate options Word contains many options that can be manipulated from within VBA.

Master It In Word, one object controls many of the options. This object has dozens of properties but no methods. Name this object.

Chapter 21

Working with Widely Used Objects in Word

In the previous chapter, you learned how to work with some of the main objects in the Word object model, such as `Document` objects, the `Selection` object, `Range` objects, and the `Options` object. This chapter shows you how to go further with VBA in Word by working with Find and Replace; with headers, footers, and page numbers; with sections, page setup, windows, and views; and with tables.

IN THIS CHAPTER, YOU WILL LEARN TO DO THE FOLLOWING:

- Use Find and Replace via VBA
- Work with headers, footers, and page numbers
- Manage sections, page setup, windows, and views
- Manipulate tables

Using Find and Replace via VBA

Word's Find and Replace tool can be useful in some macros. You can use it, for example, to quickly adjust multiple styles throughout an entire document. Or, you could automate the process of finalizing documents (spell-checking, revising corporate information, looking for out-of-date references, or whatever routinely needs to be done before publication).

To access Word's Find and Replace features via VBA, you use the `Find` and `Replacement` objects. This section illustrates how to work with the `Find` object's `Execute` method, usually the best method to employ when working with `Find`. Typically, you will specify the parameters for the `Find` operation as arguments in the `Execute` statement, but you can also specify them beforehand using properties if you prefer that approach.

Table 21.1 describes the `Find` properties that are useful for most search operations.

TABLE 21.1: Properties of the `Find` object

PROPERTY	MEANING
`Font`	Font formatting you're searching for (on either specified text or an empty string).
`Forward`	A Boolean variable-type argument specifying whether to search forward (`True`) or backward (`False`) through the document.
`Found`	A Boolean property that's `True` if the search finds a match and `False` if it doesn't.
`Highlight`	A Long variable-type argument controlling whether highlighting is included in the formatting for the replacement text (`True`) or not (`False`).
`MatchAllWordForms`	A Boolean property—`True` or `False`—corresponding to the Find All Word Forms check box.
`MatchCase`	A Boolean property corresponding to the Match Case check box. If the user has this option deselected, be sure your code deselects it after you're finished with any case-sensitive searching in your procedure. See the sidebar "Practical Searching: Remember to Clear Formatting" later in this chapter.
`MatchSoundsLike`	A Boolean property corresponding to the Sounds Like check box.
`MatchWholeWord`	A Boolean property corresponding to the Find Whole Words Only check box.
`MatchWildcards`	A Boolean property corresponding to the Use Wildcards check box.
`ParagraphFormat`	Paragraph formatting you're searching for (on either specified text or an empty string).
`Replacement`	Returns (fetches) a `Replacement` object containing the criteria for a replace operation.
`Style`	The style for the search text. Usually, you'll want to use the name of a style in the current template, but you can also use one of the built-in Word constant style names, such as `wdStyleHeading1` (Heading 1 style).
`Text`	The text you're searching for (what you'd enter in the Find What box in the Find And Replace dialog box). Use an empty string (`""`) to search only for formatting.
`Wrap`	A Long property that governs whether a search that starts anywhere other than the beginning of a document (for a forward search) or the end of a document (for a backward search), or a search that takes place in a range, *wraps* (continues) when it reaches the end or beginning of the document or the end or beginning of the selection.

Use the `Replacement` object to specify the replace criteria in a replacement operation. The `Replacement` object has the following properties, which correspond to the properties of the `Find` object (but pertain to the replacement operation instead): `Font`, `Highlight`, `ParagraphFormat`, `Style`, and `Text`.

Understanding the Syntax of the *Execute* Method

The syntax for the `Execute` method is as follows:

```
expression.Execute(FindText, MatchCase, MatchWholeWord, MatchWildcards,
   MatchSoundsLike, MatchAllWordForms, Forward, Wrap, Format,
   ReplaceWith, Replace, MatchKashida, MatchDiacritics, MatchAlefHamza,
   MatchControl, MatchPrefix, MatchSuffix, MatchPhrase, IgnoreSpace,
   IgnorePunct)
```

The final five arguments, starting with `MatchPrefix`, are not displayed in the Auto List Members tool in the Editor, nor in the MSDN parameter list. However, they can be used in code, as in, for example, `IgnoreSpace:=True`.

The most commonly used arguments for this method are explained here:

- *`expression`* is a required expression that returns a `Find` object. Usually, it's easiest to use the `Find` object itself.
- `FindText` is an optional Variant specifying the text for which to search. Although this argument is optional, you'll almost always want to specify it, even if you specify only an empty string (`""`) to allow you to search for formatting rather than text. (If you don't specify `""` for `FindText`, you will inadvertently search for the previous text searched for, and the style you want to locate will never be found unless that text is also present.)

  You can search for special characters by using the same special characters you use when using Word's Find dialog box interactively (for example, `^p` for a paragraph mark or `^t` for a tab) and for wildcards by using the traditional Windows wildcards. For wildcards to work in a macro, you need to set `MatchWildcards` to `True`. You can search for a symbol by entering a caret and a zero, followed by its character code. For example, to search for a smart double closing quote, you'd specify **`^0148`** because its character code is 148.
- `MatchCase` is an optional Variant that you can set to `True` to make the search case-sensitive.
- `MatchWholeWord` is an optional Variant that you can set to `True` to restrict the search to finding whole words rather than words contained in other words.
- `MatchWildcards` is an optional Variant that you can set to `True` to use wildcards in the search.
- `MatchSoundsLike` is an optional Variant that you can set to `True` to have Word find words that it thinks sound similar to the Find item specified.
- `MatchAllWordForms` is an optional Variant that you can set to `True` to have Word find all forms of the Find item specified (for example, different forms of the same verb or noun).

- `Forward` is an optional Variant that you can set to `True` to have Word search forward (from the beginning of the document toward the end) or `False` to have Word search backward.
- `Wrap` is an optional Variant that governs whether a search that begins anywhere other than the beginning of a document (for a forward search) or the end of a document (for a backward search), or that takes place in a range, *wraps* (continues) when it reaches the end or beginning of the document. Word offers various options for `Wrap`, as detailed in Table 21.2.

TABLE 21.2: Options for `Wrap` offered by Word

CONSTANT	VALUE	MEANING
`wdFindAsk`	2	Word searches the selection or range—or from the insertion point to the end or beginning of the document—and then displays a message box prompting the user to decide whether to search the rest of the document.
`wdFindContinue`	1	Word continues to search after reaching the end or beginning of the search range or the end or beginning of the document.
`wdFindStop`	0	Word stops the `Find` operation upon reaching the end or beginning of the search range or the end or beginning of the document.

- `Format` is an optional Variant that you can set to `True` to have the search operation find formatting as well as (or instead of) any Find text you've specified.
- `ReplaceWith` is an optional Variant specifying the replacement text. You can use an empty string for `ReplaceWith` to simply remove the `FindText` text; you can also use special characters for `ReplaceWith` as you can for the `FindText` argument. To use a graphic object, copy it to the Clipboard and then specify **`^c`** (which stands for the contents of the Clipboard).

HOW TO USE GRAPHIC OBJECTS WITH `ReplaceWith`

To use a graphic object as described in the bulleted item that explains the `ReplaceWith` argument, the graphic needs to be in the text layer (not floating over text). If the graphic is floating over text, `^c` pastes in the previous text contents of the Clipboard.

- `Replace` is an optional Variant that controls how many replacements the `Find` operation makes: one (`wdReplaceOne`), all (`wdReplaceAll`), or none (`wdReplaceNone`).
- `MatchPrefix` is an optional Variant that allows you to search for a string of characters at the start of words, but not if any other character(s) precede the string. Here's how it works: If you leave `MatchPrefix` and `MatchWholeWord` set to `False` and then search for **real**, you'll

get results with any word that contains that string, such as *real*, sur*real*, *real*time, bo*real*, and so on. Any word with *real* in it will be a hit. But set `MatchWholeWord` to `True`, and only the specific word itself, **real**, will result in a hit. Leave `MatchWholeWord` set to `False` but set `MatchPrefix` to `True`, and only words that *begin* with *real* will hit, such as *real* and *real*time. Words like sur*real* fail to qualify because they don't begin with the target string.

- `MatchSuffix` is an optional Variant that works the same way as `MatchPrefix`, except `MatchSuffix` allows you to search for a string of characters at the *end* of a word but not if any other characters follow the string. Using the example in the previous bullet, with `MatchSuffix` set to `True`, you would get hits on sur*real* and bo*real* but not *real*time.
- `MatchPhrase` is an optional Variant that when set to `True` ignores any control characters (such as paragraph or tab characters) or white space (one or more space characters) between words.

  This

  phrase

  becomes equivalent to

  this phrase.
- `IgnoreSpace` is an optional Variant that ignores any white space between words but that does not ignore control characters.
- `IgnorePunct` is an optional Variant that ignores all punctuation characters between words in a search phrase.

Real World Scenario

Practical Searching: Remember to Clear Formatting

One behavior in Word that can puzzle even experienced users and developers results from the fact that Find settings *persist*. For example, say that you search for a style such as *Heading1*. All goes well, you find the headings, and you close the Find And Replace dialog box (or if you're searching using VBA code, your macro finishes execution).

Then somewhat later you run another macro that searches or replaces—or you use the Find And Replace dialog box in Word to look for a word such as *program*. You know that the word *program* appears many times in your document, but the Find utility displays a message stating that "The search item was not found." What's wrong?

The problem is that your original search for that headline style persists during your session with Word. Even switching to a different document during the current session will not clear the search criteria—including any style, font, or other special search criteria, such as `MatchCase`, that may have been previously employed.

Continues

Continued

In other words, you're now searching for the word *program* but *also* for the style *Heading 1*. So, none of the instances of *program* in regular body text will trigger hits because they are not in the specified style.

If you search for a style but fail to click the No Formatting button in the Find And Replace dialog box when you've finished, that style search remains active.

Likewise, when you use the `Find` object and the `Replacement` object in a macro, you'll often need to use the `ClearFormatting` method, which clears any formatting specified under the Find What box or the Replace With box. Using the `ClearFormatting` method has the same effect as clicking the No Formatting button with the focus on the Find What box or the Replace With box. The following statements (here used within a `With` structure) clear formatting from the `Find` and `Replacement` objects, respectively:

```
With ActiveDocument.Content.Find
    .ClearFormatting
    .Replacement.ClearFormatting
End With
```

It's a good idea to get into the habit of using the `ClearFormatting` method at the *start* of any macro that searches for anything. Sometimes unnecessary? Sure. But clearing previous search settings is good insurance against this common and puzzling bug.

A similar situation occurs when you employ the `Execute` method, as described earlier in this chapter. Remember that when using `Execute`, you should almost always specify the `FindText` argument—even if you specify only an empty string (`""`) to allow you to search for formatting. If you don't specify `FindText`, you run the risk of searching inadvertently for the string searched for previously.

Putting Find and Replace to Work

The simplest way to use Find and Replace is to specify only as many parameters as you need in an `Execute` statement, leaving out any optional parameters that are irrelevant to your search. With long argument lists, it's always better to use the named-argument approach, like this:

```
FindText:="National Velvet"
```

This example replaces all pairs of paragraph marks (thereby removing empty lines) in the active document with single paragraph marks; you could search for **`^p^p`** and replace it with **`^p`** with the following statement:

```
ActiveDocument.Content.Find.Execute FindText:="^p^p",
  ReplaceWith:="^p", _
    Replace:=wdReplaceAll
```

By executing this statement within a loop, you could replace all extra paragraph marks in the document. You would have to employ a loop here because the `wdReplaceAll` constant specifies that the find-and-replace activity should go through the entire document once.

It's necessary to loop here because you might have multiple paragraph marks in clusters, such as four in a row: ^p^p^p^p. The first pass through the document would replace those four with two (^p^p), so you'd need to go through again to reduce these to the desired single ^p. In other words, in this case you must search and replace more than once.

You can also use a `With` statement to specify the properties for a `Find` and `Replace` operation. Listing 21.1 shows an example of this. The code changes all bold formatting in the open document named `Example.docm` to italic formatting.

LISTING 21.1: Using `With` to specify properties

```
1.  With Documents("Example.docm").Content.Find
2.      .ClearFormatting
3.      .Font.Bold = True
4.      With .Replacement
5.          .ClearFormatting
6.          .Font.Bold = False
7.          .Font.Italic = True
8.      End With
9.      .Execute FindText:= "", ReplaceWith:= "", _
            Format:=True, Replace:=wdReplaceAll
10. End With
```

- Here, line 1 identifies the `Document` object (`Example.docm` in the `Documents` collection) with which to work and begins a `With` statement with its `Find` object.
- Line 2 uses the `ClearFormatting` method to clear any formatting from the `Find` object.
- Line 3 then sets the `Bold` property of its `Font` object to `True`.
- Lines 4 through 8 contain a nested `With` statement for the `Replacement` object.
- Line 5 uses the `ClearFormatting` method to clear formatting from the `Replacement` object,
- Line 6 sets its `Bold` property to `False`.
- Line 7 sets its `Italic` property to `True`.
- Line 9 then uses the `Execute` method to execute the replacement operation. Both `FindText` and `ReplaceWith` here are specified as empty strings to cause Word to work with formatting only; `Format` is set to `True` to activate the formatting set in the `Find` and `Replacement` objects, and `Replace` is set to `wdReplaceAll` to replace all instances of the bold formatting with the italic formatting.
- Line 10 ends the outer `With` statement.

Working with Headers, Footers, and Page Numbers

The following sections show you how to work with headers and footers in Word documents. You'll also learn how to use VBA to manipulate page numbers when they're included in headers and footers.

Understanding How VBA Implements Headers and Footers

You can create several types of headers and footers in a Word document: the primary header and footer, special headers and footers that appear only on the even pages, unique first-page-only headers and footers, and even different sets of headers and footers for each of the sections in a document if need be.

Every document automatically gets a primary header and a primary footer, even if you don't put anything in them. You can then create different first-page and even-page headers by changing the Page Setup options for the section. (Click the Page Layout tab on the Ribbon, and then click the small arrow in the lower-right corner of the Page Setup zone. This opens the Page Setup dialog box; click the Layout tab. Note, however, that the primary header and footer features are accessed from the Insert tab on the Ribbon.)

VBA uses the following objects for headers and footers:

- Both headers and footers are contained in `HeaderFooter` objects. You access headers through the `Headers` property and footers through the `Footers` property.
- The `HeadersFooters` collection contains all the `HeaderFooter` objects in a given section of a document. Because each section of a document can have headers and footers unique to it, you reach any given header or footer by going through the section.
- To return the `HeadersFooters` collection, you use the `Headers` property or the `Footers` property of the appropriate `Section` object in the appropriate `Document` object. Alternatively, you can use the `HeaderFooter` property of the `Selection` object to return a single `HeaderFooter` object, but this approach tends to be more limited in its use.
- The `HeaderFooter` object gives access to the `Range` object, the `Shapes` collection, and the `PageNumbers` collection.

Getting to a Header or Footer

You access a header or footer through the appropriate *section* within the document. For example, the following statement displays a message box containing the text in the first-page footer that's in the second section of an open document named `Transfer.docm`:

```
MsgBox Documents("Transfer.docm").Sections(2). _
    Footers(wdHeaderFooterFirstPage).Range.Text
```

The following statements declare the `HeaderFooter` object variable `myHeader` and assign to it the primary header in the first section in the active document:

```
Dim myHeader As HeaderFooter
Set myHeader = ActiveDocument.Sections(1).Headers _
    (wdHeaderFooterPrimary)
```

Checking to See If a Header or Footer Exists

Recall that Word automatically creates a primary header and primary footer for each document, so these objects always exist. To find out whether other types of headers or footers exist, check the Exists property of the application HeaderFooter object. The following statements check to see if the even-pages footer exists in each section in turn in the active document and create a generic header (containing the section number and the full name of the document) formatted with the style named Footer (which exists by default in most Word documents):

```
Dim cSection As Section
With ActiveDocument
    For Each cSection In .Sections
        cHeader = cSection.Headers(wdHeaderFooterEvenPages)
        If Not cSection.Headers(wdHeaderFooterEvenPages).Exists Then
            cSection.PageSetup.OddAndEvenPagesHeaderFooter = True
            cSection.Headers(wdHeaderFooterEvenPages).Range.Text _
                = "Section " & cSection.Index & " of " & .FullName
            cSection.Headers(wdHeaderFooterEvenPages).Range. _
                Style = "Even Footer"
        End If
    Next cSection
End With
```

Linking to the Header or Footer in the Previous Section

By default, Word links the header and footer in each section after the first to the header and footer in the previous section. To break the link, set the LinkToPrevious property of the header or footer to False; to create the link, set this property to True. The following statement unlinks the primary footer in the third section of the active document from the corresponding footer in the second section:

```
ActiveDocument.Sections(3).Footers _
(wdHeaderFooterPrimary).LinkToPrevious = False
```

Creating a Different First-Page Header

To create a different header on the first page of a section, set the DifferentFirstPageHeaderFooter property of the PageSetup object for the section to True. The following statements check to see if the tenth section of the active document contains a first-page header and create one if it doesn't:

```
With ActiveDocument.Sections(10)
    If .Headers(wdHeaderFooterFirstPage).Exists = False Then _
        .PageSetup.DifferentFirstPageHeaderFooter = True
End With
```

Creating Different Odd- and Even-Page Headers

To employ different headers for odd and even pages of your document (other than the first page), create an even-page header. The primary header by default appears on both odd and even pages until you create an even-page header, at which point the primary header becomes the odd-page header.

As with the first-page header, you work through the `PageSetup` object to create a different even-page header, setting the `OddAndEvenPagesHeaderFooter` property to `True`, as in the following statement:

```
ActiveDocument.Sections(1).PageSetup.OddAndEvenPagesHeaderFooter = True
```

> **USE NESTED LOOPS TO MODIFY HEADERS AND FOOTERS**
>
> If you write procedures to format documents, you may need to check or change all the headers and footers in a document. The easiest way to do so is to use two `For Each...Next` loops, the outer loop working through each `Section` object in the `Sections` collection and the inner loop working through each `HeaderFooter` object in the `HeaderFooters` collection within that section.

Adding Page Numbers to Your Headers and Footers

A header or footer of a document often contains a page number: either a simple number in a straightforward format (1, 2, 3, and so on) or a more complex number denoting the chapter and page within it, separated by a separator character.

VBA implements page numbers through a `PageNumbers` collection that you return by using the `PageNumbers` property of the appropriate `HeaderFooter` object within the appropriate section of the document.

ADDING PAGE NUMBERS TO ONE OR MORE SECTIONS OF A DOCUMENT

To add page numbers to a document, use the `Add` method with the `PageNumbers` collection for the appropriate section of the document.

The syntax for the `Add` method is as follows:

```
expression.Add PageNumberAligment, FirstPage
```

Here, *`expression`* is a required expression that returns a `PageNumbers` collection. Usually, you'll use the `PageNumbers` collection itself.

`PageNumberAlignment` is an optional Variant argument specifying the alignment for the page numbers being added. Table 21.3 lists the constants and values you can use.

TABLE 21.3: `PageNumberAlignment` constants and values

CONSTANT	VALUE	RESULTING ALIGNMENT
`wdAlignPageNumberLeft`	0	Left
`wdAlignPageNumberCenter`	1	Centered
`wdAlignPageNumberRight`	2	Right (default)

TABLE 21.3: `PageNumberAlignment` constants and values *(CONTINUED)*

CONSTANT	VALUE	RESULTING ALIGNMENT
wdAlignPageNumberInside	3	Inside margin (right on left-hand pages, left on right-hand pages)
wdAlignPageNumberOutside	4	Outside margin (left on left-hand pages, right on right-hand pages)

`FirstPage` is an optional Variant argument that you can set to `False` to make the header and footer on the first page suppress the page number. If you omit the `FirstPage` argument, the `DifferentFirstPageHeaderFooter` property of the `PageSetup` object controls whether the header and footer on the first page are the same as or different than they are on the other pages in the section.

Both the `PageNumberAlignment` argument and the `FirstPage` argument are optional, but you'll usually want to specify at least the `PageNumberAlignment` argument.

The following subprocedure adds page numbers to all the headers in each section of a document by using two `For Each...Next` loops:

```
Sub AddPageNumbersToAllHeadersAndSections()
    Dim cHeader As HeaderFooter, cSection As Section
    With Documents("Headers and Footers.docm")
        For Each cSection In .Sections
            For Each cHeader In cSection.Headers
                cSection.Headers(wdHeaderFooterPrimary).PageNumbers.Add _
                PageNumberAlignment:=wdAlignPageNumberRight, FirstPage:=True
            Next cHeader
        Next cSection
    End With
End Sub
```

REMOVING PAGE NUMBERS FROM ONE OR MORE SECTIONS OF A DOCUMENT

To remove a page number from a page, specify the `PageNumber` object and use the `Delete` method. The following subprocedure removes each `PageNumber` object from the current section of the active document:

```
Sub RemovePageNumbersFromCurrentSection()
    Dim ThisHeader As HeaderFooter
    Dim ThisPageNumber As PageNumber
    With Selection.Sections(1)
        For Each ThisHeader In .Headers
            For Each ThisPageNumber In ThisHeader.PageNumbers
                ThisPageNumber.Delete
            Next ThisPageNumber
        Next ThisHeader
    End With
End Sub
```

Finding Out If a Section of a Document Has Page Numbers

The easiest way to find out if any given page number exists is to check the `Count` property for the `PageNumbers` collection for the appropriate section. For example, the following statement adds centered page numbers to the even-pages header in the current section if the header doesn't already have them:

```
If Selection.Sections(1).Headers(wdHeaderFooterEvenPages) _
    .PageNumbers.Count = 0 Then Selection.Sections(1) _
    .Headers(wdHeaderFooterEvenPages).PageNumbers.Add _
    PageNumberAlignment:=wdAlignPageNumberCenter
```

Changing the Page Numbering for a Section

To change the page numbering for a section, you work with the `StartingNumber` property, using the `RestartNumberingAtSection` property, the `IncludeChapterNumber` property, and the `ChapterPageSeparator` property as necessary.

The `StartingNumber` property is a Long property that contains the starting page number for the section when the `RestartNumberingAtSection` property is set to `True`. When the `RestartNumberingAtSection` property is set to `False`, `StartingNumber` returns `0` (zero). The following statements set the page numbering for the primary header in the fourth section of the active document to start at 55 if it doesn't currently have a starting number assigned:

```
With ActiveDocument.Sections(4).Headers(wdHeaderFooterPrimary)
    If .PageNumbers.StartingNumber = 0 Then
        .PageNumbers.RestartNumberingAtSection = True
        .PageNumbers.StartingNumber = 55
    End If
End With
```

To add the chapter number to the page numbers, use heading numbering in your document. Set the `IncludeChapterNumber` property to `True`, and specify the separator to use (for example, `wdSeparatorEnDash` for an en dash):

```
With ActiveDocument.Sections(4).Headers(wdHeaderFooterPrimary) _
    .PageNumbers
    .IncludeChapterNumber = True
    .ChapterPageSeparator = wdSeparatorEnDash
End With
```

Suppressing the Page Number for the First Page

To suppress the page number for the first page in a section, set the `ShowFirstPageNumber` property for the appropriate `HeaderFooter` object in the appropriate section to `False`:

```
ActiveDocument.Sections(1).Footers(wdHeaderFooterPrimary).PageNumbers_
    .ShowFirstPageNumber = False
```

Formatting Page Numbers

You can format page numbers in two ways: by setting the format in which they're displayed (for instance, as regular Arabic numbers or as lowercase Roman numerals) and by formatting the font in which that format is displayed.

To choose the format in which the page numbers are displayed, set the `NumberStyle` property of the `PageNumbers` collection in question. For example, the following statement formats the page numbers in the primary header in the fourth section of the active document as lowercase letters:

```
ActiveDocument.Sections(4).Headers(wdHeaderFooterPrimary) _
    .PageNumbers.NumberStyle = wdPageNumberStyleLowercaseLetter
```

Once the page numbers are in the header or footer, you can format them in any of several ways. One easy way to set the font in which a given page number is formatted is to use the `Select` method to select the `PageNumber` object and then apply formatting to it as you would any other selection, as in the following statements:

```
ActiveDocument.Sections(4).Headers(wdHeaderFooterPrimary) _
    .PageNumbers(1).Select
    With Selection.Font
        .Name = "Impact"
        .Size = 22
        .Bold = True
    End With
```

Creating "Page X of Y"-Type Page Numbers

You can also implement page numbering by using Word's field codes in the header or footer. This technique is especially useful when you want to number the pages with an "X of Y" numbering scheme—"Page 168 of 192" and so on. The following statements select the primary header for the final section of the active document, apply center alignment, and enter the text and fields to produce this type of numbering:

```
ActiveDocument.Sections(ActiveDocument.Sections.Count) _
    .Headers(wdHeaderFooterPrimary).Range.Select
With Selection
    .Paragraphs(1).Alignment = wdAlignParagraphCenter
    .TypeText Text:="Page "
    .Fields.Add Range:=Selection.Range, Type:=wdFieldEmpty, Text:= _
        "PAGE ", PreserveFormatting:=True
    .TypeText Text:=" of "
    .Fields.Add Range:=Selection.Range, Type:=wdFieldEmpty, Text:= _
        "NUMPAGES ", PreserveFormatting:=True
End With
```

If you insert a page number by using a field in this way, you can still access the page number by using the appropriate PageNumber object. (In this case, the PageNumber object consists of the PAGE field, not of the NUMPAGES field.)

Working with Sections, Page Setup, Windows, and Views

Each Word document contains at least one section by default and can contain multiple sections as needed for its contents and layout. The section of the document controls the page layout so that different sections of a document can use different page layouts if necessary.

Adding a Section to a Document

You can add a section to a document either by using the Add method with the Sections collection or by using the InsertBreak method with a Range or Selection object.

The Add method has the following syntax:

```
expression.Add Range, Start
```

Here, *expression* is a required expression that returns a Sections collection. Range is an optional Variant argument specifying the range at the beginning of which to insert the break. (If you omit Range, VBA inserts the break at the end of the document.) Start is an optional Variant argument used to specify the type of section break to insert:

- wdSectionContinuous (0) for a continuous break
- wdSectionEvenPage (3) for an even-page break
- wdSectionOddPage (4) for an odd-page break
- wdSectionNewColumn (1) for a new-column break
- wdSectionNewPage (2, the default) for a new-page break

The following statement adds a new-page section to the active document, placing it before the second paragraph:

```
ActiveDocument.Sections.Add _
Range:=.Range(Start:=.Paragraphs(2).Range.Start, _
        End:=.Paragraphs(2).Range.Start), Start:=wdSectionNewPage
```

The InsertBreak method takes the following syntax:

```
expression.InsertBreak Type
```

Here, *expression* is a required expression that returns a Selection or Range object. Type is an optional Variant argument specifying the type of section break to be inserted:

- wdSectionBreakNextPage (2) for a new-page break
- wdSectionBreakContinuous (3) for a continuous break
- wdSectionBreakEvenPage (4) for an even-page break

- `wdSectionBreakOddPage` (5) for an odd-page break
- `wdColumnBreak` (8) for a new-column break

The following statement inserts a continuous section break before the second paragraph in the active document:

```
ActiveDocument.Paragraphs(2).Range.InsertBreak _
 Type:=wdSectionBreakContinuous
```

Changing the Page Setup

To change the page setup of a document or a section, you work with the `PageSetup` object of the application `Document` object or `Section` object. For example, the following statements work with the `PageSetup` object of the document named `Planning.docm`, setting letter-size paper, portrait orientation, mirror margins, and margin measurements (in points):

```
With Documents("Planning.docm").PageSetup
    .PaperSize = wdPaperLetter
    .Orientation = wdOrientPortrait
    .TopMargin = 1
    .BottomMargin = 1
    .LeftMargin = 1
    .RightMargin = 1.5
    .MirrorMargins = True
End With
```

Opening a New Window Containing an Open Document

To open a new window containing an open document, use the `Add` method. Its syntax is straightforward:

```
expression.Add window
```

Here, *`expression`* is an expression that returns a `Windows` collection, and *`window`* is an optional Variant argument specifying the window containing the document for which you want to open a new window. If you omit *`window`*, VBA opens a new window for the active document.

Understanding the Two Windows Collections

There are two `Windows` collections: one for the application and one for the windows displaying the document with which you're working. The `Windows` collection for the `Document` object can be useful if you have multiple windows open for the same document (as you can do by clicking the Ribbon's View tab and then clicking the New Window button in the Window section of the Ribbon), but usually you'll want to use the `Windows` collection for the `Application` object. `Windows` is a creatable object, so you don't need to specify the `Application` object.

For example, the following statements open a new window for the first window open for the active document, assigning the window to the variable `myWindow`:

```
Dim myWindow As Window
Set myWindow = Windows.Add(Window:=ActiveDocument.Windows(1))
```

Closing All Windows Except the First for a Document

Occasionally, it's useful to open one or more new windows for a document. If you do so, sooner or later you'll need to close all the secondary windows to give yourself more room to maneuver. The following statements close all windows except the first for the active document:

```
Dim myWin As Window, myDoc As String
myDoc = ActiveDocument.Name
For Each myWin In Windows
    If myWin.Document = myDoc Then _
        If myWin.WindowNumber <> 1 Then myWin.Close
Next myWin
```

Splitting a Window

To split a window in two parts horizontally, set its `Split` property to `True`. To specify the split percentage (which controls how far down the window, measuring vertically, the split is placed), set the `SplitVertical` property. The following statements split the active window 70 percent of the way down the window:

```
With ActiveWindow
    .Split = True
    .SplitVertical = 70
End With
```

To remove the split from the window, set the `Split` property to `False`:

```
ActiveWindow.Split = False
```

TRY SNAPPING WINDOWS

In all versions of Windows 7, 8, and 10, you'll find a nice feature that you might want to use instead of Word's internal split window. Drag a window by its title bar to the left side of the screen. Drag another window to the right side. They snap and automatically take up half the screen each. Or, you can press Windows key + ← (or →) to split the screen.

Displaying the Document Map for a Window

To display the Document Map for a window at the Document Map's previous width percentage (of the entire window), set the `DocumentMap` property to `True`:

```
ActiveWindow.DocumentMap = True
```

To display the Document Map at a different width, or to change the width of the Document Map, set the DocumentMapPercentWidth property to a suitable percentage of the window's width:

```
ActiveWindow.DocumentMapPercentWidth = 25
```

To hide the Document Map again, set the DocumentMap property to False or set the DocumentMapPercentWidth property to 0.

Scrolling a Window

To scroll a window up, down, left, or right, use either the LargeScroll method or the SmallScroll method.

The LargeScroll method is analogous to clicking within the scroll bar (not on a thumb—the arrows at the top and bottom of the scroll bar); this scrolls the contents of the window by one entire "screen." The SmallScroll method is analogous to clicking a thumb; this scrolls the contents of the window up or down by one line. If you're working with a horizontal scroll bar, the contents move left or right by a small scroll increment.

The syntax for the LargeScroll method is as follows:

```
expression.LargeScroll(Down, Up, ToRight, ToLeft)
```

The syntax for the SmallScroll method is almost identical:

```
expression.SmallScroll(Down, Up, ToRight, ToLeft)
```

Here, *expression* is a required expression that returns a Window object. Down, Up, ToRight, and ToLeft are optional Variant arguments that specify the number of screens (for LargeScroll) or lines or horizontal movement units (for SmallScroll) to scroll the contents of the window in the directions their names indicate.

The following statement scrolls the active window up two screens:

```
ActiveWindow.LargeScroll Up:=2
```

Arranging Windows

To arrange a number of windows, use the Arrange method. The syntax for the Arrange method is as follows:

```
expression.Arrange ArrangeStyle
```

Here, *expression* is an expression that returns a Windows collection, and ArrangeStyle is an optional Variant argument that specifies how to arrange the windows: as icons (wdIcons, 1) or tiled (wdTiled, 0). The default is wdTiled.

For example, the following statement tiles the open windows:

```
Windows.Arrange ArrangeStyle:=wdTiled
```

Positioning and Sizing a Window

To position a window on the monitor, set its Left and Top properties, as in this example:

```
ActiveWindow.Left = 100
ActiveWindow.Top = 200
```

To size a window, set its `Height` and `Width` properties:

```
With ActiveWindow
    .Height = 300
    .Width = 400
End With
```

To maximize, minimize, or "restore" a window, set its `WindowState` property to `wdWindowStateMaximize`, `wdWindowStateMinimize`, or `wdWindowStateNormal`, respectively. The following statements maximize the window containing the document named `Example.docm` if the window is minimized:

```
With Documents("Example.docm").Windows(1)
    If .WindowState = wdWindowStateMinimize Then _
        .WindowState = wdWindowStateMaximize
End With
```

Making Sure an Item Is Displayed in the Window

After opening or arranging windows, you'll often need to make sure an item you want the user to see—a range, some text, a graphic or other shape, or a field—is displayed in the window. The easiest way to do so is to use the `ScrollIntoView` method of the `Window` object. This method moves the view but not the selection, so if you need the selection to move as well, you'll need to write additional code to move it there.

The `ScrollIntoView` method takes the following syntax:

```
expression.ScrollIntoView(Obj, Start)
```

Here, *`expression`* is a required expression that returns a `Window` object. `Obj` is a required argument specifying a `Range` or `Shape` object. `Start` is an optional Boolean argument that you can set to `True` (the default) to have the upper-left corner of the range or shape displayed, or `False` to have the lower-right corner displayed. Specify `False` for `Start` when you need to make sure the end of a range or shape that may be larger than the window is displayed.

The following statements position the selection at the end of the last paragraph in the first list in the active document, ready to add a new paragraph to the list:

```
Dim rngFirstList As Range
Set rngFirstList = ActiveDocument.Lists(1).Range
ActiveDocument.Windows(1).ScrollIntoView Obj:=rngFirstList,
   Start:=False
rngFirstList.Select
Selection.Collapse Direction:=wdCollapseEnd
Selection.MoveLeft Unit:=wdCharacter, Count:=1, Extend:=wdMove
```

Changing a Document's View

To change a document's view, set the `Type` property of the `View` object for the appropriate window to `wdConflictView`, `wdMasterView`, `wdNormalView`, `wdOutlineView`, `wdPrintPreview`, `wdPrintView`, `wdReadingView`, or `wdWebView`. For example, the following statement changes the view for `Sample.docm` to Print Layout view:

```
Documents("Sample.docm").Windows(1).View.Type = wdPrintView
```

Switching to Read Mode

Read mode hides the Ribbon, any markup, and nearly everything else except the text itself. Panes, however, such as Navigation and Thesaurus, do remain visible. The text itself is usually displayed as two pages or three (depending on your zoom level) side by side as in a book. You cannot edit in this view. Here's how to switch to Read mode:

```
ActiveDocument.ActiveWindow.View.Type = wdReadingView
```

Read mode is thoughtfully designed to make the content as easy to read and remember as possible. For example, the zoom feature (lower right) adjusts the font size but repaginates (reflows) so you never have the struggle with moving a horizontal scroll bar to show hidden text. There *is* a scroll bar, but it's never needed to display text that's out of view because of the zoom level. The zoom bar is strictly for global document navigation and as an indicator of your current position.

Read mode also gives you some control over column width. Most people find it easier to read shorter lines of text, so you can adjust line length in the View menu. The Esc key exits Read mode.

Zooming the View to Display Multiple Pages

To zoom Print Layout view or Print Preview to display multiple pages, set the `PageColumns` and `PageRows` properties of the appropriate `View` object. (Change the view first if necessary.) The following statement displays `Sample.docm` in Print Layout view with six pages displayed (three across by two deep):

```
With Documents("Sample.docm").Windows(1).View
    .Type = wdPrintView
    With .Zoom
        .PageColumns = 3
        .PageRows = 2
    End With
End With
```

Working with Tables

Many people need to work with tables in their Word documents, either creating them from scratch or manipulating existing tables.

VBA uses a `Table` object to represent each individual table. If there is more than one `Table` object, they are gathered together into the `Tables` collection. To work with tables, you use the `Tables` property to return the `Tables` collection for the `Document`, `Range`, or `Selection` object in question.

Here is a sample of the collections and objects that are members of the `Tables` collection and the `Table` object:

- The `Rows` collection contains the rows in the table. Each row is represented by a `Row` object.
- The `Columns` collection contains the columns in the table. Each column is represented by a `Column` object.

- The `Cell` object provides access to a specified cell directly from the `Table` object. You can also reach the cells in the table by going through the row or column in which they reside.
- The `Range` object provides access to ranges within the table.
- The `Borders` collection contains all the borders for the table.
- The `Shading` object contains all the shading for the table.

For a complete list of the members of the `Table` object, see this web page:

`http://msdn.microsoft.com/en-us/library/office/ff195902.aspx`

The members of the `Tables` collection can be found here:

`http://msdn.microsoft.com/en-us/library/office/ff822892.aspx`

Creating a Table

To create a new table from scratch (rather than converting existing text to a table), use the `Add` method with the `Tables` collection. The `Add` method takes the following syntax for the `Tables` collection:

```
expression.Add(Range, NumRows, NumColumns, DefaultTableBehavior, AutoFitBehavior)
```

The arguments are as follows:

- *`expression`* is a required expression that returns a `Tables` collection. Typically, you'll want to use the `Tables` collection for the appropriate document.
- `Range` is a required argument supplying the range where you want to insert the table. If the range is a selection (rather than being a collapsed selection, or insertion point), the table replaces the range.
- `NumRows` is a required Long argument specifying the number of rows the table is to have.
- `NumColumns` is a required Long argument specifying the number of columns the table is to have.
- `DefaultTableBehavior` is an optional Variant argument specifying whether the table autofits its columns to their contents or to the window when you change the contents or the window width. Use `wdWord9TableBehavior` to have the table autofit its columns or `wdWord8TableBehavior` (the default) to have the columns retain their width.
- `AutoFitBehavior` is an optional Variant argument specifying the autofit behavior for the table. This argument applies only when `DefaultTableBehavior` is `wdWord9TableBehavior`. Use `wdAutoFitContent` to resize the columns to their contents, `wddAutoFitWindow` to resize the columns to the window width, or `wdAutoFitFixed` to use a fixed column width.

For example, the following statement inserts a new, blank, non-autofitting table containing 10 rows and 5 columns at the current position of the insertion point in the active document:

```
ActiveDocument.Tables.Add Range:=Selection.Range, NumRows:=10, _
    NumColumns:=5, DefaultTableBehavior:=wdWord8TableBehavior
```

Selecting a Table

To select a table, specify the `Document`, `Range`, or `Selection` object involved, and then identify the `Table` object and use the `Select` method. This method takes no arguments.

The following statement selects the first table in the active document:

```
ActiveDocument.Tables(1).Select
```

The following statements declare the variable `tempTable` and then select the first table in the document named `Log.docm` and assign its `Range` object to `tempTable`:

```
Dim tempTable
Documents("Log.docm").Tables(1).Select
Set tempTable = Selection.Tables(1).Range
```

The following statement selects the second table in the range named `tempRange`:

```
tempRange.Tables(2).Select
```

This statement selects the first table in the current selection:

```
Selection.Tables(1).Select
```

Converting Text to a Table

To convert ordinary text to a table (as opposed to inserting a new table from scratch), use the `ConvertToTable` method with an appropriate `Range` or `Selection` object. The `ConvertToTable` method takes the following syntax:

```
expression.ConvertToTable(Separator, NumRows, NumColumns,
   InitialColumnWidth, Format, ApplyBorders, ApplyShading, ApplyFont,
   ApplyColor, ApplyHeadingRows, ApplyLastRow, ApplyFirstColumn,
   ApplyLastColumn, AutoFit, AutoFitBehavior, DefaultTableBehavior)
```

The arguments are as follows:

- *`expression`* is a required argument specifying an expression that returns a `Range` object or a `Selection` object.
- `Separator` is an optional Variant argument specifying the separator character (also known as the *delimiter* character) to use to mark where the column divisions were. You can use these values for `Separator`:
  - `wdSeparateByCommas` separates column information at commas.
  - `wdSeparateByDefaultListSeparator` separates column information at the currently specified Other list separator character (the character shown in the text box alongside the Other option button in the Convert Table To Text dialog box).
  - `wdSeparateByParagraphs` separates column information at the paragraph marks.
  - `wdSeparateByTabs` (the default separator if you don't specify one) separates column information at tabs.

  - Alternatively, you can specify a single separator character of your choice as a string or between double quotation marks. For example, enter **`Separator:="|"`** to use a vertical bar [|] as the separator.
- `NumRows` is an optional Variant argument specifying the number of rows the table should have. If you omit the `NumRows` argument, Word decides the number of rows in the table based on the number of columns specified and/or the number of the chosen separator characters it finds.
- `NumColumns` is an optional Variant argument specifying the number of columns the table should have. As with `NumRows`, if you omit the `NumColumns` argument, Word decides the number of columns in the table based on the number of rows specified and/or the number of the chosen separator characters it finds.
- `InitialColumnWidth` is an optional Variant argument that you can use to specify the initial width (in points) of each column in the table. If you omit the `InitialColumnWidth` argument, Word uses the full width of the page—from margin to margin—and allocates an equal width to each column, regardless of the relative widths of the contents of the columns. The `InitialColumnWidth` argument is useful primarily for restraining tables from using the full width of the page automatically. In many cases, autofitting the columns provides a better solution.
- `Format` is an optional Variant argument that you can use to specify one of Word's built-in autoformat styles for tables. To use the `Format` argument, specify the appropriate `WdTableFormat` constant (such as `wdTableFormatElegant` to specify the Elegant autoformat style). If you choose to apply a format, you can specify which properties of the autoformat style to apply to the table by using the following optional Variant arguments:
  - Set `ApplyBorders` to `True` to apply the border formatting, or to `False` not to apply it.
  - Set `ApplyShading` to `True` to apply the shading, or to `False` not to apply it.
  - Set `ApplyFont` to `True` to apply the font formatting, or to `False` not to apply it.
  - Set `ApplyColor` to `True` to apply the color formatting, or to `False` not to apply it.
  - Set `ApplyHeadingRows` to `True` to apply any heading-row formatting, or to `False` not to apply it.
  - Set `ApplyLastRow` to `True` to apply any last-row formatting, or to `False` not to apply it.
  - Set `ApplyFirstColumn` to `True` to apply any first-column formatting, or to `False` not to apply it.
  - Set `ApplyLastColumn` to `True` to apply any last-column formatting, or to `False` not to apply it.
- `AutoFit` is an optional Variant argument you can set to `True` to have Word adjust the column width to best fit whatever contents are in the cells. When autofitting, Word doesn't increase the overall width of the table—it either reduces or retains the table's width.
- `AutoFitBehavior` and `DefaultTableBehavior` are as described in the section "Creating a Table," earlier in the chapter.

The following statement converts the current selection to a five-column table, *delimiting* (separating) the information at commas. It applies autofitting to the table based on cell content and sets the cells to resize automatically:

```
Set myTable = Selection.ConvertToTable(wdSeparateByCommas, _
    Selection.Paragraphs.Count, 5, , , , , , , , , , , True, _
    wdAutoFitContent, wdWord9TableBehavior)
```

Ensuring That a Selection Is Within a Table

Before running any procedure that is intended to manipulate a table, it's a good idea to make sure the current selection actually is within a table. Use the `wdWithInTable` argument of the `Information` property for the selection. `wdWithInTable` is Boolean, returning `True` if the selection is in a table and `False` if it isn't. Here's an example:

```
If Selection.Information(wdWithInTable) = True Then
    'take actions here
End If
```

Finding Out Where a Selection Is Within a Table

In addition to establishing whether the selection is in a table, you can use the `Information` property to find out other information that can be useful when working with tables via a `Range` object or `Selection` object.

Once you've established that the selection is within a table (probably by using the `wdWithInTable` argument), check whether the selection is at an end-of-row marker rather than being in a cell. If the selection is at an end-of-row marker, certain actions fail. For example, attempting to select the current cell or column fails because the selection is outside any cell or column, but attempting to select the current row succeeds.

To check whether the selection is at the end-of-row marker, use the `AtEndOfRowMarker` argument for the `Information` property. The following statement moves the selection left one character (into the last cell in the same row) if the selection is at the end-of-row marker:

```
If Selection.Information(wdAtEndOfRowMarker) = True Then _
    Selection.MoveLeft Unit:=wdCharacter, Count:=1
```

If the selection contains the end-of-row marker rather than being a collapsed selection (an insertion point) before the marker, the `wdAtEndOfRowMarker` argument returns `False`. To avoid a selected end-of-row marker causing problems in your procedures, collapse the selection if it isn't collapsed before checking whether it's at the end-of-row marker. The following statements do this, using a variable named `curSel` to restore the selection it collapses unless collapsing the selection leaves the selection at an end-of-row marker:

```
Dim curSel
With Documents("Communications.docm")
    If Selection.Type <> wdSelectionIP Then
        Set curSel = Selection.Range
        Selection.Collapse Direction:=wdCollapseStart
    End If
```

```
    If Selection.Information(wdAtEndOfRowMarker) = True Then
        Selection.MoveLeft Unit:=wdCharacter, Count:=1, Extend:=wdMove
    Else
        If curSel <> "" Then curSel.Select
        Set curSel = Nothing
    End If
End With
```

After establishing that the selection is safely in a table, you can retrieve six useful pieces of information about the table:

- wdStartOfRangeColumnNumber returns the number of the column in which the beginning of the selection or range falls. The following statement selects the column in which the current selection begins:

  ```
  Selection.Tables(1).Columns(Selection.Information _
      (wdStartOfRangeColumnNumber)).Select
  ```

- wdEndOfRangeColumnNumber returns the number of the column in which the end of the selection or range falls. The following statements delete the column in which the range testRange ends if the range is more than one column wide:

  ```
  With testRange
      If .Information(wdStartOfRangeColumnNumber) <> _
          .Information(wdEndOfRangeColumnNumber) Then _
          .Tables(1).Columns(.Information _
          (wdEndOfRangeColumnNumber)).Delete
  End With
  ```

- wdStartOfRangeRowNumber returns the number of the row in which the beginning of the selection or range falls.
- wdEndOfRangeRowNumber returns the number of the row in which the end of the selection or range falls.
- wdMaximumNumberOfColumns returns the highest number of columns in any row in the selection or range.
- wdMaximumNumberOfRows returns the highest number of rows in the specified selection or range in the table.

Sorting a Table

To sort a table, identify the table and use the Sort method. Sort takes the following syntax with the Table object:

```
expression.Sort(ExcludeHeader, FieldNumber, SortFieldType, SortOrder,
   FieldNumber2, SortFieldType2, SortOrder2, FieldNumber3,
   SortFieldType3, SortOrder3, CaseSensitive, BidiSort, IgnoreThe,
   IgnoreKashida, IgnoreDiacritics, IgnoreHe, LanguageID)
```

The arguments are as follows:

- *expression* is an expression that returns a `Table` object.
- `ExcludeHeader` is an optional Variant argument that you can set to `True` to exclude the first row in the table (which is often the table header row) from the sort, or to `False` to include the first row in the table.
- `FieldNumber`, `FieldNumber2`, and `FieldNumber3` are optional Variant arguments specifying the first, second, and third fields by which to sort (respectively). Usually you'll want to specify at least `FieldNumber`; if you don't, Word performs an alphanumeric sort on the table.
- `SortFieldType`, `SortFieldType2`, and `SortFieldType3` are optional Variant arguments specifying the type of sorting you want to use for `FieldNumber`, `FieldNumber2`, and `FieldNumber3`, respectively. For U.S. English, the options are alphanumeric sorting (`wdSortFieldAlphanumeric`, the default), numeric sorting (`wdSortFieldNumeric`), and date sorting (`wdSortFieldDate`).
- `SortOrder`, `SortOrder2`, and `SortOrder3` are optional Variant arguments specifying the sorting order for `FieldNumber`, `FieldNumber2`, and `FieldNumber3`. Use `wdSortOrderAscending` to specify an ascending sort (the default) or `wdSortOrderDescending` to specify a descending sort.
- `CaseSensitive` is an optional Variant argument that you can set to `True` to specify case-sensitive sorting. The default setting is `False`.
- The next five arguments (`BidiSort`, `IgnoreThe`, `IgnoreKashida`, `IgnoreDiacritics`, and `IgnoreHe`) are for specialized sorting (such as right-to-left languages, Arabic, and Hebrew).
- `LanguageID` is an optional Variant argument that you can use to specify the language in which to sort. For example, to sort in Lithuanian, you could specify `wdLithuanian` for `LanguageID`. For sorting in your default language, you can omit this argument.

Adding a Column to a Table

To add a column to a table, use the `Add` method with the `Columns` collection for the appropriate `Table` object. The `Add` method takes the following syntax for the `Columns` collection:

```
expression.Add [BeforeColumn]
```

Here, *expression* is a required expression that returns a `Columns` collection, and `BeforeColumn` is an optional Variant argument specifying the column to the left of which you want to insert the new column.

The following example uses the `Count` property to check the number of columns in the first table in the active document. If this table contains fewer than five columns, one or more columns are added to bring the number of columns up to five. Each new column is added before (to the left of) the existing last column in the table:

```
With ActiveDocument.Tables(1)
    .Select
```

```
    If .Columns.Count < 5 Then
        Do Until .Columns.Count = 5
            .Columns.Add BeforeColumn:=.Columns(.Columns.Count)
        Loop
    End If
End With
```

Deleting a Column from a Table

To delete a column, identify it (for example, use the number 1 as in the following statement), and then use the `Delete` method. `Delete` takes no arguments. The following statement deletes the first column in the table referenced by the object variable `myTable`:

```
myTable.Columns(1).Delete
```

Setting the Width of a Column

You can set the width of a column by using the `AutoFit` method, by using the `SetWidth` method, or by specifying the `Width` property for the column.

The `AutoFit` method resizes each column automatically to a width suitable to its contents. `AutoFit` takes no arguments. The following statement uses the `AutoFit` method to resize each column in the first table in the active document:

```
ActiveDocument.Tables(1).Columns.AutoFit
```

The `SetWidth` method allows you to set the width of one or more columns and specify how the other columns in the table should change as a result. The syntax for the `SetWidth` method is as follows:

```
expression.SetWidth ColumnWidth, RulerStyle
```

Here, *`expression`* is an expression that returns the `Columns` collection or `Column` object that has the width you want to set. `ColumnWidth` is a required Single argument specifying the width of the column or columns, measured in points. `RulerStyle` is a required Long argument that specifies how Word should adjust the width of the columns:

- The default value, `wdAdjustNone`, sets all the specified columns to the specified width, moving other columns to the left or right as necessary. This argument is analogous to Shift+dragging a column border when working interactively.
- `wdAdjustFirstColumn` applies the specified width to the first specified column, adjusting only as many columns to the right of this column as necessary. For example, widening the first column in a table slightly causes Word to narrow the second column but leave the third and subsequent columns unchanged. Widening the first column significantly causes Word to narrow the second and third columns, leaving the fourth and subsequent columns unchanged. This argument is analogous to dragging a column border when working interactively.
- `wdAdjustProportional` applies the specified width to the first specified column, keeping the right edge of the table in its previous position and adjusting all nonspecified columns proportionally to accommodate the change.

- `wdAdjustSameWidth` applies the specified width to the first specified column, keeping the right edge of the table in its previous position and adjusting all the other columns to an identical width to accommodate the change. This argument is analogous to Ctrl+dragging a column border when working interactively.

The following statement sets the width of the second column in the first table in the active document to 50 points, adjusting the columns to the right of the second column proportionally:

```
ActiveDocument.Tables(1).Columns(2).SetWidth ColumnWidth:=50, _
    RulerStyle:=wdAdjustProportional
```

The `Width` property lets you change the width of a column without worrying about the effect on the other columns. Specify the width you want in points, as in this example:

```
ActiveDocument.Tables(11).Columns(44).Width = 100
```

Selecting a Column

To select a column, use the `Select` method with the appropriate `Column` object. `Select` takes no arguments. The following statement selects the second column in the third table in the document named `Originals.docm`:

```
Documents("Originals.docm").Tables(3).Columns(2).Select
```

Adding a Row to a Table

To add a row, use the `Add` method with the `Rows` collection for the table. The `Add` method takes the following syntax for the `Rows` collection:

```
expression.Add [BeforeRow]
```

Here, *`expression`* is a required expression that returns a `Rows` object, and `BeforeRow` is an optional Variant argument specifying the row before which you want to add the new row. If you omit `BeforeRow`, VBA adds the new row after the last row in the table.

The following statement adds a new first row to the table referenced by the object variable `myTable`:

```
myTable.Rows.Add BeforeRow:=1
```

You can also insert a row into a table at the current selection, using the `InsertRowsBelow` or `InsertRowsAbove` method. You specify how many rows. In this example, one row is inserted below the current selection:

```
Selection.InsertRowsBelow 1
```

Deleting a Row from a Table

To delete a row, use the `Delete` method with the appropriate `Row` object. The `Delete` method takes no arguments. The following statement deletes the first row in the table referenced by the object variable `myTable`:

```
myTable.Rows(1).Delete
```

Setting the Height of One or More Rows

You can set the height of rows by letting Word set the row height automatically, by using the `SetHeight` method to specify an exact height or a minimum height, or by setting the `Height` property of the row or rows directly.

To have Word set the height of a row automatically, set the row's `HeightRule` property to `wdRowHeightAuto`. Word then adjusts the height of the row to accommodate the cell with the tallest contents. The following statement sets the `HeightRule` property for the second row in the fourth table in the active document to `wdRowHeightAuto`:

```
ActiveDocument.Tables(4).Rows(2).HeightRule = wdRowHeightAuto
```

To specify an exact height or a minimum height for one or more rows, use the `SetHeight` method with the row or rows. The syntax for the `SetHeight` property is as follows:

```
expression.SetHeight RowHeight, [HeightRule]
```

Here, *expression* is an expression that returns a `Row` object or a `Rows` collection. `HeightRule` is a required Variant argument specifying the rule for setting the row height: use `wdRowHeightAtLeast` to specify a minimum height or `wdRowHeightExactly` to specify an exact height. (The third setting for `HeightRule` is `wdRowHeightAuto`, which specifies automatic row height and which you won't want to use in this case.)

Instead of using the `SetHeight` method, you can set the `Height` property of the row or rows in question by specifying the height in points:

```
Documents("Tables.docm").Tables(3).Rows(3).Height = 33
```

Selecting a Row

To select a row, use the `Select` method for the appropriate `Row` object. The `Select` method takes no arguments. The following statement selects the last row in the last table in the document named `Tables.docm`:

```
Documents("Tables.docm").Tables(.Tables.Count).Rows.Last.Select
```

Inserting a Cell

To insert a cell, use the `Add` method with the `Cells` collection. The `Add` method takes the following syntax for the `Cells` collection:

```
expression.Add [BeforeCell]
```

Here, *expression* is an expression that returns a `Cells` collection, and `BeforeCell` is an optional Variant argument that specifies the cell to the left of which the new cell should be inserted. (If you omit the `BeforeCell` argument, VBA adds a new row of cells to the end of the table if you're using the `Cells` collection of the `Columns` collection, or it adds a new cell to the first row in the table if you're using the `Cells` collection of the `Rows` collection.)

The following statement inserts a cell before the second cell in the first row of the first table in the document named `Tables.docm`:

```
Documents("Tables.docm").Tables(1).Rows(1).Cells.Add _
    BeforeCell:=Documents("Tables.docm").Tables(1).Rows(1).Cells(2)
```

Returning the Text in a Cell

To return (fetch) the contents of a cell, use the Text property of the Range object for the cell. The following statement returns the text in the first cell in the second row of the third table in the active document and assigns it to the variable strCellText:

```
strCellText = ActiveDocument.Tables(3).Rows(2).Cells(1).Range.Text
```

Because the Text property includes the end-of-cell marker (which takes up two characters), you'll usually want to strip off the last two characters when assigning the Text property to a string, like this:

```
strCellText = ActiveDocument.Tables(3).Rows(2).Cells(1).Range.Text
strCellText = Left(strCellText, Len(strCellText) - 2)
```

When using the Range object, you can work with any of the objects and collections it contains. For example, to work with the paragraphs in a cell, use the Paragraphs collection.

Entering Text in a Cell

To enter text in a cell, assign the text to the Text property of the Range object for the cell. The following statements enter text in the first three cells in the first row of the current selection:

```
With Selection.Tables(1).Rows(1)
    .Cells(1).Range.Text = "Sample text in first cell."
    .Cells(2).Range.Text = "Sample text in second cell."
    .Cells(3).Range.Text = "Sample text in third cell."
End With
```

Deleting Cells

To delete cells, use the Delete method with the appropriate Cell object or Cells collection. When you delete one or more cells, you must specify what happens to the rest of the table—whether the cells to the right of those you deleted move to the left or whether the cells below those you deleted move up.

The syntax for the Delete method for the Cells collection and the Cell object is as follows:

```
expression.Delete [ShiftCells]
```

Here, *expression* is an expression that returns a Cells collection or a Cell object. ShiftCells is an optional Variant argument that specifies how the cells below or to the right of the deleted cell or cells should move. Use these values:

- wdDeleteCellsEntireColumn deletes the whole column in which the specified cell (or cells) is located.
- wdDeleteCellsEntireRow deletes the whole row.
- wdDeleteCellsShiftLeft moves cells across to the left to fill the gap.
- wdDeleteCellsShiftUp moves cells up to fill the gap.

The following statement deletes the first cell in the first row of the first table in the active document and shifts the other cells in the first row to the left to fill the gap:

```
ActiveDocument.Tables(1).Rows(1).Cells(1).Delete _
    ShiftCells:=wdDeleteCellsShiftLeft
```

For macros that rely on the user to make a selection within a table, you may want to determine how many rows or columns are in the selection before deciding how to shift the cells. The following example checks the number of rows and columns in a selection. If the selection is only one cell, or if the selection is all in one column, the code deletes the cell or cells and moves the other cells in the row to the left. If the selection is multiple cells in one column, the code deletes the cells and moves the other cells in the column up. If the selection spans columns and rows, the code displays a message box asking the user to make a selection in only one row or only one column:

```
With Selection
    If .Columns.Count > 1 And .Rows.Count > 1 Then
        MsgBox "Please select cells in only one row " _
            & "or only one column."
        End
    Else
        If .Cells.Count > 1 Then
            If .Columns.Count > 1 Then
                .Cells.Delete ShiftCells:=wdDeleteCellsShiftUp
            Else
                .Cells.Delete ShiftCells:=wdDeleteCellsShiftLeft
            End If
        Else
            .Cells.Delete ShiftCells:=wdDeleteCellsShiftLeft
        End If
    End If
End With
```

Selecting a Range of Cells

To select a range of cells within a table, declare a Range variable, assign to it the cells you want to select, and then select the range. The following example declares the Range variable `myCells`, assigns to it the first four cells in the first table in the active document, and then selects the range:

```
Dim myCells As Range
With ActiveDocument
    Set myCells = .Range(Start:=.Tables(1).Cell(1, 1).Range.Start, _
        End:=.Tables(1).Cell(1, 4).Range.End)
    myCells.Select
End With
```

Converting a Table or Rows to Text

To convert an entire table or a row or number of rows to text, specify the table, row, or rows and use the `ConvertToText` method. This is frequently useful if you're copying and pasting from Internet pages; they often contain tables and you just want the contents, the text, not the table structure itself. Due to the limitations of the HTML language used to describe web page layout, HTML tables are sometimes used for spacing and other reasons unrelated to displaying actual tabular data. These faux "tables" can look bizarre when pasted as text into Word or other body text. To see how to get rid of these annoying artifacts, see the example macro at the end of this section. It's a useful macro to add to your Normal project in Word's VBA Editor.

The `ConvertToText` method takes the following syntax:

```
expression.ConvertTotext(Separator, Nested Tables)
```

Here, *`expression`* is a required expression that returns a `Table` object, a `Row` object, or a `Rows` collection. `Separator` is an optional Variant argument specifying the separator character (also known as the *delimiter* character) to use to mark where the column divisions were. The possible values are as follows:

- `wdSeparateByCommas` separates column information by commas.
- `wdSeparateByDefaultListSeparator` separates column information by the currently specified Other list-separator character (the character shown in the text box alongside the Other option button in the Convert Table To Text dialog box).
- `wdSeparateByParagraphs` separates column information with paragraph marks.
- `wdSeparateByTabs` (the default separator if you don't specify one) separates column information by tabs.
- Alternatively, you can specify a separator character of your choice as a string or between double quotation marks. For example, enter **`Separator:="|"`** to use a vertical bar [|] as the separator. (Although you can supply more than one separator character here, Word uses only the first character.)

The following statement converts the first table in the current selection to text using an asterisk (*) as the separator character:

```
Selection.Tables(1).ConvertToText Separator:="*"
```

You can use the `ConvertToText` method with a `Table` object, a `Row` object, or a `Rows` collection. The following statement converts only the first row of the selected table to tab-delimited text:

```
Selection.Tables(1).Rows(1).ConvertToText Separator:=wdSeparateByTabs
```

If you need to continue working with the contents of the table once you've converted it, assign a range to the table as you convert it. You can then work with the `Range` object afterward to manipulate the information. For example, the following statements convert the first table in the document named `Cleveland Report.docm` to text separated by paragraphs and assign the range exTable to the converted information and then copy the range, create a new document, and paste in the information:

```
Dim exTable As Range
Set exTable = Documents("Cleveland Report.docm").Tables(1). _
    ConvertToText(Separator:=wdSeparateByParagraphs)
exTable.Copy
Documents.Add
Selection.Paste
```

Often when you copy and paste information from a web page, it's in a tabular format. If you paste such tables into Word, it usually doesn't look right, is too bulky, and can be difficult to edit or format. In other words, you want to remove the web-page table definitions but leave the data in a usable format within Word.

The following macro does just that:

```
Sub Untable()

On Error Resume Next

   Selection.Rows.ConvertToText Separator:=wdSeparateByCommas, NestedTables:= _
     True
   Selection.MoveDown Unit:=wdLine, Count:=1

If Err Then MsgBox "No table was detected, dude."

End Sub
```

To use this macro, click somewhere within the text you've pasted from the Internet to put the insertion cursor in a table (or a suspected table; they often don't look like tables, merely like an area of bizarre formatting), and then execute the macro. You may need to execute this macro more than once to completely eliminate all the tabular formatting debris left over from the original HTML. The macro tells you when all table structures have been destroyed, and not only that—it calls you "dude."

The Bottom Line

Use Find and Replace via VBA. Word's Find and Replace utilities are frequently valuable to the VBA programmer. You'll want to master them and also some subtleties associated with their use.

Master It Sometimes when replacing, you need to go through a document more than once—using a loop structure. Why would you ever need to repeatedly search and replace the same document? Doesn't the Replace All setting in fact *replace all*?

Work with headers, footers, and page numbers. All Word documents contain headers and footers, even if they are empty. In addition, you can insert various types of headers and footers.

Master It Name two types of headers you can use in a Word document.

Manage sections, page setup, windows, and views. Among the various ways you can view a document, you sometimes want to have the document automatically scroll to a particular table, graphic, or other target.

Master It What method of the `Window` object can be used to easily accomplish this task?

Manipulate tables. When you need to manage tables in Word documents, you can employ VBA to work with the `Table` object to represent a single table. If there is more than one table, they are referenced by a collection of `Table` objects.

Master It Name two important and useful objects within the `Tables` collection or the `Table` object.

Chapter 22

Understanding the Excel Object Model and Key Objects

This chapter shows you how to start working with the Excel object model, the architecture underlying Excel. It also shows you how to perform common tasks with the most frequently useful Excel objects. These objects include the `Workbooks` collection and the `Workbook` object, the `ActiveCell` object, and `Range` objects. You'll also see how to set options in Excel.

IN THIS CHAPTER, YOU WILL LEARN TO DO THE FOLLOWING:

- Work with workbooks
- Work with worksheets
- Work with the active cell or selection
- Work with ranges
- Set options

Getting an Overview of the Excel Object Model

As with the other Office applications, it's not necessary (or even possible for most people) to understand how the entire Excel object model fits together in order to work with VBA in Excel. However, you'll find that knowing a bit about the main objects in the object model is helpful. And as usual, the code examples in the Help system's object-model reference are invaluable—showing you how and where to employ objects in your own programming.

To see the Excel object-model reference, follow these steps:

1. Launch or activate Excel, and then press Alt+F11 to launch or activate the VBA Editor.
2. In the Editor, choose Help ➤ MSDN On The Web.
3. Click the magnifying glass in the upper-right corner of the MSDN home page, type **excel 2015 object model**, and press Enter.
4. Click the Object model (Excel VBA reference) link. You'll now have access (in the left pane of this web page) to the whole collection of syntax specifications, useful descriptions, and code examples, as shown in Figure 22.1.

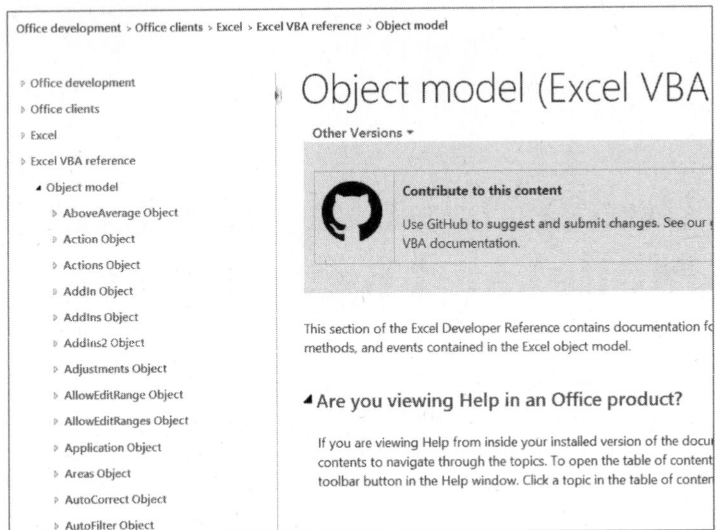

FIGURE 22.1
The entries in the Excel object model reference will help you write your own VBA code.

HELP WHEN MIGRATING LEGACY CODE FROM EARLIER OFFICE PROJECTS

If you've inherited VBA code written in earlier versions of Office, those procedures might contain objects, methods, and properties that have since been changed. It's unlikely, but possible. Remember that modifications to object models are generally few, but some incompatibilities can crop up and "break" the code so it won't run correctly. Fortunately, you can download a free utility, the Office Code Compatibility Inspector, which will flag objects and their members that have changed. It does a text comparison of the current Office object model against VBA code written in earlier versions of Office. After checking the system requirements and installation information, you can download the Compatibility Inspector from this web page:

`www.microsoft.com/en-us/download/details.aspx?id=15001`

Understanding Excel's Creatable Objects

Excel *exposes* (makes available for your use in code) various *creatable* objects, meaning that you can employ most of the important objects in its object model without explicitly going through (mentioning) the `Application` object. For most programming purposes, these creatable objects are the most commonly used objects. Here's a list:

- The `Workbooks` collection contains the `Workbook` objects that represent all the open workbooks. Within a workbook, the `Sheets` collection contains the `Worksheet` objects that represent the worksheets and the `Chart` objects that represent chart sheets. On a sheet, the

Range object gives you access to ranges, which can be anything from an individual cell to a complete worksheet. Remember that, because the workbooks object is creatable, you need not write Application.Workbooks in your code. You can leave off the Application and merely write Workbooks.

- The ActiveWorkbook object represents the currently active workbook.
- The ActiveSheet object represents the active worksheet.
- The Windows collection contains the Window objects that represent all the open windows.
- The ActiveWindow object represents the active window. When using this object, be sure to check that the window it represents is the type of window you want to manipulate, because the object returns whatever window currently has the focus.
- The ActiveCell object represents, you guessed it, the active cell. This object is especially valuable for simple procedures (for example, those that compute values or correct formatting) that work on a cell selected by the user.

Managing Workbooks

In many of your Excel procedures, you'll need to manipulate workbooks: creating new workbooks, saving them in various locations and formats, opening, closing, and printing them. To accomplish these tasks, you employ the Workbooks collection, which contains a Workbook object for each open workbook in Excel.

Creating a Workbook

To create a new workbook, use the Add method with the Workbooks collection. The syntax is as follows:

```
Workbooks.Add(Template)
```

Here, Template is an optional Variant argument that specifies how to create the workbook. The following subsections discuss the available options.

Creating a New Blank Workbook

To create a blank workbook (same as if you'd clicked the File tab on the Ribbon and then clicked the New button), omit the Template argument:

```
Workbooks.Add
```

The new workbook receives the number of sheets specified in the Excel Options dialog box. (Click the File tab on the Ribbon, and then choose Options to display the When Creating New Workbooks section of the dialog box—you'll see a field where you can specify the Include This Many Sheets option. The default is one.)

You can get or set this value in VBA by using the SheetsInNewWorkbook property of the Application object. For example, the following macro declares an Integer variable named mySiNW, stores the current SheetsInNewWorkbook property in it, sets the SheetsInNewWorkbook property to 12, creates a new workbook (with those 12 worksheets), and then restores the `SheetsInNewWorkbook` setting to its previous value:

```
Sub MVBA_New_Workbook_with_12_Sheets()
    Dim mySiNW As Integer
    mySiNW = Application.SheetsInNewWorkbook
    Application.SheetsInNewWorkbook = 12
    Workbooks.Add
    Application.SheetsInNewWorkbook = mySiNW
End Sub
```

Creating a New Workbook Based on a Template

To create a workbook based on a template, specify the full path and name of the template file. For example, the following statement creates a new workbook based on the template `Balance Sheet.xlt` in a network folder `\\server\template\excel`:

```
Workbooks.Add Template:= "\\server\template\excel\Balance Sheet.xlt"
```

Creating a New Workbook Based on an Existing Workbook

To create a workbook based on an existing workbook, specify the full name and path of the workbook file. For example, the following statement creates a new workbook based on the existing workbook named `Personnel.xlsx` in the `C:\Business` folder:

```
Workbooks.Add Template:= "C:\Business\Personnel.xlsx"
```

Creating a Chart Workbook, a Macro Sheet, or a Worksheet

You can also create a workbook that contains a single chart, macro sheet, or worksheet by using the constants shown in Table 22.1 with the `Template` argument.

Table 22.1: Constants for creating a chart workbook, macro sheet, or worksheet

Constant	Creates a Workbook Containing
`xlWBATChart`	A chart sheet
`xlWBATExcel4IntlMacroSheet`	An international macro sheet
`xlWBATExcel4MacroSheet`	A macro sheet
`xlWBATWorksheet`	A worksheet

For example, the following statement creates a workbook containing a single chart sheet:

```
Workbooks.Add Template:=xlWBATChart
```

Saving a Workbook

The first time you save a workbook, you must specify the path and filename to use (this is the SaveAs option). After that, you can save the workbook under the same name and path by default, or you can specify a different path, name, format, or all three (this is the Save option).

SAVING A WORKBOOK FOR THE FIRST TIME OR AS A DIFFERENT FILE

To save a workbook for the first time, or to save a workbook using a different path, name, or format, use the SaveAs method. The syntax is as follows:

```
expression.SaveAs(FileName, FileFormat, Password, WriteResPassword,
   ReadOnlyRecommended, CreateBackup, AccessMode, ConflictResolution,
   AddToMru, TextCodePage, TextVisualLayout, Local)
```

The components of the syntax are as follows:

- *expression* is a required expression that returns a Workbook object.
- FileName is an optional Variant argument that specifies the name for the workbook. If you omit FileName, VBA uses the current folder and the default filename of Book*n*.xlsx for a workbook, where *n* is the next available number (for example, Book5.xlsx).

  VBA uses the default file format, which is specified in the Options dialog box's Save page. (Click the File tab on the Ribbon, then click Options to display the Options dialog box, and then click the Save button on the left. You'll see a Save Files In This Format drop-down list.)

  You can get and set the default save format by using the DefaultSaveFormat property of the Application object. For example, the following statement sets the default save format to xlNormal, the "Excel Workbook" format:

  ```
  Application.DefaultSaveFormat = xlNormal
  ```

- FileFormat is an optional Variant argument that specifies the format in which to save the workbook. Table 22.2 lists the XlFileFormat constants for specifying commonly used formats.

> **BE CAREFUL NOT TO ACCIDENTALLY OVERWRITE A FILE**
>
> When saving a workbook to a folder, you should check whether a workbook with the same name already exists in the folder. If it does, and unless you prevent it, VBA overwrites it without warning, causing data loss. See "Using the Dir Function to Check Whether a File Exists" in Chapter 9, "Using Built-In Functions," for instructions on how to check whether a file with a particular filename already exists.

- `Password` is an optional Variant argument that you can use to supply the password that is to be required to open the workbook (the "password to open"). `Password` is case-sensitive. If the user can't provide the password, Excel won't open the workbook.
- `WriteResPassword` is an optional Variant argument that you can use to supply the password that is required to open the workbook in a writable form (the "password to modify"). `WriteResPassword` is case-sensitive. If the user can't provide the password, Excel will open the workbook as read-only.
- `ReadOnlyRecommended` is an optional Variant argument that you can set to `True` to have Excel recommend that the user open the document as read-only. Such recommendations are easily ignored, so if you want to lock a workbook to prevent others from modifying it, you'd do better to employ a "password to modify."
- `CreateBackup` is an optional Variant argument that you can set to `True` to make Excel automatically create a backup of the workbook. The default setting is `False`.
- `AccessMode` is an optional argument that you can use to specify whether the workbook is shared or is in Exclusive mode. Specify `xlExclusive` for Exclusive mode, `xlShared` for Shared mode, and `xlNoChange` to leave the access mode unchanged (this is the default setting).
- `ConflictResolution` is an optional argument that you can use to specify how to resolve any conflicting changes to the workbook. Use `xlLocalSessionChanges` to accept the changes in the current Excel session, `xlOtherSessionChanges` to accept the other user's or users' changes, and `xlUserResolution` to display the Resolve Conflicts dialog box so that the user can choose how to resolve the conflicts.
- `AddToMru` is an optional Variant argument that you can set to `True` to add the workbook to the list of recently used files at the bottom of the File menu. The default setting is `False`.
- `TextCodePage` and `TextVisualLayout` are optional Variant arguments used in international versions of Excel (not in U.S. English Excel).
- `Local` is an optional Variant that controls whether the language used is that of Excel (`True`) or of VBA (`False`). (You'll seldom need to use `Local`.)

TABLE 22.2: `XlFileFormat` constants for widely used formats

CONSTANT	SAVES DOCUMENT AS
`xlNormal`	A normal workbook
`xlXMLSpreadsheet`	An XML spreadsheet
`xlWebArchive`	A single-file web page
`xlHtml`	A web page
`xlTemplate`	A template
`xlExcel9795`	An Excel workbook for Excel versions 95 and later

For example, the following statement saves the active workbook in the current folder under the name `Salaries.xlsx` and using the default save format:

```
ActiveWorkbook.SaveAs FileName:="Salaries.xlsx"
```

The following statement saves the open workbook named `Schedule.xlsx` under the name `Building Schedule.xlsx` in the folder named `\\server2\Public` using the Microsoft Excel 97–2003 & 5.0/95 format (from Excel 2003):

```
ActiveWorkbook.SaveAs Filename:="\\server2\Public\Building Schedule.xlsx", _
        FileFormat:=xlExcel9795
```

To see a complete list of all the Excel 2016 file formats, visit this web page:

`http://msdn.microsoft.com/en-us/library/office/ff198017.aspx`

Saving a Workbook That Has Already Been Saved

Once a workbook has been saved, you can just save it again with the same name by using the `Save` method. For a `Workbook` object, the `Save` method takes no arguments. For example, the following statement saves the workbook named `Data Book.xlsx`:

```
Workbooks("Data Book.xlsx").Save
```

Saving All Open Workbooks

The `Workbooks` collection doesn't have a `Save` method, but you can save all open workbooks by using a loop such as that shown in the following subroutine:

```
Sub Save_All_Workbooks()
    Dim myWorkbook As Workbook
    For Each myWorkbook In Workbooks
        myWorkbook.Save
    Next myWorkbook
End Sub
```

Note that if any of the currently opened workbooks have not been previously saved, and if they include any macros, a security message will be displayed when this procedure executes. Users are told that they must agree to save the potentially dangerous executable content in a macro-enabled file format (`.xlsm`). However, if the file has already been saved with the `.xlsm` filename extension, no message is displayed. If you want to suppress such messages, you can insert the following code at the start of this procedure:

```
Application.DisplayAlerts = False
```

However, be sure to set the `DisplayAlerts` property back to `True` as soon as you can in the code. This particular warning message is quite useful as a reminder to the user—so you likely won't want to suppress it.

Accessing Cloud Storage

Having VBA access OneDrive, Dropbox, or one of the other cloud storage systems is fairly easy. Just open from, or save a file to, the OneDrive or Dropbox folder.

The only thing to figure out is the file path, and it will look something like this: `"C:\Users\`*`Richard`*`\OneDrive\ExcelToCloudTest"`, with *`Richard`* replaced by your name.

This example saves the current document to OneDrive. Because this is a source of so many errors, I repeat: Change my name, *`Richard`*, to your username in the file path in this example code:

```
ActiveWorkbook.SaveAs ("C:\Users\Richard\OneDrive\ExcelCloudTest")
```

To save to Dropbox, it's pretty much the same:

```
ActiveWorkbook.SaveAs ("C:\Users\Richard\DropBox\ExcelCloudTest")
```

Opening a Workbook

To open a workbook, use the `Open` method with the `Workbooks` collection. The syntax is as follows:

```
expression.Open(FileName, UpdateLinks, ReadOnly, Format, Password,
   WriteResPassword, IgnoreReadOnlyRecommended, Origin, Delimiter,
   Editable, Notify, Converter, AddToMru, Local, CorruptLoad)
```

The components of the syntax are as follows:

- *`expression`* is a required expression that returns a `Workbooks` collection. Often, you'll want to use the `Workbooks` collection itself.
- `FileName` is a required String argument that supplies the path and name of the workbook to open.
- `UpdateLinks` is an optional Variant that controls how Excel updates any links in the workbook. If you leave out this argument, the user is prompted to specify how to update the links. Table 22.3 shows the values and their effects. If Microsoft Excel is opening a file in the WKS, WK1, or WK3 format and the `UpdateLinks` argument is `2`, Microsoft Excel generates charts from the graphs attached to the file. If the argument is `0`, no charts are created.
- `ReadOnly` is an optional Variant that you can set to `True` to open the workbook as read-only. The default is `False`.
- `Format` is an optional Variant that you can use to specify the delimiter character when opening a text file. Use `1` for tabs, `2` for commas, `3` for spaces, `4` for semicolons, `5` for no delimiter character, and `6` for a delimiter you specify using the `Delimiter` argument.
- `Password` is an optional Variant argument that you can use to provide the password required to open the workbook (the "password to open"). `Password` is case-sensitive. If you omit `Password` and a password is required, Excel prompts the user for it.

> **DON'T INCLUDE PASSWORDS IN YOUR PROCEDURES**
>
> It's usually best to avoid putting passwords in your code, because it may be possible for other people to read them.

- `WriteResPassword` is an optional Variant argument that you can use to provide the password required to open the workbook in a writable form (the "password to modify"). `WriteResPassword` is case-sensitive. If you omit `WriteResPassword` and a password is required, Excel prompts the user for it.
- `IgnoreReadOnlyRecommended` is an optional Variant argument that you can set to `True` to have Excel ignore a read-only recommendation on the workbook.
- `Origin` is an optional Variant argument that you can use when opening a text file to specify the operating system used to encode it and, thus, how to treat carriage-return/line-feed characters and character encoding. Use `xlWindows` to indicate Windows, `xlMacintosh` to indicate Mac OS, or `xlMSDOS` to indicate DOS.
- `Delimiter` is an optional Variant argument you can use with a `Format` value of `6` to specify one delimiter character to use when opening a text file.
- `Editable` is an optional Variant argument that you can set to `True` when `FileName` specifies a template to open the template itself rather than start a workbook based on the template (`False`). `Editable` also applies to Excel 4.0 add-ins: `True` opens the add-in in a visible window, while `False` opens the add-in hidden. However, you can't employ this option with add-ins created in Excel 5.0 or later.
- `Notify` is an optional Variant argument that you can set to `True` to have Excel add the workbook to the notification list when someone else has the workbook open for editing and VBA requests the workbook. Excel then notifies the user when the workbook becomes available. If you specify `Notify:=False`, opening the workbook fails if someone else has the workbook open.
- `Converter` is an optional Variant argument that you can use to specify the first file converter to use when opening a file.
- `AddToMru` is an optional Variant argument that you can set to `True` to add the workbook to the list of recently used files at the bottom of the File menu. The default setting is `False`.
- `Local` is an optional Variant that controls whether the language used is that of Excel (`True`) or of VBA (`False`). (You'll seldom need to use `Local`.)
- `CorruptLoad` is an optional Variant that you can use to control how Excel handles corruption it encounters when opening the workbook. Use `xlNormalLoad` to use normal behavior—first, opening the workbook as usual; second, repairing the file if there's a problem; and third, recovering the data from the workbook. Use `xrRepairFile` to go straight to the repair stage or `xlExtractData` to go straight to the recovery stage.

TABLE 22.3: Values for the `UpdateLinks` argument

VALUE	EFFECT
(If you omit this argument)	Excel prompts the user to decide how to update links.
1	User specifies how links are to be updated.

TABLE 22.3: Values for the `UpdateLinks` argument *(CONTINUED)*

VALUE	EFFECT
2	Links are never updated for this workbook when it's opened.
3	Excel always updates links for this workbook when opening it.

For example, the following statement opens the workbook named `Expenses.xlsx` stored in the `C:\Business` folder without updating links:

```
Workbooks.Open Filename:= "C:\Business\Expenses.xlsx", UpdateLinks:=0
```

The following statement opens the workbook named `Plan.xlsx` stored in the `D:\Planning` folder, providing the password for opening the workbook:

```
Workbooks.Open Filename:="D:\Planning\Plan.xlsx", Password:="s@cur1ng!"
```

The following statement opens the text file named `Data13.txt` in the folder `z:\transfer` using an exclamation point (`!`) as the delimiter character:

```
Workbooks.Open _
 Filename:="z:\transfer\Data13.txt", Format:=6,  Delimiter:="!"
```

Closing a Workbook

To close a workbook, use the `Close` method with the appropriate `Workbook` object. The syntax is as follows:

```
expression.Close(SaveChanges, Filename, RouteWorkbook)
```

The components of the syntax are as follows:

- *`expression`* is a required expression that returns a `Workbook` object or the `Workbooks` collection.
- `SaveChanges` is an optional Variant argument that lets you specify whether to save any unsaved changes in the workbook (`True`) or not (`False`). If you omit the `SaveChanges` argument, Excel prompts the user to save any workbook that contains unsaved changes.
- `Filename` is an optional Variant that you can use to specify the filename under which to save the workbook if it contains changes. In most cases, it's best to use the `SaveAs` method to save the workbook under a different name before you use the `Close` method to close it.
- `RouteWorkbook` is an optional Variant argument that you can set to `True` to route the workbook to the next recipient on its routing slip, or `False` to refrain from routing the workbook. If the workbook has no routing slip attached, `RouteWorkbook` has no effect.

For example, the following statement closes the active workbook without saving changes:

```
ActiveWorkbook.Close SaveChanges:=False
```

Closing All Open Workbooks

To close all open workbooks, use the `Close` method with the `Workbooks` collection:

```
Workbooks.Close
```

The `Close` method takes no arguments. Excel prompts you to save any workbook that contains unsaved changes. If such prompts will be inconvenient in a procedure, use a loop (for example, a `For Each…Next` loop with the `Workbooks` collection) to close each open workbook individually, using the `SaveChanges` argument to control whether Excel saves or discards any unsaved changes.

Sharing a Workbook

To determine whether a workbook is shared, check its `MultiUserEditing` property. This is a read-only Boolean property.

To share a workbook, use the `SaveAs` method (discussed in "Saving a Workbook for the First Time or as a Different File," earlier in this chapter) to save the file using the `xlShared` value for the `AccessMode` argument.

For example, the following statements share the workbook named `Brainstorming.xlsx` if it is not already shared:

```
With Workbooks("Brainstorming.xlsx")
    If MultiUserEditing = False Then
        .SaveAs Filename:=.FullName, AccessMode:=xlShared
    End If
End With
```

Protecting a Workbook

To protect a workbook, use the `Protect` method with the appropriate `Workbook` object. The syntax is as follows:

```
expression.Protect(Password, Structure, Windows)
```

The components of the syntax are as follows:

- *`expression`* is a required expression that returns a `Workbook` object.
- `Password` is an optional Variant argument that specifies the password for unprotecting the workbook. `Password` is case-sensitive. You'll almost always want to supply `Password`—if you don't, anybody who can open your workbook can unprotect it.
- `Structure` is an optional Variant argument that you can set to `True` to protect the workbook's structure (how the worksheets are positioned relative to each other) or leave at its default setting, `False`.
- `Windows` is an optional Variant argument that you can set to `True` to protect the workbook windows or omit to leave the windows unprotected.

For example, the following statement protects the structure and windows of the active workbook with the password `0llsecurd`:

```
ActiveWorkbook.Protect Password:="0llsecurd", Structure:=True, Windows:=True
```

> **YOU CAN PROTECT WORKBOOKS AGAINST BOTH WRITING (EDITING) AND READING**
>
> In addition to protecting a workbook against modifications, you can protect it against being opened and viewed. See the sidebar "Setting Passwords and Read-Only Recommendations for a Workbook" later in this chapter for details.

Working with the *ActiveWorkbook* Object

The `ActiveWorkbook` object returns a `Workbook` object that represents the active workbook (whichever workbook currently has the focus in the Excel window). The `ActiveWorkbook` object behaves like a `Workbook` object and is very useful in macros that users execute after opening the workbook they want to manipulate.

If no workbook is open, there is no `ActiveWorkbook` object, so any code that tries to use the `ActiveWorkbook` object returns an error. So, it's a good idea to verify that at least one workbook is open before trying to execute code that assumes there is an active workbook. One option is to check that the `ActiveWorkbook` object is not `Nothing` before running the code, as in the following example:

```
If ActiveWorkbook Is Nothing Then
    MsgBox "Please open a workbook and click in it before running this macro." _
        & vbCr & vbCr & "This macro will now end.", _
        vbOKOnly + vbExclamation, "No Workbook Is Open"
    End
End If
```

It's also a good idea to check that the workbook your code assumes is the active workbook actually *is* the active workbook. This problem can easily occur when a macro starts with the active workbook and then creates a new workbook to work in. The new workbook becomes the active workbook, and from this point on, the code may start accessing the wrong workbook.

If there's any doubt about which workbook you're working with, declare a `Workbook` object variable and use that object variable in your code rather than the `ActiveWorkbook` object. For example, the following statements declare a `Workbook` object variable and assign the `ActiveWorkbook` object to it. Now subsequent code can work with the object variable, which will not change to a different workbook:

```
Dim myWorkbook As Workbooks
Set myWorkbook = ActiveWorkbook
With myWorkbook
    'actions here
End With
```

Working with Worksheets

Most workbooks you need to manipulate via VBA will contain one or more worksheets. As a result, many macro procedures will need to work with worksheets—inserting them, deleting them, copying or moving them, or simply printing a range from them.

Each worksheet is represented by a `Sheet` object. The `Sheet` objects are contained within the `Sheets` collection.

Inserting a Worksheet

To insert a worksheet into a workbook, use the `Add` method with the `Sheets` collection. The syntax is as follows:

```
expression.Add(Before, After, Count, Type)
```

The components of the syntax are as follows:

- *`expression`* is a required expression that returns a `Sheets` collection. Often, you'll want to use the `Sheets` collection itself.
- `Before` is an optional Variant argument that specifies the sheet before which to add the new sheet. `After` is an optional Variant argument that specifies the sheet after which to add the new sheet. Typically, you'll want to specify either `Before` or `After`, but not both. You can also omit both arguments to make Excel insert the new sheet before the active worksheet.
- `Count` is an optional Variant argument that specifies how many sheets to add. If you omit `Count`, VBA uses the default value, `1`.
- `Type` is an optional Variant that specifies the type of sheet to insert. The default is `xlWorksheet`, a standard worksheet. You can also insert a chart sheet (`xlChart`), an Excel 4 macro sheet (`xlExcel4MacroSheet`), or an Excel 4 international macro sheet (`xlExcel4IntlMacroSheet`).

For example, the following statements declare a `Worksheet` object variable named `mySheet`, insert a worksheet before the first sheet in the first open workbook and assign the new sheet to `mySheet`, and then set the `Name` property of `mySheet` to `Summary` (the `Name` property controls the text that appears on the worksheet's tab):

```
Dim mySheet As Worksheet
Set mySheet = Workbooks(1).Sheets.Add(before:=Sheets(1))
mySheet.Name = "Summary"
```

If you run this macro, look for the new *`Summary`* worksheet on the tab at the bottom of your workbook.

The following statements insert two chart sheets after the last worksheet in the active workbook. The chart sheets receive default names, such as `Chart1` and `Chart2`:

```
ActiveWorkbook.Sheets.Add _
After:=Sheets(Sheets.Count), Count:=2, Type:=xlChart
```

Deleting a Worksheet

To delete a worksheet, use the `Delete` method of the appropriate `Sheet` object. The `Delete` method takes no arguments. For example, the following statement deletes the worksheet named `Summary` from the workbook referenced by the `myWorkbook` object variable:

```
Dim myWorkbook As Workbook
Set myWorkbook = Workbooks(1)

myWorkbook.Sheets("Summary").Delete
```

If you delete a worksheet, you lose any data stored on that worksheet; so when in interactive mode (the user is deleting via a keyboard, not a macro), Excel asks the user to confirm the deletion by default (see Figure 22.2).

However, in a macro you may want to avoid displaying this warning message. For example, in a procedure that adds a worksheet without the user's knowledge, uses it to manipulate data, and then deletes it, you simply don't need this alert dialog box. By default, it will not display when a delete is accomplished via a macro. However, if you do need your macro to suppress a dialog box, you can turn off alerts in Excel by setting the `DisplayAlerts` property of the `Application` object to `False` before executing the main macro code, and then turning alerts back on before exiting the macro, like this:

```
Application.DisplayAlerts = False
myWorkbook.Sheets("Summary").Delete
Application.DisplayAlerts = True
```

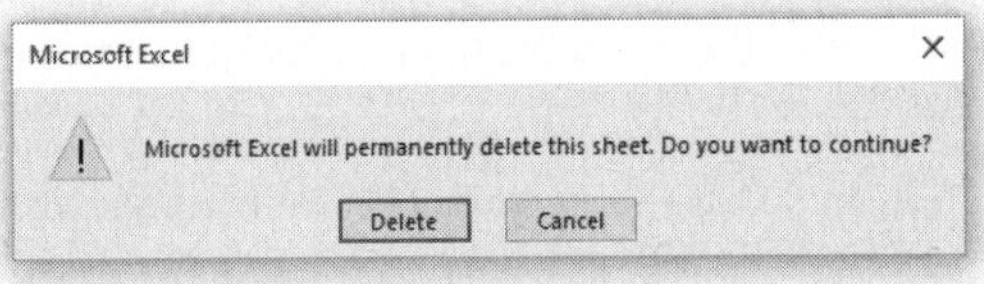

FIGURE 22.2
When deleting a worksheet by hand, Excel displays this warning dialog box.

Copying or Moving a Worksheet

To copy a worksheet, use the `Copy` method of the appropriate `Sheet` object. To move a worksheet, use the `Move` method. The syntax is as follows:

```
expression.Copy(Before, After)
expression.Move(Before, After)
```

Here, *`expression`* is a required expression that returns a `Worksheet` object. `Before` is an optional Variant argument that specifies the sheet before which to place the copy or the moved sheet. `After` is an optional Variant argument that specifies the sheet after which to place it:

- Typically, you'll want to specify either `Before` or `After`, but not both.
- You can specify another workbook by name to copy or move the worksheet to another workbook.
- You can also omit both arguments to make Excel create a new workbook containing the copied or moved sheet. The new workbook becomes the active workbook, so you can use the `ActiveWorkbook` object to start working with it or to assign it to an object variable.

For example, the following statement copies the worksheet named `Costs - Materials` in the workbook named `Building Schedule.xlsx`, placing the copy after the last of the current worksheets in the workbook:

```
Workbooks("Building Schedule.xlsx").Sheets("Costs - Materials").Copy, _
    After:=Sheets(Sheets.Count)
```

The following line of code moves the worksheet named `Homes` from the workbook named `Planning.xlsx` to the workbook named `Building Schedule.xlsx`, inserting the worksheet before the first existing worksheet in the workbook:

```
Workbooks("Planning.xlsx").Sheets("Homes").Move , _
   Before:=Workbooks("Building Schedule.xlsx").Sheets(1)
```

Printing a Worksheet

To print a worksheet, use the `PrintOut` method with the appropriate `Worksheet` object.

THE PrintOut METHOD CAN BE USED WITH SEVERAL OBJECTS

Several objects have `PrintOut` method. These objects include the `Worksheets` collection; the `Chart` object and the `Charts` collection; the `Workbook` object; the `Window` object; and the `Range` object.

The syntax for the `PrintOut` method is as follows:

```
expression.PrintOut(From, To, Copies, Preview, ActivePrinter,
   PrintToFile, Collate, PrToFileName, IgnorePrintAreas)
```

The components of the syntax are as follows:

- *`expression`* is a required expression that returns the appropriate `Worksheet` object or other object to which the `PrintOut` method applies.
- `From` is an optional Variant argument that specifies the number of the page at which to start printing. Omit `From` to start printing at the beginning of the object. Note that `From` and `To` refer to the pages in the printout, not to the overall number of pages that the object would take up.
- `To` is an optional Variant argument that specifies the number of the page at which to stop printing. Omit the `To` argument to print to the end of the object.
- `Copies` is an optional Variant argument that specifies the number of copies to print. If you omit `Copies`, Excel prints one copy.
- `Preview` is an optional Variant argument that you can set to `True` to display the object in Print Preview before printing it. Set `Preview` to `False`, or simply omit this argument, to print the object without previewing it. Use the `PrintPreview` method to display an object in Print Preview without printing it.
- `ActivePrinter` is an optional Variant argument that you can use to specify the printer on which to print.
- `PrintToFile` is an optional Variant argument that you can set to `True` to make Excel print to a print file rather than a printer. When printing to a file, you can use the `PrToFileName` property to specify the filename, or omit it and have Excel prompt the user for the filename.

- `Collate` is an optional Variant argument that you can set to `True` to have Excel print multiple copies for collation rather than printing all the copies of one page, all the copies of the next, and so on.
- `PrToFileName` is an optional Variant argument that you can use with `PrintToFile:=True` to specify the filename of the print file.
- `IgnorePrintAreas` is an optional Variant argument. Set to `False`, this argument prints the entire specified print area; when it's `True`, the entire object is printed and any print area is ignored. A *print area* can be defined in Excel and is useful as a way of printing only a specified range of cells. Once specified, the print area is retained by Excel until you either clear it or specify a new print area. You define a print area by selecting the cells you want to print and then clicking the Ribbon's Page Layout tab. Click the Print Area option in the Page Setup area of the Ribbon.

The following statement prints two copies of each page of the first worksheet in the active workbook, collating the pages:

```
ActiveWorkbook.Sheets(1).Printout Copies:=2, Collate:=True
```

The following statement prints the first two pages of the worksheet named `Summary` in the workbook named `Planning.xlsx` to a file named `Planning Summary.prn` in the network folder `\\server\to_print`:

```
Workbooks("Planning.xlsx").Sheets("Summary").PrintOut From:=1, To:=2, _
    PrintToFile:=True, _
    PrToFileName:="\\server\to_print\Planning Summary.prn"
```

Protecting a Worksheet

To protect a worksheet, use the `Protect` method with the appropriate `Worksheet` object. The syntax is as follows:

```
expression.Protect(Password, DrawingObjects, Contents, Scenarios,
   UserInterfaceOnly, AllowFormattingCells, AllowFormattingColumns,
   AllowFormattingRows, AllowInsertingColumns, AllowInsertingRows,
   AllowInsertingHyperlinks, AllowDeletingColumns, AllowDeletingRows,
   AllowSorting, AllowFiltering, AllowUsingPivotTables)
```

The components of the syntax are as follows:

- *`expression`* is a required expression that returns a `Worksheet` object.
- `Password` is an optional Variant argument that specifies the password for unprotecting the worksheet. `Password` is case-sensitive. You'll almost always want to supply `Password` to prevent unauthorized people from unprotecting the workbook.
- `DrawingObjects` is an optional Variant argument that you can set to `True` to protect shapes in the worksheet. The default setting is `False`.
- `Contents` is an optional Variant argument that protects the locked cells when set to `True`, its default value. Set `Contents` to `False` to leave the locked cells unprotected.

- `Scenarios` is an optional Variant argument that protects scenarios when set to `True`, its default value.
- `UserInterfaceOnly` is an optional Variant argument that you can set to `True` to leave macros unprotected while protecting the user interface. The default value is `False`.
- `AllowFormattingCells`, `AllowFormattingColumns`, and `AllowFormattingRows` are optional Variant arguments that you can set to `True` to allow the formatting of cells, columns, and rows, respectively. The default value for each argument is `False`.
- `AllowInsertingColumns`, `AllowInsertingRows`, and `AllowInsertingHyperlinks` are optional Variant arguments that you can set to `True` to allow the user to insert columns, rows, and hyperlinks, respectively. The default value for each argument is `False`.
- `AllowDeletingColumns` and `AllowDeletingRows` are optional Variant arguments that you can set to `True` to allow the user to delete columns or rows, respectively, where every cell in the column or row is unlocked. The default setting is `False`.
- `AllowSorting` is an optional Variant argument that you can set to `True` to allow the user to sort unlocked cells on the protected worksheet. The default setting is `False`.
- `AllowFiltering` is an optional Variant argument that you can set to `True` to allow the user to set filters or change filter criteria (but not enable or disable an autofilter) on a protected worksheet. The default setting is `False`.
- `AllowUsingPivotTables` is an optional Variant argument that you can set to `True` to allow the user to work with pivot tables on the protected worksheet. The default value is `False`.

For example, the following statement protects the worksheet referenced by the object variable `myWorksheet` using the password `no1gets1n`:

```
myWorksheet.Protect Password:="no1gets1n"
```

The following statement protects the `myWorksheet` worksheet with the same password but allows the formatting of cells and allows the sorting of unlocked cells:

```
myWorksheet.Protect Password:="no1gets1n", AllowFormattingCells:=True, _
    AllowSorting:=True
```

Working with the *ActiveSheet* Object

The `ActiveSheet` object returns the active worksheet. If you specify a workbook, the active worksheet in *that* specified workbook is returned.

If no sheet is active, `ActiveSheet` returns `Nothing`. Before executing code that depends on there being an active sheet, it's a good idea to check, as in this example:

```
If ActiveSheet Is Nothing Then End
```

Working with the Active Cell or Selection

In a procedure that manipulates a selection that the user has made, you'll typically work with either the active cell or the selection. The active cell is always a single cell, but the selection can encompass multiple cells or other objects.

Working with the Active Cell

The ActiveCell property of the Application object or the Window object returns a Range object that represents the active cell in the Excel application, or in a specified window. If you use ActiveCell without specifying a window, VBA returns the active cell in the currently active window.

For example, the following statement returns the address of the active cell in the active workbook:

```
MsgBox (ActiveCell.Address)
```

This code would return the result shown in Figure 22.3 if the currently selected cell is A1:

FIGURE 22.3 The currently active cell is fetched via the ActiveCell object.

The following statement returns the text in the active cell in the first window open on the workbook named Planning.xlsx:

```
MsgBox Workbooks("Planning.xlsx").Windows(1).ActiveCell.Text
```

If no worksheet is active, or if a chart sheet is active, there is no active cell. If you try to access ActiveCell, VBA returns an error. So before using code that assumes there is an active cell, check that ActiveCell is not Nothing:

```
If ActiveCell Is Nothing Then End
```

Getting and Setting the Value of the Active Cell

To return the value of the active cell, use the Value property. For example, the following statement sets the value of the active cell to 25:

```
ActiveCell.Value = 25
```

And the following statement retrieves the value of the active cell:

```
MsgBox ActiveCell.Value
```

Moving the Active Cell to Another Address

The ActiveCell object is often convenient to work with in your code, so sometimes you'll want to make a different cell the active cell in order to work with it via the ActiveCell object. To make a cell the active cell, use the Activate method with the appropriate Range object. For example, the following statement makes cell L7 the active cell in the worksheet identified by the object variable myWorksheet:

```
myWorksheet.Range("B5").Activate
```

Often, you'll need to move the active cell to a different range a specified number of rows or columns away (in other words, to an address *relative* to the location of the active cell—as opposed to an *absolute* address, such as C12). To do so, use the `Offset` property of the active cell object, specifying the number of rows with the `RowOffset` argument and the number of columns with the `ColumnOffset` argument. Use a positive offset to move the active cell right or down and a negative offset to move the active cell left or up. For example, the following statement moves the active cell up two rows (`RowOffset:=-2`) and four columns to the right (`ColumnOffset:=4`):

```
ActiveCell.Offset(RowOffset:=-2, ColumnOffset:=4).Activate
```

In your macros that the user triggers, it's usually a good idea to return the active cell to where it was when the user started the procedure. To do so, you can store the location of the active cell and then return it to the stored location after your procedure is finished with its tasks. Here's an example:

```
Set myActiveCell = ActiveCell
Set myActiveWorksheet = ActiveSheet
Set myActiveWorkbook = ActiveWorkbook

'take actions here

myActiveWorkbook.Activate
myActiveWorksheet.Activate
myActiveCell.Activate
```

BE CAREFUL WITH EQUATIONS THAT USE RELATIVE CELL ADDRESSES

Always test your procedures carefully with various types of data. Errors can sometimes occur when you move cells that contain equations that use relative cell addresses.

WORKING WITH THE REGION AROUND THE ACTIVE CELL

You can work with the range of cells around the active cell by using the `CurrentRegion` property to return the `CurrentRegion` object. The current region extends from the active cell to the first *blank* row above and below and to the first blank column to the left and right. In other words, if there are no blank rows or columns in the entire worksheet, then the region is all the cells in the worksheet.

For example, the following statements use the `Font` property of the `CurrentRegion` object to set the font of the current region to 12-point Times New Roman with no bold or italic:

```
With ActiveCell.CurrentRegion.Font
    .Name = "Times New Roman"
    .Size = 12
    .Bold = False
    .Italic = False
End With
```

Working with the User's Selection

In macros designed to be run by a user, you will often need to work with cells that the user has selected. For example, a user might select a range of cells and then run a macro to manipulate the contents of that range.

To work with the range the user has selected, use the `RangeSelection` property of the appropriate `Window` object. For example, you might assign the `RangeSelection` property to a range so that you could work with it in a macro and then select it again at the end of the macro, leaving the user ready to work with their selection again. Here's an example:

```
Dim myMacroRange As Range
Set myMacroRange = ActiveWindow.RangeSelection
With myMacroRange
    'take actions on the range here
End With
myMacroRange.Activate
```

Working with Ranges

Within a worksheet, you'll often need to manipulate ranges of cells. You can work with *absolute* ranges (ranges for which you specify the absolute addresses of the cells you want to affect, such as C12) or ranges relative to the active cell, where you merely describe an offset.

You can either specify a range by using the `Range` property or create a named range by using the `Names` collection. Excel also provides the `UsedRange` property for working with the used range on a worksheet, and the `SpecialCells` method of the `Range` object for working with cells that meet specific criteria.

Working with a Range of Cells

To work with a range of cells, use the `Range` property of the appropriate `Worksheet` object to specify the cells. For example, the following statement sets the value of cell C12 on the active worksheet to 44:

```
ActiveSheet.Range("C12").Value = "44"
```

Creating a Named Range

To create a named range, use the `Add` method with the `Names` collection. The syntax is as follows:

```
expression.Add(Name, RefersTo, Visible, MacroType, ShortcutKey,
   Category, NameLocal, RefersToLocal, CategoryLocal, RefersToR1C1,
   RefersToR1C1Local)
```

The components of the syntax are as follows:

- *`expression`* is a required expression that returns a `Names` object.
- `Name` is an optional Variant argument that specifies the name to assign to the named range. `Name` is required if you don't specify the `NameLocal` argument (later in this list). The name cannot be a cell reference, nor can it contain spaces.

- `RefersTo` is an optional Variant argument that specifies the range for the named range. You need to specify `RefersTo` unless you use the `RefersToLocal` argument, the `RefersToR1C1` argument, or the `RefersToR1C1Local` argument.
- `Visible` is an optional Variant argument that you can omit, set to `True` to have Excel make the name visible in the user interface (in the Go To dialog box, the Paste Name dialog box, and other locations), or set to `False` to make the name hidden.
- `MacroType` is an optional Variant argument that you can use to assign a macro type to the range: 1 for a user-defined `Function` procedure, 2 for a `Sub` procedure, and 3 or omitted for no macro.
- `ShortcutKey` is an optional Variant argument that specifies the shortcut key for a command macro assigned to the named range.
- `Category` is an optional Variant argument that specifies the category of the macro or function specified by `MacroType`. You can specify one of the categories used by the Function Wizard, or specify another name to have Excel create a new category with that name.
- `NameLocal` is an optional Variant argument that specifies the name for the range in the local language. Use `NameLocal` when you omit `Name`.
- `RefersToLocal` is an optional Variant argument that specifies the range for the named range. Use `RefersToLocal` when you omit `RefersTo`, `RefersToR1C1`, and `RefersToR1C1Local`.
- `CategoryLocal` is an optional Variant argument that you use to specify the category of the macro or function specified by `MacroType`. Use `CategoryLocal` when you omit `Category`.
- `RefersToR1C1` is an optional Variant argument that specifies the range for the named range using R1C1 notation (R1C1 would mean row 1 column 1). Use `RefersToR1C1` when you omit `RefersTo`, `RefersToLocal`, and `RefersToR1C1Local`.
- `RefersToR1C1Local` is an optional Variant argument that specifies the range for the named range using R1C1 notation in the local language. Use `RefersToR1C1Local` when you omit `RefersTo`, `RefersToLocal`, and `RefersToR1C1`.

For example, the following statement defines a range named `myRange`, which refers to the range A1:G22 on the worksheet named `Materials` in the workbook named `Building Schedule.xlsx`:

```
Workbooks("Building Schedule.xlsx").Names.Add Name:= "myRange", _
        RefersTo:="=Materials!$A$1:$G$22"
```

Deleting a Named Range

To delete a named range, use the `Delete` method with the appropriate `Name` object. For example, the following statement deletes the range named `myRange` in the workbook named `Building Schedule.xlsx`:

```
Workbooks("Building Schedule.xlsx").Names("myRange").Delete
```

Working with a Named Range

To work with a named range, specify the name with the Range object. For example, the following statements set the row height of the rows in the named range myRange to 20 points and applies 16-point Arial font to the cells:

```
With Range("myRange")
    .RowHeight = 20
    .Font.Name = "Arial"
    .Font.Size = "16"
End With
```

Working with the Used Range

If you need to work with all the cells on a worksheet, but not with any unoccupied areas of the worksheet, use the UsedRange property. For example, the following statement autofits all the columns in the used range in the active worksheet:

```
ActiveSheet.UsedRange.Columns.AutoFit
```

Working with SpecialCells

If you need to work with only some types of cells on a worksheet or in a range, use the SpecialCells method of the Range object to return the cells you need. The syntax is as follows:

```
expression.SpecialCells(Type, Value)
```

These are the components of the syntax:

- *expression* is a required expression that returns a Range object.
- Type is a required argument that specifies which cells you want. Table 22.4 lists the constants you can use.
- Value is an optional Variant argument that you can use when Type is xlCellTypeConstants or xlCellTypeFormulas to control which cells Excel includes. Table 22.5 shows the constants and what they return.

TABLE 22.4: Constants for the Type argument for the SpecialCells method

CONSTANT	RETURNS THIS KIND OF CELL
xlCellTypeAllFormatConditions	All formats
xlCellTypeAllValidation	Cells that use validation
xlCellTypeBlanks	Empty

TABLE 22.4: Constants for the `Type` argument for the `SpecialCells` method *(CONTINUED)*

CONSTANT	RETURNS THIS KIND OF CELL
`xlCellTypeComments`	Containing notes
`xlCellTypeConstants`	Containing constants
`xlCellTypeFormulas`	Containing formulas
`xlCellTypeLastCell`	The last cell in the used range
`xlCellTypeSameFormatConditions`	Having the same format
`xlCellTypeSameValidation`	Containing the same validation criteria
`xlCellTypeVisible`	All visible

TABLE 22.5: Constants for the `Value` argument for the `SpecialCells` method

CONSTANT	RETURNS CELLS CONTAINING
`xlErrors`	Errors
`xlLogical`	Logical values
`xlNumbers`	Numbers
`xlTextValues`	Text formulas

For example, the following statement activates the last cell in the worksheet referenced by the object variable `myWorksheet`:

```
myWorksheet.Cell.SpecialCells(Type:=xlCellTypeLastCell).Activate
```

The following statement identifies all the cells that contain formulas resulting in errors in the active worksheet:

```
ActiveSheet.Cells.SpecialCells(Type:=xlCellTypeFormulas, _
    Value:=xlErrors).Activate
```

Entering a Formula in a Cell

To enter a formula in a cell, set the `Formula` property of the appropriate `Cell` object. For example, the following statement enters the formula `=SUM($G$12:$G$22)` in the active cell:

```
ActiveCell.Formula = "=SUM($G$12:$G$22)"
```

Setting Options

With Word, most of the options that you find in the Word Options dialog box (click the File tab and then click Options) are available through Word's `Options` object. By contrast, most of Excel's options are located in the `Application` object. And workbook-specific options are accessed through the `Workbook` object.

Setting Options in the *Application* Object

The following sections show three examples of setting widely useful options in the `Application` object.

Controlling Excel's Calculation

In complex worksheets that perform many calculations, you may need to turn off automatic calculation so that a procedure can enter data quickly without the calculations taking place.

To do so, set the `Calculation` property of the `Application` object to `xlCalculationManual`, enter the data, and then set the `Calculation` property back to its previous value:

```
Dim varAutoCalculation As Variant
varAutoCalculation = Application.Calculation
Application.Calculation = xlCalculationManual
'enter the data here
Application.Calculation = xlCalculationAutomatic
```

Clearing the Recently Used Files List

Sometimes you may find it useful to clear all the entries from recently displayed documents (shown when you click the File tab on the Ribbon and then click Recent). Perhaps, for example, your macro creates some temporary files that you want to remove from this list.

You can do this by setting the `Maximum` property of the `RecentFiles` object to `0`. After doing so, you likely want to restore the user's previous setting, as the following example illustrates:

```
Dim myMax As Long
With Application.RecentFiles
    myMax = .Maximum 'store the user's preference, currently in effect
    .Maximum = 0
    .Maximum = myMax
End With
```

After you execute this code and then click the File tab on the Ribbon and click Recent, no files will be displayed in the Recent Documents list.

Setting a Default File Location

To set the default location for saving and opening files, use the `DefaultFilePath` property of the `Application` object, as in this example:

```
Application.DefaultFilePath = "\\server3\users\mjones\files"
```

Setting Options in a Workbook

Workbook-specific options include the following:

- Security options (such as those shown in the following section and the sidebar "Setting Passwords and Read-Only Recommendations for a Workbook")
- Whether to update remote references in the workbook (the Boolean `UpdateRemoteReferences` property) and whether to save external link values (the Boolean `SaveLinkValues` property)
- Whether to use AutoRecover (the Boolean `EnableAutoRecover` property)
- Whether to accept labels in formulas (the Boolean `AcceptLabelsInFormulas` property) and whether to use the 1904 date system (the Boolean `Date1904` property)

Forcing Excel to Remove Personal Information from the File Properties When You Save

To make Excel remove personal information from a workbook's properties when you save it, set the `RemovePersonalInformation` property of the workbook to `True`:

```
ActiveWorkbook.RemovePersonalInformation = True
```

Real World Scenario

Setting Passwords and Read-Only Recommendations for a Workbook

Office's protection works well in a typical workplace. To protect a workbook against an unauthorized user opening it or modifying it, you can set a "password to open" (for reading only) or a "password to modify" on a workbook. You can also specify that when anyone opens a workbook, Excel will recommend that they open it as read-only rather than read/write.

To set a "password to open," set the `Password` property of the `Workbook` object. For example, the following statement sets the active workbook to use the "password to open" `1mpass4`:

```
ActiveWorkbook.Password = "1mpass4"
```

To set a "password to modify," set the `WritePassword` property of the `Workbook` object. For example, the following statement sets the active workbook to use the "password to modify" `n0mods`:

```
ActiveWorkbook.WritePassword = "n0mods"
```

To apply a read-only recommendation to a workbook, set its `ReadOnlyRecommended` property to `True`:

```
Workbooks("Strategy.xlsx").ReadOnlyRecommended = True
```

Accessing OneNote

Earlier in this chapter, you saw how to access OneDrive and Dropbox. Simple enough. Dealing with OneNote is another matter because its contents are stored in the tricky XML format. When you write code to deal with XML, the words *efficient*, *straightforward*, and *sensible* do not come to mind.

VBA isn't built into OneNote, but you can access OneNote from VBA in other Office applications.

The following example gets the *metadata* (data about data) from your OneNote notebooks.

Before you try this code, choose Tools ➤ References in Excel's VBA Editor and ensure that both Microsoft OneNote 15.0 Object Library and Microsoft XML v6.0 are selected (checked) in the References dialog box.

```
1.  Sub GetMetaData()
2.
3.  'If it's not currently running, OneNote will be launched
4.  Dim ONote As oneNote.Application
5.  Set ONote = New oneNote.Application
6.
7.  Dim strXML As String
8.
9.  ONote.GetHierarchy "", hsNotebooks, strXML, xs2013 'don't use xs2016
10.
11. MsgBox strXML
12. End Sub
```

Lines 4 and 5 create a temporary instance of OneNote and assign it to the `ONote` object variable. Next, we create a string variable in line 7 to hold the metadata. Line 9 uses the `GetHierarchy` method to fill `strXML` with the metadata. `hsNotebooks` represents the collection of notebooks in OneNote. The message box displays the results.

The Bottom Line

Work with workbooks. You often need to create a new, blank workbook in a macro (mimicking a user clicking the File tab on the Ribbon and then clicking the New button). And writing code that accomplishes this is not difficult. It requires only two words.

Master It What code would you write to create a new, blank notebook?

Work with worksheets. Most workbooks you access via VBA will contain one or more worksheets, so most procedures will need to work with worksheets—inserting, deleting, copying, or moving them, or simply printing the appropriate range from them.

Master It Name the object you use in VBA code to represent a worksheet.

Work with the active cell or selection. In a procedure that manipulates a selection that the user has made, you'll typically work with either the active cell or the current selection.

Master It What is the difference between the active cell and a selection?

Work with ranges. Within a worksheet, you'll often need to manipulate ranges of cells. Excel includes a special kind of range—represented by the `UsedRange` property.

Master It What is unique about `UsedRange`?

Set options. Word employs an `Options` object to contain most of the options that you find in the Word Options dialog box (click the File tab on the Ribbon and then click Options). Excel uses a different object to contain its options.

Master It From which object do you access most of Excel's options?

Chapter 23

Working with Widely Used Objects in Excel

In the previous chapter, you learned to work with some of the main objects in the Excel object model, such as `Workbook` objects, the `ActiveCell` object, `Range` objects, and the `Options` object. This chapter shows you how to expand your programming facility with VBA in Excel by working with charts, windows, and Find and Replace.

IN THIS CHAPTER, YOU WILL LEARN TO DO THE FOLLOWING:

- Work with charts
- Work with windows
- Work with Find and Replace

Working with Charts

The following sections show you how to use VBA to create and format charts, either as entire chart sheets in a workbook or as objects on an existing worksheet.

Creating a Chart

VBA uses the `Chart` object to represent a chart on a chart sheet and a `ChartObject` object to represent an embedded chart on a worksheet. The `ChartObject` object contains a `Chart` object, which you can manipulate by accessing it through the `ChartObject` object. Confused? Object classification schemes can certainly be a bit bewildering.

When writing a macro, you create a chart or chart object in a different order than when working interactively and doing things by hand within Excel. Here are the steps you take when creating charts *programmatically* (via macro code rather than interactively via a mouse and keyboard):

1. Create a `Chart` object variable.
2. *Instantiate* (bring into existence) the `Chart` object using the `Set` command.
3. Specify the source range for its data using the `SetSourceData` method.
4. Specify the chart type using the `ChartType` property.
5. Specify any other items you need to.

Creating a Chart on a New Chart Sheet

To create a chart on a new chart sheet, use the `Add` method with the `Charts` collection. The syntax is as follows:

```
expression.Add(Before, After, Count, Type)
```

Here are the components of this syntax:

- *`expression`* is a required expression that returns a `Charts` collection.
- `Before` is an optional Variant argument that you can use to specify the sheet before which to add the new chart sheet. `After` is an optional Variant argument that you can use to specify the sheet after which to add the new sheet. Typically, you'll use either `Before` or `After`. If you omit both arguments, VBA adds the new chart sheet before the active sheet.
- `Count` is an optional Variant argument that you can use to specify how many chart sheets to add. The default is one.
- `Type` is an optional Variant argument that you can use to specify which kind of chart you want displayed. The choices are `xlWorksheet`, `xlChart`, `xlExcel4MacroSheet`, and `xl Excel4IntlMacroSheet`. The default value is `xlWorksheet`, so you have to specify `xlChart` in the following code example because it adds a chart, not an ordinary worksheet.

The following code declares an object variable named `myChartSheet` as being of the `Chart` type (a chart worksheet) and then assigns to `myChartSheet` a new chart sheet added after the last existing sheet in the active workbook:

```
Dim myChartSheet As Chart
Set myChartSheet = ActiveWorkbook.Sheets.Add _
    (After:=ActiveWorkbook.Sheets(ActiveWorkbook.Sheets.Count), _
    Type:=xlChart)
```

Creating a Chart on an Existing Worksheet

To create a chart on an existing worksheet, use the `Add` method with the `ChartObjects` collection. The syntax is as follows:

```
expression.Add(Left, Top, Width, Height)
```

Here are the components of this syntax:

- *`expression`* is a required expression that returns a `ChartObjects` collection.
- `Left` is a required Double (variable type) argument that specifies the position of the upper-left corner of the chart in points from the left edge of cell A1.
- `Top` is a required Double argument that specifies the position of the upper-left corner of the chart in points from the top edge of cell A1.
- `Width` is a required Double argument that specifies the width of the chart in points.
- `Height` is a required Double argument that specifies the height of the chart in points.

For example, the following statements declare a new `ChartObject` object named `myChartObject` and assign to it a new chart object (chart area) 400 points wide by 300 points deep, positioned 200 points from the left edge and 200 points from the top of the worksheet:

```
Dim myChartObject As ChartObject
Set myChartObject = ActiveSheet.ChartObjects.Add(Left:=200, Top:=200, _
    Width:=400, Height:=300)
```

To work with the chart inside the `ChartObject`, return the `Chart` property of the `ChartObject` object.

Specifying the Source Data for the Chart

So far, the chart (on the chart sheet or in the `Chart` object) is blank. To give it contents, specify the chart's source data by using the `SetSourceData` method of the `Chart` object. For example, the following statement specifies the range `A1:E5` on the worksheet named `Chart Data` in the active workbook as the source data of the `Chart` object in the `ChartObject` object named `myChartObject`:

```
myChartObject.Chart.SetSourceData Source:= _
    ActiveWorkbook.Sheets("Chart Data").Range("A1:E5")
```

Specifying a Chart Type

To specify a chart type, set the `ChartType` property of the `Chart` object. Excel offers too great a variety of charts to list here (73 different types), but you can easily identify the chart types from their enumeration-constant names. For example, the constant `xl3DArea` represents the 3D Area chart type, `xlColumnStacked` represents the Stacked Column chart type, and `xlDoughnut Exploded` represents the Exploded Doughnut chart type.

The following statement sets the type of the chart represented by the object variable `myChart` to the Stacked Column type:

```
myChart.ChartType = xlColumnStacked
```

Working with Series in the Chart

To work with series in a chart, you use the `SeriesCollection` collection, which contains all the series in the specified chart.

Creating a New Series

To create a new series, use the `NewSeries` method with the `SeriesCollection` collection. For example, the following statement adds a new series to the chart represented by the object variable `myChart`:

```
myChart.SeriesCollection.NewSeries
```

Adding a New Series

To add a new series to a `SeriesCollection` collection, use the `Add` method with the appropriate `SeriesCollection` object. The syntax is as follows:

```
expression.Add(Source, Rowcol, SeriesLabels, CategoryLabels, Replace)
```

Here are the components of this syntax:

- *expression* is a required expression that returns a SeriesCollection collection.
- Source is a required Variant argument that specifies the source of the data for the new series. You can supply the data either as a range or as an array of data points.
- Rowcol is an optional argument that you can set to xlRows to specify that the new values are in rows in the specified range, or you can use the default setting, xlColumns, to specify that the new values are in columns. If you omit this argument, Excel uses xlColumns.
- SeriesLabels is an optional Variant argument that you can set to True to specify that the first row or column in the source area contains the series labels, or set to False to specify that the first row or column in the source area contains the first data point for the series. If you omit this argument, Excel tries to work out whether the first row or column contains a series label. It's best to specify this argument to avoid confusion. However, if Source is an array, VBA ignores this argument.
- CategoryLabels is an optional Variant argument that you can set to True to specify that the first row or column contains the name for the category labels, or set to False to specify that it does not contain them. If you omit this argument, Excel tries to work out whether the first row or column contains a category label. It's best to specify this argument to avoid confusion. Again, if Source is an array, VBA ignores this argument.
- Replace is an optional Variant argument that you can set to True when CategoryLabels is True to make the categories replace the existing categories for the series, or set to False (the default value) to prevent the existing categories from being replaced.

The following procedure brings together several elements used in the previous code examples in this chapter. It illustrates how to create a complete chart and add a new series to the chart identified by the object variable myChart. The procedure draws the data from the range A4:K4 on the active worksheet in the active workbook, using rows:

```
Sub test()

Dim myChartObject As ChartObject
Dim MyChart As Chart

Set myChartObject = ActiveSheet.ChartObjects.Add(Left:=100, Top:=100, _
    Width:=400, Height:=300)

Set MyChart = myChartObject.Chart
MyChart.ChartType = xlConeBarStacked

MyChart.SeriesCollection.Add _
 Source:=ActiveSheet.Range("A4:K4"), Rowcol:=xlRows

End Sub
```

If you execute this example, you'll see results similar to those shown in Figure 23.1. A chart will be generated based on whatever data lies within the specified range.

Extending an Existing Series

To extend an existing series, use the `Extend` method with the appropriate `SeriesCollection` object. The syntax is as follows:

```
expression.Extend(Source, Rowcol, CategoryLabels)
```

Here are the components of this syntax:

- *`expression`* is a required expression that returns a `SeriesCollection` object.
- `Source` is a required Variant argument that specifies the source of the data for the new series. You can supply the data either as a range or as an array of data points.
- `Rowcol` is an optional argument that you can set to `xlRows` to specify that the new values are in rows in the specified range, or you can use the default setting, `xlColumns`, to specify that the new values are in columns. If you omit this argument, Excel uses `xlColumns`.
- `CategoryLabels` is an optional Variant argument that you can set to `True` to specify that the first row or column contains the name for the category labels, or you can set to `False` to specify that it does not contain them. If you omit this argument, Excel tries to work out whether the first row or column contains a category label. It's best to specify this argument to avoid confusion. If `Source` is an array, VBA ignores this argument.

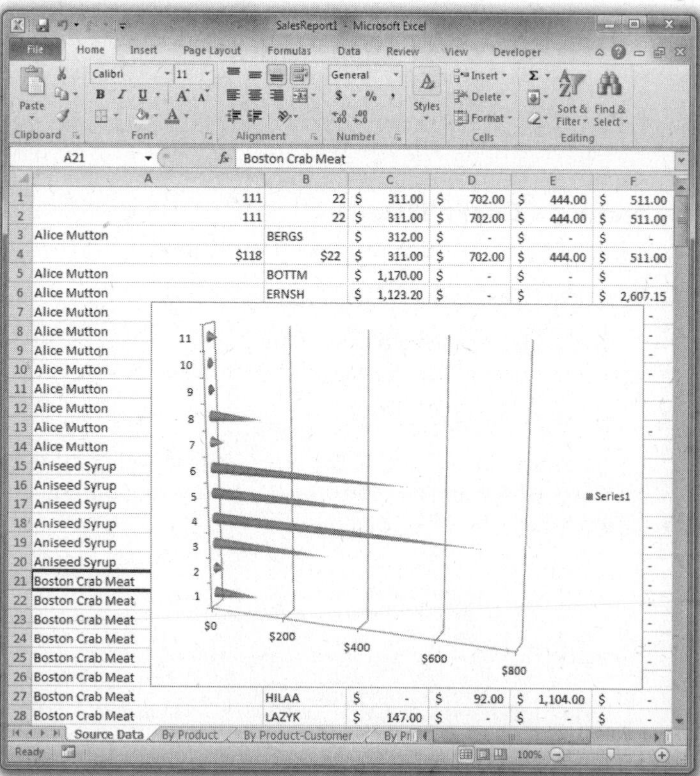

Figure 23.1 This chart was generated in a procedure, using the `Add` method of the `SeriesCollection` object.

For example, the following statement extends the series in the chart identified by the object variable myChart using the data in the cells P3:P8 on the worksheet named Chart Data:

```
myChart.SeriesCollection.Extend _
Source:=Worksheets("Chart Data").Range("P3:P8")
```

Adding a Legend to the Chart

To add a legend to the chart, set its HasLegend property to True. To manipulate the legend, work with the properties of the Legend object. Key properties include these:

- The Position property controls where the legend appears: xlLegendPositionBottom, xlLegendPositionCorner, xlLegendPositionLeft, xlLegendPositionRight, or xlLegendPositionTop.
- The Height property and the Width property control the height and width of the legend, respectively, in points.
- The Font property returns the Font object, which has properties you can set to specify the font size, name, and effects.

For example, the following statements add the legend to the chart represented by the object variable myChart and apply 16-point Arial font to it:

```
With myChart.Legend
    .HasLegend = True
    .Font.Size = 16
    .Font.Name = "Arial"
End With
```

Adding a Chart Title

To add a title to the chart, set its HasTitle property to True, as in this example:

```
myChart.HasTitle = True
```

Excel adds the title with the default text Chart Title. To change the text, set the Text property of the ChartTitle object, which represents the chart title. Here's an example:

```
myChart.ChartTitle.Text = "Industrial Mixups in North Dakota"
```

To position the title, set its Top property (specifying the number of points from the top edge of the worksheet) and its Left property (specifying the number of points from the left edge of the worksheet), as in this example:

```
With myChart.ChartTitle
    .Top = 100
    .Left = 150
End With
```

To format the text of the title, work with its `Font` object, as follows:

```
myChart.ChartTitle.Font.Name = "Arial"
```

Working with a Chart Axis

To work with an axis of a chart, use the `Axes` method to access the appropriate axis. The syntax is as follows:

```
expression.Axes(Type, Group)
```

Here, *`expression`* is a required expression that returns a `Chart` object. `Type` is an optional Variant argument that specifies the axis to return. Use `xlValue` to return the value axis, `xlCategory` to return the category axis, or `xlSeriesAxis` to return the series axis (on 3D charts only). `Group` is an optional argument that you can set to `xlSecondary` to specify the second axis group instead of `xlPrimary` (the default setting), which specifies the first axis group.

For example, the following statements work with the category axis in the primary group of the chart, applying its title, adding text, setting the font and font size, and turning major gridlines on and minor gridlines off. Note that this `With` structure should be placed within a second, outer `With` structure representing the chart itself:

```
With MyChart
    With .Axes(Type:=xlCategory, AxisGroup:=xlPrimary)
.HasTitle = True
        .AxisTitle.Text = "Years"
        .AxisTitle.Font.Name = "Times New Roman"
        .AxisTitle.Font.Size = 12
        .HasMajorGridlines = True
        .HasMinorGridlines = False
    End With

End With
```

Formatting Headers and Footers

You can manipulate headers and footers easily via VBA by using a built-in set of format and content constants. These include format specifications such as `&U` for underlining and `&C` for centering. Content constants include `&D`, which inserts the current date, `&P` for the page number, and `&F` for the document's name. The complete list of VBA header and footer constants can be found here:

```
http://msdn.microsoft.com/en-us/library/office/ff822794.aspx
```

This next code turns on italics and underlining, and on the right side of the header prints *Dr. Dancy Page* followed by the current page and the total number of pages: *Dr. Dancy Page 2 of 7.* If there is no header, one is created.

```
ActiveSheet.PageSetup.RightHeader = "&U&I Doctor Dancy  Page &P of &N"
```

Working with Windows Objects

The `Windows` collection contains a `Window` object for every open window in the Excel application. Normally, when you open a workbook, Excel opens a window so that you can see it. You can also open further windows as necessary—for example, by clicking the Ribbon's View tab and then clicking the New Window button in the Window area.

In most cases, using `Window` objects isn't a very useful way to access data via VBA because you can access it more easily using objects such as the `ActiveSheet` object or the `ActiveCell` object. However, you may want to open, close, activate, or arrange windows programmatically (via a macro rather than having the user do it by hand interactively) to display data to the user in a special way.

Opening a New Window on a Workbook

To open a new window on a workbook, use the `NewWindow` method of the appropriate `Window` object. This method takes no arguments. For example, the following statement opens a new window showing the contents of the first window open on the workbook identified by the object variable `myWorkbook`:

```
myWorkbook.Windows(1).NewWindow
```

Closing a Window

To close a window, use the `Close` method with the appropriate `Window` object. The syntax is as follows:

```
expression.Close(SaveChanges, Filename, RouteWorkbook)
```

Here, *`expression`* is a required expression that returns a `Window` object. This syntax is the same as for closing a workbook (see "Closing a Workbook" in the previous chapter). The difference is that if two or more windows are open on the same workbook, closing the second or subsequent window does not close the workbook, so the arguments are not relevant. (If the window you're closing is the workbook's last window, however, you do need to specify the windows—otherwise, Excel prompts the user to save any unsaved changes.) For example, the following statement closes all windows open on the workbook referenced by the object variable `myWorkbook` except for one window:

```
Do While myWorkbook.Windows.Count > 1
    myWorkbook.Windows(myWorkbook.Windows.Count).Close
Loop
```

Activating a Window

Activation in VBA means to give a particular window the *focus*. Only one window in an application at a time can accept user typing. It's said to have the focus. To activate a window, use the `Activate` method of the appropriate `Window` object. For example, the following statement activates the first window open on the workbook `Planning.xlsx`:

```
Workbooks("Planning.xlsx").Windows(1).Activate
```

Similarly, you can activate the previous window by using the `ActivatePrevious` method or the next window by using the `ActivateNext` method.

Arranging and Resizing Windows

To arrange windows, use the `Arrange` method with the appropriate `Windows` collection. The syntax is as follows:

```
expression.Arrange(ArrangeStyle, ActiveWorkbook, SyncHorizontal, SyncVertical)
```

Here are the components of this syntax:

- *`expression`* is a required expression that returns a `Windows` collection.
- `ArrangeStyle` is an optional argument that you can set to `xlArrangeStyleTiled` to tile the windows (the default setting), `xlArrangeStyleHorizontal` to arrange the windows horizontally, `xlArrangeStyleVertical` to arrange the windows vertically, or `xl ArrangeStyleCascade` to cascade the windows in an overlapping arrangement that lets you see the title bar of each window but the contents of only the front window.
- `ActiveWorkbook` is an optional Variant argument that you can set to `True` to make VBA arrange only the windows of the active workbook. The default value is `False`, which arranges all open windows.
- `SyncHorizontal` and `SyncVertical` are optional Variant arguments that you can set to `True` when you use `ActiveWorkbook:=True` to make the windows of the active workbook scroll horizontally or vertically in sync (when you scroll one window, the other windows scroll by the same amount in the same direction). The default is `False`.

For example, the following statement arranges the windows in the workbook `Budget.xlsx` vertically and sets synchronized scrolling on them:

```
Workbooks("Budget.xlsx").Windows.Arrange _
    ArrangeStyle:=xlArrangeStyleVertical, _
    ActiveWorkbook:=True, SyncVertical:=True
```

You can maximize, minimize, or restore the application window by setting the `WindowState` property of the `Application` object to `xlMaximized`, `xlMinimized`, or `xlNormal`. Similarly, within the application window, you can maximize, minimize, or restore a document by setting its `WindowState` property.

When a window is in a "normal" state (`xlNormal`; not maximized or minimized), you can position it by using the `Top` and `Left` properties to specify the position of the upper-left corner of the window and size it by setting its `Height` and `Width` properties. Check the `UsableWidth` property and the `UsableHeight` property of the `Application` object to find the amount of space available in the `Application` window. (Similarly, you can check the `UsableWidth` property and the `UsableHeight` of the `Window` object to see how much space is available in the window—for example, so that you can size or position an object correctly.)

The following example declares two `Window` object variables, `myWindow1` and `myWindow2`, and assigns `myWindow1` to the active window and `myWindow2` to a new window showing the same worksheet as `myWindow1`. The example then sizes and positions the two windows so that each is the full height available in the application window, with `myWindow1` taking one-quarter of the available width and `myWindow2` taking the remaining three-quarters of the available width:

```
Dim myWindow1 As Window, myWindow2 As Window
Set myWindow1 = ActiveWindow
Set myWindow2 = myWindow1.NewWindow
With myWindow1
    .WindowState = xlNormal
    .Top = 0
    .Left = 0
    .Height = Application.UsableHeight
    .Width = Application.UsableWidth * 0.25
End With
With myWindow2
    .WindowState = xlNormal
    .Top = 0
    .Left = (Application.UsableWidth * 0.25) + 1
    .Height = Application.UsableHeight
    .Width = Application.UsableWidth * 0.75
End With
```

Zooming a Window and Setting Display Options

To change the zoom, set the `Zoom` property of the appropriate `Window` object. *Zoom* in this context means merely to change the size of the window onscreen—it doesn't necessarily imply enlarging it, merely changing it.

For example, the following statement zooms the active window to 150 percent:

```
ActiveWindow.Zoom = 150
```

In some procedures, you may need to change the display of the Excel window to ensure that certain features are (or are not) available to the user. Use the Boolean properties `DisplayScrollBars`, `DisplayStatusBar`, and `DisplayFormulaBar` to control whether Excel displays the scroll bars, status bar, and formula bar. Use the `DisplayFullScreen` property to toggle full-screen view on and off.

For example, the following statements make sure that the scroll bars and status bar are hidden and that the formula bar is displayed:

```
With Application
    .DisplayScrollBars = False
    .DisplayStatusBar = False
    .DisplayFormulaBar = True
End With
```

Working with Find and Replace

Excel's Find and Replace features can be useful for locating data in your procedures. In Excel, Find and Replace are implemented through methods rather than (as in Word) through a `Find` object.

Both the `Range` object and the `WorksheetFunction` object have `Find` methods and `Replace` methods (but with different syntax). For most find and replace operations, you'll want to use the `Range` object—for example, to replace the contents of specific cells on a worksheet.

Searching with the *Find* Method

The syntax for the `Range` object's `Find` method is as follows:

```
expression.Find(What, After, LookIn, LookAt, SearchOrder, SearchDirection,
MatchCase, MatchByte, SearchFormat)
```

Here are the components of this syntax:

- *`expression`* is a required expression that returns a `Range` object.
- `What` is a required Variant argument that specifies the data to find. This data can be a string of text or any Excel data type.
- `After` is an optional Variant argument that you can use to specify the cell after which to begin searching. `After` must be a cell in the range that's being searched. If you omit `After`, Excel begins the search at the upper-left cell in the range.
- `LookIn` is an optional Variant argument that you can use to specify whether to search in formulas (`xlFormulas`), values (`xlValues`), or comments (`xlComments`).
- `LookAt` is an optional Variant argument that you can set to `xlWhole` to search for the entire contents of a cell, or to `xlPart` to search for the match within the contents of cells.
- `SearchOrder` is an optional Variant argument that you can set to `xlByRows` to search by rows, or to `xlByColumns` to search by columns.
- `SearchDirection` is an optional Variant argument that you can set to `xlNext` to search downward, or to `xlPrevious` to search upward.
- `MatchCase` is an optional Variant argument that you can set to `True` to use case-sensitive searching. The default setting is `False`.
- `MatchByte` is an optional Variant argument used only if you've installed double-byte language support.
- `SearchFormat` is an optional Variant argument that controls whether Excel searches for specified formatting (`True`) or not (`False`).

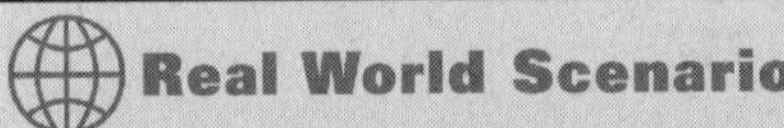

Practical Searching: Beware Persistent Settings

The `LookIn`, `LookAt`, `SearchOrder`, and `MatchByte` arguments of the `Range` object's `Find` method *persist*—Excel retains them from one search to the next. Unless you know that the settings used in the previous search are suitable for your current needs, you should set these arguments explicitly for each new search to avoid getting unexpected results.

Pay particular attention to the `LookAt` setting. This setting corresponds to the Match Entire Cell Contents check box in the Find And Replace dialog box. To see this option manually in an Excel window, click any cell, and then click the Find And Select button on the Ribbon's Home tab. Choose Replace on the menu that drops down, and then click the Options button in the Find And Replace dialog box, if necessary, to display all the options available in that dialog box.

Remember that format settings such as font and subscript persist as well. So, you might want to also specify them if you're concerned they might have been previously employed by you or the user.

And, finally, remember to always be courteous to users by restoring their settings. Users know that Find and Replace settings persist, so they expect them to remain as you found them, no matter what you might do with them while your procedure executes. So at the start of your procedure, store the user's current settings in variables. Then at the end of your procedure, save these settings back to the various options.

Excel has no global command equivalent to Word's `ClearFormatting` statement, described in Chapter 21, "Working with Widely Used Objects in Word."

The following example code searches for `2008` in formulas in cells after the active cell, without searching for formatting:

```
Cells.Find(What:="2008", After:=ActiveCell, LookIn:=xlFormulas, LookAt _
    :=xlWhole, SearchOrder:=xlByRows, SearchDirection:=xlNext, MatchCase:= _
    True, SearchFormat:=False).Activate
```

Notice that in this code each argument is named. And one, `MatchByte`, is omitted. Recall that if you leave out an argument in an argument list, you must either insert a comma as a placeholder or use named arguments. Given that Excel's `Find` arguments are persistent, it is a good idea to use named arguments here to remind yourself that they need to be restored to the user's previous settings.

Continuing a Search with the *FindNext* and *FindPrevious* Methods

After you have executed a search using the `Find` method, you can use the `FindNext` method to find the next instance of the search item, or the `FindPrevious` method to find the previous instance. The syntax is as follows:

```
expression.FindNext(After)
expression.FindPrevious(After)
```

Here, *expression* is a required expression that returns a Range object, and After is an optional Variant argument that specifies the cell after which you want to search (for the FindNext method) or before which you want to search (for the FindPrevious method). After must be a single cell.

For example, the following statement finds the next instance of the search item:

```
Cells.FindNext
```

Replacing with the *Replace* Method

To replace using VBA, use the Replace method with the Range object. The syntax is as follows:

```
expression.Replace(What, Replacement, LookAt, SearchOrder, MatchCase, MatchByte,
SearchFormat, ReplaceFormat)
```

The components of the syntax are the same as for the Search method except for the following:

- Replacement is a required Variant argument that specifies the replacement string for the search.
- ReplaceFormat is an optional Variant argument that controls whether Excel replaces formatting in the search (True) or not (False).

For example, the following statement replaces the instances of the word Sales in column B of the active worksheet with the words Sales & Marketing, using case-sensitive matching:

```
ActiveSheet.Columns("B").Replace What:="Sales", _
    Replacement:="Sales & Marketing", SearchOrder:=xlByColumns, _
    MatchCase:=True
```

Searching for and Replacing Formatting

To search for formatting, use the FindFormat property of the Application object to define the formatting, and then set the SearchFormat argument of the Find method to True. Similarly, use the ReplaceFormat property of the Application object to define the replacement formatting, and then set the ReplaceFormat property of the Replace method to True.

For example, the following statements use a With structure to set the Application .FindFormat.Font properties for which to search, a With structure to set the Application .ReplaceFormat.Font with which to replace them, and the Replace method of the Cells collection to effect the replacement:

```
With Application.FindFormat.Font
    .Name = "Arial"
    .Size = "12"
    .Bold = True
End With
With Application.ReplaceFormat.Font
    .Name = "Arial Black"
```

```
        .Bold = False
    End With
    Cells.Replace What:="5", Replacement:="5", LookAt:=xlPart, SearchOrder _
        :=xlByColumns, MatchCase:=False, SearchFormat:=True, ReplaceFormat:=True
```

Adding Shapes

It's easy to add shapes to a worksheet. Shapes can be used to draw attention to important points or liven up statistical data for a presentation. Here's an example that adds two explosion graphics to a worksheet:

```
Sub AutoShapes()

    ActiveSheet.Shapes.AddShape(msoShapeExplosion2, 425, 145, 86, 101).Select
    ActiveSheet.Shapes.AddShape(msoShapeExplosion1, 265, 224, 190, 190).Select

End Sub
```

The `AddShape` method takes the following arguments:

```
AddShape(Type, Left, Top, Width, Height)
```

The `Type` argument specifies one of a set of `msoShape` constants that can be found in Excel's VBA Editor. There are dozens of shapes, including a moon, a heart, and a tear. Press F2 to display the Object Browser. In the list box at the top left of the Object Browser, you'll likely see All Libraries displayed by default. Instead, open this list and select Office. (This list box specifies the library of objects that will be searched.) Now in the search field directly below that, type **msoshape** and click the binoculars icon next to the field.

The Bottom Line

Work with charts. You can create either full chart sheets or embedded charts within an ordinary Excel worksheet.

Master It What object is used in a procedure to represent an embedded chart?

Work with windows. To open a new window on a workbook, you use the `NewWindow` method of the appropriate `Window` object.

Master It Does the `NewWindow` method take any arguments?

Work with Find and Replace. When working with the Find and Replace features in Excel, you need to be aware of a phenomenon known as *persistence.*

Master It What is persistence, and why should it concern you?

Chapter 24

Understanding the PowerPoint Object Model and Key Objects

This chapter shows you how to start working with the PowerPoint object model, the architecture underlying PowerPoint, and how to perform common actions with the most immediately useful PowerPoint objects. These objects include the `Presentations` collection and the `Presentation` object, the `ActivePresentation` object, the `Slides` collection and `Slide` objects, `Window` objects, and `Master` objects.

IN THIS CHAPTER, YOU WILL LEARN TO DO THE FOLLOWING:

- Understand the PowerPoint object model
- Understand PowerPoint's creatable objects
- Work with presentations
- Work with windows and views
- Work with slides
- Work with masters

Getting an Overview of the PowerPoint Object Model

As with all Office applications that include VBA, you can write macros without understanding how the PowerPoint object model fits together, but most people find that familiarity with the main objects in the object model is helpful. Also, the code examples in the Help system's object-model reference can be invaluable. They show how and where to employ objects in your own programming.

To begin exploring the PowerPoint object model, follow these steps:

1. Launch or switch to PowerPoint, and then press Alt+F11 to launch or switch to the VBA Editor.
2. In the Editor, choose Help ➢ MSDN On The Web.
3. Click the magnifying glass in the upper-right corner of the MSDN home page and type **Object model (PowerPoint VBA reference)** and press Enter.

4. Click the link Object model (PowerPoint VBA reference).
5. You now see the object model on the left. You'll have access to the whole collection of syntax specifications, useful descriptions, and code examples, as shown in Figure 24.1.

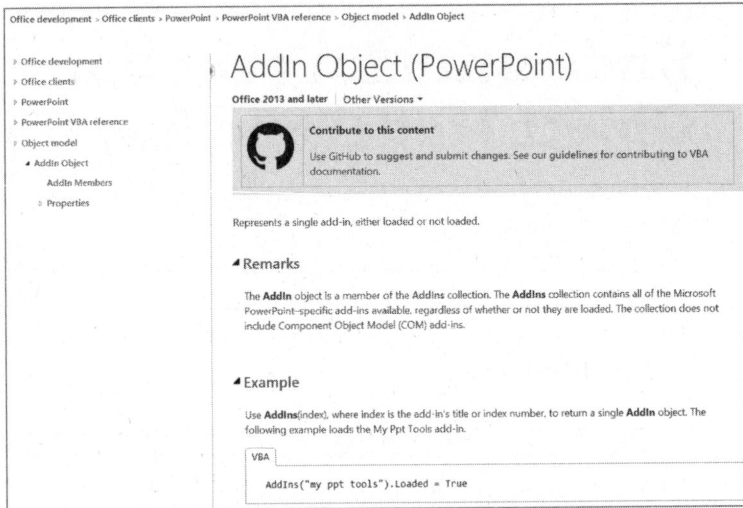

FIGURE 24.1 The entries in the PowerPoint object-model reference will help you write your own VBA code.

HELP WHEN MIGRATING LEGACY CODE FROM EARLIER OFFICE PROJECTS

If you've inherited VBA code written in earlier versions of PowerPoint, those macros might contain objects, methods, and properties that have been changed in Office 2016. Although changes to previous object models are generally few, some incompatibilities can crop up and "break" the code so it won't run correctly. Fortunately, you can download a free utility to assist you in mending the broken code. See the sidebar in Chapter 22 titled "Help When Migrating Legacy Code from Earlier Office Projects" for more information.

Understanding PowerPoint's Creatable Objects

In PowerPoint, the `Application` object gives you access to all the objects in the PowerPoint application. But for many operations, you can go directly through one of the "creatable" objects available in PowerPoint. (Recall that *creatable* merely means you can optionally leave out the word `Application` when specifying a creatable object in your code.) The four most frequently used creatable objects are listed here:

- The `ActivePresentation` object represents the active presentation, the presentation that would respond if you typed something.

- The `Presentations` collection contains the `Presentation` objects, each of which represents one of the currently open presentations.
- The `ActiveWindow` object represents the active window in the application.
- The `SlideShowWindows` collection contains the `SlideShowWindow` objects, each of which represents an open slide-show window. This collection is useful for manipulating a slide show that's currently displayed.

Within a presentation, you'll typically find yourself working with the `Slides` collection, which contains all the `Slide` objects that represent the slides. On a slide, most items are represented by `Shape` objects gathered into the `Shapes` collection. For example, the text in a typical placeholder is contained in the `Text` property of the `TextRange` object in the `TextFrame` object within a `Shape` object on a slide.

Working with Presentations

To get any work done in PowerPoint, you'll usually need to work with one or more presentations. VBA uses the `Presentation` object to represent a presentation and organizes the open `Presentation` objects into the `Presentations` collection.

Creating a New Presentation Based on the Default Template

You can create a new presentation based on the default template. This is equivalent to clicking the File tab on PowerPoint's Ribbon and then clicking the New option in PowerPoint. To do this, use the `Add` method with the `Presentations` collection. The syntax is as follows:

```
expression.Add(WithWindow)
```

Here are the components of this syntax:

- *`expression`* is a required expression that returns a `Presentations` object. Often, it's easiest to use the `Presentations` object itself.
- `WithWindow` is an optional Long argument. Set `WithWindow` to `msoFalse` to prevent the new presentation from being visible—for example, so that you can create and manipulate it without the user seeing the details. (You may want to temporarily hide the presentation so that the user doesn't have to endure the irritating flickering effect that PowerPoint tends to exhibit while creating presentation objects programmatically.) The default value is `msoTrue`, making the new presentation visible.

For example, the following statements declare an object variable of the `Presentation` type named `myPresentation`, create a new presentation, assign the new presentation to `myPresentation`, and make it *invisible* to the user:

```
Dim myPresentation As Presentation
Set myPresentation = Presentations.Add(WithWindow:=msoFalse)
```

Given that it's invisible to the users, your macro can manipulate the presentation without alarming the users or permitting them to modify it. To create a visible PowerPoint presentation, change `msoFalse` to **`msoTrue`**.

Understanding Tri-State Values

This is a bit rarefied, but let's leave no stone unturned. The `Add` method of the `Presentations` object allows you to set its `WithWindow` argument to four different states: `msoFalse`, `msoTrue`, `msoTriStateToggle`, or `msoTriStateMixed`. True and false are common and easily understood states. But PowerPoint makes extensive use of two unusual states called `MsoTriState` values, both of which represent a kind of super-Boolean state. Instead of being limited to merely `True` or `False`, a *tri-state* value can also be in special third and fourth states. `msoTriStateMixed` means that something is both true and false at the same time, like lovers. Here's an example: If a string contains three words, one of which is bold, is the string bold or not? Well, the answer in VBA is that it is a *mixed* string. `msoTriStateToggle` means that the state is potentially true or false. In other words, the user could click a two-state control resetting the status either way, or your code could reset it.

In most cases, you'll want to set a tri-state value to either `msoTrue` or `msoFalse`. In fact, I can't imagine a situation in which your code would actually ever need to *set* `msoTriState` values. However, code might sometimes need to check this value (to *read* it) to find out if the property you were dealing with contained a mixture of `msoTrue` and `msoFalse` values. Remember that *mixed* means something is true and false at the same time; *toggle* means that something is *potentially* either true or false. Actually, don't remember this, because it's so infrequently useful. I mention it only because it pervades the online documentation on PowerPoint programming.

Creating a New Presentation Based on a Template

To create a new presentation based on a template other than the default template, use the `Open` method of the `Presentations` collection. The syntax is as follows:

```
expression.Open(FileName, ReadOnly, Untitled, WithWindow)
```

The components of the syntax are explained here (`ReadOnly`, `Untitled`, and `WithWindow` are all `msoTriState` values, but pay no attention to that):

- *`expression`* is a required expression that returns a `Presentations` object. Often, it's easiest to use the `Presentations` object itself.
- `FileName` is a required String argument that specifies the path and name of the file to use as a template for the new presentation. This file can be either a template in the conventional sense or a presentation that you want to use as a template.
- `ReadOnly` is an optional argument that specifies whether the file is opened with read-only status (`msoTrue`) or with read/write status (`msoFalse`). When creating a new presentation based on a template, you don't need to specify `ReadOnly`.

- `Untitled` is an optional argument that specifies whether to open the file as itself (`msoFalse`) or as a copy (`msoTrue`). When creating a new presentation based on a template, set `Untitled` to `msoTrue`.
- `WithWindow` is an optional argument that you can set to `msoFalse` to prevent the new presentation from being visible. The default value is `msoTrue`, making the new presentation visible.

For example, the following statement creates a new presentation based on the template named `Capsules.potm` located in the `C:\Users\`*`Richard`*`\Documents\Custom Office Templates\` folder:

```
Presentations.Open _
 FileName:="C:\Users\Richard\Documents\Custom Office Templates\Presentation2.
potx", Untitled:=msoTrue
```

As usual, replace my name, *`Richard`*, with your name. Or, specify a different file path to wherever your template is located on your machine.

Opening an Existing Presentation

To open an existing presentation already on the hard drive, use the `Open` method of the `Presentations` collection. The syntax is as shown in the previous section. The difference is that you use the `FileName` argument to specify the presentation you want to open (as opposed to the file that you want to use as the template for creating a new presentation) and either omit the `Untitled` argument or set it to `msoFalse`. You may also need to use the `OpenConflictDocument` argument to specify how to handle any conflict file that exists for the presentation you're opening.

For example, the following statement opens the existing presentation named `Train Time .pptm` stored in the folder `Z:\Public`, opening the presentation for editing rather than opening it as read-only:

```
Presentations.Open FileName:="Z:\Public\Train Time.pptm", ReadOnly:=msoFalse
```

Opening a Presentation from the Cloud

Chapter 20, "Understanding the Word Object Model and Key Objects," and Chapter 22, "Understanding the Excel Object Model and Key Objects," demonstrated how to save documents to OneDrive and Dropbox. Here we'll go the other way and open a presentation that's been stored on OneDrive. The mechanics of contacting the cloud are, blessedly, handled for us by the various cloud services. There *are* security issues—particularly during transmission to and from the storage servers—which I personally am glad to leave to these companies' programmers.

All VBA programmers have to do to store to or open from the cloud is to get the file path right. It's as if you are storing something on your hard drive—which in fact you are. The only difference is that the files in this location on your hard drive are also automatically stored (synced) somewhere else in the world, in a server farm.

Let's assume you have a presentation named `PX.pptm` stored in OneDrive. The file path will normally be `"C:\Users\`***`Richard`***`\OneDrive\PX.pptm"`.

So, to open this PX presentation, you can use this code, replacing *`Richard`* with whatever your name is.

```
Presentations.Open FileName:="C:\Users\Richard\OneDrive\PX.pptm",
ReadOnly:=msoFalse
```

Saving a Presentation

The first time you save a presentation, you must specify the path and filename to use. After that, you can save the presentation under the same name or specify a different path, name, format, or all three. This is the same distinction between the Save and Save As options on the File tab of the Ribbon.

Saving a Presentation for the First Time or Under a Different Name

To save a presentation for the first time, or to save a presentation using a different path, name, or format, use the `SaveAs` method. The syntax is as follows:

```
expression.SaveAs(Filename, FileFormat, EmbedFonts)
```

Here are the components of this syntax:

- *`expression`* is a required expression that returns a `Presentation` object.
- `Filename` is a required String argument that specifies the filename under which to save the presentation. Normally, you include the path in `Filename`; if you omit the path, PowerPoint uses the current folder.
- `FileFormat` is an optional argument that specifies the file format to use. Although there are currently 30 total `SaveAs` constants, Table 24.1 lists only the seven most widely useful formats.
- `EmbedFonts` is an optional argument that you can set to `msoTrue` to embed TrueType fonts in the presentation, or to `False` (the default) to not embed them.

Table 24.1: Example `FileFormat` constants for saving PowerPoint files

Format Name	Constant
PowerPoint format	`ppSaveAsPresentation`
Default format (set on the Save tab of the Options dialog box)	`ppSaveAsDefault`
Single-file web page	`ppSaveAsWebArchive`
Web page	`ppSaveAsHTML`
Presentation	`ppSaveAsPresentation`

TABLE 24.1: Example `FileFormat` constants for saving PowerPoint files *(CONTINUED)*

FORMAT NAME	CONSTANT
Design template	`ppSaveAsTemplate`
PowerPoint show	`ppSaveAsShow`

For example, the following statement saves the presentation identified by the object variable `myPresentation` under the name `HR.pptm` in the folder `Z:\Shared\Presentations`, using the web-page format and not embedding fonts:

```
myPresentation.SaveAs FileName:="Z:\Shared\Presentations\HR.pptm", _
    FileFormat:= ppSaveAsHTML, EmbedTrueTypeFonts:=msoFalse
```

USING THE OBJECT BROWSER TO QUICKLY SEE CONSTANTS AND OBJECTS

Here's a useful reminder. When you don't need code samples or extra details, you don't need to take the time to look through the full online Help system for an object's members or constants (such as the `ppSaveAs` constants shown in Table 24.1). Instead, just press F2 in the VBA Editor to bring up the Object Browser. Then, in the search field (to the left of the binoculars icon), type the object's name, a member (property or method), or a constant name. For example, you could type **ppSaveAsPresentation** and then click the binoculars icon. You would then see the entire list of 30 `ppSaveAs` constants.

To see the full list in the online Help system, visit this web page:

`http://msdn.microsoft.com/en-us/library/office/ff746500.aspx`

SAVING A PRESENTATION UNDER ITS EXISTING NAME

To save a presentation under its existing name, use the `Save` method. This method takes no arguments because it has only one possible behavior.

The following statement saves the active presentation:

```
ActivePresentation.Save
```

If the presentation on which you use the `Save` method has never been saved, PowerPoint doesn't prompt the user to specify the filename and location. Instead, PowerPoint saves the presentation using the default name assigned to its window (for example, a presentation that has a window called `Presentation11` will be saved as `Presentation11.pptm`) and in the current folder. To avoid using this default name and file path location, you can check the `Path` property of the `Presentation` object before using the `Save` method if you need to determine whether the presentation has been saved. If it has not been saved (if `Path = ""`), then you would use the `SaveAs` method to specify the folder and title you want to use, as in this example:

```
If ActivePresentation.Path = "" Then
    ActivePresentation.SaveAs FileName:="z:\public\presentations\Corporate.pptm"
```

```
Else
    ActivePresentation.Save
End If
```

Saving a Copy of a Presentation

Instead of using the SaveAs method to save a presentation under a different name, you can use the SaveCopyAs method to save a copy of the open presentation without affecting the open presentation (the presentation remains open, and any unsaved changes remain unsaved). The syntax and arguments for the SaveCopyAs method are the same as for the SaveAs method:

```
expression.SaveAs(Filename, FileFormat, EmbedFonts)
```

For example, the following statement saves a copy of the active presentation under the name Copy 1.pptm in the folder Z:\Public\Presentations, using the same file format as the presentation currently uses:

```
ActivePresentation.SaveCopyAs FileName:="Z:\Public\Presentations\Copy 1.pptm"
```

Saving All Open Presentations

The Presentations collection doesn't have a Save method, but you can save all open presentations by using a loop such as that shown in the following subroutine. This subroutine leaves unsaved any presentation that doesn't yet have a filename assigned.

```
Sub Save_All_Presentations()
    Dim myPresentation As Presentation
    For Each myPresentation In Presentations
        If myPresentation.Path <> "" Then myPresentation.Save
    Next myPresentation
End Sub
```

Closing a Presentation

To close a presentation, use the Close method of the appropriate Presentation object. The Close method takes no arguments. For example, the following statement closes the active presentation:

```
ActivePresentation.Close
```

If the presentation you're closing contains unsaved changes, PowerPoint prompts the user to save them. To avoid prompting the user, set the Saved property of the Presentation object to True before using the Close method. Here's an example:

```
With Presentations("Karelia Industry.pptm")
    .Saved = True
    .Close
End With
```

Exporting a Presentation or Some Slides to Graphics

You can export an entire presentation, a single slide, or a range of slides by using the `Export` method of the `Presentation` object, the `Slide` object, or a `SlideRange` object. The syntax for the `Export` method with a `Presentation` object is as follows:

```
expression.Export(Path, FilterName, ScaleWidth, ScaleHeight)
```

The syntax for the `Export` method with a `Slide` object or a `SlideRange` object is almost the same:

```
expression.Export(FileName, FilterName, ScaleWidth, ScaleHeight)
```

Here are the components of this syntax:

- *`expression`* is a required expression that returns a `Presentation` object, a `Slide` object, or a `SlideRange` object, as appropriate.
- `Path` (for a `Presentation` object) is a required String argument that specifies the path of the folder in which to save the graphics files of the slides.
- `FileName` (for a `Slide` object or a `SlideRange` object) is a required String argument that specifies the filename to use for the exported graphic. Include the path in `FileName` unless you want PowerPoint to use the current folder.
- `FilterName` is a required String argument that specifies the filter to use. Use the registered filename extension (`JPG`, `TIF`, `BMP`, or `PNG`) for `FilterName`.
- `ScaleWidth` is an optional Long argument that you can include to specify the width of the graphic in pixels.
- `ScaleHeight` is an optional Long argument that you can include to specify the height of the graphic in pixels.

For example, the following statement exports all the slides in the active presentation to 800×600 JPG graphics in the `Z:\Public\Presentations` folder. PowerPoint names the graphics `Slide1`, `Slide2`, and so on:

```
ActivePresentation.Export Path:="Z:\Public\Presentations", _
    FilterName:="JPG", ScaleWidth:=800, ScaleHeight:=600
```

The following statement exports the sixth slide in the active presentation to the file named `Slide6.png` in the `Z:\Public\Presentations` folder, using the PNG format:

```
ActivePresentation.Slides(6).Export _
    FileName:="Z:\Public\Presentations\Slide6.png", FilterName:="PNG"
```

Printing a Presentation

To print a presentation, use the `PrintOut` method of the appropriate `Presentation` object. The syntax is as follows:

```
expression.PrintOut(From, To, PrintToFile, Copies, Collate)
```

Here are the components of this syntax:

- *expression* is a required expression that returns a Presentation object.
- From and To are optional Integer arguments that specify the first slide and last slide to print. If you omit From, PowerPoint prints from the first slide; if you omit To, PowerPoint prints through the last slide.
- PrintToFile is an optional String argument that you can include to make PowerPoint print to the specified file rather than to the printer.
- Copies is an optional Integer argument that specifies how many copies of the presentation or slides to print. Omit Copies to use the default value, 1.
- Collate is an optional argument that you can set to msoFalse to prevent PowerPoint from collating multiple copies (which is the default setting).

For example, the following statement prints all the slides in the active presentation:

```
ActivePresentation.PrintOut
```

The following example prints slides 5 through 12 of the presentation identified by the object variable myPresentation:

```
myPresentation.PrintOut From:=5, To:=12
```

Applying a Template to a Presentation, to a Slide, or to a Range of Slides

You can apply a design template to a presentation, to a single slide within a presentation, or to a range of slides by using the ApplyTemplate method with the Presentation object, the Slide object, or the SlideRange object. The syntax is as follows:

```
expression.ApplyTemplate(FileName)
```

Here, *expression* is a required expression that returns a Presentation object, a Slide object, or a SlideRange object. FileName is a required String argument that specifies the path and name of the design template.

For example, the following statement applies the design template named Clouds.potm stored in the C:\Users***Richard***\AppData\Roaming\Microsoft\Templates\ folder:

```
ActivePresentation.Slides(1).ApplyTemplate FileName:= _
"C:\Users\Richard\AppData\Roaming\Microsoft\Templates\Clouds.potm"
```

As usual, replace my name, *Richard*, with your name.

The following statement applies the design template named Mountain Top.potm stored in the Z:\Public\Template folder to the first slide in the presentation named Success.pptm:

```
Presentations("Success.pptm").Slides(1).ApplyTemplate FileName:= _
    "Z:\Public\Template\Mountain Top.potm"
```

The following example applies the design template named `Disaster.potm` stored in the `Z:\Public\Template` folder to a range of slides consisting of the first, fourth, and sixth slides in the active presentation:

```
ActivePresentation.Slides.Range(Array(1, 4, 6)).ApplyTemplate _
    FileName:="Z:\Public\Template \Disaster.potm"
```

Working with the Active Presentation

The `ActivePresentation` property of the `Application` object returns a `Presentation` object that represents the active presentation (the presentation in the active window). The `ActivePresentation` object can be very useful for macros run by the user.

If no window is open, trying to use the `ActivePresentation` object returns an error. Unless you're sure that there is an active presentation, it's a good idea to first check that a window is open before you access the `ActivePresentation` object, as in this example:

```
If Windows.Count = 0 Then
    MsgBox "Please open a presentation before running this macro."
    End
End If
```

Working with Windows and Views

To get the PowerPoint window into the state you want, you'll often need to work with the window and with the view. PowerPoint uses two types of windows:

- *Document windows* are windows that contain documents (presentation files) rather than slide shows. VBA considers document windows to be `DocumentWindow` objects organized into the `DocumentWindows` collection but represents them with `Window` objects organized into the `Windows` collection. (Sounds mad, but you'll see how this works shortly.)
- *Slide-show windows* are windows that contain open slide shows. VBA uses `SlideShowWindow` objects and the `SlideShowWindows` collection to represent slide-show windows.

The following sections show you how to work with document windows. You'll learn how to work with slide-show windows in "Setting Up and Running a Slide Show" in Chapter 25, "Working with Shapes and Running Slide Shows."

The `Windows` collection contains a `Window` object for every open window in the PowerPoint application. When you open a presentation while working interactively, PowerPoint opens a window so that you can see the presentation. When a macro opens a presentation via VBA, you can set the `WithWindow` argument of the `Add` method to `msoFalse` to prevent PowerPoint from displaying to the user a window for the presentation. In the user interface, you can also open further windows as necessary—for example, by clicking the New Window button in the Window section of the Ribbon's View tab.

Working with the Active Window

PowerPoint uses the `ActiveWindow` object to represent the window that is active (the window that currently has the *focus* and is, thus, the one that accepts mouse clicks or typing).

Only one window is active at a time. The active window is always the first `Window` object in the `Windows` collection—`Windows(1)`.

If no window is open at all, or all open windows are hidden, there is no active window and using the `ActiveWindow` object causes VBA to return an error. To make sure that a window is open, check whether the `Count` property of the `Windows` collection is `0`. Here's an example:

```
If Windows.Count = 0 Then MsgBox "There is no active window.", vbOkOnly + _
    vbExclamation, "No Window Is Open"
```

When you're working with presentations using VBA, you may sometimes find that the `ActiveWindow` object is a handy way to access a presentation, especially for a macro that the user runs after choosing the presentation, slide, or other object that they want to affect. In other cases, you may find that the `ActivePresentation` object is a more convenient way to access the presentation you need to work with, or you may prefer to access the presentation via the `Presentations` collection.

Opening a New Window on a Presentation

To open a new window, use the `NewWindow` method of the appropriate `Window` object. This method takes no arguments. For example, the following statement opens a new window showing the contents of the active window:

```
ActiveWindow.NewWindow
```

Closing a Window

To close a window, use the `Close` method with the appropriate `Window` object. In PowerPoint, the `Close` method takes no arguments.

BE CAREFUL WHEN CLOSING WINDOWS PROGRAMMATICALLY

Recall that *programmatically* means *by programming*, by executing your VBA macro code (as opposed to by user interaction with an application—clicking and typing). If the window you're closing is the last window open for the presentation, PowerPoint simply closes the window *without prompting the user to save* any unsaved changes. For this reason, be careful when closing windows or your code could cause the user to lose data.

For example, you might close all windows but one on a presentation:

```
Do While ActivePresentation.Windows.Count > 1
    ActivePresentation.Windows(ActivePresentation.Windows.Count).Close
Loop
```

Alternatively, you might use the Save method to save a presentation before closing its last window, as in the next example. (More simply, you could use the Close method to close the presentation itself after saving it.)

```
With ActivePresentation
    If .Path = "" Then
        MsgBox "Please save this presentation.", vbOKOnly
    Else
        .Save
        For Each myWindow In Windows
            .Close
        Next myWindow
    End If
End With
```

Activating a Window

To activate a window or one of its panes, use the Activate method of the appropriate Window object. For example, the following statement activates the first window open on the presentation Benefits.pptm:

```
Presentations("Benefits.pptm").Windows(1).Activate
```

Arranging and Resizing Windows

To arrange windows, use the Arrange method with the appropriate Windows collection. The syntax is as follows:

```
expression.Arrange(ArrangeStyle)
```

Here, *expression* is a required expression that returns a Windows collection. ArrangeStyle is a required argument that specifies how to arrange the windows: ppArrangeCascade (cascade the windows in an overlapping arrangement that lets you see the title bar of each window but the contents of only the front window) or ppArrangeTiled (tile the windows; the default setting).

You can maximize, minimize, or restore the application window by setting the WindowState property of the Application object to ppWindowMaximized, ppWindowMinimized, or ppWindowNormal. Similarly, within the application window, you can maximize, minimize, or restore a document by setting its WindowState property.

When a window is in a "normal" state (ppWindowNormal, not maximized or minimized), you can position it by using the Top and Left properties to specify the position of the upper-left corner of the window and size it by setting its Height and Width properties.

The following example maximizes the application window and cascades the document windows within it:

```
Application.WindowState = ppWindowMaximized
Windows.Arrange ArrangeStyle:=ppArrangeCascade
```

Changing the View

To change the view in a window, set the `ViewType` property of the appropriate `Window` object to one of these 12 constants: `ppViewHandoutMaster`, `ppViewMasterThumbnails`, `ppViewNormal`, `ppViewNotesMaster`, `ppViewNotesPage`, `ppViewOutline`, `ppViewPrintPreview`, `ppViewSlide`, `ppViewSlideMaster`, `ppViewSlideSorter`, `ppViewThumbnails`, or `ppViewTitleMaster`. For example, the following statement switches the active window into Slide Sorter view:

```
ActiveWindow.ViewType=ppViewSlideSorter
```

To zoom the view, specify a value from 10 to 400 for the `Zoom` property of the `View` object for the appropriate window. The value represents the zoom percentage, but you don't include a percent sign. For example, the following statement zooms the active window to 150 percent:

```
ActiveWindow.View.Zoom = 150
```

Working with Panes

The `Pane` object represents a pane of the PowerPoint window in Slide view. The Outline pane is represented by index number 1, the Slide pane by index number 2, and the Notes pane by index number 3. You can activate a pane by using the `Activate` method with the appropriate `Pane` object. The following example switches the view in the active window to Slide view and activates the Outline pane:

```
With ActiveWindow
    .ViewType = ppViewSlide
    .Panes(1).Activate
End With
```

To change the arrangement of the panes in a PowerPoint window in Slide view, use the `SplitHorizontal` property and the `SplitVertical` property of the `Window` object.

The `SplitHorizontal` property controls the percentage of the document window's width that the Outline pane occupies, and the `SplitVertical` property controls the percentage of the document window's height that the Slide pane occupies. The following example sets the Outline pane to 25 percent of the width of the document window (leaving 75 percent to the Slide pane) and the Slide pane to 75 percent of the height of the window (leaving 25 percent to the Notes pane):

```
With ActiveWindow
    .SplitHorizontal = 25
    .SplitVertical = 75
End With
```

Working with Slides

Once you have created or opened the presentation you want to affect, you can access the slides it contains by using the `Slides` collection, which contains a `Slide` object for each slide in the presentation. Each slide is identified by its index number, but you can also assign names to slides in three different ways:

Using object variables Then you can refer to each slide by its object variable name.

Using ID numbers See the section titled "Finding a Slide by Its ID Number" later in this chapter.

Using the `Name` property See the section titled "Accessing a Slide by Name" later in this chapter.

Having a unique name for a slide is especially useful when you add slides to or delete slides from a presentation, because this causes the index numbers of the slides to change. It's much easier to just name the slides than to try to keep track of their shifting index numbers.

Adding a Slide to a Presentation

To add a slide to a presentation, use the Add method with the `Slides` collection. The syntax is as follows:

```
expression.Add(Index, Layout)
```

Here are the components of this syntax:

- *`expression`* is a required expression that returns a `Slides` collection. In many cases, it's easiest to use the `Slides` collection itself.
- `Index` is a required Long argument that specifies the index number for positioning the slide in the presentation. For example, the number 2 makes the new slide the second slide in the presentation.
- `Layout` is a required Long argument that specifies the layout for the new slide. The layout names correspond closely to the names you'll see in the Insert Slide dialog box or the Slide Layout task pane. For example, `ppLayoutBlank` specifies a blank slide, `ppLayoutTitleOnly` a title-only slide, and `ppLayoutChartAndText` a chart-and-text slide. The following statements declare an object variable named `mySlide` and assign to it a new title slide added at the beginning of the active presentation:

  ```
  Dim mySlide As Slide
  Set mySlide = ActivePresentation.Slides.Add(Index:=1, _
      Layout:=ppLayoutTitle)
  ```

Understanding the "Mixed" Constants

If you look at the list of constants for the `Layout` property, you'll notice one is called `ppLayoutMixed`. There's no "Mixed" layout in PowerPoint's list of slide layouts, and if you try to apply `ppLayoutMixed` to a slide, VBA will return an error. This is because `ppLayoutMixed` is the value VBA returns for the `Layout` property of a slide range that contains multiple slides with different designs.

Other properties have similar `Mixed` values to indicate that the objects use different values. For example, `ppTransitionSpeedMixed` means that the slides or shapes use different transition speeds. However, don't try to *set* a property to a `Mixed` value, because doing so always gives an error. Put another way, you can get (read) information about a mixed value, but you can't set (write) it.

Inserting Slides from an Existing Presentation

When creating presentations automatically, it's often useful to insert slides from an existing presentation. To do so, use the `InsertFromFile` method of the `Slides` collection. The syntax is as follows:

```
expression.InsertFromFile(FileName, Index, SlideStart, SlideEnd)
```

Here are the components of this syntax:

- *`expression`* is a required expression that returns a `Slides` collection. Often, you'll want to use the `Slides` collection itself.
- `FileName` is a required String argument that specifies the file from which to insert the slides.
- `Index` is a required Long argument that specifies the slide position in the open presentation at which to insert the slides.
- `SlideStart` is an optional Long argument that specifies the first slide to insert. If you omit `SlideStart`, PowerPoint starts at the first slide.
- `SlideEnd` is an optional Long argument that specifies the last slide to insert. If you omit `SlideEnd`, PowerPoint goes up to the last slide.

For example, the following statement inserts slides 2 through 8 from the presentation named `Handbook.pptm` stored in the folder `Z:\Transfer\Presentations`, placing the slides starting at the fifth slide in the open presentation `Corporate.pptm`:

```
Presentations("Corporate.pptm").Slides.InsertFromFile _
    FileName:="Z:\Transfer\Presentations\Handbook.pptm", Index:=5, _
    SlideStart:=2, SlideEnd:=8
```

Finding a Slide by Its ID Number

When working programmatically with a presentation, it can be difficult to track which slide is which, especially when you add, delete, insert, copy, or move slides—thereby changing the slides' index numbers.

To help you, PowerPoint assigns a slide ID number to each slide when it's created. The slide ID number doesn't change when you move a slide to a different position in the presentation, unlike the index number, which always reflects the slide's position in the presentation. You can check a slide's ID number by returning the `SlideID` property of the appropriate `Slide` object.

To find a slide by its ID number, use the `FindBySlideID` method of the `Slides` collection. The syntax is as follows:

```
expression.FindBySlideID(SlideID)
```

Here, *`expression`* is a required expression that returns a `Slides` collection. `SlideID` is a required Long argument that specifies the ID number of the slide you want to return.

The following example declares a Long variable named `TargetSlide` and assigns to it a new slide added at the fifth index position in the active presentation, inserts a full presentation at the third index position, and then uses the FindBySlideID method to return the slide identified by TargetSlide and apply a different design template to it. This approach is similar to creating object variables for slides, as described earlier in this chapter. However, here you create Long variables to hold the ID numbers instead of object variables:

```
Dim TargetSlide As Long
TargetSlide = ActivePresentation.Slides.Add(Index:=5, _
    Layout:=ppLayoutFourObjects).SlideID
Presentations("Corporate.pptm").Slides.InsertFromFile _
    FileName:="Z:\Transfer\Presentations\Handbook.pptm", Index:=3
ActivePresentation.Slides.FindBySlideID(TargetSlide).ApplyTemplate _
    FileName:="C:\Program Files\Microsoft Office\Templates\Presentation
    ÂDesigns\Brain Blitz.potm"
```

Changing the Layout of an Existing Slide

To change the layout of an existing slide, set its Layout property. For example, the following statement changes the layout of the first slide in the active presentation to the clip-art-and-vertical-text layout:

```
ActivePresentation.Slides(1).Layout = ppLayoutClipArtAndVerticalText
```

When you change the layout of a slide, PowerPoint moves its existing contents to allow any new objects needed to be added to the slide.

Deleting an Existing Slide

To delete an existing slide, use the Delete method with the appropriate Slide object. For example, the following statement deletes the first slide in the active presentation:

```
ActivePresentation.Slides(1).Delete
```

Be aware that PowerPoint doesn't confirm the deletion of a slide via VBA.

Copying and Pasting a Slide

To copy a slide, use the Copy method of the appropriate Slide object. The Copy method takes no arguments. (You can also cut a slide by using the Cut method, which also takes no arguments.)

To paste a slide, use the Paste method of the Slides collection. The Paste method takes an Index argument that specifies the slide position at which to paste in the slide.

For example, the following statements copy the first slide in the active presentation and paste it in so that it is the fifth slide:

```
ActivePresentation.Slides(1).Copy
ActivePresentation.Slides.Paste Index:=5
```

Duplicating a Slide

Instead of copying and pasting, you can directly duplicate a slide by using the Duplicate method of the Slide object. This method takes no arguments and places the duplicate of the slide immediately after the original in the index-number list. For example, the following statement duplicates the fourth slide in the active presentation, placing the copy at the fifth index position:

```
ActivePresentation.Slides(4).Duplicate
```

Moving a Slide

Instead of cutting and pasting a slide, you can move it directly by using the `MoveTo` method with the appropriate `Slide` object. Moving a slide has the same ultimate effect as cutting and pasting it but has the advantage of not changing the contents of the Clipboard (which you might need to preserve for the user or for other purposes). The syntax for the `MoveTo` method is as follows:

```
expression.MoveTo(ToPos)
```

Here, *expression* is a required expression that returns a `Slide` object, and `ToPos` is a required Long argument that specifies the index position to which you want to move the slide.

For example, the following statement moves the third slide in the presentation identified by the object variable `myPresentation` to the beginning of the presentation:

```
myPresentation.Slides(3).MoveTo ToPos:=1
```

Accessing a Slide by Name

Instead of accessing a slide by its index number, you can assign a name to it by using the `Name` property of the `Slide` object. For example, the following statements assign the name `Chairman's Introduction` to the fifth slide in the active presentation and then use the `Select` method of the `Slide` object to select that slide by name:

```
ActivePresentation.Slides(1).Name = "Chairman's Introduction"
ActivePresentation.Slides("Chairman's Introduction").Select
```

Working with a Range of Slides

To work with a range of slides, use the `Range` method of the `Slides` collection to return a `SlideRange` object that represents the slides. The `SlideRange` object can represent a single slide, but you're usually better off using it to represent a range of slides. (You can access a single slide more easily by its index number or by a name you assign to it than through a `SlideRange` object.)

To return a `SlideRange` object that encompasses two or more slides, use the `Array` function with a comma-delimited list of the slides. The list can use either the index numbers or the names of the slides. For example, the following statements declare the `SlideRange` object variable `mySlideRange` and assign to it the first five slides in the open presentation named `HR.pptm`:

```
Dim mySlideRange As SlideRange
Set mySlideRange = _
Presentations("HR.pptm").Slides.Range(Array(1, 2, 3, 4, 5))
```

The following statement assigns to the SlideRange object variable mySlideRange the slides named Intro and Outro in the active presentation:

```
Set mySlideRange = ActivePresentation.Slides.Range(Array("Intro", "Outro"))
```

Formatting a Slide

You can apply a design template to a slide by using the ApplyTemplate method, as discussed in "Applying a Template to a Presentation, to a Slide, or to a Range of Slides," earlier in this chapter. You can also apply a background or a color scheme, as discussed in the following sections.

Applying a Background to One or More Slides

To apply a background to a slide or several slides, use the Background property of the appropriate Slide object or SlideRange object to return the ShapeRange object representing the background of the slide or slides. You can then use the Fill object to set a color, fill, gradient, or picture in the background.

The following example applies the picture Winter.jpg from the folder C:\Sample Pictures to the fourth slide in the presentation named Corporate.pptm. The example sets the FollowMasterBackground property to msoFalse, making the slide use a different background than the slide master; it also sets the DisplayMasterShapes property to msoFalse, preventing the slide from displaying the shapes on the slide master:

```
With Presentations("Corporate.pptm").Slides(4)
    .FollowMasterBackground = msoFalse
    .DisplayMasterShapes = msoFalse
    With .Background
        .Fill.ForeColor.RGB = RGB(255, 255, 255)
        .Fill.BackColor.SchemeColor = ppAccent1
        .Fill.UserPicture "C:\Sample Pictures\Winter.jpg"
    End With
End With
```

Applying a Color Scheme to a Slide

A color scheme is a group of eight colors that are used to create the look of the title, background, and other elements of a slide, handout, or notes page. VBA uses an RGBColor object to represent each color and a ColorScheme object to represent each color scheme. The ColorScheme objects are gathered in a ColorSchemes collection for the entire presentation.

To change the color scheme of a slide or several slides, use the ColorScheme property of the appropriate Slide object or SlideRange object to return the ColorScheme object, and then work with the Colors method to specify the color. The syntax is as follows:

```
expression.Colors(SchemeColor)
```

Here, *expression* is a required expression that returns a ColorScheme object. SchemeColor is a required argument that specifies which color in the color scheme to set—for example, ppAccent1 (for the first accent in the color scheme), ppBackground (for the background color) or ppTitle (for the title color).

The following statement sets the background color of the color scheme for the first three slides in the active presentation to black, which is RGB(0, 0, 0):

```
ActivePresentation.Slides.Range(Array(1, 2, 3)) _
    .ColorScheme.Colors(ppBackground).RGB = RGB(0, 0, 0)
```

Setting a Transition for a Slide, a Range of Slides, or a Master

To set a transition for a slide, a range of slides, or a master, use the SlideShowTransition property of the Slide object, the SlideRange object, or the Master object to return the SlideShowTransition object.

To specify the speed at which the transition runs, set its Speed property to ppTransitionSpeedFast, ppTransitionSpeedMedium, or ppTransitionSpeedSlow.

Real World Scenario

Creating Effective Transitions Between Slides

Using transitions between slides can make a presentation look smooth and professional or awkward and amateurish.

To specify which effect to use, you set the EntryEffect property to a constant. There are too many constants to list here, but their names are generally descriptive enough to be easy to decipher. For example, the ppEffectBlindsHorizontal constant generates a transition that is vaguely reminiscent of an adjustment of venetian blinds and the ppEffectDissolve constant causes a rather crude kind of melting effect.

You should avoid those two, and most of the other available transitions, unless you want to go back several decades to the clumsy, early TV transition effects. Contemporary television and movies employ smooth, subtle, and unobtrusive transitions between scenes. And slides are simple scenes. So, you should generally stay away from trick transitions like venetian blinds or crude transitions like the ppEffectDissolve, which is highly pixelated.

To discover which of the transition effects are sophisticated and discreet, try them out. You can preview all the transitions by clicking the Transitions tab on the PowerPoint Ribbon. Then click any slide transition you want to see.

The default transition is quite a good dissolve, but if you want to try another classy transition, experiment with ppEffectFade. It's similar to the default. Also try experimenting with the Animations tab on the PowerPoint Ribbon, which governs how you animate the various shape objects on a slide.

And try varying the transition speed to suit the animation to the subject of your presentation.

To control how the slide advances, set the AdvanceOnTime property to msoTrue (for automatic advancing) or msoFalse (for manual advancing). If you use automatic advancing, use the AdvanceTime property to specify the number of seconds. If you want the slide to advance when the user clicks, set the `AdvanceOnClick` property to `msoTrue`. (You can set both `AdvanceOnTime` and `AdvanceOnClick` to `msoTrue`. The slide advances manually if the user clicks before the `AdvanceTime` interval has elapsed.)

To play a preset sound effect with the transition, use the `SoundEffect` property of the `SlideShowTransition` object to return the `SoundEffect` object, use the `Name` property to specify the name of the sound effect, and then use the `Play` method to play the sound effect. You can also play any compatible sound file by using the `ImportFromFile` method of the `SoundEffect` object and using the `FullName` argument to specify the path and filename of the sound file.

PowerPoint 2016 can play any of the following audio-file types: `.aiff`, `.au`, `.mid`, `.midi`, `.mp3`, `.m4a`, `.mp4`, `.wav`, or `.wma`. But be aware that even if a file has one of these filename extensions, it still might not be playable if the proper codec isn't available. That's why everyone implores you to never give a *naked presentation*. Always first do a test run of any presentation on the equipment you'll be using for the official presentation when people are there closely watching you. You might remember certain botched Microsoft and Apple product announcement presentations that, at the very least, put a dent in *somebody's* career.

If you want the sound to loop until the next sound, set the `LoopSoundUntilNext` property of the `SlideShowTransition` object to `msoTrue`. The default value is `msoFalse`.

The following example sets up a transition for the second slide in the active presentation. The transition uses the Fade effect running at medium speed, sets advancing to either on click or after a delay of 30 seconds, and plays a sound file from an external source without looping:

```
With ActivePresentation.Slides(2)
    With .SlideShowTransition
        .EntryEffect = ppEffectFade
        .Speed = ppTransitionSpeedMedium
        .AdvanceOnClick = msoTrue
        .AdvanceOnTime = msoTrue
        .AdvanceTime = 30
        .SoundEffect.ImportFromFile _
            FileName:="d:\Sounds\Crescendo.wav"
        .LoopSoundUntilNext = msoFalse
    End With
End With
```

To see this particular effect, you can press F5 in the Code window, switch to the PowerPoint window, and then press F5 again. (You'll also need to either delete the two lines of code that refer to sound, or provide a file path to an actual sound file on your machine.)

Working with Masters

VBA uses the `Master` object to represent the various masters that PowerPoint uses: the slide master, title master, handout master, and notes master.

Working with the Slide Master

To work with the slide master for a presentation, use the `SlideMaster` property of the `Presentation` object.

To return the slide master for a slide, use the `Master` property of the appropriate `Slide` object. For example, the following statement adds a title to the slide master for the active presentation (if the slide master already has a title, VBA returns an error):

```
ActivePresentation.SlideMaster.Shapes.AddTitle.TextFrame.TextRange.Text = _
    "Orientation"
```

Working with the Title Master

To find out whether a presentation has a title master, check the `HasTitleMaster` property. If it doesn't, you can use the `AddTitleMaster` method of the `Presentation` object to add a title master, as in the following example. If the presentation already has a title master, VBA returns an error when you try to add a title master:

```
If Not ActivePresentation.HasTitleMaster Then _
ActivePresentation.AddTitleMaster
```

To return the title master for the presentation, use the `TitleMaster` property of the `Presentation` object. The following example checks that the title master exists and, if it does, formats the date and time to be visible and to use the `dMMMyy` format with automatic updating:

```
With myPresentation
    If .HasTitleMaster Then
        With .TitleMaster.HeadersFooters.DateAndTime
            .Visible = msoTrue
            .Format = ppDateTimedMMMyy
            .UseFormat = msoTrue
        End With
    End If
End With
```

Working with the Handout Master

To work with the handout master, use the `HandoutMaster` property of the `Presentation` object to return the `Master` object. The following example uses the `HandoutMaster` property of the `ActivePresentation` object to fill the background of the handout master with a picture:

```
With ActivePresentation.HandoutMaster.Background
    .Fill.ForeColor.RGB = RGB(255, 255, 255)
    .Fill.BackColor.SchemeColor = ppAccent1
    .Fill.UserPicture "d:\igrafx\dawn.jpg"
End With
```

Working with the Notes Master

To work with the notes master, use the `NotesMaster` property of the `Presentation` object to return the `Master` object. For example, the following statement clears the `HeaderFooter` objects in the notes master in the first open presentation:

```
Presentations(1).NotesMaster.HeadersFooters.Clear
```

Deleting a Master

You can delete the title master or handout master, but not the slide master or notes master. To delete the title master or handout master, use the `Delete` method of the `Master` object. The following example checks that the active presentation has a title master and then deletes it:

```
If ActivePresentation.HasTitleMaster Then _
 ActivePresentation.TitleMaster.Delete
```

The Bottom Line

Understand PowerPoint's creatable objects. Creatable objects are commonly used objects that can be employed in VBA code without requiring that you qualify them with the `Application` object. You can leave that word out of your code; it's optional and rarely used.

Master It Name one of the objects or collections that are creatable in PowerPoint macros.

Work with presentations. You can create a new presentation programmatically, but PowerPoint generates an annoying flicker on most systems while it brings the new presentation into view. You can block this unpleasant, strobelike effect to avoid disturbing your audience.

Master It How do you prevent a newly created presentation from being visible so that you can create and manipulate it in your code without the user seeing the flickering effect onscreen?

Work with windows and views. To get the PowerPoint window into the state you want, you'll often need to work with the window and with the view.

Master It PowerPoint uses two types of windows. What are they?

Work with slides. Once you have created or opened the presentation you want to manipulate, you can access the slides it contains by using the `Slides` collection. This collection contains a `Slide` object for each slide in the presentation. Each slide is identified by its index number, but you can also use object variables to refer to slides or to assign names to slides.

Master It Why would you want to assign names to slides rather than using the default index numbers that are automatically assigned to the slides?

Work with masters. Before attempting to manipulate a master in your code, you should determine whether the master actually exists in the presentation.

Master It How do you find out whether a presentation has a title master?

Chapter 25

Working with Shapes and Running Slide Shows

In the previous chapter, you learned to work with `Presentation` objects, `Slide` objects, and `Master` objects. In this chapter, you'll learn to work with `Shape` objects to manipulate the contents of slides and with `HeaderFooter` objects to control the contents of headers and footers. You'll also see how to set up and run a slide show using VBA.

IN THIS CHAPTER, YOU WILL LEARN TO DO THE FOLLOWING:

- Work with shapes
- Work with headers and footers
- Set up and run a slide show

Working with Shapes

Most of the objects on a typical PowerPoint slide are `Shape` objects. For example, a title box is a `Shape` object, as is a picture or a Word table that you've pasted in. You access the `Shape` objects through the `Shapes` collection of a `Slide` object, a `SlideRange` object, or a `Master` object.

Adding Shapes to Slides

Varying methods of the `Shapes` collection add the different types of shapes. Table 25.1 lists the `Shape` objects you can add and the methods and arguments for adding them. The following sections explain the arguments. You can find additional details about the `Shapes` object here:

```
http://msdn.microsoft.com/en-us/library/office/ff745286.aspx
```

Shared Arguments for Adding Shapes

These are arguments that are shared among various shape-adding methods:

- `BeginX` and `EndX` are required arguments (of the Single data type) that specify the horizontal starting position and ending position of the connector or line, measured in points from the left edge of the slide.
- `BeginY` and `EndY` are required Single data arguments that specify the vertical starting point and ending point of the connector or line, measured in points from the top of the slide.

- `FileName` is a required String argument used to specify the file to be used for creating the object (for example, the media file for creating a media object).
- `Left` is a required Single argument that specifies the position of the left edge of the shape from the left edge of the slide, measured in points. `Top` is a required Single argument that specifies the position of the top edge of the shape from the top edge of the slide, measured in points.
- `Height` is a required Single argument that specifies the height of the shape, measured in points. `Width` is a required Single argument that specifies the width of the shape, measured in points.
- `LinkToFile` is on optional argument that you can set to `msoTrue` to link the picture to its source file.
- `NumColumns` and `NumRows` are required Long arguments that specify the number of columns and rows in the table you're adding.
- `Orientation` is a required argument that specifies the orientation: `msoTextOrientationHorizontal` (horizontal) or `msoTextOrientationVerticalFarEast` (vertical).
- `SafeArrayOfPoints` is a required Variant argument that supplies an array of coordinate pairs that give the vertices and control points of a curve or polyline. The line begins at the first pair of coordinates and ends at the last pair.
- `SaveWithDocument` is a required argument that controls whether PowerPoint saves the linked picture in the presentation (`msoTrue`) or not (`msoFalse`). If you set `LinkToFile: =msoFalse`, you must set `SaveWithDocument: =msoTrue`.

TABLE 25.1: Shapes and the methods for adding them to slides

To Add This Shape	Use This Method and These Arguments
Callout	`AddCallout(Type, Left, Top, Width, Height)`
Chart	`AddChart(Type, Left, Top, Width, Height)`
Chart2	`AddChart(Style, Type, Left, Top, Width, Height, NewLayout)`
Comment	`AddComment(Left, Top, Width, Height)`
Connector	`AddConnector(Type, BeginX, BeginY, EndX, EndY)`
Curve	`AddCurve(SafeArrayOfPoints)`
Label	`AddLabel(Orientation, Left, Top, Width, Height)`
Line	`AddLine(BeginX, BeginY, EndX, EndY)`
Media object	`AddMediaObject(FileName, Left, Top, Width, Height)`
Media object 2	`AddMediaObject2(FileName, LinkToFile, Left, Top, Width, Height)`

TABLE 2.2: Shapes and the methods for adding them to slides *(CONTINUED)*

TO ADD THIS SHAPE	USE THIS METHOD AND THESE ARGUMENTS
Media object from embed tag	`AddMediaObjectFromEmbedTag(EmbedTag, Left, Top, Width, Height)`
OLE object	`AddOLEObject(Left, Top, Width, Height, ClassName, FileName, DisplayAsIcon, IconFileName, IconIndex, IconLabel, Link)`
Picture	`AddPicture(FileName, LinkToFile, SaveWithDocument, Left, Top, Width, Height)`
Placeholder	`AddPlaceholder(Type, Left, Top, Width, Height)`
Polyline	`AddPolyline(SafeArrayOfPoints)`
Shape	`AddShape(Type, Left, Top, Width, Height)`
Smart Art	`AddSmartArt(Layout, Left, Top, Width, Height)`
Table	`AddTable(NumRows, NumColumns, Left, Top, Width, Height)`
Textbox	`AddTextbox(Orientation, Left, Top, Width, Height)`
Text Effect	`AddTextEffect(PresetTextEffect, Text, FontName, FontSize, FontBold, FontItalic, Left, Top)`
Title	`AddTitle`

TYPE ARGUMENT FOR ADDING SHAPES

The `Type` argument is different for the various methods that use it. Here are some examples:

- `Type` for the `AddPlaceholder` method is a required argument that specifies the type of placeholder to add. The names are self-explanatory: `ppPlaceholderBitmap`, `ppPlaceholderBody`, `ppPlaceholderCenterTitle`, `ppPlaceholderChart`, `ppPlaceholderDate`, `ppPlaceholderFooter`, `ppPlaceholderHeader`, `ppPlaceholderMediaClip`, `ppPlaceholderMixed`, `ppPlaceholderObject`, `ppPlaceholderOrgChart`, `ppPlaceholderPicture`, `ppPlaceholderSlideNumber`, `ppPlaceholderSubtitle`, `ppPlaceholderTable`, `ppPlaceholderTitle`, `ppPlaceholderVerticalBody`, `ppPlaceholderVerticalObject`, `ppPlaceholderVerticalTitle`

LIMITATIONS ON PLACEHOLDERS

You can use the `ppPlaceholderVerticalBody` and `ppPlaceholderVerticalTitle` placeholders only on slides that use vertical text—the slide layouts `ppLayoutVerticalText`, `ppLayoutClipArtAndVerticalText`, `ppLayoutVerticalTitleAndText`, and `ppLayout VerticalTitleAndTextOverChart`.

- Type for the `AddCallout` method is a required argument that specifies the type of callout line to add: `msoCalloutOne` (a one-segment line that can be vertical or horizontal), `msoCalloutTwo` (a one-segment line that rotates freely), `msoCalloutThree` (a two-segment line), or `msoCalloutFour` (a three-segment line).
- Type for the `AddShape` method is a required argument that specifies the type of AutoShape to add. There are too many constants to list here, but most are easy to identify from their names. For example, `msoShapeHeart` is a heart shape, `msoShapeLightningBolt` gives a lightning bolt, and so on. To see a list of the constants, search for the `AddShape` method in the VBA Editor Help file, and then click the link for the `msoAutoShapeType` entry. Or, type **msoautoshapetype** in the Editor's Object Browser search field.
- Type for the `AddDiagram` method is a required argument that specifies the diagram type: `msoDiagramCycle` (a cycle diagram), `msoDiagramOrgChart` (an org chart), `msoDiagramPyramid` (a pyramid diagram), `msoDiagramRadial` (a radial diagram), `msoDiagramTarget` (a target diagram), or `msoDiagramVenn` (a Venn diagram).

Real World Scenario

WHAT IS *MSO*? PRACTICAL ADVICE FOR THE PERPLEXED PROGRAMMER

You may have noticed that many of the enumerations and constants you're running into in PowerPoint are prepended (the opposite of *appended*) by *mso*. This strange little acronym can stand for several things: Martha Stewart's stock market name (Martha Stewart Omnimedia), Milwaukee Symphony Orchestra, or Microsoft Office. In PowerPoint, it stands for *Microsoft Office*. And why it is prepended to PowerPoint enumerations and not to other Office 2016 enumerations is just one of those mysteries that keep all us programmers on our toes. After all, even those of us who are semiconscious are likely aware that we're using VBA in Microsoft Office.

Here's another example of a mystery. Throughout the decades of BASIC programming history, and in all other versions of BASIC and VBA, you use the words `True` and `False` to mean true and false. That makes a certain kind of sense when you think about it. However, in PowerPoint 2016, you can also use the built-in constants `msoTrue` and `msoFalse` to, for example, set the `Visible` property of a footer on a slide. Luckily, these constants are optional. You can still use the traditional `True` and `False`. There is no difference between Microsoft Office's truth and truth in general. (I'm speaking here strictly in the context of these constants.)

Mso also appears in the `MsoTriState` variable type—that bizarro uber-Boolean type that you ran into in the previous chapter.

ARGUMENTS SPECIFIC TO THE ADDTEXTEFFECT METHOD

The following arguments apply only to the `AddTextEffect` method:

- `PresetTextEffect` is a required argument that specifies the preset text effect to use. These preset text effects are identified by the constants `msoTextEffect1` through msoTextEffect30, which correspond to the order in which the samples appear in the WordArt Gallery dialog box (1 through 6 are the first row, 7 through 12 the second row, and so on).

- Text is a required String argument that specifies the text to use in the WordArt object.
- FontBold is a required argument that you set to msoTrue to make the font bold or msoFalse to make it not bold.
- FontItalic is a required argument that you set to msoTrue to make the font italic and msoFalse to make it not italic.
- FontName is a required String argument that specifies the name of the font to use.
- FontSize is a required Single argument that specifies the font size to use.

ARGUMENTS SPECIFIC TO THE *ADDOLEOBJECT* METHOD

The following arguments apply only to the AddOLEObject method:

- ClassName is an optional String argument that specifies the program ID (the ProgID) or OLE long class name for the object. You must use either ClassName or FileName, but not both. In most cases, it's easiest to use FileName.
- DisplayAsIcon is an optional argument that you can set to msoTrue to display the OLE object as an icon rather than as itself (the default).
- IconFileName is an optional String argument that you can use with DisplayAsIcon:=True to specify the filename of the icon you want to display for the object.
- IconIndex is an optional Integer argument that specifies the index of the icon to use within the icon file specified by IconFileName. If you omit the IconIndex argument, VBA uses the second icon in the icon file, the icon at position 1 (the first icon in the file is at position 0).
- IconLabel is an optional String argument that you can use to specify the caption (or label) to display under the icon.
- Link is an optional argument that you can set to msoTrue to link the OLE object to its source file when you use the FileName argument. Link must be msoFalse when you use ClassName to specify a class name.

AN EXAMPLE OF USING THE *ADDSHAPE* METHOD

The following statement uses the AddShape method to add a bent up-arrow to the upper-right corner of the last slide in the active presentation. Before executing this example, click the File tab on PowerPoint's Ribbon, and then click the New option in the left pane to see some of the available templates and themes. Double-click one of the templates so you'll have some slides to work with in this example. (In versions of PowerPoint prior to 2013, you'll have to open the Sample Templates folder before choosing a template.)

Open the Visual Basic Editor by pressing Alt+F11. Locate the project in the Project window, right-click on its name (it will be boldface), and choose Insert ➤ Module. Type the following into the new module, and then press F5 with your blinking cursor inside this subroutine to execute the code and see the effect:

```
Sub test()

ActivePresentation.Slides(ActivePresentation.Slides.Count) _
    .Shapes.AddShape Type:=msoShapeBentUpArrow, Left:=575, Top:=10, _
    Width:=150, Height:=75

End Sub
```

To see what happened, look at last slide and notice that a shape has been added to it—a bent up-arrow.

An Example of Using the *AddTextEffect* Method

The following example uses the `AddTextEffect` method to superimpose a WordArt item onto the third slide. Ensure that you have at least three slides by pressing Ctrl+M a few times to add some new slides.

This code draws the text *Questions & Answers* (on three lines) on the slide. This WordArt item is instructed in our code to use 54-point bold Garamond.

```
ActivePresentation.Slides(3).Shapes.AddTextEffect _
   PresetTextEffect:=msoTextEffect14, _
       Text:="Questions" + Chr$(CharCode:=13) + _
       "&" + Chr$(CharCode:=13) + "Answers", _
       FontName:="Garamond", FontSize:=54, FontBold:=msoTrue, _
       FontItalic:=msoFalse, Left:=230, Top:=125
```

There are 30 `msoTextEffect` constants you can experiment with. They range from `msoTextEffect1` to `msoTextEffect30`. `msoTextEffect14` is nice; it provides a kind of metallic effect. See Figure 25.1.

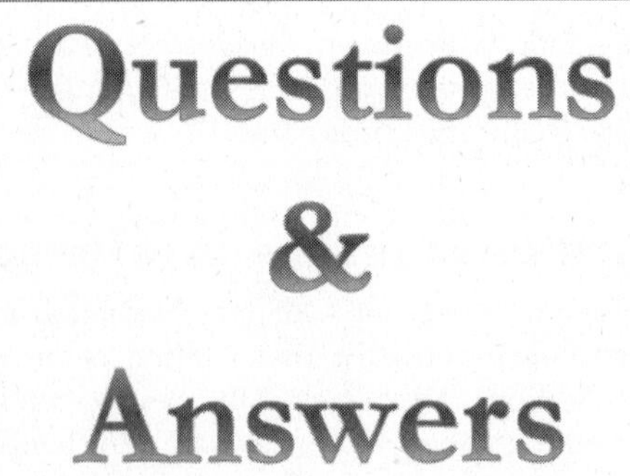

Figure 25.1
msoTextEffect 14 offers a metallic look.

AN EXAMPLE OF USING THE *ADDTEXTBOX* METHOD

The following example adds a text box to the second slide in the active presentation and assigns text to it:

```
Dim myTextBox As Shape

With ActivePresentation.Slides(2)
    Set myTextBox = .Shapes.AddTextbox _
        (Orientation:=msoTextOrientationHorizontal, Left:=100, Top:=50, _
        Width:=400, Height:=100)
    myTextBox.TextFrame.TextRange.Text = "Corrective Lenses"
End With
```

Deleting a Shape

To delete a shape, use the `Delete` method with the appropriate `Shape` object. For example, the following statement deletes the first `Shape` object on the second slide in the active presentation:

```
ActivePresentation.Slides(2).Shapes(1).Delete
```

Selecting All Shapes

To select all the shapes on a slide, use the `SelectAll` method of the appropriate `Shapes` collection. For example, the following statement selects all the `Shape` objects on the first slide in the active presentation:

```
ActivePresentation.Slides(1).Shapes.SelectAll
```

Repositioning and Resizing a Shape

To reposition a shape, set its `Left` property (to specify the distance in points from the left edge of the slide to the left edge of the shape) and its `Top` property (to specify the distance in points from the top edge of the slide to the top edge of the shape).

To change the size of a shape, set its `Width` and `Height` properties to the appropriate number of points.

For example, the following statements position the first shape on the first slide in the active presentation 200 points from the left side of the slide and 100 points from its top, and make the shape 300 points wide by 200 points high:

```
With ActivePresentation.Slides(1).Shapes(1)
    .Left = 200
    .Top = 100
    .Width = 300
    .Height = 200
End With
```

You can also move a shape relative to its current location by using the `IncrementLeft` method and the `IncrementTop` method. Rotate it by using the `IncrementRotation` method.

Note that these methods are not absolute specified locations within a slide. Instead, they are relative to the current position or rotation of the shape. Each of these methods takes an `Increment` argument:

- For the `IncrementLeft` and `IncrementTop` methods, the `Increment` argument specifies the number of points to move the shape. A negative number moves the shape to the left or upward, while a positive number moves the shape to the right or downward.
- For the `IncrementRotation` method, the `Increment` argument specifies the number of degrees to rotate the shape. A positive number rotates the shape clockwise; a negative number rotates the shape counterclockwise.

The following example works with the first shape on the third slide of the active presentation, moving it 100 points to the left and 200 points down and rotating it 90 degrees counterclockwise:

```
With ActivePresentation.Slides(3).Shapes(1)
    .IncrementLeft Increment:=-100
    .IncrementTop Increment:=200
    .IncrementRotation Increment:=-90
End With
```

Copying Formatting from One Shape to Another

Often, it's useful to be able to apply the same formatting to multiple shapes. When one shape has the formatting you want, you can use the `PickUp` method of the `Shape` object to copy the formatting from that shape and then use the `Apply` method to apply that formatting to another shape.

Neither the `PickUp` method nor the `Apply` method uses any arguments. The following example copies the formatting from the first shape on the second slide in the active presentation and applies it to the third shape on the fourth slide:

```
With ActivePresentation
    .Slides(2).Shapes(1).PickUp
    .Slides(4).Shapes(3).Apply
End With
```

Working with Text in a Shape

The text within a shape is contained in a `TextRange` object, which itself is contained in a `TextFrame` object. To work with the text in a shape, you use the `TextFrame` property of the `Shape` object to return the `TextFrame` object and then use the `TextRange` property of the `TextFrame` object to return the `TextRange` object. Got it? (Remember that some objects can have complex, one might say baffling, relationships.)

Within the `TextRange` object, the `Text` property contains the text, the `Font` object contains the font formatting, the `ParagraphFormat` object contains the paragraph formatting, and the `ActionSettings` collection contains the action settings for the text range.

Finding Out Whether a Shape Has a Text Frame

Not every shape has a text frame; so prior to manipulating text, it's a good idea to first determine whether the shape you're dealing with in fact even *has* a text frame.

To do so, check that the `HasTextFrame` property of the `Shape` object is `msoTrue`, as in this example:

```
If ActivePresentation.Slides(1).Shapes(1).HasTextFrame = msoTrue Then
    MsgBox "The shape contains a text frame."
End If
```

You may also need to check whether the text frame contains text. To do so, check that the `HasText` property of the `TextFrame` object is `msoTrue`. Here's an example:

```
With ActivePresentation.Slides(1).Shapes(1).TextFrame
    If .HasText = msoTrue Then MsgBox .TextRange.Text
End With
```

Returning and Setting the Text in a Text Range

To return (read) or set (specify) the text in a text range, you can simply use the `Text` property of the `TextRange` object. For example, the following statement sets the text in the first shape on the fourth slide in the presentation identified by the object variable `myPresentation` to `Strategic Planning Meeting`:

```
Sub Test()

Dim myPresentation As Presentation
Set myPresentation = Presentations(1)

myPresentation.Slides(4).Shapes(1).TextFrame.TextRange.Text _
    = "Strategic Planning Meeting"

End Sub
```

You can also return parts of the text by using the `Paragraphs` method, the `Sentences` method, the `Lines` method, the `Words` method, the `Characters` method, or the `Runs` method. The syntax for these methods is shown here, using the `Paragraphs` method as the example:

```
expression.Paragraphs(Start, Length)
```

The components of the syntax are as follows:

- *`expression`* is a required expression that returns a `TextRange` object.
- `Start` is an optional Long argument that specifies the first item (paragraph, sentence, line, word, character, or text run) to return.
- `Length` is an optional Long argument that specifies how many items to return—for example, two paragraphs, three sentences, or four words.

> **UNDERSTANDING TEXT RUNS**
>
> A *text run* is a sequence of characters that have the same font formatting. Text runs can be useful for picking out parts of text ranges that are formatted in a particular way.

The following code example returns the second through fifth words (the four words starting with the second word) from the first shape on the first slide in the active presentation:

```
MsgBox ActivePresentation.Slides(1).Shapes(1).TextFrame _
    .TextRange.Words(Start:=2, Length:=4)
```

The next code example sets the text of the second paragraph in the second shape on the sixth slide in the presentation identified by the object variable `myPresentation` to `VP of Business Development`:

```
myPresentation.Slides(6).Shapes(2).TextFrame.TextRange _
    .Paragraphs(Start:=2, Length:=1).Text = "VP of Business Development"
```

FORMATTING THE TEXT IN A TEXT RANGE

To format the text in a text range, use the `ParagraphFormat` object to control the paragraph formatting (including the alignment and the space before and after) and the `Font` object to control the font formatting.

These are the most useful properties of the `ParagraphFormat` object:

- The `Alignment` property controls the alignment. Use `ppAlignLeft` for left alignment, `ppAlignCenter` for centering, `ppAlignJustify` for justified alignment, `ppAlignDistribute` for distributed alignment (justified using all available space), or `ppAlignRight` for right alignment.
- The `Bullet` property returns the `BulletFormat` object, which represents the bullet formatting. See the next section for details.
- The `LineRuleBefore` property, the `LineRuleAfter` property, and the `LineRuleWithin` property determine whether the measurements set by the `SpaceBefore` property, the `SpaceAfter` property, and the `SpaceWithin` property use lines (`msoTrue`) or points (`msoFalse`).
- The `SpaceBefore` property and the `SpaceAfter` property control the amount of space before and after each paragraph. The `SpaceWithin` property controls the amount of space between base lines in a paragraph. All measurements are in points.

The following example sets left alignment, 18 points of spacing before and after paragraphs, and 12 points of spacing between lines for the second shape on the slide identified by the object variable `mySlide`:

```
Dim mySlide As Slide
Set mySlide = Presentations(1).Slides(2)

With mySlide.Shapes(2).TextFrame.TextRange.ParagraphFormat
    .Alignment = ppAlignLeft
    .LineRuleAfter = msoFalse
    .SpaceAfter = 18
    .LineRuleBefore = msoFalse
    .SpaceBefore = 18
    .LineRuleWithin = msoFalse
    .SpaceWithin = 12
End With
```

Formatting the Bullets for a Text Range

Bullets and numbers are vital to the lists used in many PowerPoint slides. To control whether and how bullets and numbers appear, use the `Bullet` property of the `TextRange` object to return the `BulletFormat` object, and then work with the `BulletFormat` object's properties and methods.

To make bullets and numbers visible, set the `Visible` property of the `BulletFormat` object to `msoTrue`; to hide bullets and numbers, set `Visible` to `msoFalse`.

To specify which type of bullet or numbering to use, set the `Type` property of the `BulletFormat` object to `ppBulletUnnumbered` (for a bullet), `ppBulletNumbered` (numbers), `ppBulletPicture` (for a picture), or `ppBulletNone` (no bullet).

> **Another Mixed Data Type**
>
> The `Type` property of the `BulletFormat` object returns the value `ppBulletMixed` when the selection includes multiple types of bullets. You can't set (write) `ppBulletMixed` to `Type`. You can only read it.

To specify the bullet character, use the `Character` property and the character number. You can find out the character number from the Symbol dialog box or the Character Map applet, which you can run by pressing the Windows key to open Start menu in Windows 10 (or reveal the icons view in Windows 8) and then typing **Character Map**.

Seeing this desktop application in previous versions of Windows is somewhat clumsier. For Windows 7 and previous, click Start ➢ All Programs ➢ Accessories ➢ System Tools ➢ Character Map.

Unfortunately, the character codes are given in the *hexadecimal* numbering system. If you look up the check-box symbol for the Wingdings font that's used in the following code example, the character map utility doesn't say 254 in our human, decimal numbering system. Instead, it says Character Code: 0xFE (the hex way of expressing 254).

This tedious holdover from the early days of computing serves no particular purpose in character codes, but you have to deal with it. Why? Because some people think that pointless complexity is cute, or it helps make programming seem somehow more mysterious than it in fact is. Complications like this can also obviously help improve job security because managers will usually be dazzled by what they assume are complicated programming mysteries like hex. Hex (short for hexadecimal) is based on 16 digits: 0 1 2 3 4 5 6 7 8 9 A B C D E F. People with eight fingers on each hand have an advantage here.

To solve the hex-character-code problem, you can either use a calculator that can translate between hex and decimal or just prepend the characters *&H* in front of the hex code and let VBA translate it for you when the macro executes.

For example, in the following code example, I used 254 (a decimal number) because I can translate hex (well, my HP programming calculator can). But if you can't, or more likely don't want to be bothered, just click the character you want to use in the Character Map dialog box and then look at its hex code in the lower left of the dialog box. In this example, it's listed as 0xFE (which means, you guessed it, decimal 254). Because the Wingdings font has only 256 characters, ignore the *0x* part and use the *FE*, like this, in your code:

```
.Character = &H FE
```

Use the `Font` property to specify the font name, size, and color. The following example sets the bullet for the first shape on the slide identified by the object variable `mySlide` to Wingdings character 254, a check box, using the color white, which is `RGB(255, 255, 255)`, and 44-point size:

```
With mySlide.Shapes(1).TextFrame.TextRange.ParagraphFormat.Bullet
    .Type = ppBulletUnnumbered
    .Character = 254
    With .Font
        .Name = "Wingdings"
        .Size = 44
        .Color = RGB(255, 255, 255)
    End With
End With
```

Color is, of course, an important element in any design. You can easily find out which RGB values you need to employ for various colors by visiting this web page:

```
http://cloford.com/resources/colours/500col.htm
```

To use your own custom picture as a bullet, set the `Type` property of the `BulletFormat` object to `ppBulletPicture` and then use the `Picture` method with the `Picture` argument, a required String argument that specifies the path and filename of the file to use as the bullet. You can use most common types of graphics files, including `.bmp`, `.eps`, `.gif`, `.jpg`, `.jpeg`, `.pcx`, `.png`, `.tiff`, and `.wmf` files. (The `.png` graphic file type allows for higher quality resolution than most other methods, so many people now prefer this way of saving images.) The following example uses the file `Face1.png` stored in the folder `Z:\Public\Pictures` as the bullet for the first shape on the slide identified by the object variable `mySlide`:

```
With mySlide.Shapes(1).TextFrame.TextRange.ParagraphFormat.Bullet
    .Type = ppBulletPicture
    .Picture Picture:="z:\Public\Pictures\Face1.png"
End With
```

Animating a Shape or a Range of Shapes

To animate a shape or a range of shapes, use the `AnimationSettings` property of the `Shape` object or the `ShapeRange` object to return the `AnimationSettings` object.

To specify the animation effect to use, set the `EntryEffect` property to the constant for the effect. Let's see how to figure out which animation effect looks best for the shape you're working with. First, click a shape in a slide to select the shape. Now display the Add Animation pane.

There are too many animation constants to list here, but their names are easy to understand from the names listed in the Add Animation pane. To open this pane, click an object within a slide that you'd like to animate (to select it) and then click the Animations tab in PowerPoint's Ribbon. Finally, click the Add Animation icon in the Advanced Animation section.

A pane drops down in PowerPoint's window, as shown in Figure 25.2.

As usual with animations, less is more. Choose subtle effects unless you're presenting to an audience of louts who will appreciate vulgarity.

To write code that creates an animation, set the `Animate` property to `msoTrue`. (To turn off an animation, set `Animate` to `msoFalse`.)

To control how the text in a shape is animated, set the `TextLevelEffect` property to `ppAnimateLevelNone` (no animation), `ppAnimateByFirstLevel`, `ppAnimateBySecond-Level`, `ppAnimateByThirdLevel`, `ppAnimateByFourthLevel`, `ppAnimateByFifthLevel`, or `ppAnimateByAllLevels`.

If you set `TextLevelEffect` to any value other than `ppAnimateByAllLevels` or `ppAnimate LevelNone`, you can use the `TextUnitEffect` property to specify how to animate the text. Use `ppAnimateByParagraph` to animate by paragraph, `ppAnimateByWord` to animate by word, or `ppAnimateByCharacter` to animate by character.

To reverse the order of the animation, set the `AnimateTextInReverse` property to `msoTrue`. (The default is `msoFalse`.)

To control how the animation advances, set the `AdvanceMode` property to `ppAdvanceOnTime` (for automatic advancing using a timing) or `ppAdvanceOnClick` (for manual advancing). If you use automatic advancing, use the `AdvanceTime` property to specify the number of seconds to wait before advancing.

To play a built-in sound effect with the transition, use the `SoundEffect` property of the `AnimationSettings` object to return the `SoundEffect` object, use the `Name` property to specify the name of the sound effect, and then use the `Play` method to play the sound effect. You can also play your own sound file by using the `ImportFromFile` method of the `SoundEffect` object and using the `FullName` argument to specify the path and filename of the sound file.

To control how a media clip is played, use the `PlaySettings` property of the `Animation Settings` object to return the `PlaySettings` object. For example, if you want the sound to loop until the next sound, set the `LoopSoundUntilNext` property of the `PlaySettings` object within the `AnimationSettings` object to `msoTrue`. The default value is `msoFalse`.

You can find all these options by pressing F2 to display the Object Browser in the VBA Editor and then searching for them. For example, search for `ppEntryEffect` to see all possible constants for the various possible lead-in animations.

The following example applies a custom animation to the first shape on the slide identified by the object variable `mySlide`. The animation uses the entry effect Fly In From Right, plays a sound effect from a file, animates the text by first-level paragraphs and by whole paragraphs, and advances when the user clicks:

```
Dim mySlide As Slide
Set mySlide = Presentations(1).Slides(2)
```

```
With mySlide.Shapes(1).AnimationSettings
    .EntryEffect = ppEffectFlyFromRight
    .AdvanceMode = ppAdvanceOnClick
    .SoundEffect.ImportFromFile FileName:="D:\Media\Whistle4.wav"
    .TextLevelEffect = ppAnimateByFirstLevel
    .TextUnitEffect = ppAnimateByParagraph
End With
```

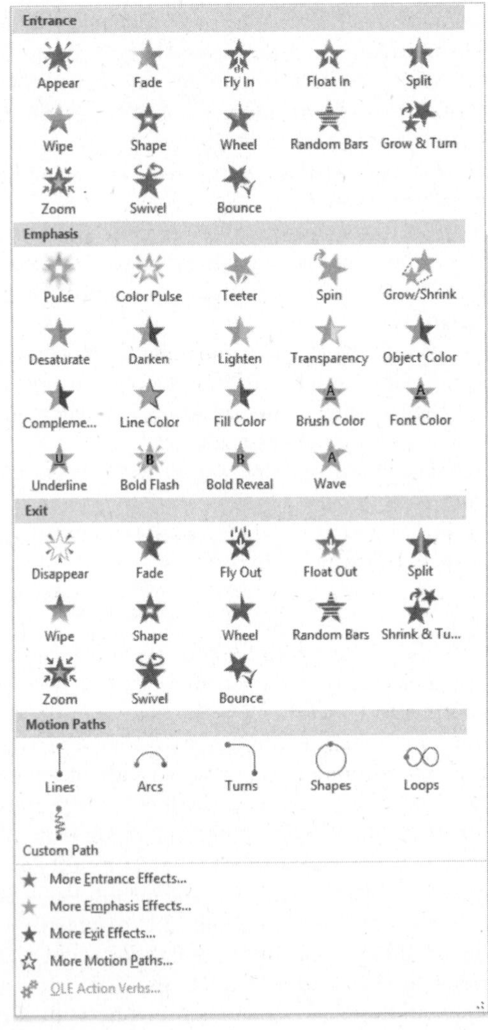

FIGURE 25.2 Here's a selection of animation effects available for use in PowerPoint.

To test this (or other code examples you try in PowerPoint), just press F5 in the main PowerPoint window, and then repeatedly click the screen to activate the various transitions and effects. Press Esc when you're done.

Working with Headers and Footers

PowerPoint uses `HeaderFooter` objects to represent the headers, footers, slide numbers, and date and time on slides. The `HeaderFooter` objects are organized into the `HeadersFooters` collection, which you access through the `HeaderFooters` property of the `Master` object, a `Slide` object, or a `SlideRange` collection.

Be warned: Before you can execute the following code examples, you must first *add a footer to the slides in your active presentation.* The code examples expect to modify an existing footer, not to create it (unlike in Excel, where a new header or footer *will* be created automatically).

So, before executing these examples, click the Insert tab on PowerPoint's Ribbon, and then in the Text area, click the Header And Footer button to open the Header And Footer dialog box. In this dialog box, click the Date And Time check box and the Footer check box. Then click the Apply To All button.

Returning the Header or Footer Object You Want

To access the object you want, use the appropriate property of the `HeaderFooter` object:

- Use the `DateAndTime` property to return the date and time.
- Use the `Footer` property to return the footer itself.
- Use the `Header` property to return the header on a notes page or handout. Slides themselves can't have a header.
- Use the `SlideNumber` property to return the slide number on a slide or the page number on a notes page or a handout.

The following example uses the `Footer` property to set the text of the `HeaderFooter` object of the first slide in the active presentation:

```
ActivePresentation.Slides(1).HeadersFooters.Footer.Text = "Sentence 102"
```

Displaying or Hiding a Header or Footer Object

To display the `HeaderFooter` object, set its `Visible` property to `msoTrue` (or just `True`). To hide the `HeaderFooter` object, set its `Visible` property to `msoFalse`. For example, the following statement hides the footer on the fifth slide in the active presentation:

```
ActivePresentation.Slides(5).HeadersFooters.Footer.Visible = False
```

Setting the Text in a Header or Footer

To set the text that you want in a `HeaderFooter` object, assign a string containing the text to the object's `Text` property. For example, the following statement sets the text of the footer of the fifth slide in the active presentation to `Confidential`:

```
ActivePresentation.Slides(5).HeadersFooters.Footer.Text = "Confidential"
```

If you executed the previous example code, executing this example will trigger an error message. That's because you made the footer for slide 5 invisible in the previous code. To be able to set the text in this slide, it must first be visible:

```
ActivePresentation.Slides(5).HeadersFooters.Footer.Visible = True
ActivePresentation.Slides(5).HeadersFooters.Footer.Text = "Confidential"
```

Setting the Format for Date and Time Headers and Footers

If your slides, notes pages, or handouts use dates and times in their footers or headers, use the `Format` property to specify how the dates and times should appear. Table 25.2 lists the constants you can use.

TABLE 25.2: `Format` property constants for date and time headers and footers

FORMAT	EXAMPLE
`ppDateTimeddddMMMMddyyyy`	Wednesday, October 05, 2016
`ppDateTimedMMMMyyyy`	5 October 2016
`ppDateTimedMMMyy`	5-Oct-16
`ppDateTimeFormatMixed`	10/5/2016
`ppDateTimeHmm`	10:17
`ppDateTimehmmAMPM`	10:17AM
`ppDateTimeHmmss`	10:17:16
`ppDateTimehmmssAMPM`	10:17:16AM
`ppDateTimeMdyy`	10/5/2016
`ppDateTimeMMddyyHmm`	10/5/2016 10:17AM
`ppDateTimeMMddyyhmmAMPM`	10/5/2016 10:17:16AM
`ppDateTimeMMMMdyyyy`	October 5, 2016
`ppDateTimeMMMMyy`	October 16
`ppDateTimeMMyy`	Oct-16

Set the UseFormat property of the HeaderFooter to msoTrue if you want the date and time to be updated automatically. Set UseFormat to msoFalse if you want the date and time to remain unchanged.

The following example displays the current date in the format Tuesday, April 12, 2016:

```
Sub SetFooter()

Dim objPresTation As Presentation
Set objPresTation = Application.ActivePresentation

With objPresTation.Slides(2).HeadersFooters.DateAndTime

     .UseFormat = True

     .Format = ppDateTimeddddMMMMddyyyy

End With


End Sub
```

Setting Up and Running a Slide Show

Not only can you assemble and format a slide show using VBA; you can also run it using VBA. To set up a slide show, use the SlideShowSettings property of the Presentation object to return the SlideShowSettings object. When you run the slide show, VBA creates a SlideShowWindow object, which you can then manipulate to control the slide show.

Controlling the Show Type

To specify the type of show, set the ShowType property of the SlideShowSettings object to ppShowTypeSpeaker (for a standard full-screen presentation presented by a speaker), ppShowTypeKiosk (for a kiosk presentation), or ppShowTypeWindow (for a "browsed by an individual" presentation that appears in a window). For a show in a window, you can use the Left and Top properties to specify the position of the upper-left corner of the window and the Height and Width properties to specify its size.

To control whether animation and narration are used, set the ShowWithAnimation property and the ShowWithNarration property of the SlideShowSettings object to msoTrue or msoFalse.

To control whether the presentation loops until stopped, set the LoopUntilStopped property of the SlideShowSettings object to msoTrue or msoFalse.

To control how the presentation advances, set the AdvanceMode property to ppSlideShowManualAdvance (for manual advancing), ppSlideShowUseSlideTimings (for automatic advancing using timings already set), or ppSlideShowRehearseNewTimings (to rehearse new timings while the show plays).

The following example sets the active presentation running as a kiosk presentation that will advance automatically using its timings and loop until it is stopped:

```
With ActivePresentation.SlideShowSettings
    .LoopUntilStopped = msoCTrue
    .AdvanceMode = ppSlideShowUseSlideTimings
    .ShowType = ppShowTypeKiosk
    .Run
End With
```

This next example sets the presentation named `Corporate.pptm` running in speaker (full-screen) mode, sizing the image to 800×600 pixels and positioning it at the upper-left corner of the screen. The show uses manual advancing:

```
With Presentations("Corporate.pptm").SlideShowSettings
    .LoopUntilStopped = msoFalse
    .ShowType = ppShowTypeSpeaker
    .AdvanceMode = ppSlideShowManualAdvance
    With .Run
        .Height = 600
        .Width = 800
        .Left = 0
        .Top = 0
    End With
End With
```

Creating a Custom Show

Custom shows within a presentation are represented by the `NamedSlideShows` collection within the `SlideShowSettings` object. Use the `NamedSlideShows` property of the `SlideShowSettings` object to return the `NamedSlideShows` collection.

To create a custom show, use the `Add` method of the `NamedSlideShows` collection. The syntax is as follows:

```
expression.Add(Name, SafeArrayOfSlideIDs)
```

Here, *`expression`* is a required expression that returns a `NamedSlideShows` object. `Name` is a required String argument that specifies the name to assign to the new custom show. `SafeArrayOfSlideIDs` is a required Variant that specifies the numbers or names of the slides to include in the custom show.

For example, the following statements declare an array of the Long data type; assign to it slides 2, 4, 5, and 10 from the open presentation named `Corporate.pptm`; and create a new custom show named `Short Show` using the following array:

```
Dim myArray(4) As Long
With Presentations("Corporate.pptm")
    myArray(1) = .Slides(2).SlideID
    myArray(2) = .Slides(4).SlideID
    myArray(3) = .Slides(5).SlideID
    myArray(4) = .Slides(10).SlideID
    .SlideShowSettings.NamedSlideShows.Add Name:="Short Show", _
        safeArrayOfSlideIDs:=myArray
End With
```

Deleting a Custom Show

To delete a custom show, use the Delete method with the appropriate NamedSlideShow object. For example, the following statement deletes the custom show named Overview from the active presentation:

```
ActivePresentation.SlideShowSettings.NamedSlideShows("Overview").Delete
```

Starting a Slide Show

To start a slide show using the whole presentation, use the Run method of the SlideShow Settings object. For example, the following statement starts the slide show running in the presentation identified by the object variable myPresentation:

```
myPresentation.SlideShowSettings.Run
```

To show only a range of slides from a presentation, set the RangeType property of the SlideShowSettings object to ppShowSlideRange, use the StartingSlide property of the SlideShowSettings object to specify the first slide and the EndingSlide property to specify the last slide, and then use the Run method to run the presentation. The following example shows slides 4 through 8 in the presentation named Corporate.pptm:

```
With Presentations("Corporate.pptm").SlideShowSettings
    .RangeType = ppShowSlideRange
    .StartingSlide = 4
    .EndingSlide = 8
    .Run
End With
```

To start running a custom show, set the RangeType property of the SlideShowSettings object to ppShowNamedSlideShow, use the SlideShowName property to specify the name of the custom show, and then use the Run method to run the custom show. The following example shows the custom show named Short Show in the active presentation:

```
With ActivePresentation.SlideShowSettings
    .RangeType = ppShowNamedSlideShow
    .SlideShowName = "Short Show"
    .Run
End With
```

When you start a slide show, VBA creates a SlideShowWindow object representing the object. You can access the SlideShowWindow object either through the SlideShowWindows collection (a creatable object that contains a SlideShowWindow object for each open slide show) or through the SlideShowWindow property of the Presentation object. If you know which presentation is running, it's easier to go through the appropriate Presentation object.

Changing the Size and Position of a Slide Show

To find out whether a slide show is displayed full screen or in a window, check the IsFullScreen property of the SlideShowWindow object. If the IsFullScreen property returns -1, the presentation is full screen; if the property returns 0, the presentation is a window.

To set the height and width of the slide-show window in pixels, use the Height property and the Width property. To set its position, use the Top property to specify the distance in pixels of the top edge of the presentation from the top of the window or screen, and the Left property to specify the distance in pixels of the left edge of the presentation from the left edge of the window or the screen.

Moving from Slide to Slide

Apart from controlling the position and size of the presentation, most of the actions you can take with a presentation involve the View object. To find out which slide is displayed, return the CurrentShowPosition property:

```
MsgBox ActivePresentation.SlideShowWindow.View.CurrentShowPosition
```

To display the first slide in the presentation, use the First method. To display the last slide, use the Last method:

```
ActivePresentation.SlideShowWindow.View.First
ActivePresentation.SlideShowWindow.View.Last
```

To display the next slide, use the Next method. To display the previous slide, use the Previous method. Here's an example:

```
ActivePresentation.SlideShowWindow.View.Previous
```

To display a particular slide in the slide show, use the GotoSlide method of the View object, using the Index argument to specify the slide number. For example, the following statement displays slide 5 in the first open slide-show window:

```
Application.SlideShowWindows(1).View.GotoSlide Index:=5
```

Pausing the Show and Using White and Black Screens

To display a white screen, set the State property to ppSlideShowWhiteScreen. To display a black screen, set the State property of the View object to ppSlideShowBlackScreen:

```
ActivePresentation.SlideShowWindow.View.State = ppSlideShowWhiteScreen
ActivePresentation.SlideShowWindow.View.State = ppSlideShowBlackScreen
```

To toggle the black screen or white screen off and start the show running again, set the State property to ppSlideShowRunning.

To pause the presentation, set the State property of the View object to ppSlideShowPaused. To start the show again, set the State property to ppSlideShowRunning, as in this example:

```
With ActivePresentation.SlideShowWindow.View
    .State = ppSlideShowPaused
    .State = ppSlideShowRunning
End With
```

Starting and Stopping Custom Shows

To start a custom show running, use the `GotoNamedShow` method and use the `SlideShowName` argument to specify the name of the custom show. For example, the following statement starts the custom show named `New Show` running:

```
SlideShowWindows(1).GotoNamedShow SlideShowName:="New Show"
```

To exit a custom show, use the `EndNamedShow` method and then use the `Next` method to advance the presentation. PowerPoint then displays the first slide in the full presentation:

```
With ActivePresentation.SlideShowWindow.View
    .EndNamedShow
    .Next
End With
```

Exiting a Slide Show

To exit the slide show, use the `Exit` method of the `View` property of the `SlideShowWindow` object. For example, the following statement exits the slide show in the active presentation:

```
ActivePresentation.SlideShowWindow.View.Exit
```

The Bottom Line

Work with shapes. PowerPoint VBA provides many ways to access and manipulate shapes.

Master It Describe what the following line of code does:
`ActivePresentation.Slides(2).Shapes(1).Delete`

Work with headers and footers. Using PowerPoint headers and footers can be a convenient way to provide continuity for presentations as well as to identify each element.

Master It In this chapter, you worked with several examples showing how to manipulate footers for slides. Why were there no examples illustrating how to manipulate headers for slides?

Set up and run a slide show. To create a custom slide show, you use the `Add` method of the `NamedSlideShows` collection.

Master It The syntax when using the `Add` method of the `NamedSlideShows` collection is
`*expression*.Add(Name, SafeArrayOfSlideIDs)`

Explain what the four components of this line of code are and what they do.

Chapter 26

Understanding the Outlook Object Model and Key Objects

In this chapter, you'll begin to come to grips with the Outlook object model and using VBA to manipulate Outlook. You'll learn where Outlook stores VBA items, meet the VBA objects for Outlook's creatable objects and main user-interface items, and work with some of the main Outlook objects. You'll explore a variety of objects, from the `Application` object that represents the entire application through the objects that represent individual messages, calendar items, and tasks. You'll also learn how to search programmatically (via macros rather than the keyboard or mouse).

IN THIS CHAPTER, YOU WILL LEARN TO DO THE FOLLOWING:

- Work with the `Application` object
- Work with messages
- Work with calendar items
- Work with tasks and task requests
- Search for items

Getting an Overview of the Outlook Object Model

Many people find Outlook harder to work with programmatically than other Office applications, so it's particularly helpful to explore the Outlook object model to see which objects Outlook uses and how they're related. Above all, when working with objects, seeing VBA code examples in the online Help system or online can be invaluable.

You can find the Outlook object-model reference by following these steps:

1. Launch or switch to Outlook, and then press Alt+F11 to launch or switch to the VBA Editor.
2. In the Editor, choose Help ➤ Microsoft Visual Basic For Applications Help F1. (Although it says that F1 is an alternative way to get to the right web page, it's not. Click instead Microsoft Visual Basic For Applications Help F1 here in the Help menu.
3. Click the Outlook VBA Reference link on the left side of the web page.

4. Click the Object Model link on the left side of the web page.
5. You'll have access to the whole collection of Outlook 2016 VBA objects, their syntax specifications, useful descriptions, and code examples (one of which is shown in Figure 26.1).

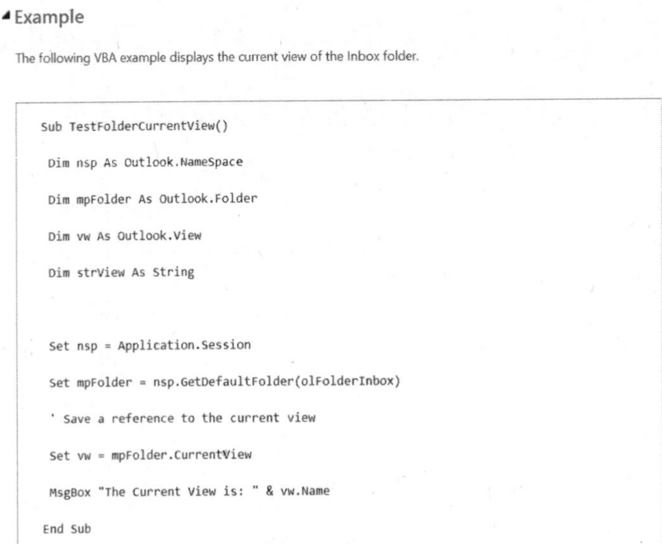

Example
The following VBA example displays the current view of the Inbox folder.
Sub TestFolderCurrentView()
Dim nsp As Outlook.NameSpace
Dim mpFolder As Outlook.Folder
Dim vw As Outlook.View
Dim strView As String
Set nsp = Application.Session
Set mpFolder = nsp.GetDefaultFolder(olFolderInbox)
' Save a reference to the current view
Set vw = mpFolder.CurrentView
MsgBox "The Current View is: " & vw.Name
End Sub

FIGURE 26.1 Sample code found in the Outlook object model reference will help you write your own VBA code.

Understanding Where Outlook Stores VBA Macros

As you saw earlier in this book, Word and Excel let you store VBA projects either in a global location (the `Normal.dotm` template in Word or the Personal Macro Workbook in Excel) or in individual templates or document files. PowerPoint lets you store VBA projects in presentation files and templates.

Outlook, by contrast, doesn't let you store VBA projects in individual items (such as Outlook's email messages or contacts). Instead, Outlook saves all projects in one file called `VbaProject.OTM`, which is stored in the following folder (instead of *`Richard`* in this path, substitute your username):

```
C:\Users\Richard\AppData\Roaming\Microsoft\Outlook
```

If the file doesn't exist (left over from the 2013 version of Office, for example), it will be created as soon as you close Outlook 2016 after having created a macro.

Understanding Outlook's Most Common Creatable Objects

In Outlook VBA, the `Application` object represents the entire Outlook application, so you can access any Outlook object by going through the `Application` object. However, Outlook also exposes various creatable objects, allowing you to reach some of the objects in its object model without explicitly going through the `Application` object. Recall that "creatable" merely means that when you're writing code involving these objects, using the word `Application` is optional. You can get the same result by using either of the following versions:

```
Application.Explorers
```

or more simply,

```
Explorers
```

Here is a list of Outlook's most common creatable objects; you'll work with most of them in more detail later in this chapter and in the next chapter:

- The `Explorers` collection contains an `Explorer` object for each window that displays the contents of a folder.
- The `Inspectors` collection contains an `Inspector` object for each window that's open displaying an Outlook item.
- The `COMAddIns` collection contains a `COMAddIn` object for each COM (Component Object Model) add-in loaded in Outlook.
- The `Reminders` collection contains a `Reminder` object for each reminder.

The most prominent objects in the Outlook user interface are represented in VBA by items with names that are descriptive of their purpose, such as these, for example:

- The `MailItem` object represents a mail item.
- The `ContactItem` object represents a contact.
- The `TaskItem` object represents a task.
- The `AppointmentItem` object represents an appointment.
- The `JournalItem` object represents a journal entry.
- The `NoteItem` object represents a note.

You'll learn how to work with these objects later in this chapter and in the next chapter.

Working with the *Application* Object

You can have only one instance of Outlook running at a time. (By contrast, you can run multiple instances of Word or Excel at the same time.) You probably won't find this a limitation when you're writing macros that work within Outlook. But if you create a procedure in another application (such as Word) that will communicate with and manipulate Outlook, you will need to check whether there is an instance of Outlook currently running in the computer before you create an instance programmatically. (See Chapter 30, "Accessing One Application from Another Application," for instructions on how to communicate between Office applications using macros.)

Introducing the *NameSpace* Object

Here is a new concept: the `NameSpace`. Among all the VBA-enabled Office applications, only Outlook employs this technique. That the NameSpace approach is unique to Outlook demonstrates beyond all doubt that the various Microsoft Office application teams work at least partly independently when building their object-model structures.

Working with Inspectors and Explorers

Many Outlook VBA activities, such as accessing email messages, tasks, or contacts programmatically, require that you use the `GetNameSpace` method of Outlook's `Application` object to return the `NameSpace` object that represents the root object of the data source. Anyway, that's the official version. Just remember that you use the following syntax to get most jobs done in Outlook VBA:

```
expression.GetNameSpace(Type)
```

Here, *`expression`* is a required expression that returns an `Application` object. `Type` is a required String argument that specifies the type of namespace you want to return. Outlook supports only the MAPI data source, so you always use `Type: = "MAPI"` with the `GetNameSpace` method. For example, the following statement returns the `NameSpace` and uses the `CurrentUser` property to display the name of the current user in a message box:

```
MsgBox Application.GetNamespace("MAPI").CurrentUser
```

What Is an API?

MAPI means Messaging Application Programming Interface. It's a collection of functions written by Microsoft that can be used in programming related to email. All kinds of APIs are used for various purposes. *API* is just another term for a library of built-in functions. Come to think of it, *namespace* is also a synonym. The general term *namespace* in computer programming means a collection of functions that is self-contained. This allows you to have functions with identical names that are distinguished by their individual namespaces. That way VBA or another language knows which function to trigger when it appears in the code. It's similar to a teacher using full names to distinguish John Thompson from John Ortega. Given that they have *John* in common, additional modification is required. In the same way, namespaces provide adjectives to distinguish between identically named functions. The term *namespace* is also used in some other contexts as well. For example, namespaces are used in XML to distinguish identically named elements or attributes.

Accessing Default Folders Within the *NameSpace* Object

The `NameSpace` object contains the folders that Outlook uses—both the collection of default folders used to store default items such as email messages, tasks, and contacts as well as any other folders created by the user or by custom procedures. These folders are represented in Outlook's VBA by `MAPIFolder` objects that are organized into a `Folders` collection.

You'd probably expect that to find out which are the current default folders, you would use a method of the `Folders` collection. Nope. Given that we're in a special situation here (dealing with email), `GetDefaultFolder` is a method of the `NameSpace` object. The syntax is as follows:

```
expression.GetDefaultFolder(FolderType)
```

Here, *`expression`* is a required expression that returns a `NameSpace` object. `FolderType` is a required argument that specifies which default folder you want to return. The constants are self-explanatory: `olFolderCalendar`, `olFolderConflicts`, `olFolderContacts`, `olFolderDeletedItems`, `olFolderDrafts`, `olFolderInbox`, `olFolderJournal`, `olFolderJunk`, `olFolderLocalFailures`, `olFolderManagedEmail`, `olFolderNotes`, `olFolderOutbox`, `olFolderRSSFeeds`, `olFolderSentMail`, `olFolderServerFailures`, `olFolderSuggestedContacts`, `olFolderSyncIssues`, `olFolderTasks`, `olFolderToDo`, or `olPublicFoldersAllPublicFolders`.

The following example creates the object variable `myCal` and assigns the default calendar folder to it:

```
Dim myCal As MAPIFolder
Set myCal = Application.GetNamespace("MAPI") _
    .GetDefaultFolder(FolderType:=olFolderCalendar)
```

ACCESSING OTHER FOLDERS WITHIN THE *NAMESPACE* OBJECT

Accessing the default folders in the `NameSpace` object via the `GetDefaultFolder` method is easy, but often you'll need to access other folders. In this case, you *do* use the `Folders` collection.

The following example displays a message box (see Figure 26.2) containing a list of all the folders contained in the namespace:

```
Sub List_All_NameSpace_Folders()
    Dim myNS As NameSpace
    Dim myFolder As MAPIFolder
    Dim mySubfolder As MAPIFolder
    Dim strFolderList As String

    strFolderList = "Your Outlook NameSpace contains these folders:" _
        & vbCr & vbCr

    Set myNS = Application.GetNamespace("MAPI")
    With myNS
        For Each myFolder In myNS.Folders
            strFolderList = strFolderList & myFolder.Name & vbCr
            For Each mySubfolder In myFolder.Folders
                strFolderList = strFolderList & "*  " & mySubfolder.Name & vbCr
            Next mySubfolder
        Next myFolder

    End With
    MsgBox strFolderList, vbOKOnly + vbInformation, "Folders in NameSpace"

End Sub
```

FIGURE 26.2
Listing the folders contained in the `NameSpace` object

Understanding Inspectors and Explorers

VBA uses two major Outlook objects that most users wouldn't recognize from working with the Outlook user interface alone:

- An `Inspector` is an object that represents a window displaying a specific Outlook item, such as an email message or an appointment.
- An `Explorer` object represents a window that displays the contents of a folder, such as a list of emails.

> **OBJECTS WITHIN OBJECTS**
>
> Unlike the behavior of many collections, an `Explorer` object is included in the `Explorers` collection even if it is not visible.

Opening an Inspector Window

To open an Inspector window for an object, use the `Display` method of the `Inspector` object. For example, the following statement displays an Inspector window for the object referenced by the object variable `myItem`:

```
myItem.Display
```

Returning the Inspector Associated with an Item

To return the inspector associated with an item, use the `GetInspector` property of the appropriate object. The following example returns the inspector for the item identified by the object variable `myItem`:

```
myItem.GetInspector
```

Returning the Active Window, Inspector, or Explorer

Unlike Word, Excel, and PowerPoint, Outlook doesn't have an `ActiveWindow` object that represents the active window. However, Outlook's `Application` object does have an `ActiveWindow` method, which returns the topmost Outlook window. (If there is no window, `ActiveWindow` returns `Nothing`.)

This window will be either an `Inspector` object or an `Explorer` object. Similarly, the `ActiveExplorer` method of the `Application` object returns the active explorer, and the `ActiveInspector` method of the `Application` object returns the active inspector. Got it?

You can use the `TypeName` function to determine which type of window is active. The following example displays a message box that states which window type is active *if* there is an active window:

```
If Not TypeName(ActiveWindow) = "Nothing" Then
    MsgBox "An " & TypeName(ActiveWindow) & " window is active."
End If
```

Notice that we say here `If Not…Nothing`. The double negative means "if the active window isn't nothing."

Working with the Active Inspector

In many procedures, you'll need to determine what the topmost inspector in the Outlook application is, either so that you can work with that inspector or so that you can restore the inspector to the topmost position at the end of a procedure that manipulates other inspectors. (Remember, you should always try to restore an application to the state it was in when your procedure started execution. This is a courtesy to the user and evidence of careful, quality programming.)

To find out which is the topmost inspector, use the `ActiveInspector` method of the `Application` object. For example, the following statement maximizes the window of the topmost inspector:

```
Application.ActiveInspector.WindowState = olMaximized
```

Note that this example attempts to maximize an Inspector window, so there must actually *be* an Inspector window open when you run the code. In other words, double-click an email message in Outlook to open it in a window separate from the Outlook window. This separate window, showing a single email, is an inspector. If you want to *trap* this error (and you should) to prevent your macro from crashing when no inspector exists, here's how to make sure there is an active inspector. You can check that the TypeName function does not return Nothing when run on the ActiveInspector method of the Application object, like this:

```
Sub MaxIt()

If TypeName(Application.ActiveInspector) = "Nothing" Then

    MsgBox "No item is currently open."
    End 'shut down the macro

Else

Application.ActiveInspector.WindowState = olMaximized

End If

End Sub
```

Creating Items

To create new items in Outlook, you use the CreateItem method or the CreateItemFromTemplate method of the Application object. The CreateItem method creates default items, while the CreateItemFromTemplate method creates items based on the templates you specify.

> **YOU CAN USE CUSTOM FORMS TO CREATE NEW OBJECTS**
>
> You can also create new objects using a custom form. To do so, use the Add method with the Items collection.

USING THE *CREATEITEM* METHOD TO CREATE DEFAULT ITEMS

The syntax for the CreateItem method is as follows:

```
expression.CreateItem(ItemType)
```

Here, *expression* is a required expression that returns an Application object. ItemType is a required argument that specifies the type of item to create: olAppointmentItem, olContactItem, olDistributionListItem, olJournalItem, olMailItem, MobileItemMMS, MobileItemSMS, olNoteItem, olPostItem, or olTaskItem.

The following example creates a new email message; assigns a recipient (by setting the To property), a subject (by setting the Subject property), and body text (by setting the Body property); and then displays the Message window:

```
Dim myMessage As MailItem
Set myMessage = Application.CreateItem(ItemType:=olMailItem)
With myMessage
    .To = "test@example.com"
    .Subject = "Test message"
    .Body = "This is a test message."
    .Display
End With
```

Quitting Outlook

To quit Outlook, use the Quit method of the Application object. This method takes no arguments:

```
Application.Quit
```

You may also want to work with the events available to the Application object. See Chapter 27, "Working with Events in Outlook," for a discussion of how to work with these application-level events and with item-level events.

Understanding General Methods for Working with Outlook Objects

Many of the objects in Outlook use the methods covered in the following sections. You'll see brief examples showing you how to use the methods, as well as further examples on the individual types of objects—email messages, appointments, contacts, tasks, and so on—later in this chapter and in the next.

Using the *Display* Method

To open an item in an Inspector window, use the Display method. The syntax is as follows:

```
expression.Display(Modal)
```

Here, *expression* is a required expression that returns the type of object you want to display—for example, a ContactItem object or a MailItem object. Modal is an optional Variant argument that you can set to True to make the window modal. A window is modeless by default, or it becomes modeless if you set Modal to False. Making the window modal means that users must close the window before they can work with another window.

Note that the Modal argument isn't available for Explorer and MAPIFolder objects.

For example, the following statement uses the Display method to display the Inbox:

```
Application.GetNamespace("MAPI").GetDefaultFolder(olFolderInbox).Display
```

Using the *Close* Method

To close a window, use the `Close` method. The syntax is as follows:

```
expression.Close(SaveMode)
```

Here, *expression* is a required expression that returns the object you want to close. `SaveMode` is a required argument that specifies whether to save changes (`olSave`), discard the changes (`olDiscard`), or prompt the user to decide whether to save the changes (`olPromptForSave`).

The following example closes the active inspector and saves any changes to its contents:

```
ActiveInspector.Close SaveMode:=olSave
```

Remember that this code requires that an inspector be currently open. See the warning earlier in this chapter in the section titled "Working with the Active Inspector."

Real World Scenario

Practical Programming: The *Items* Collection Is Unsorted

You often need to sort and search data. Be warned that the index numbers in the `Items` collection of your contacts are not ordered in any way. The collection is not alphabetical, nor is it ordered in any other fashion (by the date the contact was entered, was modified, or by any other order). Using the `Delete`, `Display`, or other methods with the `Items` collection accesses what to us, as programmers, will be a random item. In the previous example, `Items(1)` will almost certainly not be the first contact in your list of contacts. Or, as the Outlook online Help system puts it, "The items in the `Items` collection object are not guaranteed to be in any particular order."

However, you *can* sort items yourself if you like, by writing code that sorts. Then you can search the sorted list that's generated. You do this by using the `Sort` method, as the following example illustrates. These statements sort your contacts alphabetically by the Full Name field in the Contacts dialog box. You can optionally sort by due date (for tasks), by last name (for contacts), and many other ways.

```
Sub SortContacts()
    Dim strNames As String
    Dim myNameSpace As Outlook.NameSpace
    Dim myFolder As Outlook.Folder
    Dim myItem As Outlook.ContactItem
    Dim myItems As Outlook.Items

    Set myNameSpace = Application.GetNamespace("MAPI")
    Set myFolder = myNameSpace.GetDefaultFolder(olFolderContacts)
    Set myItems = myFolder.Items
    myItems.Sort "[FullName]", False
```

```
        For Each myItem In myItems

            strNames = strNames & ", " & myItem.FullName

        Next myItem

        MsgBox strNames

    End Sub
```

Notice that you could also use this `For Each...Next` loop to search for a particular item in the collection of items.

Alternatively, you can use the `AdvancedSearch` method of the `Application` object, as described in the section "Searching for Items" later in this chapter.

Using the *PrintOut* Method

To print an item, use the `PrintOut` method. This method takes no arguments. The following example prints the item with the index number `1` in the Inbox:

```
Application.GetNamespace("MAPI").GetDefaultFolder(olFolderInbox) _
    .Items(1).PrintOut
```

Using the *Save* Method

To save an item, use the `Save` method. This method takes no arguments. The following example creates a new task; assigns it a subject, start date (today), and due date (a week from today); turns off the reminder for the task; and then saves it:

```
Dim myTask As TaskItem
Set myTask = Application.CreateItem(ItemType:=olTaskItem)
With myTask
    .Subject = "Arrange Review Meeting"
    .StartDate = Date
    .DueDate = Date + 7
    .ReminderSet = False
    .Save
End With
```

This item will appear in the ToDo list of the MyTasks section of your Outlook Tasks.

Using the *SaveAs* Method

To save an item as a separate file, use the SaveAs method. The syntax is as follows:

```
expression.SaveAs(Path, Type)
```

Here, *expression* is a required expression that returns the object to be saved. Path is a required String argument that specifies the path and filename under which to save the file. Type is an optional Variant argument that you can use to control the file type used for the file, as shown in Table 26.1.

TABLE 26.1: Type arguments for the SaveAs method

ARGUMENT	TYPE OF FILE
olHTML	HTML file
olMSG	Outlook message format (.msg filename extension)
olRTF	Rich Text format
olTemplate	Template
olDoc	Word document format (email messages using WordMail)
olTXT	Text file
olVCal	vCal file
olVCard	vCard file
olICal	iCal file
olMSGUnicode	Outlook Unicode message format (.msg filename extension)

The following example saves the message open in the active inspector. So before testing this example, be sure that a message has been double-clicked and is, thus, open in its own window separate from the main Outlook window. Remember that code involving the active inspector requires that an inspector be currently open. See the warning, and a way to error-trap this, earlier in this chapter in the section titled "Working with the Active Inspector."

If the IsWordMail property of the ActiveInspector object returns True, the example saves the message as a .doc file; if the IsWordMail property returns False, the example saves the message as an .rtf file. If no Inspector window is active, the example displays a message box pointing out that problem to the user:

```
If TypeName(ActiveInspector) = "Nothing" Then
    MsgBox "This macro cannot run because " & _
        "there is no active window.", vbOKOnly, "Macro Cannot Run"
    End
Else
```

```
    If ActiveInspector.IsWordMail Then
        ActiveInspector.CurrentItem.SaveAs "c:\temp\message.doc"
    Else
        ActiveInspector.CurrentItem.SaveAs "c:\temp\message.rtf"
    End If
End If
```

To test this example, ensure that there's a `\temp` folder on your `C:\` drive.

Working with Messages

If you or your colleagues use Outlook's email capabilities extensively, you may be able to save time by programming Outlook to create or process messages automatically. The following sections show you how to create a new message, work with its contents, add an attachment, and send the message.

Creating a New Message

To create a new message, use the `CreateItem` method of the `Application` object and specify `olMailItem` for the `ItemType` argument. The following example creates a `MailItem` object variable named `myMessage` and assigns to it a new message:

```
Dim myMessage As MailItem
Set myMessage = Application.CreateItem(ItemType:=olMailItem)
```

Working with the Contents of a Message

To work with the contents of a message, set or get the appropriate properties. These are the most widely useful properties:

- `To` is the recipient or recipients of the message.
- `CC` is the recipient or recipients of copies of the message.
- `BCC` is the recipient or recipients of blind copies of the message.
- `Subject` is the subject line of the message.
- `Body` is the body text of the message.
- `BodyFormat` is the message's formatting type: `olFormatPlain` for text only, `olFormatRichText` for text with formatting, and `olFormatHTML` for HTML formatting.
- `Importance` is the relative importance of the message. Set it to `olImportanceHigh`, `olImportanceNormal`, or `olImportanceLow`.

The following example creates a new message item and assigns it to the object variable `myMessage`. It then adds an addressee, a subject, and body text; applies the HTML format; sets the importance to high; and sends the message:

```
Dim myMessage As MailItem
Set myMessage = Application.CreateItem(ItemType:=olMailItem)
```

```
With myMessage
    .To = "petra_smith@ourbigcompany.com"
    .Subject = "Preparation for Review"
    .Body = "Please drop by tomorrow and spend a few minutes" _
        & " discussing the materials we need for Darla's review."
    .BodyFormat = olFormatHTML
    .Importance = olImportanceHigh
    .Send
End With
```

When this message, shown in Figure 26.3, arrives at Petra's machine, Outlook 2016 briefly displays it in the upper-right corner:

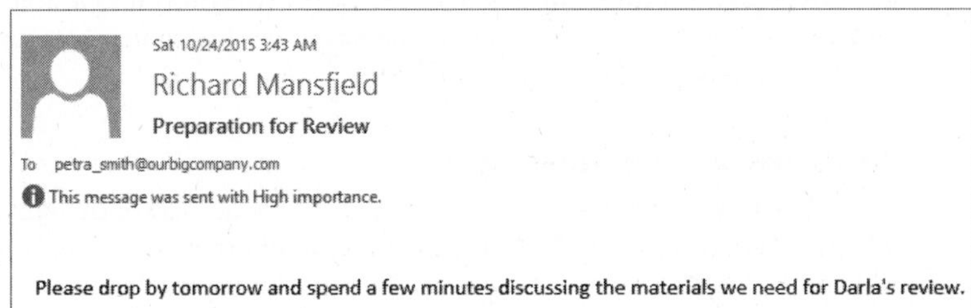

FIGURE 26.3 A portion of a message of high importance is briefly displayed in Outlook.

Adding an Attachment to a Message

To add an attachment to a message, use the Add method with the `Attachments` collection, which you return by using the `Attachments` property of the `MailItem` object. The syntax is as follows:

```
expression.Add(Source, Type, Position, DisplayName)
```

Here are the components of the syntax:

- *`expression`* is a required expression that returns an `Attachments` collection.
- `Source` is a required String argument that specifies the path and filename of the attachment.
- `Type` is an optional String argument that you can use to specify the type of attachment.
- `Position` is an optional String argument that you can use with rich-text messages to specify the character at which the attachment is positioned in the text. Use character `0` to hide the attachment, `1` to position the attachment at the beginning of the message, or a higher value to position the attachment at the specified character position. To position the attachment at the end of the message, use a number higher than the number of characters in the message.

- `DisplayName` is an optional String argument that you can specify to control the name displayed for the attachment in the message.

The following example attaches to the message referenced by the object variable `myMessage` the file `Corporate Downsizing.pptm` stored in the folder `Y:\Sample Documents`, positioning the attachment at the beginning of the message and setting its display name to `Downsizing Presentation`:

```
myMessage.Attachments.Add _
    Source:="Y:\Sample Documents\Corporate Downsizing.pptm", _
    Position:=1, DisplayName:="Downsizing Presentation"
```

To test this, insert this code into the example code from the previous section ("Working with the Contents of a Message"), like this:

```
Dim myMessage As MailItem
Set myMessage = Application.CreateItem(ItemType:=olMailItem)

myMessage.Attachments.Add _
    Source:="Y:\Sample Documents\Corporate Downsizing.pptm", _
    Position:=1, DisplayName:="Downsizing Presentation"

With myMessage
    .To = "petra_smith@ourbigcompany.com"
    .Subject = "Preparation for Review"
    .Body = "Please drop by tomorrow and spend a few minutes" _
        & " discussing the materials we need for Darla's review."
    .BodyFormat = olFormatHTML
    .Importance = olImportanceHigh
    .Send
End With
```

Sending a Message

To send a message, use the Send method. This method takes no arguments. The following example sends the message referenced by the object variable `myMessage`:

```
myMessage.Send
```

MULTIPLE SENDS

The Send method applies to the `AppointmentItem`, `MeetingItem`, and `TaskItem` objects, as well as to the `MailItem` object.

To check whether a message has been sent, check its `Sent` property. This Boolean property returns `True` if the message has been sent and `False` if it has not.

Working with Calendar Items

If you create or receive many calendar items, you may be able to save time or streamline your scheduling by using VBA. The following sections show you how to create a calendar item and work with its contents.

Creating a New Calendar Item

To create a new calendar item, use the `CreateItem` method of the `Application` object and specify `olAppointmentItem` for the `ItemType` argument. The following example creates an `AppointmentItem` object variable named `myAppointment` and assigns to it a new appointment item:

```
Dim myAppointment As AppointmentItem
Set myAppointment = Application.CreateItem(ItemType:=olAppointmentItem)
```

Working with the Contents of a Calendar Item

To work with the contents of a calendar item, set or get the appropriate properties. These are the most widely useful properties:

- `Subject` is the subject of the appointment.
- `Body` is the body text of the appointment.
- `Start` is the start time of the appointment.
- `End` is the end time of the appointment.
- `BusyStatus` is your status during the appointment: `olBusy`, `olFree`, `olOutOfOffice`, or `olTentative`.
- `Categories` is the category or categories assigned to the item.
- `ReminderSet` determines whether the appointment has a reminder (`True`) or not (`False`).
- `ReminderMinutesBeforeStart` is the number of minutes before the event that the reminder should occur.

The following example creates a new `AppointmentItem` object and assigns it to the object variable `myAppointment`. It then sets the subject, body, start date (2:30~PM on the day seven days after the present date), and end date (one hour after the start); marks the time as busy; assigns the `Personal` category; sets a reminder 30 minutes before the appointment; and saves the appointment:

```
Dim myAppointment As AppointmentItem
Set myAppointment = Application.CreateItem(ItemType:=olAppointmentItem)
With myAppointment
    .Subject = "Dentist"
```

```
        .Body = "Dr. Schmitt " & vbCr & "4436 Acacia Blvd."
        .Start = Str(Date + 7) & " 2.30 PM"
        .End = Str(Date + 7) & " 3.30 PM"
        .BusyStatus = olBusy
        .Categories = "Personal"
        .ReminderMinutesBeforeStart = 30
        .ReminderSet = True
        .Save
    End With
```

The AppointmentItem object has a grand total of 71 properties. If you want to explore more of them, take a look at this MSDN web page:

http://msdn.microsoft.com/en-us/library/office/jj900814.aspx

ALLOWING USERS TO MANUALLY ASSIGN CATEGORIES

Assigning categories to an item programmatically can be difficult, especially because many users create custom categories or assign categories in an idiosyncratic manner. In many cases, it's better to allow each user to assign their preferred categories manually by displaying the Categories dialog box at the appropriate point in your procedure. You can do so by using the ShowCategoriesDialog method of the item—for example, myAppointment.ShowCategoriesDialog for an item referenced by the object variable myAppointment.

Working with Tasks and Task Requests

VBA can automate tasks and task requests. The following sections show you how to create a task, work with the contents of a task item, and send a task request.

Creating a Task

To create a new task item, use the CreateItem method of the Application object and specify olTaskItem for the ItemType argument. The following example creates a TaskItem object variable named myTask and assigns to it a new task item:

```
Dim myTask As TaskItem
Set myTask = Application.CreateItem(ItemType:=olTaskItem)
```

Working with the Contents of a Task Item

To work with the contents of a task item, set or get the appropriate properties. These are the most widely useful properties:

- Subject is the subject of the task.
- Body is the body text of the task.

- Start is the start time of the task.
- DueDate is the due date of the task.
- Importance is the importance of the task. Set it to olImportanceHigh, olImportance Normal, or olImportanceLow.
- Status is the status of the task: olTaskNotStarted, olTaskWaiting, olTaskDeferred, olTaskInProgress, or olTaskComplete.
- PercentComplete is the percentage of the task completed.
- Companies specifies the companies associated with the task.
- BillingInformation is the company or department to bill for the task.

The following example creates a TaskItem object variable named myTask and assigns to it a new task item. It then sets the subject and body of the task, specifies a due date in the future, sets the status to olTaskInProgress and the percentage complete to 10, specifies the company involved and who to bill, sets the importance to High, and then saves the task:

```
Dim myTask As TaskItem
Set myTask = Application.CreateItem(ItemType:=olTaskItem)
With myTask
    .Subject = "Create a business plan"
    .Body = "The business plan must cover the next four years." & _
        vbCr & vbCr & "It must provide a detailed budget, " & _
        "staffing projections, and a cost/benefit analysis."
    .DueDate = Str(Date + 28)
    .Status = olTaskInProgress
    .PercentComplete = 10
    .Companies = "Acme Polyglot Industrialists"
    .BillingInformation = "Sales & Marketing"
    .Importance = olImportanceHigh
    .Save
End With
```

The TaskItem object has 69 properties. If you want to explore more of them, take a look at this MSDN web page:

http://msdn.microsoft.com/en-us/library/office/jj871952.aspx

Assigning a Task to a Colleague

To assign a task to a colleague, use the Assign method of the TaskItem object, and then use the Add method of the Recipients collection to add one or more recipients. Finally, you can use the Send method to send the task to your colleague.

The following example creates a task, uses the Assign method to indicate that it will be assigned, specifies a recipient, and sends the task:

```
Dim myTaskAssignment As TaskItem
Set myTaskAssignment = Application.CreateItem(ItemType:=olTaskItem)
```

```
With myTaskAssignment
    .Assign
    .Recipients.Add Name:="Peter Nagelly"
    .Subject = "Buy Bagels for Dress-Down/Eat-Up Day"
    .Body = "It's your turn to get the bagels on Friday."
    .Body = .Body & vbCr & vbCr & "Remember: No donuts AT ALL."
    .DueDate = Str(Date + 3)
    .Send
End With
```

Searching for Items

To search for items, use the `AdvancedSearch` method of the `Application` object. The syntax is as follows:

```
expression.AdvancedSearch(Scope, Filter, SearchSubFolders, Tag)
```

Here are the components of the syntax:

- *`expression`* is a required expression that returns an `Application` object.
- `Scope` is a required String argument that specifies the scope of the search (which items to search). Usually, you'll search a particular folder. For example, you might search the Inbox for messages that match certain criteria, or you might search the Tasks folder for particular tasks.
- `Filter` is an optional String argument that specifies the search filter. While this argument is optional, you will need to use it unless you want to return all the items within the scope you've specified.
- `SearchSubFolders` is an optional Variant argument that you can set to `True` to search through any subfolders of the folder specified by the `Scope` argument, or `False` to search only the specified folder. The default is `False`.
- `Tag` is an optional Variant argument that you can use to specify a name for the search you're defining. If you create a name, you can call the search again.

The following example searches the Inbox (`Scope: = "Inbox"`) for messages with the subject line containing *Office*. If any messages are found, the procedure produces a list of sender names, which it assigns to the String variable `strMessages` and displays in a message box.

Note that at the time of this writing, there appears to be a timing bug in the advanced search feature. If you press F5 to execute the following code, no search hits are found. However, if you press F8 repeatedly to step through the code, it works as expected and hits are found.

I'm including this code because *it should work* at normal speed. If you find a way to insert an effective delay or otherwise fix the problem, please email me at my address in the Introduction to this book. Or, perhaps by the time this book is published Microsoft will have fixed it.

```
Sub Sample_Advanced_Search()

    Dim mySearch As Search
```

```
    Dim myResults As Results
    Dim intCounter As Integer
    Dim strMessages As String
    Dim intTotal As Integer


Dim strFilter As String
strFilter = Chr(34) & "urn:schemas:httpmail:subject" & Chr(34) & " like
'%Office%'"


    Set mySearch = AdvancedSearch(Scope:="Inbox", filter:=strFilter)


    Set myResults = mySearch.Results
    intTotal = myResults.Count


    For intCounter = 1 To intTotal
        strMessages = strMessages & _
            myResults.Item(intCounter).SenderName & vbCr
    Next intCounter

    MsgBox strMessages, vbOKOnly, "Search Results"

End Sub
```

YOU CAN EXECUTE 100 SEARCHES SIMULTANEOUSLY, BUT SHOULD YOU?

If necessary, you can run two or more searches at the same time. To do so, use the `AdvancedSearch` method in successive lines of code. Actually, you can run up to 100 searches at the same time, but doing so puts a considerable load on your computer and may make it run slowly or appear to stop responding. And what's the point?

The Bottom Line

Work with the `Application` object. VBA uses two major Outlook objects that most users wouldn't recognize from working with the Outlook user interface alone.

Master It One of these objects represents a window that displays the contents of a folder. The other represents a window displaying an Outlook item, such as an email message or an appointment. What are the names of these two objects?

Work with messages. To work with the contents of a message in VBA, you set or get various properties.

Master It Name one of the most widely useful properties employed when manipulating the contents of a message in a procedure.

Work with calendar items. You can create new calendar appointment items via VBA.

Master It To create a new calendar item, you use a particular method of the `Application` object and specify `olAppointmentItem` for the `ItemType` argument. What is the method?

Work with tasks and task requests. You can assign a task to a colleague and then add one or more recipients. You can then send the task to your colleague and, optionally, the additional recipients.

Master It What methods do you use to assign, add, and send a task to others?

Chapter 27

Working with Events in Outlook

If you want to write macros to automate tasks in Outlook, you may sometimes need to write code that responds to Outlook events. Outlook has two classes of events, application-level events and item-level events, and between them, they enable your macros to respond to most anything that happens in Outlook. In this chapter, you will learn how to work with both types of events, and you will see code examples showing how to manage some of the events.

How Event-Handler Procedures Differ from Ordinary Macros

The techniques used to write and test an event-handler procedure differ from the techniques you've employed throughout this book to create and test ordinary macro procedures. If you intend to test the examples in this chapter, I suggest that you first read the sidebar titled "How to Test Event-Handler Procedures" later in this chapter.

The following points summarize the qualities of event-handler procedures that differ from ordinary procedures:

- An event handler must be located within a class module, not in an ordinary macro module. Therefore, you're entering the world of object-oriented programming (OOP). And, in spite of some useful qualities, OOP has the potential to sink us programmers into a quagmire of complexity. A complete example demonstrating how to add an event handler to Outlook and then test it can be found in the sidebar "How to Test Event-Handler Procedures."
- You must declare an object variable.
- Next, you initialize the object variable to connect it to an actual object.
- You then write code in a procedure triggered by the event you're interested in.
- You test your code differently than you would in ordinary modules. In a class module, you cannot simply test the event handler by pressing F5 to run it directly. Pressing F5 brings up the Macro dialog box. Instead, you test your code indirectly by triggering the event it's designed to service—for example, by modifying a contact in the Contacts folder.

In addition to the events discussed in this chapter, Outlook supports form events such as those discussed in "Using Events to Control Forms" in Chapter 15, "Creating Complex Forms Boxes." However, as is so often the case with Outlook and Access, the folders in Outlook are somewhat unique and are different from the VBA forms you worked with earlier in this book. Outlook's folder/form is described later in this chapter in the sidebar titled "What Is VBScript?"

As you'll see, you even use a special version of the VBA language when programming this folder-slash-form.

We'll conclude this chapter with a brief look at Outlook's Quick Steps feature. For those who don't want to, or can't, write macros, Quick Steps provides an alternative, if seriously limited, way to automate some tasks. This tool is similar to Access's Macro Designer, although even more simplistic.

IN THIS CHAPTER, YOU WILL LEARN TO DO THE FOLLOWING:

- Create event handlers
- Work with application-level events
- Work with item-level events
- Understand the Quick Steps tool

Working with Application-Level Events

By default, for security reasons, macros are disabled in Outlook 2016. To work with the examples in this chapter, or to use macros in general, you must select an enabling option in Outlook's Trust Center. To do so, follow these steps:

1. Click the File tab on the Ribbon.
2. Choose Options in the left pane of the File window.
3. Click Trust Center in the left pane of the Outlook Options dialog box.
4. Click the Trust Center Settings button.
5. Click Macro Settings in the left pane of the Trust Center dialog box.
6. Now choose one of the two lower options: Notification For All Macros (which gets old quickly) or Enable All Macros.

Recall that an event is something that *happens to* an object, such as a click, a mouse drag, a keystroke, and so on. You can write code in an event (an *event procedure*, as it's called) to respond to clicking or other events.

An application-level event is an event that happens to the Outlook application as a whole rather than to an individual item within it. For example, the `Startup` event is an application-level event that occurs when Outlook starts, and the `Quit` event is an application-level event that occurs when Outlook closes. By contrast, item-level events represent things that happen to individual items—for example, the opening of a particular email message or contact record, or a user's switching from one folder to another.

Application-level events are easier to access than the item-level events because the `Application` object is the topmost object and is always available when Outlook is running. This means that you don't have to use an event handler to create the `Application` object. It just always exists. You do, however, have to write code that creates an object for an item-level event.

To access the application-level events, you use the built-in `ThisOutlookSession` class module. It's automatically inserted into the VBA Editor. Look in the Project Explorer and expand the `Project1` item that represents the Outlook VBA project and then expand the `Microsoft Outlook Objects` item. You now see the `ThisOutlookSession` item. Double-click it to open a Code window showing its contents. (If this is the first time you've opened the `ThisOutlookSession` class module, it will have no contents.)

Each of the events described in the following sections works with the `Application` object. For simplicity, most of the following examples directly use the Outlook `Application` object itself, but you could declare an object variable and then use it to return the `Application` object if you want.

Recall that you can find the `Application` object in the drop-down list on the top left of the VBA Editor's Code window. All the events available to the `Application` object can be selected from the drop-down list on the top right of the Code window, as shown in Figure 27.1.

FIGURE 27.1
The drop-down list on the right shows all the events available in the `Application` object.

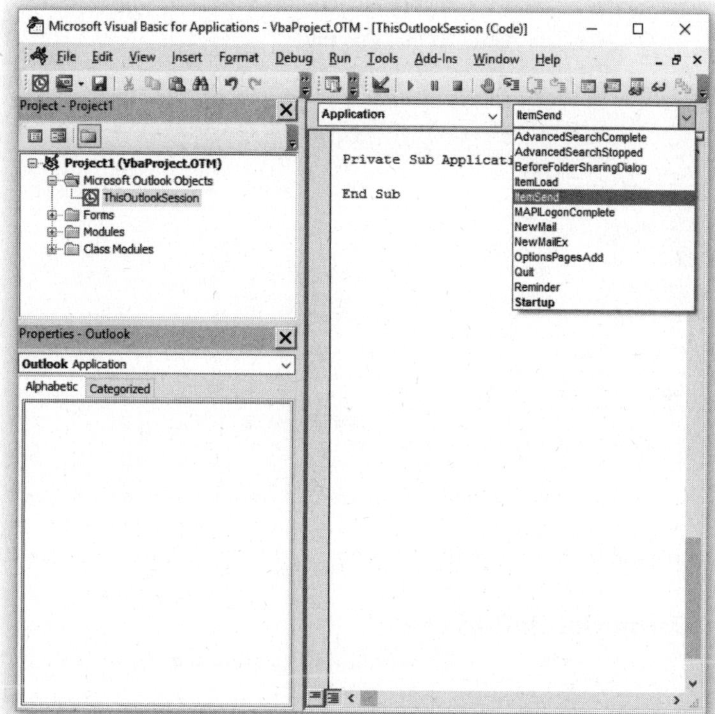

You can select these various events from the drop-down list (causing the Editor to type in the procedure structure for you) or just type the event name yourself as a sub directly in the Code window. However, if you select from the drop-down list, the VBA Editor will automatically add any necessary arguments as well. So that's the easier approach.

Also, if you declare object variables using the `WithEvents` statement, like this, the Editor's drop-down lists will include these objects and their available events:

```
Public WithEvents myInspectors As Inspectors
Public WithEvents myInspector As Inspector
```

That can be a useful shortcut while programming because you can then view every event available in an object—and also have the Editor type in the arguments. Later in this chapter you'll experiment with the Inspectors collection and the Inspector argument.

Using the *Startup* Event

The Startup event, which takes no arguments, occurs when Outlook starts. In other words, every time the user starts Outlook, any code you might have written in the Sub Application_Startup() procedure will automatically execute.

The Startup event is useful for making sure that Outlook is correctly configured for the user to start work. Say that someone always starts off by writing notes, and the first note is always a reminder about time cards. The following example creates a new NoteItem object (a note), assigns text to its Body property, and uses the Display item to display it (see Figure 27.2):

```
Private Sub Application_Startup()
    Dim myNoteItem As NoteItem
    Set myNoteItem = Application.CreateItem(ItemType:=olNoteItem)
    myNoteItem.Body = "Please start a new time card for the day."
    myNoteItem.Display
End Sub
```

FIGURE 27.2
This note automatically appears when the user first starts Outlook.

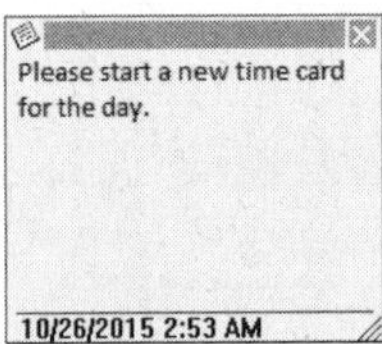

You can also put the Startup event to good use by writing code with the Set command to connect an object variable to a real object it is supposed to represent. More on this later in this chapter, in the section titled "Declaring an Object Variable and Initializing an Event."

Using the *Quit* Event

The Quit event occurs when Outlook is shut down. This event is triggered three possible ways:

- By the user choosing Exit in the File tab of the Ribbon
- By the user clicking the red X icon in the upper right of the Outlook window
- By the programmer using the Quit method of the Application object in VBA

By the time that the Quit event fires (is triggered), all of Outlook's windows have already been closed and all global variables have been released, so there's little left for a programmer to access via code in this event procedure. One possibility, however, is to display a parting message to the user, as in the following example, which displays a message on the workday that precedes a national holiday to remind the user of the holiday:

```
Private Sub Application_Quit()

    Dim strMessage As String
    Select Case Format(Date, "MM/DD/YYYY")
        Case "01/18/2016"
            strMessage = "Next Monday is Martin Luther King Day."
        Case "02/15/2016"
            strMessage = "Next Monday is President's Day."
        Case "05/23/2016"
            strMessage = "Next Monday is Memorial Day."
        Case "07/03/2016"
            strMessage = "Friday is Independence Day." & _
                " Monday is a company holiday."
        Case "08/29/2016"
            strMessage = "Next Monday is Labor Day."
        'other National Holidays here
    End Select

If strMessage = "" Then Exit Sub

MsgBox strMessage, vbOKCancel + vbExclamation, "Don't Forget…"

End Sub
```

Note that to test this macro, you need to quit Outlook. What's more, this macro can be tested only on the dates listed or by suppressing the `Exit Sub` code line (commenting it out) like this:

```
'If strMessage = "" Then Exit Sub
```

Using the *ItemSend* Event

The `ItemSend` event occurs when an item is sent, either by the user issuing a Send command (for example, by clicking the Send button in a Message window) or by executing the Send method in VBA code. The syntax for the `ItemSend` event is as follows:

```
Sub expression_ItemSend(ByVal Item As Object, Cancel As Boolean)
```

Here, *`expression`* is a required expression that returns an `Application` object. `Item` is a required argument that specifies the item that's being sent. `Cancel` is an optional Boolean argument that you can set to `False` to prevent the item from being sent.

The following example examines the `Subject` property of the `Item` object being sent. If the `Subject` property is an empty string, the message box prompts the user to add a subject line, and the `Cancel = True` statement cancels the sending of the item:

```
Private Sub Application_ItemSend(ByVal Item As Object, Cancel As Boolean)
    If Item.Subject = "" Then
        MsgBox "Please add a subject line to this message before sending it."
        Cancel = True
    End If
End Sub
```

A reminder: To test event procedure macros like these, you can't just press F5 (the way you test ordinary macros). You must instead do something in Outlook to fire the event. In this example, you must attempt to send an email message without the Subject field filled in.

Using the *NewMail* Event

The `NewMail` event occurs when one or more new mail items arrives in the Inbox. The `NewMail` event can be useful for sorting messages automatically. You can also specify custom rules to sort messages automatically. The `NewMail` event takes no arguments.

The following example displays a message box that offers to show the Inbox when new mail arrives, triggering the `NewMail` event:

```
Private Sub Application_NewMail()
    If MsgBox("You have new mail. Do you want to see your Inbox?", _
        vbYesNo + vbInformation, "New Mail Alert") = vbYes Then

        Application.GetNamespace("MAPI").GetDefaultFolder(olFolderInbox).Display
    End If
End Sub
```

> **AN ALTERNATIVE TO THE *NEWMAIL* EVENTS**
>
> Instead of using a `NewMail` or `NewMailEx` event, you can use an `ItemAdd` event with the items in the Inbox to process each new message that arrives.

Using the *AdvancedSearchComplete* and the *AdvancedSearchStopped* Events

Outlook provides two events for working with advanced searches created using the `AdvancedSearch` method. The `AdvancedSearchComplete` event fires when the `AdvancedSearch` method is run via VBA (in macro code, not by the user) and finishes searching. The `AdvancedSearchStopped` event fires when the `AdvancedSearch` method is run via VBA, and is stopped by using the `Stop` method of the search.

The syntax for the `AdvancedSearchComplete` event is as follows:

```
Private Sub expression_ AdvancedSearchComplete(ByVal SearchObject As Object)
```

Here, *expression* is a required expression that returns an Application-type object variable that has been declared with events in a class module. SearchObject is the Search object that the AdvancedSearch method returns.

The following example uses the AdvancedSearchComplete event to return the number of search results that were found by the AdvancedSearch method:

```
Private Sub Application_AdvancedSearchComplete(ByVal SearchObject As Search)
    MsgBox "The search has finished running and found " & _
        SearchObject.Results.Count & " results.", vbOKOnly + vbInformation, _
        "Advanced Search Complete Event"
End Sub
```

The following example uses the AdvancedSearchStopped event to inform the user that the search has been stopped:

```
Private Sub Application_AdvancedSearchStopped(ByVal SearchObject As Search)
    MsgBox "The search was stopped by a Stop command.", vbOKOnly
End Sub
```

Using the *MAPILogonComplete* Event

The MAPILogonComplete event occurs when the user has successfully logged on to Outlook. You can use the MAPILogonComplete event to ensure that Outlook is configured correctly for the user or simply to display some information in a message. The MAPILogonComplete event takes no arguments.

The following example of a MAPILogonComplete procedure displays a message about current trading conditions when the user has successfully logged on to Outlook. The code includes a commented line indicating where the String variables strPubDownBegin and strPubForecast would be declared and assigned data in a real-world implementation of this example:

```
Private Sub Application_MAPILogonComplete()

    Dim strMsg As String

    'strPubDowBegin and strPubForecast declared and assigned strings here

    strMsg = "Welcome to the UltraBroker Trading System!" & vbCr & vbCr
    strMsg = strMsg & "Today's starting value is " & strPubDowBegin & "." _
        & vbCr & vbCr
    strMsg = strMsg & "Today's trading forecast is " & strPubForecast & "."
    MsgBox strMsg, vbOKOnly + vbInformation, _
        "UltraBroker Trading System Logon Greeting"
End Sub
```

This macro displays a message box, but it's underneath the blue Outlook startup splash graphic. To see it, drag the splash out of the way. Unfortunately, there's no simple way to force a message box to display anywhere other than directly in the middle of the screen.

Using the *Reminder* Event

The Reminder event fires immediately before a reminder for a meeting, task, or appointment is displayed to the user. You can use the Reminder event to take an action related to the reminder. Because the reminder itself is usually by itself adequate for reminding the user, the Reminder event tends to be more useful when accessing Outlook programmatically than when a user is working interactively with Outlook. The syntax is as follows:

```
Sub expression_Reminder(ByVal Item As Object)
```

Here, *expression* is a required expression that returns an Application object, and Item is the AppointmentItem, MailItem, ContactItem, or TaskItem object associated with the reminder.

Using the *OptionsPagesAdd* Event

The OptionsPagesAdd event occurs when either the Options dialog box (Tools ➤ Options) or the Properties dialog box for a folder, such as the Inbox, is opened. (To open the Properties dialog box for a folder, right-click the folder and then choose Properties from the context menu.) You can use this event to add a custom page (which is contained in a COM [Component Object Model] add-in that you have created) to the Options dialog box or the Properties dialog box. The syntax for the OptionsPagesAdd event is as follows:

```
Sub expression_OptionsPagesAdd(ByVal Pages As PropertyPages, _
    ByVal Folder As MAPIFolder)
```

Here, *expression* is a required expression that returns an Application object or a NameSpace object. Pages is a required argument that gives the collection of custom property pages added to the dialog box. Folder is a required argument used when *expression* returns a MAPIFolder object. Folder returns the MAPIFolder object for which the Properties dialog box is being opened.

Working with Item-Level Events

In addition to the application-level events discussed so far, Outlook has a wide variety of *item-level events*—events that fire when specific items (such as tasks or notes) are manipulated, as opposed to events related to Outlook as a whole (such as shutting Outlook itself down).

You can handle item-level events in Outlook in two ways:

- By declaring an event in a class module and running an initialization procedure so that VBA then traps the event when it fires. This chapter takes this approach.
- By creating Visual Basic Script (VBScript) code and placing it in a "custom form" used by the item. Custom forms are not to be confused with the UserForms we've been working with in the VBA Editor throughout this book. You create a custom form in Outlook by clicking the Developer tab on the Ribbon and then choosing options displayed on the Custom Forms section of the Ribbon.

WHAT IS VBSCRIPT?

Script versions of computer languages were originally designed to execute when a user visits a web page. For security reasons, these languages are supposed to contain fewer capabilities than ordinary languages. For example, VBScript doesn't have a command that deletes a folder in Outlook, whereas VBA does (`FolderRemove`). You don't want to delete Outlook folders—or trigger similar damaging actions—just because you simply opened a malicious web page in your browser.

The original intent was that script languages would be lightweight, web-oriented versions of their parent languages. But as always seems to happen with mission creep, script languages have changed over time to perform various tasks and to have a variety of implementations. This sort of corruption is typical in computer software: There are many versions of "standards" like XML, HTML, and the like. They start out with the intention to be uniform across platforms, to be governed by certain rules, and so on. Then they deconstruct. It reminds you of Mae West's famous remark: "I used to be Snow White, but I drifted."

In spite of VBScript's limitations, you might want to employ it for one specialized job in Outlook: sharing items with others. VBScript code is contained within its custom form, so you can send it to other people. You can't directly export VBA to others inside items you share.

If you're interested in pursuing Outlook's Custom Forms and the VBScript that drives them, consult the useful tutorial here:

`http://msdn.microsoft.com/en-us/library/office/jj973110.aspx`

Declaring an Object Variable and Initializing an Event

Follow these steps to declare an object variable and initialize an event:

1. Use a class module to contain your object-variable declaration, in one of the following three ways:

    - Use the built-in `ThisOutlookSession` module. In the Project Explorer, expand the project name (it's in boldface and by default is named Project1). Expand the Microsoft Outlook Objects item, and double-click the `ThisOutlookSession` item to open its Code window.
    - Create a new class module by right-clicking the project name in the Project Explorer and choosing Insert ➢ Class Module from the context menu. The VBA Editor automatically opens a Code window for the class.
    - If a class module already exists, double-click it in the Project Explorer.

2. In the declarations area at the beginning of your class module (at the top of the Code window), declare a variable to represent the object to which the event applies. Use the

`WithEvents` keyword to specify that this object has events. The following example creates a public variable named `myPublicContactItem`:

```
Public WithEvents myPublicContactItem As ContactItem
```

3. Initialize the object variable by setting it to represent the appropriate object. The following example sets our `myPublicContactItem` variable to represent the first item in the default contacts folder:

```
Set myPublicContactItem = Application.GetNamespace("MAPI") _
    .GetDefaultFolder(olFolderContacts).Items(1)
```

Once you've initialized the object variable, the procedure will run after the event fires.

You can initialize the object variable manually if necessary, and you may find it convenient to do so when you're writing and testing code to handle events. But if you need to handle the event each time Outlook runs—if you want to make the macro a permanent part of your macro collection—it's obviously best to run the code to initialize the object variable automatically. For example, you might use the `Startup` event of the `Application` object (discussed in "Using the `Startup` Event," earlier in this chapter) to run event-handling initialization code automatically each time Outlook starts. In other words,

```
Private Sub Application_Startup()

Set myPublicContactItem = Application.GetNamespace("MAPI") _
    .GetDefaultFolder(olFolderContacts).Items(1)

End Sub
```

Understanding the Events That Apply to All Message Items

Table 27.1 lists the common message events. I'm using the term *message* here to refer to the `AppointmentItem`, `MailItem`, `ContactItem`, and `TaskItem` objects. In other words, Table 27.1 lists the most common events that are available to these four objects.

But be aware that there are additional "item" objects in Outlook, such as the `DocumentItem`, `DistListItem`, `JournalItem`, `MeetingItem`, and so on. To view these various items, and see descriptions of their events, visit this web page:

`http://msdn.microsoft.com/en-us/library/office/ff866465.aspx`

Also note that although Table 27.1 describes 16 common events, each of the "item" objects actually has 26 events. As an example, the complete list of events for the `MailItem` object in Outlook is provided on this web page:

`https://msdn.microsoft.com/EN-US/library/office/dn320337.aspx`

TABLE 27.1: Common item-level events

EVENT	EVENT OCCURS
`AttachmentAdd`	After an attachment is added to the item
`AttachmentRead`	When the user opens an email attachment for reading

TABLE 27.1: Common item-level events *(CONTINUED)*

EVENT	EVENT OCCURS
BeforeAttachmentSave	When the user chooses to save an attachment but before the command is executed
BeforeCheckNames	Before Outlook checks the names of the recipients of an item being sent
BeforeDelete	Before an item is deleted
Close	When an inspector is being closed but before the closing occurs
CustomAction	When the custom action of an item is executed
CustomPropertyChange	When a custom property of an item is changed
Forward	When the user forwards an item
Open	When an item is opened in an inspector
PropertyChange	When a standard property (as opposed to a custom property) in the item is changed
Read	When an item is opened for editing in an inspector window or is selected for editing in-cell
Reply	When the user issues a `Reply` command for an item
ReplyAll	When the user issues a `Reply All` command
Send	When a `Send` command has been issued, but before the item is sent
Write	When an item is saved, either explicitly by the user or implicitly by Outlook

Note that the `Close` event applies to the `Inspector` object and the `Explorer` object as well as to the objects just mentioned.

The events that fire before an action occurs allow you to cancel the action, preventing it from happening at all. The syntax for these events uses a Boolean argument named `Cancel` that you can set to `True` to prevent the action from taking place. For example, the syntax for the `BeforeDelete` event is as follows:

```
Sub expression_BeforeDelete(ByVal Item As Object, Cancel As Boolean)
```

Here, *`expression`* is a required expression that returns one of the message items to which the event applies (for example, a `TaskItem` object). The following example uses the `BeforeDelete` event to see if the `TaskItem` object that's open in an inspector is marked as complete when the user tries to delete it. If the task is not marked as complete, a message box prompts the user to complete the task, and the example then sets the `Cancel` argument to `True` to prevent the deletion:

```
Private Sub myTaskItem_BeforeDelete(ByVal Item As Object, Cancel As Boolean)
    If myTaskItem.Complete = False Then
```

```
        MsgBox "Please complete the task before deleting it.", _
            vbOKOnly + vbExclamation, "Task Is Incomplete"
        Cancel = True
    End If
End Sub
```

THE DIFFERENCE BETWEEN THE *READ* AND *OPEN* EVENTS

The Read event and the Open event both occur when the user opens an existing item for editing. The difference between the two events is that the Open event occurs only when the item is being opened in an Inspector window, whereas the Read event occurs both when the item is being opened in an Inspector window and also when it is being selected for editing in a cell.

Understanding the Events That Apply to Explorers, Inspectors, and Views

Table 27.2 lists the events that apply to explorers, inspectors, and views. Some events apply to both explorers and inspectors.

TABLE 27.2: Events that apply to explorers, inspectors, or views

EVENT	APPLIES TO	EVENT OCCURS
`BeforeFolderSwitch`	Explorer	Before the explorer displays a new folder
`BeforeItemCopy`	Explorer	When the user issues a Copy command but before the Copy operation takes place
`BeforeItemCut`	Explorer	When an item is cut from a folder
`BeforeItemPaste`	Explorer	Before an item is pasted
`BeforeViewSwitch`	Explorer	Before the view changes in the Outlook window
`Close`	Explorer, Inspector	When an explorer is closing
`FolderSwitch`	Explorer	After an explorer displays a new folder
`SelectionChange`	Explorer	When the focus is moved to a different item in a folder, or when Outlook itself automatically selects the first item in a folder because the user has selected that folder

TABLE 27.2: Events that apply to explorers, inspectors, or views *(CONTINUED)*

EVENT	APPLIES TO	EVENT OCCURS
`AttachmentSelectionChange`	Explorer, Inspector	When a new or different attachment is selected
`ViewSwitch`	Explorer	When the view changes in the explorer window
`Activate`	Explorer, Inspector	When an Explorer window or an Inspector window is activated (becomes the active window)
`Deactivate`	Explorer, Inspector	When an Explorer window or an Inspector window is deactivated (stops being the active window)
`BeforeMaximize`	Explorer, Inspector	When the user maximizes the explorer or inspector but before maximization takes place
`BeforeMinimize`	Explorer, Inspector	When the user minimizes the explorer or inspector but before minimization takes place
`BeforeMove`	Explorer, Inspector	When the user moves an Explorer window or an Inspector window but before the action takes place
`BeforeSize`	Explorer, Inspector	When the user resizes the Explorer window or Inspector window but before the resizing takes place
`PageChange`	Inspector	When the active form page changes
`InlineResponse`	Explorer	When an inline response appears in the reading pane
`InlineResponseClose`	Explorer	When an inline response in the reading pane closes
`NewExplorer`	Explorers	When a new Explorer window is opened
`NewInspector`	Inspectors	When a new Inspector window is opened
`ViewAdd`	Views	When a view is added to the `Views` collection
`ViewRemove`	Views	When a view is removed from the `Views` collection

If you work on a small screen (for example, a laptop screen), you might prefer to use the `NewInspector` event to maximize each Inspector window you open and to hide any toolbars you don't need. The first procedure in the following example (which includes the necessary declarations) uses the `NewInspector` event to make sure the Standard toolbar is displayed, hide the Advanced toolbar, and assign the `Inspector` object representing the new inspector to the `Public` object variable `myInspector`. The second procedure uses the `Activate` event of the `myInspector` object to maximize its window by setting the `WindowState` property to `olMaximized`.

The net effect of these two event procedures is to configure the toolbars as described earlier and maximize the Inspector window. Put more simply, if you, for example, double-click an email, it opens in a new window. That window is the "inspector" object. The `Activate` event procedure is necessary because the `NewInspector` event runs before the Inspector window is displayed, which means the `NewInspector` event procedure cannot maximize the Inspector window.

```
Public WithEvents myInspectors As Inspectors
Public WithEvents myInspector As Inspector

Private Sub myInspectors_NewInspector(ByVal Inspector As Outlook.Inspector)
    With Inspector
        With .CommandBars
            .Item("Standard").Visible = True
            .Item("Advanced").Visible = False
        End With
        Set myInspector = Inspector
    End With
End Sub

Private Sub myInspector_Activate()
    myInspector.WindowState = olMaximized
End Sub
```

Real World Scenario

How to Test Event-Handler Procedures

You don't test event handlers the same way that you test ordinary VBA modules. In an ordinary module, you click to put the blinking insertion cursor inside the macro you want to execute and then you press F5 to execute that procedure.

In a *class* module, by contrast, pressing F5 merely opens the Macros dialog box rather than directly running the code.

If you are confused about where to put handler code, and how to test it, don't be discouraged. An event handler must be put into a class module. And whenever you use classes, you're venturing into OOP. OOP, whatever its merits, always adds a layer of complexity for the programmer. So, let's briefly review this topic so you'll see how to write, and then test, event handlers.

In this next example, you want to respond to any changes the user might make to one of the user's contacts. In other words, you need to write some code in the `ItemChange` event of the Contacts folder. Perhaps you want your code to alert the user that they need to make further changes. Or, that they need to send this new information to their assistant. Whatever the reason, your purpose is to write code that executes when a Contact item changes—when the user modifies a contact and then clicks the Save button, thereby triggering the `ItemChange` event.

"Handling" an event (writing your own code that executes when an event takes place) requires that you take three steps:

1. **Create an object variable—using the `WithEvents` command—that will represent the object whose event you want to handle.** Where does this code go? At the top of a class module in the General Declarations section above any subs. Outlook has that special built-in class module named `ThisOutlookSession`. So instead of creating a new class module, let's keep things simple and just use the existing `ThisOutlookSession` class module to declare our object variable.
2. **Point or connect (`Set`) your new object variable to the actual object whose event you want to handle.** In our example, we want to handle the `Items` collection of Outlook's Contacts folder. Where does this code go? It could be put into a macro. Or, because we want to have this connection made automatically, let's put it in Outlook's startup event. That way the connection is made whenever the user runs Outlook. Remember that the various Office applications have specially reserved names: If you name a procedure in Word `AutoExec`, for example, its code executes when you start Word. If you name a procedure `Application_Startup` in Outlook, that's the equivalent of Word's `AutoExec`.
3. **Write the event-handler code—the actions you want taken when this event occurs.** Where does this code go? In the same class module where you declared the object variables (step 1, above).

There are other ways to handle events, but this is a straightforward example. To keep it simple, we'll put the code for all three steps in Outlook's built-in `ThisOutlookSession` class module. Now let's follow the preceding steps, only this time we'll insert the actual code:

1. First, open Outlook's VBA Editor by pressing Alt+F11. Expand Project1 in the Project window until you see the ThisOutlookSession class module (under Microsoft Outlook Objects). Double-click ThisOutlookSession to open its Code window.
2. At the top of the ThisOutlookSession Code window, type the object variable's declaration:

```
Public WithEvents objContacts As Items
```

3. Now, in the Application Startup event, we'll write code that connects the object variable to the real Outlook object we're interested in, which is the Items collection of the Contacts folder:

```
Private Sub Application_Startup()

    Set objContacts = Application.GetNamespace("MAPI") _
        .GetDefaultFolder(olFolderContacts).Items

End Sub
```

4. Finally, we'll write the event-handler code that does the job we want to do. This code also goes in the ThisOutlookSession module:

```
Private Sub objContacts_ItemChange(ByVal Item As Object)

    MsgBox "This Contact Item Has Been Changed"

End Sub
```

Continues

Continued

Now, to test this event handler, first, shut Outlook down and then restart it. This is necessary to execute the `Application_Startup` procedure that hooks our object variable into the Contacts folder's Items collection (described in item 3 in the list above).

Now in Outlook, open your Contacts folder. In Outlook 2013 and 2016, this folder is named *People* and is found in the lower-left corner next to the Mail and the Calendar icons. Double-click some random contact. Click Edit in the upper right of the window, click Notes, and type something in the Notes field. Finally, click the Save button in the lower-right corner. This should cause your event-handler code to execute, displaying a message telling you that the contact info has changed, as shown in Figure 27.3:

FIGURE 27.3
Using OOP, we indirectly triggered this message box.

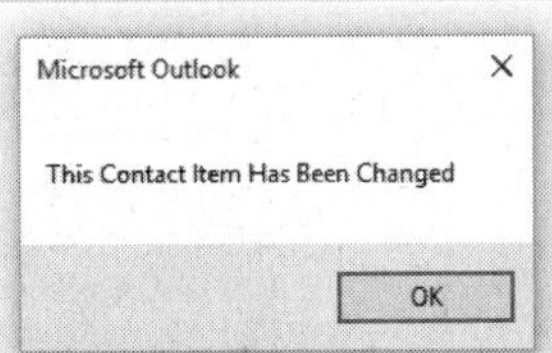

I'm not going to pretend that any of this is easy. Although OOP has its merits, writing code employing OOP rules can be a real wrestling match—sometimes far more labyrinthine than this example. Complexities involving diction, punctuation, reference, scope, precedence, and other issues will often draw you into a world of multiplying interactions—leading to unpredictable and perplexing test-code-retest cycles. Your best bet when working with class modules is to try to find online some working example code that's close to what you're trying to accomplish and then modify it to suit your purposes.

Understanding the Events That Apply to Folders

Outlook provides three events (see Table 27.3) that apply to folders.

TABLE 27.3: Events that apply to folders

EVENT	EVENT OCCURS
`FolderAdd`	When a folder is added to the specified `Folders` collection
`FolderChange`	When a folder in the specified `Folders` collection is changed
`FolderRemove`	When a folder is removed from the specified `Folders` collection

Understanding the Events That Apply to Items and Results Objects

Table 27.4 lists the events that apply to items and results.

TABLE 27.4: Events that apply to items and results

EVENT	EVENT OCCURS
`ItemAdd`	When one or more items are added to the collection but not when many items are added all at once
`ItemChange`	When an item in the `Items` collection or the `Results` collection is changed
`ItemRemove`	When an item is deleted from the `Items` collection or the `Results` collection but not when 16 or more items are deleted at once from a Personal Folders file, an Exchange mailbox, or an Exchange public folder; also not when the last item in a Personal Folders file is deleted

The example in the sidebar "How to Test Event-Handler Procedures" earlier in this chapter employs the `ItemChange` event to monitor when any contact is changed in the Contacts folder.

Understanding the Events That Apply to Reminders

Table 27.5 explains the events that Outlook provides for reminders. You can use these events to take actions when a reminder fires, before the reminder dialog box appears, when the user clicks the Snooze button to dismiss a reminder, or when reminders are added, changed, or removed.

TABLE 27.5: Events that apply to reminders

EVENT	EVENT OCCURS
`BeforeReminderShow`	Before Outlook displays the Reminder dialog box
`ReminderAdd`	When a reminder is added
`ReminderChange`	After a reminder has been changed
`ReminderFire`	Before a reminder is executed
`ReminderRemove`	When a reminder is removed from the `Reminders` collection
`Snooze`	When the user dismisses a reminder by clicking the Snooze button

Understanding the Events That Apply to Synchronization

If you write procedures to synchronize Outlook, you may need to use the three events that apply to the `SyncObject` object, which represents a Send/Receive group for a user. (You can access the `SyncObject` object by using the `SyncObjects` property of the `NameSpace` object to return the `SyncObjects` collection.) Table 27.6 explains the events that apply to the `SyncObject` object.

TABLE 27.6: Events that apply to the `SyncObject` object

EVENT	EVENT OCCURS
`SyncStart`	When Outlook starts synchronizing a user's folders
`Progress`	Triggers periodically during the synchronization of Outlook folders
`SyncEnd`	After synchronization ends
`OnError`	When an error occurs during synchronization

The following example uses the `OnError` event with the object variable `mySyncObject`. If an error occurs during synchronization of the `SyncObject` represented by `mySyncObject`, this procedure displays an error message giving the error code and description:

```
Private Sub mySyncObject_OnError(ByVal Code As Long, _
    ByVal Description As String)

    Dim strMessage As String
    strMessage = "An error occurred during synchronization:" & vbCr & vbCr
    strMessage = strMessage & "Error code: " & Code & vbCr
    strMessage = strMessage & "Error description: " & Description
    MsgBox strMessage, vbOKOnly + vbExclamation, "Synchronization Error"

End Sub
```

Understanding Quick Steps

A Quick Steps feature allows nonprogrammers to combine actions in Outlook without having to record a macro (Outlook has no recorder anyway) or write a procedure using VBA.

Although not nearly as flexible and powerful as writing macros in VBA, for a common task you might consider seeing if it's possible to create a Quick Step.

While looking at the Mail page in Outlook, click the Home button on the Ribbon. You'll see the Quick Steps area right in the middle of the Ribbon.

The reason to use this Quick Steps feature is the same as for writing or recording macros: After you've specified and saved a set of actions, you won't need to manually repeat those actions in the future—you can merely run the macro (or Quick Steps "program") and the behaviors will be carried out automatically.

Quick Steps is similar to Access's Macro Designer: You're presented with a list of common actions and you can choose to combine two or more of them into a macro-like little "program." And, like a macro, a Quick Steps one-click button saves time by launching its "program" anytime the user chooses. Nonprogrammers can build the Quick Steps "programs" out of actions that they frequently perform—thus saving time.

Some sample Quick Steps are already available in the Ribbon; and when you first click them, you're asked to customize their behavior to suit your way of working. Click, for example, the MoveTo: ? sample, and the First Time Setup dialog box opens, as shown in Figure 27.4.

FIGURE 27.4
You can experiment with the sample Quick Steps to get an idea how to create and customize them.

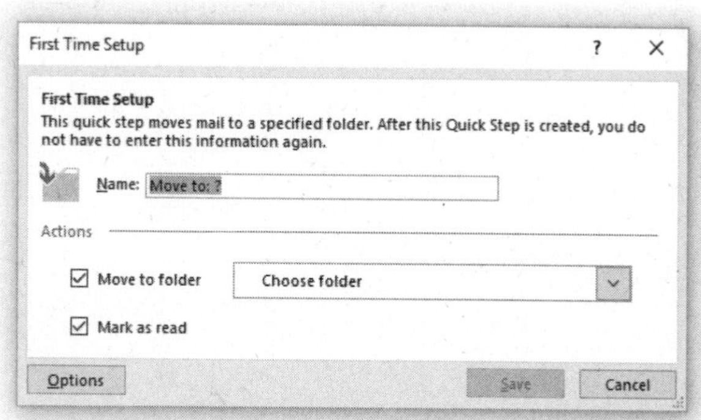

As you see in Figure 27.4, you're allowed to customize this Quick Step by changing its name, specifying the target folder, and deciding whether or not to mark it as read. So this little program performs two actions at the click of a button. That could be a time-saver if you frequently store read email in a particular folder. Also notice the Options button where you can further modify the behavior of this Quick Step. You can add more actions, delete actions, specify a shortcut key, and write a tooltip.

Quick Steps makes 20 actions available to you, so it's no competition for the tens of thousands of things you can do with VBA. Nonetheless, you might want to consider employing the Quick Steps tool for quick and easy automation of common mail-related tasks in Outlook.

The Bottom Line

Create event handlers. Event handlers are procedures that contain code that responds to an event. In other words, if a user modifies one of their contacts, an event can detect this modification and execute code you've written to respond to the modification.

Master It Event-handler procedures are unlike ordinary macro procedures in several ways. Name one of the differences.

Work with application-level events. Application-level events happen to Outlook as a whole.

Master It Name an important Outlook application-level event.

Work with item-level events. Outlook has two primary kinds of events.

Master It What are the two types of events in Outlook? And how do they differ?

Understand the Quick Steps tool. With Outlook's Quick Steps feature, you can build a set of actions the user can later trigger to automate a frequently repeated task. This is quite similar to the nature and purpose of macros.

Master It What is the key difference between a Quick Step and a macro?

Chapter 28

Understanding the Access Object Model and Key Objects

If you work with Access databases, forms, or reports, you'll find that customizing Access using VBA can streamline your work and that of your colleagues. For example, you can program Access to automatically extract datasets you need, to create custom reports on a regular schedule, and to perform many other tasks.

Even if your work in Access consists simply of entering data into databases and checking that it is correct, you may want to create macros to make mundane tasks less onerous. For example, you can use VBA to simplify data entry or to validate data that the user enters to avoid problems further down the line.

However, because Access implements VBA in a different way from the other applications this book has discussed, we'll begin this chapter showing you how to get started using VBA in Access. You'll then come to grips with the Access object model and learn about its most important creatable objects. After that, the chapter will show you how to open and close databases, set startup properties for a database, work with the `Screen` object, and use the important `DoCmd` object to run Access commands.

The next chapter discusses how to manipulate the data in an Access database via VBA.

IN THIS CHAPTER, YOU WILL LEARN TO DO THE FOLLOWING:

- Become familiar with how VBA works in Access
- Understand Access-style macros
- Open and close databases
- Work with the `Screen` object
- Use the `DoCmd` object to run Access commands

Getting Started with VBA in Access

Access implements VBA differently than the other Office applications do. Here are the main differences:

- Collections in Access are zero-based—the first item in a collection is numbered `0` (zero) rather than `1`. For example, `Forms(0).Name` returns the `Name` property of the first `Form` object in the `Forms` collection. It's like visiting a country where the first floor is called zero rather than one. So if you're trying to get to the fifth floor, you have to make the mental adjustment that in the elevator you must press the 4 button. Crazy, but you just have to deal with it. Zero-based collections make your job as a programmer a bit more difficult, particularly when employing loops.

- The term *macro* is used in a special way in Access, unlike the way it's used in other Office applications, not to mention all other forms of computing. An Access "macro" is a historical entity—a holdover from the early days of this database system. Some consider the whole approach rather harebrained because it's limited to only a subset of the available programming statements, and it's not nearly as useful or flexible or efficient (in most cases) as just writing VBA code. To build what Access calls a "macro," you enter a list of actions that you want to perform by using a special utility—the Macro Designer (formerly known as the Macro Builder)—that's built into Access. You choose these actions from a list and then type arguments into the next cell in a table displayed by the Macro Designer. So, it's all a bit like filling in a form and not that much like real programming. It's similar to Outlook's Quick Steps tool described in Chapter 27, "Working with Events in Outlook." But we can imagine that sometime in the early days, somebody said that people who work with databases will be comfortable with entering data into tables.
- Access's "macros" are created by clicking the Table tab on the Ribbon, clicking the Named Macros option, and clicking Create Named Macro. From now on, we'll call these self-styled "macros" *Access-style macros* to distinguish them from the true macros we've worked with throughout this book.
- Fortunately, Access also offers VBA. When you write VBA code in the Access VBA Editor—as you would in the other Office 2016 applications—you create true macros, properly so called. (Just remember that the Access literature generally doesn't describe these VBA macros as *macros*. You just have to get used to the difference in terminology.) We'll focus our attention on the VBA capabilities in Access rather than on the legacy Macro Designer.
- To make it possible for a user to execute one of your macro `Subs` in Access, you must first create an Access-style function that calls the subprocedure. While you, the programmer, are working on a macro in the VBA Editor, you can debug and run the subprocedure by using the VBA Editor's usual commands (for example, press F5 to run and test the subprocedure). But a user will not be able to run the macro directly from the Access user interface. Instead, you must employ a `RunCode` command, as you'll see. There is, however, one exception to this rule. In Chapter 31, "Programming the Office 2016 Ribbon" (see the section titled "Direct Communication with VBA"), you'll learn how to modify the Access Ribbon to let users directly trigger VBA code via the Ribbon.

The following sections provide a complete, start-to-finish example of how to work with VBA in Access. Briefly, you first create a module, then write a macro procedure in that module, and finally, use the Macro Designer to create an Access-style macro whose sole purpose is to start the execution of a true macro (the VBA procedure).

Before going further, let's ensure that macros are, in fact, enabled in Access. Follow these steps to enable Access macros:

1. Click the File tab on the Ribbon.
2. Click Options in the left pane.

3. Click Trust Center in the Access Options dialog box.
4. Click the Trust Center Settings button.
5. Click Macro Settings in the left pane of the Trust Center dialog box.
6. Click the Enable All Macros option button.
7. Click OK twice to close the dialog boxes.

Recall that by taking these steps you have now exposed your machine to possible harmful macros that could automatically execute upon loading into Access. Now you can test and explore the Access macros in this book. However, if you plan to work with unknown or unreliable Access content, repeat the above steps, but in Step 6, choose to disable all macros.

Creating a Module in the VBA Editor

To create a module where you can write VBA macro code, open an Access database and click the Ribbon's Database Tools tab. Click the Visual Basic button on the Ribbon (or simply press Alt+F11).

The VBA Editor opens. Choose Insert ➢ Module in the VBA Editor or right-click the project's name (it's boldface) in the Project Explorer pane, and choose Insert ➢ Module from the shortcut menu.

Creating a Function

After creating a VBA module in the VBA Editor, you can create a function within it as described earlier in this book. The following example creates a function named `Standard_Setup` that simply displays a message box to indicate that it is running (however, the next section uses this macro as an example):

```
Public Function Standard_Setup()
    'put your choice of commands here
    MsgBox "The Standard_Setup macro is running."
End Function
```

You can test this code as usual by clicking somewhere inside the procedure and then pressing F5.

After creating the function, switch back to Access by pressing Alt+F11 or clicking the View Microsoft Access button on the far left of the Standard toolbar in the VBA Editor. Of course, you could also use the traditional Windows Alt+Tab or Windows key+Tab shortcuts.

Using the Macro Designer

Although this and the next chapter focus on automating Access via the more flexible and powerful VBA language, some readers may be interested to know how to work with the Macro Designer tool. So, we'll explore it briefly before moving on to VBA examples.

Creating an Access-Style Macro to Run a Function

Recall that a user can't directly trigger a VBA procedure interactively from the main Access interface (although you, the programmer, can press F5 to test procedures in the VBA Editor as we just did in the previous example function).

You'll find no Macros dialog box like the one in Word and other Office 2016 applications. True, there *is* a Run Macro button on the Database Tools tab of the Access Ribbon, but this feature cannot directly trigger a true macro procedure in VBA. It only triggers an Access-style macro.

For a user to run a VBA procedure, you have to create an Access-style macro that was built using Access's Macro Designer. You use the `RunCode` action (command) to call the VBA procedure. We'll see how to do that now:

1. Display the Database window if it's not already displayed. For example, click the word *View* (the *word* with the small black down-arrow, not the icon) on the Ribbon's Home tab, and then select Datasheet View from the options displayed.

2. Click the Macro button on the Ribbon's Create tab to open the Macro Designer window (see Figure 28.1). This also opens a Design tab on the Ribbon.

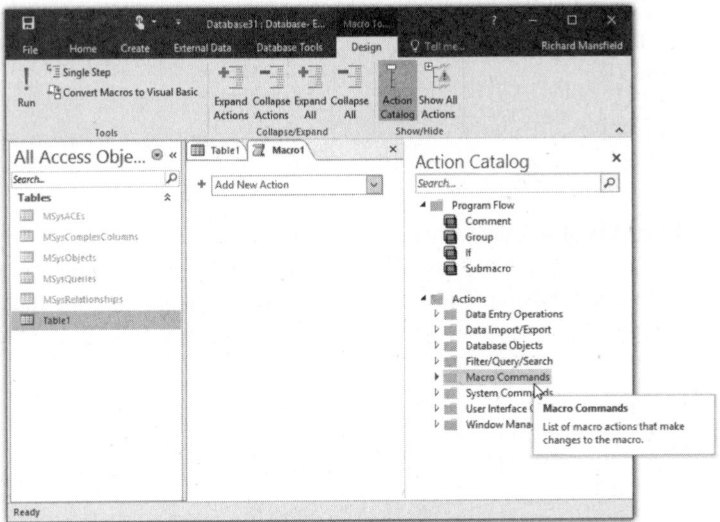

FIGURE 28.1 Use the Macro Designer window to create a new Access-style "macro" in Access.

3. In the Action Catalog pane on the right, open the Macro Commands folder and double-click the `RunCode` item. This inserts the `RunCode` command into the middle pane. (The `RunMacro` option command can execute only Access-style macros. Likewise, if you try to add a button to the Quick Access Toolbar above the Ribbon, it too can execute only Access-style macros.)

4. In the Function Name field, type **Standard_Setup()**, the name of the VBA test function you created earlier in this chapter. *The empty parentheses are required, so don't omit them.*

5. Click the Save icon in the Quick Access Toolbar above the Ribbon, or press Ctrl+S.

6. Type the name **test** in the Save As dialog box, and click the OK button. (Tip: If you modify the macro later and want to change its name, choose File ➢ Save As ➢ Save Object As, and

then click the Save button. Access can be remarkably roundabout sometimes. Or, you can right-click the macro's name in the left pane of the main Access window and then choose Rename.)

7. Now test this macro (and consequently the VBA procedure it triggers) by clicking the Run icon on the Ribbon. It's the icon with the red exclamation point. This icon appears only when the Macro Designer is active in the Design tab of the Ribbon. You now see the message box telling you that your macro is running.

The user can execute Access-style macros when the Macro Designer is closed. Just double-click *test* in the All Access Objects list (the pane on the left side of the main window).

Or alternatively, the user can click the Database Tools tab of the Ribbon and then click the Run Macro icon on the Macro section (it too has a red exclamation point). Access's Run Macro dialog box opens. Select *test* as the macro name you want to run and then click OK to close the dialog box and execute your macro.

Three Ways to Execute an Access-Style Macro

To sum up, a user can execute an Access-style macro only three ways:

- Choose the Run Macro option from the Ribbon's Database Tools tab. This opens a small Run Macro dialog box from which you can select an Access-style macro and execute it.
- Double-click the Access-style macro's name in the All Access Objects list in the left pane of the main Access window.
- Add a button to the Quick Access Toolbar that will execute the Access-style macro.

You add a button to the Quick Access Toolbar by following these steps:

1. Click the Customize Quick Access Toolbar button (the down arrow icon on the right of the Quick Access Toolbar at the top left of the Access window).
2. Click the More Commands option in the drop-down list. The Access Options dialog box opens.
3. Select Macros in the Choose Commands From drop-down list.
4. Double-click your macro's name to move it into the list on the right side (where the toolbar's displayed items are listed).
5. Click OK to close the dialog box and put your macro on the toolbar.

Note that you can't trigger a macro from a keyboard shortcut (Access doesn't permit you to create custom keyboard shortcuts).

Translating an Access-Style Macro into a VBA Macro

Given that VBA is far more powerful than the Access-style macros, you might want to convert an Access-style macro into VBA to enhance it. You can have Access automatically translate Access-style macros into VBA functions. Follow these steps:

1. Display the Database window if it's not already displayed. For example, click the word *View* (the *word* with the small black down-arrow, not the icon) on the Ribbon's Home tab, and then select Datasheet View from the options displayed.
2. Right-click your *test* macro in the All Access Objects pane on the left. Click Design View in the context menu that opens. You want to view the Access-style macro you created earlier in this chapter (see Figure 28.1).
3. On the left side of the Ribbon, click Convert Macros To Visual Basic.
4. You see a dialog box where you can optionally refuse to include error handling or comments.
5. Click the Convert button.
6. The VBA Editor opens.
7. In the Navigation pane, locate and double-click the module named *Converted Macro-test*. You now see the translated code:

```
'------------------------------------------------------------
' test
'
'------------------------------------------------------------
Function test()
On Error GoTo test_Err

    Standard_Setup


test_Exit:
    Exit Function


test_Err:
    MsgBox Error$
    Resume test_Exit

End Function
```

If you opted to avoid the error trapping and commenting, it's simpler:

```
'------------------------------------------------------------
' test1
'
'------------------------------------------------------------
Function test1()

    Run_SampleProcedure

End Function
```

Using an *AutoExec* Macro to Initialize an Access Session

To set up preconditions for an Access session, you can use an `AutoExec` macro. When Access starts running, it checks to see if there is a macro named `AutoExec`. If so, that macro is executed (runs) automatically when Access opens. This AutoExec feature is also available in other Office applications, such as Word. (By the way, people who want to do you damage by triggering a virus or other harmful code use an `AutoExec` to store their trickery.)

But you might decide to use `AutoExec` to run useful initialization code. For example, you might choose to maximize the Application window, open a particular item such as a table, or display a particular record. Note that `AutoExec` must be the name of an Access-style macro, not a VBA procedure (as it would be in other Office applications).

By the way, you can prevent an `AutoExec` macro from running when you open a database by holding down the Shift key while the database opens.

To create an `AutoExec` macro, start a new Access-style macro as described in the previous section, add to it the actions that you want the macro to perform, and save it with the special reserved name **`AutoExec`**. The macro will run the next time you open the database.

We'll now turn our attention to regular VBA programming, but if you're interested in learning more about the Macro Designer, see the tutorial on this web page:

```
https://msdn.microsoft.com/en-us/library/office/gg435977(v=office.14).aspx
```

Running a Subprocedure

Until now in this book, you've mostly created traditional subs when writing or recording a macro. And for consistency, the Access VBA code examples in this chapter and elsewhere will also be subs.

But beware! If you want to permit the user to execute Access VBA procedures, they must be turned into functions. Just replace the word `Sub` with `Function` in your code. VBA will then automatically change the line at the end of your procedure from `End Sub` to `End Function`. Easy enough.

So, once again just remember that Access differs from other Office applications in this way, and in many others. When you're writing a VBA macro in Access, there's no good reason to create Access VBA code in a subprocedure rather than in a function because a sub cannot be triggered directly in Access.

Only functions can be directly triggered, as the example in the previous section illustrated. If you feel you must create a sub, the only way to execute it is to create a function that, in turn, has the single job of executing your subprocedure. So what is the point?

The process of triggering functions indirectly is clumsy, but it can be made to work if for some unimaginable reason you want to use a subprocedure. Here is a simple example:

1. In the VBA Editor, create a subprocedure that performs the actions you want:

```
Sub SampleProcedure()
    MsgBox "The subprocedure named Sample Procedure is running."
End Sub
```

2. Still in the VBA Editor, create a function that runs the subprocedure:

```
Public Function Run_SampleProcedure()
    Call SampleProcedure
End Function
```

3. Then switch to Access and create an Access-style macro that uses the `RunCode` action to run the function that runs the subprocedure. (See the section earlier in this chapter titled "Creating an Access-Style Macro to Run a Function.")

Understanding the *Option Compare Database* Statement

When you launch the VBA Editor in Access (by pressing Alt+F11 or clicking the Visual Basic button on the Ribbon's Database Tools tab) and then insert a code module, you'll notice that Access automatically enters an `Option Compare Database` statement in the General Declarations area at the top of the Code window.

As an aside, recall that if you've selected the Require Variable Declaration check box on the Editor tab of the VBA Editor Options dialog box (Tools ➤ Options) to make the VBA Editor force you to declare all variables explicitly, you'll see an `Option Explicit` statement in the General Declarations area as well.

Access supports three different ways of comparing text strings: `Option Compare Database`, `Option Compare Binary`, and `Option Compare Text`. Here's what these options mean:

- `Option Compare Database` is the default comparison type for Access databases, and it performs string comparisons using the sort order for the locale that Windows is using (for example, U.S. English). Sorting is not case-sensitive. Access automatically inserts an `Option Compare Database` statement in the declarations section of each module that you insert. You can delete the `Option Compare Database` statement, in which case Access will use `Option Compare Binary` instead.
- `Option Compare Binary` performs case-sensitive sorting. To use `Option Compare Binary`, either delete the `Option Compare Database` statement in the declarations section or change it to an `Option Compare Binary` statement.
- `Option Compare Text` performs case-insensitive sorting. To use `Option Compare Text`, change the `Option Compare Database` or `Option Compare Binary` statement to an `Option Compare Text` statement.

Getting an Overview of the Access Object Model

It's not crucial to understand how the Access object model fits together in order to work with VBA in Access, but most people find it helpful to know the main objects in the object model. And sometimes the code examples in the Help system's object-model reference prove invaluable—showing you how to employ objects in your own programming.

To explore the Access object model, follow these steps:

1. Launch or activate Access, and then press Alt+F11 to launch or activate the VBA Editor.
2. In the Editor, choose Help ➤ Microsoft Visual Basic For Applications Help.

3. In the pane on the left side of this web page, click the link Access VBA Reference.
4. In the pane on the left side of this Access VBA Reference web page, click the Object Model link. You now see the list of primary Access objects, as shown in Figure 28.2.

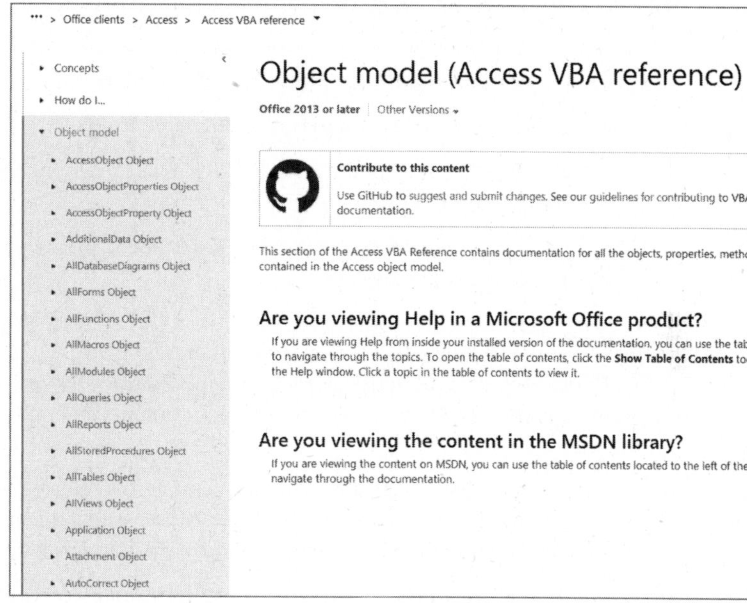

FIGURE 28.2 The entries in the Access object-model reference will help you write your own VBA code.

Understanding Creatable Objects in Access

Access *exposes* (makes available for your use in code) various *creatable* objects, meaning that you can employ most of the important objects in its object model without explicitly going through (mentioning in your code) the `Application` object.

For most programming purposes, these creatable objects are the most commonly used objects. The main creatable objects in Access are as follows:

- The `Forms` collection contains all the `Form` objects, which represent the open forms in a database. Because it's creatable, you need not write `Application.Form` in your code. You can leave off the `Application` and merely write `Form`.
- The `Reports` collection contains all the `Report` objects, which represent the open reports in a database.
- The `DataAccessPages` collection contains all the `DataAccessPage` objects, which represent the open data access pages in a project or a database. (An Access *project* is a file that connects to a SQL Server database.)
- The `CurrentProject` object represents the active project or database in Access.

- The `CurrentData` object represents the objects stored in the current database.
- The `CodeProject` object represents the project containing the code database of a project or database.
- The `CodeData` object represents the objects stored in the code database.
- The `Screen` object represents the screen object that currently has the focus (the object that is receiving input or ready to receive input). The object can be a form, a report, or a control.
- The `DoCmd` object enables you to run Access commands.
- The `Modules` collection contains the `Module` objects, which represent the code modules and class modules in a database.
- The `References` collection contains the `Reference` objects, which represent the references set in the Access application.
- The `DBEngine` object represents the Microsoft Jet Database Engine and is the topmost object in the Data Access Objects (DAO) hierarchy. The `DBEngine` object provides access to the `Workspaces` collection, which contains all the `Workspace` objects available to Access, and to the `Errors` collection, which contains an `Error` object for each operation involving DAO.
- The `Workspace` object contains a named session for a given user. When you open a database, Access creates a workspace by default and assigns the open database to it. You can work with the current workspace or create more workspaces as needed.
- The `Error` object contains information about the data-access errors that have occurred in a DAO operation.

Opening and Closing Databases

The following sections show you how to open and close databases in a macro. You can use the `CurrentDb` method to return the current database, open a database and treat it as the current database, or even open multiple databases at once. You can also create and remove workspaces.

Using the *CurrentDb* Method to Return the Current Database

To work with the database that's currently open in Access, use the `CurrentDb` method on the `Application` object or an object variable representing the `Application` object. The `CurrentDb` method returns a `Database` object variable representing the currently open database that has the *focus* (can be interacted with by the user—typed into, or clicked).

The following example declares an object variable of the `Database` type named `myDatabase` and then uses the `CurrentDb` method to assign the active database to it:

```
Dim myDatabase As Database
Set myDatabase = Application.CurrentDb
```

Closing the Current Database and Opening a Different Database

In Access, you can choose from among several ways of opening and closing a database. This section discusses the simplest method of opening and closing a database—by treating it as the current database. This method is similar to opening and closing a database when working interactively in Access. See the next section for another method of opening and closing databases that lets you have two or more databases open at the same time.

To open a database as the current database, use the `OpenCurrentDatabase` method of the `Application` object. The syntax is as follows:

```
expression.OpenCurrentDatabase(Filepath, Exclusive, bstrPassword)
```

Here are the components of the syntax:

- *`expression`* is a required expression that returns an `Application` object.
- `Filepath` is a required String argument that specifies the path and filename of the database to open. You should specify the filename extension; if you omit it, Access assumes the extension is `.accdb`.
- `Exclusive` is an optional Boolean argument that you can set to `True` to open the database in Exclusive mode rather than in Shared mode (the default, or the result of an explicit `False` setting).
- `bstrPassword` is an optional String argument that specifies the password required to open the database.

To close the current database, use the `CloseCurrentDatabase` method with the `Application` object. This method takes no arguments.

You can run the `CloseCurrentDatabase` method from the current database, but you can't do anything after that because the code stops running once VBA executes the `CloseCurrentDatabase` method. The database containing the code immediately closes, so any subsequent code in that macro cannot be executed.

To close the current database and open another by using the `OpenCurrentDatabase` method, you must run the code from outside the databases involved—for example, by using automation from another application. Chapter 30, "Accessing One Application from Another Application," describes this technique. (The section "Communicating Between Office Applications" later in this chapter provides an example as well.)

Real World Scenario

PREPARE THE NORTHWIND DATABASE TO USE WITH THIS BOOK'S EXAMPLES

To test and experiment with some of the Access code examples in this and the following chapters, you need to do a little preliminary housekeeping. Put simply, we all need to be experimenting with the same database so we get the same results.

Traditionally, when authors have written about Access, they've employed a sample database named *Northwind* that Microsoft included with Access. Northwind employs a variety of Access's features and, therefore, is a useful example database. It can be particularly valuable when you want to experiment with Access but don't want to use your own database (both to keep it safe and because your database might not exercise some of Access's capabilities).

Continues

Continued

I'll use Northwind in some of the examples in this book so that all readers can be working with the same data and the same structures. Therefore, before you test some of the upcoming code examples, please put a copy of the `Northwind.accdb` file in your `C:\Temp` directory so the example code in this book can locate it. If you don't have a `C:\Temp` directory, create one.

You may already have Northwind on your hard drive. To see if you do, press the Start button to display the Windows 8 or 10 Start page, and type **Northwind.accdt**. If it shows up in the search, right-click its name, choose Open File Location, copy it, and paste it into your `C:\Temp` directory.

However, if you don't have a copy of `Northwind.accdb`, follow these steps to get it:

1. Open Microsoft Access 2016.
2. You should see a selection of template icons on the right. If you don't see this, choose File ➤ New to display the templates.
3. Locate the Search For Online Templates field at the top of the screen.
4. Type **Northwind** into this field and press Enter.
5. Single-click the Desktop Northwind 2007 Sample Database icon shown in the results of your search.
6. Type **Northwind.accdb** in the File Name field.
7. Look at the filepath listed just below the File Name field. This is where on your hard-drive Access stores your database files. Make a note of this location so you can find `Northwind.accdb` in step 12.
8. Click the Create button. Access will download the Northwind database and create your copy, storing it in the default database location you noted in step 7.
9. The Northwind database will also open automatically in Access after it's created.
10. Click the Login [*sic*] button to open the database if you see a Login [*sic*] dialog box. [*Sic*] because as most people know, but not Microsoft, the verb form is *log in*, not *login*. You wouldn't write: *Walkin* the park.
11. You now want to copy the `Northwind.accdb` file to your `C:\Temp` directory, so close Access.
12. Locate the `Northwind.accdb` file where Access stores your database files (see step 7).
13. Copy `Northwind.accdb` file and paste it into the `C:\Temp` directory.

Now the code examples in this book can reference this file path to open Northwind, like this:

```
filepath:="C:\Temp\Northwind.accdb"
```

Next, you'll want to remove the default Login dialog box so you can work with the database more easily from code. Open `Northwind.accdb` by double-clicking its name in Windows Explorer.

By default, a Login dialog box appears asking you to select one of the employees from this imaginary company. So, you must click the Login button to close the dialog box before you can see Northwind in Access. We don't want to have to deal with this in our code examples. So, let's remove it.

Start Access running by using File Explorer to go to your `C:\Temp` folder and double-clicking `Northwind.accdb`. Log in by clicking that Login button. If it's not already open, click the >> symbol in Access's left pane to open the *Navigation pane*. Locate the Supporting Objects entry in the Navigation pane and click it to expand it. Scroll down until you locate the macro named `AutoExec`. (It's near the bottom of the list, next to the macro symbol, a golden scroll.) Right-click `AutoExec`, choose Cut from the context menu, and then close Access. (If you're warned that the Clipboard will be emptied, go ahead and let it happen.)

Now that Login dialog box won't interrupt you any more when you open the Northwind example database.

Communicating Between Office Applications

There's a special requirement when you're writing code that communicates *between* Office applications. You can't simply declare an object variable to point to an application object, like this:

```
Dim myAccess As Access.Application
```

Code like this will run only if you first provide a *reference* in the host application. For example, if you're trying to manipulate Access from VBA code within a Word macro, you need to set a reference in Word's VBA Editor.

The following example illustrates a way to contact and manipulate Access from another VBA host—for example, from Excel or from Word. But before you can execute this code from Word or some other application, you must first choose Tools ➤ References in the Word VBA Editor, then scroll down, locate, and double-click *Microsoft Access 16.0 Object Library* in the drop-down list. Click OK to close this dialog box. (In case you reopen this References dialog box in the future, you'll see this reference listed at the top, but its name will be *Microsoft Access 15.0 Object Library*, not the 16.0 you chose. But don't worry, it will work fine. It's just one of those things … just one of those crazy things.)

Note that to test the following example, you must also have a database currently loaded and running in an instance of Access. But open some database other than Northwind. You'll see why shortly.

This next example declares the object variable `myAccess` as the `Access.Application` type and the object variable `myDatabase` as the `Object` type. The example uses the `GetObject` method to assign to `myAccess` the copy of Access that's running, uses the `CloseCurrentDatabase` method to close this database, and then uses the `OpenCurrentDatabase` method to open another database, namely Northwind, in Exclusive mode. The final statement uses the `CurrentDb` method to assign the open database to the `myDatabase` object variable. Copy and paste this into Word's VBA Editor:

```
Sub ContactAccess()
Dim myAccess As Access.Application
```

```
Dim myDatabase As Object

Set myAccess = GetObject(, "Access.Application")
myAccess.CloseCurrentDatabase
myAccess.OpenCurrentDatabase _
    filepath:="C:\Temp\Northwind.accdb", Exclusive:=True
Set myDatabase = myAccess.CurrentDb
End Sub
```

When you test this code by pressing F5 to execute it in the Word VBA Editor, you'll know it works because when you look at Access, whatever database was open in Access will have been replaced by Northwind (if you don't see this, look at the "Prepare the Northwind Database to Use with This Book's Examples" sidebar earlier in this chapter).

When running this code, you might get an error message saying "User-defined type not defined." And the Editor will highlight this line of code:

```
Dim myAccess As Access.Application
```

This means that the Editor can't locate the object named `Access`. For reasons unknown, a newly added library is sometimes *deselected* in the References. It's just *another* one of those things. To fix this problem, repeat the steps described previously to use the Word VBA Editor's Tools ➢ References dialog box to add a reference to the *Microsoft Access 15.0 Object Library* again. This time it should stay put.

Opening Multiple Databases at Once

Instead of using the `OpenCurrentDatabase` method to open a database as the current database, you can use the `OpenDatabase` method of the `Workspace` object to open another database and return a reference to the `Database` object representing it. The syntax for the `OpenDatabase` method is as follows:

```
Set database = workspace.OpenDatabase (Name, Options, ReadOnly, Connect)
```

Creating New Databases, Forms, and Reports in Access

The discussions of the other Office applications in this part of the book (Part 6) have emphasized creating and saving new files—for example, creating new documents in Word or new workbooks in Excel and saving them under suitable names and in the appropriate formats.

Access, too, has its own VBA commands for programmatically creating new databases, forms, reports, tables, and other objects:

- To create a new database, use the `NewCurrentDatabase` method of the `Application` object.
- To create a new form, use the `CreateForm` method. To place controls on the form, use the `CreateControl` method.
- To create a new report, use the `CreateReport` method. To place controls on the report, use the `CreateReportControl` method.

While programmatically creating a new database is quite feasible, it is not only complex but also something that you probably won't ever need to do. In most cases, the goal of your Access VBA programming will be to manipulate existing databases and objects that you have built manually.

Here are the components of the syntax:

- `database` is an object variable that will represent the database you open.
- `workspace` is an optional object variable that specifies the workspace in which you want to open the database. If you omit `workspace`, Access opens the database in the default workspace. Although you can open the database in the default workspace without problems, you may find it more convenient to create another workspace and use it to keep the database separate. See "Creating and Removing Workspaces" later in this chapter for details.
- `Name` is a required String argument that specifies the name of the database to open. An error results if the database doesn't exist or isn't available or if another user has opened the database for exclusive access.
- `Options` is an optional Variant argument that specifies any options you want to set for the database. For an Access database, you can specify `True` to open the database in Exclusive mode or `False` (the default) to open it in Shared mode. For ODBCDirect workspaces, you can use other options; see the Access Visual Basic Help file for details.
- `ReadOnly` is an optional Variant argument that you can set to `True` to open the database in Read-only mode. The default value is `False`, which opens the database in Read/write mode.
- `Connect` is an optional Variant that you can use to pass any necessary connection information, such as a password for opening the database.

The following example "opens" the Northwind database in a special sense of the word *open*: It's opened behind the scenes to allow our code to contact it and be able to manipulate its data, structure, and other features. But *it is not opened in Access where the user can see it*. In technical terms: An *instance* of the database is fully *exposed* to our code, but the instance is invisible. It has no user interface. There's no display in Access of the Northwind database. For this reason, I've included a message box in the next code example to prove to you that the code example has actually opened Northwind and fetched some data from it.

Also, when you use this invisible database technique, it's a good idea to finish up by closing any recordsets or other objects you've opened, as well as closing the database instance itself. This way, unattached and useless entities aren't left floating as ghosts in your computer's memory.

This example will not work if you have Northwind open in Access. You must test this code while a different database is open in Access. So prepare Access by first opening some other database.

This example declares a `Workspace` object variable named `myWorkspace` and a `Database` object variable named `myDatabase`. It then assigns to `myWorkspace` the first `Workspace` object in the `Workspaces` collection (the default workspace), and it assigns to `myDatabase` the database `Northwind.accdb`, which it opens in Exclusive mode with read/write access.

To show you that Northwind did come into existence, we fetch the city data from the first record in the Customers table. Finally, we display the city name and then clean up memory by closing both the recordset and the database instance.

You can try this by entering this code in a module in the Access VBA Editor, but remember to do this while some database other than Northwind is open in Access. Press F5, and you'll see the city data. The database currently in Access will remain undisturbed.

```
Sub test()

Dim myWorkspace As Workspace
```

```
Set myWorkspace = DBEngine.Workspaces(0)

Dim myDatabase As Database
Dim RecSet As Recordset


Set myDatabase = myWorkspace.OpenDatabase _
    (Name:="C:\temp\northwind.accdb", _
    Options:=True, ReadOnly:=False)

Set RecSet = myDatabase.OpenRecordset("Customers", dbOpenDynaset)

MsgBox ("Hi! I got this city datum from an invisible instance of Northwind: " &
RecSet!City)

 RecSet.Close
 myDatabase.Close


End Sub
```

Closing a Database

To close a database that you've opened by using the `OpenDatabase` method, use the `Close` method of the object variable to which you've assigned the database. For example, the following statement closes the database assigned to the object variable `myDatabase`:

```
myDatabase.Close
```

Creating and Removing Workspaces

To keep different databases in separate sessions, you can create a new workspace as needed and remove it when you have finished working with it.

Creating a New Workspace

To create a new workspace, use the `CreateWorkspace` method of the `DBEngine` object.

The syntax is as follows:

```
Set workspace = CreateWorkspace(Name, UserName, Password, UseType)
```

Here are the components of the syntax:

- *`workspace`* is the object variable to which you want to assign the workspace you're creating.
- `Name` is a required String argument that specifies the name to assign to the new workspace.
- `UserName` is a required String argument that specifies the owner of the new workspace.

- `Password` is a required String argument that specifies the password for the new workspace. The password can be up to 14 characters long. Use an empty string if you want to set a blank password.
- `UseType` is an optional argument that indicates the type of workspace to create. Use `dbUseJet` to create a Microsoft Jet workspace. Use `dbUseODBC` to create an ODBCDirect workspace. Omit this argument if you want the `DefaultType` property of the `DBEngine` object to determine the type of data source connected to the workspace.

The following example declares an object variable named `myWorkspace` of the `Workspace` type and assigns to it a new Jet workspace named `Workspace2`. The example makes the `admin` account the owner of the new workspace:

```
Dim myWorkspace As Workspace
Set myWorkspace = CreateWorkspace(Name:="Workspace2", _
    UserName:="admin", Password:="", UseType:=dbUseJet)
```

After creating a new workspace, you can use it to open a new database (as described earlier in this chapter).

Removing a Workspace

Before removing a workspace from the `Workspaces` collection, you must close all the open connections and databases. You can then use the `Close` method to close the `Workspace` object. For example, the following statement closes the `Workspace` object identified by the object variable `myWorkspace`:

```
myWorkspace.Close
```

Working with the *Screen* Object

If you've used VBA in the other Office applications, you've probably written code that works with whichever object is currently active (has the *focus*, meaning it's the one affected by typing or clicking).

In Word you can use the `ActiveDocument` object to work with the active document or the `Selection` object to work with the current selection. In PowerPoint you can work with the `ActivePresentation` object to work with whichever presentation happens to be active.

But in Access, you can use the `Screen` object to work with the form, report, or control that has the focus. The `Screen` object has various properties, including the following:

- The `ActiveForm` property returns the active form. If there is no active form, trying to use the `ActiveForm` property returns the error 2475.
- The `ActiveDatasheet` property returns the active datasheet. If there is no active datasheet, trying to use the `ActiveDatasheet` property returns the error 2484.
- The `ActiveReport` property returns the active report. If there is no active report, trying to use the `ActiveReport` property returns the error 2476.

- The `ActiveDataAccessPage` property returns the active data access page. If there is no active data access page, trying to use the `ActiveDataAccessPage` property returns the error 2022.
- The `ActiveControl` property returns the active control. If there is no active control, trying to use the `ActiveControl` property returns the error 2474.
- The `PreviousControl` property lets you access the control that previously had the focus.

To avoid errors, you should check to see that your target object is currently the active one before trying to manipulate it by using the `Screen` object. The following example uses the error numbers listed above to determine whether a form, report, datasheet, or data access page is active, and then it displays a message box identifying the item and giving its name:

```
On Error Resume Next

Dim strName As String
Dim strType As String
strType = "Form"
strName = Screen.ActiveForm.Name
If Err = 2475 Then
    Err = 0
    strType = "Report"
    strName = Screen.ActiveReport.Name
    If Err = 2476 Then
        Err = 0
        strType = "Data access page"
        strName = Screen.ActiveDataAccessPage.Name
        If Err = 2022 Then
            Err = 0
            strType = "Datasheet"
            strName = Screen.ActiveDatasheet.Name
        End If
    End If
End If

MsgBox "The current Screen object is a " & strType & vbCr _
    & vbCr & "Screen object name: " & strName, _
    vbOKOnly + vbInformation, "Current Screen Object"
```

If you test this, use the Create tab on the Ribbon (and click the Form icon) to ensure that there is a form active in Access.

Using the *DoCmd* Object to Run Access Commands

The `DoCmd` object enables you to execute normal Access commands, such as Find or Rename, in your VBA code.

To run a command, you use one of the methods of the `DoCmd` object. Table 28.1 lists the 66 `DoCmd` methods available in Access 2016 and explains briefly what they do.

The following sections include examples showing how to use some of the methods described in Table 28.1.

TABLE 28.1: Methods of the `DoCmd` object

METHOD	EXPLANATION
`AddMenu`	Adds a menu to the global menu bar or to a custom menu bar.
`ApplyFilter`	Applies a filter so that only records that match certain criteria are displayed.
`Beep`	Makes the computer beep—for example, to attract the user's attention when an error has occurred.
`BrowseTo`	`BrowseTo` is an Access-style macro action that helps you either create a custom user interface on top of an existing wizard navigation control or build your own.
`CancelEvent`	Cancels the event that has occurred.
`ClearMacroError`	Use after you handle an Access-style macro error to reset the data about the error so you can check for any future errors (in the `MacroError` object) while the macro continues to execute.
`Close`	Closes the specified object—for example, a form or a report.
`CloseDatabase`	Closes the database, just as if you'd clicked the File tab on the Ribbon and chosen the Close Database option. A Save dialog box will appear if necessary, asking for your disposition of any unsaved objects.
`CopyDatabaseFile`	Copies the database connected to the current project to a SQL Server file.
`CopyObject`	Copies the specified object (for example, a query or a table) into the specified database (or to a new table in the current database).
`DeleteObject`	Deletes the specified object from the database.
`DoMenuItem`	Performs a command from a menu or toolbar. This is an older command that has been replaced by the `RunCommand` method (described later in this table).
`Echo`	Provides backward compatibility for running the `Echo` action in earlier versions of VBA. It's better to use `Application.Echo` now.
`FindNext`	Finds the next record matching the search criteria specified by the `FindRecord` method.

TABLE 28.1: Methods of the DoCmd object *(CONTINUED)*

METHOD	EXPLANATION
FindRecord	Performs a search for a record that matches the specified criteria.
GoToControl	Moves the focus to the specified control or field in a form or datasheet.
GoToPage	Moves the focus to the specified page of a form.
GoToRecord	Makes the specified record the current record.
Hourglass	Changes the mouse pointer to an hourglass (a wait pointer) or back to a normal pointer.
LockNavigationPane	This option prevents the user from right-clicking a database object displayed in the left pane (Navigation pane) and then selecting the Cut or Delete option from the context menu that appears. Other options on that menu, such as Copy and Paste, are still enabled.
Maximize	Maximizes the active window.
Minimize	Minimizes the active window.
MoveSize	Moves or resizes (or both) the active window.
NavigateTo	Allows you to specify how objects are displayed in the Navigation pane (left pane). For example, you could reorganize the list of objects, or even prevent some objects from being displayed at all.
OpenDataAccessPage	Opens the specified data access page in the specified view.
OpenDiagram	Opens the specified database diagram.
OpenForm	Opens the specified form and optionally applies filtering.
OpenFunction	Opens the specified user-defined function in the specified view (for example, datasheet view) and mode (for example, for data entry).
OpenModule	Opens the specified VBA module at the specified procedure.
OpenQuery	Opens the specified query in the specified view and mode.
OpenReport	Opens a report in Design view or Print Preview. Alternatively, you can use this method to print a hard copy of the report.
OpenStoredProcedure	A macro action that opens a stored procedure in Design view, Datasheet view, or Print Preview.
OpenTable	Opens the specified table in the specified view and mode.

TABLE 28.1: Methods of the `DoCmd` object *(CONTINUED)*

METHOD	EXPLANATION
`OpenView`	Opens the specified view in the specified view and mode.
`OutputTo`	Outputs the data in the specified object (for example, a report or a data access page) in the specified format.
`PrintOut`	Prints the specified object.
`Quit`	Provides backward compatibility with Access 95. With later versions of Access, use `Application.Quit` instead.
`RefreshRecord`	Refreshes a record.
`Rename`	Renames the specified object with the name given.
`RepaintObject`	Repaints the specified object, completing any screen updates that are pending.
`Requery`	Updates the data in the specified control by querying the data source again.
`Restore`	Restores the active window to its nonmaximized and nonminimized size.
`RunCommand`	Runs the specified built-in menu command or toolbar command.
`RunDataMacro`	Calls a named data macro.
`RunMacro`	Runs the specified macro.
`RunSavedImportExport`	Runs a saved import or export specification.
`RunSQL`	Runs an Access action query using the specified SQL statement.
`Save`	Saves the specified object or (if no object is specified) the active object.
`SearchForRecord`	Searches for a specific record in a table, form, query, or report.
`SelectObject`	Selects the specified object in the database window or in an object that's already open.
`SendObject`	Sends the specified object (for example, a form or a report) in an email message.
`SetDisplayedCategories`	Specifies which categories are displayed under the Navigate To Category option in the Navigation pane. If you click anywhere in the Navigation pane's title bar, you'll see the various options.

TABLE 28.1: Methods of the DoCmd object *(CONTINUED)*

METHOD	EXPLANATION
SetFilter	Can be used to change the WHERE clause to update a URL.
SetMenuItem	Sets the state of a menu item—for example, enabling or disabling a menu item.
SetOrderBy	Change an order by. In other words, sort records in ascending or descending order.
SetParameter	Sets the values of parameters.
SetProperty	Sets various properties of a control or field, such as BackColor, Width, Enabled, and Caption.
SetWarnings	Turns system messages on or off.
ShowAllRecords	Removes any existing filters from the current form, query, or table.
ShowToolbar	Displays or hides the specified toolbar.
SingleStep	Pauses the currently executing macro and displays a Macro Single Step dialog box.
TransferDatabase	Imports data into or exports data from the current database or project.
TransferSharePointList	Imports (or links) data from a Microsoft Windows SharePoint Services 3.0 site.
TransferSpreadsheet	Imports data from or exports data to a spreadsheet.
TransferSQLDatabase	Transfers the specified SQL Server database to another SQL Server database.
TransferText	Imports data from or exports data to a text file.

Using the OpenForm Method to Open a Form

To open a form, use the OpenForm method of the DoCmd object. The syntax is as follows:

```
expression.OpenForm(FormName, View, FilterName, WhereCondition, DataMode,
WindowMode, OpenArgs)
```

Here are the components of the syntax:

- *expression* is a required expression that returns a DoCmd object. In many cases, it's easiest to use the DoCmd object itself.
- FormName is a required Variant argument that specifies the name of the form you want to open. The form must be in the current database.

- `View` is an optional argument that specifies the view to use: `acNormal` (the default), `acDesign`, `acFormDS`, `acFormPivotChart`, `acFormPivotTable`, or `acPreview`.
- `FilterName` is an optional Variant argument that you can use to specify the name of a query. The query must be stored in the current database.
- `WhereCondition` is an optional Variant that you can use to specify a SQL `WHERE` clause. Omit the word `WHERE` from the clause.
- `DataMode` is an optional argument for specifying the mode in which to open the form: `acFormPropertySettings`, `acFormAdd`, `acFormEdit`, or `acFormReadOnly`. `acFormPropertySettings` is the default setting and opens the form using the mode set in the form.
- `WindowMode` is an optional argument for specifying how to open the form. The default is `acWindowNormal`, a normal window. You can also open the form as a dialog box (`acDialog`) or as an icon (`acIcon`) or keep it hidden (`acHidden`).
- `OpenArgs` is an optional Variant that you can use to specify arguments for opening the form—for example, to move the focus to a particular record.

The following example uses the `DoCmd` object to open a form in the Northwind sample database (you must have this database open in Access for this to work). Press Alt+F11 to open Access's VBA Editor, and then type in this code. When you execute the code by pressing F5, Access displays the first record for which the `Employee` field matches `Jan Kotas`:

```
Sub test ()

DoCmd.OpenForm FormName:="Sales Analysis Form", View:=acNormal, _
WhereCondition:="Employee ='Jan Kotas'"

End Sub
```

Using the *PrintOut* Method to Print an Object

To print an object, use the `PrintOut` method. The syntax is as follows:

```
expression.PrintOut(PrintRange, PageFrom, PageTo, PrintQuality, Copies,
CollateCopies)
```

Here are the components of the syntax:

- *`expression`* is a required expression that returns a `DoCmd` object.
- `PrintRange` is an optional argument that specifies what to print: all of the object (`acPrintAll`, the default), specific pages (`acPages`), or the selection (`acSelection`).
- `PageFrom` and `PageTo` are optional Variant arguments that you use with `PrintRange: = acPages` to specify the starting and ending page numbers of the print range.
- `PrintQuality` is an optional argument that you can use to specify the print quality. The default setting is `acHigh`, but you can also specify `acLow`, `acMedium`, or `acDraft` (draft quality, to save ink and time).

- `Copies` is an optional Variant argument that you can use to specify how many copies to print. The default is `1`.
- `CollateCopies` is an optional Variant argument that you can set to `True` to collate the copies, and `False` not to. The default setting is `True`.

The following example prints one copy (the default) of the first page in the active object at full quality without collating the copies:

```
DoCmd.PrintOut PrintRange:=acPages, _
PageFrom:=1, PageTo:=1, CollateCopies:=False
```

Be sure to trap this code for an error in case you've requested a printout of something that doesn't exist—such as a range of 1 to 4 for a single-page form. In fact, it's always a good idea to trap errors in code that contacts peripherals such as printers or hard drives. What if the printer isn't turned on or the hard drive is full? Your code should anticipate and manage situations like these.

Using the *RunMacro* Method to Run an Access-Style Macro

To run an Access-style macro, use the `RunMacro` method. The syntax is as follows:

```
expression.RunMacro(MacroName, RepeatCount, RepeatExpression)
```

Here are the components of the syntax:

- *`expression`* is a required expression that returns a `DoCmd` object.
- `MacroName` is a required Variant argument that specifies the macro name.
- `RepeatCount` is an optional Variant argument that you can use to specify an expression to control the number of times that the macro should run. The default is `1`.
- `RepeatExpression` is an optional Variant argument that contains a numeric expression to be evaluated each time the macro runs. The macro stops when this expression evaluates to `0` (`False`).

The following example runs an Access-style macro named `RemoveDuplicates`:

```
DoCmd.RunMacro "RemoveDuplicates"
```

The Bottom Line

Become familiar with how VBA works in Access. Access allows you to write macros in a VBA Editor using VBA code. But it also features a legacy Macro Designer utility (formerly known as the Macro Builder) with which you create an entirely different kind of macro, what we've been calling an *Access-style macro.*

Master It The term *macro* is used in a special way in Access (referring to only one of the two types of custom procedures Access permits you to construct: VBA and Macro Designer). This usage of *macro* is unlike the way the term *macro* is used in other Office applications, not to mention all other forms of computing. Describe what Access means by the term *macro*.

Open and close databases. Access permits you to open a database in several ways.

Master It Two common commands that open a database in Access are `OpenCurrentDatabase` and `OpenDatabase`. What is the difference between these two commands?

Work with the `Screen` object. You became familiar with using `ActiveDocument` objects in Word to access the document that currently has the focus. Or, you used the `ActivePresentation` object to work with whichever presentation happened to be active in PowerPoint. Access, however, employs the `Screen` object as the parent of whatever object has the focus.

Master It The `Screen` object represents the screen object that currently has the focus in Access (that is, the object that is receiving input or ready to receive input). Three types of common Access objects can have the focus when you employ the `Screen` object. What are they?

Use the `DoCmd` object to run Access commands. Many of the tools that Access makes available to users, such as printing a report or maximizing a window, are also available to the programmer via the methods of the `DoCmd` object.

Master It The `DoCmd` object has 66 methods in Office 2016. Describe the purpose of the `DoCmd` object's `Beep` method.

Chapter 29

Manipulating the Data in an Access Database via VBA

This chapter shows you how to use VBA to manipulate data in an Access database. You can also manage Access databases from within another VBA-enabled application—for example, from Excel or from Word. However, here we'll focus on Access VBA.

There are two main ways to manage data in an Access database: via Data Access Objects (DAO) or via ActiveX Data Objects (ADO). DAO, now *deprecated* (no longer approved of), is the older technology, and it works for both Microsoft Jet databases (also now deprecated) and ODBC-compliant data sources. (ODBC is Open Database Connectivity, a long-existing standard for accessing databases. ODBC is also useful for accessing open-source solutions, such as MySQL.) ADO, the newer technology, is a high-level programming interface that can be used with a wide range of data sources.

Access offers you the choice of methods, but you will probably find it easier to use ADO than DAO. Additional information about choosing between these two approaches can be found at the following location:

```
http://msdn.microsoft.com/en-us/library/aa164825(office.10).aspx
```

IN THIS CHAPTER, YOU WILL LEARN TO DO THE FOLLOWING:

- Open a recordset
- Access a particular record in a recordset
- Search for a record
- Edit a record
- Insert and delete records

Understanding How to Proceed

Here are the primary steps to manipulate the data in an Access database:

1. Add a reference to the object library you'll be using.
2. Create a recordset that contains the records with which you want to work.
3. Work with the records in the recordset.
4. Close the recordset.

All the steps work in more or less the same way for ADO and DAO, except that you create the recordset in different ways. The following sections take you through these steps, splitting the path where necessary to cover the differences in ADO and DAO. Note that we're still covering DAO in this chapter because, although deprecated, it still works with Access. And many companies, in fact, do still use it.

Preparing to Manage the Data in a Database

Given that there are two distinct ways to manage data in Access—ADO and DAO—you have to specify which one you're planning to employ. They have different *libraries* (collections of prewritten functions).

Why bother fooling around with multiple libraries? The answer is that there can't be a single, massive, all-purpose library because, among other issues, there would be name confusion. Two different functions in two different libraries might well employ the same name. But they could perform different tasks or perform the same task differently. It's like having various libraries in a large university. The word *positive* means an entirely different thing in the law library than it does in the medical library.

Note that some of the following code examples will work just fine no matter which library you are currently referencing.

However, to ensure consistency and avoid bugs, create a reference to the object library you want to use (ADO or DAO). And in your code you'll specify the appropriate connection to the data source—the Microsoft ActiveX Data Objects 6.1 Library for an ADO connection or Microsoft DAO 3.6 Object Library for a DAO connection. (Note that these 6.1 and 3.6 version numbers might not match the versions of these libraries available on your machine. Just choose the latest, highest version number you see.)

Adding a Reference to the Appropriate Object Library

To create a reference to the object library you need, follow these steps:

1. Launch Access.
2. Launch or activate the VBA Editor by pressing Alt+F11.
3. In the VBA Editor, choose Tools ➢ References to display the References dialog box.
4. Scroll down the Available References list box to the appropriate object library item, and then select its check box and click OK to close the References dialog box:
   - For an ADO connection, select the check box for the Microsoft ActiveX Data Objects 6.1 Library item.
   - For a Data Access Object, select the check box for Microsoft DAO 3.6 Object Library.

You can't select both libraries at the same time. And if you don't include the correct library, you'll get a compile error when you try to execute one of the objects in that library (such as a `DAO.Recordset`). The message will refer to this as a "user-defined" object because it can't find the object in the currently referenced libraries—so the Editor thinks it's a new object introduced by you, the programmer, but that you forgot to declare it.

Establishing a Connection to the Database

It's possible to establish connections to databases in a variety of ways, but in this chapter we'll use a simple, direct line of code. In Chapter 28, "Understanding the Access Object Model and Key Objects," you saw what steps to take to go online and download the `Northwind.accdb` sample database and where to store it on your hard drive (in a `C:\test` folder) so you could experiment with the example code in these final chapters of the book. If you haven't already taken those steps, see the sidebar in Chapter 28 titled "Prepare the Northwind Database to Use with This Book's Examples."

To open a connection (but not make it visible to the user in Access) to the Northwind sample database, you can use this code if you're employing DAO:

```
Dim myDatabase As DAO.Database
Set myDatabase = DBEngine.OpenDatabase("C:\temp\Northwind.accdb")
```

You'll see this approach used in examples later in this chapter. You'll also see how to manipulate Northwind while it's loaded into Access where the user can see it. Recall from the previous chapter that you can open a database two ways: to get to its data but not display it to the user, or to load it into Access and make it visible to the user.

GOING BEYOND NORTHWIND

Although in this book we're going to focus only on the Northwind database, more advanced Access users might be interested in also working with SQL and a set of sample databases for that technology. Here's a link where you can obtain and explore the AdventureWorks database, along with scripts for it:

`http://msftdbprodsamples.codeplex.com/`

SQL databases will work with Access, and some readers might want to investigate AdventureWorks as the backend database for Access.

Opening a Recordset

To get to the records in the database to which you're establishing the connection, you must open a recordset. ADO and DAO use different approaches. The following subsections give you the details.

Opening a Recordset Using ADO

To open a recordset using ADO, you use the `Open` method of the `RecordSet` object. The syntax for the `Open` method is as follows:

```
recordset.Open Source, ActiveConnection, CursorType, LockType, Options
```

Here are the components of the syntax:

- *recordset* is the RecordSet object that you want to open. Often, you'll use an object variable that references the RecordSet object.
- Source is an optional Variant argument that specifies the table, command, SQL statement, or file that contains the recordset.
- ActiveConnection is an optional Variant argument. This can be either an object variable of the Connection type or a Variant/String containing parameters for the connection.
- CursorType is an optional argument for specifying the type of cursor to use in the recordset. Table 29.1 explains the cursor types.
- LockType is an optional argument for specifying how to lock the recordset while it is open. Table 29.2 explains the lock options.
- Options is an optional Long argument that you can use to control how the Source value is evaluated if it is not a Command object. Table 29.3 explains the available constants, which fall into two categories: command-type options and execute options. You can use two or more constants for the Options argument.

An Alternative to Providing Arguments for the *Open* Method

Instead of specifying the arguments with the Open method, you can set the Source, ActiveConnection, CursorType, and LockType properties of the RecordSet object you're opening and then use the Open method without arguments. You may find that this approach makes your code easier to read.

Table 29.1: Cursor-type constants for opening a recordset

Constant	Cursor Type and Explanation
adOpenForwardOnly	Forward-only cursor. You can scroll through the recordset only forward. This is the default cursor and provides the best performance when you need to go through the records only once.
adOpenDynamic	Dynamic cursor. You can move freely through the recordset, and you can see changes that other users make to records.
adOpenKeyset	Keyset cursor. You can move freely through the recordset and see changes that other users make to records. You cannot see records that other users add, and records that other users delete are inaccessible.
adOpenStatic	Static cursor. You can't see changes that other users make. Use a static cursor when you need to only search for data or create reports from the data that exists when you open the recordset.

TABLE 29.2: Lock options for opening a recordset via ADO

CONSTANT	OPENS THE RECORDSET WITH
`adLockReadOnly`	Data in read-only mode, so you cannot alter it. Use this constant if you need to search or analyze the data but not manipulate it.
`adLockOptimistic`	Optimistic locking, which locks a record only when you run the `Update` method to update it explicitly.
`adLockBatchOptimistic`	Optimistic batch locking, which enables you to perform a simultaneous update on several records that you've changed.
`adLockPessimistic`	Pessimistic locking, which locks a record immediately after you change it.

TABLE 29.3: Choices for the `Options` argument when opening a recordset

CONSTANT	EXPLANATION
COMMAND-TYPE OPTIONS	
`adCmdText`	Evaluates `Source` as text specifying a command or stored procedure call.
`acCmdTable`	Evaluates `Source` as the name of a table consisting of columns returned by an internally generated SQL query.
`acCmdStoredProc`	Evaluates `Source` as the name of a stored procedure.
`acCmdFile`	Evaluates `Source` as the filename of a stored recordset.
`acCmdTableDirect`	Evaluates `Source` as a table name and returns all columns of the table. Do not use with `adAsyncExecute`.
`adCmdUnknown`	This means that the type is unknown. This is the default.
EXECUTE OPTIONS	
`adAsyncExecute`	Executes the command asynchronously. Does not work with `acCmdTableDirect`.
`adAsyncFetch`	Retrieves the rows specified by the `CacheSize` property synchronously and the remaining rows asynchronously.
`adAsyncFetchNonBlocking`	Prevents the main thread from blocking other data access while retrieving data.
`adExecuteRecord`	The `CommandText` (`adCmdText`, described earlier in this table) is a stored procedure or a command that fetches a single row of data. It is returned as a `Record` object.

TABLE 29.3: Choices for the `Options` argument when opening a recordset *(CONTINUED)*

CONSTANT	EXPLANATION
`adExecuteNoRecords`	Used to improve performance when you know that no records will be returned (for example, you're merely adding, not fetching, data).
`adExecuteStream`	Treats the data returned by `Source` as a single row that becomes a `Record` object.

You'll see examples of opening a recordset a little later in this chapter. First, you must decide which approach you want to use to access the data in the recordset. The easiest methods are to use an existing table or a SQL `SELECT` statement.

Choosing How to Access the Data in an ADO Recordset

How you actually get to the data in the recordset you open depends on whether you want to fetch all the data in a table or just part of it. If you want all the data in a table, you can use a table object to access the data. If you want to return only a subset of particular records, you can use a SQL `SELECT` statement to fetch them.

USING A TABLE TO ACCESS THE DATA IN AN ADO RECORDSET

To open in a recordset a whole table from a database, specify the table name as the `Source` argument in the `Open` statement. The following example declares a `RecordSet` object variable, uses a `Set` statement to assign the appropriate recordset type to it, uses the `ActiveConnection` method to connect to the currently active database (whatever you have loaded into Access at the time), and then uses the `Open` method to open the entire `Customers` table. We'll use the Northwind sample database (that you installed in Chapter 28), which has a `Customers` table.

This next example demonstrates how to bring into an ADO recordset the data from an entire table and then move around within this recordset. Your code will not need to instantiate a database object but instead will work with the Northwind database that's currently loaded into Access. (This is a very simple example to illustrate some basic concepts. Normally when accessing a database, you'll want to employ a SQL statement and check for recordset boundary conditions—using `BOF` and `EOF` properties. SQL and `BOF`/`EOF` are described later in this chapter. For now, just consider the following example code an illustration of elementary principles, to which you'll add real-world maneuvers demonstrated in the code examples later in this chapter.)

As always, it's necessary for you to first ensure that the ADO library is referenced. So in the VBA Editor, choose Tools ➢ References and select the check box next to Microsoft ActiveX Data Objects 6.1 Library. Finally, by hand, load the `Northwind.accdb` sample database into Access. Then you can paste this code into an Access VBA Module, press F5 with the blinking insertion cursor located within the code, and watch the various message boxes demonstrate that the code is in fact working:

```
1.   Sub ExploreRecordset()
2.       Dim myRecordset As ADODB.Recordset
3.       Set myRecordset = New ADODB.Recordset
4.
5.  'point to the currently loaded database
6.       myRecordset.ActiveConnection = CurrentProject.Connection
7.       myRecordset.CursorType = adOpenStatic
8.       myRecordset.Open Source:="Customers"
9.
10.  'Display the First Name from the first row
11.      MsgBox myRecordset("First Name")
12.
13.  'Move to the last row and show the Last Name
14.      myRecordset.MoveLast
15.      MsgBox myRecordset("Last Name")
16.
17.  'Move to the previous row and display the Job Title
18.      myRecordset.MovePrevious
19.      MsgBox myRecordset("Job Title")
20.
21.  'Move back to the first row and display the Phone Number
22.      myRecordset.MoveFirst
23.      MsgBox myRecordset("Business Phone")
24.
25.  'Move to the next row and show the Last Name
26.      myRecordset.MoveNext
27.     MsgBox myRecordset("Last Name")
28.
29.
30.     myRecordset.Close
31.     Set myRecordset = Nothing
32. End Sub
```

In this code, you first declare a recordset variable, and in line 6 you point it to the database currently loaded in Access. Line 7 defines the cursor type as static, and line 8 loads the data—the entire Customers table—into your recordset.

Line 11 doesn't move anywhere within the recordset, so by merely supplying the recordset's name, MyRecordset, along with one of the table's field names, Last Name, to a `MsgBox` function, you can display the first record in the table.

Line 14 does move to a different record within the recordset—the last record—before displaying the data in that record's Last Name field. Line 18 moves to the penultimate record, line 22 moves to the first record, and line 26 moves to the second record. Finally, line 30 closes the recordset, and line 31 assigns `Nothing` to the object variable, which has the effect of eliminating it.

Real World Scenario

WHAT IS A "FIRST RECORD" IN A TABLE?

It's important for beginners to understand the practical difference between a table of raw data in a database and an organized *recordset* extracted from that database. The concept of a "first record" within a relational database is essentially meaningless until you use a SQL statement to organize (sort or group) the table's records in some fashion.

Records in a relational database (the type of database Access employs) are not necessarily organized. For example, they are not necessarily alphabetized by any particular field (such as `LastName`) or numerically listed by an `ID` number, or organized using any other scheme. True, data is stored in tables, and a table *does* have structure: Its fields separate the data into logical categories such as LastName, Address, CellPhone, and so on. But its records (the rows of actual data) are *not necessarily* maintained in any particular order.

A set of records (a *recordset*) is extracted from a database when you execute a SQL statement. This statement allows you to specify how you want to see the records organized (grouped by city, alphabetized, or whatever). SQL is flexible: You can organize records in many ways when you extract a recordset from a database. You can sort records by any of their fields; you can also sort in either ascending (the default) or descending order (specify `DESC` for descending). Which record ends up being first after you query the data table also depends on which field you sort your new recordset, as specified in the `ORDER BY` statement.

In the example in the section "Using a Table to Access the Data in an ADO Recordset" in this chapter, the records are moved into the recordset unsorted. As each action is carried out in this code—moving forward and backward through the recordset—message boxes display the records in their unsorted order. However, perhaps you want to organize the records in alphabetical order by each customer's last name. To do that, you would modify the query that fetches the records. You would add an `ORDER BY` keyword to your SQL statement, like this:

```
myRecordset.Open "Select * from Customers
ORDER BY 'Last Name'
"
```

You *can* get a recordset without even specifying a SQL statement, like this:

```
myRecordset.Open Source:="Customers"
```

But the concept of a "first record" in this recordset probably will have no meaning.

However, you can get a recordset by using a SQL statement, like this:

```
myRecordset.Open strSQL
```

In this case, the "first record" will have meaning *to you*—based on the criteria you specified in the SQL statement (`strSQL` here in this code would be a string you previously defined that contains a SQL statement). The section titled "Using a SQL `SELECT` Statement to Access a Subset of the Data in an ADO Recordset," later in this chapter, explains how to use a SQL statement.

Using a SQL *SELECT* Statement to Access a Subset of the Data in an ADO Recordset

If you want to add to your recordset not the entire table, but only those records that match criteria you specify, use a SQL `SELECT` statement. `SELECT` statements can be constructed in complex ways, but you can also create straightforward statements with a little practice using this syntax:

```
SELECT [DISTINCT] fields FROM table WHERE criteria ORDER BY fields [DESC]
```

The words in uppercase are the SQL keywords, and the words in lowercase italics are placeholders for the data you supply, such as the actual name of a real table. Here are the details:

- The `SELECT` keyword indicates that you're creating a statement to select records (as opposed to, say, delete records).
- You can include the optional `DISTINCT` keyword (the brackets indicate that it is optional) to make the statement return only unique records, discarding any duplicates that the statement would otherwise return. If you omit `DISTINCT`, you get any duplicates as well.
- *`fields`* is a list of the fields that you want to have appear in the recordset. If you use two or more field names, separate them with commas—for example, `contact, company, address`. To return all field names, enter an asterisk (*).
- `FROM` *`table`* specifies the name of the table from which to draw the data.
- `WHERE` *`criteria`* specifies the criteria for filtering the records. Enter the field name, an equal sign, a single straight quote, the value you're looking for, and another single straight quote. For example, `WHERE City = 'Taos'` returns only the results where `Taos` appears in the City field.
- `ORDER BY` *`fields`* specifies the field or fields on which to sort the results. If you use two or more fields, put them in the order of precedence you want (the first sort field first, the second sort field second, and so on) and separate them with commas. The default sort order is ascending, but you can force a descending sort by adding the `DESC` keyword. For example, `ORDER BY Zip DESC` produces a descending sort by the Zip field, while `ORDER BY State, City` produces an ascending sort by the State field and, within that, by City.

Because SQL `SELECT` statements contain so many elements, putting a `SELECT` statement as an argument in an `Open` statement can create uncomfortably long lines of code. You can break the lines of code in the Editor with the underscore symbol as usual, but you may find it easier to use the properties of the `RecordSet` object to specify the details of the recordset rather than using the `Open` arguments.

Another way to avoid using a large SQL statement as an argument for the `Open` method is to first assign the `SELECT` statement to a String variable and then use that string to supply the argument. The following code illustrates that approach.

In this code, we'll assign a SQL statement to a string and then use that string as the argument for the `Open` statement. Before executing this example, press Ctrl+G in the VBA Editor to open the Immediate window, where the results will be displayed.

```
Sub SubSet()

    Dim strSQL As String
```

```
    Dim myRecordset As ADODB.Recordset
    Set myRecordset = New ADODB.Recordset
    myRecordset.ActiveConnection = CurrentProject.Connection
    strSQL = "Select * FROM Customers WHERE ID > 17"
    myRecordset.Open strSQL

    Do Until myRecordset.EOF
        Debug.Print myRecordset("Last Name")
        myRecordset.MoveNext
    Loop

End Sub
```

In this example, you want to import into the recordset only those records that have an ID higher than 17, so you set up a SQL statement that specifies that condition. Then you looped through the recordset until EOF (end of file), displaying each last name in the Immediate window.

Note that we use the Immediate window here because displaying the results of testing this code would be clumsy via repeated message boxes. There are too many results to make the message box approach tolerable.

Opening a Recordset Using DAO

When working with DAO, you use a different approach than the ADO techniques explored so far in this chapter. You use the `OpenRecordset` method of the `Database` object to create a new recordset and add it to the `Recordsets` collection.

The syntax for the `OpenRecordset` method is as follows:

```
Set recordset = object.OpenRecordset (Name, Type, Options, LockEdit)
```

Here are the components of the syntax:

- *`recordset`* is an object variable representing the `RecordSet` object you're opening.
- *`object`* is an object variable representing the database from which to create the new `RecordSet` object.
- `Name` is a required String argument that specifies the table, query, or SQL statement that provides the records for the recordset. If you're using a Jet database and returning a table-type recordset, you can use only a table name for the `Name` argument.
- `Type` is an optional argument that you can use to specify the type of recordset you're opening. Table 29.4 explains the constants you can use for `Type`.
- `Options` is an optional argument that you can use to specify constants that control how Access opens the recordset. Table 29.5 explains the constants you can use for `Options`.
- `LockEdit` is an optional constant that you can use to specify how the recordset is locked. Access 2013 stopped supporting ODBCDirect workspaces. So if you need to connect to external data stores directly (not through Access's database engine), then you must use ADO rather than DAO. Table 29.6 explains the constants you can use for `LockEdit`.

Table 29.4: Constants for the `Type` argument for the `OpenRecordSet` method

Constant	Opens This Type of Recordset
`dbOpenTable`	Table-type. This works only in Microsoft Jet workspaces. This is the default setting if you open a recordset in a Jet workspace without specifying the `Type`.
`dbOpenDynamic`	Dynamic-type. This works only in ODBCDirect workspaces. The recordset is similar to an ODBC dynamic cursor and enables you to add, remove, or edit rows from a database table.
`dbOpenDynaset`	Dynaset-type. This recordset is similar to an ODBC keyset cursor and enables you to add, remove, or edit rows from a database table. You can also move freely through the rows in the dynaset.
`dbOpenSnapshot`	Snapshot-type. This recordset is similar to an ODBC static cursor. It opens a snapshot of the records but does not update them when other users make changes. To update the snapshot, you must close the recordset and reopen it.
`dbOpenForwardOnly`	Forward-only. You can move only forward through the recordset.

Table 29.5: Constants for the `Options` argument

Constant	Explanation	Limitations
`dbAppendOnly`	Users can add new records but cannot edit or delete existing records.	Jet dynaset-type recordsets only
`dbSQLPassThrough`	Passes a SQL statement to an ODBC data source connected via Jet.	Jet snapshot-type recordsets only
`dbSeeChanges`	Causes a runtime error if a user attempts to change data that another user is already editing.	Jet dynaset-type recordsets only
`dbDenyWrite`	Prevents other users from adding or modifying records.	Jet recordsets only
`dbDenyRead`	Prevents other users from reading data.	Jet table-type recordsets only
`dbForwardOnly`	Forces a forward-only recordset. This is an older option included for backward compatibility. Use `Type: = dbOpenForwardOnly` instead.	Jet snapshot-type recordsets only
`dbReadOnly`	Prevents users from changing the recordset. This is an older option included for backward compatibility. Use `LockEdits: = dbReadOnly` instead. If you must use `Options: = dbReadOnly`, do not include the `LockEdits` argument.	Jet recordsets only

TABLE 29.5: Constants for the `Options` argument *(CONTINUED)*

CONSTANT	EXPLANATION	LIMITATIONS
`dbRunAsync`	Runs a query asynchronously (so that some results are returned while others are still pending).	ODBCDirect workspaces only
`dbExecDirect`	Runs a query by calling `SQLExecDirect`.	ODBCDirect workspaces only
`dbInconsistent`	Permits inconsistent updates, enabling you to update a field in one table of a multitable recordset without updating another table in the recordset. You can use either this constant or `dbConsistent`, but not both.	Jet dynaset-type and snapshot-type recordsets only
`dbConsistent`	Permits only consistent updates so that shared fields in tables underlying a multitable recordset must be updated together. You can use either this constant or `dbInconsistent`, but not both.	Jet dynaset-type and snapshot-type recordsets only
`dbFailOnError`	If an error occurs, updates are rolled back.	Jet recordsets only

TABLE 29.6: Constants for the `LockEdit` argument

CONSTANT	EXPLANATION	DEFAULT OR LIMITATIONS
`dbPessimistic`	Uses pessimistic locking, which locks a record immediately after you change it.	Default for Jet workspaces
`dbOptimistic`	Uses optimistic locking, which locks a record only when you run the `Update` method to update it explicitly.	
`dbOptimisticValue`	Uses optimistic concurrency, comparing the data values in old and new records to find out if changes have been made since the record was last accessed. The concurrency is based on row values.	ODBCDirect workspaces only
`dbOptimisticBatch`	Uses optimistic batch locking, which enables you to perform a simultaneous update on several records that you've changed.	ODBCDirect workspaces only

Opening a DAO Recordset Using a Table

The easiest way to open a DAO recordset is to open an entire table by specifying the table name for the Name argument and using Type: = dbOpenTable to explicitly state that you're opening a table. The following example declares the object variable myRecordset as a DAO.Recordset object and then assigns to it the records from the Customers table in the database identified by the myDatabase object variable:

```
Sub DAOTest()
Dim myRecordset As DAO.Recordset
Dim myDatabase As DAO.Database

   'Open the copy of Northwind on the hard drive
   Set myDatabase = DBEngine.OpenDatabase("C:\temp\Northwind.accdb")

   'Create the DAO-style Recordset

Set myRecordset = myDatabase.OpenRecordset(Name:="Customers", _
    Type:=dbOpenTable)

   MsgBox myRecordset("ID")
   MsgBox myRecordset("Company")
   MsgBox myRecordset("Address")
   MsgBox myRecordset("City")

   Set myRecordset = Nothing
End Sub
```

Opening a DAO Recordset Using a SQL *SELECT* Statement

If you want to return only a subset of records rather than an entire table, use a SQL SELECT statement to open the DAO recordset. (See "Using a SQL SELECT Statement to Access a Subset of the Data in an ADO Recordset," earlier in this chapter, for an explanation of the essentials of SQL SELECT statements.)

Specify the SQL statement as the Name argument for the OpenRecordset method, as the following example illustrates. This code declares a Database object variable, assigns the Northwind sample database to it, declares a RecordSet object variable, and then assigns to the object variable the results of a SELECT statement run on the database:

```
Sub DAOSelect()

Dim myDatabase As DAO.Database
   Set myDatabase = DBEngine.OpenDatabase("C:\temp\Northwind.accdb")

Dim myRecordset As DAO.Recordset
   Set myRecordset = myDatabase.OpenRecordset _
```

```
     (Name:="SELECT * FROM Customers WHERE City ='Boston'", _
     Type:=dbOpenDynaset)
    Do Until myRecordset.EOF
        Debug.Print myRecordset("Last Name")
        myRecordset.MoveNext
     Loop

    Set myRecordset = Nothing
End Sub
```

Note that the results in this example are printed in the VBA Editor's Immediate window, so if that window isn't visible, press Ctrl+G to open it before pressing F5 to test this procedure.

Accessing a Particular Record in a Recordset

Once you've fetched a recordset, you can manipulate the records inside it. To locate a particular record within a recordset, you can either write some code to move through (loop) the records until you find the one you want or search for the record using `Seek` or `Find` methods. The `RecordSet` object includes these methods for moving about the records in the recordset:

Method	**Moves to Record**
`MoveFirst`	First
`MoveNext`	Next
`MovePrevious`	Previous
`MoveLast`	Last
`Move`	Move to a specified record

Using the *MoveFirst*, *MoveNext*, *MovePrevious*, and *MoveLast* Methods

The `MoveFirst` method and `MoveLast` method are always safe to use because as long as the recordset contains one or more records, there's always a first record and a last record. (If the recordset contains only one record, that record is considered both first and last.)

But if you use the `MovePrevious` method from the first record in the recordset or the `MoveNext` method from the last record, you move beyond the recordset, accessing what is sometimes called a "phantom record"—one that isn't there. When you try to access the contents of such a record, VBA gives the runtime error 3021 ("No current record"). Figure 29.1 shows this error.

`BOF` means beginning of file, and `EOF` means end of file. Note that you can visualize the end of a recordset as a point just beyond the last record. `EOF`, therefore, is not the same as the last record. `BOF`, likewise, is not the first record, but a point just before it. (I mention this because we have a tendency to view the first item in a set as the "beginning" of the set, just as we would consider the first float as the beginning of a parade. Recordsets aren't like that.)

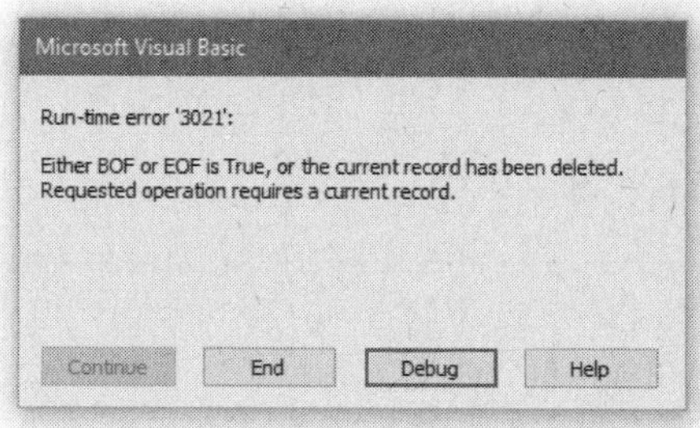

FIGURE 29.1 The runtime error "No current record" usually means that you've moved outside the recordset.

To check whether you're at the beginning or end of the recordset, use the `BOF` property or the `EOF` property of the `RecordSet` object. The `BOF` property returns `True` when the current record is at the beginning of the file, and the `EOF` property returns `True` when the current record is at the end of the file. To avoid errors, after using the `MovePrevious` method, check whether the beginning of the file has been reached, as in this example:

```
With myRecordset
    .MovePrevious
    If .BOF = True Then .MoveNext
End With
```

Similarly, after using the `MoveNext` method, check whether the end of the file has been reached:

```
myRecordset.MoveNext
If myRecordset.EOF Then myRecordset.MovePrevious
```

Using the *Move* Method to Move Past Multiple Records

To move several records at once, but not to the first record or last record in the recordset, use the `Move` method. The syntax for ADO differs from that used with DAO.

Here's the syntax for the `Move` method with ADO:

```
recordset.Move NumRecords, Start
```

The syntax for the `Move` method with DAO is as follows:

```
recordset.Move Rows, StartBookmark
```

Here, *`recordset`* is the recordset involved, `NumRecords` or `Rows` is the number of records by which to move (use a positive number to move forward or a negative number to move back), and `Start` or `StartBookmark` is an optional argument that you can use to specify a bookmark from which you want to start the movement. If you omit `Start` or `StartBookmark`, movement starts from the current record.

For example, the following statement moves 10 records forward from the current record in an ADO recordset:

```
myRecordset.Move NumRecords:=10
```

The following statement moves five records backward from the current record in a DAO recordset:

```
myRecordset.Move Rows:=-5
```

To create a bookmark, move to the record that you want to mark, and then use the `Bookmark` property of the `RecordSet` object. The following example declares a Variant variable named `myBookmark` and then assigns to it a bookmark representing the current record in an ADO recordset:

```
Dim myBookmark As Variant
myBookmark = myRecordset.Bookmark
```

After setting a bookmark, you can use it as the starting point of a move. For example, the following statement moves to the eighth record after the bookmark `myBookmark` in an ADO recordset:

```
myRecordset.Move NumRecords:=8, Start:=myBookmark
```

Searching for a Record

The process of searching for a record in a recordset differs in ADO and in DAO. The following sections show you how to search using either technology.

> **ALSO CONSIDER THE Seek METHOD**
>
> Both ADO recordsets and DAO recordsets include a method called `Seek`, which is more complex and more powerful than the `Find` method for ADO and the four `Find` methods for DAO discussed here. Consult the Access VBA Help file for additional details on the `Seek` method.

Searching for a Record in an ADO Recordset

To search for a record in an ADO recordset, you can use the `Find` method of the `RecordSet` object. The syntax is as follows:

```
recordset.Find Criteria, SkipRows, SearchDirection, Start
```

Here are the components of the syntax:

- *`recordset`* is the recordset involved.
- `Criteria` is a required String argument that specifies the column name, type of comparison, and value to use. For example, to locate a record where the state is California, you could specify that the `State` column is equal (=) to `CA`.

- SkipRows is an optional Long value that you can use to specify an offset from the current row (or from the bookmark specified by the Start argument) at which to start searching instead of starting from the current row. For example, an offset of 3 starts the search three rows later than the current row.
- SearchDirection is an optional argument for specifying whether to search forward or backward. The default is adSearchForward; specify adSearchBackward to search backward instead.
- Start is an optional Variant argument that specifies the bookmark from which to start the search or the offset. If you omit Start, the search starts from the current row.

When you run the search, it stops at the first matching record. If no record matches and you're searching forward, it stops at the end of the recordset; if you're searching backward, it stops at the beginning of the recordset. If the end or beginning of the recordset is reached, you know that there was no match for the search.

The following example begins by moving to the first record in the recordset that is represented by the object variable myRecordset. Then the code searches for the first record that matches the criterion "City = 'Denver'". The example checks the EOF property to ensure that the end of the recordset has not been reached. If it has not, this means we found a record containing Denver in the City field, so the example displays a message box with the last name data for the record matching Denver. However, if the end of the recordset has been reached, the example displays a message box stating that no match was found:

```
Sub SearchADO()

    Dim strSQL As String

    Dim myRecordset As ADODB.Recordset
    Set myRecordset = New ADODB.Recordset
    myRecordset.ActiveConnection = CurrentProject.Connection

    myRecordset.Open Source:="Select * from Customers", _
        Options:=adCmdText

    With myRecordset
    .MoveFirst
    .Find Criteria:="City='Denver'"

    If Not .EOF Then
        MsgBox .Fields("Last Name")
    Else
        MsgBox "No matching record was found."
    End If

End With

End Sub
```

To continue your search for the same criteria, you can use the `SkipRows` argument to specify an offset so that you don't simply find the current record again. For example, you'll likely want to move ahead just one row, like this:

```
myRecordset.Find Criteria="City='Denver'", SkipRows:=1
```

Searching for a Record in a DAO Recordset

To search for a record in a DAO recordset, you can use one of these four methods:

- The `FindFirst` method starts searching at the beginning of the recordset and searches forward.
- The `FindNext` method starts searching at the current record and searches forward.
- The `FindPrevious` method starts searching at the current record and searches backward.
- The `FindLast` method starts searching at the end of the recordset and searches backward.

The syntax for these four methods is as follows:

```
recordset.FindFirst Criteria
recordset.FindNext Criteria
recordset.FindPrevious Criteria
recordset.FindLast Criteria
```

Here, *`recordset`* is a required object variable that represents the `RecordSet` object involved. *`Criteria`* is a required String argument that specifies the criteria for the search. *`Criteria`* works in the same way as the `WHERE` clause in a SQL statement, except that it does not use the word `WHERE`.

The following example uses the `FindFirst` method to search from the beginning of the recordset for the first record that matches the criterion `City = 'Las Vegas'`:

```
Sub DAOSearch()

Dim myDatabase As DAO.Database
Set myDatabase = DBEngine.OpenDatabase("C:\temp\Northwind.accdb")
Dim myRecordset As DAO.Recordset
Set myRecordset = myDatabase.OpenRecordset _
    (Name:="SELECT * FROM Customers", _
    Type:=dbOpenDynaset)

myRecordset.FindFirst "City = 'Las Vegas'"

MsgBox myRecordset("Last Name")

   Set myRecordset = Nothing
End Sub
```

When you start a search in a DAO recordset using one of the four `Find` methods, the `NoMatch` property of the `RecordSet` object is set to `True`. If the method finds a match, the `NoMatch` property is set to False. So you can test the NoMatch property to tell whether or not the search found a match, as in this example:

```
If myRecordset.NoMatch = False Then
   MsgBox myRecordset("Last Name")
End If
```

Returning the Fields in a Record

Once you've moved to a record, you can return the fields it contains by using the appropriate Field object from the Fields collection. Field is the default property for the RecordSet object, so you can omit it if you choose. For example, both the following statements return the Last Name field from the current record:

```
myRecordset.Fields("Last Name")
myRecordset("Last Name")
```

Editing a Record

To change the data in a record, first use the Edit method to specify the value you want to store in the field, and then use the Update method of the RecordSet object to update the data in the underlying table. The following example prepares a record for editing with the Edit method, changes the value in the Last Name field to Schmidtz, and then uses the Update method to update it:

```
With myRecordset
    .Edit
    .Fields("Last Name").Value = "Schmidtz"
    .Update
End With
```

Inserting and Deleting Records

To insert a new record, use the AddNew method of the RecordSet object. You can then assign data to the fields in the record. After that, use the Update method to save the data to the table in the database. The following example uses a With statement to perform these actions:

```
Sub AddOne()

Dim myDatabase As DAO.Database
Set myDatabase = DBEngine.OpenDatabase("C:\temp\Northwind.accdb")
Dim myRecordset As DAO.Recordset
Set myRecordset = myDatabase.OpenRecordset _
    (Name:="SELECT * FROM Customers", _
    Type:=dbOpenDynaset)
```

```
With myRecordset
     .AddNew
     .Fields("ID").Value = 32
     .Fields("Last Name").Value = "Murphy"
     .Fields("First Name").Value = "Andrea"
     .Fields("Company").Value = "Company RP"
     .Fields("City").Value = "City of Industry"
     'add data for the other fields here
     .Update
End With

   Set myRecordset = Nothing

End Sub
```

After you press F5 in the VBA Editor to test this code, switch to Access, display the Customers table, *and then you will need to press F5 to refresh the view in Access before you can see this new record.*

To delete a record, identify it by either moving to it or searching for it, and then use the `Delete` method followed by the `Update` method. The following example deletes the current record and then updates the table:

```
myRecordset.Edit
myRecordset.Delete
myRecordset.Update
```

Closing a Recordset

After working with an object, you should close it. To close a recordset, use the `Close` method with the appropriate `RecordSet` object or the object variable that represents the `RecordSet` object. The following example closes the recordset represented by the object variable `myRecordset`:

```
myRecordset.Close
```

After closing the recordset, set its object variable to `Nothing` to release the memory it occupied:

```
Set myRecordset = Nothing
```

Saving a Recordset to the Cloud

You might want to store a recordset on your hard drive or in the cloud. As you've seen in cloud-access examples in previous chapters, saving files to the cloud is much the same as saving to an ordinary hard-drive folder. In fact, you *are* saving to your hard drive when you send something to the cloud in a system like Dropbox. You just save locally, and then Dropbox handles the updating and saving (*syncing*) to its cloud.

By the way, this example also illustrates how to use the Save method of the `RecordSet` object:

```
1.  Sub SaveToCloud()
2.
3.      Dim myRecordset As ADODB.Recordset
4.      Set myRecordset = New ADODB.Recordset
5.      myRecordset.ActiveConnection = CurrentProject.Connection
6.
7.      Dim strSQL As String
8.      Dim strFilepath As String
9.      strFilepath = "C:\Users\Richard\OneDrive\Cities.xml"
10.
11.         strSQL = "SELECT city FROM Employees"
12.         myRecordset.Open strSQL
13.
14.         myRecordset.Save strFilepath, adPersistXML
15.
16.     Set myRecordset = Nothing
17.
18. End Sub
```

To test this, open Northwind and press Alt+F11 to open the VBA Editor. Paste this code into a module, but change *Richard* in line 9 to your own name.

Most of this code should be understandable from previous examples in this chapter. Line 9 specifies the location on my hard drive where files move to OneDrive automatically after being saved there. You could just as easily save this recordset to any ordinary hard-drive folder, like this:

```
myRecordset.Save "c:\temp\Cities.xml", adPersistXML
```

The save command we're using stores this recordset in the XML format, about which I'll have much more to say in Chapter 31, "Programming the Office 2016 Ribbon."

However, for the curious, here's what this recordset looks like in the XML format, showing the city data for the nine records in the Employees table:


```
<xml xmlns:s='uuid:BDC6E3F0-6DA3-11d1-A2A3-00AA00C14882'
     xmlns:dt='uuid:C2F41010-65B3-11d1-A29F-00AA00C14882'
     xmlns:rs='urn:schemas-microsoft-com:rowset'
     xmlns:z='#RowsetSchema'>
<s:Schema id='RowsetSchema'>
     <s:ElementType name='row' content='eltOnly'>
          <s:AttributeType name='city' rs:number='1' rs:nullable='true'
rs:maydefer='true' rs:writeunknown='true'>
               <s:datatype dt:type='string' dt:maxLength='50'/>
          </s:AttributeType>
          <s:extends type='rs:rowbase'/>
     </s:ElementType>
</s:Schema>
<rs:data>
```

```
        <z:row city='Seattle'/>
        <z:row city='Bellevue'/>
        <z:row city='Redmond'/>
        <z:row city='Kirkland'/>
        <z:row city='Seattle'/>
        <z:row city='Redmond'/>
        <z:row city='Seattle'/>
        <z:row city='Redmond'/>
        <z:row city='Seattle'/>
</rs:data>
</xml>
```

The Bottom Line

Open a recordset. You can open an ADO recordset in two different ways.

> **Master It** One way to open an ADO recordset is to provide an argument list following the `Open` method. What is the other way to open an ADO recordset, which doesn't involve using arguments? Some people say that this second approach makes their code easier to read.

Access a particular record in a recordset. Both ADO and DAO technologies have methods that allow you to move around within a recordset.

> **Master It** One method you can use to traverse a recordset is the `MoveFirst` method. It takes you to the first record in the recordset. What does the *first record* mean in a recordset in a relational database? Is it the record that's the lowest numerically, the lowest alphabetically, or what?

Search for a record. Both ADO and DAO offer methods to directly search for a particular record.

> **Master It** ADO offers a `Find` method. How many methods does DAO offer, and what are they?

Edit a record. When editing a record, you first use the `Edit` method, and then you can change the value in a field.

> **Master It** After you have made a change to a value in a record, what method do you use to save this change to make it part of the database?

Insert and delete records. It's not difficult to insert new records or delete existing ones. In both situations, you use the `Update` method when finished to save the changes to the database.

> **Master It** To insert a new record into a recordset, what method do you use before you can assign data to the fields in the new record?

Chapter 30

Accessing One Application from Another Application

So far, this book has focused on how to work with VBA to perform actions *within* a VBA host application, such as Word or Access.

But you might sometimes need to communicate between applications as well. This chapter demonstrates four tools you can use to contact and manipulate one application from another: Automation, data objects, Dynamic Data Exchange (DDE), and `SendKeys`.

IN THIS CHAPTER, YOU WILL LEARN TO DO THE FOLLOWING:

- Use Automation to transfer information
- Use the `Shell` function to run an application
- Use data objects to store and retrieve information
- Communicate via DDE
- Communicate via `SendKeys`

Understanding the Tools Used to Communicate Between Applications

The Office applications that this chapter uses as examples offer several tools for communicating with other applications:

Automation Formerly known as Object Linking and Embedding (OLE), Automation is usually the most effective method for transferring information from one Windows application to another. If the applications you're using support Automation, use it in preference to the alternatives, DDE and `SendKeys`.

Dynamic Data Exchange (DDE) An older method of transferring information between applications that remains a good fallback when Automation isn't available. DDE is offered in only some applications.

`SendKeys` The oldest and most primitive method of communicating between applications, `SendKeys` relies on sending keystroke equivalents to the other application. It's an attempt to pretend that someone is typing on the keyboard. But this approach can cause timing and other issues. Nonetheless, even though it's rudimentary by comparison to Automation and DDE, `SendKeys` can still be effective in some situations.

Beyond these three communications tools, this chapter discusses the `DataObject` object, which you can use to store information and to transfer information to and from the Windows Clipboard.

DON'T FORGET THE COMMAND LINE

If an application doesn't offer any of the control methods discussed in this chapter, you may be able to control it through the command line. For example, you can use the `/p` command-line switch in many applications to print a file without any user interaction. Search the Web for "command line, vba" and the application's name to find relevant tutorials.

Using Automation to Transfer Information

Automation is the most powerful and efficient way to communicate between applications. Each application that supports Automation offers one or more Component Object Model (COM) objects that you can access programmatically—usually an object representing the application, an object representing the various types of files the application uses, objects representing its major components, and so on.

For any Automation transaction, there's a *server application* that provides the information or tools and a *client application* that receives or employs them. (There's also another pair of terms that distinguish between two communicating applications: The server application is also sometimes known as the *object application*, and the client application is known as the *controlling application*.)

Automation lets the client application harness the built-in capabilities of the server application. For example, Excel has better calculation features than Word and can generate useful charts, data maps, and so on based on its calculations and data. By using Automation, Word can borrow Excel's calculation engine and then insert the results into a Word document. Or, Word could use Excel to create a chart that it then inserts into a document as well. Word can also take more-limited actions, such as causing Excel to open a workbook, copy a group of cells from a spreadsheet in it, and paste-link them into a document.

To use Automation through VBA, you create an object in VBA that references the application you want to work with. You use the `CreateObject` function to create a new object in another application and the `GetObject` function to retrieve an existing object in another application.

When using Automation, you can choose whether to display the server application or keep it hidden from the user. For some procedures, you'll need to display it—for example, the user might need to choose a file or a folder or make another choice that requires live intervention. In other situations, it can be best to keep the server application hidden so that the user isn't distracted by an application suddenly launching itself spontaneously and robotically carrying out actions in front of the user's startled eyes. This can make some users uneasy, as if the computer has gotten out of control. A colleague of mine, something of a prankster, used to torment new hires by inserting a procedure in their word processor that caused individual characters in a document to start swinging and then drop off the bottom of the screen as if they'd "come loose." Then he would walk over and tell them that this wouldn't be a problem as long as they didn't jar their desk while typing.

But even if you decide to hide a server application from the user when the procedure runs, in most cases it's helpful to display the server application to yourself while you're writing and testing the procedure. That makes it much easier to see what's going wrong if your code doesn't work as expected.

Understanding Early and Late Binding

When you use Automation to access another application, you can choose which type of *binding* to use—that is, how to establish the connection between the client application and the server application.

Early binding involves adding a reference to the application's object library by using the References dialog box (Tools ➤ References) and then declaring an object at the start of the code by using a `Dim` statement that declares the specific object class type rather than declaring the object generically `As Object`.

For example, the following code connects to a slide within a PowerPoint presentation by using early binding:

```
Dim myPowerPoint As PowerPoint.Application
Dim myPresentation As Presentation
Dim mySlide As Slide
Set myPowerPoint = CreateObject("PowerPoint.Application")
Set myPresentation = myPowerPoint.Presentations.Add
Set mySlide = myPresentation.Slides.Add(Index:=1, Layout:=ppLayoutTitleOnly)
```

With late binding, you create an object that references the other application on the fly when the code executes. If you declare the object explicitly, you declare it as a generic object—`As Object`—rather than declare it as a specific object class type.

For example, the following statements declare the Object variable `myOutlook` and then assign to it a reference to an `Outlook.Application` object:

```
Dim myOutlook As Object
Set myOutlook = CreateObject("Outlook.Application")
```

EARLY BINDING ISN'T UNIVERSAL

Not all applications that support Automation support early binding. Some applications cannot provide direct access to their functions at design time (while you're writing your code), as is required for early binding. They provide access to their functions only at runtime (when the code is executing). With such applications, you have no choice. You must use late binding.

If the server application you're using supports early binding, use it in preference to late binding. There are three advantages to early binding:

- Once you've added to the project the reference to the application's object library, you can dynamically work in your code with the outside (server) application's objects, properties, and methods through the VBA Editor in the client application. This makes it much easier to use the Editor's built-in IntelliSense features to find the objects, properties, and methods you need in the application you're referring to, and to avoid mistakes such as typos and missing arguments.

- Because you specify the particular type of object when you declare the object variable, you're less likely to attempt to work with the wrong object by mistake.
- Because VBA can compile more information about the object, elements of its methods and properties need not be resolved during runtime. So it runs faster.

On the other hand, late binding can avoid object-library issues such as having to make the right references and other library-version problems.

Creating an Object with the *CreateObject* Function

The `CreateObject` function creates and returns a reference to an Automation object exposed to other applications. The syntax is as follows:

```
CreateObject(class [,servername])
```

Here, *`class`* is a required argument specifying the class (the formal definition) of the object to create. The *`class`* argument consists of the name of the library that will provide the object and the type of object to be provided, so it looks like this:

```
applicationname.objecttype
```

For example, to specify the Excel `Application` object as a class, use a *`class`* argument of `Excel.Application`. Here, `Excel` is the name of the application that provides the object, and `Application` is the type of object that we want Excel to provide. Likewise, `Excel.Sheet` would specify a worksheet object in Excel.

`servername` is an optional string Variant that specifies the name of the network server on which to create the object. If you merely want to connect to an application located on the user's machine (in other words, if both applications—the client and server applications—are located on the same hard drive), omit *`servername`* or specify an empty string. To connect with an application located on a remote server machine, you must have DCOM (the Distributed Component Object Model) installed, and the object on the server computer must be configured to allow remote creation.

Typically, you'll use a `CreateObject` function with a `Set` statement to assign to an object variable the object that you create. For example, the following statements declare an object variable named `myNewSheet` and assign an Excel worksheet object to it:

```
Dim myNewSheet As Object
Set myNewSheet = CreateObject("Excel.Sheet")
```

CREATEOBJECT CAN BE USED WITH ANY COM OBJECT

You can use the `CreateObject` function with any COM object on your computer system, not just with application objects.

Returning an Object with the *GetObject* Function

The `GetObject` function returns a reference to an existing Automation object. The syntax is as follows:

```
GetObject([pathname] [, class])
```

You can provide either argument—but you must provide *one* of them. Here, *pathname* is an optional string Variant specifying the full path and name of the file that contains the object you want to retrieve. *pathname* is optional, but if you don't specify it, you must specify the *class* argument. *class* (which is optional if you specify *pathname*, but required if you don't) is a string Variant specifying the class of the object you want to return.

As with `CreateObject`, typically, you'll use a `GetObject` function with a `Set` statement to assign to an object variable the object that you return with the `GetObject` function. For example, in the second of the following statements, the `GetObject` function returns an object consisting of the workbook `Z:\Finance\Revenue.xlsm`. The `Set` statement assigns this object to the object variable named `Revenue` declared in the first statement:

```
Dim Revenue As Object
Set Revenue = GetObject("Z:\Finance\Revenue.xlsm")
```

Here, the workbook is associated with Excel. When this code runs, VBA starts Excel if it isn't already running and activates the workbook. You can then reference the object by referring to its object variable; in this example, you could manipulate the `Revenue` object to affect the `Z:\Finance\Revenue.xlsm` workbook.

Examples of Using Automation with the Office Applications

The following sections show three examples of using Automation with Office applications.

Transferring Information from an Excel Spreadsheet to a Word Document

This example transfers information from an Excel spreadsheet to a Word document.

First, you need to add to the target Word project (the client project that will contain the code that accesses Excel) a reference to the Excel object library. Follow these steps:

1. Start or activate Word, and then press Alt+F11 to launch the VBA Editor.
2. In the Project Explorer, click the project to which you want to add the reference. For example, if the procedure or procedures will reside in the `Normal.dotm` template, select the Normal project in the Project Explorer before adding the reference. Or, just choose Insert ➢ Module to create a brand-new module to play around with.
3. Choose Tools ➢ References to display the References dialog box.
4. Select the check box for the Microsoft Excel 16.0 Object Library item.
5. Click the OK button to close the References dialog box.

Once you've added the reference, you can use the VBA Editor's Object Browser to browse Excel objects. Display the Object Browser as usual by pressing F2 or choosing View ➤ Object Browser, and then choose Excel in the Object Browser's Project/Library drop-down list. The Object Browser will display the contents of the Excel object library, as shown in Figure 30.1. You can display the help (code examples, syntax) for a selected Excel object by clicking the Help button (the question-mark icon) in the Object Browser.

To create and test the next code example, first set up in Excel the preconditions that this procedure expects: namely, a range object named `SalesTotal`. To do this, open Excel, and right-click a cell anywhere in the displayed sheet in Book1 (the default name of the first blank workbook). If you don't see a workbook named Book1, choose File ➤ New, and then click the blank workbook icon in the displayed templates.

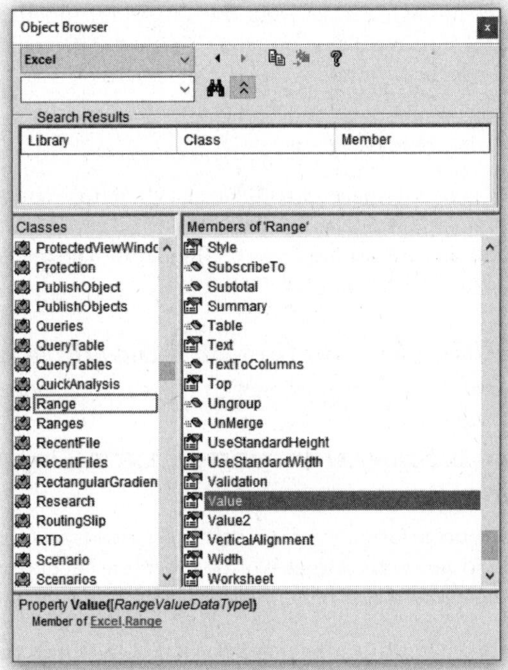

FIGURE 30.1 Once you've loaded the Excel object library, you can view its contents in the Object Browser from the VBA Editor session launched from the host application (in this case, Microsoft Word).

In the context menu that opens when you right-click a cell in Book1, choose the Define Name option. In the New Name dialog box that opens, type **SalesTotal** in the Name field. Then click OK to close the dialog box.

Now double-click the same cell you just named and type in **145** or some other value. It's this value that your macro in Word will pluck from this workbook. Now click the File tab in the Ribbon, choose Save As, and save this workbook as **`Book1.xlsx`** in the `C:\temp` subdirectory. (Note that you're saving it as an `.xlsx` file.) Now you can either leave Excel running or just close it. It won't matter because your macro will open the file on the hard drive.

Okay, now in Word's VBA Editor, add the code. Because you used early binding, you have available the Editor's IntelliSense assistance and code-completion features. Create the procedure shown in Listing 30.1. This procedure uses the `GetObject` function to retrieve the information from the specified cell in the Excel spreadsheet you previously created and inserts this data in the active Word document at the current insertion point (where the blinking cursor is).

LISTING 30.1: Getting data from an Excel cell and inserting it into Word

```
1.  Sub Return_a_Value_from_Excel()
2.
3.          Dim mySpreadsheet As Excel.Workbook
4.          Dim strSalesTotal As String
5.
6.          Set mySpreadsheet = _
7.              GetObject("C:\Temp\Book1.xlsx")
8.
9.          strSalesTotal = mySpreadsheet.Application.Range("SalesTotal").Value
10.
11.         Set mySpreadsheet = Nothing
12.
13.         Selection.TypeText "Current sales total: $" & strSalesTotal & "."
14.
15.         Selection.TypeParagraph
16.
17.     End Sub
```

This macro retrieves one piece of information from an Excel spreadsheet that's on the hard drive in the `C:\temp` directory. Here's what happens in the macro:

- Line 3 declares the object variable `mySpreadsheet` of the type `Excel.Workbook`. Line 4 declares the String variable `strSalesTotal`.
- Line 6 uses a `Set` statement and the `GetObject` function to make `mySpreadsheet` reference the spreadsheet `C:\Temp\Book1.xlsm`.
- Line 9 assigns to the String variable `strSalesTotal` the `Value` property (the actual data) of the `Range` object named `SalesTotal` in the Excel `Application` object. You defined the `SalesTotal` range as a single cell, so `strSalesTotal` receives the value of that cell.
- Line 11 assigns to the `mySpreadsheet` object the special value `Nothing`, releasing the memory it occupied. (Because the procedure ends almost immediately afterward, this statement isn't necessary here. VBA will destroy it at the end of execution of the procedure. But, it's good practice to free the memory assigned to an object when you no longer need to use the object, just to get into the habit.)

- Line 13 uses the `TypeText` method of the `Selection` object in Word to enter a string of text and the `strSalesTotal` string at the current selection. Line 14 uses the `TypeParagraph` method to insert a paragraph after the text.

If you have trouble getting this example to work, double-check the following:

- Choose Tools ➤ References in the Editor to ensure that the check box next to Microsoft Excel 16.0 Object Library is checked.
- If you see an error message stating "Run-time error '432': File name or class name not found during Automation operation," it means that there's something wrong in this line of code:

  ```
  Set mySpreadsheet = _
      GetObject("C:\Temp\Book1.xlsx")
  ```

  Either you've mistyped this path in your code (such as typing `C:\Docs` rather than `C:\Temp`) or you have not saved an Excel file named `Book1.xlsx` to this folder.

- If you see an error message stating "Run-time error '1004': Method 'Range' of object '_Application' failed," this is an error in the following line of code:

  ```
  strSalesTotal = mySpreadsheet.Application.Range("SalesTotal").Value
  ```

  If this code fails, either you've got a typo in the code, such as specifying the wrong range name, or there is no range by the name SalesTotal in the Excel workbook you're opening. Try renaming the cell and renaming it in the code. Then resave the workbook. Remember, the workbook is opened by this macro as a file on the hard drive—not accessed in the Excel application itself.

Transferring Information from a Word Document to an Excel Workbook

We managed to send data from Excel to Word in the previous section. Now let's go the other way.

This next procedure (Listing 30.2) runs as a macro in Word. The procedure requires that Excel be currently running, so the macro checks for the possibility that Excel isn't executing and, if necessary, handles the problem itself by starting Excel if necessary. The procedure creates a new Excel workbook and then transfers information from Word to the workbook.

For this example to work, you must store a Word `.docm` file named `test.docm` in your `C;\temp` directory.

As before, you'll find creating this procedure easier if you first add to the current Word project a reference to the Excel object library. (See the previous section for instructions.)

Listing 30.2: Sending data from Word to Excel

```
Sub Send_Word_Count_to_Excel_Spreadsheet()

    Dim WordCount As Variant
    Dim strPath As String
    Dim strFile As String
```

```
    Dim docCurDoc As Document
    Dim myXL As Excel.Application
    Dim myXLS As Excel.Workbook
    Const errExcelNotRunning = 429
    Const errDocNotAvailable = 5174

    On Error GoTo Handle

    ' open the Word document:
    strPath = "C:\temp"
    strFile = "test.docm"
    Set docCurDoc = Documents.Open(strPath & "\" _
        & strFile, AddToRecentFiles:=False)


    'is Excel already running?
    Set myXL = GetObject(, "Excel.application")

    myXL.Visible = True
    Set myXLS = myXL.Workbooks.Add
    myXL.ActiveCell.Range("A1").Select
    myXL.ActiveCell = "Word Count"

    WordCount = docCurDoc _
        .BuiltInDocumentProperties(wdPropertyWords)

        myXL.ActiveCell.Range("A2").Select
        myXL.ActiveCell = WordCount

        docCurDoc.Close SaveChanges:=wdDoNotSaveChanges

Shutdown:
    Set myXL = Nothing
    Set myXLS = Nothing

    Exit Sub

Handle:
     If Err.Number = errExcelNotRunning Then
        'If no instance of Excel is running then, run it:
        Set myXL = CreateObject("Excel.Application")
        Err.Clear
        Resume Next
    ElseIf Err.Number = errDocNotAvailable Then
        MsgBox "No Word Document named Test.docm Found"
        GoTo Shutdown
    Else
```

```
53.             Resume Next
54.         End If
55.
56. End Sub
```

Here's what happens in Listing 30.2:

- Line 2 is a spacer. In fact, all blank lines are just spacers—so I won't mention them again.
- Line 3 declares the Variant variable that will be assigned the number of words in a Word document. Later, in line 33, this same variable assigns its value to an Excel cell. Line 4 declares the String variable `strPath` that will hold the file path to the Word document, and line 5 declares the String variable `strFile` that will hold the Word document's filename.
- Line 6 declares the `Document` variable `docCurDoc`; it will point to the Word document when it is opened using the `Open` method of the `Documents` object. Line 7 declares an `Excel.Application` object variable `myXL`, and line 8 declares an `Excel.Workbook` object variable `myXLS`.
- Line 9 declares the constant `errExcelNotRunning`, setting its value to `429`. This error number indicates that the procedure attempted to manipulate Excel while no instance of Excel was currently executing. Line 10 declares the constant `errDocNotAvailable`, setting its value to `5174`. This error number indicates that the Word document your procedure attempted to open could not be found.
- Line 12 starts error handling for the procedure, directing execution to the code below the label `Handle` in the event of an error.
- Line 17 opens the Word document specified by `strPath`, a backslash, and `strFile`, assigning the document object to the `docCurDoc` variable. If the document isn't available, an error occurs and execution is transferred to the error-handler code that starts in line 43. This error number matches the constant defined in the procedure as `errDocNotAvailable`, so a message box informs the user that the Word document wasn't found. Then execution is transferred to the `Shutdown` label where the two object variables are destroyed and the procedure is exited.
- Line 22 can also potentially trigger an error condition. It attempts to assign a currently executing instance of Excel to the object variable `myXL`. However, if this attempt fails, execution is transferred to the `Handle` label. If Excel isn't running at this point, error 429 ("ActiveX component cannot create object") occurs, so line 44 in the error handler checks for this error by using the constant `errExcelNotRunning`. If it matches the error number, line 46 assigns to `myXL` a *new* instance of Excel that it creates by using the `CreateObject` function. Line 47 then uses an `Err.Clear` statement to clear the error, and line 48 contains a `Resume Next` statement to cause VBA to resume execution back up at the next statement following the offending statement.
- One way or another, by the time line 24 is executed, `myXL` refers to a running instance of Excel. Line 24 sets the `Visible` property of `myXL` to `True` so that it appears onscreen.

- Line 25 assigns to `myXLS` a new workbook created by using the `Add` method of the `Workbooks` object in `myXL`.
- Line 26 positions the insertion pointer in the first cell.
- Line 27 assigns to the active cell in `myXL` the text `Word Count`.
- Line 29 assigns the document's word count value to the variable `WordCount`. This value is accessed by using the `wdPropertyWords` property from the `BuiltInDocumentProperties` collection of `docCurDoc`.
- Line 32 moves the insertion cursor down one row in Excel to cell A2, and line 33 displays the word count in that cell.
- Finally, line 35 closes the Word document without saving any changes that may have been made to it while it was opened for inspection.
- Line 41 contains an `Exit Sub` statement to exit the procedure at this point—to avoid permitting execution to continue down into the zone where the error-handling statements are. Using an `Exit Sub` like this is common when a procedure includes an error handler at the end.

Placing a PowerPoint Slide in an Outlook Message

The next procedure shows how to communicate between PowerPoint and Outlook. This procedure, run from PowerPoint, returns the existing instance of Outlook or (if there is none) creates a new instance. The procedure then uses PowerPoint to send a message that gives details drawn from the presentation.

Listing 30.3 shows the procedure. There's one complication: Because PowerPoint doesn't have a central macro storage project like Word's `Normal.dotm` or Excel's Personal Macro Workbook, the code must be stored in an open presentation. This could be the presentation that is the subject of the email, but it is much more convenient to maintain a code-only presentation that you open at the beginning of all PowerPoint sessions that require the use of code. This becomes your own personal macro-storage system.

In any case, you need some slides from which to pick information that will be sent (and you also need to provide your email address), so follow these steps to set up the necessary preconditions for the upcoming example.

First, prepare the target PowerPoint project (the project that will contain the code that accesses Outlook and will contain the slides you're accessing):

1. Start PowerPoint. In the search field at the top of PowerPoint's start page, type **Photo Album** and then press Enter. Click the Contemporary Photo Album presentation, and then click the Create button to load it into PowerPoint.
2. Launch the PowerPoint VBA Editor by pressing Alt+F11.
3. In the VBA Editor, choose Insert ➢ Module to open a code module where you can put a macro.
4. Choose Tools ➢ References to display the References dialog box.

5. Select the check box for the Microsoft Outlook 16.0 Object Library item.
6. Click OK to close the References dialog box.

Now enter the code from Listing 30.3 into the module you inserted in step 3. Be sure to replace my email address in line 23 with your email address.

LISTING 30.3: Placing a PowerPoint Slide in an Outlook Message

```
1.  Sub Notify_of_New_Presentation()
2.
3.      Dim myPresentation As Presentation
4.      Dim strPresentationFilename As String
5.      Dim strPresentationTitle As String
6.      Dim strPresentationPresenter As String
7.      Dim myOutlook As Outlook.Application
8.      Dim myMessage As Outlook.MailItem
9.      Const errOutlookNotRunning = 429
10.
11.     On Error GoTo ErrorHandler
12.
13.     Set myPresentation = ActivePresentation
14.     With myPresentation
15.         strPresentationFilename = .FullName
16.         strPresentationTitle = _
                .Slides(1).Shapes(3).TextFrame.TextRange.Text
17.         strPresentationPresenter = _
                .Slides(1).Shapes(1).TextFrame.TextRange.Text
18.     End With
19.
20.     Set myOutlook = GetObject(, "Outlook.Application")
21.     Set myMessage = myOutlook.CreateItem(ItemType:=olMailItem)
22.     With myMessage
        ' replace the following line with your email address:
23.          .To = "richard41@pri.r.com"
24.
25.         .Subject = "Presentation for review: " & strPresentationTitle
26.         .BodyFormat = olFormatHTML
27.         .Body = "Please review the following presentation:" & _
                vbCr & vbCr & "Title: " & strPresentationTitle & vbCr & _
                "Presenter: " & strPresentationPresenter & vbCr & vbCr & _
                "The presentation is in the file: " & _
                strPresentationFilename
28.         .Send
29.     End With
30.
31.     myOutlook.Quit
```

```
32.
33.     Set myMessage = Nothing
34.     Set myOutlook = Nothing
35.     Exit Sub
36. ErrorHandler:
37.     If Err.Number = errOutlookNotRunning Then
38.         Set myOutlook = CreateObject("Outlook.Application")
39.         Err.Clear
40.         Resume Next
41.     Else
42.         MsgBox Err.Number & vbCr & Err.Description, vbOKOnly + _
                vbCritical, "An Error Has Occurred"
43.   End If
44.
45. End Sub
```

Here's what happens in Listing 30.3:

- Line 3 declares a `Presentation` object variable named `myPresentation`. Line 4 declares a String variable named `strPresentationFilename`, which is used for storing the path and filename of the presentation. Line 5 declares a String variable named `strPresentationTitle`, which is used to store the title of the presentation. Line 6 declares a String variable named `strPresentationPresenter`, which is used to store the name of the presenter of the presentation.
- Line 7 declares an `Outlook.Application` object variable named `myOutlook` that is used to represent the Outlook application. Line 8 declares an `Outlook.MailItem` object variable named `myMessage` that is used to represent the message that the procedure creates. Line 9 declares a constant named `errOutlookNotRunning` and assigns to it the number `429`, the error number returned if no instance of Outlook is available when the `GetObject` function tries to access it.
- Line 11 starts error handling for the procedure, directing execution to the label `ErrorHandler` (in line 36) in the event of an error.
- Line 13 assigns the active presentation to the `myPresentation` object variable. Lines 14 through 18 contain a `With` structure that works with `myPresentation`. Line 15 assigns the `FullName` property of `myPresentation` to `strPresentationFilename`.
- Line 16 assigns to `strPresentationTitle` the `Text` property of the `TextRange` object in the `TextFrame` object in the third `Shape` object on the first `Slide` object—in other words, the text from the first placeholder shape on the first slide in the presentation. Similarly, line 17 assigns to `strPresentationPresenter` the text from the second shape on the second slide.
- Line 20 assigns to `myOutlook` the current instance of Outlook, which it returns using the `GetObject` function. If Outlook isn't running at this point, error 429 ("ActiveX component cannot create object") occurs, so line 37 in the error handler checks for this error by using the constant `errOutlookNotRunning`. If it matches, line 38 assigns to `myOutlook` a new

instance of Outlook that it creates by using the `CreateObject` function. Line 39 then uses an `Err.Clear` statement to clear the error, and line 40 contains a `Resume Next` statement to cause VBA to jump back up in the code and resume execution where it left off (at the statement after the offending statement).

- Line 21 uses the `CreateItem` method of the Outlook `Application` object (represented by `myOutlook`) to create a new mail item (a new email), which it assigns to `myMessage`. Lines 22 through 29 contain a `With` structure that works with `myMessage`.
- Line 23 assigns recipients by setting the `To` property. *(You should change this line to your own email address so you can test this code and receive the message it sends.)*
- Line 24 is a placeholder.
- Line 25 enters text for the `Subject` property. Line 26 specifies that the message use HTML formatting (`.BodyFormat = olFormatHTML`). Line 27 assigns text to the body of the message by using the `Body` property. Line 28 then uses the `Send` method to send the message.
- Line 31 uses the `Quit` method to close `myOutlook`.
- Line 33 sets `myMessage` to `Nothing`, releasing the memory it occupied. Similarly, line 34 sets `myOutlook` to `Nothing`. Line 35 then exits the procedure.
- As discussed earlier in this list, the primary function of the error handler is to launch an instance of Outlook if none is currently running. If any error other than error 429 occurs, execution branches to the `Else` statement in line 41, and line 42 displays a message box that gives the error number and description.

If you test this example, be sure to remember to change line 23 from my email address to your email address. When the procedure finishes execution, look in your Inbox in Outlook for the new email message.

Using the *Shell* Function to Run an Application

Instead of using the `CreateObject` function to start an application and return a reference to it, you can use the `Shell` function to run an application. `Shell` can run any executable program, and its syntax is straightforward:

```
Shell(pathname[,windowstyle])
```

Here, `pathname` is the file path and program name of the program you want the `Shell` command to execute. Also include in the `pathname` any necessary command-line switches or arguments required by that program.

This example opens Internet Explorer, maximizes its window, and then switches the focus to it:

```
Sub OpenIE()

Dim id
```

```
id = Shell("c:\program files\internet explorer\iexplore.exe", vbMaximizedFocus)

End Sub
```

Shell Can Launch Applications via Filename Extensions

`Shell` can also start an application based on a file whose filename extension is associated with that program. It's as if you had double-clicked on a file in Windows Explorer, causing Windows to see if any application is associated with that file's extension.

For example, say that you specify a `.txt` filename extension as the argument for `Shell`: `Shell "testfile.txt"`. A file with a `.txt` extension usually starts Notepad because Notepad is usually associated with the filename extension `.txt`. (I say *usually* because Windows users are free to reassign filename extensions to alternative applications.) If `Shell` can't find the specified application or file, it returns a runtime error.

`windowstyle` is an optional integer Variant that you use to specify the type of window in which to run the application and to switch focus to the newly launched application. Table 30.1 lists the constants and values for `windowstyle`.

Real World Scenario

Using the *Sleep* Function to Avoid Problems with *Shell's* Asynchrony

The `Shell` function runs other programs *asynchronously* rather than *synchronously*. In other words, `Shell` doesn't halt all other activity in the computer until it is finished with its job. So when VBA executes a `Shell` statement, it registers the statement as an action to be performed—but that action may not necessarily be finished before the next statement in your VBA code executes.

This asynchrony can cause errors in your procedures if subsequent VBA statements depend on the `Shell` statement having already been executed. Should you run into this type of problem, a crude but often-effective fix is to just allow extra time for the `Shell` function to execute before taking any dependent action. For example, you might run the `Shell` function earlier in the procedure than you otherwise would have done rather than running it right before the dependent actions. But a better solution is to use an API call (such as `Sleep`) to delay the execution of further statements for a few seconds so that the `Shell` function can finish executing. Place this declaration in the declarations section at the top of the Code window:

```
Public Declare Sub Sleep Lib "kernel32" (ByVal dwMilliseconds As Long)
```

Then call the `Sleep` function at the appropriate point in your code, specifying the number of miliseconds you want the code to wait. The following statement uses `Sleep` to implement a 2-second delay:

```
Sleep (2000)
```

TABLE 30.1: Constants and values for the `windowstyle` argument

CONSTANT	VALUE	WINDOW STYLE
`vbHide`	0	Minimized and hidden, but with focus
`vbNormalFocus`	1	Normal ("restored") with focus
`vbMinimizedFocus`	2	Minimized with focus (the default)
`vbMaximizedFocus`	3	Maximized with focus
`vbNormalNoFocus`	4	Normal ("restored") without focus
`vbMinimizedNoFocus`	6	Minimized without focus

Using Data Objects to Store and Retrieve Information

As you've seen so far in this book, you can store information in many places using VBA. But there's also a uniquely useful *data object* with the ability to copy information to, and retrieve information from, the Clipboard. This chapter is all about ways to communicate between applications, and the Clipboard is one such way.

A data object is attached to a `UserForm` object in the Microsoft Forms object model, but you can use a data object by itself with no user form displayed. This is similar to the way that you can create and manipulate a hidden Access database with no visible interface displayed to the user. (This technique is described in the section titled "Opening Multiple Databases at Once" in Chapter 28.)

A data object, which is represented in VBA by the `DataObject` object, is used to store data. Each data object can hold multiple pieces of text information, and each piece must be in a defined format. You can create and use multiple data objects to store multiple pieces of data in the same format, or you can be tricky and tell VBA that information is in a different format when really it's not.

At any given time, the Clipboard can contain one text item and one item in another format, such as a picture. If you copy another text item to the Clipboard, that item will overwrite the previous text item, but any graphical item on the Clipboard will remain unscathed. Likewise, if you copy a picture to the Clipboard, it will overwrite any previous graphical item (or indeed *any* type of nontext item) stored in the Clipboard, but any text item in the Clipboard will be unaffected.

The data object works in a way similar to the Clipboard. However, a data object can't store graphical information. It *can* store multiple pieces of text information, each defined as being in a different format.

Creating a Data Object

To create a data object, declare an object variable of the `DataObject` type and then use a `Set` statement to assign a new `DataObject` object to it. For example, the following statements declare a `DataObject` variable named `myDObj` and assign a new `DataObject` to it:

```
Dim myDObj As DataObject
Set myDObj = New DataObject
```

Storing Information in a Data Object

To store information in a data object, use the SetText method, which has the following syntax:

```
object.SetText(StoreData [,format])
```

The components of the syntax are as follows:

- *object* is a required argument specifying a valid object.
- StoreData is a required argument specifying the data to store in the data object.
- format is an optional argument containing an Integer value or a String specifying the format of the information in StoreData. A value of 1 indicates text format; a value other than 1 or a String indicates a user-defined format.

For example, the following statement stores the text Sample text string in the DataObject named myDObj:

```
myDObj.SetText "Sample text string"
```

The following statement stores the text Sample formatted text string in the DataObject named myDObj, defining and using the custom format myFormat:

```
myDObj.SetText "Sample formatted text string", "myFormat"
```

Once the custom format has been defined and stored in the data object, you can access the data stored in that format by specifying the format. In this case, no formatting is actually involved—the code simply uses the format argument to create and identify a different data slot in the data object so that the new string doesn't overwrite the existing text string. It's a trick.

Returning Information from a Data Object

To return information from a data object, use the GetText method of the DataObject object. The GetText method has the following syntax:

```
object.GetText([format])
```

The components of the syntax are as follows:

- *object* is a required argument specifying a valid object.
- format is an optional argument containing a String or an Integer specifying the format of the data to retrieve.

For example, the following statement displays a message box containing the plain-text string stored in the DataObject named myDObj:

```
MsgBox myDObj.GetText
```

The following statement assigns to the String variable strTemp the text stored with the myFormat format in the DataObject named myDObj:

```
strTemp = myDObj.GetText("myFormat")
```

Here's a working code example that illustrates how to create a data object and then uses it to store and retrieve information. First, choose Tools ➢ References in the Editor to ensure that the check box next to Microsoft Forms 2.0 Object Library is checked. Note that it's likely this library will not be in its correct alphabetic location in the list of libraries in the References dialog box. Instead, it will probably be checked already and, thus, found in the first 10 or so libraries at the top of the References list. Once a library is selected, it moves to the top of the list.

Type this working example into an application's VBA Editor, and press F5 to see it execute:

```
Sub StoreText()

   Dim myDObj As DataObject

   Set myDObj = New DataObject

   myDObj.SetText "Sample text string"

   MsgBox myDObj.GetText


End Sub
```

Assigning Information to the Clipboard

To assign text to the Clipboard from a data object, use the `PutInClipboard` method of the `DataObject`. For example, the following example creates a new data object named `myDO`, assigns to it the text `Nasta Louise Gomes`, and then assigns that text to the Clipboard:

```
Sub ManageClipboard()

Dim myDO As New MSForms.DataObject

myDO.SetText "Nasta Gomes"
myDO.PutInClipboard

myDO.GetFromClipboard
MsgBox myDO.GetText


End Sub
```

To fetch whatever text information is in the Clipboard and store it in a data object, use the `GetFromClipboard` method of the `DataObject` object. The previous example uses the data object referenced by the variable `myDO`, assigns to it the text from the Clipboard, and then displays the text.

To return formatted information from the Clipboard and store it in a data object, use the `GetFormat` method of the `DataObject` object.

Finding Out Whether a Data Object Contains a Given Format

To find out whether a data object contains a given format, use the `GetFormat` method of the `DataObject` object. The syntax for the `GetFormat` method is as follows:

```
object.GetFormat(format)
```

Here are the components of the syntax:

- *`object`* is a required argument that returns a valid `DataObject` object.
- `format` is an Integer or String specifying the format you're looking for. If the `DataObject` contains the format, `GetFormat` returns `True`; if not, `GetFormat` returns `False`.

For example, the following statement checks to see if the `DataObject` named `myDO` contains the format `myHTML` and assigns the format's contents to the string `strHTMLText` if it does:

```
If myDO.GetFormat("myHTML") = True Then _
    strHTMLText = myDO.GetText(Format:="myHTML")
```

Communicating via DDE

If the application with which you want to communicate doesn't support Automation, you can try Dynamic Data Exchange (DDE). DDE is a protocol that establishes a channel between two applications through which they can automatically exchange data. DDE can be tricky to set up, but once you get it working, it is usually reliable.

Not all applications support DDE. Among the Office applications, Word, Excel, and Access support DDE, but PowerPoint and Outlook do not. What's more, Microsoft warns that DDE is not a secure technology. So use it only in situations where you aren't vulnerable to outside intrusion.

In the following descriptions of DDE statements, I'll use the term *method* in its more generic, non-OOP sense. Long, long ago when DDE was introduced (in Windows 3.0!), object-oriented programming wasn't yet fashionable.

A typical DDE conversation can contain the following actions:

- Using the `DDEInitiate` method to start a DDE connection and establish the channel on which the connection operates
- Using the `DDERequest` method to return text from the other application or the `DDEPoke` method to send text to the other application
- Using the `DDEExecute` method to execute a command in the other application
- Using the `DDETerminate` method to close the current DDE channel or using the `DDETerminateAll` method to close all the DDE channels

Using *DDEInitiate* to Start a DDE Connection

To start a DDE connection, you use the `DDEInitiate` method. The `DDEInitiate` method employs the following syntax:

```
expression.DDEInitiate(App, Topic)
```

The components of the syntax are as follows:

- *`expression`* is an optional expression specifying an `Application` object.

- `App` is a required String argument specifying the name of the application with which the DDE connection is to be started.
- `Topic` is a required String argument specifying the DDE topic (such as an open file) in the application. To discover the list of topics available for an application, you send a DDE request (via the `DDERequest` method, discussed in the next section) to the `System` object in the application.

`DDEInitiate` returns the number of the DDE channel established. You then use this number for subsequent DDE calls.

For example, the following statements declare the Long variable `lngDDEChannel1` and assign to it a DDE channel established with the workbook `Sales Results.xlsm` in Excel:

```
Dim lngDDEChannel1 As Long
lngDDEChannel1 = DDEInitiate("Excel", "Sales Results.xlsm")
```

Using *DDERequest* to Return Text from Another Application

To return a string of text from another application, you use the `DDERequest` method. The `DDERequest` method has the following syntax:

```
expression.DDERequest(Channel, Item)
```

The components of the syntax are as follows:

- *`expression`* is an optional expression that returns an `Application` object.
- `Channel` is a required Long argument specifying the DDE channel to use for the request.
- `Item` is a required String argument specifying the item requested.

To get the list of topics available via DDE, request the `Topics` item from the `System` topic. For example, the following statements establish a DDE channel to FrontPage (by using `DDEInitiate`) and return the list of DDE topics, assigning the list to the String variable `strDDETopics`:

```
Dim lngDDE1 As Long
Dim strDDETopics As String
lngDDE1 = DDEInitiate(App:="FrontPage", Topic:="System")
strDDETopics = DDERequest(Channel:=lngDDE1, Item:="Topics")
```

Open Excel, click the File tab on the Ribbon, and then click the New option. In the search field at the top, type **Monthly Family Meal Planner**. Click that template to select it, and then click the Create button.

Now open Word's VBA Editor and type in the following procedure. The following statements establish a DDE channel to the workbook `SalesReport1.xlsm` in Excel and return the contents of cell C7 (R7C3) in the String variable `strResult`:

```
Sub DDEtoExcel()

Dim lngDDEChannel1 As Long, strResult As String
lngDDEChannel1 = DDEInitiate("Excel", "Monthly family meal planner1")
```

```
strResult = DDERequest(lngDDEChannel1, "R11C4")
MsgBox strResult
DDETerminateAll

End Sub
```

Don't save this workbook. Press F5 to test this, and you should see a message box displaying "Beef and Mushroom Skillet Supper," which sounds pretty nasty.

For DDE to work, you have to use the correct, full name of the target document as it appears in the title bar of the application. In this case, your target document is an Excel workbook named *Monthly family meal planner1*.

The previous code works only *if you haven't yet saved* the `Monthly family meal planner1` workbook because before it's saved, a new workbook has no filename extension appended to its name. However, if you *have* already saved this workbook, you must append whatever filename extension you employed, such as `.xlsm`. Here's an example:

```
lngDDEChannel1 = DDEInitiate("Excel", "Monthly family meal planner1.xlsx")
```

The `DDETerminateAll` statement is explained shortly.

Using *DDEPoke* to Send Text to Another Application

To send text to another application, use the `DDEPoke` method. The `DDEPoke` method has the following syntax:

```
expression.DDEPoke(Channel, Item, Data)
```

The components of the syntax are as follows:

- *`expression`* is an optional expression that returns an `Application` object.
- `Channel` is a required Long argument specifying the DDE channel to use.
- `Item` is a required String argument specifying the item to which to send the data.
- `Data` is a required String argument specifying the data to be sent.

Continuing to use the previous example, the following statements use the `DDEPoke` method to assign the data Potato Salad Surprise to cell R11 C4 in the worksheet:

```
Sub DDEPokeExcel()

Dim lngDDEChannel1 As Long, strResult As String

lngDDEChannel1 = DDEInitiate("Excel", "Monthly family meal planner1")
strResult = DDERequest(lngDDEChannel1, "R11C4")


DDEPoke Channel:=lngDDEChannel1, Item:="R11C4", _
    Data:="Potato Salad Surprise"
DDETerminateAll

End Sub
```

Now look at the Excel worksheet and you'll see that "Beef and Mushroom Skillet Supper" has been replaced with the even more dubious-sounding "Potato Salad Surprise."

Using *DDEExecute* to Have One Application Execute a Command in Another

To execute a command in another application, use the `DDEExecute` method. The `DDEExecute` method has the following syntax:

```
expression.DDEExecute(Channel, Command)
```

The components of the syntax are as follows:

- *`expression`* is an optional expression that returns an `Application` object.
- `Channel` is a required Long argument specifying the DDE channel to use.
- `Command` is a required String argument specifying the command or series of commands to execute.

For example, the following statements establish a DDE channel to Excel and issue a `Close` command to close the active workbook:

```
Sub DDEExec()

Dim lngMyChannel
lngMyChannel = DDEInitiate(App:="Excel", Topic:="System")
DDEExecute lngMyChannel, Command:="[Close]"

End Sub
```

If the workbook you're closing has unsaved data, Excel will display a message box prompting you to save it first—thus, preventing it from closing until the prompt is satisfied.

Using *DDETerminate* to Close a DDE Channel

When you've finished a DDE communication, use the `DDETerminate` method to close the DDE channel you opened. The syntax for the `DDETerminate` method is as follows:

```
expression.DDETerminate(Channel)
```

Here are the components of the syntax:

- *`expression`* is an optional expression that returns an `Application` object.
- `Channel` is a required Long argument specifying the DDE channel to close.

The following statements employ the previous example, closing the DDE channel that was opened:

```
Dim lngMyChannel
lngMyChannel = DDEInitiate(App:="Excel", Topic:="System")
DDEExecute lngMyChannel, Command:="[Close]"
DDETerminate lngMyChannel
```

Using *DDETerminateAll* to Close All Open DDE Channels

To close all open DDE channels, use the `DDETerminateAll` method:

```
DDETerminateAll
```

Because VBA doesn't automatically close DDE channels when a procedure ends, it's a good idea to use a `DDETerminateAll` statement to make sure you haven't inadvertently left any DDE channels open.

Communicating via *SendKeys*

The `SendKeys` statement is a basic and limited form of communication between applications. You may find `SendKeys` useful if neither Automation nor DDE works with the target application. But `SendKeys` does have shortcomings, as you'll see momentarily.

`SendKeys` transmits specified keystrokes to the destination application. It impersonates someone typing at the keyboard.

For example, to use `SendKeys` to send the command to create a new file in Notepad, you send the keystrokes for Alt+F, N (to execute the File ➢ New command), and Notepad reacts as if you had pressed the keys manually. In Office 2016 applications, Alt+F opens the File tab on the Ribbon.

`SendKeys` works only with currently running Windows applications: You can't use `SendKeys` to start another application running (for that you need to use the `Shell` command, as discussed earlier in this chapter), nor can you use `SendKeys` to communicate with DOS applications running in a virtual DOS machine under Windows.

The syntax for the `SendKeys` statement is as follows:

```
SendKeys string[, wait]
```

Here, `string` is a required String expression specifying the keystrokes to be sent to the destination application. `wait` is an optional Boolean value specifying whether to wait after sending the keystrokes until the application has executed them (`True`) or to immediately return control to the procedure sending the keystrokes (`False`, the default setting). The `True` setting, however, can prevent some kinds of timing problems.

Typically, `string` consists of a series of keystrokes (rather than a single keystroke). All alphanumeric characters that appear on the regular keyboard are represented by the characters themselves: To send the letter *H*, you specify **H** in the string, and to send the word *Hello*, you specify **Hello** in the string. To denote the movement (arrow) and editing keys, `SendKeys` uses keywords enclosed within braces ({}), as described in Table 30.2.

TABLE 30.2: `SendKeys` keywords for movement and editing keys

KEY	CODE
Down arrow	{DOWN}
Left arrow	{LEFT}
Right arrow	{RIGHT}

TABLE 30.2: SendKeys symbols for meta keys *(CONTINUED)*

KEY	CODE
Up arrow	`{UP}`
Backspace	`{BACKSPACE}`, `{BS}`, or `{BKSP}`
Break	`{BREAK}`
Caps Lock	`{CAPSLOCK}`
Delete	`{DELETE}` or `{DEL}`
End	`{END}`
Enter	`{ENTER}`
Esc	`{ESC}`
F1, F2, etc.	`{F1}`, `{F2}`, etc. (up to `{F16}`)
Help	`{HELP}`
Home	`{HOME}`
Insert	`{INSERT}` or `{INS}`
NumLock	`{NUMLOCK}`
Page Down	`{PGDN}`
Page Up	`{PGUP}`
Print Screen	`{PRTSC}`
Scroll Lock	`{SCROLLLOCK}`
Tab	`{TAB}`

To send Shift, Control, and Alt, use the symbols shown in Table 30.3.

TABLE 30.3: SendKeys symbols for meta keys

KEY	CODE
Shift	+
Ctrl	^
Alt	%

SendKeys automatically assigns the keystroke after the meta key to the meta key, thereby imitating pressing and holding the Alt key—for example, while simultaneously pressing S.

In other words, to send a Ctrl+O keystroke combination, you would specify **^O**, and SendKeys imitates holding down Ctrl while pressing O. Then, the next keystroke after the *O* is considered to be struck separately. If you need to assign multiple keystrokes to the meta key, enter the keystrokes in parentheses after the meta key. For example, to send Alt+F, I, I, you'd write **%(FII)**, not **%FII**.

As you can see, SendKeys has special uses for the plus sign (+), caret (^), percent sign (%), and parentheses (). The tilde (~) gets special treatment as well. To use these characters to merely represent themselves instead of their special uses, enter them within braces: `{=}` sends a regular = sign, `{^}` a regular caret, `{%}` a percent sign, {~} a tilde, and `{()}` parentheses. Likewise, you must enclose brackets (which have a special meaning in DDE in some applications) within braces; braces themselves also go within braces.

Using SendKeys is much less complex than these details initially make it appear—but with that reassurance, there's one more trick you should know: To repeat a key, enter the key and the number of repetitions in braces. For example, to send five up-arrow keystrokes, you'd specify `{UP 5}`; to send 10 zeroes, you'd specify `{0 10}`.

Listing 30.4 shows an example of how to use SendKeys to send some text to Notepad after first starting it with the Shell command.

> **WARNINGS ABOUT *SENDKEYS***
>
> SendKeys is an old technology, and it has two serious drawbacks. First, you can run into timing issues. SendKeys was created when computers ran far more slowly than they do today. For this reason, in some circumstances, executing the code in Listing 30.4 creates a problem when it displays the Save dialog box. Execution stops, failing to complete the file-saving. Or, the filename is saved as *og file* rather than *log file*. These are timing problems. The second drawback relates to testing your code. Because SendKeys needs to activate the target application, you can't step through your code (repeatedly pressing F8) in the VBA Editor. The Editor just grabs the focus back at the wrong point, becomes perplexed, and the sent keystrokes are dumped into the Editor rather than into Notepad, the intended target. Instead, you must run the procedure either from the VBA Editor (by pressing F5) or from the host application as a macro. Technically, this second behavior—absorbing keystrokes into the Editor rather than Notepad—is a result of what SendKeys is actually doing: It's pushing keystrokes into the computer's key buffer. Then they pop back out wherever they can.

LISTING 30.4: Automating Notepad with SendKeys

```
Sub Send_to_Notepad()
    Dim strLogDate As String
    Dim strSaveLog As String
    Dim strMsg As String
    Dim appNotepad As Variant
    strMsg = "Sample log text here."
```

```
7.         strLogDate = Month(Now) & "-" & Day(Now) & "-" & Year(Now)
8.         strSaveLog = "Log file for " & strLogDate & ".txt"
9.         appNotepad = Shell("notepad.exe", vbNormalFocus)
10.        AppActivate appNotepad
11.        SendKeys strMsg & "%FS" & strSaveLog & "{Enter}" & "%{F4}", True
12.    End Sub
```

Here's how the code works:

- The `Send_to_Notepad` procedure starts by declaring (in lines 2, 3, and 4) three String variables—`strLogDate`, `strSaveLog`, and `strMsg`—and (in line 5) one Variant variable, `appNotepad`.
- Line 6 then assigns to `strMsg` a sample string of text.
- Line 7 assigns to `strLogDate` a date built of the `Day`, `Month`, and `Year` values for `Now` (which returns the current date and time). For example, if the date is July 11, 2016, `Month(Now)` will return 7, `Day(Now)` will return `11`, and `Year(Now)` will return `2016`, so the `strLogDate` string will contain `7-11-2016`.
- Line 8 then assigns to the `strSaveLog` string (which will be used to supply the filename for the log file) text describing the file, the `strLogDate` string, and the `.txt` filename extension (to continue our example, `Log file for 7-11-2016.txt`).
- In line 9, the procedure finally gets down to business, using the `Shell` statement to run Notepad in a "normal" (not maximized or minimized) window with focus and storing the task ID of the Notepad session in the variable `appNotepad`.
- Line 10 then uses an `AppActivate` statement to activate Notepad.
- Line 11 uses a `SendKeys` statement to send to Notepad the following:
  - The information contained in the String variable `strMsg`.
  - An Alt=F keystroke (to pull down the File menu), followed by an S keystroke to choose the Save item on the menu. This keystroke displays the Save As dialog box with the File Name text box selected.
  - The `strSaveLog` String variable, which is entered in the File Name text box.
  - An Enter keystroke to choose the Save button in the Save As dialog box.
  - An Alt=F4 keystroke to quit Notepad.
- Line 12 ends the procedure.

When you run this procedure (again, remember that you need to run the procedure by pressing F5 rather than stepping into it with F8), you'll see the following:

1. Notepad springs to life.
2. The contents of the `Msg` string appear in the Notepad window.

3. The Save As dialog box displays itself, enters the filename in the File Name text box, and then dismisses itself.

4. Notepad closes. The `.txt` file is saved to the currently active folder on your hard drive.

   (To locate the currently active folder, open Notepad by hand and choose File ➤ Save As. You might also find that timing problems have changed the name of the file from the intended *Log file for 1-13-2016.txt* to something like *g file for 1-13-2016.txt*.)

Because `SendKeys` was historically most often employed to open an application's menus and select an option from the menus (the way that Notepad still behaves), you might think that applications since Vista—which are largely menu-free and employ the Ribbon instead—would seriously curtail the flexibility of the `SendKeys` technique. However, this isn't true. Many of the features of the Ribbon, for example, are accessible via key combinations. Try pressing the sequence Alt, W, Q, 2, and the Enter key in Word; it will switch to the View tab on the Ribbon, select the Zoom option, and switch to a 200 percent zoom.

The difference here is that instead of employing the traditional approach of simultaneously pressing the Alt key while pressing other keys (such as Alt+V to open a View menu), in current Windows operating systems you press and release Alt by itself and then you press the W key to switch to the View tab on the Ribbon. At this point, additional keystrokes are possible to activate the various options on the View tab. To exit from this mode, press Esc.

Here's another code example, which illustrates how to manipulate Ribbon-based applications. This time Excel, not Notepad, is the target, and the Ribbon, not a menu, is manipulated. The code sends an Alt key by itself (this activates the shortcut key feature on the Ribbon and the Quick Access Toolbar as well, displaying a variety of keys you can choose from). Then the code switches to the View tab (a W does that), and finally full-screen mode is turned on by sending an E:

```
Sub Send_to_Excel()

    Dim appExcel As Variant

    appExcel = Shell("Excel.exe", vbNormalFocus)
    AppActivate appExcel

        SendKeys "%", True 'send Alt by itself
    SendKeys "W", True 'W for the View tab
    SendKeys "E", True 'E for full screen mode

 End Sub
```

Before pressing F5 to test this code, close Excel.

Going Beyond VBA

VBA is not limited to its own library of functions. In this chapter, you've seen how to use the Editor's Tools ➤ References feature to make Office applications' object libraries available to VBA's built-in capabilities. But wait! There's more.

VBA can also access the entire Windows API (application programming interface). This isn't as simple as adding a library via Tools ➤ References. And the necessary code is verbose. But if you want to have complete control over Windows's internals to, for example, perfectly manage timing issues such as waiting for an outside application to complete its task and other advanced techniques, the Windows API functions are up to such jobs (and plenty more besides).

Windows API programming is beyond the scope of this book, but if you're interested, copy and paste the sample code from this MSDN web page:

`http://msdn.microsoft.com/en-us/library/office/bb258148(v=office.12).aspx`

That sample code works fine in Word's or Access's VBA Editors. And the links provided on that web page are your doorways into further, deeper study of the topic. If, like me, you have major geek tendencies, it's great fun to wander around and experiment in an immense compendium like the API. You can make Windows do things you wouldn't believe.

The Bottom Line

Use Automation to transfer information. Automation sets up communication between two applications, designating one of them as the *server* and the other as the *client.*

> **Master It** Of the various ways to communicate between applications, which is generally the most effective?

Use the `Shell` function to run an application. Although the `Shell` function can prove useful in a variety of inter-application communication situations, `Shell` can also present the programmer with a timing problem.

> **Master It** Describe the timing issues that the `Shell` function raises, and describe a good solution to this problem.

Use data objects to store and retrieve information. This book has described a variety of ways to store and retrieve information when working with the VBA language. Using data objects is one of these useful techniques.

> **Master It** How is the data-object technology special as a way of storing and retrieving information? What can a data object do that's unique?

Communicate via DDE. Dynamic Data Exchange (DDE) is a technology introduced back in May 1990 with Windows 3.0. Use it if other, more efficient communication technologies are unavailable to the applications you are working with.

> **Master It** Not all applications support DDE. Which Office 2016 applications don't support DDE communication?

Communicate via `SendKeys`. Using `SendKeys` is a fairly simple, but rather awkward and limited, way to communicate between applications. It imitates typing in keystrokes, thereby allowing your code to manipulate an application by accessing some of its features using, for example, Alt+key combinations such as Alt+F to open the File tab on the Ribbon.

> **Master It** `SendKeys` was historically most often employed to open an application's menus and select an option from the menus. Since Vista, Windows applications have largely done away with traditional menus, so is `SendKeys` of even more limited use now than in the past?

Chapter 31

Programming the Office 2016 Ribbon

VBA programmers may want to customize the Office applications' Ribbons programmatically (via macro code as opposed to the user manually manipulating the Options dialog box). Perhaps your organization wants to perform tasks like these:

- Hide certain features in Excel
- Add a step-through wizard to Word
- Create a Ribbon that is custom-designed for working with a particular presentation
- Add a special tab containing capabilities relevant to your business
- Otherwise automate management of this major part of the user interface.

Or, you might want to create dynamic Ribbon effects, such as hiding, disabling, revealing, or modifying Ribbon elements—labels, groups, controls, or whatever—based on the user's behaviors in the application or on some other criterion.

This chapter explores all aspects of Ribbon customization so you'll be able to fully exploit the Ribbon's capabilities programmatically.

Note that the Ribbon can be programmatically modified in two ways: The most efficient approach is to create XML code and make it interact with VBA procedures. This chapter employs this technique and describes how to customize the Ribbon in Word, Excel, and PowerPoint. A second, more complex approach requires writing COM add-ins, a technique that is beyond the scope of this book.

The Access Ribbon can't be modified in the same way that you modify the Ribbon in Word, Excel, and PowerPoint. Access requires a unique approach, including creating a specialized table to hold the XML code that modifies the Ribbon. Modifying the Access Ribbon is covered at the end of this chapter.

The Office Ribbon's contents are described in the XML language, but you don't need to know how to write XML to manipulate the Ribbon. Throughout this chapter, you can just copy and paste XML code examples, making modifications to them to suit your needs.

As you'll see shortly, there's also a handy utility you can download that helps you avoid several tedious steps when modifying the Ribbon and verifies that your XML statements are "well formed" (that they follow the structural rules of XML).

IN THIS CHAPTER, YOU WILL LEARN TO DO THE FOLLOWING:

- Understand what XML is
- Hide a group on the Ribbon
- Add a new, custom group
- Create callbacks for event handling
- Manipulate the Access Ribbon
- Debug Ribbon programming

What Is XML?

XML means *extensible markup language*. It's a way to surround data with descriptions of that data.

Think of a file cabinet holding various documents, each of which is stored in a folder with a label describing the meaning of its document: Telephone Bill, Boat Insurance, Bobby's Arrest, and so on.

But XML takes this a step further, becoming more *granular* (more finely detailed) in its marking (labeling) of data. Each paragraph, sentence, or even individual word can be contained within descriptive "tags," like this:

```
<firstarrest>
      <dateofarrest>12,1,2016</dateofarrest>
      <location>sao paulo, brazil
      </location>
</firstarrest>
<secondarrest>
<dateofarrest>12,14,2016</dateofarrest>
      <location>miami airport
      </location>
<secondarrest>

...
```

You get the idea: descriptive tags, then the data contained, followed by closing tags. For example, `<location>` is a tag presumably containing some kind of geographical data. `</location>` is a tag with a backslash, meaning that this is the end of the information about location. Any opening tag must be paired with a closing tag, and they, thus, surround the data that they describe.

Notice, too, that data in XML is *nested* (structured). Within the parent elements `<first arrest>` and `<secondarrest>` are nested, subsidiary, child elements `<dateofarrest>` and `<location>`. So the position of elements within an XML "tree" structure tells you something about their relationships—described most often as *parent, child, sibling,* and *ancestor*.

One final word of caution about XML: its tags are case-sensitive. `<ThisTag>` is entirely different from `<Thistag>`. We'll look at this issue more later in this chapter in the section titled "A Word of Warning."

XML is "extensible," meaning anybody can make up their own tags. XML is a way of storing information along with descriptions (the tags) of the meaning of that information.

Contrast this with HTML (the markup language that underlies web pages), which describes only how to *display* information and contains standardized tags, such as `<i> </i>` for italic, understood by all browsers.

If you want to know more about XML, you'll find a good introductory tutorial here:

`http://w3schools.com/xml/`

Hiding the Clipboard Group on the Word Ribbon

To get an idea of how to modify the Ribbon, let's assume that you want to remove the Clipboard group in the Word Ribbon's Home tab. This group does things you don't need to activate via the Ribbon, such as cutting, copying, pasting, and format painting. You decide that you just don't need to display these options because you never click them via the mouse. Instead, you use the keyboard shortcuts such as Ctrl+C for copy, Ctrl+V for paste, and so on. Format painting can be selected via a context menu that appears when text is selected.

To you, this Clipboard group is useless, just wasting valuable space on the Ribbon.

To hide the Clipboard group on the Ribbon, follow these steps:

1. First, you'll want to download a free utility that makes working with the Ribbon much easier. Go to

   `http://openxmldeveloper.org/blog/b/openxmldeveloper/archive/2010/08/10/23248.aspx`

   and download and install the Office Custom UI Editor tool. This utility (it works fine with Office 2016) can be downloaded via the `OfficeCustomUIEditorSetup.zip` link on this web page. (The file icon is just above the comments.) When you extract the contents of this zip file, you'll have an installer (`.msi`) file. Just double-click it to install the Custom UI Editor.

2. Start Word.

3. Press Alt, F, N, (or click the File tab, and then click the New option). Then click the blank document template.

4. Press Alt, F, A and save the document as `RibbonMod.docm` to your Desktop (or some other location such as `C:\temp` where you can easily locate it). When the Save As dialog box opens, ensure that below the filename field, the Save As Type field says *Word Macro-Enabled document (*.docm)*.

5. Press Alt, F, C to close this document. Closing the document is necessary because if it's still open when you attempt to store your XML code in it (by choosing File ➢ Save in the Custom UI Editor for Microsoft Office), you'll get an error message.

Why You Should Use Macro-Enabled File Types

Note that you could also save the document as the default `.docx` file type, but in this chapter you'll always use the macro-enabled `.docm` type (and the other "m" types, such as `.xlsm` for macro-enabled Excel files and `.pptm` for PowerPoint). These types of files can include macros, and in some of the examples in this chapter, you'll need to write procedures to handle events—triggered when the user clicks a control that you've added to the Ribbon.

6. Run the Custom UI Editor for Microsoft Office.
7. Choose File ➤ Open.
8. Browse to the `RibbonMod.docm` file that you saved in step 4, and open it.
9. In the right pane of the Custom UI Editor, type the following XML code:

```
<customUI xmlns="http://schemas.microsoft.com/office/2009/07/customui">
  <ribbon>
     <tabs>
        <tab idMso="TabHome">
           <group idMso="GroupEditing" visible="false" />
        </tab>
     </tabs>
  </ribbon>
</customUI>
```

Identifiers (`idMso`), images (`imageMso`), and other attributes in Ribbon XML code can have an `Mso` suffix. `Mso` is short for Microsoft Office, and when appended to an attribute, it means *built-in*. So, a tab with an `idMso` attribute is one of the tabs on the Ribbon by default. A tab with a plain `id` attribute is a new tab you've added to the Ribbon. Likewise, an `imageMso` is one of the set of built-in Office 2016 icons, but an `image` is an icon you created by importing a graphics file (see "Creating Your Own Icons" later in this chapter).

Real World Scenario

Watch Out for Special Characters

XML will choke on special characters—it expects plain vanilla text with none of those curly quotation marks (called *smart quotes*) or other fancy formatting. You used to be able to paste code into Notepad, copy it from Notepad, and paste it into the VBA Editor or the Custom UI Editor. When text was dipped into Notepad like this, all special characters were stripped off. Curly quotation marks (which are two distinct characters, open and close quotes) turned into one, stripped-down quotation-mark character. This was quite a good way to wash text. No more. Those at Microsoft who fiddle with good tools and make them less useful decided to justify their salaries by *not leaving Notepad alone*. After all, they're getting paid to do *something*, so they get restless. Until this unfortunate "improvement," Notepad had been left alone, unchanged for decades.

So, how *do* you get rid of characters such as smart quotes (“ and ”) that XML (and the VBA Editor) cannot work with, replacing them with straight quotes (")? There are three ways, but number 3 is the best:

1. Hand-edit each bad character by selecting it and then pressing the " key. If you press this key in Notepad or a Code Editor, it will appear as the correct " simple quotation mark (no curls).
2. If you're working with a large piece of code with many quotation marks, paste it into Notepad and then press Ctrl+H to open the Replace dialog box. Paste one of the bad, open-quote (“) curly quotation-mark characters into the Find What field, then click the Replace With field, and press the " key. (Notepad by default uses the straight-quotes character.) Note that you'll have to repeat this process with the close-quote (“) curly quotation-mark character.
3. What do we do when faced with a repetitive and tedious task? Anyone?

   Yes. Write a macro. Here's a macro that opens a new, blank Word document, pastes in the text that needs changing, and then makes the necessary replacements:

```
Sub StraightenQuotes()
' Changes smart quotes (slanted) to straight quotes

On Error GoTo Problem
Dim aDO As DataObject
Set aDO = New DataObject
aDO.GetFromClipboard
aDO.GetText

Dim bQuotesOn As Boolean
bQuotesOn = Options.AutoFormatAsYouTypeReplaceQuotes

Options.AutoFormatAsYouTypeReplaceQuotes = False

Documents.Add Template:="Normal", NewTemplate:=False, DocumentType:=0

Selection.Paste

    Selection.WholeStory

    Selection.Find.ClearFormatting
    Selection.Find.Replacement.ClearFormatting

    With Selection.Find
        .Text = ChrW(8221)
        .Replacement.Text = """"
        .Wrap = wdFindStop
        .Forward = True
    End With
    Selection.Find.Execute Replace:=wdReplaceAll
```

Continues

Continued

```
31.
32.     Selection.Find.ClearFormatting
33.     Selection.Find.Replacement.ClearFormatting
34.
35.     With Selection.Find
36.         .Text = ChrW(8220)
37.         .Replacement.Text = """"
38.         .Wrap = wdFindStop
39.         .Forward = True
40.         End With
41.     Selection.Find.Execute Replace:=wdReplaceAll
42.
43. Options.AutoFormatAsYouTypeReplaceQuotes = bQuotesOn
44.
45. Exit Sub
46.
47. Problem:
48. MsgBox "There was a problem. Be sure that you have copied some text
into the Clipboard before executing this macro."
49.
50. End Sub
```

To test this, just copy some text that contains some of those unwanted curly quotation marks into the Windows Clipboard (select the text, and then press Ctrl+C). Then run the macro. Here's what the code does:

- Line 4 says that if something goes wrong, jump down to the label named `Problem` at the end of the procedure. The most likely problem is that the user has a graphic in the Clipboard (they pressed PrtScn, for example) rather than text.
- Lines 5–8 fetch the text from the Clipboard.
- Lines 10 and 11 save the user's setting for smart quotes so we can restore it at the end of the macro.
- Line 13 turns off Word's Smart Quotes feature so when in our code the slanted quotation marks are replaced by straight quotation marks, Word will permit this. Line 15 opens a new, blank document. This is important because you might currently also be working on a second, ordinary text document where you want smart quotes.
- Line 17 pastes the text from the Clipboard into the blank document.
- Lines 21 through 41 carry out the find and replace. Remember, this code must be executed twice, once for the open-quote and a second time for the close-quote characters.
- Line 43 restores the user's setting for the Smart Quotes option.
- Line 45 exits the procedure so we don't fall into the error handler after successfully running the procedure without error.

- Line 47's label identifies the error-handler code.
- Line 48 handles the error by reminding the user that there must be text in the Clipboard for this macro to work.

Yes, I used Word's Macro Recorder to help me write this code. Having been programming in BASIC and writing books on it for 25 years, I'm by now almost freakishly proficient in the language. But I had only a vague idea what kind of code would turn off Word's Smart Quotes feature. So, I turned on the Macro Recorder, then went to File ➢ Options in Word, and turned off Smart Quotes. VBA created this code:

```
Options.AutoFormatAsYouTypeReplaceQuotes = False
```

So I just copied the code into my macro. I used the same trick to get the code that opens a new document and does the finding and replacing. Unless you're Martha Stewart and can remember everything you've ever read or done, you'll need to rely on the Macro Recorder and online code samples to write macros of even moderate complexity.

10. In the Custom UI Editor, click the icon with the red check mark.

    This tool validates your XML code (a handy feature).

    If you don't see the message "Custom UI XML is well formed," you've made a typo in the XML code or included bad special characters. Retype it (or better yet, copy and paste it from this book's web page—see this book's Introduction for information on copying code).

    If you see an error message stating " "" is an unexpected token…," you need to fix the quotation marks in the XML code to make them straight, not "smart" quotation marks, as described in the sidebar in this chapter titled "Watch Out for Special Characters."

    You should always validate your XML code because if there *is* an error of some kind, your Ribbon customization simply won't happen. You will be given no error message or other warning when executing the customization itself. It just won't work. (Browsers and other applications that you feed XML generally do not provide error messages if they can't parse (understand) XML. Instead, they usually do nothing at all.)

11. In the Custom UI Editor, choose File ➢ Save (which saves your Word document with the changes to the Ribbon), and then select File ➢ Exit to close the UI Editor.

12. Now, to see the effect, open the RibbonMod document by clicking the File tab on Word's Ribbon and then clicking Open. In the list of recent documents, choose `RibbonMod.docm` (or double-click that filename in File Explorer).

If you entered the correct XML code, you'll see a Ribbon like the one on the bottom of Figure 31.1.

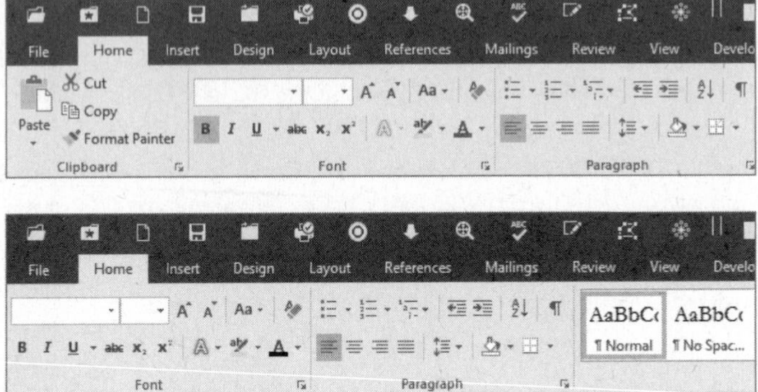

FIGURE 31.1
Word's Ribbon with (top) and without its Clipboard group (bottom)

The key lines in the XML code are these:

```
<tab idMso="TabHome">
      <group idMso="GroupEditing" visible="false" />
```

The line of code that begins with `<tab` specifies the tab on the Ribbon you want to modify—in this case, it's the Home tab. The `group` element specifies which group within the tab you are targeting. In this case, it's the Clipboard group. Finally, the code specifies that the Clipboard group's `Visible` attribute should be set to `false`. (I'll define the XML terms *element* and *attribute* shortly.)

Real World Scenario

DECIDING WHAT TO INCLUDE ON THE RIBBON

Practical Ribbon programming can require a little planning. When you modify the Ribbon, you'll want to include utilities or features that you use frequently, and perhaps hide those you'll never need.

Here's a useful tip: Real estate on the Ribbon is valuable. Notice that when you removed the Clipboard group, the Ribbon automatically expanded the options visible for the Styles group, or otherwise freed up some extra space. So, if you're planning to add some new options or a new group of your own (as described later in this chapter), consider making room for them by hiding a group you don't need.

Also, Office applications are mature software and by now contain a quite large number of features. Microsoft had to leave many tools off the Ribbon, relegated to dialog boxes that appear when you click the small arrow icon found in the bottom right of many Ribbon groups.

But Microsoft's choices of what to show or hide are unlikely to completely match your preferences. To see if there is a feature missing from Word's default Ribbon that you want to add to it, right-click the Ribbon and choose Customize The Ribbon. The Word Options dialog box opens. In the Choose Commands From drop-down list, select Commands Not In The Ribbon. You'll see a list—a long list.

A Word of Warning

There's a major problem to be aware of when you're working with XML code. When XML was being designed, some crack committee decided that this new language would be *case-sensitive.* That decision has caused countless problems for programmers over the years. It's easy to generate bugs in languages that are case-sensitive because `ThisVariableName` is not the same as `ThisVariablename`, even though they look quite alike. The capital `N` in the first version means that these two words refer to two completely different variables (even though, of course, the programmer intended them to represent the same variable, but accidentally mistyped). And since the two versions look very much the same, it can be difficult to locate and fix this bug. Your XML code won't work if you don't precisely match capitalization. Validating XML code (as we did earlier with the Custom UI Editor) can flag *some* case-error typos, but not all.

Fortunately and sensibly, VBA *isn't* case-sensitive, so you never have to worry about this kind of error in VBA code. But if you're getting an error when attempting to modify the Ribbon using XML, make sure there isn't a case mismatch somewhere in all that code. A good rule is to simply *always use lowercase* when writing XML code. If you create names without any capitalization—and stick to that practice—you'll avoid the case-related debugging headaches that XML programmers have struggled with for years.

See the section at the end of this chapter titled "What to Look For If Things Go Wrong" for additional possible problems when working with the Ribbon and XML.

XML Terminology

To understand the descriptions of XML code examples in this chapter, you need to know just a bit more about XML.

In XML, the order of the elements matters. XML is hierarchical (also known as *nested* or a *tree*), meaning that you need to put elements inside each other in the proper order, as with a Russian doll set.

When working with the Microsoft Ribbon, the order of the element tags is `Ribbon`, `tabs`, `tab`, `group`, `button` (or other control), as you can see in this code:

```
<customUI xmlns="http://schemas.microsoft.com/office/2009/07/customui">
     <ribbon>
          <tabs>
               <tab idMso="TabView">
                    <group id="CustomViewsGroup"
                     label="Next Window"
                     insertAfterMso="GroupWindow">
                         <labelControl id="null"/>
                         <button idMso="WindowNext"/>
                    </group>
               </tab>
          </tabs>
     </ribbon>
</customUI>
```

If you violate this nesting structure—by putting a `group` tag outside a `tab` tag, for example—you'll get an error message ("The name in the end tag must match the name in the start tag"):

```
<button idMso="WindowNext"/>
    </tab>
</group>
```

Or, if you leave out one of the closing tags (signified by the `/>`), you'll get the same error message (here the closing `</tab>` tag is missing):

```
                </group>
            </tabs>
```

Using Built-In Icons

The `imageMso` "galleries" can be downloaded from this web page:

```
www.microsoft.com/downloads/details.aspx?FamilyID=2D3A18A2-2E75-4E43-8579-D543C19
D0EED&displaylang=e&displaylang=en?
```

Load this `.docx` file into Word. Choose Enable Editing if asked. Then you'll see a mystery message in boldface: "**Images are in the *ImageMso 0* and *ImageMso 1* tabs in the Backstage.**" Are you among the few who know what the term *backstage* means in relation to Office applications? It means, "Click the File tab on the Ribbon." But it's so much more fun to have everybody guessing.

After clicking the File tab, you'll see two new items listed on the left side under Options: ImageMso 0 and ImageMso 1. Click these to see a complete list of icons and the names you can use to reference them in your XML code, like this: `imageMso="diamond"`.

Working with Excel and PowerPoint

To modify Excel's or PowerPoint's Ribbons, you use the same techniques demonstrated with Word's Ribbon in the previous section. To illustrate this, the following example hides PowerPoint's Ink group in the Ribbon's Review tab.

1. Start PowerPoint. Click the Blank Presentation template.
2. Click the File tab on the Ribbon; then click Save As, and save the document as `PPMod.pptx` to your Desktop (or another location where you can easily locate it).
3. Click the File tab on the Ribbon and click Close to close this document.
4. Run the Custom UI Editor for Microsoft Office.
5. Choose File ➢ Open.
6. Browse to the `PPMod.pptx` file that you saved in step 2, and open it.
7. In the Custom UI tab of the Editor, type the following XML code:

```
<customUI xmlns="http://schemas.microsoft.com/office/2009/07/customui">
  <ribbon>
```

```
        <tabs>
          <tab idMso="TabReview">
            <group idMso="GroupInk" visible="false" />
          </tab>
        </tabs>
      </ribbon>
    </customUI>
```

8. Click the icon with the red check mark to validate your XML code. If you don't see the message "Custom UI XML is well formed," you've made a typo in the XML code. Retype it (or copy and paste it from this book's web page).
9. Choose File ➤ Save, and then select File ➤ Exit to close the UI Editor.

At this point, open `PPMod.pptx` and click the Review tab. The Ink group should now be hidden.

Undoing Ribbon Modifications

In the previous two sections, you modified the Ribbon: first by hiding a group in Word and then by hiding a group in PowerPoint. In other examples later in this chapter, you'll add new groups to the Ribbon.

But what if you want to undo the changes you made to the Ribbon or modify those changes? It's quite easy. Just open the document, presentation, workbook, or template in the Custom UI Editor for Microsoft Office. You will see the XML code that represents your customization. Delete it or modify it, and then simply validate and save it (overwriting it) back to your hard drive. If you explore the Ribbon technology in depth—working directly with `.zip` and other files that are part of an Office 2016 document—you'll come to appreciate all the tedious and error-prone steps that the Custom UI Editor saves you.

Selecting the Scope of Your Ribbon Customization

Recall that where you put your VBA macros determines their scope: You can embed a macro in a single document, in a template used by multiple documents, or (for Word) in the `Normal.dotm` file.

When you create XML code to manipulate the Ribbon, where you store your code determines its scope—much the same as the way scope works with macros. Here are your options, listed in increasing size of scope:

- To apply your Ribbon customization to only a single document, just embed it in that document, as illustrated in the two previous examples.
- To use the custom Ribbon for all documents based on a particular template, put the XML code in a macro-enabled template file type (file types with the `.dotm`, `.xltm`, and `.potm` filename extensions).
- Add the XML code to `Normal.dotm` if you want the custom Ribbon automatically available to all Word documents. Just follow the same steps as in the first example in this chapter,

but instead of modifying the `RibbonMod.docm` file in the Custom UI Editor for Microsoft Office, modify `Normal.dotm`.

(`Normal.dotm` can be found in a path similar to this: `C:\Users\`**`Richard`**`\AppData\Roaming\Microsoft\Templates`. However, replace *`Richard`* with your username.)

Recall that you add custom Ribbons to *individual* PowerPoint or Excel documents much the same way that you add them to Word—by adding XML code and using the Custom UI Editor. However, it's not that simple to add a *global* custom Ribbon to PowerPoint or Excel documents because they don't have a direct equivalent to `Normal.dotm`. Instead, with Excel and PowerPoint, you must create an add-in file to globally customize the Ribbon.

Adding a New Group

In this next example, you'll see how to specify where on the Ribbon you want to place a new, custom element and also where to find the correct control identifier (`idMso` attribute) for built-in dialog boxes, commands, and controls.

Cautions About Customizing

When customizing the Ribbon for coworkers, you could, of course, hide an entire group and then replace it by adding a new group of your own—reproducing some or all of Microsoft's original buttons on the group and adding some new ones. But you should think twice before taking this approach because lots of study has gone into these groupings and most people will find them well organized if not totally intuitive. What's more, people get used to the Ribbon's organization.

Of course, if you're just customizing the Ribbon for yourself and your coworkers won't use it, you can more freely rearrange things.

Back to the 1950s

As an aside, we're using the term *button* here because that's the technical term. However, on the Ribbon and introduced elsewhere with the Windows 8 Modern interface, there's no visual button that the user clicks. In an effort to provide us with what some think is a "modern" aesthetic (actually, it's a 1950s look), the photorealism (now derided as *skeuomorphism*) that reached its zenith in Windows 7 has been stripped away by Microsoft's design team. The user interface is now flattened. Pretty much gone are gradients, dimensional effects, reflections, textures, subtle colors, buttons, highlights, opacity, serif typefaces, and shadowing. Figure 31.2 illustrates the difference. (Interestingly, however, Windows 10 restores drop shadows around certain elements such as dialog boxes.)

I frequently like to cycle through open Word documents, and that requires the Next Window feature. The Word Ribbon displays a Switch Windows drop-down list on the View tab, but I don't want to choose from a list; I want to just click a button to open each active document in turn (like the way you can switch to each active Windows application by pressing Alt+Tab).

The Next Window command is listed in the Commands Not In The Ribbon list in the Word Options dialog box. Normally, you want to avoid filling up the Ribbon with new groups because some of the Ribbon's built-in buttons must be hidden in order to make room for your custom groups. This can force the user to have to click the Ribbon to reveal what is perhaps a favorite, frequently used button. But in Word's View tab, there's plenty of room to add a new group. Figure 31.2 shows how the new group will look in the new "modern" Windows 8 style.

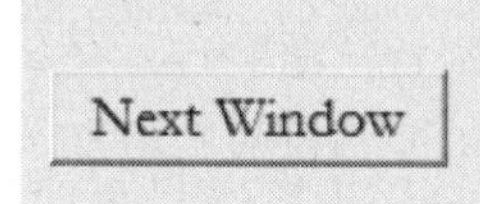

FIGURE 31.2 A traditional button control on a VBA form (left) compared to the simplified "button" on Word's Ribbon (right)

A good place for our new tab, which we will call *Shuffle,* is just to the right of the built-in Window group (on the View tab). This will leave the Macros group on the far right of the View tab, as it is in the default Ribbon arrangement.

To create a new group (called Shuffle) and a new button (called Next Window) in that group, follow the steps in the first example in this chapter. But replace the XML code in step 9 with this XML code:

```
<customUI xmlns="http://schemas.microsoft.com/office/2009/07/customui">
      <ribbon>
            <tabs>
                  <tab idMso="TabView">
                        <group id="CustomViewsGroup" label="Shuffle"
insertAfterMso="GroupWindow">
                              <labelControl id="null"/>
                              <button idMso="WindowNext"/>
                        </group>
                  </tab>
            </tabs>
      </ribbon>
</customUI>
```

There are several things to notice in this code. Each element in the Ribbon (the `group`, `label`, and `button`) is given an identifier, an `id`—a unique string. And there are two types of IDs: the `idMso` and the plain `id`. An `idMso` refers to a built-in Microsoft command, control, or dialog box (such as the Next Window command or a Font dialog box). A plain `id` refers to a customized element you are adding to the Ribbon, such as a customized group, a new tab, a button that triggers one of your macros, and so on.

Note that I added a *button* control to the Ribbon (there are other controls you can place on the Ribbon, such as a label, as you'll see in another example shortly).

The code in this example illustrates how to use the XML element `id`:

```
group id="CustomViewsGroup"
```

You can also use it like this:

```
labelControl id="null"
```

The `id` name that you give to these objects (such as `CustomViewsGroup`) is not displayed; it's for internal programming purposes only. So name them as you like.

Note that I added a Label control but didn't provide any text caption (I included no `Label` attribute). Used this way, a Label control acts as a spacer, pushing the Next Window button to the middle of the group area. Without it, the button would be displayed at the top of the Ribbon. Add two of these captionless Label spacer controls if you want to push the button to the bottom of the Ribbon.

In this code, the View tab is specified as the tab we're going to use (`<tab idMso="TabView">`). The caption that will be displayed on the Ribbon to describe our new group is Next Window, thanks to this code: `label="Shuffle"`. The position of our new item on the Ribbon is specified as being to the right of the built-in Window group: `insertAfterMso="GroupWindow">`.

Two Ways to Find the Correct *idMso*

How did I know that the proper Microsoft name for this Next Window command is `WindowNext`? Right-click the Ribbon and click Customize The Ribbon. If you look up the command in the Choose Commands From drop-down list (Commands Not In The Ribbon) in the Word Options dialog box, it is displayed as Next Window. But if you use `Next Window` in the code for the `idMso` (Microsoft built-in command ID), nothing will be displayed on the Ribbon because `Next Window` is not the correct internal ID. This won't work:

```
<button idMso="Next Window"/>
```

You must use this:

```
<button idMso="WindowNext"/>
```

The quickest way to identify the correct internal Microsoft ID (`idMso`) for any control or command is to pause your mouse pointer on top of the command in the Options dialog box's Choose Commands From drop-down list, as shown in Figure 31.3. The control name appears in parentheses at the far right of the tooltip that is displayed when you hover your mouse pointer over any command in the list.

If you prefer, you can download a more detailed list of the commands and controls to use with the `idMso` attribute. To download tables (that can be viewed in Excel) of all the built-in Office 2016 controls—such as the font dialog box or the Clipboard task pane (`ShowClipboard`)—go to this web page:

```
www.microsoft.com/en-us/download/details.aspx?id=36798
```

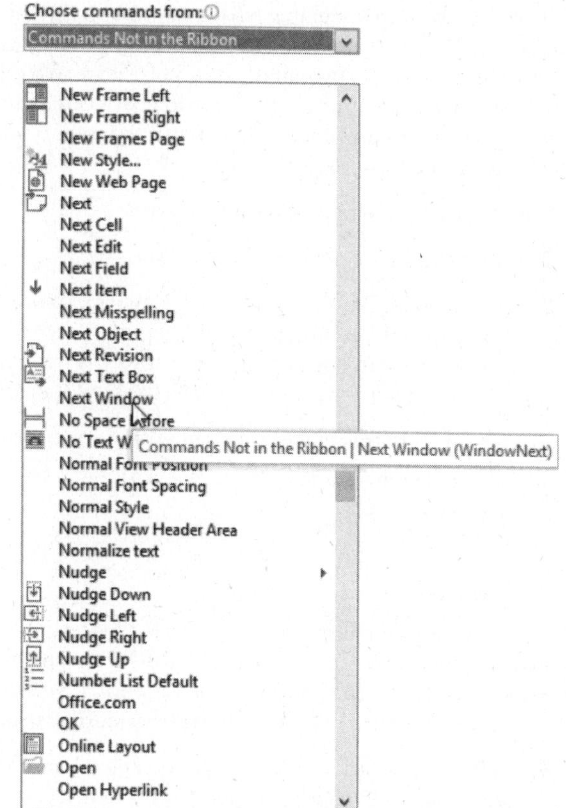

FIGURE 31.3 Hover your mouse pointer over any command in this list to see the correct ID to use in your XML code. In this example, you can see that the Next Window command has an ID of `WindowNext`.

Adding Callbacks

Now it's time to employ some VBA code to respond when the user interacts with the Ribbon. In the previous example we added a button that triggered one of Word's built-in features (Next Window). But now we'll add a button that triggers one of your own macros.

To run your own VBA code, you insert a *callback* in the XML code to execute whatever VBA macro you specify. When the user clicks a control, such as a button, the XML code that services this control sends a message to the Office application, telling it that a response is needed (this is very similar to the triggering of a `Click` event in ordinary VBA programming). The Office application then "calls back" to trigger the macro that's specified by the `onAction` attribute you write in the XML code.

Put another way, to create a callback, you type in an attribute in the XML code, specifying which macro you want to execute. It looks like this:

```
onAction="module1.test"
```

If you add this attribute to a Button control on the Ribbon, it means that when the user clicks that button, the macro named `test` located in module1 is executed. In addition to the Button control, the CheckBox, ToggleButton, and Gallery controls also have `OnAction` attributes.)

To see exactly how this communication between a button and a VBA macro works, follow these steps (refer to the first example in this chapter if you need additional information about how to carry out these steps):

1. Create a new, empty Word document.
2. Press Alt+F11 to open the VBA Editor.
3. Double-click *ThisDocument* in the Project Explorer to open the Code window for your new, empty Word document. (Make sure you're clicking the correct ThisDocument project if more than one document currently is open in Word. It will be the ThisDocument in the project with the same name as the new Word document you just created.)
4. Now type in this macro that you will execute via a button on the Ribbon:

```
Sub test(control As IRibbonControl)

MsgBox "Hi!"

End Sub
```

Notice the argument for this procedure: `control As IRibbonControl`. This argument is necessary when you're interacting with the Ribbon using a button (or any of the large number of other controls that can be put on the Ribbon). If you don't include this argument, you'll get a "Wrong number of arguments, or invalid property assignment" error message.

5. Go back to Word itself and click the File tab on the Ribbon. Choose Save As to save this document as `RibbonTest.docm`. (Make sure to save it as a `.docm` file.) Then close the document.
6. Run the Custom UI Editor for Microsoft Office.
7. Choose File ➢ Open.
8. Browse to the `RibbonTest.docm` file that you saved in step 5 and open it.
9. In the Custom UI tab of the Editor, type the following XML code:

```
<customUI xmlns="http://schemas.microsoft.com/office/2009/07/customui">
<ribbon>
  <tabs>
    <tab id="t1" label="Execute">
      <group id="g1" label="Run Test">

<button id="b1"
       label="See Message"
onAction="ThisDocument.test" />

      </group>
    </tab>
```

```
    </tabs>
  </ribbon>
  </customUI>
```

10. Click the icon with the red check mark to validate the XML code. If the code isn't well formed according to the validation test, you've made a typo in the XML code. Retype it (or better, copy and paste it from this book's web page).
11. Choose File ➤ Save, and then select File ➤ Exit to close the UI Editor.
12. Now, to see your new tab, group, and button, open `RibbonTest.docm` in Word, click the new Execute tab at the far right of the button, and click the See Message "button."

You should see a message box appear with the message "Hi!" in it. If you don't, check out the section "What to Look For If Things Go Wrong" later in this chapter.

Try modifying the code in the previous example to see the effect of some other attributes of the Button control. That control has the following attributes: `description`, `enabled`, `id`, `idMso`, `idQ`, `image`, `imageMso`, `insertAfterMso`, `insertAfterQ`, `insertBeforeMso`, `insertBeforeQ`, `keytip`, `label`, `ScreenTip`, `showImage`, `showLabel`, `size`, `supertip`, `tag`, and `visible`.

Adding Attributes

As you can see, the Ribbon is quite dramatically modifiable; in fact, you can re-create the Ribbon from scratch. In this section, you'll explore some additional ways to modify the Ribbon. For this and the remaining examples in this chapter, we'll use Word because it's the most popular Office application and because modifying the Excel or PowerPoint Ribbons works much the same way, as the second example in this chapter illustrated.

Using Built-In Icons and ScreenTips

Try following the steps in the previous section again; but this time, modify the XML code for the button element by adding two additional attributes, like this:

```
<button id="b1"
        label="See Message"
        imageMso= "ShowTimeZones"
        screentip="Say Hi!"
        onAction="module1.test" />
```

When you load the `.docm` file and click the Execute tab that you've added to the Ribbon, you'll see two changes from the previous example, reflecting the two attributes you added to the `button` element. First, there is a globe icon (one of the built-in `imageMso` icons).

Also, when you pause your mouse cursor on top of the button, a tooltip (now called a *ScreenTip* by Microsoft) is displayed. You can employ this attribute to remind the user of the purpose of the button. There are actually two elements to a ScreenTip: The `ScreenTip` attribute displays a heading in boldface and the `supertip` attribute displays a normal-font "body text" message. You can use either or both. Adding a supertip produces the result shown in Figure 31.4:

```
screentip="Run a Macro"
supertip="Click this button to execute the test macro."
```

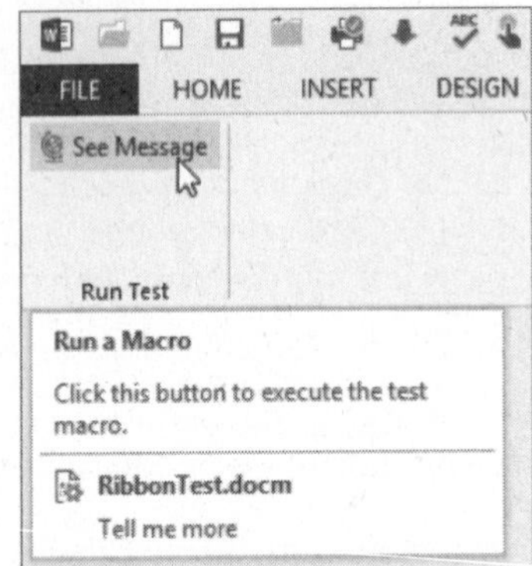

Figure 31.4 The `ScreenTip` attribute is shown on top in boldface. The `supertip` attribute displays the body text in a regular font, below.

Creating Your Own Icons

Although Microsoft provides an extensive collection of built-in icons, you can also create your own. You can use any `.png`, `.tif`, `.bmp`, `.jpg`, or `.ico` file. The attribute for a custom icon is `image` rather than `imageMso`.

The Custom UI Editor for Microsoft Office provides an easy way to find and employ custom icons. To see how this works, open `RibbonTest.docm` in the UI Editor, and then click the middle icon in the UI Editor (its ScreenTip is *Insert Icons*). An Insert Custom Icons dialog box opens. Browse your hard drive until you locate the graphics file you want to use. All permitted graphics file types will be displayed in the browser.

It's not necessary to reduce the size of a large graphics file. It will automatically be reduced for you when displayed.

When you find the file you want, double-click it. The dialog box closes and a picture of the image as well as its name are displayed in the left panel of the UI Editor. You have to click the small + next to the customUI entry in the left pane to see the image. Right-click the image to delete it or to change its ID.

Notice that the filename extension, such as `.jpg`, is stripped off in the UI Editor. This reminds you that you don't use the extension when you add this image to the XML code. A photo of a rose is used as an icon in the following code.

The file on the hard drive is `rose.jpg`, but notice that in the code it's referred to merely as `rose`:

```
<button id="b1"
          label="See Message"
          image="Rose"
          size="large"
      screentip="Say Hi!"
      onAction="module1.test" />
```

Using Menus and Lists

Although the button is the most common control employed on the Ribbon (or indeed in any user interface), you can use other controls as well. For example, if you want to offer the user multiple options—such as choosing between executing three different macros—a drop-down list box or a menu might be preferable to using up Ribbon space by adding three buttons on the *top level* (what's always visible in a tab) of the Ribbon.

Adding Menus

Here's how to add to the Ribbon a menu that, when clicked, displays three buttons—each of which launches a different macro:

1. Open `RibbonTest.docm` in the Custom UI Editor.
2. Type this XML code into the Custom UI Editor:

```
<customUI xmlns="http://schemas.microsoft.com/office/2009/07/customui">
<ribbon>
  <tabs>
    <tab id="t1" label="Execute">
      <group id="g1"  label="Favorite Macros">

<menu id="m1" label="Choose a Macro">
 <button id="b1"
     imageMso="InkDeleteAllInk"
     label="Convert Case"
     onAction="ThisDocument.ConvertCase" />
 <button id="b2"
     imageMso="DataRefreshAll"
     label="Replace 5pt with 10pt"
     onAction="ThisDocument.UpSize" />
 <button id="b3"
     imageMso="PictureBrightnessGallery"
     label="Memo Format"
     onAction="ThisDocument.Memo" />
</menu>

      </group>
    </tab>
  </tabs>
</ribbon>
</customUI>
```

   Note that I chose `imageMso` icons that symbolize the various actions taken by these macros (see Figure 31.5).

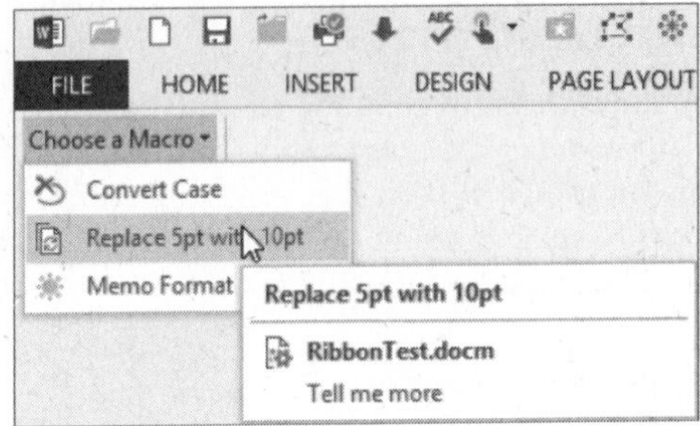

FIGURE 31.5 Click the Choose A Macro menu, and the menu items are displayed as a set of buttons, ready to launch various macros when clicked.

3. Click the Validate button in the Custom UI Editor, and if the message says your code has no typos (meaning it is well formed), choose File ➤ Save in the UI Editor to store this XML code in the `RibbonTest.docm` file.
4. Open `RibbonTest.docm` in Word and press Alt+F11 to open the VBA Editor. Ensure that you have three macros in the `ThisDocument` module, named `ConvertCase`, `UpSize`, and `Memo`. They should look like this:

```
Sub ConvertCase(control As IRibbonControl)

  MsgBox "convert"

End Sub

Sub UpSize(control As IRibbonControl)

  MsgBox "upsize"

End Sub

Sub Memo(control As IRibbonControl)

  MsgBox "memo"

End Sub
```

(These message boxes are mere stubs for testing purposes; your actual procedure will, of course, contain real macros that convert case, resize fonts, and display a memo form.)

You can now return to the document `RibbonTest.docm` and try out the new menu. Click the Execute tab, and notice the Choose A Macro menu in the Favorite Macros group. A menu is indicated in the Ribbon by a down-arrow icon that the user clicks to display the menu items, as shown in Figure 31.5.

If you prefer, you can send all the menu buttons to a single macro and then choose between them in that macro's VBA code by testing their `id` attribute (which is passed to the VBA code by the `ID` property of the control object). The VBA code would look like this:

```
Sub choosemacro(control As IRibbonControl)

    Select Case control.ID
        Case "b1"
```

```
            MsgBox ("button1")
        Case "b2"
            MsgBox ("button2")
        Case "b3"
            MsgBox ("button3")
    End Select

End Sub
```

For this select-case technique to work, you also need to modify the XML code in this example so that each button executes this same `choosemacro` procedure:

```
<menu id="m1" label="Choose a Macro">
    <button id="b1"
            imageMso="InkDeleteAllInk"
            label="Convert Case"
            onAction="ThisDocument.choosemacro" />
    <button id="b2"
            imageMso="DataRefreshAll"
            label="Replace 5pt with 10pt"
            onAction="ThisDocument.choosemacro" />
    <button id="b3"
            imageMso="PictureBrightnessGallery"
            label="Memo Format"
            onAction="ThisDocument.choosemacro" />
</menu>
```

Adding a DropDown List Control

You can employ a DropDown List control much as you would a menu when you want to offer the user a set of choices. Here's an example of XML code that displays a drop-down list on the Ribbon. This example displays the same choices (three macros) to the user as the previous example. But here we use a drop-down list rather than a menu:

```
<customUI xmlns="http://schemas.microsoft.com/office/2009/07/customui">
<ribbon>
   <tabs>
      <tab id="t1" label="Execute">
         <group id="g1"  label="Favorite Macros">

<dropDown id="ddlist1"


getSelectedItemIndex="setfirst"

           label="Favorite Macros"
           onAction="ThisDocument.test">

     <item id="i1" label="Convert Case"/>
     <item id="i2" label="Replace 5pt with 10pt"/>
```

```
        <item id="i3" label="Memo Format"/>

</dropDown>

          </group>
        </tab>
      </tabs>
</ribbon>
</customUI>
```

You create a DropDown List control by adding a `dropDown` element in the XML code and then adding as many `item` child elements as you want within the parent `dropDown` element. (Remember that XML is very particular about capitalization. If you try to use `dropdown` rather than `dropDown`, you'll cause an error because your XML code will not be well formed.)

You should include a `getSelectedItemIndex` attribute, as illustrated earlier, so the DropDown List control's text box will not initially be blank, confusing the user. This attribute executes a macro named `setfirst`, which you must write. This macro returns the index number of the item you want to initially display in the DropDown List control's text box. In this example, the macro returns a zero (which means to display the first item). So in this example, Convert Case will be displayed. Here's the macro that causes this to happen by setting the return value argument (passed back in the variable named *x*) to zero:

```
Sub setfirst(ByVal control As IRibbonControl, ByRef x)
    x = 0
End Sub
```

Pay particular attention to this `GetSelectedItemIndex` attribute. Recall that this attribute transfers execution to a VBA procedure when the document is being loaded (before the user sees the Ribbon), so it is a form of initialization. (For other kinds of initialization, you can use other attributes in the set of built-in `get` attributes, including `getEnabled`, `getImageMso`, `get Label`, and `getVisible`.)

One additional macro must be written as well. This second macro (pointed to by the `onAction` attribute in the XML code) responds appropriately when the user clicks an item in the list:

```
Sub test(control As IRibbonControl, id As String, index As Integer)

    Select Case index

        Case 0
            MsgBox ("item1")
        Case 1
            MsgBox ("item2")
        Case 2
            MsgBox ("item3")
    End Select

End Sub
```

When the user clicks an item in the list, the values of both that item's `id` and `index` attributes are passed to the macro. So you can use either one to decide what code to execute. In this example, I'm using the index number, but you could just as easily use the ID string (such as `Case "i1"`) to detect the ID of each item.

Using a DialogBoxLauncher

Some of the Ribbon's built-in groups display a small arrow in the lower-right corner (see the Font group on Word's Home tab for an example). Click that arrow, and a dialog box or task pane appears. This is a way to conserve space on the Ribbon if displaying a whole slew of options at all times would be impractical.

If you want to add a dialog box to one of your custom groups, use the DialogBoxLauncher control by writing some XML code like this:

```
<customUI xmlns="http://schemas.microsoft.com/office/2009/07/customui">
<ribbon>
   <tabs>
      <tab id="t1" label="Execute">
           <group id="g1"
               imageMso="StartAfterPrevious"
               label="Insert Date">

<dialogBoxLauncher>

     <button id="b1"
     onAction="test" />

</dialogBoxLauncher>

         </group>
      </tab>
   </tabs>
</ribbon>
</customUI>
```

This DialogBoxLauncher merely transfers execution to a macro (named `Test` in this example). So, when the user clicks the small arrow at the bottom of the custom group named Execute, the `test` macro displays whatever built-in dialog box is appropriate. Write this code, and the macro displays the Date And Time dialog box:

```
Sub test(control As IRibbonControl)

    Dialogs(wdDialogInsertDateTime).Show

End Sub
```

The VBA Editor will show you a list of the available dialog boxes as soon as you type the left parenthesis in `Dialogs(`. (This assumes that you've got the handy Auto List Members feature turned on in the VBA Editor. Choose Tools ➤ Options, and then click the Editor tab in the Options dialog box.)

Test this example. It will insert the current date, formatted as the user chooses by selecting an option in the Date And Time dialog box.

Toggling with a Toggle-Button Control

A toggle button used to look like a regular button, but with the introduction of the Windows 8 interface, it's now just text, like a hyperlink. The button, when clicked, used to animate itself. Shadows were displayed behind a clicked toggle button to make the button look like it had been pressed. With Office 2010, however, the shadowing was, for some reason, removed. When toggled, an Office 2010 button startlingly turned yellow! I guess that's somebody's idea of improving this visual cue. As we all know, when you press something it does turn yellow.

With Office 2013, a pressed toggle button changed again. Clicking it resulted in a surprising blue background around the button's label. In Office 2016, we have yet another curious effect: A "depressed" toggle button is now symbolized (we can't use the word *animated*) by a dark gray background.

What's next? Fuchsia? We can hope that sooner or later things will settle down and we can get accustomed to cues that last longer than each revision of Office and that, at long last, make some kind of visual sense.

VBA Escapes the Visual Flattening Due to Neglect

Fortunately, VBA's forms have consistently retained over the years the same shadowed, realistic buttons and other three-dimensional controls (see Figure 31.2). This, however, is most likely a matter of neglect rather than common sense on Microsoft's part. For now at least, their decision-makers appear to be generally uninterested in any form of the Basic language, including VBA. They tolerate it for backward compatibility and, I suppose, because of the millions of people who like to use Basic in their Office applications and in other contexts (see Microsoft's Visual Studio for ways to use Visual Basic to create stand-alone applications). In spite of Microsoft's negligence, VBA remains a vital tool in offices all over the world.

If you need to add an on-off control to the Ribbon, you can use either a check-box control or a toggle button. Both visually cue users about their status: the check box with a check and the toggle button by changing color and adding a frame.

Either of these controls can be used for two-state situations, such as allowing the user to choose between italic text or non-italic text. Here's an example showing how to employ the toggle button. When the user clicks it, the button lights up and looks as if it's been pressed into the Ribbon. When the button is clicked a second time, the yellow lighting effect is turned off.

Your VBA procedure can detect the status of the button—pressed or not—by examining a Boolean argument I named down that is passed to your procedure. Here's how to use it in your VBA code:

```
Sub test(control As IRibbonControl, down As Boolean)

    If down Then
```

```
        MsgBox "Button Down"
    Else
        MsgBox "Button Up"
    End If

End Sub
```

This VBA procedure will respond to the following XML code you can store in your document by using the UI Editor as described in the various step-through examples throughout this chapter:

```
<customUI xmlns="http://schemas.microsoft.com/office/2009/07/customui">
<ribbon>
   <tabs>
      <tab id="t1" label="Execute">
         <group id="g1" label="Run Test">

<toggleButton id="tbutton1"
   label="Click to Toggle"
   imageMso="DeclineInvitation"
   onAction="ThisDocument.test" />

         </group>
      </tab>
   </tabs>
</ribbon>
</customUI>
```

Modifying the Ribbon in Access

As you've doubtless noticed in previous examples in this book, Access often takes its own, sometimes rather meandering, path to accomplish a given task. Ribbon customization is no exception.

You can still use the Custom UI Editor for Microsoft Office (or any other XML Editor) to enter and validate your XML code, but you can't use it to automatically save the XML in an Access database the way you've stored XML in Word and PowerPoint in previous examples in this chapter.

With Access, you must store XML by hand, in a cell in a special table. Let's call it less than elegant, to avoid saying *kludge*.

In the following example, you'll see how to modify the Access Ribbon by adding a new tab, group, and toggle button—just as we added these elements to Word's Ribbon in the previous section. When the Access Ribbon has been modified, you can click the new toggle button and see the message "Button Down" or "Button Up." The result is the same as in the previous section, "Toggling with a Toggle-Button Control," but the steps to achieve that result in Access are quite dissimilar from those you took to add a toggle button to Word's Ribbon.

Follow these steps:

1. Open a new blank database by running Access, clicking the Blank Desktop Database template, typing in the name **R.accdb**, and then clicking the Create button.

(You could also open Northwind or any other database and modify its Ribbon following these steps, but for simplicity, let's stick with a blank database for this example.)

2. Right-click the Navigation pane's title bar where it says All Access Objects. (The Navigation pane is on the left side.)
3. Choose Navigation Options from the context menu.
4. Check the Show System Objects check box in the Navigation Options dialog box. Then click OK to close the dialog box. You're going to create a special table named USysRibbons, and it won't be visible in the Navigation pane if this check box isn't checked.
5. Now you want to make sure you see some error messages if there's a bug in your Ribbon-customization programming. To do this, follow these steps:
    a. Click the File tab on the Ribbon.
    b. Click Options.
    c. Click the Client Settings button in the left pane of the Access Options dialog box. Scroll down until you locate the General section near the bottom.
    d. Check the Show Add-in User Interface Errors check box. If you're using Access 2010, this option is enabled by default. In Access 2013 it's disabled by default, as it is in Word and the other Office 2013 applications. However, in the Office 2016 applications, happy day it's back, enabled by default again. Is it possible that somebody has more job than work to fill it?
    e. Click OK to close the dialog box.
6. Next, you'll create the required special table. Click the Ribbon's Create tab, and then click the Table Design button in the Tables group on the Ribbon.
7. In the first column of the first row, type **ID** for the field name, and in the second column, choose AutoNumber as the data type.
8. In the second row, type **RibbonName** and choose Short Text as the data type.
9. In the third row, type **RibbonXml** and choose Long Text as the data type.
10. Click the cell where you typed in **ID** to select it, and then click the Primary Key button in the Tools group on the Ribbon. (You may need to click a tab at the very top named Table Tools.)

    A key symbol is displayed in the record selector.
11. Click the File tab, and then click Save to save your new table. Be sure to name the table **USysRibbons**. Click the Yes button in the two message boxes that are displayed.
12. Now that you've designed the structure of this special table, it's time to add the data that modifies the Ribbon. Locate on your hard drive the `.accdb` file you just created and double-click it to open it in Access. Double-click UsysRibbons in the left pane. Then right-click the USysRibbons tab and select Datasheet View.
13. Ignore the ID field; it will automatically generate ID numbers for you.

14. Click the RibbonName cell and type **Toggle**—this is the name that will identify your custom Ribbon (you can choose any name that you like, but for the purpose of this example, use Toggle).

15. Enlarge the row both vertically and horizontally to make enough room to view the XML code you'll add to the RibbonXml cell. (See Figure 31.6.) This step isn't absolutely necessary, but it makes it easier for you to test and modify the XML code. So, in the title bar between the labels RibbonXml and Click To Add, drag to the right to widen the RibbonXml column.

16. Right-click the record selector (the yellow area just to the right of the Navigation pane and just above an asterisk symbol). Choose Row Height from the context menu. Type **300** and click OK to close the Row Height dialog box.

17. Type the following code into the RibbonXml cell:

```
<customUI xmlns="http://schemas.microsoft.com/office/2009/07/customui">
 <ribbon
startFromScratch="false">
  <tabs>
    <tab id="t1" label="Execute">
      <group id="g1" label="Run Test">

<toggleButton id="tbutton1"
label="Click to Toggle"
imageMso="DeclineInvitation"
onAction="togtest"/>

      </group>
    </tab>
  </tabs>
</ribbon>
</customUI>
```

Note that in Access, unlike in other applications, it is necessary to set the `startFromScratch` attribute to `false` in the XML code. (This attribute specifies whether you're creating a brand-new Ribbon or modifying the default Ribbon.)

18. Right-click the table's tab (it reads **USysRibbons** in boldface) and choose Close. Answer Yes when asked if you want to save changes to the layout.

19. Click the File tab and choose Close.

Testing Your New Ribbon

Now you're ready to choose your new Ribbon as the default Ribbon for this database. You have to specifically select the custom Ribbon you named Toggle. Follow these steps:

1. Open the database that you closed in step 19 in the previous exercise.
2. Click the File tab, and then choose Options to open the Access Options dialog box.
3. Click the Current Database button.

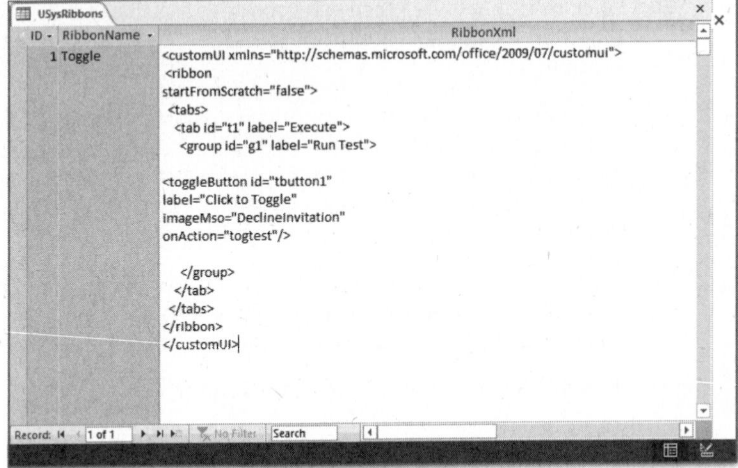

FIGURE 31.6 Here's the special table you can use in Access to store your XML code when modifying the Ribbon.

4. Scroll down until you locate the Ribbon And Toolbar Options section in the dialog box.
5. Open the Ribbon Name drop-down list box and select Toggle. (If you didn't name your table USysRibbons in step 11 in the previous exercise, the Toggle option will not appear in the drop-down list.)
6. Click OK to close the dialog box.
7. A message informs you that you must close then reopen this database for this new option to take effect. Do so.
8. Now you should see a new tab named Execute on the Ribbon, as shown in Figure 31.7.
9. Click the Execute tab. You should then see the Run Test group and your Click To Toggle button. At this point, just *look*, but don't *touch*. Don't click the button yet—you've not yet provided a macro named `togtest` that will act as an event handler (a callback) for this button. Recall that you have this line of code in your XML: `onAction="togtest"`. That means *When I'm clicked, execute the VBA procedure named togtest.* But you haven't yet created that procedure in a VBA module. You'll do that in the next section.

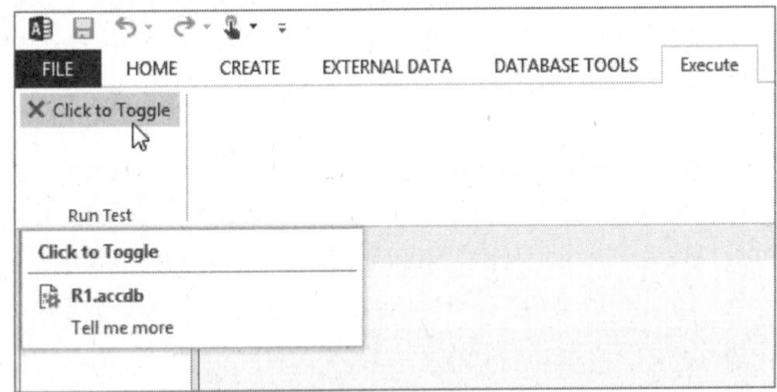

FIGURE 31.7 Now you've modified the Access Ribbon, add a new tab named Execute.

Adding a Callback in Access

In the previous section, you modified the Ribbon by adding three elements to it: a tab, a group, and a control. Now it's time to see how to add a callback. Follow these steps:

1. Open the database that contains your special Execute tab on its Ribbon that you used in the previous step-through.
2. Press Alt+F11 to open the VBA Editor in Access. Before you can communicate from the Ribbon's controls to a VBA procedure in Access, you must specify a reference to an object library (this step is not required in the other Office 2016 applications).
3. Choose Tools ➤ References in the VBA Editor. Notice that the Microsoft Office 15.0 Access database engine Object Library is selected by default. However, you must scroll down until you find Microsoft Office 16.0 Object Library and select its check box. Fail to take this step, and your VBA callbacks will not work—you'll see the error message "Microsoft Office cannot run the macro or callback function 'togtest'. Make sure the macro or function exists and takes the correct parameters."

I'm harping on this because not adding the Office 16.0 Object Library is an easy mistake to make (at least it was for me—it took me hours to figure this one out). I had read that a reference to that library was necessary, but when I opened the References dialog box and glanced at it, I saw *Microsoft Access 15.0 Object Library* and thought that was it. So I just closed the dialog box without adding the essential reference to the *Office 16.0* library.

4. Click OK to close the References dialog box.
5. Double-click Module1 in the VBA Editor Project Explorer. If there is no Module1, choose Insert ➤ Module.
6. Type this procedure into the module:

```
Sub togtest(control As IRibbonControl, down As Boolean)

  If down Then
     MsgBox "Button Down"
  Else
     MsgBox "Button Up"
  End If

End Sub
```

   This procedure looks at the argument named `down`, and if it returns a value of `True`, that means the toggle button has been pressed on the Ribbon. If a value of `False` is returned, that means the toggle button has popped back out. The code `If down Then` is just a shorter version of `If down = True Then`.

7. Now click your Click To Toggle button on the Execute tab of the Access Ribbon. You should see a message box saying "Button Down."

DIRECT COMMUNICATION WITH VBA

You may recall from Chapter 28, "Understanding the Access Object Model and Key Objects," that the user can't directly execute a VBA procedure from a button on the Quick Access Toolbar. Instead, you must first create an old-style Access "macro" that employs the `RunCode` command to execute the VBA procedure. However, the callback technique you learned in this section permits the user to click a button (or other control) on the Ribbon that directly executes a VBA function—without going through an old-style Access "macro."

What to Look For If Things Go Wrong

Ribbon customization—though useful and important—is new territory for many programmers. You have to deal with XML as a code platform, some unusual programming techniques (such as writing descriptive "markup" code in the XML and traditional programming code in VBA), communication between the XML and VBA via callbacks, new controls, new enumerations (such as the set of icons you can use with `ImageMso`), and so on.

Bugs happen even when writing code in a technology that you may have been using for decades, such as Visual Basic. So it's no surprise that Ribbon programming—with its several unique features—is pretty much guaranteed to bother you with bugs. The following sections describe some strategies for dealing with common Ribbon-related bugs.

Employ Error-Message Tools

Here are two preliminary steps to take in your effort to avoid, or cure, bugs.

First, turn on an error-reporting feature that's off by default. It allows you to see certain kinds of error messages if something is wrong with your Ribbon customization. Click the File tab on the Ribbon, and then choose Options to open the application's Options dialog box. Click the Advanced button (or if you're working in Access, click the Client Settings button). Scroll down to the General section and ensure that the Show Add-in User Interface Errors check box is selected.

XML itself doesn't display error messages or crash—it just *does nothing* if there's a problem, and generally so do browsers if you feed bad XML to them. In other words, whatever effect you're after doesn't happen: A new tab doesn't appear, a built-in tab isn't hidden, expected formatting changes in a browser aren't seen, and so on. But if you turn on the Show Add-in User Interface Errors feature, you'll see a descriptive explanation of why a Ribbon was not modified. It will look something like the message displayed in Figure 31.8.

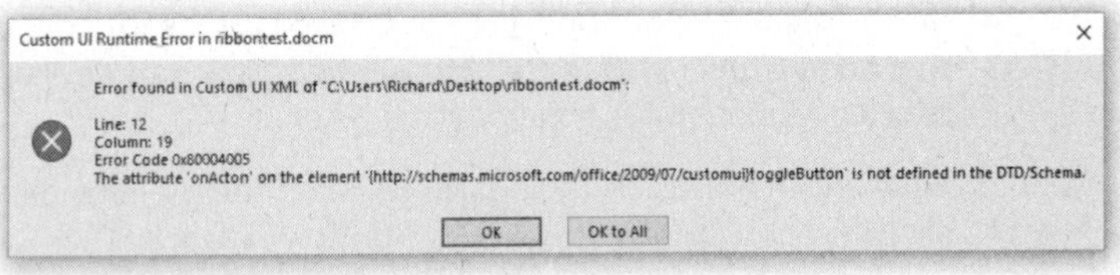

FIGURE 31.8
Error messages are your first line of defense against bugs.

This error message tells you that your error in the XML is located in line 12 in the following code:

```
1.  <customUI xmlns="http://schemas.microsoft.com/office/2009/07/customui">
2.  <ribbon>
3.     <tabs>
4.        <tab id="t1" label="Execute">
5.           <group id="g1" label="Run Test">
6.
7.
8.            <toggleButton id="tb1"
9.                    label="Change me."
10.                   supertip="Dynamically changes this button's label"
11.
12.                   onActon="tix"
13.                  />
14.          </group>
15.       </tab>
16.    </tabs>
17. </ribbon>
18. </customUI>
```

The message also says that the `toggleButton` element has no attribute named `onActon`, which indeed it doesn't. You meant to type `onAction`, so this a typo. However, more often this error message is caused by *improper case.* For example, you've spelled the attribute or other code element correctly, but you typed `OnAction` rather than the "proper" `onAction`. Remember that XML cares about capitalization and insists that it match exactly. Recall that this irrational case-sensitivity is the source of a many XML bugs. Always check capitalization when you're tracking down an XML problem. A case mismatch is easily overlooked.

The second preliminary step to take when fixing bugs is to use an XML Editor capable of validating XML code. Such an Editor is included with some versions of Visual Basic (such as VB Express, which is not the VBA built into Office applications, but rather the stand-alone version of the Basic programming language in Microsoft's Visual Studio).

You can also find free XML Editors for download from places like MajorGeeks.com. Or, just use the Custom UI Editor for Microsoft Office tool you downloaded earlier in this chapter. XML Editors can give you useful error messages if your XML code is faulty—the specific line where a problem is and, sometimes, a good description of the error. There is overlap between XML-validation error messages and those displayed by the Show Add-In User Interface Errors option you turned on in the previous step. But when it comes to fixing bugs, the more messages the merrier.

Cure Common User-Interface Programming Problems

Now let's explore some common error messages and what you can do about them.

Callback Problems: Bad Reference, Missing VBA Procedure, or Security Issues

The first error message we'll look at tells you that there's a problem with a callback you're attempting. The XML code can't execute the `onAction` attribute (see Figure 31.9). This error message can be caused because you haven't set a reference to the Microsoft Access 16.0 Object Library, as described in step 3 in the section "Adding a Callback in Access" earlier in this chapter (a variation on this error message is described in that section).

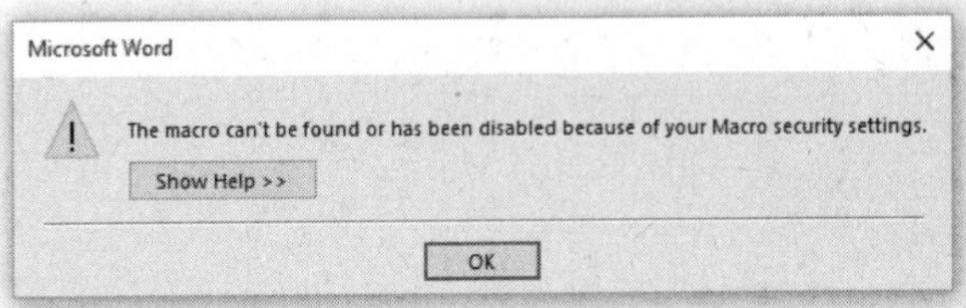

FIGURE 31.9 When you click your new button on the Ribbon to test it, you might see this error message.

This error message can also be caused by the two problems mentioned in the error message. First, you either mistyped or never wrote the procedure that you're referencing. For example, there is no procedure named `tix`:

```
onActon="tix"
```

Or, second, you need to enable macros by clicking the File tab on the Ribbon, clicking Options, then clicking the Trust Center button in the dialog box, clicking the Trust Center Settings button, and clicking one of the check boxes that permit macros.

OTHER CALLBACK PROBLEMS

The next error message (see Figure 31.10) means either one of two things. First, you've neglected to put in the required argument IRibbonControl.

You've put in

```
Sub trigger()
```

rather than

```
Sub trigger(IRibbonControl)
```

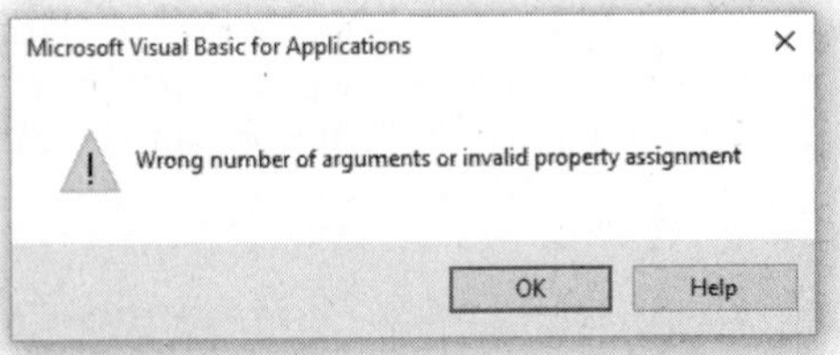

FIGURE 31.10 This error message results when you don't provide necessary arguments.

Or, second, you've neglected to provide additional required arguments. For example, the Toggle Button control passes two arguments to VBA, the `IRibbonControl` (which all callbacks always pass) and the status of the button, up or down, a Boolean value, like this:

```
Sub test(control As IRibbonControl, down As Boolean)
```

XML Mistakes

The next error I'll describe is easy to make. If you violate the XML nesting structure—by putting a `group` tag outside a `tab` tag, for example—you'll get the error message shown in Figure 31.11:

```
        <button idMso="WindowNext"/>
            </tab>
      </group>
```

Figure 31.11 When XML tags aren't in the proper order, you'll see this error message.

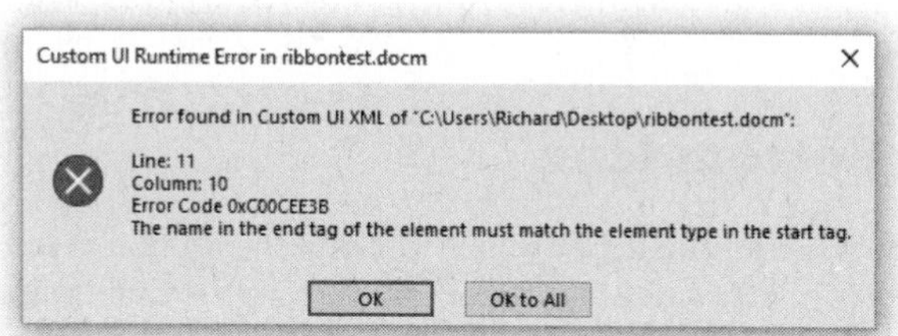

The `group` is supposed to be inside a `tab`, not vice versa. Or, if you leave out one of the closing tags (signified by the `/>`), you'll get the same error message. Here the closing `</tab>` tag is missing:

```
            </group>
        </tabs>
```

However, if you validate your XML code in an XML Editor like the Custom UI Editor for Microsoft Office, the Editor itself will flag certain problems such as this incorrect nesting.

Where to Go from Here

As you've seen, the Ribbon can be customized programmatically in a variety of ways. This chapter shows you the essential techniques. However, there's more to explore. You can experiment with the interesting Gallery control or create dynamic Ribbon effects, such as disabling, hiding, or changing the label on a control while your macro is executing, as conditions warrant. In fact, you can create an entirely new Ribbon from scratch using the `startFromScratch` attribute.

If you're interested in going deeper into Ribbon programming, here are some useful online resources:

Download the RibbonX Visual Designer. This powerful utility can assist you in all types of modifications to the Ribbon. Take a tour of its features at

`www.andypope.info/vba/ribboneditor.htm`

Try MSDN white papers. Take a look at Microsoft's online help system for developers—MSDN. It includes a lengthy, three-part tutorial on Ribbon programming, which can be found at

`http://msdn2.microsoft.com/en-us/library/aa338202.aspx`

This helpful tutorial covers advanced topics such as using COM add-ins and dynamic Ribbon updating; a helpful FAQ; and a complete reference to the many attributes, callbacks, and child elements involved in Ribbon programming. Or, take a look here:

`http://msdn.microsoft.com/en-us/library/office/ff862537.aspx`

Visit the Windows Ribbon Development Forum. The Windows Ribbon Development Forum is filled with questions and answers on Ribbon programming. If you run into a roadblock, post your question here and experts will respond.

`http://social.msdn.microsoft.com/Forums/en-US/windowsribbondevelopment`

The Bottom Line

Hide a tab on the Ribbon. Modifying the Ribbon involves employing XML attributes—similar to methods and properties—of various Ribbon elements such as tabs, groups, and buttons.

Master It Some Ribbon-related attributes include the suffix `Mso`. Examples include `idMso` and `imageMso`. What does the `Mso` mean, and what kind of attributes' names are appended with `Mso`?

Hide a group. You might want to make an entire Ribbon group invisible. For example, the Clipboard group on the Home tab includes features that most people trigger via shortcut keys. So there's no point in having this group take up space on the Ribbon.

Master It What XML attribute of a group do you set to `false` to remove that group from the Ribbon?

Create callbacks for event handling. To execute VBA code, you insert a callback in the XML code that will run whatever VBA macro you specify. When the user clicks a control, such as a button, the XML code that services this control sends a message to the Office application, telling it that a response is needed.

Master It What XML attribute do you use to create a callback?

Manipulate the Access Ribbon. Access often does things differently from the majority of Office applications, and Ribbon programming is no different. You can manipulate the Access Ribbon as freely as in the other applications, but several of the programming techniques differ.

Master It Where can you store the XML code when programming the Access Ribbon?

Debug Ribbon programming. Most Ribbon programming involves writing two types of code: XML and VBA. Strategies for fixing bugs in XML include *validation*.

Master It What is XML validation?

Appendix

The Bottom Line

Each of "The Bottom Line" sections in the chapters suggests exercises to deepen skills and understanding. Sometimes there is only one possible solution, but often you are encouraged to use your skills and creativity to create something that builds on what you know and lets you explore one of many possible solutions.

Chapter 1: Recording and Running Macros in the Office Applications

Record a macro. The easiest way to create a macro is to simply record it. Whatever you type or click—all your behaviors—are translated into VBA automatically and saved as a macro.

Master It Turn on the Macro Recorder in Word and create a macro that moves the insertion cursor up three lines. Then turn off the Macro Recorder and test the new macro.

Solution Click the Developer tab on the Ribbon (if that tab isn't visible, press Alt+F, I and select Show Developer Tab in the Ribbon). Click the Record Macro button on the Developer tab, then give the macro a name, such as **temporary**, and, if necessary, change the Store Macros In target to All Documents (Normal.dotm). Click OK to close the Record Macro dialog box. This begins the recording process. Press the up-arrow key three times. That's what you want to record.

Now click the Stop Recording button on the Developer tab or on the status bar at the bottom of the screen. Press Alt+F11 to open the Visual Basic Editor. Open Normal, then Modules, and double-click NewMacros in the left (Project) pane of the Editor. Scroll the Code window until you locate your new macro. The macro code should look something like this:

```
Sub temporary()
'
' temporary Macro
'
'
    Selection.MoveUp Unit:=wdLine, Count:=3
End Sub
```

Assign a macro to a button or keyboard shortcut. You can trigger a macro using three convenient methods: clicking an entry on the Ribbon, clicking a button in the Quick Access Toolbar, or using a keyboard shortcut. You are responsible for assigning a macro to any or all of these methods.

Master It Assign an existing macro to a new Quick Access Toolbar button.

Solution Press Alt+F, I. Click Customize in the left pane of the Word Options dialog box. In the Choose Commands From list, select Macros. Click a macro's name to select it in the list. Click the Add button to insert this macro's name in the Customize Quick Access Toolbar list. Click OK to close the dialog box. Now you see a new button on the toolbar that, when clicked, launches your macro.

Run a macro. Macros are most efficiently triggered via a Ribbon entry, by clicking a button on the Quick Access Toolbar, or by pressing a shortcut key combination such as Alt+N or Ctrl+Alt+F. When you begin recording a macro, the Record Macro dialog has buttons that allow you to assign the new macro to a shortcut key or toolbar button. However, if you are using the Visual Basic Editor, you can run a macro by simply pressing F5.

Master It Execute a macro from within the Visual Basic Editor.

Solution Open the Visual Basic Editor by pressing Alt+F11. Click to put the insertion cursor anywhere in the code within one of your macros in the right pane (between the `Sub` and `End Sub` lines of code). Press F5 to execute the macro.

Delete a macro. It's useful to keep your collection of macros current and manageable. If you no longer need a macro, remove it. Macros can be directly deleted from the Visual Basic Editor or by clicking the Delete button in the Macros dialog (opened by pressing Alt+F8).

Master It Temporarily remove a macro and then restore it using the Visual Basic Editor.

Solution Press Alt+F11 to open the Visual Basic Editor. The code within this Editor is just text, similar to Notepad. Locate a macro within the Editor. Each macro is the code that starts with `Sub` and concludes with `End Sub`. So drag your mouse to select an entire macro, including its `Sub…End Sub` lines. (Note that the Editor displays a horizontal line between each macro, so you can easily see where each macro's code begins and ends.) Press Ctrl+C to copy the macro's code. Then press Delete to delete the macro. Close the Visual Basic Editor and press Alt+F8 to open the Macros dialog box and see your list of macros. Scroll this list and notice that the macro you deleted in the Editor no longer exists.

Now close the Macros dialog box. Restore the macro by pressing Alt+F11 to reopen the Editor. Then click on a blank line at the very top of the right pane where the macro code is. However, you want to put the blinking insertion cursor *outside* of any other macro's `Sub…End Sub` code area. Finally, press Ctrl+V to paste the macro you previously deleted. It's restored. Remember, this Visual Basic Editor merely accepts ordinary, plain text for its source code—so you can freely cut, copy, and paste code. In fact, you can copy and paste all the code examples from this book at the book's website: `www.sybex.com/go/masteringvba2016`.

Chapter 2: Getting Started with the Visual Basic Editor

Open the Visual Basic Editor. When you want to create a new macro by hand-programming (as opposed to recording) or need to modify or test a macro, the Visual Basic Editor is a powerful tool.

Master It Open the Visual Basic Editor in Word and create a simple macro.

Solution Press Alt+F11.

Open a Macro in the Visual Basic Editor. You edit and test macro code in the Code window of the Visual Basic Editor.

Master It Open the Visual Basic Editor and display a particular macro in the Code window.

Solution Press Alt+F8 to open the Macros dialog box, click the name of the macro you want to work with, and then click the Edit button.

The Project Explorer window displays a tree of current projects. You can choose between viewing only the files or the folders and files.

Understand the Project Explorer's two views. The Project Explorer window displays a tree of current projects. You can choose between viewing only the files or the folders and files.

Master It Switch between folder and contents view in the Project Explorer.

Solution Click the icon on the right side (a picture of a folder) just under the Project Explorer's title bar.

Set properties for a project. You can specify a project's name, an associated Help file, and other qualities of a project.

Master It Lock a project so others can't modify or even read its contents.

Solution Right-click the project's name in the Project Explorer to open the shortcut menu. Choose <ProjectName> Properties. Click the Protection tab and select the Lock project for viewing text box. In the Password to View Project Properties group box, enter a password for the project in the Password text box, and then enter the same password in the Confirm Password text box. Click the OK button and close the project.

Customize the Visual Basic Editor. The Visual Basic Editor can be customized in many ways, including personalizing classic menus and toolbars.

Master It Undock the Properties window and change its size. Then redock it.

Solution Double-click the title bar of the Properties window to undock it. Position your mouse pointer in the lower-right corner until the pointer changes to a double arrow. Then drag the window to resize it. Restore the Properties window to its default docked position by double-clicking its title bar again.

Chapter 3: Editing Recorded Macros

Test a macro in the Visual Basic Editor. When you need to modify or debug a macro, the Visual Basic Editor is your best friend. It's filled with tools to make your job easier.

Master It Open a macro; then step through it to see if anything goes wrong.

Solution Press Alt+F8 to open the Macros dialog box. Select the macro's name that you want to test, and then click the Step Into button. The Visual Basic Editor opens and the insertion cursor is located within the chosen macro, thereby making it the currently active one (the one with which the Editor's features—such as the Step tool—will work). The first line is highlighted, indicating that it is the next line that will execute. Press F8 to execute the first line; then press F8 repeatedly to step down through each line of code. See if any problems occur—either problems you observe in the behavior of the macro in your application, or problems that VBA notifies you of by displaying an error-message box.

Set breakpoints and use comments. Setting breakpoints allows you to press F5 to execute a macro, but forces the Editor to enter Break mode when execution reaches the line where the breakpoint resides. Comments help you understand the purpose of code—they describe it but are ignored during execution of the macro's code. "Commenting out" a line of code allows you to temporarily render it inactive to see what effect this has during execution. This is sometimes a good way to see if that line is causing the bug you're tracking down.

Master It Set a breakpoint in, and add a comment to, a macro.

Solution Set a breakpoint by clicking in the gray, margin indicator bar to the left of a line of code where you want to halt execution. The line of code on which you set a breakpoint is shaded brown by default. You can set as many breakpoints as you like. Now type in a line such as **'The following With block describes the format for this new paragraph**. Because you've started this line with a single-quote symbol, the line will be ignored when the Editor executes the macro.

Edit a recorded macro. Make some changes to a Word macro.

Master It With the Visual Basic Editor open, choose a macro and modify it.

Solution Click a line between the `Sub` and `End Sub` lines that envelop the macro you want to modify. This puts the insertion cursor where you want it. Now simply type in whatever adjustments you want to make to the code.

Chapter 4: Creating Code from Scratch in the Visual Basic Editor

Set up the Visual Basic Editor for creating procedures. How you arrange the various components of the Visual Basic Editor is your personal choice, but while using this book, it's easiest if you set up the Editor to resemble the way it appears in the book's figures. Besides, this arrangement is quite close to the default layout, which has proven to be the most effective one for the majority of programmers (according to various focus groups and polls) for the decades that Visual Basic has been used.

Master It Press a single key to display the Properties window.

Solution Press F4 to display the Properties window.

Create a procedure for Word. Using the Help feature in any VBA-enabled application allows you to find code examples that you can copy and paste into your own code.

Master It Open the Code window and use Help to find a code example.

Solution Press F7 to open the Code window, and then press F1 to open Help. Click the Word Object Model Reference link. Scroll down until you see the Line Numbering Object link. Click it; then click the Line Numbering Object link in this newly displayed information. You'll find a code example that adds line numbers to the active document. Select and copy this code, and then paste it into the Visual Basic Editor. Note that many code examples are not full procedures but merely snippets of code, so it's up to you to add the `Sub... End Sub` envelope. Your final procedure in the Visual Basic Editor should look like this:

```
Sub AddLines()

With ActiveDocument.Sections(1).PageSetup.LineNumbering
```

```
        .Active = True
        .CountBy = 5
        .RestartMode = wdRestartPage
    End With


    End Sub
```

I named it AddLines; name it whatever you want. But keep in mind that to be able to execute it—for it to be a formal macro—you must include the Sub…End Sub.

Press F5 to try it out, and then look at the document and see the line numbers.

Remove the line numbers from the document by clicking the Line Numbers option in the Page Setup section of the Page Layout tab on the Ribbon and choosing None.

Create a procedure for Excel. Certain procedure names are special. In a previous Excel exercise, you added line numbering and gave that procedure a name of your own choice. But some procedure names have a special meaning—they are triggered by an *event* in Excel itself. They will execute *automatically* when that event takes place (you don't have to run events by choosing Run from the Macro dialog box or by assigning the macro to a keyboard shortcut or Quick Access Toolbar button). One such event is Excel's Auto_Open procedure.

Master It Display a message to the user when Excel first executes.

Solution Press F7 to open the Code window in Excel's Visual Basic Editor. Locate VBAProject (*theprojectname*) in the Project Explorer, double-click it to open its contents, and then double-click ThisWorkbook under the project. An empty Sub (an open event) appears in the Code window. Type the highlighted code into the procedure:

```
Private Sub Workbook_Open()
    MsgBox "Opened"
End Sub
```

Close and then reopen the workbook to see the message automatically displayed.

Create a procedure for PowerPoint. As you type a procedure, the Visual Basic Editor provides you with lists of objects' members (the Auto List Members feature) and with syntax examples, including both required and optional arguments (the Auto Quick Info feature). These tools can be invaluable in guiding you quickly to the correct object and syntax for a given command.

Master It Use the Auto List Members and Auto Quick Info features to write a macro that saves a backup copy of the currently active presentation.

Solution Create a new presentation based on a template of your choosing. Press Alt+F11 to open the Visual Basic Editor. Choose Tools ➤ Options and ensure that the Auto List Members and Auto Quick Info check boxes are selected.

Right-click the name of the presentation in the Project Explorer; then choose Insert Module so you'll have a place to write a macro.

Type the following line of code to create a macro:

```
Sub SaveTemp()
```

When you press the Enter key, the Visual Basic Editor automatically adds End Sub.

Now type **`Application.`** in the macro. As soon as you press the period (`.`), a list of properties and methods of the `Application` object is displayed. Choose `ActivePresentation`. Again, when you press the period key, a list of the `ActivePresentation` object's members appears. Choose `SaveCopyAs`. Press the spacebar to insert a space after `SaveCopyAs`, and you'll see that this method has only one required argument: a filename string (meaning you must provide a literal filename within quotes, or a string variable or constant). In this case, just type **`"temporary"`**, and then press the F5 key to execute the macro. You didn't specify a path, so you can find your file in your Documents folder, where it is saved by default.

Your macro should look like this:

```
Sub SaveTemp()

Application.ActivePresentation.SaveCopyAs "temporary"

End Sub
```

Create a procedure for Access. Although Access includes a variety of macro-related features that are unique (such as its Macro Builder/Designer), its Visual Basic Editor is quite similar to the Visual Basic Editors in the other Office applications.

Master It Open the Visual Basic Editor in Access and write a macro that displays today's date using the `Date` function rather than the `Now` function. Use the Access Visual Basic Editor Help system to understand the difference between these two functions.

Solution In Chapter 4, you wrote a macro in Access that displays today's date and time. Here you will display the date only.

1. Start Access.
2. Click the Blank Database button, and then click the Create button.
3. Press Alt+F11 to open the Visual Basic Editor.
4. Right-click the database name in the Project Explorer, and then choose Insert Module to open a new module in the Code window.
5. In the Code window, type the following macro:

```
Sub ShowDateOnly()

MsgBox Date

End Sub
```

6. Press F5 to execute the macro. You should see a message box that displays the current date.

Chapter 5: Understanding the Essentials of VBA Syntax

Understand the basics of VBA. VBA includes two types of procedures, used for different purposes.

Master It Name the two types of procedures used in VBA (and indeed in most computer languages), and describe the difference between them.

Solution A *function* always returns a value after it finishes executing. For example, you can display a message box, and when the user clicks a button to close that box, the value returned represents which button the user clicked. When the statement that called (invoked) the `MsgBox` function gets that value, it can respond in whatever way the programmer finds appropriate. Often, it's something like this: *If the user clicked OK, then check the spelling, or if the user clicked Cancel, then close the document.*

A *subprocedure* (or subroutine) does not return a value. It does a job and then quits without sending back any information to the code or action that triggered it. Events are always subprocedures.

Work with subs and functions. A procedure (a sub or function) is a container for a set of programming statements that accomplish a particular job.

Master It Write a sub in the Visual Basic Editor that displays a message to the user. Then execute that sub to test it.

Solution In the Visual Basic Editor Code window, type code similar to this:

```
Sub showmessage()

MsgBox "Hi, user."

End Sub
```

Execute this code by clicking within the subprocedure to position the insertion point there and then pressing F5.

Use the Immediate window to execute individual statements. When you're writing code, you often want to test a single line (a statement) to see if you have the syntax and punctuation right or if it produces the expected result.

Master It Open the Immediate window, type in a line of code, and then execute that line.

Solution Press Ctrl+G to open the Immediate window; then type a line of VBA code. When you've finished, press the Enter key to execute that statement.

Understand objects, properties, methods, and events. Object-oriented programming (OOP) means working with objects in your programming. OOP has become the fundamental paradigm upon which large programming projects are built. Generally speaking, macros are not large and, therefore, they usually don't profit from the clerical, security, and other benefits that OOP offers—these features particularly benefit people who write large applications as a team.

However, in your programming, you'll make frequent use of code libraries. All VB's commands are part of these libraries, such as the vast VBA set of objects and their members (not to mention the even vaster .NET libraries that tap into the power of the operating system itself). These libraries *are* written by large groups of people and written at different times. What's more, the libraries themselves are huge. They are so large that there must be a way to organize their objects and functions—to categorize them and allow you to execute the methods and manage their properties and arguments in your own macros. As a result, another aspect of OOP—taxonomy—is quite valuable even when writing brief macros. It's a way to quickly locate the members you're interested in.

Master It Look up the Document object in the Visual Basic Editor's Help system; then look at its methods.

Solution With the Visual Basic Editor the active window, choose Help ➤ Microsoft Visual Basic Help. Click the Word Object Model Reference link in the Help dialog box. Maximize the Help dialog box so you can see the large lists of objects and members. Scroll down until you see the Document object link. Click that link, and then click the link Document Object Members. As you scroll down, you'll see the many methods, properties, and events for this object. Click any of them to get a description, syntax, and, usually, a helpful code example you can cut and paste into your Code window.

Chapter 6: Working with Variables, Constants, and Enumerations

Understand what variables are and what you use them for. Variables are a cornerstone of computer programming; they are extremely useful for the same reason that files are useful in the real world. You give a name to a variable for the same reason that you write a name to identify a file folder. And a file can, over time, contain various different papers, just as the value contained in a programming variable can vary. In both cases, the contents vary; the name remains the same. It's good practice to always specifically name a variable before using it in your code. This is called *explicit declaration.*

Master It Explicitly declare a variable named CustomersAge.

Solution This code explicitly declares a variable:

```
Dim CustomersAge
```

If you decided to declare the variable as an Integer type, it would look like this:

```
Dim CustomersAge As Integer
```

Create and use variables. When creating (declaring) a new variable, you should avoid using words or commands that are already in use by VBA, such as Stop or End. There are also restrictions such as not using special characters.

Master It The following variable name cannot be used, for two reasons. Fix it so it is a legitimate variable name:

```
Dim 1Turn! as Integer
```

Solution

```
Dim Turn as Integer
```

You can't begin a variable name with a digit, nor can you use an exclamation point anywhere in the name.

Specify the scope and lifetime of a variable. Variables have a range of influence, depending on how you declare them.

Master It Create a variable named AnnualSales that will be available to any procedure within its own module but not to other modules.

Solution Constants, like variables, are named locations in memory that contain a value. Unlike variables, however, the value in a constant does not change during program execution.

Work with constants. Constants, like variables, are named locations in memory that contain a value. Unlike with variables, however, the value in a constant does not change during program execution.

Master It Define a string constant using the `Dim` command. Name your constant `FirstPrez`, and assign it the value `George Washington`.

Solution This code line defines a constant, and assigns a value to it:

```
Const FirstPrez As String = "George Washington"
```

Work with enumerations. Enumerations provide a handy name for each item in a list, often a list of properties.

Master It In the Project Explorer, click the `ThisDocument` object to select it. Then locate the `JustificationMode` property in the Properties window, and choose one of that property's enumerated constants by clicking the small down-arrow that appears and then clicking one of the constants in the drop-down list.

Solution You'll see the drop-down list of enumerated values for the `JustificationMode` property, as illustrated in the following screenshot.

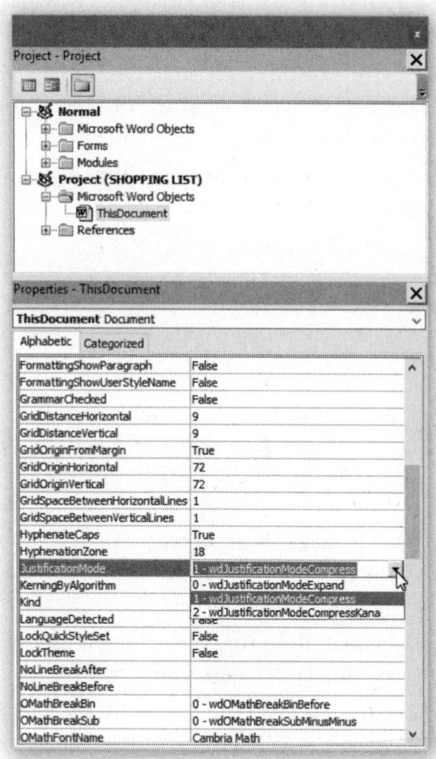

Chapter 7: Using Array Variables

Understand what arrays are and what you use them for. Arrays play an important role in computer programming. In some ways they resemble a mini-database, and organized data is central to computing. Computers are sometimes called data processors for good reason, and arrays make it easier for you to manipulate variable data.

Master It What is the difference between an array and an ordinary variable?

Solution An ordinary (scalar) variable can contain only a single value; an array can contain multiple values, identified by index numbers.

Create and use arrays. When you create a new array, you *declare* it and, optionally, specify the number of values it will contain.

Master It There are four keywords that can be used to declare arrays. Name at least three of them.

Solution Arrays can be declared using the same keywords that are employed to declare ordinary variables: `Dim`, `Private`, `Public`, or `Static`.

Redimension an array. If you want to resize an existing dynamic array, you can redimension it.

Master It Redimensioning an array with the `ReDim` statement causes you to lose any values that are currently in that array. However, you can preserve these values using a special keyword. What is it?

Solution To preserve values when redimensioning an array, use the `Preserve` command, like this:

```
ReDim Preserve arrTestArray(5)
```

Erase an array. You can erase all the values in a fixed-size array or completely erase a dynamic array.

Master It Write a line of code that erases the contents of an array named `arrMyArray`.

Solution Use the `Erase` statement with the name of an array you want to erase. The following statement erases the contents of the fixed-size array named `arrMyArray`:

```
Erase arrMyArray
```

Find out whether a variable is an array. An array is a type of variable, and you may occasionally need to check whether a particular variable name denotes an array or an ordinary *scalar variable* (a variable that isn't an array).

Master It Which built-in function can you use in VBA to find out whether a variable is an array or an ordinary, single-value variable?

Solution Use the `IsArray` function with the variable's name to see if a variable is an array. For example, the following statement checks the variable `MyVariable` to see if it's an array:

```
If IsArray(MyVariable) = True Then
```

Sort an array. Visual Basic .NET includes array objects with built-in search and sort methods. In VBA, however, you must write a bit of code to search and sort the values in an array.

Master It Name a popular, understandable, but relatively inefficient sorting technique.

Solution The bubble sort is easy to visualize, but relatively inefficient.

Search an array. Searching through an array can be accomplished in two primary ways. If you have a relatively small array, you can use the simpler, but less efficient technique. With large amounts of data, though, it's best to use the more robust approach.

Master It Name two common search algorithms.

Solution You can use either the simple linear search or the binary search, which requires that an array be sorted first.

Chapter 8: Finding the Objects, Methods, and Properties You Need

Understand and use objects, properties, and methods. Contemporary programming employs a hierarchical method of organization known as object-oriented programming (OOP). At the very top of the hierarchy for any given application is the `Application` object. You go through this object to get to other objects that are lower in the hierarchy.

Master It By using *creatable* objects, you can often omit the `Application` object when referencing it in code. What are creatable objects?

Solution Because you'd have to go through the `Application` object to get to pretty much anything in the application, most applications include a number of *creatable* objects—objects that you can access without referring explicitly to the `Application` object. These creatable objects are usually the most-used objects for the application, and by using them, you can access most of the other objects without having to refer to the `Application` object. For example, Excel exposes the `Workbooks` collection as a creatable object, so you can use the following statement, which doesn't use the `Application` object:

```
Workbooks(1).Sheets(1).Range("A1").Select
```

Use collections of objects. Collections are containers for a group of related objects, such as the `Documents` collection of `Document` objects.

Master It Are collections objects? Do they have their own methods and properties?

Solution Yes, collections are themselves objects—in the same sense that a flower vase contains a group of flower objects but the vase, too, is an object. A collection can have its own properties and methods, although collections usually have fewer properties and methods than other objects.

Find objects, properties, and methods. The Visual Basic Editor offers several ways to locate objects' members and add them to your programming code. There's an extensive Help system, the Object Browser, a List Properties/Methods tool, and the Auto List Members tool.

Master It How do you employ Auto List Members to find out which properties and methods are available for Word's `Document` object?

Solution Type **Document.** in the Code window, and as soon as you type the period, a list of the Document object's members appears.

Use Object variables to represent objects. You can create variables that contain objects rather than typical values like strings or numbers.

Master It What keywords do you use to declare an Object variable?

Solution The same keywords are used to declare Object variables as you use for any other variable. To create an Object variable, declare it using a `Dim`, `Private`, or `Public` statement. For example, the following statement declares the Object variable `objMyObject`:

```
Dim objMyObject As Object
```

However, you assign a value to an ordinary variable by using the = sign:

```
strMyString = "Harry"
```

You assign an object to an Object variable using the `Set` command in addition to the = sign, like this:

```
Dim wksSheet1 As Worksheet
Set wksSheet1 = ActiveWorkbook
```

Chapter 9: Using Built-In Functions

Understand what functions are and what they do. A function is a unit of code, a procedure, that performs a task *and returns a value.*

You can write your own functions by writing code between `Function` and `End Function` in the VBA Editor. Chapter 10, "Creating Your Own Functions," explores how to write such custom functions. But in addition to functions you might write, there are many functions already prewritten in VBA—ready for you to call them from your macros to perform various tasks.

Master It A function in VBA is quite similar to a subroutine, but there is a significant difference. What is it?

Solution Subroutines don't return a value; functions do.

Use functions. In a macro, you can call a built-in function by merely typing in its name and providing any required arguments.

Master It You can combine multiple functions in a single line of code. The `MsgBox` function displays a message box containing whatever data you request. The only required argument for this function is the *prompt*. The `Now` function returns the current date and time. Write a line of code that calls the `MsgBox` function and uses the `Now` function as its argument.

Solution:

```
MsgBox Now
```

The `MsgBox` function displays a message box which, in this case, is the date and time returned by the `Now` function.

Use key VBA functions. VBA offers the services of hundreds of built-in functions. You'll find yourself using some of them over and over. They are *key* to programming.

Master It What built-in function is used quite often to display information in a dialog box to the user while a procedure runs?

Solution Both the `MsgBox` and `InputBox` functions are used to display information to the user in a dialog box.

Convert data from one type to another. It's sometimes necessary to change a value from one data type to another. Perhaps you used an input box to ask the user to type in a String variable, but then you need to change it into an Integer type so you can do some math with it. (You can't add pieces of text to each other.)

Master It What built-in function would you use to convert a string such as `"12"` (which, in reality, is two text *characters*, the digits 1 and 2) into an Integer data type, the actual *number* 12, that you can manipulate mathematically?

Solution The built-in function `CInt` transforms other data types into an Integer type. Here's an example

```
intMyVar = CInt(varMyInput)
```

Manipulate strings and dates. VBA includes a full set of functions to manage text and date data.

Master It Which built-in function would you use to remove any leading and trailing space characters from a string? For example, you want to turn

```
"  this          "
```

into

```
"this"
```

Solution Use the `Trim` function. The following example displays two message boxes. The first shows you the length of the string before the `Trim` function is applied. The second displays the number of characters in the string after `Trim` does its job.

```
Dim s As String
s = "   this          "
MsgBox Len(s)
s = Trim(s)
MsgBox Len(s)
```

Chapter 10: Creating Your Own Functions

Understand the components of a function statement. Arguments can be passed from the calling code to a function in one of two ways: by reference or by value.

Master It Describe the difference between passing data by reference and passing data by value.

Solution The memory address of the actual value is passed to the function when passed *by reference*. This means that the value can be changed by the function. When passed *by value*, a copy of the data is sent to the function, leaving the original data unmodifiable by the called function. By reference is the default.

Create a generic function. You can write, and save (File ➤ Export File), sets of generic functions that work in any VBA-enabled application.

Master It Create a function that displays the current year in a message box. This function will require no arguments, nor will it return any value.

Solution

```
Function ShowYear()

    MsgBox (Year(Now))

  End Function
```

Create a function for Word. Word contains a whole set of objects and members unique to word-processing tasks. Functions that are specific to Word employ one or more of these unique features of the Word object model.

Master It Write a function that displays the number of hyperlinks in the currently active document. Use Word's `Hyperlinks` collection to get this information.

Solution

```
Function FindHyperCount()

    MsgBox (ActiveDocument.Hyperlinks.Count)

End Function
```

Create a function for Excel. Excel uses an `ActiveWorkbook` object to represent the currently selected workbook. You can employ a full set of built-in methods to manipulate the features of any workbook.

Master It Using the `Sheets` collection of Excel's `ActiveWorkbook` object, write a function that displays the number of sheets in the current workbook.

Solution

```
Function SheetsCount()

MsgBox (ActiveWorkbook.Sheets.Count)

End Function
```

Create a function for PowerPoint. PowerPoint's object model includes an `ActivePresentation` object, representing the currently selected presentation. Functions can make good use of this object and its members.

Master It Write a function that returns how many slides are on a presentation. Pass the `ActivePresentation` object as an argument to this function; then display the number of slides the presentation contains. Call this function from a subroutine.

Solution

```
Option Explicit

Function CountSlides(objPresentation As Presentation) As Integer
    CountSlides = objPresentation.Slides.Count
```

```
End Function

Sub SeeNumber()
    MsgBox (CountSlides(ActivePresentation))
End Sub
```

Notice that your `CountSlides` function is called from within the `SeeNumber` sub. The `ActivePresentation` object is passed as an argument. The `CountSlides` function's argument list includes a variable of the *Presentation* type. And the entire function is defined as an Integer type, meaning it will pass back Integer data to the caller. `CountSlides` is assigned the Integer value provided by the `Count` method and, thus, returns this value to the calling subroutine.

Create a function for Access. Access often works a little differently from other VBA-enabled Office applications. For example, some common tasks are carried out by using methods of the special `DoCmd` object rather than methods of a `Form` or `Table` object.

Master It Write a function that closes Access by using the `DoCmd` object's `Quit` method. Ensure that all data is saved by employing the `acQuitSaveAll` constant as an argument for the `Quit` method.

Solution This function closes Access with the `DoCmd` object's `Quit` method.

```
Function QuitApp()

DoCmd.Quit (acQuitSaveAll)

End Function
```

Chapter 11: Making Decisions in Your Code

Use comparison operators. Comparison operators compare items using such tests as *greater than or not equal to.*

Master It Write a line of code that uses a *less than* comparison to test whether a variable named `Surplus` is less than 1200.

Solution Here's an example of the *less than* comparison operator:

```
If Surplus < 1200 Then
```

Compare one item with another. You can compare strings using *less than* and *more than* comparison operators.

Master It What symbol do you use to determine if `VariableA` is lower in the alphabet than `VariableB`?

Solution You use the *less than* symbol (<), like this:

```
If VariableA < VariableB Then
```

Test multiple conditions. To test multiple conditions, you use VBA's *logical operators* to link the conditions together.

Master It Name two of the most commonly used logical operators.

Solution The most often-used logical operators are `And`, `Or`, and `Not`. Tests can be combined using these operators, like this:

```
If A < B AND C = F Then
```

Use `If` blocks. `If` blocks are among the most common programming structures. They are often the best way to allow code to make decisions. To test two conditions, use `If…Else…EndIf`.

Master It Write an `If…Else…End If` block of code that displays two message boxes. If the temperature (the variable `Temp`) is greater than 80, tell the user that it's hot outside. Otherwise, tell the user that it's not that hot.

Solution Your code may vary somewhat from this, but see if you've followed the basic structure:

```
Sub tempShow()

  Dim Temp As Integer
  Temp = 66

  If Temp > 80 Then
    MsgBox "Hey, it's hot outside!"
  Else
    MsgBox "It's not that hot."
  End If

End Sub
```

Use `Select Case` blocks. `Select Case` structures can be a useful alternative to `If` blocks.

Master It When should you use a `Select Case` structure?

Solution `Select Case` is often more readable than a lengthy, complex `If…ElseIf…ElseIf…` multiple-test decision-making block.

Use the `Select Case` statement when the decision you need to make in the code depends on one variable (or expression) that has more than two or three different values that you need to evaluate.

Chapter 12: Using Loops to Repeat Actions

Understand when to use loops. Loops come in very handy when you need to perform a repetitive task, such as searching through a document for a particular word.

Master It What is the alternative to looping if you are carrying out repetitive tasks in a macro?

Solution You can copy the repeated code and then paste it into the Visual Basic Editor as many times as you want to repeat the task. Programmers, however, frown on repeated code because they consider it a redundancy, which it often is. If some behavior needs to be repeated, you can almost always employ some form of loop structure.

Use `For...` loops for fixed repetitions. `For...` loops are the most common loop structures in programming. You specify the number of iterations the loop must make, and the loop is exited when that number is reached.

Master It Write a `For...Next` loop that counts up to 100, but use the `Step` command to increment by twos.

Solution This code increments its *counter* variable (`i`) by twos:

```
For i = 1 To 100 Step 2

Next
```

Use `Do...` loops for variable numbers of repetitions. A `Do...` loop iterates until or while a condition exists and then exits from the loop when the condition no longer exists.

Master It There are two categories of `Do...` loops. `Do While...Loop` and `Do Until...Loop` loops test a condition before performing any action. What is the other category?

Solution The second type of `Do...` loop includes loops that perform an action before testing a condition. `Do...Loop While` and `Do...Loop Until` fall into this category.

Nest one loop within another loop. You can put loops inside other loops.

Master It Think of a programming task where nested loops would be useful.

Solution Nested loops would come in handy if you're accessing a multidimensional array or a table of data, for example. You could use one loop to search through each row in the table, and another loop to search through all the columns. The example of nested loops given in this chapter is that you need to create a number of folders, each of which contains a number of subfolders. Structurally, this subfolders-within-folders example resembles a multidimensional array or a table of data.

Avoid infinite loops. An infinite loop causes your macro to continue execution indefinitely—as if the macro had stopped responding and was "frozen."

Master It How can you avoid creating an infinite loop?

Solution Be sure that it is possible for your loop to terminate at some point. Ensure that a condition will occur that ends the looping.

Chapter 13: Getting User Input with Message Boxes and Input Boxes

Display messages on the status bar. The information bar at the bottom of the window in many applications is a useful, unobtrusive way of communicating with the user. The status bar is frequently used by applications to indicate the current page, zoom level, active view (such as *datasheet* in Access), word count, and so on. However, you, too, can display information on the bar.

Master It Write a small sub in the Visual Basic Editor that displays the current date and time in the status bar.

Solution This procedure shows how to display information in the status bar.

```
Sub Experimentation_Zone()

Application.StatusBar = Now

End Sub
```

Display message boxes. Message boxes are commonly used to inform or warn the user. By default, they appear in the middle of the screen and prevent the user from interacting with the host application until a button on the message box is clicked, thereby closing it.

Master It Write a small sub in the Visual Basic Editor that displays the current date and time using a message box.

Solution Here's how to display information in a message box.

```
Sub Experimentation_Zone()

MsgBox Now

End Sub
```

Display input boxes. An input box is similar to a message box, except the former can get more information from the user. An input box allows the user to type in a string, which is more data than the simple information provided by which button the user clicked in a message box.

Master It Write a small sub in the Visual Basic Editor that asks users to type in their name. Use the `InStr` function to see if there are any space characters in the returned string. If not, it means either they are Madonna or they have typed in only one name—so display a second input box telling them to provide both their first and last names.

Solution You can handle this several ways, but this example code uses a `Do...Loop Until` structure to repeatedly display an input box until the user types in at least two words:

```
Sub Get_Name()

Dim response As String

response = InputBox("Please type in your full name:", _
   "Enter Name")

If Not InStr(response, " ") Then 'found no space character

    Do

        response = InputBox _
 ("You entered only one name. Please type in your full name:", _
 "Enter First and Last Names Please")

    Loop Until InStr(response, " ")
```

```
End If


End Sub
```

Understand the limitations of message boxes and input boxes. For even moderately complex interaction with the user, message and input boxes are often too limited. They return to the VBA code, for example, only a single user response: a button click or a single piece of text. So you can't conveniently use an input box to ask for multiple data—such as an address *and* a phone number—without displaying multiple input boxes. That's ugly and disruptive.

Master It In addition to the limitations on the amount of information you can retrieve from the user, what are the two other major limitations of message boxes and input boxes?

Solution You are limited in the formatting and the amount of information you can display to the user.

Chapter 14: Creating Simple Custom Dialog Boxes

Understand what you can do with a custom dialog box. Custom dialog boxes—user interfaces you design as forms in the Visual Basic Editor—are often needed in macros and other kinds of Office automation. You might, for example, want to display a dialog box that allows the user to specify whether to let a macro continue beyond a certain point in its code or cease execution. Perhaps your macro is searching through a document for a particular phrase; then when it finds that phrase, it displays a dialog box to users asking if they want to continue further.

Master It Which VBA statement would you use to stop a macro from continuing execution?

Solution The `End` command halts execution.

Create a custom dialog box. You use the Visual Basic Editor to both design a custom dialog box (form) and write code for macros. You can attach the various controls to a form and then enter code *behind* the dialog box.

Master It How do you switch between the form-design window (sometimes called the object window) and the Code window in the Visual Basic Editor?

Solution The easiest way is to press F7 to display the Code window and press Shift+F7 to display the Design window. However, you can also use the View menu, or double-click the module name in the Project Explorer (to switch to design mode), or double-click the form or one of its controls (to switch to the Code window).

Add controls to a dialog box. It's easy in the Visual Basic Editor to add various controls—such as command buttons and text boxes—to a user form (a custom dialog box).

Master It How do you add a command button to a custom dialog box?

Solution If the Visual Basic Editor Toolbox isn't visible, click the form. Or you can choose View ➢ Toolbox. Or click the Toolbox button on the Standard toolbar to display the Toolbox. Then click the command-button icon and click the form. If you want to add more than one command button, double-click the command-button icon in the Toolbox. Move your mouse cursor (notice that it now displays a small button icon) to the location in the dialog box where you want to place the command button. Click the form to place the new button on the form.

Link dialog boxes to procedures. Buttons, check boxes, option buttons—displaying various controls to the user is fine, but unless you write some code *behind* these various user-interface objects, what's the point? Your macro's user shouldn't discover that clicking a button *does nothing.*

Dialog boxes often display objects with which users can communicate their wants to your code. Therefore, you write code that reads the values the user enters into controls, and responds.

Master It Create a small custom dialog box that displays a message in a label control saying, "Would you like to know the current date and time?" Put an OK button and a Cancel button on this form. Write code that simply ends the procedure if the user presses the Cancel button but that displays the date and time in the label if the user clicks the OK button. If the user clicks OK a second time, end the procedure.

Solution After you've placed the label with its `Caption` property set to "Would you like to know the current date and time?" and put two appropriately captioned buttons on the form, double-click the Cancel button to open the Code window. Name the label **`lblShowTime`**.

In the Cancel button's `Click` procedure, type **End**. Now use the Object drop-down list (on the top left of the Code window) to select the OK button.

In the OK button's `Click` procedure, type the code shown here:

```
1.  Private Sub btnCancel_Click()
2.      End
3.  End Sub
4.
5.  Private Sub btnOK_Click()
6.
7.      If Label1.Caption = "Would you like to see the current date
       and time?" Then
8.          Label1.Caption = Now
9.      Else
10.         End
11.     End If
12.
13. End Sub
```

Here's how the code works:

- Line 2 closes the dialog box using the `End` statement. You could also use the `UnLoad` statement.
- Line 7 tests the value in the label's `Caption` property. This is how the procedure knows if this is the first time the user has clicked the OK button. If the label displays the original caption ("Would you like to see the current date and time?"), then you

know the user has not previously clicked OK. However, if this original caption is not displayed (because the date and time are), that means the user is clicking OK a second time and wants to close the dialog box.

- Line 8 displays the date and time in the label.
- Line 10 exits the procedures, which also has the effect of removing the dialog box.

There are other ways to test whether the user has clicked OK twice. You could create a `Static` Boolean variable type that is set to `True` the first time the OK button is clicked. Line 7 would then test the value of this variable in the following way:

```
If blnToggle = True Then
```

Retrieve the user's choices from a dialog box. A major task of most dialog boxes is retrieving values that the user has specified in various controls by selecting check boxes and so on. Then you write code to carry out the user's wants based on these retrieved values. This interaction via dialog box is the typical way that a user communicates with your procedures, and vice versa.

Master It Create a new dialog box that contains three option buttons captioned Small, Medium, and Large and named `optSmall`, `optMedium`, and `optLarge`. Write code in each option button's `Click` procedure to change the button's caption to boldface when the button is clicked.

Solution The following code shows how to employ the `Font` object's `Bold` property to turn boldface on and off in a caption on a dialog box:

```
Private Sub optSmall_Click()
    optSmall.Font.Bold = True
    optMedium.Font.Bold = False
    optLarge.Font.Bold = False
End Sub

Private Sub optMedium_Click()
    optSmall.Font.Bold = False
    optMedium.Font.Bold = True
    optLarge.Font.Bold = False
End Sub

Private Sub optLarge_Click()
    optSmall.Font.Bold = False
    optMedium.Font.Bold = False
    optLarge.Font.Bold = True
End Sub
```

With code, there are always various ways to achieve a given result. You could write this code a different way by creating a function that accepted `small`, `medium`, or `large` as an argument and then used a `Select Case` structure to make the appropriate caption boldface. That solution would look like this:

```
Private Sub optSmall_Click()
    ChangeSize ("small")
```

```
End Sub

Private Sub optMedium_Click()
    ChangeSize ("medium")
End Sub

Private Sub optLarge_Click()
    ChangeSize ("large")
End Sub


Function ChangeSize(strChoice As String)

Select Case strChoice

Case Is = "small"

optSmall.Font.Bold = True
optMedium.Font.Bold = False
optLarge.Font.Bold = False


Case Is = "medium"

optSmall.Font.Bold = False
optMedium.Font.Bold = True
optLarge.Font.Bold = False

Case Is = "large"

optSmall.Font.Bold = False
optMedium.Font.Bold = False
optLarge.Font.Bold = True

End Select

End Function
```

Chapter 15: Creating Complex Forms

Understand what a complex dialog box is. Simple dialog boxes tend to be static, but complex dialog boxes are dynamic—they change during execution in response to clicks or other interaction from the user.

Master It Describe two types of dynamic behavior typical of complex dialog boxes.

Solution The following types of dynamic behavior are typical of complex dialog boxes:

- The application changes the information in the dialog box to reflect choices that the user has made.
- The dialog box displays a hidden section of secondary options when the user clicks a button in the primary area of the dialog box.
- The application uses the dialog box to keep track of a procedure and to guide the user to the next step by displaying appropriate instructions and by activating the relevant control.

Reveal and hide parts of a dialog box. Dialog boxes need not display everything at once. Word's Find And Replace dialog box illustrates how useful it can be to display an abbreviated dialog box containing the most common tasks and expand the box to reveal less-popular options if the user needs access to them.

Master It Name the two most common techniques you can use to display additional options in a dialog box.

Solution The two most common techniques for displaying additional options in a dialog box are as follows:

- Set the `Visible` property to `False` during design time to initially hide a control on a form. Then set its `Visible` property to `True` when you want to display the control.
- Increase the height or width (or both) of the dialog box to reveal an area containing further controls.

Create multipage dialog boxes. VBA includes the MultiPage control, which enables you to create multipage dialog boxes. Word's Font dialog box is an example of one. You can access any page (one at a time) by clicking its tab at the top of the page.

Master It How does the TabStrip control differ from the MultiPage control? What are the typical uses for each?

Solution A MultiPage control allows the user to switch among different virtual *pages* (with differing controls and varied layouts). The MultiPage control is most often employed to display a set of property pages for a feature (such as fonts) that includes many possible options and settings. You, therefore, can subdivide all these options among multiple pages in the form: one page for font properties and another page for character spacing, for example.

A TabStrip control contains multiple *tabs* but not multiple pages. In other words, the layout of the rest of the dialog box (apart from the tab strip itself) stays the same no matter which tab on the tab strip the user clicks. This is useful for displaying records from a database because the fields (such as text boxes) remain identical no matter which record the user is viewing.

Create modeless dialog boxes. A *modeless* dialog box can be left visible onscreen while the user continues to work in an application. For example, the Find And Replace dialog box in Access, Word, and Excel is modeless, as is the Replace dialog box in PowerPoint. A *modal* dialog box, by contrast, must be closed by users before they can continue to interact with the application.

Master It How do you make a user form modeless?

Solution Set its `ShowModal` property to `False`. The default is `True`.

Work with form events. Events are actions that happen to controls (or the form itself) while a program is executing. By using events, you can monitor what the user does and take action accordingly or even prevent the user from doing something that doesn't seem like a good idea.

Master It Name two of the three most commonly used events in VBA programming.

Solution The three most commonly useful events for VBA programming are `Click`, `Initialize`, and `Change`.

Chapter 16: Building Modular Code and Using Classes

Arrange your code in modules. Rather than use a single lengthy, complex procedure that accomplishes many tasks at once, programmers usually subdivide their code into smaller, self-contained procedures—dedicated to a single, discrete task.

Master It Shorter, self-contained, single-task procedures offer the programmer several advantages. Name three.

Solution The advantages of shorter, self-contained, single-task procedures are as follows:

- Modular code is often easier to write because you create a number of short procedures, each of which performs a specific task.
- You can usually debug shorter procedures relatively easily.
- Short procedures are more readable because you can more easily follow what they do.
- By breaking your code into procedures, you can repeat their tasks at different points in a sequence of procedures without needing to repeat the lines of code.
- By reusing whole procedures, you reduce the amount of code you have to write.
- If you need to change an item in the code, you can make a single change in the appropriate procedure instead of having to make changes at a number of locations in a long procedure.
- You can easily reuse short, dedicated, single-task procedures in other code in the future.

Call a procedure. You execute a procedure by calling it from within your programming code.

Master It How do you call a procedure?

Solution You can use the optional `Call` statement, like this, to call a procedure named `FormatDocument`:

```
Call FormatDocument
```

But most programmers omit the `Call` keyword, using just the name of the procedure, like this:

```
FormatDocument
```

Pass information from one procedure to another. Sometimes a procedure requires that you pass it some information. For example, a procedure that searches text and makes some style changes to it will require that you pass the text you want to modify.

Sometimes a procedure passes back information to the procedure that called it. For example, it might pass back a message describing whether the actions taken in the procedure were (or were not) accomplished successfully.

Master It What kind of procedure can pass back information to the caller?

Solution Only functions can pass back information to a caller. Subroutines can accept data (arguments) like functions, but subroutines cannot pass data back to the caller.

Understand what classes are and what they're for. Contemporary computer programs employ classes for various reasons—to help organize large programs, to make code more easily reusable, to provide certain kinds of security, or as a superior substitute for public variables. But beginners sometimes have a hard time wrapping their minds around the concept, particularly the relationship between classes and objects.

Master It What is the difference between a class and an object?

Choose the correct answer (only one answer is correct):

1. A class is like a cookie and an object is like a cookie cutter.
2. A class is like a programmer and an object is like a module.
3. A class is like a blueprint and an object is like a house built from that blueprint.

Solution The answer is 3. A class is like a blueprint and an object is like a house built from that blueprint.

Create a class. The VBA Editor employs a special kind of module for containing classes.

Master It How do you create a class module in the VBA Editor?

Solution There are three ways to create a class module:

- Right-click the name of the target project in the Project Explorer (or right-click one of the items contained within the project). Then choose Insert ➢ Class Module from the context menu.
- Click the Insert button on the Standard toolbar and choose Class Module from the drop-down list.
- Choose Insert ➢ Class Module from the menu bar.

Chapter 17: Debugging Your Code and Handling Errors

Understand the basic principles of debugging. A major aspect of programming is testing your code. Debugging can be enjoyable if you think of it as a puzzle you can solve. But whether or not you enjoy it, debugging is essential if you want to preserve a reputation as a professional.

Master It When testing your code, try to imagine ways that the code could fail. Describe a situation that can produce unanticipated results.

Solution A user may try to run a document-formatting procedure without first opening a document.

Or, the user might try to open a file and trigger certain errors—perhaps the file doesn't exist; or is currently in use by another computer; or is on a network drive, floppy drive, CD-ROM drive, or removable drive that isn't available at the time.

You'll also run into other peripheral-related errors if the user tries to use a printer or other remote device (say, a scanner or a digital camera) that's not present, connected, powered up, or configured correctly.

Similarly, any procedure that deals with a particular object in a document (for example, a chart in Excel) will run into trouble if that object is not present or not available.

Recognize the four different types of errors you'll create. Experts have concluded that there are four primary categories of error in programs.

Master It Name two of the four basic types of programming errors.

Solution Here are the four basic types of programming errors:

- Language errors
- Compile errors
- Runtime errors
- Program logic errors

Employ VBA's debugging tools. The VBA Editor and VBA include a generous assortment of debugging tools to help you track down and remove bugs from your procedures. The main windows you'll employ for debugging are the Immediate window, the Locals window, and the Watch window.

Master It The Watch window is especially useful because you can set watch expressions (also known as conditional breakpoints). Describe this debugging tactic.

Solution Watch expressions are flexible and powerful debugging tools. You can ask the VBA Editor to break on any kind of expression you can think up, such as any line that causes a variable to exceed a certain value, go below zero, change to a shorter string length, and so on.

You specify a condition (a watch expression such as `X < 0`), and the VBA Editor automatically halts execution and displays the line where this occurs.

Deal with runtime errors You can trap some runtime errors (errors that show up while a procedure is executing) while debugging your code. But others show up only while your user is interacting with your program—and you're probably not there to help them. There is a way, though, to soften the blow and, in some cases, even fix a problem by adding error handlers to your programs.

Master It Error handlers are special statements and sections of code that detect and then manage runtime errors. What VBA statement detects a runtime error?

Solution VBA's `On Error` statement triggers when there is a runtime error, allowing you to write code that responds to the error.

Chapter 18: Building Well-Behaved Code

Understand the characteristics of well-behaved procedures. Well-behaved procedures don't annoy or alarm the user either during or after their execution.

Master It Name two ways programmers can write procedures that don't annoy users.

Solution Here are some ways programmers can avoid annoying users by their procedures' actions:

- Make no durable or detectable changes to the user environment—other than changes the procedure is designed to make. In other words, restore the previous settings.
- Present the user with relevant choices for the procedure and relevant information once the procedure has finished running.
- Show or tell the user what is happening while the procedure is running.
- Make sure whenever possible that conditions are appropriate for the procedure to run successfully—before the procedure takes any actions.
- Anticipate or trap errors to avoid a crash. But if the procedure does crash, handle the situation as gracefully as possible and minimize damage to, or loss of, the user's work.
- Leave users in the optimal position to continue their work after the procedure finishes executing.
- Delete any scratch documents, folders, or other debris that the procedure created in order to perform its duties but that are no longer needed.

Retain and restore the user environment. Users quite rightly don't appreciate it if your procedure leaves the state of their application's or operating system's environment modified. Find ways to restore the user environment before your procedure finishes execution.

Master It Assume that you are writing a procedure that employs Word's Search and Replace feature. This feature retains its settings between uses so the user can repeatedly trigger the same search or replace actions. How can you temporarily store the status of the user's last search or replace so that you can restore this data after your procedure is finished executing?

Solution To store such information, you can use private variables, public variables, or custom objects.

Let the user know what's happening. Particularly when a procedure is doing a lengthy "batch job" such as updating dozens of files, it's important to let the user know that the computer hasn't frozen. People need to be told that execution is continuing as expected even though nothing appears to be happening.

Master It Describe a way to let the user know that a procedure isn't frozen—that activity is taking place during execution.

Solution You can tell users via a message box before starting a lengthy process that they should anticipate a delay. Alternatively, you can display messages on the status bar.

Or, you could disable screen updating for parts of a procedure and turn it back on, or refresh it, for other parts.

Check that the procedure is running under suitable conditions. Another important element of creating a well-behaved procedure is to check that it's running under suitable conditions. This ideal is nearly impossible to achieve under all circumstances, but you should take some basic steps.

Master It If a procedure accesses data from a file, name an error that could occur and, thus, should be trapped.

Solution You should trap errors in case a file being accessed hasn't been opened, doesn't exist (has been deleted or moved), or doesn't contain data that the procedure expects to find in it.

Clean up after a procedure. A well-behaved procedure avoids leaving unneeded files or other temporary items behind. In other words, a procedure should clean up after itself.

Master It Cleaning up involves three major tasks. Name one.

Solution The three main ways that a procedure cleans up after itself are as follows:

- Undoing any changes that the procedure had to make to enable itself to run
- Closing any files that no longer need to be open
- Removing any scratch files or folders that the procedure has created to achieve its effects

Chapter 19: Exploring VBA's Security Features

Understand how VBA implements security. Microsoft takes a multipronged approach to protecting users from malicious VBA code embedded in documents and capable of launching itself when the user simply opens the document.

Master It Name two ways that users are protected from malicious VBA code.

Solution Users are protected from malicious VBA code in the followings ways:

- The default file type for Office documents simply cannot contain any embedded macros at all (these files' filename extensions end in `x`, such as `.docx`).
- Macro-enabled documents can be stored in a trusted area on the hard drive.
- The user can specify various trust settings for both macros and other executables, such as add-ins and ActiveX controls. For example, the user can forbid the execution of any controls unless the user is first notified. Another setting prompts the user for permission before allowing a control to be loaded.
- The user can modify a list of "trusted publishers"—companies whose documents are considered safe.

- Developers can digitally sign their own projects, thereby making themselves "trusted publishers."
- The types of files that an application can access can be more specifically controlled via file blocking.
- A Trusted Documents feature allows users to specify individual documents as reliable.
- Files are scanned before being opened.
- Files can be opened in a sandbox called Protected View.

Sign a macro project with a digital signature. You can add a digital signature to your projects by creating your own certification, getting it from your company, or getting it from certification authorities such as VeriSign.

Master It Describe the limitations of self-certifying a VBA macro project—without obtaining a certificate from your company or a commercial certification authority.

Solution The quickest and easiest way of getting a digital certificate is to create one yourself. However, this kind of certification works only on the computer on which the certificate was created, and it's the least trustworthy type of digital signature. A digital certificate you create yourself is of little value to people other than you and those who personally trust you.

Get a digital certificate. Commercial certification authorities provide the greatest level of security, but their certification is also more difficult to attain than self-certification or certification from your company.

Master It Name some of the ways you may be required to prove your identity when obtaining a digital signature from a commercial certification authority.

Solution The procedure for proving your identity varies depending on the commercial certification authority and the type of certificate you want. Generally speaking, the greater the degree of trust that the certificate is intended to inspire, the more proof you'll need to supply. For example, you can get a basic certificate on the strength of nothing more than a verifiable email address, but this type of certificate is unlikely to make people trust you. Other certificate types require you to appear in person before a registration authority with full documentation (such as a passport, driver's license, or other identity documents). Such certificates carry more trust.

Choose the appropriate security level. When choosing the right security level to use VBA macros safely, you or a user of your code must achieve a balance. The security level must be set high enough to avoid malicious or incompetent code but low enough that it doesn't prevent you from running useful, safe code.

Master It To set a suitable level of security for your purposes, open the Trust Center in Access, Word, Excel, or PowerPoint. You'll see four settings. Which one of the following five settings is *not* available:

- Disable All Macros Without Notification
- Disable All Macros With Notification

- Disable All Macros Except Digitally Signed Macros
- Enable All Macros With Notification
- Enable All Macros

Solution There is no Enable All Macros With Notification option.

Lock your code. You can protect your source code in the VBA Editor from others. You can add a password to a project (projects are in boldface in the Project Explorer) so that others can't open your VBA procedures for reading or modifying.

Master It What is one drawback to locking your code?

Solution The lock requires an extra step to access the modules and forms in the project because you must first provide the password. However, for the protection you gain by locking your code, this small extra effort can be well worth the trouble.

Chapter 20: Understanding the Word Object Model and Key Objects

Understand Word's creatable objects. Word contains a set of creatable objects that VBA programmers will frequently employ in their code.

Master It What is a creatable object?

Solution A *creatable object* is simply one that doesn't require you to use the term `Application` when invoking it. It's a kind of shorthand. For example, the `Documents` collection object is creatable, so the word `Application` is optional in this code: `Application.Documents.Count` does the same thing as `Documents.Count`.

Work with the `Documents` collection and the `Document` object. The `Documents` collection represents all the currently open documents. Using VBA, you can manipulate this collection in a variety of ways.

Master It Here is the syntax for adding a new document to the `Documents` collection:

```
Documents.Add Template, NewTemplate, DocumentType, Visible
```

If you merely want to add a new, empty document (based on the default `Normal.dotm` template) to the documents currently open in Word, the code is quite simple. What is the code that you would write in VBA to accomplish this?

Solution The code is as follows:

```
Documents.Add
```

Work with the `Selection` object. The `Selection` object represents the current selection in the active document in Word. The user can select a zone by dragging the mouse or by using various key combinations (such as pressing Shift and an arrow key). A selection can include one or more objects—one or more characters, one or more words, one or more paragraphs, a graphic, a table, and so on. Or, it can include a combination of these objects.

Master It One kind of selection is described as a *collapsed selection*. What is that?

Solution A collapsed selection is an insertion point (the blinking cursor). Nothing is visibly selected. The insertion point, however, is still thought of as technically a selection (pointing to a place within the document), even though this special kind of selection has no contents.

Create and use ranges. In Word, a *range* is a named area of a document with a defined starting and ending point. The typical use of ranges in Word VBA is similar to how you use bookmarks when working interactively with Word: to mark a location in a document that you want to be able to access quickly or manipulate easily.

Master It Although a range is similar to a bookmark, what is the significant difference between them?

Solution The main difference between a range and a bookmark involves their lifetimes. A range exists only as long as the VBA procedure that defines it is executing. A bookmark is persistent: it is saved with the document or template that contains it and can be accessed at any time (whether or not a procedure is running).

Manipulate options Word contains many options that can be manipulated from within VBA.

Master It In Word, one object controls many of the options. This object has dozens of properties but no methods. Name this object.

Solution The `Options` object controls many of the options in Word.

Chapter 21: Working with Widely Used Objects in Word

Use Find and Replace via VBA. Word's Find and Replace utilities are frequently valuable to the VBA programmer. You'll want to master them and also some subtleties associated with their use.

Master It Sometimes when replacing, you need to go through a document more than once—using a loop structure. Why would you ever need to repeatedly search and replace the same document? Doesn't the Replace All setting in fact *replace all?*

Solution In some situations, the act of replacing actually generates new instances of the target of the replacement activity. Let's say you want only single-space strings in a document. (For example, you want sentences separated by only a single space character, but sometimes a typist accidentally presses two or more spaces.) You set up a search and replace that looks for double-space character strings and replaces them with single-space characters. You have to take into account that there can also be some multiple-space-character strings. Consider a string of six adjacent space characters. During the first pass, your double-to-single search and replace reduces the six-space string to a three-space string (three instances of double spaces would reduce to three instances of single spaces). The second pass through a loop would reduce it to a two-space string, requiring yet a third pass through the loop to achieve the desired single space. This same situation can apply to multiple-paragraph spacing (multiple blank lines) and tabs.

Work with headers, footers, and page numbers. All Word documents contain headers and footers, even if they are empty. In addition, you can insert various types of headers and footers.

Master It Name two types of headers you can use in a Word document.

Solution Here are the major types of Word headers: the primary header, different first-page headers, different even-page headers, and different sets of headers for each of the sections in the document.

Manage sections, page setup, windows, and views. Among the various ways you can view a document, you sometimes want to have the document automatically scroll to a particular table, graphic, or other target.

Master It What method of the `Window` object can be used to easily accomplish this task?

Solution The `ScrollIntoView` method of the `Window` object moves the view to a target you specify.

Manipulate tables. When you need to manage tables in Word documents, you can employ VBA to work with the `Table` object to represent a single table. If there is more than one table, they are referenced by a collection of `Table` objects.

Master It Name two important and useful objects within the `Tables` collection or the `Table` object.

Solution Some of the most useful objects within a `Table` object or a `Tables` collection are as follows:

- The `Rows` collection contains the rows in the table. Each row is represented by a `Row` object.
- The `Columns` collection contains the columns in the table. Each column is represented by a `Column` object.
- The `Cell` object provides access to a specified cell directly from the `Table` object. You can also reach the cells in the table by going through the row or column in which they reside.
- The `Range` object provides access to ranges within the table.
- The `Borders` collection contains all the borders for the table.
- The `Shading` object contains all the shading for the table.

Chapter 22: Understanding the Excel Object Model and Key Objects

Work with workbooks. You often need to create a new, blank workbook in a macro (mimicking a user clicking the File tab on the Ribbon and then clicking the New button). And writing code that accomplishes this is not difficult. It requires only two words.

Master It What code would you write to create a new, blank notebook?

Solution To create a blank workbook, omit the `Template` argument, like this:

```
Workbooks.Add
```

Work with worksheets. Most workbooks you access via VBA will contain one or more worksheets, so most procedures will need to work with worksheets—inserting, deleting, copying, or moving them, or simply printing the appropriate range from them.

Master It Name the object you use in VBA code to represent a worksheet.

Solution Each worksheet is represented by a `Sheet` object. The `Sheet` objects are contained within the `Sheets` collection.

Work with the active cell or selection. In a procedure that manipulates a selection that the user has made, you'll typically work with either the active cell or the current selection.

Master It What is the difference between the active cell and a selection?

Solution The active cell is always a single cell, but the selection can either be a single cell or encompass multiple cells or other objects.

Work with ranges. Within a worksheet, you'll often need to manipulate ranges of cells. Excel includes a special kind of range—represented by the `UsedRange` property.

Master It What is unique about `UsedRange`?

Solution If you need to work with all the cells on a worksheet (but not with any unoccupied areas of the worksheet), use the `UsedRange` property. `UsedRange` ignores empty areas of a worksheet.

Set options. Word employs an `Options` object to contain most of the options that you find in the Word Options dialog box (click the File tab on the Ribbon and then click Options). Excel uses a different object to contain its options.

Master It From which object do you access most of Excel's options?

Solution You access most of Excel's options from the `Application` object. However, you can access the workbook-specific properties that appear in the Excel Options dialog box through the appropriate `Workbook` object.

Chapter 23: Working with Widely Used Objects in Excel

Work with charts. You can create either full chart sheets or embedded charts within an ordinary Excel worksheet.

Master It What object is used in a procedure to represent an embedded chart?

Solution VBA uses the `ChartObject` object to represent an embedded chart on a worksheet.

Work with windows. To open a new window on a workbook, you use the `NewWindow` method of the appropriate `Window` object.

Master It Does the `NewWindow` method take any arguments?

Solution No, the `NewWindow` method takes no arguments. For example, the following statement opens a new window showing the contents of the first window open on the workbook identified by the object variable `myWorkbook`:

```
myWorkbook.Windows(1).NewWindow
```

Work with Find and Replace. When working with the Find and Replace features in Excel, you need to be aware of a phenomenon known as *persistence*.

Master It What is persistence, and why should it concern you?

Solution The `LookIn`, `LookAt`, `SearchOrder`, and `MatchByte` arguments of the `Range` object's `Find` method *persist*. This means that Excel retains their settings from one search to the next (until this session with Excel ends and you shut it down). So, if you don't know that the settings used in the last search (either programmatically in a procedure or by the user) are suitable for your current needs, you should set these arguments explicitly in each search to avoid getting unexpected results. Format settings such as font and subscript also persist.

Chapter 24: Understanding the PowerPoint Object Model and Key Objects

Understand PowerPoint's creatable objects. Creatable objects are commonly used objects that can be employed in VBA code without requiring that you qualify them with the `Application` object. You can leave that word out of your code; it's optional and rarely used.

Master It Name one of the objects or collections that are creatable in PowerPoint macros.

Solution Objects or collections that are creatable in PowerPoint procedures include the `ActivePresentation` object, the `Presentations` collection, the `ActiveWindow` object, and the `SlideShowWindows` collection.

Work with presentations. You can create a new presentation programmatically, but PowerPoint generates an annoying flicker on most systems while it brings the new presentation into view. You can block this unpleasant, strobelike effect to avoid disturbing your audience.

Master It How do you prevent a newly created presentation from being visible so that you can create and manipulate it in your code without the user seeing the flickering effect onscreen?

Solution `WithWindow` is an optional Long argument of the `Add` method of the `Presentations` collection. Set `WithWindow` to `msoFalse` to hide the presentation so that the user doesn't have to endure the irritating flickering effect that PowerPoint tends to exhibit while creating presentation objects programmatically. The default value is `msoTrue`, making the new presentation visible.

Work with windows and views. To get the PowerPoint window into the state you want, you'll often need to work with the window and with the view.

Master It PowerPoint uses two types of windows. What are they?

Solution PowerPoint uses document windows and slide-show windows.

Work with slides. Once you have created or opened the presentation you want to manipulate, you can access the slides it contains by using the `Slides` collection. This collection contains a `Slide` object for each slide in the presentation. Each slide is identified by its index number, but you can also use object variables to refer to slides or assign names to slides.

Master It Why would you want to assign names to slides rather than using the default index numbers that are automatically assigned to the slides?

Solution Assigning names to slides is useful because if you add slides to, or delete them from, the presentation, the index numbers of the slides will change. You don't want to have to keep track of readjusted index numbers as you manipulate the collection. If they have names, you can access the slides directly, without worrying that their index numbers might have changed.

Work with masters. Before attempting to manipulate a master in your code, you should determine whether the master actually exists in the presentation.

Master It How do you find out whether a presentation has a title master?

Solution Check the `HasTitleMaster` property. If the presentation already has a title master, VBA returns an error when you try to add a title master. So check, like this:

```
If ActivePresentation.HasTitleMaster Then
       'take further action based on the If...Then test
```

Chapter 25: Working with Shapes and Running Slide Shows

Work with shapes. PowerPoint VBA provides many ways to access and manipulate shapes.

Master It Describe what the following line of code does:

```
ActivePresentation.Slides(2).Shapes(1).Delete
```

Solution The code example deletes the first `Shape` object on the second slide in the active presentation.

Work with headers and footers. Using PowerPoint headers and footers can be a convenient way to provide continuity for presentations as well as to identify each element.

Master It In this chapter, you worked with several examples showing how to manipulate footers for slides. Why were there no examples illustrating how to manipulate headers for slides?

Solution Slides can't have headers, only footers. Notes pages or handouts can have headers.

Set up and run a slide show. To create a custom slide show, you use the `Add` method of the `NamedSlideShows` collection.

Master It The syntax when using the `Add` method of the `NamedSlideShows` collection is

```
expression.Add(Name, SafeArrayOfSlideIDs)
```

Explain what the four components of this line of code are and what they do.

Solution The components are as follows:

- *`expression`* is a required expression that returns a `NamedSlideShows` object.
- `Add` is the method (of the `NamedSlideShows` object) that adds the slides to the new show.
- `Name` is a required String argument that specifies the name to assign to the new custom slide show.
- `SafeArrayOfSlideIDs` is also a required argument. It's a Variant argument that specifies the numbers or names of the slides to include in the custom show.

Chapter 26: Understanding the Outlook Object Model and Key Objects

Work with the `Application` object. VBA uses two major Outlook objects that most users wouldn't recognize from working with the Outlook user interface alone.

Master It One of these objects represents a window that displays the contents of a folder. The other represents a window displaying an Outlook item, such as an email message or an appointment. What are the names of these two objects?

Solution An `Inspector` object is an object that represents a window displaying an Outlook item, such as an email message or an appointment.

An `Explorer` object represents a window that displays the contents of a folder.

Work with messages. To work with the contents of a message in VBA, you set or get various properties.

Master It Name one of the most widely useful properties employed when manipulating the contents of a message in a procedure.

Solution The most commonly useful properties when accessing a message in VBA are `To`, `CC`, `BCC`, `Subject`, `Body`, `BodyFormat`, and `Importance`.

Work with calendar items. You can create new calendar appointment items via VBA.

Master It To create a new calendar item, you use a particular method of the `Application` object and specify `olAppointmentItem` for the `ItemType` argument. What is the method?

Solution To create a new calendar item, you use the `CreateItem` method of the `Application` object. This example creates an `AppointmentItem` object variable named `myAppointment` and assigns to it a new appointment item:

```
Dim myAppointment As AppointmentItem
Set myAppointment = Application.CreateItem(ItemType:=olAppointmentItem)
```

Work with tasks and task requests. You can assign a task to a colleague and then add one or more recipients. You can then send the task to your colleague and, optionally, the additional recipients.

Master It What methods do you use to assign, add, and send a task to others?

Solution To assign, add, and send a task to others, use the `Assign`, `Add`, and `Send` methods.

Chapter 27: Working with Events in Outlook

Create event handlers. Event handlers are procedures that contain code that responds to an event. In other words, if a user modifies one of their contacts, an event can detect this modification and execute code you've written to respond to the modification.

Master It Event-handler procedures are unlike ordinary macro procedures in several ways. Name one of the differences.

Solution Both the construction of an event-handler procedure and its testing differ somewhat from the techniques you've been employing throughout this book when creating and testing ordinary macro procedures:

- An event handler must be located within a class module, not an ordinary macro module.
- An object variable must be declared that can point to the event.
- The object variable must be initialized (connected to an object).
- You cannot simply test the event handler by pressing F5 to run it directly (you must instead run it indirectly by triggering the event it's designed to service—for example, by modifying a contact in the Contacts folder).

Work with application-level events. Application-level events happen to Outlook as a whole.

Master It Name an important application-level event.

Solution The `Startup` and `Quit` events are common application-level events.

Work with item-level events. Outlook has two primary kinds of events.

Master It What are the two types of events in Outlook? And how do they differ?

Solution The two types of events in Outlook are application-level and item-level events. Application-level events apply to Outlook as a whole (for example, an event that triggers when the application is closed). Item-level events apply to individual items within Outlook, such as a contact or an email message in the Inbox.

Understand the Quick Steps tool. Outlook's Quick Steps feature can be used to specify a set of actions that can later be triggered by the user to automate these actions. This is very similar to creating macros.

Master It How do an Outlook's Quick Steps differ from macros?

Solution Quick Steps are not nearly as flexible and powerful as macros. To create a Quick Step you simply choose from a list of common actions to combine two or more of them into a little "program."

Chapter 28: Understanding the Access Object Model and Key Objects

Become familiar with how VBA works in Access. Access allows you to write macros in a VBA Editor using VBA code. But it also features a legacy Macro Designer utility (formerly known as the Macro Builder) with which you create an entirely different kind of macro, what we've been calling an Access-style macro.

Master It The term *macro* is used in a special way in Access (referring to only one of the two types of custom procedures Access permits you to construct: VBA and Macro Designer). This usage of *macro* is unlike the way the term *macro* is used in other Office applications, not to mention all other forms of computing. Describe what Access means by the term *macro*.

Solution Instead of defining macros as VBA procedures, Access uses the term *macro* to describe a technology unique to Access. You create these Access "macros" by clicking the Macro button on the Create tab (in the Macros And Code section of the Ribbon) to open the Macro Designer window.

An Access "macro" is a historical entity—a holdover from the early days of this database system. Access macros are limited to a subset of the available programming statements.

Using the Macro Designer, you enter a list of actions that you want to perform. You choose these actions from a list and then type in arguments in the next cell in a table displayed by the Macro Designer.

Open and close databases. Access permits you to open a database in several ways.

Master It Two common commands that open a database in Access are `OpenCurrentDatabase` and `OpenDatabase`. What is the difference between these two commands?

Solution Instead of using the `OpenCurrentDatabase` method to open a database as the current database, you can use the `OpenDatabase` method of the `Workspace` object to open another database and return a reference to the `Database` object representing it. Using this method, you can open multiple databases. The `OpenCurrentDatabase` method, by contrast, can open only a single database at a time.

Work with the `Screen` object. You became familiar with using `ActiveDocument` objects in Word to access the document that currently has the focus. Or you used the `ActivePresentation` object to work with whichever presentation happened to be active in PowerPoint. Access, however, employs the `Screen` object as the parent of whatever object has the focus.

Master It The `Screen` object represents the screen object that currently has the focus in Access (that is, the object that is receiving input or ready to receive input). Three types of common Access objects can have the focus when you employ the `Screen` object. What are they?

Solution The object can be a form, a report, or a control.

Use the `DoCmd` object to run Access commands. Many of the tools that Access makes available to users, such as printing a report or maximizing a window, are also available to the programmer via the methods of the `DoCmd` object.

Master It The `DoCmd` object has 66 methods in Office 2016. Describe the purpose of the `DoCmd` object's `Beep` method.

Solution The `Beep` method makes the computer emit a sound. This can be used in conjunction with an error message to alert the user that an error has occurred.

Chapter 29: Manipulating the Data in an Access Database via VBA

Open a recordset. You can open an ADO recordset in two different ways.

Master It One way to open an ADO recordset is to provide an argument list following the `Open` method. What is the other way to open an ADO recordset, which doesn't involve using arguments? Some people say that this second approach makes their code easier to read.

Solution Instead of specifying arguments for the `Open` method, you can set the `Source`, `ActiveConnection`, `CursorType`, and `LockType` properties of the `RecordSet` object you're opening and then use the `Open` method without arguments. You may agree with those who feel this approach makes the code easier to read.

Access a particular record in a recordset. Both ADO and DAO technologies have methods that allow you to move around within a recordset.

Master It One method you can use to traverse a recordset is the `MoveFirst` method. It takes you to the first record in the recordset. What does the *first record* mean in a recordset in a relational database? Is it the record that's the lowest numerically, the lowest alphabetically, or what?

Solution The concept of a "first record" within a relational database is essentially meaningless, unless you sort the records in some fashion. You can sort them by any of their fields and either ascending (the default) or descending (specify `DESC`). Which record is first depends on the field by which you sort the recordset. But *you* must sort them. They can't be assumed to be sorted in any way within the database itself.

Search for a record. Both ADO and DAO offer methods to directly search for a particular record.

Master It ADO offers a `Find` method. How many methods does DAO offer, and what are they?

Solution There are four `Find` methods for DAO: `FindFirst`, `FindNext`, `FindPrevious`, and `FindLast`.

Edit a record. When editing a record, you first use the `Edit` method, and then you can change the value in a field.

Master It After you have made a change to a value in a record, what method do you use to save this change to make it part of the database?

Solution You use the `Update` method to save the changes you made to a recordset.

Insert and delete records. It's not difficult to insert new records or delete existing ones. In both situations, you use the `Update` method when finished to save the changes to the database.

Master It To insert a new record into a recordset, what method do you use before you can assign data to the fields in the new record?

Solution You use the `AddNew` method of the `RecordSet` object to create a new, empty record.

Chapter 30: Accessing One Application from Another Application

Use Automation to transfer information. Automation sets up communication between two applications, designating one of them as the *server* and the other as the *client*.

Master It Of the various ways to communicate between applications, which is generally the most effective?

Solution Automation is the most powerful and efficient way to communicate between applications.

Use the `Shell` function to run an application. Although the `Shell` function can prove useful in a variety of inter-application communication situations, `Shell` can also present the programmer with a timing problem.

Master It Describe the timing issues that the `Shell` function raises, and describe a good solution to this problem.

Solution The `Shell` function runs other programs *asynchronously* rather than synchronously. In other words, `Shell` doesn't halt all other activity until it has finished with its job. So when VBA executes a `Shell` statement, it registers the statement as an action to be performed—but that action may not necessarily be finished before the next statement in the procedure executes.

This asynchrony can cause errors in your procedures if subsequent commands depend on the `Shell` statement having already been executed. If you run into this type of problem, a crude but often-effective fix is to just allow extra time for the `Shell` function to execute before taking any dependent action. You can employ the `Sleep` function to pause execution of your procedure to allow any necessary commands to be carried out.

Use data objects to store and retrieve information. This book has described a variety of ways to store and retrieve information when working with the VBA language. Using data objects is one of these useful techniques.

Master It How is the data-object technology special as a way of storing and retrieving information? What can a data object do that's unique?

Solution The data object has the ability to copy information to and retrieve information from the Windows Clipboard.

Communicate via DDE. Dynamic Data Exchange (DDE) is a technology introduced back in May 1990 with Windows 3.0. Use it if other, more efficient communication technologies are unavailable to the applications you are working with.

Master It Not all applications support DDE. Which Office 2016 applications don't support DDE communication?

Solution PowerPoint and Outlook do not support DDE.

Communicate via `SendKeys`. Using `SendKeys` is a fairly simple but rather awkward and limited way to communicate between applications. It imitates typing in keystrokes, thereby allowing your code to manipulate an application by accessing some of its features using, for example, Alt+key combinations, such as Alt+F to open the File tab on the Ribbon.

Master It `SendKeys` was historically most often employed to open an application's menus and select an option from the menus. Since Vista, Windows applications have largely done away with traditional menus, so is `SendKeys` of even more limited use now than in the past?

Solution No, `SendKeys` must simply send some different keystrokes to access recent Office applications' features. Many of the features of the Ribbon, for example, are accessible via key combinations. For example, pressing the sequence Alt, W, Q, 2, and the Enter key in Word will switch to the View tab on the Ribbon, select the Zoom option, and switch to a 200 percent zoom. The difference here is that instead of employing the older approach of simultaneously pressing the Alt key while pressing other keys (such as Alt+V to open a View menu), in today's applications you press and release Alt by itself to activate the Ribbon; then you press the W key to switch to the View tab on the Ribbon. At this point, additional keystrokes can be sent to trigger the various options on the View tab.

Chapter 31: Programming the Office 2016 Ribbon

Hide a tab on the Ribbon. Modifying the Ribbon involves employing XML attributes—similar to methods and properties—of various Ribbon elements such as tabs, groups, and buttons.

Master It Some Ribbon-related attributes include the suffix `Mso`. Examples include `idMso` and `imageMso`. What does the `Mso` mean, and what kind of attributes' names are appended with `Mso`?

Solution `Mso` stands for Microsoft Office, and it means that a tab, icon, or other element is built in—such as a tab that is, by default, visible on the Ribbon.

Hide a group. You might want to make an entire Ribbon group invisible. For example, the Clipboard group on the Home tab includes features that most people trigger via shortcut keys. So there's no point in having this group take up space on the Ribbon.

Master It What XML attribute of a group do you set to `false` to remove that group from the Ribbon?

Solution You can set any group's `visible` attribute to `false`, thereby hiding it from the user.

Create callbacks for event handling. To execute VBA code, you insert a callback in the XML code that will run whatever VBA macro you specify. When the user clicks a control, such as a button, the XML code that services this control sends a message to the Office application, telling it that a response is needed.

Master It What XML attribute do you use to create a callback?

Solution You use the `onAction` attribute to create a callback.

Manipulate the Access Ribbon. Access often does things differently from the majority of Office applications, and Ribbon programming is no different. You can manipulate the Access Ribbon as freely as in the other applications, but several of the programming techniques differ.

Master It Where can you store the XML code when programming the Access Ribbon?

Solution You store the XML code when programming the Access Ribbon in a special table you create, named USysRibbons.

Debug Ribbon programming. Most Ribbon programming involves writing two types of code: XML and VBA. Strategies for fixing bugs in XML include *validation*.

Master It What is XML validation?

Solution XML validation is a feature built into XML Code Editors that checks to ensure that the XML is *well formed* (free of certain kinds of errors). A validation looks for tags that are missing, out of order, improperly punctuated, use the wrong capitalization, are not part of the schema (aren't listed as attributes or elements in the document that defines the particular XML version being used), and so on. Some errors can't be detected during validation (such as pointing an `onAction` attribute to a VBA procedure that doesn't exist). But many common errors—such as typos—can be spotted by validation, which is an automatic scan of XML code.

Index

Note to the reader: Throughout this index boldfaced page numbers indicate primary discussions of a topic. *Italicized* page numbers indicate illustrations.

B

C

E

F

I

M

N

Q

R

T

U

V

X

Y

Z